CAMBRIDGE
EDUCATIONAL SERVICES, INC.®

ACT • PLAN • EXPLORE
TestPrep PLUS™

SAT • ACT • PSAT • PLAN • EXPLORE • GRE • GMAT • LSAT • MCAT • TOEFL • GED • PRAXIS • ITBS • College Prep

Published by Cambridge Publishing, Inc.

Cambridge Educational Services, Inc.
2720 River Road, Suite 36
Des Plaines, IL 60018
(847) 299-2930

Manufactured in the United States of America.
6 7 8 9 10
Edited by Julie M. Lengle & David P. Waldherr.

CHICAGO HEADQUARTERS • 2720 RIVER ROAD • DES PLAINES, ILLINOIS 60018 • PHONE: (847) 299-2930 • FAX: (847) 299-2933

WWW.CAMBRIDGEED.COM • TESTPREP@CAMBRIDGEED.COM

About This Book

You are about to begin your ACT preparation. We have examined the ACT question by question and answer choice by answer choice. We have literally taken each test apart, analyzed every component, and then put the pieces back together again. The result of all of our efforts is a proven plan. We call it the Cambridge Six-Step Approach™. It is a sure-fire method that has worked for thousands of students at hundreds of schools.

By working your way through these pages with your instructor, you will get a complete course covering all the key points you need to raise your ACT score. You will review all of the topics and concepts that are tested on the ACT, and you will learn powerful strategies for answering every question-type.

How to Use this Book

This textbook is for use in a course with an instructor utilizing the Cambridge TestPrep PLUS™ textbook and teacher guide. Some portions of this book will be completed in class under your teacher's direction, while other portions will be completed on your own. This book has a flexible format, so be sure to follow your teacher's direction to get the most from your preparation.

This book contains:

In-class lessons
Advanced in-class problem solving and quizzes
Special strategy drills
Basic math and grammar review
Admissions help
Test anxiety material
Full-length practice tests

CAMBRIDGE
EDUCATIONAL SERVICES, INC.®

Acknowledgements

Many thanks to all the hardworking teachers, authors, and educators who have helped make Cambridge Educational Services the largest campus-based TestPrep™ in the United States. Ever since Cambridge was started in 1990, our mission has been to provide schools across America with the highest quality test preparation at an affordable price. Now teachers all over America are teaching their own students TestPrep™ strategies. Over five thousand teachers have put forth an extraordinary effort to make our mission come true.

My special thanks to the Cambridge Curriculum Committee, made up of teachers, principals, authors, and scholars; and Tom, senior author and chair of the Cambridge Curriculum Committee; Julie, my senior editor, who has been here from the beginning; Sally, who has personally talked with thousands of teachers; Jeff, for his creativity and exceptional vision in designing this book; Matthew, for his outstanding work on Cambridge web courses and CD-ROMs; Rick, director of diagnostic assessment services; my new son, Andrew, for his constant inspiration; and my wife, Kathy, for her extraordinary insight as a mathematics teacher. I also wish to thank my dedicated staff, especially Roger, Vivian, Jenny, Janet, Dominic, Natalya, Kristine, Maggie, and last but not least, Brad, who I can always count on when I need him most.

And of course to the hundreds of high schools, colleges, and universities across the United States who choose Cambridge materials for their campus-based test preparation programs. Your devotion and loyalty have truly launched a TestPrep™ revolution.

Thank you for being a part of Cambridge Educational Services.

David P. Waldherr

David P. Waldherr
President

ACT • PLAN • EXPLORE
TEXTBOOK

Table of Contents

APPLYING TO COLLEGE—WINNING STRATEGIES 3

OVERCOMING TEST ANXIETY—WINNING STRATEGIES 13

ACT • PLAN • EXPLORE ENGLISH
Cambridge Course Concept Outline—English 25
Section One—English Review 27
Section Two—English Problem-Solving 32
Section Three—English Quizzes 43
Section Four—English Testing Points Exercise 55
Section Five—English Error Identification Exercise 57
English Answer Key 60
Strategy Summary Sheet—English 62

ACT • PLAN • EXPLORE MATHEMATICS
Cambridge Course Concept Outline—Mathematics 67
Section One—Mathematics Review 69
Section Two—Mathematics Problem-Solving 94
Section Three—Mathematics Quizzes 105
Section Four—Trigonometry Exercise 114
Section Five—Calculator Exercise 117
Mathematics Answer Key 119
Strategy Summary Sheet—Mathematics 121

ACT • PLAN • EXPLORE READING
Cambridge Course Concept Outline—Reading 125
Section One—Reading Review 127
Section Two—Reading Problem-Solving 132
Section Three—Reading Quizzes 153
Reading Answer Key 159
Strategy Summary Sheet—Reading 160

ACT • PLAN • EXPLORE SCIENCE REASONING
Cambridge Course Concept Outline—Science Reasoning 165
Section One—Science Reasoning Review 167
Section Two—Science Reasoning Problem-Solving 182
Section Three—Science Reasoning Quizzes 198
Science Reasoning Answer Key 205
Strategy Summary Sheet—Science Reasoning 207

APPENDIX A (Red Section): ACT PRACTICE TESTS

PREFACE
Diagnostic Test Score Form (Student Copy) A-3
Homework Progress Reports (Student Copy) A-4
Homework Progress Reports (Instructor Copy) A-5
Diagnostic and Final Test Score Forms (Instructor Copy) A-7

ACT PRACTICE TEST I
English Test A-10
Mathematics Test A-20
Reading Test A-28
Science Reasoning Test A-35
Answer Key A-42
Explanatory Answers A-44
Answer Sheet A-59

ACT PRACTICE TEST II
English Test A-62
Mathematics Test A-73
Reading Test A-81
Science Reasoning Test A-87
Answer Key A-95
Explanatory Answers A-97
Answer Sheet A-111

ACT PRACTICE TEST III
English Test A-114
Mathematics Test A-125
Reading Test A-134
Science Reasoning Test A-141
Answer Key A-149
Explanatory Answers A-151
Answer Sheet A-167

ACT PRACTICE TEST IV
English Test A-170
Mathematics Test A-184
Reading Test A-192
Science Reasoning Test A-201
Answer Key A-210
Explanatory Answers A-212
Answer Sheet A-223

APPENDIX B (Blue Section): ACT • PLAN • EXPLORE BASIC MATH REVIEW

Real Number System B-3
Whole Numbers B-4
  Exercise One—Whole Numbers B-7
Fractions B-10
  Exercise Two—Fractions B-16
Decimals B-19
  Exercise Three—Decimals B-24
Percents B-27
  Exercise Four—Percents B-31
Negative Numbers B-37
  Exercise Five—Negative Numbers B-41
Mean, Median, and Mode B-44
  Exercise Six—Mean, Median, and Mode B-46
Ratios and Proportions B-49
  Exercise Seven—Ratios and Proportions B-53
Exponents and Radicals B-56
  Exercise Eight—Exponents and Radicals B-63

Algebraic Operations B-67
Exercise Nine—Algebraic Operations B-74
Equations and Inequalities B-79
Exercise Ten—Equations and Inequalities B-85
Geometry B-88
Exercise Eleven—Geometry B-96
Coordinate Geometry B-105
Exercise Twelve—Coordinate Geometry B-109
Problem-Solving B-110
Exercise Thirteen—Problem-Solving B-117
Answer Key B-120

ACT • PLAN • EXPLORE MATH EXPRESS B-135

APPENDIX C (Yellow Section): ACT • PLAN • EXPLORE BASIC GRAMMAR REVIEW

Parts of Speech C-3
Exercise One—Parts of Speech C-5
Common Grammatical Errors C-7
Exercise Two—Common Grammatical Errors C-18
Analyzing Sentence Structure C-20
Exercise Three—Analyzing Sentence Structure C-27
Problems of Logical Expression C-32
Exercise Four—Problems of Logical Expression C-38
Idioms and Clarity of Expression C-43
Exercise Five—Idioms and Clarity of Expression C-52
Punctuation C-56
Exercise Six—Idioms and Clarity of Expression C-63
Explanatory Answers C-64

CAMBRIDGE
EDUCATIONAL SERVICES, INC.®

AMERICA'S #1 CAMPUS-BASED TESTPREP

Introduction to the

CAMBRIDGE ACT • PLAN • EXPLORE REVIEW COURSE

The Cambridge ACT • PLAN • EXPLORE Review Course is designed to provide you with complete preparation for the ACT (American College Testing) Assessment, PLAN, and EXPLORE tests. The course includes classroom lessons, practice tests, skill reviews and exercises, and actual test simulation. Each of these program components has been carefully designed to maximize the effectiveness of the Cambridge ACT • PLAN • EXPLORE Review Program.

- **COLLEGE APPLICATION PREPARATION:** The first chapter of this textbook is "Applying to College—Winning Strategies." This chapter was written with the goal of helping you get into the college of your choice. Information given includes: how the admissions process works, where to apply, the top 25 national universities and colleges, advice on creating your application, and how to maximize effectiveness of letters of recommendation.

- **OVERCOMING TEST ANXIETY:** This textbook's second chapter is "Overcoming Test Anxiety—Winning Strategies." This chapter was written with the goal of helping you manage test anxiety and the damaging effects it can have on test scores due to inducing negative stress reactions. Included is an introduction to test anxiety and its causes, exercises for physical and mental relaxation, minimizing the influence of negative test associations and auto-suggestions, and a host of suggestions for maximizing your performance on test day.

- **CLASSROOM LESSONS:** The classroom lessons are a combination of review of skills and tested concepts, easy-to-difficult problem-solving, and timed quizzes. The classroom lessons provide you with a complete substantive review of the ACT • PLAN • EXPLORE testing materials, detailed explanations of the in-class problems in this textbook, powerful test-taking strategies, and testprep shortcuts. All review of substantive concepts and skills, strategies, tips, and explanatory answers are given in class. You must attend each class!

- **PRACTICE TESTS:** Appendix A has four full-length simulated ACT practice tests. After each lesson, problems from these tests are assigned as homework to be done both timed and untimed. Your progress in the course will be tracked using the Diagnostic and Final Test Score Forms and Homework Progress Reports (Appendix A preface). It is important for you to complete your homework assignments to reach your highest test score possible. Practice and even more practice using key strategies and problem-solving skills is the key to success on the ACT!

- **MATH SKILLS REVIEW:** Appendix B is the Basic Math Review, a complete and in-depth self-tutorial of the basic math concepts essential for studying the quantitative ACT materials. Following the Basic Math Review is the Basic Math Express, a brief summary of important math concepts and formulas to prepare for the ACT mathematics.

- **GRAMMAR REVIEW:** Appendix C is the Basic Grammar Review, a complete and in-depth self-tutorial of the basic grammar concepts essential for successful study of the ACT English materials.

- **ACTUAL TEST SIMULATION:** In long-version classroom programs, practice tests are administered in class, using official past-administered ACT tests. These timed-test simulations are administered at the beginning (Diagnostic Test) and end of the course (Final Test). In intensive course programs, you will take your Diagnostic and Final Tests at home. Extended course schedules include a Post-Test Review. Some courses may use one or more of the ACT Practice Tests (Appendix A) for in-class test simulation.

Once enrolled in the Cambridge ACT • PLAN • EXPLORE Review Course, the textbook and exams are yours to keep. As directed, you'll find it helpful to tear out answer keys and answer sheets, as well as the Diagnostic and Final Test Score Forms and Homework Progress Reports. Be sure to keep class notes or write in your textbook, as all problem explanations and course strategies are given in class! It is vital to your success in the Cambridge ACT • PLAN • EXPLORE Review Course that you attend each class and testing session.

CAMBRIDGE
EDUCATIONAL SERVICES, INC.®

APPLYING TO COLLEGE
–Winning Strategies–

APPLYING TO COLLEGE
–Winning Strategies–

Helping you get into the college of your choice is the goal of this six-part section. We have advised tens of thousands of students, interviewed college admissions officers across the country, and attended annual advisors' conferences. Thus, the descriptions, conclusions, and suggestions contained herein have been distilled from a variety of sources.

This section is intended for a range of readers—for those who are already actively working on their applications as well as for those who are only thinking of applying to college. Therefore, some of the points we make are very general and others are very specific. Some information may already be familiar, while other points and tips may surprise you. No matter what your status, you will find the following six-part section immediately useful for applying to college and getting into the college of your choice.

1. INTRODUCTION

In order to create the most effective application you can, you must understand and appreciate the function of the admissions process as a social and economic process. Many prospective applicants view the filing of a college application only from their own individual perspective and consider themselves as outsiders or spectators who are merely the beneficiaries of or perhaps the victims of a bureaucratic juggernaut. From those who share this point of view, we offer the following comments:

> *Colleges only care about your ACT score.*
> *You can't get into a really good school unless you know someone.*
> *They really don't read your personal statement.*

Such comments reflect an attitude that is based on a misreading of the admissions process as a social and economic process. Let us examine this process from two perspectives: yours and that of a college.

First, from your perspective, you must keep in mind that the college admissions process is much more than merely answering a few questions about your educational background and employment history. Rather, the application process is just the first step on a career path that will last for most of the rest of your life. Decisions you make at this stage may have implications for your life 30 or 40 years from now. An easy way of realizing this is to imagine the different courses your life might follow if you get into college and if you don't, or to compare your career prospects if you get accepted by your first choice school or if you do not.

Now, this is not to say that not getting into a certain school spells disaster. Obviously, becoming a psychologist, engineer, biochemist, computer scientist, economist, chemist, teacher, historian, musician, physicist, geologist, political scientist or sociologist is not for everyone. Rather, we are simply trying to stress the importance of the admissions process to you as an individual. Indeed, to appreciate the effect that the admissions process will have on you, you don't have to look far into the future. Your decisions at this point will determine where you are likely to live for the next four years.

Additionally, you must appreciate the financial commitment that you are making. In the first instance, the cost of the application process alone could easily exceed $200. The fees that you pay to take the ACT Assessment for score reports could be as much as $100. Furthermore, the application fees charged by schools run between $25 and $40. Assuming that you apply to ten schools, you could easily spend $450 on application fees. In addition, you will probably spend at least $100 on administrative details such as document preparation, copying, postage, and long distance telephone calls. Add another $300 or so for test preparation for the ACT, and you have already committed $1,000 or more.

On top of application expenses, most schools require that you respond to an acceptance offer by a certain deadline with a non-refundable deposit. You may find yourself in the uncomfortable position of paying such a deposit to ensure that you have a college seat even though you have not yet heard from some other schools. But these sums pale in comparison to the cost of tuition—as much as $35,000. And when the expense of room and board for four years is taken into account, the entire expense to obtain your college degree could exceed $100,000.

Don't let those numbers frighten you. We are not trying to dissuade you from pursuing a college degree. We are trying to dramatize a point: the decision to apply to college has significant social and economic implications for you as an individual.

On the other side of the coin, from the perspective of the college, there are also social and economic implications. A college, like any educational institution, is a corporate individual, and its admissions decisions reflect social and economic policies adopted by the corporation. Consider first some of the economic implications for a college to accept or reject an applicant.

The college has to be run as any other business entity. It has employees; it owns or rents property; it operates a library; it buys furniture and office equipment; it pays utility bills; and so on. A large part of those expenses are paid using student tuition. A college, therefore, is absolutely dependent on a steady flow of tuition income. So admissions decisions must be made in the context of budgetary constraints. A college simply cannot afford to have large numbers of students dropping out of school. So one concern of a college admissions officer is to ensure that those applicants who are accepted are committed to completing the course of study. Additionally—though this may not be an explicit concern—colleges rely heavily on alumni donations. So it would not be surprising to learn that an applicant who shows considerable professional promise would be considered favorably. And a school that graduates successful BAs or BSs gets a reputation for being a good school and such a reputation in turn tends to attract highly qualified applicants.

We do not mean to give you the impression that an admission decision is made solely on economic considerations. That is far from the truth. Colleges also have a sense of the social responsibility they bear as educators of BAs or BSs—two of the most influential groups of people in our society. They meet this responsibility in some fairly obvious ways such as actively seeking applications from groups who are underrepresented in the professional community and by establishing programs to train professionals for positions of special need.

The admissions process, then, is the interface between these two perspectives. The process is designed to match individuals and institutions that can mutually satisfy each other's needs. This matching function, however, is somewhat skewed. For decades there have been more people interested in pursuing professional careers than there are seats available at accredited colleges. In recent times, there have been over two applicants for each available seat. As a consequence, applicants are competing for college entrance.

Given the mismatch between the number of available slots and the number of applicants, the application process is turned into a competition. You will have to compete against others for a college seat (or at least for a spot at the college of your choice). To do this, you must make yourself attractive to a college. You must persuade the admission committee that you will help them satisfy their economic and social needs. And that thought must guide you as you create your application.

Using the information in this section, you will create an application that will position you for acceptance. That is, an application that will give a college an affirmative reason for accepting you. In addition to this section, you may also want to consider some other sources. For general information about the accredited colleges in this country, you should buy the *College Handbook*. The book is published by College Entrance Examination Board and contains summaries of important aspects of the approximately 3,200 two and four-year colleges. For each school in which you have even a passing interest, request that school's information bulletin. Read those bulletins carefully. They provide listings of faculty members and their qualifications, descriptions of any special programs, information about student activities and campus life, catalogues of financial aid, and much more.

2. HOW THE ADMISSIONS PROCESS WORKS

If we read the title to this section literally, then anything we say about it must be false. Why? This is because there is no "the" admissions process. Rather, each college has its own individual admissions process, and its process differs in ways more or less important from that of every other college in the country.

On the other hand, we cannot talk about the details of the admissions process at each of the approximately 3,200 U.S. Colleges and Universities offering hundreds of degree program areas. Indeed, almost all schools regard the mechanics of the decision-making process as a highly sensitive matter and don't share the details of that process with outsiders. In any event, you cannot exercise any control over the way a college makes its decision. As you will see, you don't need "inside" information to create an effective application.

As noted above, the "admissions process" varies from school to school. Faculty committees may make the decisions by majority vote or unanimous agreement and may be required before an acceptance is extended to an applicant. A single professional admissions officer or officers who may not themselves be B.A.s, B.S.s, or Ph.D.s or a Dean of Admissions who has a graduate degree but is not a faculty member may make the decision. A committee of members drawn from both administration and faculty may make the decisions. Finally, students themselves may have some input into admissions decisions.

We won't dwell on these different possibilities for two reasons. One, they are outside of your control. Two, regardless of the formal structure of the admissions process, the process is designed to satisfy the institution's social and economic goals—as we noted above.

Despite the variety of formal structures, one generalization is possible:

> *Every college relies to some extent on the applicant's Grade Point Average (GPA) and ACT score, but there are few (if any) colleges that rely only on these quantitative factors.*

This statement contains two ideas. Let us look at each.

First, most colleges use the GPA and the ACT score. Again, the exact use of these numbers varies from school to school, but many use a formula that combines the two together into an index. The formula is designed to weight the two numbers approximately equally to give admissions officers some idea of how the applicant stacks up against other applicants.

Second, at the opposite extreme are schools that claim to minimize the importance of the ACT and the GPA. They claim that the ACT is the very last factor that is looked at. Such schools have a very flexible admissions process.

Most schools fall somewhere in between these extremes. Many schools use the ACT and the GPA as a screening device to determine how much attention will be given to an application. Applications with very low test scores and grades will receive little attention. The schools reason that unless there is something obvious and compelling in the application to offset the low numbers, then the applicant should be rejected. Applications with very high test scores and grades will also receive little attention. The reasoning is that unless there is something obvious and compelling in the application to reject it, it should be accepted. On this theory, the applications with test scores and grades in the middle receive the greatest attention. These are applications from candidates who are at least competitive for the school but who do not command an automatic acceptance. It is in this pool that competition is the most severe.

Here is a table that illustrates what happens at most colleges:

	ACT SCORE (Percentile)			
GPA	*61–70%*	*71–80%*	*81–90%*	*90–100%*
3.75+	$\frac{2}{19}$	$\frac{49}{101}$	$\frac{102}{116}$	$\frac{72}{79}$
3.74–3.50	$\frac{6}{112}$	$\frac{75}{275}$	$\frac{301}{361}$	$\frac{120}{129}$
3.50–0	$\frac{10}{160}$	$\frac{90}{601}$	$\frac{375}{666}$	$\frac{201}{250}$

The fractions represent the total number of accepted applicants divided by the total number of applicants.

The categories in the table show what this college did with applications with certain ACT scores (shown in percentile terms) and grade point averages. In the category in the upper right hand corner are candidates with scores above the 90th percentile and GPAs above 3.75. The table shows that 72 of the 79 were accepted and seven rejected.

What is obvious from the table is that some candidates with higher indices were rejected in favor of candidates with lower numbers. For example, of those candidates with scores between the 81st and 90th percentiles, 74 more candidates were accepted with a GPA below 3.49 than the higher GPA between 3.5 and 3.74.

Why would a college reject an applicant with higher numbers for one with lower numbers? The answer lies in our analysis of the admissions process in the introduction above. Apparently, there were factors in the applications of those who were accepted that suggested to the admission committee that those applicants would better meet the social and economic goals of the institution. Those factors are the unquantifiable ones such as motivation, commitment, leadership, experience, and so on.

As you prepare your applications, you are, of course, saddled with your GPA and your ACT score. There is nothing you can do to change those factors. (Below we take up the question of retaking the ACT.) This means that the only real control you will have over your application will be those unquantifiable factors. And we will show you how to maximize their impact.

There is one final point that needs to be made about the mechanics of the application process: rolling admissions. Rolling admissions is a device used by many colleges that regulates the release of acceptances. A typical college application season opens in October and closes in May or perhaps June. Applications will be received throughout the application season, and decisions are made on an ongoing basis.

Rather than saving all applications until the deadline for applications is past and then making decisions, rolling admissions allows colleges to notify applicants on an ongoing basis. This is accomplished by targeting an entering class. Based on its admissions history, a college will estimate what it thinks will be the range of ACT scores and the range of GPAs of the students it will accept in the upcoming year. Then, as it receives applications (say, month by month), it will act on them. Students with very strong applications compared with the target group will receive acceptances; students with weak ones receive rejections. Applications in the middle will be carried over—no notification or notification that the application is still pending.

The rolling admissions process has advantages for both the college and the applicant. From the applicant's point of view, the earlier the notification of the disposition of an application, the better. That is, you know whether you were accepted or rejected and can go on from there. From the college's viewpoint, the entering class, and therefore the stability of the budget, begin to take shape as early as possible.

The rolling admissions process is also a tool you can use to your advantage: apply early. Obviously, schools have greater flexibility earlier in the admission season than later. There are more seats available earlier in the year.

We do not mean to imply that if you apply late in the season you will be rejected. In fact, it is impossible to quantify exactly the advantage that applications received earlier rather than later enjoy. Still, if you want to maximize your chances of acceptance, apply early!

3. WHERE TO APPLY

Given the economic commitment that you will be making, one of the obvious questions on your mind will be "Where should I apply?" Let us give two answers to this question. First, you should apply to a group of schools such that, given your economic resources, you maximize your chances of gaining admission to the colleges of your choice.

To apply to a college, you must remit a non-refundable application fee. This means that you are, to speak crudely, gambling with your money. You pay the fee, but you don't know in advance whether you will win or lose. So hedge your bets. In a gambling situation, a bettor will have several choices. Some will be long shots, others will be almost sure things, and others will lie somewhere in between. The long shots will pay handsome dividends and the sure things a reasonable return. The others will fall in between.

Let's assume that you have the resources to apply to ten schools and that you have an above average GPA and ACT score. Depending on the exact numbers, you may very well have a chance at one of the top colleges. But those are your long shot schools. You are almost a sure thing at many schools. And there is a long list of schools in the middle where your application will almost surely receive serious consideration but is not guaranteed for acceptance.

Given these considerations, you should select two or perhaps three "long shot" schools. As the term "long shot" implies, the odds of your being accepted at these schools are not very good, but the potential payoff justifies the gamble. On the other hand, you should also select one or two "sure thing" schools. To do this, you may have to apply to a school in your geographical area that doesn't enjoy a particularly good reputation or to a school that is located in another part of the country. The rest of your applications should go to your "good bet" schools—schools for which the chances for acceptance are 40% to 75%.

This strategy of "stacking" your applications will maximize your chances of acceptance at a school you want while minimizing the chance that you won't get into any school. Of course, the way the strategy gets implemented will vary from person to person. For people who are lucky enough to have a high GPA and a top ACT score, the middle and bottom tier schools collapse into a single tier. And at the other extreme, those who are unlucky enough to have a GPA and ACT score that are below what most schools accept will have to work with the second and third tiers.

As you prepare to implement the strategy, make a realistic assessment of your chances. Candidates unfortunately tend to overestimate the importance of what they believe to be their own interesting or unique factors. For example, we often hear candidates make statements such as "Well sure my GPA is a little low, but I had to work part-time while I was in school" and "I know my ACT score is not that good, but I was a member of the high school Student Council." These are valid points and are usually taken into consideration by admissions officers. But the question is how much weight they will be given for they (or some similar point) are true of most of the people who are applying to college. For example, if your are thinking of applying to a program requiring an average GPA of 3.8 and average ACT score of 90 percentile, then there had better be something really special in your background—such as an Olympic medal.

A question related to the "Where should I apply?" question is "What are the top undergraduate schools in the country?" Since there is no single criterion for "best school" that would be accepted by everyone, it is arguable that this question simply cannot be given a meaningful answer. But even though no unequivocal answer can be given, it is possible to get an approximate answer. The "U.S. News & World Report" Year 2000 survey of college school deans lists the following top twenty-five national universities and top-twenty-five national colleges. Entries on the list may change each year, as may the rankings.

TOP 25 NATIONAL UNIVERSITIES

1. California Institute of Technology
2. Harvard University (MA)
3. Massachusetts Inst. of Technology
4. Princeton University (NJ)
5. Yale University (CT)
6. Stanford University (CA)
7. Duke University (NC)
7. John Hopkins University (MD)
7. University of Pennsylvania
10. Columbia University (NY)
11. Cornell University (NY)
11. Dartmouth College (NH)
13. University of Chicago
14. Brown University (RI)
14. Northwestern University (IL)
14. Rice University (TX)
17. Washington University (MO)
18. Emory University (GA)
19. University of Notre Dame (IN)
20. Univ. of California—Berkeley
20. Vanderbilt University (TN)
22. University of Virginia
23. Carnegie Mellon Univ. (PA)
23. Georgetown University (DC)
25. U. of California—Los Angeles
25. U. of Michigan—Ann Arbor

TOP 25 NATIONAL LIBERAL ARTS COLLEGES

1. Swarthmore College (PA)
2. Amherst College (MA)
3. Williams College (MA)
4. Wellesley College (MA)
5. Haverford College (PA)
5. Middlebury College (CT)
7. Pomona College (CA)
8. Carleton College (MN)
9. Bowdoin College (ME)
10. Wesleyan University (CT)
11. Davidson College (NC)
11. Grinnell College (IA)
13. Smith College (MA)
14. Claremont McKenna College (CA)
15. Washington and Lee Univ. (VA)
16. Mount Holyoke College (MA)
17. Vassar College (NY)
18. Bryn Mawr College (PA)
18. Colby College (ME)
18. Colgate University (NY)
18. Hamilton College (NY)
22. Trinity College (CT)
23. Bates College (ME)
24. Macalester College (MN)
25. Barnard College (NY)
25. Colorado College
24. Connecticut College
25. Oberlin College (OH)
25. University of the South (TN)

4. CREATING YOUR APPLICATION

The title of this section echoes our analysis of the admissions process given above. To maximize your chances of success, you must create an application that satisfies the needs of the school to which you are applying. This does not mean that you create an application out of whole cloth, but it does mean that you organize and present your experiences in a way that depicts you in the most favorable light.

Most of the questions you will be asked need only short answers, for example, "Did you work while you were in school," "What clubs did you join," and "What honors or awards did you receive?" You don't have much room to maneuver here. But you should try to communicate as much information as possible in your short answers. Compare the following pairs of descriptions:

Member of Orchestra
Second Violinist of the Orchestra

Played Intra-Mural Volleyball
Co-captain of the Volleyball Team

Member of the AD's CSL
One of three members on the Associate Dean's Committee on Student Life

Worked at Billy's Burger Barn
Assistant Manager at Billy's Burger Barn (25 hours/week)

In addition to the short answer questions, most applications invite you to make a personal statement. Some applications ask for very little, for example, "In a paragraph explain to us why you want to go to college." Other applications are open-ended: "On a separate sheet of paper, tell us anything else you think we ought to know about you." The point of the question is to give you the opportunity to give the admissions committee any information that might not be available from the test scores, GPA, and short-answer questions.

For two reasons, you should consider the personal statement to be the most important part of your application. First, the personal statement should be your argument to the admissions committee for your acceptance. It should give the reasons to accept you. Second, the personal statement is the one aspect of the application over which you can exercise any real control. Your GPA is already settled. Your work experience was accumulated over years; your ACT has been scored. Those are aspects of the application that cannot be easily manipulated. The personal statement, however, is under your control.

What should go into a personal statement? You should include arguments that interpret your academic, employment, and personal history in such a way to indicate that you have the ability to complete college and that you are committed to studying and later to pursuing a career in your chosen area of study. Importantly, the personal statement must not be a simple restatement of facts already in the application. Imagine, for example, a personal statement that reads as follows:

> *I went to high school where I got a 3.5 GPA. I was a member of the Associate Dean's Committee on Student life, and I worked as the assistant manager on the night shift at Billy's Burger Barn. Then I took the ACT and got a 24. I know I will make a really good BA candidate and will enjoy my job.*

This is not very interesting. Furthermore, all of that information is already included in your answers to the standard questions on the application. There is no point in simply repeating it.

Instead, you *interpret* the facts of your life to make them *reasons* for accepting you. Let's start with the GPA. Try to bring out facts that suggest that the GPA is really better than it looks. Did you have one particularly bad semester during which you took Physics, Calculus, and Latin that pulled your average down? Was there a death in the family or some other difficult time that interfered with your studies? How many hours did you work in an average week? What extracurricular or family commitments took time away from your studies? Did you follow an unusual course of study such as an honors program? Was your major a particularly challenging one? Did you participate in any unusual courses such as field research?

These are the points that the admissions committee wants to hear. For example:

> *The committee will see that my final GPA is 3.5. I should point out that the average would have been higher had I not had to work 20 hours each week to save for my college education. Additionally, my grades in the first semester of my junior year were disappointing because my grandmother, who lived with my family and with whom I was very close, died. Finally, in order to fulfill the requirements for the honors program, I wrote a 20 page honors thesis on the Dutch fishing industry of the*

> *18th century. I have included with this application a copy of the introduction to this paper.*

You should take the same approach to your work experience. For example:

> *During my junior and senior years in high school, I worked an average of 20 hours per week at Billy's Burger Barn as the manager on the night shift. I would report to work at midnight and get off at four a.m. As night manager, I supervised eight other employees and was responsible for making emergency repairs on kitchen equipment. For example, once I was able to keep the deep fryer in operation by using a length of telephone cable to repair a faulty thermostat. The night manager was also responsible for maintaining order. It's no easy job to convince intoxicated students who become too rowdy to leave without calling the police. And we were robbed at gunpoint not once but twice.*

Of course, if you have considerable work experience, e.g., if you graduated from high school several years ago, you still want to go into that experience in more detail than if you had only student work experience.

Can you say anything about the ACT? Probably not much—the ACT score is fairly simple and not usually open to interpretation. But there are some exceptions. One such exception is a history of poor scores on standardized exams. Consider the following two examples:

> *I believe that my ACT score of 24 understates my real ability for I have never had much success on aptitude tests. Yet, I finished high school with a 3.6 GPA.*

> *The committee will see that I have two ACT scores, 18 and 24. During the first test, I had the flu and a fever and simply could not concentrate.*

These are the two most common excuses for a disappointing ACT score.

Finally, you must also persuade the admissions committee that you are serious about obtaining your college degree. You must be able to show the committee something in your background that explains why you want to go to college. Also, it will help your case if you can suggest what you might do with a college degree. For example:

> *As a prospective science major, I interned with the Student Environmental Association. Working with private company executives, who had themselves satisfied E.P.A. admission standards, we convinced the University to stop polluting the Ten-Mile Run Creek. From this experience, I learned how business helps to protect our environment. I plan to make environmental resources my area of study and I hope to work for the government or a private agency to protect the environment through cooperative efforts with private industry.*

A word of warning is in order here. Your career objectives have to be believable. It won't do to write: "I plan to solve the environmental problems of American industry." That's much too abstract. Nor are college admissions officers interested in a general discourse on the advantages of democracy or the hardship of poverty. If you write: "I want to eliminate damage to the planet; and to help private industry environmentally help themselves," then there had better be something in your experience that makes this believable.

Finally, with regard to motivation, don't imagine that there is a preferred political position that you should adopt. College admissions officers span the political spectrum. To be sure, some are political liberals but there are also conservatives. You don't have to make up a "tear-jerker" to get accepted.

Thus far we have discussed the issues of ability and motivation. You may also wish to include in your personal statement information that shows that you have something that will help the school create a diverse student body. This additional information can be something dramatic:

> *One morning, a patron choked on a burger and lost consciousness. I used the Heimlich maneuver to dislodge the food and performed CPR until a team of paramedics arrived. The patron recovered fully in large part, according to her doctors, because of my first aid.*

Or the information may not be dramatic:

> *My parents are Armenian immigrants, so I am fluent in Armenian as well as English. I would enjoy meeting others who share an interest in the politics, legal developments, and culture of that part of the world.*

But don't overestimate the value of this kind of information. It is, so to speak, the icing on the cake. It makes you a more interesting individual and might tip the scale in your favor when all other things are equal. It will not, however, get you an acceptance at a school for which you are not otherwise competitive in terms of ACT and GPA.

Now we turn our attention to matters of style. When you marshal your arguments for acceptance, you need to present them in an organized fashion. There is no single preferred format, but you might start with the following outline:

I. I have the ability
  A. My high school studies are good
    1. I had one bad semester
    2. I was in the accelerated program
    3. I wrote a thesis
  B. My work experience is good
    1. I was promoted to shift leader at my job
    2. I worked while in high school
II. I want to earn my college degree
  A. I worked with PhDs on the pollution problem during my internship
  B. I would become a specialist in environmental chemistry
III. There is something interesting about me

The prose you use should be your own natural style of writing. Don't try something cute. Admissions officers detest essays that try to look like manuscripts and refer to the footnoted "documentary evidence." You should create your outline, using all the arguments you can think of. Then you must begin to edit. For most people, the final document should not be more than a page to a page and a half—typed of course! During the editing process, you will strive for an economy of language, so that you can convey as much information as possible. Additionally, you will be forced to make considered judgments about the relative importance of various points. You will be forced to delete those ideas that aren't really that compelling. To obtain a really good personal statement, it may be necessary to reduce five or six pages to a single page, and the process may require more than 20 drafts.

5. LETTERS OF RECOMMENDATION

Perhaps the best advice that we can give you about so-called letters of recommendation is to think of them as evaluations rather than recommendations. Indeed, many admissions officers refer to letter-writers as evaluators. These letters can be very important factors in an application, so who should write them?

First of all, some schools require a letter from the dean of students (or some similar functionary) at your high school. This is not optional on your part. Even if you never met the dean, you have to get this letter. But colleges don't really expect the dean to have much to say. The requirement is in essence an inquiry to the school about your behavior. It is intended to evoke any information about disciplinary problems that might not otherwise surface. So the best letter from a dean, and the one that most people get, is just a statement to the effect that there is nothing to say about you. In addition to the dean's letter, most schools require or at least permit you to submit two or three letters of evaluation from other sources. Who should write these? First, let us dispose of a common misunderstanding. A letter of evaluation does not have to come from a famous person. How effective is the following letter:

Francis Scott
Chairperson of the Board

To the Admissions Committee:

I am recommending Susan Roberts for college. Her mother is a member of our board of directors. Susan's mother earned her doctorate at the University of Chicago and she regularly makes significant contributions to our corporate meetings. Susan, following in her mother's footsteps, will make a fine college candidate.

Sincerely,
Francis Scott

The letterhead holds out great promise, but then the letter itself is worthless. It is obvious that the letter-writer doesn't really have any basis for her conclusion that the candidate will make a good college candidate.

The best letters of evaluation will come from people who know you very well, *e.g.*, a teacher with whom you took several courses, your intern supervisor, or an associate with whom you have worked closely. A good evaluation will incorporate the personal knowledge into the letter and will make references to specific events and activities. For example:

Mary P. Weiss
White, Waste, and Blanche

To the Admissions Committee:

White, Waste, and Blanche is a consulting firm that advises corporations on environmental concerns. Susan Roberts has worked for us as an intern for the past two summers. Her work is outstanding, and she is an intelligent and genial person.

Last summer, as my assistant, Susan wrote a 5-page report that outlined a way of altering a client's exhaust stack to reduce sulfur emissions. The report was organized so that it was easy to follow and written in a style that was clear and easy to understand. Additionally, Susan assisted with a live presentation during a meeting with the client's board of directors and engineers. She was confident and handled some very difficult questions in an easy manner.

Finally, Susan made an important contribution to our company softball team. The team finished in last place, but Susan played in every game. Her batting average wasn't anything to brag about, but her enthusiasm more than made up for it.

Sincerely,
Mary Weiss

To get a letter such as this, you will have to ask someone who knows you well.

6. TAKING THE ACT

We have already emphasized the important role that the ACT plays in the admissions process. It is only common sense, then, that you do everything you can to maximize your score. You should not take the ACT until you are certain you are ready to do your best. Colleges receive all of your ACT test scores—not just your best one, and many colleges average multiple scores. You're already heading in the right direction by taking the Cambridge ACT Review Course—we will provide you with everything you need to succeed on the ACT. The rest is up to you! Good luck!

CAMBRIDGE

EDUCATIONAL SERVICES, INC.®

OVERCOMING TEST ANXIETY

–Winning Strategies–

OVERCOMING TEST ANXIETY
–Winning Strategies–

Test anxiety comes in various forms, from the common occurrences of butterflies in the stomach, mild sweating, or nervous laughter, to the more extremes of overwhelming fear, anxiety attacks, and unmanageable mental worry. While some mild anxiety before or during testing is normal for everyone, more intense worry, fear, or tension distracts students like you from successfully navigating standardized tests. Some experts who study human performance suggest that light stress may help focus a person's concentration. However, stress that reaches beyond minimum levels, and remains for a long period of time, blocks the ability to quickly recall facts, remember strategies, think through complex problems, and creatively tackle difficult questions. Taking tests in a relaxed and calm state that promotes clear and logical thinking is essential. The advice that follows provides practical hints and strategies for those who experience milder forms of test anxiety. Using these steps should help alleviate debilitating test anxiety.

1. PLAN...HAVE A STUDY PLAN AND STICK TO IT

Putting off important test review assignments until the last minute naturally causes high stress in anyone seriously anticipating test day. Even the brightest student experiences nervousness when he or she walks into a test totally unprepared or under prepared. Therefore, stress reduction begins weeks or even months before sitting down to take the test. By beginning to review materials early, you will reduce anxiety, because prepared test-takers are more relaxed, confident, and composed test-takers.

Warning! There is almost no chance of successfully cramming for a test like the ACT, SAT, GRE, GMAT or LSAT. Knowing that you have waited until the day or week before the test to begin studying will elevate your anxiety level. Cramming may have worked for you in the past for quizzes or less comprehensive tests, but last minute intensive learning will not work to prepare you for long, comprehensive, standardized tests. Trying to cram will leave you feeling frustrated, unprepared, and nervous about the pending test day.

The key is to plan ahead to combat test anxiety caused by a lack of preparation. Do not procrastinate; have a study plan, start early, and stick to it. Develop a study plan, which is simply a written set of daily goals that will help you track the content and the sequence of your test review. In a study plan, you tell yourself what, when, where, and how much you will study.

Plan your work. Work your plan. Here are some tips on producing your own study plan.

➢ ***Record a plan on paper.***

Write out a study plan. A written plan is more real, concrete, and firm than one that simply rattles around in your head. Take a piece of paper and pen and write out a plan for reviewing all the essential materials necessary for succeeding on the test. Record important items and dates on your calendar. Post the plan in a place where you will see it often. When you accomplish a goal from your plan, (for example, taking a timed practice exam or reviewing a certain number of problems) check it off. This will give you a sense of accomplishment.

➢ ***Break the test into pieces.***

Segment the test into sections and study these smaller sections. Do not try to learn every test strategy at once or review the whole test in one day. Do not try to learn all the quantitative sections or the entire verbal portion in one sitting. The subject matter covered is far too broad to learn in a few short minutes. Attack the review by studying small pieces of the test sections. Also, vary the sections you study in order to ward off boredom. On one day, study a quantitative section, on the next, study a verbal section. In addition, remember to review sections you have already studied. This will keep all the sections fresh in your mind for test day. Remember that no two learners are identical. Some can learn huge chunks of information at once, while others need to take smaller bites over time. Find the amount of material you can adequately cover in one day, and then, each day, attack that amount of material.

➢ ***Do some studying or preparation every day.***

Yes—every single day—study something. Once you get the "study snowball" rolling, the momentum will help you overcome the desire to quit. Be consistent. It is far better to study sixty minutes per day for seven straight days, than to study seven straight hours in one day, only once per week.

➢ ***Study at the same time and place.***

Find somewhere quiet where there are few distractions. Provide yourself a place that has good lighting and is comfortable. Since most tests are given either at desks, tables, or at computer terminals, avoid studying in bed or in a lounge chair. Simulate the test conditions by studying at a desk or table. Turn off the TV and music. Unplug the phone. Power down the computer (unless of course you are using it as a study tool). Give yourself quality, uninterrupted time to study. Find a consistent time and lock it into you schedule. Don't let yourself off the hook. Be consistent, and study each day at the same time and place.

➢ ***Set goals and reward yourself.***

Set a weekly goal for the amount of time you will study, and the amount of material you will review. When you meet these weekly goals, reward yourself. Brag about your study accomplishments to your family and friends. Offer yourself special incentives that will motivate you to reach your next goal.

➢ ***Find a study partner, or someone to hold you accountable for your progress.***

There really is strength in numbers. Find at least one person to help you stay on course with your goals. Have this person ask you every few days whether or not you are sticking to your plan. Consider finding a "study buddy." Push each other to set and reach high test-preparation goals.

Early and consistent test preparation means you will walk confidently and calmly into the testing center on test day, knowing that you have done your very best to prepare for the test.

2. POSITIVE...REPLACE ANXIETY BY THINKING POSITIVE, BEING POSITIVE

Positive thinking helps overcome test anxiety. For years, psychologists have studied how attitudes affect and alter achievement. These studies suggest that students with positive attitudes consistently score higher than students with negative attitudes. Thus, to overcome test anxiety, start today to immerse yourself in positive thinking.

Here are some practical ways to start thinking positively.

➢ ***Talk Positively to Yourself***

Success comes in a "can," not a "cannot." Learn to think positively by mentally replacing "cannots" with "cans." Negative statements such as, "I will never pass this test," "I know I can't get this," or "I'm not smart enough to get a good score," are counterproductive, and they hinder the study and test taking process. To cancel negative thoughts, take note of them when you first have them, and then take steps to eliminate them! Use the positive mental attitude replacement process. As soon as you recognize a negative thought, replace it immediately with a positive thought. It's easy. In your mind, whenever you hear phrases such as "I can't do this," or "I'm not smart enough," say to yourself, "I can do this," "I will understand this," or "I am smart enough." Furthermore, as you walk into the classroom on the day of the test, repeatedly say to yourself: "I have studied," I will do my best," and "I will succeed."

➢ ***Think Positively about Yourself***

Think and be positive with the help of visualization. Try this. While in a relaxed mood, close your eyes and envision a picture of yourself walking into the test room perfectly calm and confident. See yourself having no problems with the test. Imagine yourself taking each section of the test with great calmness. See yourself answering the questions quickly and correctly. Watch yourself exiting the test area with confidence because you performed extremely well. By visualizing, you can mentally and emotionally practice taking the test in a confident and calm manner. Practice visualization at any time. Many students find that it works well close to bedtime. Coaches encourage peak performing athletes to use daily visualization exercises to increase their abilities in running, jumping, shooting, etc. Every single day, from now to the test day, practice visualization and picture yourself taking the test quickly, easily, confidently and calmly. Visualization can help you overcome test anxiety. Get the picture?

➢ ***Act Positively to Yourself***

On the day of the test, act positively. Even if you don't "feel" completely confident, stride into the testing classroom with your head held high and with a bounce in your step. Show that you are at ease and in complete control of the situation. Present yourself to everyone as someone who knows that he or she will be successful. Acting confidently will actually help you feel confident.

Practice these strategies to instill within yourself a positive mental attitude. Positive thinking means believing in yourself. Believe that somehow, sometime, somewhere, you can achieve your highest goal. Know that you can do it. Dare to try.

3. POWER UP PHYSICALLY...RELEASE STRESS WITH PHYSICAL EXERCISE

Physical exercise is an excellent way to reduce anxiety levels and prepare yourself to cope with the effects of stress. Start a regular program of healthy exercise that includes stretching and cardio-vascular exercises. Check with a doctor or a health professional about the best program for you.

4. PUT AWAY NEGATIVE THOUGHTS...THEY FUEL TEST ANXIETY

Since you will be practicing positive thinking, you should also learn to recognize and eliminate distorted or twisted thinking. Avoid thinking the following distorted things about yourself.

I must always be perfect. The reality surrounding perfection is that everyone makes mistakes. In testing situations, perfectionists mentally fuss and fume about a single mistake, instead of celebrating all the correct answers. Dwelling on mistakes wastes time and creates more tension. Push past mistakes behind you and move forward to the next set of questions. Remember, we all reserve the right to get smarter and to learn and grow.

I failed the last *times, so I'll fail this time.* Past failure does not lead to future failure. People do get better the more they practice. Because you did poorly on something in the past does not simply guarantee poor achievement this time. Use this test as an opportunity for a fresh start. Forget yesterday's failures and imagine that today is a brand new beginning, because it is.

People won't like me if I do poorly. It is preferable to have good relations with people, to have them approve of you, even to love you—but it is not necessary. You will not be unhappy unless you make yourself unhappy. Rely on self-approval, not other's approval. Do your best, because you want to, and you can, not because you want to please someone else.

I have been anxious when taking tests before, therefore, I'll always be anxious. You can learn to control your anxiety. This twisted thought implies that you have no control over your behavior, but you do. You can change. It will take time and hard work to change twisted thinking, but you can do it.

5. PRACTICE BEING CALM...LEARN TO MENTALLY AND PHYSICALLY RELAX

You may not realize that mental and physical relaxation is a significant part of the studying process. Clearing your mind and body of stress and anxiety refreshes mental and physical energy. Spend quality time studying and reviewing for the test. Spend time relaxing your mind and body so that you are re-energized to study again.

Practice these relaxation exercises:

➢ ***Physical Relaxation Exercise***

Pick a quiet room where you will find few distractions. Shut off all intrusive lights. Sit or lie down. If you wear glasses, take them off. Get comfortable. Loosen any tight or binding clothing. Close your eyes. Take a deep breath. Blow out all the air in your lungs and then breathe in deeply. Now, focus on your tense muscles and consciously relax them. Start by focusing on your toes, your feet, and your calves. Tense and release the muscles to fully relax them. Then move upward through each muscle group in your body, up to and including your facial muscles. Continue to breathe slowly, steadily, and fully during this exercise. Repeat this process, while consciously relaxing tense muscles, until you relax your entire body. Rest in this state for a few minutes. When completed, open your eyes. Remain sitting or reclining for another minute or two before rising.

➢ ***Breathing Exercise***

Deep and relaxed breathing will calm your nerves and reduce stress. Whenever you start feeling anxious, take time out to perform this simple breathing exercise. Place you hands upon your stomach and breath in slowly and deeply through the nose, feeling your rib cage rise. Pause and hold your breath for a second and think, "I am calm." Release this breath slowly and fully, blowing it out through your mouth. Repeat the exercise eight to ten times. Perform this exercise whenever you feel nervous or anxious.

➢ ***Mental Relaxation Exercise***

Meditation, in various forms, has been practiced to allow the mind to release stressful thoughts. Many types of meditation can be learned and practiced. A popular type of meditation is the permissive form. Begin meditation after your body is in a relaxed state. Concentrate on something monotonous until your mind becomes quiet. You may choose to concentrate on a sound, a word, or an object. Observe your thoughts without controlling them. Gently refocus back on the sound, word, or object. Passively observe your thoughts when they come, then gently refocus back upon the sound, word, or object.

6. PREPARE...DON'T LEAVE LAST MINUTE ITEMS UNTIL THE LAST MINUTE

On the day of the test, you want to remain as relaxed as possible. In order to eliminate that last minute, frantic rushing to find that one thing you cannot locate, make a list of the items you need for the test day. Set out those important items the night before in order to efficiently and effectively speed you own your way toward the testing center.

➢ ***Determine the items you are expected to bring.***

Carefully read the test packet materials so you know exactly what you should and should not bring to the test center. You may need to bring an eraser, personal I.D., calculator, or pencils. However, some test centers do not allow food, scratch paper, or alarms. Determine what things to bring and what to leave home.

➢ ***Check working condition of calculator, watch, etc.***

This might sound silly, but make sure that your watch and calculator (if allowed) are in good working condition. Replace old calculator batteries with new ones. Sharpen pencils prior to arriving at the test center.

➢ ***Pack the items you need.***

Set out the items you need the night before the test so you are sure you have them. This will save you the anxiety of trying to find them at the last minute.

➢ ***Know the directions to the test center.***

If you have not been to the test center before, have specific and clear directions provided to you as soon as possible. If you are confused in the least about how get to the test center, call the test center immediately and clarify the directions.

➢ ***To study or not to study.***

Should you study the night before? Well, you certainly should not attempt to cram for the test. You may want to review a few strategies, but you do not want to attempt to learn a great deal of new material. Instead, take some time to review, and then find some entertaining activity. Go to the gym or see a movie with friends. Also, laughing is a great way to reduce stress, so find something humorous to do or watch.

➢ ***Sleep well.***

A good night of sleep will help reduce the stress on test day. Do not stay out late the night before the test.

➢ ***Get to the test site early enough.***

Your anxiety will rise if you arrive at the test center late, stand in line to register, run to a seat, and then immediately begin the test. Arrive at the test center early enough to find the room, register, find your seat, set out necessary items (pencil, calculator), and still have a few minutes to relax and compose yourself. You may also need time to locate the restrooms and drinking fountains. Do not arrive at the test center too early though. Students who wait a long time with nothing to do, except think about the coming test, typically get nervous and anxious. Find the balance between too early and too late that works best for you.

➢ ***Watch your diet.***

What you eat is one physical cause of stress you can control. Eat a healthy breakfast the day of the test. Restrict you levels of sugar, salt, and caffeine. Remember, sugar and caffeine are found in coffee, cola, cocoa, and tea. These substances trigger a stress response in your body. High levels of sugar and caffeine are associated with nervousness, dizziness, irritability, headache, and insomnia. Additionally, smoking has been found to decrease a person's ability to handle stress. Cigarettes are a stimulant because of their nicotine content and will increase stress levels.

➢ ***Dress comfortably.***

Wear comfortable clothes to the testing center. The good news is that you are going to a test, not a fashion show. Choose clothes that are not overly binding or tight. Dressing in layers is always a good idea, since testing rooms are notoriously too hot or too cold.

7. PAUSE...RELEASE PHYSICAL AND MENTAL ANXIETY BEFORE THE TEST

As you have already read, relaxation allows you to focus your full attention and energy on the task at hand, rather than being distracted by tension and stress. Right before the test, release as much tension and anxiety as possible.

➢ ***Release and relax.***

Having arrived early at the test site, take the last few minutes to relax. Do not attempt to study or review at this point. Instead, use a simple relaxation technique. Close your eyes. Breathe in deeply through your nose. Hold that breath for a few seconds. Next, release that breath through your mouth. Repeat this in and out breathing. Try to slow the pace of the in-and-out motion of your breathing. Visualize yourself at a place you find peaceful and relaxing, such as the beach, the woods, or some other favorite spot. Continue this for a few minutes until you feel yourself becoming relaxed and calm.

➢ ***Do some low-level physical exercise.***

Take a brisk walk. For many, walking helps lower high-stress levels while positively easing the mind from worrying about the upcoming test. Others find that stretching exercises help loosen tense muscles. Just remember to be back to register and sit down for the test in plenty of time.

➢ ***Massage tension away.***

While waiting for the test, sit comfortably in your chair. Notice places in your body that are tense—generally the shoulders, neck, or back. Gently massage tense areas for a few minutes.

8. PUSH...CONCENTRATE ON CURRENT QUESTION, NOT THE LAST, OR NEXT

Dwelling on answers to previous sections will elevate test anxiety, so avoid worrying about those sections or questions that you have finished. The strategy to use to avoid worrying about previous sections is actually quite simple.

➢ ***Focus on one question at a time.***

Your task on any test is to get the questions correct, one question at a time. Good test-takers focus on the answer to the question they are currently working on. Poor test-takers worry about the answer to the questions they just answered or the questions in the upcoming section. Try to stay "in the moment" by concentrating on one question at a time.

9. PROUD...WALK OUT WITH YOU HEAD HELD HIGH.

➢ ***Know that you've done your best.***

If you have followed the strategies listed in this section, if you've attended the test preparation classes, and if you've spent time reviewing and studying on your own, you have most likely done your very best. As you walk out of the test, remind yourself that you have indeed done your best.

➢ ***Watch the labels.***

After the test, never label yourself as a "failure," "loser," or "under-achiever." Instead, if you did not do as well as you expected, use the experience to learn about the test and about yourself. Students do re-take standardized tests, so reflect upon what you can do better next time, not how poorly you think you did this time.

10. PERSPECTIVE...KEEP LIFE IN PERSPECTIVE.

Keep life in perspective. Yes, the test you will take is important, but other things in life are important too. Remember that this test is a means to an end—getting into college, graduate school, a profession—and not the end itself.

11. POST THOUGHTS...DON'T LET STRESS OVERWHELM YOU.

Some test-takers, even after applying all the strategies above, still experience debilitating stress. Intense anxiety or stress that causes nausea, headaches, overwhelming emotional fears, or other severe symptoms may need special attention and care that goes beyond the strategies in these pages. Ask your high school or university counseling office what resources are available to help overcome severe test anxiety.

CAMBRIDGE

EDUCATIONAL SERVICES, INC.®

ACT • PLAN • EXPLORE
ENGLISH

CAMBRIDGE
EDUCATIONAL SERVICES, INC.®

AMERICA'S #1 CAMPUS-BASED TESTPREP

Cambridge Course Concept Outline
ACT • PLAN • EXPLORE—ENGLISH

I. ENGLISH REVIEW (p. 27)

A. PRELIMINARIES
1. TEACHING THE ENGLISH LESSON
2. FORMATS OF THE ACT, PLAN, AND EXPLORE TESTS
3. DIRECTIONS FOR ENGLISH PROBLEMS
4. WHAT IS TESTED

B. GRAMMAR
1. SUBJECT-VERB AGREEMENT (Review Question #1)
    a. MATERIAL INSERTED BETWEEN SUBJECT AND VERB (Review Questions #2-5)
    b. INVERTED SENTENCE STRUCTURE (Review Questions #6-7)
    c. COMPOUND SUBJECTS (Review Questions #8-9)
2. PRONOUN USAGE
    a. PRONOUNS MUST HAVE AN ANTECEDENT (Review Questions #10-11)
    b. ANTECEDENTS MUST BE CLEAR (Review Question #12)
    c. PRONOUN-ANTECEDENT AGREEMENT (Review Questions #13-16)
    d. PRONOUNS MUST HAVE PROPER CASE (Review Questions #17-18)
3. ADJECTIVES VERSUS ADVERBS
    a. LINKING VERBS
    b. ADJECTIVES MODIFY NOUNS, ADVERBS MODIFY VERBS (Review Questions #19-20)
    c. WATCH FOR ADJECTIVES POSING AS ADVERBS
4. DOUBLE NEGATIVES (Review Questions #21-22)
5. NOUNS AND NOUN CLAUSES (Review Questions #23-24)

C. ANALYZING SENTENCE STRUCTURES
1. FAULTY PARALLELISM (Review Questions #25-27)
2. INCOMPLETE SPLIT CONSTRUCTIONS (Review Questions #28-29)
3. VERB TENSE
    a. PRINCIPAL PARTS OF VERBS
    b. WHEN TO USE THE PERFECT TENSE
    c. THE SUBJUNCTIVE MOOD

D. PROBLEMS OF LOGICAL EXPRESSION
1. FAULTY OR ILLOGICAL COMPARISONS (Review Questions #30-36)
2. SEQUENCE AND VERB TENSE (Review Questions #37-40)
3. UNINTENDED MEANINGS (Review Questions #41-42)
4. CONCISENESS
    a. AVOID AWKWARD SENTENCES AND WEAK PASSIVE VERBS
    b. AVOID NEEDLESSLY WORDY SENTENCES (Review Questions #43-47)
5. MISPLACED MODIFIERS (Review Questions #48-49)

E. IDIOMS AND CLARITY OF EXPRESSION

1. **WRONG PREPOSITION** (Review Questions #50-51)
2. **DICTION** (Review Questions #52-53)
3. **GERUND VERSUS INFINITIVE** (Review Questions #54-55)
4. **AMBIGUITY IN SCOPE** (Review Question #56)
5. **LOW-LEVEL USAGE** (Review Question #57)
6. **ISOLATED ERRORS** (Review Questions #58-59)

F. PUNCTUTATION ERRORS

1. **COMMAS** (Review Questions #60-80)
2. **SEMICOLONS** (Review Questions #81-84)
3. **COLONS** (Review Questions #85-88)
4. **PERIODS** (Review Question #89)
5. **DASHES** (Review Questions #90-92)
6. **HYPHENS** (Review Question #93)
7. **QUOTATION MARKS** (Review Question #94)
8. **PUNCTUATING FOR CLARITY** (Review Question #95)

G. ENGLISH USAGE CHECKLIST

II. ENGLISH PROBLEM-SOLVING (p. 32)

III. ENGLISH QUIZZES (p. 43)

IV. ENGLISH TESTING POINTS EXERCISE (p. 55)

V. ENGLISH ERROR IDENTIFICATION EXERCISE (p. 57)

SECTION ONE—ENGLISH REVIEW

DIRECTIONS: The questions in this section accompany the in-class review of the principles of grammar, sentence structure, and usage tested by the ACT, PLAN, and EXPLORE. These questions do not necessarily reflect the format of questions on the exam. You will work through the questions and answers with your instructor in class.

1. The professor were traveling in Europe when she received notice of her promotion.

2. The professor voted Teacher of the Year by the students were traveling in Europe when she received notice of her promotion.

3. Most teachers, unless they have an appointment to a prestigious university, earns relatively less as a teacher than they might in business.

4. Many nutritionists now believe that a balanced diet and not large doses of vitamins are the best guarantee of health.

5. Television comedies in which there is at least one really detestable character captures the interest of viewers.

6. Although this is the wealthiest country in the world, within a few blocks of the White House there is scores of homeless people who live on the streets.

7. Just a few miles from the factories and skyscrapers stand a medieval castle, that looks exactly as it did in the twelfth century.

8. John, his wife, and the rest of his family plans to attend the awards dinner to be given by the company for the employees with the most seniority.

9. Either the governor or one of his close aides prefer not to have the senator at the head table.

10. During her rise to fame, she betrayed many of her friends; and because of it, very few people trust her.

11. In New York City, they are brusque and even rude but quick to come to one another's assistance in a time of crisis.

12. Ten years ago, the United States imported ten times as much French wine as Italian wine; today, Americans are drinking more of it.

13. Although a police officer used to be a symbol of authority, today they receive little respect from most people.

14. The Abbot was an effective administrator who attempted to assign each monk a task particularly suited to their talents and training.

15. After three years of college education, a person should be allowed to apply to graduate school, because by that time you are ready to choose a profession.

16. If one wishes to apply for a scholarship, you must submit a completed application by May 1.

17. The judges were unable to make a final decision on a single winner, so they divided first prize between John and he.

18. Although Peter had been looking forward to the debate for weeks, a sore throat prevented him taking part.

19. Some psychologists maintain that a child who has seen violence on television is more likely to react violent in situations of stress.

20. The recent created commission has done nothing to address the problem except to approve a new brand of stationery.

21. Not hardly a sound could be heard in the auditorium when the speaker approached the dais to announce the result of the contest.

22. Although she had been hired by the magazine to write book reviews, she knew scarcely nothing about current fiction.

23. The reason Harriet fired her secretary is because he was frequently late and spent too much time on personal phone calls.

24. The reason the manager changed catchers was because he hoped that the opposing side would put in a left-handed batter.

25. To abandon their homes, leave behind their families, and traveling across the ocean required great courage on the part of the immigrants who moved to America.

26. The review praised the wit, charm, and interpreting of the recitalist but never once mentioned her voice.

27. To acknowledge that one has something to learn is taking the first step on the road to true wisdom.

28. The students are critical of the dean because he either is unfamiliar or doesn't care about the urgent need for new student housing on campus.

29. Baseball has and probably always will be the sport that symbolizes for people in other countries the American way of life.

30. The great pianist Vladimir Horowitz played the music of the romantic era better than any pianist in history.

31. Educators are now expressing their concern that American schoolchildren prefer watching television to books.

32. The novels of Nathaniel Hawthorne contain characters that are every bit as sinister and frightening as the master of cinematic suspense, Alfred Hitchcock.

33. A Japanese firm has developed a computer so small that users can carry it in their briefcase.

34. Carlos has a very pleasant personality and he is a talented musician; therefore, he gets good grades in school.

35. John had already been granted three extensions of the deadline; moreover, the dean refused to grant him another.

36. A poll of students shows that Helen is the top choice for student body president. Helen, however, is likely to win the election.

37. The teacher began to discuss the homework assignment when he will be interrupted by the sound of the fire alarm.

38. The conductor announced that the concert would resume as soon as the soloist replaces the broken string on her violin.

39. Many patients begin to show symptoms again after they stopped taking the drug.

40. Postmodern art, with its vibrant colors and bold shapes, taking its inspiration from artists such as Cézanne but reacting against the pastel indistinctness of the Impressionist canvases.

41. Mary Lou was awarded the gold medal because she scored more points than any child participating in the field day.

42. Appearing in his first American tour, the British singer's album rose to the top of the charts.

43. After months of separation, Gauguin finally joined Van Gogh in Arles in October of 1888, Gauguin left a few weeks later.

44. The nineteenth-century composers Wagner and Mahler did more than just write music, they conducted their own works.

45. Since only the ruling party is allowed to vote, its members are able to maintain the existing status quo.

46. Each year, the geese make their annual migration from Northern Canada to their winter habitats in the United States.

47. Although the committee met for over two weeks and issued a 50-page report, its findings were of little importance or consequence.

48. Wrapped in several thicknesses of newspaper, packed carefully in a strong cardboard carton, and bound securely with tape, the worker made sure that the fragile figurines would not be broken.

49. Riding in a coach and wearing the crown jewels, the crowd cheered the royal couple.

NOTES AND STRATEGIES

50. In contrast of the prevailing opinion, the editorial places the blame for the strike on the workers and their representatives.

51. Although ballet and modern dance are both concerned in movement in space to musical accompaniment, the training for ballet is more rigorous than that for modern dance.

52. By midnight the guests still had not been served anything to eat and they were ravishing.

53. The raise in the number of accidents attributable to drunk drivers has prompted a call for stiffer penalties for driving while intoxicated.

54. The idea of trying completing the term paper by Friday caused Ken to cancel his plans for the weekend.

55. Psychologists think that many people eat satisfying a need for affection that is not otherwise fulfilled.

56. Along with an end to featherbedding and no-show jobs, the new head of the Transit Authority has eliminated many other inefficient employment practices.

57. Being that the hour was late, we agreed to adjourn the meeting and reconvene at nine o'clock the following morning.

58. John, having took his seat at the head of the table, announced that the dinner would feature specialties from Thailand.

59. The winter was so severe that several of Hilary's prize rosebushes had sustained serious damage.

60. I think that Doré's illustrations of Dante's *Divine Comedy* are excellent, but my favorite drawing is "Don Quixote in His Library."

61. Practically all nitrates are crystalline and readily soluble, and they are characterized by marked decrepitation when heated on charcoals by a blowpipe.

62. The door was ajar, and the house had been ransacked.

63. Because many diseases and insects cause serious damage to crops, special national legislation has been passed to provide for the quarantine of imported plants; and under provisions of various acts, inspectors are placed at ports of entry to prevent smugglers from bringing in plants that might be dangerous.

64. A full train crew consists of a motorman, a brakeman, a conductor, and two ticket takers.

65. The procedure requires that you open the outer cover plate, remove the thermostat, replace the broken switch, and then replace the thermostat.

66. After Peter finished painting the bird feeder, he and Jack hung it from a limb of the oak tree.

67. When Pat explained to his mother that ten was the highest mark given on the entrance test, she breathed a sigh of relief.

68. Tim hopes to score well on the exam because he plans to go to an Ivy League school.

69. In this impoverished region with its arid soil, a typical diet may contain only 800 calories per day.

70. At the height of the moral war against sensational journalism, Horace Greeley moved into the forefront of the journalistic picture.

71. Begun in 1981 and completed in 1985, the bridge provided the first link between the island and the mainland.

72. To slow the bleeding, Van tied a tourniquet around the lower portion of the leg.

73. Niagra Falls, which forms part of the border between the United States and Canada, was the site of a saw mill built by the French in 1725.

74. The second Nicene Council, the seventh ecumenical council of the Church, was summoned by the Empress Irene and her son Constantine.

75. The last hope of the French expired when Bazaine surrendered Metz, along with 180,000 soldiers.

76. Secretary of State Acheson, however, made a reasoned defense of the treaty.

77. Until the end of the 18th century, the only musicians in Norway, were simple unsophisticated peasants who traveled about.

78. Prizes will be awarded in each event, and the participant, who compiles the greatest overall total, will receive a special prize.

79. Since learning of the dangers of caffeine, neither my wife nor I have consumed any beverage, containing caffeine.

80. After months of separation, Gauguin finally joined Van Gogh in Arles in October of 1888, Gauguin left a few weeks later.

81. He grew up on a farm in Nebraska; he is now the captain of a Navy ship.

82 The Smithtown players cheered the referee's decision; the Stonybrook players booed it.

83. When John entered the room; everyone stood up.

84. Clem announced that the prize would be donated to Harbus House; a well-known charity.

85. The teacher announced that the course would require three papers: one on Shakespeare, one on Dickens, and one on a contemporary writer.

86. Will's suggestion was truly democratic: let everyone serve as chair for one meeting.

87. The seemingly tranquil lane has been the scene of many crimes including: two assaults, three robberies, and one murder.

88. In addition to test scores, college admissions officers take into consideration many other factors such as: grades, extracurricular activities, and letters of recommendation.

89. Peter notified Elaine. The guidance counselor, that he had been accepted.

90. Careful attention to the details of one's personal appearance—neatly pressed clothing, shined shoes, and a neat haircut—is an important part of preparing for a job interview.

91. Many colleges—including the nation's top schools—set aside a certain number of freshman seats for students who show academic promise in spite of low test scores.

92. Peanuts—blanched or lightly roasted, add an interesting texture and taste to garden salads.

93. The optimist feels that his glass is one-half full; the pessimist feels that his glass is one-half empty

94. The first chapter of *The Scarlet Letter* is "The Custom House."

95. On Monday (slight pause) Mark received a letter of acceptance from State College (full stop) He immediately called his mother (slight pause) herself a graduate of State College (slight pause) to tell her about his acceptance (full stop) When he told her he had also been awarded a scholarship (slight pause) she was very excited (full stop) After hanging up (slight pause) Mark's mother decided to throw a surprise party for Mark (full stop) She telephoned his brother (slight pause) his sister (slight pause) and several of his friends (full stop) Because the party was supposed to be a surprise (slight pause) she made them all promise not to say anything to Mark (full stop) Mark (slight pause) however (slight pause) had a similar idea (pause) a party for his mother to celebrate his acceptance at her alma mater (full stop) He telephoned his brother (slight pause) his sister (slight pause) and several of his parents' friends to invite them to a party at his house on Saturday night (pause) and he made them all promise to say nothing to his mother (full stop) On Saturday night (slight pause) both Mark and his mother were surprised (full stop)

SECTION TWO—ENGLISH PROBLEM-SOLVING

DIRECTIONS: The questions in this section reflect both the format and difficulty range of ACT English questions. You will work through these questions with your instructor in class. In the passages that follow, certain parts and phrases are underlined and numbered. In the right-hand column, you will find alternatives for each underlined part. You are to choose the one that best expresses the idea, makes the statement appropriate for standard written English, or is worded more consistently with the style and tone of the passage as a whole. If you think the original version is the best, choose "NO CHANGE."

You will also find questions about a section of the passage, or about the passage as a whole. These questions do not refer to an underlined portion of the passage, but rather are identified with a note.

For each question, choose the alternative you consider best. Read each passage through once before you begin to answer the questions that accompany it. You cannot determine most answers without reading several sentences beyond the question. Be sure that you have read far enough ahead each time you choose an alternative. Answers are on page 60.

Passage I

The first Europeans who adopted Appalachia as home, followed [1] the trails pounded out by those earliest mountain engineers: the [2] buffalo, elk, deer, and other wild game. (Later they found the great traces forged by the Indian tribes on their trading and fighting forays.) [3] Gradually, these first Europeans hewed out passages that become part of [4] America's history, and portions of which may still be discovered along today's interstates and backroads. Their very names connect us to [5] the past in the region: The Great Warrior's Trail, Boone's Trace (which became the Wilderness Road), and the Cumberland Gap.

1. (A) NO CHANGE
(B) home followed
(C) home: followed
(D) home; followed

2. (F) NO CHANGE
(G) engineers, the
(H) engineers the
(J) engineers. The

3. (A) NO CHANGE
(B) Great traces forged by the Indian tribes, however, were later found on their trading and fighting forays.
(C) (Finding later, great traces forged by the Indian tribes, on their trading and fighting forays.)
(D) Later they found the great traces forged by the Indian tribes on their trading and fighting forays.

4. (F) NO CHANGE
(G) will become a part of
(H) became a part of
(J) became part

5. (A) NO CHANGE
(B) connecting us to
(C) connected us to
(D) connect us

NOTES AND STRATEGIES

Geographic isolation greatly influenced the region's culture. From the beginning, numerous ethnic groups contributed to Appalachian settlement. During the late 1600's and into the next century, Germans from the Rhineland settled in the Great Appalachian Valley. Building fat barns and tight houses on the fertile fields of Pennsylvania, Maryland, Virginia, and North Carolina. They were called "Pennsylvania Dutch."

6. (F) NO CHANGE
(G) Geographically isolated
(H) Isolated geographically
(J) Isolated geography

7. (A) NO CHANGE
(B) Valley, building
(C) Valley: building
(D) Valley,

The German settlers made important contributions. One of the important contributions made by German settlers to frontier life was the Pennsylvania rifle—also called the Kentucky rifle and the Long rifle. A weapon born of necessity and economy, its extended barrel assured greater accuracy and precision than could be achieved with the old muskets, and its smaller bore required less powder and lead for each shot (precious commodities). Such rifles were highly prized possessions, and their manufacture was one of the central industries of pioneer Appalachia.

8. (F) NO CHANGE
(G) (Place in parentheses.)
(H) (Place in quotation marks.)
(J) OMIT

9. (A) NO CHANGE
(B) accuracy as well as precision
(C) accuracy plus precision
(D) accuracy

10. (F) NO CHANGE
(G) (Place immediately after *powder*)
(H) (Place immediately after *lead*)
(J) (Place immediately after *each*)

Passage II

Art of the Middle Ages is first, and foremost, a sacred script, the symbols and meanings of which are well settled. A circular halo placed vertically behind the head of a figure signifies sainthood, meanwhile the halo impressed with a cross signifies divinity.

11. (A) NO CHANGE
(B) is well settled
(C) are settled well
(D) would be settled

12. (F) NO CHANGE
(G) sainthood, because
(H) sainthood because
(J) sainthood, while

A tower[13] with a window indicates a village; and should an angel be watching from the battlements, that city is thereby identified as Jerusalem.

Mathematics too is an important element of this iconography. "The Divine Wisdom," wrote Saint Augustine, "reveals itself everywhere in numbers." A doctrine[14] derived from the Neoplatonists who[15] revived the teachings of Pythagoras. And numbers require symmetry. At Chartres, a stained-glass window shows the four prophets Isaac, Ezekiel, Daniel, and Jeremiah carrying on their shoulders the four evangelists Matthew, Mark, Luke, and John.

Every painting[16] is also an allegory, showing us one thing and inviting us to see another. In this respect, the artist was[17] asked to imitate God, who had hidden a profound meaning behind[18] the literal and who wished nature to be a moral lesson to man. In a painting of the final judgment, the foolish virgins can be seen by us[19] at the left hand of Jesus and the wise on the right, and we understand that this symbolizes those who are lost and those that have been saved[20].

13. (A) NO CHANGE
(B) (Do NOT begin a new paragraph) A tower
(C) Towers
(D) Having a tower

14. (F) NO CHANGE
(G) numbers," which
(H) numbers," a doctrine
(J) numbers" which

15. (A) NO CHANGE
(B) Neoplatonists that
(C) Neoplatonist's that
(D) Neoplatonist's who

16. (F) NO CHANGE
(G) (Do NOT begin a new paragraph) Every painting
(H) (Begin a new paragraph) However, every painting
(J) (Do NOT begin a new paragraph) However, every painting

17. (A) NO CHANGE
(B) Furthermore, the artist was
(C) The artist, however, was
(D) Generally, artists are

18. (F) NO CHANGE
(G) meaning which was behind
(H) meaning being behind
(J) meaning behind and in back of

19. (A) NO CHANGE
(B) OMIT
(C) by each of us
(D) by all of us

20. (F) NO CHANGE
(G) those who have been saved
(H) those who are saved
(J) the saved

Within such a system even the most mediocre talent was elevated by the genius of centuries, and the first artist of the Renaissance broke with the tradition at great risk. Even when they are great, medieval artists are no more than the equals of the old masters who passively followed the sacred rules; and when they are not outstanding, they scarcely avoid banality and insignificance in their religious works

21. (A) NO CHANGE
(B) (Do NOT begin a new paragraph) Within such a system
(C) (Do NOT begin a new paragraph) Inside of such a system
(D) (Do NOT begin a new paragraph) To be inside such a system

22. (F) NO CHANGE
(G) with
(H) however
(J) since

23. (A) NO CHANGE
(B) always
(C) ever
(D) OMIT

Items 24-26 pose questions about the passage as a whole.

24. The author most likely wrote this article for which of the following?

(F) A scholarly art journal
(G) A book tracing the history of mathematics
(H) A history of the Catholic Church
(J) A book that surveys the history of Western art

25. The author relies on which of the following to develop the passage?

(A) Examples
(B) Extensive quotations from other authorities
(C) Statistics
(D) Personal experience

26. The author probably quotes Saint Augustine in order to

(F) ridicule his position.
(G) emphasize the importance of numbers and symmetry.
(H) prove the importance of Church teaching.
(J) illustrate Augustine's knowledge of art.

Passage III

A persistent and universal symbol in the mythology of virtually every culture, is that of a bottomless pit or an engulfing whirlpool. It was the maw of the abyss: and those venturing too close were dragged inward toward chaos by an irresistible force.

27. (A) NO CHANGE
(B) culture is
(C) culture are
(D) cultures are

28. (F) NO CHANGE
(G) abyss, and those
(H) abyss meanwhile those
(J) abyss due to the fact that

NOTES AND STRATEGIES

Socrates (a Greek philosopher who committed suicide) [29] talked of a chasm that pierced the world straight through from side to side. Ulysses also encountering it [30] as did a mythical Cherokee who escaped, but not before he was drawn down to the narrowest circle of the maelstrom where he could peer into the nether world of the dead. Many primitive cultures bury their dead with tools in the belief that the tools will be useful to them in the afterlife. [31]

On the other hand, the search [32] for a solution to one of astronomys' [33] most persistent and perplexing riddles, black holes, could be viewed by one [34] as a continuation of the search for [35] the whirlpool that is the maw of the abyss, a depth our telescopes cannot reach and from which nothing will have returned [36]. What is incredible to contemplate, and what sets us [37] apart from the ancients, is that we think we have a fair idea not only as to [38] how they are formed, but also how large they are and so forth. A combination of theory

29. (A) NO CHANGE
(B) OMIT
(C) (a Greek philosopher who had committed suicide)
(D) (a philosopher from Greece who committed suicide)

30. (F) NO CHANGE
(G) also encountered it
(H) also encountered them
(J) encountered them also

31. (A) NO CHANGE
(B) (Move to before *Ulysses*)
(C) (Move to the end of the passage)
(D) OMIT

32. (F) NO CHANGE
(G) (Do NOT begin a new paragraph) The search
(H) (Begin a new paragraph) The search
(J) (Begin a new paragraph) Also, the search

33. (A) NO CHANGE
(B) astronomy's
(C) astronomy
(D) astronomys

34. (F) NO CHANGE
(G) OMIT
(H) by those
(J) by one astronomer

35. (A) NO CHANGE
(B) a continuing the search of
(C) continuation to the search for
(D) continuation for the search for

36. (F) NO CHANGE
(G) will return
(H) returns
(J) returning

37. (A) NO CHANGE
(B) setting us
(C) and that sets us
(D) and we are set

38. (F) NO CHANGE
(G) about
(H) not about
(J) OMIT

and observation <u>have led to</u> 39 the growing suspicion among astrophysicists that the nucleus of virtually every galaxy harbors a massive black hole.

39. (A) NO CHANGE
(B) has led to
(C) has led
(D) led

Passage IV

Instead of casting aside traditional values during the Meji Restoration of 1888, those who strove to dismantle feudalism and to modernize the country chose to preserve three traditions as the foundations <u>on which they could build a modern Japan upon</u> 40.

40. (F) NO CHANGE
(G) on which they could be building a modern Japan upon
(H) on which they could build a modern Japan
(J) upon which they someday could probably build a modern Japan

The <u>older</u> 41 tradition and basis of the entire Japanese value system was <u>respect for and even worshipping</u> 42 the Emperor. During the early centuries of Japanese history the Shinto cult, in which <u>the imperial family traced its ancestry to the Sun Goddess</u> 43, became the people's sustaining faith. <u>Being later subordinated</u> 44 to imported Buddhism and Confucianism, Shintoism was perpetuated in Ise and Izumo, the great shrines of the Imperial family, until the Meji modernizers established it as a quasi state religion to unify the people and restore the Emperor as the symbol of national unity

41. (A) NO CHANGE
(B) oldest
(C) old
(D) OMIT

42. (F) NO CHANGE
(G) respecting and even worshipping
(H) respect for and even worship of
(J) respect and even worship

43. (A) NO CHANGE
(B) the imperial family got its ancestry traced back to the Sun Goddess
(C) the imperial family's ancestry was traced back to the Sun Goddess
(D) the Sun Goddess was considered to be the ancestor of the imperial family

44. (F) NO CHANGE
(G) Later subordinated
(H) Later subordinated,
(J) Subordinated later,

and the object of loyalty <u>to the Japanese</u>.(45)

<u>Another tradition that was enduring</u>(46) was the hierarchical system of social relations based on feudalism. Confucianism prescribed <u>a pattern by</u>(47) ethical conduct between groups of people within a fixed hierarchy. Four of five Confucian relationships <u>(those between ruler and subject, husband and wife, father and son, and elder brother and younger brother)</u>(48) <u>were</u>(49) <u>vertical since they</u>(50) required loyalty and obedience from the inferior toward the superior <u>and benevolence and protection from the superior to the inferior</u>.(51) Only the fifth <u>relationship, that</u>(52) between friend and friend—was horizontal. <u>A</u>(53) third tradition was respect

45. (A) NO CHANGE
(B) the Japanese had
(C) by the Japanese
(D) for the Japanese

46. (F) NO CHANGE
(G) (Begin a new paragraph) Another tradition
(H) (Do NOT begin a new paragraph) Another tradition
(J) (Begin a new paragraph) The other tradition

47. (A) NO CHANGE
(B) patterns by
(C) a pattern for
(D) patterns with

48. Is the author's use of parentheses here appropriate?

(F) Yes, because the examples are irrelevant to the passage.
(G) Yes, because although the information is relevant, the material is not part of the main development of the passage.
(H) No, because the material is irrelevant to the passage.
(J) No, because the material is essential to the reader's understanding of the passage.

49. (A) NO CHANGE
(B) was
(C) are
(D) could be

50. (F) NO CHANGE
(G) vertical, they
(H) vertical, since it
(J) vertical, being they

51. (A) NO CHANGE
(B) and also benevolence and protection from the superior to the inferior
(C) with the benevolence and protection being from the superior to the inferior
(D) and from the superior to the inferior, the benevolence and protection

52. (F) NO CHANGE
(G) relationship that
(H) relationship—that
(J) relationship

53. (A) NO CHANGE
(B) (Begin a new paragraph) A
(C) (Do NOT begin a new paragraph) Further, a
(D) (Begin a new paragraph) Also a

NOTES AND STRATEGIES

for learning, another basic idea of Confucius.[54] In traditional Japan, study was the absolute duty of man. It was a religious mandate as well[55] as a social duty and was a means of promoting a harmonious and stable society. The individual's behavior[56] was strictly prescribed by law and custom. Only the Samurai had the right to retaliate with force if they were displeased. But his[57] primary duty was to the lord.

54. (F) NO CHANGE
    (G) Confucius idea
    (H) idea of Confucianism
    (J) Confucianism idea

55. (A) NO CHANGE
    (B) mandate as well as being
    (C) mandate as well,
    (D) mandate,

56. (F) NO CHANGE
    (G) An individual behavior
    (H) Behavior by individual's
    (J) The individuals behavior

57. (A) NO CHANGE
    (B) But their
    (C) Being that their
    (D) Because their

Item 58 poses a question about the passage as a whole.

58. The best description of the development of this article would be

    (F) argument and rebuttal.
    (G) a personal narrative.
    (H) a three-part exposition.
    (J) question and answer.

SECTION THREE—ENGLISH QUIZZES

DIRECTIONS: This section contains three English quizzes. In the passages that follow, certain parts and phrases are underlined and numbered. In the right-hand column, you will find alternatives for each underlined part. You are to choose the one that best expresses the idea, makes the statement appropriate for standard written English, or is worded more consistently with the style and tone of the passage as a whole. If you think the original version is the best, choose "NO CHANGE." Complete each quiz while being timed. Answers are page 60.

QUIZ I (32 questions; 20 minutes)

Passage I

No writer can please many readers and please them for a long time excepting by [1] the accurate representation of human nature. Shakespeare, however, [2] is above all writers, the poet of human nature, the writer who holds up to his readers a faithful and true [3] mirror of manners and life.

Shakespeare's characters are not modified by the customs of particular places unknown to the rest of the world, by peculiarities of study or professions known to just a few, or [4] by the latest fashions or popular opinions.

Shakespeare's characters are each [5] genuine representations of common humanity. Hamlet and Othello act and speak [6] according to the general passions and principles that affect all of us. In the writings of other poets, whoever they may be, [7] a character is too often an individual; in that of Shakespeare [8] it is commonly a species.

1. (F) NO CHANGE
   (G) except by
   (H) except for
   (J) excepting

2. (A) NO CHANGE
   (B) moreover
   (C) therefore
   (D) furthermore

3. (F) NO CHANGE
   (G) faithful
   (H) faithfully true
   (J) true and real

4. (A) NO CHANGE
   (B) about by only a few, and
   (C) to just a few, but
   (D) to only a few, since

5. (F) NO CHANGE
   (G) every
   (H) all
   (J) each one a

6. (A) NO CHANGE
   (B) acting and speaking
   (C) acted and spoke
   (D) acted and spoken

7. (F) NO CHANGE
   (G) whoever they may be
   (H) whomever they may be,
   (J) OMIT

8. (A) NO CHANGE
   (B) the one of Shakespeare
   (C) those of Shakepeare's
   (D) those of Shakespeare

Other dramatists can gain attention only by using exaggerated characters. Shakespeare <u>has no heroes; his</u> [9] scenes <u>only</u> [10] are occupied by persons who act and speak as the reader thinks he or she <u>would of spoken</u> [11] or acted on the same occasion.

This therefore, is the praise of <u>Shakespeare that</u> [12] his drama is the mirror of life. [13]

9. (F) NO CHANGE
   (G) has no heroes: his
   (H) has no heroes his
   (J) has no heroes, his

10. (A) NO CHANGE
    (B) (place after *act*)
    (C) (Place before *act*)
    (D) (Place after *occupied*)

11. (F) NO CHANGE
    (G) would have speaked
    (H) would have spoken
    (J) would speak

12. (A) NO CHANGE
    (B) Shakespeare,
    (C) Shakespeare. That
    (D) Shakespeare:that

13. Is the final sentence of the article an appropriate ending?

    (F) Yes, because it makes a final point about Shakespeare not previously mentioned and so leaves the reader with something to think about.
    (G) Yes, because it is a summary of what was said in the introductory paragraph and so gives the reader a sense of closure.
    (H) No, because it is irrelevant to the article and will leave the reader confused.
    (J) No, because it is so repetitious that it will make the reader impatient.

Items 14-17 pose questions about the passage as a whole.

14. What assumption is the author of the article making?

    (A) Everyone believes Shakespeare is a good writer.
    (B) No one has ever heard of Shakespeare.
    (C) An accurate representation of human nature is important for great art.
    (D) We could not understand Shakespeare's characters in the twentieth century.

15. Where might you find this article published?

    (F) In a book of literary criticism
    (G) In a journal for Renaissance scholars
    (H) In a Shakespeare biography
    (J) In a sociology textbook

16. Which of the following is NOT one of the strategies used by the author to make his/her point?

(A) Comparison
(B) Argument
(C) Examples
(D) Personal anecdote

17. Which of the following would most strengthen the author's argument that Shakespeare is the poet of human nature?

(F) A discussion of Shakespeare's poetry
(G) An analysis of the characters Hamlet and Othello
(H) Biographical background on Shakespeare
(J) A description of Shakespeare's Globe Theater

Passage II

> The three paragraphs in this passage may or may not be in the most logical order. Each paragraph is numbered in brackets, and item 31 will ask you to choose the sequence of paragraphs that will make the essay most logical.

[1]

In the course of billions of years, millions of stars may <u>sometimes occasionally</u> [18] be concentrated into a region, or regions, only a few light years across, <u>and in these crowded conditions colliding</u> [19] with one another. Some of these collisions <u>would occur</u> [20] at high speeds, in which case the stars are partially or completely torn apart. Other collisions are gentle <u>bumps, but the stars coalesce</u> [21]. The bigger the star <u>becomes, the more likely</u> [22] it is to be hit again and the faster it grows until it reaches instability, collapses on itself, <u>and forms a black hole</u> [23].

[2]

When most of the stars and gas in the core of a

18. (A) NO CHANGE
(B) sometimes, occasionally
(C) occasionally
(D) off and on

19. (F) NO CHANGE
(G) colliding
(H) and in these crowded conditions they collide
(J) which causes them to collide

20. (A) NO CHANGE
(B) will occur
(C) to occur
(D) occur

21. (F) NO CHANGE
(G) bumps, since the stars
(H) bumps, and the stars coalesce
(J) bumps, with the stars coalescing

22. (A) NO CHANGE
(B) becomes the more
(C) becomes the more,
(D) becomes; the more

23. (F) NO CHANGE
(G) and a black hole is formed
(H) and when this happens a black hole is formed
(J) and thus a black hole is formed at this very moment

galaxy has been swallowed up by the black hole, the nucleus of the galaxy settles down to a relative quiet existence. This is probably the state of the nucleus of our own galaxy, but every hundred million years or so it may flare upto a brightness 100 times its present level when a globular cluster or especially large gas cloud of enormous size spirals into the nucleus.

[3]

Once formed, a central "seed" black hole grows mainly through the accretion of gas accumulated in the nucleus; gas obtained from disrupted stars, from supernova explosions, or from stars torn apart by the gravitational field of the black hole. Perhaps an entire galaxy can collide with another galaxy, and the result would be the transfer of large amounts of gas from one galaxy to each other.

24. (A) NO CHANGE
(B) have been
(C) will have been
(D) would have been

25. (F) NO CHANGE
(G) to a relatively
(H) for a relative and
(J) relatively

26. (A) NO CHANGE
(B) up
(C) up to
(D) OMIT

27. (F) NO CHANGE
(G) of great enormity
(H) which is huge
(J) OMIT

28. (A) NO CHANGE
(B) nucleus, gas
(C) nucleus. Gas
(D) nucleus gas

29. (F) NO CHANGE
(G) galaxy to result in
(H) galaxy. Such a collision could result in
(J) galaxy with the results that

30. (A) NO CHANGE
(B) to the other
(C) an other
(D) and another

Items 31 and 32 are about the passage as a whole.

31. Which of the following represents the most logical sequence for the paragraphs?

(F) 1,2,3
(G) 1,3,2
(H) 2,3,1
(J) 3,1,2

32. The author's intended audience is most probably:

(A) astronomers.
(B) young children.
(C) high school students.
(D) physicists.

QUIZ II (29 questions; 20 minutes)

Passage I

Georgia O'Keeffe, who's [1] death at age ninety-eight [2] closed one of the most fertile chapters of American creativity and flourished [3] as a maverick in her life and work. Since other [4] painters spent a season or two in the country trying to come to terms with the scenes and settings of the Southwest—O'Keeffe stayed a lifetime. When the canvases of other artists, working in the region [5] faded from view and then were neglected in the chronicle of American visual history [6], her stylized images made an indelible and permanent [7] impression on countless eyes.

Between 1900 and 1945, the region now called New Mexico both fascinated and also it perplexed [8] two generations of American artists. Despite successes, [9] many of those artists wearied of the industrial world of

1. (A) NO CHANGE
   (B) which
   (C) that
   (D) whose

2. (F) NO CHANGE
   (G) at the old age of ninety-eight
   (H) at the age of ninety-eight years
   (J) when she was ninety-eight years old

3. (A) NO CHANGE
   (B) creativity, and flourished
   (C) creativity—flourished
   (D) creativity, flourished

4. (F) NO CHANGE
   (G) Because other
   (H) In that other
   (J) Other

5. (A) NO CHANGE
   (B) artists working in the region,
   (C) artists working in the region
   (D) artists, who worked in the region

6. (F) NO CHANGE
   (G) got neglected then in the chronicle of American visual history
   (H) were also then neglected in the American visual history chronicle
   (J) then they were also totally neglected in the chronicle of American visual history

7. (A) NO CHANGE
   (B) indelible
   (C) indelible—and permanent—
   (D) indelible but permanent

8. (F) NO CHANGE
   (G) and perplexed
   (H) while perplexing
   (J) but perplexed

9. (A) NO CHANGE
   (B) Despite successes
   (C) In spite of their successes
   (D) Ensuring successes,

the east. The vast expanse of the west offered a promise for inspiration [10]. For these artists, life and art, so separate in New York and Paris, seemed inextricably bounded [11] in Southwestern cultures. Painters of every persuasion were convinced [12] that sampling this mysterious phenomenon will strengthen [13] and enrich their own work. Most were touched by what D. H. Lawrence called the "spirit of the place." Besides the scenic beauty bathed in clear golden light. The [14] rich traditions of New Mexico's Indian and Hispanic people who were living there [15] became frequent subjects of the artists who traveled to Taos and Santa Fe.

10. (F) NO CHANGE
(G) America's west, with its vast expanse, offered an inspiring promise.
(H) America's vast expanse of the west offered a promise for inspiration.
(J) Offering a promise of inspiration to the artists, was the vast expanse of the American west.

11. (A) NO CHANGE
(B) inextricably bound
(C) inextricable bounding
(D) inextricably bounding

12. (F) NO CHANGE
(G) could be convinced
(H) will be convinced
(J) are convincing

13. (A) NO CHANGE
(B) would strengthen
(C) strengthens
(D) strengthening

14. (F) NO CHANGE
(G) light, the
(H) light the
(J) light: the

15. (A) NO CHANGE
(B) who lived there
(C) living there
(D) OMIT

Items 16 and 17 pose questions about the passage as a whole.

16. Is the author's quote of D. H. Lawrence in the last paragraph appropriate?

(F) Yes, because the author is talking about how this spirit inspired artists and the quote strengthens his argument.
(G) No, because the author has already made his point about the spirit and the quote is redundant.
(H) No, because the author does not make it clear that Lawrence is an authority on the subject.
(J) Yes, because it is always a good idea to end an article with a quotation.

17. How might the author have developed the passage so that it was more interesting?

(A) The author could have told an anecdote about D. H. Lawrence.
(B) The author could have eliminated all mention of Georgia O'Keeffe.
(C) The author could have discussed the settling of New Mexico.
(D) The author could have been more specific about the other artists who went to the Southwest.

Passage II

Early in November 1850, the work of a logging detail from Fort Gaines in the Minnesota Territory was interrupted by a party of Chippewa warriors who demanded payment for the timber. <u>The loggers refused, so</u> [18] the Indians, <u>acting at the direction of Chief Hole-in-the-Day</u> [19] confiscated the government's oxen. The loggers had established their camp on Chippewa lands <u>without his authorizing it</u> [20]. <u>Therefore</u> [21], in a move designed to force reimbursements for the timber, Hole-in-the-Day <u>was ordering</u> [22] his braves to seize the oxen.

Captain John Todd, the commanding officer at Fort Gaines, demanded <u>that the cattle had to be returned to them</u> [23]. The chief's reply was firm, <u>and at the same time, it was friendly</u> [24]. In his message to Captain Todd, Hole-in-the-Day explained that he had <u>delayed to seize</u> [25] the cattle until he could meet Todd in council and had sent a messenger to the officer requesting a conference at Crow Wing. When Todd did not come, he <u>acted, additionally</u> [26] he later decided that since the army had not paid for timber cut the previous winter, he intended to keep

18. (F) NO CHANGE
    (G) The loggers refused—
    (H) The loggers refused:
    (J) The loggers refused so

19. (A) NO CHANGE
    (B) that acted at the direction of Chief Hole-in-the-Day,
    (C) acting at the direction of Chief Hole-in-the-Day,
    (D) (acting at the direction of Chief Hole-in-the-Day),

20. (F) NO CHANGE
    (G) without his authorization
    (H) without their authorizing it
    (J) without his authorization of it

21. (A) NO CHANGE
    (B) Henceforth
    (C) Since
    (D) On the contrary

22. (F) NO CHANGE
    (G) gave orders that
    (H) orders
    (J) ordered

23. (A) NO CHANGE
    (B) the return of the cattle
    (C) the cattle's returning
    (D) that they return the cattle

24. (F) NO CHANGE
    (G) but, at the same time, it was friendly
    (H) yet friendly
    (J) at the same time—friendly

25. (A) NO CHANGE
    (B) delayed to have seized
    (C) had delayed to seized
    (D) delayed seizing

26. (F) NO CHANGE
    (G) acted but additionally
    (H) acted. Additionally,
    (J) acted additionally,

the oxen until the tribe <u>was reimbursed by</u> [27] all the timber taken for the fort. Hole-in-the-Day concluded by saying: "Do not think hard of me, but I do as others would—the timber is mine." [28]

27. (A) NO CHANGE
(B) reimbursed for
(C) reimbursed
(D) was reimbursed for

28. Is the author's use of the quote in the final passage appropriate?

(F) Yes, because it neatly summarizes the main point of the passage.
(G) No, because the chief's thoughts were irrelevant to the events.
(H) Yes, but the author should have included a quotation from Captain Todd.
(J) No, because quotations have no place in expository writing.

Item 29 poses a question about the passage as a whole.

29. Which of the following best describes the overall character of the passage?

(A) Description of a scene
(B) Narration of events
(C) Comparison of two theories
(D) Argument for a change

QUIZ III (31 questions; 20 minutes)

Passage I

Most people have a certain crime <u>that one believes</u> [1] should be ranked as the worst of all crimes. For some <u>its'</u> [2] murder; for others it may be selling drugs to children. I believe, <u>moreover</u>, [3] that the worst of all crimes may be the confidence scheme.

The confidence scheme may seem an <u>odd</u> [4] choice for the worst crime since con games are usually <u>nonviolent. Although,</u> [5] it is a crime that ranks in heartlessness. Con artists are the most devious, the most harmful, and the most disruptive of society because <u>they break</u> [6] down the most important bonds of the social <u>order, honesty and trust</u> [7].

The con games themselves are <u>simplistic almost infantile</u> [8]. They work <u>on account of a con artist can</u> [9] win complete confidence, talk fast enough to keep the victim slightly confused, <u>and dangling</u> [10] enough temptation to suppress any suspicion or skepticism. The primary targets of these criminals

1. (A) NO CHANGE
   (B) that they believe
   (C) which one believes
   (D) that you believe

2. (F) NO CHANGE
   (G) they are
   (H) it's
   (J) its

3. (A) NO CHANGE
   (B) however
   (C) further
   (D) therefore

4. (F) NO CHANGE
   (G) obvious
   (H) irrelevant
   (J) apt

5. (A) NO CHANGE
   (B) nonviolent, though
   (C) nonviolent, but
   (D) nonviolent, and

6. (F) NO CHANGE
   (G) it breaks
   (H) of its breaking
   (J) of them breaking

7. (A) NO CHANGE
   (B) order, honesty, and trust
   (C) order: honesty and trust
   (D) order: honesty, and trust

8. (F) NO CHANGE
   (G) simplistic; almost infantile
   (H) simplistic, almost infantile
   (J) simplistic, yet almost infantile

9. (A) NO CHANGE
   (B) on account of a con artist's ability to
   (C) owing to a con artist's ability to
   (D) because a con artist can

10. (F) NO CHANGE
    (G) and dangles
    (H) and has dangled
    (J) and dangle

will be[11] the elderly and women. (And they prefer to work where there are large crowds.)[12]

11. (A) NO CHANGE
(B) to be
(C) are
(D) is

12. (F) NO CHANGE
(G) women, and they prefer to work in large crowds.
(H) women, preferring of course, to work in large crowds.
(J) women (who prefer to work in large crowds).

Items 13-17 pose questions about the passage as a whole.

13. Which of the following is most probably the author's opinion rather than a fact?

(A) Con artists are the most disruptive of society.
(B) Most con games are nonviolent
(C) Most of the targets are the elderly and women.
(D) Most con games are simple.

14. What would be the most logical continuation of the article?

(F) A description of some confidence games
(G) An account of the elderly as crime victims in society
(H) An account of the author's experience with con artists
(J) An explanation of crowd psychology

15. What would strengthen the author's contention that con games rank first in heartlessness?

(A) Statistics to show the number of people who were taken in by the con artist
(B) A discussion of the way the police handle the problem
(C) An example to show how the con artist breaks down honesty and trust
(D) An example to illustrate that con games are nonviolent and simple

---

Passage II

Elizabeth I had a sensuous and indulgent nature that she inherited from her mother, Anne Boleyn (who was beheaded by Henry VIII).[16]

16. (F) NO CHANGE
(G) (having been beheaded by Henry VIII)
(H) beheaded by Henry VIII
(J) OMIT

Splendor and pleasure is[17] the very air she breathed.

17. (A) NO CHANGE
(B) is,
(C) were
(D) were,

She loved gaiety, laughter, and wit. Her vanity remained even, to old age. The[18] vanity of a coquette.

18. (F) NO CHANGE
(G) remains, even to old age, the
(H) remains, even to old age the
(J) remained, even to old age, the

The statesmen who she outwitted [19] believed, almost to the end, that Elizabeth I was little more than a frivolous woman who was very vain [20]. But the Elizabeth whom they saw was far from being [21] all of Elizabeth. The willfulness of Henry and the triviality of Anne played over the surface of a nature so hard like [22] steel—a purely intellectual temperament. Her vanity and caprice carried no weight whatsoever [23] in state affairs. The coquette of the presence chamber had became [24] the coolest and hardest of politicians at the council board.

It was this part that gave her her marked superiority over [25] the statesmen of her time. No more nobler a group [26] of ministers ever gathered round the council board than those of Elizabeth, but she was the instrument of none. She listened and she weighed, but her policy, as a whole, was her own. It was the policy of good sense, not genius, she [27] endeavored to keep her throne, to keep England out of war, and she wanted [28] to restore civil and religious order.

19. (A) NO CHANGE
    (B) that she outwitted
    (C) whom she outwitted
    (D) who she was outwitting

20. (F) NO CHANGE
    (G) and she was also very vain
    (H) known for her great vanity
    (J) OMIT

21. (A) NO CHANGE
    (B) to be
    (C) having been
    (D) OMIT

22. (F) NO CHANGE
    (G) as hard as
    (H) so hard as
    (J) as hard like

23. (A) NO CHANGE
    (B) no matter what
    (C) whatever, at all
    (D) whatever, despite everything

24. (F) NO CHANGE
    (G) became
    (H) used to become
    (J) becomes

25. (A) NO CHANGE
    (B) superiority in regard to
    (C) superiority about
    (D) superior quality to

26. (F) NO CHANGE
    (G) nobler a group,
    (H) nobler group
    (J) more nobler of a group,

27. (A) NO CHANGE
    (B) not genius she
    (C) not genius. She
    (D) —not genius, she

28. (F) NO CHANGE
    (G) wanting
    (H) and wanting
    (J) and

Items 29-31 pose questions about the passage as a whole.

29. What might logically have preceded this passage in the entire article?

(A) Some biographical background on Elizabeth I
(B) A discussion of the wives of Henry VIII
(C) A discussion of the politics of Tudor England
(D) A discussion of the policies of Elizabeth's ministers

30. This passage is most probably taken from a:

(F) scholarly work on Renaissance England.
(G) biography of Elizabeth I.
(H) diary kept by one of Elizabeth's ministers.
(J) political science textbook.

31. Which of the following would most strengthen the passage?

(A) Knowing who the ministers were and what their policies were
(B) Examples of Elizabeth's dual nature
(C) A discussion of Henry VIII's policies
(D) A discussion of the role of the woman in Tudor England

SECTION FOUR—ENGLISH TESTING POINTS EXERCISE

DIRECTIONS: Choose the letter of the underlined portion of each sentence that is incorrect and write the structural testing point for each question. Choose the testing point from the following list:

1. Word Form
2. Wrong Word
3. Parallel Construction
4. Additional Word
5. Verb Tense
6. Omission of Word
7. Singular/Plural Noun
8. Word Reversal
9. Preposition
10. Article

Not all of the above testing points are used in the questions below, and some of the testing points are repeated. If you are not sure which testing point to choose, guess. Sometimes a testing point fits more than one category. Answers are on page 61.

1. A Bay Meadows jockey can be suspended [A] for [B] two years for carrying [C] an illegal electrical device while [D] a race.

   Testing Point: ______________________

   Answer: ____

2. For the first time in [A] three decades, Californians drank [B] less beer, winery [C], and hard liquor this year than they [D] did last year.

   Testing Point: ______________________

   Answer: ____

3. Many universities are calling for [A] additional ethnic studies [B] courses and changes in other courses give [C] more credit to [D] minority people.

   Testing Point: ______________________

   Answer: ____

4. A flammable liquid it [A] was used to ignite [B] a fire that [C] burned part of the [D] blighted Nairobi Shopping Center.

   Testing Point: ______________________

   Answer: ____

5. Twelve workers at a small semiconductor plant [A] were evacuated after [B] a container of gas poisonous [C] was accidently disconnected [D].

   Testing Point: ______________________

   Answer: ____

6. Some politicians share [A] lunch and jokes after electing [B] even though a few weeks before [C] they may have been throwing insults at [D] each other.

   Testing Point: ______________________

   Answer: ____

7. To help [A] with the [B] waste disposal problem, many Americans had sorted [C] their garbage for [D] recycling.

   Testing Point: ______________________

   Answer: ____

8. A [A] strong economies [B] makes imports cheap [C] and exports more expensive [D].

   Testing Point: ______________________

   Answer: ____

9. While (A) a strong defend (B) is important to any country, it cannot be more important than the (C) livelihood of its (D) citizens.

Testing Point: ____________________________

Answer: ____

10. In 1919 the California Assembly approve (A) plans to build (B) Highway One through (C) the central coast region known (D) as Big Sur.

Testing Point: ____________________________

Answer: ____

EXERCISE FIVE—ENGLISH ERROR IDENTIFICATION EXERCISE

DIRECTIONS: Without the aid of answer choices, identify and correct any and all errors in the underlined portion of the sentence only. Rewrite the underlined portion of the sentences correctly if they are incorrect. Answers are on page 61.

1. Quintus Marcius, the Roman legate in the war against Persius, wanted to gain time for the reason that he needed to wait for reinforcements to arrive.

2. It was us Americans who first became obsessed with the idea of physical fitness, but the madness has now spread to Europe.

3. The new tax reform bill may be as important, if not more important than, any other piece of legislation introduced in the Congress in the past decade.

4. Much of the Wall Street jargon one reads in the financial pages are taken from the game of poker such as the phrase "blue chip" stocks.

5. The primary aims of the Greenback Party, formed in 1875, was the adoption of a new monetary policy and the federal issuance of paper currency not backed by gold.

6. There is new evidence to suggest that a child's personality is developed more by everyday interactions rather than by traumatic events.

7. Required by law to register by the end of the year, the post office was crowded with legal aliens attempting to comply with the law before the deadline.

8. One of the greatest enterprises of modern times was the laying of the first transatlantic cable.

9. Throughout the New Deal era, the economic troubles of the nation's people spurred our political leaders on constantly to new, creative heights in social legislation.

10. Many experts agree that the rise in the number of street crimes reported due to increased unemployment and homelessness is a problem that can be solved only by providing jobs and homes to those who need them.

11. Although many tantalizing clues were found and the manhunt intensive, the infamous killer Jack the Ripper eluded the police.

12. Being that she was Oriental and a woman, she was denied several promotions that were later given to men.

13. Pets such as turtles and iguanas, which require very little personal attention, and are rapidly becoming popular in families having everyone working or in school.

14. It is only through the cooperation of all the forces of production and distribution that we can obtain a higher standard of living and ensuring a better future for our children.

15. Fought on April 19, 1775, Concord, Massachusetts, was the first serious engagement of the American Revolution.

16. Other desirable qualities of concrete, the only major building material that can be delivered to the job site in a pliable state, include its strength, economy, and the fact that it lasts a long while.

17. Though the sun has been the subject of scientific study for decades, there is no agreement among scientists for what caused the sun's beginning.

18. If enacted into law, the Compassion Pain Relief Act would allow American physicians prescribing heroin to the terminally ill in a hospital or hospice, a course of treatment which has long been available to British physicians.

19. As the first order of business, we were advised of the importance of regular and timely class attendance, told we could not smoke in the classroom, and were admonished to stay current with the reading at all times.

20. Advances in metallurgy have often been inspired by war, since Bessemer steel was the direct outcome of the attempts to correct the deficiencies of the artillery used in the Crimean War.

21. A plant turns toward a light because the light reduces the concentration of auxin, a growth hormone, on the more brightly lighted side of the stem.

22. The flavor of coffee is not diminished by the escape of coffee vapors, new research published by industrial chemists shows; rather, contact with oxygen is a far more important factor in flavor deterioration than the loss of vapors.

23. The origin of the expression "to get one's goat" comes from the practice of stabling a goat with high-strung racehorses in order to keep the animal calm.

24. The recent discovery of papers previously thought destroyed shows that Freud based some of his conclusions on a now discredited theory of genetics.

25. It is too early to say yet how the warnings of the Federal Reserve Board have been taken to heart by investors.

ENGLISH ANSWER KEY

SECTION TWO—ENGLISH PROBLEM-SOLVING (p. 32)

1. B
2. F
3. D
4. H
5. A
6. F
7. B
8. J
9. D
10. H
11. A
12. J
13. B
14. H
15. A
16. F
17. A
18. F
19. B
20. H
21. A
22. F
23. A
24. J
25. A
26. G
27. B
28. G
29. B
30. G
31. D
32. H
33. B
34. G
35. A
36. H
37. A
38. F
39. B
40. H
41. B
42. H
43. A
44. G
45. D
46. G
47. C
48. G
49. A
50. F
51. A
52. H
53. B
54. H
55. A
56. F
57. B
58. H

SECTION THREE—ENGLISH QUIZZES (p. 43)

QUIZ I

1. G
2. A
3. G
4. A
5. H
6. A
7. J
8. D
9. F
10. D
11. H
12. D
13. G
14. C
15. F
16. D
17. G
18. C
19. H
20. D
21. H
22. A
23. F
24. B
25. G
26. C
27. J
28. B
29. H
30. B
31. G
32. C

QUIZ II

1. D
2. F
3. D
4. J
5. C
6. F
7. B
8. G
9. A
10. F
11. B
12. F
13. B
14. G
15. D
16. F
17. D
18. F
19. C
20. G
21. A
22. J
23. B
24. H
25. D
26. H
27. D
28. F
29. B

QUIZ III

1. B
2. H
3. B
4. F
5. C
6. F
7. C
8. H
9. D
10. J
11. C
12. G
13. A
14. F
15. C
16. J
17. C
18. J
19. C
20. F
21. A
22. G
23. A
24. G
25. A
26. H
27. C
28. J
29. A
30. G
31. B

SECTION FOUR—ENGLISH TESTING POINTS EXERCISE (p. 55)

1. D	3. C	5. C	7. C	9. B
2. C	4. A	6. B	8. B	10. A

SECTION FIVE—ENGLISH ERROR IDENTIFICATION EXERCISE (p. 57)

1. Quintus Marcius, the Roman legate in the war against Persius, wanted to gain time because he was waiting for reinforcements to arrive.
2. It was we Americans who first became obsessed with the idea of physical fitness, but the madness has now spread to Europe.
3. The new tax reform bill may be as important as, if not more important than, any other piece of legislation introduced in the Congress in the past decade.
4. Much of the Wall Street jargon one reads in the financial pages, such as "blue chip" stocks, is taken from the game of poker.
5. The primary aims of the Greenback Party, formed in 1875, were the adoption of a new monetary policy and the federal issuance of paper currency not backed by gold.
6. There is new evidence to suggest that a child's personality is developed more by everyday interactions than by traumatic events.
7. Legal aliens, who are required by law to register by the end of the year, crowded into the post office in an attempt to comply with the law before the deadline.
8. The sentence is correct as written.
9. Throughout the New Deal era, the economic troubles of the nation's people constantly spurred on our political leaders to new, creative heights in social legislation.
10. Many experts agree that the rise in the number of reported street crimes, which is attributable to increased unemployment and homelessness, is a problem that can be solved only by providing jobs and homes to those who need them.
11. Although many tantalizing clues were found, and though the manhunt was intensive, the infamous killer Jack the Ripper eluded the police.
12. Because she was Oriental and a woman, she was denied several promotions that were later given to men.
13. Pets such as turtles and iguanas, which require very little personal attention, are rapidly becoming popular in families in which everyone is either working or in school.
14. It is only through the cooperation of all the forces of production and distribution that we can obtain a higher standard of living and ensure a better future for our children.
15. The first serious engagement of the American Revolution was the Battle of Concord, Massachusetts, fought on April 19, 1775.
16. Other desirable qualities of concrete, the only major building material that can be delivered to the job site in a pliable state, include its strength, economy, and durability.
17. Though the sun has been the subject of scientific study for decades, there is no agreement among scientists as to the origin of the sun.
18. If enacted into law, the Compassion Pain Relief Act would allow American physicians the option of prescribing heroin to the terminally ill in a hospital or hospice, a course of treatment which has long been available to British physicians.
19. As the first order of business, we were advised of the importance of regular and timely class attendance, told we could not smoke in the classroom, and admonished to stay current with the reading at all times.
20. Advances in metallurgy have often been inspired by war; Bessemer steel, for example, was the direct outcome of the attempts to correct the deficiencies of the artillery used in the Crimean War.
21. The original sentence is correct.
22. According to new research published by industrial chemists, the escape of coffee vapors is not the only factor that diminishes the taste of coffee; rather, contact with oxygen is a far more important factor in flavor deterioration than the loss of vapors.
23. The expression "to get one's goat" derives from the practice of stabling goats with high-strung racehorses to keep the animals calm.
24. Papers recently discovered, which had previously been thought destroyed, show that Freud based some of his conclusions on a now discredited theory of genetics.
25. It is too early to say whether the warnings of the Federal Reserve Board have been taken to heart by investors.

Strategy Summary Sheet
ACT • PLAN • EXPLORE—ENGLISH

STRUCTURE OF ENGLISH TESTS: The English section is the first of four sections on the ACT, PLAN, and EXPLORE. The English section is 45 minutes, in which you must answer 75 multiple-choice English questions, accompanying five prose passages. The PLAN is 50 items, 30 minutes; the EXPLORE is 40 items, 30 minutes. Some items refer to underlined portions of the text and offer four alternatives including "NO CHANGE" (A or F). Other items refer to sections of the text or the passage as a whole. The following summarizes how many items test each content area on the three tests:

		ACT (75 questions)	PLAN (50 questions)	EXPLORE (40 questions)
Usage/Mechanics:	Punctuation	10	7	6
	Basic Grammar/Usage	12	9	8
	Sentence Structure	18	14	11
Rhetorical Skills:	Strategy	12	6	5
	Organization	11	7	5
	Style	12	7	5

GENERAL STRATEGY: This is neither a test of reading nor vocabulary. Don't get hung up on unfamiliar words or topics; just isolate errors and fix them. Also, remember that some of the underlined portions are correct. Don't create errors where they don't exist. Unless one of the other choices fixes a definite error, choose "NO CHANGE."

1. Read the passage, anticipating errors and appropriate corrections.

2. Decide what, if anything, is wrong with the underlined portion.

3. Without looking at the answer choices, suggest an appropriate correction.

4. Look for your suggestion among the answer choices. If it's there, choose it, if not, examine how the choices address the error you identified. Eliminate answer choices that correct the original errors, but introduce additional new problems.

5. Read your choice back into the passage to make sure it fits.

6. If you cannot find the right answer, eliminate any obviously wrong (often wordy or just plain silly) choices and *guess.* Incorrect answers are not penalized on the ACT, PLAN, or EXPLORE.

CHECKLIST FOR POSSIBLE ENGLISH ERRORS:

1. *Verbs:* Does the sentence have a main verb? If not, is there a verb form underlined that could be changed into a main verb? If any verbs are underlined, do they agree with their subjects? Are they in the correct tense?

2. *Pronouns:* If any pronouns are underlined, do they have clearly identifiable referents? Do they agree with their referents? Do the underlined pronouns have correct case?

3. *Adjectives and Adverbs:* If an adjective or adverb is underlined, is it correctly modifying a verb or another adjective? Is the use of a specific adjective or adverb appropriate?

4. *Prepositions:* If a preposition is underlined, is its use idiomatic?

5. *Conjunctions:* If a conjunction is underlined, is its use consistent with the logic of the sentence?

6. *Modifier:* If the sentence has a modifier, is it close to what it modifies? Is the idea clearly and logically presented?

7. *Comparisons:* If the sentence makes a comparison, are like things being compared? Is the idea clearly and logically presented?

8. *Parallelism:* If the sentence includes a series of ideas, do the ideas have the same form?

9. *Diction:* Do the underlined words mean what the sentence intends for them to mean?

10. *Conciseness:* Does the sentence use more words than necessary? Does the proposed answer choice eliminate this wordiness without introducing additional errors?

11. *Directness:* Can the sentence be worded more directly? Does the proposed answer choice eliminate this indirectness without introducing additional errors?

ADDITIONAL NOTES AND STRATEGIES FROM IN-CLASS DISCUSSION:

CAMBRIDGE

EDUCATIONAL SERVICES, INC.®

ACT • PLAN • EXPLORE MATHEMATICS

CAMBRIDGE
EDUCATIONAL SERVICES, INC.®

AMERICA'S #1 CAMPUS-BASED TESTPREP

Cambridge Course Concept Outline
ACT • PLAN • EXPLORE—MATHEMATICS

I. MATHEMATICS REVIEW (p. 69)

A. MATHEMATICS PRELIMINARIES
1. **TEACHING THE MATHEMATICS LESSON**
2. **FORMAT OF THE ACT, PLAN, AND EXPLORE TESTS**
3. **DIRECTIONS FOR MATHEMATICS PROBLEMS**
4. **WHAT IS TESTED**
   a. **ARITHMETIC MANIPULATION** (Review Question #1)
   b. **ARITHMETIC APPLICATION** (Review Question #2)
   c. **ALGEBRA MANIPULATION** (Review Question #3)
   d. **ALGEBRA APPLICATION** (Review Question #4)
   e. **GEOMETRY MANIPULATION** (Review Question #5)
   f. **GEOMETRY APPLICATION** (Review Question #6)
   g. **TRIGONOMETRY APPLICATION** (Review Question #7)
5. **IMPORTANT FACTS ABOUT THE ANSWER CHOICES**
   a. **THE CHOICES ARE ARRANGED IN ORDER**
   b. **WRONG CHOICES CORRESPOND TO CONCEPTUAL ERRORS** (Review Question #8)
6. **READ THE PROBLEM CAREFULLY** (Review Questions #9-12)
7. **THE MATHEMATICS LADDER OF DIFFICULTY** (Review Questions #13-22)
8. **ADDITIONAL HELPFUL HINTS**

B. ARITHMETIC REVIEW AND STRATEGIES
1. **SIMPLE MANIPULATIONS—JUST DO IT!** (Review Questions #23-24)
2. **COMPLICATED MANIPULATION—LOOK FOR SHORTCUTS**
   a. **SIMPLIFYING** (Review Question #25)
   b. **FACTORING** (Review Questions #26-27)
   c. **APPROXIMATION** (Review Questions #28-30)
   d. **THE FLYING X**
   e. **DECIMAL/FRACTION EQUIVALENTS** (Review Questions #31-32)
3. **SOLVING COMPLICATED ARITHMETIC APPLICATION PROBLEMS** (Review Questions #33-34)
4. **COMMON ARITHMETIC PROBLEMS**
   a. **PROPERTIES OF NUMBERS** (Review Questions #35-43)
   b. **ABSOLUTE VALUES** (Review Question #44)
   c. **COMPLEX NUMBERS** (Review Questions #45-46)
   d. **PERCENTS** (Review Questions #47-53)
   e. **RATIOS** (Review Questions #54-55)
   f. **AVERAGES** (Review Questions #56-60)
   g. **MEDIAN** (Review Question #61)
   h. **MODE** (Review Question #62)
   i. **PROPORTIONS** (Review Questions #63-65)
5. **"TEST-THE-TEST"** (Review Questions #66-71)

C. ALGEBRA REVIEW AND STRATEGIES

1. **SIMPLE ALGEBRAIC MANIPULATIONS—JUST DO IT!** (Review Questions #72-73)
2. **MANIPULATION OF ALGEBRAIC EXPRESSIONS**
   a. **EVALUATING EXPRESSIONS** (Review Questions #74-77)
   b. **EXPONENTS** (Review Questions #78-79)
   c. **FACTORING** (Review Questions #80-82)
3. **FUNCTION MATH** (Review Questions #83-85)
4. **SOLVING EQUATIONS**
   a. **ONE EQUATION WITH ONE VARIABLE** (Review Question #86)
   b. **ONE EQUATION WITH TWO VARIABLES** (Review Question #87)
   c. **TWO EQUATIONS WITH TWO VARIABLES** (Review Questions #88-92)
   d. **EQUATION WITH ABSOLUTE VALUES** (Review Question #93)
   e. **QUADRATIC EQUATIONS** (Review Question #94-98)
5. **"TEST-THE-TEST"** (Review Questions #99-110)
6. **COORDINATE GEOMETRY**
   a. **COORDINATE PLANE** (Review Question #111)
   b. **SLOPE OF A LINE** (Review Question #112)
   c. **SLOPE-INTERCEPT FORM OF A LINEAR EQUATION** (Review Question #113)
   d. **THE DISTANCE FORMULA** (Review Question #114)
   e. **GRAPHING LINEAR EQUATIONS IN TWO VARIABLES USING SOLUTIONS** (Review Question #115)
   f. **GRAPHING FIRST-DEGREE INEQUALITIES** (Review Question #116)
   g. **GRAPHING QUADRATIC EQUATIONS** (Review Questions #117-118)

D. GEOMETRY REVIEW AND STRATEGIES

1. **ANGLES** (Review Questions #119-123)
2. **TRIANGLES** (Review Questions #124-129)
3. **RECTANGLES AND SQUARES** (Review Questions #130-132)
4. **CIRCLES** (Review Question #133)
5. **COMPLEX FIGURES** (Review Questions #134-139)
6. **ALTERNATIVE STRATEGIES**
   a. **GUESTIMATING** (Review Questions #140-142)
   b. **MEASURING** (Review Questions #143-144)
   c. **MEASTIMATING** (Review Questions #145-146)

D. TRIGONOMETRY REVIEW AND STRATEGIES

1. **DEFINITION OF SIX TRIGONOMETRIC FUNCTIONS** (Review Questions #147-148)
2. **DETERMINING TRIGONOMETRY VALUES**
3. **TRIGONOMETRIC RELATIONSHIPS** (Review Questions #149-150)

II. MATHEMATICS PROBLEM-SOLVING (p. 94)

III. MATHEMATICS QUIZZES (p. 105)

IV. TRIGONOMETRY EXERCISE (p. 114)

V. CALCULATOR EXERCISE (p. 117)

SECTION ONE—MATHEMATICS REVIEW

DIRECTIONS: The questions in this section accompany the in-class review of the Mathematics concepts and skills tested by the ACT, PLAN, and EXPLORE tests. You will work through the questions with your instructor in class. Solve each problem and choose the correct answer. Answers are on page 119.

Note: Unless otherwise stated, all of the following should be assumed.

- Illustrative figures are NOT necessarily drawn to scale.
- Geometric figures lie in a plane.
- The word *line* indicates a straight line.
- The word *average* indicates arithmetic mean.

1. What is the average of 8.5, 7.8, and 7.7?

(A) 8.3
(B) 8.2
(C) 8.1
(D) 8.0
(E) 7.9

2. If the price of fertilizer has been decreased from 3 pounds for $2 to 5 pounds for $2, how many more pounds of fertilizer can be purchased for $10 than could have been purchased before?

(F) 2
(G) 8
(H) 10
(J) 12
(K) 15

3. If $\frac{2x-5}{3} = -4x$, then $x = ?$

(A) -1
(B) $-\frac{5}{14}$
(C) 0
(D) $\frac{5}{14}$
(E) 1

4. A vending machine dispenses k cups of coffee, each at a cost of c cents, every day. During a period d days long, what is the amount of money in *dollars* taken in by the vending machine from the sale of coffee?

(F) $\frac{100kc}{d}$
(G) kcd
(H) $\frac{dk}{c}$
(J) $\frac{kcd}{100}$
(K) $\frac{kc}{100d}$

5. If a circle has a radius of 1, what is its area?

(A) $\frac{\pi}{2}$
(B) π
(C) 2π
(D) 4π
(E) π^2

6. In the figure below, a triangle is inscribed in a circle with center O. What is the area of the circle?

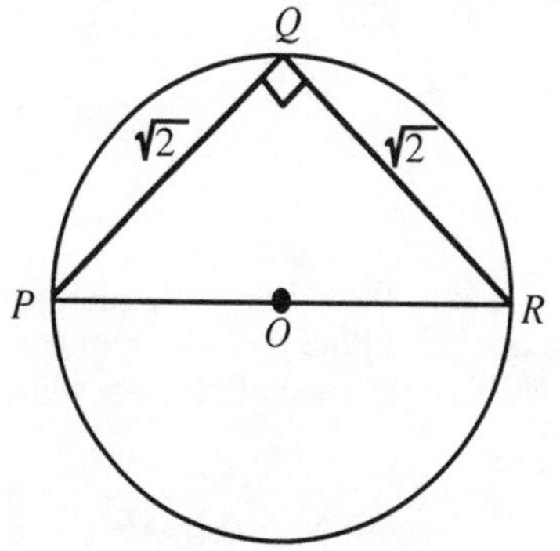

(F) $\frac{\pi}{2}$
(G) $\frac{\pi}{\sqrt{2}}$
(H) π
(J) $\pi\sqrt{2}$
(K) 2π

7. In the figure below, sin A = ?

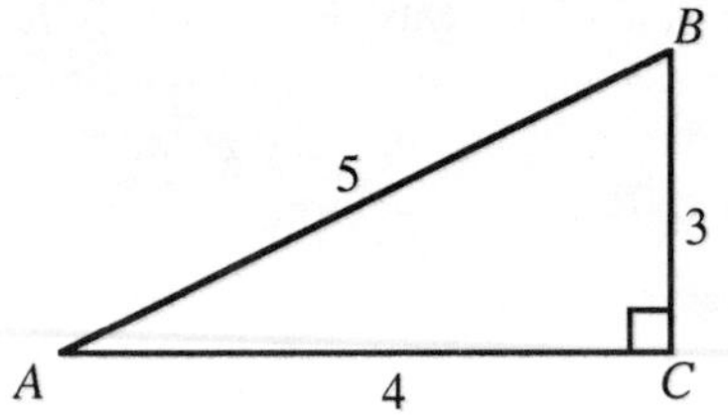

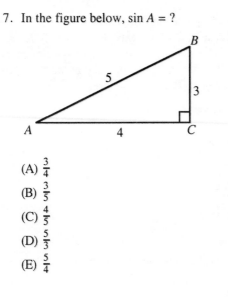

(A) $\frac{3}{4}$
(B) $\frac{3}{5}$
(C) $\frac{4}{5}$
(D) $\frac{5}{3}$
(E) $\frac{5}{4}$

8. In a certain year, the number of girls who graduated from City High School was twice the number of boys. If $\frac{3}{4}$ of the girls and $\frac{5}{6}$ of the boys went to college immediately after graduation, what fraction of the graduates that year went to college immediately after graduation?

(F) $\frac{5}{36}$
(G) $\frac{16}{27}$
(H) $\frac{7}{9}$
(J) $\frac{29}{36}$
(K) $\frac{31}{36}$

9. A jar contains black and white marbles. If there are ten marbles in the jar, which of the following could NOT be the ratio of black to white marbles?

(A) 9:1
(B) 7:3
(C) 1:1
(D) 1:4
(E) 1:10

10. If n is a negative number, which of the following is the LEAST?

(F) $-n$
(G) $n - n$
(H) $n + n$
(J) n^2
(K) n^4

11. If a machine produces 240 thingamabobs per hour, how many *minutes* are needed for the machine to produce 30 thingamabobs?

(A) 6
(B) 7.5
(C) 8
(D) 12
(E) 12.5

12. Of the 120 people in a room, $\frac{3}{5}$ are women. If $\frac{2}{3}$ of the people are married, what is the maximum number of women in the room who could be *unmarried*?

(F) 80
(G) 72
(H) 48
(J) 40
(K) 32

13. Three friends are playing a game in which each person simultaneously displays one of three hand signs, a clenched fist, an open palm, or two extended fingers. How many different combinations of the signs are possible?

(A) 3
(B) 9
(C) 10
(D) 12
(E) 27

14. If $\frac{1}{3}$ of the girls at a school equals $\frac{1}{5}$ of the total number of students, then what is the ratio of girls to boys at the school?

(F) 5:3
(G) 3:2
(H) 2:5
(J) 1:3
(K) 1:5

NOTES AND STRATEGIES

15. Peter walked from point P to point Q and back again, a total distance of 2 miles. If he averaged 4 miles per hour on the trip from P to Q and 5 miles per hour on the return trip, what was his average walking speed for the entire trip?

(A) $2\frac{2}{9}$
(B) 4
(C) $4\frac{4}{9}$
(D) $4\frac{1}{2}$
(E) 5

16. After a 20-percent decrease in price, the cost of an item is D dollars. What was the price of the item before the decrease?

(F) $0.75D$
(G) $0.80D$
(H) $1.20D$
(J) $1.25D$
(K) $1.5D$

17. On a certain trip, a motorist drove 10 miles at 30 miles per hour, 10 miles at 40 miles per hour, and 10 miles at 50 miles per hour. What portion of her total driving time was spent driving 50 miles per hour?

(A) $\frac{5}{7}$
(B) $\frac{5}{12}$
(C) $\frac{1}{3}$
(D) $1\frac{13}{51}$
(E) $\frac{12}{47}$

18. What is the largest number of non-overlapping sections that can be created when a circle is crossed by three straight lines?

(F) 3
(G) 4
(H) 5
(J) 6
(K) 7

19. At Glenridge High School, 20 percent of the students are seniors. If all of the seniors attended the school play, and 60 percent of all the students attended the play, what percent of the *non-seniors* attended the play?

(A) 20%
(B) 40%
(C) 50%
(D) 60%
(E) 100%

20. The water meter at a factory displays the reading below. What is the MINIMUM number of cubic feet of water the factory must use before four of the five digits on the meter are the same?

Water Usage in Cubic Feet

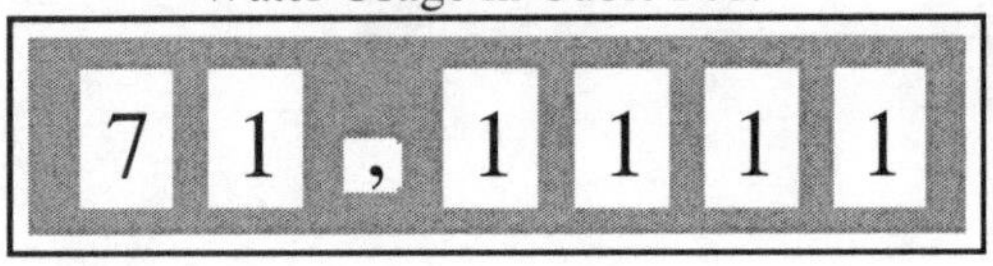

(F) 10,000
(G) 1,000
(H) 999
(J) 666
(K) 9

21. A telephone call from City X to City Y costs \$1.00 for the first three minutes and \$0.25 for every minute thereafter. What is the maximum length of time (in minutes) that a caller could talk for \$3.00?

(A) 8
(B) 10
(C) 11
(D) 12
(E) 13

22. In the figure below, $m + n + o + p + q + r = ?$

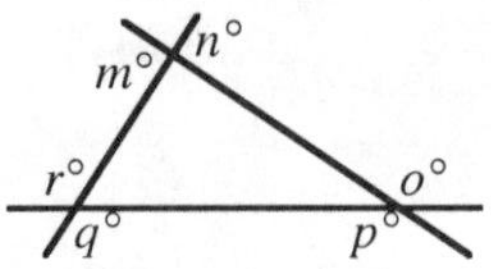

(F) 360
(G) 540
(H) 720
(J) 900
(K) Cannot be determined from the information given.

23. $\frac{8}{9} - \frac{7}{8} = ?$

(A) $\frac{1}{72}$
(B) $\frac{15}{72}$
(C) $\frac{1}{7}$
(D) $\frac{1}{8}$
(E) $\frac{15}{7}$

24. $\sqrt{1 - \left(\frac{2}{9} + \frac{1}{36} + \frac{1}{18}\right)} = ?$

(F) $\frac{1}{5}$
(G) $\sqrt{\frac{2}{3}}$
(H) $\frac{5}{6}$
(J) 1
(K) $\sqrt{3}$

25. $\frac{1}{2} \bullet \frac{2}{3} \bullet \frac{3}{4} \bullet \frac{4}{5} \bullet \frac{5}{6} \bullet \frac{6}{7} \bullet \frac{7}{8} = ?$

(A) $\frac{1}{56}$
(B) $\frac{1}{8}$
(C) $\frac{28}{37}$
(D) $\frac{41}{43}$
(E) $\frac{55}{56}$

26. 86(37) – 37(85) = ?

(F) 0
(G) 1
(H) 37
(J) 85
(K) 86

27. Which of the following is the prime factorization of 120?

(A) (2)(2)(15)
(B) (2)(3)(4)(5)
(C) (2)(2)(3)(10)
(D) (2)(2)(2)(3)(5)
(E) (2)(2)(3)(3)(5)

28. $\frac{0.2521 \bullet 8.012}{1.014}$ is approximately equal to what?

(F) 0.25
(G) 0.5
(H) 1.0
(J) 1.5
(K) 2.0

29. Which of the following fractions is the largest?

(A) $\frac{111}{221}$
(B) $\frac{75}{151}$
(C) $\frac{333}{998}$
(D) $\frac{113}{225}$
(E) $\frac{101}{301}$

30. –4.01(3.2) + 0.2(0.4) = ?

(F) –12.752
(G) –4.536
(H) 0.432
(J) 1.251
(K) 12.783

31. 0.125 • 0.125 • 64 = ?

(A) 0.625
(B) 0.125
(C) 0.5
(D) 1
(E) 8

32. $\frac{0.111 \bullet 0.666}{0.166 \bullet 0.125}$ is approximately equal to what?

(F) 6.8
(G) 4.3
(H) 3.6
(J) 1.6
(K) 0.9

33. If the senior class has 360 students, of whom $\frac{5}{12}$ are women, and the junior class has 350 students, of whom $\frac{4}{7}$ are women, how many more women are there in the junior class than in the senior class?

(A) $(350 - 360)(\frac{4}{7} - \frac{5}{12})$

(B) $\frac{(350 - 360)(\frac{4}{7} - \frac{5}{12})}{2}$

(C) $(\frac{4}{7} - \frac{5}{12})(360 - 350)$

(D) $(\frac{4}{7} \bullet 350) - (\frac{5}{12} \bullet 360)$

(E) $(\frac{5}{12} \bullet 350) - (\frac{4}{17} \bullet 350)$

34. If the price of candy increases from 5 pounds for \$7 to 3 pounds for \$7, how much less candy (in pounds) can be purchased for \$3.50 at the new price than at the old price?

(F) $\frac{2}{7}$
(G) $1\frac{17}{35}$
(H) $3\frac{34}{35}$
(J) 1
(K) 2

35. If n is any integer, which of the following is always an odd integer?

(A) $n - 1$
(B) $n + 1$
(C) $n + 2$
(D) $2n + 1$
(E) $2n + 2$

36. Which of the following represents the product of two consecutive integers?

(F) $2n + 1$
(G) $2n + n$
(H) $2n^2$
(J) $n^2 + 1$
(K) $n^2 + n$

37. If n is an integer, which of the following must be even?

I. $2n$
II. $2n + n$
III. $2n \bullet n$

(A) I only
(B) II only
(C) III only
(D) I and II only
(E) I and III only

38. If n is the first number in a series of three consecutive even numbers, which of the following represents the sum of the three numbers?

(F) $n + 2$
(G) $n + 4$
(H) $n + 6$
(J) $3n + 6$
(K) $6(3n)$

39. If n is an odd number, which of the following represents the third odd number following n?

(A) $n + 3$
(B) $n + 4$
(C) $n + 6$
(D) $3n + 3$
(E) $4n + 4$

40. If n is an odd integer, which of the following must also be odd?

I. $n + n$
II. $n + n + n$
III. $n \bullet n \bullet n$

(F) I only
(G) II only
(H) III only
(J) II and III only
(K) I, II, and III

NOTES AND STRATEGIES

41. If n is a negative number, which of the following must be positive?

I. $2n$
II. n^2
III. n^5

(A) I only
(B) II only
(C) III only
(D) I and II only
(E) II and III only

42. If $0 < x < 1$, which of the following is the largest?

(F) x
(G) $2x$
(H) x^2
(J) x^3
(K) $x + 1$

43. If $-1 < x < 0$, which of the following is the largest?

(A) -1
(B) x
(C) $2x$
(D) x^3
(E) $x - 1$

44. What is $|5| - |-5| + |-3|$?

(F) -8
(G) -3
(H) 3
(J) 8
(K) 13

45. $(3 + i)(4 - 3i) = ?$

(A) $12 + 3i^2$
(B) $12 - 3i^2$
(C) $9 - 5i^2$
(D) $9 - 5i$
(E) $15 - 5i$

46. $\frac{1}{2-i} = ?$

(F) -2
(G) -1
(H) $\frac{2+i}{5}$
(J) $\frac{2-i}{5}$
(K) $\frac{2+i}{3}$

47. If a jar contains 24 white marbles and 48 black marbles, then what percent of all the marbles in the jar are black?

(A) 10%
(B) 25%
(C) $33\frac{1}{3}\%$
(D) 60%
(E) $66\frac{2}{3}\%$

48. Three friends shared the cost of a tape recorder. If Andy, Barbara, and Donna each paid \$12, \$30, and \$18, respectively, then Donna paid what percent of the cost of the tape recorder?

(F) 10%
(G) 30%
(H) $33\frac{1}{3}\%$
(J) 50%
(K) $66\frac{2}{3}\%$

49. If 20 people attended Professor Rodriguez's class on Monday and 25 attended on Tuesday, then the number of people who attended on Tuesday was what percent of the number who attended on Monday?

(A) 5%
(B) 20%
(C) 25%
(D) 80%
(E) 125%

50. If the population of a town was 20,000 in 1970 and 16,000 in 1980, what was the percentage decline in the town's population?

(F) 50%
(G) 25%
(H) 20%
(J) 10%
(K) 5%

Questions #51-53 are based on the following table.

NUMBER OF FIRES IN CITY *Y*

Year	Number of Fires
1982	100
1983	125
1984	140
1985	150
1986	135

51. The number of fires in 1982 was what percent of the number of fires in 1983?

(A) 25%
(B) $66\frac{2}{3}$%
(C) 80%
(D) 100%
(E) 125%

52. The number of fires in 1986 was what percent of the number of fires in 1985?

(F) 90%
(G) 82%
(H) 50%
(J) 25%
(K) 10%

53. What was the percent decrease in the number of fires from 1985 to 1986?

(A) 10%
(B) 25%
(C) 50%
(D) 82%
(E) 90%

54. A groom must divide 12 quarts of oats between two horses. If Dobbin is to receive twice as much as Pegasus, how many quarts of oats should the groom give to Dobbin?

(F) 4
(G) 6
(H) 8
(J) 9
(K) 10

55. If the ratio of John's allowance to Lucy's allowance is 3:2, and the ratio of Lucy's allowance to Bob's allowance is 3:4, what is the ratio of John's allowance to Bob's allowance?

(A) 1:6
(B) 2:5
(C) 1:2
(D) 3:4
(E) 9:8

56. If the average of 35, 38, 41, 43, and x is 37, what is x?

(F) 28
(G) 30
(H) 31
(J) 34
(K) 36

57. In a certain shipment, the average weight of six packages is 50 pounds. If another package is added to the shipment, the average weight of the seven packages is 52 pounds. What is the weight (in pounds) of the additional package?

(A) 2
(B) 7
(C) 52
(D) 62
(E) 64

58. For a certain student, the average of ten test scores is 80. If the high and low scores are dropped, the average is 81. What is the average of the high and low scores?

(F) 76
(G) 78
(H) 80
(J) 81
(K) 82

59. In a certain course, a student's final exam grade is weighted twice as heavily as his midterm grade. If a student receives a score of 84 on his final exam and 90 on his midterm, what is his average for the course?

(A) 88
(B) 87.5
(C) 86
(D) 86.5
(E) 85

60. In a group of children, three children are ten years old and two are five years old. What is the average age in years of the children in the group?

(F) 6
(G) 6.5
(H) 7
(J) 7.5
(K) 8

61. The number of employment applications received by a certain firm per month during 1994 was:

8, 3, 5, 3, 4, 3, 1, 0, 3, 4, 0, 7

What is the median number of applications?

(A) 3
(B) 4
(C) 5
(D) 6
(E) 7

62. The monthly electric bills for a given year were as follows: $40, 38, 36, 38, 34, 34, 30, 32, 34, 37, 39, and 40. What is the mode?

(F) 33
(G) 34
(H) 35
(J) 36
(K) 37

63. If 4.5 pounds of chocolate cost $10, how many pounds of chocolate can be purchased for $12?

(A) $4\frac{3}{4}$
(B) $5\frac{2}{5}$
(C) $5\frac{1}{2}$
(D) $5\frac{3}{4}$
(E) 6

64. At a certain school, 45 percent of the students bought a yearbook. If 540 students bought yearbooks, how many students did not buy a yearbook?

(F) 243
(G) 540
(H) 575
(J) 660
(K) 957

65. Walking at a constant rate of 4 miles per hour, it takes Jill exactly one hour to walk home from school. If she walks at a constant rate of 5 miles per hour, how many minutes will the trip take?

(A) 48
(B) 54
(C) 56
(D) 72
(E) 112

66. Which of the following is the larger of two numbers whose product is 600 and whose sum is five times their difference?

(F) 10
(G) 15
(H) 20
(J) 30
(K) 50

67. If $\frac{1}{3}$ of a number equals 3 more than $\frac{1}{4}$ of the number, then what is the number?

(A) 18
(B) 24
(C) 30
(D) 36
(E) 48

68. If $\frac{3}{5}$ of a number equals 4 more than $\frac{1}{2}$ of the number, then what is the number?

(F) 20
(G) 28
(H) 35
(J) 40
(K) 56

NOTES AND STRATEGIES

69. When both 16 and 9 are divided by n, the remainder is 2. What is n?

(A) 3
(B) 4
(C) 5
(D) 6
(E) 7

70. The sum of the digits of a three-digit number is 16. If the tens digit of the number is 3 times the units digit, and the units digit is $\frac{1}{4}$ of the hundreds digit, then what is the number?

(F) 446
(G) 561
(H) 682
(J) 862
(K) 914

71. If the sum of five consecutive integers is 40, what is the smallest of the five integers?

(A) 4
(B) 5
(C) 6
(D) 7
(E) 8

72. If $a^3 + b = 3 + a^3$, then $b = ?$

(F) 3^3
(G) $3\sqrt{3}$
(H) 3
(J) $\sqrt[3]{3}$
(K) $-\sqrt{3}$

73. Which of the following is equivalent to $4a + 3b - (-2a - 3b)$?

(A) $2a$
(B) $12ab$
(C) $2a + 6b$
(D) $6a + 6b$
(E) $8a + 9b$

74. If $x = 2$, what is the value of $x^2 + 2x - 2$?

(F) –2
(G) 0
(H) 2
(J) 4
(K) 6

75. If $x = 2$, then $\frac{1}{x^2} + \frac{1}{x} - \frac{x}{2} = ?$

(A) $-\frac{3}{4}$
(B) $-\frac{1}{4}$
(C) 0
(D) $\frac{1}{4}$
(E) $\frac{1}{2}$

76. If $\frac{1}{3}(x) = 10$, then $\frac{1}{6}(x) = ?$

(F) $\frac{1}{15}$
(G) $\frac{2}{3}$
(H) 2
(J) 5
(K) 30

77. If $p = 1$, $q = 2$, and $r = 3$, then $\frac{(q \bullet r)(r - q)}{(q - p)(p \bullet q)} = ?$

(A) –3
(B) –1
(C) 0
(D) 3
(E) 6

78. $\frac{9(x^2y^3)^6}{(3x^6y^9)^2} = ?$

(F) 1
(G) 3
(H) x^2y^3
(J) $3x^2y^3$
(K) $x^{12}y^{12}$

79. $2^0 + 2^1 + 2^{-2} = ?$

(A) -2
(B) $-\frac{1}{2}$
(C) 0
(D) $2\frac{3}{4}$
(E) $3\frac{1}{4}$

80. $\frac{x^2 - y^2}{x + y} = ?$

(F) $x^2 - y^2$
(G) $x^2 + y^2$
(H) $x^2 + y$
(J) $x + y^2$
(K) $x - y$

81. $\frac{x^2 - x - 6}{x + 2} = ?$

(A) $x^2 - \frac{1}{2}x - 3$
(B) $x^2 - 2$
(C) $x - 2$
(D) $x - 3$
(E) x

82. Which of the following is the factorization of $6x^2 + 4x - 2$?

(F) $(6x + 1)(x - 3)$
(G) $(6x + 3)(x - 1)$
(H) $(3x - 1)(2x - 2)$
(J) $(2x + 2)(3x - 1)$
(K) $(2x + 4)(3x - 2)$

83. If $f(x) = x^2 - x$ for all integers, then $f(-2) = ?$

(A) -6
(B) -2
(C) 0
(D) 4
(E) 6

84. If $f(x) = x^2 - x$, then $f(f(3)) = ?$

(F) 27
(G) 30
(H) 58
(J) 72
(K) 121

85. If $f(x) = x + 3$ and $g(x) = 2x - 5$, what is $f(g(2))$?

(A) -2
(B) 0
(C) 2
(D) 4
(E) 10

86. If $(2 + 3)(1 + x) = 25$, then $x = ?$

(F) $\frac{1}{5}$
(G) $\frac{1}{4}$
(H) 1
(J) 4
(K) 5

87. If $x + y = 3$, then $2x + 2y = ?$

(A) $\frac{2}{3}$
(B) $\frac{1}{2}$
(C) $\frac{2}{3}$
(D) 6
(E) Cannot be determined from the information given.

88. If $2x + y = 8$ and $x - y = 1$, then $x = ?$

(F) -2
(G) -1
(H) 0
(J) 1
(K) 3

89. If $7x = 2$ and $3y - 7x = 10$, then $y = ?$

(A) 2
(B) 3
(C) 4
(D) 5
(E) 6

90. If $2x + y = 8$ and $x - y = 1$, then $x + y = ?$

(F) –1
(G) 1
(H) 2
(J) 3
(K) 5

91. If $4x + 5y = 12$ and $3x + 4y = 5$, then $7(x + y) = ?$

(A) 7
(B) 14
(C) 49
(D) 77
(E) 91

92. Which of the following equations correctly describes the relationship between the values x and y in the table below?

x	–2	–1	0	1	2
y	$\frac{10}{3}$	$\frac{8}{3}$	2	$\frac{4}{3}$	$\frac{2}{3}$

(F) $3x + 2y = 6$
(G) $3x - 2y = 3$
(H) $3x + 3y = -6$
(J) $6x + 4y = 7$
(K) $2x + 3y = 6$

93. Which of the following express all, and only, the values of x that satisfy $|2x + 4| < 4$?

(A) $x > -4$
(B) $x < -4$
(C) $x > 0$
(D) $0 < x < 4$
(E) $-4 < x < 0$

94. What are the solutions for the equation $2x^2 - 2x = 12$?

(F) $\{-3, -2\}$
(G) $\{-2, 3\}$
(H) $\{\frac{2}{3}, 3\}$
(J) $\{\frac{3}{2}, 2\}$
(K) $\{2, 3\}$

95. If $x^2 - 3x = 4$, then which of the following shows all the possible values of x?

(A) $\{4, 1\}$
(B) $\{4, -1\}$
(C) $\{-4, 1\}$
(D) $\{-4, -1\}$
(E) $\{-4, 1, 4\}$

96. If $x^2 - y^2 = 0$ and $x + y = 1$, then $x - y = ?$

(F) –1
(G) 0
(H) 1
(J) 2
(K) 4

97. What is the solution set for the following equation: $3x^2 + 3x = 6$?

(A) $\{1, -2\}$
(B) $\{1, 2\}$
(C) $\{\frac{1}{2}, 1\}$
(D) $\{\frac{1}{2}, \frac{1}{3}\}$
(E) $\{-1, -2\}$

98. Which of the following is the complete solution set to the equation $2x^2 - 3x = 2$?

(F) $\{\frac{1}{2}, \frac{1}{2}\}$
(G) $\{-\frac{1}{2}, -\frac{1}{2}\}$
(H) $\{-\frac{1}{2}, -2\}$
(J) $\{2, -2\}$
(K) $\{2, 4\}$

99. Diana spent $\frac{1}{2}$ of her allowance on a book and another \$3 on lunch. If she still had $\frac{1}{6}$ of her original allowance, how much is Diana's allowance?

(A) \$24
(B) \$18
(C) \$15
(D) \$12
(E) \$9

NOTES AND STRATEGIES

100. In a certain game, a player had five successful turns in a row, and after each one the number of points added to his total score was double what was added the preceding turn. If the player scored a total of 465 points, how many points did he score on the first play?

(F) 15
(G) 31
(H) 93
(J) 155
(K) 270

101. At a certain firm, d gallons of fuel are needed per day for each truck. At this rate, g gallons of fuel will supply t trucks for how many days?

(A) $\frac{dt}{g}$
(B) $\frac{gt}{d}$
(C) dgt
(D) $\frac{t}{dg}$
(E) $\frac{g}{dt}$

102. Y years ago Paul was twice as old as Bob. If Bob is now 18 years old, how old is Paul in terms of Y?

(F) $36 + Y$
(G) $18 + Y$
(H) $18 - Y$
(J) $36 - Y$
(K) $36 - 2Y$

103. After filling the car's fuel tank, a driver drove from P to Q and then to R. She used $\frac{2}{5}$ of the fuel driving from P to Q. If she used another 7 gallons to drive from Q to R and still had $\frac{1}{4}$ of a tank left, how many gallons does the tank hold?

(A) 12
(B) 18
(C) 20
(D) 21
(E) 35

104. If pencils cost x cents each, how many pencils can be purchased for y dollars?

(F) $\frac{100}{xy}$
(G) $\frac{xy}{100}$
(H) $\frac{100y}{x}$
(J) $\frac{y}{100x}$
(K) $100xy$

105. A merchant increased the original price of an item by 10 percent. If she then reduces the new price by 10 percent, the final result in terms of the original price is equal to which of the following?

(A) a decrease of 11 percent
(B) a decrease of 1 percent
(C) no net change
(D) an increase of 1 percent
(E) an increase of 11 percent

106. Harold is twice as old as Jack, who is three years older than Dan. If Harold's age is five times Dan's age, how old in years is Jack?

(F) 2
(G) 4
(H) 5
(J) 8
(K) 10

107. A tank with capacity T gallons is empty. If water flows into the tank from Pipe X at the rate of X gallons per minute, and water is pumped out by Pipe Y at the rate of Y gallons per minute, and X is greater than Y, in how many minutes will the tank be filled?

(A) $\frac{T}{Y-X}$
(B) $\frac{T}{X-Y}$
(C) $\frac{T-X}{Y}$
(D) $\frac{X-Y}{60T}$
(E) $\frac{60T}{XY}$

108. Machine X produces w widgets in five minutes. Machine X and Machine Y, working at the same time, produce w widgets in two minutes. How long will it take Machine Y working alone to produce w widgets?

(F) 2 minutes, 30 seconds
(G) 2 minutes, 40 seconds
(H) 3 minutes, 20 seconds
(J) 3 minutes, 30 seconds
(K) 3 minutes, 40 seconds

109. If a train travels m miles in h hours and 45 minutes, what is its average speed in miles per hour?

(A) $\frac{m}{h+\frac{3}{4}}$
(B) $\frac{m}{1\frac{3}{4}h}$
(C) $m\left(h+\frac{3}{4}\right)$
(D) $\frac{m+45}{h}$
(E) $\frac{h}{m+45}$

110. In a playground, there are x seesaws. If 50 children are all riding on seesaws, two to a seesaw, and five seesaws are not in use, what is x?

(F) 15
(G) 20
(H) 25
(J) 30
(K) 35

111. In the figure below, what is the length of PQ?

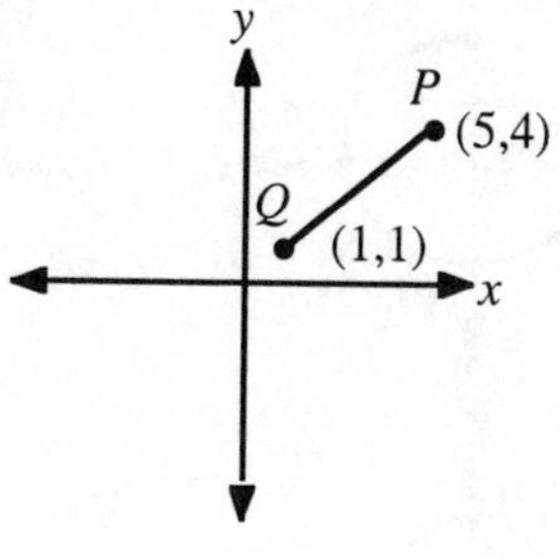

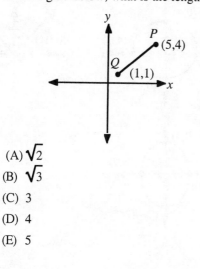

(A) $\sqrt{2}$
(B) $\sqrt{3}$
(C) 3
(D) 4
(E) 5

112. In the figure below, what is the slope of the line?

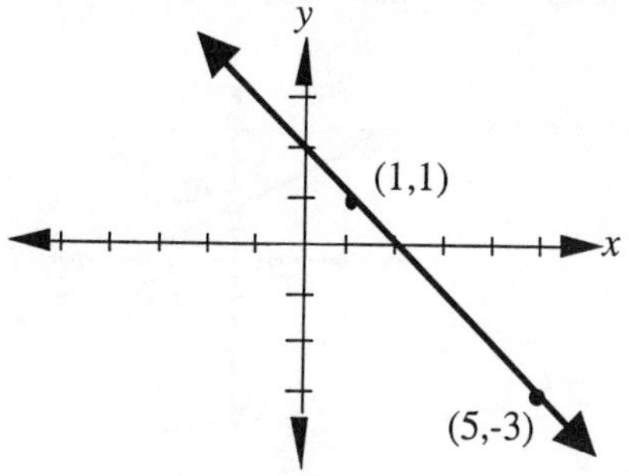

(F) –3
(G) –2
(H) –1
(J) 1
(K) 2

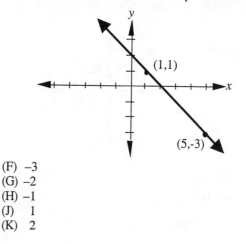

113. A line includes the points (2, 3) and (3, 6). What is the equation of the line?

(A) $y = 2x - 3$
(B) $y = 3x - 3$
(C) $y = \frac{3x-3}{2}$
(D) $y = 3x + 3$
(E) $y = x - 3$

114. What is the distance between the points (–3, –2) and (3, 3)?

(F) $\sqrt{3}$
(G) $2\sqrt{3}$
(H) 5
(J) $\sqrt{29}$
(K) $\sqrt{61}$

115. The figure below is the graph of which of the following equations?

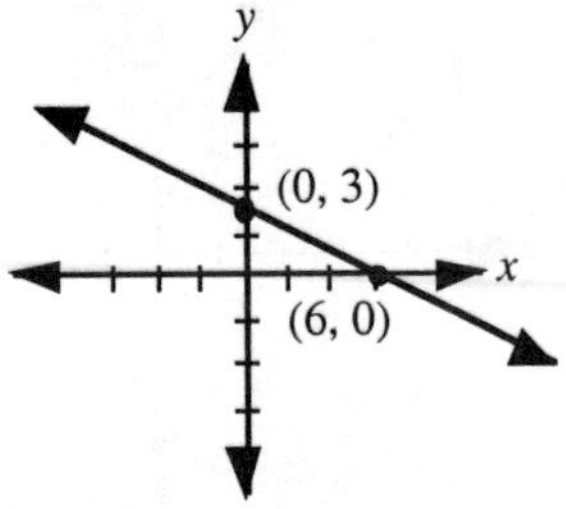

(A) $x + 2y = 6$

(B) $2x + y = 6$

(C) $x + \frac{1}{2}(y) = 6$

(D) $\frac{1}{2}(x) + y = 2$

(E) $x - 3y = 2$

116. Which of the following is the graph of the inequality $y \geq 2x$?

(F)
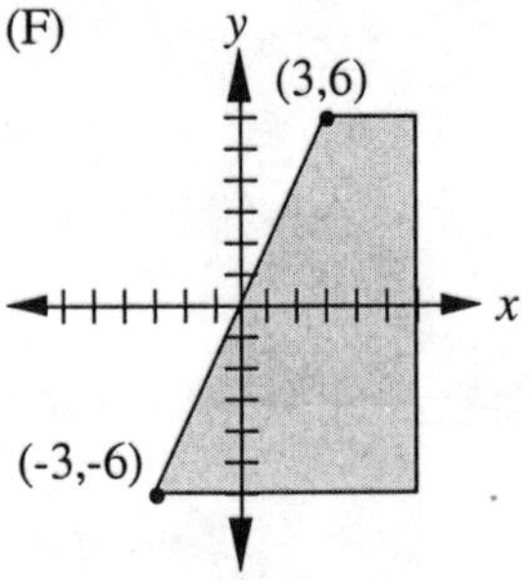

(J)
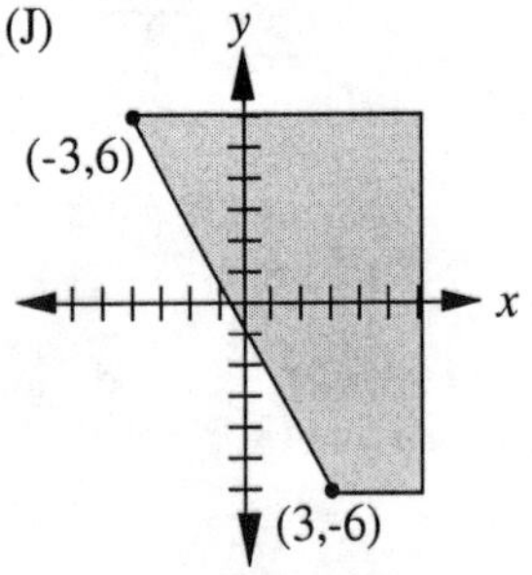

(G)
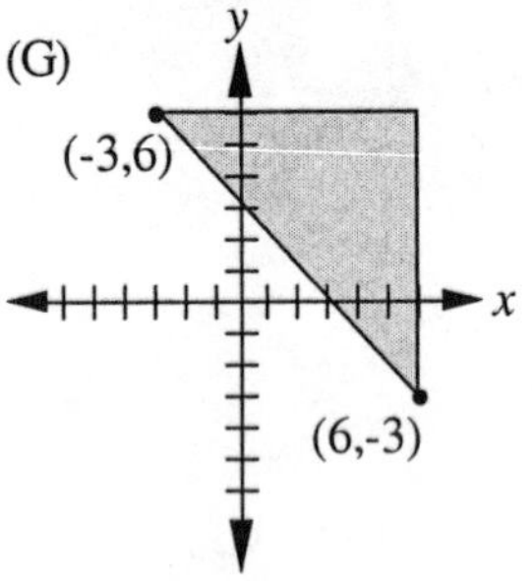

(K)
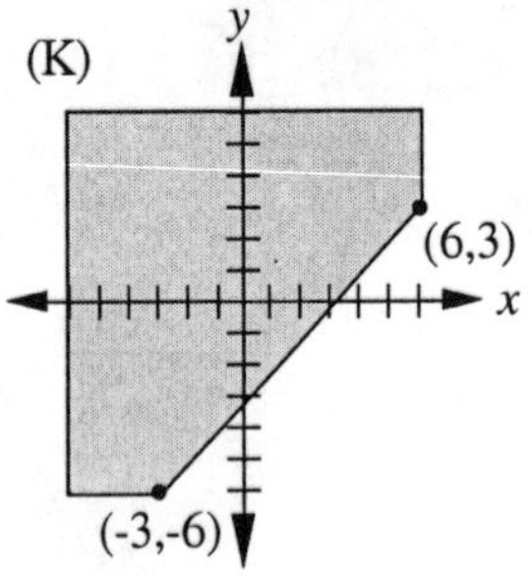

(H)
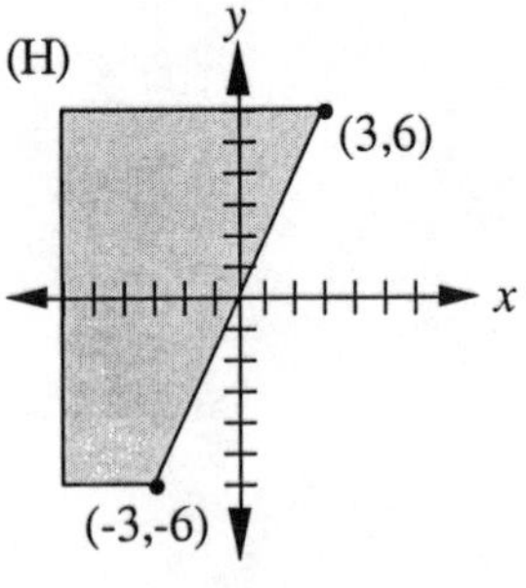

117. Which of the following is a graph of $(x - 1)^2 + y^2 = 4$?

(A)
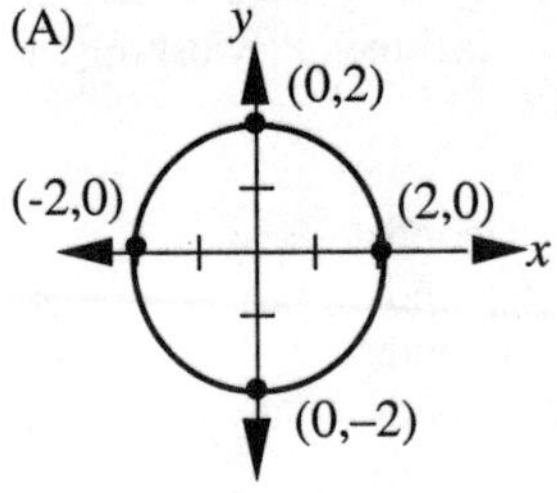

(D)
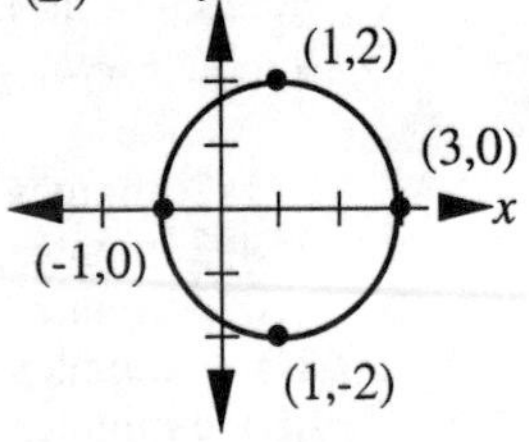

(B)
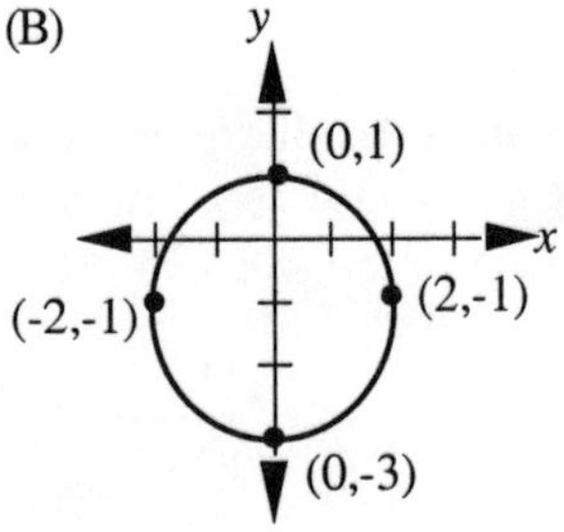

(E)
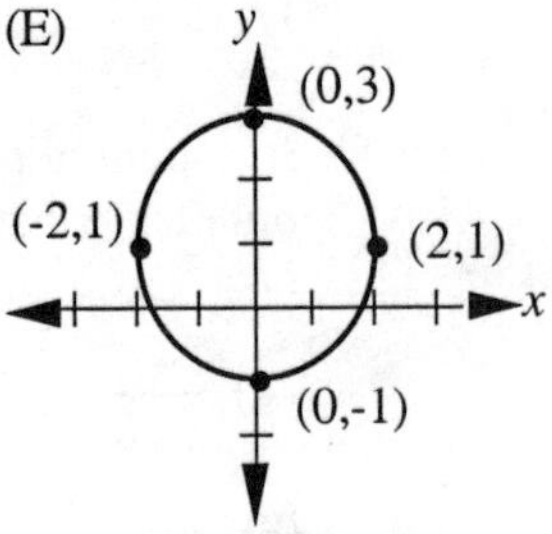

(C)
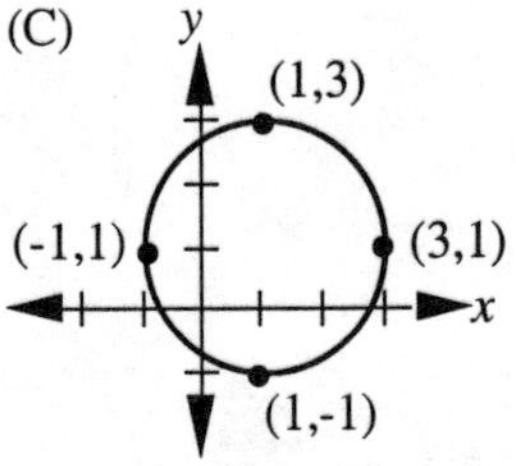

118. Which of the following is the graph of $\frac{x^2}{9} + \frac{y^2}{16} = 1$?

(F)
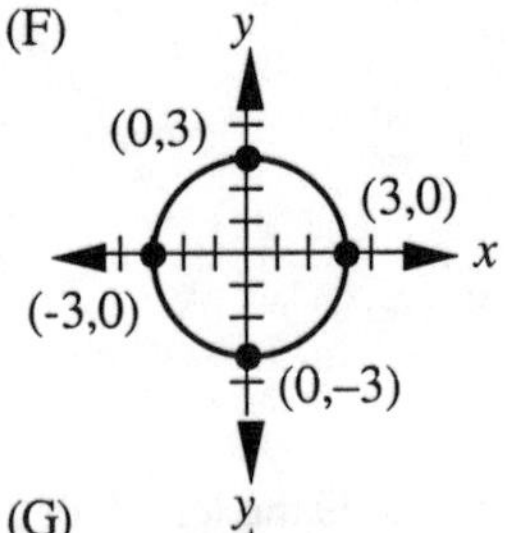

(J)
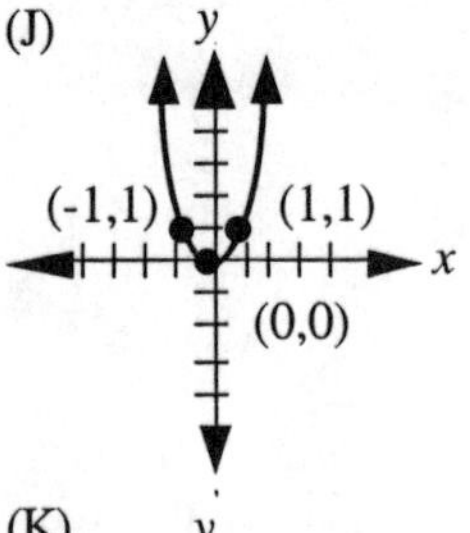

(G)
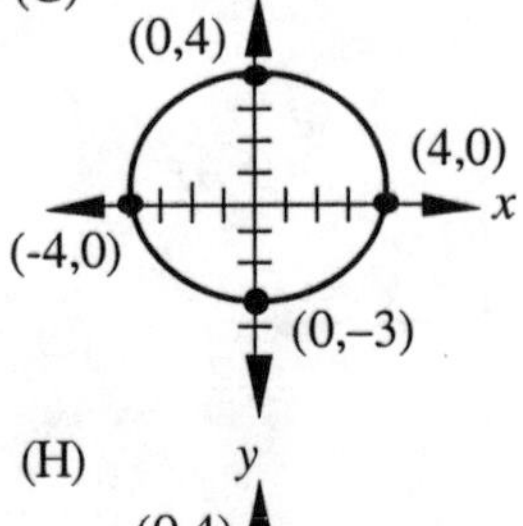

(K)
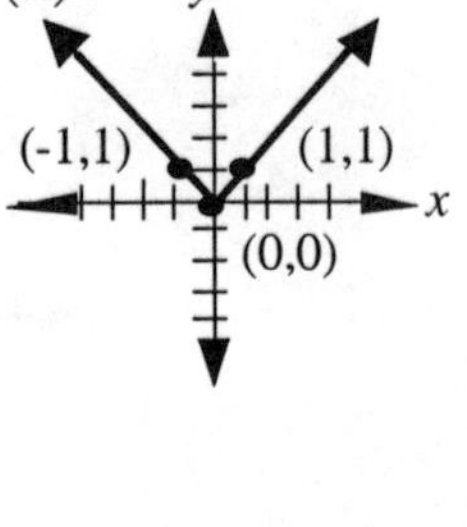

(H)
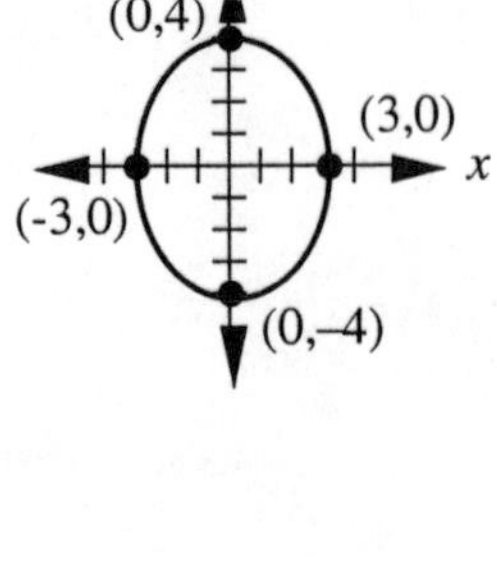

NOTES AND STRATEGIES

119. In the figure below, $x = ?$

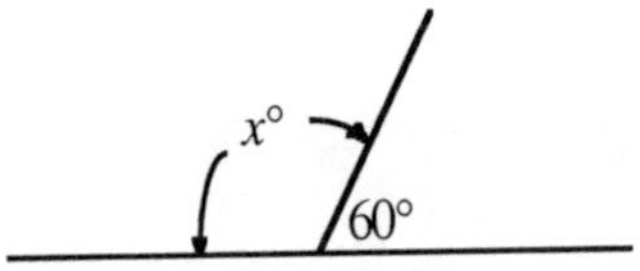

(A) 45
(B) 60
(C) 75
(D) 90
(E) 120

120. In the figure below, $x = ?$

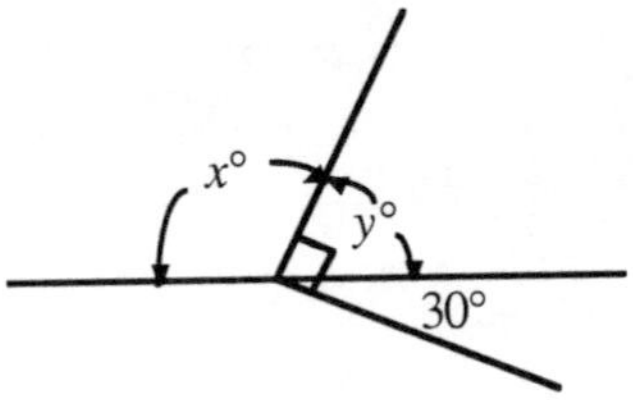

(F) 45
(G) 60
(H) 90
(J) 105
(K) 120

121. In the figure below, l_1 is parallel to l_2. Which of the following must be true?

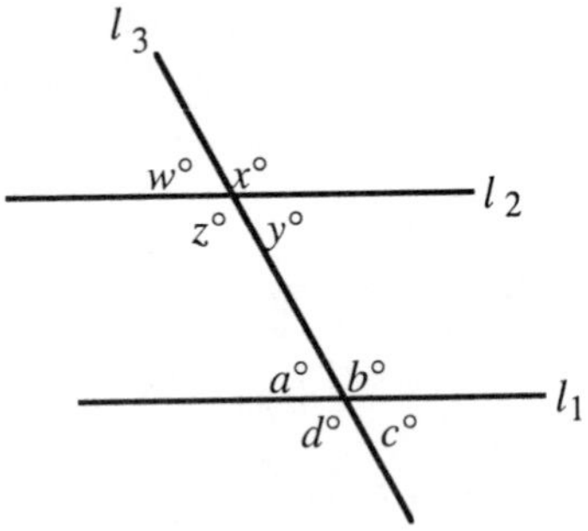

I. $w = a$
II. $y + b = 180°$
III. $x + d = 180°$

(A) I only
(B) II only
(C) I and II only
(D) II and III only
(E) I, II, and III

122. In the figure below, $x = ?$

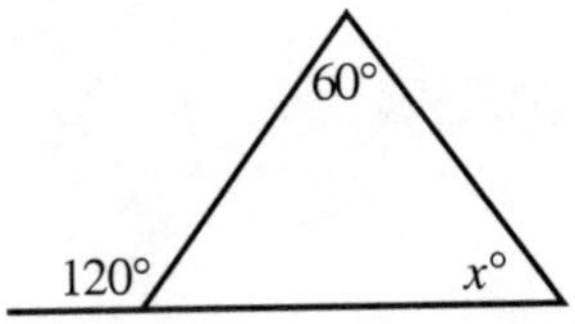

(F) 30
(G) 45
(H) 60
(J) 75
(K) 90

123. In the figure below, what is the sum of the indicated angles?

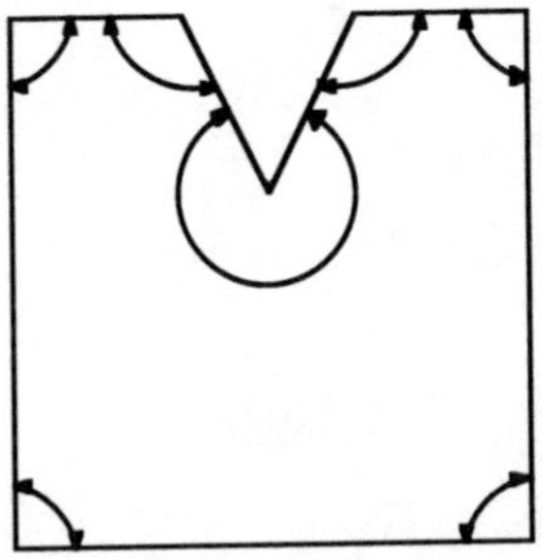

(A) 540
(B) 720
(C) 900
(D) 1,080
(E) 1,260

124. In the figure below, $AB = ?$

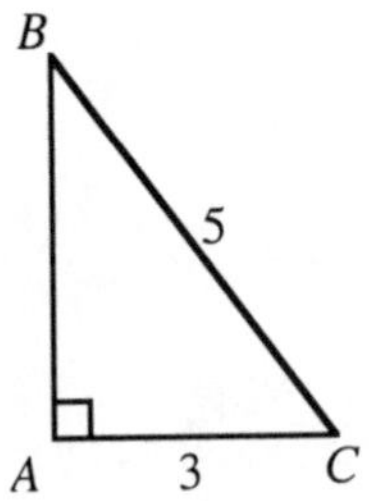

(F) 2
(G) $2\sqrt{3}$
(H) 4
(J) $4\sqrt{2}$
(K) 8

125. In the figure below, $PQ = ?$

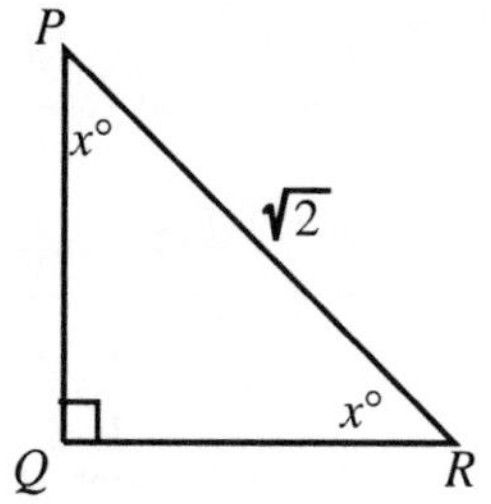

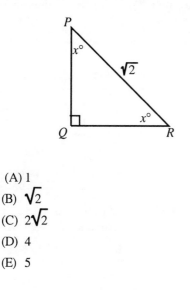

(A) 1
(B) $\sqrt{2}$
(C) $2\sqrt{2}$
(D) 4
(E) 5

126. In a right isosceles triangle, the hypotenuse is equal to which of the following?

(F) half the length of either of the other sides.
(G) the length of either of the other sides multiplied by the square root of two.
(H) twice the length of either of the other sides.
(J) the sum of the lengths of the other two sides.
(K) the sum of the lengths of the other two sides multiplied by the square root of two.

127. In the triangle below, what is the length of AC?

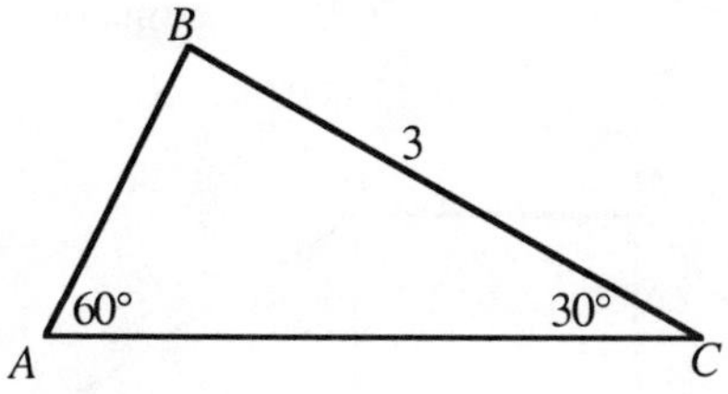

(A) 2
(B) $\sqrt{3}$
(C) $2\sqrt{3}$
(D) $3\sqrt{3}$
(E) 6

128. In the figure below, the perimeter of triangle $PQR = ?$

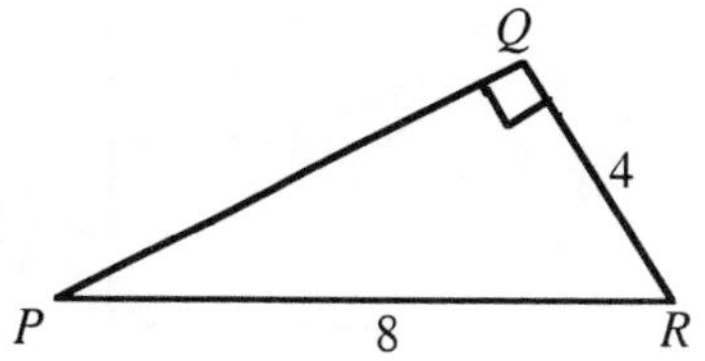

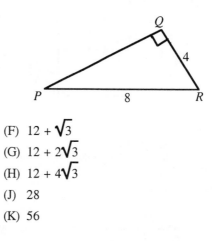

(F) $12 + \sqrt{3}$
(G) $12 + 2\sqrt{3}$
(H) $12 + 4\sqrt{3}$
(J) 28
(K) 56

129. What is the area of triangle MNO?

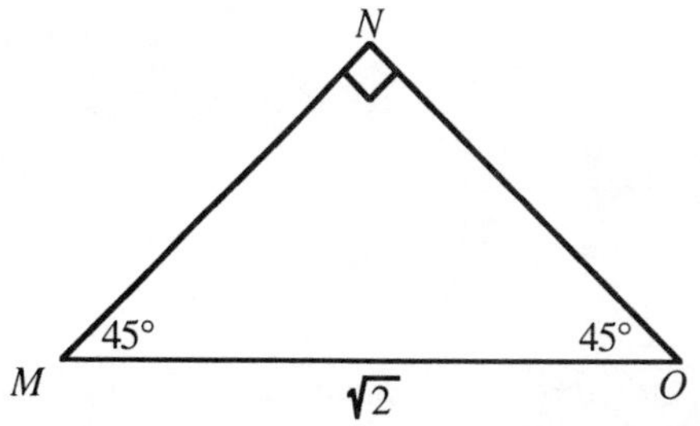

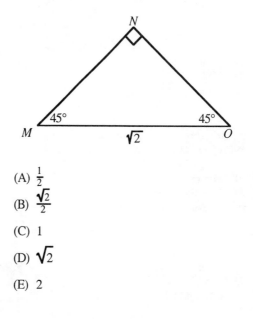

(A) $\frac{1}{2}$
(B) $\frac{\sqrt{2}}{2}$
(C) 1
(D) $\sqrt{2}$
(E) 2

130. If the area of the rectangle below is 18, what is the perimeter?

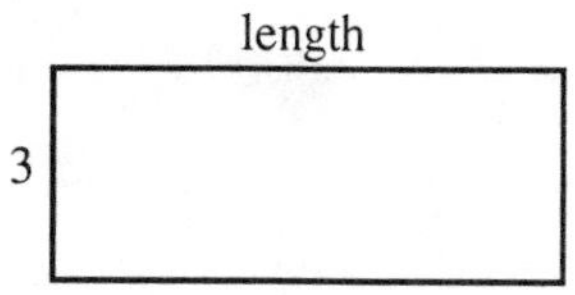

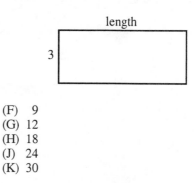

(F) 9
(G) 12
(H) 18
(J) 24
(K) 30

131. In the figure below, $PQRS$ is a rectangle. If $PR = 5$, then what is the area of the rectangle?

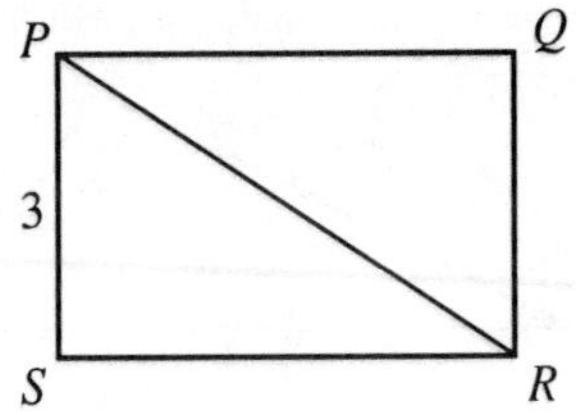

(A) 2
(B) 3
(C) 4
(D) 8
(E) 12

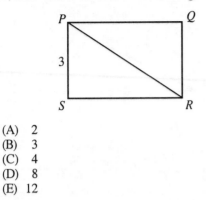

132. If the width of a rectangle is increased by 10 percent and the length of the rectangle is increased by 20 percent, the area of the rectangle increases by what percent?

(F) 2%
(G) 10%
(H) 15%
(J) 32%
(K) 36%

133. If the area of a circle is 9π, which of the following is (are) true?

I. The radius is 3.
II. The diameter is 6.
III. The circumference is 6π.

(A) I only
(B) II only
(C) III only
(D) I and II only
(E) I, II, and III

134. If a circle of radius 1 is inscribed in a square, what is the area of the square?

(F) 1
(G) $\frac{\sqrt{2}}{2}$
(H) $\sqrt{2}$
(J) 2
(K) 4

135. An isosceles right triangle is inscribed in a semicircle with radius 1. What is the area of the triangle?

(A) $\frac{1}{2}$
(B) $\frac{\sqrt{2}}{3}$
(C) 1
(D) $\sqrt{2}$
(E) $2\sqrt{2}$

136. In the figure below, if $BCDE$ is a square with an area of 4, what is the perimeter of triangle ABE?

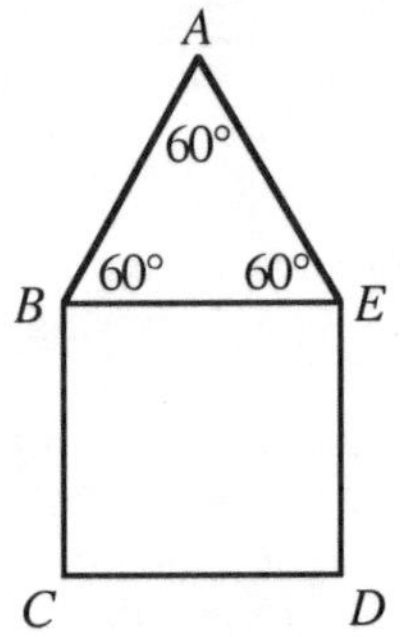

(F) 3
(G) 4
(H) 6
(J) 8
(K) 12

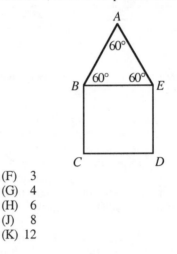

137. In the figure below, if $QRST$ is a square and $PQ = \sqrt{2}$, what is the length of RU?

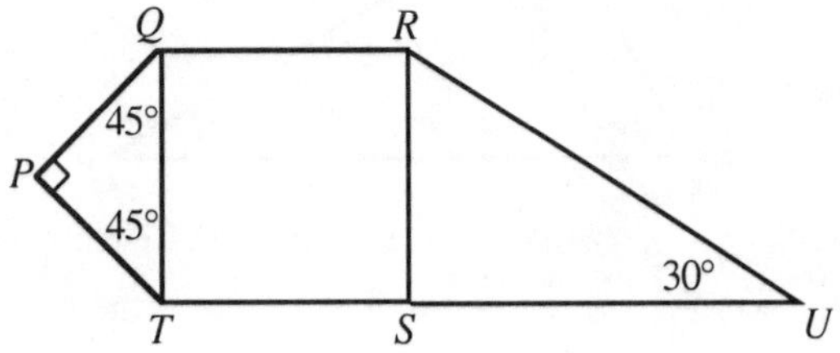

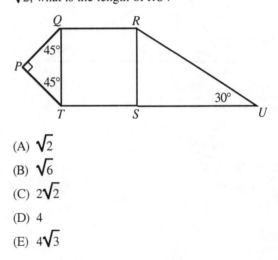

(A) $\sqrt{2}$
(B) $\sqrt{6}$
(C) $2\sqrt{2}$
(D) 4
(E) $4\sqrt{3}$

NOTES AND STRATEGIES

138. In the figure below, $PQRS$ is a square, and PS is the diameter of a semicircle. If $PQ = 2$, what is the area of the shaded portion of the diagram?

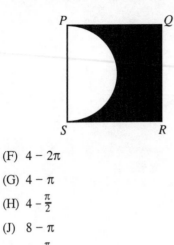

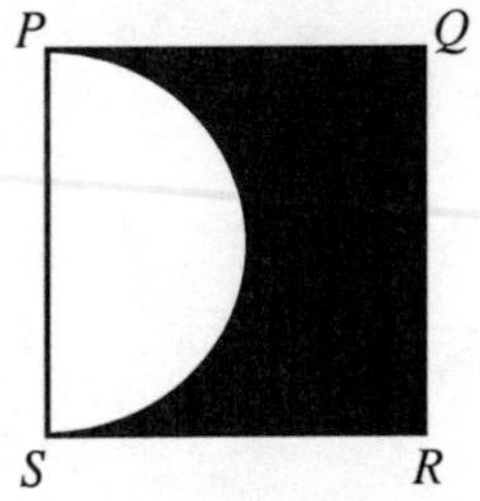

(F) $4 - 2\pi$

(G) $4 - \pi$

(H) $4 - \frac{\pi}{2}$

(J) $8 - \pi$

(K) $8 - \frac{\pi}{2}$

139. What is the area of the quadrilateral below?

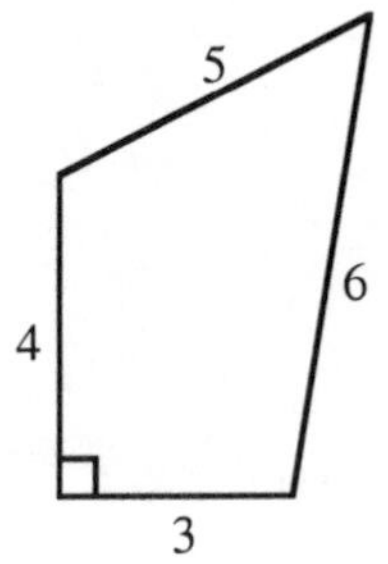

(A) 6

(B) $6 + \sqrt{3}$

(C) 12

(D) 18

(E) 24

140. What is the perimeter of the triangle below?

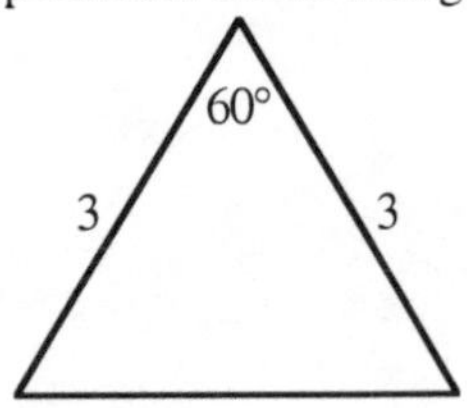

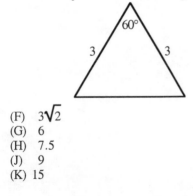

(F) $3\sqrt{2}$
(G) 6
(H) 7.5
(J) 9
(K) 15

141. In the figure below, $x = ?$

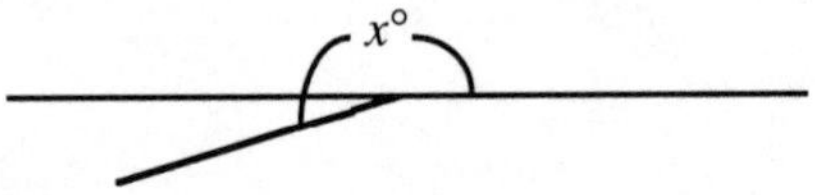

(A) 120
(B) 150
(C) 180
(D) 210
(E) 240

142. In the figure below, $x = ?$

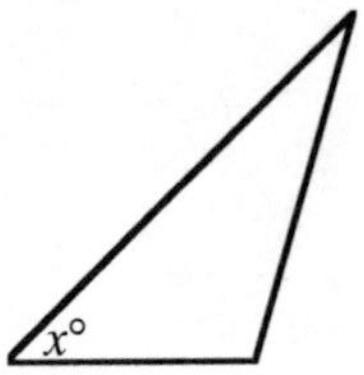

(F) 30
(G) 45
(H) 60
(J) 75
(K) 90

143. In the figure below, $AC = ?$

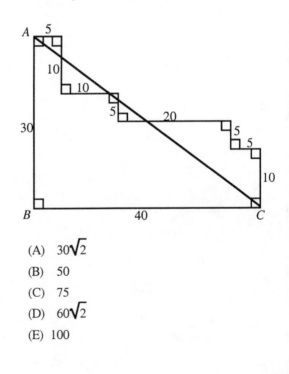

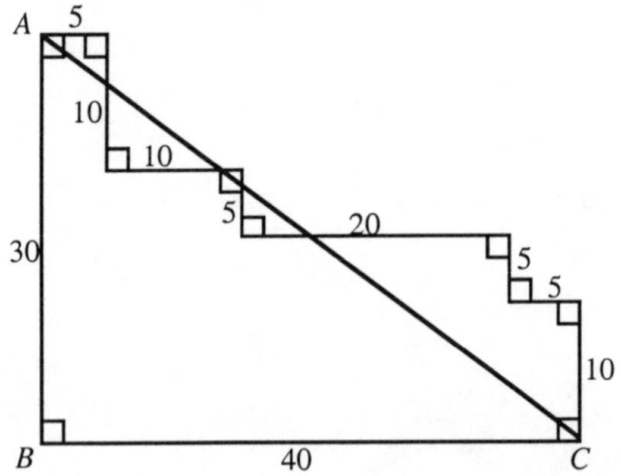

(A) $30\sqrt{2}$

(B) 50

(C) 75

(D) $60\sqrt{2}$

(E) 100

144. In the figure below, what is the area of square $ABCD$?

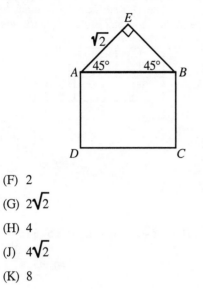

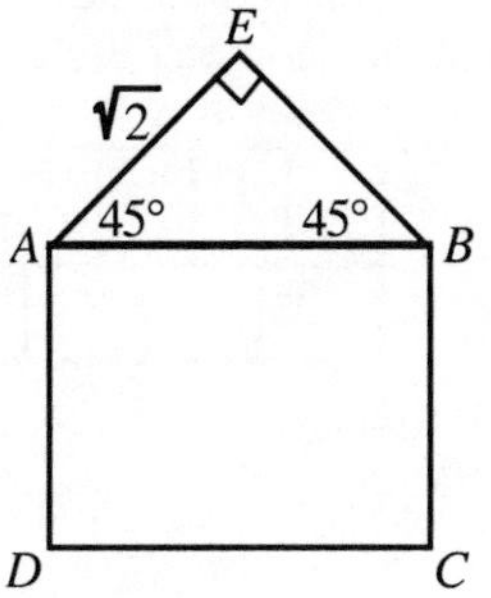

(F) 2

(G) $2\sqrt{2}$

(H) 4

(J) $4\sqrt{2}$

(K) 8

145. In the figure below, which of the following is the best approximation of the length of AC?

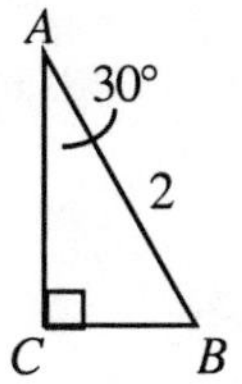

(A) 0.8
(B) 1.0
(C) 1.7
(D) 1.9
(E) 2.3

146. For the figure below, $\sin \theta = \frac{12}{13}$. Which of the following is INCORRECT?

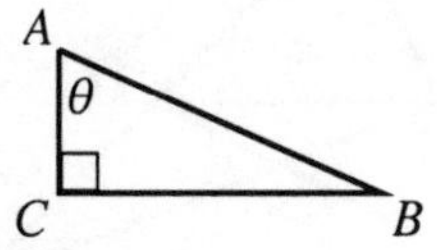

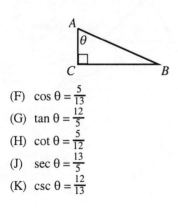

(F) $\cos \theta = \frac{5}{13}$

(G) $\tan \theta = \frac{12}{5}$

(H) $\cot \theta = \frac{5}{12}$

(J) $\sec \theta = \frac{13}{5}$

(K) $\csc \theta = \frac{12}{13}$

147. In the right triangle shown below, the length of AB is 5, A measures 30°, and $\sin 30° = 0.5$. What is the length of BC?

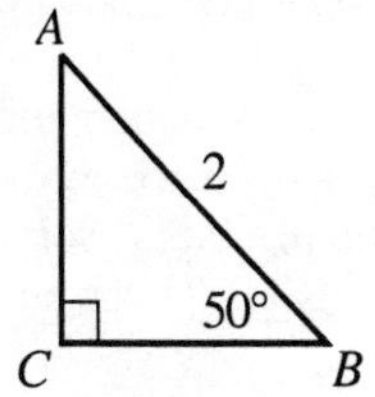

(A) 4

(B) $3\frac{1}{2}$

(C) $2\frac{3}{4}$

(D) $2\frac{1}{2}$

(E) 2

148. If $\sin 60° = \frac{\sqrt{3}}{2}$, what is the value of $\sin^2 30° + \cos^2 30°$?

(F) $\frac{\sqrt{3}+1}{2}$

(G) $\sqrt{5}$

(H) $\frac{\sqrt{5}}{2}$

(J) $\frac{3}{4}$

(K) 1

149. Which of the following is equivalent to $\frac{\sin A}{\cos A}$?

(A) $\tan A$

(B) $\cot A$

(C) $\sec A$

(D) $\csc A$

(E) $\frac{1}{\tan A}$

SECTION TWO—MATHEMATICS PROBLEM-SOLVING

DIRECTIONS: The questions in this section reflect both the format and difficulty range of ACT Mathematics questions—though difficult problems are emphasized. You will work through these questions with your instructor in class. Solve each problem and choose the correct answer. Answers are on page 119.

Note: Unless otherwise stated, all of the following should be assumed.

- Illustrative figures are NOT necessarily drawn to scale.
- Geometric figures lie in a plane.
- The word *line* indicates a straight line.
- The word *average* indicates arithmetic mean.

1. A company bought a load of water-damaged copy paper, estimating that $\frac{2}{3}$ of the reams could be salvaged, in which case the cost per salvageable ream would be \$0.72. If it later turned out that $\frac{3}{4}$ of the reams were salvageable, then what was the actual cost per salvageable ream?

(A) \$0.56
(B) \$0.60
(C) \$0.64
(D) \$0.68
(E) \$0.80

2. If each of the dimensions of a rectangle is increased 100%, the area is increased

(F) 100%
(G) 200%
(H) 300%
(J) 400%
(K) 500%

3. Three valves, when opened individually, can drain the water from a certain tank in 3, 4, and 5 minutes respectively. What is the greatest part of the tank that can be drained in one minute by opening just two of the valves?

(A) $\frac{3}{20}$
(B) $\frac{1}{5}$
(C) $\frac{7}{12}$
(D) $\frac{2}{3}$
(E) $\frac{3}{4}$

4. Nine playing cards from the same deck are placed as shown in the figure below to form a large rectangle of area 180 sq. in. How many inches are there in the perimeter of this large rectangle?

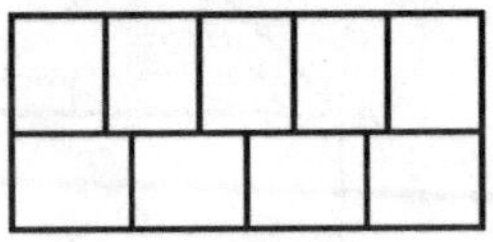

(F) 29
(G) 58
(H) 64
(J) 116
(K) 210

5. What is 10% of $\frac{1}{3}(x)$ if $\frac{2}{3}(x)$ is 10% of 60?

(A) 0.1
(B) 0.2
(C) 0.3
(D) 0.4
(E) 0.5

6. A cube has an edge four inches long. If the edge is increased by 25%, then the volume is increased by approximately

(F) 25%
(G) 48%
(H) 73%
(J) 95%
(K) 122%

7. In the figure below, M and N are midpoints of the sides PR and PQ, respectively, of ΔPQR. What is the ratio of the area of ΔMNS to that of ΔPQR?

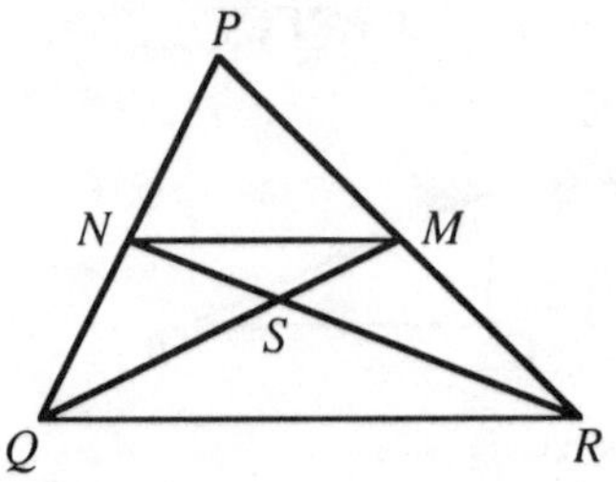

(A) 2:5
(B) 2:9
(C) 1:4
(D) 1:8
(E) 1:12

NOTES AND STRATEGIES

8. The average of 8 numbers is 6; the average of 6 other numbers is 8. What is the average of all 14 numbers?

(F) 6
(G) $6\frac{6}{7}$
(H) 7
(J) $7\frac{2}{7}$
(K) $8\frac{1}{7}$

9. The front wheels of a wagon are 7 feet in circumference and the back wheels are 9 feet in circumference. When the front wheels have made 10 more revolutions than the back wheels, what distance, in feet, has the wagon gone?

(A) 126
(B) 180
(C) 189
(D) 315
(E) 630

10. A pound of water is evaporated from 6 pounds of seawater containing 4% salt. The percentage of salt in the remaining solution is

(F) 3.6%
(G) 4%
(H) 4.8%
(J) 5.2%
(K) 6%

11. Doreen can wash her car in 15 minutes, while her younger brother Dave takes twice as long to do the same job. If they work together, how many minutes will the job take them?

(A) 5
(B) $7\frac{1}{2}$
(C) 10
(D) $22\frac{1}{2}$
(E) 30

12. In the figure below, the side of the large square is 14. Joining the midpoints of each opposite side forms the four smaller squares. Find the value of Y.

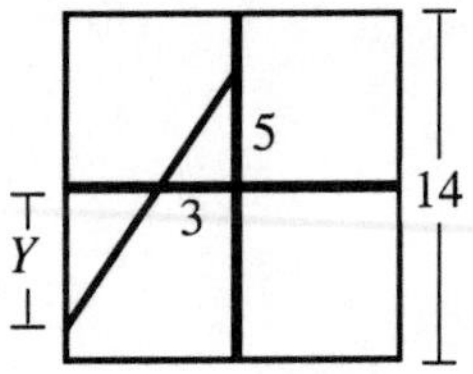

(F) 5
(G) 6
(H) $6\frac{5}{8}$
(J) $6\frac{2}{3}$
(K) 6.8

13. A cylindrical container has a diameter of 14 inches and a height of 6 inches. Since one gallon equals 231 cubic inches, the capacity of the tank in gallons is approximately

(A) $\frac{2}{3}$
(B) $1\frac{1}{7}$
(C) $2\frac{2}{7}$
(D) $2\frac{2}{3}$
(E) 4

14. In the figure below, $PQRS$ is a parallelogram, and $ST = TV = VR$. What is the ratio of the area of triangle SPT to the area of the parallelogram?

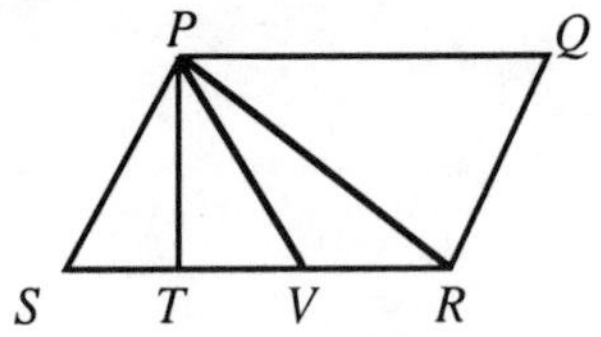

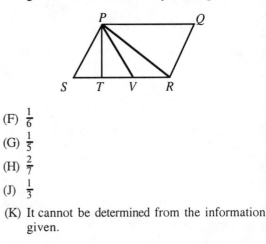

(F) $\frac{1}{6}$
(G) $\frac{1}{5}$
(H) $\frac{2}{7}$
(J) $\frac{1}{3}$
(K) It cannot be determined from the information given.

15. If $p > q$ and $r < 0$, which of the following is (are) true?

I. $pr < qr$
II. $p + r > q + r$
III. $p - r < q - r$

(A) I only
(B) II only
(C) I and III only
(D) I and II only
(E) I, II and III

16. John is now three times Pat's age. Four years from now John will be x years old. In terms of x, how old is Pat now?

(F) $\frac{x+4}{3}$
(G) $3x$
(H) $x + 4$
(J) $x - 4$
(K) $\frac{x-4}{3}$

17. The figure below is a possible graph for which of the following equations?

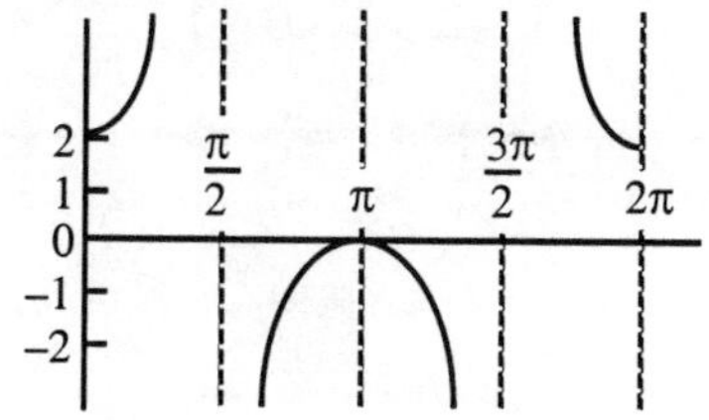

(A) $y = 2 \sin x$
(B) $y = \sin x + 2$
(C) $y = \csc x + 1$
(D) $y = \csc x - 1$
(E) $y = \sec x + 1$

18. If θ is an acute angle and $\cos \theta = \frac{b}{c}$, $b > 0$ and $c > 0$ and $b \neq c$, then $\sin \theta$?

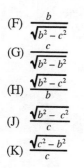

(F) $\frac{b}{\sqrt{b^2 - c^2}}$
(G) $\frac{c}{\sqrt{b^2 - b^2}}$
(H) $\frac{\sqrt{b^2 - c^2}}{b}$
(J) $\frac{\sqrt{b^2 - c^2}}{c}$
(K) $\frac{\sqrt{c^2 - b^2}}{c}$

19. In the figure below, what percent of the area of rectangle $PQRS$ is shaded?

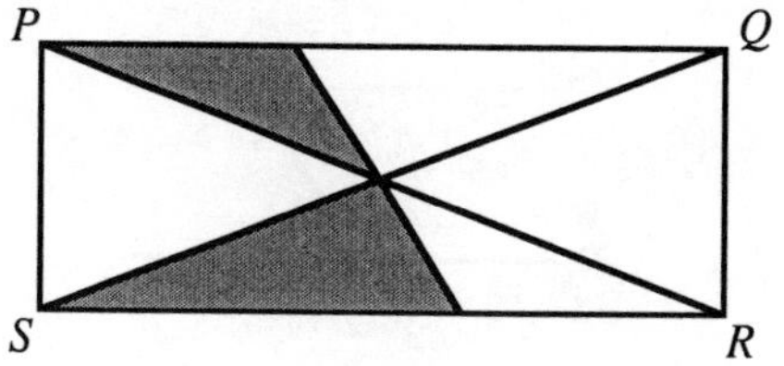

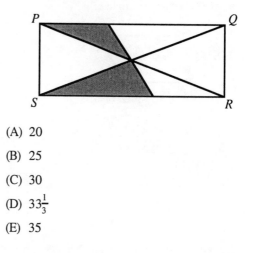

(A) 20
(B) 25
(C) 30
(D) $33\frac{1}{3}$
(E) 35

20. A train running between two towns arrives at its destination 10 minutes late when it goes 40 miles per hour and 16 minutes late when it goes 30 miles per hour. The distance in miles between the towns is

(F) $8\frac{6}{7}$
(G) 12
(H) 192
(J) 560
(K) 720

21. In the figure below, $PQRS$ is a square and PTS is an equilateral triangle. How many degrees are there in angle TRS?

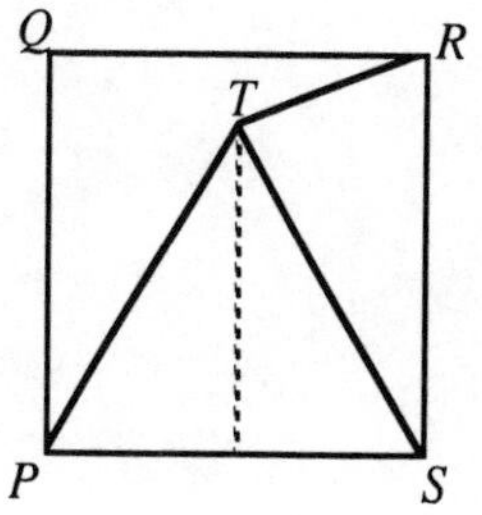

(A) 60°
(B) 75°
(C) 80°
(D) 90°
(E) It cannot be determined from the information given.

22. In the figure below, line PQ is parallel to line RS, angle $y = 60°$, and angle $z = 130°$. How many degrees are there in angle x?

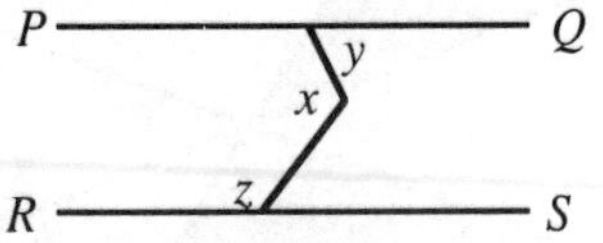

$y = 60°$
$z = 130°$

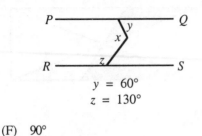

(F) 90°
(G) 100°
(H) 110°
(J) 120°
(K) 130°

23. If Paul can paint a fence in 2 hours and Fred can paint the same fence in 3 hours, Paul and Fred working together can paint the fence in how many hours?

(A) 5
(B) $2\frac{1}{2}$
(C) $1\frac{1}{5}$
(D) 1
(E) $\frac{5}{6}$

24. A motorist drives 60 miles to her destination at an average speed of 40 miles per hour and makes the return trip at an average rate of 30 miles per hour. Her average speed in miles per hour for the entire trip is

(F) 17
(G) $34\frac{2}{7}$
(H) 35
(J) $43\frac{1}{3}$
(K) 70

25. In the coordinate plane, the graph of which of the following lines is perpendicular to the graph of the line $y = \frac{3}{2}(x) + 1$?

(A) $y = \frac{3}{2}(x) - 1$
(B) $y = \frac{3}{4}(x) + 1$
(C) $y = \frac{3}{4}(x) - 1$
(D) $y = -\frac{2}{3}(x) + 2$
(E) $y = -\frac{3}{2}(x) - 1$

26. Which graph represents the solution set of the inequality $(x - 1)(x + 3) < 0$?

(F)
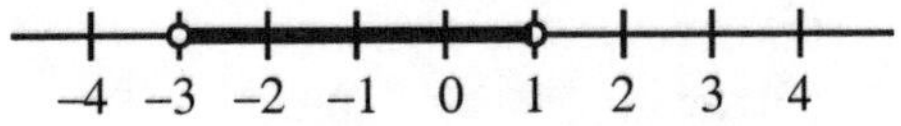

(G)
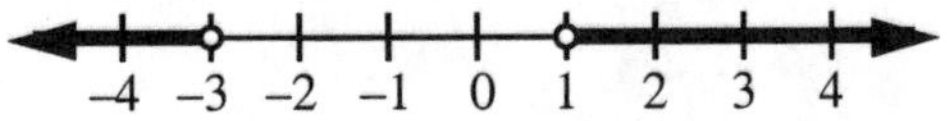

(H)
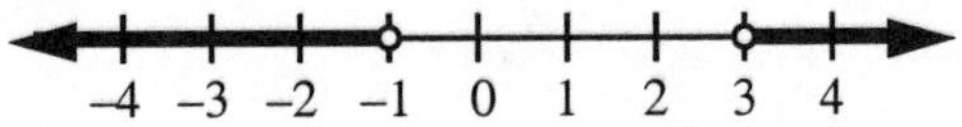

(J)
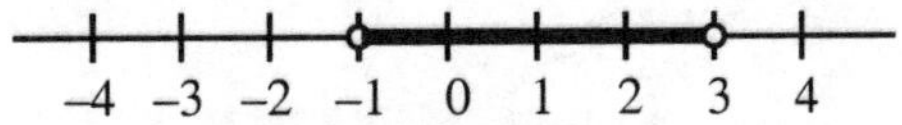

(K)
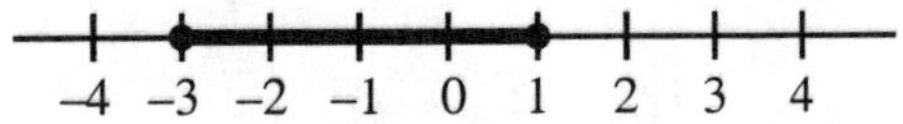

27. If $(x + 1)(x - 2)$ is positive, then

(A) $x < -1$ or $x > 2$
(B) $x > -1$ or $x < 2$
(C) $-1 < x < 2$
(D) $-2 < x < 1$
(E) $x = -1$ or $x = 2$

28. An ice-cream truck runs down a certain street 4 times a week. This truck carries 5 different flavors of ice-cream bars, each of which comes in 2 different designs. Considering that the truck runs Monday through Thursday, and Monday was the first day of the month, by what day of the month could a person, buying one ice-cream bar each truck run, purchase all of the different varieties of ice-cream bars?

(F) 11th
(G) 16th
(H) 21st
(J) 24th
(K) 30th

NOTES AND STRATEGIES

29. If $N! = N(N-1)(N-2)\ldots[N-(N-1)]$, what does $\frac{N!}{(N-2)!}$ equal?

(A) $N^2 - N$
(B) $N^5 + N^3 - N^2 + \frac{N}{N^2}$
(C) $N + 1$
(D) 1
(E) 6

30. In the figure below, equilateral triangle ABC has a perpendicular line drawn from point A to point D. If the triangle is "folded over" on the perpendicular line so that points B and C meet, the perimeter of the new triangle is approximately what percent of the perimeter of the triangle before the fold?

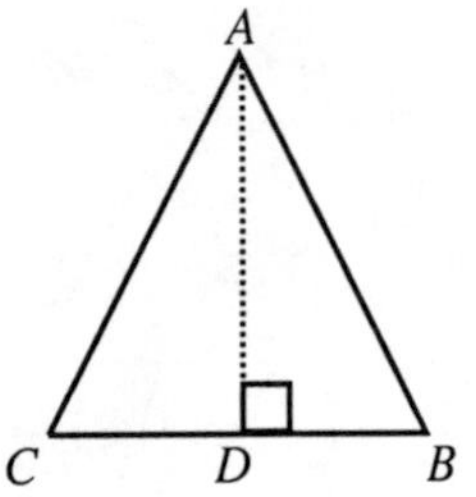

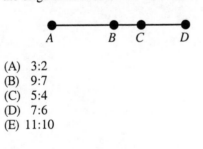

(F) 100%
(G) 78%
(H) 50%
(J) 32%
(K) It cannot be determined from the information given.

31. In the figure below, segment AB is three times longer than segment BC, which is two times as long as segment CD. If segment BC is removed from the line and the other two segments are joined to form one line, then what is the ratio of the original line AD to the new line AD?

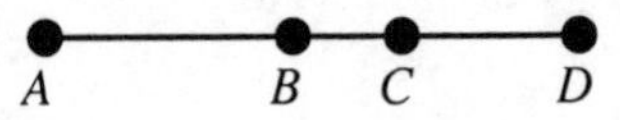

(A) 3:2
(B) 9:7
(C) 5:4
(D) 7:6
(E) 11:10

32. If s, t, and u are different positive integers and $\frac{s}{t}$ and $\frac{t}{u}$ are also positive integers, which of the following cannot be a positive integer?

(F) $\frac{s}{u}$
(G) $s \bullet t$
(H) $\frac{u}{s}$
(J) $(s + t)u$
(K) $(s - u)t$

33. In the figure below, $AD = DC$. What is $AD + DC$?

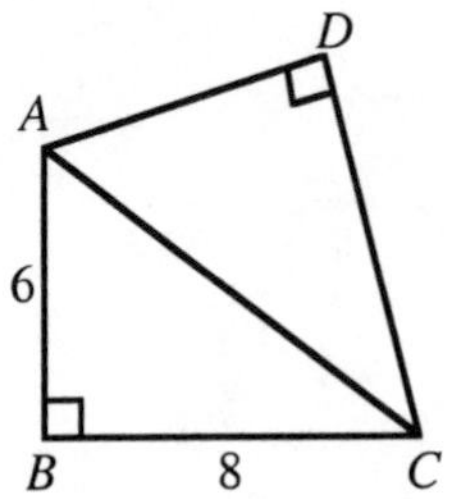

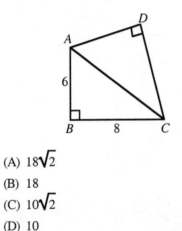

(A) $18\sqrt{2}$
(B) 18
(C) $10\sqrt{2}$
(D) 10
(E) $6\sqrt{2}$

34. In the figure below, $AB = BC = CA$. What is the value of y?

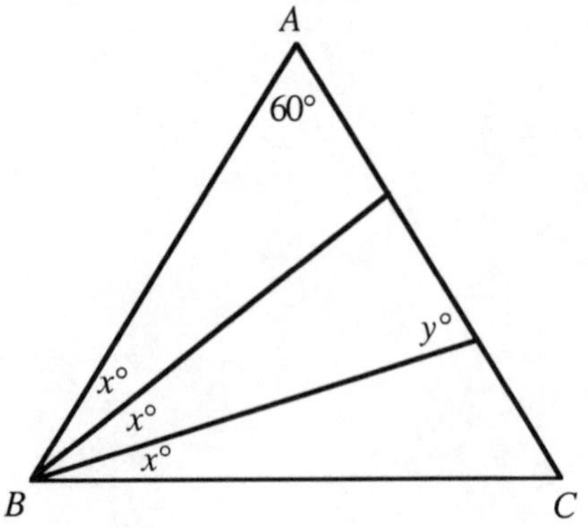

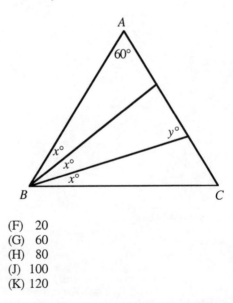

(F) 20
(G) 60
(H) 80
(J) 100
(K) 120

35. In the figure below, O is the center of the circle with radius 1. What is the area of the shaded region?

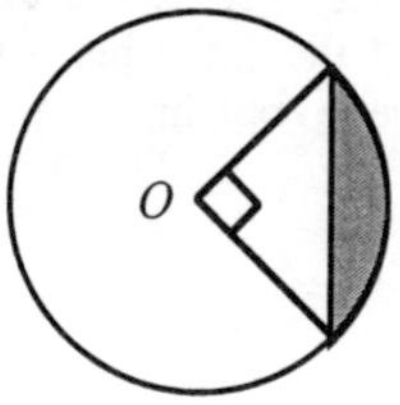

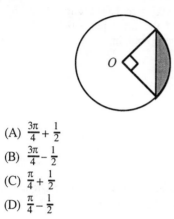

(A) $\frac{3\pi}{4} + \frac{1}{2}$
(B) $\frac{3\pi}{4} - \frac{1}{2}$
(C) $\frac{\pi}{4} + \frac{1}{2}$
(D) $\frac{\pi}{4} - \frac{1}{2}$
(E) $\pi - 1$

36. Which is true for the set of numbers {4, 7, 12}?

(F) A range of 3 and a median of 7
(G) A range of 8 and a median of 7
(H) A range of 12 and a median of $7\frac{2}{3}$
(J) A range of 8 and a median of $7\frac{2}{3}$
(K) An average of $7\frac{2}{3}$ and a median of 8

37. If $z = \frac{x+y}{x}$, $1 - z =$

(A) $\frac{1-x+y}{x}$
(B) $\frac{x+y-1}{x}$
(C) $\frac{1-x-y}{x}$
(D) $-\frac{y}{x}$
(E) $1 - x - y$

38. In a list of the first one hundred positive integers, the digit 9 appears how many times?

(F) 9
(G) 10
(H) 11
(J) 19
(K) 20

39. Which of the following graphs is NOT the graph of a function?

(A)
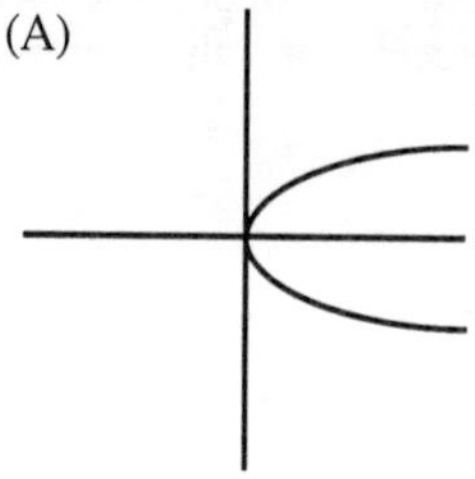

(D)
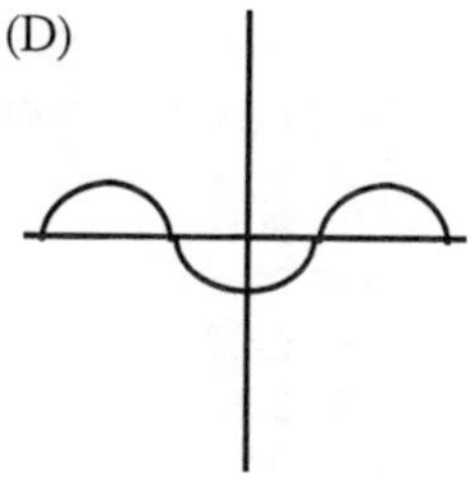

(B)
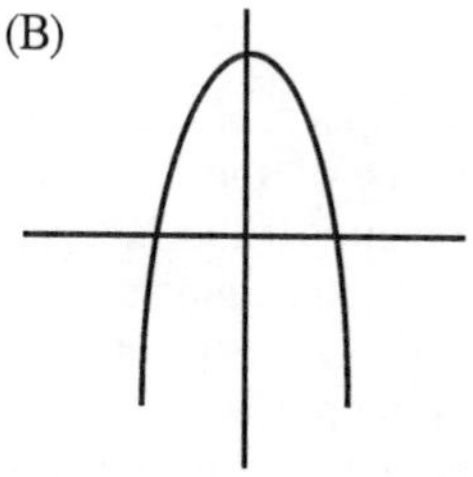

(E)
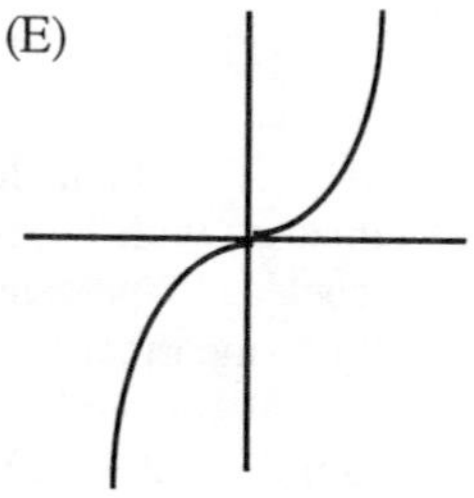

(C)
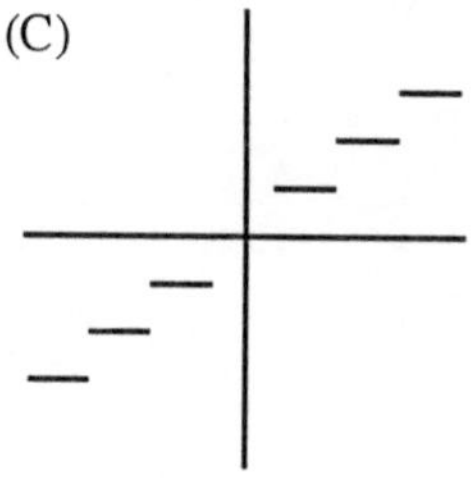

40. In the figure below, what is the area of the quadrilateral?

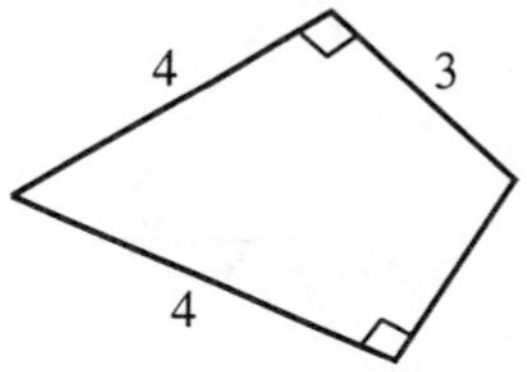

(F) 18
(G) 15
(H) 12
(J) 9
(K) 8

41. The average weight of the 8 packages in a certain shipment is 6 pounds. If the heaviest package is removed, the average weight of the remaining packages is 5 pounds. What is the weight, in pounds, of the heaviest package?

(A) 6
(B) 8
(C) 10
(D) 13
(E) 15

42. In the Excel Manufacturing Company, 46 percent of the employees are men. If 60 percent of the employees are unionized and 70 percent of these are men, what percent of the non-union employees are women?

(F) 90%
(G) 87.5%
(H) 66.7%
(J) 50%
(K) 36%

43. An accrediting agency set up a proficiency test for a lab in which 20 percent of the samples were injected with a contaminant. If the lab correctly labeled 80 percent of the contaminated samples but incorrectly labeled 5 percent of the uncontaminated samples, then what percent of the samples labeled by the lab as uncontaminated were actually contaminated?

(A) 4%
(B) 5%
(C) 10%
(D) 20%
(E) 25%

44. For the figure below, which of the following statements is true?

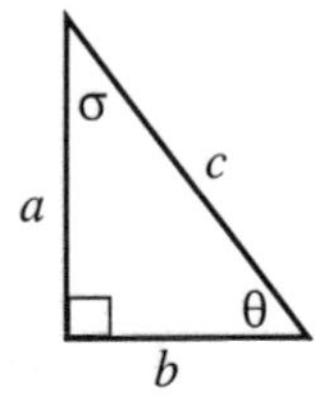

(F) $\sin\theta = \frac{b}{c}$

(G) $\tan\sigma = \frac{a}{b}$

(H) $\cos\theta = \frac{c}{a}$

(J) $\sin\theta = \cos\sigma$

(K) $\cot\sigma = \tan\sigma$

45. A study of a city's water-use patterns shows that for every $8x$ percent increase in the price of water, usage drops by x percent. If the price for water is currently \$1.05 per 1,000 cubic feet, by how much should the price per 1,000 cubic feet be raised in order to obtain a reduction in usage of 2 percent?

(A) \$0.042
(B) \$0.105
(C) \$0.168
(D) \$0.199
(E) \$0.225

46. In the figure below, each side of PQR has length 4. If $QS = 3$, what is the area of $PQST$?

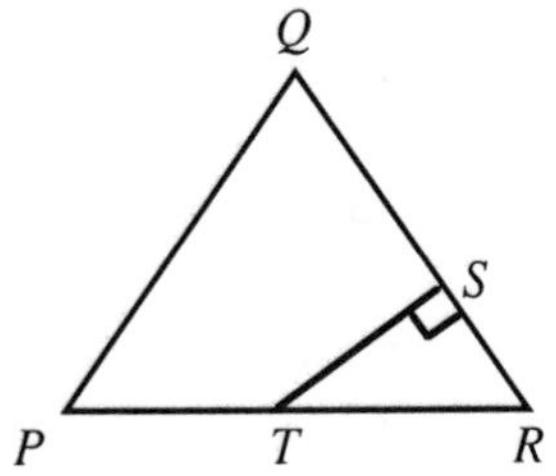

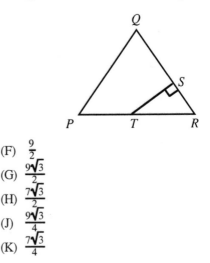

(F) $\frac{9}{2}$
(G) $\frac{9\sqrt{3}}{2}$
(H) $\frac{7\sqrt{3}}{2}$
(J) $\frac{9\sqrt{3}}{4}$
(K) $\frac{7\sqrt{3}}{4}$

47. The fountain in the illustration below is located exactly at the center of the circular path. How many cubic feet of gravel are required to cover the circular garden path six inches deep with gravel?

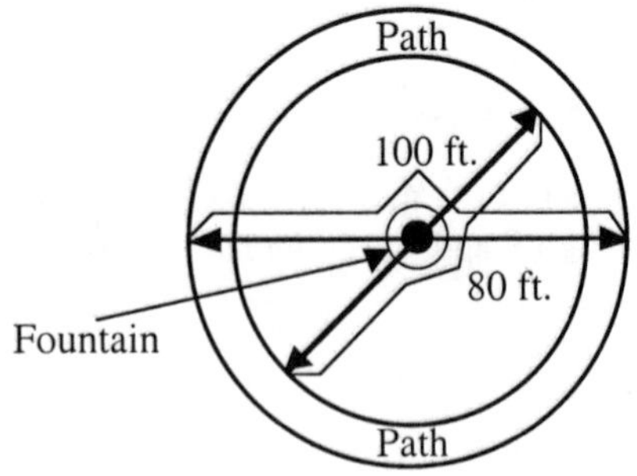

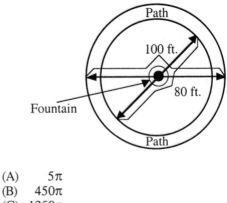

(A) 5π
(B) 450π
(C) 1250π
(D) 4500π
(E) 5400π

NOTES AND STRATEGIES

48. In the figure below, if arcsin s = 2 arcsin d, then $x = ?$

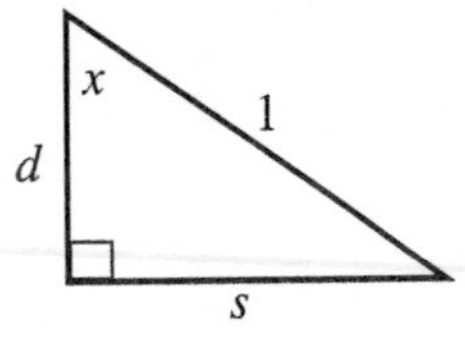

(F) 15
(G) 30
(H) 45
(J) 60
(K) 75

49. In the figure below, if AC is a diameter of the circle, B is a point on the circle, and $\sin\theta = \frac{1}{2}$, then $\sin\phi = ?$

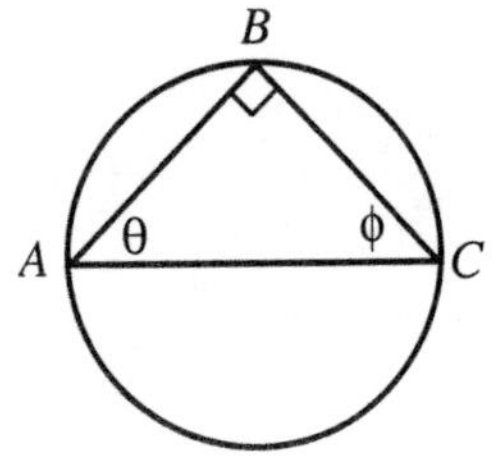

(A) $\frac{\sqrt{2}}{3}$
(B) $\frac{\sqrt{3}}{3}$
(C) $\frac{\sqrt{3}}{2}$
(D) $\frac{2\sqrt{2}}{3}$
(E) $\frac{2\sqrt{3}}{2}$

50. What is the equation of the hyperbola graphed below?

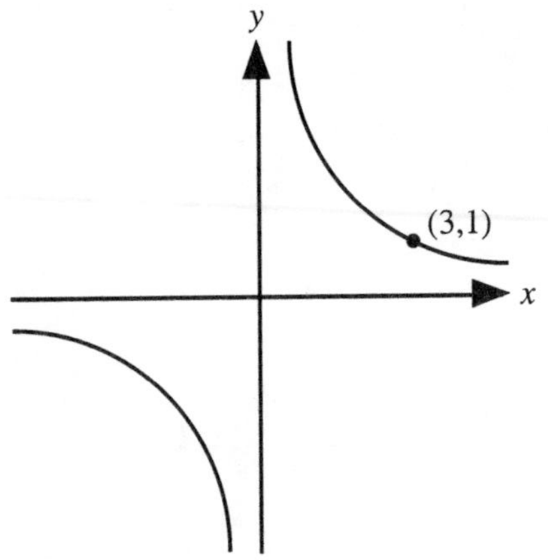

(F) $\frac{x^2}{3} + \frac{y^2}{1} = 1$
(G) $\frac{x^2}{9} + \frac{y^2}{1} = 1$
(H) $xy = 3$
(J) $xy = -3$
(K) $3x^2 + y^2 = 1$

SECTION THREE—MATHEMATICS QUIZZES

DIRECTIONS: This section contains three Mathematics quizzes. Complete each quiz while being timed. Answers are on page 120.

Note: Unless otherwise stated, all of the following should be assumed.

- Illustrative figures are NOT necessarily drawn to scale.
- Geometric figures lie in a plane.
- The word line indicates a straight line.
- The word average indicates arithmetic mean.

QUIZ I (20 questions; 20 minutes)

1. A jar contains between 50 and 60 marbles. If the marbles are counted out 3 at a time, 1 is left over; if they are counted out 4 at a time, 3 are left over. How many marbles are in the jar?

(A) 52
(B) 54
(C) 55
(D) 58
(E) 59

2. In the triangle below, $x = ?$

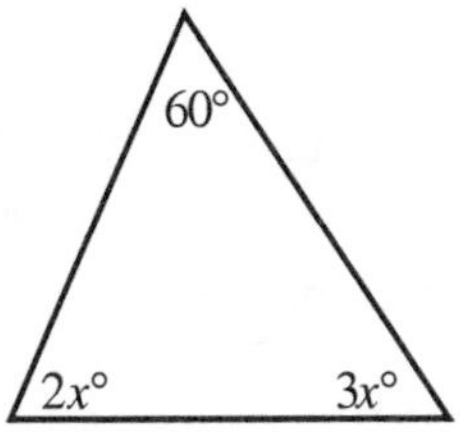

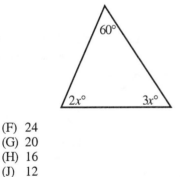

(F) 24
(G) 20
(H) 16
(J) 12
(K) 10

3. A normal dozen contains 12 items, and a baker's dozen contains 13 items. If x is a number of items that could be measured either in a whole number of normal dozens or in a whole number of baker's dozens, what is the minimum value of x?

(A) 1
(B) 12
(C) 13
(D) 25
(E) 156

4. Starting from points 200 kilometers apart, two trains travel toward each other along two parallel tracks. If one train travels at 70 kilometers per hour and the other at 80 kilometers per hour, how much time, in hours, will elapse before the trains pass each other?

(F) $\frac{3}{4}$
(G) 1
(H) $\frac{4}{3}$
(J) $\frac{3}{2}$
(K) 2

5. A student begins heating a certain substance with a temperature of 50 degrees Celsius over a bunsen burner. If the temperature of the substance will rise 20 degrees Celsius for every 24 minutes it remains over the burner, what will be the temperature, in degrees Celsius, of the substance after 18 minutes?

(A) 52
(B) 56
(C) 60
(D) 65
(E) 72

6. How many of the two-element subsets of the set below do NOT contain the pair red and green?

{red, green, yellow, blue}

(F) 2
(G) 4
(H) 5
(J) 6
(K) 10

7. If the ratio of men to women in a meeting is 8 to 7, what fractional part of the people at the meeting are women?

(A) $\frac{1}{56}$
(B) $\frac{1}{15}$
(C) $\frac{1}{7}$
(D) $\frac{7}{15}$
(E) $\frac{8}{7}$

8. In a certain direct mail center, each of x computers addresses y letters every z minutes. If every computer works without interruption, how many hours are required for the center to address 100,000 letters?

(F) $\frac{100{,}000z}{60xy}$
(G) $\frac{100{,}000x}{60yz}$
(H) $\frac{100{,}000xy}{60z}$
(J) $\frac{60xy}{100{,}000z}$
(K) $\frac{60y}{100{,}000xz}$

9. The object of a certain board game is to use clues to identify a suspect and the weapon used to commit a crime. If there are three suspects and six weapons, how many different solutions to the game are possible?

(A) 2
(B) 3
(C) 9
(D) 12
(E) 18

10. The average weight of three boxes is $25\frac{1}{3}$ pounds. If each box weighs at least 24 pounds, what is the greatest possible weight, in pounds, of any one of the boxes?

(F) 25
(G) 26
(H) 27
(J) 28
(K) 29

11. If n subtracted from $\frac{13}{2}$ is equal to n divided by $\frac{2}{13}$, what is the value of n?

(A) $\frac{2}{3}$
(B) $\frac{13}{15}$
(C) 1
(D) $\frac{13}{11}$
(E) 26

12. If $x = 6 + y$ and $4x = 3 - 2y$, what is the value of x?

(F) 4
(G) $\frac{11}{3}$
(H) $\frac{5}{2}$
(J) $-\frac{2}{3}$
(K) $-\frac{7}{2}$

13. If $\frac{2}{3}$ is written as a decimal to 101 places, what is the sum of the first 100 digits to the right of the decimal point?

(A) 66
(B) 595
(C) 599
(D) 600
(E) 601

14. If $i = \sqrt{-1}$, $(2 + i)(3 + 2i) = ?$

(F) $4 + 7i$
(G) $5 + 5i$
(H) $6 - 5i$
(J) $6 + 5i$
(K) $6 + 6i$

15. A jar contains 5 blue marbles, 25 green marbles, and x red marbles. If the odds of drawing at random a red marble are $\frac{1}{4}$, what is the value of x?

(A) 25
(B) 20
(C) 15
(D) 12
(E) 10

16. $\frac{1}{10^{25}} - \frac{1}{10^{26}} = ?$

(F) $\frac{9}{10^{25}}$
(G) $\frac{9}{10^{26}}$
(H) $\frac{1}{10^{25}}$
(J) $-\frac{9}{10^{25}}$
(K) $-\frac{1}{10}$

17. In the figure below, $ABCD$ is a rectangle with sides AB, BC, and CD touching the circle with center O. If the radius of the circle is 2, what is the area of the shaded region?

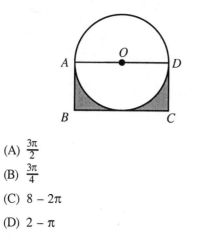

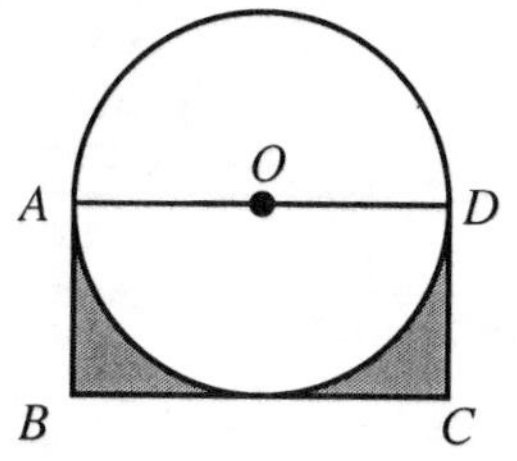

(A) $\frac{3\pi}{2}$

(B) $\frac{3\pi}{4}$

(C) $8 - 2\pi$

(D) $2 - \pi$

(E) $\pi - 1$

18. If Yuriko is now twice as old as Lisa was 10 years ago, how old is Lisa today if Yuriko is now n years old?

(F) $\frac{n}{2} + 10$

(G) $\frac{n}{2} - 10$

(H) $n - 10$

(J) $2n + 10$

(K) $2n - 10$

19. In a certain community, the property tax is solely a function of the tax rate and assessed value of the property. If the assessed value of a property is decreased by 25 percent while the tax rate is increased by 25 percent, what is the net effect on the taxes on the property?

(A) An increase of 18.75 percent
(B) An increase of 6.25 percent
(C) No net change
(D) A decrease of 6.25 percent
(E) A decrease of 18.75 percent

20. For the figure below, which of the following statements is NOT correct?

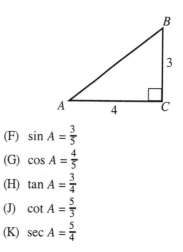

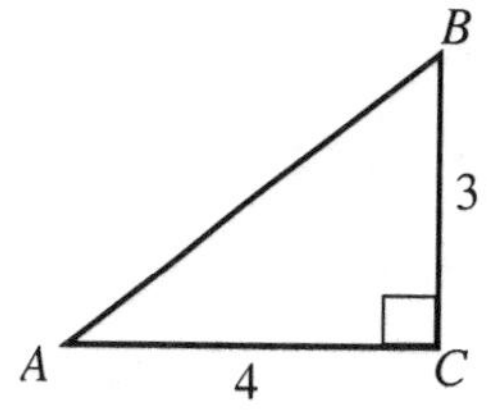

(F) $\sin A = \frac{3}{5}$

(G) $\cos A = \frac{4}{5}$

(H) $\tan A = \frac{3}{4}$

(J) $\cot A = \frac{5}{3}$

(K) $\sec A = \frac{5}{4}$

QUIZ II (20 questions; 20 minutes)

1. If $x + 3 = 3 + 12$, what is the value of x?

(A) 0
(B) 3
(C) 6
(D) 9
(E) 12

2. Which of the following CANNOT be written as the sum of two negative numbers?

(F) -5
(G) $-3\sqrt{2}$
(H) -1
(J) $-\frac{1}{2}$
(K) 0

3. If $x + 2y = 3$, what is the value of $2x + 4y$?

(A) -3
(B) 0
(C) 2
(D) 6
(E) 9

4. The average (arithmetic mean) of three numbers is 6. If the sum of two of the numbers is 11, then the third number is equal to which of the following?

(F) 5
(G) 6
(H) 7
(J) 8
(K) 9

5. Joan had exactly \$9 before Jerry repaid her \$6 that he had borrowed. After the debt was repaid, both Joan and Jerry have the same amount of money. How much money did Jerry have before the debt was repaid?

(A) \$3
(B) \$9
(C) \$15
(D) \$21
(E) \$24

6. The figure below is a plan that shows two views of a solid set of steps to be constructed from concrete blocks of equal size. How many blocks are needed to construct the steps?

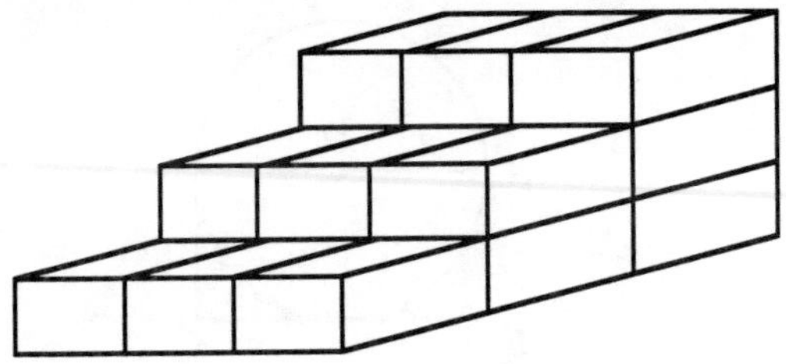

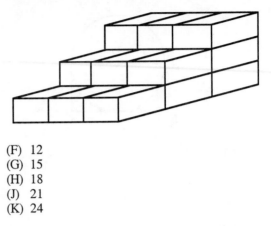

(F) 12
(G) 15
(H) 18
(J) 21
(K) 24

7. In the figure below, what is the value of x?

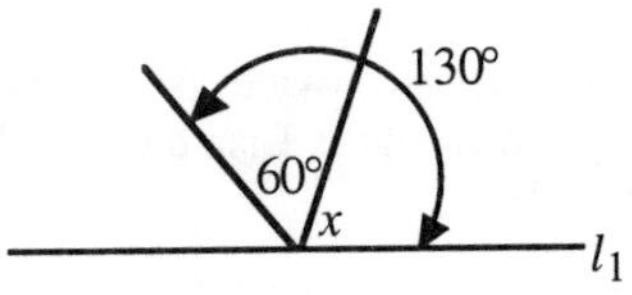

(A) 70
(B) 60
(C) 50
(D) 40
(E) 30

8. If $2^{x+1} = 4^{x-1}$, what is the value of x?

(F) 1
(G) 2
(H) 3
(J) 4
(K) 5

9. Of the actors in a certain play, 5 are in Act I, 12 are in Act II, and 13 are in Act III. If 10 of the actors are in exactly two of the three acts and all of the other actors are in just one act, how many actors are in the play?

(A) 17
(B) 20
(C) 24
(D) 30
(E) 38

10. Under certain conditions, a bicycle traveling k meters per second requires $\frac{k^2}{20} + k$ meters to stop. If $k = 10$, how many meters does the bicycle need to stop?

(F) 10
(G) 12
(H) 15
(J) 20
(K) 30

11. What percent of 125 is 100?

(A) 75%
(B) 80%
(C) 120%
(D) 125%
(E) 150%

12. The sum of two integers is 72. If the integers are in a ratio of 4:5, what is the value of the smaller integer?

(F) 32
(G) 36
(H) 40
(J) 42
(K) 48

13. If $n = \frac{x}{12} + \frac{x}{12} + \frac{x}{12}$ and n is an integer, then the least possible value of x is?

(A) 2
(B) 3
(C) 4
(D) 5
(E) 6

14. An album contains x black-and-white photographs and y color photographs. If the album contains a total of 24 photographs, then all of the following can be true EXCEPT which of the following?

(F) $x = y$
(G) $x = 2y$
(H) $x = 3y$
(J) $x = 4y$
(K) $x = 5y$

Questions #15-16 are based on the following number line in which the letters represent a series of consecutive integers.

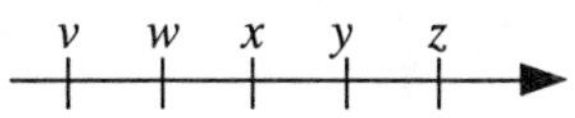

15. $y - w = ?$

(A) 0
(B) 1
(C) 2
(D) 3
(E) 4

16. In terms of v, $v + x + z = ?$

(F) $3v + 2$
(G) $3v + 3$
(H) $3v + 4$
(J) $3v + 5$
(K) $3v + 6$

17. For all positive integers x:

♣ $(x) = x^2$ if x is even

♣ $(x) = \sqrt{x}$ if x is odd

What is the value of ♣ $(7 + 1)$?

(A) 64
(B) 50
(C) 25
(D) $2\sqrt{2}$
(E) $\sqrt{7}$

18. If $2a = 3b = 4c$, then in terms of a, what is the average (arithmetic mean) of a, b, and c?

(F) $\frac{13a}{18}$
(G) $\frac{13a}{9}$
(H) $\frac{8a}{3}$
(J) $\frac{4a}{3}$
(K) $2a$

19. Which of the following is the graph of $(x-1)^2 + y^2 = 9$?

(A)

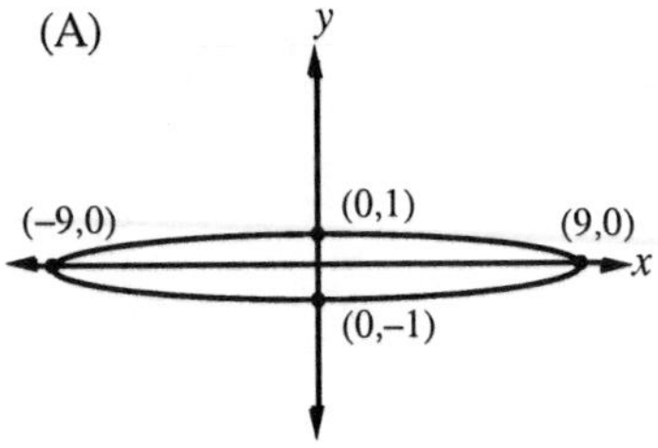

(B)

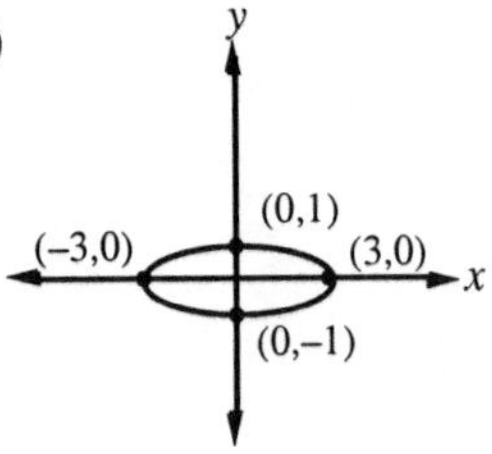

(C)

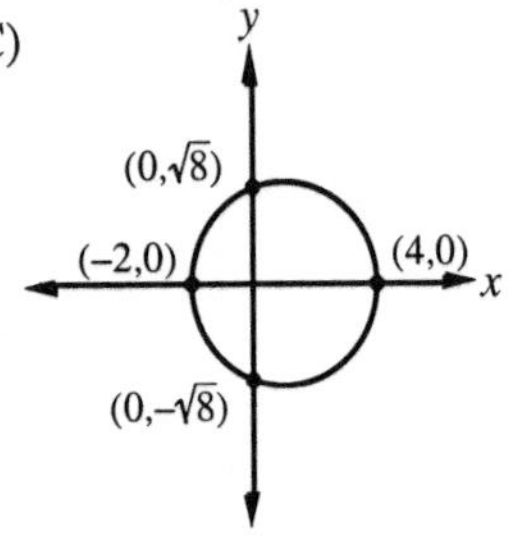

(D)

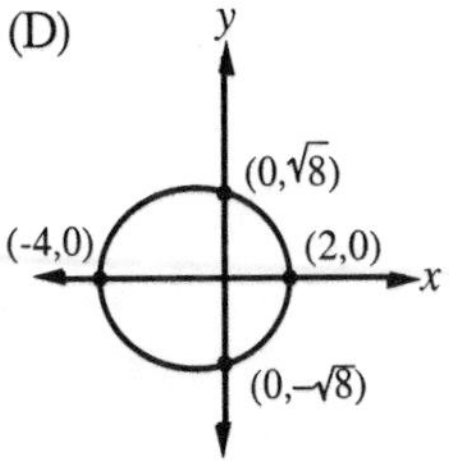

(E)

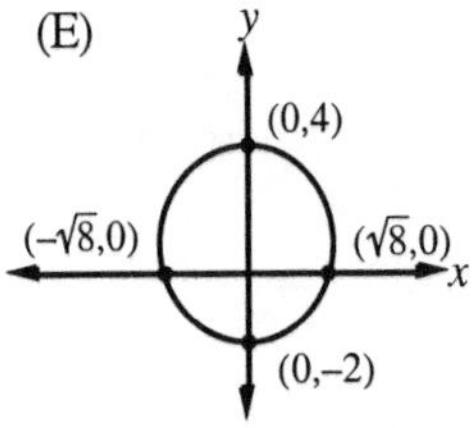

20. Which of the following best approximates the length of BC ($\tan 22° \approx 0.4$.)?

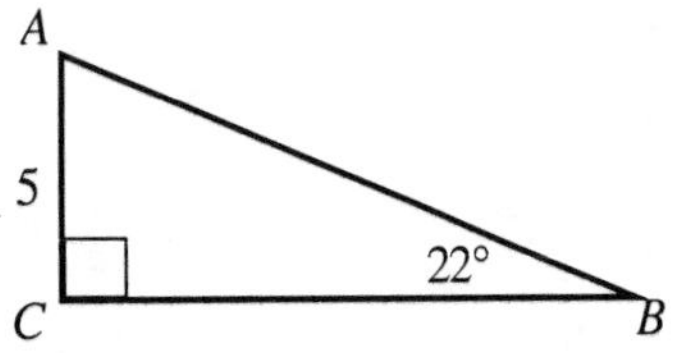

(F) 2.0
(G) 3.0
(H) 7.5
(J) 12.5
(K) 16

QUIZ III (20 questions; 20 minutes)

1. If a recipe that will produce 8 servings of a dish uses 2 eggs, then how many eggs are needed to produce 12 servings of the dish?

(A) 12
(B) 8
(C) 6
(D) 4
(E) 3

2. If $x + 5$ is an even integer, then x could be which of the following?

(F) –4
(G) –1
(H) 0
(J) 2
(K) 4

3. If $(x + 2)(9 - 4) = 25$, then $x = ?$

(A) 1
(B) 2
(C) 3
(D) 4
(E) 5

4. $\sqrt{1+2+3+4+1+2+3+4+1+2+3+4+1+2+3} = ?$

(F) $3\sqrt{2}$
(G) $3\sqrt{3}$
(H) 4
(J) 5
(K) 6

5. What is the average (arithmetic mean) of all integers 6 through 15 (inclusive)?

(A) 6
(B) 9
(C) 10.5
(D) 11
(E) 21

6. In the figure below, if $x = 50$, then $y = ?$

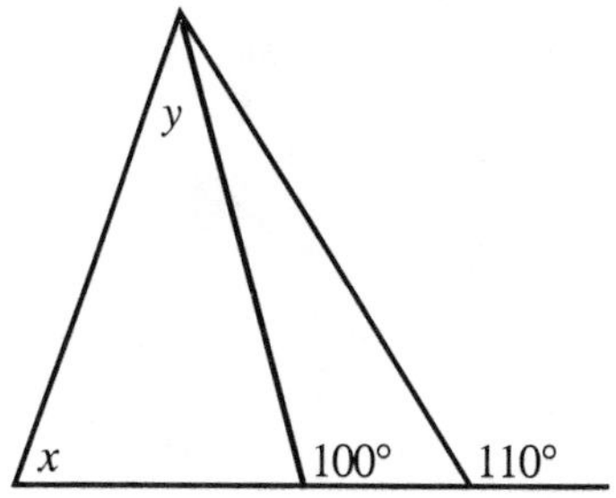

(F) 30
(G) 45
(H) 50
(J) 60
(K) 75

7. Of the following, which number is the greatest?

(A) 0.08
(B) 0.17
(C) 0.171
(D) 0.1077
(E) 0.10771

8. If the rectangle below has an area of 72, then $x = ?$

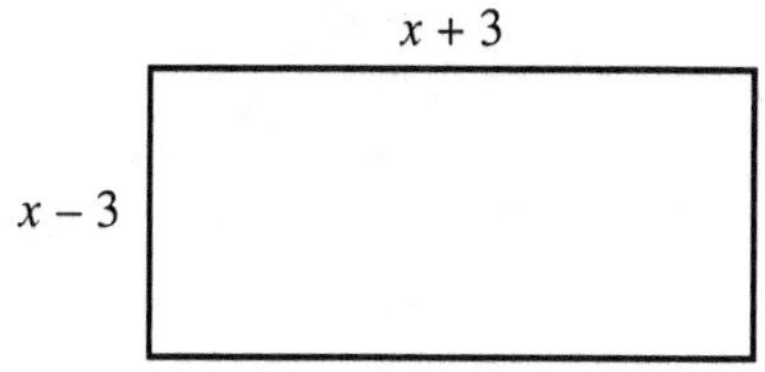

(F) 3
(G) 4
(H) 6
(J) 8
(K) 9

9. Machine X produces 15 units per minute and machine Y produces 12 units per minute. In one hour, X will produce how many more units than Y?

(A) 90
(B) 180
(C) 240
(D) 270
(E) 360

10. Two circles with radii r and $r + 3$ have areas that differ by 15π. What is the radius of the *smaller* circle?

(F) 4
(G) 3
(H) 2
(J) 1
(K) $\frac{1}{2}$

11. The average (arithmetic mean) of Pat's scores on three tests was 80. If the average of her scores on the first two tests was 78, what was her score on the third test?

(A) 82
(B) 84
(C) 86
(D) 88
(E) 90

12. In the figure below, $a + c - b$ is equal to which of the following?

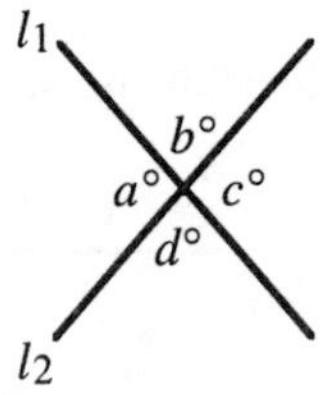

(F) $2a - d$
(G) $2a + d$
(H) $2d - a$
(J) $2a$
(K) 180

13. If $i = \sqrt{-1}$, then $\frac{2}{3-2i} = ?$

(A) $\frac{6+4i}{3}$
(B) $\frac{6+4i}{13}$
(C) $\frac{7+3i}{3}$
(D) $\frac{8+4i}{2}$
(E) $\frac{8+5i}{3}$

14. If x, y, and z are integers, $x > y > z > 1$, and $xyz = 144$, then what is the greatest possible value of x?

(F) 8
(G) 12
(H) 16
(J) 24
(K) 36

15. On the first day after being given an assignment, a student read $\frac{1}{2}$ the number of pages assigned and on the second day 3 more pages. If the student still has 6 more pages to read, how many pages were assigned?

(A) 15
(B) 18
(C) 24
(D) 30
(E) 36

16. For all integers, $x \spadesuit y = 2x + 3y$. Which of the following must be true?

I. $3 \spadesuit 2 = 12$
II. $x \spadesuit y = y \spadesuit x$
III. $0 \spadesuit (1 \spadesuit 2) = (0 \spadesuit 1) \spadesuit 2$

(F) I only
(G) I and II only
(H) I and III only
(J) II and III only
(K) I, II, and III

17. The sum of two positive consecutive integers is n. In terms of n, what is the value of the larger of the two integers?

(A) $\frac{n-1}{2}$
(B) $\frac{n+1}{2}$
(C) $\frac{n}{2} + 1$
(D) $\frac{n}{2} - 1$
(E) $\frac{n}{2}$

18. If a polygon with all equal sides is inscribed in a circle, then the measure in degrees of the minor arc created by adjacent vertices of the polygon could be all of the following EXCEPT which one?

(F) 30
(G) 25
(H) 24
(J) 20
(K) 15

19. Which of the following is the graph of $y = \frac{x^2}{2}$?

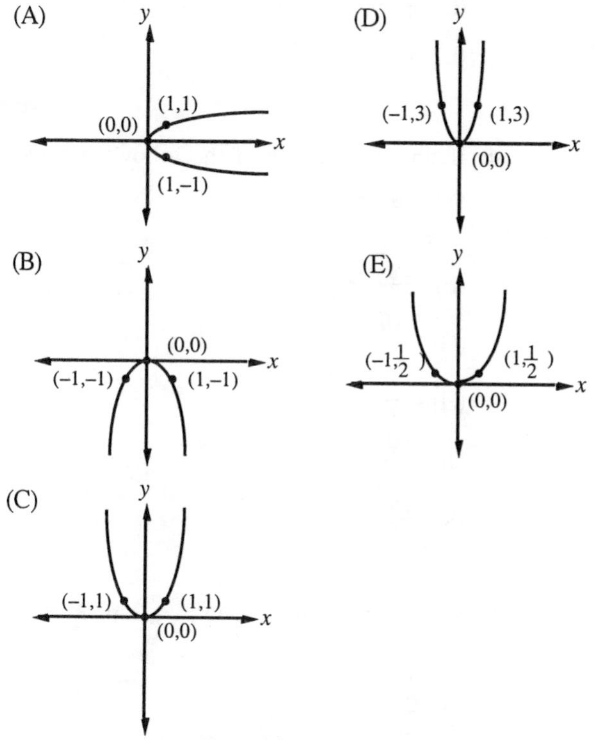

20. Cos 45° ≈ 0.7. Which of the following best approximates the length of BC?

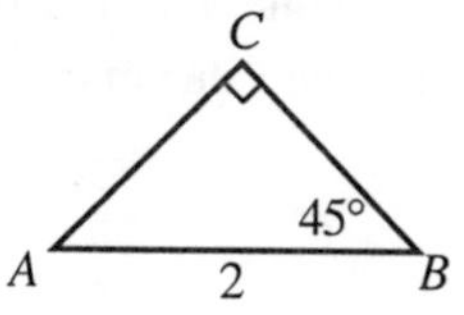

(F) 0.7
(G) 1.2
(H) 1.4
(J) 2.9
(K) 3.4

SECTION FOUR—TRIGONOMETRY EXERCISE

DIRECTIONS: This exercise consists of additional trigonometry review problems designed to further familiarize you with the basic trigonometry concepts. Note that while these questions do not include trigonometric values, values will be provided on the ACT Mathematics test. Answers are on page 120.

1. In the figure below, what is the value of $\sin B$?

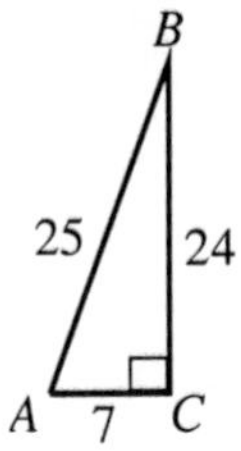

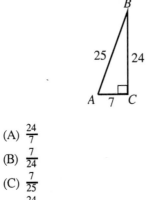

(A) $\frac{24}{7}$
(B) $\frac{7}{24}$
(C) $\frac{7}{25}$
(D) $\frac{24}{25}$
(E) $\frac{25}{24}$

2. For the figure below, which of the following statements is NOT correct?

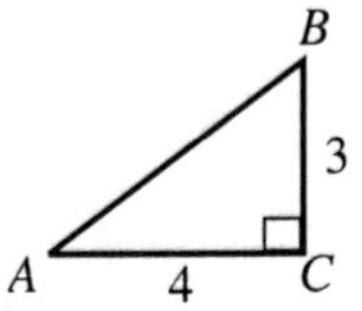

(F) $\sin A = \frac{3}{5}$
(G) $\cos A = \frac{4}{5}$
(H) $\tan A = \frac{3}{4}$
(J) $\cot A = \frac{5}{3}$
(K) $\sec A = \frac{5}{4}$

3. In the figure below ΔLMN has its right angle at M. If $\tan L = \frac{4}{3}$, what is the value of $\sin N$?

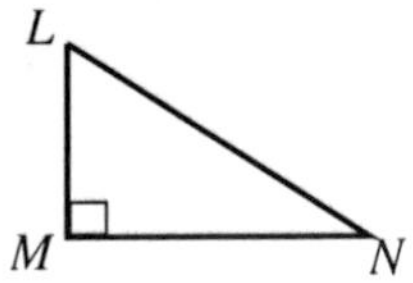

(A) $\frac{3}{5}$
(B) $\frac{4}{5}$
(C) $\frac{3}{4}$
(D) $\frac{4}{3}$
(E) $\frac{5}{3}$

4. If $\sin x = \frac{5}{7}$, which of the following could be the value of $\frac{1}{\tan x}$?

(F) $\frac{2\sqrt{6}}{7}$
(G) $5\frac{\sqrt{6}}{7}$
(H) $\frac{5}{7}$
(J) $\frac{5\sqrt{6}}{12}$
(K) $\frac{2\sqrt{6}}{5}$

5. What is the value of $2\sin^2 3x + 2\cos^2 3x$?

(A) 1
(B) 2
(C) 3
(D) 4
(E) 9

6. In triangle NJL, angle J is the right angle. If $\sin N = \frac{2}{3}$, what is the value of $\cos N$?

(F) $\frac{1}{3}$
(G) $\frac{8}{9}$
(H) $\frac{3\sqrt{5}}{5}$
(J) $\frac{\sqrt{5}}{2}$
(K) $\frac{\sqrt{5}}{3}$

7. In the figure below, $\sin x$ is $\frac{3}{5}$. What is the length of BC?

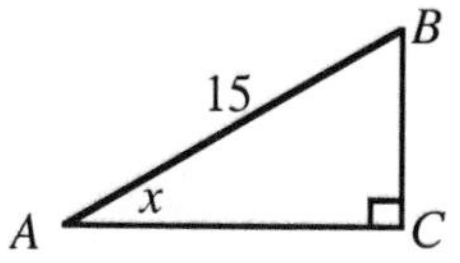

(A) 3
(B) 6
(C) 9
(D) 12
(E) 15

8. $(1 - \sin x)(1 + \sin x)$ is equal to what?

(F) $\sin x$
(G) $\cos^2 x$
(H) $\tan x$
(J) 1
(K) $\sin^2 x$

9. In right triangle RST, S is the right angle. If $\sin R = \frac{1}{4}$, what is the value of $\tan T$?

(A) 4
(B) $\sqrt{15}$
(C) 1
(D) $\frac{4\sqrt{15}}{15}$
(E) $\frac{\sqrt{15}}{16}$

10. $\frac{(\cos x)(\tan x)}{\sin x} = ?$

(F) $\sin x$
(G) $\cos x$
(H) $\tan x$
(J) $(\sin x)(\cos x)$
(K) 1

11. Angle A and angle B are acute angles of right triangle ABC. $\sin A = ?$

(A) $\frac{1}{\sin B}$
(B) $\frac{1}{\cos B}$
(C) $\frac{1}{\sec B}$
(D) $\frac{1}{\csc B}$
(E) $\frac{1}{\tan B}$

12. For $0° < \theta < 90°$, $\sin \theta \cdot \csc \theta = ?$

(F) $\cos \theta$
(G) $\sec \theta$
(H) $\sin^2\theta$
(J) $\sqrt{3}$
(K) 1

13. From the below figure, $\tan A = ?$

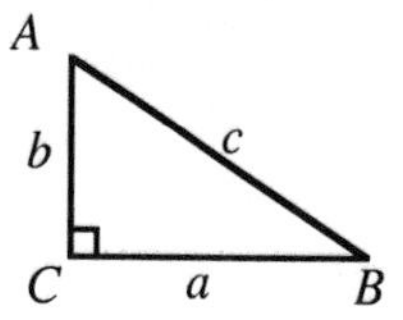

(A) $\frac{\sin C}{\cos C}$
(B) $\frac{\cos B}{\sin B}$
(C) $\frac{\sin B}{\cos B}$
(D) $\frac{\cos A}{\sin A}$
(E) $\frac{\sin A}{\cos B}$

14. $\sin 150° = ?$

(F) $\frac{\sqrt{3}}{2}$
(G) $\frac{\sqrt{2}}{2}$
(H) $\frac{1}{2}$
(J) $-\frac{1}{2}$
(K) $-\frac{\sqrt{3}}{2}$

15. cos 150° = ?

(A) $\frac{\sqrt{3}}{2}$
(B) $\frac{\sqrt{2}}{2}$
(C) $-\frac{1}{2}$
(D) $-\frac{1}{2}$
(E) $-\frac{\sqrt{3}}{2}$

16. tan 240° = ?

(F) $\sqrt{3}$
(G) $3\sqrt{3}$
(H) $\frac{\sqrt{3}}{2}$
(J) $-\frac{\sqrt{3}}{3}$
(K) $-\sqrt{3}$

17. If $\sin\theta = -\frac{1}{2}$ and $\tan\theta > 0$, then $\cos\theta = ?$

(A) $\sqrt{3}$
(B) $\frac{\sqrt{3}}{2}$
(C) $\frac{1}{2}$
(D) $-\frac{1}{2}$
(E) $-\frac{\sqrt{3}}{2}$

18. If $\sec\theta = 2$ and $\sin\theta < 0$, then $\tan\theta = ?$

(F) $\sqrt{3}$
(G) $\frac{\sqrt{3}}{2}$
(H) $\frac{1}{2}$
(J) $-\frac{\sqrt{3}}{2}$
(K) $-\sqrt{3}$

SECTION FIVE—CALCULATOR EXERCISE

DIRECTIONS: Although no question on the ACT requires the use of a calculator, you may find a calculator helpful for some questions. A calculator may be useful for any question that involves complex arithmetic computations; however, it cannot take the place of understanding how to set up a mathematical problem. This exercise is designed to illustrate when and when not to use a calculator on the ACT. The degree to which you can use your calculator will depend on the type of calculator.

Label each of the following problems from the in-class Mathematics Review according to the following categories: 1) a calculator would be very useful (it would save valuable test time), 2) calculator might or might not be useful, or 3) calculator would be counter-productive (it would waste valuable test time). Answers are on page 120.

1. What is the average of 8.5, 7.8, and 7.7?

   (A) 8.3
   (B) 8.2
   (C) 8.1
   (D) 8.0
   (E) 7.9

2. If $0 < x < 1$, which of the following is the largest?

   (F) x
   (G) $2x$
   (H) x^2
   (J) x^3
   (K) $x + 1$

3. If 4.5 pounds of chocolate cost $10, how many pounds of chocolate can be purchased for $12?

   (A) $\frac{3}{4}$
   (B) $5\frac{2}{5}$
   (C) $5\frac{1}{2}$
   (D) $5\frac{3}{4}$
   (E) 6

4. $\frac{8}{9} - \frac{7}{8} = ?$

   (F) $\frac{1}{72}$
   (G) $\frac{5}{72}$
   (H) $\frac{1}{7}$
   (J) $\frac{1}{8}$
   (K) $\frac{15}{7}$

5. Which of the following fractions is the largest?

   (A) $\frac{111}{221}$
   (B) $\frac{75}{151}$
   (C) $\frac{333}{998}$
   (D) $\frac{113}{225}$
   (E) $\frac{101}{301}$

6. $0.125 \cdot 0.125 \cdot 64 = ?$

   (F) 0.625
   (G) 0.125
   (H) 0.5
   (J) 1
   (K) 8

7. What is the solution set for the equation $3x^2 + 3x = 6$?

   (A) $\{1, -2\}$
   (B) $\{1, 2\}$
   (C) $\{\frac{1}{2}, 1\}$
   (D) $\{\frac{1}{2}, \frac{1}{3}\}$
   (E) $\{-1, -2\}$

8. In the triangle below, what is the length of AC?

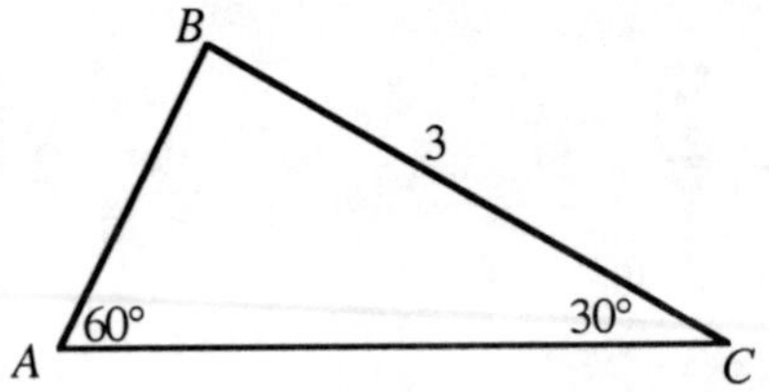

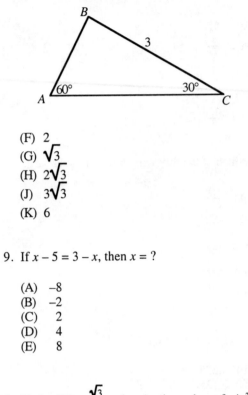

(F) 2
(G) $\sqrt{3}$
(H) $2\sqrt{3}$
(J) $3\sqrt{3}$
(K) 6

9. If $x - 5 = 3 - x$, then $x = ?$

(A) −8
(B) −2
(C) 2
(D) 4
(E) 8

10. If $\sin 60° = \frac{\sqrt{3}}{2}$, what is the value of $\sin^2 30° + \cos^2 30°$?

(A) $\frac{\sqrt{3}+1}{2}$
(B) $\sqrt{5}$
(C) $\frac{\sqrt{5}}{2}$
(D) $\frac{3}{4}$
(E) 1

MATHEMATICS ANSWER KEY

SECTION ONE—MATHEMATICS REVEW (p. 69)

1. D	31. D	61. A	91. C	121. C
2. H	32. H	62. G	92. K	122. H
3. D	33. D	63. B	93. E	123. C
4. J	34. J	64. J	94. G	124. H
5. B	35. D	65. A	95. B	125. A
6. H	36. K	66. J	96. G	126. G
7. B	37. E	67. D	97. A	127. C
8. H	38. J	68. J	98. G	128. H
9. E	39. C	69. E	99. E	129. A
10. H	40. J	70. J	100. F	130. H
11. B	41. B	71. C	101. E	131. E
12. J	42. K	72. H	102. J	132. J
13. C	43. D	73. D	103. C	133. E
14. G	44. H	74. K	104. H	134. K
15. C	45. E	75. B	105. B	135. C
16. J	46. H	76. J	106. H	136. H
17. E	47. E	77. D	107. B	137. C
18. K	48. G	78. F	108. H	138. H
19. C	49. E	79. E	109. A	139. D
20. J	50. H	80. K	110. J	140. J
21. C	51. C	81. D	111. E	141. D
22. H	52. H	82. J	112. H	142. G
23. A	53. A	83. E	113. B	143. B
24. H	54. H	84. G	114. K	144. H
25. B	55. E	85. C	115. A	145. C
26. H	56. F	86. J	116. H	146. K
27. D	57. E	87. D	117. D	147. D
28. K	58. F	88. K	118. H	148. K
29. A	59. C	89. C	119. E	149. A
30. F	60. K	90. K	120. K	

SECTION TWO—MATHEMATICS PROBLEM-SOLVING (p. 94)

1. C	9. D	17. E	25. D	33. C
2. H	10. H	18. K	26. F	34. H
3. C	11. C	19. B	27. A	35. D
4. G	12. J	20. G	28. G	36. G
5. C	13. E	21. B	29. A	37. D
6. J	14. F	22. H	30. G	38. K
7. E	15. D	23. C	31. B	39. A
8. G	16. K	24. G	32. H	40. H

41. D	43. B	45. C	47. B	49. C
42. F	44. J	46. H	48. J	50. H

SECTION THREE—MATHEMATICS QUIZZES (p. 105)

QUIZ I

1. C	5. D	9. E	13. D	17. C
2. F	6. H	10. J	14. F	18. F
3. E	7. D	11. B	15. E	19. D
4. H	8. F	12. H	16. G	20. J

QUIZ II

1. E	5. D	9. B	13. B	17. A
2. K	6. H	10. H	14. J	18. F
3. D	7. A	11. B	15. C	19. C
4. H	8. H	12. F	16. K	20. J

QUIZ III

1. E	5. C	9. B	13. B	17. B
2. G	6. H	10. J	14. J	18. G
3. C	7. C	11. B	15. B	19. E
4. K	8. K	12. F	16. F	20. H

SECTION FOUR—TRIGONOMETRY EXERCISE (p. 114)

1. C	5. B	9. B	13. B	17. E
2. J	6. K	10. K	14. H	18. K
3. A	7. C	11. C	15. E	
4. K	8. G	12. K	16. F	

SECTION FIVE—CALCULATOR EXERCISE (p. 117)

1. 1	3. 2	5. 1	7. 2	9. 3
2. 2	4. 2	6. 1	8. 2	10. 3

Strategy Summary Sheet
ACT • PLAN • EXPLORE—MATHEMATICS

STRUCTURE OF ACT MATHEMATICS TEST: The ACT Assessment includes one Mathematics Test: 60 minutes in which to answer 60 multiple-choice questions. The PLAN is 40 items, 40 minutes; the EXPLORE is 30 items, 30 minutes. Figures are not necessarily drawn to scale, but usually are. Answer choices are arranged in sequential order unless requesting testing largest or smallest value. While there is no definite ladder of difficulty (increasing difficulty with increasing problem number), more advance concepts tend to be tested towards the end of test. The following summarizes how many items test each content area on the three tests (ACT summary is approximate):

	ACT *(60 questions)*	PLAN *(40 questions)*	EXPLORE *(30 questions)*
Pre-Algebra	15	14	10
Elementary Algebra	14	8	9
Plane Geometry	17	7	7
Statistics/Probability	1	–	4
Coordinate Geometry	9	11	–
Trigonometry	4	–	–

MATHEMATICS GENERAL STRATEGIES: Pay attention to thought-reversers (capitalized and underlined words). When guessing on difficult questions, eliminate "simple answers" and the "Cannot be determined" response. Don't jump at easy answers unless reasoned. If you can see your way to an elegant, quick solution, solve the problem directly, based on subject knowledge. Translate, use pictures, and substitute useful numbers into story problems. Plug-and-chug—especially on algebra questions. Use the "good enough" principle and approximation—the correct answer is among the choices. "Test-the-Test," starting with (C) or (H). If you do not understand a question or cannot think of a way to solve the problem, guess quickly.

CHECKLIST OF CONCEPTS & SKILLS TESTED:

ARITHMETIC:

1. Simplifying: Fractions, Collecting Terms
2. Approximation
3. The Flying-X
4. Decimal/Fraction Equivalents
5. Properties of Numbers: Odd, Even, Negative, Positive, Consecutive Numbers
6. Percentages: Change, Original Amount, Price Increase
7. Ratios: Two-Part, Three-Part, Weighted
8. Averages: Simple, Weighted
9. Median and Mode
10. Proportions: Direct, Inverse

ALGEBRA:

11. Absolute Value
12. Complex Numbers
13. Exponents
14. Functions
15. Factoring

16. Solving Equations: Linear, Quadratic, and Simultaneous Equations
17. Special Problems: Work, Averages
18. Conic Sections: Lines, Parabolas, Circles, Ellipses
19. Permutations
20. Radicals
21. Evaluation of Expressions

COORDINATE GEOMETRY:

22. Coordinate Plane
23. Slope of a Line
24. Slope-Intercept Form of Linear Equation
25. Distance Formula
26. Graphing Linear Equations
27. Graphing First-Degree Inequalities
28. Graphing Quadratic Equations

GEOMETRY:

29. Lines & Angles: Perpendicular, Parallel, and Intersecting Lines
30. Triangles: Equilateral, Isosceles, Acute, Obtuse, Perimeter, Area, Altitudes, Pythagorean Theorem
31. Quadrilaterals: Squares, Rectangles, Rhombuses, Parallelograms, Trapezoids, Perimeter, Area
32. Polygons: Sum of Interior Angles
33. Circles: Radius, Diameter, Circumference, Area, Others (chords, tangents)
34. Solids (Three Dimensional): Cubes, Cylinders, Spheres, Volumes, Surface Areas
35. Complex Figures

TRIGONOMETRY:

36. Definitions of: sin θ, cos θ, tan θ, csc θ, sec θ, and cot θ
37. Trigonometric values for $\theta = 0°, 30°, 45°, 60°$, and $90°$
38. Trigonometric Relationships
39. Angle Measure: Degree and Radian
40. Trigonometric Graphs

ADDITIONAL NOTES AND STRATEGIES FROM IN-CLASS DISCUSSION:

CAMBRIDGE

EDUCATIONAL SERVICES, INC.®

ACT • PLAN • EXPLORE
READING

CAMBRIDGE
EDUCATIONAL SERVICES, INC.®

AMERICA'S #1 CAMPUS-BASED TESTPREP

Cambridge Course Concept Outline
ACT • PLAN • EXPLORE—READING

I. READING REVIEW (p. 127)

A. READING PRELIMINARIES
1. TEACHING THE READING LESSON
2. FORMAT OF THE ACT, PLAN, AND EXPLORE READING TESTS
3. DIRECTIONS FOR READING PROBLEMS
4. WHAT IS TESTED
5. WHY THE READING TEST IS DIFFICULT
   a. PASSAGES CAN TREAT ANY SUBJECT
   b. PASSAGES ARE EDITED

B. THE THREE QUESTION TYPES AND READING LEVELS
1. MAIN IDEA QUESTIONS TEST APPRECIATION OF GENERAL THEME (Review Questions #1-2)
2. SPECIFIC DETAIL QUESTIONS TEST UNDERSTANDING OF SPECIFIC POINTS (Review Questions #3-5)
3. EVALUATION QUESTIONS TEST EVALUATION OF TEXT (Review Questions #6-10)
4. ROMAN NUMERAL QUESTIONS
5. ADDITIONAL ADVICE ON QUESTION TYPES

C. STRATEGIES FOR READING PASSAGES
1. LABEL PASSAGES AS EASY OR HARD
2. PREVIEW FIRST AND LAST SENTENCES OF SELECTION
3. PREVIEW QUESTION STEMS
4. READ THE PASSAGE
5. ANSWER THE QUESTIONS (Review Questions #11-19)

II. READING PROBLEM-SOLVING (p. 132)

A. SOCIAL STUDIES (Problem-Solving Questions #1-20)

B. NATURAL SCIENCES (Problem-Solving Questions #21-44)

C. PROSE FICTION (Problem-Solving Questions #45-69)

D. HUMANITIES (Problem-Solving Questions #70-89)

III. READING QUIZZES (p. 153)

SECTION ONE—READING REVIEW

DIRECTIONS: The questions in this section accompany the in-class review of the reading concepts and skills tested by the ACT, PLAN, and EXPLORE. You will work through the questions with your instructor in class. Each of the following passages is followed by several questions. After reading a passage, choose the best answer to each question. You may refer to the passage as often as necessary. Answers are on page 160.

Questions 1-10 are based on the following passage.

To broaden their voting appeal in the presidential election of 1796, the Federalists selected Thomas Pinckney, a leading South Carolinian, as running mate for the New Englander John Adams. But Pinckney's Southern friends chose to ignore their party's intentions and regarded Pinckney as a presidential candidate, creating a political situation that Alexander Hamilton was determined to exploit. Hamilton had long been wary of Adams' stubbornly independent brand of politics and preferred to see his running mate, over whom he could exert more control, in the President's chair.

The election was held under the system originally established by the Constitution. At that time there was but a single tally, with the candidate receiving the largest number of electoral votes declared President and the candidate with the second largest number declared Vice-President. Hamilton anticipated that all the Federalists in the North would vote for Adams and Pinckney equally in an attempt to ensure that Jefferson would not be either first or second in the voting. Pinckney would be solidly supported in the South while Adams would not. Hamilton concluded if it were possible to divert a few electoral votes from Adams to Pinckney, Pinckney would receive more votes than Adams would yet both Federalists would outpoll Jefferson.

Various methods were used to persuade the electors to vote as Hamilton wished. In the press, anonymous articles were published attacking Adams for his monarchical tendencies and Jefferson for being overly democratic, while pushing Pinckney as the only suitable candidate. In private correspondence with state party leaders the Hamiltonians encouraged the idea that Adams' popularity was slipping, that he could not win the election, and that the Federalists could defeat Jefferson only by supporting Pinckney.

Had sectional pride and loyalty not run as high in New England as in the Deep South, Pinckney might well have become Washington's successor. New Englanders, however, realized that equal votes for Adams and Pinckney in their states would defeat Adams; therefore, eighteen electors scratched Pinckney's name from their ballots and deliberately threw away their second votes to men who were not even running. It was fortunate for Adams that they did, for the electors from South Carolina completely abandoned him, giving eight votes to Pinckney and eight to Jefferson.

In the end, Hamilton's interference in Pinckney's candidacy lost him even the Vice-Presidency. Without New England's support, Pickney received only 59 electoral votes, finishing third to Adams and Jefferson. He might have been President in 1797, or as Vice-President a serious contender for the Presidency in 1800; instead, stigmatized by a plot he had not devised, he served a brief term in the United States Senate and then dropped from sight as a national influence.

1. The main purpose of the passage is to:

   (A) propose reforms of the procedures for electing the President and Vice-President.
   (B) condemn Alexander Hamilton for interfering in the election of 1796.
   (C) describe the political events that led to John Adams' victory in the 1796 presidential election.
   (D) contrast the political philosophy of the Federalists to that of Thomas Jefferson.

2. The author is primarily concerned with:

   (F) the failure of Alexander Hamilton's plan for Thomas Pinckney to win the 1796 presidential election.
   (G) the roots of Alexander Hamilton's distrust of John Adams and New England politics.
   (H) important issues in the 1796 presidential campaign as presented by the Federalist candidates.
   (J) the political careers of Alexander Hamilton, John Adams, and Thomas Pinckney.

3. According to the passage, which of the following was true of the presidential election of 1796?

   (A) Thomas Jefferson received more electoral votes than did Thomas Pinckney.
   (B) John Adams received strong support from the electors of South Carolina.
   (C) Alexander Hamilton received most of the electoral votes of New England.
   (D) Thomas Pinckney was selected by Federalist party leaders to be the party's presidential candidate.

4. According to the passage, Hamilton's plan included all BUT which of the following?

   (F) Articles published in newspapers to create opposition to John Adams
   (G) South Carolina's loyalty to Thomas Pinckney
   (H) Private contact with state officials urging them to support Thomas Pinckney
   (J) John Adams' reputation as a stubborn and independent New Englander

5. In 1796, the Federalist candidate for president was:

   (A) Alexander Hamilton.
   (B) Thomas Pinckney.
   (C) John Adams.
   (D) George Washington.

6. The passage suggests that some electors voted for John Adams because they were:

   (F) persuaded to do so by Hamilton.
   (G) afraid South Carolina would not vote for Pinckney.
   (H) concerned about New England's influence over the South.
   (J) anxious to have a president from their geographical region.

7. Which of the following can be inferred from the passage?

   (A) Thomas Pinckney had a personal dislike for Jefferson's politics.
   (B) The Federalists regarded themselves as more democratic than Jefferson.
   (C) The Hamiltonians contacted key Southern leaders to persuade them to vote for Adams.
   (D) Electors were likely to vote for candidates from their own geographical region.

8. It can be inferred that had South Carolina not cast any electoral votes for Jefferson, the outcome of the 1796 election would have been a:

   (F) larger margin of victory for John Adams.
   (G) victory for Thomas Jefferson.
   (H) Federalist defeat in the Senate.
   (J) victory for Pinckney.

9. The electors who scratched Pinckney's name from their ballots behaved most like which of the following people?

   (A) A newspaper publisher who adds a special section to the Sunday edition to review the week's political events
   (B) A member of the clergy who encourages members of other faiths to meet to discuss solutions to the community's problems
   (C) An artist who saves preliminary sketches of an important work even after the work is finally completed
   (D) A general who orders his retreating troops to destroy supplies they must leave behind so the enemy cannot use them

10. Hamilton's strategy can best be summarized as:

    (F) divide and conquer.
    (G) retreat and regroup.
    (H) feint and counterattack.
    (J) hit and run.

NOTES AND STRATEGIES

Questions 11-15 are based on the following passage.

The liberal view of democratic citizenship that developed in the 17th and 18th centuries was fundamentally different from that of the classical Greeks. The pursuit of private interests with as little interference as possible from government was seen as the road to human happiness and progress rather than the public obligations and involvement in the collective community that were emphasized by the Greeks. Freedom was to be realized by limiting the scope of governmental activity and political obligation and not through immersion in the collective life of the *polis*. The basic role of the citizen was to select governmental leaders and keep the powers and scope of public authority in check. On the liberal view, the rights of citizens against the state were the focus of special emphasis.

Over time, the liberal democratic notion of citizenship developed in two directions. First, there was a movement to increase the proportion of members of society who were eligible to participate as citizens—especially through extending the right of suffrage—and to ensure the basic political equality of all. Second, there was a broadening of the legitimate activities of government and a use of governmental power to redress imbalances in social and economic life. Political citizenship became an instrument through which groups and classes with sufficient numbers of votes could use the state power to enhance their social and economic well being.

Within the general liberal view of democratic citizenship, tensions have developed over the degree to which government can and should be used as an instrument for promoting happiness and well being. Political philosopher Martin Diamond has categorized two views of democracy as follows. On the one hand, there is the "libertarian" perspective that stresses the private pursuit of happiness and emphasizes the necessity for restraint on government and protection of individual liberties. On the other hand, there is the "majoritarian" view that emphasizes the "task of the government to uplift and aid the common man against the malefactors of great wealth." The tensions between these two views are very evident today. Taxpayer revolts and calls for smaller government and less government regulation clash with demands for greater government involvement in the economic marketplace and the social sphere.

11. The author's primary purpose is to:

(A) study ancient concepts of citizenship.
(B) contrast different notions of citizenship.
(C) criticize modern libertarian democracy.
(D) describe the importance of universal suffrage.

12. It can be inferred from the passage that the Greek word *polis* means:

(F) family life.
(G) military service.
(H) marriage.
(J) political community.

13. The author cites Martin Diamond because the author:

(A) regards Martin Diamond as an authority on political philosophy.
(B) wishes to refute Martin Diamond's views on citizenship.
(C) needs a definition of the term "citizenship."
(D) is unfamiliar with the distinction between libertarian and majoritarian concepts of democracy.

14. According to the passage, all of the following are characteristics of the liberal idea of government that would distinguish it from the Greek idea of government EXCEPT:

(F) the emphasis on the rights of private citizens.
(G) the activities government may legitimately pursue.
(H) the obligation of citizens to participate in government.
(J) the size of the geographical area controlled by a government.

15. A majoritarian would be most likely to favor legislation that would:

(A) eliminate all restrictions on individual liberty.
(B) cut spending for social welfare programs.
(C) provide greater protection for consumers.
(D) lower taxes on the wealthy and raise taxes on the average worker.

Questions 16-19 are based on the following passage.

The place of public education within a democratic society has been widely discussed and debated through the years. Perhaps no one has written more widely on the subject in the United States than John Dewey, sometimes called "the father of public education," whose theories of education have a large social component, that is, an emphasis on education as a social act and the classroom or learning environment as a replica of society.

Dewey defined various aspects or characteristics of education. First, it was a necessity of life inasmuch as living beings needed to maintain themselves through a process of renewal. Therefore, just as humans needed sleep, food, water, and shelter for physiological renewal, they also needed education to renew their minds, assuring that their socialization kept pace with physiological growth.

A second aspect of education was its social component, which was to be accomplished by providing the young with an environment that would provide a nurturing atmosphere to encourage the growth of their as yet undeveloped social customs.

A third aspect of public education was the provision of direction to youngsters, who might otherwise be left in uncontrolled situations without the steadying and organizing influences of school. Direction was not to be of an overt nature, but rather indirect through the selection of the school situations in which the youngster participated. Finally, Dewey saw public education as a catalyst for growth. Since the young came to school, capable of growth, it was the role of education to provide opportunities for that growth to occur. The successful school environment is one in which a desire for continued growth is created—a desire that extends throughout one's life beyond the end of formal education. In Dewey's model, the role of education in a democratic society is not seen as a preparation for some later stage in life, such as adulthood. Rather, education is seen as a process of growth that never ends, with human beings continuously expanding their capacity for growth. Neither did Dewey's model see education as a means by which the past was recapitulated. Instead education was a continuous reconstruction of experiences, grounded very much in the present environment.

Since Dewey's model places a heavy emphasis on the social component, the nature of the larger society that supports the educational system is of paramount importance. The ideal larger society, according to Dewey, is one in which the interests of a group are all shared by all of its members and in which interactions with other groups is free and full. According to Dewey, education in such a society should provide members of the group a stake or interest in social relationships and the ability to negotiate change without compromising the order and stability of the society.

Thus, Dewey's basic concept of education in a democratic society is based on the notion that education contains a large social component designed to provide direction and assure children's development through their participation in the group to which they belong.

16. The main idea of this passage can best be stated as:

(F) The role of education is extremely complex.
(G) Dewey's notion of education contains a significant social component.
(H) Dewey's model of education is not relevant today.
(J) Direction provided in education must not be overt.

17. The phrase "a continuous reconstruction of experience" (line 44) used in reference to education means that education is

(A) based in life experiences
(B) a never ending process
(C) a meaning-based endeavor
(D) an individual pursuit

18. While not directly stated, the passage suggests that:

(F) true education fosters the desire for lifelong learning.
(G) a truly educated person has an understanding of physics.
(H) Dewey was a radical philosopher.
(J) education must cease at some point.

19. The tone of this passage can best be described as

(A) humorous
(B) serious
(C) dramatic
(D) informal

SECTION TWO—READING PROBLEM-SOLVING

DIRECTIONS: Each of the following passages is followed by several questions. After reading a passage, choose the best answer to each question. You may refer to the passage as often as necessary. Answers are on page 159.

Questions 1-5 are based on the following passage.

In 1792 there was no contest for the presidency. George Washington received the unanimous vote of the electors, Federalist and Republican alike. But the struggle over the vice-presidency hinted at the rekindling of old divisions and antagonisms sparked by Alexander Hamilton's system. Southern planters who in 1789 had been ready, in fact eager, to cooperate with the moneyed men of the North, parted with them when they realized that the policies designed to benefit Northern merchants and bankers brought no profit to them as landed aristocrats. Even more, they saw themselves paying for a system that contributed to another section's prosperity. Although in 1792 they were willing to continue with Washington, they were not as willing to go along with Vice-President John Adams, who represented the commerce, shipbuilding, fisheries, and banking institutions of New England and the North. If the Federalists were to have the first office, then the followers of Jefferson—who had already come to call themselves Republicans in contra-distinction to the unpopular term anti-Federalist, insisted that they were to command the second office.

Appealing to the shopkeepers, artisans, laboring men, and farmers of the North on the basis of their sympathy with the French Revolution, and to the Southern planters with their agrarian bias, the Republicans waged a gallant but losing campaign for the second office. But the campaign served notice to the overconfident Federalists that when the Republicans became better organized nationally, they would have to be more seriously considered. This did not take long. In 1793 England went so far as to declare war with republican France over the guillotining of Louis XVI and in 1794 John Jay's treaty terminating the United States' difficulties with Britain seemed to suggest a sympathetic policy toward monarchical and conservative England, instead of republican, liberty-loving France. The treaty intensified party spirit and gave the Republicans a sense of mission that legitimized their existence. The contest was now between the Republican "lovers of liberty" and the Monocrats.

1. Which of the following titles best describes the content of the passage?

   (A) The Origins of Jefferson's Republican Party
   (B) Jefferson's Defeat in the 1792 Election
   (C) The Legacy of Hamilton's Political System
   (D) Political Differences between the Rich and the Poor

2. According to the passage, all of the following are true of the Republicans EXCEPT:

   (F) they opposed the monied interests of the North.
   (G) they were led by Thomas Jefferson.
   (H) they disapproved of the French Revolution.
   (J) they and the Federalists supported the same candidate for president in 1792.

3. It can be inferred that the term "Monocrats" (line 41) was a term:

   (A) used by John Jay in his treaty to refer to France's King Louis XVI.
   (B) invented by the Federalists to refer to the aristocratic landowners of the South.
   (C) coined by the Republicans to disparage the Federalist's support of England.
   (D) employed by Republicans to describe their leader, Thomas Jefferson.

4. The passage implies that Thomas Jefferson was unsuccessful in his 1792 bid for the vice-presidency because the Republican Party:

   (F) did not have its own presidential candidate.
   (G) was not as well organized as the Federalists.
   (H) refused to support John Adams.
   (J) appealed to workers in the North.

5. The tone of the passage can best be described as:

   (A) enthusiastic and impassioned.
   (B) scholarly and neutral.
   (C) opinionated and dogmatic.
   (D) argumentative and categorical.

NOTES AND STRATEGIES

Questions 6-14 are based on the following passage.

Friends and fellow citizens:—I stand before you tonight under indictment for the alleged crime of having voted at the last presidential election, without having a lawful right to vote. It shall be my work this evening to prove to you that in thus voting, I not only committed no crime, but, instead, simply exercised *my citizen's rights,* guaranteed to me and all United States citizens by the National Constitution, beyond the power of any State to deny. The preamble of the Federal Constitution says:

"We, the people of the United States, in order to form a more perfect union, establish justice, insure *domestic* tranquility, provide for the common defense, promote the general welfare, and secure the blessings of liberty to ourselves and our posterity, do ordain and establish this Constitution for the United States of America."

It was we, the people, not we, the white male citizens; but we, the whole people, who formed the Union. And we formed it, not to give the blessings of liberty, but to secure them; not to the half of ourselves and the half of our posterity but to the whole people—women as well as men. And it is a downright mockery to talk to women of their enjoyment of the blessings of liberty while they are denied the use of the only means of securing them provided by this democratic—republican government—the ballot.

For any State to make sex a qualification that must ever result in the disfranchisement of one entire half of the people is a violation of the supreme law of the land. By it the blessings of liberty are forever withheld from women and their female posterity. To them this government has no just powers derived from the consent of the governed. To them this government is not a democracy. It is not a republic. It is a hateful oligarchy of sex. An oligarchy of learning, where the educated govern the ignorant, might be endured; but this oligarchy of sex, which makes father, brothers, husband, sons, the oligarchs or rulers over the mother and sisters, the wife and daughters of every household—which ordains all men sovereigns, all women subjects, carries dissension, discord and rebellion into every home of the nation.

Webster's Dictionary defines a citizen as a person in the United States, entitled to vote and hold office.

The only question left to be settled now is, Are women persons? And I hardly believe any of our opponents will have the hardihood to say we are not. Being persons, then, women are citizens; and no State has a right to make any law, or to enforce any old law, that shall abridge their privileges or immunities. Hence, every discrimination against women in the constitutions and laws of the several States is today null and void.

Adapted from "A Citizen Is Entitled to Vote," by Susan (B) Anthony.

6. The nineteenth-century feminist leader Susan B. Anthony fought long and hard to guarantee women the right to vote. In this speech, Anthony talks as if she were a:

   (F) defendant on trial.
   (G) chairperson of a committee.
   (H) legislator arguing for a new law.
   (J) judge ruling at a trial.

7. Anthony broadens her appeal to her audience by showing how her case could affect all:

   (A) existing laws.
   (B) United States citizens.
   (C) women.
   (D) uneducated persons.

8. Anthony quotes the preamble to the Constitution in order to:

   (F) impress the audience with her intelligence.
   (G) utilize a common legalistic trick.
   (H) point out which part of the preamble needs to be changed.
   (J) add force to her argument.

9. According to Anthony, who formed the Union?

   (A) Only one-half of the people
   (B) The whole people
   (C) White male citizens only
   (D) White female citizens

10. When Anthony says that the blessings of liberty are forever withheld from women and their female posterity, she means that:

    (F) all classes of women are discriminated against.
    (G) women of the past have been victimized.
    (H) female children of the poor will be the only ones affected.
    (J) women of the present and the future will suffer.

11. Anthony argues that a government that denies women the right to vote is not a democracy because its powers do not come from:

    (A) the Constitution of the United States.
    (B) the rights of the states.
    (C) the consent of the governed.
    (D) the vote of the majority.

12. According to this speech, an oligarchy of sex would cause:

(F) women to rebel against the government.
(G) men to desert their families.
(H) problems to develop in every home.
(J) the educated to rule the ignorant.

13. In this speech, a citizen is *defined* as a person who has the right to vote and also the right to:

(A) acquire wealth.
(B) speak publicly.
(C) hold office.
(D) pay taxes.

14. Anthony argues that state laws which discriminate against women are:

(F) being changed.
(G) null and void.
(H) helpful to the rich.
(J) supported by the Constitution.

Questions 15-20 are based on the following passage.

International commerce is woven thoroughly into the fabric of the American economy. Exports and imports amounted to more than 11 percent of the U.S. gross domestic product (GDP) in 1991, up dramatically from 7.5 percent just 5 years before. More than 7 million American jobs are related to exports, and millions more depend on the overall economic activity generated by export trade. Export-related jobs pay more—almost 17 percent more than the average American job.

Exports are vital to the economic health of many key sectors of the manufacturing economy. For instance, makers of computers, aerospace and heavy earthmoving equipment, and farm implements are increasingly dependent on export markets. For these exports, slow growth abroad translates to declining vitality at home. The same picture is true of agriculture, where roughly one in four farm acres is now harvested for the export market. International sales of business-related services—construction, finance, insurance, and engineering, among others—amount to tens of billions of dollars each year.

In the early years of the post-World War II era, the United States stood virtually alone as the industrial and technological leader of the world. At that time, the U.S. produced almost half of the world's GDP, including much of the world's manufactured goods, and had roughly 80 percent of the world's hard currency reserves. Today, while the U.S. remains the world's leading economy, its share of world GDP has shrunk to about 24 percent, and its share of world manufacturers is even lower. Experts agree that, relative to the size of the economy and the diversity of its industrial and technological base, the U.S. has lagged far behind its export potential.

Meanwhile, the potential for growth in U.S. exports is enormous. Markets in Europe and Japan are huge and relatively stable. There is growing promise in Asia's $5.7 trillion economy and Latin America's $1 trillion economy. These markets are generating a rapidly growing demand for infrastructure investment, aircraft, and high-technology capital goods—all areas in which the U.S. has real or potential strengths. In addition, new entrants into the world economy, such as Central and Eastern Europe and the countries of the former Soviet Union, show real promise as potential markets for U.S. exports.

Growing world markets, however, do not automatically translate into U.S. export sales. The fierce competition for international markets comes first and foremost from the more innovative firms in Europe and Japan. In particular, Japanese companies have set the pace with a mix of aggressive business practices and a virtually economy-wide commitment to quality, rapid time to market, ongoing innovation, and customer satisfaction. American companies are beginning to try to meet the competition. In corporate parlance, they have had to benchmark to the best, whether that best is in Chicago, Frankfurt, or Osaka.

The new realities of international competition yield lessons for the U.S. government as well. Persistent economic diplomacy and high-level advocacy, competitive and well-focused export financing, and improved efforts at information-gathering have become necessary components of an export promotion policy. Many foreign governments have been more aggressive and more focused than the U.S. government in working with their firms to secure export sales. Senior government officials up to and including the president or prime-minister often will travel to support the sale of their home country's goods and services. The U.S. government needs to begin to measure its export strategy against the flexibility and effectiveness of the competition. Exports are central to growth, jobs, and a rising standard of living for all Americans. Our role in building a better America at home and acting as an economic leader abroad is dependent on our ability to develop a coherent, aggressive, and effective national export strategy.

15. Which of the following sectors of the U.S. economy has declined most seriously since World War II?

(A) Agriculture
(B) Manufacturing
(C) High-technology products
(D) Business-related services

16. Which of the following best expresses the central point of the passage?

(F) Exports drive the U.S. economy.
(G) U.S. exports have declined since shortly after World War 11.
(H) Exports are so important to the U.S. economy that steps should be taken to increase U.S. exports worldwide.
(J) The U.S. government should encourage U.S. corporations to expand into markets in Asia and Latin America.

17. Which of the following areas is NOT mentioned in the passage as a potential market for U.S. goods abroad?

(A) Asia
(B) Latin America
(C) Central Europe
(D) Northern Africa

18. The passage suggests that both U.S. corporations and the U.S. government should:

(F) discourage imports in favor of exports.
(G) focus on improving the quality of American products.
(H) imitate the most successful of their counterparts abroad.
(J) take steps to reduce the economy's dependence on exports.

19. With which of the following explanations for the decline in the United States' share of world GDP would the author be most likely to agree?

I. Other countries are relatively uninterested in purchasing the goods and services the U.S. has to offer.
II. Other governments have done more to encourage their countries' exports than has the U.S. government.
III. Companies in some other countries have been more enterprising in producing high-quality goods and services.

(A) II only
(B) I and II only
(C) I and III only
(D) II and III only

20. According to the passage, an increase in U.S. exports abroad would generate:

(F) more high-paying jobs for American workers.
(G) increased profits for American farmers.
(H) greater diversity in American industry.
(J) resentment among foreign competitors.

Questions 21-25 are based on the following passage.

An atom consists of a nucleus (containing protons and neutrons) surrounded by electrons. Each proton has a positive charge of +1, and each electron has a negative charge of a –1. A neutron has no charge. The number of protons in their nuclei determines the identities of the different elements. For example, hydrogen atoms have only one proton, while oxygen atoms have eight protons. The total number of protons in the nucleus is the *atomic number* of that element. The total number of protons and neutrons in the nucleus is the *atomic mass* of the atom. Different atoms of the same element may contain a different number of neutrons, and so have different atomic masses. (But they will have the same number of protons and the same atomic number.) Atoms of the same element with different atomic masses are called isotopes of that element.

Certain elements are radioactive—they emit various types of radiation from their atomic nuclei. Two common types of radiation are alpha particles and beta particles. An alpha particle—which is the equivalent of a helium nucleus—consists of two protons and two neutrons. It is written ${}^{4}_{2}He$ (the superscript 4 is the mass number of the particle, and the subscript 2 is its atomic number). A beta particle is an electron traveling at high speed. It is written ${}^{0}_{-1}e$. Both types of radiation are emitted at a very high speed and can easily penetrate other substances.

When atoms of a substance emit radiation, they are said to undergo radioactive decay. When this happens, the result is a different element with a different atomic number and a different mass number. For example, when a radium atom emits an alpha particle, it decays into an atom of radon. This reaction is shown in the following equation:

$${}^{226}_{88}Ra \rightarrow {}^{4}_{2}He + {}^{222}_{86}Rn$$

Note that the equation is balanced. That is, the atomic number of the original atom on the left side of the equation equals the sum of the atomic numbers of the products on the right side of the equation. Similarly, the mass number of the original atom equals the sum of the mass numbers of the products. Every nuclear reaction balances in this same manner.

Some types of nuclear radiation take place very slowly; other types are very rapid. The rate of radiation is measured in half-lives. A half-life is the time required for one-half the amount of a given radioactive substance to decay.

NOTES AND STRATEGIES

21. As radium emits alpha particles, the mass of radium will:

(A) increase.
(B) decrease.
(C) stay the same.
(D) either increase or decrease depending on condition.

22. In nuclear chemistry notation, two isotopes (forms) of cobalt are written $^{59}_{27}Co$ and $^{60}_{27}Co$. The difference between the two isotopes is:

(F) an alpha particle.
(G) a beta particle.
(H) a proton.
(J) a neutron.

23. An alpha particle has:

(A) no electric charge.
(B) a positive electric charge.
(C) a negative electric charge.
(D) a variable electric charge.

24. A beta particle has:

(F) no electric charge.
(G) a positive electric charge.
(H) a negative electric charge.
(J) a variable electric charge.

25. When an atom emits a beta particle, the mass of the atom will:

(A) increase.
(B) decrease.
(C) stay the same.
(D) either increase or decrease depending on conditions.

Questions 26-35 are based on the following passage.

In 1866, Gregor Mendel published the results of his studies on the breeding of different races of pea plants. Through his experiments, Mendel discovered a pattern of inheritance and subsequently developed the concept of a "unit of inheritance."

Mendel started with pure stock of pea plants that had recognizably different characteristics. He artificially cross-pollinated the different races of plants and noted the characteristics of the different offspring over several generations. Mendel concluded that a pair of discrete "factors" governed each trait and that they segregated upon the formation of the gametes. This pair of factors is now known as the maternally and paternally derived alleles on homologous chromosomes that first come together at fertilization and later segregate during meiosis.

Subsequent studies have shown that new genes could appear as mutations of existing genes and that crossing over and recombination could redistribute maternal and paternal characteristics. Genes can occur in a linear sequence, and groups of genes that segregate together are called *linkage groups.* The chromosome is the carrier of the linear array of genes and the physical basis of the linkage groups.

It was originally thought that proteins were the genetic carrier. In contrast to nucleic acids, proteins were known to mediate complex reactions and to be composed of a variety of different building blocks. There are approximately 20 different amino acids in a protein, but only 4 different nucleotides in a nuclear acid molecule. It wasn't until 1944 that Avery *et al.* noted that deoxyribonucleic acid (DNA) was the genetic carrier, not protein. Avery and his co-workers conducted experiments on the transformation in pneumococcus. Two strains of the bacteria had been isolated: one produced colonies having a smooth (s) appearance and was able to cause pneumonia in a suitable host; the other grew into rough (r) colonies as a result of a defect in its capsule and was nonvirulent. When a cell-free extract of the S bacteria was added to the medium in which the R strain was growing, a few of the R bacteria grew into smooth colonies and were virulent. They had become transformed. From the time of transformation, the progeny of that cell continued to have the properties of the S strain. The transformation was a stable genetic change. Avery and his co-workers purified the contents of cells in detergent after their disruption and found that among the contents of the cells, only the purified DNA was capable of causing the transformation. As a result of these and future experiments, it was determined that in order for transformation to occur, DNA fragments entered the recipient cell intact and substituted in the bacterial chromosome for the original DNA, which was eliminated. This process resulted in the creation of a genetically different microorganism.

DNA is a very long, fibrous molecule with a backbone composed of alternate sugar and phosphate groups joined by 3', 5' phosphodiester linkages. Attached to each sugar is one of four possible nitrogenous bases. There are two types of bases: the pyrimidines, cytosine (C) and thymine (T); and the purines, adenine (A) and guanine (G). The amount of purine equals the amount of pyrimidine, and, more specifically, the amount of adenine equals the amount of thymine, and the amount of guanine equals the amount of cytosine.

In 1953 Watson and Crick proposed that DNA was made of two chains of nucleotides coiled around a common axis, with the sugar-phosphate backbone on the outside and the bases pointing in toward the axis, and that the two chains were held together by hydrogen bonds. The hydrogen bonds occur between each base of one chain and an associated base on the other chain. Based on the 20-angstrom width of the fiber, a pyrimidine from one chain is always paired with a purine from the other chain. Adenine is the only purine capable of bonding to thymine and guanine is the only purine capable of bonding to cytosine.

Watson and Crick proposed that the information in DNA was coded for by the linear sequence of the base pairs. They theorized that a mutation could be accounted for by a chance mistake in the formation of the sequence during duplication. Another major aspect of the Watson and Crick model was the proposed complementarity between hydrogen-bonded nucleotides. For example, adenine is complementary to thymine, AGC is complementary to TCG, and one chain is complementary to the other. If the base sequence of one chain is known, then the base sequence of the complementary chain can be derived. The concept of complementarity of nucleic acids in DNA and RNA chains is the basis of most research in which these classes of molecules are involved.

26. Mendel conducted his studies using the method known as:

(F) cloning.
(G) genetic mapping.
(H) cross-pollination.
(J) transformation.

27. Mendel's findings were important because they indicated that:

(A) DNA fragments can replace original DNA
(B) specific units, handed down from one generation to the next, govern traits in organisms.
(C) proteins are composed of approximately 20 different amino acids.
(D) All of the above.

28. Avery *et al.* discovered that, contrary to earlier beliefs,

(F) there are only four different nucleotides in DNA
(G) pneumonia can be passed from host to host.
(H) genes can mutate.
(J) DNA, not protein, carries genetic information.

29. If you witnessed R strain pneumococcus infected with S extract, and you saw a few R strain pneumococcus transformed to S strain, you would expect:

(A) the remaining R strain pneumococcus to transform later.
(B) only the new S strain cells to survive.
(C) offspring of those transformed cells to be S strain as well.
(D) a few S strain pneumococcus to transform to R strain.

30. The word *nonvirulent* (line 39) is used by the author to mean:

(F) harmless.
(G) toxic.
(H) bacterial.
(J) sweet.

31. In contrast to the paragraphs before, paragraph 5 (lines 57-67) is intended primarily to:

(A) provide historical information about genetic research.
(B) describe the results of Mendel's experiments.
(C) speculate on the future of genetic research.
(D) provide a definition for an essential element in genetic research.

32. A chain of DNA with the pattern CAG would bond with a chain with the pattern:

(F) GAC
(G) TGA
(H) GTC
(J) Cannot be determined from the information given.

33. Which of these is a purine?

(A) cytosine
(B) guanine
(C) thymine
(D) both (F) and (G)

34. Watson and Crick's contribution to the study of genetics was:

    (F) information about transfer of genes across membranes.
    (G) the notion that pairs of genes could work together.
    (H) a suggestion about the structure of DNA
    (J) All of the above.

35. The concept of complementarity in DNA is apparently important because:

    (A) it contradicts the notion that proteins are the basis for genetic transformation.
    (B) the nucleotides are connected by hydrogen bonds.
    (C) if maternally and paternally derived alleles were not complementary, life could not exist.
    (D) if you know one chain's sequence, you can determine that of the other.

Questions 36-44 are based on the following passage.

Lakes arise from sources that are almost entirely geologic in nature. Once they have formed, lakes are doomed. Because of the concave nature of the lake basin, there is a trend toward demise as the basin fills in with sediment. A lake lives through youthful stages to maturity, senescence, and death when the basin is finally full. This procedure does not always follow a direct course. Periods of rejuvenation occasionally occur in some lakes. Eventually, marshes, swampy meadows, and forests appear where lakes once existed. Large lakes may be far from death as a result of shoaling, but climatic changes or geologic events that result in drying out or drainage eventually lead to their ends.

The *littoral* zone of a lake is the region of the shallows. The shallows are subject to fluctuating temperatures and erosion of the shoreline through wave action and the effects of weather. The shallows are usually well lit and serve as home to rooted aquatic plants. The littoral region is the region from the shoreline to the depth where the "weeds" disappear. Sometimes wave action is so extreme that most aquatic vegetation is absent and only algae are present, marking the outer regions of the littoral region. The *littoral benthos* is the bottom region of the littoral region. This region contains many species and taxonomic groups. A high diversity and high annual production set this community apart from other regions of the lake.

The *sublittoral* zone extends from the outer region of the littoral region. Sediments in the sublittoral zone are finer grained than those of the littoral zone. Although this region is dimly lit, it is usually well oxygenated. The sublittoral zone community contains fewer species than does the littoral zone. This is due mainly to the reduced number of habitats.

In some lakes the old shells of gastropods and pelecypods that inhabit the littoral zone are found accumulated in the sublittoral zone. These shell zones are thought to mark the place where weather interactions and currents have carried and dropped these remains.

The *profundat* zone is defined as the regions in lakes where summer temperature stratification is apparent. Under such conditions a deep cold region is formed where currents are at a minimum and where light is greatly reduced. The temperature is mostly uniform throughout this region, and under some conditions oxygen is almost completely absent, but CO_2 and methane are prevalent. The hydrogen ion concentration is high because of the presence of carbonic acid. This stratum of water is characterized by the existence of decayed matter rather than by the production of organic matter.

As solar radiation passes down from the surface of the lake, it disappears exponentially, and the heating wavelengths are usually absorbed very fast. At the end of the yearly heating period, one might expect the temperature stratum to resemble the light curve; however, due to weather conditions—for example, wind—the temperature profiles of lakes are altered. The temperature difference is readily explained by the wind mixing the upper layers of water and distributing downward the heat that has been absorbed by the surface layers of water.

Direct stratification occurs when dense cold water lies beneath lighter warm layers of water. Direct stratification divides a lake into three regions. The upper warm region, mixed completely by wind to produce a region which is almost at a uniform temperature throughout, is called the *epilimnion.* At the bottom is a colder, heavier region of water, which is unaffected by wind action and therefore remains stagnant. This region is called the *hypolimnion.* Separating these two regions is the *thermocline,* a region of water where temperature drops quickly with increasing depth.

Dimictic lakes are lakes which have two mixing periods, the vernal and the autumnal. The typical dimictic lake stratifies directly during the warm months. When the cold months arrive, the surface water starts to cool, which eventually destroys the stratification and initiates complete circulation. During the fall mixing, chilling of the entire water mass continues until the water mass achieves a uniform temperature of about 4 degrees Celsius.

Polymictic lakes are lakes which have many mixing periods or which have continuous circulation throughout the year. Polymictic lakes are influenced more by fluctuations in temperature from day to night than by seasonal changes.

Meromictic lakes circulate at times, but

NOTES AND STRATEGIES

incompletely. The entire water mass does not participate in the mixing. A dense region of water at the bottom remains stagnant and anaerobic. The three regions of a meromictic lake have their own names. The bottom layer, which is basically stagnant and contains a greater concentration of dissolved substances, is called the *monimolimnion*. The upper layer is mixed by the wind, is more dilute, and shows seasonal changes. This region is called the *mixolimnion.* Between the monimolimnion and the mixolimnion is a region where salinity increases quickly with depth. This region is called the *chemocline.*

36. The author uses the word *doomed* in line 3 to indicate that:

    (F) he regrets the event.
    (G) the lakes have a limited future.
    (H) people will destroy the lakes.
    (J) All of the above.

37. Unlike the sublittoral zone, the littoral zone:

    (A) has fine-grained sediment.
    (B) contains many varied habitats.
    (C) contains aquatic vegetation.
    (D) is well oxygenated.

38. Why is aquatic vegetation absent in some lakes?

    (F) Extreme wave action might uproot plants.
    (G) Some lakes have no littoral or sublittoral regions.
    (H) Algae takes over the littoral region.
    (J) The lakes are fully mature.

39. The remains of gastropods are deposited in the sublittoral zone by:

    (A) currents.
    (B) wind.
    (C) Both (A) and (B).
    (D)Neither (A) nor (B).

40. The profundat zone is marked by:

    (F) shells of organisms, low vegetation, and high diversity.
    (G) solar radiation and a vernal mixing period.
    (H) increased temperatures in summer and production of organic matter.
    (J) cold temperatures, low light, and a lack of oxygen.

41. In October, you would expect a northern dimictic lake to:

    (A) be warmer on the surface than it was in May.
    (B) cool from the surface to achieve a uniform temperature.
    (C) begin to stratify directly.
    (D) slowly freeze across the surface.

42. A polymictic lake might be coldest:

    (F) at night.
    (G) in autumn.
    (H) after sunrise.
    (J) in spring.

43. The chemocline in a meromictic lake is equivalent to:

    (A) the littoral zone in a senescent lake.
    (B) the profundat zone in a dimictic lake.
    (C) the thermocline in a dimictic lake.
    (D) the epilimnion in a polymictic lake.

44. Which of these conclusions can you NOT draw from this article?

    (F) Deep lakes are unaffected by weather.
    (G) Lakes have geologic derivations.
    (H) Lakes vary in temperature.
    (J) All lakes will eventually die.

Questions 45-49 are based on the following passage.

It still lacked a half hour of sunrise when Miss Hepzibah—we will say awoke, it being doubtful whether the poor old lady had so much as closed her eyes during the brief night of midsummer—but, at all events, arose from her solitary pillow, and began the adornment of her person. She was alone in the old house—quite a house by itself, indeed—with locks, bolts, and oaken bars on all the intervening doors. Inaudible, consequently, were poor Miss Hepzibah's gusty sighs, inaudible the creaking joints of her stiffened knees, as she knelt down by the bedside. And inaudible too, by mortal ear, that almost agony of prayer—now whispered, now a groan, now a struggling silence—wherewith she sought the Divine assistance through the day! Evidently this is to be the day of more than ordinary trial to Miss Hepzibah, who for above a quarter of a century gone by has dwelt in strict seclusion, taking no part in the business of life, and just as little in its intercourse and pleasures.

Here comes Miss Hepzibah. Forth she steps into the dusky, time-darkened passage a tall figure, clad in black silk, with a long and shrunken waist, feeling her way towards the stair like a nearsighted person, which in truth she is.

Her scowl—as the world persisted in calling it—her scowl had done Miss Hepzibah every ill office, in establishing her character as an ill-tempered old maid; nor does it appear improbable that, by often gazing at herself in a dim looking glass, and perpetually encountering her own frown within its ghostly sphere, she had been led to interpret the expression almost unjustly as the world did. But her heart never frowned.

45. According to the passage, Miss Hepzibah is all of the following EXCEPT:

(A) elderly.
(B) reclusive.
(C) religious.
(D) vain.

46. The author's portrait of Miss Hepzibah is:

(F) critical and disparaging.
(G) loving and intimate.
(H) sarcastic and mocking.
(J) interested and sympathetic.

47. It can be inferred that Miss Hepzibah views the day's coming events with:

(A) apprehension.
(B) confidence.
(C) eagerness.
(D) boredom.

48. Which of the following correctly describes the scene as set by the passage

I. The season is summer.
II. The weather is threatening.
III. The time is morning.

(F) I only
(G) III only
(H) I and II only
(J) I and III only

49. In the last paragraph, the author implies that Miss Hepzibah is:

(A) old and wicked.
(B) affable and outgoing.
(C) good-hearted but misunderstood.
(D) sincere but blasphemous.

Questions 50-59 are based on the following passage.

The poor little woman looked as if she needed rest but was not likely to get it; for the room was in a chaotic state, the breakfast table presented the appearance of having been devastated by a swarm of locusts, the baby began to fret, little Polly set up her usual whine of "I want sumpin to do," and a pile of work loomed in the comer waiting to be done.

"I don't see how I ever shall get through it all," sighed the despondent matron as she hastily drank a last cup of tea, while two great tears rolled down her cheeks, as she looked from one puny child to the other, and felt the weariness of her own tired soul and body more oppressive than ever.

"A good cry" was impending, when there came a brisk ring at the door, a step in the hall, and a large, rosy woman came bustling in, saying in a cheery voice as she set a flower-pot down upon the table, "Good morning! Nice day, isn't it? Came in early on business and brought you one of my Lady Washingtons, you are so fond of flowers."

"Oh, it's lovely! How kind you are. Do sit down if you can find a chair; we are all behind hand today, for I was up half the night with poor baby, and haven't energy enough to go to work yet," answered Mrs. Bennet, with a sudden smile that changed her whole face, while baby stopped fretting to stare at the rosy clusters, and Polly found employment in exploring the pocket of the newcomer, as if she knew her way there.

"Let me put the pot on your stand first, girls are so careless, and I'm proud of this. It will be an ornament to your parlor for a week," and opening a door Mrs. Gay carried the plant to a sunny bay window where many others were blooming beautifully.

Mrs. Bennet and the children followed to talk and admire, while the servant leisurely cleared the table. "Now give me that baby, put yourself in the easy chair, and tell me all about your worries," said Mrs. Gay, in the brisk, commanding way which few people could resist.

"I'm sure I don't know where to begin," sighed Mrs. Bennet, dropping into the comfortable seat while baby changed bearers with great composure.

"I met your husband and he said the doctor had ordered you and these chicks off to Florida for the winter. John said he didn't know how he should manage it, but he meant to try."

"Isn't it dreadful? He can't leave his business to go with me, and we shall have to get Aunt Miranda to come and see to him and the boys while I'm gone, and the boys can't bear her strict, old-fashioned ways, and I've got to go that long journey all alone and stay among strangers, and these heaps of fall work to do first, and it will cost an immense sum to send us, and I don't know what is to become of me."

Here Mrs. Bennet stopped for breath, and Mrs. Gay asked briskly, "What is the matter with you and the children?"

"Well, baby is having a hard time with his teeth and is croupy, Polly doesn't get over scarlet fever well, and I'm used up; no strength or appetite, pain in my side and low spirits. Entire change of scene, milder climate, and less work for me, is what we want, the doctor says. John is very anxious about us, and I feel regularly discouraged."

"I'll spend the day and cheer you up a bit. You just rest and get ready for a new start tomorrow; it is a saving of time to stop short now and then and see where to begin next. Bring me the most pressing job of work. I can sew and see to this little rascal at the same time."

From "Mrs. Gay's Prescription." by Louisa May Alcott.

50. The "little woman" referred to in line 1 is:

(F) Lady Washington.
(G) a servant.
(H) Mrs. Bennet.
(J) Mrs. Gay.

51. When Alcott compares the breakfast table to something "devastated by a swarm of locusts" (line 4), she means:

(A) that it is a mess left by an uncaring mob.
(B) that children are no more meaningful than insects to Mrs. Bennet.
(C) to illustrate the horror of Mrs. Bennet's life.
(D) that the Bennets are pests.

52. Had Mrs. Gay not arrived when she did, the author leads us to suspect that:

(F) Mrs. Bennet would have gone back to bed.
(G) the children would have continued to cry.
(H) Mrs. Bennet would have accomplished little all day.
(J) sickness would have overtaken the entire family.

53. The "rosy clusters" in lines 26-27 are:

(A) Mrs. Gay's cheeks.
(B) Mrs. Bennet's cheeks.
(C) candies from Mrs. Gay's pockets.
(D) flowers.

NOTES AND STRATEGIES

54. In lines 30-33 the author:

(F) reveals Mrs. Bennet's only talent.
(G) uses the sunny parlor as a symbol of hope.
(H) contrasts Mrs. Gay's sunniness with Mrs. Bennet's dullness.
(J) contrasts Mrs. Bennet's plants with her children.

55. When Mrs. Bennet says that she's "used up" (line 60), she means that she:

(A) has no energy.
(B) is abused.
(C) is exploited.
(D) has spent all her money.

56. The word *pressing* (line 68) means:

(F) heavy.
(G) ardent.
(H) forceful.
(J) important.

57. Mrs. Bennet's friend's disposition is indicated by:

I. her name.
II. her speech.
III. her clothing.

(A) I only
(B) III only
(C) I and II only
(D) I and III only

58. The author implies that Mrs. Bennet's real problem is:

(F) her inability to cope.
(G) a touch of fever.
(H) the cold winter weather.
(J) a lack of common sense.

59. Mrs. Gay's primary quality seems to be her:

(A) lethargy.
(B) anxiety.
(C) dignity.
(D) practical nature.

Questions #60-69 are based on the following passage.

At the end of what seemed a tedious while, I had managed to pack my head full of islands, towns, bars, "points," and bends; and a curiously inanimate mass of lumber it was, too. However, inasmuch as I could shut my eyes and reel off a good long string of these names without leaving out more than ten miles of river in every fifty, I began to feel that I could make her skip those little gaps. But of course my complacency could hardly get start enough to lift my nose a trifle into the air, before Mr. Bixby would think of something to fetch it down again. One day he turned on me suddenly with this settler:—

"What is the shape of Walnut Bend?"

He might as well have asked me my grandmother's opinion of protoplasm. I reflected respectfully, and then said I didn't know it had any particular shape. My gunpowdery chief went off with a bang, of course, and then went on loading and firing until he was out of adjectives.

I had learned long ago that he only carried just so many rounds of ammunition, and was sure to subside into a very placable and even remorseful old smooth-bore as soon as they were all gone. That word "old" is merely affectionate; he was not more than thirty-four. I waited. By and by he said:—

"My boy, you've got to know the *shape* of the river perfectly. It is all there is left to steer by on a very dark night. Everything else is blotted out and gone. But mind you, it hasn't the same shape in the night that it has in the daytime."

"How on earth am I ever going to learn it, then?"

"How do you follow a hall at home in the dark? Because you know the shape of it. You can't see it."

"Do you mean to say that I've got to know all the million trifling variations of shape in the banks of this interminable river as well as I know the shape of the front hall at home?"

"On my honor, you've got to know them *better* than any man ever did know the shapes of the halls in his own house."

"I wish I was dead!"

"Now I don't want to discourage you, but"—

"Well, pile it on me; I might as well have it now as another time."

"You see, this has got to be learned; there isn't any getting around it. A clear starlight night throws such heavy shadows that, if you didn't know the shape of a shore perfectly, you would claw away from every bunch of timber, because you would take the black shadow of it for a solid cape; and you see you would be getting scared to death every fifteen minutes by the watch. You would be fifty yards from shore all the time when you ought to be within fifty feet of it. You can't see a snag in one of those shadows, but you know exactly where it is, and the shape of the river tells you when you are coming to it. Then there's your pitchdark night; the river is a very different shape on a pitchdark night from what it is on a starlit night. All shores seem to be straight lines, then, and mighty dim ones, too; and you'd *run* them for straight lines, only know better. You boldly drive your boat right into what seems to be a solid straight wall (you knowing very well that in reality there is a curve there), and that wall falls back and makes way for you. Then there's your gray mist. You take a night when there's one of these grisly, drizzly, gray mists, and then there isn't any particular shape to a shore. A gray mist would tangle the head of the oldest man that ever lived. Well, then different kinds of *moonlight* change the shape of the river in different ways.

"From Old Times on the Mississippi," by Mark Twain.

60. In line 12, the word *settler* is used to mean:

(F) a pioneer.
(G) a perch on the railing.
(H) a remark that decides the issue.
(J) a humbling problem.

61. When the narrator compares Bixby's question to asking his "grandmother's opinion of protoplasm" (line 15), he means that:

(A) the question is inane.
(B) the speaker is very old.
(C) he does not know the answer.
(D) his grandmother would be able to respond.

62. Comparing the chief to a gun (lines 17-19) points out the chief's:

(F) accuracy.
(G) peppery temper.
(H) love of hunting.
(J) violet past.

63. When Twain writes that Mr. Bixby "carried just so many rounds of ammunition," he means that:

(A) Bixby used a pistol to settle arguments.
(B) Bixby loaded and fired his gun at random.
(C) Bixby was impossible to work for.
(D) Bixby's hot temper would soon subside.

64. The narrator's reaction to Mr. Bixby's insistence on the need to know the river at night is:

(F) despair.
(G) elation.
(H) puzzlement.
(J) anger.

65. In the phrase, "Pile it on me" (line 44), *it* refers to:

(A) clothing.
(B) information.
(C) the river.
(D) the shoreline.

66. The word *cape* (line 51) means:

(F) cloak.
(G) robe.
(H) peninsula.
(J) waterway.

67. Mr. Bixby is shown to be extremely:

(A) knowledgeable.
(B) rude.
(C) condescending.
(D) fearful.

68. What is the purpose of including the lengthy explanation provided in the last paragraph of the selection?

I. To show how well Bixby speaks
II. To show how much a riverboat captain must know
III. To show the many modes of the river

(F) I only
(G) II only
(H) I and III only
(J) II and III only

69. According to the passage, which of the following is true?

(A) A riverboat should always be within 50 feet of the shore.
(B) On a clear, starlit night the shoreline is easy to see.
(C) On a pitch-dark night, the pilot can't discern the curve of the shoreline.
(D) The river's shape gives no hint of underwater snags.

Questions 70-74 are based on the following passage.

Georgia O'Keeffe, whose death at age 98 closed one of the most fertile chapters of American artistic creativity, flourished as a maverick in her life and work. While other painters spent a season or two in the country trying to come to terms with the scenes and settings of the Southwest, O'Keeffe stayed a lifetime. When the canvases of other artists working in the region faded from view, and then were neglected in the chronicle of American visual history, her stylized images, skeletal, floral, and geological motifs made an indelible impression on countless eyes.

Between 1900 and 1945, the region now called New Mexico both fascinated and perplexed two generations of American artists—luminaries such as Stuart Davis, Marsden Hartley, and John Sloan, whose reputations were built largely on depictions of gritty, modern life in Eastern urban centers. Despite successes, many of these artists wearied of the industrial world of the East. The vast expanse of the American West offered a promise for inspiration. It was an ancient yet new world to their eyes—an enchanted land far removed from urban conventions.

For these artists, life and art, so separate in New York and Paris, seemed inextricably bound in Southwestern cultures. Painters of every persuasion were convinced that sampling this mysterious phenomenon would strengthen and enrich their own work. Most were touched by what D.H. Lawrence called the "spirit of the place." Besides the scenic possibilities bathed in clear golden light, the rich traditions of New Mexico's Native American and Latino people—their dress, crafts, adobe pueblos, plaza life, rituals, and simple dignity—became frequent subjects of the artists who traveled to Taos and Santa Fe.

Some of the artists were traditionalists—local color realists; some were modernists—like O'Keeffe, avant-garde painters of the abstract. Their varied talents coupled with the attractions of the land gave New Mexico's art centers a status unrivaled among other American summer colonies and contributed to their heyday in the early twentieth century.

70. This passage deals primarily with:

(F) life of Georgia O'Keeffe.
(G) major trends of American modern art.
(H) mystery and spirit of the Southwest.
(J) artists in the American Southwest.

71. The author implies that the Southwest attracted artists for all of the following reasons EXCEPT:

(A) the quality of life was different from that of large urban centers.
(B) the inhabitants and culture provided interesting subject matter.
(C) New Mexico was the only state to support young, avant-garde painters.
(D) the region offered unusual geological features and landscapes.

72. The author implies that most of the artists who painted in the Southwest:

(F) originally studied in Paris.
(G) lived there only temporarily.
(H) painted only landscapes.
(J) received considerable recognition.

73. The author mentions which of the following facts about Georgia O'Keeffe?

I. She resided permanently in the Southwest.
II. She enjoyed considerable and lasting fame.
III. She created modern, abstract paintings.

(A) I only
(B) II only
(C) I and III only
(D) I, II, and III

74. Stuart Davis, Marsden Hartley, and John Sloan were painters who painted mainly in:

(F) Paris.
(G) New Mexico.
(H) cities in the Eastern United States.
(J) Rome.

NOTES AND STRATEGIES

Questions 75-82 are based on the following passage.

Were we to estimate the learning of the English by the number of books that are every day published among them, perhaps no country, not even China itself, could equal them in this particular. I have reckoned not less than twenty-three new books published in one day, which, upon computation, makes eight thousand three hundred and ninety-five in one year. Most of these are not confined to one single science, but embrace the whole circle. History, politics, poetry, mathematics, metaphysics, and the philosophy of nature are all comprised in a manual not larger than that in which our children are taught the letters. If then, we suppose the learned of England to read but an eighth part of the works which daily come from the press (and surely none can pretend to learning upon less easy terms), at this rate every scholar will read a thousand books in one year. From such a calculation, you may conjecture what an amazing fund of literature a man must be possessed of, who thus reads three new books every day, not one of which but contains all the good things that ever were said or written.

And yet I know not how it happens, but the English are not, in reality, so learned as would seem from this calculation. We meet but few who know all arts and sciences to perfection; whether it is that the generality are incapable of such extensive knowledge, or that the authors of those books are not adequate instructors. In China, the Emperor himself takes cognizance of all the doctors in the kingdom who profess authorship. In England, every man may be an author, that can write; for they have by law a liberty, not only of saying what they please, but of being also as dull as they please.

Yesterday, I testified my surprise, to the man in black, where writers could be found in sufficient number to throw off the books I daily saw crowding from the press. I at first imagined that their learned seminaries might take this method of instructing the world. But, to obviate this objection, my companion assured me that the doctors of colleges never wrote, and that some of them had actually forgot their reading. "But if you desire," continued he, "to see a collection of authors, I fancy I can introduce you to a club, which assembles every Saturday at seven…." I accepted his invitation; we walked together, and entered the house some time before the usual hour for the company assembling.

My friend took this opportunity of letting me into the characters of the principal members of the club….

"The first person," said he, "of our society is Doctor Nonentity, a metaphysician. Most people think him a profound scholar, but, as he seldom speaks, I cannot be positive in that particular; he generally spreads himself before the fire, sucks his pipe, talks little, drinks much, and is reckoned very good company. I'm told he writes indexes to perfection: he makes essays on the origin of evil, philosophical inquiries upon any subject, and draws up an answer to any book upon 24 hours' warning…."

From an essay by Oliver Goldsmith published in bookform as "The Citizen of the World," 1762.

75. Goldsmith's disdainful attitude toward English authors is best explicated in:

 (A) lines 1-4.
 (B) lines 12-17.
 (C) lines 30-33.
 (D) lines 42-44.

76. Goldsmith believes that:

 (F) we can tell how knowledgeable English authors are by counting the number of books they publish.
 (G) the number of books published in England is not up to standards set in China.
 (H) the number of books published in England says nothing about English scholarship.
 (J) every English scholar reads a thousand books a year.

77. Why does Goldsmith calculate the number of books published in England?

 (A) To impress his readers with English erudition
 (B) To make the point that anyone can be an author
 (C) As defense for his argument that England is better than China
 (D) As a comparison with publication quotas in other lands

78. The tone of paragraph two may best be described as:

 (F) self-satisfied.
 (G) awestruck.
 (H) affectionate.
 (J) sardonic.

79. Goldsmith first assumes that English writers come from:

 (A) foreign lands.
 (B) seminaries.
 (C) China.
 (D) clubs.

80. The word *obviate* (line 39) means:

(F) clarify.
(G) obscure.
(H) turn.
(J) negate.

81. Goldsmith's opinion of the first member of the club is illuminated by which of the following?

I. His conversation with the character
II. His name for the character
III. His friend's description of the character

(A) I only
(B) II only
(C) I and III only
(D) II and III only

82. One of Goldsmith's major objections to English authors is to their:

(F) deficiency in language skills.
(G) inclination to drink.
(H) tendency to write about everything at once.
(J) inability to retain information.

Questions 83-88 are based on the following passage.

For nearly a century, the houses and other artificial structures of the Appalachian region have played a prominent role in its representation in books, magazines, and film. From nineteenth-century magazine illustrations of single-room log cabins to twentieth-century television programs focusing on unpainted, one- or two-room company houses, the dominant image of the region has been the dilapidated, weather-beaten Appalachian home. While some of these presentations are authentic, some are contrived, and nearly all are selective. Interpreters of Appalachian culture have tended to focus on extremes and, as a result, have misrepresented Appalachian life. A survey of the New River Gorge area in West Virginia revealed a much more diverse landscape than has been described in the past. While project researchers did locate log cabins and abandoned coal towns, they also found considerable architectural variety. Contrary to past reports, the New River Gorge cultural landscape reflects the history of a community that designed, built, and used its buildings—according to individual tastes and principles.

The territory is dotted with homes whose original appearances have been altered to suit the occupant. These individually styled facades may appear quirky to the outsider, but their meaning is revealed through an understanding of the local history. Many of the homes were originally constructed by coal companies for their workers. Whole towns of box houses (cheap, fast to build, and temporary) were constructed at one time. While the floor plans varied, the basic construction technique did not. Vertical boards attached to sills and plates formed both the interior and exterior walls, as well as the buildings' weight-bearing supports. Today, West Virginians commonly call box houses "Jinn Linns." One local resident related a story concerning the origin of the term. Jenny Lynn, a coal camp resident, decided to distinguish her home from the other identical box houses in her camp by nailing narrow strips over the spaces between the vertical boards, creating the board and batten siding now characteristic of these houses. Soon many others followed her example and eventually named the house type after her.

Unlike Jenny Lynn, most coal camp residents were required to maintain their box houses according to strict company standards or risk eviction. As the coal boom declined, however, companies began selling the homes to their tenants. Having obtained the freedom to maintain their homes according to their own standards, residents altered facades or added rooms or porches, resulting in the variety of box houses visible in the region today. Others decided to leave the company camps altogether. Many purchased modern prefabricated houses, for example, the Lustron, an all-steel factory-made home manufactured in Ohio between 1948 and 1950. The Lustron was a one-story, gable-roof ranch house with an exterior and interior skin of enameled steel panels bolted to a structural-steel frame and a concrete slab foundation. Unlike the Jinn Linn, the home was durable, easy to maintain, and strong.

Innovative construction materials are also produced locally. Bluish cinder blocks and "red dog" blocks, both byproducts of the coal industry, have been used to construct homes, churches, gymnasiums, and barns throughout the Gorge. These and other colorful materials, including glazed tile, are often used in striking combinations, and an unusual amount of care is given to decorative detail. For example, yellow and red bricks and stones are often used for window and door trims, quoins, and belt courses (projecting horizontal strips around the outside of a building).

The complex balance between formal design and personal expression is a striking feature of the New River Gorge landscape. Like the quilts made in the region, much of the architecture is pieced together from locally made and recycled materials. Materials rarely used in combination in other areas are carefully pieced together into a landscape filled with personal meaning.

83. In saying that popular representations of Appalachian architecture are "selective" (line 11), the author means that they:

(A) present only one facet of Appalachian architecture.
(B) focus on public buildings rather than on private homes.
(C) show only the most attractive side of Appalachian architecture.
(D) represent the perceptions only of the residents themselves.

84. With which of the following aspects of New River Gorge houses described in the passage would the interpreters mentioned in line 11 be most surprised?

(F) Their uniformity
(G) Their unusually large size
(H) The ease with which they were built and maintained
(J) The attention given to decorative detail in constructing them

85. Which of the following best expresses the author's main point in telling the story of Jenny Lynn in lines 37-43?

(A) Residents of the coal camps modified their originally identical homes to suit their own preferences.
(B) The person who most influenced architecture in the New River Gorge was Jenny Lynn.
(C) Box houses are the most common type of house in the New River Gorge because they were inexpensive to construct.
(D) Coal companies had a great deal of control over the architecture of the New River Gorge.

86. Which of the following is NOT a difference between Lustron houses and Jinn Linn houses?

(F) Lustron houses were tougher than were Jinn Linn houses.
(G) Lustron houses were easier to keep up than were Jinn Linn houses.
(H) Lustron houses were made of steel while Jinn Linn houses were made of wood.
(J) Lustron houses came in several different floor plans while Jinn Linn houses always had the same plan.

87. According to the passage, Lustron houses were:

(A) less expensive than box houses.
(B) more common in Ohio than in West Virginia.
(C) ready-made in one place to be put up elsewhere.
(D) extremely popular among former coalcamp residents.

88. In what way is the architecture of the New River Gorge like the quilts made there (lines 74-78)?

I. Both use designs or plans that originally come from outside the region.
II. Both are made from available materials used in innovative ways.
III. Both express the personal tastes of the makers or users.

(F) I and II only
(G) II only
(H) II and III only
(J) I, II, and III

89. Which of the following aspects of Appalachian architecture does the author appear to value most highly?

(A) Its beauty
(B) Its diversity
(C) Its practicality
(D) Its durability

SECTION THREE—READING QUIZZES

DIRECTIONS: This section contains three Reading Quizzes. Below each of the following reading passages is a series of questions. Choose the best answer to each question, interpreting what is stated or implied by the passage in the light of your own background in the subject. You may refer back to the passage as often as necessary, though the answers to some questions may not be found expressly in the passage. Complete each quiz while being timed. Answers are on page 159.

QUIZ I (10 questions; 9 minutes)

"Heartily tired" from the brutal, almost daily conflicts that erupted over questions of national policy between himself and Alexander Hamilton, Thomas Jefferson resigned his position as Secretary of State in 1793. Although his Federalist opponents were convinced that this was merely a strategic withdrawal to allow him an opportunity to plan and promote his candidacy for the presidency should Washington step down in 1796, Jefferson insisted that this retirement from public life was to be final.

But even in retirement, the world of politics pursued him. As the election grew nearer and it became apparent that Washington would not seek a third term, rumors of Jefferson's presidential ambitions grew in intensity. Reacting to these continuous insinuations in a letter to James Madison, Jefferson admitted that while the idea that he coveted the office of chief executive had been originated by his enemies to impugn his political motives, he had been forced to examine his true feelings on the subject for his own peace of mind. In so doing he concluded that his reasons for retirement—the desire for privacy, and the delight of family life—coupled with his now failing health were insuperable barriers to public service. The "little spice of ambition" he had in his younger days had long since evaporated and the question of his Presidency was forever closed.

Jefferson did not actively engage in the campaign on his own behalf. The Republican party, presaging modern campaign tactics, created a grass roots sentiment for their candidate by directing their efforts toward the general populace. In newspapers, Jefferson was presented as "the uniform advocate of equal rights among the citizens" while Adams was portrayed as the "champion of rank, titles, heredity, and distinctions."

Jefferson was not certain of the outcome of the election until the end of December. Under the original electoral system established by the Constitution, each presidential elector cast his ballot for two men without designating between them as to office. The candidate who received the greater number of votes became the president; the second highest, the vice-president. Jefferson foresaw on the basis of his own calculations that the electoral vote would be close. He wrote to Madison that in the event of a tie, he wished for the choice to be in favor of Adams. The New Englander had always been his senior in public office, he explained, and the expression of public will being equal, he should be preferred for the higher honor. Jefferson, a shrewd politician, realized that the transition of power from the nearly mythical Washington to a lesser luminary in the midst of the deep and bitter political divisions facing the nation could be perilous, and he had no desire to be caught in the storm that had been brewing for four years and was about to break. "This is certainly not a moment to covet the helm," he wrote to Edward Rutledge. When the electoral vote was tallied, Adams emerged as the victor. Rejoicing at his "escape," Jefferson was completely satisfied with the decision. Despite their obvious and basic political differences, Jefferson genuinely respected John Adams as a friend and compatriot. Although he believed that Adams had deviated from the course set in 1776, Jefferson never felt a diminution of confidence in Adam's integrity and was confident he would not steer the nation too far off its Republican tack. Within two years, Jefferson's views would be drastically altered as measures such as the Alien and Sedition Acts of 1798 convinced him of the need to wrest control of the government from the Federalists.

1. The phrase "heartily tired" (line 1) is most probably a quotation from:

   (A) Alexander Hamilton.
   (B) Thomas Jefferson.
   (C) George Washington.
   (D) John Adams.

2. The "escape" mentioned in the passage in line 58 refers to the fact that Jefferson:

   (F) was no longer Secretary of State.
   (G) would not be burdened with the problems of the presidency.
   (H) fled the country following the election.
   (J) was hoping that the votes would be recounted.

3. According to the passage, the Republican party appealed primarily to:

   (A) wealthy landowners.
   (B) ordinary people.
   (C) prosperous merchants.
   (D) high society.

4. The author states that all of the following were reasons Jefferson resigned as Secretary of State EXCEPT:

(F) He disliked Madison.
(G) He wanted to spend time with his family.
(H) He was weary of the demands of public service.
(J) He wished for greater privacy.

5. The author is primarily concerned with revealing the:

(A) feud between Alexander Hamilton and Thomas Jefferson.
(B) difference between the Federalists and the Republicans.
(C) strategies used by early American political parties.
(D) character and personality of Thomas Jefferson.

6. The author relies on which of the following in developing the selection?

I. Personal correspondence
II. Newspapers
III. Voter registration rolls

(F) I only
(G) II only
(H) I and II only
(J) I and III only

7. One reason for Jefferson's retirement was his disagreement with:

(A) Alexander Hamilton.
(B) George Washington.
(C) James Madison.
(D) Edward Rutledge.

8. In the context of the passage, the phrase "covet the helm" (line 57) means:

(F) aspire to be president.
(G) desire to purchase a boat.
(H) wish to be left in peace.
(J) hope to become wealthy.

9. The passage suggests that two years after the 1796 election Jefferson would:

(A) ally himself with Alexander Hamilton.
(B) ally himself with John Adams.
(C) disagree with John Adams.
(D) disagree with Edward Rutledge.

10. The newspaper depicted Jefferson and Adams as:

(F) conservative and liberal, respectively.
(G) liberal and conservative, respectively.
(H) conservatives.
(J) liberals.

QUIZ II (10 questions; 9 minutes)

In the summer of 999, Leif Ericsson voyaged to Norway and spent the following winter with King Olaf Tryggvason. Substantially the same account is given by both the Saga of Eric the Red and the Flat Island Book. Of Leif's return voyage to Greenland the latter says nothing, but according to the former it was during this return voyage that Leif discovered America. The Flat Island Book, however, tells of another and earlier landfall by Biarni, the son of a prominent man named Heriulf, and makes this Leif's inspiration for the voyage to the new land. In short, like Leif, Biarni and his companions sight three countries in succession before reaching Greenland, and to come upon each new land takes one "doegr" more than the last until Biarni comes to land directly in front of his father's house in the last-mentioned country.

This narrative has been rejected by most later writers, and they may be justified. Possibly, Biarni was a companion of Leif when he voyaged from Norway to Greenland via America, or it may be that the entire tale is but a garbled account of that voyage and Biarni another name for Leif. It should be noted, however, that the stories of Leif's visit to King Olaf and Biarni's to that king's predecessor are in the same narrative in the Flat Island Book, so there is less likelihood of duplication than if they were from different sources. Also, Biarni landed on none of the lands he passed, but Leif apparently landed on one, for he brought back specimens of wheat, vines, and timber. Nor is there any good reason to believe that the first land visited by Biarni was Wineland. The first land was "level and covered with woods," and "there were small hillocks upon it." Of forests, later writers do not emphasize them particularly in connection with Wineland, though they are often noted incidentally; and of hills, the Saga says of Wineland only "wherever there was hilly ground, there were vines."

Additionally, if the two narratives were from the same source we should expect a closer resemblance of Helluland. The Saga says of it: "They found there hellus" (large flat stones). According to the Biarni narrative, however, "this land was high and mountainous." The intervals of one, two, three and four "doegr" in both narratives are suggestive, but mythic formulas of this kind may be introduced into narratives without altogether destroying their historicity. It is also held against the Biarni narrative that its hero is made to come upon the coast of Greenland exactly in front of his father's home. But it should be recalled that Heriulfsness lay below two high mountains that served as landmarks for navigators.

I would give up Biarni more readily were it not that the story of Leif's voyage, contained in the supposedly more reliable Saga, is almost as amazing. But Leif's voyage across the entire width of the North Atlantic is said to be "probable" because it is documented in the narrative of a preferred authority, while Biarni's is "improbable" or even "impossible" because the document containing it has been condemned.

1. The author's primary concern is to demonstrate that:

   (A) Leif Ericsson did not visit America.
   (B) Biarni might have visited America before Leif Ericsson.
   (C) Biarni did not visit Wineland.
   (D) Leif Ericsson visited Wineland first.

2. The passage provides information that defines which of the following terms?

   I. Doegr
   II. Hellus
   III. Heriulfsness

   (F) I only
   (G) II only
   (H) I and II only
   (J) II and III only

3. It can be inferred from the passage that scholars who doubt the authenticity of the Biarni narrative make all of the following objections BUT:

   (A) Biarni might have accompanied Leif Ericsson on the voyage to America, and that is why a separate, erroneous narrative was invented.
   (B) The similarity of the voyages described in the Saga and in the Flat Island Book indicates that there was but one voyage, not two voyages.
   (C) It seems very improbable that a ship, having sailed from America to Greenland could have found its way to a precise point on the coast of Greenland.
   (D) Both the Saga of Eric the Red and the Flat Island Book make use of mythical formulas, so it is probable that the same person wrote them both.

4. The author mentions the two high mountains (lines 50-51) in order to show that it is:

(F) reasonable for Biarni to land precisely at his father's home.
(G) possible to sail from Norway to Greenland without modern navigational equipment.
(H) likely that Biarni landed on America at least 100 years before Leif Ericsson.
(J) probable that Leif Ericsson followed the same course as Biarni.

5. All of the following are mentioned as similarities between Leif Ericsson's voyage and Biarni's voyage EXCEPT:

(A) both visited Norway.
(B) on the return voyage, both visited three different lands.
(C) both returned to Greenland.
(D) both sighted Wineland.

6. It can be inferred that the author regards the historicity of the Biarni narrative as:

(F) conclusively proved.
(G) almost conclusively proved.
(H) possibly true.
(J) highly unlikely.

7. In the final paragraph, the author suggests some authorities who regard the Saga as authentic are guilty of which of the following errors in reasoning?

(A) Oversimplification
(B) Logical contradiction
(C) False analogy
(D) Circular reasoning

8. According to the passage, Heriulf is:

(F) Leif Ericsson's son.
(G) one of Leif Ericsson's sailors.
(H) Biarni's father.
(J) King Olaf Tryggvason's son.

9. According to the author, most authorities regard the Biarni narrative as:

(A) conclusively demonstrated.
(B) probably true.
(C) probably untrue.
(D) an attempted fraud.

10. Biarni's home was in:

(F) Norway.
(G) Greenland.
(H) Wineland.
(J) Flat Island.

QUIZ III (10 questions; 9 minutes)

Whether used to control airplane traffic, detect speeding automobiles, or track a hurricane, radar is a very useful tool. Developed during World War II, this technology allows for remote sensing, that is, locating objects that are not seen directly. The word *radar* is a contraction of "radio detection and ranging." It works in much the same way as an echo. When you shout toward a cliff or a large building, part of the sound bounces back. In radar, waves of electromagnetic radiation are sent out. When they strike an object, they bounce back and are picked up by a receiver. The returning signal indicates the direction of the object; the time it takes for the signal to return indicates the distance to the object. Radar waves detect objects by their varying densities. They are not deflected by atmospheric layers and therefore always travel in a straight line—in all weather, both day and night.

Radar waves are electromagnetic waves, as are light waves, electric waves, x-rays, cosmic rays, and radio waves. All electromagnetic waves travel at 300,000 kilometers per second—the speed of light. Waves differ from each other in the number of times they vibrate per second; this variable is known as frequency and is usually expressed as cycles per second. Waves also differ in their size, or wavelength. The speed, frequency, and wavelength of a wave are related by the wave equation in which:

$$\text{speed} = \text{frequency} \cdot \text{wavelength}$$

This shows that the product of the frequency and wavelength of any given wave is always a constant—the speed of light. To find the wavelength of a wave knowing the frequency, this formula is used:

$$\text{wavelength} = \frac{\text{speed}}{\text{frequency}}$$

For example, if a radio station broadcasts waves at 600,000 cycles per second (cps), wavelength would be calculated this way:

$$\begin{aligned}\text{wavelength} &= 300{,}000 \text{ km per sec}/600{,}000 \text{ cps}\\ &= 0.5 \text{ km or } 500 \text{ m}\end{aligned}$$

If the frequency of the wave were doubled to 1,200,000 cycles per second, its wavelength would be cut in half to 250 meters. Since frequencies are so high, the unit *megahertz* is usually used; 1 megahertz = 1,000,000 cycles per second.

Wavelengths within the electromagnetic spectrum vary greatly. Radar has wavelengths that measure from approximately one centimeter (0.01 m) up to one meter. Each kind of wave has a range of wavelengths. The table compares some sample wavelengths of several kinds of electromagnetic waves.

Type of Wave (meters)	*Sample Wavelength*
cosmic rays	0.0000000000000001
x-rays	0.0000000001
ultra-violet rays	0.00000001
visible light	0.000001
infrared heat	0.0001
microwaves	0.001
radar	0.1
television	1.0
radio	100
long radio waves	10,000
electric power	1,000,000

1. Radio waves and radar waves have the same:

(A) frequency.
(B) wavelength.
(C) cycles per second.
(D) speed.

2. A radar signal having a frequency of 3,000 megahertz would have a wavelength of:

(F) 0.001 km.
(G) 0.01 km.
(H) 10 m.
(J) 0.1 m.

3. A radar set could not locate an airplane if it were flying:

(A) faster than the speed of sound.
(B) above a heavy storm.
(C) above the atmosphere.
(D) below the horizon.

4. It is possible to find the distance to an object from a radar set because the:

(F) wavelength of radar is known.
(G) frequency of radar is known.
(H) speed of radar is 300,000 kilometers per second.
(J) set operates at 10 megahertz.

5. The relationship between the frequency and wavelength of a wave is:

(A) constant.
(B) directly proportional.
(C) exponential.
(D) inverse.

6. An antenna picks up a signal that has a wavelength of about one meter. It is likely to be:

(F) in the visible spectrum.
(G) an ultraviolet ray.
(H) a television signal.
(J) an x-ray.

7. Radio waves will not penetrate the ionosphere, but microwaves will. Would you expect X-rays to penetrate the ionosphere?

(A) Yes, because they have a shorter wavelength than microwaves and radio waves.
(B) Yes, because they have a lower frequency than microwaves and radio waves.
(C) No, because they travel more slowly than microwaves.
(D) No, because they have fewer cycles per second than microwaves or radio waves.

8. Compared to cosmic rays, the frequency value of visible light waves is:

(F) higher.
(G) lower.
(H) the same.
(J) impossible to determine from the information given.

9. Which factor would be most important in order for radar to detect and track storms?

(A) Radar signals travel in straight lines.
(B) The densities of moist air masses are different from those of dry air masses.
(C) The atmosphere does not deflect radar signals.
(D) Radar signals travel much faster than storm tracks.

10. Like a radar reflection, an echo can be used to determine the distance of an object. This must be because:

(F) sound is a form of radar.
(G) sound travels at a relatively fixed rate.
(H) sound waves have different frequencies.
(J) sound waves are invisible.

READING ANSWER KEY

SECTION ONE—READING REVIEW (p. 127)

1. C	5. C	9. D	13. A	17. B
2. F	6. J	10. F	14. J	18. F
3. A	7. D	11. B	15. C	19. B
4. J	8. F	12. J	16. G	

SECTION TWO—READING PROBLEM-SOLVING (p.132)

1. A	19. D	37. B	55. A	73. D
2. H	20. F	38. F	56. J	74. H
3. C	21. B	39. C	57. C	75. C
4. G	22. J	40. J	58. F	76. H
5. B	23. B	41. B	59. D	77. B
6. F	24. H	42. F	60. J	78. D
7. B	25. C	43. C	61. C	79. B
8. J	26. H	44. F	62. G	80. J
9. B	27. B	45. D	63. D	81. D
10. J	28. J	46. J	64. F	82. H
11. C	29. C	47. A	65. B	83. A
12. H	30. F	48. J	66. H	84. J
13. C	31. D	49. C	67. A	85. A
14. G	32. H	50. H	68. J	86. J
15. B	33. B	51. A	69. C	87. H
16. H	34. H	52. H	70. J	88. C
17. D	35. D	53. D	71. C	
18. H	36. G	54. G	72. G	

SECTION THREE—READING QUIZZES (p. 153)

QUIZ I

1. B	3. B	5. D	7. A	9. C
2. G	4. F	6. H	8. F	10. G

QUIZ II

1. B	3. D	5. D	7. D	9. C
2. J	4. F	6. H	8. H	10. G

QUIZ III

1. D	3. D	5. D	7. A	9. B
2. J	4. H	6. H	8. G	10. G

CAMBRIDGE
EDUCATIONAL SERVICES, INC.®

AMERICA'S #1 CAMPUS-BASED TESTPREP

Strategy Summary Sheet

ACT • PLAN • EXPLORE—READING

STRUCTURE OF READING TEST: The ACT Reading Test contains four 500-600 word reading passages from each of the four content areas: social studies, natural sciences, prose fiction, and humanities. The PLAN is 25 items in 20 minutes; the EXPLORE is 30 items in 30 minutes. Each passage is followed by 10 questions. Questions are multiple-choice with four answer choices. The section is 35 minutes long with 40 questions.

	ACT (40 questions)	**PLAN** (25 questions)	**EXPLORE** (30 questions)
Social Studies	10	8	10
Natural Sciences	10	–	–
Prose Fiction	10	8	10
Humanities	10	9	10

GENERAL STRATEGY: This is not an exact science. Practice is essential to master the following techniques:

1. *Read the first two sentences of each of the passages.* Grade as E (for easy) or H (for hard). Analyze the easier passages first.

2. *Preview the first and last sentences of selection.* If the selection is more than one paragraph long, begin with a preview of the first sentence of each paragraph.

3. *Preview the question stems for a given passage.* Label as follows:

   a. *Main Idea Questions (MI)—Level 1:* Main idea questions test the first level of reading—appreciation of the general theme. Main idea questions ask about the central theme that unifies the passage and the overall development of the passage.

   Examples: Which of the following is the main point of the passage? The main argument the author makes about...is that.... What is the main theme of the third paragraph?

   b. *Specific Detail (SD)—Level 2:* Specific detail questions test your ability to read at the intermediate level—understanding of specific points. Specific detail questions ask about details and the logical role of those details that are explicitly mentioned in the passage. Typically, these questions will direct you to refer to a specific part of the passage with key words, line number references, or reference to a particular paragraph.

   Examples: The author mentions which of the following? According to the fourth paragraph, ... Why does the author mention...?

   c. *Evaluation (E)—Level 3:* Evaluation questions ask not just for understanding—they ask for a judgment about or an evaluation of what you read. These questions test the highest level of reading. You can't evaluate a text unless you understand the specific points that are made. The third level is the most difficult because it presupposes that you understand the first two levels.

   Examples: The author suggests that.... With which of the following would the author agree? The passage is probably taken from what source? In the passage, the term "—" means which of the following?

4. *Read the passage.* Ask what the author is attempting to describe, especially if there are evaluation questions. Some advice is to read the first sentence in each paragraph prior to reading the entire selection. This is optional, depending on the ease of the selection, your personal preference, and time available. Bracket difficult material. Instead of wasting time rereading, simply attempt to understand the context in which the author introduced those concepts.

5. *Answer the questions.* Circle answers to questions in test booklet. Transcribe the answers to all the questions for a passage to answer sheet at one time. Alter this strategy for the last passage when time pressure applies. In this case, directly transcribe your answers to the answer sheet, so as not to lose credit for your work when time expires.

ADDITIONAL NOTES AND STRATEGIES FROM IN-CLASS DISCUSSION:

CAMBRIDGE

EDUCATIONAL SERVICES, INC.®

ACT • PLAN • EXPLORE SCIENCE REASONING

CAMBRIDGE
EDUCATIONAL SERVICES, INC.®

AMERICA'S #1 CAMPUS-BASED TESTPREP

Cambridge Course Concept Outline

ACT • PLAN • EXPLORE—SCIENCE REASONING

I. SCIENCE REASONING REVIEW

(*Cambridge ACT • PLAN • EXPLORE Textbook*, Science Reasoning Section One, p. 167)

A. SCIENCE REASONING PRELIMINARIES

1. **TEACHING THE SCIENCE REASONING LESSON**
2. **FORMAT OF THE ACT, PLAN, AND EXPLORE TESTS**
3. **DIRECTIONS FOR SCIENCE REASONING PROBLEMS**
4. **WHAT IS TESTED**

B. THREE TYPES OF SCIENCE REASONING PASSAGES

1. **DATA REPRESENTATION PASSAGES**
    - a. **GRAPHS**
        - i. **STRAIGHT LINES**
        - ii. **PARABOLIC CURVES**
        - iii. **GRAPH READING STRATEGIES** (Review Questions #1-3)
    - b. **TABLES** (Review Questions #4-9)
    - c. **TYPICAL DATA REPRESENTATION QUESTIONS** (Review Questions #10-14)
2. **RESEARCH SUMMARY PASSAGES**
    - a. **DESIGN QUESTIONS**
    - b. **PREDICTION QUESTIONS**
    - c. **EVALUATION QUESTIONS**
    - d. **TYPICAL RESEARCH SUMMARY QUESTIONS** (Review Questions #15-25)
3. **CONFLICTING VIEWPOINT PASSAGES**
    - a. **PREDICTION QUESTIONS**
    - b. **SPOT THE ASSUMPTIONS QUESTIONS**
    - c. **PICK THE BEST ARGUMENT QUESTIONS**
    - d. **TYPICAL CONFLICTING VIEWPOINT QUESTIONS** (Review Questions #26-36)

C. THREE TYPES OF SCIENCE REASONING QUESTIONS

1. **COMPREHENSION QUESTIONS**
2. **ANALYSIS QUESTIONS**
3. **APPLICATION QUESTIONS**

D. STRATEGIES FOR THE SCIENCE REASONING TEST

1. **GENERAL SCIENCE REASONING STRATEGIES**
    - a. **PLAN YOUR ATTACK—EASIEST PASSAGES FIRST**
    - b. ***DON'T* PREVIEW QUESTION STEMS BEFORE READING PASSAGE**
    - c. **UNDERLINE KEY WORDS AND PHRASES**
    - d. **PAY ATTENTION TO WHAT IS THERE, NOT WHAT ISN'T**
    - e. **PAY ATTENTION TO DIFFERENCES**
    - f. **WATCH FOR ASSUMPTIONS**
    - g. **LOOK FOR TRENDS**
    - h. **TRANSCRIBE ANSWERS IN GROUPS**

2. **DATA REPRESENTATION STRATEGIES** (Review Questions #36-41)
3. **RESEARCH SUMMARY STRATEGIES** (Review Questions #42-47)
4. **CONFLICTING VIEWPOINT STRATEGIES** (Review Questions #48-54)

II. SCIENCE REASONING PROBLEM-SOLVING

(*Cambridge ACT • PLAN • EXPLORE Textbook*, Science Reasoning Section Two, p. 182)

A. DATA REPRESENTATION PASSAGES (Problem-Solving Questions #1-27)

B. RESEARCH SUMMARIES PASSAGES (Problem-Solving Questions #28-51)

C. CONFLICTING VIEWPOINTS PASSAGES {Problem-Solving Questions #52-79)

III. SCIENCE REASONING QUIZZES

(*Cambridge ACT • PLAN • EXPLORE Textbook*, Science Reasoning Section Three, p. 198)

SECTION ONE—SCIENCE REASONING REVIEW

DIRECTIONS: The questions in this section accompany the in-class review of the Science Reasoning skills tested by the ACT, PLAN, and EXPLORE tests. Each passage is followed by several questions. After reading a passage, choose the best answer to each question. You may refer to the passages as often as necessary. Answers are on page 205.

PASSAGE I

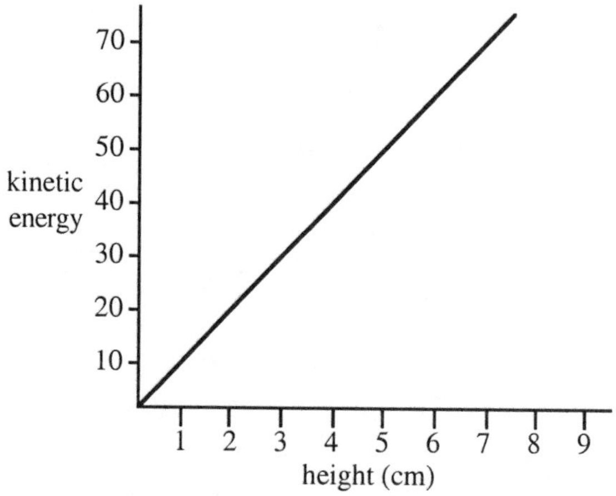

The kinetic energy of an object with mass m (measured in grams) after a fall from a height h (measured in cm) was recorded for different heights. A graph was made representing the kinetic energy versus height.

1. If the kinetic energy is given in units of g cm^2/s^2, what units must the slope have?

(A) g cm/s
(B) g cm/s^2
(C) s cm/g
(D) s^2/(g cm)

2. It is discovered that if we redo the experiment with an object with twice the mass, the kinetic energy obtained for every height is doubled. The slope of the new set of experiments can be obtained by doing what to the old slope?

(F) Multiplying by 2
(G) Dividing by 2
(H) Squaring
(J) Taking the square root

3. What would be the kinetic energy in g cm^2/s^2 of an object of mass m if it was dropped from a height of 4.5 cm?

(A) 45
(B) 4.5
(C) 90
(D) 9.0

PASSAGE II

A scientist investigated the variables that affect the age at which a female of the animal species *taedi periculum* first gives birth. Some of the results of this study are summarized in the table below.

Experiment	*Temperature (°C)*	*Average food intake (g)*	*Age when first gave birth (mo.)*
1	25	15	7
2	25	30	6
3	25	45	4
4	35	15	5
5	35	30	3
6	35	45	3

4. Which of the following would be good animals to use for the experiment?

(F) Adult females
(G) Newborn females
(H) Newborn males
(J) Adult males

5. Which of the pairs of experiments listed below would be useful for studying the effect of temperature on age of first birth?

(A) 1and 2
(B) 1and 5
(C) 1and 4
(D) 2 and 6

6. If all other variables are kept constant, which of the following will result in an increase in the age at which the animals give birth?

(F) Increase in temperature from 25°C to 35°C
(G) Increase in food from 15g to 45g
(H) Decrease in food from 30g to 15g
(J) Increase in temperature from 25°C to 30°C

7. Which experiment was the control for temperature for Experiment 5?

(A) Experiment 1
(B) Experiment 2
(C) Experiment 3
(D) Experiment 6

8. If an experiment was set up with the temperature set at 30°C and the food intake at 30g, which of the following would be a reasonable prediction of the age in months of the animals when they first gave birth?

(F) 7.5
(G) 6.0
(H) 4.5
(J) 2.5

9. Which of the following conclusions is consistent with the data presented in Table 1?

(A) The weight of the firstborn is proportional to the food intake.
(B) The weight of the firstborn is related to the temperature.
(C) The age of the mother at time of first offspring's birth increases with decreasing food intake.
(D) The age of the mother at time of first offspring's birth decreases with decreasing food intake.

NOTES AND STRATEGIES

PASSAGE III

The chart below shows the average blood pressure and relative total surface area associated with the different types of human blood vessels.

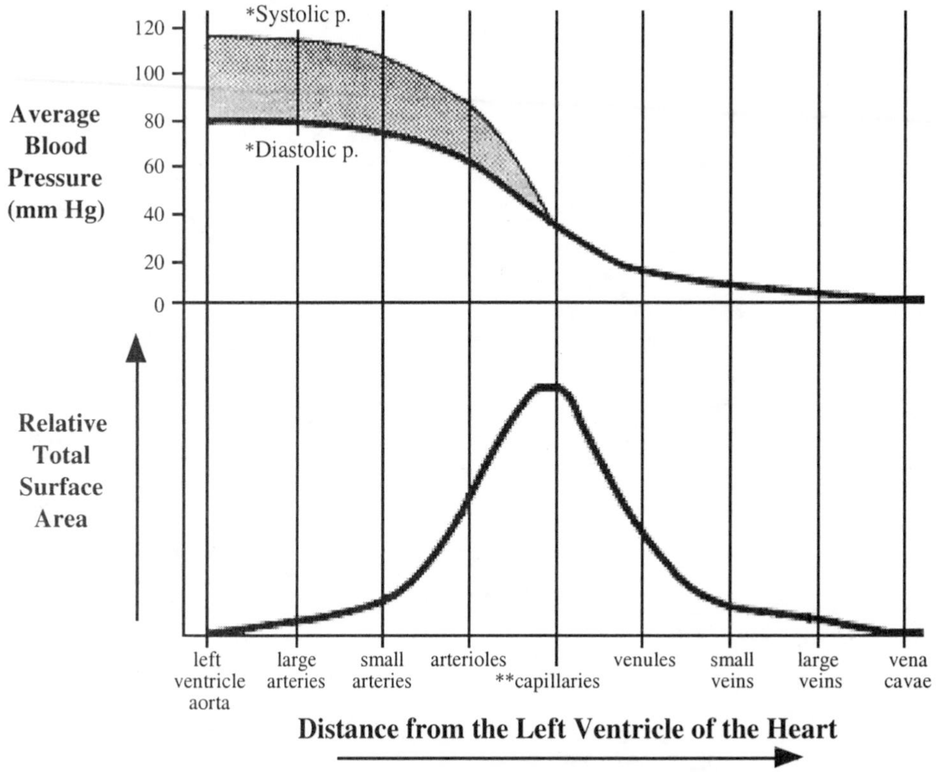

*Pulse is the difference between systolic and diastolic pressure.
**Blood velocity is lowest in the capillaries (averaging 3 cm/sec.).

10. According to the diagram, pulse pressure can be detected:

(F) in large arteries only.
(G) in large arteries as well as in large veins.
(H) in blood vessels between the aorta and the capillaries.
(J) primarily in the arterioles, capillaries, and venules.

11. Based on the information in the diagram, which of the following conclusions about average blood pressure is correct?

(A) The average blood pressure decreases continuously as it gets further away from the left ventricle.
(B) The average blood pressure remains approximately the same as it passes through the different blood vessels of the body.
(C) Starting at the aorta, average blood pressure first increases and then decreases.
(D) The average blood pressure is highest in the blood vessels with the greatest relative total surface area.

12. Which of the following correctly states the relationship between the relative total surface area of different blood vessels and their average blood pressure?

    (F) As relative total surface area decreases, average blood pressure increases.
    (G) As relative total surface area decreases, average blood pressure decreases.
    (H) As relative total surface area decreases, average blood pressure may increase or decrease.
    (J) Average blood pressure always changes in the opposite direction as the relative total surface area changes.

13. Which of the following conclusions can be drawn from the information provided in the diagram?

    (A) As the distance of blood vessels from the left ventricle increases, their relative total surface area decreases.
    (B) As the distance of blood vessels from the left ventricle increases, their pulse pressure increases.
    (C) Blood vessels with the greatest relative total surface area have the highest pulse pressure.
    (D) Blood vessels closest to and farthest away from the left ventricle have the smallest relative total surface area.

14. A physician examining a newly discovered tribe of people deep in the Amazon jungles found that the relative total surface area of their capillaries was greater than that previously reported for any other people. If the physician were to predict the average velocity of blood through their capillaries, which of the following values would be most reasonable?

    (F) 2cm/sec
    (G) 3cm/sec
    (G) 4cm/sec
    (J) 5cm/sec

PASSAGE IV

To test the hypothesis that all antibiotics are equally effective in preventing bacterial growth, the following three experiments were carried out using clear plastic plates filled with nutrient agar (a mixture of ingredients that supports the growth of bacteria).

Experiment 1

Three plates (A, B, and C) of agar were set up, each with an equal amount of bacterial culture (Bacterium X) spread over the agar surface. Plate A had a small paper disk soaked in Antibiotic I placed on the agar surface in the center of the bacterial culture. Plate B was treated identically except that the paper disk was soaked in Antibiotic II. For plate C, the paper disk was soaked in plain water. After incubation overnight at 37°C (body temperature), Plates A and B had a clear area, 2" in diameter surrounding the paper disk, but beyond this 2" region, the plates were cloudy. Plate C was entirely cloudy, including the area adjacent to the paper disk. When bacteria reproduce successfully, colonies form on the agar, giving it a cloudy appearance.

Experiment 2

Identical procedures were followed except that Plates A, B, and C were incubated overnight at 22°C (room temperature). After incubation, Plate A again had a clear area, 2" in diameter, surrounding the paper disk. However, Plates B and C were entirely cloudy.

Experiment 3

Procedures identical to those in Experiment 2 were followed except that the concentrations of Antibiotic I (Plate A) and Antibiotic II (Plate B) were made twice as strong. After incubation overnight at 22°C, Plates A and B both had clear, 2" areas around the paper disk, while Plate C remained entirely cloudy.

15. After incubation, a clear area around a previously soaked paper disk represents:

    (A) a region where agar had washed away.
    (B) a region decomposed by high incubation temperatures.
    (C) a region where bacterial growth did not occur.
    (D) a region where bacteria grew best.

16. Which statement is supported by the results of Experiment 1 alone?

    (F) Antibiotic I, Antibiotic II, and water are equally effective as inhibitors (preventers) of bacterial growth at 37°C.
    (G) Dry paper disks can be effective in controlling bacterial growth at 37°C.
    (H) The concentration of an antibiotic may influence its effectiveness in controlling bacterial growth at 37°C.
    (J) Both Antibiotics I and II can inhibit bacterial growth at 37°C.

17. In the described experiments, which of the following results would indicate that the antibiotics being tested have nothing to do with the control of bacterial growth?

(A) A clear, 2" region was always observed around the disks soaked in water.
(B) All results remained the same at the two experimental temperatures and at the two antibiotic concentration levels.
(C) Plates A and B always remained completely clear.
(D) The disks soaked in water were not used in the experiments at all.

18. The results of Experiment 2 and Experiment 3 lead to which of the following conclusions?

(F) Antibiotics I and II have similar effects on bacterial growth, regardless of their concentrations.
(G) Antibiotic II and water have similar effects on bacterial growth, regardless of their concentrations.
(H) The effectiveness of Antibiotic I at 22°C depends on its concentration.
(J) The effectiveness of Antibiotic II at 22°C depends on its concentration.

19. Which hypothesis best explains the observation that the agar plates never appear clear beyond a 2" area surrounding the soaked paper disks?

(A) The bacteria cannot grow well within 2" of any moist paper disks.
(B) The antibiotics cannot seep through the agar beyond a distance of 2".
(C) At the experimental incubation temperatures used, the two antibiotics interfere with each other's effectiveness.
(D) The paper disks can absorb nutrients out of the agar from the distance of 2".

20. If either Antibiotic I or Antibiotic II could be prescribed for internal use to prevent the spread of Bacterium X infections, which recommendation, based on the results of the experiments, is appropriate if the *cost due to the amount of antibiotic used per dose* is the most critical factor?

(F) Antibiotic I or Antibiotic II can be taken at equal cost.
(G) Antibiotic I would be less expensive than Antibiotic II.
(H) Antibiotic II would be less expensive than Antibiotic I.
(J) Neither Antibiotic I nor Antibiotic II would be effective in preventing the spread of Bacterium X.

PASSAGE V

To investigate the hypothesis that the quality of the detail of a fossil depends on the size of the particles that make up the rock surrounding the fossil, three experiments were performed using a particular type of leaf with many fine veins.

Experiment 1

A leaf was placed on a flat bed made of a paste of extra-fine plaster. The leaf was then completely covered with more of the same plaster paste. A glass cover with a five-pound weight was placed on top of the paste for one hour, until the plaster set. The plaster was then baked for 30 minutes at 25°C. When the cast was opened, the imprint of the leaf showed all of the veins, including the finest ones.

Experiment 2

A leaf was placed on a flat bed made of a paste of fine grade plaster. The leaf was then completely covered with more of the same plaster paste. A glass cover with a five-pound weight was placed on top of the plaster for one hour. The plaster was then baked for 30 minutes at 25°C. When the cast was opened, all the main veins were visible, but only isolated traces of the finer veins were found.

Experiment 3

A leaf was placed on a flat bed made of a paste of coarse grain plaster. The leaf was then completely covered with more of the same plaster paste. A glass cover with a five-pound weight was placed on top of the plaster for one hour. The plaster was then baked for 30 minutes at 25°C. When the cast was opened, only the thickest veins were visible, and some of the edge of the leaf was difficult to discern.

NOTES AND STRATEGIES

21. Should the investigator have used a different type of leaf in each experiment?

(A) Yes, because different types of structure could be studied.
(B) Yes, because in real life many different types of fossils are found.
(C) No, because the leaf served as a controlled variable.
(D) No, because the nature of the leaf is not important.

22. When a fossil is formed, the sediment that surrounds it is normally compressed by the tons of earth deposited over it. What part of the model simulates this sediment?

(F) The five-pound weight
(G) The glass
(H) The upper layer of paste
(J) The baking oven

23. A fourth experiment was set up the same way as the previous three, except that the paste was, made by mixing equal amounts of very coarse sand with the extra-fine plaster. The investigator is likely to discover:

(A) no change from Experiment I because only the plaster counts.
(B) no change because the same kind of leaf is used.
(C) the imprint is better than Experiment 1 because the sand provides air pockets.
(D) the imprint is worse than Experiment 1 because the average particle size is bigger.

24. Which of the following hypotheses are supported by the results of Experiment 1 alone?

(F) The finer the sediment the greater the detail of the resulting fossil.
(G) Hardened sediment can preserve the imprint of a specimen.
(H) All fossils must have been baked at high temperatures.
(J) Only organic material can leave imprints in sediment.

25. Which of the following changes in the experiments would have permitted a test of the hypothesis that the quality of a fossil imprint depends on the pressure applied?

(A) Repeat the experiments except for using a ten-pound weight in Experiment 2, and a twenty-pound weight in Experiment 3.
(B) Choose one of the plasters, and run experiments using the same plaster in all trials while varying the weights.
(C) Rerun all the experiments without the glass.
(D) Vary the depth of the leaf in each new trial, because in nature increased pressure means the fossil is at a greater depth.

PASSAGE VI

Theory 1

Early in the twentieth century, many chemists believed that the stability of the molecule methane, CH_4, could be explained by the "octet" rule, which states that stability occurs when the central atom, in this case carbon, is surrounded by eight "valence," or outer, electrons. Four of these originally came from the outer electrons of the carbon itself, and four came from the four surrounding hydrogen atoms (the hydrogen itself was considered to be an exception to the rule since it was known to favor a closed shell of two electrons as helium has.) According to the octet rule, neither CH_3 nor CH_5 should exist as stable compounds, and this prediction has been born out by experiment.

Theory 2

While the octet rule predicted many compounds accurately, it also had shortcomings. Ten electrons, for example, surround the compound PC_{15}. The greatest shock to the octet rule concerned the "noble gases" such as krypton and xenon, which have eight electrons surrounding them in their atomic states, and therefore should not form compounds since no more electrons would be needed to make an octet. The discovery in 1960 that xenon could form compounds such as XeF_4 forced consideration of a new theory, which held that (a) compounds formed when electrons were completely paired, either in bonds or in nonbonded pairs; (b) the total number of shared electrons around a central atom varied, and could be as high as twelve; (c) the shapes of compounds were such as to keep the pairs of electrons as far from each other as possible.

For example, since six electrons in the atomic state surround sulfur, in the compound SF_6 it acquired six additional shared electrons from the surrounding fluorines for a total of twelve electrons. The shape of the compound is "octahedral," as shown below, since this conformation minimizes the overlap of bonding pairs of electrons.

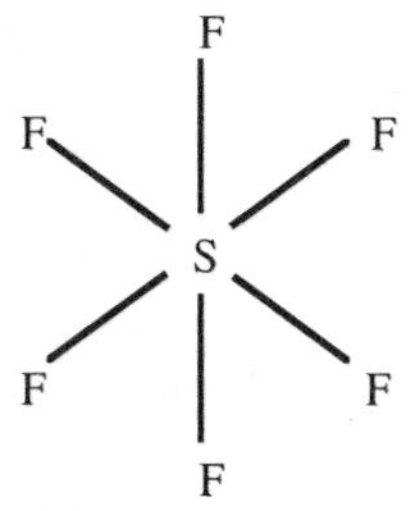

26. According to Theory 1, the compound CH_2Cl_2:

(F) should have eight electrons surrounding the carbon atom.
(G) cannot exist since the original carbon atom does not have eight electrons.
(H) should have eight electrons surrounding each hydrogen atom.
(J) requires more electrons for stability.

27. According to Theory 1, the compound XeF_4:

(A) exists with an octet structure around the xenon.
(B) should not exist since the xenon is surrounded by more than eight electrons.
(C) will have similar chemical properties to CH_4.
(D) exists with the xenon surrounded by twelve electrons.

28. The atom boron has three outer electrons, and in bonding to boron, a fluorine atom donates one electron. The BF_3 molecule is known to exist. Which of the following is true?

(F) BF_3 obeys Theory 1.
(G) The existence of BF_3 contradicts Theory 2.
(H) According to Theory 2, the structure of BF_3 is a pyramid:

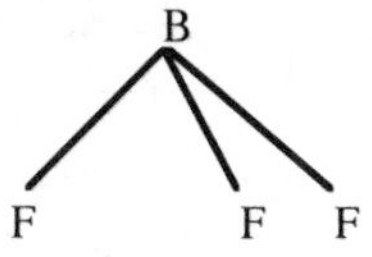

(J) According to Theory 2, the structure of BF_3 is triangular and planar:

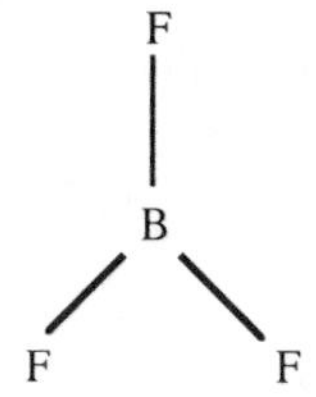

29. A scientist seeking to explain why Theory 2 has more predictive power than Theory 1 might argue that:

(A) eight electrons shall represent a "closed shell."
(B) while eight electrons represent a "closed shell" for some atoms, for others the closed shell may be six, ten, or twelve.
(C) it is incorrect to assume that a given atom always has the same number of electrons around it.
(D) CH_4 is not as important a compound as XeF_4.

30. Theory 2 could be threatened by evidence of:

(F) the existence of SF_4.
(G) the existence of XeF_5.
(H) molecules with stable octets.
(J) the existence of SF_6.

PASSAGE VII

Scientist 1

The atmosphere of the earth was at one time almost totally lacking in oxygen. One piece of evidence supporting this assertion is the very fact that life got started at all. The first chemical reactions that are necessary for the origin of life, the formation of amino acids, require ultraviolet light. Most of the ultraviolet light coming from the sun is now absorbed by oxygen in the atmosphere. If there were as much oxygen in the atmosphere then as now there would have been too little ultraviolet light available to enable life to begin. Also, the oldest bacteria, the ones which have the shortest DNA, are almost all anaerobes—they either do not need oxygen or die if exposed to oxygen. Most of the oxygen that exists now entered the atmosphere later from volcanic fumes.

Scientist 2

The prevailing opinion is that the atmosphere, though thicker now than it was in the past, is not essentially different in composition. The argument that the earth must originally have been deficient in oxygen is flawed. First of all, the presence of iron and other oxides in the rocks from this time indicates that there was oxygen available. Secondly, the requirement for a great deal of ultraviolet light holds only if there is a low concentration of the starting materials in the water. If the water in some prehistoric lake began to freeze, the starting materials would be concentrated in a small volume of unfrozen water. The high concentration of the starting materials would offset the so-called deficiency of ultraviolet light, and life could begin.

31. According to the hypothesis of Scientist 1, which of the following would have been among the last living things to evolve?

(A) Anaerobes
(B) Plants
(C) Insects
(D) Viruses

32. According to the information presented by Scientist 1, if his theory of the origin of oxygen in the atmosphere is correct, the total amount of oxygen in the air over the next million years, on the average, should:

(F) decrease, then increase.
(G) increase, then decrease.
(H) increase.
(J) decrease.

33. Underlying the argument of Scientist 2 is the assumption that the oxygen in the oxides in the rocks was:

(A) always tied up in the rocks.
(B) involved in biological reactions.
(C) all gaseous during the early days of the atmosphere.
(D) proportional to the oxygen in the atmosphere at the time.

34. Underlying Scientist 1's suggestion that the evolutionary record supports the idea of an oxygen deficiency on the early earth is the assumption that the oldest living things:

(F) have the shortest DNA.
(G) have the most fragmented DNA.
(H) have changed radically.
(J) must have died out.

35. Which of the following is the strongest argument Scientist 1 could use to counter Scientist 2's suggested mechanism for the origin of life?

(A) There wasn't enough ultraviolet light available.
(B) Chemical reactions occurred differently then.
(C) The temperature at the surface of the earth at that time was always above 35°C because of geothermal heat release.
(D) Most lakes would not have covered large enough areas to guarantee that all the essential building blocks were present.

36. To refute Scientist 1's hypothesis, Scientist 2 might best show that:

(F) the amount of oxide in rocks has changed little over the past four billion years.
(G) there are ways of making the biologically important molecules without ultraviolet light.
(H) there are complex anaerobic bacteria.
(J) the atmospheric pressure hasn't changed over the earth's history.

PASSAGE VIII

Ocean water contains "salt"—actually a mixture of ions, primarily sodium, chloride, potassium, calcium, magnesium, bicarbonate, and sulfate. The solid-line graph below indicates the percentage of these ions ("salinity") in a slab of ice that lies over sea water on a cold ocean surface. The arrow and dashed line indicate the salinity of the water beneath the ice.

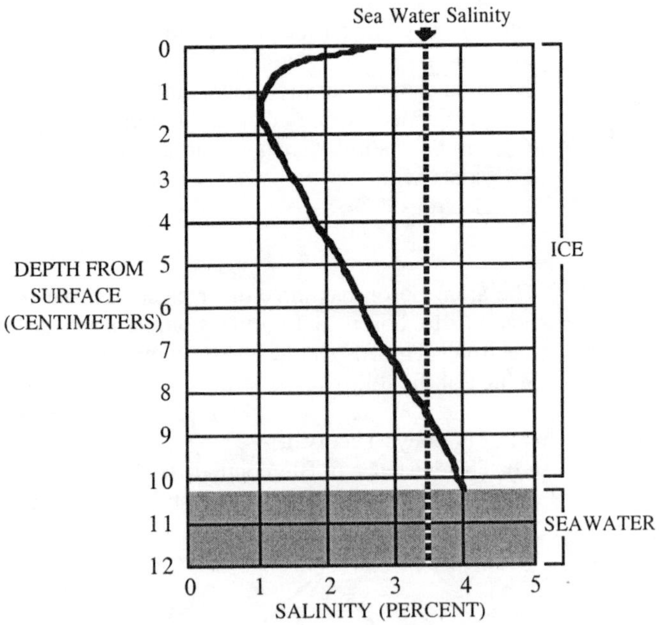

37. According to this figure the salt content of the ice above the ocean water:

(A) equals 0.
(B) is constant at all depths.
(C) generally decreases with greater depth.
(D) generally increases with greater depth.

NOTES AND STRATEGIES

38. Compared to the ocean water below it, the salinity of the ice is:

(F) generally lower.
(G) about the same.
(H) generally higher.
(J) unable to be determined.

39. The salinity of the ice at the surface of the slab is equal to the salinity of:

(A) ice at a depth of approximately 1.5 cm.
(B) ice at a depth of approximately 7.0 cm.
(C) ice at a depth of approximately 9.0 cm.
(D) the water beneath the ice.

40. An experimenter wants to take a sample of ice that is one half the salinity of the sea water below. At what depth should he sample?

(F) Between 1 and 2 cm
(G) Between 4 and 5 cm
(H) Either between 0 and 1 cm or 3 and 4 cm
(J) Between 5 and 6 cm

41. The investigator takes a 1-g sample of ice from a depth of 10 cm, and wishes to take a sample of ice from 1.3 cm depth that will contain the same weight of total salts. How large a sample is needed?

(A) 0.25 g
(B) 1.0 g
(C) 4.0 g
(D) 10 g

PASSAGE IX

The term erosion refers to the processes that wear down rocks and soil, as well as the processes that transport the worn-away materials to other locations. Although in the real world, these processes usually show their effects gradually (over geologic time), laboratory models can be designed to investigate which environmental factors affect erosion rate.

Three experimental "sandboxes" were set up that were identical in size (10 feet • 15 feet), had identical types of soil and rocks, and were filled to equal depths (3 feet). The sandboxes were kept for two weeks in large environmental chambers, each maintained at a constant temperature, with a continuous wind flow of 5 mph.

Sandbox 1

One half was kept bare (just soil and rocks), while the other half had a variety of grasses and weeds planted among the soil and rocks. After two weeks, the bare half had small channels (ruts) running along its length that averaged 1 inch in width. The planted half had few channels, and those that were found averaged less than 1 inch wide.

Sandbox 2

The conditions were identical to those of Sandbox 1, with the addition that both halves were subjected to light, 15-minute showers of water every twelve hours. After two weeks, the bare half had channels averaging 4 inches wide, while the planted half had fewer channels averaging 2 inches wide.

Sandbox 3

The conditions were identical to those of Sandbox 2, with the addition that the entire box was mechanically raised to rest at an angle of 15° to stimulate a steep slope. After two weeks, the bare half had channels averaging 7 inches wide, while channels in the planted half were less common and averaged 4 inches in width.

42. Results from all three experimental sandboxes indicate that:

(F) different types of soils and rocks are affected differently by environmental factors.
(G) under all tested conditions, plants reduce erosion.
(H) changing wind and temperature conditions can affect erosion patterns.
(J) water from short periods of rain has little or no effect on erosion patterns.

43. Sudden cloudbursts are known to cause more erosion than longer periods of mild rains. How could the present experiments be changed to examine this idea?

(A) Raise the angle in Sandbox 3 to produce a steeper slope.
(B) Add the "rain conditions" from Sandbox 2 to the conditions in Sandbox 1.
(C) Include light, 15-minute showers every six hours instead of every twelve hours.
(D) Every twelve hours allow the same total volume of water to fall in a 5-minute span rather than in a 15-minute span.

44. Should the investigator have used different soil types in each sand box experiment?

(F) Yes, because different soils may erode differently.
(G) Yes, because a different group of plants could have been used in each sandbox as well.
(H) No, because some soils can be washed completely away within the 2-week experiment.
(J) No, because the soil type was a controlled variable in all three experiments.

45. Which statement does the design and results of the experiments NOT support?

(A) Light winds have no erosive effect.
(B) Steep slopes undergo more erosion than level surfaces.
(C) Water has major erosive effects.
(D) The effects of changing temperature remain unanswered.

46. Sandbox 3 specifically demonstrates the role of which particular variable in the set of experiments?

(F) Rain
(G) Wind
(H) Gravity
(J) Temperature

47. If another sandbox was set up, which of the following conditions would probably cause *wider and deeper* channels in the soil than was observed in Sandbox 3?

(A) Steeper angles for the sandbox
(B) A greater volume of water during the 15-minute showers every twelve hours
(C) Removal of plants from soil
(D) All of the above

PASSAGE X

In the 1940's, 1950's, and 1960's, the growing field of animal behavior maintained an ongoing debate about the origin of observed behavior in many different animal species. Two extreme viewpoints were at the center of this "Nature vs. Nurture" debate.

Viewpoint 1 (Nature)

Many behaviors or instincts are literally programmed by one or more genes. Genes serve as "blueprints" that enable an individual to carry out a particular stereotyped behavior (Fixed Action Pattern) as soon as the appropriate stimulus (releaser) is observed. Other individuals do not have to be observed performing the behavior. The releasing stimulus need never have been seen before. At first view of the releaser and every time thereafter, the Fixed Action Pattern will be carried out to completion in the exact same way- even if the releaser is removed before the Fixed Action Pattern is finished! Examples include: a) the pecking of baby gulls at the red spot on their mother's bill (which causes the mother gull to regurgitate food), b) song birds producing their species song without ever having heard it before, and c) a male stickle-back fish defending its territory by attacking anything red because other breeding males always have red underbellies.

Viewpoint 2 (Nurture)

Many behaviors are determined by experience and/or learning during an individual's lifetime. Genes provide the limits of the "blank slate" that each individual starts out as, but then various experiences will determine the actual behavior patterns within the individual genetic range of possibilities. In other words, behavior can be modified. Examples include: a) positive ("reward") reinforcement and punishment causing a behavior to increase and decrease (respectively), and b) song birds producing their species song only after having heard it performed by other individuals of their species.

48. A food seeking bluejay captured a distinctively colored butterfly that had a very bad-tasting substance in its tissues. After spitting out the butterfly, that particular bluejay never again tried to capture a similarly colored butterfly. This incident seems to support:

(F) Viewpoint 1.
(G) Viewpoint 2.
(H) both viewpoints.
(J) neither viewpoint, since the incident is irrelevant.

49. The red spot on a mother gull's bill is called a(n):

(A) Fixed Action Pattern.
(B) instinct.
(C) releaser.
(D) stereotyped response.

50. To refute the strict "genetic blueprint" ideas of Viewpoint 1, a scientist could show that:

(F) baby gulls peck at a stick with a red spot on it.
(G) baby gulls will peck at mother gulls' red spot as soon as they hatch out of their eggs.
(H) baby gulls pecking at the red spot happens exactly the same way each time.
(J) baby gulls' accuracy in pecking at mother gulls' red spot improves with practice.

51. Which of the following examples clearly provides support for Viewpoint 1?

(A) A rat reaches the end of a maze by exactly the same route, but finishes faster after each trip through.
(B) Monkey A watches other monkeys wash sweet potatoes before eating them, and then Monkey A always washes sweet potatoes before he eats them.
(C) A male stickleback fish attacks a picture of a red mailbox held in front of his aquarium.
(D) A bird performs its species song after hearing the song only once.

52. If baby chickens peck at grains of food on the ground when hungry, but not as much after they have recently eaten:

(F) this supports Viewpoint 1.
(G) this supports Viewpoint 2.
(H) this does not refer to behavior.
(J) this is irrelevant to the Nature vs. Nurture argument.

53. In some species, it is believed that birds "learn" to fly. This statement is based on observations of young birds fluttering and flapping their wings (a kind of practice) at the nest until they reach the age when flight is possible. In Species X, nestlings were kept in harmless, but tight plastic tubes in which they could not carry out such "practice movements." When they reached their age of flight, they were released. Viewpoint 1 predicts that the birds will fly:

(A) after fluttering their wings for a time.
(B) after watching other individuals flutter their wings.
(C) after watching other individuals flutter and fly.
(D) immediately.

54. A song bird can sing its species song after it hears other individuals of its own species singing. But, if it hears the song from a different species, the bird will not sing the "foreign" song. This suggests that:

(F) genetic "programming" and experience play a role in this species' ability to sing its song.
(G) the song in this species is a Fixed Action Pattern.
(H) song development in this species is strictly a learned behavior with no genetic component.
(J) genes appear to be far more important than experience in this example.

NOTES AND STRATEGIES

SECTION TWO—SCIENCE REASONING PROBLEM-SOLVING

DIRECTIONS: The questions in this section reflect both the format and difficulty range of ACT Science Reasoning questions. You will work through these questions with your instructor in class. Each passage is followed by several questions. After reading a passage, choose the best answer to each question. You may refer to the passages as often as necessary. Answers are page 205.

PASSAGE I

The graph of the medium-thickness line below shows the hearing sensitivity of female moths. The auditory characteristics of certain sounds important to moth survival are also included.

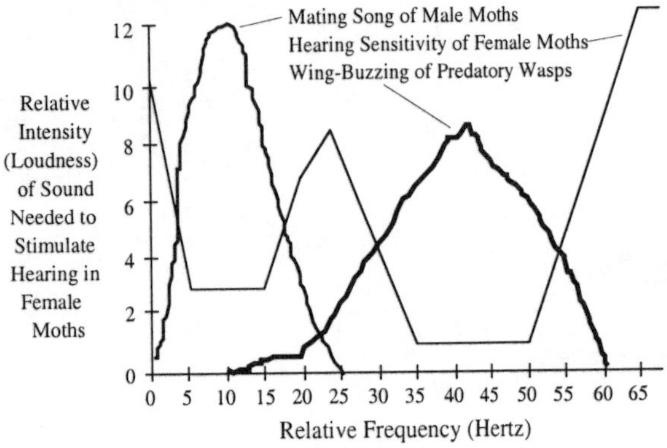

1. According to the graph, female moths are *most sensitive* to sounds between:

   (A) 0-5 hertz.
   (B) 5-15 hertz.
   (C) 20-25 hertz.
   (D) 35-50 hertz.

2. The nervous system of female moths may be set up to allow them to respond in different ways to sounds of different frequencies. Based on the information in the graph, which statement best describes the appropriate responses of female moths?

   (F) Approach sounds between 5-15 hertz, withdraw from sounds between 35-50 hertz.
   (G) Approach sounds between 35-50 hertz, withdraw from sounds between 5-15 hertz.
   (H) Approach sounds between 5-15 hertz and 35-50 hertz.
   (J) Withdraw from sounds between 5-15 hertz and 35-50 hertz.

3. Which statement is supported by the information in the graph?

   (A) The wing-buzzing sounds of wasps occur at a narrower range of frequencies than the range of the male moth mating song.
   (B) The frequency range of the male moth mating song is narrower than the range of wasp wing-buzzing sounds.
   (C) Female moths cannot hear sounds with relative intensities less than 3.
   (D) Male moths are less sensitive to sounds than predatory wasps.

4. Which statement accurately describes the relationship between male moth mating song and female moth hearing sensitivity?

   (F) The frequency range of the male song coincides with the frequency range at which females are maximally sensitive to any sound.
   (G) Females need not be maximally sensitive at the frequency range of the male song because of the extremely high intensity of the song.
   (H) Females cannot hear the male song if its intensity level is less than 10.
   (J) The male song does not extend to an intensity level above 10.

5. If a new species of wasp were introduced into the moths' environment, which wing-buzzing characteristic would make it the most successful predator of female moths?

   (A) Extreme high intensity at relative frequencies between 35-50 hertz
   (B) An intensity level of 7-8 at relative frequencies between 20-25 hertz
   (C) Low intensity at relative frequencies above 60 hertz
   (D) Extreme high intensity at relative frequencies above 60 hertz

6. A "new male" comes to town having a mating song with a frequency range between 20-25 hertz and an intensity level of 4. What are his chances of finding a mate?

   (F) Excellent
   (G) Poor
   (H) Good, if no wasps are present
   (J) Cannot be determined

PASSAGE II

Graph I shows the relationship between the relative rates of activity of enzymes A and B and temperature. Graph II shows the relationship between the relative rates of activity of enzymes A and B and pH.

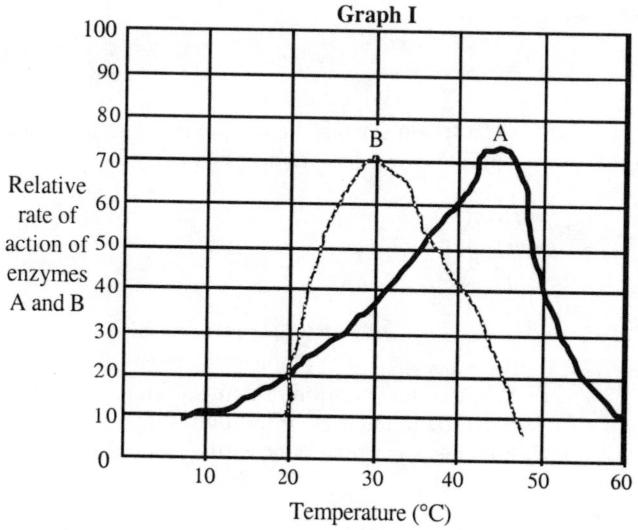

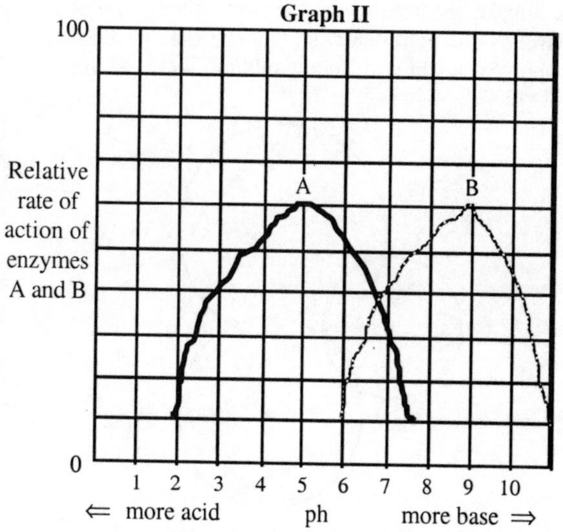

7. Under which conditions is enzyme A most effective?

(A) 40°C and a pH of 5
(B) 45°C and a pH of 5
(C) 45°C and a pH of 9
(D) 50°C and a pH of 9

8. The optimum environment for enzyme B is:

(F) acidic.
(G) basic.
(H) either acidic or basic.
(J) neutral.

9. At which one of the following temperatures do A and B exhibit the same relative rate of action?

(A) 6.9°C
(B) 10°C
(C) 37°C
(D) 47°C

10. At which pH do A and B exhibit the same relative rate of action?

(F) 6.9
(G) 10
(H) 37
(J) 47

11. At what temperature does A have half the activity of B?

(A) 20°C
(B) 25°C
(C) 42°C
(D) 53°C

12. At what temperature does B have half the activity of A?

(F) 20°C
(G) 30°C
(H) 42°C
(J) 53°C

13. Over what range of pH will both A and B be active?

(A) 1 to 3
(B) 3 to 6
(C) 6 to 8
(D) 8 to 10

14. At what pH will A and B both be at their maximum activity?

(F) 2
(G) 5
(H) 8.5
(J) No such pH

PASSAGE III

A seismographic station can detect how far away an earthquake occurred, but not the direction. Any given station can therefore report that the epicenter of an earthquake occurred somewhere on the circumference of a circle. The map below shows the data recorded for an earthquake at three different seismic stations, or: A, B, and C.

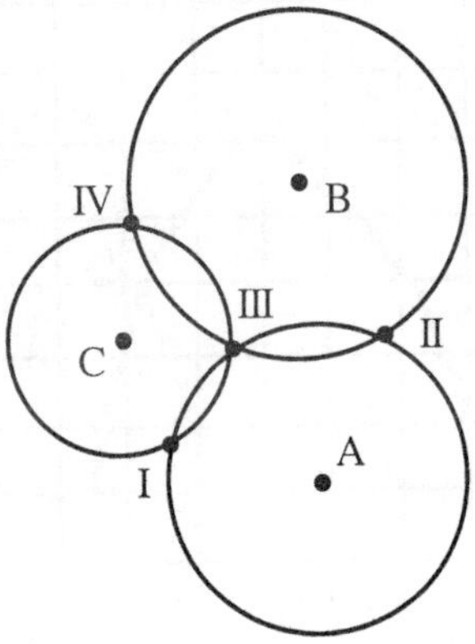

15. Which station was closest to the epicenter?

(A) A
(B) B
(C) C
(D) Can't be determined from data

16. Given the information from stations A and B only, which site(s) is (are) possible for the epicenter?

(F) I only
(G) III only
(H) II and III
(J) I and III

17. Given the information from stations A and C only, which site(s) is (are) possible for the epicenter?

(A) I only
(B) III only
(C) II and III
(D) I and III

18. Given the information from all three stations, which site(s) is (are) possible for the epicenter?

(F) I only
(G) III only
(H) I and III
(J) II and III

19. If a fourth seismic station gave a report, at what point must its curve meet A's curve?

(A) I
(B) II
(C) III
(D) IV

20. If a fourth seismic station gave a report, at what point must its curve meet C's curve?

(F) I
(G) II
(H) III
(J) IV

21. What is the minimum number of points where two circumferences from two seismic stations, both measuring the same earthquake, can meet?

(A) 1
(B) 2
(C) 3
(D) Infinite

PASSAGE IV

A scientist investigated the number of fossils per cubic foot through several feet in a quarry. The results are presented below.

Layer	Fish	Shells	Plants	Land Reptile
1 (TOP)	0	0	3	1
2	0	1	8	2
3	1	10	4	0
4	5	18	1	0
5	7	20	0	0

22. When was the site most likely above water?

(F) During the formation of Layers 1 and 2
(G) During the formation of Layers 2 and 3
(H) During the formation of Layers 1 and 4
(J) During the formation of Layer 3

23. Was the site most recently above or below water?

(A) Above
(B) Below
(C) Borderline
(D) Not enough data

NOTES AND STRATEGIES

24. What assumption is made to relate the fossil record to the environment?

(F) No assumption
(G) That fossils don't affect the environment
(H) That the fossils are mostly from plants and animals that lived in the region
(J) That only animal fossils are important

25. No trilobite fossils were found. This proves:

(A) that no trilobites were in the region.
(B) that the layers were formed before trilobites existed.
(C) that the layers were formed after the trilobites died out.
(D) nothing about the presence of the trilobite in the region.

26. A nautilus shell was found in Layer 3. This proves that:

(F) Layer 3 formed while the nautilus still existed.
(G) Layer 3 is newer than Layer 2.
(H) Layer 3 is older than Layer 2.
(J) the nautilus once lived on land.

27. Where will the newest layer form?

(A) Under Layer 4
(B) Over Layer 1
(C) Across all the layers
(D) Layers no longer form

PASSAGE V

To investigate the factors affecting the rate at which starch is broken down to sugar by the digestive enzyme salivary amylase, two experiments were performed. In both experiments, starch (in the form of a cracker) was mixed in a beaker with the enzyme, and the samples were removed every three minutes. Dipping special sugar indicators in the sample revealed the presence of starch in a sample (indicating that the cracker had not yet been completely digested).

Experiment 1

To test the effects of different pH levels on enzyme activity rate, one cracker and a standard amount of enzyme were placed in three beakers, each containing buffers of different pH. This procedure was repeated using standard amounts of water in place of the enzyme. All tests were carried out at optimal temperature. Starch and sugar levels (starch/sugar) from selected samples are shown in Table 1.

Table 1

CONTENTS OF BEAKERS	APPROXIMATE pH LEVELS	LEVELS OF STARCH/SUGAR After 3 min.	After 9 min.	After 15 min.	After 60 min.
cracker + enzyme + buffer	5	high/none	high/none	high/low	moderate/moderate
	7	moderate/moderate	low/high	none/high	none/high
	9	high/none	high/none	high/low	moderate/moderate
cracker + water + buffer	5	high/none	high/none	high/none	high/none
	7	high/none	high/none	high/none	high/none
	9	high/none	high/none	high/none	high/none

Experiment 2

To test the effects of temperature on enzyme activity rate, one cracker and a standard amount of enzyme were placed in 3 beakers, each kept at different temperatures. This was also repeated using standard amounts of water in place of the enzyme. All tests were carried out at optimal pH. Starch and sugar levels (starch/sugar) from selected samples are shown in Table 2.

Table 2

CONTENTS OF BEAKERS	TEMP-ERATURES	LEVELS OF STARCH/SUGAR *After 3 min.*	*After 9 min.*	*After 15 min.*	*After 60 min.*
cracker + enzyme	25°C	high/none	high/none	high/low	moderate/moderate
	37°C	moderate/moderate	low/high	none/high	none/high
	45°C	high/none	high/none	high/low	moderate/moderate
cracker + water	25°C	high/none	high/none	high/none	high/none
	37°C	high/none	high/none	high/none	high/none
	45°C	high/none	high/none	high/none	high/none

28. Under what conditions does salivary amylase appear to work best?

(F) Any pH greater than 5 and any temperature greater than 25°C
(G) Any pH greater than 5 and any temperature less than 45°C
(H) pH: 9 and temperature: 37°C
(J) pH: 7 and temperature: 37°C

29. The ingredient used as a control for both experiments is the:

(A) cracker.
(B) water.
(C) enzyme.
(D) starch/sugar level.

30. Which of the following hypotheses is supported by the results of Experiment 1?

(F) At the appropriate pH, water can break down starch, but at a slower rate than salivary amylase can.
(G) At any one-time interval, no differences in the effects of the three buffers on salivary amylase activity should be detectable.
(H) Salivary amylase can show activity at each of the three pH levels tested.
(J) The duration of time in which starch and enzyme remain in the beakers should have no effect on the amount of sugar produced.

31. Which of the following experimental designs would test the hypothesis that enzyme concentration can affect the rate of starch digestion?

(A) Using the same pH, temperature, and enzyme levels in all beakers, test additional samples at 90 minutes, 120 minutes, and 240 minutes.
(B) Using different pH, temperature, and enzyme levels in all beakers, test additional samples at 90 minutes, 120 minutes, and 240 minutes.
(C) Using the same pH and temperatures in all beakers, test additional samples with the enzyme at $\frac{1}{2}$ • strength, 2 • strength, and 4 • strength.
(D) Using the same pH, temperature, and enzyme levels in all beakers, test additional samples after stirring for 3 minutes, 9 minutes, 15 minutes, and 60 minutes.

32. In Experiment 2, an additional beaker was tested at 70°C (cracker + enzyme). After 60 minutes, the sample showed high levels of starch and no sugar. Which of the following best explains this result?

(F) All the starch was destroyed at this high temperature.
(G) The enzyme does not work at all at this high temperature.
(H) Starch cannot be detected at this high temperature.
(J) Iodine and sugar indicators cannot function properly at this high temperature.

33. On the basis of the results of Experiment 1, what would probably occur if Experiment 2 were carried out at a pH level of 5?

(A) Digestion of starch to sugar would slowly begin in the beakers containing cracker + water.
(B) Overall, digestion of starch to sugar would probably take place less efficiently.
(C) Overall, digestion of starch to sugar would probably take place more efficiently.
(D) Results would not change.

PASSAGE VI

A chemistry student wishes to study weight relationships between compounds before and after they take part in reactions. Two experiments were conducted to investigate two different reactions. The reactions are shown below, together with the amount (grams) of each substance before and after each reaction has proceeded. Equations are balanced to show the number of each type of atom before and after the reactions.

Experiment 1					
	NaBr +	$AgNO_3$	⇒	AgBr +	$NaNO_3$
Initial Wt.	103	170		0	0
Final Wt.	0	0		188	85

Experiment 2						
	Na_2CO_3 +	2HCl	⇒	2NaCl +	H_2O (g) +	CO_2
Initial Wt.	106	72		0	0	(?)
Final Wt.	0	0		117	18	(?)

(The student has measured the quantities he could, but was unable to weigh the CO_2 because it is a gas. Since it is a gas, he assumes it has negligible weight.)

34. In Experiment 1, the data indicate that after the reaction has proceeded:

(F) all of the Na originally present has been converted to Ag.
(G) there are fewer molecules of $NaNO_3$ than there were molecules of $AgNO_3$ at the outset.
(H) no NaBr remains.
(J) no AgBr remains.

35. In Experiment 1, the data indicate that for this reaction, there is conservation:

(A) of mass only.
(B) of mass and atoms.
(C) of $AgNO_3$.
(D) None of the above

36. In Experiment 2, the mass of the weighed products is:

(F) 0.
(G) less than the mass of reactants.
(H) equal to the mass of reactants.
(J) greater than the mass of reactants.

37. Experiment 2 differs from Experiment 1 in that:

(A) the number of atoms is not conserved.
(B) the reaction does not go to completion.
(C) there are no ionic compounds involved.
(D) gas is evolved.

38. Assuming the student is right in neglecting the weight of one of the products in Experiment 2, he can conclude from the data that:

(F) mass is consumed as the reaction proceeds.
(G) mass is produced as the reaction proceeds.
(H) energy is consumed as the reaction proceeds.
(J) mass is conserved as the reaction proceeds.

39. The student is advised of a means to weigh the CO_2 gas produced in the reaction, and finds this weight to be 61 g. The student can now state that the two experiments:

(A) lead to similar conclusions: neither mass nor atoms are conserved.
(B) lead to similar conclusions: both mass and atoms are conserved.
(C) lead to different conclusions: the number of molecules is not the same for the reactants as for the products.
(D) lead to different conclusions: gases have negligible weight.

PASSAGE VII

A series of three experiments was designed to investigate the interrelationships between various factors known to influence gases (temperature, pressure, volume, and the number of moles). Commonly used units for these factors include the following: temperature (degrees Kelvin), pressure (atmospheres), and volume (liters).

Experiment 1

A gas at 200°K and a volume of 0.30 liters was found to have a pressure of 0.40 atm. After the temperature was raised to 400°K while keeping the volume the same, the pressure was found to be 0.80 atm.

NOTES AND STRATEGIES

Experiment 2

A gas at 200°K had a pressure of 0.50 atm. when its volume was 1 liter. Its volume was then increased to 2 liters at constant temperature. The resulting pressure was 0.25 atm.

Experiment 3

Two moles of a gas were found to occupy 44.8 liters at 1 atm. pressure and 273° K. Four moles of the same gas are added to the system with temperature and pressure held constant, resulting in a new volume of 134.4 liters.

40. The results of Experiment 1 support the hypothesis that:

(F) the pressure of the gas is proportional to its volume at constant temperature.
(G) the volume of the gas is proportional to its temperature at constant pressure.
(H) the pressure of a gas is proportional to its temperature at constant volume.
(J) None of the above

41. The results of Experiment 2 support the hypothesis that if the temperature of a gas is held constant:

(A) pressure increases as volume increases.
(B) pressure decreases as volume increases.
(C) pressure does not depend strongly on volume.
(D) None of the above.

42. The result of Experiment 3 supports the hypothesis that with pressure and temperature held constant:

(F) volume varies inversely with the number of moles of gas.
(G) volume varies directly with the number of moles of gas.
(H) adding additional gas raises the volume to a maximum value of 134.4 liters.
(J) None of the above.

43. An experimenter put 0.08 moles of gas into a 4-liter flask at 273°K and 0.448 atm. pressure. She allowed 0.02 moles of the gas to escape, and put the remaining gas into a smaller flask that caused the pressure to remain at 0.448 atm. pressure, while the temperature was kept constant as well. According to Experiment 3, the volume of the smaller flask must be:

(A) 0.06 liter.
(B) 0.448 liters.
(C) 3 liters.
(D) Cannot be determined.

44. Six moles of a gas originally at 0.1 atm. pressure and 273°K occupy a volume of 13.4 liters. The temperature is then changed to 300°K and the volume changed to 10.0 liters. To predict the final pressure on the six moles of gas, a student should use the results of Experiment(s):

(F) 1.
(G) 2.
(H) 1 and 2.
(J) 1 and 3.

45. The final pressure of the gas described in question #44 above will be:

(A) less than 0.1 atm. pressure.
(B) equal to 0.1 atm. pressure.
(C) greater than 0.1 atm pressure.
(D) Cannot be determined.

PASSAGE VIII

Using electrical circuits, three experiments were performed to investigate the relationship between voltage (volts), resistance (ohms) (total resistance equals sum of individual resistances), and current (amperes.) Each experiment was set up with the following circuit design:

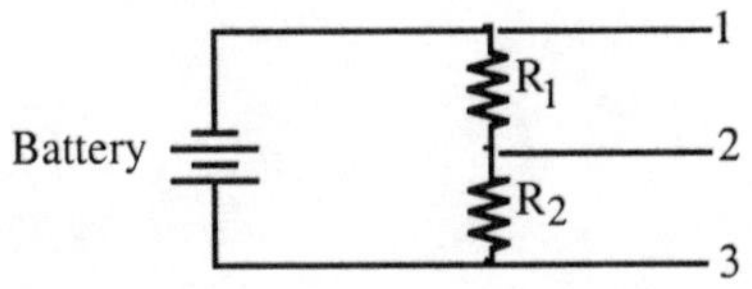

Experiment 1

Using a 6-volt battery (far left), and two resistors (R_1 and R_2), each equaling 1,000 ohms, the voltages from point 1 to point 2, and from point 2 to point 3, were found to be 3 volts.

Experiment 2

When the battery voltage was increased to 12 volts, and the resistors were kept the same (1,000 ohms each), the voltages from point 1 to point 2, and from point 2 to point 3, were found to be 6 volts each.

Experiment 3

Using the original 6-volt battery, R_1 was replaced with a resistor that measured 2,000 ohms. The voltage measured from point 1 to point 2 was 4 volts; it measured 2 volts between point 2 and point 3.

46. Judging from the results in Experiment 1 and Experiment 2, if the battery voltage were changed to 1.5 volts, what voltage would be expected between point 1 and point 2?

(F) 0.75 volts
(G) 1.5 volts
(H) 3.0 volts
(J) 6.0 volts

47. The experimenter studies this measurement, as well as those made earlier in Experiments 1, 2, and 3, and hypothesizes that:

(A) voltage measured across a resistor is inversely proportional to the value of that resistor.
(B) voltage measured across a resistor is directly proportional to the value of that resistor.
(C) voltage measured across a resistor is not related to the value of that resistor.
(D) voltage measured across a resistor equals the battery voltage.

48. When the experimenter recorded the current in the circuit of Experiment 1, it measured 0.003 amp. In Experiment 3, however, the current measured 0.002 amp. These results show that current and total resistances are:

(F) directly proportional.
(G) inversely proportional.
(H) equal.
(J) unrelated.

49. Which of the following formulas for the current in the circuit best summarizes the above results? (The battery voltage is given by V_B and the total resistance is given by R.)

(A) V_bR
(B) $\frac{R}{V_b}$
(C) $\frac{V_b}{R}$
(D) $V_b + R$

50. A new circuit is set up, similar in design to those in the experiments. The battery voltage and the size of the resistors are unknown, but the current measures 0.001 amp. If the battery voltage is doubled and one of the two resistors is replaced with one having a smaller value, which answer most accurately describes the new current?

(F) It will be smaller than 0.001.
(G) It will be unchanged.
(H) It will be greater than 0.001.
(J) It cannot be determined without more information.

51. Which of the following single changes to Experiment 2 would produce a current of 0.004 amp.?

(A) Decrease the voltage to 8 volts.
(B) Increase the resistance to 3,000 ohms.
(C) Neither change will create a current of 0.004 amp.
(D) Either change will create a current of 0.004 amp.

PASSAGE IX

The process of biological evolution was hypothesized by Jean Baptiste Lamarck before Charles Darwin was born. Aspects of some of their ideas are presented below.

Lamarckism

Observations of the fossil record led Lamarck to believe that several lines of descent led to Nature's broad diversity of organisms. Old fossils and more recent fossils showed patterns leading to the characteristics of modern species. He believed that newer forms were more complex and more "perfectly" adapted to their environment. New adaptations could arise as the environment changed. Organs of the body that were used to cope with the environment became stronger and larger, while those not used deteriorated. For example, giraffes stretching their necks to reach higher leaves would develop longer necks. In addition, such changes in structure could then be passed on to offspring (these acquired characteristics could be inherited).

Darwinism

Based on the fossil and geologic record, Darwin also came to believe that various modern species were related through descent from common ancestors. He also noted that the great diversity of organisms that he observed during his travels were all very well adapted to their environments. The adaptations, however, did not come about through "coping" or usage. Instead, individuals from a population can each show slight genetic or "heritable" differences (variability) in a trait. If such differences, by chance alone, give the individual some reproductive advantage, i.e., he or she can successfully produce more offspring than other members of the population, then more individuals with that trait will make up the next generation. Through this "natural selection" of individuals with characteristics that give them a slight advantage in their particular environment, species appear to become very well suited to their natural world. However, "perfection" is not a useful term since the environment is constantly changing. The adaptations that are advantageous "today" may not be advantageous "tomorrow" under different conditions.

52. A major difference between Lamarck and Darwin relates to their views on:

(F) the diversity of organisms in the natural world.
(G) the significance of fossils.
(H) the importance of adaptations to the environment.
(J) the way adaptations come about.

53. Which viewpoint supports the idea that present-day species are descended from earlier forms?

(A) Lamarckism
(B) Darwinism
(C) Both viewpoints
(D) Neither viewpoint

54. Which statement might be used by a Darwinist to explain the extinction of a species?

(F) The environment changed, and not enough individuals had traits or adaptations well suited to the new conditions.
(G) The environment changed, and body parts could not be manipulated enough to adapt to new conditions.
(H) As the environment changed, the individuals present were not "perfect" enough.
(J) As the environment changed, there was no "natural selection."

55. One way that Darwin might dispute the Lamarckian idea of inheriting acquired characteristics would be to point out that:

(A) giraffes with short necks may do just as well as those with long necks.
(B) giraffes that break a leg and walk around on three legs all their lives still do not produce three-legged offspring.
(C) giraffes had shorter necks millions of years ago.
(D) giraffes that break a leg would not be able to reach the highest leaves.

56. Many species of moles live underground, in the dark. These species often have small, almost nonfunctional eyes. Which statement(s) would a Lamarckian thinker use to explain this phenomenon?

(F) Disuse of eyes in the dark led to their deterioration in mole species.
(G) Eye deterioration can be transferred to a mole's genes, which are then passed on to the next generation.
(H) Both statements
(J) Neither statement

57. Which factor is vital to Darwin's ideas, but not to those of Lamarck?

(A) The fossil record
(B) An examination of modern species
(C) The inheritance of adaptations
(D) Chance

NOTES AND STRATEGIES

58. A few individuals in a population have an adaptation that enables them to tolerate extremely cold temperatures. In their lifetimes, the environment never reaches such extremes. If all other traits are the same among individuals, what would a Darwinist predict about the number of offspring left in the next generation by these individuals, compared to the number left by other members of the population?

(F) These individuals will leave approximately the same number of offspring.
(G) These individuals will leave more offspring.
(H) These individuals will leave fewer offspring.
(J) These individuals will probably not leave any offspring.

PASSAGE X

How did life originate on the planet earth? Two opposing views are presented.

Scientist 1

The idea that earth could have given rise to life independently is mistaken. Life on this planet must have come from elsewhere for several reasons. First of all, complex life appears very suddenly in the geological record. Secondly, all life on earth has a very similar biochemistry. If life originated on earth, one would expect regional variations in biochemistry, similar to the variations in species spread over large areas. Finally, the time when life first appeared in the geological record was also a time when large numbers of meteorites struck the earth. The meteorites must have caused life to appear on the earth. The simplest hypothesis is that the meteorites brought life with them.

Scientist 2

Life need not have been imported from outer space. The chemicals required for life existed on the surface of the earth at the time life first appeared. The fact that all life has a similar biochemistry can be explained by considering that any group of chemicals that won the race to life would probably have used the almost-living as food. Since we can offer explanations for what happened without relying on a meteorite of unknown composition that might have fallen to earth, we should stick to hypotheses that have fewer unknowns.

59. Which of the following is an assumption of Scientist 1?

(A) Complex life forms can develop quickly.
(B) Meteorites bum up as soon as they hit the earth's atmosphere.
(C) There is a cause-and-effect relationship between meteors falling and the origin of life.
(D) The changes on the earth's surface due to the presence of life attracted meteor showers.

60. Which of the following, if true, strengthens Scientist 2's argument the most?

(F) Only 5% more meteors than normal fell on the earth during the time life began.
(G) Only 5% of the meteorites studied contained organic molecules.
(H) A simulation of early earth chemistry showed the spontaneous formation of complex biomolecules.
(J) Meteorites containing amoebas have been found.

61. Which of the following, if true, strengthens Scientist 1's argument the most?

(A) Only 5% more meteors than normal fell on the earth during the time life began.
(B) Only 5% of the meteorites studied contained organic molecules.
(C) A simulation of early earth chemistry showed the spontaneous formation of complex biomolecules.
(D) Meteorites containing amoebas have been found.

62. Which explanation of the similar biochemistry of all life on earth would Scientist 1 most likely agree with?

(F) A single chemical pathway to life exists.
(G) Life arose from a single source.
(H) Life is not varied.
(J) Meteors are simple.

63. Which explanation of the similar biochemistry of all life on earth would Scientist 2 most likely agree with?

(A) A single chemical pathway to life exists.
(B) Life arose from a single source.
(C) Life is not varied.
(D) Meteors are simple.

64. Which scientist would be likely to disagree with the idea that life on different planets could have different biochemistries?

(F) Scientist 1
(G) Scientist 2
(H) Both
(J) Neither

65. Which of the following questions would be the most difficult for Scientist 1 to defend his theory against?

(A) Why was there more meteorite activity earlier in earth's history?
(B) Why haven't other meteors brought other life based on a different biochemistry?
(C) Why did complex life emerge suddenly?
(D) Why should meteor activity have any connection to the origin of life?

66. Could Scientist 2 believe that life exists on other planets without affecting his hypothesis?

(F) Yes, as long as he believes that life elsewhere has a different biochemistry.
(G) Yes, because wherever the chemicals required for life exist, life can begin.
(H) No, because then he has to admit that meteorites brought life from these planets.
(J) No, because then he has to admit that meteorites that came from pieces of similar planets brought life to the earth.

PASSAGE XI

What will the end of the universe be like? Two opposing views are presented.

Scientist 1

The universe will die out with a whimper because the energy of the big bang that created the universe will spread itself out over larger and larger regions of space. Since there is only so much energy in the universe, every cubic foot must hold, on the average, less energy as time goes on. In the end everything will get so cold that all motion will stop. That will be the true end of time.

Scientist 2

The idea that the universe will spread itself too thin and freeze is seriously flawed. Such theories do not take into account the gravitational attractions of the bits of matter in the universe for each other. Gravity can act as a cosmic glue to keep the universe from dissolving into nothingness.

67. Which of the following is a major assumption of Scientist 1?

(A) All matter consists of atoms.
(B) There is a limited amount of energy in the universe.
(C) Gravity doesn't exist in interstellar space.
(D) The universe is contracting.

68. Which of the following facts, if true, does not help Scientist 2's hypothesis?

(F) It is shown that the galaxies are moving away from each other with a constant speed.
(G) It is shown that the galaxies are moving towards each other with a constant speed.
(H) It is shown that the galaxies are moving towards each other with a constant acceleration.
(J) It is shown that the galaxies are not moving at all relative to each other.

69. It has been calculated that if the universe has a mass greater than or equal to m, then the universe will eventually collapse on itself. Scientist 1 would be most likely to say that the mass of the universe:

(A) is equal to m.
(B) is less than or equal to m.
(C) is greater than m.
(D) is less than m.

70. If Scientist 2 claims that the universe is contracting, what would he expect the average temperature of the universe to be ten billion years from now?

(F) Higher than now
(G) Lower than now
(H) Same as now
(J) No comparison possible

71. What must be true about the energy content of the universe if Scientist 1 is correct?

(A) It is increasing.
(B) It is decreasing.
(C) It is a constant.
(D) It increased at the moment of the big bang, and decreased afterwards.

72. What would happen if the forces moving the galaxies farther out were exactly balanced by forces pulling them together?

(F) The galaxies would stop moving.
(G) The galaxies would move in a straight line with constant speed.
(H) The galaxies would move in a straight line with constant acceleration.
(J) The galaxies would move back and forth in a straight line.

PASSAGE XII

How old is the earth? Two opposing views are presented.

Scientist 1

The earth is approximately five billion years old. We know this to be true because of radioactive dating. Some chemical elements are unstable and will fall apart into smaller pieces overtime. This disintegration occurs over a period of time that is very regular for the particular element. In general, we talk about the half-life of the element, which is the time necessary for one-half of the material to disintegrate. This time is constant whether we have an ounce or a ton of the material. So, by measuring the relative amounts of the material left and the disintegration products, we can form an accurate idea of how old the earth is by determining how many half-lives have occurred.

Scientist 2

The argument that supports the hypothesis that the earth is only five billion years old is seriously flawed. What the argument fails to take into account is that the earth is the constant recipient of a shower of cosmic debris in the form of meteorites. These meteorites replenish the stock of radioactive material on the surface of the earth, making it seem as though the earth has gone through fewer half-lives than it really has. Therefore, all estimates of the age of the earth based on radioactive dating are too low.

73. Which of the following is a major assumption of Scientist 1?

(A) The earth has life that recycles carbon-14.
(B) The earth is five billion years old.
(C) The radioactive material was formed at the same time as the earth.
(D) There is no longer any radioactivity on the earth.

74. Which of the following is a major assumption of Scientist 2?

(F) The meteorites that land on the earth are radioactive.
(G) Few meteorites have landed on the earth.
(H) The earth is greater than five billion years old.
(J) The earth is highly radioactive.

75. Which of the following, if true, would best refute Scientist 2's argument?

(A) Recent meteorites have been found to be radioactive.
(B) The earth has a greater amount of radioactive material on the surface than in the mantle.
(C) The earth's orbit intersects the orbits of a number of meteorites.
(D) Few meteorites have been found to contain radioactive material.

76. Which of the following would be most likely if Scientist 2's hypothesis were correct?

(F) The amount of radioactive material and its disintegration products on the earth has decreased over time.
(G) The amount of radioactive material and its disintegration products has increased over time.
(H) The amount of radioactive material and its disintegration products has stayed essentially the same over time.
(J) The earth will reach a critical mass and explode.

77. Which of the following would be most likely if Scientist 1's hypothesis were correct?

(A) The amount of radioactive material and its disintegration products has decreased over time.
(B) The amount of radioactive material and its disintegration products increase over time.
(C) The amount of radioactive material and its disintegration products has stayed essentially the same over time.
(D) The earth will reach a critical mass and explode.

78. Which of the following conditions, if true, would prevent an estimation of the earth's age by Scientist 1's method?

(F) No radioactive disintegration has occurred.
(G) Only some of the radioactive material has disintegrated.
(H) Eighty percent of the radioactive material has disintegrated.
(J) All of the radioactive material has disintegrated.

SECTION THREE—SCIENCE REASONING QUIZZES

DIRECTIONS: This section contains three Science Reasoning quizzes. Each passage is followed by several questions. After reading a passage, choose the best answer to each question. You may refer to the passages as often as necessary. Complete each quiz while being timed. Answers are on page 206.

QUIZ I (10 questions; 9 minutes)

PASSAGE I

The ecological pyramid below shows the relative biomass* of organisms at each trophic feeding level of a marine food chain.

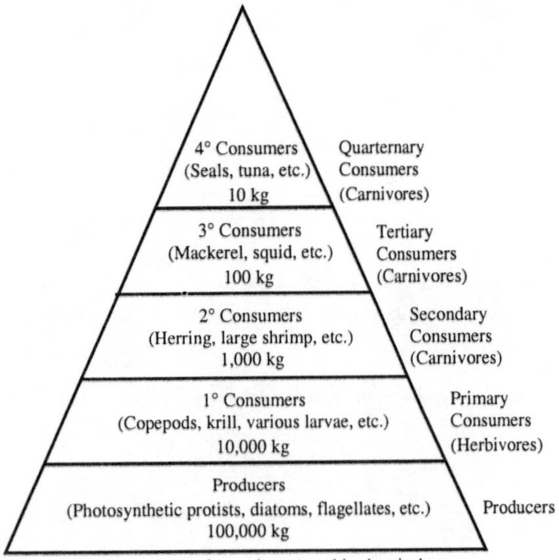

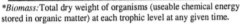

**Biomass:* Total dry weight of organisms (useable chemical energy stored in organic matter) at each trophic level at any given time.

1. According to the diagram, the trophic level with the largest relative biomass is the:

(A) 4° consumers.
(B) 1° consumers.
(C) producers.
(D) 3° and 2° consumers.

2. From the information in the diagram, one can conclude that at any given time:

(F) 10 seals may be found for every mackerel.
(G) The relative dry weight of all carnivores combined is far greater than that of the herbivores alone.
(H) Only 1% of all producers live long enough to be eaten by a mackerel.
(J) The relative dry weight of every consumer trophic level is usually less than that of the trophic level on which they feed.

3. Organisms from which trophic level are most likely to be found near the water surface where light can penetrate?

(A) 4° consumers
(B) producers
(C) 2° consumers
(D) 3° consumers

4. If there were an additional trophic level of carnivores (5° consumers), its relative biomass at any given time would be approximately:

(F) 11 kg.
(G) 1,000,000 kg.
(H) 1 kg.
(J) 111 kg.

5. The best explanation for biomass being measured as dry weight is:

(A) If water weight were included, efficiency ratios at each trophic level would be unpredictable.
(B) Body fluids contribute little to the mass of marine organisms.
(C) Water molecules contain little or no useable chemical energy.
(D) Each trophic level contains a different amount of water.

PASSAGE II

The table below shows various characteristics of different layers of the atmosphere.

Approximate Altitude (km)	*Layers of the Atmosphere*	*Approximate Mean Temperature (° C)*	*Clouds*
60,000			
6,000			
	THERMOSPHERE		
600		1200	
80		–90	
	MESOSPHERE		
50		–3	
	STRATOSPHERE		Cirrus
12		–50	
5	TROPOSPHERE		Cirrostratus Altostratus Nimbostratus
0		18	

6. Which statement accurately describes the relationship between the approximate altitude and the approximate mean temperature of the layers of the atmosphere?

   (A) As altitude increases, temperature increases.
   (B) As altitude increases, temperature decreases.
   (C) As altitude increases, temperature first decreases then continuously increases.
   (D) As altitude increases, temperature first decreases, then increases, then decreases, and then increases.

7. Based on the information in the table, the atmospheric layer with the narrowest range of altitude is:

   (F) thermosphere.
   (G) troposphere.
   (H) mesosphere.
   (J) stratosphere.

8. The type of cloud(s) most likely to consist of ice crystals is(are):

   (A) nimbostratus only.
   (B) nimbostratus and altostratus.
   (C) cirrus and cirrostratus.
   (D) cirrostratus only.

9. The absorption of solar heat energy increases as the gases of the atmosphere become rarefied. The layer of the atmosphere that appears most rarefied is the:

   (F) thermosphere.
   (G) mesosphere.
   (H) stratosphere.
   (J) troposphere.

10. According to the table, which atmospheric layer shows a decrease in temperature of approximately 3 degrees for every 1-kilometer increase in altitude?

    (A) thermosphere
    (B) mesosphere
    (C) stratosphere
    (D) troposphere

QUIZ II (10 questions; 9 minutes)

PASSAGE I

The chart below shows in outline form a common means of analyzing a sample solution for various cations (positive ions). Ions above the horizontal arrows are those that are suspected to be present in the sample solution; the substances in the boxes are the reagents added as tests (0.3 M H^+ is acidic, NH_4OH is alkaline); the products shown next to the arrows pointing downward are solid precipitates resulting from the tests. Tests for specific ions need not always start from the beginning of the sequence.

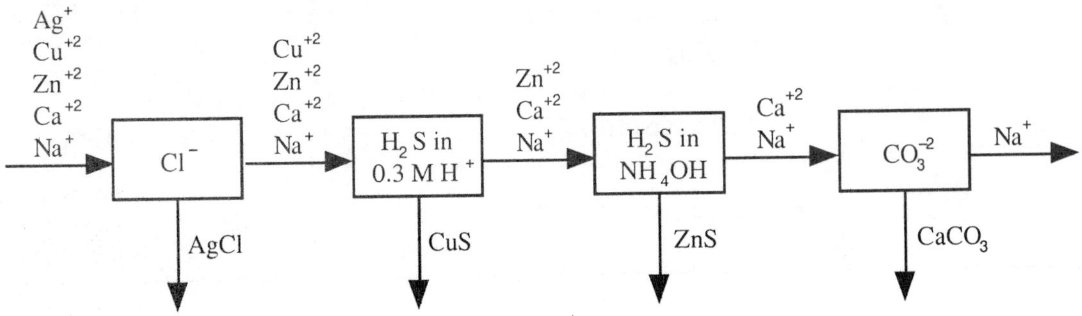

1. According to the chart, if silver (Ag) is present in the sample, it will be indicated by a precipitate of:

   (A) AgCl.
   (B) Ag.
   (C) CuS.
   (JD ZnS.

2. If a solution containing silver (Ag) nitrate and cupric (Cu) nitrate is tested according to this scheme, an experimenter will:

   (F) first observe AgCl on treatment with Cl^-, and next observe CuS on treatment with H_2S.
   (G) first observe CuS on treatment with Cl^-, and next observe AgCl on treatment with H_2S.
   (H) first observe $CaCO_3$ on treatment with CO_3^{-2}, and next observe AgCl on treatment with Cl^-.
   (J) observe no reactions, since the scheme does not test for nitrate.

3. A student is told that an unknown solution may contain no positive ions except Cu^{+2} or Zn^{+2}, but not both. The minimum number of tests that must be run in order to confirm the composition is:

   (A) 1.
   (B) 2.
   (C) 3.
   (D) 4.

4. Which statement is most correct concerning the separation of Cu^{+2} from Zn^{+2} in the same solution?

   (F) Completely different test reagents are used in each of the two steps.
   (G) The same test reagents are used in each of the two steps.
   (H) The same test reagents are used, but the first step must be in an alkaline environment while the second step must be in an acidic environment.
   (J) The same test reagents are used, but the first step must be in an acidic environment while the second step must be in an alkaline environment.

5. A clear solution is found, by a method not discussed here, to contain chloride ion (Cl^-). From the information given here, what ion could not be present in the solution?

   (A) Carbonate (CO^{-2})
   (B) Cupric (Cu^{+2})
   (C) Silver (Ag^+)
   (D) Zinc (Zn^{+2})

PASSAGE II

The chart below shows the flavor preferences of white-tailed deer when offered various fluids to drink at different ages.

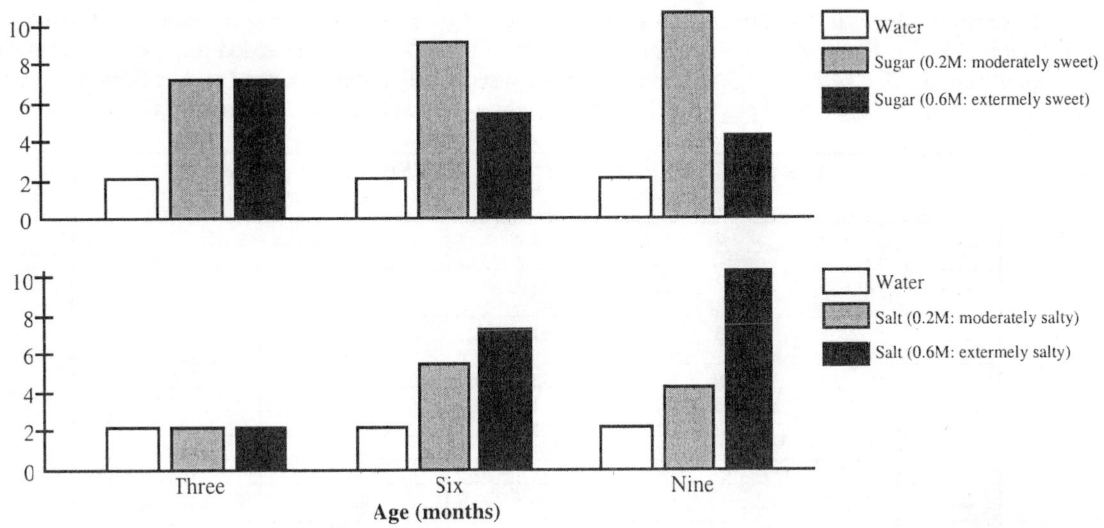

6. Which category on the chart shows no preference between water and the experimental flavor?

(F) Three months of age/sugar
(G) Six months of age/salt
(H) Three months of age/salt
(J) Nine months of age/sugar

7. Which statement about white-tailed deer is supported by the information in the chart?

(A) As age increases, the preference for all tested sugars increases.
(B) As age increases, the preference for all tested salts increases.
(C) As age increases, differences between sugars cannot be detected, and differences between salts cannot be detected.
(D) As age increases, differences between sugars can be detected, and differences between salts can be detected.

8. Which of the following conclusions about water is *not* consistent with the data presented in the chart?

(A) Water is never preferred to any tested flavors.
(B) Before the age of six months, white-tailed deer cannot taste the difference between water and sugar or between water and salt.
(C) At the age of three months, both salty fluids are equally preferred to water.
(D) As age increases, the volume of water swallowed remains the same.

9. Based on the trends shown in the chart, which of the following predictions is most reasonable for one-year-old white-tailed deer?

(A) Moderately sweet and moderately salty will be most preferred.
(B) Extremely sweet and extremely salty will be most preferred.
(C) Moderately sweet and extremely salty will be most preferred.
(D) Extremely sweet and moderately salty will be most preferred.

10. The flavor preference that fluctuates most irregularly with age is:

(F) moderately salty.
(G) moderately sweet.
(H) extremely salty.
(J) extremely sweet.

QUIZ III (11 questions; 9 minutes)

PASSAGE I

The table below shows the first three "ionization energies" for the atoms hydrogen through potassium. The first ionization energy, "E_1," is the energy (in kilocalories per mole of atoms) that must be added in order to remove the first electron from the atom. "E_2" is the energy required to remove a second electron once the first has been removed, and "E_3" is the energy needed to remove a third electron. If an atom lacks a second or third electron, no value is given in the table.

IONIZATION ENERGIES OF THE ELEMENTS (kcal/mole)

Atomic No.	*Element*	E_1	E_2	E_3
1	H	313.6	-	-
2	He	566.8	1254	-
3	Li	124.3	1744	2823
4	Be	214.9	419.9	3548
5	B	191.3	580.0	874.5
6	C	259.6	562.2	1104
7	N	335.1	682.8	1094
8	O	314.0	810.6	1267
9	F	401.8	806.7	1445
10	Ne	497.2	947.2	1500
11	Na	118.5	1091	1652
12	Mg	176.3	346.6	1848
13	Al	138.0	434.1	655.9
14	Si	187.9	376.8	771.7
15	P	241.8	453.2	695.5
16	S	238.9	540	807
17	Cl	300.0	548.9	920.2
18	Ar	363.4	637	943.3
19	K	100.1	733.6	1100

1. For a given element, the ionization energies increase in the order:

(F) E_3, E_2, E_1.
(G) E_2, E_1, E_3.
(H) E_1, E_2, E_3.
(J) Order varies.

2. A student suspects that there may be an atom for which the second ionization energy is roughly twice that of the first, and the third is roughly twice that of the second. Which of the following atoms fits this relationship the best?

(A) Be
(B) C
(C) Ne
(D) Ar

3. As atomic number increases, the trend in the values of E_2 is:

(F) generally upward.
(G) generally downward.
(H) upward for a few values, then suddenly downward, followed by an increase again, etc.
(J) downward for a few values, then suddenly upward, followed by a decrease again, etc.

4. If the chart were continued to the element having atomic number 20, its value for E_1 would be expected to be closest to:

(A) 20.
(B) 90.
(C) 140.
(D) 730.

5. An experimenter has at her disposal a means of providing an atom with any energy up to 200 kcal/mole. From how many different atoms could she remove one electron?

(F) 7
(G) 8
(H) 11
(J) 12

PASSAGE II

A physics student performed two sets of experiments designed to examine the factors that influence the motion of falling objects.

Experiment 1

A stone was dropped from a steep cliff while a camera, mounted on a tripod on the ground, took photographs at 1-second intervals. Back in the laboratory, the same procedure was repeated in the absence (nearly) of air inside a huge vacuum chamber.

Experiment 2

The experiments were repeated (on the cliff and inside the vacuum chamber) using a stone and a cork with identical masses dropped at the same time. At the cliff, the stone hit the ground first. In the vacuum chamber, both objects hit the ground together.

6. Assuming that air acts to resist the downward acceleration of the stone, how will the total time required to reach the ground in the vacuum chamber compare to the time required to reach the ground from the cliff?

   (A) Longer time in air than in vacuum chamber
   (B) Longer time in vacuum chamber than in air
   (C) Same time in each
   (D) Cannot be determined

7. In Experiment 1, gravity accelerates the stone as it falls from the cliff, causing it to pick up speed as it drops. Which of the following series of pictures most resembles how the stone appears as it drops?

(F)
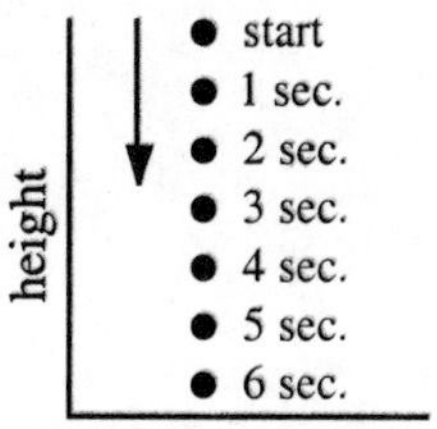

(G)
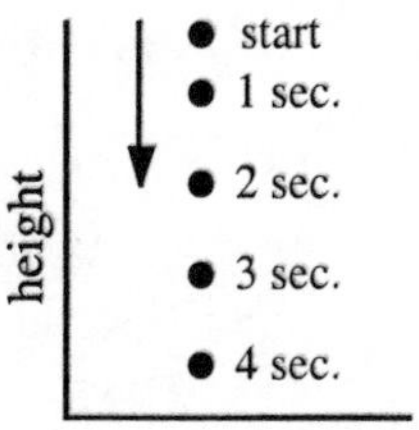

(H)
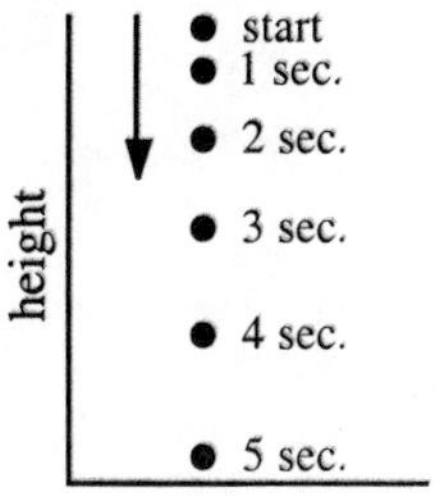

(J)
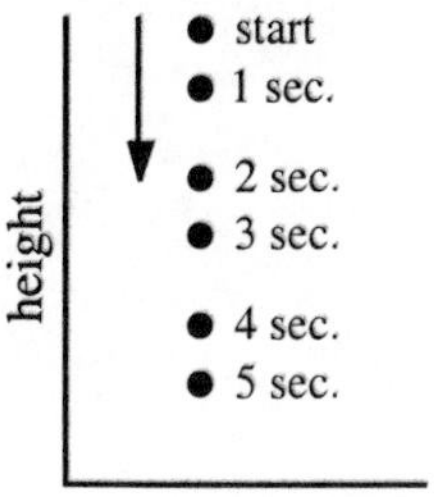

8. In Experiment 2, the observed results can be explained by the hypothesis that:

   (A) heavier objects fall more rapidly than lighter ones.
   (B) a cork of the same mass as a stone is smaller than the stone, and it encounters more air resistance.
   (C) a cork of the same mass as a stone is larger than the stone, and it encounters more air resistance.
   (D) the gravitational acceleration of objects toward the ground diminishes when air is not present.

9. If part of Experiment 1 were repeated on the moon, where the pull of gravity is one sixth that of the Earth, the stone's downward speed would increase as it falls (i.e., it would accelerate) but the rate of increase in speed would only be one sixth as great as on the Earth. When the photos taken at 1-second intervals on the moon are compared to the photos taken on Earth, the series of moon pictures of the stone will be:

   (F) closer together.
   (G) farther apart.
   (H) identical.
   (J) closer at some times and farther apart at others.

10. The experimenter devises a means of suspending the Earth's gravity for short periods of time. Armed with this technique, he drops the stone (on Earth, in air, under conditions of normal gravity), and then suspends gravity 2 seconds after the stone has been falling and leaves it off for the next minute. Recalling that gravity causes the stone's downward speed to increase continually, choose the "photo" that best illustrates, in 1-second intervals, this experiment.

(A)

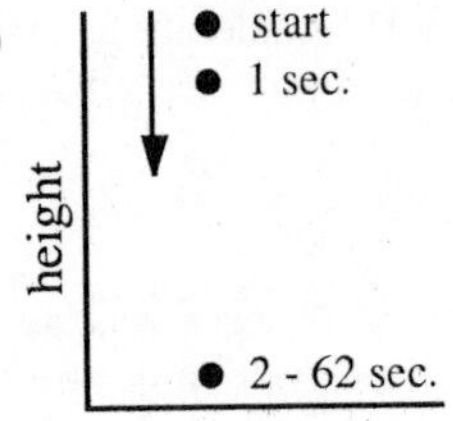

(B)

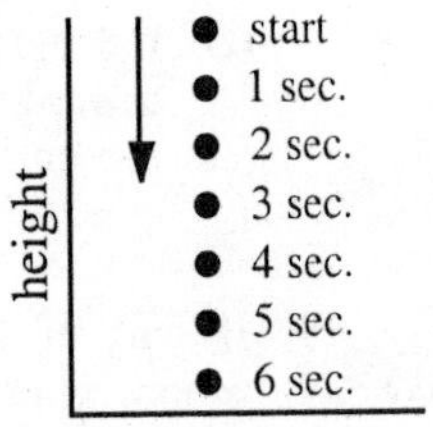

(C)

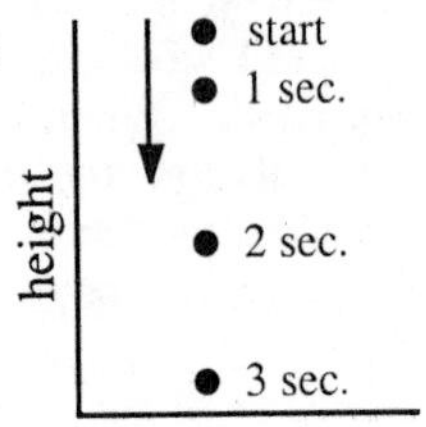

(D)

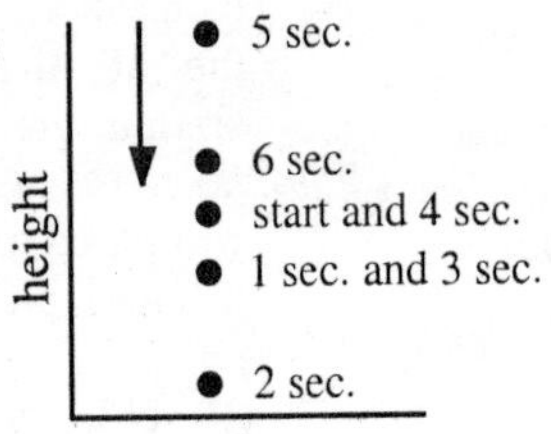

11. If Experiment 2 were repeated on the airless moon, which prediction would be correct?

(F) The cork would fall more slowly than on the Earth.
(G) The cork would fall as rapidly as the stone.
(H) Both predictions are correct.
(J) Neither prediction is correct.

SCIENCE REASONING ANSWER KEY

SECTION ONE—SCIENCE REASONING REVIEW (p. 167)

1. B	12. H	23. D	34. F	45. A
2. F	13. D	24. G	35. C	46. H
3. A	14. F	25. B	36. G	47. D
4. G	15. C	26. F	37. D	48. G
5. C	16. J	27. B	38. F	49. C
6. H	17. A	28. J	39. B	50. J
7. D	18. J	29. B	40. H	51. C
8. H	19. B	30. G	41. C	52. F
9. C	20. F	31. C	42. G	53. D
10. H	21. C	32. H	43. D	54. F
11. A	22. F	33. D	44. J	

SECTION TWO—SCIENCE REASONING PROBLEM-SOLVING (p. 182)

1. D	17. D	33. B	49. C	66. G
2. F	18. G	34. H	50. H	67. B
3. B	19. C	35. B	51. D	68. F
4. G	20. H	36. G	52. J	69. D
5. C	21. A	37. D	53. C	70. F
6. G	22. F	38. F	55. F	71. C
7. B	23. A	39. B	56. H	72. G
8. G	24. H	40. H	57. D	73. C
9. C	25. D	41. B	58. F	74. F
10. F	26. F	42. G	59. C	75. D
11. B	27. B	43. C	60. H	76. G
12. H	28. J	44. H	61. D	77. C
13. C	29. B	45. C	62. G	78. J
14. J	30. H	46. F	63. B	
15. C	31. C	47. B	64. J	
16. H	32. G	48. G	65. B	

SECTION THREE—SCIENCE REASONING QUIZZES (p. 198)

QUIZ I

1. C	3. B	5. C	7. G	9. F
2. J	4. H	6. D	8. C	10. B

QUIZ II

1. A	3. A	5. C	7. D	9. C
2. F	4. J	6. H	8. G	10. F

QUIZ III

1. C	4. H	7. C	10. H
2. G	5. A	8. H	11. C
3. C	6. G	9. A	

CAMBRIDGE
EDUCATIONAL SERVICES, INC.®

AMERICA'S #1 CAMPUS-BASED TESTPREP

Strategy Summary Sheet

ACT • PLAN • EXPLORE—SCIENCE REASONING

STRUCTURE OF ACT SCIENCE REASONING TEST: The ACT Assessment includes one Science Reasoning Test: 35 minutes in which to answer 40 multiple-choice questions. (The PLAN is 30 items in 25 minutes; the EXPLORE is 28 items in 30 minutes). There will be about seven reading passages divided among biology, earth/space sciences, chemistry, and physics. While there is no general ladder of difficulty (increasing difficulty with increasing problem number), the questions within a question group tend to get harder towards the end of the group of questions. There will be six to eight groups with five to seven questions each, preceded by a scientific discussion.

	ACT (40 questions)	**PLAN** (30 questions)	**EXPLORE** (28 questions)
Data Representations	15	8	12
Research Summaries	18	–	10
Conflicting Viewpoints	7	8	6

SCIENCE REASONING GENERAL STRATEGIES: This section tests your reasoning skills, not your scientific knowledge. Most of the passages have all of the information you will need to answer the questions. In some cases, background information at the level of your high school general science courses is required, but do not imply data that is not given. The following are basic general Science Reasoning strategies:

- *Pacing is important.* Remember that within the 35-minute limit you'll have to read and think about seven reading passages and the accompanying question sets. In other words, you'll have an average of just five minutes per passage. You'll need to work quickly to answer every question.

- Before reading any passage, quickly *glance over each passage and code each according to passage type* to determine the order you will attack the passages. Identifying and coding each passage should take no more than five seconds.

- *Don't preview the question stems.* Previewing the Science Reasoning question stems will only confuse you and slow you down, since they tend to be confusing without having first read the passage.

- It is important to only *read the passage thoroughly once*, rather than skimming it several times. The material can be difficult to understand, thus it is important to read thoughtfully and carefully. Be an active reader. Use your pencil to underline key words and points of information. That way, you'll be able to locate them easily when answering the questions.

- When a reading passage includes tables or graphs, make sure you *read and understand the labels* on axes, columns, and rows. You need to know what information is being presented and what units of measure are being used.

- Tables and graphs present results, often of observations or experiments. Questions will usually ask you to spot patterns in the data, so *look for trends* such as upward movement, downward movement, inverse variation, and the like.

- Many passages will contain much more information than you need to answer a particular question. In your search for a logical conclusion, *don't be misled by data that do not relate to the question at hand.*

- The experiments described in Research Summary questions are based on scientific assumptions. However, if an assumption is faulty, the experiment may not prove what it claims to prove, and conclusions drawn from it may be invalid. Therefore, for questions that ask about the validity of a scientific conclusion, *consider the validity of underlying assumptions.*

- The arguments presented in Conflicting Viewpoint questions are also based on scientific assumptions. Again, *if the assumption is wrong, the entire argument is open to challenge.* Assumptions that are based on scientific fact add strength to an argument; faulty assumptions weaken it.

- Offering the assumptions you started with as proof of your argument is called circular reasoning, and it is not an acceptable proof. For that reason, any conclusions discussed in Science Reasoning passages or offered as answer choices must be based on additional evidence (*e.g.*, experiments) to be valid. *Beware of any that are nothing more than a restatement of an underlying premise.*

- All the information you need to answer the questions is provided in the passage—don't imply any information not given or relate previous experience to the passage. *Pay attention to material noted with an asterisk.*

- *Transcribe your answers from the test booklet to the answer sheet by groups* (by passage). However, when you get to the last passage, transcribe each answer as it is determined.

STRATEGES FOR EACH PASSAGE TYPE:

1. *Data Representation:* When given data in the form of a graph or a chart, pay particular attention to the scale, units, legend, and other noted information.

2. *Research Summary:* When given multiple experiments, identify the controls and variables. Note that the controls must remain the same and that variables can only change one at a time in all experiments.

3. *Conflicting Viewpoints:* When given two points of view on a topic, identify the main points of difference and the logical value of the arguments. After you understand the nature of the passage, attack the questions.

STRATEGIES FOR EACH QUESTION TYPE:

1. *Comprehension:* Recognize basic concepts. For comprehension questions, read carefully. Make sure your answers consider appropriate scales and units. Also note the difference between absolute and percentage changes.

2. *Analysis:* Identify relationships and trends. Analysis questions ask you to identify relationships and trends. Pay particular attention to direct and inverse relationships.

3. *Application:* Draw conclusions, predict outcomes, and synthesize new information. In answering application questions, beware of "all, none, always, never." Remember that a single case of contradictory evidence is all that is necessary to disprove an absolute theory.

ADDITIONAL NOTES AND STRATEGIES FROM IN-CLASS DISCUSSION:

ACT APPENDIX A: PRACTICE TESTS

CAMBRIDGE

EDUCATIONAL SERVICES, INC.®

ACT • PLAN • EXPLORE

Appendix A

ACT PRACTICE TESTS

ACT DIAGNOSTIC TEST SCORE FORM

(Student Copy)

DIRECTIONS: Check your answer sheet against the answer key. Count and record the number of correct answers for each test section below—these are your raw scores. Use the "% Correct Chart" to determine the percent correct for each test section and record in the "% Correct" column. Use Table 1 from your test booklet and your raw score to determine the scale score for each test section. Total the four scale scores. Divide this sum by four. This is your ACT Composite Score, which ranges from 1 (lowest) to 36 (highest). Transfer the information to the Diagnostic Test Score Form (Instructor Copy) and turn in that copy to your instructor. Keep this copy, your answer sheet, and your test booklet.

ACT DIAGNOSTIC TEST SCORE CALCULATION

	Total #	*Raw Score*	*% Correct*	*Scale Score*
TEST 1: ENGLISH	75			
TEST 2: MATHEMATICS	60			
TEST 3: READING	40			
TEST 4: SCIENCE REASONING	40			
			SUM OF SCALE SCORES	
			ACT COMPOSITE SCORE (Sum of Scale Scores ÷ 4)	

% CORRECT CHART

Raw Score	*40 Questions Total*	*60 Questions Total*	*75 Questions Total*	*Raw Score*	*40 Questions Total*	*60 Questions Total*	*75 Questions Total*
1	3%	2%	1%	39	98%	65%	52%
2	5%	3%	3%	40	100%	67%	53%
3	8%	5%	4%	41		68%	55%
4	10%	7%	5%	42		70%	56%
5	13%	8%	7%	43		72%	57%
6	15%	10%	8%	44		73%	59%
7	18%	12%	9%	45		75%	60%
8	20%	13%	11%	46		77%	61%
9	23%	15%	13%	47		78%	63%
10	25%	17%	14%	48		80%	64%
11	28%	18%	15%	49		82%	65%
12	30%	20%	17%	50		83%	67%
13	33%	22%	18%	51		85%	68%
14	35%	23%	19%	52		87%	69%
15	38%	25%	20%	53		88%	71%
16	40%	27%	21%	54		90%	72%
17	43%	28%	23%	55		92%	73%
18	45%	30%	24%	56		93%	75%
19	48%	32%	25%	57		95%	76%
20	50%	33%	27%	58		97%	77%
21	53%	35%	28%	59		98%	79%
22	55%	37%	29%	60		100%	80%
23	58%	38%	31%	61			81%
24	60%	40%	32%	62			83%
25	63%	42%	33%	63			84%
26	65%	43%	35%	64			85%
27	68%	45%	36%	65			87%
28	70%	47%	37%	66			88%
29	73%	48%	39%	67			89%
30	75%	50%	40%	68			91%
31	78%	52%	41%	69			92%
32	80%	53%	43%	70			93%
33	83%	55%	44%	71			95%
34	85%	57%	45%	72			96%
35	88%	58%	47%	73			97%
36	90%	60%	48%	74			99%
37	93%	62%	49%	75			100%
38	95%	63%	51%				

ACT HOMEWORK PROGRESS REPORT

(Student Copy)

DIRECTIONS: This progress report is designed to help you monitor your homework progress. Following each class, your instructor will assign specific parts of the ACT Practice Tests. Complete the problems corresponding to each in-class lesson before the next class. Problems from Practice Tests I and II should be done without timing; problems from Practice Test III should be done with timing. Correct your answers and indicate the number and percent correct. Transfer the information to the Homework Progress Report (Instructor Copy) and give that copy to your instructor at the next class session.

ACT PRACTICE TEST I SCORE CALCULATIONS *(untimed)*	Total #	Raw Score	% Correct	Scale Score
TEST 1: ENGLISH (p. A-10)	75			
TEST 2: MATHEMATICS (p. A-20)	60			
TEST 3: READING (p. A-28)	40			
TEST 4: SCIENCE REASONING (p. A-35)	40			

ACT PRACTICE TEST II SCORE CALCULATIONS *(untimed)*	Total #	Raw Score	% Correct	Scale Score
TEST 1: ENGLISH (p. A-62)	75			
TEST 2: MATHEMATICS (p. A-73)	60			
TEST 3: READING (p. A-81)	40			
TEST 4: SCIENCE REASONING (p. A-87)	40			

ACT PRACTICE TEST III SCORE CALCULATIONS *(timed)*	Total #	Raw Score	% Correct	Scale Score
TEST 1: ENGLISH (p. A-114)	75			
TEST 2: MATHEMATICS (p. A-125)	60			
TEST 3: READING (p. A-134)	40			
TEST 4: SCIENCE REASONING (p. A-141)	40			

ACT PRACTICE TEST IV SCORE CALCULATIONS *(timed)*	Total #	Raw Score	% Correct	Scale Score
TEST 1: ENGLISH (p. A-170)	75			
TEST 2: MATHEMATICS (p. A-184)	60			
TEST 3: READING (p. A-192)	40			
TEST 4: SCIENCE REASONING (p. A-201)	40			

ACT HOMEWORK ASSIGNMENT 1 PROGRESS REPORT

(Instructor Copy)

Name ______________________ Section ______________ Date ______________

Homework Subject (check one): ☐ English ☐ Mathematics ☐ Reading ☐ Science Reasoning

	% Correct
ACT PRACTICE TEST I	
ACT PRACTICE TEST II	
ACT PRACTICE TEST III	
ACT PRACTICE TEST IV	

ACT HOMEWORK ASSIGNMENT 2 PROGRESS REPORT

(Instructor Copy)

Name ______________________ Section ______________ Date ______________

Homework Subject (check one): ☐ English ☐ Mathematics ☐ Reading ☐ Science Reasoning

	% Correct
ACT PRACTICE TEST I	
ACT PRACTICE TEST II	
ACT PRACTICE TEST III	
ACT PRACTICE TEST IV	

ACT HOMEWORK ASSIGNMENT 3 PROGRESS REPORT

(Instructor Copy)

Name ______________________ Section ______________ Date ______________

Homework Subject (check one): ☐ English ☐ Mathematics ☐ Reading ☐ Science Reasoning

	% Correct
ACT PRACTICE TEST I	
ACT PRACTICE TEST II	
ACT PRACTICE TEST III	
ACT PRACTICE TEST IV	

ACT HOMEWORK ASSIGNMENT 4 PROGRESS REPORT

(Instructor Copy)

Name ______________________ Section ______________ Date ______________

Homework Subject (check one): ☐ English ☐ Mathematics ☐ Reading ☐ Science Reasoning

	% Correct
ACT PRACTICE TEST I	
ACT PRACTICE TEST II	
ACT PRACTICE TEST III	
ACT PRACTICE TEST IV	

ACT DIAGNOSTIC TEST SCORE FORM

(Instructor Copy)

Name ______________________ Section ____________ Date ____________

DIRECTIONS: Copy the information needed below from the ACT Diagnostic Test Score Form (Student Copy) and return to your instructor.

ACT DIAGNOSTIC TEST SCORE CALCULATION	*Total #*	*Raw Score*	*% Correct*	*Scale Score*
TEST 1: ENGLISH	75			
TEST 2: MATHEMATICS	60			
TEST 3: READING	40			
TEST 4: SCIENCE REASONING	40			
			SUM OF SCALE SCORES	
			ACT COMPOSITE SCORE (Sum of Scale Scores ÷ 4)	

ACT FINAL EXAM SCORE FORM

(Instructor Copy)

Name ______________________ Section ____________ Date ____________

DIRECTIONS: Fill in the following information about your Final Exam and return to your instructor after you have taken your Final Exam.

ACT FINAL EXAM SCORE CALCULATION	*Total #*	*Raw Score*	*% Correct*	*Scale Score*
TEST 1: ENGLISH	75			
TEST 2: MATHEMATICS	60			
TEST 3: READING	40			
TEST 4: SCIENCE REASONING	40			
			SUM OF SCALE SCORES	
			ACT COMPOSITE SCORE (Sum of Scale Scores ÷ 4)	

CAMBRIDGE

EDUCATIONAL SERVICES, INC.®

ACT • PLAN • EXPLORE

Appendix A

ACT PRACTICE TEST I

1 1 1 1 1 1 1 1 1 1 1 1

ENGLISH

45 Minutes—75 Questions

DIRECTIONS: In the five passages that follow, certain parts and phrases are underlined and numbered. In the right-hand column, you will find alternatives for each underlined part. You are to choose the one that best expresses the idea, makes the statement appropriate for standard written English, or is worded more consistently with the style and tone of the passage as a whole. If you think the original version is the best, choose "NO CHANGE."

You will also find questions about a section of the passage, or about the passage as a whole. These questions do not refer to an underlined portion of the passage, but rather are identified with a note.

For each question, choose the alternative you consider best. Read each passage through once before you begin to answer the questions that accompany it. You cannot determine most answers without reading several sentences beyond the question. Be sure that you have read far enough ahead each time you choose an alternative.

Passage I

The challenge <u>to start to begin to make</u> (1) timely progress toward removing the threat of nuclear war is today the most important challenge in international relations. Three general principles guide our defense and negotiating policies toward such a goal, principles based on the technical realities of nuclear war.

First, nuclear weapons are <u>fundamentally different than</u> (2) non-nuclear weapons. These weapons of mass destruction <u>that could do a lot of harm</u> (3) have a long and deadly radioactive <u>memory, the</u> (4) unknowns of nuclear conflict dwarf the predictable consequences. The

1. A. NO CHANGE
   B. to begin making
   C. to begin the making of
   D. of beginning the making of

2. F. NO CHANGE
   G. different than fundamentally
   H. different from fundamentally
   J. fundamentally different from

3. A. NO CHANGE
   B. (and they could also do a great deal of harm)
   C. (owing to the fact that they could do a lot of harm)
   D. OMIT

4. F. NO CHANGE
   G. memory. The
   H. memory the
   J. memory; the

GO ON TO THE NEXT PAGE

number of deaths resulting from injuries and the unavailability of medical care [5] and the economic damage as a result from [6] disruption and disorganization would be even more devastating than [7] the direct loss of life and property.

Second, the sole purpose [9] of nuclear weapons must be to deter nuclear war, it is [10] neither a substitute for maintaining adequate conventional military forces to meet vital national security goals but [11] an effective defense against the almost total mutual annihilation and devastation that results from a full-scale nuclear war. Third, [12] arms control is an essential part of our national security. Thus far, we have had no effective controls on offensive nuclear weaponry, and it is clear that each step forward in the arms race toward more and

5. A. NO CHANGE
   B. from injuries and also from the unavailability of medical care
   C. from the unavailability of injuries and medical care
   D. both from injuries and also from the unavailability of medical care as well

6. F. NO CHANGE
   G. as a result to
   H. resulting from
   J. with a result of

7. A. NO CHANGE
   B. is even more devastating than
   C. are even more devastating as
   D. might be more devastating even as

Item 8 poses a question about Passage I as a whole.

8. Which of the following would be an appropriate final sentence for the second paragraph?
   F. And so I believe nuclear weapons to be a challenge.
   G. Nuclear war could have no winners.
   H. Nuclear conflict is very dangerous.
   J. Nuclear conflict would be rather wasteful.

9. A. NO CHANGE
   B. solely, the purpose
   C. the solely purpose
   D. the purpose solely

10. F. NO CHANGE
    G. war. They are
    H. war they are
    J. war; it is

11. A. NO CHANGE
    B. and
    C. nor
    D. including

12. F. NO CHANGE
    G. (Do NOT begin a new paragraph.) Third
    H. (Begin a new paragraph.) Third
    J. (Begin a new paragraph.) Third,

GO ON TO THE NEXT PAGE

improved weapons has made less[13] our security. Before deploying additional weapons, they must develop[14] a coherent arms control strategy.

13. A. NO CHANGE
    B. has lessened
    C. have lessened
    D. have made less of

14. F. NO CHANGE
    G. the development is necessary of
    H. it is necessary to develop
    J. it is necessarily to be developed,

Items 15 and 16 pose questions about Passage I as a whole.

15. Which of the following best describes the overall structure of the passage?
    A. A three-part argument
    B. A two-part narrative
    C. A three-part comparison
    D. A four-part argument

16. Which of the following is the thesis of this essay?
    F. Nuclear weapons are fundamentally different from non-nuclear weapons.
    G. The sole purpose of nuclear weapons must be to deter nuclear war.
    H. There are three principles that guide our effort to remove the threat of nuclear war.
    J. Nuclear war is a frightening possibility.

Passage II

The founders of the Republic viewing their[17] revolution primarily in political terms rather as[18] in economic terms. Therefore,[19] they viewed the kind of education needed for the new Republic largely in political terms instead of as a means to[20] academic excellence or individual self-fulfillment. Talking about[21] education as a bulwark for liberty, equality, popular

17. A. NO CHANGE
    B. having viewed its
    C. viewed its
    D. viewed their

18. F. NO CHANGE
    G. rather than
    H. but
    J. OMIT

19. A. NO CHANGE
    B. Since
    C. However
    D. On the contrary

20. F. NO CHANGE
    G. as a means or a way to
    H. to
    J. as

21. A. NO CHANGE
    B. Talking
    C. With the talking about
    D. They talked about

GO ON TO THE NEXT PAGE

consent, and devotion to the public good goals[22] that took precedence over[23] the uses of knowledge for self-improvement or occupational preparation. Over and over again, the Revolutionary generation, both liberal and conservative in outlook—assert their[24] faith that the welfare of the Republic tested upon an educated citizenry.

All agreed that the principal ingredients of a civic education was[25] literacy and inculcation of patriotic and moral virtues some[26] others added the study of history and the study of the principles of the republican government itself. The founders, as was the case of almost all their successors, were long on exhortation and rhetoric regarding the value of civic education; since[27] they left it to the textbook writers to distill the essence of those values for school children. Texts in American history and government appeared as early as the 1790s. The textbook writers turned out being[28] very largely of conservative persuasion, more likely Federalist in outlook than Jeffersonian, and universally almost agreed[29] that political virtue must rest upon moral and religious precepts. Since most textbook writers were New Englanders, this meant that the texts had a decided Federalist slant.

22. F. NO CHANGE
    G. good. Goals
    H. good, goals
    J. good; goals

23. A. NO CHANGE
    B. precede
    C. precede over
    D. took precedence on

24. F. NO CHANGE
    G. outlook, asserted its
    H. outlook; asserted its
    J. outlook asserts their

25. A. NO CHANGE
    B. being
    C. were
    D. were like

26. F. NO CHANGE
    G. virtues—some
    H. virtues, some
    J. virtues; some

27. A. NO CHANGE
    B. education. And
    C. education. Since
    D. education, but

28. F. NO CHANGE
    G. turned out to be
    H. turning out to be
    J. having turned out to be

29. A. NO CHANGE
    B. almost, agreed universally
    C. almost universally agreed
    D. almost universally, agreed

GO ON TO THE NEXT PAGE

In the first half of the Republic, civic education in the schools emphasized the inculcation of civic values, put less emphasis on political knowledge, and no attempt to develop[30] political skills. The development of political skills was left to the local parties, town meetings, churches, coffeehouses, and ale houses where men gathered to talk. [31]

30. F. NO CHANGE
G. made no attempt to develop
H. none at all on the development of
J. none was put at all on developing

31. Which of the following correctly describes how the last paragraph of the article functions?

A. It contradicts much of what was said before.
B. It continues the logical development of the essay.
C. It reiterates what was said in the first paragraph.
D. It is a transitional paragraph to introduce a new topic.

Item 32 poses a question about Passage II as a whole.

32. This passage would most likely be published in

F. a history textbook
G. a political science journal
H. a journal for educators
J. a biography of Jefferson

Passage III

The following paragraphs may or may not be in the most logical order. Each paragraph is numbered in brackets, and item 45 will ask you to choose the sequence of paragraph numbers that is most logical.

[1]

The contribution of women[33] on the home front during World War I was varied. It included a large range of activities from knitting and the operation of[34] drill presses and engaged a cross section of the female population from housewives to society girls. World

33. A. NO CHANGE
B. Women, their contribution
C. The contribution of woman
D. Woman's contribution

34. F. NO CHANGE
G. from knitting with the operation of
H. from knitting and operating
J. from knitting to operating

GO ON TO THE NEXT PAGE

War I marked the first time [35] in the history of the United States that a systematic effort was made, through organizations like the League for Women's Service, to utilize [36] the capabilities of women in all regions of the country.

[2]

While much of this volunteer work falls within [37] the established bounds of women's club work, many women entered areas of industrial work previously reserved by [38] the male population. Women put on the uniforms of elevator operators, streetcar conductors, postmen, and industrial workers. However, they were employed [39] in aircraft and munitions plants as well as in shipbuilding yards and steel mills.

[3]

Much of the work fell into the traditional realm of volunteer activity knitting [40] garments for the boys overseas, canning for Uncle Sam, planting Victory gardens, etc. Through these activities, every homemaker could demonstrate their [41] patriotism while still fulfilling her role as homemaker. Women with more time volunteered to hostess at canteens: make [42] bandages, and organize food and clothing drives. The Women's Land Army, dressed in bloomer uniforms and armed with such slogans as "The Woman with the Hoe Must Defend the Man with the Musket," was dispatched [43] to assist farmers in processing crops.

35. A. NO CHANGE
    B. has marked the first time
    C. is the first time it is marked
    D. was marked, the first time

36. F. NO CHANGE
    G. being able to utilize
    H. utilizing
    J. and utilize

37. A. NO CHANGE
    B. fell within
    C. having fallen within
    D. fell in

38. F. NO CHANGE
    G. having previously been reserved
    H. previously reserved for
    J. reserved previous to then

39. A. NO CHANGE
    B. workers. They were employed
    C. workers, but they were employed
    D. workers. Since they were employed

40. F. NO CHANGE
    G. activity—knitting
    H. activity: knitting
    J. activity, knitting

41. A. NO CHANGE
    B. be demonstrating
    C. have demonstrated their
    D. demonstrate her

42. F. NO CHANGE
    G. canteens make
    H. canteens, make
    J. canteens; make

43. A. NO CHANGE
    B. Musket," which was then dispatched
    C. Musket," and it was dispatched
    D. Musket," and it got dispatched

GO ON TO THE NEXT PAGE

[4]

Women performed ably during the war and laid the foundation (44) for more specialized jobs, increased wages, better working conditions, and a more competitive job status in the labor market.

44. F. NO CHANGE
G. the foundation was laid
H. the foundation was lain
J. laying the foundation

Items 45 and 46 pose questions about Passage III as a whole.

45. Which of the following represents the most logical sequence for the paragraphs?

A. 1, 4, 3, 2
B. 1, 3, 4, 2
C. 1, 3, 2, 4
D. 2. 4, 3, 1

46. Is the use of the sample slogan appropriate to the passage?

F. Yes, because it helps the reader to understand one of the points being made.
G. Yes, because all general statements should be illustrated with an example.
H. No, because it does not help the reader to understand the point being made.
J. No, because it is needlessly distracting,

Passage IV

Following the end of World War II, substantial changes undertaken (47) in Japan to liberate the individual from authoritarian restraints. The new democratic value system was acceptable by (48) many teachers, students, intellectuals, and old liberals, and (49) it was not immediately embraced by the society as a whole. Japanese traditions were dominated by group values, (50) and notions of personal freedom and individual rights being (51) unfamiliar.

47. A. NO CHANGE
B. will be undertaken
C. have been undertaken
D. were undertaken

48. F. NO CHANGE
G. accepted by
H. excepted by
J. excepted to

49. A. NO CHANGE
B. liberals, since
C. liberals, but
D. liberals; consequently

50. F. NO CHANGE
G. Dominated by group values were the Japanese traditions
H. Group values were always dominating the Japanese traditions
J. Dominating Japanese traditions were group values

51. A. NO CHANGE
B. were
C. was
D. are

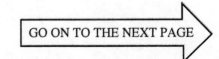

GO ON TO THE NEXT PAGE

Today, the triumph of[52] democratic processes is clear[53] evident in the widespread participation of the Japanese in social and political life. Furthermore,[54] there is no universally accepted and stable value system, values being[55] constantly modified by strong infusions of Western ideas. School textbooks expound democratic principles, and so emphasizing[56] equality over hierarchy and rationalism over tradition, but in practice these values are often sometimes distorted[57] particularly by the youth that translated[58] the individualistic and humanistic goals of democracy into egoistic and materialistic ones. [59]

52. F. NO CHANGE
    G. (Do NOT begin a new paragraph) Today the triumph, of
    H. (Begin a new paragraph) Today, the triumph, of
    J. (Do NOT begin a new paragraph) Today, owing to the fact that

53. A. NO CHANGE
    B. is
    C. is clear and also
    D. are clearly

54. F. NO CHANGE
    G. Therefore,
    H. So,
    J. Yet,

55. A. NO CHANGE
    B. system with that values are
    C. system since that values are
    D. system since values are

56. F. NO CHANGE
    G. principles, emphasizing
    H. principles and the emphasis of
    J. principles with the emphasis that

57. A. NO CHANGE
    B. had been misinterpreted and distorted often
    C. often misinterpreted and distorted
    D. are often misinterpreted and distorted

58. F. NO CHANGE
    G. that translate
    H. who translate
    J. translate

59. What type of discussion might logically follow this last paragraph?
    A. A discussion of goals of Japanese youth
    B. A discussion of Western democratic principles
    C. A discussion of Western education
    D. A discussion of World War II

GO ON TO THE NEXT PAGE

Passage V

From the beginning, humankind always has shared [60] some sort of link with the animal world. The earliest and most primitive was surely that of hunter and prey—with humans possibly playing the fatal role of victim. Later, of course, humans reversed the roles as they became more skillful and intelligenter [61]. The later domestication of certain animals and also [62] the discovery of agriculture, made for a more settled and stable existence and was an essential step in the not-so-orderly and very chaotic [63] process of becoming civilized. However, the intellectual distance between regarding an animal as the source of dinner or of material comfort and to consider them [64] a worthy subject for study, is considerable.

Not until Aristotle did the animal world become a subject for serious scientific study. Although he seemingly writes on [65] every subject, Aristotle's work [66] in zoology—studying animals as animals—is considered his most successful. He seemed to have had a natural affinity for and curiosity about all the living creatures of the world, and [67] he took special interest in marine life.

Aristotle's zoological writings reveal him to be a remarkably astute observer of the natural world, wedding his [68] observations to what might be called speculative reason. He was therefore a theorist as well.

60. F. NO CHANGE
G. have always shared
H. is always sharing
J. has always shared

61. A. NO CHANGE
B. so intelligent
C. and more intelligent
D. but intelligent

62. F. NO CHANGE
G. animals, also
H. animals, along with
J. animals; along with

63. A. NO CHANGE
B. (and very chaotic)
C. yet very chaotic
D. OMIT

64. F. NO CHANGE
G. considering it
H. considering them
J. then to consider them

65. A. NO CHANGE
B. he wrote (seemingly) on
C. writing seemingly on
D. he wrote on seemingly

66. F. NO CHANGE
G. subject; Aristotles work
H. subject Aristotles' work
J. subject: Aristotle's work

67. A. NO CHANGE
B. so
C. but
D. because

68. F. NO CHANGE
G. who was wedded to
H. in that he wedded
J. with the wedding of

GO ON TO THE NEXT PAGE

His overall theory was simple. In the works of [69] Nature," he said, "purpose and not accident is predominant." A thing is known then, when we know what it is for. He linked and combined [70] theory and practice by saying that interpretation of an observed phenomenon must always be made in light of its purpose [71]. His zoological theory was thus a reflection of the essentially teleological nature of his overall philosophy. [72]

69. A. NO CHANGE
    B. simple—in
    C. simple. "In
    D. simply. "In

70. F. NO CHANGE
    G. combining
    H. to combine
    J. OMIT

71. A. NO CHANGE
    B. always keeping its purpose in mind
    C. without ever forgetting what its purpose is
    D. given an understanding of what its purpose is

72. Is the quote from Aristotle in the last paragraph appropriate?

    A. Yes, because it is important to quote the works of people you are talking about.
    B. Yes, because it is a succinct statement of Aristotle's theory.
    C. No, because the quote is irrelevant to what the author is talking about in that paragraph.
    D. No, because it is wrong to quote when you can express the idea in your own words.

Items 73-75 pose questions about Passage IV as a whole.

73. The author probably had which audience in mind for this article?

    F. Zoologists
    G Students who are studying Aristotle
    H. The average person interested in science
    J. Teachers of marine biology

74. What is the actual thesis of this passage?

    A. People have always liked animals.
    B. Animals and people reversed roles.
    C. Aristotle was interested in the natural world.
    D. The animal world became a source of serious study because of Aristotle.

75. How does the first paragraph of this passage function?

    F. It poses questions to be answered.
    G. It provides general background for the rest of the passage.
    H. It introduces an argument.
    J. It provides an anecdote related to the rest of the passage.

IF YOU FINISH BEFORE TIME IS CALLED, YOU MAY CHECK YOUR WORK ON THIS TEST ONLY. DO NOT WORK ON ANY OTHER TEST SECTION. **STOP**

2 2 2 2 2 2 2 2 2 2 2 2

MATHEMATICS

60 Minutes—60 Questions

DIRECTIONS: Solve each problem, choose the correct answer, and then blacken the corresponding oval on your answer sheet. Do not linger over problems that take too much time. Solve as many as you can, then return to the others in the time you have left for this test.

Note: Unless otherwise stated, all of the following should be assumed:

1. Illustrative figures are NOT necessarily drawn to scale.
2. Geometry figures lie in a plane.
3. The word *line* means straight line.
4. The wôrd *average* means arithmetic mean.

---

1. If $\frac{1}{x} + \frac{1}{x} = 8$, then $x = ?$

A. $\frac{1}{4}$
B. $\frac{1}{2}$
C. 1
D. 2
E. 4

2. If $x = 2$ and $y = -1$, then $3x - 4y = ?$

F. −5
G. −1
H. 0
J. 2
K. 10

3. In a certain school, there are 600 boys and 400 girls. If 20 percent of the boys and 30 percent of the girls are on the honor roll, how many of the students are on the honor roll?

A. 120
B. 175
C. 240
D. 250
E. 280

4. If p, q, r, s, and t are whole numbers, the expression $t(r(p + q) + s)$ *must* be an even number when which of the five numbers is even?

F. p
G. q
H. r
J. s
K. t

5. A student conducting a lab experiment finds that the population of flies in a bottle increases by a certain multiple from week to week. If the pattern shown in the table continues, how many flies can the student expect to find in the bottle in week 5?

Results of Biology Project Conducted by Student X					
Week	1	2	3	4	5
# of Flies in Bottle	3	12	48	192	?

A. 195
B. 240
C. 384
D. 564
E. 768

GO ON TO THE NEXT PAGE

6. Three students are each scheduled to give a short speech at an assembly. In how many different orders can the speeches be scheduled?

F. 12
G. 9
H. 6
J. 4
K. 3

7. If points P and Q lie in the xy-plane and have the coordinates shown below, what is the midpoint of PQ?

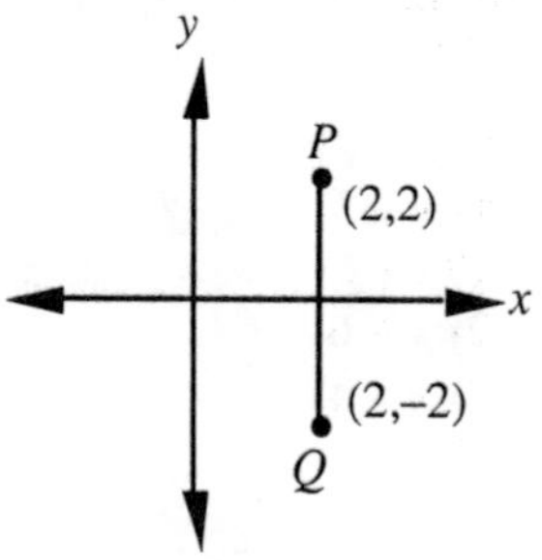

A. (–2, 0)
B. (–2, 2)
C. (0 ,2)
D. (2, 0)
E. (2, 2)

8. If $xy = |xy|$ and $xy \neq 0$, which of the following CANNOT be true?

F. $x > y > 0$
G. $y > x > 0$
H. $x > 0 > y$
J. $0 > x > y$
K. $0 > y > x$

9. In the scale drawing of the floor of a rectangular room shown below, the scale used was 1 centimeter = 4 meters. What is the actual area, in square meters, of the floor of the room?

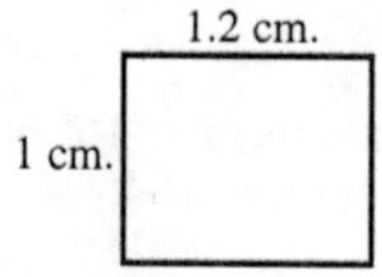

A. 9.6
B. 13.6
C. 15
D. 19.2
E. 38.4

10. If $30{,}000 \cdot 20 = 6 \cdot 10^n$, then n = ?

F. 4
G. 5
H. 6
J. 7
K. 8

11. Karen purchased a total of 4 pounds of candy, some of which were chocolates and some of which were caramels. If chocolates cost \$3 per pound and caramels cost \$2 per pound, and if Karen spent a total of \$10.00, how many pounds of chocolates did she buy?

A. 1
B. 2
C. 2.5
D. 3
E. 3.5

12. The average (arithmetic mean) of Al's scores on three tests was 80. If the average of his scores on the first two tests was also 80, what was his score on the third test?

F. 90
G. 85
H. 80
J. 75
K. 72

13. A book contains 10 photographs, some in color and some in black and white. Each of the following could be the ratio of color to black-and-white photographs EXCEPT:

A. 9:1
B. 4:1
C. 5:2
D. 3:2
E. 1:1

14. If $\frac{4}{5} = \frac{x}{4}$, then x = ?

F. 5
G. $\frac{16}{5}$
H. $\frac{5}{4}$
J. $\frac{4}{5}$
K. $\frac{5}{16}$

GO ON TO THE NEXT PAGE

15. In the figure below, three equilateral triangles have a common vertex, $x + y + z = ?$

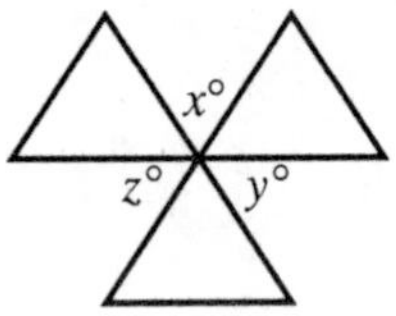

A. 60
B. 90
C. 120
D. 180
E. 240

16. Peter spent $\frac{1}{4}$ of his allowance on Monday and $\frac{1}{3}$ of the *remainder* on Tuesday. What part of the allowance does Peter still have?

F. $\frac{1}{12}$
G. $\frac{1}{4}$
H. $\frac{1}{2}$
J. $\frac{3}{4}$
K. $\frac{11}{12}$

17. If 100 identical bricks weigh p pounds, then in terms of p, 20 of these bricks weigh how many pounds?

A. $\frac{p}{20}$
B. $\frac{p}{5}$
C. $20p$
D. $\frac{5}{p}$
E. $\frac{20}{p}$

18. If the distances between points P, Q, and R are equal, which of the following could be true?

I. P, Q, and R are points on a circle with center O.
II. P and Q are points on a circle with center R.
III. P, Q, and R are vertices of an equilateral triangle.

F. I only
G. I and II only
H. I and III only
J. II and III only
K. I, II, and III

19. In the table below, the percent increase in the price of the item was greatest during which of the following periods?

Year	1950	1955	1960	1965	1970	1975
Price	\$2	\$4	\$7	\$12	\$20	\$30

A. 1950-1955
B. 1955-1960
C. 1960-1965
D. 1965-1970
E. 1970-1975

20. Which of the following is a factorization of $x^2 + 4x - 12$?

F. $(x - 6)(x + 2)$
G. $(x - 4)(x + 3)$
H. $(x - 2)(x + 6)$
J. $(x + 2)(x + 6)$
K. $(x + 3)(x + 4)$

21. Two cartons weigh $3x - 2$ and $2x - 3$. If the average weight of the cartons is 10, the heavier carton weighs how much more than the lighter carton?

A. 2
B. 4
C. 5
D. 6
E. 10

22. A group of 15 students took a test that was scored from 0 to 100. If exactly 10 students scored 75 or more on the test, what is the *lowest* possible value for the average of the scores of all 15 students?

F. 25
G. 50
H. 70
J. 75
K. 90

23. For all real numbers x, 16^x is equal to which of the following expressions?

A. x^{16}
B. 2^{3x}
C. 4^{2x}
D. 8^{2x}
E. 8^{4x}

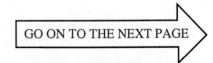

GO ON TO THE NEXT PAGE

24. If the figure below is a square, what is the perimeter of the figure?

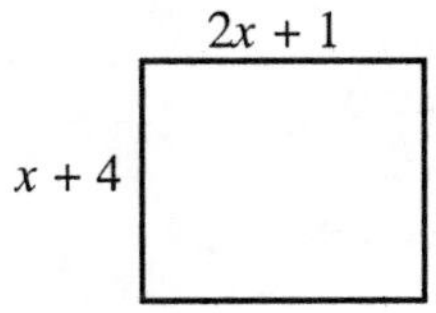

F. 28
G. 16
H. 9
J. 3
K. 2

25. If a certain rectangle has a length that is twice its width, what is the ratio of the area of the rectangle to the area of an isosceles right triangle with a hypotenuse equal to the width of the rectangle?

A. $\frac{1}{8}$
B. $\frac{1}{4}$
C. $\frac{1}{2}$
D. $\frac{4}{1}$
E. $\frac{8}{1}$

26. In the coordinate plane, what is the shortest distance between the point with (x, y) coordinates $(1, 3)$ and the line with the equation $x = -2$?

F. 1
G. 3
H. 4
J. 6
K. 9

27. If 5 pounds of coffee cost \$12, how many pounds of coffee can be purchased for \$30?

A. 7.2
B. 10
C. 12.5
D. 15
E. 18

28. If the two triangles below are equilateral, what is the ratio of the perimeter of the smaller to that of the larger?

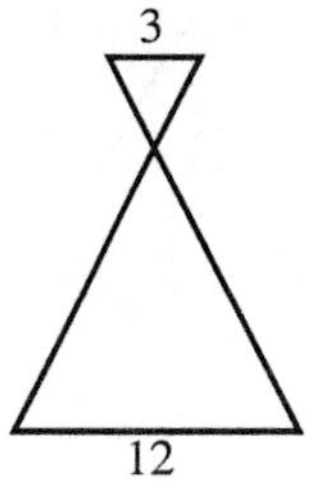

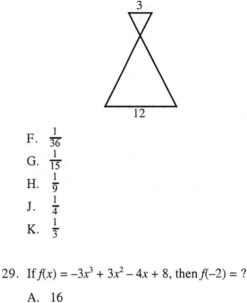

F. $\frac{1}{36}$
G. $\frac{1}{15}$
H. $\frac{1}{9}$
J. $\frac{1}{4}$
K. $\frac{1}{3}$

29. If $f(x) = -3x^3 + 3x^2 - 4x + 8$, then $f(-2) = ?$

A. 16
B. 22
C. 28
D. 36
E. 52

30. A merchant pays \$120 wholesale for a dress and then adds a 30% markup. Two weeks later, the dress is put on sale at 40% off the retail price. What is the sale price of the dress?

F. \$102.40
G. \$97.30
H. \$93.60
J. \$89.40
K. \$87.00

31. If $\frac{1}{3}$ of a number is 2 more than $\frac{1}{5}$ of the number, then which of the equations can be used to find the number x?

A. $\frac{1}{3}(x) + 2 = -\frac{1}{5}(x)$
B. $\frac{1}{3}(x) - 2 = -\frac{1}{5}(x)$
C. $\frac{1}{3}(x) - \frac{1}{5}(x) = 2$
D. $\frac{1}{3}(x) - \frac{1}{5}(x) = -2$
E. $5\left(\frac{1}{3}(x) + 2\right) = 0$

GO ON TO THE NEXT PAGE

32. In the figure below, if the triangle is equilateral and has a perimeter of 12, then the perimeter of the square = ?

F. 9
G. 12
H. 16
J. 20
K. 24

33. If one solution of the equation $12x^2 + kx = 6$ is $\frac{2}{3}$, then k = ?

A. 1
B. $\frac{3}{2}$
C. 2
D. 5
E. 9

34. If a six-sided polygon has two sides of length $x - 2y$ each and four sides of length $2x + y$ each, what is its perimeter?

F. $6x - 6y$
G. $6x - y$
H. $5x$
J. $6x$
K. $10x$

35. At the first stop on her route, a driver unloaded $\frac{2}{5}$ of the packages in her van. After she unloaded another three packages at her next stop, $\frac{1}{2}$ of the original number of packages in the van remained. How many packages were in the van before the first delivery?

A. 10
B. 18
C. 25
D. 30
E. 36

36. For all x and y, $12x^3y^2 - 8x^2y^3$ = ?

F. $4x^2y^2(2xy)$
G. $4x^2y^2(3xy)$
H. $4x^2y^2(3x - 2y)$
J. $2x^2y^2(4x - y)$
K. $x^3y^3(12xy - 8xy)$

37. $\dfrac{1}{1 + \frac{1}{x}}$ is equal to which of the following?

A. $x + 1$
B. $\frac{1}{x+1}$
C. $\frac{x}{x+1}$
D. $\frac{x+1}{x}$
E. $x^2 + x$

38. If S is 150% of T, then T is what percent of $S + T$?

F. $33\frac{1}{3}$%
G. 40%
H. 50%
J. 75%
K. 80%

39. In ΔPQR, the lengths of PQ and QR are equal, and the measure of $\angle Q$ is 3 times that of $\angle P$. What is the measure of $\angle R$?

A. 24°
B. 30°
C. 36°
D. 45°
E. 60°

40. If the cost of b books is d dollars, which of the following equations can be used to find the cost, C, in dollars, of x books at the same rate?

F. $C = xd$
G. $C = \frac{dx}{b}$
H. $C = \frac{bd}{x}$
J. $C = bx$
K. $C = \frac{bx}{d}$

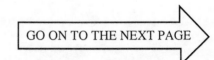

GO ON TO THE NEXT PAGE

41. An article is on sale for 25% off its regular price of \$64. If the merchant must also collect a 5% sales tax on this reduced price, what is the total cost of the article including sales tax?

A. \$42.10
B. \$44.20
C. \$49.60
D. \$50.40
E. \$56.70

42. If $\frac{x}{z} = k$ and $\frac{y}{z} = k - 1$, then $x = ?$

F. $y - 1$
G. $y + 1$
H. $y + z$
J. $z - y$
K. $\frac{y}{z}$

43. If x is 25 percent of y, then y is what percent of x?

A. 400%
B. 300%
C. 250%
D. 125%
E. 75%

44. If x is an integer that is a multiple of both 9 and 5, which of the following must be true?

I. x is equal to 45.
II. x is a multiple of 15.
III. x is odd.

F. I only
G. II only
H. III only
J. II and III only
K. I, II, and III

45. If a cube has an edge of length 2, what is the distance from any vertex to the center of the cube?

A. $\frac{\sqrt{2}}{2}$
B. $\sqrt{3}$
C. $2\sqrt{2}$
D. $2\sqrt{3}$
E. $\frac{3}{2}$

46. The figure below shows two right circular cylinders, C and C'. If $r = kr'$ and $h = kh'$, then what is the ratio of $\frac{\text{Volume of } C}{\text{Volume of } C'}$. (Volume of a cylinder $= \pi r^2 h$.)

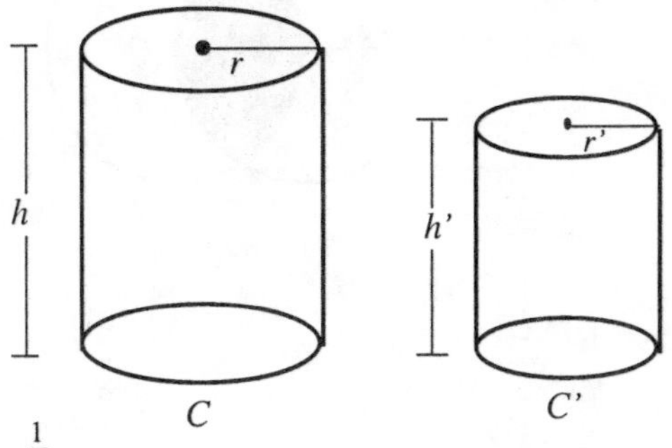

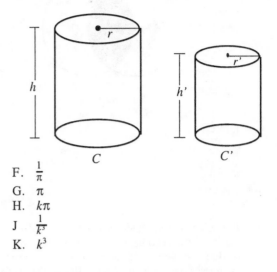

F. $\frac{1}{\pi}$
G. π
H. $k\pi$
J $\frac{1}{k^3}$
K. k^3

47. In the figure below, if the triangle has an area of 1, then the area of the circle is:

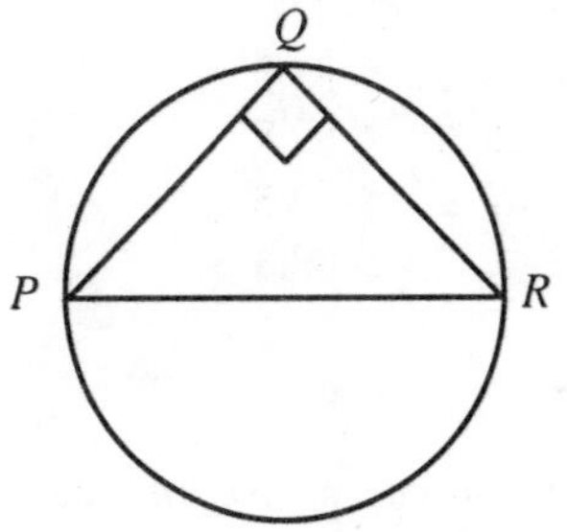

$PQ = QR$

A. π
B. 2π
C. $2\sqrt{3}\pi$
D. 4π
E. $4\sqrt{3}\pi$

GO ON TO THE NEXT PAGE

48. In the figure below, the radius of the circles is 1. What is the *perimeter* of the shaded part of the figure?

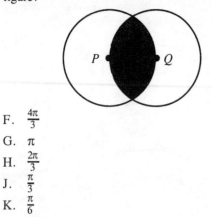

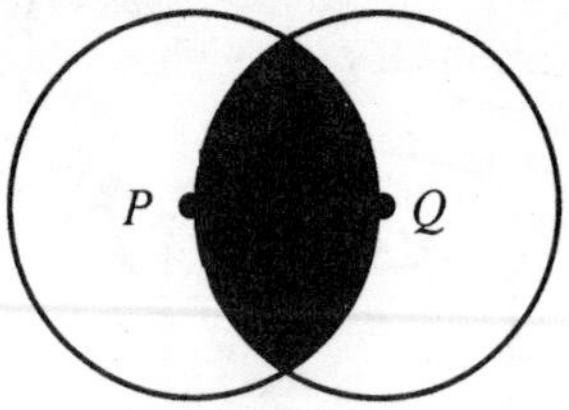

F. $\frac{4\pi}{3}$
G. π
H. $\frac{2\pi}{3}$
J. $\frac{\pi}{3}$
K. $\frac{\pi}{6}$

49. A student's final grade in a certain course is the average of his scores on ten tests graded on a scale of 0 to 100, inclusive. For the first six tests, the student's scores averaged 83. If x is the student's final grade for the course, then which of the following is true?

A. $8.3 \le x \le 83.0$
B. $49.8 \le x \le 83.0$
C. $49.8 \le x \le 89.8$
D. $54.7 \le x \le 89.8$
E. $83.0 \le x \le 89.8$

50. Which of the following represents the multiplicative inverse of the complex number $2 - i$?

F. $2 + i$
G. $i - 2$
H. $\frac{2+i}{3}$
J. $\frac{2-i}{3}$
K. $\frac{2+i}{5}$

51. $\log_3\sqrt{3} = ?$

A. -1
B. $\frac{1}{3}$
C. $\frac{1}{2}$
D. $\frac{2}{3}$
E. 2

52. $f(x) = (x - 1)^2 + 2$, what value for x creates the minimum value for $f(x)$?

F. -3
G. -2
H. 0
J. 1
K. 2

53. If, for all n, $2^n + 2^n + 2^n + 2^n = x(2^{n+1})$, then $x = ?$

A. 2
B. 4
C. 2^n
D. 2^{2n}
E. 2^{n+1}

54. If $f(x) = x^2 + 2x + 1$, then the set of all k for which $f(k) = f(-k)$ is?

F. {0}
G. {1}
H. {2}
J. {1, 2}
K. All real numbers

55. What is $\lim_{x \to 1} \frac{x^2 - 1}{x - 1}$?

A. -1
B. 0
C. 1
D. 2
E. The limit does not exist.

56. If $0 \le x \le \pi$ and $\cos x = -1$, then $\cos \frac{x}{2} = ?$

F. $-\frac{\sqrt{3}}{2}$
G. $-\frac{1}{2}$
H. 0
J. $\frac{1}{2}$
K. $\frac{\sqrt{3}}{2}$

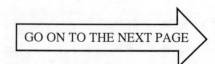

GO ON TO THE NEXT PAGE

57. Which of the following defines the range of the function $f(x) = \frac{1-x}{x}$?

A. All real numbers
B. All real numbers except –1
C. All real numbers except 0
D. All real numbers except 1
E. All real numbers greater than –1

58. Which of the following figures represents the graph of $x = 3 \sin \theta$ and $y = 2 \cos \theta$?

F.
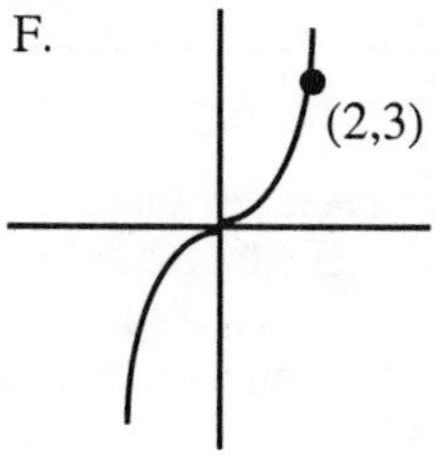

J.
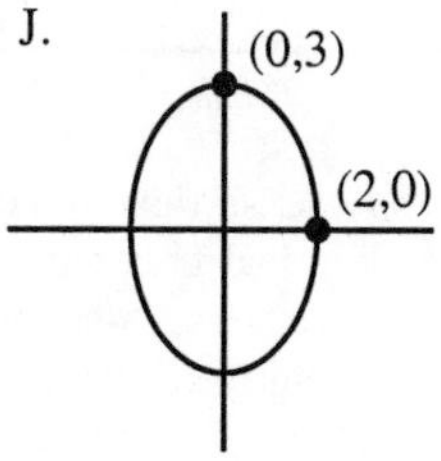

G.
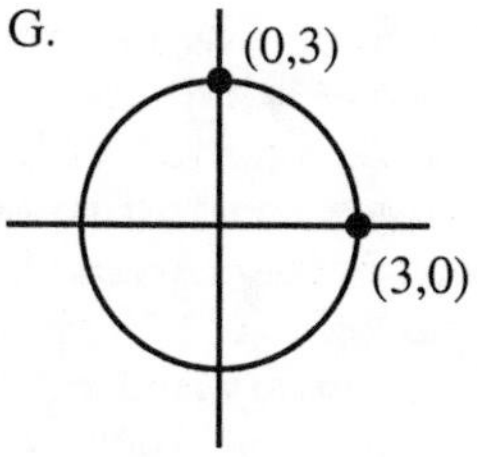

K.
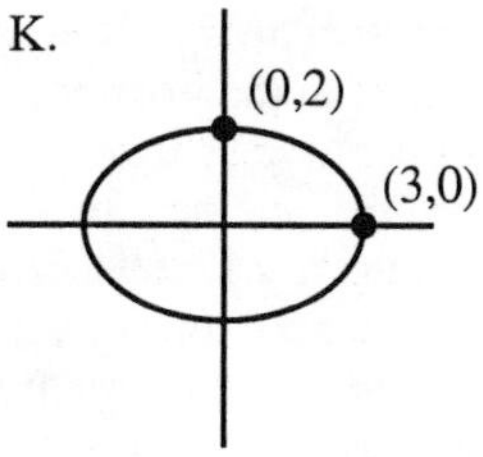

H.
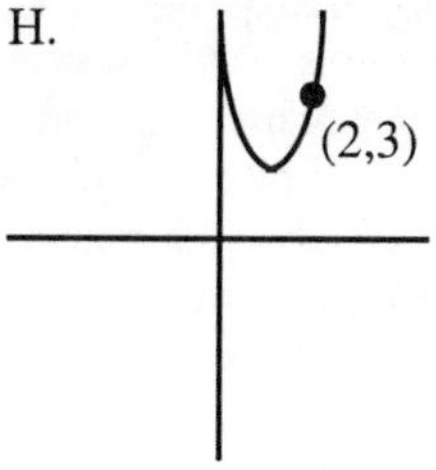

59. For all θ such that $0° < \theta° < 90°$, which of the following is equal to $\sin \theta \bullet \csc \theta$?

A. 1
B. $\sqrt{2}$
C. $\tan \theta$
D. $\cot \theta$
E. $\sec \theta$

60. In ΔABC below, the measures of $\angle ABC$, $\angle BCA$, and $\angle CAB$ are 90°, 40°, and 50°, respectively. If AB is 3 units long, how many units long is BC?

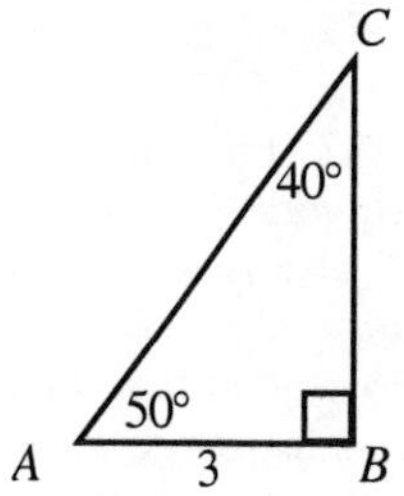

F. 4
G. 5
H. sin 10°
J. 3 tan 50°
K. 3 tan 40°

IF YOU FINISH BEFORE TIME IS CALLED, YOU MAY CHECK YOUR WORK ON THIS TEST ONLY. DO NOT WORK ON ANY OTHER TEST SECTION. **STOP**

3 3 3 3 3 3 3 3 3 3 3 3

READING

35 Minutes—40 Questions

DIRECTIONS: There are four passages in this test. Each passage is followed by several questions. After reading each passage, choose the best answer to each question and blacken the corresponding oval on your answer sheet. You may refer to the passages as often as necessary.

Passage I (SS): This passage discusses Frederick Turner's hypothesis of the American Frontier.

In July of 1893 Frederick Jackson Turner, a historian from the University of Wisconsin, presented a paper to a group of historians convening in Chicago during the Columbian Exposition. Entitled "The Significance of the American Frontier in History," Turner's paper drew little immediate reaction. Yet no theory of history has had a greater influence on the direction and methodology of inquiry and the issues of debate in American history. Later historians took issue with some of Turner's interpretations; some of his own students were among those whose research proved certain of his views wrong. Yet these debates merely serve to illustrate the importance of Turner's hypothesis.

Turner's was an overarching hypothesis about how the settlement of the frontier had shaped the American experience and character. As with all general hypotheses in any field of study, it gave a coherent interpretation to many facts that had been largely ignored by historians up to that time.

Turner used statistical evidence from the 1880 census as the basis for a startling conclusion: Prior to 1880 there had been a frontier to be settled. By 1890, Turner pointed out, there was no longer any area of wilderness completely untouched by settlements. The frontier had disappeared. The passing of the frontier, Turner concluded, was a historic moment.

Turner further claimed that the frontier experience had produced a distinctively American character, which was not explainable simply as the predictable behavioral traits molded by English political institutions. Frontier settlers developed inquisitiveness, inventiveness, energy, and a great passion for freedom. These attributes defined a new American character, one evidenced in nationalism, independence, and democracy. This new sense of national identity derived from the fact that people from every section of the country mixed at the Western frontier. Economic independence could be traced to the fact that the settlers no longer depended on England for goods but had become self-sufficient. In addition, the frontier settlers, whose basic social unit was the family, enjoyed freedom from direct governmental interference. Frontier life thus reinforced the fundamental ideals of populist democracy.

Turner also argued that the frontier fostered democracy in the cities of the East. The availability of free land at the frontier provided a "safety-valve" against possible social unrest: those discontented with social inequities and economic injustice could strike out and settle the free land available in frontier territories.

Turner's thesis was thus original in both what it said and in the methodology that Turner used in formulating it. Up to the time of Turner's essay, history had been essentially the history of politics. A Midwesterner, Turner challenged this traditional approach of Eastern historians by incorporating techniques of the social sciences, showing how factors of geography, economics, climate, and society influenced the development of the American West. Although now common among historians, at the time this interdisciplinary approach was novel.

1. Turner's essay challenged the views of:

   A. frontier writers such as Mark Twain.
   B. other American historians of his time.
   C. sociologists.
   D. European critics of America.

2. Turner's methods were original in that he:

   F. utilized research techniques from a variety of other academic fields.
   G. insulted other historians.
   H. refused to encourage further research.
   J. ignored the need for a unifying view.

GO ON TO THE NEXT PAGE

3. Turner's evidence for the disappearance of the American frontier drew on:

   A. interviews with settlers.
   B. his reading of Karl Marx.
   C. diaries.
   D. the census of 1880.

4. Turner's essay affected:

   F. the reputations of American historians in Europe.
   G. future settlements in the West.
   H. the way in which population was counted.
   J. the subsequent focus of inquiry in American history.

5. One fact that would cast a doubtful light on Turner's view that the West was settled by individuals looking for escape from the pressures of Eastern city life would be if:

   A. many Western towns had few inhabitants.
   B. few people settled in mountain country.
   C. much of the land in the West and Midwest was actually bought by wealthy land speculators from the East.
   D. many people chose to settle along the banks of the Mississippi.

6. Which of the following items, if true, would prove that Turner's "safety-valve" theory was false?

   F. Population movements showed that more people actually left the farms for the cities than left cities to move to the frontier.
   G. Much of the West had a desert climate.
   H. The transcontinental railroad was completed in 1869.
   J. The numbers of buffalo dropped markedly during the late nineteenth century.

7. A theory would best be defined as:

   A. a foolish notion founded on questionable data.
   B. an idle speculation that may have no basis in fact.
   C. a hypothesis that explains a large number of isolated facts.
   D. a somewhat questionable view of factual data.

8. The frontier line of America moved essentially from:

   F. the South to the East.
   G. the West to the East.
   H. the East to the West.
   J. the North to the South.

9. The economic independence of Americans arose, Turner said, from the fact that:

   A. Americans rarely bought anything.
   B. many pioneers had few relatives left in Europe.
   C. Americans were buying American goods rather than English goods.
   D. few settlers ever voted in local elections.

10. Which of the following quotations captures the approach of historians at the time when Turner read his paper?

   F. "This history of the world is but the biography of great men."
   G. "History is past Politics and Politics is present History.
   H. "Those who do not heed the lessons of history are doomed to repeat them."
   J. "Anybody can make history. Only a great man can write it."

GO ON TO THE NEXT PAGE

Passage II (H): In this selection, the author expresses his opinion regarding the role of philosophy.

The service of philosophy towards the human spirit is to startle it into sharp and eager observation. Every moment, and for that moment only, some form grows perfect in hand or face; some tone on the hills or the sea is choicer than the rest. Not the fruit of experience, but experience itself is the end. Only a counted number of pulses is given to us of a variegated, dramatic life. How shall we pass most, quickly from point to point, and be present always at the focus where the greatest number of vital forces unite in their purest energy?

To burn always with this hard, gemlike flame, to maintain this ecstasy, is success in life. It is only the roughness of the eye that makes any two persons, things, or situations seem alike. While all melts under our feet, we may well catch at any exquisite passion, or any knowledge that seems by a lifted horizon to set the spirit free for a moment, or any stirring of the senses, strange dyes, strange colors, curious odors, or work of the artist's hands or the faces of one's friends. Not to discriminate every moment some passionate attitude in those about us, and in the brilliancy of their gifts some tragic dividing of forces of their ways is, on this short day of the frost and sun, to sleep before evening. With this sense of the splendor of our experience and of its awful brevity, gathering all we are into one desperate effort to see and touch, we shall hardly have time to make theories about the things we see and touch.

We are all under sentence of death but with a sort of indefinite reprieve; we have an interval and then our place knows us no more. Some spend this interval in listlessness, others in high passions, the wisest—at least among the "children of this world"—in art and song. For our one chance lies in expanding this interval, in getting as many pulsations as possible into the given time. Great passions may give us this quickened sense of life, ecstasy, sorrow, and love, the various forms of enthusiastic activity. Of this wisdom, the poetic passion, the desire of beauty, the love of art for art's sake has most; for art comes to you professing frankly to give nothing but the highest quality to your moments as they pass, and simply for the sake of those moments.

11. Which of the following best describes the overall structure of the passage?

A. The author raises a question and then provides an answer.
B. The author presents a theory, which he then proves.
C. The author studies a widely held belief and then rejects it.
D. The author defines a term and then provides examples.

12. In the passage, the author uses the word "pulsations" (line 35) to mean:

F. children.
G. lives.
H. death.
J. experiences.

13. According to the author, the function of art is to:

A. depict reality accurately.
B. stimulate strong emotions.
C. encourage social reform.
D. express the artist's feelings.

14. With which of the following statements would the author most likely agree?

F. A person's lifetime is merely preparation for what comes after death.
G. Only an artist can truly enjoy life.
H. The original experience is more important than the memory of it.
J. A perceptive person understands that all experience is repetitious.

15. The tone of the passage can best be described as:

A. impassioned.
B. scholarly.
C. informative.
D. speculative.

16. In the context of this passage, the phrase "short day of the frost and sun" refers to:

F. the transient effect of poetry.
J. a brief moment of passion.
H. the life of a person.
J. stimulation of the senses.

17. The phrase "awful brevity" in line 26 means that:

A. philosophy is not really useful.
B. art may not satisfy everyone.
C. life is short.
D. passion is the greatest virtue.

18. The "children of this world" (line 33) are NOT:

F. passionate.
G. wise.
H. lovers of art and song.
J. listless.

GO ON TO THE NEXT PAGE

19. The greatest passion according to the author is the love of:

A. beauty.
B. one's spouse.
C. wealth.
D. security.

20. The phrase "then our place knows us no more" (lines 29-30) means that we:

F. move to another town.
G. have children.
H. die.
J. divorce.

Passage III (NS): This passage explains how energy becomes usable through photosynthesis.

Every living cell must acquire energy in a usable form. According to the First Law of Thermodynamics, energy, which is the capacity to work, can be converted from one into another without any net gain or loss. An organism must have an outside source of usable energy. The Second Law of Thermodynamics states that every transformation of energy results in a reduction of the free (usable) energy of the system. Living cells primarily use chemical energy derived from complex organic compounds.

Photosynthesis is the process by which green plants transform sunlight into a usable energy source. Green plants utilize the energy of light to combine carbon dioxide with water to form organic material (sugar) and oxygen.

$$6CO_2 + 12H_2O + \text{light} \xrightarrow{\text{chlorophyll}} 6O_2 + C_6H_{12}O_6 + 6H_2O$$

Photosynthesis is a reduction reaction. Reduction is the addition of one or more electrons to an atom or molecule. Oxidation is the removal of electrons from an atom or molecule. Reduction stores energy, while oxidation releases it. Biological systems rely on the addition or removal of an electron from hydrogen. Photosynthesis is based on two key processes. Light energy is trapped and stored, and hydrogen atoms are transformed from water to carbon dioxide to form carbohydrate.

Photosynthesis takes place within the chloroplasts. The pigments within the chloroplasts are precisely arranged within the membranes of flattened sacs called thylakoids. Thylakoids often lie close together in sacks called grana. The light reactions of photosynthesis take place within the thylakoid membranes, while the dark reactions take place in the colorless matrix (stroma) surrounding the thylakoids.

Different wavelengths of light, especially red and blue light, are trapped by various pigment molecules contained within chloroplasts. When a photon of light strikes a pigment molecule and is absorbed, the energy is transferred to an electron, which is raised to a high energy state. A specialized form of chlorophyll passes the energized electron to an acceptor molecule, X, which has a high affinity for electrons. X passes the electron to a series of acceptor molecules, each at a slightly lower energy level. After being passed from molecule to molecule, the electron may return to the chlorophyll from which it started. Some of the energy released as the electron is passed down the energy gradient is used to synthesize the compound *ATP* from *ADP* and inorganic phosphate.

ATP is a universal energy packet used by cells to do work. ATP is synthesized from ADP and inorganic phosphate in a process called phosphorylation. Phosphorylation is a very high energy demanding process. *Cyclic photophosphorylation* occurs when the energy used for ATP synthesis comes from light-energized electrons as they are returned to the chlorophyll molecules from which they originated.

Another process which occurs in green plants is noncyclic photophosphorylation. In this reaction some electrons are passed from the chlorophyll to a different type of acceptor molecule called $NAPD_{ox}$, which retains the electron and is therefore reduced to become $NAPD_{re}$.

The ATP and $NADP_{re}$ produced in the light reaction are used to reduce carbon dioxide to carbohydrate in a series of reactions called the *Calvin cycle* (dark reaction). Basically, a five-carbon sugar, ribulose diphosphate (RuDP), is combined with CO_2. This process is called carboxylation. The products are then phosphorylated by ATP and reduced by $NAPD_{re}$ to form PGAL, a three-carbon sugar.

Under certain conditions RuDP is oxidized by the very same enzyme that under more agreeable conditions would facilitate its carboxyilation. This process, called photorespiration, is seemingly a wasteful process since no ATP is created. Photorespiration predominates over photosynthesis when CO_2 levels are low and O_2 levels are high.

Some angiosperm plants of tropical origin have unique leaf structure known as *Kranz* anatomy (C_4 plants). In Kranz plants, the bundle-sheath cells have numerous chloroplasts (other plants usually do not), and the mesophyll cells are clustered in a ringlike arrangement around the bundle sheath. These plants can carry out photosynthesis under conditions of high temperature and concentrated light, when loss of water induces closure of the stomata. When the stomata close, the concentration of CO_2 in the air spaces inside the leaf falls, and the concentration of O_2 rises. Under

GO ON TO THE NEXT PAGE

these conditions most plants (C_3) would experience a net loss of CO_2 because of photorespiration. Kranz plants (C_4) do not because of their specialized way of intially fixing CO_2. They combine CO_2 with a three-carbon compound in the mesophyll cells to form a four-carbon compound that passes into the bundle-sheath cells, where the CO_2 is regenerated. Therefore, Krans plants can maintain a CO_2 level in the bundle-sheath cells that allows carboxilation of RuDP in the Calvin cycle to predominate over its oxidation in photorespiration.

21. According to this passage, "the capacity to do work" is the definition of:

A. photosynthesis
B. energy.
C. oxidation.
D. thermodynamics.

22. In the equation in line 16, $C_6H_{12}O_6$ apparently names:

F. oxygen.
G. carbon dioxide.
H. a sugar.
J. photosynthesis.

23. Which of these could be considered the reverse of reduction?

A. Oxidation
B. Photosynthesis
C. Transformation
D. Phosphorylation

24. Which of the following conclusions is (are) suggested by the third paragraph (lines 17-26)?

I. Photosynthesis involves the addition of electrons.
II. Photosynthesis involves action on hydrogen.
III. Photosynthesis is a form of energy release.

F. I only
G. II only
H. III only
J. I and II only

25. Paragraph 5 (lines 35-50) deals mainly with:

A. defining terms related to plant growth.
B. comparing one reduction reaction to another.
C. explaining the process of photosynthesis.
D. expressing the author's opinion.

26. Which statement is NOT true about ATP?

F. It mixes with phosphate to make ADP.
G. It is created through photophosphorylation.
H. It serves a purpose in the Calvin cycle.
J. It is used by cells to do work.

27. The Calvin cycle involves:

A. the combination of carbon dioxide and a five-carbon sugar, with a three-carbon sugar as the result.
B. the combination of oxygen and a three-carbon sugar, with a five-carbon sugar as the result.
C. a mix of ATP and sugar to create carbon dioxide.
D. are duction of carbohydrate to form carbon dioxide.

28. By "more agreeable conditions" (line 73), the author probably means:

F. conditions that produce higher levels of oxygen.
G. conditions that produce higher levels of CO_2.
H. conditions with higher temperatures.
J. conditions with longer growing periods.

29. Which statement names a difference between photorespiration and photosynthesis?

A. Photorespiration involves RuDP.
B. In photosynthesis, ATP is synthesized.
C. Photorespiration is a reduction reaction.
D. All of the above.

30. Unlike the preceding paragraphs, the final paragraph discusses:

F. plants that do not photosynthesize.
G. living matter other than plants.
H. plants with an unusual structure.
J. plants that transform carbon dioxide into carbohydrate.

GO ON TO THE NEXT PAGE

Passage IV (PF): In this selection, a young country boy, alone in town for the first time, tries to find a relative, Major Molineux.

It was near nine o'clock of a moonlight evening, when a boat crossed the ferry with a single passenger, who had obtained his conveyance at that unusual hour by the promise of extra fare. He was a youth of barely eighteen years, evidently country-bred, and now upon his first visit to town. The youth finally drew from his pocket a little province bill of five shillings, which, in depreciation in that sort of currency, satisfied the ferryman's demand with the addition of a sex-angular piece of parchment, valued at three pence. He then walked forward into the town with as light a step as if his day's journey had not already exceeded thirty miles, and with as eager an eye as if he were entering London city, instead of the little metropolis of a New England colony. Before Robin had proceeded far, however, it occurred to him that he knew not whither to direct his steps; so he paused, and looked up and down the narrow street, scrutinizing the small and mean wooden buildings that were scattered on either side.

"This low hovel cannot be my kinsman's dwelling," thought he, "nor yonder old house; and truly I see none hereabouts that might be worthy of him. It would have been wise to inquire my way of the ferryman and doubtless he would have gone with me, and earned a shilling from the Major for his pains. But the next man I meet will do as well."

He resumed his walk, and was glad to perceive that the street now became wide, and the houses were more respectable in their appearance. He soon discerned a figure moving on moderately in advance, and hastened his steps to overtake it. Robin laid hold of the skirt of the man's old coat, just when the light from the open door and windows of a barber's shop fell upon both their figures.

"Good evening to you, honored sir," said he, making a low bow, and still retaining hold of the skirt. "I pray you tell me whereabouts is the dwelling of my kinsman, Major Molineux."

The citizen answered him in a tone of excessive anger and annoyance. "Let go my garment, fellow! I tell you, I know not the man you speak of. What! I have the authority, I have—hem, hem— authority; and if this be the respect you show for your betters, your feet shall be brought acquainted with the stocks by daylight, tomorrow morning!"

Robin released the old man's skirt, and hastened away, pursued by an ill-mannered roar of laughter from the barber's shop. He was at first considerably surprised by the result of his question, but, being a shrewd youth, he soon thought himself able to account for the mystery.

"This is some country representative," was his conclusion, "who has never seen the inside of my kinsman's door, and lacks the breeding to answer a stranger civilly. Ah, Robin, Robin! Even the barber's boys laugh at you for choosing such a guide! You will be wiser in time, friend Robin."

31. In the final paragraph the young man is talking to:

A. the Major.
B. the man in the coat.
C. himself.
D. the barbers.

32. The total cost of the young man's passage on the ferry boat was:

F. five shillings.
G. three pence.
H. five shillings less three pence.
J. five shillings plus three pence.

33. The young man believes that his relative is a:

A. barber.
B. wealthy person.
C. constable.
D. builder.

34. The incidents described in the passage take place:

F. in the late morning.
G. in the early afternoon.
H. in the late afternoon.
J. at night.

35. The passage suggests that 30 miles is:

A. a long distance to travel in one day.
B. easily traveled in a single day.
C. easily traveled in an hour.
D. a long ferryboat ride.

36. The young man believes that the barbers laughed at him because:

F. his clothes clearly show that he is from the country.
G. he asked a question of a stranger who obviously would not know the answer.
H. he badly needs a haircut and a shave.
J. the stranger he questioned is actually the man he is looking for.

37. The scenes in the passage are most likely set in which of the following time periods?

A. Eighteenth century
B. Nineteenth century
C. Early twentieth century
D. Present time

GO ON TO THE NEXT PAGE

38. The young man approaches the stranger in the coat:

F. respectfully.
G. rudely.
H. coyly.
J. stealthily.

39. The young man is the only passenger on the ferry boat because:

A. he paid the ferryman extra for a private charter.
B. no one else was traveling at that hour.
C. the Major had sent the boat especially for him.
D. the ferryman was a good friend of the young man.

40. Just after he gets off the ferry the young man finds himself in a:

F. poorer neighborhood.
G. wealthy neighborhood.
H. forest.
J. large city.

IF YOU FINISH BEFORE TIME IS CALLED, YOU MAY CHECK YOUR WORK ON THIS TEST ONLY. DO NOT WORK ON ANY OTHER TEST SECTION.

STOP

4 4 4 4 4 4 4 4 4 4 4 4

SCIENCE REASONING

35 Minutes—40 Questions

DIRECTIONS: There are seven passages in this test. Each passage is followed by several questions. After reading a passage, choose the best answer to each question and blacken the corresponding oval on your answer sheet. You may refer to the passages as often as necessary.

Passage I

The chart below shows several physical properties of compounds called alkanes, which are long "chains" of carbons to which hydrogen atoms are attached. As an example, the compound propane, which has three carbons, has the structural formula:

$$CH_3—CH_2—CH_3$$

PHYSICAL PROPERTIES OF STRAIGHT-CHAIN ALKANES

Name	*# of Carbons*	*Boiling Point (°C)*	*Melting Point (°C)*	*Density*
methane	1	−162	−183	0.47
ethane	2	−89	−183	0.57
propane	3	−42	−188	0.50
butane	4	0	−138	0.58
pentane	5	36	−130	0.56
hexane	6	69	−95	0.66
heptane	7	98	−91	0.68
octane	8	126	−57	0.70
nonane	9	151	−54	0.72
decane	10	174	−30	0.74

1. The *general* trends shown in the chart are:

   A. as the number of carbons increases, all properties increase in value (with occasional exceptions).
   B. as the number of carbons increases, boiling points and melting points decrease, while density increases.
   C. as the number of carbons increases, density decreases and other properties increase.
   D. as the number of carbons increases, all properties decrease.

2. The change in boiling point is greatest:

   F. from methane to ethane.
   G. from propane to butane.
   H. from butane to pentane.
   J. from nonane to decane.

3. For alkanes with more than one carbon, the change in melting point tends to be greater:

   A. from an even number of carbons to the next odd number.
   B. from an odd number of carbons to the next even number.
   C. makes no difference.
   D. cannot be determined.

4. Considering the alkane properties listed, if alkane *X* has a higher boiling point than alkane *Y*, then without exception, it must also have a:

   F. higher melting point.
   G. higher density.
   H. higher number of carbons.
   J. longer name.

5. The greatest percentage increase in density occurs from:

   A. ethane to propane.
   B. propane to butane.
   C. pentane to hexane.
   D. hexane to heptane.

GO ON TO THE NEXT PAGE

Passage II

A student performs a set of physics laboratory experiments, in which objects of different masses glide "frictionlessly" along a smooth surface, collide, then continue to glide. The momentum of each object is defined as its "mass • velocity." The momentum of a system of objects is the sum of the individual momenta.

Experiment 1

The light mass moves toward the stationary, heavy mass, and both stick together and continue to move. Table 1 shows the relevant information.

Table 1

	Object 1	*Object 2*
Mass	2 kg	5 kg
Initial velocity	4 m/sec	0
Final velocity	1.14 m/sec	1.14 m/sec

Experiment 2

The student performs a similar experiment in which the objects do not stick together, but collide "elastically"—that is, rebound from each other with no loss in energy. Table 2 shows the results.

Table 2

	Object 1	*Object 2*
Mass	2 kg	5 kg
Initial velocity	4 m/sec	0
Final velocity	–1.71 m/sec	2.29 m/sec

(Note that positive velocities indicate motion to the right, negative velocities indicate motion to the left.)

6. In Experiment 1, the momentum of Object 1 before the collision is:

F. 0.
G. 2.
H. 4.
J. 8.

7. After the collision in Experiment 1, the momentum of the combined masses is:

A. much less than the initial total momentum of the two masses.
B. about equal to the initial total momentum of the two masses.
C. much greater than the initial total momentum of the two masses.
D. Cannot be determined from the information given.

8. After the collision in Experiment 2:

F. both objects are moving to the right.
G. both objects are moving to the left.
H. Object 1 is moving to the left and Object 2 to the right.
J. Object 2 is moving to the right and Object 2 to the left.

9. In Experiment 2, if Object 2 were replaced by another object that was far more massive than Object 1, its final velocity would be closest to:

A. 4.0 m/sec.
B. 2.3 m/sec.
C. –1.7 m/sec.
D. 0.

10. Under the conditions described in question 9, the final velocity of Object 1 would be closest to:

F. –2 m/sec.
G. –1.7 m/sec.
H. 0.
J. 2 m/sec.

11. Kinetic energy is defined as $\frac{1}{2}mv^2$. During the collision described in Experiment 1, the kinetic energy of Object 1:

A. increases.
B. remains the same.
C. decreases.
D. cannot be determined.

GO ON TO THE NEXT PAGE

Passage III

The table below shows how an increase (+) or a decrease (–) in one or more plant hormones and environmental factors can affect various plant activities. The activities listed on the left occur when the combinations of conditions to the right exist at the same time. Hormones (H) are numbered; e.g., H_1, H_2, etc.

Activities	H_1	H_2	H_3	H_4	H_5	*Da yLength*	*Temperature*
Plant growth	+ +		+ +				
No plant growth	+ +		+ +	+ +			
No plant growth	+ +		+ +		+ +		
Seed germination			+ +				
Flowering			+ +		+ +	*(+ + *or* – –)	+ +
Flower drop-off	– –	+ +					
Fruit drop-off	– –	+ +					
Leaf drop-off	– –	+ +					– –

*Different species of plants require different combinations of light and darkness to stimulate flowering.

12. Based on the information in the table, a drop in temperature will help cause:

    F. flowering.
    G. loss of leaves, fruit, and flowers.
    H. loss of leaves only.
    J. seed germination.

13. The hormones that can inhibit (prevent) plant growth are:

    A. 1 and 3.
    B. 1, 3, and 4.
    C. 1, 3, and 5.
    D. 4 and 5.

14. Which conclusion is correct about the various factors affecting plant activities?

    F. Hormone 3 influences more plant activities than any other factor.
    G. Seed germination is influenced by the fewest factors, whereas flowering is influenced by the most.
    H. For Hormone I to have an effect on any plant activity, it must be changing in the opposite direction of at least one other hormone.
    J. Temperature changes can affect all plant activities.

15. Which activity would most likely be affected by changing a house plant's growing conditions from 12 hours light/12 hours darkness to constant light?

    A. Plant growth
    B. Loss of leaves
    C. Flowering
    D. All of these

16. Which statement best describes the relationship between Hormone 1 and Hormone 2?

    F. Hormone 2 must change in the opposite direction of Hormone 1 for plant growth to occur.
    G. When Hormone 1 and Hormone 2 affect a plant activity together, no other factors influence that activity.
    H. As Hormone I goes up, Hormone 2 always goes down; and as Hormone 1 goes down, Hormone 2 always goes up.
    J. Hormone 2 only affects plant activities when Hormone 1 is also involved.

GO ON TO THE NEXT PAGE

Passage IV

In order to examine the factors that affect the flow of substances across cell membranes, three experiments were carried out. In each experiment, semi-permeable bags (bags with small pores that allow some substances to pass through, but not others) were partially filled with a fluid, tied, and then weighed (first weighing). The bags were then submerged into a large beaker of water, and at 10-minute intervals, removed from the beaker of water and re-weighed.

Experiment 1

A bag containing a 30% red dye solution (30% red dye and 70% water) weighed 100 g. The bag was then submerged in a beaker of pure water. After 20 minutes, the bag weighed 110 g. The beaker water remained clear.

Experiment 2

A second bag containing 40% red dye solution (40% red dye and 60% water) weighed 100 g before being submerged in a beaker of pure water. After only 10 minutes, the bag weighed 110 g. The beaker water remained clear.

Experiment 3

A third bag containing only pure water and weighing 100 g was submerged in a beaker of 50% red dye solution (50% red dye and 50% water). After 20 minutes, the bag weighed 70 g. The bag water remained clear.

17. In Experiment 1, a gain in bag weight suggests that:

A. material passed out from bag to beaker faster than it passed in from beaker to bag.
B. material passed in from beaker to bag faster than it passed out from bag to beaker.
C. material passed in and out of the bag at approximately the same rate.
D. materials did not move at all.

18. Which of the following hypotheses is supported by the results of all three experiments?

F. Red dye can leave the bag but not enter.
G. Red dye can enter the bag but not leave.
H. Red dye can enter or leave the bag.
J. Red dye cannot enter or leave the bag.

19. Which of the following represents the best approximation for the weight of the bag in Experiment 2 after 20 minutes?

A. 90 g
B. 100 g
C. 110 g
D. 120 g

20. Which of the following questions is the entire set of experiments designed to answer?

F. How does concentration of red dye affect rate and direction of water flow?
G. How does concentration of water affect rate and direction of red dye flow?
H. How does rate of red dye flow affect direction of water movement?
J. How does direction of red dye movement affect rate of water flow?

21. A control experiment was set up to confirm the investigation's conclusion. A bag containing pure water and weighing 100 g was submerged in a beaker of pure water. What is expected to occur?

A. The bag will slowly gain weight.
B. The bag will slowly lose weight.
C. The bag will remain approximately the same weight.
D. The bag will eventually become empty, and the water level in the beaker will rise.

22. Assuming that salts cannot freely pass across a cell's membrane, what would happen to human red blood cells (approximately 1% salt and 99% water) submerged in sea water (approximately 5% salt and 95% water)?

F. The cells would shrink due to a loss of water.
G. The cells would shrink due to a loss of salt.
H. The cells would swell up due to a gain of water.
J. The cells would swell up due to a gain of salt.

GO ON TO THE NEXT PAGE

Passage V

The chart below shows various physical characteristics of different types of soil.

PHYSICAL CHARACTERISTICS OF SOIL				
Types of Soil	*Diameter of Particles (μm)*	*Relative* Ability to Hold Positively Charged Minerals (Ca^{+2}, K^+, Mg^{+2})*	*Relative* Ability to Maintain Air Spaces*	*Relative* Ability to Retain Water*
Clay	less than 2	1	4	1
Silt	2–20	2	3	2
Sand	20–200	3	2	3
Coarse Sand	200–2,000	4	1	4

*Soils with relative abilities of 1 are best (most able), 4 are worst (least able).

23. The soil type that is least able to hold substances such as magnesium (Mg^{+2}) is:

    A. sand.
    B. coarse sand.
    C. silt.
    D. clay.

24. Based on the information in the chart, which of the following statements best describes the relationship between a soil's particle size and its other physical characteristics?

    F. As particle size increases, the ability to hold positively charged minerals increases.
    G. As particle size decreases, the ability to retain water decreases.
    H. As particle size decreases, the ability to maintain air spaces increases.
    J. As particle size increases, the ability to retain water decreases.

25. The size of particles in the soil type that is neither best nor worst at any of the listed abilities *must be:*

    F. less than 20 micrometers.
    G. more than 20 micrometers.
    H. between 2 and 200 micrometers.
    J. between 2 and 2,000 micrometers.

26. Loam is a type of soil that is mostly clay, but also contains some sand and silt particles. Which prediction is most likely to be accurate about the ability of loam to support plant growth?

    A. Plants will *grow well* because loam *primarily* has small particles that can hold minerals and retain water, yet it also has enough large particles to provide air spaces containing oxygen.
    B. Plants will *grow* well because loam *primarily* has large particles that can provide air spaces containing oxygen, yet it also has enough small particles that can hold minerals and retain water.
    C. Plants will *not grow well* because although loam is *excellent* at maintaining air spaces for oxygen, it will not hold enough minerals or water.
    D. Plants will *not grow well* because although loam has enough minerals and air spaces for oxygen, it *cannot* retain enough water.

27. On the basis of the information provided in the chart, which of the following conclusions about soil types is *not correct?*

    A. Soils best at retaining water are also best at holding positively charged minerals.
    B. No two soil types have the exact same combination of relative abilities.
    C. Clay and coarse sand are the soil types that are most different in every physical characteristic.
    D. A different type of soil is best at each listed ability.

GO ON TO THE NEXT PAGE

Passage VI

Theory 1

The rate of a chemical reaction is defined as the number of moles of a specified reactant consumed in one second. Since reactants must collide in order for a reaction to occur, it might seem that rates would depend upon the concentration of reactants—since the more reactants that are present, the greater the likelihood of a collision. This is in fact the case, as a concrete example will make clear. For the reaction: $2NO + O_2 \Rightarrow 2NO_2$ the rate is proportional to the amount of NO and O_2 present. We may express this fact as a "rate law" as follows: rate $= k[NO]^2[O_2]^1$ where k is called the rate constant, and the powers (exponents) in the rate law reflect the coefficients in front of the reactants in the chemical reaction. This relationship between numbers of reactant molecules and exponents in the rate law is a general one.

Theory 2

Theory 1 is very often true, for it expresses the reasonable insight that the greater the concentration of reactants, the greater the likelihood of a reaction. It has a great shortcoming, however, in its assumption that all reactions proceed in one fell swoop rather than in several skirmishes.

For example, let letters A, B, C, *etc*., stand for molecules. In the reaction: $A + 2B \Rightarrow C$. Theory 1 predicts a rate law as follows: rate $= k[A][B]^2$. However, if the reaction actually proceeds in two stages, with the first one being: $A + B \Rightarrow AB$ followed by: $AB + B \Rightarrow C$.

Theory 2 implies, then, that we must understand the details of the reaction, including the relative speeds of the various subreactions, in order to predict a rate law. Theory 1 is not totally wrong, just incomplete.

28. Theory 1 relates:

F. the rate of a reaction to the concentration of products.
G. the rate of a reaction to the concentration of reactants.
H. the relative amounts of products to each other.
J. the rate of a reaction to the individual rates of various stages of that reaction.

29. According to Theory 1, the rate of the reaction $3M + 2N \Rightarrow 4P$ will be given by:

A. $k[M][N]$.
B. $k[M]^3[N]^2$.
C. $k[M]^3[N]^2[P]^4$.
D. $k([M]^3 + [N]^2)$.

30. According to a proponent of Theory 2:

F. Theory 1 can never give a correct prediction for a rate law.
G. Theory 1 will give a correct result if the reactant coefficients are all equal to 1.
H. Theory 1 will give a correct result for a single-stage reaction.
J. Theory 1 is in error because it claims that collisions are necessary for reactions to take place.

31. A chemist studies the rate of the reaction $2NO_2 + F_2 \Rightarrow 2NO_2F$. According to Theory 1, the rate of the reaction is proportional to:

A. the first power of NO_2 and the first power of F_2
B. the second power of NO_2 and the second power of NO_2F.
C. the second power of NO_2 and the second power of F_2.
D. the second power of NO_2 and the first power of F_2.

32. Supporters of Theory 2 would best be able to defend their positions if:

F. they could show that the reaction occurs in more than one stage.
G. they slowed the reaction down by cooling the reactants.
H. they sped the reaction up with additional heat.
J. they eliminated all collisions.

33. According to Theory 2, if in a two-stage reaction, Stage 1 is much slower than Stage 2, then the overall reaction rate will be:

A. primarily determined by the rate of Stage 1.
B. primarily determined by the rate of Stage 2.
C. undeterminable unless all collisions are counted.
D. undeterminable unless the rate law is measured experimentally.

34. When discussing the rates of reactions that have more than one stage, Theory 2 would not be necessary if:

F. all stages went quickly.
G. all stages had different rates.
H. the sum of the rates of each stage always equaled the rate of the reaction as a whole.
J. the sum of the rates of each stage was never equal to the rate of the reaction as a whole.

GO ON TO THE NEXT PAGE

Passage VII

Closely related species of butterflies are often found living in very different environments. A pair of experiments was performed in which butterfly species previously captured in either desert areas or mountain areas were tested in laboratory incubators to determine the conditions at which they could carry out important life functions such as mating, oviposition (egg-laying), and pupation (the stage in which the stationary cocoon undergoes its final development into an adult).

Experiment 1

Under conditions of 100% relative humidity (maximum moisture content of the air), 100 desert butterflies (Species D) and 100 mountain butterflies (Species M) were tested at temperature intervals of 2°C (from 0°C to 40°C) to determine if they could mate, oviposit, and pupate. Each species achieved at least 90% success at the following range of temperatures:

Table 1

TEMPERATURE RANGES (°C)			
	Mating	*Oviposition*	*Pupation*
Species D	10–34	14–34	4–38
Species M	6–30	10–28	4–34

Experiment 2

The experiment was repeated at 0% relative humidity (minimum moisture content of the air). The species achieved at least 90% success at the following range of temperatures:

Table 2

TEMPERATURE RANGES (°C)			
	Mating	*Oviposition*	*Pupation*
Species D	10–34	14–34	4–38
Species M	6–24	10–22	4–28

35. Results of Experiments 1 and 2 indicate that the life function with the narrowest range of temperature at which both species achieve 90% success is:

A. mating.
B. oviposition.
C. pupation.
D. The life function with the narrowest range of temperatures in Experiment 1 is different from that in Experiment 2.

36. Which condition has most detrimental effects on Species M for mating, oviposition, and pupation?

F. Moist air at low temperatures
G. Moist air at high temperatures
H. Dry air at low temperatures
J. Dry air at high temperatures

37. A third experiment was conducted at 100% relative humidity in which the temperature range *for caterpillar survival* (another life function) was tested in Species D and Species M. Species D achieved 90% success at 12°C–36°C, while Species M achieved 90% success at 8°C–30°C. Which range of temperatures is likely a good prediction of caterpillar survival in *Species D under dry conditions?*

A. 8°C–30°C
B. 8°C–24°C
C. 12°C–36°C
D. 12°C–30°C

38. If an investigator wanted to set up an experiment to determine the effects of light and dark on mating ability in Species D and Species M at 100% relative humidity, which set of conditions would provide the most complete results?

F. Test both species at 6°C in the light and 6°C in the dark.
G. Test both species at 20°C in the light and 20°C in the dark.
H. Test both species at 34°C in the light and 34°C in the dark.
J. Test both species at 34°C in the light and 30°C in the dark.

39. Which hypothesis is *not supported* by the results of Experiment 1 and Experiment 2?

A. For all tested life functions, dry conditions only affect Species M at the high end of its temperature ranges.
B. For all tested life functions, dry conditions have no effects on the temperature ranges of the desert species.
C. Species D does better than Species M at high temperatures in all tested life functions.
D. Species M does better than Species D at low temperatures for pupation.

40. Which of the following statements best explains the broad range of temperatures for pupation observed in both butterfly species?

F. Since the cocoon is stationary, it must be able to survive changing temperature conditions until the adult butterfly emerges.
G. Deserts can get very hot and mountains can get very cold.
H. Mountain butterflies would not survive long in the desert, and desert butterflies would not survive long in the mountains.
J. The stationary cocoon must be able to survive under light and dark conditions until the adult butterfly emerges.

IF YOU FINISH BEFORE TIME IS CALLED, YOU MAY CHECK YOUR WORK ON THIS TEST ONLY. DO NOT WORK ON ANY OTHER TEST SECTION. **STOP**

Answer Key

DIRECTIONS: For the *correct* answers in each ACT Test Subject, check the corresponding unshaded box. (Correct answers correspond to unshaded boxes.) Then, for each test, total the number of checkmarks in each column (subject category) and add to determine the raw scores.

TEST 1: ENGLISH (p. A-10)

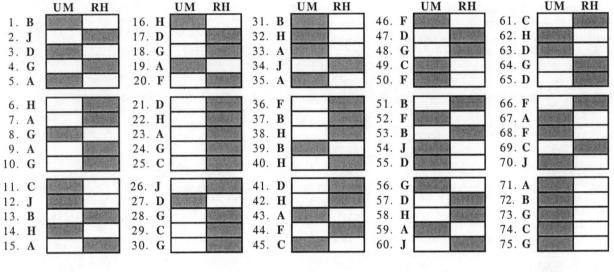

		UM	RH
1.	B	■	☐
2.	J	☐	■
3.	D	■	☐
4.	G	☐	■
5.	A	■	☐
6.	H	☐	■
7.	A	☐	■
8.	G	■	☐
9.	A	☐	■
10.	G	☐	■
11.	C	■	☐
12.	J	■	☐
13.	B	☐	■
14.	H	■	☐
15.	A	☐	■
16.	H	■	☐
17.	D	☐	■
18.	G	☐	■
19.	A	■	☐
20.	F	☐	■
21.	D	☐	■
22.	H	☐	■
23.	A	☐	■
24.	G	☐	■
25.	C	☐	■
26.	J	☐	■
27.	D	■	☐
28.	G	☐	■
29.	C	☐	■
30.	G	☐	■
31.	B	■	☐
32.	H	■	☐
33.	A	■	☐
34.	J	☐	■
35.	A	■	☐
36.	F	☐	■
37.	B	☐	■
38.	H	☐	■
39.	B	■	☐
40.	H	☐	■
41.	D	☐	■
42.	H	☐	■
43.	A	■	☐
44.	F	☐	■
45.	C	■	☐
46.	F	■	☐
47.	D	☐	■
48.	G	☐	■
49.	C	■	☐
50.	F	■	☐
51.	B	☐	■
52.	F	■	☐
53.	B	☐	■
54.	J	■	☐
55.	D	■	☐
56.	G	■	☐
57.	D	☐	■
58.	H	☐	■
59.	A	■	☐
60.	J	☐	■
61.	C	☐	■
62.	H	■	☐
63.	D	■	☐
64.	G	☐	■
65.	D	☐	■
66.	F	☐	■
67.	A	■	☐
68.	F	■	☐
69.	C	☐	■
70.	J	■	☐
71.	A	■	☐
72.	B	■	☐
73.	G	■	☐
74.	C	■	☐
75.	G	■	☐

Usage/Mechanics (UM): ______/39 Rhetorical Skills (RM): ______/36 English Raw Score (UM + RH): ______/75

TEST 2: MATHEMATICS (p. A-20)

		EA	AG	GT
1.	A	☐	■	■
2.	K	☐	■	■
3.	C	☐	■	■
4.	K	☐	■	■
5.	E	☐	■	■
6.	H	☐	■	■
7.	D	■	☐	■
8.	H	■	☐	■
9.	D	■	■	☐
10.	G	☐	■	■
11.	B	■	☐	■
12.	H	☐	■	■
13.	C	☐	■	■
14.	G	☐	■	■
15.	D	■	■	☐
16.	H	☐	■	■
17.	B	■	☐	■
18.	K	■	■	☐
19.	A	☐	■	■
20.	H	■	■	☐
21.	D	■	☐	■
22.	G	☐	■	■
23.	C	■	☐	■
24.	F	■	■	☐
25.	E	■	■	☐
26.	G	■	☐	■
27.	C	☐	■	■
28.	J	■	■	☐
29.	E	☐	■	■
30.	H	☐	■	■
31.	C	☐	■	■
32.	H	■	■	☐
33.	A	■	☐	■
34.	K	■	■	☐
35.	D	☐	■	■
36.	H	☐	■	■
37.	C	■	☐	■
38.	G	☐	■	■
39.	C	■	■	☐
40.	G	■	☐	■
41.	D	☐	■	■
42.	H	☐	■	■
43.	A	☐	■	■
44.	G	☐	■	■
45.	B	■	■	☐
46.	K	■	■	☐
47.	A	■	■	☐
48.	F	■	■	☐
49.	C	■	☐	■
50.	K	■	☐	■
51.	C	■	☐	■
52.	J	■	☐	■
53.	A	■	☐	■
54.	F	■	☐	■
55.	D	■	☐	■
56.	H	■ x	■	☐
57.	B	■	☐	■
58.	K	■	■	☐
59.	A	■	■	☐
60.	J	■	■	☐

Pre-Algebra/Elementary Algebra (EA): ______/24

Intermediate Algebra/Coordinate Geometry (AG): ______/18

Plane Geometry/Trigonometry (GT): ______/18

Total Raw Score (EA + AG + GT): ______/60

TEST 3: READING (p. A-28)

#	Answer	SS	S	H	PF
1.	B		■	■	■
2.	F		■	■	■
3.	D		■	■	■
4.	J		■	■	■
5.	C		■	■	■
6.	F		■	■	■
7.	C		■	■	■
8.	H		■	■	■
9.	C		■	■	■
10.	G		■	■	■
11.	A	■	■		■
12.	J	■	■		■
13.	B	■	■		■
14.	H	■	■		■
15.	A	■	■		■
16.	H	■	■		■
17.	C	■	■		■
18.	J	■	■		■
19.	A	■	■		■
20.	H	■	■		■
21.	B	■		■	■
22.	H	■		■	■
23.	A	■		■	■
24.	J	■		■	■
25.	C	■		■	■
26.	F	■		■	■
27.	A	■		■	■
28.	G	■		■	■
29.	B	■		■	■
30.	H	■		■	■
31.	C	■	■	■	
32.	J	■	■	■	
33.	B	■	■	■	
34.	J	■	■	■	
35.	A	■	■	■	
36.	G	■	■	■	
37.	A	■	■	■	
38.	F	■	■	■	
39.	B	■	■	■	
40.	F	■	■	■	

Social Studies (SS): ______/10

Sciences (S): ______/10

Humanities (H): ______/10

Prose Fiction (PF): ______/10

Reading Raw Score (SS + S + H + PF): ______/40

TEST 4: SCIENCE REASONING (p. A-35)

#	Answer	B	C	P	ES
1.	A	■		■	■
2.	F	■		■	■
3.	B	■		■	■
4.	H	■		■	■
5.	C	■		■	■
6.	J	■	■		■
7.	B	■	■		■
8.	H	■	■		■
9.	D	■	■		■
10.	F	■	■		■
11.	C	■	■		■
12.	H		■	■	■
13.	D		■	■	■
14.	G		■	■	■
15.	C		■	■	■
16.	J		■	■	■
17.	B		■	■	■
18.	J		■	■	■
19.	D		■	■	■
20.	F		■	■	■
21.	C		■	■	■
22.	F		■	■	■
23.	B	■	■	■	
24.	J	■	■	■	
25.	H	■	■	■	
26.	A	■	■	■	
27.	D	■	■	■	
28.	G	■		■	■
29.	B	■		■	■
30.	H	■		■	■
31.	D	■		■	■
32.	F	■		■	■
33.	A	■		■	■
34.	H	■		■	■
35.	B		■	■	■
36.	J		■	■	■
37.	C		■	■	■
38.	G		■	■	■
39.	D		■	■	■
40.	F		■	■	■

Biology (B): ______/17

Chemistry (C): ______/12

Physics (P): ______/6

Earth Science (ES): ______/5

Science Reasoning Raw Score (B + C + P + ES): ______/40

Explanatory Answers

TEST 1: ENGLISH (p. A-10)

1. (B) The original is needlessly repetitious: to begin is to start. (B) eliminates the unnecessary repetition.

2. (J) The original contains an error of diction. The correct word for making the comparison intended by the original is *from,* not *than.* (*Than* is a conjunction, and conjunctions are used to introduce clauses. What follows the underlined part of the sentence is a noun phrase—not a clause.) (G) fails to make the needed correction. (H) makes the needed correction but introduces a new error. In general, a modifier should be placed as close as possible to what it modifies. Here, *fundamentally* must modify *are different,* but the placement of *fundamentally* after *from* suggests that it is intended to modify *weapons.* Thus, (H) would result in an ambiguous sentence.

3. (D) The underlined material is needlessly repetitious. A weapon of *mass destruction* is one that could do *a great deal of harm.* Eliminate the surplus material.

4. (G) The original is a run-on sentence. (G) solves the problem by starting a new sentence at an appropriate point.

5. (A) The original is correct. (B) destroys the logic of the sentence. (C) ambiguously implies that injuries are unavailable. And (D) is needlessly wordy.

6. (H) The original is not idiomatic. (H) is idiomatic with *resulting from.* (G) and (J) are simply not idiomatic.

7. (A) The original is correct as written. The use of the subjunctive *would* correctly suggests that a nuclear war might or might not occur. (B) and (C) are both wrong because the indicative mood (*is* and *are*) doesn't have this meaning. Additionally, either (B) or (C) must be wrong because one uses a singular and the other a plural verb. The subject of the sentence is the compound subject *Number of deaths...and economic damage,* and a compound subject requires a plural verb. Thus (B) is wrong for yet another reason. In (D), although *might* preserves the element of contingency suggested by the subjunctive *would* the phrasing *more devastating even as* is not idiomatic.

8. (G) In the second paragraph the author is arguing that nuclear weapons are fundamentally different than conventional weapons because of their massive destructive power. (G) correctly summarizes this point.

9. (A) The original is correct. The other choices introduce errors in modification.

10. (G) The original has two mistakes. The original is a run-on sentence. Also, *it* is singular but refers to *weapons,* which is plural. (G) makes both the needed corrections.

11. (C) The original is not idiomatic. The correct idiom is *neither...nor,* not *neither...but.*

12. (J) The original is incorrect because a new paragraph should be started here. In the opening paragraph, the author announces that he or she will make three points. The second paragraph is devoted to the first point—the other two points should be presented in separate paragraphs.

13. (B) The original is awkward. (B) is more concise and reads better than the original. (C) is incorrect because the subject of the sentence is the singular verb *step.* (D) has the original errors and includes a plural verb.

14. (H) The original contains an ambiguous pronoun: who is they? The other choices all eliminate the ambiguous pronoun, but (H) is the most directly and concisely worded.

15. (A) In the initial paragraph, the author announces that three considerations should guide our formulation of a defense policy. The author then proceeds to address each consideration.

16. (H) Again, the author argues that three principles should guide our defense policy.

17. (D) The original lacks a main verb. (C) and (D) supply the verb, but (B) doesn't. (*Having viewed* is a participle form and cannot be a main verb.) In (C), *its* is intended to refer to *founders,* but *founders* is plural.

18. (G) The original is not idiomatic. The correct idiom is *rather than,* not *rather as.* Both (H) and (J) are wrong because they too are not idiomatic.

19. (A) This question tests whether you understand the relationship between ideas in the passage. The idea discussed in the second sentence of the passage is the result or effect of the idea discussed in the first sentence.

20. (F) The original is correct as written. (G) is needlessly wordy, so the original is preferable. (H) completely destroys the logical structure of the sentence. The resulting construction would read: *The founders viewed education in political terms instead of to academic excellence.* And (J) changes the intended meaning of the sentence by implying that the founders could have chosen to view education as academic excellence—rather than as a means to academic excellence.

21. (D) The problem with the sentence as originally written is that it lacks a conjugated or main verb. *Talking* is a participle and cannot function as a main verb. Only (D) supplies a conjugated verb form.

22. (H) The original is incorrectly punctuated. *Goals* is an appositive that refers to *liberty*, etc. The correct punctuation is a comma preceding the appositive. (G) is wrong because the period completely isolates the appositive from the sentence that supports it and turns everything following the comma into a sentence fragment. (J) is also incorrectly punctuated. The semicolon is too powerful—it signals that an independent clause will follow. An appositive, however, is dependent for its existence on the nouns that come before it, so a comma provides enough separation from the main body of the sentence without being too powerful.

23. (A) The original is correct as written. To *take precedence over* is an English idiom meaning to be more important than something else. (B) distorts the intended meaning of the original. To *precede* means to come before in time, so the resulting sentence would make no sense. (C) is simply not idiomatic.

24. (G) The original contains three errors. First, the parenthetical expression signaled by the comma following *generation* must be closed by a comma, not a dash. (You can use dashes or commas to set off such remarks—but not a mixture of both.) Second, the subject of the sentence is *generation,* which is singular. So the plural noun *assert* is wrong. Third, *their* refers to *generation* and so fails to agree in number with its referent. (G) makes all three changes. (H) makes two of the changes, but the semicolon is a mistake. The semicolon would be used to separate two clauses, but what follows the semicolon used in (H) is not a clause. Finally, (J) fails to correct the third error mentioned above and is incorrectly punctuated. (You need that second comma.) Additionally, (J) uses the present tense verb *asserts,* which is inconsistent with the other verbs in the selection.

25. (C) The verb *was* is singular and fails to agree with its plural subject, *ingredients.* (C) corrects this problem. (B) eliminates the problem of agreement. *Being* is a participle and doesn't show number. Unfortunately, since *being* is a participle, the resulting construction lacks a main verb, and the sentence becomes a sentence fragment. Finally, (D) distorts the intended meaning of the original. The author does not mean to say the principal ingredients of a civic education were similar to literacy and inculcation of patriotic and moral virtues.

26. (J) The original is a run-on sentence. You have two clauses run together without any punctuation and with no conjunction. (J) is one way of solving the problem: use a semicolon to separate the two clauses. (You could also use a comma and a coordinate conjunction such as *and.*) The dash cannot be used to separate two clauses, so (G) is wrong. As for (H), a comma by itself is just not strong enough to do the job.

27. (D) The original contains an error of illogical subordination compounded by a punctuation mistake. The two ideas joined at the underlined part have equal importance. One should not be subordinated to the other, but *since* always signals a subordinate idea. Additionally, a semicolon cannot be used to join a subordinate clause to an independent or main clause. (B) solves the subordination problem, but *and* signals a continuation of a thought. The second idea here contrasts with the first and should be signaled by a word like *but.* (C) eliminates the punctuation mistake but creates a sentence fragment of the second half of the sentence. *Since* introduces a subordinate clause that must be joined to an independent or main clause.

28. (G) The original sentence is not idiomatic. The correct idiom here requires the use of the infinitive *to be* rather than the gerund *being.* (H) and (J) both correct this error, but (H) and (J) also eliminate the only conjugated verb in the clause. The result is a fragment rather than a complete sentence.

29. (C) The placement of *almost* is not idiomatic. Given its proximity to *agreed, almost* seems to modify *agreed* rather than *universally.* But the intended meaning of the sentence is that *almost* modifies *universally.* (C) provides the correct and idiomatic placement of *almost.* (B) is also not idiomatic. As for (D), although the words are in the correct order, the comma between *universally*, an adverb, and the word it modifies, *agreed,* disrupts the logical flow of the sentence.

30. (G) The underlined part is incorrect because it destroys the parallelism of the sentence. You have a series of three elements: *emphasized, put*, and *attempt*. The third element is a noun rather than a verb. (G) restores the parallelism of the sentence by supplying a verb. (H) fails to provide a verb. Finally, although (J) includes a verb, it also includes a subject. The result is a clause, and the clause is not parallel to the verb forms.

31. (B) The final paragraph contains a new thought that extends the development of the essay: this is the content of the textbooks.

32. (H) The passage is a discussion of old textbooks. What audience would be most interested in old textbooks? Surely *teachers.*

33. (A) The original is correct as written. (B) destroys the logic of the sentence. (C) and (D) are illogical because the sentence intends to refer generally to the contribution of women as a whole—not to the contribution of any particular individual.

34. (J) The original is not idiomatic. (J) provides the correct idiom: *range from...to*. (G) and (H) fail to correct this problem.

35. (A) The original is correct as written. It is idiomatic, and the past tense verb *marked* is consistent with the other past tense verbs in the selection. (B) is wrong because the present-perfect *has marked* implies an action that began in the past but continues into the present. (C) is wordy and awkward. As for (D), the use of the passive voice completely destroys the logic of the sentence.

36. (F) The original is correct as written: *effort was made...to utilize.* (G) and (H) are simply not idiomatic—*effort was made...being able to utilize, effort was made...utilizing.* Finally, (J) destroys the logical structure of the sentence: *effort was made...and utilize.*

37. (B) The original uses an incorrect verb tense. The present tense *falls* conflicts with the other past tense verbs of the selection. (B) and (D) both make the needed correction, but (D) is not idiomatic. The correct idiom is *falls within a category.* Although *falls in* is idiomatic, *falls in* has a meaning that is not appropriate here. (C) is grammatically incorrect because it eliminates the only conjugated verb in the clause introduced by *while.*

38. (H) The original is not idiomatic. The correct idiom is *reserved for,* not *reserved by. Reserved by* has a meaning that is not appropriate here. (G) is needlessly wordy and ambiguous. (G) is ambiguous because it is not clear what the phrase is intended to modify. It seems to modify *women*, but the intent of the sentence is that the phrase modify *work*. (J) is also wordy and awkward.

39. (B) The original uses an illogical transition word. *However* is used to signal a contrast, but the sentence that is introduced by *however* is actually a continuation of the thought contained in the previous sentence. (B) is correct because, since there is no transition word, the reader will naturally assume that the next sentence will continue the train of thought. (C) is wrong because the use of *but* tells the reader to expect a contrasting thought. Finally, (D) eliminates the only conjugated verb in the sentence, so the result is a fragment rather than a complete sentence.

40. (H) The original is incorrectly punctuated. Since there is no punctuation between *activity* and *knitting,* a reader won't pause after *activity.* Consequently, *knitting* seems to be a participle that somehow modifies *activity.* The author intends, however, for *knitting* to be a gerund in the series including *knitting, canning,* and *planting.* The correct punctuation in a series like this is the colon.

41. (D) The original contains an error of pronoun usage. The pronoun *their* refers to *homemaker*—the singular *her* should be used. (B) eliminates the problem by using no pronoun at all. The resulting structure is a bit awkward (*demonstrate patriotism*) but not incorrect. But the verb in (B) is not acceptable. The *could be demonstrating* is inconsistent with the other verbs in the paragraph. (C) is incorrect—the verb *could have demonstrated* implies that a woman might or might not have demonstrated her patriotism, but this is not the intended meaning. The author means to assert

definitely that women did demonstrate their patriotism. (C) is also wrong because it fails to correct the pronoun problem.

42. (H) The original is incorrectly punctuated. The colon seems to signal a clarification of the idea of hostessing at canteens. Instead, the hostessing is one of a group of activities women volunteered to do. So the correct punctuation is a comma.

43. (A) The material between the commas is an adjective phrase: "...*Army, dressed...and armed...with the Musket, was dispatched.*" The other choices destroy this logic.

44. (F) The original is correct as written. The other choices disrupt the parallelism of the sentence. Since the two verbs *performed* and *laid* have a similar function in the sentence, they should both have similar forms. (G) and (H) use the passive voice and are not parallel to the active voice *performed.* (J) is the participle and is not parallel to *performed,* a conjugated verb.

45. (C) One way of fixing the order of the paragraphs is to recognize that neither [2] nor [3] can be the first paragraph. The *this* in the first sentence of [2] clearly refers to something that has come before. Similarly, the phrase *much of the work* in the first sentence of [3] also refers to something that has come before. [1] appears to be the best choice for the first paragraph, because [4] seems to be a summary or conclusion. Only (C) has [4] as the conclusion, so pick it! As for [2] and [3], [2] must follow [3] because [2] is intended to contrast with [3]: most of the work was traditional but some was not. But a reader cannot understand the importance of the contrast suggested by [2] without the information provided by [3].

46. (F) Examples are often helpful. They enable readers to understand a general point in a more concrete fashion.

47. (D) *Undertaken* is the past participle of the verb *to undertake.* A past participle is not itself a complete verb. (D) solves this problem by creating a sentence that uses the passive voice: *changes were undertaken.*

48. (G) The original is not idiomatic. The sentence means to say that the new values were embraced by some people, and that is the sense of (G). (H) and (J) are also wrong because they are not idiomatic.

49. (C) The two ideas joined at the underlined part contrast with each other: these did something; the others did not. To signal this contrast, you must use something other than *and. But* is an acceptable choice, so (C) is correct. (B) and (D) are incorrect because *since* and *consequently* signal a relationship in which one idea follows from or is the consequence of another.

50. (F) The original is correct. By comparison the other choices are needlessly wordy and awkward.

51. (B) The comma and *and* signal that the last half of the sentence must be a clause. The original, however, contains no main verb. (B) supplies a main verb in the right tense that also agrees in number with its subject *notions.*

52. (F) The original is correct. This is the proper place at which to begin a new paragraph since the author is shifting from talking about the past to a discussion of the present. Since you need a new paragraph here, (G) and (J) are wrong. And (J) is wrong for the additional reason that the use of *owing to* in place of *because of* is low-level usage. Finally, although (H) correctly begins a new paragraph, the second comma illogically isolates the subject of the sentence from its verb.

53. (B) In the original, *clear* is intended to modify *evident.* But that is a job that can be done only by the adverb *clearly.* In any event, clear and evident are synonyms, so you don't need both.

54. (J) The transitional word here must signal a contrast between two ideas. The best choice is *yet.*

55. (D) *Being* is a participle that can function as an adjective. But there is no noun that can logically be modified by *being.* What the sentence means to assert is that the cause of the lack of a stable value system is the influence of Western ideas.

56. (G) The *and so* distorts the logical structure of the sentence. It seems to introduce another clause, but what follows lacks a main verb. By eliminating the *and so,* (G) allows *emphasizing,* a participle, to function as an adjective modifying *textbooks.* (Note: Although you ordinarily want your modifiers close to what they modify, here there is no possibility of misunderstanding.) (H) results in a sentence that is distorted because the *and* seems to join another verb to the first verb *expound. But emphasis* is a noun, not a

verb. Thus, with (H) you get: *textbooks expound...and emphasis.* As for (J), *that* seems to introduce a relative clause, but no verb follows.

57. (D) *Often sometimes* is not a possible phrase in English because the two words have opposite meanings. You have to eliminate one or the other. All of the choices make this correction. (B), however, uses a verb tense that is inconsistent with the other tenses in the paragraph. As for (C), *distorted* is a past participle and cannot stand alone. It requires another verb such as *are.*

58. (H) The original contains two errors. First, the past tense *translated* is inconsistent with the present tense verbs in the rest of the paragraph. Second, *who* should replace *that* since it refers to people. Only (H) makes both corrections.

59. (A) In the last paragraph, the author introduces the topic of Japanese youth; it would be appropriate for the discussion to continue along these lines.

60. (J) The original doesn't contain a grievous error, but on balance it is not as idiomatic as (J). The placement of *always* directly before the main element of the verb instead of before the *have* is preferable to the original. (G) is wrong because *have* does not agree with the singular *humankind.* And (H) is wrong because the present tense is inconsistent with the introductory phrase *from the beginning.*

61. (C) In English, if an adjective has more than one or two syllables, we form the comparative using more rather than by adding *-er*.

62. (H) The comma following *agriculture* a few words after the underlined portion has no logical function in the sentence as written. (H) solves this problem by allowing it to mark the close of a parenthetical expression introduced by a first comma in front of *along.* (G) attempts the correction, but (G) is wrong because the resulting phrase has no clear logical connection with the rest of the sentence. The resulting phrase consists of a noun modified by a prepositional phrase, but the noun can't just sit there—it has to do something. But because of the punctuation, the noun can't do its natural job, which would be to function as the subject of the sentence. ([H] doesn't have this problem. In [H], the noun *discovery* is the object of a preposition, and the prepositional phrase is connected to the rest of the sentence as a modifier of *domestication.*) (J) destroys the logical structure of the sentence by isolating the subject from the verb. The semicolon is too strong.

63. (D) The underlined material is repetitious.

64. (G) The original contains two errors. First, it lacks parallelism. As written, it reads: *between regarding...and to consider.* Second, the pronoun *them* does not agree in number with its antecedent *animal.* Only (G) corrects both of these problems. (H) solves the problem of parallelism but fails to eliminate the wrong pronoun. And (J) doesn't correct either mistake.

65. (D) The original contains two errors. First, the placement of *seemingly* is incorrect. *Seemingly* is intended to modify *every*, which in turn modifies *subject.* But its placement in the verb seems to suggest that Aristotle wrote in a style that could be called *seemingly.* Second, the present tense *writes* is inconsistent with the other verbs in the sentence; e.g., *seemed* and *was.* (Note: the present tense verbs are used to describe our attitudes today. Although Aristotle wrote in the past, we currently have certain attitudes about those writings.) (B) corrects the one problem but not the other. Simply putting *seemingly* into parentheses does not clarify what the word is supposed to modify. As for (C), while this eliminates the problem of verb tense by reducing the verb to a participle modifying *Aristotle,* you still have the ambiguity created by *seemingly.*

66. (F) The original is correct as written. The comma following *subjects* marks the end of the introductory dependent clause. You do need punctuation at that point, so (H) is wrong. The correct punctuation is a comma—the semicolon and the colon are both too powerful, so (G) and (J) are wrong as well.

67. (A) The transition word here must connect the two ideas: Aristotle was interested in all life; he was particularly interested in marine life. *And* correctly coordinates these two ideas. Had the passage gone on to discuss marine life in particular, then the contrast set up by the *but* in (C) makes that the better choice.

68. (F) The original is correct as written. *Wedding is* a participle that modifies *observer.* (G) distorts the intended meaning of the original by suggesting that Aristotle was himself joined to something. The sentence means to say that Aristotle joined two ideas. (H) is needlessly wordy and awkward compared to

the original. Finally, (J) creates a prepositional phrase that doesn't clearly modify any other element in the sentence.

69. (C) The original is incorrectly punctuated. You must use quotation marks to indicate the start of the quotation. (B) fails to make this correction and makes another error of punctuation. The dash cannot be used in place of the period. (D) is wrong because the adverb simply cannot be used as a predicate complement; that is, *simply* cannot modify the subject of the sentence.

70. (J) The original is needlessly wordy. *Link* and *combine* both have the meaning of *join*, so you should get rid of one or the other.

71. (A) The original is correct. By comparison, the other choices are needlessly wordy and awkward.

72. (B) The author's use of Aristotle's own words is particularly forceful. It lets Aristotle make the point for himself.

73. (G) The passage is expository but not overly technical. Its main topic is Aristotle.

74. (C) The focus of the passage is Aristotle and his interest in the natural world.

75. (G) The function of the first paragraph is to place Aristotle in a certain context.

TEST 2: MATHEMATICS (p. A-20)

1. (A) With a single equation with one variable, solve for x: $\frac{1}{x} + \frac{1}{x} = 8 \Rightarrow \frac{2}{x} = 8 \Rightarrow x = \frac{1}{4}$. Or, reason that $\frac{1}{x}$ and $\frac{1}{x}$ are equal, and since their sum is 8, x must be 4. So the value of x must be $\frac{1}{4}$.

2. (K) Evaluate the expression: $3x - 4y = 3(2) - 4(-1) = 6 - (-4) = 6 + 4 = 10$.

3. (C) This question asks about percents. 20% of 600 boys = 120 boys on honor roll. 30% of 400 girls = 120 girls on honor roll. Therefore, 120 boys + 120 girls = 240 students on honor roll.

4. (K) Since an even number times any other whole number yields an even number, the correct answer is (K). None of the other letters guarantees an even result. If this insight escapes you, you can experiment with some values. For each letter, assume that that letter only is even and that all other numbers are odd. Only t generates an even result under those circumstances.

5. (E) This is a long question but it is not that difficult. You must see that the number of flies in each successive week is four times the number of the previous week. So the final count should be $4 \cdot 192 = 768$.

6. (H) You can use the formula for finding the number of permutations to solve this question: $3! = 3 \cdot 2 \cdot 1 = 6$. Or you could count the number of possibilities: ABC, ACB, BAC, BCA, CAB, CBA.

7. (D) This question tests basic coordinate geometry. Since the x-coordinate of both points is 2, the line runs parallel to the y-axis. The x-coordinate of the midpoint will also be 2. As for the y-coordinate, the midpoint is halfway between 2 and –2—0.

8. (H) Since the absolute value of xy is positive, xy itself must be positive (since $|xy| = xy$). Therefore, both x and y have the same sign. They might both be positive, or they might both be negative.

And it doesn't make any difference which is larger. So (F), (G), (J), and (K) can all be true. x and y cannot, however, have different signs, because a positive times a negative yields a negative result. And, of course, you could have tried substituting numbers. If $x > 0 > y$, then x could be 1 and y could be –1, and $1 \cdot -1 = -1$.

9. (D) Just convert the dimensions shown to real dimensions. Since 1 centimeter is equal to 4 meters, the width of the room is 4 meters, and the length is 4.8. So the area of the room is $4 \cdot 4.8 = 19.2$.

10. (G) This question tests powers. $30{,}000 \cdot 20 = 600{,}000 = 6 \cdot 10^5$. (One power of ten for each zero.)

11. (B) Solve this problem with simultaneous equations. Let x be the quantity of chocolates and y the quantity of caramels: $x + y = 4$ and $3x + 2y = 10 \Rightarrow y = 4 - x \Rightarrow 3x + 2(4 - x) = 10 \Rightarrow 3x + 8 - 2x = 10 \Rightarrow x = 10 - 8 = 2$.

Or you can test the answers, starting with (C). If Karen buys 2.5 pounds of chocolates, she bought 4 – 2.5 = 1.5 pounds of caramels and the total cost would be $(2.5 \cdot 3) + (1.5 \cdot 2) = 7.50 + 3 = \$10.50$. This is too much money and wrong. Since chocolates are more expensive than caramels, Karen bought less than 2.5 pounds of chocolates. So try (B): 2 pounds of chocolates and 2 pounds of caramels would cost $(2 \cdot 3) + (2 \cdot 2) = 10$.

12. (H) You can use the procedure you learned for finding a missing element of an average. The total of all three numbers is 3 • 80 = 240. The total of the two numbers you know is 2 • 80 = 160. So the missing number is 240 – 160 = 80. Or, you might have used the "above and below" method. Since 80 is neither above nor below the average, the first two 80s are equal to the average, so the final number can be neither above nor below the average. It must be 80.

13. (C) The total number of ratio parts in the ratio 5:2 is 7, and 10 is not evenly divisible by 7.

14. (G) You can treat this equation as a proportion. Cross-multiply and solve for x: $\frac{4}{5} = \frac{x}{4} \Rightarrow 4(4) = 5x \Rightarrow x = \frac{16}{5}$.

15. (D) Let us label the unlabeled angles:

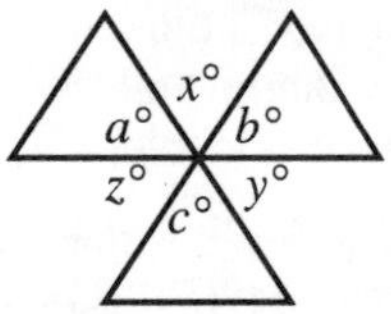

Since the measure of the degrees in a circle is 360, the sum of x, y, and z plus the sum of a, b, and c is 360. What is the value of the angles inside the triangles? Since they are equilateral triangles, each angle is 60°: $3(60) + x + y + z = 360 \Rightarrow x + y + z = 180$.

16. (H) This is just an exercise in multiplying fractions. If Peter spent $\frac{1}{4}$ of his allowance on Monday, he had $\frac{3}{4}$ of his allowance left. Then, he spent $\frac{1}{3}$ of that $\frac{3}{4}$ on Tuesday: $\frac{1}{3} \cdot \frac{3}{4} = \frac{1}{4}$. After spending the additional $\frac{1}{4}$, he has left $\frac{3}{4} - \frac{1}{4} = \frac{1}{2}$ of the original allowance. Of course, you could have substituted numbers but the arithmetic would have been the same.

17. (B) There are three ways of arriving at the solution. The simplest and most direct is to reason that if 100 bricks weigh p pounds, 20 bricks, which is $\frac{1}{5}$ of 100, must weigh $\frac{1}{5}$ of p.

This same reasoning can be expressed using a direct proportion. The more bricks, the greater the weight, so $\frac{100}{20} = \frac{p}{x} \Rightarrow 100x = 20p \Rightarrow x = \frac{20p}{100} \Rightarrow x = \frac{p}{5}$.

Finally, you could have substituted numbers. Assume that 100 bricks weigh 100 pounds, which is 1 pound apiece. 20 bricks weigh 20 pounds. On the assumption that p = 100, the correct formula will generate the number 20.

18. (K) The following drawings show that I, II, and III are possible.

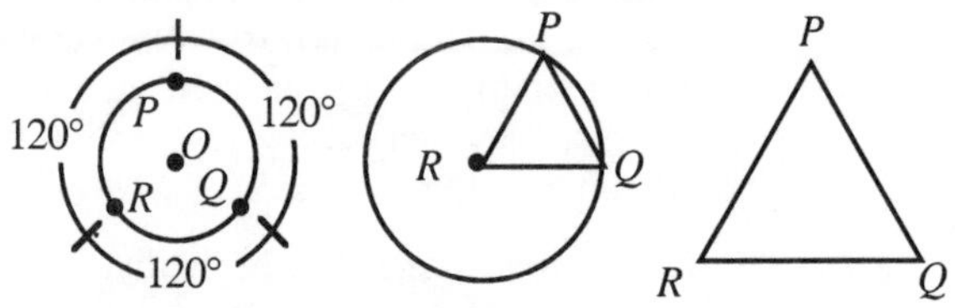

The thing to watch for here is the test-prep blunder. Both I and III are fairly obvious possibilities; II is more subtle.

19. (A) This problem can be solved with the "changeover" principle. But, you object, that is five different calculations. True, so look for an escape route: approximation. The percent increase in the period 1950–1955 was $\frac{4-2}{2}$ = 100 percent. For the next period it was $\frac{3}{4}$, which is less than 100 percent. For the next, $\frac{8}{12} = \frac{2}{3}$, which is less than 100 percent. And for the last, it was $\frac{10}{20}$, which is less than 100 percent. The answer is (A).

20. (H) The easiest approach is just to perform the multiplication for the answer choices:

F.	$(x-6)(x+2) = x^2 - 4x - 12$	X
G.	$(x-4)(x+3) = x^2 - x - 12$	X
H.	$(x-2)(x+6) = x^2 + 4x - 12$	√
J.	$(x+2)(x+6) = x^2 + 8x + 12$	X
K.	$(x+3)(x+4) = x^2 + 7x + 12$	X

21. (D) The best approach to this question is just to do the algebra. Since the average of $3x - 2$ and $2x - 3$ is 10, their sum is 20: $3x - 2 + 2x - 3 = 20 \Rightarrow 5x - 5 = 20 \Rightarrow 5x = 25 \Rightarrow x = 5$. So one of the packages weighs $3(5) - 2$ = 13 pounds and the other weighs $2((5) - 3 = 7$ pounds. So the difference between their weights is 6.

22. (G) This question is a variation on the theme of an average with missing elements. Since ten students have scores of 75 or more, the total of their scores is at minimum 10 • 75 = 750. Then, even assuming the other five students each scored zero, the average for the 15 would be at least 750 ÷ 15 = 50.

23. (C) Since $16 = 4^2$, $16^x = (4^2)^x = 4^{2x}$. You could reach the same conclusion by assuming a value for x, say, 1. On that assumption, $16^x = 16^1 = 16$. Now substitute 1 for x in the answer choices. The correct choice will yield the value 16:

A. $1^{16} = 1$	X
B. $2^{3(1)} = 2^3 = 8$	X
C. $4^{2(1)} = 4^2 = 16$	√
D. $8^{2(1)} = 8^2 = 64$	X
E. $8^{4(1)} = 8^4$	X

24. (F) The figure is a square, so the two sides are equal: $2x + 1 = x + 4 \Rightarrow x = 3$. Each side is $x + 4 = 3 + 4 = 7$; the perimeter is $4(7) = 28$.

25. (E) You can work this out algebraically. Let w be the width of the rectangle. The length of the rectangle is twice that, or $2w$. So the rectangle has an area of $w \bullet 2w = 2w^2$. Then, w is also the length of the hypotenuse of a 45-45-90 triangle. Each of the other two sides (the ones that form the right angle) is $\frac{1}{2} \bullet w \bullet \sqrt{2} = \frac{\sqrt{2}w}{2}$. (Since the two sides form a right angle, they can be the altitude and base.) So the area of the triangle is $\frac{1}{2} \bullet$ altitude $\bullet$ base $= \frac{1}{2} \bullet \frac{\sqrt{2}w}{2} \bullet \frac{\sqrt{2}w}{2} = \frac{1}{2} \bullet \frac{w^2}{4}$. And the ratio of the area of the rectangle to that of the triangle is $\frac{2w^2}{\frac{w^2}{4}} = \frac{2}{\frac{1}{4}} = \frac{8}{1}$.

It's true the explanation above is difficult to follow without a diagram—therefore draw a figure when one is not provided:

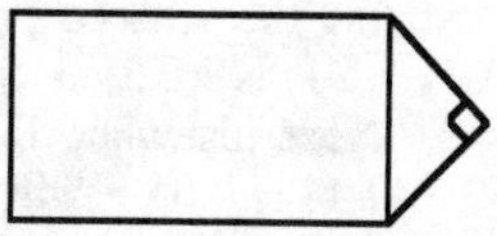

Now the explanation will not only be easier to follow; you can dispense with it altogether. In the first place, the rectangle is obviously bigger than the triangle, so you can eliminate three choices: (A), (B), and (C). Next, a quick addition to the figure shows that the area of the triangle is less then $\frac{1}{4}$ of the area of the rectangle:

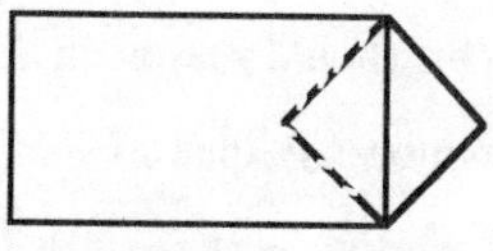

By the process of elimination, (E) is correct.

26. (G) No diagram is provided, so sketch one:

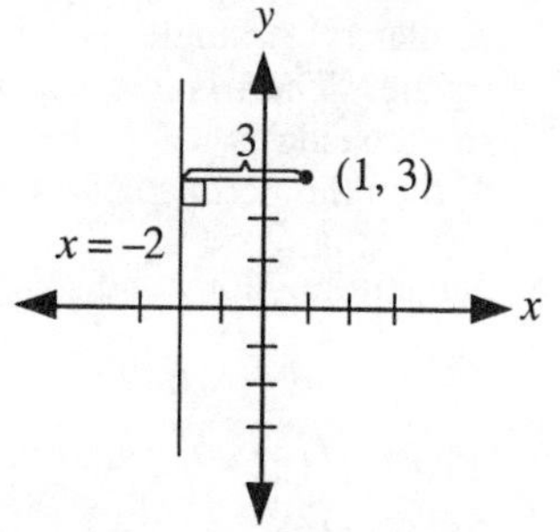

27. (C) This question can be answered using "supermarket math." You find out how much coffee costs per pound: $\frac{\$12}{5 \text{ pounds}} = \$2.40$ per pound. Then you divide \$30 by \$2.40: $\$30 \div \$2.40 = 12.5$. The steps of the process can all be represented in a single proportion: $\frac{\text{Cost } X}{\text{Cost } Y} = \frac{\text{Pounds } X}{\text{Pounds } Y} \Rightarrow \frac{\$12}{\$30} = \frac{5}{x} \Rightarrow 12x = 5(30) \Rightarrow x = \frac{150}{12} = 12.5$.

28. (J) Attack the question directly. Find the perimeter of each triangle. Since the triangles are equilateral, the smaller one has a perimeter of $3 + 3 + 3 = 9$, and the larger one has a perimeter of $12 + 12 + 12 = 36$. And $\frac{9}{36} = \frac{1}{4}$.

Alternatively, you might have reasoned that since the triangles are equilateral, the ratio of their perimeters is the same as the ratio of their sides. So the ratio of their perimeters will also be $\frac{3}{12}$, or $\frac{1}{4}$.

The second line of reasoning is more elegant (simpler), but who needs elegance when the first line of attack is easily managed anyway?

29. (E) Substitute –2 for x in the function: $f(-2) = -3(-2)^3 + 3(-2)^2 - 4(-2) + 8 = -3(-8) + 3(4) - (-8) + 8 = 24 + 12 + 8 + 8 = 52$.

30. (H) First add 30 percent to the \$120 wholesale price: \$120 + (0.30 • \$120) = \$120 + \$36 = \$156. Now find the sale price: \$156 – (0.40 • \$156) = \$156 – \$62.40 = \$93.60.

31. (C) You should reason in English that $\frac{1}{3}$ of the number is equal to $\frac{1}{5}$ of the number plus 2. Therefore: $\frac{1}{3}(x) = \frac{1}{5}(x) + 2 \Rightarrow \frac{1}{3}(x) - 2 = \frac{1}{5}(x)$ or $\frac{1}{3}(x) - \frac{1}{5}(x) = 2$.

32. (H) This is a composite figure. One side of the equilateral triangle is also a side of the square. The triangle has a perimeter of 12, so each side is 4. If the square has a side of 4, then the perimeter is 4 + 4 + 4 + 4 = 16.

33. (A) Substitute $\frac{2}{3}$ for x and solve for k:

$$12\left(\tfrac{2}{3}\right)^2 + k\left(\tfrac{2}{3}\right) = 6$$
$$12\left(\tfrac{4}{9}\right) + k\left(\tfrac{2}{3}\right) = 6$$
$$4\left(\tfrac{4}{3}\right) + k\left(\tfrac{2}{3}\right) = 6$$
$$k\left(\tfrac{2}{3}\right) = 6 - \left(\tfrac{16}{3}\right)$$
$$k\left(\tfrac{2}{3}\right) = \left(\tfrac{18}{3}\right) - \left(\tfrac{16}{3}\right)$$
$$k\left(\tfrac{2}{3}\right) = \left(\tfrac{2}{3}\right)$$
$$k = 1$$

34. (K) The perimeter equals the sum of the lengths of the sides: $2(x - 2y) + 4(2x + y) = (2x - 4y) + (8x + 4y) = 2x + 8x - 4y + 4y = 10x$.

Alternatively, substitute numbers. Assume that $x = 3$ and $y = 1$. The two short sides are each $3 - 2(1) = 1$, for a total of 2. And the four long sides are $2(3) + 1 = 7$, for a total of 28. The perimeter is $28 + 2 = 30$. So if $x = 3$ and $y = 1$, the correct formula will generate the number 30. Only (K) produces the correct value.

35. (D) Set up an equation. Let x be the number of packages in the van before the driver makes her first delivery: $\left(x - \frac{2}{5}x\right) - 3 = \frac{1}{2}(x) \Rightarrow \frac{3}{5}(x) - 3 = \frac{1}{2}(x) \Rightarrow \frac{3}{5}(x) - \frac{1}{2}(x) = 3 \Rightarrow \frac{1}{10}(x) = 3 \Rightarrow x = 30$.

Alternatively, this is a perfect question for test-the-test. Try an easy value like 25, then 30.

36. (H) The largest common factor of 12 and 8 is 4, so you can factor out a 4 from the coefficients of the two terms. Then, you can also factor out x^2 and y^2. The result is: $4x^2y^2(3x - 2y)$.

37. (C) Rewrite the expression:

$$\frac{1}{1+\frac{1}{x}} = \frac{1}{\frac{x+1}{x}} = 1\left(\frac{x}{x+1}\right) = \frac{x}{x+1}$$

Or substitute numbers. If $x = 1$, then:

$$\frac{1}{1+\frac{1}{x}} = \frac{1}{1+\frac{1}{1}} = \frac{1}{1+1} = \frac{1}{2}$$

On the assumption that $x = 1$, (B) and (C) both generate the result $\frac{1}{2}$. So try another number, say, $x = 2$. If $x = 2$, the correct answer should generate the value $\frac{2}{3}$. Now you eliminate (B), and (C) must be correct.

38. (G) You can solve this problem using S and T as unknowns. Since S is 150 percent of T, S equals $1.5T$. Then the question asks you to express $\frac{T}{S+T}$ as a percent. Just substitute $1.5T$ for S: $\frac{T}{1.5T+T} = \frac{T}{2.5T} = \frac{1}{2.5} = 40$ percent.

If you don't like working with letters, then pick some numbers. Let S be 15 and T be 10. Then $\frac{T}{S+T} = \frac{10}{10+15} = \frac{10}{25} = 40\%$.

39. (C) No figure is provided, so sketch one:

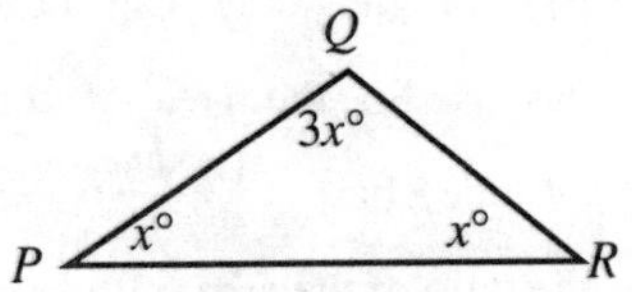

$x + x + 3x = 180 \Rightarrow 5x = 180 \Rightarrow x = 36$.

40. (G) Use a direct proportion: $\frac{b}{x} = \frac{d}{C} \Rightarrow bC = dx \Rightarrow C = \frac{dx}{b}$.

41. (D) First find the reduced price: \$64 – (25% of \$64) = \$64 – (0.25 • \$64) = \$64 – \$16 = \$48. Next, calculate the sales tax on \$48: 5% of \$48 = 0.05 • \$48 = \$2.40. Now find the total cost: \$48.00 + \$2.40 = \$50.40.

42. (H) Use the method for solving simultaneous equations: $\frac{y}{z} = k - 1 \Rightarrow k = \frac{y}{z} + 1$. And since $\frac{x}{z} = k$: $\frac{x}{z} = \frac{y}{z} + 1 \Rightarrow x = z\left(\frac{y}{z} + 1\right) = y + z$.

43. (A) If $x = 0.25y$, then $y = \frac{x}{0.25} = 4x$. So y is 400 percent of x.

44. (G) Since 3 is a factor of 9 and 5 is a factor of 5, any multiple of both 9 and 5 will be a multiple of 15. So (II) belongs in the correct choice. (I), however, is not correct. x could

be any multiple of 45, e.g., 90, which also proves that (III) does not belong in the correct choice.

45. (B) The neat thing about a cube is that if you have any one feature; e.g., volume, edge, diagonal of a face, diagonal of the cube, surface area, you can calculate every other feature. It is for this reason that cubes are often the focus of test problems. Given that the edge has a length of 2, we can use the Pythagorean Theorem to find length of the diagonal of a face:

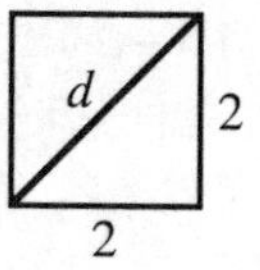

$d^2 = 2^2 + 2^2 = 4 + 4 = 8 \Rightarrow d = 2\sqrt{2}$. Now we can find the length of the diagonal of the cube:

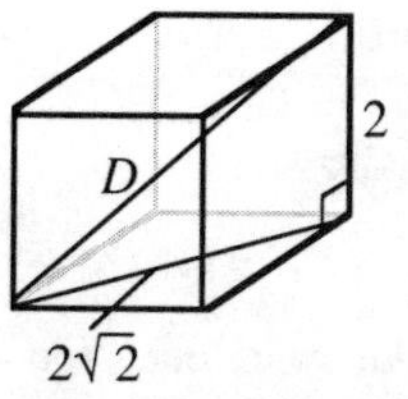

$D^2 = 2^2 + (2\sqrt{2})^2 = 4 + 8 = 12 \Rightarrow D = 2\sqrt{3}$. That is the length of the entire diagonal of the cube. The point that is the center of the cube is the midpoint of the diagonal of the cube and is $\sqrt{3}$ from each vertex.

46. (K) The formula for calculating the volume of a cylinder is: $V = \pi r^2 h$. So the volume of the larger cylinder is just that. Now we redefine the dimensions of the smaller cylinder in terms of r and h: $r = kr'$ so $r' = \frac{r}{k}$ and $h = kh'$ so $h' = \frac{h}{k}$. And the volume of the smaller cylinder is: $V = \pi(\frac{r}{k})^2(\frac{h}{k}) = \frac{\pi r^2 h}{k^3}$. And the ratio is: $\frac{\pi r^2 h}{\frac{\pi r^2 h}{k^3}} = k^3$.

As an alternative, you could assume some numbers. Let the radius and height of the larger cylinder be 4 and 4, respectively, and those of the smaller cylinder 2 and 2. Since $r = kr'$ and $h = kh'$, k must be 2. Now the larger cylinder has a volume of: $V = \pi(4)^2 4 = 64\pi$. And the smaller cylinder a volume of: $V = \pi(2)^2 2 = 8\pi$. And the ratio 64π to 8π is 8 to 1 or simply 8. Now, using (K) = 2, find an answer choice that has the value 8:

F. $\frac{1}{\pi}$ X
G. π X
H. 8π X
J. $\frac{1}{8}$ X
K. 8 √

47. (A) Since this is a right triangle, the adjacent sides intercept an arc of 180 degrees. (An inscribed angle intercepts twice the arc.) So the hypotenuse of the triangle is also the diameter of the circle. And given any bit of information about a right isosceles triangle; e.g., either side, the hypotenuse, or the area, we can find the other information. If we designate the two adjacent sides as s and use them as altitude and base: Area $= \frac{1}{2}(s)(s) \Rightarrow 1 = \frac{1}{2}s^2 \Rightarrow s^2 = 2 \Rightarrow s = \sqrt{2}$. And the length of the hypotenuse is equal to the length of the side multiplied by $\sqrt{2}$. So the hypotenuse/diameter is equal to $\sqrt{2}$. Thus, the radius of the circle is 1, and the area of the circle: area $= \pi(1)^2 = \pi$.

You can arrive at this same conclusion in a slightly different manner:

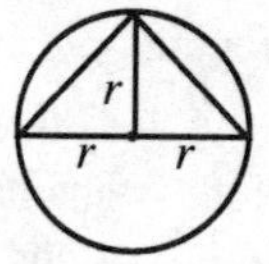

r is now the length of the altitude of the triangle and $2r$ the *length* of the base: Area $= \frac{1}{2} \bullet (r)(2r) \Rightarrow 1 = \frac{1}{2} \bullet (r)(2r) \Rightarrow 2 = 2r^2 \Rightarrow r^2 = 1 \Rightarrow r = 1$. Again, the area of the circle is just π.

Finally, a little common sense can get you through this problem without any math. The triangle, which has an area of 1, takes up slightly less than half the circle:

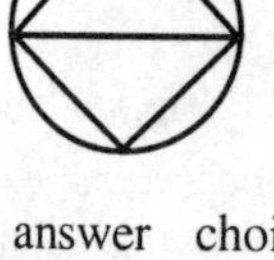

So the correct answer choice must be something that's a bit larger than 2. Only one of the answer choices qualifies. (B) says, for example, that the triangle is less than 1/6 of the circle. So (B), and with it the other choices that are larger, have to be incorrect.

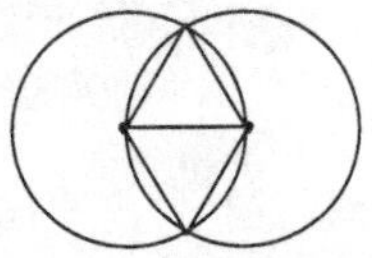

48. (F) This is a good exercise in organized problem solving. Look at the figure and ask yourself what you already know. You know the radius of the circle. Additionally, you know that the perimeter of the shaded area consists of two arcs. There must be some way to use the information about the radius to find the length of the arcs. Arcs can be measured in terms of length or in terms of degrees.

Since the sides of the triangles are all radii, the triangles must be equilateral. This means that the degree measure of each arc is 120. Since the circles have radii of 1, they have circumferences of $2\pi(1) = 2\pi$. And since each arc is a third that long: $\frac{2\pi}{3}$. And since there are two such arcs, the perimeter of the shaded area is $2 \cdot \frac{2\pi}{3} = \frac{4\pi}{3}$.

49. (C) For the first six tests the student has accumulated a total point count of $6 \cdot 83 = 498$. If the student scores zero on each of the remaining four tests, the total point count will remain 498 and the average will be $\frac{498}{10} = 49.8$. If the student scores 100 on each of the four remaining tests, the total point count will be 898 and the average will be $\frac{898}{10} = 89.8$.

50. (K) Let x be the multiplicative inverse of $2 - i$: $x(2 - i) = 1 \Rightarrow x = \frac{1}{2-i}$. And rationalize the right side of the equation: $x = \frac{1}{2-i} \cdot \frac{2+i}{2+i} = \frac{2+i}{4-i^2}$. Since $i = \sqrt{-1}$, $i^2 = -1$, so: $x = \frac{2+i}{4-(-1)} = \frac{2+i}{5}$.

51. (C) By definition, the logarithm of a number, to a given base, is the exponent that is used with the base to obtain that number: $b^e = n \Rightarrow e = \log_b n$. Here the base, b, is 3, and the number, n, is $\sqrt{3}$. So all you need to do is rewrite the statement in its equivalent exponential form: 3 to what power equals $\sqrt{3}$? Since the fractional exponent $\frac{1}{2}$ indicates "square root," the statement should read: 3 to the $\frac{1}{2}$ power equals $\sqrt{3}$.

52. (J) One way to attack this problem is to study the structure of f. Under what circumstance will the function have its minimum value? Essentially, this is like asking for the minimum value of $(x - 1^2)$, and that expression is least when x is equal to 1. So the minimum value of the function is $(1 - 1)^2 + 2 = 2$.

Alternatively, you can just test answer choices:

F. $(-3 -)^2 + 2 = 18$	X
G. $(-2 - 1)^2 + 2 = 11$	X
H. $(0 - 1)^2 + 2 = 3$	X
J. $(1 - 1)^2 + 2 = 2$	√
K. $(2 - 1)^2 + 2 = 3$	X

53. (A) $2^n + 2^n + 2^n + 2^n = x(2^{n+1})$
$2^2(2^n) = x(2^{n+1})$
$2^{n+2} = x(2^{n+1})$
$x = 2^{n+2} \div 2^{n+1} = 2^{(n+2)-(n+1)} = 2^1 = 2$

54. (F) $f(k)$ will equal $f(-k)$ when:
$(k)^2 + 2(k) + 1 = (-k)^2 - 2k + 1$
$k^2 + 2k + 1 = k^2 - 2k + 1$
$2k = -2k$
$4k = 0$
$k = 0$

Alternatively, you can work backwards from the answer choices. Use first the value 0: $(0) + 2(0) + 1 = (-0) + 2(0) + 1 \Rightarrow 1 = 1$. So 0 is part of the solution set—eliminate (G), (H), and (J). Now, the only question that remains is whether the correct answer is (K). Take another value, say 1: $(1)^2 + 2(1) + 1 = (-1)^2 + 2(-1)^2 + 2(-1) + 1 \Rightarrow 1 \neq -1$. And this proves that the answer is (F).

55. (D) $\frac{x^2 - 1}{x - 1} = \frac{(x+1)(x-1)}{x-1} = x + 1$. As x approaches 1, $x + 1$ approaches 2. (Note: Although the expression is not defined at $x = 1$, we are not concerned with what happens at that point.)

56. (H) Given the restrictions on x, since $\cos x = -1$, x must equal π (180°). And $\cos \pi/2 = 0$.

You can also reach this same conclusion if you visualize the graph of the cosine function (or graph it on your calculator):

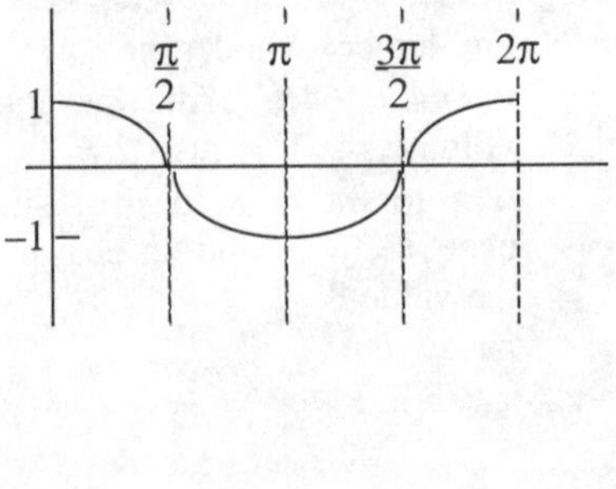

57. (B) Sketch a graph of the function (or use your graphing calculator):

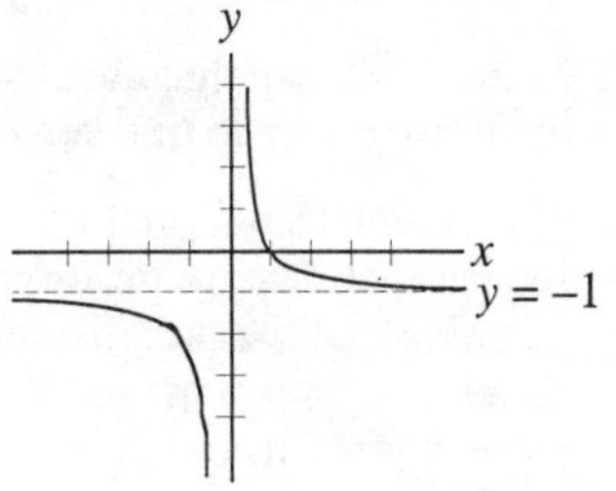

58. (K) Since $x = 3 \sin \theta$ and $y = 2 \cos \theta$, $\sin \theta = \frac{x}{3}$ and $\cos \theta = \frac{y}{2}$. Since $\sin^2 \theta + \cos^2 \theta = 1$: $\left(\frac{x}{3}\right)^2 + \left(\frac{y}{2}\right)^2 = 1 \Rightarrow \frac{x^2}{9} + \frac{y^2}{4} = 1$ is the equation of an ellipse with center (0, 0) that passes through the points (3, 0) and (0, 2).

Alternatively, you can try some values for θ. For $\theta = 0$, $x = 3 \sin 0 = 3(0) = 0$. For $\theta = \pi/2$, $x = 3 \sin \pi/2 = 3(1) = 3$ and $y = 2 \cos \pi/2 = 2(0) = 0$.

So the graph must include the points (3, 0) and (0, 2). The only graph given that contains both of those points is (K).

59. (A) Sine and cosecant are reciprocal functions, so the product of the sine of any angle and the cosecant of that angle is 1.

If you forget this fact during the exam, you can quickly derive it from the definitions of sine and cosecant. Sketch a triangle with sides a and b and hypotenuse c. Let θ be opposite side b. Now the $\sin \theta = b/c$ and $\csc \theta = c/b$. Therefore $\sin \theta \bullet \csc \theta = 1$.

60. (J) There are several different ways of expressing the length of BC: as a number, as a function of $\angle ABC$, and as a function of $\angle CAB$. Test-the-test is the easiest option, and some exam wisdom can help you out. First, you don't fall for (F) or (G). Aside from the easily remembered values covered in the lesson, you aren't expected to know values of trigonometric functions at particular angles. Since 40° and 50° aren't easily remembered values, the answer is not going to be 4 or 5. The answer will be expressed using a trigonometric function. (J) is correct: $\tan A = \frac{BC}{AB} \Rightarrow BC = \tan 50° \bullet 3 = 3 \tan 50°$.

TEST 3: READING (p. A-28)

1. (B) As stated in the last paragraph of the passage, Turner's essay challenged the views of other American historians of his time.

2. (F) Turner was the first historian to use the techniques of the social sciences to formulate and investigate historical questions. He studied the effects of economic, geographical, and sociological factors on the settlement of the American West. In addition, Turner redirected the focus of historical inquiry away from politics and political leaders, centering it instead on the lives of people in a national setting. In doing so, Turner identified what he considered to be the attributes of the American character.

3. (D) As noted in the third paragraph of the passage, Turner's evidence for the disappearance of the American frontier drew on the census of 1880.

4. (J) As stated in the first paragraph of the passage, Turner's essay affected the subsequent direction and methodology of inquiry in American history.

5. (C) The fact that much of the land in the West and Midwest was bought by wealthy land speculators from the East cast doubt on Turner's view that the West was settled by individuals looking to escape from the pressure of city life in the East.

6. (F) In contrast to Turner's theory that the West served as a safety valve by providing a means for the dissipation of social dissatisfaction stemming from the frustration of city life, demographic data show that more people actually left the farms for the cities than left the cities to move to the frontier.

7. (C) A theory can be defined as a hypothesis that contains an assumed explanation of a large number of isolated facts. A theory can be tested and thus can be proved or disproved.

8. (H) The frontier line of America moved from the East, where the first English colonies were founded, to the West, where the last settlements were established.

9. (C) According to Turner, the change from the American pattern of buying goods made in England to buying goods made in the United States culminated in the economic independence of Americans.

10. (G) As stated in the last paragraph of the passage, before Turner turned his attention to studying the people and the settlements of the American frontier, American historians had restricted the boundaries of American history to the history of politics and the roles played by past American political leaders.

11. (A) At the end of the first paragraph, the author raises a question, which he or she then proceeds to answer. (A) correctly describes this development. (B) is incorrect because the author does not present a theory as such. Though you might argue that we, the readers, can learn from the passage about the author's theory of life, but the author does not explicitly state a theory of life as such. As for (C), the author does not contrast his or her own views with other views. As for (D), the author does not define a term.

12. (J) What does the author mean by the word *pulsations?* In the final paragraph, the author explains that life is much too short. The author introduces the discussion by stating that experience is the end or goal of life—to get the most out of life, one must pack it with as many pulsations as possible. We can infer that the author means experiences.

13. (B) The discussion of art is found in the closing sentences of the passage. Having said that the best life is one packed with experiences (pulsations), the author goes on to say how one can have these intense experiences. This is one function of art, he or she says—to do nothing but provoke feelings—not to depict reality, (A); not to encourage reform, (C); not as a means of expression, (D).

14. (H) Experience is everything according to the author, so he or she would probably agree with (H). It is the feeling of the moment, not the memory of the feeling, that is important. Once the feeling is past, you should be looking for new feelings, not thinking about past ones.

15. (A) The writing is highly impassioned. The intensity of the writing is evident in every sentence. The issues are those of life and death. The author uses phrases such as "awful brevity" and "splendor of experience."

16. (H) In the second paragraph, the author argues that the best life is one filled with experiences of every sort. Not to seek after a variety of experiences is, in the author's words, "on this short day of the frost and sun, to sleep before evening." The phrase "to sleep before evening" must mean to stop living even before death. So the "short day of the frost and sun" must refer to a person's life.

17. (C) The author emphasizes the importance of living life to the fullest. In line 25, the awful, meaning terrible, brevity refers to the shortness of life.

18. (J) In the final paragraph, the author contrasts those who are listless with those who are the children of the world. The children of the world are high in passion, and are wise and love art and song.

19. (A) Lines 37-42 say that the desire for beauty has the most power to quicken our sense of life.

20. (H) The author says that we are all under a sentence of death with an indefinite reprieve, meaning that we are all mortal. We have an "interval," meaning our life; and then "our place knows us no more," meaning we are gone from the earth, that is, we are dead.

21. (B) The answer appears in line 3.

22. (H) Paragraph 2 states that the result of the process is a mix of sugar and oxygen. O_2 names oxygen, and H_2O names water, so $C_6H_{12}O_6$ names a sugar.

23. (A) Lines 19-21 define both terms. Reduction is the addition of electrons, and oxidation is their removal.

24. (J) Lines 17-19 states that photosynthesis involves the addition of electrons, making (I) correct. Lines 23-26 state that photosynthesis involves action on hydrogen, meaning that (II) is also correct. Since lines 20-21 state that "reduction stores energy, while oxidation releases it," and line 17 states that "photosynthesis is a reduction reaction," (III) cannot be correct. Because (I) and (II) are correct, the answer is (J).

25. (C) The paragraph gives a step-by-step analysis of the process defined in preceding paragraphs.

26. (F) (G) is supported by lines 51-52, (H) is supported by lines 64-67, (J) is stated in lines 50-51. (F) states the reverse of the truth; it is ADP that is mixed with phosphate to form ATP (see lines 51-52).

27. (A) A careful reading of lines 64-72 can lead to no other conclusion. A five-carbon sugar (RuDP) is combined with carbon dioxide (CO_2), ultimately resulting in the formation of a three-carbon sugar (PGAL).

28. (G) Growing periods (J) are never discussed. Higher temperatures (H), as indicated in the final paragraph, can lead to disagreeable conditions. Lines 75-79 state that the photorespiration, with its "seemingly wasteful" result, occurs when CO_2 levels are low. You can infer that a higher level of CO_2 would be a more agreeable condition. Also, more agreeable conditions facilitate carboxyilation. This process involves combining CO_2. Therefore, more CO_2 means an increase in carboxyilation.

29. (B) As stated in line 17, photosynthesis is a reduction reaction, which makes (C) an incorrect choice. Lines 73-76 indicate that RuDP is used in both processes, making (A) incorrect as well. The main difference, as stated in line 75, is that no ATP is created via photorespiration.

30. (H) The angiosperm plants discussed in the final paragraph *do* photosynthesize ((F) and (J)), but they do it in an unusual way, using their specialized leaf structure.

31. (C) In the final paragraph, the young man, whose name is Robin, is trying to explain to himself why the barbers laughed at him. So he is talking to himself.

32. (J) The five shillings was not enough to satisfy the ferryman for having to make a special trip. The young man was forced to pay an additional three pence, bringing the total fare to five shillings and three pence.

33. (B) Just after the young man gets off the ferryboat he finds himself in a neighborhood of hovels and old houses which, he concludes, could not belong to his relative. Therefore, we infer that the young man must think his relative is well-to-do.

34. (J) The scene is at night: the boat crosses at nine o'clock in the evening, the lights are on in the barber shop, and the stranger in the coat threatens to have the young man put in the stocks by morning.

35. (A) In the first paragraph, the narrator remarks that the young man sets off on foot with a light step—as though he had not already traveled more than 30 miles. Thus, 30 miles is a long way to travel in a day.

36. (G) The young man finally concludes that the barbers laugh at him for approaching the stranger in the coat because it should have been obvious to him that the stranger in the coat would not know the Major.

37. (A) The currency used to pay the ferryman and the length of a day's journey are suggestive. And the reference to a "New England colony" clearly places the action sometime before the end of the eighteenth century.

38. (F) The young man bows to the stranger and addresses him as "honored Sir" in order to show respect.

39. (B) The passage states that nine o'clock in the evening was an unusual time for anyone to be using the ferryboat. This is why the young man was its only passenger.

40. (F) The neighborhood near the ferry landing is characterized by "small and mean wooden buildings." The next paragraph also mentions a hovel and an old house.

TEST 4: SCIENCE REASONING (p. A-35)

1. (A) All three of the tabulated properties generally increase with the number of carbons.

2. (F) The change from methane (–162°C) to ethane (–89°C) is greatest (73°C).

3. (B) This property can be seen by looking at propane (3 carbons: –188°C) to butane (4 carbons: –138°C), pentane (5 carbons: –130°C) to hexane (6 carbons: –95°C), etc.

4. (H) Only boiling points and number of carbons increase without exception.

5. (C) Pentane (0.56) to hexane (0.66) is an increase of 0.10 (0.10/0.56 = 18%).

6. (J) Momentum = mass • velocity = $2 \text{ kg} \cdot 4 \frac{\text{m}}{\text{sec}}$.

7. (B) The momenta of the two masses are initially 8 and 0; afterward, the momentum of the combined mass is 7.98.

8. (H) You must note the minus sign on the final velocity for Object 1, and the note in the text about the meaning of negative velocity.

9. (D) Since no actual value is given in the phrase "far more massive," it is unlikely that an explicit calculation is needed. To be successful, a reader needs to visualize a collision of a very light object with a massive one; the large one won't budge.

10. (F) The lighter object would recoil even *faster* than the observed –1.71 m/sec.

11. (C) Using the formula given, initial kinetic is found to be 16.0; the final kinetic energy has decreased to about 4.5. The problem is easily misread as referring to Experiment 2, where the kinetic energy remains the same.

12. (H) An increase in temperature influences *flowering,* while a *decrease* in temperature is one factor that causes leaves to drop off.

13. (D) The table shows that plant growth occurs when Hormones 1 and 3 increase. Yet, even if these two hormones increase, a similar increase in either H_4 or H_5 will lead to no plant growth—H_4 and H_5 inhibit growth.

14. (G) Looking across the table, you can see the various factors that influence each plant activity. *Seed germination* is influenced by only one factor (H_3), while *flowering* is influenced by four different factors (H_3 and H_5, Daylength, and Temperature).

15. (C) Changing a house plant's growing conditions from 12 hours light/12 hours dark to constant light is an example of altering daylength, which only affects *flowering*.

16. (J) H_2 only affects *flower drop-off, fruit drop-off,* and *leaf drop-off.* For each of these activities, H_1 must also play a role (as H_2 increases, H_1 decreases).

17. (B) The only way the bag can gain weight between weighings is if additional fluid has moved inside. In this case, water moved inside (by osmosis) faster than it moved out.

18. (J) The fluid compartment (bag or beaker) that starts out with only water (no red dye) never gets red. It always remains clear. This indicates that the red dye is not free to pass across the bag's "membrane."

19. (D) In Experiment 2, the bag has gained 10 grams after only 10 minutes (water has entered the bag faster than in Experiment 1). By 20 minutes, more water will have entered and the bag should be even heavier.

20. (F) The experiments show that water will flow *toward* the compartment containing red dye. The more concentrated the red dye, the faster the flow of water will be.

21. (C) Water is free to flow into or out of the bag. Since there is no dye in the bag or the beaker, water will flow at an equal rate in both directions and the bag's weight should remain the same.

22. (F) Since salts are not able to enter or leave the cell, only water will move—in a direction that tends towards balanced concentrations. The water will flow toward the greater concentration of salt (from red blood cell to sea water), causing a shrinkage of the cells.

23. (B) Magnesium is a positively charged mineral (Mg^{+2}). The soil that has the worst relative ability to hold such minerals is coarse sand.

24. (J) As particles get bigger (from less than 2 micrometers to 200–2,000 micrometers) their relative ability to retain water decreases (goes from 1 to 4).

25. (H) Soils that are neither best nor worst at any ability cannot be ranked 1 or 4. The only soils that are never ranked 1 or 4 are silt (2–20 micrometers) and sand (20–200 micrometers). The total size range, therefore, is between 2–200 micrometers.

26. (A) Since loam is *mostly* clay, it primarily has small particles, which hold minerals and water well. The larger silt and sand particles in loam are adequate at maintaining air spaces containing oxygen. None of the other predictions fit the data in the chart.

27. (D) Clay is best (relative ability: 1) at both holding positively charged minerals and retaining water.

28. (G) Concentrations of reactants, not products, determine rate in both theories.

29. (B) Here you must have understood the relation of numbers of reactants in the overall equation to exponents in the rate law.

30. (H) This question tests critical comprehension of the passage, and requires you to understand the relationship of the two theories.

31. (D) The coefficients of the reactants determine their exponents in the rate law.

32. (F) This question tests comprehension of the differences between the theories.

33. (A) If the first stage is very slow and the second stage is much quicker, the overall rate is essentially that of the first stage.

34. (H) If the sum of the rates of each stage always equaled the rate of the reaction taken as a whole, there would be no need to analyze each subreaction.

35. (B) Temperature range for a life function is the high temperature minus the low temperature. For both species and both humidity conditions, oviposition always has the narrowest range.

36. (J) For each life function, Species M achieved 90% success at the same low temperatures in moist or dry air. At high temperatures, however, dry air was detrimental (under dry conditions, 90% success was not achieved at the same high temperatures as when conditions were moist!)

37. (C) Since dry conditions had no effect on Species D for mating, oviposition, or pupation, one may predict that dry conditions will have little effect on caterpillar survival in Species D as well. The temperature range would, therefore, be the same as observed at 100% relative humidity.

38. (G) Mating success in the light and in the dark should be compared at the same temperature. It should be a temperature at which both species can successfully mate. Otherwise, additional variables confuse the issue.

39. (D) Species M and Species D are both equally successful at low temperatures for pupation.

40. (F) (G) and (H) are not relevant to the question. (J) only refers to light conditions. (F) is a hypothesis supported by the results.

Answer Sheet

Name ______________________ Student ID Number ______________________

Date ______________ Instructor ______________________ Course/Session Number ______________

TEST 1—ENGLISH

1 A B C D	16 F G H J	31 A B C D	46 F G H J	61 A B C D
2 F G H J	17 A B C D	32 F G H J	47 A B C D	62 F G H J
3 A B C D	18 F G H J	33 A B C D	48 F G H J	63 A B C D
4 F G H J	19 A B C D	34 F G H J	49 A B C D	64 F G H J
5 A B C D	20 F G H J	35 A B C D	50 F G H J	65 A B C D
6 F G H J	21 A B C D	36 F G H J	51 A B C D	66 F G H J
7 A B C D	22 F G H J	37 A B C D	52 F G H J	67 A B C D
8 F G H J	23 A B C D	38 F G H J	53 A B C D	68 F G H J
9 A B C D	24 F G H J	39 A B C D	54 F G H J	69 A B C D
10 F G H J	25 A B C D	40 F G H J	55 A B C D	70 F G H J
11 A B C D	26 F G H J	41 A B C D	56 F G H J	71 A B C D
12 F G H J	27 A B C D	42 F G H J	57 A B C D	72 F G H J
13 A B C D	28 F G H J	43 A B C D	58 F G H J	73 A B C D
14 F G H J	29 A B C D	44 F G H J	59 A B C D	74 F G H J
15 A B C D	30 F G H J	45 A B C D	60 F G H J	75 A B C D

TEST 2—MATHEMATICS

1 A B C D E	13 A B C D E	25 A B C D E	37 A B C D E	49 A B C D E
2 F G H J K	14 F G H J K	26 F G H J K	38 F G H J K	50 F G H J K
3 A B C D E	15 A B C D E	27 A B C D E	39 A B C D E	51 A B C D E
4 F G H J K	16 F G H J K	28 F G H J K	40 F G H J K	52 F G H J K
5 A B C D E	17 A B C D E	29 A B C D E	41 A B C D E	53 A B C D E
6 F G H J K	18 F G H J K	30 F G H J K	42 F G H J K	54 F G H J K
7 A B C D E	19 A B C D E	31 A B C D E	43 A B C D E	55 A B C D E
8 F G H J K	20 F G H J K	32 F G H J K	44 F G H J K	56 F G H J K
9 A B C D E	21 A B C D E	33 A B C D E	45 A B C D E	57 A B C D E
10 F G H J K	22 F G H J K	34 F G H J K	46 F G H J K	58 F G H J K
11 A B C D E	23 A B C D E	35 A B C D E	47 A B C D E	59 A B C D E
12 F G H J K	24 F G H J K	36 F G H J K	48 F G H J K	60 F G H J K

TEST 3—READING

1 A B C D	9 A B C D	17 A B C D	25 A B C D	33 A B C D
2 F G H J	10 F G H J	18 F G H J	26 F G H J	34 F G H J
3 A B C D	11 A B C D	19 A B C D	27 A B C D	35 A B C D
4 F G H J	12 F G H J	20 F G H J	28 F G H J	36 F G H J
5 A B C D	13 A B C D	21 A B C D	29 A B C D	37 A B C D
6 F G H J	14 F G H J	22 F G H J	30 F G H J	38 F G H J
7 A B C D	15 A B C D	23 A B C D	31 A B C D	39 A B C D
8 F G H J	16 F G H J	24 F G H J	32 F G H J	40 F G H J

TEST 4—SCIENCE REASONING

1 A B C D	9 A B C D	17 A B C D	25 A B C D	33 A B C D
2 F G H J	10 F G H J	18 F G H J	26 F G H J	34 F G H J
3 A B C D	11 A B C D	19 A B C D	27 A B C D	35 A B C D
4 F G H J	12 F G H J	20 F G H J	28 F G H J	36 F G H J
5 A B C D	13 A B C D	21 A B C D	29 A B C D	37 A B C D
6 F G H J	14 F G H J	22 F G H J	30 F G H J	38 F G H J
7 A B C D	15 A B C D	23 A B C D	31 A B C D	39 A B C D
8 F G H J	16 F G H J	24 F G H J	32 F G H J	40 F G H J

CAMBRIDGE

EDUCATIONAL SERVICES, INC.®

ACT • PLAN • EXPLORE

Appendix A

ACT PRACTICE TEST II

1 1 1 1 1 1 1 1 1 1 1 1

ENGLISH

45 Minutes—75 Questions

DIRECTIONS: In the five passages that follow, certain parts and phrases are underlined and numbered. In the right-hand column, you will find alternatives for each underlined part. You are to choose the one that best expresses the idea, makes the statement appropriate for standard written English, or is worded more consistently with the style and tone of the passage as a whole. If you think the original version is the best, choose "NO CHANGE."

You will also find questions about a section of the passage, or about the passage as a whole. These questions do not refer to an underlined portion of the passage, but rather are identified with a note.

For each question, choose the alternative you consider best. Read each passage through once before you begin to answer the questions that accompany it. You cannot determine most answers without reading several sentences beyond the question. Be sure that you have read far enough ahead each time you choose an alternative.

Passage I

[1]

Botany is surely <u>the more gentler of</u> (1) sciences. The careful observation of a flower is a calm, <u>ostentatious</u> (2) action—the peaceful contemplation of a beautiful object. Reduced to its <u>essentials, it</u> (3) requires no laboratory <u>but the natural world</u> (4), a few tools and the naked eye. Botany in its most scientific or purest form <u>consists about</u> (5) seeking to know more about the plant simply for the sake of that knowledge. Plants have not always been regarded as worthy <u>of knowing</u> (6) or studying in and of themselves, not on their merits as sources of food or drugs but as lifeforms. In fact, the

1. A. NO CHANGE
   B. the most gentle of
   C. the gentler of
   D. the gentlest in the

2. F. NO CHANGE
   G. unobtrusive
   H. violent
   J. chaotic

3. A. NO CHANGE
   B. essentials; it
   C. essentials; botany
   D. essentials, botany

4. F. NO CHANGE
   G. but you do need the natural world
   H. and the natural world is needed
   J. but the natural world is necessary

5. A. NO CHANGE
   B. consists of
   C. consists in
   D. consist of

6. F. NO CHANGE
   G. for knowledge
   H. of knowledge
   J. to know

GO ON TO THE NEXT PAGE

history of botany can be viewed in terms of repeated rediscoveries of this one theme—that plants are worthy of study in and of themselves, quite apart from any use they might have for mankind.
7

7. A. NO CHANGE
B. by themselves
C. themselves
D. by and for themselves

[2]

8 The practical motives behind plant study should not be disparaging—the bulk of our medical history, for instance, is made up of accounts of herbal remedies.
9

8. Beginning paragraph 2 with which of the following might make the transition from paragraph 1 to paragraph 2 clearer?

F. However,
G. Since
H. Heretofore
J. Hence

9. A. NO CHANGE
B. disparaged—the bulk
C. disparaging, the bulk
D. disparaged; the bulk

Nonetheless, the study of the medicinal properties of plants contained a self-limiting mechanism: if a plant seemed to have no utilitarian value, it was disregarded, and no further study of it is made. The Renaissance attitude towards nature changed this overly practical bent and initiated the scientific study of plants.
10
11

10. F. NO CHANGE
G. Consequently
H. Thus
J. Moreover

11. A. NO CHANGE
B. had been made
C. were made
D. was made

[3]

Botany, as a pure science, has certain characteristics and makes certain assumptions that prove thought-provoking and interesting. One of its unspoken or basic assumptions is an implicit respect and regard for all living things. The botanist who studies a plant's structure or tries to have understood their functions confronts nature on its own terms. Investigations of how a plant thrives or reproduces, or studies of the purposefulness of a flower's coloration and structure, are almost implicitly egalitarian and
12
13

12. F. NO CHANGE
G. because
H. and thus
J. yet

13. A. NO CHANGE
B. to understand its
C. understanding its
D. having understood their

GO ON TO THE NEXT PAGE

tautological. The botanist studies the flower because they exist, but [14] because it exists, it is worthy of study.

14. F. NO CHANGE
    G. it exists, but
    H. it exists and
    J. it exists, and

Item 15 poses a question about Passage I as a whole.

15. The last sentence of the passage is actually a restatement of which of the following ideas?
    A. The study of the medicinal properties of plants has a self-limiting mechanism.
    B. The botanist who tries to understand a plant's function confronts nature on its own terms.
    C. Botany is a gentle science.
    D. The study of plants and flowers is egalitarian and tautological.

Passage II

The main characteristic of poverty is, of course, [16] lack of money. A family is defined as poor when its annual income falls below a certain dollar amount, [17] calculated by the Federal Government to be the minimum a family of their [18] size would need to maintain a minimally decent standard of living. In certain areas of rural America, consequently, [19] poverty is the rule rather than the exception. As many as 50 percent of

16. The use of the phrase "of course" is:
    F. appropriate because someone who is poor obviously lacks money.
    G. appropriate because it is not obvious that someone who is poor lacks money.
    H. questionable since someone might be poor in spirit.
    J. appropriate because it disrupts the flow of the sentence.

17. A. NO CHANGE
    B. falls and is under a certain dollar amount,
    C. is under a certain specified dollar amount,
    D. OMIT

18. F. NO CHANGE
    G. there
    H. its
    J. it's

19. A. NO CHANGE
    B. and therefore, as a result of this,
    C. moreover, due to this fact,
    D. OMIT

GO ON TO THE NEXT PAGE

the families may earn less than [20] the poverty level, and some may manage to subsist somehow on amounts even less than half the official poverty level income. [21]

Although [22] lack of money is the defining characteristic of poverty, poverty is more than simply lack of money. Poverty is an entire complex of symptoms. Low levels of formal schooling among adults parallel [23] low income levels. Additionally, in families below the poverty level, the number of children and aged who depend on those who work is in general higher than the national average for all families. As a consequence, [24] fewer workers support a greater number of nonworkers than in other, more prosperous families.

Often, the schooling provided in low-income areas are as inadequate like incomes [25]. In particular, rural children get poorer schooling than city children, and many rural poor are severely handicapped by it [26]. The general rural average is only 8.8 years of school completed. Moreover, low educational levels seem to just keep repeating and repeating themselves [27]. If the head of a rural poor family have [28] little schooling, the children are often handicapped in their efforts to get an

20. F. NO CHANGE
G. lower than
H. less as
J. lower as

21. The first paragraph provides which of the following?
A. a definition
B. an argument
C. a comparison
D. a narrative

22. F. NO CHANGE
G. (Do NOT begin a new paragraph.) Although
H. (Begin a new paragraph.) Since
J. (Do NOT begin a new paragraph.) Since

23. A. NO CHANGE
B. go along with
C. are a lot like
D. very often go together with

24. F. NO CHANGE
G. However,
H. Surprisingly,
J. Fortunately,

25. A. NO CHANGE
B. is—like family income, inadequate
C. is so inadequate as family income
D. is, like family income, inadequate

26. F. NO CHANGE
G. education
H. their education
J. their lack of education

27. A. NO CHANGE
B. be self-perpetuating of themselves
C. be self-perpetuating
D. cause the same thing to happen all over again

28. F. NO CHANGE
G. have had
H. has had
J. was to have

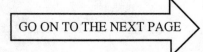

GO ON TO THE NEXT PAGE

education. It is especially difficult for people who are handicapped educationally to acquire new skills, get new jobs, or otherwise adjust to an increasingly urbanized society. This is as true on the farm rather than [29] in urban industry since modern farming of the present day [30] requires skills that poor educated [31] people lack. Lacking in education, the rural poor either take low-paying jobs on the farm or elsewhere in rural areas or swell the ranks of the unemployed or underemployed.

29. A. NO CHANGE
    B. rather as
    C. as they are
    D. as it is

30. F. NO CHANGE
    G. of the present
    H. presently
    J. OMIT

31. A. NO CHANGE
    B. poorly educated
    C. educated poor
    D. poor education

Item 32 poses a question about Passage II as a whole.

32. The author does NOT use which of the following in the development of the passage?
    F. definitions
    G. explanation
    H. statistics
    J. personal experience

Passage III

One out of every four children who entered the fifth grade in the fall of 1966 fail to graduate [33] with his or her class. The total number that should of [34] graduated was 4.1 million, but approximately 900,000 fell by the wayside.

Those who do not make it are called school dropouts. (Official statistics define a dropout as a person who has not yet attained the age of 16 and

33. A. NO CHANGE
    B. failed to graduate
    C. failed graduation
    D. fails to graduate

34. F. NO CHANGE
    G. that should of been
    H. who should of
    J. who should have

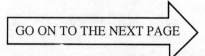

GO ON TO THE NEXT PAGE

leaves school before graduation for any reason except transfer.) School officials who work with dropouts who leave school (35) say a student will usually starting thinking (36) about dropping out about two years before he or she ceases to attend school: roughly (37) at age 14. Absenteeism, class cutting, lack of motivation, and lack of interest in school is often (38) early signs of the potential dropout. Also, (39) many students drop out mentally very early in their school career, despite their physical presence until graduation.

The dropout is most often a boy who mostly, frequently (40) leaves school at the age of 16 while in the tenth grade. He is most likely than those (41) who stay in school to score low on an intelligence test and is likely to be failing in school at the time of him dropping out. (42) Yet most dropouts are really not less bright (43) than students who remain in school until graduation. The dropout typically comes from the lower-income class and most often leaves school for financial reasons. His absences from school increasing noticeably (44) during the eighth grade and he participates

35. A. NO CHANGE
B. who have left school
C. who are leaving school
D. OMIT

36. F. NO CHANGE
G. usually will be starting thinking
H. starts usually thinking
J. usually starts to think

37. A. NO CHANGE
B. school but roughly
C. school and roughly
D. school, roughly

38. F. NO CHANGE
G. is oftentimes
H. are often
J. were often

39. A. NO CHANGE
B. dropout also
C. dropout many
D. dropout but also

40. F. NO CHANGE
G. frequently and often
H. most frequently
J. sometimes often

41. A. NO CHANGE
B. more likely than those
C. most likely as one
D. more likely than one

42. F. NO CHANGE
G. he drops out
H. of his having dropped out
J. he dropped out

43. A. NO CHANGE
B. really they are no less bright than are the students who remain
C. are, than the students who remain, really no less bright
D. than the students who remain are really no less bright

44. F. NO CHANGE
G. increase so that
H. increase noticeably
J. increased to the point where it was noticed

GO ON TO THE NEXT PAGE

little <u>or none</u> [45] in extracurricular activities. The reasons a student drops out of school <u>goes deeper as</u> [46] a mere desire to be rid of school. Dropping out is a symptom; the roots of the problem are usually below the surface.

[47]

45. A. NO CHANGE
    B. and not at all
    C. or not much
    D. or not at all

46. F. NO CHANGE
    G. go more deeply than
    H. go deeper as
    J. go deeper than

47. What would be a logical continuation of the article?
    A. A discussion of the financial reasons a student might leave school
    B. A discussion of a student's lack of motivation
    C. A discussion of possible extracurricular activities
    D. A discussion of why students might drop out of school

Item 48 poses a question about Passage III as a whole.

48. Is the use of the official definition of *dropout* in the first paragraph appropriate?
    F. Yes, because without a definition, the article would not be understandable.
    G. Yes, because the nature of a "dropout" is one of the central themes of the passage.
    H. No, because the definition has nothing to do with what the author is discussing in the second paragraph.
    J. No, because the author then redefines the word.

Passage IV

The idea of generating electricity with wind power is not new. But the kind of attention that idea is getting today, in terms of research and <u>development, are</u> [49] both new and encouraging to planners looking for renewable energy sources <u>satisfying</u> [50] growing national demands. An effort is being made in the United States

49. A. NO CHANGE
    B. development, is
    C. developing, is
    D. development are

50. F. NO CHANGE
    G. that would have satisfied
    H. to satisfy
    J. with the satisfaction of

GO ON TO THE NEXT PAGE

to use one of humankind's oldest energy sources to solve one of its [51] most modern problems, to find [52] reliable and cost-effective ways to harness the wind to produce electricity.

Wind machines are not the simple devices that they may be appearing to be, [53] and the lessons they teach seldom come easy. On the other hand, [54] the potential reward to a nation that needs more energy from a renewable source is beyond calculation. Rewards for using wind power have been gathered [55] by civilizations and cultures since early in recorded history.

No record survives of the earliest wind machine. It may have been built [56] in China more than three thousand years ago. It may have been built on the windy plains of Afghanistan. History hints at some sort of wind power used in the Pharaoh's Egypt for the drawing of water [57] for agriculture long before the birth of Christ. Hammurabi may have taken time out from developing a legal code about 2,000 BC to sponsor development of some sort of wind machine. The earliest confirmed wind machines are in that same region. Persian writers described gardens irrigated through the means of [58] wind-driven water lifts several [59] centuries before the birth of Christ. Ultimately,

51. A. NO CHANGE
    B. their
    C. it's
    D. your

52. F. NO CHANGE
    G. problems: to find
    H. problems, finding
    J. problems. To find

53. A. NO CHANGE
    B. they may be
    C. it may seem to be
    D. they may appear to be

54. F. NO CHANGE
    G. Therefore,
    H. As a consequence
    J. This means that

55. A. NO CHANGE
    B. has been gathering
    C. is gathering
    D. will have been gathered

56. F. NO CHANGE
    G. may have been
    H. was being built
    J. has been building

57. A. NO CHANGE
    B. to draw water
    C. in order that water be drawn
    D. in order to draw water

58. F. NO CHANGE
    G. irrigated by means of
    H. which were then irrigated by means of
    J. irrigated by

59. A. NO CHANGE
    B. lifts several,
    C. lifts but several
    D. lifts and several

GO ON TO THE NEXT PAGE

we can only guess at the origin of the windmill. [60]

60. F. NO CHANGE
G. the origin of the windmill can only be guessed at
H. the origin of the windmill can only be guessed at by us
J. the origin of the windmill could only be guessed at

Persian machines were horizontal devices, [61] carousel-like contraptions that revolved around a center pole and that caught the wind with bundles of reeds.

61. A. NO CHANGE
B. (Begin a new paragraph) Since Persian machines were
C. (Do NOT begin a new paragraph)
D. (Begin a new paragraph) It was discovered that Persian machines were horizontal devices,

The carousel is perhaps the more simple design for capturing [62] the wind; it cares nothing for the direction of the breeze, but revolves no matter where on the compass the wind may originate. From the Middle East, wind-machine technology may have been carried to Europe by returning Crusaders. Accurate records do not exist, but soon after the Crusades windmills appeared in northern Europe and soon were found on the British Isles.

62. F. NO CHANGE
G. most simplest design for capturing
H. simpler design to capture
J. simplest design for capturing

For a while, windmills flourished in Europe, but with the advent of steam power they come close to [63] extinction for the wind is real iffy. [64] It can fail to blow just when it is needed the most or it can rage into a gale when it isn't needed at all.

63. A. NO CHANGE
B. came close to
C. are coming closer to
D. come close upon

64. F. NO CHANGE
G. likely to blow sometimes and not to others
H. here today and gone tomorrow isn't
J. capricious

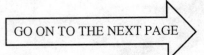

GO ON TO THE NEXT PAGE

Item 65 poses a question about Passage IV as a whole.

65. The author's use of the phrase "rage into a gale" is
   A. appropriate because it creates a vivid image.
   B. appropriate because it minimizes the importance of weather.
   C. inappropriate because images are out of place in scientific writing.
   D. inappropriate because wind is sometimes calm.

Passage V

Television and its programs do not just happen. It is (66) planned products of a huge, wealthy, and highly competitive commercial enterprise. The television industry, which includes stations, networks, production companies, actors, and writers, are (67) responsible for selecting, creating, and distributing programs. The three most popular programs are the episodic series, the (68) made-for-television movies, and the mini-series.

In the 1970s, the episodic series, both dramatic and comic, was the most (69) popular of these. With the advent (70) of cable and pay television and of video disks and tapes, the television movie is rapidly gaining in (71)

66. F. NO CHANGE
   G. They are
   H. They would be
   J. It was

67. A. NO CHANGE
   B. writers, is
   C. writers are
   D. writers-is

68. F. NO CHANGE
   G. episodic series the
   H. episodic, series the
   J. episodic series the,

69. A. NO CHANGE
   B. was the more
   C. were the most
   D. were the more

70. F. NO CHANGE
   G. Including the advent
   H. Notwithstanding the advent
   J. With the beginning of the advent

71. A. NO CHANGE
   B. has rapidly gained in
   C. is rapidly gaining
   D. will rapidly gain in

GO ON TO THE NEXT PAGE

popularity. The past ten years <u>have seen</u> [72] several changes in television drama. The action-adventure police drama has lost and the situation comedy <u>has grew</u> [73] in popularity. Topics previously considered taboo <u>emerged. Unmarried</u> [74] couples living together, divorces, and single parents. Even topics that are <u>politically controversy</u> [75] can now be the focus of programs.

72. F. NO CHANGE
    G. see
    H. will see
    J. would be seeing

73. A. NO CHANGE
    B. has grown
    C. grew
    D. grow

74. F. NO CHANGE
    G. emerged, unmarried
    H. emerged unmarried
    J. emerged: unmarried

75. A. NO CHANGE
    B. politically controversial
    C. politics controversy
    D. political controversy

IF YOU FINISH BEFORE TIME IS CALLED, YOU MAY CHECK YOUR WORK ON THIS TEST ONLY. DO NOT WORK ON ANY OTHER TEST SECTION.

STOP

2 2 2 2 2 2 2 2 2 2 2 2

MATHEMATICS

60 Minutes—60 Questions

DIRECTIONS: Solve each problem, choose the correct answer, and then blacken the corresponding oval on your answer sheet. Do not linger over problems that take too much time. Solve as many as you can, then return to the others in the time you have left for this test.

Note: Unless otherwise stated, all of the following should be assumed:

1. Illustrative figures are NOT necessarily drawn to scale.
2. Geometry figures lie in a plane.
3. The word *line* means straight line.
4. The word *average* means arithmetic mean.

---

1. $121{,}212 + (2 \cdot 10^4) = ?$

A. 312,212
B. 141,212
C. 123,212
D. 121,412
E. 121,232

2. If $6x + 3 = 21$, then $2x + 1 = ?$

F. 1
G. 2
H. 3
J. 6
K. 7

3. At a recreation center, it costs $3 per hour to rent a ping-pong table and $12 per hour to rent a lane for bowling. For the cost of renting a bowling lane for two hours, it is possible to rent a ping-pong table for how many hours?

A. 4
B. 6
C. 8
D. 18
E. 36

4. If j, k, l, and m are natural numbers and $j < k < l < m$, which of the following *could* be true?

F. $k = k + l$
G. $j = l + m$
H. $j + k = l + m$
J. $j + k + m = l$
K. $j + m = k + l$

5. Of the following, which is greater than $\frac{1}{2}$?

A. $\frac{9}{19}$
B. $\frac{7}{15}$
C. $\frac{4}{9}$
D. $\frac{6}{11}$
E. $\frac{3}{7}$

6. Out of a group of 360 students, exactly 18 are on the track team. What percent of the students are on the track team?

F. 5%
G. 10%
H. 12%
J. 20%
K. 25%

GO ON TO THE NEXT PAGE

7. In the figure below, three lines intersect as shown. Which of the following must be true?

I. $a = x$
II. $y + z = b + c$
III. $x + a = y + b$

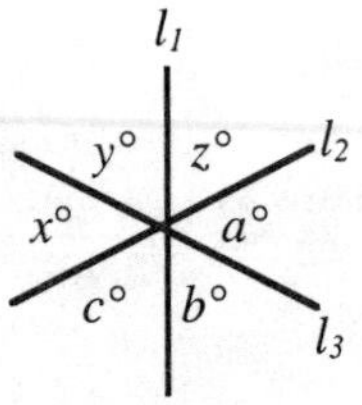

A. I only
B. II only
C. I and II only
D. I and III only
E. I, II, and III only

8. In the figure below, $x = ?$

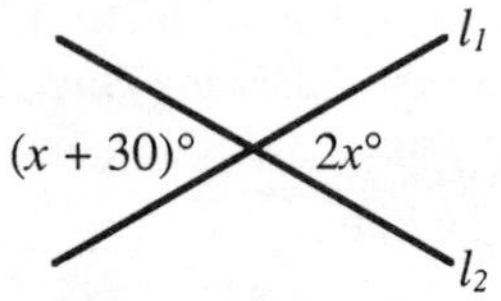

F. 15
G. 30
H. 45
J. 60
K. 90

9. Which of the following is the prime factorization of 60?

A. (2)(3)(10)
B. (3)(4)(5)
C. (2)(2)(3)(5)
D. (2)(2)(3)(6)
E. (3)(3)(3)(5)

10. The average (arithmetic mean) height of four buildings is 20 meters. If three of the buildings have a height of 16 meters, what is the height, in meters, of the fourth building?

F. 32
G. 28
H. 24
J. 22
K. 18

11. In the figure below, what is the value of x?

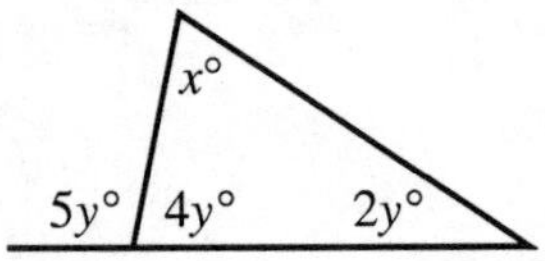

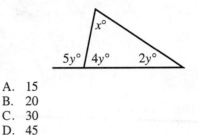

A. 15
B. 20
C. 30
D. 45
E. 60

12. In the figure below, what is the length of PQ?

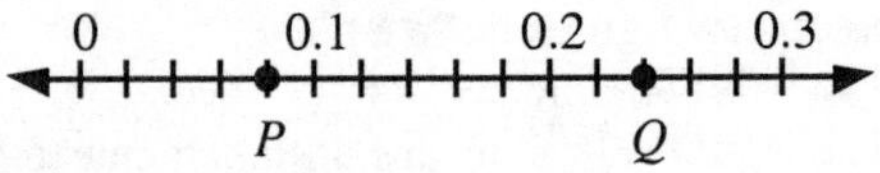

F. 0.12
G. 0.16
H. 0.13
J. 0.11
K. 0.09

13. What is the perimeter of the rectangle below?

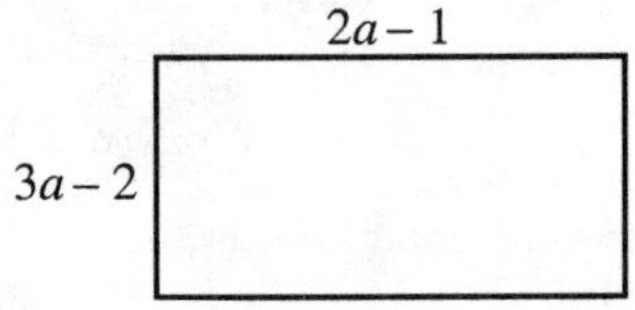

A. $10a - 6$
B. $10a - 3$
C. $6a - 3$
D. $5a - 6$
E. $5a - 3$

14. If the average (arithmetic mean) of x, x, x, 56, and 58 is 51, then $x = ?$

F. 43
G. 47
H. 49
J. 51
K. 53

15. For how many integers x is $-2 \le 2x \le 2$?

A. 1
B. 2
C. 3
D. 4
E. 5

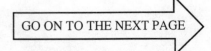

GO ON TO THE NEXT PAGE

16. For all real numbers x, 8^x equals which of the following?

F. $8x$

G. x^8

H. 2^{2x}

J. $x^{\frac{2}{3}}$

K. 2^{3x}

17. What is the sum of the areas of two squares with sides of 2 and 3, respectively?

A. 1
B. 5
C. 13
D. 25
E. 36

18. If the rectangular solid shown below has a volume of 54, then x = ?

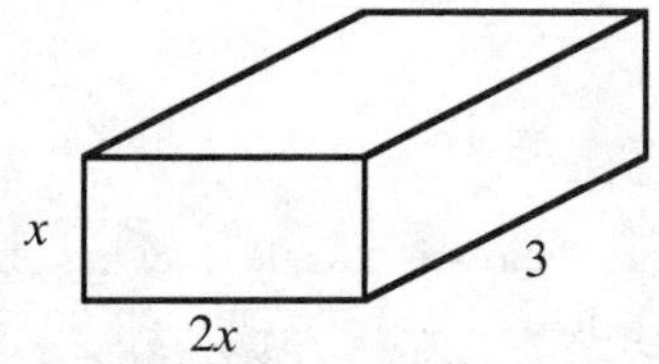

F. 2
G. 3
H. 6
J. 9
K. 12

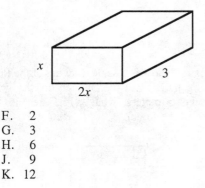

19. If x is 80 percent of y, then y is what percent of x?

A. $133\frac{1}{3}\%$
B. 125%
C. 120%
D. 90%
E. 80%

20. From which of the following statements can it be deduced that $m > n$?

F. $m + 1 = n$
G. $2m = n$
H. $m + n > 0$
J. $m - n > 0$
K. $mn > 0$

21. If $f(x) = x^2 + x$, then what is the value of $f(f(2))$?

A. 42
B. 38
C. 32
D. 18
E. 4

22. The circle below with center O has a radius of length 2. If the total area of the shaded regions is 3π, then x = ?

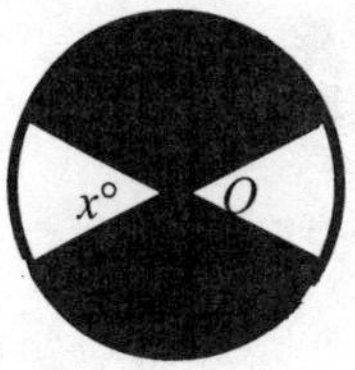

F. 270
G. 180
H. 120
J. 90
K. 45

23. If a bar of metal alloy consists of 100 grams of tin and 150 grams of lead, what percent of the entire bar, by weight, is tin?

A. 10%
B. 15%
C. $33\frac{1}{3}\%$
D. 40%
E. $66\frac{2}{3}\%$

24. If $\frac{1}{x} + \frac{1}{y} = \frac{1}{z}$, then z = ?

F. $\frac{1}{xy}$

G. xy

H. $\frac{x+y}{xy}$

J. $\frac{xy}{x+y}$

K. $\frac{2xy}{x+y}$

GO ON TO THE NEXT PAGE

25. $|-5| + |-12| - |-2| + (-6) = ?$

A. 2
B. 3
C. 6
D. 9
E. 14

26. If the average of $2x$, $2x + 1$, and $2x + 2$ is $x - 1$, which of the following equations could be used to find x?

F. $6x + 3 = x - 1$
G. $6x + 3 = 3(x - 1)$
H. $3(6x + 3) = x - 1$
J. $(6x + 3) + (x - 1) = 3$
K. $(6x + 3)(x - 1) = 3$

27. Members of a civic organization purchase boxes of candy for \$1 apiece and sell them for \$2 apiece. If no other expenses are incurred, how many boxes of candy must they sell to earn a net profit of \$500?

A. 250
B. 500
C. 1,000
D. 1,500
E. 2,000

28. $(-2)^2 - (-2)^3 = ?$

F. 16
G. 12
H. 2
J. –2
K. –8

29. The sum, the product, and the average (arithmetic mean) of three different integers are equal. If two of the integers are x and $-x$, the third integer is:

A. $\frac{x}{2}$
B. $2x$
C. –1
D. 0
E. 1

30. In a school with a total enrollment of 360, 90 students are seniors. What percent of all students enrolled in the school are seniors?

F. 25%
G. $33\frac{1}{3}\%$
H. 50%
J. $66\frac{2}{3}\%$
K. 75%

31. The perimeter of the square below is:

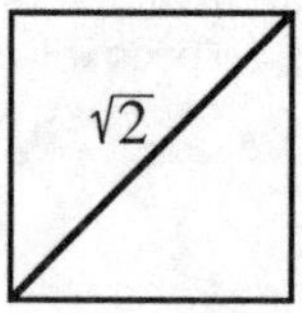

A. 1
B. $\sqrt{2}$
C. 4
D. $4\sqrt{2}$
E. 8

32. The figure below is a scale drawing of the floor of a dining hall. If 1 centimeter on the drawing represents 5 meters, what is the area, in square meters, of the floor?

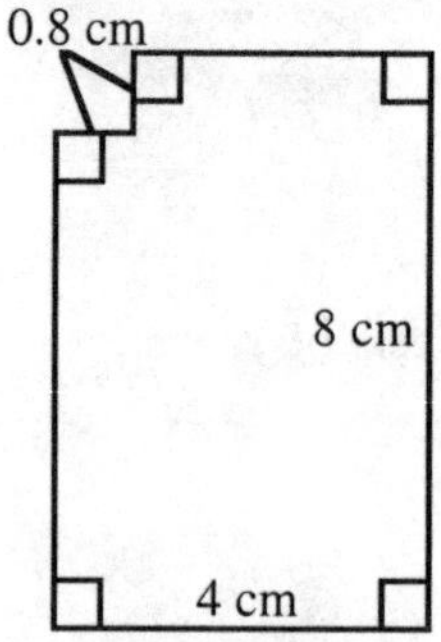

F. 144
G. 156
H. 784
J. 796
K. 844

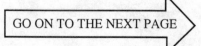

GO ON TO THE NEXT PAGE

33. If two straight lines intersect as shown, what is the value of x?

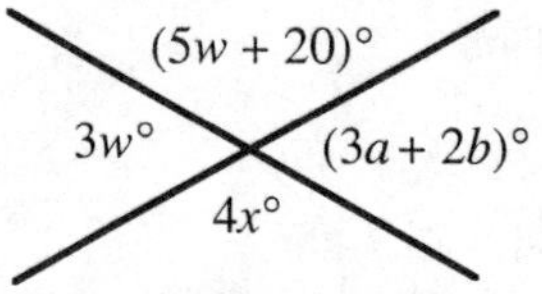

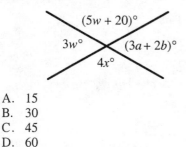

A. 15
B. 30
C. 45
D. 60
E. 75

34. A triangle has one side of length 4 and another side of length 11. What are the greatest and least possible *integer* values for the length of the remaining side?

F. 7 and 4
G. 11 and 4
H. 14 and 8
J. 15 and 7
K. 16 and 7

35. Which of the following is the solution set for the equation $-x^2 = 3 - 4x$?

A. (–3, –1)
B. (–3, 1)
C. (1, 3)
D. (1, 4)
E. (3, 5)

36. A school club spent $\frac{2}{5}$ of its budget for one project and $\frac{1}{3}$ of what remained for another project. If the club's entire budget was equal to \$300, how much of the budget was left after the two projects?

F \$60
G \$90
H. \$120
J. \$180
K. \$240

37. If the cost of n nails is c cents, which of the following equations could be used to determine d, the cost in dollars, of x nails?

A. $d = 100cnx$
B. $d = 100\frac{cx}{n}$
C. $d = \frac{100nx}{c}$
D. $d = \frac{nx}{100c}$
E. $d = \frac{cx}{100n}$

38. If $a^2b^3c < 0$, then which of the following must be true?

F. $b^3 < 0$
G. $b^2 < 0$
H. $b < 0$
J. $c < 0$
K. $bc < 0$

39. If the figure below is an equilateral triangle, what is its perimeter?

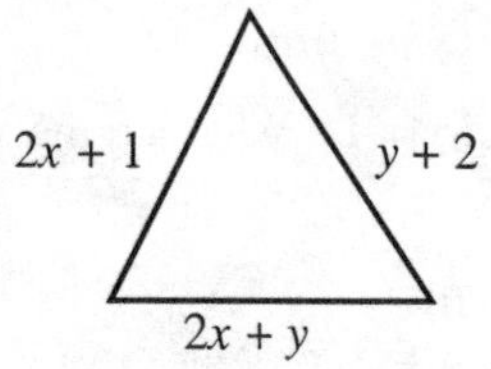

A. 1
B. 3
C. 9
D. 12
E. 15

40. In the coordinate plane, what is the distance between the point with (x, y) coordinates (2, 1) and the point with (x, y) coordinates (5, 5)?

F. $\sqrt{3}$
G. $2\sqrt{3}$
H. 5
J. $3\sqrt{2}$
K. 6

41. $\sqrt{45} - \sqrt{20} + \sqrt{5} = ?$

A. $2 - \sqrt{5}$

B. 0

C. $2 + \sqrt{5}$

D. $2\sqrt{5}$

E. 10

42. What is the least positive integer x for which $12 - x$ and $15 - x$ will be nonzero and have opposite signs?

F. 3
G. 4
H. 11
J. 12
K. 13

43. The solution set to the pair of equations:

$$mx + ny = 15$$
$$nx + my = 13$$

is $x = 3$ and $y = 1$. What are the values of m and n?

A. $m = 5; n = 3$
B. $m = 4; n = 3$
C. $m = 3; n = 4$
D. $m = 3; n = 5$
E. $m = 2; n = 6$

44. In the figure below, equally spaced points are joined by line segments that intersect each other at 90 degrees. If the total length of all line segments in the figure is 24, what is the area of the shaded part?

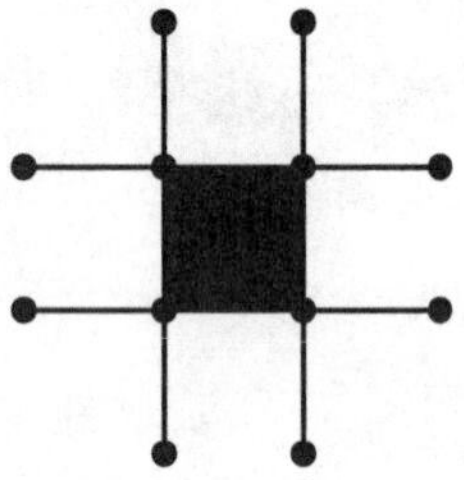

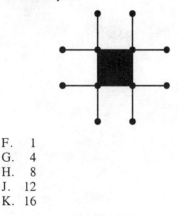

F. 1
G. 4
H. 8
J. 12
K. 16

45. All of the following are true for all real numbers EXCEPT:

A. $|a| = |-a|$
B. $|a - b| = |b - a|$
C. $|a - b| = -|b - a|$
D. $|a + b| \le |a| + |b|$
E. $|a - b| \le |a| + |b|$

46. $\text{Arccos}\left(\cos \frac{\pi}{2}\right) = ?$

F. 0
G. $\frac{\pi}{4}$
H. $\frac{\pi}{2}$
J. $\frac{3\pi}{2}$
K. π

47. Triangle ABC has coordinates A (–1, –2), B (0, 4), and C (3, –1). Which of the following, provides the coordinates of triangle $A'B'C'$, respectively, the image of triangle ABC after a reflection in the line $y = -x$?

A. (2, 1), (–4, 0), (1, –3)
B. (1, 2), (0, –4), (–3, 1)
C. (2, 1), (4, 0), (1, –3)
D. (3, 2), (5, 1), (2, –2)
E. (4, 0), (3, –1), (–1, –2)

48. If $\sin x = \cos x$, then x could terminate only in the:

F. first quadrant.
G. second quadrant.
H. first or third quadrants.
J. second or third quadrants.
K. second or fourth quadrants.

49. If the line $x = k$ is tangent to the circle $(x - 2)^2 + (y + 1)^2 = 4$, then the point of tangency is?

A. (–6, –1) or (2, –1)
B. (–2, –1) or (6, –1)
C. (0, –1) or (4, –1)
D. (0, 1) or (4, 1)
E. (2, 1) or (6, 1)

GO ON TO THE NEXT PAGE

50. What is the last term in the expansion $(2x + 3y)^4$?

F. y^4
G. $9y^4$
H. $27y^4$
J. $81y^4$
K. $(xy)^4$

51. Which of the following could be a graph of the equation $y = ax^2 + bx + c$, where $b^2 - 4ac = 0$?

A.
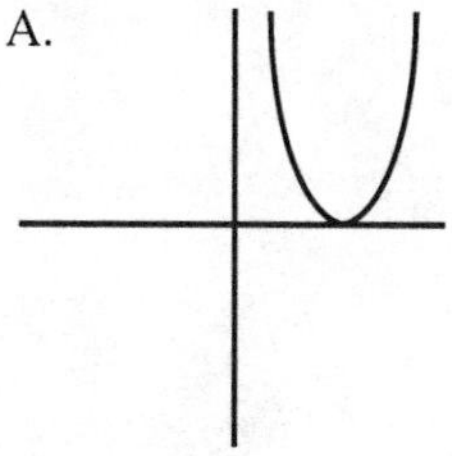

B.
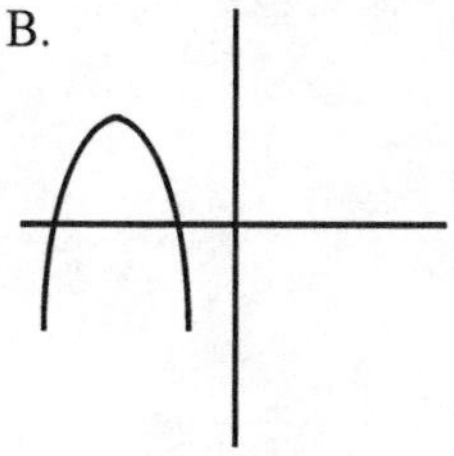

C.
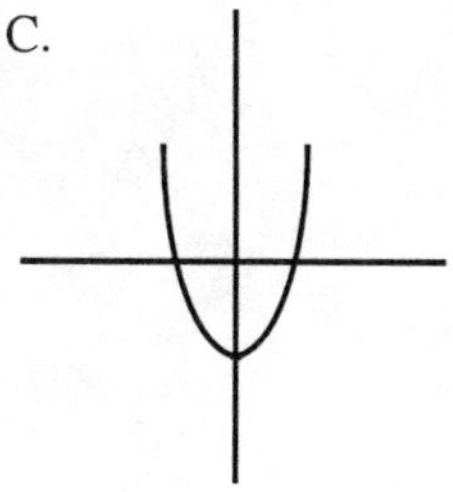

D.
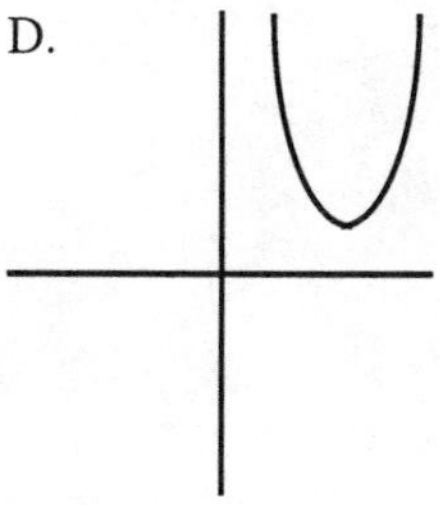

E.
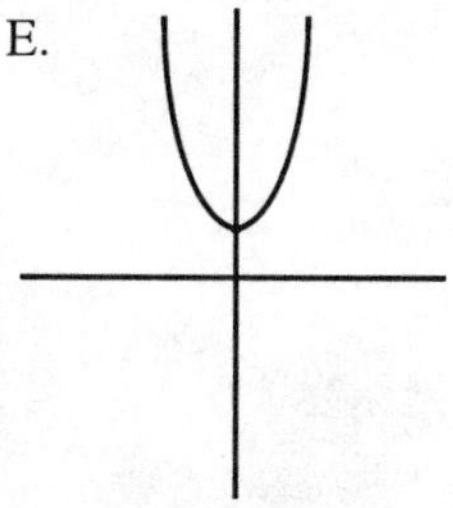

52. For any acute angle θ, which of the following is equal to $\frac{\sin\theta}{\cos\theta}$?

F. 0.5
G. 1
H. $\tan\theta$
J. $\cot\theta$
K. $\sec\theta$

53. An angle that measures $\frac{3}{2}\pi$ radians measures how many degrees?

A. 60
B. 90
C. 120
D. 180
E. 270

54. What is the solution set for $|2x - 1| = 3$?

F. All real numbers
G. The empty set
H. $\{-1\}$
J. $\{2\}$
K. $\{-1, 2\}$

55. The end points of line 1 have coordinates of (2, 5) and (2, –4). What are the coordinates of the midpoint of line 1?

A. (0,1)
B. $(2, \frac{1}{2})$
C. (2,1)
D. (2,9)
E. (4,9)

56. What is the slope of the line with the equation $2x + 3y - 2 = 0$?

F. $-\frac{3}{2}$
G. $-\frac{2}{3}$
H. $\frac{2}{3}$
J. 4
K. 6

57. $\frac{1}{\sqrt{3} - 1} = ?$

A. $\frac{\sqrt{3} - 1}{4}$
B. $\frac{\sqrt{3} - 1}{3}$
C. $\frac{\sqrt{3} - 1}{2}$
D. $\frac{\sqrt{3} + 1}{2}$
E. $\sqrt{3 + 1}$

GO ON TO THE NEXT PAGE

58. $(-2)^2 - 2^{-2} = ?$

F. –5
G. –3
H. 3
J. $3\frac{3}{4}$
K. $4\frac{1}{4}$

59. One root of the equation $x^2 + 3x + 1 = 0$ is $\frac{-3+\sqrt{5}}{2}$. What is the other root?

A. $\frac{3+\sqrt{5}}{2}$
B. $\frac{3-\sqrt{5}}{2}$
C. $\frac{-3-\sqrt{5}}{2}$
D. $3 + \frac{\sqrt{5}}{2}$
E. $3 - \frac{\sqrt{5}}{2}$

60. The figure below represents which of the following equations?

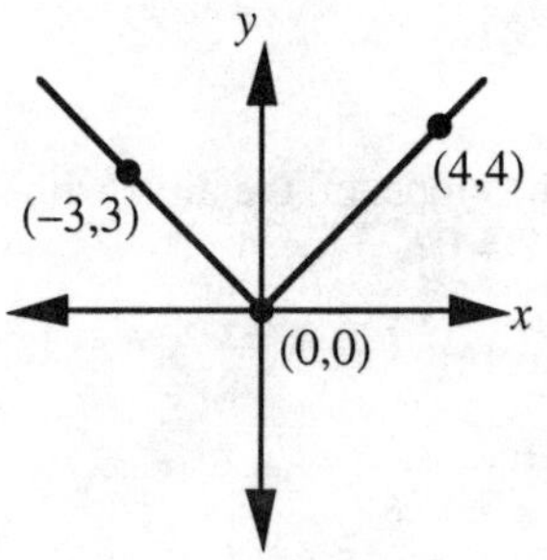

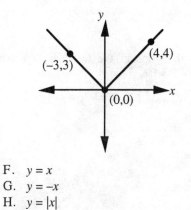

F. $y = x$
G. $y = -x$
H. $y = |x|$
J. $y = 2x$
K. $y = x^2$

IF YOU FINISH BEFORE TIME IS CALLED, YOU MAY CHECK YOUR WORK ON THIS TEST ONLY. DO NOT WORK ON ANY OTHER TEST SECTION. **STOP**

3 3 3 3 3 3 3 3 3 3 3 3

READING

35 Minutes—40 Questions

DIRECTIONS: There are four passages in this test. Each passage is followed by several questions. After reading each passage, choose the best answer to each question and blacken the corresponding oval on your answer sheet. You may refer to the passages as often as necessary.

Passage I (PF): In this selection, the narrator shares his exasperation with and sympathy for an employee.

Turkey was a short, pursy Englishman, of about my own age—that is, somewhere not far from sixty. In the morning, one might say, his face was of a fine florid hue, but after twelve o'clock, meridian—his dinner hour—it blazed like a grate full of Christmas coals; and continued blazing—but, as it were, with a gradual wane—till six o'clock p.m., or thereabouts; after which, I saw no more of the proprietor of the face, which, gaining its meridian with the sun, seemed to set with, to rise, culminate, and decline the following day, with the like regularity and undiminished glory. There are many singular coincidences I have known in the course of my life, not the least among which was the fact that, exactly when Turkey displayed his fullest beams from his red and radiant countenance, just then, too, at that critical moment, began the daily period when I considered his business capacities as seriously disturbed for the remainder of the twenty-four hours.

Not that he was absolutely idle, or averse to business then; far from it. The difficulty was, he was apt to be altogether too energetic. There was a strange, inflamed, flurried, flighty recklessness of activity about him. He would be incautious in dipping his pen into his inkstand. All his blots upon my documents were dropped there after twelve o'clock, meridian. Indeed, not only would he be reckless, and sadly given to making blots in the afternoon, but, some days, he went further, and was rather noisy. At such times, too, his face flamed with augmented blazonry, as if cannel coal had been heaped upon anthracite. He made an unpleasant racket with his chair; spilled his sand box; in mending his pens, impatiently split them all to pieces, and threw them on the floor in a sudden passion; stood up, and leaned over his table, boxing the papers about in a most indecorous manner, very sad to behold in an elderly man like him.

Nevertheless, as he was in many ways a most valuable person to me, and all the time before twelve o'clock, meridian, was the quickest, steadiest creature, too, accomplishing a great deal of work in a style not easily to be matched—for these reasons, I was willing to overlook his eccentricities, though, indeed, occasionally, I remonstrated with him. I did this very gently, however, because, though the civilest, nay, the blandest and most reverential of men in the morning, yet, in the afternoon, he was disposed, upon provocation, to be slightly rash with his tongue—in fact, insolent. Now, valuing his morning services as I did, and resolved not to lose them—yet, at the same time, made uncomfortable by his inflamed ways after twelve o'clock-and being a man of peace, unwilling by my admonitions to call forth unseemly retorts from him, I took upon me, one Saturday noon (he was always worse on Saturdays) to hint to him, very kindly, that perhaps, now that he was growing old, it might be well to abridge his labors; in short, he need not come to my chambers after twelve o'clock, but, dinner over, had best go home to his lodgings, and rest himself till teatime. But no; he insisted upon his afternoon devotions. His countenance became intolerably fervid, as he oratorically assured me—gesticulating with a long ruler at the other end of the room—that if his services in the morning were useful, how indispensable, then, in the afternoon?

"With submission, sir," said Turkey, on this occasion, "I consider myself your right-hand man. In the morning I but marshall and deploy my columns; but in the afternoon I put myself at their head, and gallantly charge the foe, thus"—and he made a violent thrust with the ruler.

"But the blots, Turkey," intimated I.

"True; but, with submission sir, behold these hairs! I am getting old. Surely, sir, a blot or two of a warm afternoon is not to be severely urged against gray hairs. Old age—even if it blot the page—is honorable. With submission, sir, we *both* are getting old."

This appeal to my fellow-feeling was hardly to be resisted. At all events, I saw that go he would not. So, I made up my mind to let him stay, resolving, nevertheless, to see to it that, during the afternoon, he had to do with my less important papers.

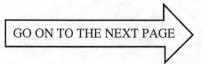

GO ON TO THE NEXT PAGE

1. The narrator is Turkey's:

   A. older brother.
   B. physician.
   C. employer.
   D. co-worker.

2. The passage suggests that Turkey is a:

   F. copyist.
   G. painter.
   H. fencing instructor.
   J. sales clerk.

3. A logical explanation for Turkey's behavior is that he:

   A. becomes fatigued.
   B. is growing old.
   C. drinks alcohol.
   D. dislikes the narrator.

4. The "fellow-feeling" mentioned in the final paragraph is based on the fact that:

   F. Turkey is the narrator's right-hand man.
   G. Turkey and the narrator are the same age.
   H. the narrator also makes ink blots.
   J. the ink blots are not very serious.

5. The narrator's final resolution of the problem is to:

   A. find a replacement for Turkey.
   B. give Turkey Saturdays off.
   C. give Turkey afternoons off.
   D. give Turkey less important work after noon.

6. According to the narrator, Turkey's face is reddest:

   F. in early morning.
   G. at noon.
   H. in midafternoon.
   J. in early evening.

7. It can be inferred that when cannel coal is heaped on anthracite, a fire:

   A. burns more intensely.
   B. burns less intensely.
   C. goes out altogether.
   D. begins to sputter and spit.

8. The narrator's attitude toward Turkey's afternoon behavior is one of:

   F. amusement.
   G. discomfort.
   H. indifference.
   J. outrage.

9. The narrator finds Turkey's work in the mornings to be:

   A. entirely satisfactory.
   B. frequently unsatisfactory.
   C. almost always unsatisfactory.
   D. inconsistent.

10. Turkey's behavior in the afternoon is NOT characterized by which of the following?

    F. Frenzied activity
    G. Excessive carelessness
    H. Idleness
    J. Verbal insolence

Passage II (SS): This passage discusses the appropriate punishment for individuals who have violated the law.

Justice in society must include both a fair trial to the accused and the selection of an appropriate punishment for those proved guilty. Because justice is regarded as one form of equality, we find in its earlier expressions the idea of a punishment equal to the crime. Recorded in the Old Testament is the expression "an eye for an eye, and a tooth for a tooth." That is, the individual who has done wrong has committed an offense against society. To atone for this offense, society must get even. This can be done only by inflicting an equal injury upon him. This conception of retributive justice is reflected in many parts of the legal codes and procedures of modern times. It is illustrated when we demand the death penalty for a person who has committed murder.

This philosophy of punishment was supported by the German idealist, Hegel. He believed that society owed it to the criminal to administer a punishment equal to the crime committed. The criminal had by his own actions denied his true self, and it is necessary to do something to restore the self that has been denied. To the murderer, nothing less than giving up his own life will pay his debt. The exaction of the death penalty is a right the state owes the criminal, and it should

GO ON TO THE NEXT PAGE

not deny him his due.

Modern jurists have tried to replace retributive justice with the notion of corrective justice. The aim of the latter is not to abandon the concept of equality but to find a more adequate way to express it. It tries to preserve the ideal of equal opportunity for each individual to realize the best that is in him. The criminal is regarded as being socially ill and in need of treatment that will enable him to become a normal member of society. Before treatment can be administered, the causes that led to antisocial behavior must be found. If the causes can be removed, provisions must be made to have this done.

Only those criminals who are incurable should be permanently separated from the rest of society. This does not mean that criminals will escape punishment or be quickly returned to take up careers of crime. It means that justice is to heal the individual, not simply to get even with him. If severe punishment is the only adequate means for accomplishing this, it should be administered. However, the individual should be given every opportunity to assume a normal place in society. His conviction of crime must not deprive him of the opportunity to make his way in the society of which he is a part.

11. The best title for this selection is:

A. Fitting Punishment to the Crime.
B. Approaches to Just Punishment.
C. Improvement in Legal Justice.
D. Attaining Justice in the Courts.

12. Hegel would view the death sentence for murder as:

F. inadequate justice.
G. the best way for society to get revenge.
H. the most efficient method of removing a known danger.
J. an inalienable right of the murderer.

13. The passage implies that the basic difference between retributive justice and corrective justice is the:

A. type of crime that was committed.
B. severity of the punishment.
C. reason for the sentence.
D. outcome of the trial.

14. The punishment that would be most inconsistent with the views of corrective justice is:

F. forced brain surgery.
G. solitary confinement.
H. life imprisonment.
J. the electric chair.

15. The Biblical expression "an eye for an eye, and a tooth for a tooth" was presented in order to:

A. justify the need for punishment as a part of law.
B. give moral backing to retributive justice.
C. show that humanity has long been interested in justice as a form of equality.
D. indicate the lack of social development during Biblical times.

16. The concept of retributive justice still reflected in many modern legal codes is:

F. giving the accused a fair trial.
G. rehabilitating the criminal.
H. separating incurable criminals from the rest of society.
J. inflicting equal injury on the criminal.

17. A major goal of modern jurists is to:

A. ensure that criminals do not escape punishment.
B. preserve the notion of equality.
C. restore states' rights.
D. select an appropriate punishment for a crime.

18. Under the notion of corrective justice, assuming "a normal place in society" (paragraph 4) most likely means:

F. acting in one's own best interests.
G. denying one's true self.
H. curing antisocial behavior.
J. accepting punishment.

19. The author's tone in the passage is best described as:

A. argumentative.
B. sympathetic.
C. explanatory.
D. conciliatory.

20. According to the author, criminals cannot be treated until:

F. they have been punished properly for their crime.
G. they have received a fair trial.
H. a legal code for treatment has been established.
J. the causes of antisocial behavior have been found.

GO ON TO THE NEXT PAGE

Passage III (H): This passage describes events leading to and the effects of World War I.

The event that touched off World War I occurred in Sarajevo, the capital of the Austro-Hungarian province of Bosnia, on June 28, 1914. There the Archduke Francis Ferdinand, the Hapsburg heir to the throne of the Austro-Hungarian Empire, was shot and killed by a young Serbian nationalist seeking revenge against the Austrians for their annexation of Bosnia. Austria issued an ultimatum to Serbia. The Serbians acquiesced, in an attempt to stave off war. Austria, however, was intent on exacting retribution and in July of that year declared war on Serbia.

For almost a century, since the Congress of Vienna in 1815, European diplomats had prevented any real threat to the delicate balance of power achieved by the Congress. This time, though, they seemed powerless to stop the movement toward war. The assassination provoked a fateful series of failed diplomatic attempts that led suspicious Russia to mobilize its armed forces as Serbia's ally. Austria sought and received the mobilization aid of its ally Germany. The other members of the Triple Entente, France and Great Britain soon joined their ally Russia against Austria. In 1917, the United States was drawn into the battle as an ally of France and Great Britain.

World War I was unlike any other war fought before or since then. The profound shock it generated dramatically affected the progression of life in Europe and America and changed the course of world politics. Moreover, the war shocked millions of people throughout Europe into confronting the terrible losses and the grim and brutal realities of modern war. The few wars that had been fought since 1815 were distant colonial wars. Europeans had always been victorious, and the battles seemed nothing more than skirmishes that offered chances to experience adventure and to demonstrate bravery and heroism. The trenches and battlefields of Europe introduced millions of young men and women to a world of pain and death that they had never imagined.

The war altered the collective social sensibility of the people of Europe. It destroyed the spirit of optimism that had prevailed in the nineteenth century. Civilized, polite behavior now seemed archaic and utterly hypocritical. Moreover, the impression that there appeared to be no sane way to end the carnage only added to the sense of futility. The war changed relationships between members of the same social class. Before the war, the upper classes of Europe felt a common bond that united them across national borders. After the war, national boundaries defined social consciousness in a way that destroyed the solidarity of class.

World War I produced several dramatic changes in the political landscape of Europe. The breakup of the Austro-Hungarian, Russian, and German empires led to the reemergence of the state of Poland and the formation of other independent nation states in Europe. The war acted as a catalyst for European revolutionaries. The Russian Revolution of 1917 set the stage for the Bolshevik seizure of power, the exercise of total power by the Communist party; and the rise of Stalin as the absolute dictator of the Russian state (renamed the Union of Soviet Socialist Republics). World War I bore bitter fruit in Central and Southern Europe as well. The rise of Nazism in Germany and fascism in Italy led many historians to conclude that World War II, which was begun by Nazi Germany in 1939, was in actuality the continuation of the Great War that destroyed the social fabric of Europe in 1914.

21. The precipitating cause of World War I was:

    A. an assassination.
    B. a coronation.
    C. a rebellion.
    D. a plebiscite.

22. The event occurred in the city of:

    F. Sarajevo in Bosnia.
    G. Vienna in Austria.
    H. Trieste in Italy.
    J. Budapest in Hungary.

23. Before World War I, a balance of power had existed for:

    A. nearly 15 years.
    B. almost a quarter century.
    C. almost 100 years.
    D. nearly 10 years.

24. The chief reason European countries other than Austria and Serbia were drawn into the conflict was that:

    F. they were members of the two alliance systems to which the combatants belonged.
    G. they feared the Hapsburgs.
    H. they wanted to ensure freedom of the seas.
    J. they wanted the land of neighboring countries.

25. Mobilization for war resulted swiftly when:

    A. the United States declared war.
    B. attempts at diplomacy failed.
    C. Russia refused to help Serbia.
    D. Italy joined the conflict.

GO ON TO THE NEXT PAGE

26. The way in which class relationships changed as a result of the outbreak of World War I suggests that:

F. nationalism might have weakened had the war never occurred.
G. the middle classes had no real love of country.
H. the upper classes had eagerly anticipated war.
J. everyone sanctioned the war.

27. The forces of militant nationalism that were unleashed during World War I culminated in the breakup of the Russian Empire and the German Empire. The political regimes that came to power in Germany and the Soviet Union before World War II were:

A. democracies that isolated themselves from world politics.
B. ruthless dictatorships dedicated to world conquest.
C. weak states allied with the United States.
D. members of a Europe-wide common market.

28. The sense of futility felt throughout Europe during and after World War I would be evident in a study of:

F. American investment policies.
G. statistics concerning foreign language study in America.
H. European literature of the 1920s, 1930s, and 1940s.
J. the number of transatlantic voyages between 1920 and 1930.

29. World War I and its aftermath suggest the idea that:

A. nationalism has little to do with world conflict.
B. war feeds on nationalist sympathies.
C. the cause of peace is best aided by reinvigorating the spirit of nationalism.
D. diplomacy never works.

30. Archduke Francis Ferdinand, as the heir to the Austro-Hungarian Empire, was a member of the:

F. Hohenzollern family.
G. Hanover family.
H. Hapsburg family.
J. Stuart family.

Passage IV (NS): This selection discusses the information gathered about the planet Uranus by the Voyager 2 spacecraft.

When the Voyager 2 spacecraft flew past Uranus and its moons in 1986, it gathered startling new information about these extraordinary celestial objects. Uranus had long been known to be different from all the other planets in one important respect: it lies tipped over on its side and instead of spinning like a top, it rolls like a ball along the path of its orbit. Its geographic poles, instead of being on the top and bottom of the planet as Earth's are, are located on either side, one facing the sun and one facing away—as if they were the ends of a gigantic axle. Voyager found still another oddity: Uranus' magnetic poles, instead of lying close to the geographic poles as Earth's do, are located not far from the planet's equator, 600 away from the geographic poles. Still another discovery is that the clouds in the Uranian atmosphere move in the same direction as the planet rotates; that is, from top to bottom and back to top, rather than horizontally, as Earth's clouds move.

The Uranian moons proved to have equally striking features. Miranda, the moon nearest the planet, bears tremendous markings where terrains of totally different types appear to have been wedged together. On Ariel, the next moon out, the landscape has been stretched apart, creating huge faults where the ground has broken apart and sunk inward. However, there is no evidence of any geological activity. Umbriel, the third moon, seems to be "painted" with some dark substance. On one side of Umbriel is a large, round bright marking called the "donut." It is presumably some type of impact crater. Each of Uranus' other seven moons is equally odd and unlike the others. Furthermore, between the orbit of Miranda and the planet's surface are up to one hundred charcoal-colored rings, ringlets, and bands of dust, and between some of these rings are still more tiny moonlets.

The moons and rings of Uranus are odd in still another way. Like the clouds in the planet's atmosphere, they circle Uranus in the same direction as the planet rotates. That is, they orbit over the top and bottom of the planet rather than around the sides, as Earth's moon does.

GO ON TO THE NEXT PAGE

31. Because of the odd way in which Uranus rotates, one geographic pole:

A. alternates between daylight and darkness.
B. receives only indirect sunlight.
C. varies between heat from the sun and cold.
D. is always in darkness.

32. The warmest spot on Uranus would most likely be located at:

F. one of the magnetic poles.
G. the equator.
H. one of the geographic poles.
J. a spot midway between a geographic pole and the equator.

33. On Uranus, a surface location that receives sunlight:

A. will alternate between daylight and darkness.
B. will always be in daylight.
C. will occasionally be in darkness.
D. must be near one of the magnetic poles.

34. The Uranian equator extends:

F. around the planet horizontally, as Earth's does.
G. around the planet through the geographic poles.
H. around the planet from top to bottom.
J. around the planet through the magnetic poles.

35. An observer at the Uranian equator would most likely experience:

A. a regular succession of days and nights.
B. constant, indirect sunlight.
C. a regular succession of warmth and cold.
D. only darkness.

36. Auroras are sky phenomena that generally appear near a planet's magnetic poles. On Earth, auroras can be seen at extreme north or south latitudes. On Uranus, auroras would most likely:

F. be visible near the planet's geographic poles.
G. never be visible.
H. be visible not far from the planet's equator.
J. be visible from everywhere on the planet's surface.

37. On Earth, atmospheric circulation patterns are largely controlled by the varying amounts of sunlight received at different latitudes. On Uranus:

A. atmospheric circulation functions in an identical way.
B. there is no atmospheric circulation.
C. the atmosphere circulates from one geographic pole to the other.
D. some other factor besides sunlight controls atmospheric circulation.

38. It has been suggested that the moon Miranda was shattered into pieces by a collision with some other object. Gravity then caused the pieces to reassemble; however, great "seam" marks most likely remained because:

F. the gravitational forces involved were weak.
G. the lack of atmosphere meant that no erosion ever took place.
H. the second object remained nearby, exerting gravitational pull.
J. the force of the collision was so great.

39. The great faults observed on the moon Ariel could have been caused by:

A. moonquakes.
B. continental drift.
C. the gravitational pull of other nearby moons.
D. volcanic activity.

40. Uranus has how many moons?

F. 3
G. 7
H. 10
J. 12

IF YOU FINISH BEFORE TIME IS CALLED, YOU MAY CHECK YOUR WORK ON THIS TEST ONLY. DO NOT WORK ON ANY OTHER TEST SECTION.

STOP

SCIENCE REASONING

35 Minutes—40 Questions

DIRECTIONS: There are seven passages in this test. Each passage is followed by several questions. After reading a passage, choose the best answer to each question and blacken the corresponding oval on your answer sheet. You may refer to the passages as often as necessary.

Passage I

The table below shows selected elements from the periodic table, together with their atomic radii in angstrom units (Å) and their electronegativities (second number):

H 0.37 Å 2.20						
Li 1.35 Å 0.98	Be 0.90 Å 1.57	B 0.80 Å 2.04	C 0.77 Å 2.55	N 0.70 Å 3.04	O 0.66 Å 3.44	F 0.64 Å 3.98
Na 1.54 Å 0.93	Mg 1.30 Å 1.31	Al 1.25 Å 1.61	Si 1.17 Å 1.90	P 1.10 Å 2.19	S 1.04 Å 2.58	Cl 0.99 Å 3.16
K 1.96 Å 0.82						Br 1.14 Å 2.96
Rb 2.11 Å 0.82						I 1.33 Å 2.66

When two atoms form a covalent bond, the approximate bond length may be calculated by adding together the two atomic radii.

The electronegativity has important chemical significance. If two atoms form a bond, the difference in the two electronegativities indicates the degree to which the bond is covalent (indicated by a small difference) or ionic (indicated by a large difference).

1. According to the chart, as one moves down a column in the table, which of the following occur?

   A. the radii decrease and the electronegativities decrease
   B. the radii increase and the electronegativities increase
   C. the radii decrease and the electronegativities increase
   D. the radii increase and the electronegativities decrease

2. The greatest electronegativity in the table is:

   F. fluorine (F).
   G. chlorine (Cl).
   H. rubidium (Rb).
   J. hydrogen (H).

3. The bond length in the P-Cl bond is:

   A. 0.11 angstroms.
   B. 0.97 angstroms.
   C. 2.09 angstroms.
   D. 5.35 angstroms.

4. The bond between which of the following is likely to have the most covalent character?

   F. Sodium (Na) and iodine (I)
   G. Magnesium (Mg) and oxygen (O)
   H. Sulphur (S) and oxygen (O)
   J. Carbon (C) and nitrogen (N)

5. The table indicates that bonds of greatest ionic character occur:

   A. between elements by each other in a row.
   B. between elements that are near each other in a column but far apart along a row.
   C. between elements that are far apart along a column but close in a row.
   D. between elements far apart along a column and far apart in a row.

6. The element cesium (Cs) lies directly below rubidium (Rb) in the Periodic Table. The electronegativity difference in CsF is likely to be:

   F. less than 3.16.
   G. equal to 3.16.
   H. greater than 3.16.
   J. Cannot be determined

GO ON TO THE NEXT PAGE

Passage II

It is known that during photosynthesis, leaf pigments absorb light energy that eventually results in the production of glucose and other carbohydrates to be used by the green plant. Oxygen gas (O_2) is also produced during the process. Various factors affecting the rate of photosynthesis were investigated by counting the number of oxygen bubbles produced under the conditions described in the following three experiments.

Experiment 1

A sample of leaf extract (a mixture of pigments previously separated from other leaf components) from the pond plant *Elodea* was placed in a beaker containing water and a standard concentration of carbon dioxide (both are necessary ingredients for photosynthesis). Light of varying intensity was used to illuminate the beaker, and the number of oxygen bubbles emitted by the plant each minute was recorded. The results are described in Figure 1.

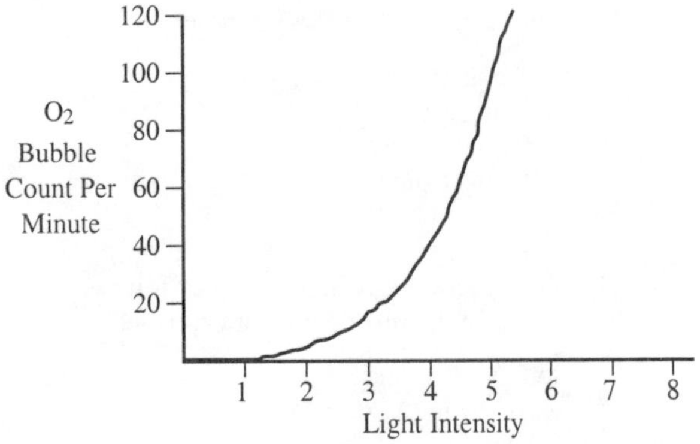

Figure 1

Experiment 2

An identical experiment was conducted in which the concentration of leaf extract was reduced four-fold (the mixture was one-fourth as concentrated as in Experiment 1). The results are described in Figure 2.

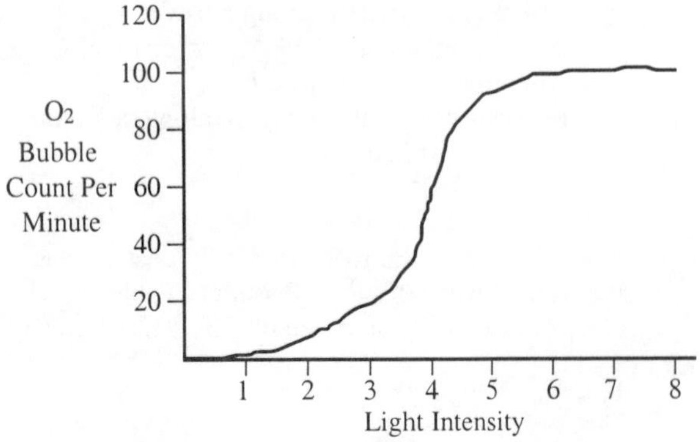

Figure 2

Experiment 3

Visible light consists of many different colors, or light wavelengths. Only those wavelengths that are absorbed by leaf pigments can provide the energy to maintain photosynthesis in the leaf. Different wavelengths of light were used separately to illuminate two samples of leaf extract, each containing a different *Elodea* leaf pigment. Oxygen (O_2) bubbles were again counted as a measure of the rate of photosynthesis. Figure 3 shows the results.

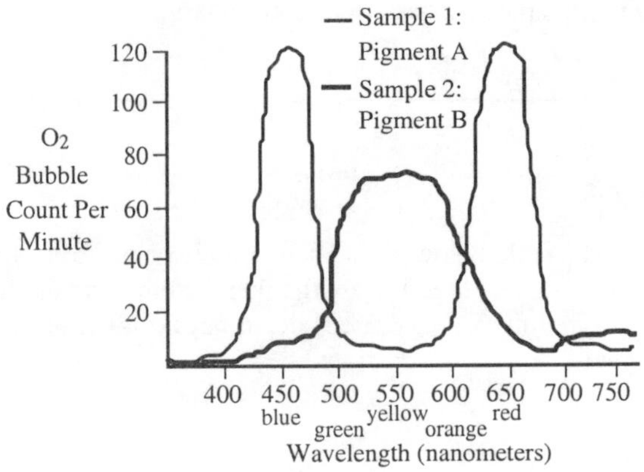

Figure 3

7. Which of the following changes in Experiment 1 of carbon dioxide affects the rate of photosynthesis?
   A. Repeat the experiment using the same concentration of carbon dioxide in the beaker of water, but with different species of green plants.
   B. Repeat the experiment using first no carbon dioxide and then varying concentrations of carbon dioxide in the beaker of water.
   C. Repeat the experiment using different levels of water in the beaker containing a standard concentration of carbon dioxide.
   D. Repeat the experiment using additional light intensities.

8. The results in Experiments 1 and 2 demonstrate that in order to maintain a continued increase in the photosynthesis rate:
   F. adequate amounts of light are needed.
   G. adequate amounts of carbon dioxide are needed.
   H. adequate amounts of oxygen are needed.
   J. adequate amounts of leaf pigments are needed.

GO ON TO THE NEXT PAGE

9. Based on the information in Figure 3, which would permit a test of the hypothesis that the level statement is correct?

   A. Pigment A primarily absorbs light at 450 and 650 manometers, while Pigment B absorbs light at 500-575 manometers.
   B. Pigment B primarily absorbs light at 450 and 650 manometers, while Pigment A primarily absorbs light at 500-575 manometers.
   C. Pigment A can influence the rate of photosynthesis, while Pigment B cannot.
   D. Pigment B can influence the rate of photosynthesis, while Pigment A cannot.

10. If the concentration of *Elodea* leaf extract was increased in Experiment 2, which of the following results could be expected?

    F. A decrease in the number of oxygen bubbles
    G. An increase in the number of oxygen bubbles
    H. No change in the number of oxygen bubbles
    J. A gradual dimming of light intensity

11. In Experiments 1 and 2, approximately how many oxygen bubbles/minute were produced at a light intensity level of 4?

    A. 20-30
    B. 30-40
    C. 40-50
    D. Between 0 and 10

12. According to the information in Figure 3, if an additional experiment were conducted, which condition would be *least effective* in maintaining photosynthetic rate in *Elodea*?

    F. Using blue light only
    G. Using green light only
    H. Using yellow light only
    J. Using orange light only

Passage III

A set of experiments was carried out to investigate the relative sizes of the planets of our solar system and their relative distances from the Sun. Table 1 was given to all students performing the experiments.

Experiment 1

Using a simple compass, ruler, and paper (11 in. • 14 in.), students were asked to compare the sizes of the planets. Calling the size of Earth 1.00 (1 earth diameter = 5 in.), a circle was drawn by inserting the point of the compass in the exact center of the paper. The circle had a radius of 2.5 in. (to produce a circle with a diameter of 5 in. representing the Earth). All other planets were drawn to scale based on the size of their diameters relative to one earth diameter (Table 1).

Experiment 2

Using the equipment from Experiment 1, students were also asked to compare planetary distances from the Sun. The Earth is 93 million miles from the Sun. This distance is called 1.00 Astronomical Unit (1 A.U. = 0.5 in.), and was used as a reference distance when the other planets were drawn at their proper distances (Table 1) from the Sun (a planet twice as far as the Earth is from the Sun would be drawn 2 A.U., or 1.0 in., from the Sun).

TABLE 1

Planet	*Approximate Diameter (in Earth diameters)*	*Approximate Distance from the Sun (A.U.)*
Mercury	0.38	0.40
Venus	0.95	0.70
Earth	1.00	1.00
Mars	0.54	1.50
Jupiter	11.20	5.20
Saturn	9.50	9.50
Uranus	3.70	19.20
Neptune	3.50	30.00
Pluto	0.47	40.00

13. In Experiment 1, the two planets that would be represented by circles most similar in size on the paper are:

    A. Earth and Venus.
    B. Mars and Pluto.
    C. Uranus and Neptune.
    D. Mercury and Pluto.

GO ON TO THE NEXT PAGE

14. Which of the following statements is supported by the data in Table 1?

F. The larger the planet, the greater is its distance from the Sun.
G. The smaller the planet, the greater is its distance from the Sun.
H. Only planets larger than the Earth are farther away from the Sun.
J. There is no consistent pattern between a planet's size and its distance from the Sun.

15. In Experiment 2, if the paper were held the "long way" and the Sun were represented by the left-hand edge of the paper, which planet(s) would not fit on the paper?

A. Uranus, Neptune, and Pluto
B. Neptune and Pluto
C. Pluto only
D. All planets *would* fit on the paper.

16. A planet's "year" is based on how long it takes to orbit the Sun. This time period is related to the distance of that planet from the Sun. If *asteroids* are found 2.8 A.U. from the Sun, which hypothesis best describes an "asteroid year"? It should be:

F. longer than a "Mars year" but shorter than a "Jupiter year."
G. longer than an "Earth year" but shorter than a "Mars year."
H. longer than an "Earth year" but shorter than a "Neptune year."
J. longer than a "Neptune year" but shorter than a "Uranus year."

17. In Experiment 1, how large would a circle representing the Sun be if its diameter is approximately 110 times greater than that of the Earth?

A. It would have a radius of approximately 550 inches.
B. It would have a diameter of approximately 550 inches.
C. It would have a radius of approximately 55 inches.
D. It would have a diameter of approximately 55 inches.

18. A third experiment was conducted in which the *mass* of each planet was described relative to the mass of the Earth (Jupiter had the greatest mass, Saturn had the next largest mass, Mercury and Pluto had the smallest masses). If the planets were *placed in an order* based on how they compared to Earth for the variables measured in all three experiments, which *two orders* would be expected to be most similar?

F. Diameter and distance from the Sun
G. Mass and distance from the Sun
H. Diameter and mass
J. All three orders would be similar.

GO ON TO THE NEXT PAGE

Passage IV

The accompanying figure shows how the world records for various footraces have improved during a portion of this century. Speeds are given in both meters/minute and minutes/mile.

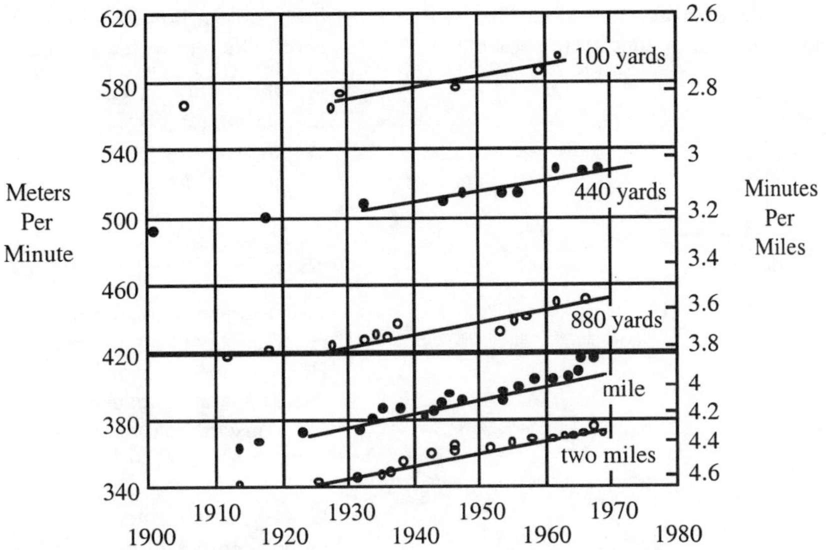

Modified from:, H.W. Ryder, H.J. Carr, and P. Herget. 1976. Future performance in footracing. *Sci. Amer.* 234 (6): 109-114.

19. In what race and in what year was the greatest speed in meters/minute achieved?

A. The 6-mile run in 1900
B. The 440-yard dash in 1968
C. The 100-yard dash in 1962
D. The 15-mile run in 1947

20. The trend in the graphs of meters/minute for the various distances shows:

F. roughly a linear increase.
G. roughly a linear decrease.
H. a linear increase for short distances and a linear decrease for long distances.
J. no systematic pattern.

21. For 1960, the ratio of minutes/mile values for the 1-mile run to that for the 440-yard dash is roughly:

A. 3/4.
B. 4/5.
C. 5/4.
D. 4/3.

22. The increase in speed (in meters/minute) for the 2-mile run from 1925 to 1967 is roughly:

F. 0.3.
G. 10.
H. 30.
J. 100.

23. If the trends shown can be expected to hold for later years, then the value of minutes per mile for the 880-yard run in 1980 is expected to be:

A. 3.5.
B. 3.8.
C. 420.
D. 460.

GO ON TO THE NEXT PAGE

Passage V

Two experiments were performed in which constant amounts of heat were added continuously to samples over a period of time. The temperatures of the samples were monitored while the heat was added. The results from Experiment 1 and Experiment 2 are shown below.

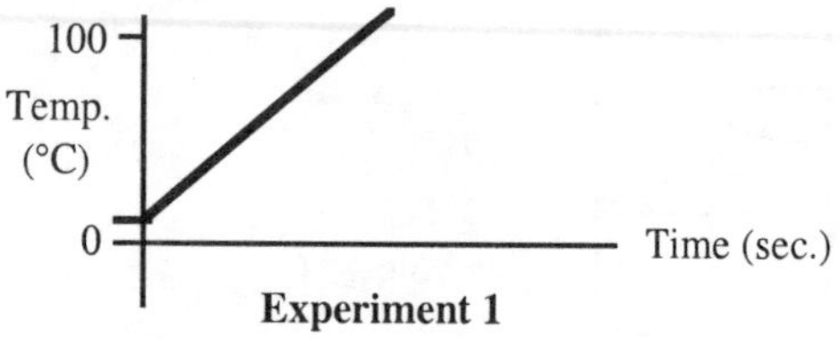

Experiment 1

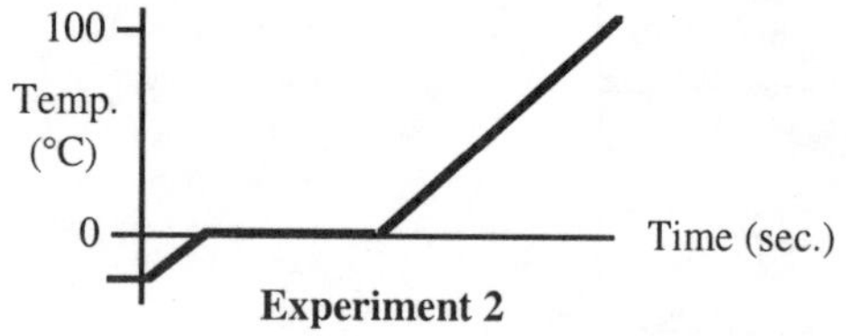

Experiment 2

24. The results of Experiment 1 may be interpreted to show that:

F. it takes longer to heat a hot sample than a cold one.
G. the temperature of the sample rises proportionately with time as heat is applied.
H. temperature is not related to heat.
J. temperature and time measure the same thing.

25. Experiment 2 differs from Experiment 1 in that:

A. only the starting temperature is different in the two experiments.
B. since the graph in Experiment 2 is not a straight line, there must have been experimental error.
C. Experiment 2 has a lower starting temperature, and also has a time period when the temperature does not rise.
D. in Experiment 2, the heat went off for a while in the middle of the experiment.

26. The experimenter wants to explain the flat part of the graph from Experiment 2. It could represent:

F. a period when the clock was turned off.
G. a period when the heat was turned off.
H. a period when heat was added but some process that did not occur in the first experiment (such as absorption of heat), caused the temperature to remain constant.
J. a period when temperature was added but the heat did not change.

27. The experimenter forms the hypothesis that the flat part of the graph in Experiment 2 results from absorption of heat by the sample, which changes the "phase" of the sample (an example of a phase change is the melting of a solid, or the boiling of a liquid). From the temperature data given, the phase change might be:

A. the boiling of water.
B. the melting of ice.
C. the melting of iron.
D. the boiling of iron.

28. The results of these experiments demonstrate that:

F. heat and temperature are basically the same.
G. heat and temperature are not the same.
H. a pause in heating can lead to a pause in temperature change.
J. constant heating leads to constant change.

29. If the experimenter extends the experiment to higher temperatures, using water as a sample, which graph best illustrates the expected results?

A.
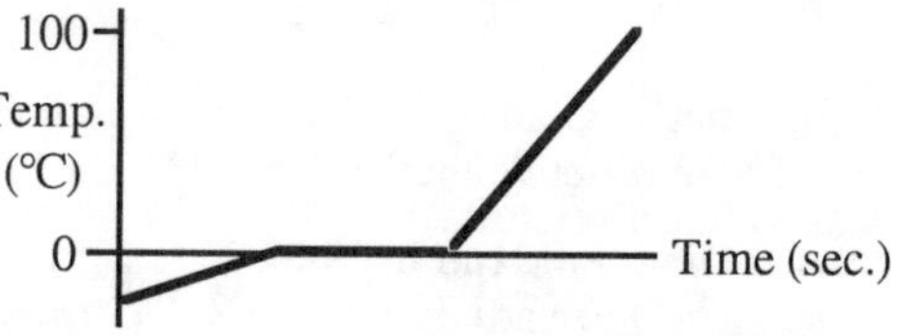

B.
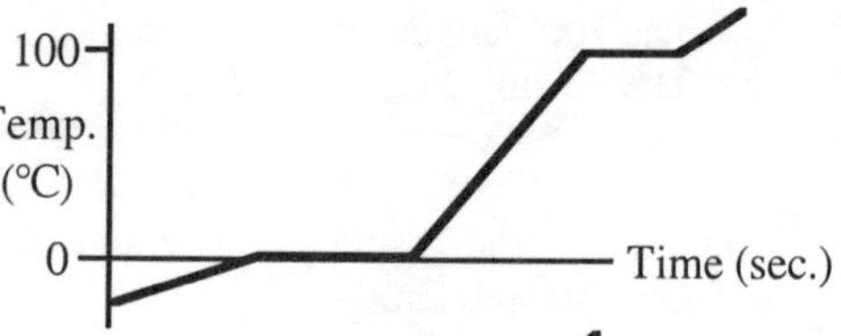

C.
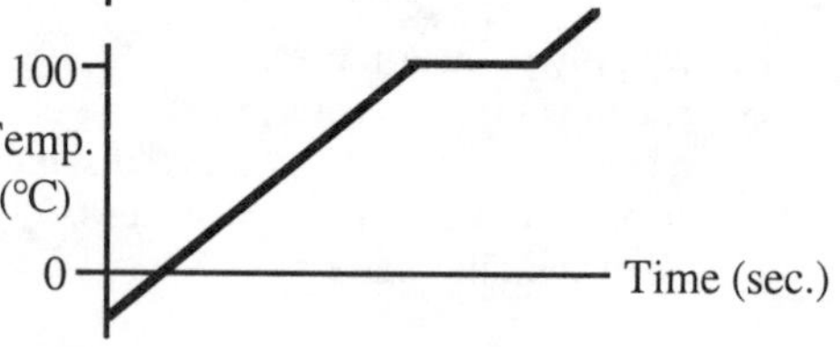

D.
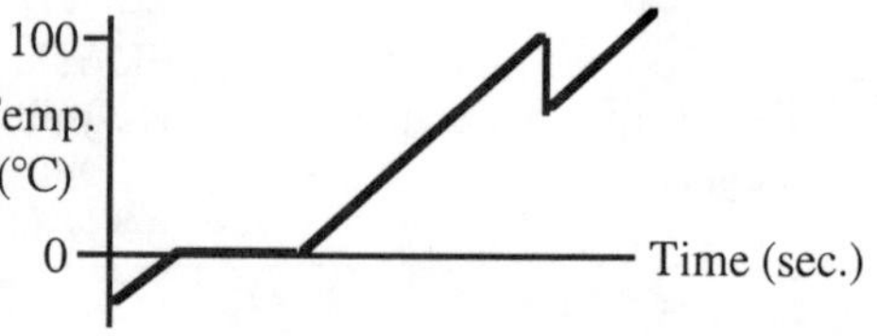

GO ON TO THE NEXT PAGE

Passage VI

The following chart shows the generalized sequence of early developmental stages (terms in boxes) observed in most vertebrates.

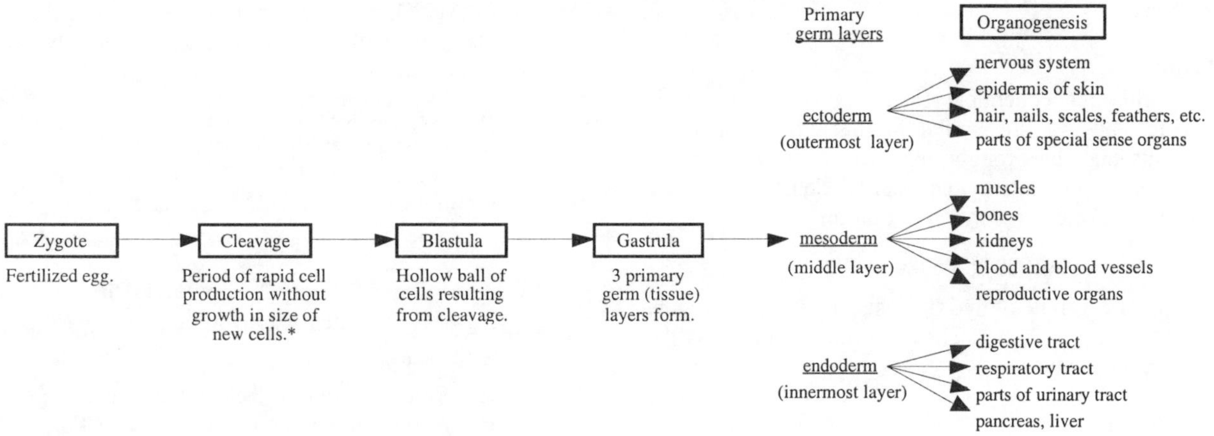

*New cells form as the zygote and its subsequent daughter cells divide and redivide.

30. According to the diagram, the stage of development when the three primary tissue layers form is:

F. cleavage.
G. blastula.
H. gastrula.
J. organogenesis.

31. Differentiation refers to a period of cell maturation during which time cells become specialized in structure and function. At which stage of development would most differentiation be expected to occur?

A. Cleavage
B. Blastula
C. Gastrula
D. Organogenesis

32. Based on the information in the diagram, which conclusion is *not correct?*

F. Vertebrates develop three primary germ layers.
G. Most bones develop from the innermost primary germ layer.
H. Diverse structures such as scales, feathers, and hair always develop from the same primary germ layer.
J. Before an organism can form different primary tissue layers, it must go through a stage in which it is in the form of a hollow ball of cells.

33. If a species of monkey were found to have extraordinary vision due to special receptor cells that were highly sensitive to different colors of light, from which primary germ layer(s) would you predict such cells to develop?

A. Endoderm
B. Mesoderm
C. Ectoderm
D. A combination of endoderm and mesoderm

34. On the basis of the information provided, the stage of development that probably has the smallest cells is:

F. zygote.
G. cleavage.
H. gastrula.
J. adult.

GO ON TO THE NEXT PAGE

Passage VII

The following are two theories regarding the proportions of chemicals that will react to form products.

Theory 1

Although a chemical reaction is more than simple mixing, the two are similar in that any amounts of reactants may be brought together to form chemical products that contain the same elements as the reactants. For example, in the reaction

$$\text{hydrogen} + \text{oxygen} \Rightarrow \text{water}$$

we may use 1 mole of hydrogen and 1 mole of oxygen, or 2 to 1, or 1 to 2, etc. The reaction will adjust to the proportions given.

Theory 2

Only certain proportions of reactants will combine chemically. For example, when hydrogen and oxygen are reacted, the amounts that will combine will be *exactly* 2 g of hydrogen for every 32 g of oxygen. We can show, using molecular weights, that these weights of reactants (which correspond to 2 moles of hydrogen and 1 mole of oxygen), imply the following reaction:

$$2H_2 + O_2 \Rightarrow 2H_2O$$

From this statement about the proportions of hydrogens and oxygens that react with each other, we can conclude that two hydrogen molecules must react with a single oxygen molecule to form two molecules of water.

35. Which of the following is NOT predicted by Theory 1?

A. 2 moles of zinc may react completely with 2 moles of sulfur.
B. 2 moles of zinc may react completely with 3 moles of sulfur.
C. 7 moles of zinc may react completely with 4 moles of sulfur.
D. If 3 moles of zinc were mixed with 4 moles of sulfur, 1 mole of sulfur would be left unreacted.

36. According to Theory 1, how many moles of water would be produced by the reaction of 2 moles of hydrogen and 1 mole of oxygen?

F. 1
G. 2
H. 4
J. Cannot be determined

37. An experimenter finds that when 170 g of $AgNO_3$ is reacted with 58.5 g of NaCl to form products, none of the original reactants remain in appreciable amounts. When the original amount of $AgNO_3$ is increased to 175 g, then all of the NaCl is used up, but 5 g of $AgNO_3$ remains. This result is:

A. consistent with Theory 1.
B. consistent with Theory 2.
C. consistent with both Theory 1 and Theory 2.
D. not consistent with either theory.

38. According to Theory 2, how might the remaining 5 g of $AgNO_3$ be used up?

F. Add more of the reactant NaCl.
G. Remove some of the reactant NaCl.
H. Add even more of the reactant $AgNO_3$.
J. There is no mechanism for using the 5g of $AgNO_3$.

39. An experimenter wishes to determine which theory better fits her data for an experiment in which iron (Fe) is chemically combined with oxygen (O). She finds that 2 moles of Fe will react completely with 2 moles of O; she also finds that 2 moles of Fe will react completely with 3 moles of O. At this point she is confident that Theory 1, which is in opposition to the idea of "definite proportions," is correct. What further experiment might she do to test the success of Theory 1 over Theory 2?

A. Add 1 mole of Fe to 1 mole of O.
B. Add 2 moles of Fe to 4 moles of O.
C. Add 3 moles of Fe to 4.5 moles of O.
D. Add 4 moles of Fe to 4 moles of O.

40. According to Theory 1, the product of the reaction of hydrogen and oxygen:

F. is H_2O
G. could be anything.
H. must contain hydrogen and oxygen, but lacks a specific formula.
J. has a definite proportion of hydrogen to oxygen.

IF YOU FINISH BEFORE TIME IS CALLED, YOU MAY CHECK YOUR WORK ON THIS TEST ONLY. DO NOT WORK ON ANY OTHER TEST SECTION. **STOP**

Answer Key

DIRECTIONS: For the *correct* answers in each ACT Test Subject, check the corresponding unshaded box. (Correct answers correspond to unshaded boxes.) Then, for each test, total the number of checkmarks in each column (subject category) and add to determine the raw scores.

TEST 1: ENGLISH (p. A-62)

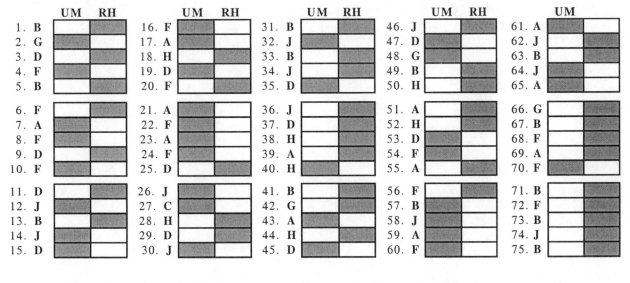

	UM	RH
1. **B**		■
2. **G**	■	
3. **D**		■
4. **F**	■	
5. **B**		■
6. **F**		■
7. **A**	■	
8. **F**	■	
9. **D**		■
10. **F**	■	
11. **D**		■
12. **J**	■	
13. **B**		■
14. **J**	■	
15. **D**	■	

	UM	RH
16. **F**	■	
17. **A**	■	
18. **H**		■
19. **D**	■	
20. **F**		■
21. **A**	■	
22. **F**	■	
23. **A**	■	
24. **F**	■	
25. **D**		■
26. **J**	■	
27. **C**	■	
28. **H**		■
29. **D**		■
30. **J**	■	

	UM	RH
31. **B**		■
32. **J**	■	
33. **B**		■
34. **J**		■
35. **D**	■	
36. **J**		■
37. **D**		■
38. **H**		■
39. **A**		■
40. **H**	■	
41. **B**		■
42. **G**		■
43. **A**	■	
44. **H**		■
45. **D**	■	

	UM	RH
46. **J**		■
47. **D**	■	
48. **G**	■	
49. **B**		■
50. **H**		■
51. **A**		■
52. **H**		■
53. **D**	■	
54. **F**	■	
55. **A**		■
56. **F**		■
57. **B**	■	
58. **J**	■	
59. **A**	■	
60. **F**	■	

	UM	
61. **A**	■	
62. **J**		■
63. **B**		■
64. **J**	■	
65. **A**	■	
66. **G**		■
67. **B**		■
68. **F**		■
69. **A**		■
70. **F**	■	
71. **B**		■
72. **F**		■
73. **B**		■
74. **J**		■
75. **B**		■

Usage/Mechanics (UM): ____/39 Rhetorical Skills (RM): ____/36 English Raw Score (UM + RH): ____/75

TEST 2: MATHEMATICS (p. A-73)

	EA	AG	GT
1. **B**		■	■
2. **K**		■	■
3. **C**		■	■
4. **K**		■	■
5. **D**		■	■
6. **F**		■	■
7. **C**	■	■	
8. **G**	■	■	
9. **C**		■	■
10. **F**		■	■
11. **E**	■	■	
12. **G**	■	■	
13. **A**	■	■	
14. **G**		■	■
15. **C**		■	■

	EA	AG	GT
16. **K**	■		■
17. **C**	■	■	
18. **G**		■	
19. **B**		■	■
20. **J**		■	■
21. **A**	■		■
22. **K**	■	■	
23. **D**		■	■
24. **J**	■		■
25. **D**		■	■
26. **G**		■	■
27. **B**		■	■
28. **G**		■	■
29. **D**		■	■
30. **F**		■	■

	EA	AG	GT
31. **C**	■	■	
32. **H**	■	■	
33. **B**	■	■	
34. **H**	■	■	
35. **C**		■	■
36. **H**		■	■
37. **E**	■		■
38. **K**	■		■
39. **C**	■	■	
40. **H**	■		■
41. **D**		■	■
42. **K**		■	■
43. **B**	■		■
44. **G**	■	■	
45. **C**	■		■

	EA	AG	GT
46. **H**	■	■	
47. **A**	■		■
48. **H**	■	■	
49. **C**	■		■
50. **J**	■		■
51. **A**	■		■
52. **H**	■	■	
53. **E**	■	■	
54. **K**	■		■
55. **B**	■		■
56. **G**	■		■
57. **D**	■		■
58. **J**	■		■
59. **C**	■		■
60. **H**	■		■

Pre-Algebra/Elementary Algebra (EA): ______/24 Intermediate Algebra/Coordinate Geometry (AG): ______/18

Plane Geometry/Trigonometry (GT): ______/18 Total Raw Score (EA + AG + GT): ______/60

TEST 3: READING (p. A-81)

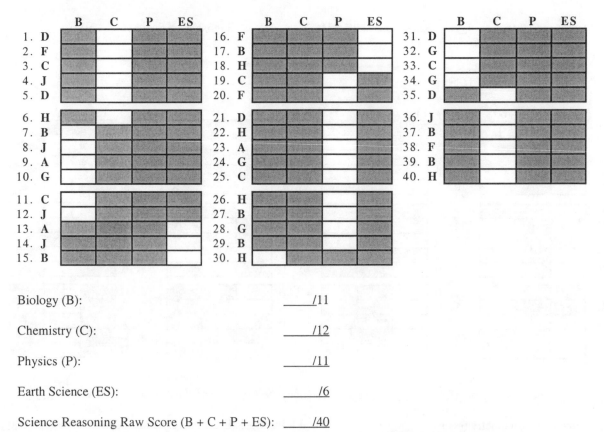

#	Answer	SS	S	H	PF
1.	C				☐
2.	F				☐
3.	C				☐
4.	G				☐
5.	D				☐
6.	G				☐
7.	A				☐
8.	G				☐
9.	A				☐
10.	H				☐
11.	B			☐	
12.	J			☐	
13.	C			☐	
14.	J			☐	
15.	C			☐	
16.	J			☐	
17.	B			☐	
18.	F			☐	
19.	C			☐	
20.	J			☐	
21.	A	☐			
22.	F	☐			
23.	C	☐			
24.	F	☐			
25.	B	☐			
26.	J	☐			
27.	B	☐			
28.	H	☐			
29.	B	☐			
30.	H	☐			
31.	D		☐		
32.	H		☐		
33.	B		☐		
34.	H		☐		
35.	B		☐		
36.	H		☐		
37.	D		☐		
38.	G		☐		
39.	C		☐		
40.	H		☐		

Social Studies (SS): ____/10

Sciences (S): ____/10

Humanities (H): ____/10

Prose Fiction (PF): ____/10

Reading Raw Score (SS + S + H + PF): ____/40

TEST 4: SCIENCE REASONING (p. A-87)

#	Answer	B	C	P	ES
1.	D		☐		
2.	F		☐		
3.	C		☐		
4.	J		☐		
5.	D		☐		
6.	H		☐		
7.	B	☐			
8.	J	☐			
9.	A	☐			
10.	G	☐			
11.	C	☐			
12.	J	☐			
13.	A				☐
14.	J				☐
15.	B				☐
16.	F				☐
17.	B				☐
18.	H				☐
19.	C			☐	
20.	F			☐	
21.	D			☐	
22.	H			☐	
23.	A			☐	
24.	G			☐	
25.	C			☐	
26.	H			☐	
27.	B			☐	
28.	G			☐	
29.	B			☐	
30.	H	☐			
31.	D	☐			
32.	G	☐			
33.	C	☐			
34.	G	☐			
35.	D		☐		
36.	J		☐		
37.	B		☐		
38.	F		☐		
39.	B		☐		
40.	H		☐		

Biology (B): ____/11

Chemistry (C): ____/12

Physics (P): ____/11

Earth Science (ES): ____/6

Science Reasoning Raw Score (B + C + P + ES): ____/40

Explanatory Answers

TEST 1: ENGLISH (p. A-62)

1. (B) The original is incorrect for two reasons. First, just as a matter of grammar, the phrase *more gentler* is wrong. The *more* is redundant of the *-er* suffix. Second, the rest of the passage makes it clear that the author means to say that botany is the most gentle of sciences. (C) is wrong because the rest of the passage makes it clear that the author intends the superlative *most*, and (D) is wrong because it is not idiomatic.

2. (G) The word *ostentatious* means "showy," a word not appropriate here. *Unobtrusive* is a better fit.

3. (D) The original is incorrect because the pronoun *it* doesn't have a clear and unambiguous referent. Although you can see that it must refer to *botany,* on first reading it seems that it might refer to *flower.* (D) eliminates the potential for misreading. (B) fails to make the needed correction. (C), like (D), makes the needed correction, but (C) is incorrectly punctuated. The introductory phrase is a participial phrase introduced by *reduced,* and it modifies the first noun in the main clause, botany. The correct punctuation is a comma to show that *that* is where the introductory phrase stops and the main clause begins. The problem with a semicolon is that it is too powerful.

4. (F) The original is the most direct and concise phrasing available.

5. (B) The original is not idiomatic. The correct idiom is *consists of,* not *consists about.* (C) and (D) are wrong because they too are not idiomatic. And (D) is wrong for the additional reason that it uses a plural verb with a singular subject.

6. (F) The original is correct as written. The other choices are not idiomatic and destroy the parallelism between *knowing* and *studying.*

7. (A) The original is the best phrasing. The phrase *in and of themselves* serves to emphasize the thought that plants are intrinsically worth studying.

8. (F) The second paragraph sets up a contrast with the first. In the first, the author states that plants are intrinsically worthy of study. Here the author says that we should not discount entirely their practical value.

9. (D) The original contains two errors. First, you need the past participle rather than the present participle following *should.* (*Disparaged,* not *disparaging.*) Second, the dash disrupts the logical flow of the sentence. It seems to signal an aside or a clarifying remark, but what follows is actually another clause. (D) is the best choice; it uses the correct verb form, and the semicolon is a correct choice of punctuation to separate two clauses when no coordinate conjunction is used. (B) corrects the verb but not the punctuation error. (C) suffers from both errors.

10. (F) The *nonetheless* sets up a contrast between the idea that plants have practical value and the idea that this very fact imposes limits on the study of plants.

11. (D) The present tense conflicts with the other verbs in the sentence. They are all in the simple past tense. Only (D) makes the required change. (B) is wrong because there is no reason to use the past-perfect. (*Had been made* suggests that one past event occurred and was completed before another past event, but that is not the intended meaning of the original.) (C) is wrong because the subject is *study,* a singular noun.

12. (J) The *or* implies that the two ideas are alternatives. But an assumption can be basic and still unspoken. What the author intends to say is that these ideas are very basic but no one ever makes them explicit.

13. (B) The original contains two mistakes. First, *to have understood* is inconsistent with the other verb forms in the paragraph, for it suggests something that will occur at a future time before some other action. (For example, "John hopes to have finished his homework before his mother comes home.") Additionally, *their* is a plural pronoun and cannot substitute for the singular *plant.* (B) makes both of the needed corrections.

14. (J) The original contains two errors. First, *they* is a plural pronoun and cannot substitute for the singular noun *flower*. Second, the *but* illogically suggests a contrast where none is

intended. Only (J) corrects both of these problems without creating new ones. (G) fails to correct the second problem. (H) corrects both problems but is incorrectly punctuated. Without a comma (*it exists, and*) the result is a run-on sentence.

15. (D) The author states that one must study plants simply because they exist, and further, that simply because they exist they are worthy of study. This circularity is characteristic of a tautology.

16. (F) The author inserts the *of course* to acknowledge that the point being made is an obvious one: of course, poverty means lack of money.

17. (A) The original is correct. (B) and (C) are awkward or wordy by comparison. And (D) destroys the structure of the sentence.

18. (H) The original contains an error of pronoun usage. *Their* is intended to refer to *family,* which might be either plural or singular. But there is already another pronoun in the sentence that refers to *family,* and it is singular. So the first *its* determines that the author will treat *family* as a singular noun. (G) is wrong because *there* is not a pronoun. Finally, (J) is the contraction for *it is* and not a pronoun at all.

19. (D) The logic of the sentence does not support the use of the transitional word *consequently*. *Consequently* is used to show that one idea follows logically from another idea or that one event follows from another event as a matter of causality. Neither of these notions is implied by the sentence. The author has not yet explained why one would find more poverty in rural America than in other regions. The best course is simply to drop the word entirely.

20. (F) The original is correct as written. (G) is wrong because *lower* cannot be substituted for *less*. The phrase *may earn lower than* is not idiomatic. (H) is wrong because the correct idiom for making a comparison like this is *less than,* not *less as.* And, finally, (J) combines the errors of both (G) and H.

21. (A) In the first paragraph the author provides the definition of *poor.*

22. (F) The original is correct as written. You do need a new paragraph here because the other is taking up a new topic. So (G) and (J) are wrong. As for (H), *since,* which means "because of," destroys the logic of the sentence.

23. (A) The single word *parallel* nicely expresses the thought that lack of education is associated with low income. By comparison the alternatives are wordy. Notice also that the wrong choices use phrases that would seem out of place given the formal style of the passage.

24. (F) The last sentence of the paragraph expresses an idea that follows from or is the result of the idea that precedes it. The phrase *as a consequence* signals the reader that the second idea is the result of the first.

25. (D) The original contains two errors. First, the plural verb *are* does not agree with its subject, *schooling.* Second, the phrase *as inadequate like* is not idiomatic. (B) corrects both errors but is punctuated incorrectly. You can treat the phrase *like family incomes* as an aside, but you cannot mark the limits of the aside with one dash and one comma. Either you must use two dashes or two commas. (C) is guilty of illogical expression, for (C) seems to imply that schooling is supposed to function *as* family income. (D) is the right choice because it corrects the problems of the original and is correctly punctuated.

26. (J) The *it* has no antecedent. (J) corrects this by supplying a noun. The other two wrong choices make illogical statements.

27. (C) The original is needlessly wordy. (C) is more concise and more in keeping with the formal tone of the selection.

28. (H) The original is incorrect because the plural verb have does not agree with its singular subject, *head.* (G) fails to correct this problem. (H) and (J) are both singular verbs, but the *was to have* in (J) implies a condition that was never fulfilled (such as, "He was to have received an award but did not"). This suggestion of an unfulfilled condition is out of place here. (H) is the correct choice. The past perfect is acceptable because it indicates a past action (the head of the family finished school) that occurred before some other action (the children begin their education.) It would also be acceptable to use the present tense: *If the head...has little schooling, the children are....*

29. (D) The original is incorrect because the expression *as...rather than in* is not idiomatic. An idiomatically correct alternative is supplied by (D): *is as true...as.* (B) fails to correct the problem of the original. As for (C), though this is

idiomatic, they does not agree with the demonstrative pronoun, *this,* to which it refers.

30. (J) The underlined phrase is redundant of *modern.* Just omit it.

31. (B) The original is incorrect because the adjective poor cannot be used to modify another adjective (educated). You need the adverb poorly for that. (B) makes the correction. (C) is wrong because it changes the intended meaning of the sentence. The author is talking about poor people who are not educated, not *educated poor people.* Finally, (D) is grammatically incorrect. The noun, *education,* cannot modify a noun.

32. (J) The author supplies a definition and a number in the first paragraph. And throughout the selection the author offers explanations.

33. (B) The original is wrong because the present tense *fail* is not consistent with the other verb in the sentence. The other verb describes a past action. Additionally, *fail* is a plural verb, but the subject of the sentence is *one,* a singular noun. (B) corrects the problem of tense (and the problem of agreement since there is only one form in the simple past). (C) makes the needed corrections, but the resulting phrase is not idiomatic. Finally, (D) does address the problem of agreement, but you still have the problem of tense.

34. (J) The original contains two errors. First, it uses *that* rather than *who* to refer to people. Second, it is not idiomatic. The correct idiom is *should have,* not *should of.* (*Of* is not a verb at all.) (G) corrects neither of these errors. (H) corrects the first but not the second. Only (J) corrects both errors.

35. (D) The underlined phrase is redundant of *dropout.* Delete it.

36. (J) The original is both grammatically incorrect and not idiomatic. First, *will starting* is not an English verb form at all. Second, in English, we use an infinitive (the to form) after a verb ending in *-ing* rather than the gerund (the *-ing* form). So *starting to think* is more idiomatic than *starting thinking.* (J) corrects both the problems of the original. (G) does not solve the problem of idiom, and (H) is ambiguous. The placement of *usually* suggests that *usually* is intended to modify *thinking* rather than *starts.*

37. (D) The original is incorrectly punctuated; if, for clarity, you set the final prepositional phrase apart, you must use a comma. The semicolon is too powerful and isolates the prepositional phrase from the rest of the sentence. (B) and (C) are wrong because connecting the preposition phrase to the rest of the sentence with a coordinate conjunction gives it an importance equal to that of the verb: *he or she ceases...and roughly at the age of 14.*

38. (H) The original is incorrect because the singular verb *is* does not agree with its subject. The subject is a compound subject (a series of elements joined by *and*), which is plural. (G) fails to correct this mistake. (H) and (J) correct the error, but the use of the past tense in (J) is incorrect. The author is describing a current problem using the present tense.

39. (A) The original is correct. Each of the wrong answer choices creates a run-on sentence. In general, when you have two independent clauses, you can do one of three things. One, join them using a comma and a coordinate conjunction such as *and* or *but.* Two, join them using a semicolon. Three, put them in separate sentences.

40. (H) The two words have the same meaning. (H) eliminates the needless repetition.

41. (B) The original contains a grammatical mistake. It uses most rather than *more* to compare two things. (The sentence compares a boy with a group. So *more* is the correct form; e.g., *John is taller than his classmates.*) Both (B) and (D) make the needed correction. (D) is wrong, however, because the singular one will not agree with its verb *stay.*

42. (G) The original is wrong for two reasons. First, it uses the objective-case pronoun *him* to modify the gerund *dropping.* (You must use the possessive case *his.*) Second, the use of the gerund is in any case awkward. It is much more direct simply to say *at the time he drops out.* (G) corrects the original and is more direct and concise as well. (J) would be correct except that it uses the past tense. The author uses present tense verbs to describe an ongoing problem, so you should also use the present here.

43. (A) The original is the best rendering. Compared to it, the other choices are awkward and wordy.

44. (H) The original is incorrect because the sentence lacks a conjugated or main verb. *Increasing* is a participle and cannot function as a main

verb. Each of the other choices uses a conjugated form of *to increase* and so avoids this error. (G), however, is incorrect because *so that* seems to introduce a clause, but what follows is not a clause: *so that during the eighth grade....* (J) is wrong because it is needlessly wordy and indirect. Additionally, the past tense in (J) is inconsistent with the other verbs in this paragraph.

45. (D) In the original *none* is a pronoun. What is required, however, is an adverb to explain how the dropout participates in activities: not at all. (B) uses the correct idiom, but the and results in a contradictory statement. How could one participate a little and not at all? (C) is incorrect because *not much* is equivalent to *little*, so the resulting statement doesn't create the "either/or" situation intended by the original.

46. (J) The original contains two errors. First, *goes* is a singular verb and does not agree with the subject of the sentence, *reasons.* Second, the phrase *goes deeper as* is not idiomatic. (J) corrects both of these problems. (G) and (H) do correct the problem of subject-verb agreement, but (G) and (H) are not idiomatic.

47. (D) In the final sentence, the author notes that dropping out is a symptom that has other root causes. It would be appropriate for the author to continue the discussion by talking about those causes.

48. (G) The word *dropout* is a fairly familiar one, so the passage would not be incomprehensible without the definition. But the definition does serve to tighten up the discussion.

49. (B) In the original, the verb *are* does not agree with its subject, *kind.* Both (B) and (C) make the needed correction, but (C) makes a change that disrupts the parallelism of the sentence: research and developing. Since *research and development* have similar functions in the sentence (they are both objects of the preposition *or*) you should use the noun *development.*

50. (H) The original is not idiomatic. The correct idiom is *look for something to do something* (to satisfy), not *look for something doing something.* (G) is incorrect because the subjunctive *would have* suggests that an anticipated past event did not occur because of some other event. (John would have come to the party, but he was taken ill.) Finally, (J) is ambiguous. *With the satisfaction of* is a prepositional phrase but it is not clear what the phrase is supposed to modify.

51. (A) The original is correct as written. *Its* refers to *humankind.* (B) is incorrect because *humankind* is singular. (C) is wrong because *it's* is the contraction of *it is* and not a pronoun at all. Finally, *your* cannot be substituted for *humankind.* (This is the problem of shifting point of view.)

52. (H) In the original the infinitive *to find* does not have a clear logical relationship to any other part of the sentence. Thus, it's just sitting there on its own. (H) solves this problem by turning to *find into finding,* which can then function as an appositive for one ("one of the problems"). (G) doesn't solve the problem of the orphaned phrase and, if anything, just makes matters worse because a colon is more powerful than a comma. Finally, (J) just creates a sentence fragment of everything that follows the period.

53. (D) The original is needlessly wordy, as you can see by comparing it to the correct choice, (D). (D) is more concise and more direct. (B) is very concise, but (B) destroys the sense of the sentence: that they may be (what?). (C) is wrong because it is a singular pronoun and cannot refer to *machines.*

54. (F) The author intends here to contrast two ideas: wind is difficult to harness but on the other hand, it is valuable.

55. (A) The original is correct as written. (B) is wrong because the singular *has* would not agree with the subject *rewards.* (C) is wrong for this reason and for the further reason that the author clearly intends to make a statement about the past, not the present. Finally, (D), which uses the future tense, must be wrong as well.

56. (F) The original is correct as written. Notice how the next sentence parallels the structure of this sentence. (G) is wrong because it eliminates this stylistic feature. (G is also wrong because the resulting sentence is ambiguous. Does the author mean to say the machine was located in China, was built in China, or was simply in China one day passing through?) (H) is wrong for the same reasons that (G) is wrong and for the additional reason that the verb tense is illogical. Finally, (J) is wrong because *has* switches to the active voice and implies that the machine was building something.

57. (B) The original doesn't contain a grammatical mistake, but it is somewhat awkward. By comparison, (B) is more concise and more direct than any of the other choices.

58. (J) Here too we have an original that doesn't contain an error but is needlessly wordy. You can render the thought more concisely and more directly by substituting **by** for *through the means of.*

59. (A) The original is correct as written. (B) is wrong because the comma separates the adjective several from the noun it modifies, *centuries.* (C) is wrong because the *but* suggests a contrast that is not intended by the author. Finally, (D) is wrong because the use of *and* suggests that what follows is similar to what comes before. But *water lift* is not like *centuries.*

60. (F) The original is correct as written. It uses the active voice and is therefore more direct than any of the alternatives.

61. (A) The original is correct. The author takes up a new topic at this point, so a new paragraph is appropriate. (B) is wrong because it creates a sentence fragment from what is otherwise a complete sentence. And (D) is wrong because it is needlessly wordy.

62. (J) The original is incorrect because it implies a comparison of two machines. In fact, the author means to compare one machine with all other such machines, and for that you need the superlative *most.* (G) does use the superlative, but *most simplest* is redundant. Use one or the other, but not both. (H) fails to correct the problem of the original.

63. (B) The original suffers from a lack of parallelism. The third in the series of two verbs should have the same form as the first: flourished, and came. Only (B) makes the needed correction.

64. (J) The original and the other two choices are needlessly wordy. The one word *capricious* will do the job and is consistent with the formal style of the passage.

65. (A) The phrase *rage into a gale* has an appropriate meaning for the sentence and adds a little spice to the prose.

66. (G) The original contains an error of pronoun usage. It refers to both *television and products,* so a plural pronoun is required. (J) fails to make the needed correction. Both (G) and (H) make the corrections, but (H) introduces a new error. The use of the subjunctive *would be* implies that an event is contingent upon the occurrence of some other event. But there is no such other event mentioned in the selection.

67. (B) The original contains an error of subject-verb agreement. The subject of the sentence is *industry,* so the verb should be singular: *industry is.* The relative clause introduced by *which* is not part of the simple subject. (C) fails to make the needed correction. (D) corrects the original but is incorrectly punctuated. The relative clause should be marked with two commas, not one comma and a dash.

68. (F) The original is correctly punctuated. (G) is incorrect because you must use a comma to separate the first two elements in a series of three or more elements. (H) is wrong because the comma separates an adjective from the noun it modifies. Finally, (J) is wrong because it separates the definite article *the* from the noun it modifies.

69. (A) The original is correct as written. The subject of the verb is *the episodic series,* a singular noun. And since three items are being compared, *most* is the correct choice.

70. (F) The original is correct as written. *With the advent* of is an idiom that identifies a certain point in time. The remaining choices are simply not idiomatic.

71. (B) The original uses the wrong verb tense. The phrase *with the advent of* pegs the time as belonging to the past. So you need some form of the past tense. Only (B) supplies a verb that refers to a past event.

72. (F) The original is correct as written. The verb *have* correctly agrees with its plural subject. Also, some form of the past tense is required here since the sentence obviously refers to events that belong to the past. Thus, the other choices are incorrect.

73. (B) The past participle of *to grow* is *grown.* (B) makes the needed change. (C) and (D) are incorrect because their forms are not parallel to the other verb form *has lost.*

74. (J) In the original, everything following the period is a sentence fragment. The list contains no main verb. One use of a colon is to introduce a list, and that is what (J) does. (G) is wrong because the comma incorrectly suggests that the elements of the list will be verbs. (H) is wrong because it fails to mark the transition from the main part of the sentence to the list.

75. (B) The original is incorrect because *controversy* is intended to be an adjective modifying topics. But *controversy* is a noun—not an adjective. (B) makes the needed correction.

TEST 2: MATHEMATICS (p. A-73)

1. (B) $2 \bullet 10^4 = 20{,}000$, and $121{,}212 + 20{,}000 = 141{,}212$.

2. (K) Solve for x: $6x + 3 = 21 \Rightarrow 6x = 18 \Rightarrow x = 3$. So $2x + 1 = 2(3) + 1 = 7$.

3. (C) There is no trick to this question. Just use "supermarket" math. Find out how much the one thing would cost. Then, using that cost, find out how much of the other you can buy. The cost of renting a bowling lane for 2 hours is $2 \bullet \$12 = \$24$. And for \$24 you can rent a ping-pong table for $\$24 \div \$3 = 8$ hours.

4. (K) (F) is incorrect since k cannot equal itself plus a number. The same reasoning applies to (G), (H), and (J). (K), however, could be true—if j is 5 and k is 10, and if l is 15 and m is 20, then $5 + 20 = 10 + 15$.

5. (D) Use $\frac{1}{2}$ as a benchmark. And reason in this way: eliminate (A). Since $\frac{9}{18}$ is $\frac{1}{2}$, $\frac{9}{19}$ is less than $\frac{1}{2}$. Continue eliminating choices until you are left with (D).

6. (F) Use the "this-of-that" strategy: $\frac{\text{this}}{\text{of that}} = \frac{\text{students on track team}}{\text{total students}} \Rightarrow \frac{18}{360} = \frac{1}{20} = 5\%$.

7. (C) (I) must be true because a and x are vertically opposite each other. Similarly, (II) must be true because y and b are equal and z and c are equal. (III), however, is not necessarily true. x and a are equal and y and b are equal, but you don't have information on which to base a conclusion about the relationship between x and y or the relationship between a and b.

8. (G) You can set up an equation: $x + 30 = 2x \Rightarrow x = 30$.

9. (C) First eliminate any choice that contains a number that is not a prime. This eliminates (A), (B), and (D). Then multiply the remaining choices:

   C. $2 \bullet 2 \bullet 3 \bullet 5 = 60$ √
   E. $3 \bullet 3 \bullet 3 \bullet 5 = 135$ X

10. (F) Use the method for finding the missing element of an average. Since the average height of all four buildings is 20, the sum of the heights of all four is $4 \bullet 20 = 80$. The three known heights total $3 \bullet 16 = 48$. So the missing value is $80 - 48 = 32$.

11. (E) First find the value of y: $5y + 4y = 180 \Rightarrow 9y = 180 \Rightarrow y = 20$. Next find the value of x: $4y + 2y + x = 180 \Rightarrow 6y + x = 180 \Rightarrow 6(20) + x = 180 \Rightarrow 120 + x = 180 \Rightarrow x = 60$.

12. (G) Each of the marks between the numbered marks is $\frac{1}{5}$ of the distance between the numbered marks. The distance between each numbered mark is 0.1, so each of the others is worth $0.1 \div 5 = 0.02$. So $PQ = 0.02 + 0.1 + 2(0.02) = 0.16$.

13. (A) The perimeter is: $2(3a - 2) + 2(2a - 1) = 6a - 4 + 4a - 2 = 10a - 6$. That's a fairly simple algebraic manipulation; but if you insist on avoiding algebra altogether, you can assume a value for a. For example, if $a = 2$, then the length of the figure is $3(2) - 2 = 4$, and the width of the figure is $2(2) - 1 = 3$. The perimeter would be $4 + 4 + 3 + 3 = 14$. Substituting 2 for a into the correct formula yields the value 14. And only (A) does that.

14. (G) Use the technique for finding the missing elements of an average. The average of the five numbers is 51, so their sum is $5 \bullet 51 = 255$. The two known values total 114. So the remaining three numbers total $255 - 114 = 141$. And $141 \div 3 = 47$.

15. (C) x could be -1, or zero, or $+1$.

16. (K) $8 = 2^3$, so $8^x = (2^3)^x = 2^{3x}$.

17. (C) One square has an area of $2 \bullet 2 = 4$, the other an area of $3 \bullet 3 = 9$, and the sum of their areas is $4 + 9 = 13$.

18. (G) You can set up an equation: $x(2x)(3) = 54 \Rightarrow 2x^2 = 18 \Rightarrow x^2 = 9 \Rightarrow x = \sqrt{9} = \pm 3 = 3$ since distances are always positive. Or, you can "test the test." Try each answer choice as the value of x until you find one that generates a volume of 54.

19. (B) Since x is 80 percent of y, $x = 0.8y$, and $y = \frac{x}{0.8} = 1.25x$. So y is 125% of x. Or test the test. Assume that y is 100. If $y = 100$, then $x = 80\%$ of $y = 80$. Finally, find what percent y is of x: $\frac{100}{80} = \frac{5}{4} = 1.25 = 125\%$.

20. (J) You can rewrite $m - n > 0$ by adding n to both sides: $m > n$. As for (F), this proves that $m < n$. As for (G), this proves nothing about m and n, since m and n might be either negative or positive. The same is true of (H), which is the equivalent to $m > -n$.

Finally, as for (K), you have neither relative values for m and n nor their signs.

21. (A) First, find $f(2)$: $f(2) = (2)^2 + 2 = 4 + 2 = 6$. Next, find $f(6)$: $f(6) = (6)^2 + 6 = 36 + 6 = 42$. So $f(f(2)) = 42$.

22. (K) First, find the area of the circle: $\pi r^2 = \pi(2)^2 = 4\pi$. Since the shaded area is equal to 3π, it accounts for $\frac{3\pi}{4\pi} = \frac{3}{4}$ of the circle. So the unshaded area accounts for $\frac{1}{4}$ of the circle. This means that angle x plus the angle vertically opposite x are equal to $\frac{1}{4}$ of $360° = 90°$. So $2x = 90$, and $x = 45$.

23. (D) Use the "this-of-that" strategy: $\frac{\text{this}}{\text{of that}} = \frac{\text{tin}}{\text{entire bar}} = \frac{100}{100 + 150} = \frac{100}{250} = \frac{2}{5} = 40\%$.

24. (J) Rewrite the equation: $\frac{1}{x} + \frac{1}{y} = \frac{1}{z}$. Add the fractions using the "flying x": $\frac{y + x}{xy} = \frac{1}{z}$. Multiply both sides by z: $z \bullet \frac{y + x}{xy} = 1$. Multiply both sides by $\frac{xy}{y + x}$: $z = \frac{xy}{y + x} = \frac{xy}{x + y}$.

Or, just assume some values. Assume that $x = 1$ and $y = 1$. On that assumption, $z = \frac{1}{2}$. Then substitute 1 for x and 1 for y into the choices. Only (J) generates the value $\frac{1}{2}$.

25. (D) $|-5| = 5$, $|-12| = 12$, and $|-2| = 2$. So: $5 + 12 - 2 + (-6) = 15 - 6 = 9$.

26. (G) Treat this average as you would any other. Add the three elements and divide by 3: $\frac{(2x) + (2x + 1) + (2x + 2)}{3} = x - 1 \Rightarrow \frac{2x + 2x + 1 + 2x + 2}{3} = x - 1 \Rightarrow \frac{6x + 3}{3} = x - 1 \Rightarrow 6x + 3 = 3(x - 1)$.

27. (B) The profit on each box of candy is $\$2 - \$1 = \$1$. To earn a total profit of \$500, it will be necessary to sell $\$500 \bullet \$1 = 500$ boxes.

28. (G) Perform the indicated operations: $(-2)^2 - (-2)^3 = 4 - (-8) = 12$.

29. (D) You can reason that if the product of three different integers is zero, one of them is zero. Of x and $-x$, one is positive and the other negative, so they cannot be zero. The missing number must be zero.

You can also set up equations, but that seems unnecessarily complicated. You would be better off using a third method, just substituting some values for x. You'll find that the missing number must be zero.

30. (F) This is a simple percent question. Use the "this-of-that" strategy. The "of that" is "of all students enrolled." The other number, the "this," is seniors: $\frac{\text{seniors}}{\text{total}} = \frac{90}{360} = \frac{1}{4} = 25\%$.

31. (C) The diagonal of a square creates an isosceles right triangle. A side of the square is equal to $\frac{1}{2} \bullet \sqrt{2} \bullet \sqrt{2} = 1$. Thus the perimeter of the square is $4(1) = 4$.

Alternatively, the side of the square could have be found from the Pythagorean Theorm: $s^2 + s^2 = h^2 \Rightarrow \sqrt{2}^2 = 2s^2 \Rightarrow s = 1 \Rightarrow$ perimeter $= 4s = 4$.

32. (H) If the floor were a perfect rectangle, it would cost have a width of $4 \bullet 5 = 20$ meters, a length of $8 \bullet 5 = 40$ meters, and a total area of $20 \bullet 40 = 800$ square meters. But the floor is not a perfect rectangle. Its actual area is smaller. Subtract the area of the missing "corner." It has dimensions of $0.8 \bullet 5 = 4$. So its actual area is 16. $800 - 16 = 784$.

33. (B) The angles labeled $3w$ and $(5w + 20)$ form a straight line: $3w + (5w + 20) = 180 \Rightarrow 8w + 20 = 180 \Rightarrow 8w = 160 \Rightarrow w = 20$. And the angles labeled $3w$ and $4x$ also form a straight line: $3w + 4x = 180 \Rightarrow 3(20) + 4x = 180 \Rightarrow 60 + 4x = 180 \Rightarrow 4x = 120 \Rightarrow x = 30$.

34. (H) The difference between 11 and 4 is 7, so 7 marks the limit of the shorter side of a triangle with sides of 11 and 4. But the side must be an integer. So the shortest possible side is 8. Conversely, the sum of 4 and 11 is 15. So 15 marks the limit of the longer side. Since the longer side must have an integral value, its maximum length is 14.

35. (C) One approach to this item is to put the equation in standard form, factor, and solve for x: $-x^2 = 3 - 4x \Rightarrow 0 = 3 - 4x + x^2 \Rightarrow x^2 - 4x + 3 = 0 \Rightarrow (x - 3)(x - 1) = 0$. So either $x - 3 = 0$ and $x = 3$ or $x - 1 = 0$ and $x = 1$. The solution set is (1, 3). Alternatively, you could simply substitute the values given for x back into the equation. The only values that work are 1 and 3.

36. (H) If the club spent $\frac{2}{5}$ of the budget on the first project, it was left with $\frac{3}{5}$ of $\$300 = \$180$. If it spent $\frac{1}{3}$ of \$180, it was left with $\$180 - \$60 = \$120$.

37. (E) Since n nails cost c cents, x nails will cost $\frac{cx}{n}$ cents. And since a dollar contains 100 cents, the cost of x nails in dollars is $\frac{cx}{100n}$. $d = \frac{cx}{100n}$.

Or, you can use the technique of assuming some values for the variables. Assume, for example, that nails cost 5 cents each and you want to buy 20 of them. On that assumption, the cost is \$1. So if $n = 1$, $c = 5$, and $x = 20$, then $d = 1$:

A. $1 = 100(5)(1)(20)$ X
B. $1 = \frac{100(5)(20)}{1}$ X
C. $1 = \frac{100(1)(20)}{5}$ X
D. $1 = \frac{(1)(20)}{100(5)}$ X
E. $1 = \frac{(5)(20)}{100(1)} = 1$ √

38. (K) Since the expression is less than zero, either one or three of the factors must be negative. a^2 cannot be negative. So either b^3 is negative or c is negative, but not both. And this means either b or c is negative, but not both. So bc must be negative. You can eliminate (F), (G), (H), and (J) since they might be, but are not necessarily, true.

39. (C) Since this is an equilateral triangle, the sides are equal. Set up equations: $2x + 1 = 2x + y$, so $y = 1$. And: $2x + y = 2y + 1 \Rightarrow 2x + (1) = 2(1) + 1 \Rightarrow 2x + 1 = 2 + 1 \Rightarrow 2x = 2 \Rightarrow x = 1$. Now pick any side: $2x + y = 2(1) + 1 = 3$. The perimeter of the triangle is $3(3) = 9$.

40. (H) Use the distance formula or the Pythagorean Theorem:

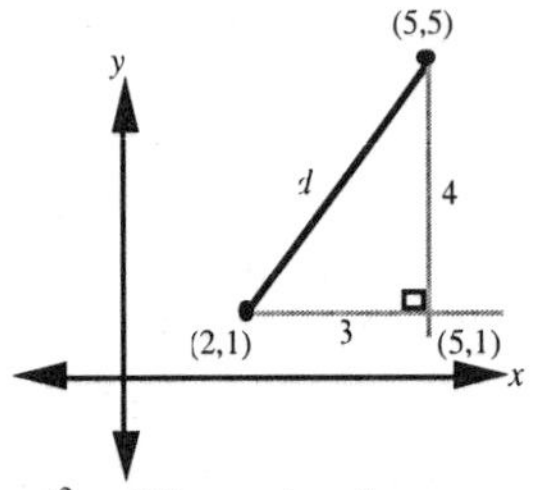

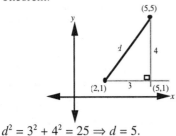

$d^2 = 3^2 + 4^2 = 25 \Rightarrow d = 5$.

41. (D) Use common sense. There must be something you can do with these expressions to combine them. And the key is $\sqrt{5}$. 45 and 20 are both multiples of 5: $\sqrt{9 \bullet 5} - \sqrt{4 \bullet 5} + \sqrt{5} = 3\sqrt{5} - 2\sqrt{5} + \sqrt{5} = 2\sqrt{5}$.

42. (K) Here is a good problem on which to use one of our alternative strategies. Test answer choices:

F. $12 - 3 = 9$ and $15 - 3 = 12$ X
G. $12 - 4 = 8$ and $15 - 4 = 11$ X
H. $12 - 11 = 1$ and $15 - 11 = 4$ X
J. $12 - 12 = 0$ and $15 - 12 = 3$ X
K. $12 - 13 = -1$ and $15 - 13 = 12$ √

Four of the choices have been eliminated, so the one that remains has to be the correct answer to the test question.

43. (B) Treat the equations as a system of simultaneous equations: $3m + n = 15$ and $3n + m = 13$. Use the first equation to solve for n: $n = 15 - 3m$. Substitute this expression for n in the second equation: $3(15 - 3m) + m = 13 \Rightarrow 45 - 9m + m = 13 \Rightarrow 8m = 32 \Rightarrow m = 4$. Only (B) has $m = 4$.

44. (G) Since the four segments total 24, each segment is $24 \div 4 = 6$ units long. Each segment is divided into 3 equal parts, so each part is $6 \div 3 = 2$ units long. The shaded area is bounded by a square with side of 2. So the area of the shaded part is $2 \bullet 2 = 4$.

Alternatively: total length = 24; count of line segments = 12; each line segment = $24 \div 12 = 2$. Area of square $= 2^2 = 4$.

45. (C) $|a - b| = -|b - a|$ only when $a - b = 0$. If you find yourself getting bogged down in a problem like this, try substituting some numbers for a and b: $|3 - 2| = -|2 - 3| \Rightarrow |1| = -|1| \Rightarrow 1 \neq -1$.

46. (H) This problem asks "What is the angle whose cosine is the cosine of $\frac{\pi}{2}$?" In other words: $\cos x = \cos \frac{\pi}{2}$. So $x = \frac{\pi}{2}$. (Remember that $0 \leq \arccos \leq \pi$.)

47. (A) A reflection in the line $x = -y$ maps a point P with coordinates (x, y) onto point P' with coordinates $(-y, -x)$:

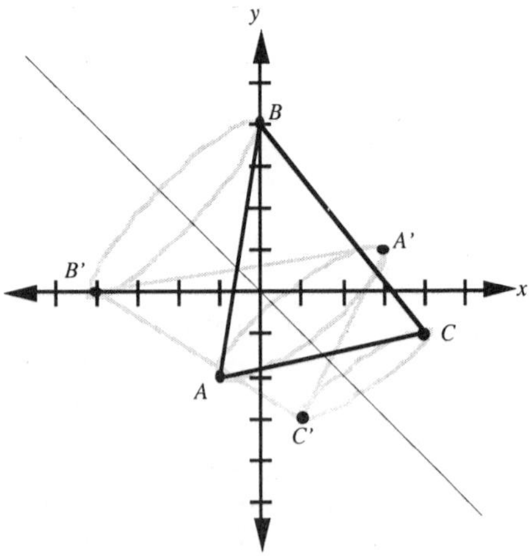

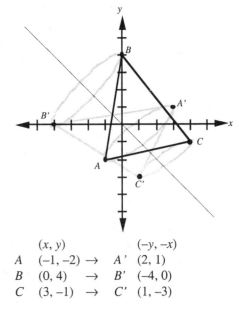

	(x, y)			$(-y, -x)$
A	$(-1, -2)$	→	A'	$(2, 1)$
B	$(0, 4)$	→	B'	$(-4, 0)$
C	$(3, -1)$	→	C'	$(1, -3)$

48. (H) You can answer this question by visualizing the graph of the sine and cosine functions:

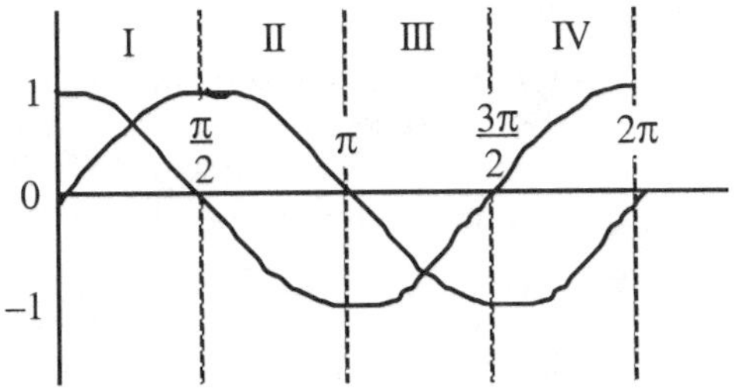

49. (C) The general form of the equation of a circle is: $(x - h)^2 + (y - k)^2 = r^2$ where (h, k) is the center of the circle and r its radius. The circle described in the question stem has a radius of 2 and has its center at $(2, -1)$:

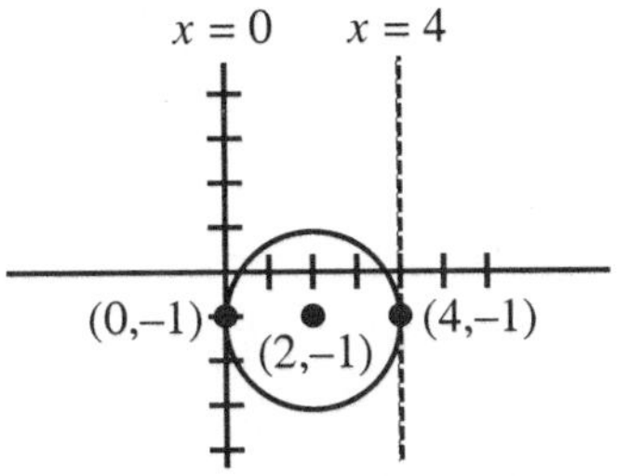

If a line of the form $x = k$ (a vertical line) is tangent to this circle, it passes through points $(0, -1)$ or $(4, -1)$.

50. (J) According to the Binomial Theorem, the last term in the expansion of a binomial having the form $(a + b)^n$ is b^n. So the last term of the expansion will be $(3y)^4 = 81y^4$.

51. (A) The Quadratic Formula: $x = \frac{-b \pm \sqrt{b^2 - 4ac}}{2a}$ is used to find the roots of a quadratic equation having the form $ax^2 + bx + c$. $b^2 - 4ac$ is called the discriminant because it discriminates among three possibilities:

1. When $b^2 - 4ac = 0$, the equation one root.
2. When $b^2 - 4ac > 0$, the equation has two unequal real roots.
3. When $b^2 - 4ac < 0$, the equation has no real roots.

Therefore, for the equation given in the question stem, $ax^2 + bx + c = 0$, has only one root. The graph given in choice (A) is the only one that has only one point on the x-axis (where $y = 0$).

52. (H) This is one of the quotient identities you were given in the trigonometry lesson: $\frac{\sin\theta}{\cos\theta} = \tan\theta$. If, during the exam, you can't recall this fact, you can easily derive it yourself. (Or, sometimes easier yet, plug-and-chug with your calculator to figure it out!) Sketch a right triangle with sides a and b and hypotenuse c. Let θ be the angle opposite side b. Using the definitions of sine and cosine: $\sin\theta = \frac{\text{opp}}{\text{hyp}} = \frac{b}{c}$ and $\cos\theta = \frac{\text{adj}}{\text{hyp}} = \frac{a}{c}$. Therefore: $\frac{\sin\theta}{\cos\theta} = = \frac{b}{c} / \frac{a}{c} = \frac{b}{c} \bullet \frac{c}{a} = \frac{b}{a}$. And for θ: $\frac{b}{a} = \frac{\text{opp}}{\text{adj}} = \tan\theta$.

53. (E) Use a simple proportion: $\frac{2\pi}{\frac{3}{2}\pi} = \frac{360°}{x°}$. Cross-multiply: $2\pi(x) = 360 \bullet \frac{3}{2\pi}$. Divide both sides by 2π: $x = 270$.

54. (K) We reviewed the technique for solving equations involving absolute value in the lesson on intermediate algebra. Since $|n| = n$ for all $n \geq 0$ and $|n| = -n$ for all $n < 0$, $2x - 1$ is equal either to 3 or to -3:

$2x - 1 = 3$ or $2x - 1 = -3$
$2x = 4$ $\quad$ $2x = -2$
$x = 2$ or $x = -1$

If you substitute the two solutions into the original equations, you will find that both are actual solutions.

55. (B) Notice that the two points have the same x-coordinate. The line, therefore, is parallel to the y-axis and the midpoint will have x-coordinate of 2. The length of the line is $5 - -4 = 9$, and half of 9 is $4\frac{1}{2}$. The y-coordinate of the midpoint is $5 - 4\frac{1}{2} = \frac{1}{2}$.

56. (G) To find the slope, you must rewrite the equation so that it has the form $y = mx + b$, where m is the slope and b is the y-intercept: $2x + 3y - 2 = 0 \Rightarrow 3y = -2x + 2 \Rightarrow y = \frac{-2x + 2}{3} = -\frac{2}{3}(x) + \frac{2}{3}$.

57. (D) This problem requires that we rationalize the fraction; that is, remove the radical from the denominator: $\frac{1}{\sqrt{3} - 1} \bullet \frac{\sqrt{3} + 1}{\sqrt{3} + 1} = \frac{\sqrt{3} + 1}{3 + \sqrt{3} - \sqrt{3} - 1} = \frac{\sqrt{3} + 1}{2}$.

58. (J) Perform the indicated operations: $(-2)^2 = -2 \bullet -2 = 4 \Rightarrow 2^{-2} = \frac{1}{2^2} = \frac{1}{4} \Rightarrow 4 - \frac{1}{4} = 3\frac{3}{4}$.

59. (C) One way to find the roots or solutions of a quadratic equation of the form $ax^2 + bx + c = 0$ is to use the quadratic formula: $x =$

$\frac{b \pm \sqrt{b^2 - 4ac}}{2a}$. The root given in the question stem has the "plus" form of the "plus or minus" formula. So the other root will have a minus sign.

60. (H) One way of solving this problem is to examine each choice to determine what the graph would look like. The graph of the equation $y = x$ is a straight line passing through the origin with a slope of +1. The graph of the equation $y = -x$ is a straight line passing through the origin with a slope of −1. The graph of the equation $y = |x|$ will look like the graph of $y = x$ for all $x > 0$ and will look like the graph of $y = x$ for all $x < 0$. And that is the correct answer. The graph of the equation $y = 2x$ is a straight line passing through the origin with a slope of +2. Thus, the graph of $y = x^2$ is a parabola.

    As an alternative, test the values given on the graph in each equation. Only the equation $y = |x|$ will accept both values.

TEST 2: READING (p. A-81)

1. (C) The passage never specifically describes the relationship between Turkey and the narrator, but it does suggest that it is employee-employer. The narrator is judging Turkey in his professional capacity and apparently has the authority to discharge him (if necessary).
2. (F) Turkey uses pen and ink and has a bad habit of spilling ink during the afternoons. That is suggestive of a copyist.
3. (C) The explanation that Turkey gives to the narrator for his eccentric behavior is age, but the behavior is more than coincidental. After his lunch, Turkey's face becomes a brilliant red, he becomes careless in his work, and his behavior becomes erratic. All of these facts are suggestive of the conclusion that Turkey's lunch is a liquid one.
4. (G) In the preceding paragraph, Turkey asks the narrator to excuse his behavior on account of his age and reminds the narrator that he too is growing older. (And the narrator has already told us that he and Turkey are of the same age.) Thus, the fellow-feeling must refer to the similarity of their ages.
5. (D) In the final paragraph, the narrator decides to continue to employ Turkey but resolves that in the afternoon Turkey won't do anything important.
6. (G) In the first paragraph, the narrator says that at noon, Turkey's lunch hour, his face veritably blazes.
7. (A) The narrator compares the augmented or increased redness of Turkey's face to dropping cannel coal on anthracite. Thus, we infer that the result is a more intense fire.
8. (G) The narrator specifically says that although Turkey is a good worker in the morning, his afternoon antics cause the narrator to feel uncomfortable.
9. (A) The narrator refers to Turkey of the morning as quick and steady and a valuable asset.
10. (H) The narrator specifically says that Turkey does not become lethargic in the afternoon. Rather, he seems to become overly active.
11. (B) (B) is the best title for this selection, as it discusses two approaches to punishment—retributive and corrective. (A) is incorrect because it is basically concerned with the retributive punishment and not with corrective. The answers represented by (C) and (D) are not at all appropriate to the subject of the selection.
12. (J) The last sentence of paragraph 1 clearly illustrates that the death penalty is a right of the murderer. The author's discussion of Hegel's views further substantiates this argument. (F) and (G) are in opposition to Hegel's views. (H), although a good answer and acceptable to Hegel, does not indicate the death penalty as a right of the murderer and is therefore insufficient as an answer.
13. (C) (C) is the best choice for this question. The philosophy of equal injury in retributive justice differs from the philosophy, in corrective justice, of treating the criminal to conform with normal society. The reason for each type of justice, therefore, is quite different. (A) is wrong because both kinds of justice can be applied to any type of crime. (D) has no bearing on the question. (B) is incorrect because the severity of punishment can be the same with either form of justice.
14. (J) The philosophy behind corrective justice is one of treatment and rehabilitation, not death. (F), (G), and (H), although forms of punishment in varying degrees, do not result in death, so they would be consistent with the philosophy of corrective justice. These answers are thus wrong. (J) is the answer that should be selected, as the electric chair results in death and is therefore inconsistent with the philosophy of corrective justice.

15. (C) In lines 6-10, the author uses the Biblical expression "an eye for an eye, and a tooth for a tooth" to show that the idea of justice as one form of equality is expressed as early as in the Bible.

16. (J) This is clear from the sixth sentence of paragraph 1: "This can be done only by inflicting an equal injury upon him." A fair trial (F), rehabilitation (G), and separation (H) are concepts associated with corrective justice rather than retributive justice.

17. (B) The key is in paragraph 3. None of the other answers can be inferred from the passage.

18. (F) Denying the true self, (G), and accepting punishment, (J), are parts of the code of retributive justice. Curing antisocial behavior, (H), is a means of enabling the criminal to act in his own best interests. Choice (F) best embodies the notion of "normal" in corrective justice systems.

19. (C) The author's goal is to explain the differences between ancient and modern systems of justice.

20. (J) The fifth sentence of paragraph 3 states this explicitly. A fair trial (G) and a legal code (H) do not apply to treating the criminal. Punishment (F) is a last resort of the corrective justice system. Choice (J) is the most appropriate answer.

21. (A) The precipitating cause of World War I was an assassination. On June 28, 1914, Archduke Francis Ferdinand, the heir to the throne of the Austro-Hungarian Empire, was assassinated by a Serbian nationalist.

22. (F) The assassination occurred in the city of Sarajevo in Bosnia. Claimed by Serbia, Bosnia was annexed by Austria, provoking the rage of the government and the people of Bosnia and Serbia.

23. (C) Before the outbreak of World War I, a balance of power had existed for almost 100 years. World War I shattered the balance of power that had been established by the Congress of Vienna in 1815.

24. (F) Russia, the protector of Serbia, and Austria were members of competing alliance systems. When war broke out between them, the member states of their alliances were drawn into the conflict. Germany intervened on the side of Austria, its alliance member, and Great Britain and France joined forces with Russia, with which both countries were allied.

25. (B) Lines 16-24 describe how suspicions enkindled by the failure of diplomacy sparked the order to mobilize the Russian armed forces. German mobilization was ordered after the Russian order was issued.

26. (J) A spirit of nationalism, not class solidarity, animated the people of the individual nation states that fought against one another in World War I. No longer did the upper classes of Europe act as a unified class. Instead, they joined with their compatriots of the middle and lower classes to wage war against people in other countries with whom they had once shared values, beliefs, and a way of life.

27. (B) The Nazi regime that came to power in Germany in 1933 and the regime of Stalin that tyrannized the Soviet people from 1927 to 1953 were ruthless dictatorships dedicated to world conquest.

28. (H) The sense of futility felt throughout Europe during and after World War I would be evident in European literature of the 1920s, 1930s, and 1940s. It is a fair assumption that the art of a particular period mirrors as well as illuminates the spirit of the age.

29. (B) World War I and its aftermath suggest the idea that war feeds on nationalist sympathies. The sense of affront felt by the Austrian people when the heir to the throne of their empire was assassinated did not allow the Austrian leaders to adopt a moderate stance in their dealings with the government of Serbia. Similarly, the sympathies evident in the pan-slavic brand of nationalism that animated the rulers of Russia to undertake the protection of Serbia led the Russians to perceive the Austrians as their implacable enemies, setting in motion the chain of events that led to the outbreak of war. Moreover, the militantly nationalistic forces that came to power in Germany, Italy, and Japan in the period between the two world wars undertook conquests that precipitated World War II.

30. (H) Archduke Francis Ferdinand, as the heir to the Austro-Hungarian Empire, was a member of the Hapsburg family.

31. (D) Since Uranus "rolls like a ball along the path of its orbit" with the geographic poles located like axles on either side, one pole is always in direct sunlight and the other is always in darkness.

32. (H) The location on Uranus that would be warmest would be the one that receives the most direct sunlight. Of the choices, the one with the most direct sunlight would be the geographic pole in the center of the planet's daylight side.

33. (B) Because of the way Uranus rotates, one side is always in daylight and the other is always in darkness. A location on the daylight side is not necessarily near the magnetic poles, which lie in indirect sunlight near the planet's equator.

34. (H) A planet's equator is by definition located midway between the geographic poles. Since on Uranus these are on the sides of the planet, the equator must ring the planet from top to bottom.

35. (B) The Uranian equator, ringing the planet from top to bottom, is located at the juncture of the planet's daylight and dark sides. An observer at the equator would most likely experience constant indirect sunlight.

36. (H) Auroras appear near a planet's magnetic poles. Since on Uranus these are located near the equator and nowhere near the geographic poles, the equator would be the most likely place to see auroras.

37. (D) On Uranus, the daylight side receives varying amounts of sunlight at different latitudes. However, this appears to have no effect on atmospheric circulation, which instead flows along the equator around the top and bottom of the planet. Clearly, some other factor besides sunlight is in operation.

38. (G) Lack of an atmosphere to create erosion is the only possible choice. Gravity was obviously strong enough to reassemble the planet, and in any case, gravity cannot wear away surface features. As for the possibility that the second object remained nearby, any collision strong enough to shatter Miranda most likely destroyed that object; in any case, the passage makes no mention of it.

39. (C) Choice (C) is the only possibility, since the passage states that there is no evidence of geological activity on Ariel.

40. (H) The second paragraph mentions three moons by name—Miranda, Ariel, and Umbriel—and then notes that there are seven other moons.

TEST 4: SCIENCE REASONING (p. A-87)

1. (D) The radii increase (0.37, 1.35, 1.54, etc.) and the electronegativities decrease (2.20, 0.98, 0.93, etc.) as one goes down each column.

2. (F) Here, it is essential to remember that the second number means electronegativity. For fluorine (F), it is 3.98.

3. (C) The bond length is the sum of the radii for each of the bonded atoms (1.10 + 0.99).

4. (J) Carbon and nitrogen have the smallest electronegativity difference, 0.49.

5. (D) Electronegativities increase steadily across each row and decrease steadily along each column, so the most widely separated elements have the most ionic bonds, or greatest ionic character.

6. (H) Several choices include the value 3.16, which is the electronegativity difference in RbF. Since Cs is below Rb, it may be expected to have an electronegativity below the value of 0.82, which is found for Rb, a prediction that leads to an electronegativity difference for CsF that is greater than 3.16.

7. (B) If carbon dioxide is the variable in question, all factors except carbon dioxide should remain fixed. Only then can the effects of various carbon dioxide levels be evaluated.

8. (J) The only difference between Experiments 1 and 2 is that the concentration of leaf extract (containing a mixture of pigments) was reduced in Experiment 2. Using the lower concentration of pigments, the rate of photosynthesis leveled off, suggesting that the amount was inadequate to maintain the previously observed increase in rate.

9. (A) The description of Experiment 3 states that wavelengths must be *absorbed* to maintain photosynthesis (which is measured by counting oxygen bubbles). The bubble counts (and therefore, peak absorption) for Pigment A are at 450 and 650 manometers. For Pigment B, peak count is between 500-575 manometers.

10. (G) Since the reduced concentration of pigments in Experiment 2 led to a leveling off in bubble count, an increase in pigment concentration should lead to an increase in the rate of photosynthesis and an associated increase in bubbles.

11. (C) Proper interpretation of the graphs in Figures 1 and 2 reveals that at light intensity level of 4, 40-50 bubbles/minute are produced.

12. (J) Fig. 3 shows that at 600 nm. (orange light), both Pigments A and B show very little absorption, as measured by the low oxygen bubble count. Since light must be *absorbed* to provide energy for photosynthesis, orange light would be *least effective.*

13. (A) Venus is only 0.05 units smaller in diameter than Earth (0.95 Earth diameters).

14. (J) As planets get farther from the Sun (A.U. column), some are larger than the Earth (Jupiter and Saturn have larger diameters)

while others are smaller than the Earth (Mars and Pluto have smaller diameters).

15. (B) 1 A.U. equals 0.5 inches in the scale used in Exp. 2. The paper is only 14 inches long. Neptune's distance is 30 A.U. (30 • 0.5 = 15 inches) and would not fit on the paper (nor would Pluto, which is even farther away!).

16. (F) If the asteroids are 2.8 A.U. away from the Sun, they'd be found between Mars and Jupiter. Thus an *asteroid year* is longer than that on Mars but shorter than that on Jupiter.

17. (B) If the Sun's diameter is 110 times greater than that of the Earth, its *diameter* would be 110 • 5 inches (Experiment 1 uses a scale where I earth diameter = 5 inches).

18. (H) The relative mass information given in the question is very similar to the order of planets based on their relative diameters (Table 1: Earth diameters column).

19. (C) The meters/minute scale increases from bottom to top. The highest point on the chart shows the fastest speed to be approximately 590-600 meters/minute.

20. (F) The lines represent the best-fitting slopes of points, which show how running speed has increased.

21. (D) In 1960, the ratio is based on 4 minutes/mile (1-mile run) to approximately 3.1 minutes/mile (440-yard dash).

22. (H) The speeds for the 2-mile run are all between 340-380 meters/minute. The gain in speed *must* be closest to the "30 meter/minute" choice.

23. (A) This problem, requiring the right-hand scale, asks for an extrapolation beyond the given data. The 880-yard line crosses the 1980 axis at approximately 3.5 minutes/mile.

24. (G) Temperature rises at an even rate during the time that the sample is heated.

25. (C) Experiment 1 starts above 0°C, whereas Experiment 2 starts below 0°C. In addition, the temperature in Experiment 2 stabilizes along the "*x*-axis" for a while.

26. (H) The passage states that heat was added constantly (ruling out [G]), yet the graph shows no increase in temperature.

27. (B) Ice melts at 0°C. This is the temperature at which the graph temporarily levels off.

28. (G) The experiment utilized constant heating. Yet temperature change was not constant.

29. (B) At the boiling point of water (100°C) there should be another flat section corresponding to the heat absorbed by the liquid in order to convert it to vapor.

30. (H) An examination of the diagram reveals that primary tissue layers and primary germ layers are names for the same developing parts. This information is part of the description of the *gastrula* stage.

31. (D) The diagram arrows show the changes that occur as each developmental stage follows the previous one. The greatest amount of differentiation in structure and function clearly occurs *during organogenesis* as the primary germ layers in the gastrula become the many specialized systems, organs, and related structures of the organism.

32. (G) The arrows show that during organogenesis, the body's bones develop from the middle primary germ layer (mesoderm), not the innermost layer (endoderm).

33. (C) Structures (receptor cells) that contribute to visual abilities in the monkey would develop as parts of the eye, "a special sense organ." The arrows show that parts of the special sense organs arise from the *ectoderm.*

34. (G) The asterisk indicates that during cleavage, the many new cells that form from the zygote and its materials do not grow. Thus, as the zygote's material is simply subdivided, the resulting cells must be extremely small.

35. (D) Theory 1 allows all proportions of reactants.

36. (J) Theory 1 simply states that any proportion of reactants may mix. It does not explain the relation of the amounts of reactants to the amounts of product produced by the reaction.

37. (B) Theory 2 states that a certain proportion of reactants will react; if the proportions are otherwise, one or another reactant will fail to react completely.

38. (F) Both reactants must be in the appropriate proportions to be used in the process of forming more product.

39. (B) This is the only response that provides a ratio of Fe to O that is different from the two ratios that proved successful in the problem.

40. (H) Theory 1 only states that products contain the original elements.

Answer Sheet

Name ____________________ Student ID Number ____________________

Date ____________ Instructor ____________________ Course/Session Number ____________

TEST 1—ENGLISH

1 A B C D	16 F G H J	31 A B C D	46 F G H J	61 A B C D
2 F G H J	17 A B C D	32 F G H J	47 A B C D	62 F G H J
3 A B C D	18 F G H J	33 A B C D	48 F G H J	63 A B C D
4 F G H J	19 A B C D	34 F G H J	49 A B C D	64 F G H J
5 A B C D	20 F G H J	35 A B C D	50 F G H J	65 A B C D
6 F G H J	21 A B C D	36 F G H J	51 A B C D	66 F G H J
7 A B C D	22 F G H J	37 A B C D	52 F G H J	67 A B C D
8 F G H J	23 A B C D	38 F G H J	53 A B C D	68 F G H J
9 A B C D	24 F G H J	39 A B C D	54 F G H J	69 A B C D
10 F G H J	25 A B C D	40 F G H J	55 A B C D	70 F G H J
11 A B C D	26 F G H J	41 A B C D	56 F G H J	71 A B C D
12 F G H J	27 A B C D	42 F G H J	57 A B C D	72 F G H J
13 A B C D	28 F G H J	43 A B C D	58 F G H J	73 A B C D
14 F G H J	29 A B C D	44 F G H J	59 A B C D	74 F G H J
15 A B C D	30 F G H J	45 A B C D	60 F G H J	75 A B C D

TEST 2—MATHEMATICS

1 A B C D E	13 A B C D E	25 A B C D E	37 A B C D E	49 A B C D E
2 F G H J K	14 F G H J K	26 F G H J K	38 F G H J K	50 F G H J K
3 A B C D E	15 A B C D E	27 A B C D E	39 A B C D E	51 A B C D E
4 F G H J K	16 F G H J K	28 F G H J K	40 F G H J K	52 F G H J K
5 A B C D E	17 A B C D E	29 A B C D E	41 A B C D E	53 A B C D E
6 F G H J K	18 F G H J K	30 F G H J K	42 F G H J K	54 F G H J K
7 A B C D E	19 A B C D E	31 A B C D E	43 A B C D E	55 A B C D E
8 F G H J K	20 F G H J K	32 F G H J K	44 F G H J K	56 F G H J K
9 A B C D E	21 A B C D E	33 A B C D E	45 A B C D E	57 A B C D E
10 F G H J K	22 F G H J K	34 F G H J K	46 F G H J K	58 F G H J K
11 A B C D E	23 A B C D E	35 A B C D E	47 A B C D E	59 A B C D E
12 F G H J K	24 F G H J K	36 F G H J K	48 F G H J K	60 F G H J K

TEST 3—READING

1 A B C D	9 A B C D	17 A B C D	25 A B C D	33 A B C D
2 F G H J	10 F G H J	18 F G H J	26 F G H J	34 F G H J
3 A B C D	11 A B C D	19 A B C D	27 A B C D	35 A B C D
4 F G H J	12 F G H J	20 F G H J	28 F G H J	36 F G H J
5 A B C D	13 A B C D	21 A B C D	29 A B C D	37 A B C D
6 F G H J	14 F G H J	22 F G H J	30 F G H J	38 F G H J
7 A B C D	15 A B C D	23 A B C D	31 A B C D	39 A B C D
8 F G H J	16 F G H J	24 F G H J	32 F G H J	40 F G H J

TEST 4—SCIENCE REASONING

1 A B C D	9 A B C D	17 A B C D	25 A B C D	33 A B C D
2 F G H J	10 F G H J	18 F G H J	26 F G H J	34 F G H J
3 A B C D	11 A B C D	19 A B C D	27 A B C D	35 A B C D
4 F G H J	12 F G H J	20 F G H J	28 F G H J	36 F G H J
5 A B C D	13 A B C D	21 A B C D	29 A B C D	37 A B C D
6 F G H J	14 F G H J	22 F G H J	30 F G H J	38 F G H J
7 A B C D	15 A B C D	23 A B C D	31 A B C D	39 A B C D
8 F G H J	16 F G H J	24 F G H J	32 F G H J	40 F G H J

CAMBRIDGE
EDUCATIONAL SERVICES, INC.®

ACT • PLAN • EXPLORE
Appendix A

ACT PRACTICE TEST III

1 1 1 1 1 1 1 1 1 1 1 1

ENGLISH

45 Minutes—75 Questions

DIRECTIONS: In the five passages that follow, certain parts and phrases are underlined and numbered. In the right-hand column, you will find alternatives for each underlined part. You are to choose the one that best expresses the idea, makes the statement appropriate for standard written English, or is worded more consistently with the style and tone of the passage as a whole. If you think the original version is the best, choose "NO CHANGE."

You will also find questions about a section of the passage, or about the passage as a whole. These questions do not refer to an underlined portion of the passage, but rather are identified with a note.

For each question, choose the alternative you consider best. Read each passage through once before you begin to answer the questions that accompany it. You cannot determine most answers without reading several sentences beyond the question. Be sure that you have read far enough ahead each time you choose an alternative.

Passage I

The first three paragraphs in this passage may or may not be in the most logical order. Each paragraph is numbered in brackets, and item 15 will ask you to choose the sequence of paragraphs that will make the essay most logical.

[1]

In 1849, San Francisco became the first official port of entry on the Pacific Coast. In 1851, <u>on account of</u> [1] the rapid growth of lumbering activity and a corresponding expansion of population in the Northwest Territory, the government established the Puget Sound District of the Bureau of Customs. <u>Nonetheless,</u> [2] smuggling grew rapidly, fostered by the tempting proximity of British havens and the natural cover afforded by vast forested areas and by the coves and inlets of <u>countless heavy</u> [3] timbered islands.

1. A. NO CHANGE
   B. since
   C. because of
   D. for

2. F. NO CHANGE
   G. Therefore,
   H. Consequently,
   J. On the contrary,

3. A. NO CHANGE
   B. countless, heavy
   C. countless, heavily
   D. countlessly heavy

GO ON TO THE NEXT PAGE

[2]

Such fears were well foundationed [4]. In 1851, U.S. customs officers seize [5] the Hudson Bay Company's steamer *Beaver* for a technical violation of the revenue laws [6]. This incident signaled an end to the era of unrestricted trade in the Pacific Northwest and drove some traders on both sides of the international border into illicit commercial arrangements. British wool, blankets, and liquor were the principle articles [7] of this trade.

[3]

In fact, [8] so much British wool was smuggled into the San Juan Islands selling [9] as domestic wool by American sheepmen one [10] naive textbook writer credited San Juan sheep with a world's record annual production of 150 pounds of wool per animal.

[4]

Although [11] American settlers in the Northwest Territory welcomed [12] the assertion of national control to the forty-ninth parallel, they were less amenable to restrictions on the trade with Vancouver Island. They wanted the duty-free rum and woolens offered by the

4. F. NO CHANGE
   G. well founded
   H. founded well
   J. well found

5. A. NO CHANGE
   B. seized
   C. were seizing
   D. have seized

6. F. NO CHANGE
   G. on account of violating the revenue laws
   H. for technically being in violation of the revenue laws
   J. in that they were in technical violation of the revenue laws

7. A. NO CHANGE
   B. were the principal articles
   C. was the principle article
   D. was the principal article

8. F. NO CHANGE
   G. Furthermore,
   H. Moreover,
   J. On the contrary,

9. A. NO CHANGE
   B. and sold
   C. and would be sold
   D. to sell

10. F. NO CHANGE
    G. sheepmen, one
    H. sheepmen that one
    J. sheepmen, and a

11. A. NO CHANGE
    B. Since
    C. Therefore
    D. Thus

12. F. NO CHANGE
    G. welcoming
    H. would welcome
    J. were welcomed by

GO ON TO THE NEXT PAGE

British but were fearing [13] that the imposition and enforcement of permanent tariffs on goods from British North America might be resulting in the losing [14] of British markets for American products.

13. A. NO CHANGE
B. and were fearing
C. and was fearful
D. but feared

14. F. NO CHANGE
G. might result in the losing
H. might result in the loss
J. results in the loss

Items 15-16 pose questions about Passage I as a whole.

15. Which of the following represents the most logical sequence of the first three paragraphs?

A. 1, 2, 3
B. 1, 3, 2
C. 2, 3, 1
D. 3, 1, 2

16. Which of the following does NOT represent a technique used in the development of the passage?

F. Narrative
G. Example
H. Statistics
J. Quotations

Passage II

One of the beauties of astronomy is that one does not have to be an expert to enjoy it [17]. Anyone can step outside on a clear, moonless night, gaze at thousands of stars shining across the vast interstellar spaces, and then one can become [18] intoxicated by a heady mix of grandeur and existential chill. The same questions come to mind time and again, how [19] far away are the stars? How many are there? Are they strewn endlessly through space, or are we a part of an island universe of suns ending [20] abruptly somewhere out there in the black ocean of space?

It has been the sometimes heroic and often frustrating task of astronomers since the dawn of science to chart [21] our position in the cosmic ocean. In

17. A. NO CHANGE
B. is the not having to be an expert to enjoy it
C. is that the enjoying of it does not have to be done by an expert
D. is that one doesn't necessarily have to be an expert in order to derive some enjoyment from it

18. F. NO CHANGE
G. spaces-and became
H. spaces, and become
J. spaces and becomes

19. A. NO CHANGE
B. again and how
C. again how
D. again. How

20. F. NO CHANGE
G. that ends
H. that end
J. ended

21. A. NO CHANGE
B. charting
C. having charted
D. who charted

GO ON TO THE NEXT PAGE

the twentieth century, significant progress had been made [22] in constructing an accurate map of the cosmos. We know, for example, that our solar system is part of a much larger system of hundreds of billions of stars. As such, this [23] system is the Milky Way Galaxy, a huge disk of stars and gas. We also know that ours is not the only galaxy in the universe. As far as the largest telescopes in the world can see, there are galaxies in every direction. The [24] nearest galaxies to our own are the Magellanic Clouds; the "crown" [25] jewels of the southern skies.

Since they are so near, they offer a laboratory in which astronomers can study the evolution of stars and galaxies. The nearest large galaxy to the Milky Way is the Andromeda Galaxy, which is about two million light years away. It is a giant spiral galaxy, much like [26] our own in size, shape, and number and type of stars. This nearby sister galaxy provides to us [27] an opportunity to get a bird's eye view of a galaxy much like our own—in effect, to see ourselves as others do [28].

22. F. NO CHANGE
    G. has been made
    H. is made
    J. will be made

23. A. NO CHANGE
    B. Obviously, this
    C. Doubtless, this
    D. This

24. F. NO CHANGE
    G. (Do NOT begin a new paragraphs.) These
    H. (Begin a new paragraph here but not after *skies*.) The
    J. (Begin a new paragraph here but not after *skies*.) As the

25. A. NO CHANGE
    B. Clouds, the crown
    C. Clouds which is the "crown
    D. Clouds, the "crown"

26. F. NO CHANGE
    G. much as
    H. like much
    J. much the same like

27. A. NO CHANGE
    B. provides us
    C. provide us
    D. providing to us

28. F. NO CHANGE
    G. to see ourselves the way other people tend to see us
    H. so that we would be seeing ourselves the way other people would be seeing us
    J. so that in this way we would see ourselves as others do

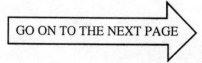

GO ON TO THE NEXT PAGE

Item 29 poses a question about Passage II as a whole.

29. Which of the following is NOT one of the reasons the author poses a series of questions in the first paragraph?
   A. To give the reader a sense of the "grandeur and existential chill"
   B. To stimulate the reader's interest in astronomy
   C. To give specific examples of questions about the cosmos that are still unanswered
   D. To alert the reader that answers to these questions will follow later in the passage

---

Passage III

[1]

The first astronauts entered the Mercury program in April 1959. They were volunteer, military pilots, graduated (30) of test pilot schools. Each were required having (31) a bachelor's degree in engineering (or its equivalent) and at least 1,500 hours of jet time. Of the first group of sixty candidates called to Washington to hear about the program, more than 80 percent volunteered. Only seven got (32) chosen. (Officials assumed that no more than seven men would have the opportunity to fly.) [33] These men were true pioneers, they (34) volunteered at a time when the plans for space travel were only on paper and no one knew what the chance of success was.

30. F. NO CHANGE
   G. pilots graduates
   H. pilots; graduates
   J. pilots, graduates

31. A. NO CHANGE
   B. was required to have
   C. required having
   D. had been required to have

32. F. NO CHANGE
   G. were
   H. had been
   J. has been

33. Is the second use of parentheses in the first paragraph appropriate?
   A. Yes, because the information explains something the author said but is not vital to the understanding of the passage.
   B. Yes, because the information contained in the parentheses is irrelevant to the passage.
   C. No, because the material is vital to the understanding of the author's main argument.
   D. No, because an entire sentence should never be placed in parentheses.

34. F. NO CHANGE
   G. pioneers but
   H. pioneers yet
   J. pioneers. They

GO ON TO THE NEXT PAGE

[2]

Scientists [35] were able to learn from each failure.

35. Which of the following phrases would best replace "Scientists" in paragraph [2] to provide a transition from the first to the second paragraph?

A. It was lucky that the men volunteered because scientists
B. There were failures as well as successes in the Mercury program, but scientists
C. Since the chances for success were unknown, scientists
D. Since the volunteers were also engineers, scientists

Fortunately they had these failures [36] early in the program. The astronauts and the animal passengers as well were flown without mishap when their time came for them [37].

36. F. NO CHANGE
G. Fortunately, they had these failures occurring
H. These failures occurred fortunately
J. Fortunately, these failures occurred

37. A. NO CHANGE
B. the time for them finally came
C. their time finally came for them
D. their time came

[3]

The most spectacular failure in the Mercury program came to be known as the "tower flight." [38] The escape tower, the parachutes, and the peroxide fuel were all deployed on the launching pad in front of the domestic and international press. A relatively simple [39] ground-circuit defect in the Redstone launch vehicle caused the main rocket engine to ignite and then shutting [40] down immediately after liftoff from the launching pad. The "flight" lasted only a second and covered a distance of inside only two inches. [41]

38. Is the use of the word *spectacular* in the first sentence of the third paragraph appropriate?

F. Yes, because the author is using the word in an ironic sense.
G. Yes, because the author obviously disapproves of the Mercury program.
H. No, because the reader might be misled about goals of the Mercury program.
J. No, because the failure cited was caused by a simple defect.

39. A. NO CHANGE
B. relative and simple
C. relative simple
D. simple relatively

40. F. NO CHANGE
G. and then will shut
H. and then they shut
J. and then to shut

41. Why does the author put the word *flight* quotation marks?

A. Because the article is quoting from another source.
B. Because there was no real flight at all.
C. Because the word is a technical term used by astronauts.
D. Because the word is often repeated in the passage.

GO ON TO THE NEXT PAGE

[4]

One of the requirements (42) of the Mercury program was that an animal had to precede man into space (43). The flight of Ham, the chimpanzee, was a major milestone in the program. Again, there were some problems. The pickup of the spacecraft was delayed, and water had leaked into (44) the capsule. Ham, however, was eventually rescued unharmed (45).

[5]

Sending a man into zero gravity was among the greatest medical experiments of all time. Fortunately, all astronauts found the weightlessness to be no problem. All returning (46) to earth with no medical difficulties whatsoever. In this area, the only question left unanswered by the Mercury program was how long man will tolerate (47) weightlessness. It seemed like, (48) however, that longer flights would require only that astronauts to have (49) suitable methods of exercise and nutrition. [50]

42. F. NO CHANGE
G. (Do NOT begin a new paragraph.) One of the requirements
H. (Do NOT begin a new paragraph.) One requirement
J. (Do NOT begin a new paragraph.) A requirement

43. A. NO CHANGE
B. had to be the one to precede man in space
C. was going to have to go into space before man
D. needed to be the one to go into space before man did

44. F. NO CHANGE
G. water leaked into
H. water leaks in
J. leaking water into

45. A. NO CHANGE
B. Place before *was.*
C. Place before *eventually.*
D. Place before *rescued.*

46. F. NO CHANGE
G. return
H. returned
J. will return

47. A. NO CHANGE
B. will be able to tolerate
C. was able to tolerate
D. could tolerate

48. F. NO CHANGE
G. seemed,
H. seemed as,
J. seemed to be,

49. A. NO CHANGE
B. have
C. had had
D. are sure to have

GO ON TO THE NEXT PAGE

50. Which of the following might be an appropriate concluding sentence for the passage?

F. Although the Mercury program experienced some failures, it was on the whole a successful part of the space program.
G. Although the Mercury program experienced some successes, it was on the whole a failure.
H. Many people have objected that it is immoral to use animals in testing programs.
J. Science fiction writers have often written about space travel.

Passage IV

[1]

It was not until the nineteenth century that medicine was able, in any broad and real way, to help [51] the suffering individual. During this century, technical advances aided the diagnostician and also [52] the surgeon, and the beginnings of an understanding of the fundamental mechanisms of disease had been emerging [53]. All aspects of medicine—from the research laboratory to the operating table—was enjoying [54] the benefits of the rigorous application of the scientific method.

[2]

By the end of the nineteenth century, a person's chances were fairly good that his doctor could not only give a name to his medical complaint yet probably had [55] an elementary understanding of what it was and how it progressed. With somewhat more luck, the doctor could select the proper treatment and he could also mitigate [56] the symptoms if not cure the disease altogether.

51. A. NO CHANGE
B. way of help
C. way to help
D. way, of helping

52. F. NO CHANGE
G. as well as
H. with
J. as opposed to

53. A. NO CHANGE
B. was emerging
C. were emerging
D. emerged

54. F. NO CHANGE
G. were enjoying
H. is enjoying
J. enjoys

55. A. NO CHANGE
B. but probably had
C. consequently probably has
D. but, probably would have

56. F. NO CHANGE
G. but could mitigate
H. and mitigate
J. and can mitigate

GO ON TO THE NEXT PAGE

[3]

This transition to modern medicine depended on three important advances. First, it required an understanding of the true nature and origin of disease. Second, it required that an organized body of standard medical practice <u>be available to</u> [57] guide physicians in diagnosis and treatment of disease. Last, <u>it presupposes</u> [58] a degree of medical technology never before available.

[4]

<u>Among the more dramatic</u> [59] nineteenth-century medical advances were those in the field of human physiology. [60] In 1822, an obscure American army camp surgeon practicing medicine <u>near where the Canadian frontier is</u> [61] was transformed almost overnight into a specialist on the mechanism of human digestion. The physician, William Beaumont, was called to treat a young trapper, accidentally shot in the stomach. <u>Beaumont's operating skill</u> [62] saved the boy's life but the patient was left with an abnormal opening leading to the stomach. To Beaumont's credit, he recognized this unique opportunity to study the human digestive

57. A. NO CHANGE
 B. was available to
 C. is available for
 D. be available as

58. F. NO CHANGE
 G. it is presupposed
 H. it presupposed
 J. they presuppose

59. A. NO CHANGE
 B. (Do NOT begin a new paragraph.) Among the more dramatic
 C. (Begin a new paragraph.) Since
 D. (Do NOT begin a new paragraph.) Since

60. Which of the following correctly describes the function of the first sentence of paragraph [4]?

 F. It introduces a topic that has nothing to do with the material discussed in the first three paragraphs.
 G. It introduces material that will contradict what was discussed in the first three paragraphs.
 H. It provides a transition that sets up a contrast to the material that came before.
 J. It provides a transition that moves from a general discussion to a more specific, but related topic.

61. A. NO CHANGE
 B. near where the Canadian frontier is,
 C. near where the Canadian frontier was
 D. near the Canadian frontier

62. F. NO CHANGE
 G. (Begin a new paragraph.) Beaumont's operating skill
 H. (Begin a new paragraph.) The skill of Beaumont at operating
 J. (Do NOT begin a new paragraph.) The skill of Beaumont at operating

GO ON TO THE NEXT PAGE

process, but for the next ten years he conducted hundreds of experiments with the reluctant cooperation of his not-so-willing patient. [63]

From his experiments, Beaumont was able to describe the physiology of digestion, demonstrating the characteristics of gastric motility and describe the properties of gastric juice. [64] He determined that the stomach contained hydrochloric acid and that it broke down food by a chemical process and not by maceration or putrefaction. Beaumont's pioneering work made him a famous man. The young trapper did not fare as well; he was forced to tour medical schools as "the man with the window in his stomach."

63. A. NO CHANGE
    B. process, and
    C. process,
    D. process. But

64. F. NO CHANGE
    G. to describe
    H. that describe
    J. and describing

Passage V

Newborn babies are not the passive creatures most people assume him to be. [65] Recent research shows that the newborn comes well-endowed of [66] charm and full potential for social graces. His eyes are equipped with surprisingly good vision. Shortly after birth he begins to watch his mother's face, which he soon comes to recognize. He also learns to know her voice and will turn toward her when he hears it. This [67] is about the time when affection begins. The infant's cry alerts the mother and causes a biological including [68] an emotional reaction. The infant's ability to cling and cuddle

65. A. NO CHANGE
    B. he was
    C. them to be
    D. it is

66. F. NO CHANGE
    G. for
    H. with
    J. by

67. A. NO CHANGE
    B. it, this
    C. it this
    D. it

68. F. NO CHANGE
    G. and
    H. with
    J. but

GO ON TO THE NEXT PAGE

communicates a pleasurable warmth to the mother and the infant's odor, too, is pleasant and uniquely its own. The newborn also smiles. The human infant, <u>unfortunately</u>,[69] <u>is in possession of</u>[70] a collection of attributes that <u>are guaranteeing</u>[71] its attractiveness.

Although there is some argument about whether the child sparks the development of love <u>or whether or not</u>[72] a special physiological state of the mother prompts her to interact with the new <u>infant. But most</u>[73] researchers agree that the newborn does mold or trigger adult behavior. The neonate organizes the mother's behavior by crying, and by eye-to-eye contact. The newborn is not a passive creature at all. [74]

69. A. NO CHANGE
    B. on the other hand
    C. nevertheless
    D. in fact

70. F. NO CHANGE
    G. possessed
    H. possesses
    J. are in possession of

71. A. NO CHANGE
    B. guaranteed
    C. guarantees
    D. guarantee

72. F. NO CHANGE
    G. or whether
    H. and whether if
    J. or whether if

73. A. NO CHANGE
    B. infant: but most
    C. infant. Most
    D. infant, most

74. Which of the following best describes the function of the last sentence of the passage?

    F. It introduces a new topic for the reader to investigate.
    G. It contradicts everything that was said before.
    H. It reiterates the main theme of the passage.
    J. It establishes the author as an authority.

Item 75 poses a question about Passage V as a whole.

75. Which of the following best describes the overall development of the passage?

    A. A comparison and contrast using anecdotes
    B. A narrative using examples
    C. A description using statistics
    D. An argument using examples

IF YOU FINISH BEFORE TIME IS CALLED, YOU MAY CHECK YOUR WORK ON THIS TEST ONLY. DO NOT WORK ON ANY OTHER TEST SECTION. **STOP**

2 2 2 2 2 2 2 2 2 2 2 2

MATHEMATICS

60 Minutes—60 Questions

DIRECTIONS: Solve each problem, choose the correct answer, and then blacken the corresponding oval on your answer sheet. Do not linger over problems that take too much time. Solve as many as you can; then return to the others in time you have left for this test.

Note: Unless otherwise stated, all of the following should be assumed:

1. Illustrative figures are NOT necessarily drawn to scale.
2. Geometry figures lie in a plane.
3. The word *line* means straight line.
4. The word *average* means arithmetic mean.

---

1. A barrel contained 5.75 liters of water and 4.5 liters evaporated. How many liters of water remain in the barrel?

   A. 0.75
   B. 1.25
   C. 1.75
   D. 2.25
   E. 13.25

2. Which of the following expressions correctly describes the mathematical relationship below?

   3 less than the product of 4 times x

   F. $4x - 3$
   G. $3x - 4$
   H. $4(x - 3)$
   J. $3(4x)$
   K. $\frac{4x}{3}$

3. If $\frac{3}{4}$ of x is 36, then $\frac{1}{3}$ of x = ?

   A. 9
   B. 12
   C. 16
   D. 24
   E. 42

4. In the figure below, what is the value of $x + y$?

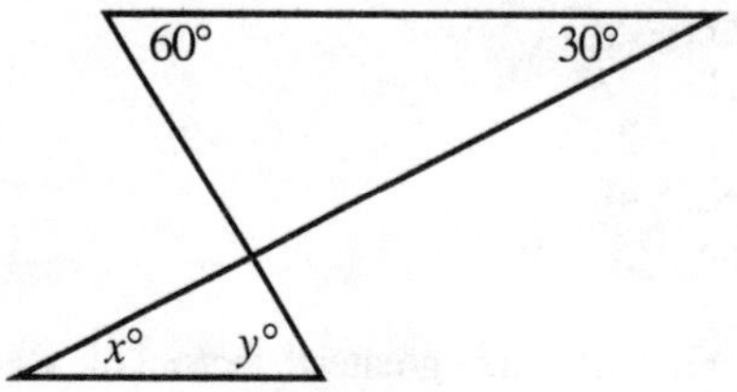

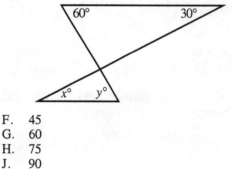

   F. 45
   G. 60
   H. 75
   J. 90
   K. 120

5. If n is a multiple of 3, which of the following is also a multiple of 3?

   A. $2 + n$
   B. $2 - n$
   C. $2n - 1$
   D. $2n + 1$
   E. $2n + 3$

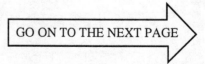

GO ON TO THE NEXT PAGE

6. Which of the following is NOT equal to the ratio of two whole numbers?

F. $\left(\frac{1}{5}\right)^2$
G. $\frac{1}{5}$
H. 0.20
J. 5%
K. $\frac{\sqrt{5}}{1}$

7. If the area of a square is 16, what is the perimeter?

A. 2
B. 4
C. 8
D. 16
E. 32

8. If $12 + x = 36 - y$, then $x + y = ?$

F. −48
G. −24
H. 3
J. 24
K. 48

9. What is the greatest factor of the following expression?

$$3x^2y^3z + 6x^3yz^3 + 2xy^2z^2$$

A. $3x^2y^2z^2$
B. $2x^2y^2z^2$
C. $x^3y^3z^3$
D. xyz
E. xz

10. Depending on the value of k, the expression $3k + 4k + 5k + 6k + 7k$ may or may not be divisible by 7. Which of the terms, when eliminated from the expression, guarantee that the resulting expression is divisible by 7 for every positive integer k?

F. $3k$
G. $4k$
H. $5k$
J. $6k$
K. $7k$

11. If $\frac{1}{3} < x < \frac{3}{8}$, which of the following is a possible value of x?

A. $\frac{1}{2}$
B. $\frac{3}{16}$
C. $\frac{17}{48}$
D. $\frac{9}{24}$
E. $\frac{5}{12}$

12. If $x^2 - y^2 = 3$ and $x - y = 3$, then $x + y = ?$

F. 0
G. 1
H. 2
J. 3
K. 9

13. If n is a positive integer, which of the following must be an even integer?

A. $n + 1$
B. $3n + 1$
C. $3n + 2$
D. $n^2 + 1$
E. $n^2 + n$

14. If the area of a square inscribed in a circle is 16, what is the area of the circle?

F. 2π
G. 4π
H. 8π
J. 16π
K. 32π

15. Ellen bought a tape recorder that usually sells for \$120 on sale for 25 percent off the usual price. If the store also collected an 8-percent sales tax on the sale price of the tape recorder, how much did Ellen pay for the tape recorder including sales tax?

A. \$106.30
B. \$101.40
C. \$97.20
D. \$95.10
E. \$88.44

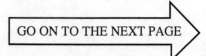

GO ON TO THE NEXT PAGE

16. A certain mixture of gravel and sand consists of 2.5 kilograms of gravel and 12.5 kilograms of sand. What percent of the mixture, by weight, is gravel?

F. 10%
G. $16\frac{2}{3}$%
H. 20%
J. 25%
K. $33\frac{1}{3}$%

17. The figure below is the top-view of a folding room divider, hinged at P and Q. If sections PR and QS are moved as shown until R and S meet, what will be the area, in square feet, enclosed? (Ignore the thickness of the hinges and the screen's sections.)

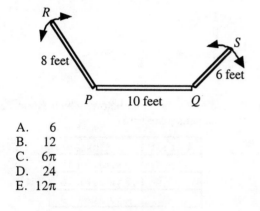

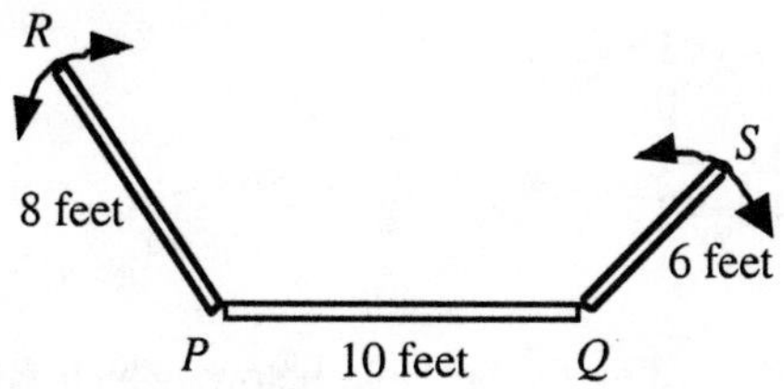

A. 6
B. 12
C. 6π
D. 24
E. 12π

18. Motorcycle X averages 40 kilometers per liter of gasoline while Motorcycle Y averages 50 kilometers per liter. If the cost of gasoline is \$2 per liter, what will be the difference in the cost of operating the two motorcycles for 300 kilometers?

F. \$3
G. \$6
H. \$12
J. \$15
K. \$20

19. If $f(x) = x^2 - 2x + 1$, then what is $f(f(3))$?

A. 3
B. 9
C. 14
D. 27
E. 39

20. For a positive integer k, which of the following equals $6k + 3$?

F. $\frac{1}{2}(k + 1)$
G. $\frac{1}{k} + 4$
H. $2k + 1$
J. $3(k + 1)$
K. $3(2k + 1)$

21. To mail a letter costs x cents for the first ounce and y cents for every additional ounce or fraction of an ounce. What is the cost, *in cents*, to mail a letter weighing a whole number of ounces, w?

A. $w(x + y)$
B. $x(w - y)$
C. $x(x - 1) + y(w - 1)$
D. $x + wy$
E. $x + y(w - 1)$

22. $|-3| \bullet |2| \bullet |-\frac{1}{2}| + (-4) = ?$

F. –1
G. 0
H. 1
J. $\frac{3}{2}$
K. 4

23. In the figure below, if the area of the square $OPQR$ is 2, what is the area of the circle with center O?

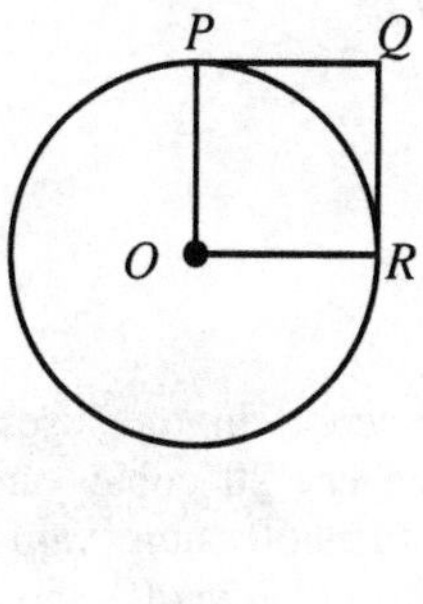

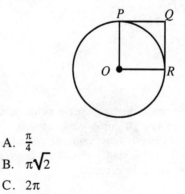

A. $\frac{\pi}{4}$
B. $\pi\sqrt{2}$
C. 2π
D. $2\sqrt{2}\pi$
E. 4π

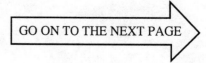

GO ON TO THE NEXT PAGE

24. Which of the following is (are) always an odd number?

I. The product of a prime number and a prime number
II. The sum of a prime number and a prime number
III. The product of an odd number and another odd number

F. I only
G. III only
H. I and II only
J. II and III only
K. I, II, and III

25. What is the area of the shaded portion of the figure below, expressed in terms of a and b?

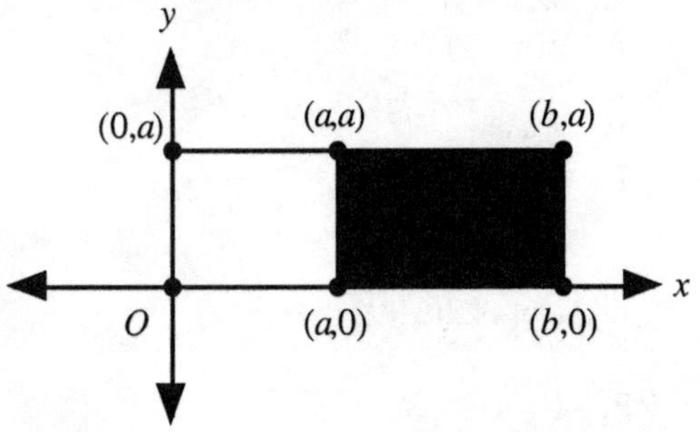

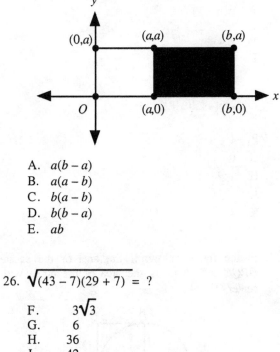

A. $a(b - a)$
B. $a(a - b)$
C. $b(a - b)$
D. $b(b - a)$
E. ab

26. $\sqrt{(43 - 7)(29 + 7)} = ?$

F. $3\sqrt{3}$
G. 6
H. 36
J. 42
K. 1,296

27. A certain concrete mixture uses 4 cubic yards of cement for every 20 cubic yards of grit. If a contractor orders 50 cubic yards of cement, how much grit (in cubic yards) should he order if he plans to use all of the cement?

A. 250
B. 200
C. 100
D. 80
E. 10

28. In the figure below, $QT = QR$. If $x = 120°$, then $y = ?$

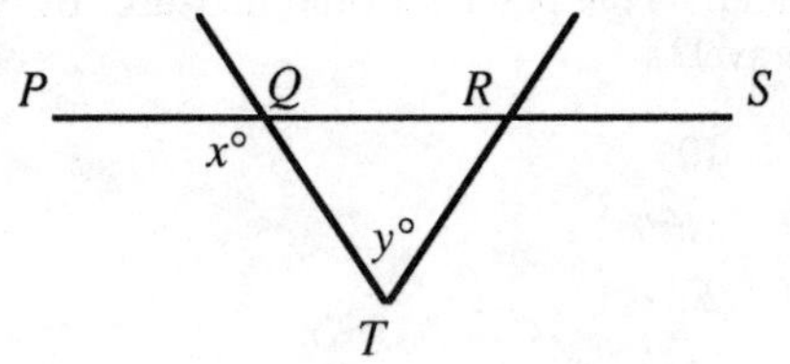

F. 30
G. 60
H. 75
J. 90
K. 120

29. If $\frac{x}{y} = -1$, then $x + y = ?$

A. 2
B. 1
C. 0
D. –1
E. –2

30. According to the table below, which fabric costs the *least* per square yard?

Fabric	Cost
F	3 yards for $8
G	2 yards for $6
H	4 yards for $9
J	5 yards for $7
K	6 yards for $4

F. F
G. G
H. H
J. J
K. K

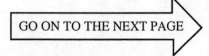

GO ON TO THE NEXT PAGE

31. In triangle PQR below, if $PQ \parallel$ to ST, then $y = ?$

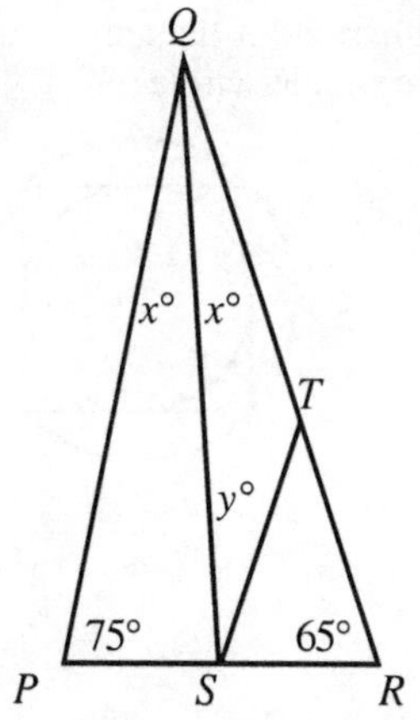

A. 20
B. 40
C. 45
D. 50
E. 55

32. $\frac{10^3(10^5 + 10^5)}{10^4} = ?$

F. 10^4
G. 10^6
H. $2(10^2)$
J. $2(10^4)$
K. $2(10^9)$

33. What is the solution set for the following equation: $x^2 - 5x + 4 = 0$?

A. $\{-4, -1\}$
B. $\{-3, -1\}$
C. $\{-1, 3\}$
D. $\{1, 4\}$
E. $\{2, 3\}$

34. The average of seven different positive integers is 12. What is the greatest that any one of the integers could be?

F. 19
G. 31
H. 47
J. 54
K. 63

35. If $x = b + 4$ and $y = b - 3$, then in terms of x and y, $b = ?$

A. $x + y - 1$
B. $x + y + 1$
C. $x - y - 1$
D. $\frac{x + y + 1}{2}$
E. $\frac{x + y - 1}{2}$

36. If $5x = 3y = z$, and x, y, and z are positive integers, all of the following must be an integer EXCEPT:

F. $\frac{z}{xy}$
G. $\frac{z}{5}$
H. $\frac{z}{3}$
J. $\frac{z}{15}$
K. $\frac{x}{3}$

37. What is the width of a rectangle with area $48x^2$ and a length of $24x$?

A. 2
B. $2x$
C. $24x$
D. $2x^2$
E. $3x^2$

38. In the figure below, if the area of the triangle is 54, then $x = ?$

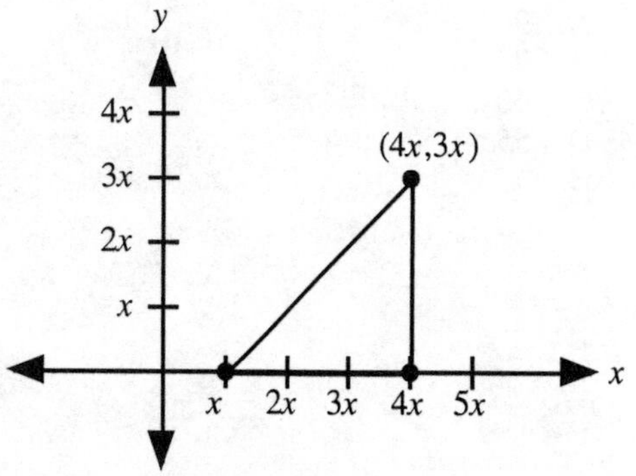

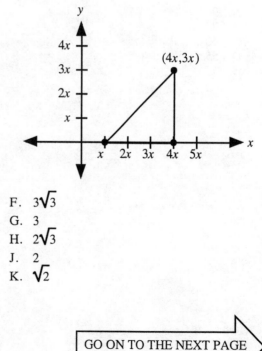

F. $3\sqrt{3}$
G. 3
H. $2\sqrt{3}$
J. 2
K. $\sqrt{2}$

GO ON TO THE NEXT PAGE

39. If $x = \frac{1}{y+1}$ and $y \neq 1$, then $y = ?$

A. $x + 1$

B. x

C. $\frac{x+1}{x}$

D. $\frac{x-1}{x}$

E. $\frac{1-x}{x}$

40. A drawer contains four green socks, six blue socks, and ten white socks. If socks are pulled out of the drawer at random and not replaced, what is the minimum number of socks that must be pulled out of the drawer to *guarantee* that two of every color have been pulled out of the drawer?

F. 6
G. 7
H. 11
J. 12
K. 18

41. In the figure below, the circle with center O has a radius of 4. If the area of the shaded region is 14π, what is the value of x?

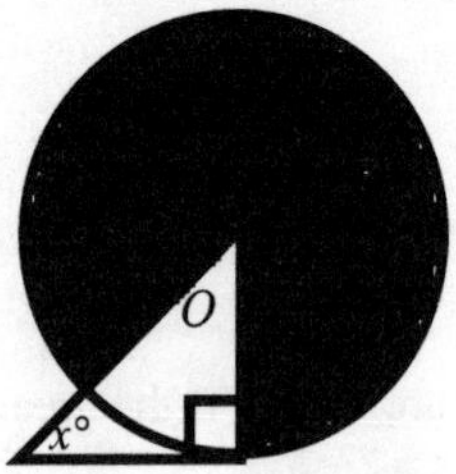

A. 90
B. 75
C. 60
D. 55
E. 45

42. In the figure below, a circle is inscribed in a square that is in turn inscribed in a larger circle. What is the ratio of the area of the larger circle to that of the smaller circle?

F. 8/1

G. 4/1

H. $\frac{2\sqrt{2}}{1}$

J. 2/1

K. $\frac{\sqrt{2}}{1}$

43. $2^0 + 2^3 - 2^{-2} = ?$

A. 4

B. $6\frac{1}{4}$

C. 7

D. $8\frac{3}{4}$

E. $9\frac{3}{4}$

44. The graph of $y = x^2 - 3$ is a parabola with axis of symmetry given by the equation $x = 0$. Which of the following are the (x, y) coordinates of the point on the parabola that is symmetric with respect to the axis of symmetry to the point with coordinates $(-1, -2)$?

F. $(-2, -1)$
G. $(-1, 2)$
H. $(0, -3)$
J. $(1, -2)$
K. $(1, 2)$

45. If 2 lines with equations $y = m_1x + b_1$ and $y = m_2x + b_2$ are perpendicular, which of the following must be true?

A. $m_1 = m_2$
B. $m_1m_2 = 1$
C. $m_1m_2 = -1$
D. $b_1 = b_2$
E. $b_1b_2 = -1$

GO ON TO THE NEXT PAGE

46. What is the area of the figure below?

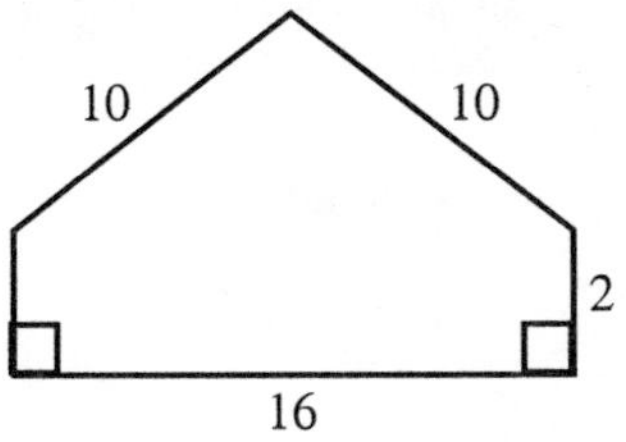

F. 36
G. 48
H. 56
J. 64
K. 80

47. For all $x > 0$ and $y > 0$, the radical expression $\frac{\sqrt{x}}{2\sqrt{x}-\sqrt{y}}$ is equivalent to:

A. $\frac{2\sqrt{x}-\sqrt{y}}{2}$
B. $\frac{2\sqrt{x}+\sqrt{y}}{4xy}$
C. $\frac{2x+\sqrt{xy}}{2x-y}$
D. $\frac{2x+\sqrt{xy}}{4x-y}$
E. $\frac{4x+\sqrt{xy}}{4x-y}$

48. In the figure below, if $l_1 \parallel l_2$, then $x = ?$

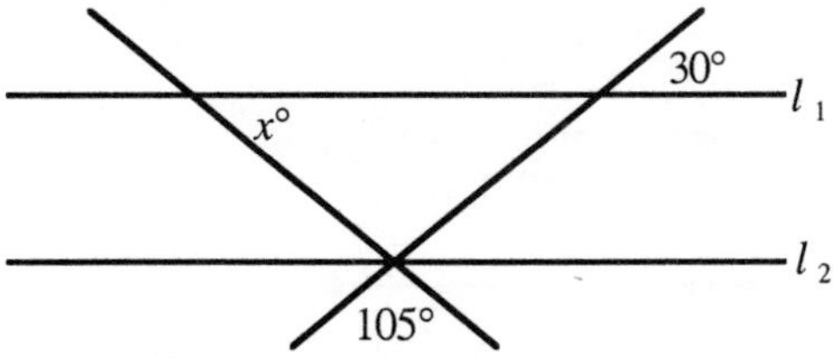

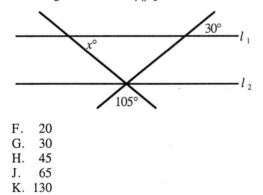

F. 20
G. 30
H. 45
J. 65
K. 130

49. The graph of $y = 2\cos 2x + 2$ intersects the y-axis where $y = ?$

A. 0
B. 2
C. 3
D. 4
E. 5

50. In the figure below, *PQRS* is a square, and each of the four circles has a radius of r. What fractional part of the area of the square is shaded?

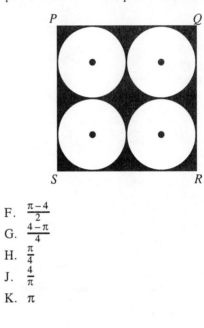

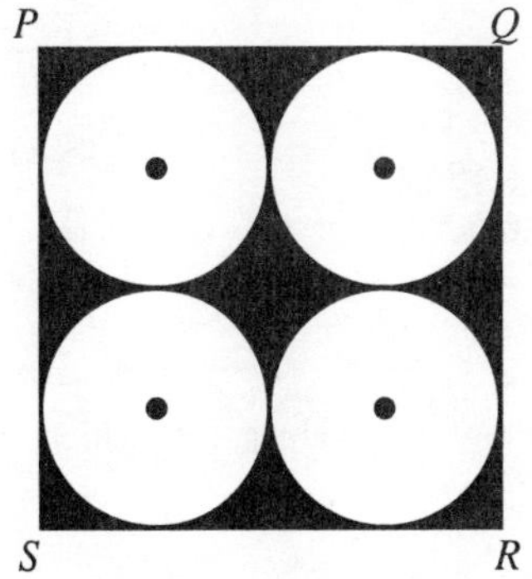

F. $\frac{\pi-4}{2}$
G. $\frac{4-\pi}{4}$
H. $\frac{\pi}{4}$
J. $\frac{4}{\pi}$
K. π

51. If $0° < \theta° < 90°$, $\frac{\sin^2\theta + \cos^2\theta}{\sin\theta}$ is equivalent to:

A. $\sin\theta$
B. $\cos\theta$
C. $\csc\theta$
D. $\tan\theta$
E. $\cot\theta$

GO ON TO THE NEXT PAGE

52. In the figure below, ABC is a triangle, $\angle ABC = 35°$, $\angle BCA = 90°$, $\angle CAB = 55°$, and the length of BC is 6 units. If $\sin 35° \approx 0.57$ and $\tan 55° \approx 1.4$, which of the following is the best approximation of the length of AC?

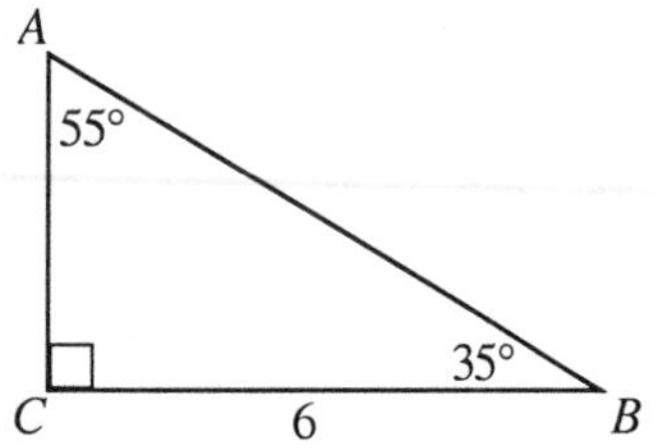

F. 3.42
G. 4.28
H. 8.57
J. 10.50
K. 12.25

53. What are the values for which $\frac{x(x + 3)}{(x - 1)(x + 2)}$ is undefined?

A. −3 only
B. −2 only
C. 1 only
D. −2 and 1 only
E. −3, −2, and 1

54. What is the maximum value of $3y$ for x and y satisfying the system of inequalities below?

$$x \geq 0$$
$$y \geq 0$$
$$x + y \leq 6$$

F. −3
G. 0
H. 6
J. 12
K. 18

55. Which of the following graphs in the standard (x, y) coordinate plane correctly shows the points on the graph of $y = |x^2 - 3|$ for $x = -1, 0,$ and 1?

A.
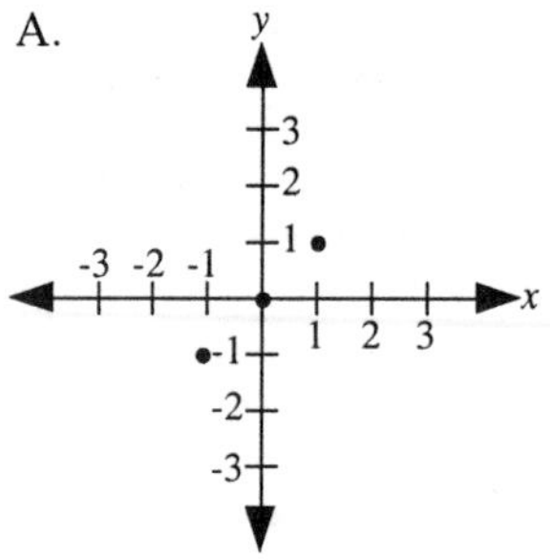

B.
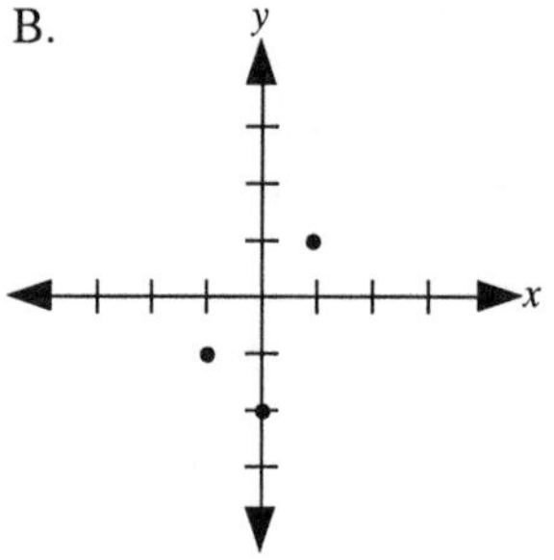

C.
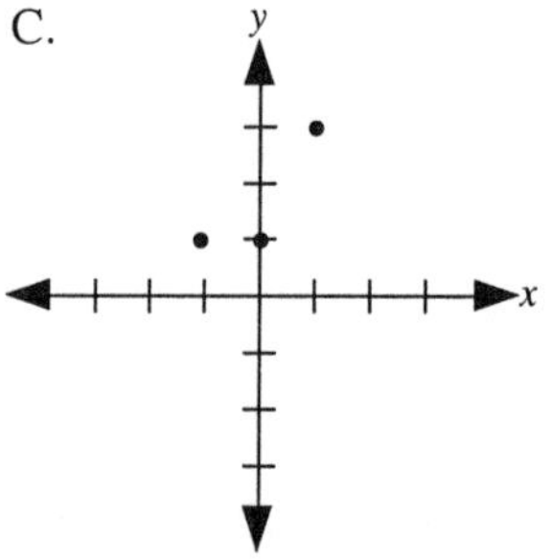

D.
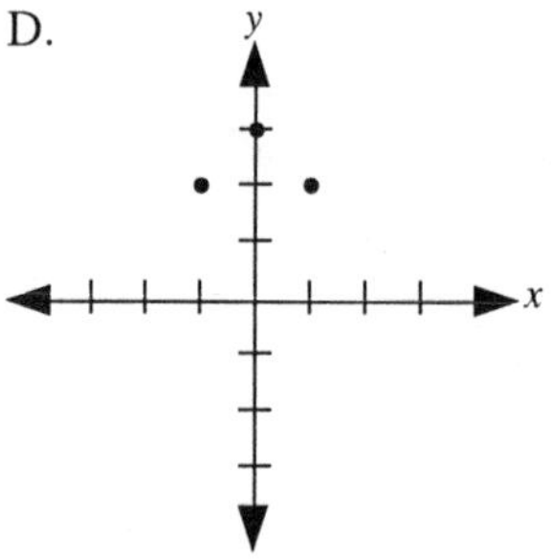

E.
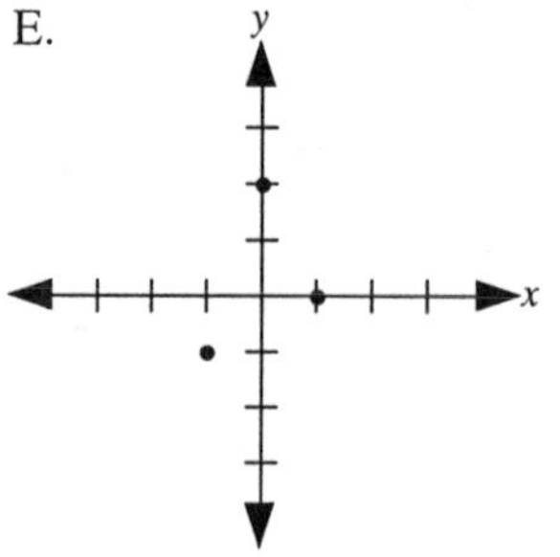

GO ON TO THE NEXT PAGE

56. The figure below is a graph of which of the following equations?

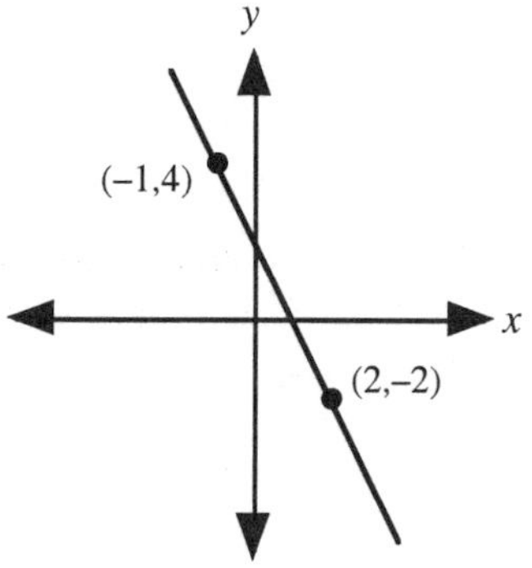

F. $y = -3x + 5$
G. $y = -2x + 2$
H. $y = -\frac{3}{2}x - 2$
J. $y = \frac{2}{3}x + 3$
K. $y = x + 2$

57. The roots of an equation of the form $ax^2 + bx + x = 0$ are $\frac{-3+\sqrt{5}}{2}$ and $\frac{-3-\sqrt{5}}{2}$. Which of the following could be the equation?

A. $x^2 + 3x + 1 = 0$
B. $x^2 - 3x + 1 = 0$
C. $x^2 + 3x - 1 = 0$
D. $x^2 - 3x - 1 = 0$
E. $-x^2 + 3x + 1 = 0$

58. The relation defined by the set of ordered pairs {(0, 3), (2, 1), (3, 0), (–1, 2), (0, 5), and (–2, 5)} is NOT a function. Deleting which of the ordered pairs will make the resulting set a function?

F. (0, 3)
G. (2, 1)
H. (3, 0)
J. (–1, 2)
K. (–2, 5)

59. Trapezoid *ABCD* has lengths, in units, and angle measures as marked in the figure below. What is the area of the trapezoid *ABCD*?

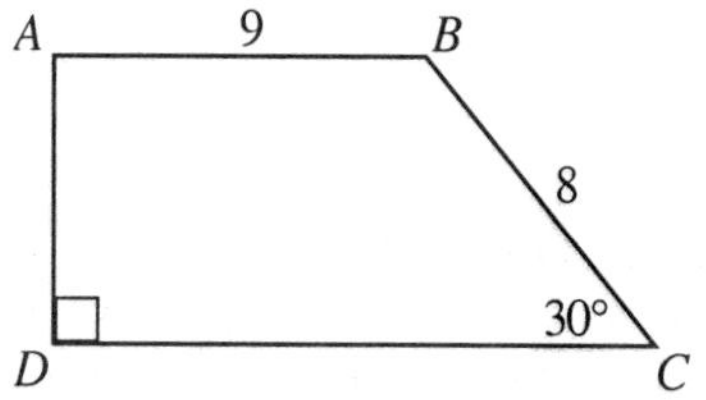

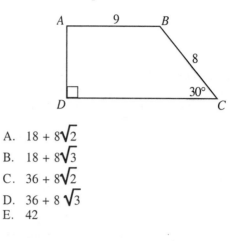

A. $18 + 8\sqrt{2}$
B. $18 + 8\sqrt{3}$
C. $36 + 8\sqrt{2}$
D. $36 + 8\sqrt{3}$
E. 42

60. What is $\tan\theta$ if $\sin\theta = \frac{3}{5}$ and $\cot\theta = \frac{4}{3} = $?

F. $\frac{9}{20}$
G. $\frac{3}{4}$
H. $\frac{7}{8}$
J. $\frac{5}{3}$
K. $\frac{20}{9}$

IF YOU FINISH BEFORE TIME IS CALLED, YOU MAY CHECK YOUR WORK ON THIS TEST ONLY. DO NOT WORK ON ANY OTHER TEST SECTION. **STOP**

3 3 3 3 3 3 3 3 3 3 3 3

READING

35 Minutes—40 Questions

DIRECTIONS: There are four passages in this test. Each passage is followed by several questions. After reading each passage, choose the best answer to each question and blacken the corresponding oval on your answer sheet. You may refer to the passages as often as necessary.

Passage I (H): The author of this passage explores the contributions of Josquin des Prez to Western music.

Until Josquin des Prez (1440-1521), Western music was liturgical, designed as an accompaniment to worship. Like the intricately carved gargoyles perched atop medieval cathedrals beyond sight of any human, music was composed to please God before anybody else; its dominant theme was reverence. Emotion was there, but it was the grief of Mary standing at the foot of the Cross, the joy of the faithful hailing Christ's resurrection. Even the secular music of the Middle Ages was tied to predetermined patterns that sometimes seemed to stand in the way of individual expression.

While keeping one foot firmly planted in the divine world, Josquin stepped with the other into the human. He scored magnificent masses, but also newly expressive motets such as the lament of David over his son Absalom or the "Deploration d'Ockeghem," a dirge on the death of Ockeghem, the greatest master before Josquin, a motet written all in black notes, and one of the most profoundly moving scores of the Renaissance. Josquin was the first composer to set psalms to music. But alongside *Benedicite omnia opera Domini Domino* ("Bless the Lord, all ye works of the Lord") he put *El Grillo* ("The cricket is a good singer who manages long poems") and *Allegez moy* ("Solace me, sweet pleasant brunette"). Josquin was praised by Martin Luther, for his music blends respect for tradition with a rebel's willingness to risk the horizon. What Galileo was to science, Josquin was to music. While preserving their allegiance to God, both asserted a new importance for man.

Why then should Josquin languish in relative obscurity? The answer has to do with the separation of concept from performance in music. In fine art, concept and performance are one; both the art lover and the art historian have thousands of years of paintings, drawings and sculptures to study and enjoy. Similarly with literature: Poetry, fiction, drama, and criticism survive on the printed page or in manuscript for judgment and admiration by succeeding generations. But musical notation on a page is not art, no matter how lofty or excellent the composer's conception; it is, crudely put, a set of directions for producing art.

Being highly symbolic, musical notation requires training before it can even be read, let alone performed. Moreover, because the musical conventions of other days are not ours, translation of a Renaissance score into modern notation brings difficulties of its own. For example, the Renaissance notation of Josquin's day did not designate the tempo at which the music should be played or sung. It did not indicate all flats or sharps; these were sounded in accordance with musicianly rules, which were capable of transforming major to minor, minor to major, diatonic to chromatic sound, and thus affect melody, harmony, and musical expression. A Renaissance composition might include several parts—but it did not indicate which were to be sung, which to be played, nor even whether instruments were to be used at all.

Thus, Renaissance notation permits several interpretations and an imaginative musician may give an interpretation that is a revelation. But no matter how imaginative, few modern musicians can offer any interpretation of Renaissance music. The public for it is small, limiting the number of musicians who can afford to learn, rehearse, and perform it. Most of those who attempt it at all are students organized in collegia musica whose memberships have a distressing habit of changing every semester, thus preventing directors from maintaining the year-in, year-out continuity required to achieve excellence of performance. Finally, the instruments used in Renaissance times—krummhorns, recorders, rausch-pfeifen, shawms, sackbuts, organettos—must be specially procured.

1. The primary purpose of the passage is to:
   - A. introduce the reader to Josquin and account for his relative obscurity.
   - B. describe the main features of medieval music and show how Josquin changed them.
   - C. place Josquin's music in an historical context and show its influence on later composers.
   - D. enumerate the features of Josquin's music and supply critical commentary.

GO ON TO THE NEXT PAGE

2. The passage contains information that would help answer all of the following questions EXCEPT:

F. What are the titles of some of Josquin's secular compositions?
G. What are the names of some Renaissance musical instruments?
H. Who was the greatest composer before Josquin?
J. What are the names of some of Josquin's most famous students?

3. It can be inferred from the passage that modern musical notation has which of the following characteristics?

I. The tempo at which a composition is to be played is indicated in the notation.
II. Whether a note is sharp or a flat is indicated in the notation.
III. The notation indicates which parts of the music are to be played by which instruments.

A. I only
B. II only
C. I and III only
D. I, II, and III

4. The author would most likely agree with which of the following statements?

F. Music is a more perfect art form than painting or sculpture.
G. Music can be said to exist only when it is being performed.
H. Josquin was the greatest composer of the Middle Ages.
J. Renaissance music is superior to music produced in modern times.

5. The passage leads most logically to a proposal to:

A. establish more *collegia musica.*
B. study Josquin's compositional techniques in greater detail.
C. include Renaissance music in college studies.
D. provide funds for musicians to study and play Josquin.

6. The author cites all of the following as reasons for Josquin's relative obscurity EXCEPT:

F. the difficulty one encounters in attempting to read his musical notation.
G. the inability of modern musicians to play instruments of the Renaissance.
H. the difficulty of procuring unusual instruments needed to play the music.
J. the lack of public interest in Renaissance music.

7. The author's attitude toward Galileo can best be described as:

A. admiring.
B. critical.
C. accepting.
D. analytical.

8. Which of the following statements about liturgical music is consistent with the selection?

F. Liturgical music is lacking in any emotion.
G. Liturgical music is written to entertain people.
H. Liturgical music is intended to be reverential.
J. Liturgical music treats primarily nonreligious themes.

9. Which of the following is NOT an example of fine art as that term is used in the passage?

A. A ballet
B. A novel
C. A poem
D. A mural

10. Josquin des Prez is important in the history of music because he:

F. wrote motets using only black notes.
G. wrote only nonliturgical music.
H. wrote both liturgical and nonliturgical music.
J. invented new musical instruments for his music.

GO ON TO THE NEXT PAGE

Passage II (PF): In this selection, the character Miss Mix experiences an exciting robbery and learns a great deal about her employer, Mr. Rawjester.

My pupil was a bright little girl, who spoke French with a perfect accent. She said to me: "Miss Mix, did you ever have the *grande passion*? Did you ever feel a fluttering here?" and she placed her hand upon her small chest. "There is to be company here tomorrow," she added, rattling on with childish naiveté, "and papa's sweetheart—Blanche Marabout—is to be here. You know they say she is to be my mamma."

What thrill was this shot through me? But I rose calmly, and administering a slight correction to the child, left the apartment.

Blunderbore House, for the next week, was the scene of gaiety and merriment. That portion of the mansion closed with a grating was walled up, and the midnight shrieks no longer troubled me.

But I felt more keenly the degradation of my situation. I was obliged to help Lady Blanche at her toilette and help her to look beautiful. For what? To captivate him? Oh-no, no—but why this sudden thrill and faintness? Did he really love her? I had seen him pinch and swear at her. But I reflected that he had thrown a candlestick at my head, and my foolish heart was reassured.

It was a night of festivity, when a sudden message obliged Mr. Rawjester to leave his guests for a few hours. "Make yourselves merry, idiots," he said, under his breath, as he passed me. The door closed and he was gone.

A half-hour passed. In the midst of the dancing a shriek was heard, and out of the swaying crowd of fainting women and excited men, a wild figure strode into the room. One glance showed it to be a highwayman, heavily armed, holding a pistol in each hand.

"Let no one pass out of this room!" he said, in a voice of thunder. "The house is surrounded and you cannot escape. The first one who crosses yonder threshold will be shot like a dog. Gentlemen, I'll trouble you to approach in single file, and hand me your purses and watches."

Finding resistance useless, the order was ungraciously obeyed.

"Now, ladies, please to pass up your jewelry and trinkets."

This order was still more ungraciously complied with. As Blanche handed to the bandit captain her bracelet, she endeavored to conceal a diamond necklace, the gift of Mr. Rawjester, in her bosom. But, with a demoniac grin, the powerful brute tore it from its concealment.

It was now my turn. With a beating heart, I made my way to the robber chieftain and sank at his feet. "Oh, sir, I am nothing but a poor governess, pray let me go."

"Oh, ho! A governess? Give me your last month's wages, then. Give me what you have stolen from your master!" and he laughed fiendishly.

I gazed at him quietly, and said, in a low voice, "I have stolen nothing from you, Mr. Rawjester!"

"Ah, discovered! Hush! listen, girl!" he hissed in a fiercer whisper, "utter a syllable to frustrate my plans and you die—aid me, and—" but he was gone.

In a few moments the party, with the exception of myself, were gagged and locked in the cellar. The next moment torches were applied to the rich hangings, and the house was in flames. I felt a strong hand seize me, and bear me out in the open air and place me upon the hillside, where I could overlook the burning mansion. It was Mr. Rawjester.

"Burn!" he said, as he shook his fist at the flames. Then sinking on his knees before me, he said hurriedly:

"Mary Jane, I love you; the obstacles to our union are or will be soon removed. In yonder mansion were confined my three crazy wives. One of them, as you know, attempted to kill me! Ha! This is vengeance! But will you be mine?"

I fell, without a word, upon his neck.

11. The name of the narrator is:

  A. Blanche Blunderbore.
  B. Blanche Mix.
  C. Mary Jane Mix.
  D. Mary Jane Rawjester.

12. Mr. Rawjester leaves the party in order to:

  F. obtain more refreshments for his guests.
  G. attend to an urgent business matter.
  H. disguise himself and return to the party as a robber.
  J. check on the whereabouts of his daughter.

13. The degradation the narrator describes in the fourth paragraph comes from:

  A. having to help the fiancé of the man she loves.
  B. having to tutor a small child who speaks French.
  C. her inability to earn more money.
  D. her inability to sleep through the night without being disturbed.

14. What is the narrator's position at Blunderbore house?

  F. The master's wife
  G. The master's mistress
  H. The child's governess
  J. Blanche Marabout's sister

GO ON TO THE NEXT PAGE

15. Mr. Rawjester's attitude towards his guests is one of:

A. warmth.
B. revulsion.
C. indifference.
D. admiration.

16. The child believes that:

F. Blanche Marabout is her natural mother.
G. Blanche Marabout is to marry her father.
H. the narrator is her natural mother.
J. her father dislikes the narrator.

17. It can be inferred that the narrator:

A. denounces Mr. Rawjester to his guests.
B. cooperates with Mr. Rawjester.
C. defends herself against Mr. Rawjester's attack.
D. gives the highwayman her month's wages.

18. The purpose of the visit of the highwayman is to:

F. obtain valuable jewelry.
G. kidnap the narrator.
H. kill the child.
J. deflect suspicion from Mr. Rawjester.

19. Blanche was unable to hide the diamond necklace because:

A. the highwayman had given it to her and knew she had it.
B. the narrator told the highwayman where it was hidden.
C. some of the other guests insisted that she give it up.
D. the child whispered its location to the highwayman.

20. The exchange between the narrator and the highwayman that takes place in the house was heard:

F. only by those two persons.
G. by the child.
H. by Blanche.
J. by every guest in the room.

Passage III (SS): This passage explores the need for regulatory legislation concerning corporate takeovers.

American financial markets are regulated by the federal government through the Securities and Exchange Commission and by various state agencies. In recent years, there has been considerable discussion of the need for more regulation because of the increased number of corporate takeovers. Many observers of the economic scene argue that much of this activity has had harmful effects not only on stockholders but on the economy as a whole.

Many corporate takeovers are hostile; that is, an outside group or company tries to seize control of an existing company whose management opposes the takeover. Most hostile takeovers begin with a tender offer in which the outside raiders offer to buy a sufficient amount of the company's outstanding stock at a stated price—usually well above the current market price. Another takeover strategy is to orchestrate a proxy battle in which a vote of shareholders of record on a specific date is taken to approve or reject a new slate of directors put forth by the raiders. The raiders generally argue that the new directors will make the company more profitable and thereby enhance the value of the stock for the existing stockholders.

Regardless of the takeover strategy employed, most raiders must purchase a significant portion of the company's stock at a price above its current market value. Outsiders usually finance such large purchases of stock through the sale of bonds that pay a very high rate of interest. The raiders argue that the debt to be incurred can easily be paid off by selling parts of the targeted company or by drawing on the additional profits that the new management insists it can make.

In 1986 and 1987, charges came to light that individuals within Wall Street firms specializing in raising capital for corporate takeovers were, in fact, selling inside information about future takeover attempts. Some of the individuals involved have already been sentenced to jail terms. In addition, such scandals have added to pressure on Congress and the Securities and Exchange Commission to provide more effective regulation of the financial aspects of attempted corporate takeovers.

GO ON TO THE NEXT PAGE

Critics of hostile corporate takeovers believe that the managers of the company to be taken over usually engage in short-term activities that have very negative long-term effects. In order to avoid hostile takeovers, managers of companies generally take measures to make the takeovers less desirable. For instance, they may insert a *golden parachute clause* in employment contracts. This clause requires a company to pay very large bonuses to any management members who are fired after a takeover. Another tactic, the *poison pill,* restructures the financial base of the corporation so that an attempted takeover would make the company less profitable. Yet another anti-raid tactic is to pay *greenmail* to the raiders; that is, the target of the takeover pays the raiders, who have acquired a significant percentage of the stock at a premium, to sell those shares back to the targeted company at a much higher price. This prevents the takeover, but it usually adds a substantial sum to the company's debt.

Supporters of corporate raiders counterargue that, in fact, it is the threat of a takeover that makes managers more efficient. For instance, it may cause managers to sell parts of the corporation that they are not managing well in order to raise the money to fend off the takeover. In addition, those who believe that takeovers are good argue that the existing shareholders always do better in a hostile takeover, since they invariably get a higher price for each share of stock than the current market value.

21. Which statement expresses the main idea of this passage?

    A. The government is regulating the financial aspects of corporate takeovers adequately.
    B. There has been recent debate over the need for additional government regulation of corporate takeovers.
    C. Hostile corporate takeovers are beneficial to the targeted corporation.
    D. Trading insider secrets has become a common problem in hostile corporate takeovers.

22. A corporation's board of directors votes to approve a new company policy. According to the plan, each member of the board and of upper management would receive severance of from two to five years' pay if the new owner fired the member after a corporate takeover. This action would be considered:

    F. a poison pill.
    G. a golden parachute.
    H. greenmail.
    J. a hostile takeover.

23. What is the most important difference between a hostile and a nonhostile takeover?

    A. In a hostile takeover, stockholders must pay greenmail to the existing directors.
    B. In a nonhostile takeover, raiders sell bonds with high interest rates.
    C. In a hostile takeover, the existing management is opposed to the takeover.
    D. In a nonhostile takeover, existing management uses golden parachutes.

24. According to the passage, which of the following parties in a hostile takeover will likely incur new debt?

    F. The raiders, because they need money to buy large blocks of stock
    G. The Securities and Exchange Commission, because it must oversee the transactions more closely
    H. The stockholders, because they must furnish additional funds works
    J. The critics of hostile takeovers, because they make less money in the stock market

25. According to the passage, a poison pill strategy involves:

    A. paying the raiders high prices to buy back the company's stock from them.
    B. paying high bonuses to the members of the old management who are fired by the new management.
    C. more regulation by the Securities and Exchange Commission.
    D. restructuring the financial base of the company so that it will be less profitable or valuable to the raiders.

26. According to the passage, supporters of corporate takeovers believe that:

    F. the shareholders always lose money because a takeover profits only the raiders.
    G. fear of being targeted for a takeover makes managers more efficient.
    H. insider trading should be made legal.
    J. a proxy fight is the best way to win control.

GO ON TO THE NEXT PAGE

27. According to the passage, in a proxy fight:

A. the raiders sell bonds to buy the targeted company's stock.
B. the raiders offer to buy stock at a higher-than-market price.
C. insider information is traded illegally.
D. a stockholders' meeting is called to vote for approval or rejection of a new board of directors put forth by the raiders.

28. The management of a business recently targeted for takeover decides to sell two of its unprofitable subsidiaries to raise cash and cut expenses. Supporters of corporate takeovers would say that this action:

F. is an example of how the greenmail strategy works.
G. is an example of how a golden parachute strategy works.
H. is an example of how the fear of a takeover makes managers more efficient.
J. is an example of how the poison pill strategy works.

29. The Securities and Exchange Commission is a:

A. state regulatory agency that polices financial markets.
B. federal regulatory agency that polices financial markets.
C. source of funding for hostile takeovers.
D. board of business executives who promote fair business practices.

30. Some individuals working on Wall Street have been sentenced to jail terms for:

F. attempting to greenmail other companies.
G. forcing companies to swallow a poison pill.
H. selling inside information about takeover attempts.
J. agreeing to pay greenmail to corporate raiders.

Passage IV (NS): This passage discusses supernova explosions and their effects.

About twice every century, the light reaches us from one of the massive stars in our galaxy that blew apart millions of years ago in a supernova explosion that sends massive quantities of radiation and matter into space and generates shock waves that sweep through the arms of the galaxy. The shock waves heat the interstellar gas, evaporate small clouds, and compress larger ones to the point at which they collapse under their own gravity to form new stars. The general picture that has been developed for the supernova explosion and its aftermath goes something like this. Throughout its evolution, a star is much like a leaky balloon, it keeps its equilibrium figure through a balance of internal pressure against the tendency to collapse under its own weight. The pressure is generated by nuclear reactions in the core of the star that must continually supply energy to balance the energy that leaks out in the form of radiation. Eventually the nuclear fuel is exhausted, and the pressure drops in the core. With nothing to hold it up, the matter in the center of the star collapses inward, creating higher and higher densities and temperatures, until the nuclei and electrons are fused into a superdense lump of matter known as a neutron star.

As the overlying layers rain down on the surface of the neutron star, the temperature rises until, with a blinding flash of radiation, the collapse is reversed. A thermonuclear shock wave runs through the now expanding stellar envelope, fusing lighter elements into heavier ones and producing a brilliant visual outburst that can be as intense as the light of 10 billion suns. The shell of matter thrown off by the explosion plows through the surrounding gas, producing an expanding bubble of hot gas, with gas temperatures in the millions of degrees. This gas will emit most of its energy at x-ray wavelengths, so it is not surprising that x-ray observatories have provided some of the most useful insights into the nature of the supernova phenomenon. More than twenty supernova remnants have now been detected in x-ray studies.

Recent discoveries of meteorites with anomalous concentrations of certain isotopes indicate that a supernova might have precipitated the birth of our solar system more than four and a half billion years ago. Although the cloud that collapsed to form the Sun and the planets was composed primarily of hydrogen and helium, it also contained carbon, nitrogen, and oxygen, elements essential for life as we know it. Elements heavier than helium are manufactured deep in the interior of stars and would, for the most part, remain there if it were not for the cataclysmic supernova explosions that blow giant stars apart. Additionally, supernovas produce clouds of high-energy particles called cosmic rays. These high-energy particles continually bombard the Earth and are responsible for many of the genetic mutations that are the driving force of the evolution of species.

GO ON TO THE NEXT PAGE

31. According to the passage, we can expect to observe a supernova in our galaxy about:

A. twice each year.
B. 100 times each century.
C. once every 50 years.
D. once every other century.

32. According to the passage, all of the following are true of supernovas EXCEPT that they:

F. are extremely bright.
G. are an explosion of some sort.
H. emit large quantities of x-rays.
J. are caused by the collision of large galaxies.

33. The author employs which of the following to develop the first paragraph?

A. Analogy
B. Deduction
C. Generalization
D. Example

34. It can be inferred from the passage that the meteorites mentioned by the author at line 40:

F. contain dangerous concentrations of radioactive materials.
G. give off large quantities of x-rays.
H. include material not created in the normal development of our solar system.
J. are larger than the meteors normally found in a solar system like ours.

35. The author implies that:

A. it is sometimes easier to detect supernovas by observation of the x-ray spectrum than by observation of visible wavelengths of light.
B. life on Earth is endangered by its constant exposure to radiation forces that are released by a supernova.
C. recently discovered meteorites indicate that the Earth and other planets of our solar system survived the explosion of a supernova several billion years ago.
D. lighter elements are formed from heavier elements during a supernova as the heavier elements are tom apart.

36. According to the passage, what is the first event in the sequence that leads to the occurrence of a supernova?

F. An ordinary star begins to emit tremendous quantities of x-rays.
G. A neutron star is enveloped by a superheated cloud of gas.
H. An imbalance between light and heavy elements causes an ordinary star to collapse.
J. An ordinary star exhausts its supply of nuclear fuel and begins to collapse.

37. According to the passage, a neutron star is:

A. a gaseous cloud containing heavy elements.
B. an intermediate stage between an ordinary star and a supernova.
C. the residue that is left by a supernova.
D. the core of an ordinary star that houses the thermonuclear reactions.

38. The author is primarily concerned with:

F. speculating about the origins of our solar system.
G. presenting evidence proving the existence of supernovas.
H. discussing the nuclear reaction that occurs in the core of a star.
J. describing a theory about the causes of supernovas.

39. How long ago was our galaxy formed?

A. 100 million years
B. 1 billion years
C. 2 billion years
D. Over 4.5 billion years

40. What is the connection between supernovas and the evolution of species on earth?

F. There is no connection.
G. Cosmic radiation from supernovas retards evolution.
H. Cosmic radiation from supernovas drives evolution.
J. Evolution makes possible future supernovas.

IF YOU FINISH BEFORE TIME IS CALLED, YOU MAY CHECK YOUR WORK ON THIS TEST ONLY. DO NOT WORK ON ANY OTHER TEST SECTION.	**STOP**

4 4 4 4 4 4 4 4 4 4 4 4

SCIENCE REASONING

35 Minutes—40 Questions

DIRECTIONS: There are seven passages in this test. Each passage is followed by several questions. After reading a passage, choose the best answer to each question and blacken the corresponding oval on your answer sheet. You may refer to the passages as often as necessary.

Passage I

Before making their historic first powered flight, the Wright Brothers made extensive lift tests in 1901 using a glider. Their data differed from that obtained twelve years earlier by the German, Otto Lilienthal.

Results of both tests (Wright: thin line; Lilienthal: thick line) are shown below. "Lift" is the force that pulls the wing away from the earth, in a direction perpendicular to the flight path, and the "angle of incidence" is the angle that the flight path makes with the horizon.

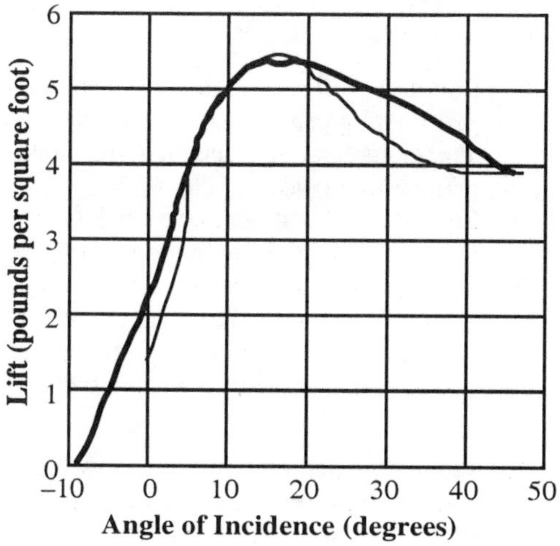

Modified from: Culick, F.E.C. 1979. The Wright "Flyer" was the outcome of an intensive program of research. *Sci. Amer. 241* (1): 86-100.

1. The two curves differ chiefly in that:

   A. the Wright's data were more accurate.
   B. lift was generally greater in the Wright's experiments.
   C. lift was generally greater in Lilienthal's experiments.
   D. the peak value for lift was greater in Lilienthal's experiments.

2. In the Wright's experiments, the greatest lift occurred at an angle of incidence of about:

   F. 5.5 degrees.
   G. 0 degrees.
   H. 16 degrees.
   J. 46 degrees.

3. At an angle of incidence of 50 degrees, by how much would you expect the two experiments to show a difference in lift?

   A. 0–1 pound/sq. ft.
   B. 1–2 pound/sq. ft.
   C. 2–3 pound/sq. ft.
   D. 3–4 pound/sq. ft.

4. The two sets of experiments differed most in lift at which of the following angles?

   F. 10 degrees
   G. 15 degrees
   H. 30 degrees
   J. 40 degrees

5. The widest range of angles (in degrees) over which of the Lilienthal values for lift continuously exceeded the Wright's values was:

   A. 10.
   B. 19.
   C. 25.
   D. 43.

GO ON TO THE NEXT PAGE

Passage II

Two experiments were performed to determine the effects of temperature on the rate of cellular respiration* in germinating peas.

*Summary Equation: $C_6H_{12}O_6 + 6O_2 \Rightarrow 6CO_2 + 6H_2O$
(glucose) (oxygen) (carbon dioxide)(water)

Experiment 1

A simple respirometer was used, primarily consisting of a large test tube partially filled with germinating peas. The peas were covered with a layer of cotton and a small amount of potassium hydroxide (KOH), a substance that can absorb and remove carbon dioxide from the tube. The remainder of the tube, with its starting volume of air sealed inside (200 milliliters), was closed to the outside with a rubber stopper. Attached was a meter designed to detect and measure any changes in gas volume in the tube during the experiment. The experiment was conducted at room temperature (22°C), and the respirator was monitored for 15 minutes. At the end of 15 minutes, the volume of gas inside the tube had *decreased* to 120 ml.

Experiment 2

An identical experiment was conducted at 30°C. At this temperature, the volume of gas inside the tube after 15 minutes had decreased from 200 ml (starting volume) to 60 ml.

6. Separate control experiments were performed alongside Experiments 1 and 2. The control contained plastic beads (the same size as peas) instead of germinating peas. All other conditions were identical. Any decrease in gas volume inside the control tube would suggest that:

F. plastic beads utilize oxygen at approximately the same rate as germinating peas.
G. plastic beads produce carbon dioxide at about the same rate as germinating peas.
H. plastic beads carry out all aspects of cellular respiration at approximately the same rate as germinating peas.
J. factors having nothing to do with cellular respiration must be responsible.

7. If potassium hydroxide (KOH) were not included in the tubes, what would happen to the volume of gas during each experiment?

A. Final volumes would be higher than starting volumes.
B. Final volumes would decrease faster than what was observed in Experiments 1 and 2.
C. Final volumes would approximately be the same as starting volumes.
D. Results would not be different from what was observed in Experiments 1 and 2.

8. In both experiments, the decrease in volume in the tube was mainly due to a change in the volume of what specific gas?

F. Oxygen
G. Carbon dioxide
H. Potassium hydroxide
J. All of the above

9. Experiment 2 showed a greater decrease in gas volume in the tube because:

A. at higher temperatures, peas use oxygen slower.
B. at higher temperatures, peas produce carbon dioxide faster.
C. at higher temperatures, peas use oxygen faster.
D. at lower temperatures, peas use oxygen slower than they produce carbon dioxide.

10. An additional set of experiments with germinating peas is conducted in the *dark* at 22°C and 30°C. All other conditions are identical to those in Experiments 1 and 2. After 15 minutes, if the final gas volume inside the tube at 22°C is 120 ml, and the final gas volume inside the tube at 30°C is 60 ml, which hypothesis best explains the results?

F. Darkness affects cellular respiration in germinating peas the same way that a rise in temperature affects cellular respiration in germinating peas.
G. Light/dark conditions have little or no effect on cellular respiration in germinating peas.
H. Cellular respiration in germinating peas occurs faster in the light than in the dark.
J. Cellular respiration in germinating peas occurs faster in the dark than in the light.

11. The summary equation (above) shows that during cellular, respiration, germinating peas must consume glucose. In Experiments 1 and 2, glucose molecules:

A. were in the peas.
B. were not available.
C. were consumed at equal rates.
D. were available but not consumed at all.

GO ON TO THE NEXT PAGE

Passage III

The chart below shows a set of "energy levels" that an electron in molecule X can occupy. The value of the energy in each level is shown to the right.

Energy Levels

E_5---------2.07
E_4---------1.75
E_3---------1.52
E_2---------1.20
E_1---------0.60

An electron can move from one level to the next (transition) in two ways:

a) the molecule can absorb a particle of light, called a "photon," of just the right energy to lift the electron to a higher level. For example, an electron in level 4 can be raised to level 5 if the molecule absorbs a photon whose energy is 0.32.

b) the molecule can emit, or give off, a photon of just the right energy necessary to lower an electron to another level. For example, an electron in level 4 can move to level 3 if the molecule emits a photon whose energy is 0.23.

12. A sample containing many X molecules absorbs light, each photon of which carries 0.60 units of energy. As the light is absorbed:

F. an electron moves from level 1 to level 2.
G. an electron moves from level 2 to level 4.
H. an electron moves from level 2 to level 1.
J. an electron moves from level 4 to level 2.

13. A sample of molecule X emits light, each photon of which carries 0.32 units of energy. Which of the following statements best explains this observation?

A. An electron has moved from level 3 to level 2.
B. An electron has moved from level 2 to level 3.
C. An electron has moved from level 5 to level 4.
D. An electron has moved from level 3 to level 2, or from level 5 to level 4.

14. A sample of molecule X emits light whose photons each carry 0.92 units of energy. As the light is emitted:

F. an electron moves from level 5 to level 2.
G. an electron moves from level 1 to level 5.
H. an electron moves from level 1 to level 3.
J. an electron moves from level 3 to level 1.

15. Suppose that in a sample of molecule X, all of the electrons are in level 1. Based on the information in the chart, photons of *how many different* energies could be absorbed by the sample?

A. 1
B. 2
C. 3
D. 4

16. Assume that each of the molecules in a sample of molecule X has only 1 electron, whose level is not known. Light is passed through the sample, and photons, each of energy 0.23, are absorbed. A very short time later, photons of the same energy are emitted. It is likely that:

F. electrons are being promoted from level 1 to level 2.
G. electrons are moving from level 4 to level 3, and then back again to level 4.
H. electrons are moving from level 3 to level 4, then back again to level 3.
J. electrons are moving from level 5 to level 4.

17. If photons whose individual energies are each 2.07 encounter a sample of molecule A, then:

A. electrons will be promoted from level 1 to level 5.
B. electrons will be promoted from all levels to level 5.
C. electrons will drop from level 5 to level 1.
D. no electron transitions will occur.

GO ON TO THE NEXT PAGE

Passage IV

Two different views of the earth's past are presented below.

Scientist 1

The history of our planet has been marked by sudden spectacular events that have no counterpart in the natural processes observed today (Catastrophism). Today's valleys formed during periods of downward slippage by fragments of the earth's crust. Mountains rose due to gigantic upheavals of land during the earth's beginnings. The three major types of rock formed when one worldwide ocean precipitated out great masses of different materials during three sudden and separate events. Substances such as granite were precipitated first (today's igneous rocks), while materials in the flat upper layers precipitated last (today's sedimentary rocks). This was followed by the disappearance of much of this great ocean's water (perhaps by evaporation during years of intensive heat). Distinct assemblages of animal and plant fossils, found in successive rock layers of a region, can be explained by local catastrophic events, such as massive fires or floods wiping out living forms and new forms replacing the old, as a result of repopulation by foreign species that immigrated from other geographic areas.

Scientist 2

Processes now in operation are adequate to account for changes in the Earth's past (Principle of Uniform Change). Although today's processes seem to have negligible effects on the landscape, great changes can result from ongoing processes, if given long enough periods of time. Valleys form as flowing water from streams and the debris streams carry cut through the sides and bottom of the land and rock they pass across. Rocks and mountains can be formed, destroyed and reformed by processes still going on today such as volcanic activity, heat and pressure under the earth's surfaces, erosion, weathering, and even shifts and movements that can lift massive areas below the land and ocean surfaces to high elevation. Different fossil types in successive layers of rocks represent the changes in form that can take place among related organisms as a result of evolutionary processes over vast periods of time.

18. One major difference between the views of Scientist 1 and Scientist 2 relates to:

F. where fossils are found.
G. when the processes that shape the earth take place.
H. the size of mountain ranges.
J. whether water played a role in forming any of the earth's characteristics.

19. Which of the following provides the strongest evidence against Scientist 1's point about mountain formation?

A. The beginnings of the earth are not well documented.
B. Floods and fires have never been massive enough to eliminate fossils from all mountain areas.
C. Volcanic activity, weathering, and erosion are believed to be less common today than in years past.
D. Fossils of recent sea creatures can be found in rocks on mountain peaks.

20. Based on the differences between Scientist 1 and Scientist 2 stated above, which description is most accurate concerning their views about the time span needed for the earth's geologic characteristics to form?

F. Scientist 1 makes references to time span and suggests a longer earth history than Scientist 2.
G. Scientist 2 makes no reference to time span, but implies, a shorter earth history than Scientist 1.
H. Scientist 2 makes references to time span and suggests a longer earth history than Scientist 1.
J. Neither scientist refers to time span or implies any difference in length of earth history.

21. According to Scientist 1, which of the major types of rocks should be found at the lowest levels?

A. Igneous (granite)
B. Metamorphic (marble)
C. Sedimentary (limestone)
D. Cannot be determined

22. According to the views of Scientist 1, the number of major rock types will most likely:

F. remain unchanged.
G. decrease.
H. increase.
J. Cannot be determined

GO ON TO THE NEXT PAGE

23. To refute Scientist 2's point of view about strictly uniform processes of change, Scientist 1 could argue that:

A. the streams of today are not measurably effective in cutting through the sides and bottoms of rock they pass across.
B. fossils are not found everywhere today.
C. at some early point in time, the actual formation of the earth had to involve very different processes from those now in evidence.
D. no mountain ranges have formed in our lifetime.

24. Which argument does *not* support the views of Scientist 2?

F. There are many regions of lava where no volcanoes are present today.
G. There are three major types of rock that exist today.
H. Many rivers today are flowing far below their former channels.
J. Distinctive fossils in upper layers of rock show similarities to those in lower layers, yet are never found in any other geographic areas.

Passage V

Cold-blooded animals (poikilotherms) cannot regulate their body temperatures internally. Their body temperature varies as the environmental temperature varies. As a consequence, the rates of many bodily processes also vary as outside temperatures change (as environmental temperatures increase, body temperature as well as the rates of bodily processes also may increase). Warm-blooded animals (homeotherms), on the other hand, can maintain their body temperatures internally. Therefore, the rates of their bodily processes can remain relatively stable when environmental temperatures change.

Experiments were set up to determine how the bodily process, heart rate, may be affected by different temperatures in two species of live laboratory animals.

Experiment 1

Ten individuals from Species A and ten individuals from Species B were kept in 20 separate containers at room temperature (22°C) for 30 minutes. Their heart rates (heart beats/minute) were recorded every 10 minutes. Average heart rates for the entire experiment were then calculated for each species. Results were as follows: Species A had an average heart rate of 150 beats/minute, while Species B averaged 100 beats/minute.

Experiment 2

Identical procedures were used to repeat the original experiment except that the containers holding the individuals of each species were placed in an incubator set at 35°C. At the end of 30 minutes, the average heart rate for both species was 148 beats/minute.

25. How many values were used to calculate the average heart beats for each species in each of these experiments?

A. 1
B. 10
C. 20
D. 30

26. Which of the following hypotheses is supported by the results of both experiments?

F. Species A is most likely poikilothermic.
G. Species B is most likely poikilothermic.
H. Both species are most likely poikilothermic.
J. Neither species is poikilothermic.

27. Which of the following statements best explains why ten individuals of each species were used in the experiments?

A. In case a few died, there would still be others available for testing.
B. If only one individual was used, it would be lonely.
C. An average value for ten individuals reduces the chance of getting an extreme value for any one individual.
D. If only one individual was chosen from each species, it would be difficult to show differences.

GO ON TO THE NEXT PAGE

28. If a third experiment were conducted at 6°C, which set of results for average heart rates is closest to what might be expected?

F. Species A: 146 beats/minute, Species B: 146 beats/minute.
G. Species A: 50 beats/minute, Species B: 146 beats/minute.
H. Species A: 50 beats/minute, Species B: 50 beats/minute.
J. Species A: 146 beats/minute, Species B: 50 beats/minute.

29. Which statement is accurate concerning Species A and Species B?

A. At 22°C, Species A has a higher average heart rate than Species B.
B. Species A has a larger average size than Species B.
C. As environmental temperature increases, average heart rate increases more for Species A than Species B.
D. As environmental temperature decreases, average heart rate increases more for Species A than Species B.

30. If the average body temperature for the ten individuals of each species were recorded during Experiment 1 and Experiment 2, which results would be expected?

F. Species A: Temperature stays the same in both experiments, Species B: Temperature increases in Experiment 2.
G. Species A: Temperature increases in Experiment 2, Species B: Temperature stays the same in both experiments.
H. Both Species: Temperature increases in Experiment 2.
J. Both Species: Temperature stays the same in both experiments.

Passage VI

A student performs a set of three experiments, in which a light beam passes through water and air. The "refraction angles" are the angles that the light beam makes with a vertical line. In the water, this angle is called θ_1. When the beam leaves the water and passes into air, a second angle, θ_2, can be measured. Figure 1 illustrates θ_1 and θ_2.

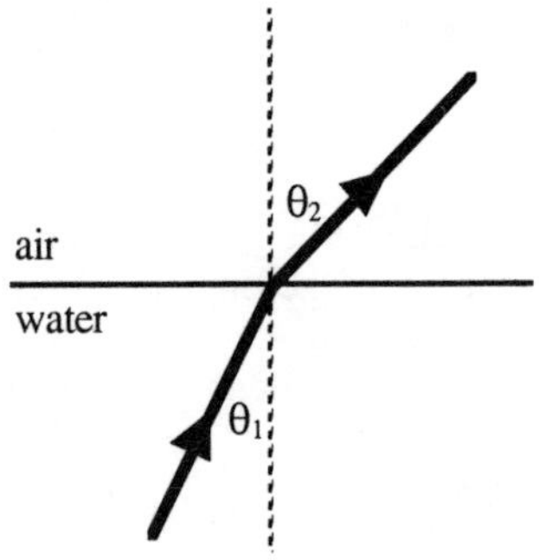

Figure 1

Experiment 1

The entry angle, θ_1, and the exit angle, θ_2, are both equal to zero.

Experiment 2

The angles observed are shown in Figure 2.

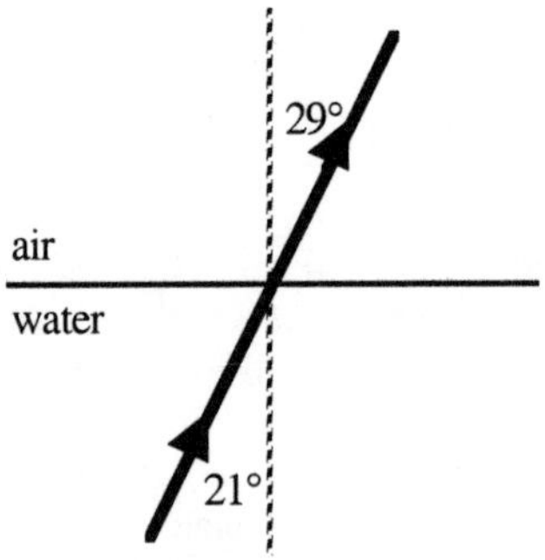

Figure 2

GO ON TO THE NEXT PAGE

Experiment 3

The angles observed are shown in Figure 3.

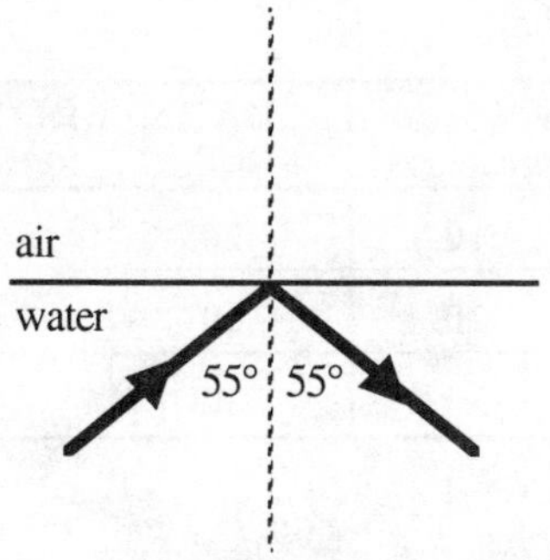

Figure 3

31. Which of the following diagrams could represent the observations of Experiment 1?

A.

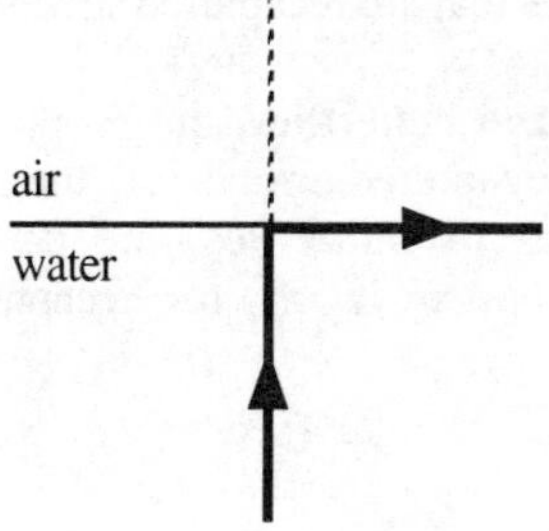

B.

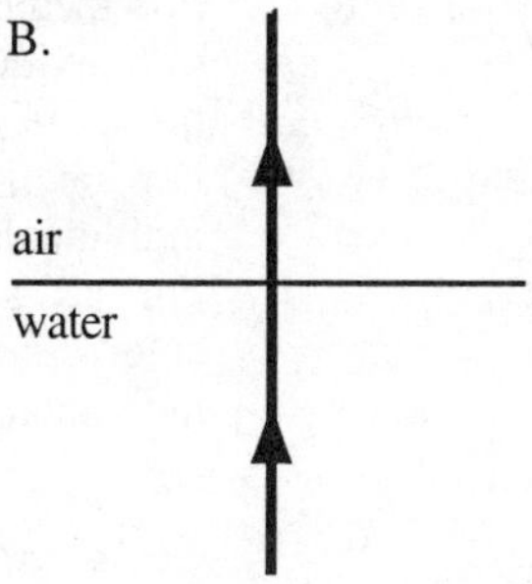

C.

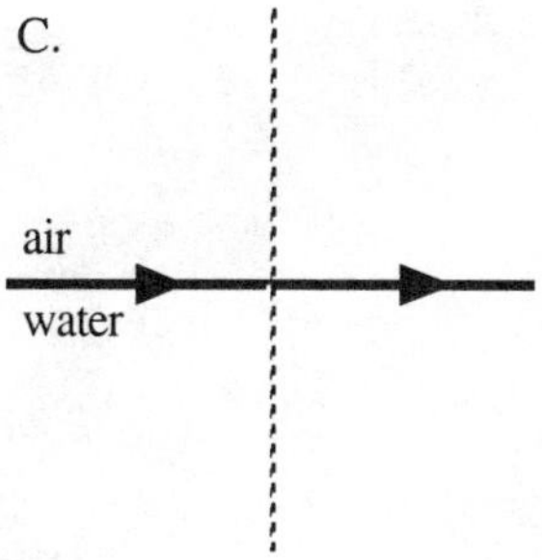

D.

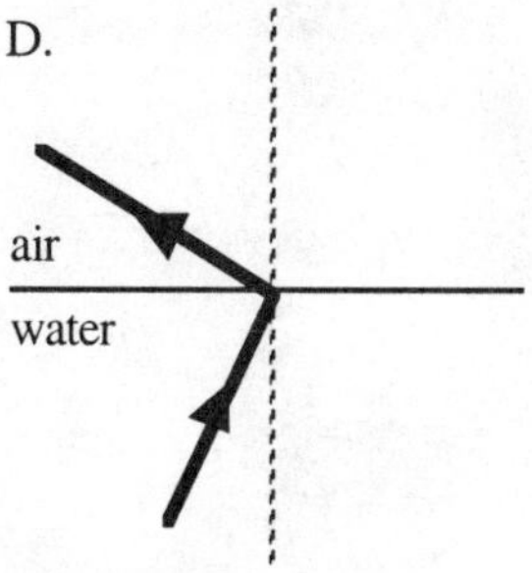

32. The student attempts to draw a conclusion from Experiments 1 and 2 that may apply to all other measurements as well. Which of the following is justified by the data?

F. Refraction angles in water are greater than those in air.
G. Refraction angles in water are less than those in air.
H. Refraction angles are equal in air and in water.
J. Refraction angles in water are equal to or less than those in air.

33. In Experiment 3, the beam travels through the water and:

A. is reflected back down from the surface of the water.
B. enters the air.
C. is absorbed completely.
D. is reflected back on itself.

34. An observer in the air attempts to see the beam of light in Experiments 2 and 3. She will:

F. be able to observe the light in each experiment, provided she is in the right place.
G. be unable to observe the light in either experiment, regardless of position.
H. be able to observe the light in Experiment 2 but not Experiment 3.
J. be able to observe the light in Experiment 3 but not Experiment 2.

35. A student attempts to summarize the results of all three experiments. Which of the following is most consistent with the observations?

A. The angle of refraction in water is less than that in air.
B. The angle of refraction in air is less than that in water.
C. The angle of refraction in water is less than or equal to that in air, but at high angles in the water, the light is reflected back into the water.
D. The angle of refraction in water is less than or equal to that in air.

GO ON TO THE NEXT PAGE

Passage VII

The table below presents the results of a study in which butterflies of different size and color were captured in flight for marking with a chemical, and then recaptured in flight a few weeks later.

SIZE	WHITE # marked	WHITE Recaptured	TAN # marked	TAN Recaptured	DARK BROWN # marked	DARK BROWN Recaptured
Small (less than 20 mm)	35	30	40	10	20	10
Medium (20–40 mm)	30	15	40	20	20	10
Large (greater than 40 mm)	50	25	60	30	30	10

36. For all sizes of butterflies, the color that seems most difficult to capture for marking is:

F. white.
G. tan.
H. dark brown.
J. Both tan and dark brown are almost equally difficult.

37. The specific type of butterfly that is easiest to recapture after being marked is:

A. between 10–20 mm and tan,
B. greater than 40 mm and tan.
C. greater than 40 mm and dark brown.
D. less than 20 mm and white.

38. Based on the information in the table, which statement best represents the relationship between a butterfly's size and its tendency to be captured for marking?

F. The larger the butterfly, the harder it is to be captured for marking.
G. The larger the butterfly, the easier it is to be captured for marking.
H. Medium-sized butterflies are consistently the easiest to capture for marking.
J. The smaller the butterfly, the easier it is to be captured for marking.

39. The chemical used to mark all the butterflies was found to be poisonous to one specific type because it was being absorbed through the wings. Based on the data in the table, which type of butterfly appears most likely to have suffered from the effects of the marking chemical?

A. Greater than 40 mm and white
B. Less than 20 mm and tan
C. Greater than 40 mm and dark brown
D. Less than 20 mm and white

40. Which conclusion is correct concerning the information in the table?

F. For tan butterflies, the proportion of individuals that are recaptured always stays the same.
G. For medium-sized butterflies, the proportion of individuals that are recaptured always stays the same.
H. For small-sized butterflies, the proportion of individuals recaptured always stay the same.
J. For all sizes of butterflies, the darker the color the easier it is to recapture an individual.

GO ON TO THE NEXT PAGE

Answer Key

DIRECTIONS: For the *correct* answers in each ACT Test Subject, check the corresponding unshaded box. (Correct answers correspond to unshaded boxes.) Then, for each test, total the number of checkmarks in each column (subject category) and add to determine the raw scores.

TEST 1: ENGLISH (p. A-114)

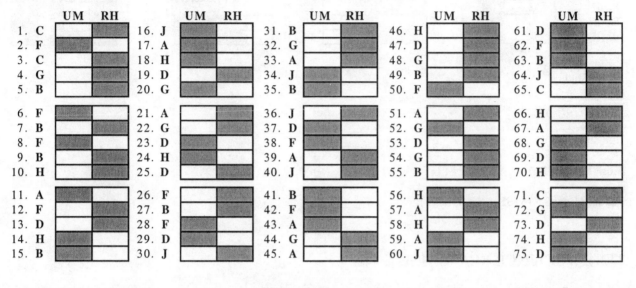

1. C	16. J	31. B	46. H	61. D
2. F	17. A	32. G	47. D	62. F
3. C	18. H	33. A	48. G	63. B
4. G	19. D	34. J	49. B	64. J
5. B	20. G	35. B	50. F	65. C
6. F	21. A	36. J	51. A	66. H
7. B	22. G	37. D	52. G	67. A
8. F	23. D	38. F	53. D	68. G
9. B	24. H	39. A	54. G	69. D
10. H	25. D	40. J	55. B	70. H
11. A	26. F	41. B	56. H	71. C
12. F	27. B	42. F	57. A	72. G
13. D	28. F	43. A	58. H	73. D
14. H	29. D	44. G	59. A	74. H
15. B	30. J	45. A	60. J	75. D

Usage/Mechanics (UM): ____/39 Rhetorical Skills (RM): ____/36 English Raw Score (UM + RH): ____/75

TEST 2: MATHEMATICS (p. A-125)

1. B	16. G	31. A	46. K
2. F	17. D	32. J	47. D
3. C	18. F	33. D	48. H
4. J	19. B	34. K	49. D
5. E	20. K	35. E	50. G
6. K	21. E	36. F	51. C
7. D	22. F	37. B	52. G
8. J	23. C	38. H	53. D
9. D	24. G	39. E	54. K
10. G	25. A	40. K	55. D
11. C	26. H	41. E	56. G
12. G	27. A	42. J	57. A
13. E	28. G	43. D	58. F
14. H	29. C	44. J	59. D
15. C	30. K	45. C	60. G

Pre-Algebra/Elementary Algebra (EA): ____/24 Intermediate Algebra/Coordinate Geometry (AG): ____/18

Plane Geometry/Trigonometry (GT): ____/18 Total Raw Score (EA + AG + GT): ____/60

TEST 3: READING (p. A-134)

#	Answer	SS	S	H	PF
1.	A			□	
2.	J			□	
3.	D			□	
4.	G			□	
5.	D			□	
6.	G			□	
7.	A			□	
8.	H			□	
9.	A			□	
10.	H			□	
11.	C				□
12.	H				□
13.	A				□
14.	H				□
15.	B				□
16.	G				□
17.	B				□
18.	J				□
19.	A				□
20.	F				□
21.	B	□			
22.	G	□			
23.	C	□			
24.	F	□			
25.	D	□			
26.	G	□			
27.	D	□			
28.	H	□			
29.	B	□			
30.	H	□			
31.	C		□		
32.	J		□		
33.	A		□		
34.	H		□		
35.	A		□		
36.	J		□		
37.	B		□		
38.	J		□		
39.	D		□		
40.	H		□		

Social Studies (SS): ____/10

Sciences (S): ____/10

Humanities (H): ____/10

Prose Fiction (PF): ____/10

Reading Raw Score (SS + S + H + PF): ____/40

TEST 4: SCIENCE REASONING (p. 141)

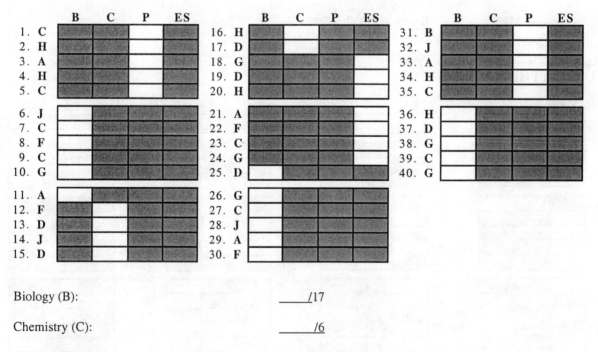

#	Answer	B	C	P	ES
1.	C			□	
2.	H			□	
3.	A			□	
4.	H			□	
5.	C			□	
6.	J	□			
7.	C	□			
8.	F	□			
9.	C	□			
10.	G	□			
11.	A	□			
12.	F		□		
13.	D		□		
14.	J		□		
15.	D		□		
16.	H		□		
17.	D		□		
18.	G				□
19.	D				□
20.	H				□
21.	A				□
22.	F				□
23.	C				□
24.	G				□
25.	D	□			
26.	G	□			
27.	C	□			
28.	J	□			
29.	A	□			
30.	F	□			
31.	B			□	
32.	J			□	
33.	A			□	
34.	H			□	
35.	C			□	
36.	H	□			
37.	D	□			
38.	G	□			
39.	C	□			
40.	G	□			

Biology (B): ____/17

Chemistry (C): ____/6

Physics (P): ____/10

Earth Science (ES): ____/7

Science Reasoning Raw Score (B + C + P + ES): ____/40

Explanatory Answers

TEST 1: ENGLISH (p. A-114)

1. (C) The original contains low-level usage. You should not use *on account of* as a substitute for *because of.* (C) makes the needed correction. (B) is wrong because *since* is a conjunction that introduces a dependent clause, but the material that follows is not a clause—it contains no verb. As for (D), although *for* can be a preposition, its meaning is not appropriate in this context.

2. (F) The sentence is correct as written. *Nonetheless* has the meaning of "in spite of this." (G) and (H) are both wrong because the author means to say that smuggling grew in spite of government efforts—not because of government efforts. Finally, as for (J), although *on the contrary* does signal an opposition, it does not have the "in spite of" meaning needed here.

3. (C) The original contains two errors. First, *timbered* is an adjective, and it takes an adverb to modify an adjective. So *heavy* should be *heavily.* Second, since *countless* is intended to modify *islands* and not *heavily timbered,* you must place a comma after *countless.* Only (C) makes both of these corrections.

4. (G) The original and (H) and (J) are not idiomatic. The correct idiom is *well founded.*

5. (B) The tense of the verb in the original is not consistent with the other verbs in the paragraph. The author is describing past events, so you should use the past tense *seized.* Although (C) and (D) can be used to refer to past actions, they have meanings that are inappropriate in this context. First, *were seizing* (the progressive form of the past tense) implies an action that continued for some time in the past, e.g., during this period, customs officials were seizing tons of wool each month. Second, *have seized* (the present perfect) implies an action that began in the past but continues into the present; e.g., the British have repeatedly seized our ships.

6. (F) The original is correct. By comparison, (G) and (J) are awkward and needlessly wordy. In choice (H), *technically* modifies *being,* whereas *technical* modifies the *violation.*

7. (B) The original contains an error of diction. *Principle* means "rule"; *principal* means "main" or "important." (C) fails to correct this problem. (D) makes the needed correction, but the verb *was* will not agree with the subject of the sentence. The subject of the sentence is a compound subject—a series of elements joined by *and*—so you have to use a plural verb.

8. (F) *In fact* signals an idea that will provide an illustration of or give special emphasis to a point that came just before. This is exactly what the author does. As for (G) and (H), these words are used to alert the reader that what follows is a continuation of an idea and that the following idea has the same status as the first idea. Thus, (G) and (H) are not suited to this sentence. Finally, as for (J), *on the contrary* signals a contrast of ideas, but the author does not intend to present contrasting ideas.

9. (B) The only conceivable role for *selling* in the original would be that of an adjective, but there is nothing for *selling* to modify. (B) corrects this problem by converting *selling* to a conjugated form. Now the sentence reads: *was smuggled...and sold.* (C) is wrong because *would be sold* is not parallel to *smuggled.* Finally, (D) suffers from the same problem as the original. There is no logical role for the infinitive *to sell* in the sentence.

10. (H) In the original, the idiom *so much...that* is never completed. (H) completes the idiom: *so much was smuggled and sold...that one....* (G) and (J) fail to complete the expression.

11. (A) The original is correct. The *although* sets up the contrast intended by the author between the ideas *settlers welcomed national control* and *they did not like the restrictions.*

12. (F) The original is correct as written. The simple past tense is consistent with the other verbs in the passage. (G) is wrong because it eliminates the only conjugated verb in the clause introduced by *although.* (H) is wrong because the tense is

inconsistent with the other tenses in the paragraph. Finally, (J) destroys the logic of the sentence.

13. (D) The original is not idiomatic—the correct idiom is *were fearful,* not *were fearing.* (D) avoids the problem by using *feared,* and the past tense is parallel to the other verb in the sentence, *wanted.* (B) fails to correct the problem of the original. (C) uses the correct idiom, but the verb *was* does not agree with the subject of the sentence, *they.*

14. (H) The original contains two errors. First, the underlined verb is in the present tense and is therefore inconsistent with the use of the past tense in the rest of the paragraph. Second, *in the losing of* is not idiomatic. More idiomatic is the phrase *in the loss of.* (H) makes both the needed corrections. (G) makes one correction but not the other. Finally, (J) uses the indicative *results.* But the indicative lacks the element of contingency "they feared that this results." You need a verb that suggests something might or might not occur: "they feared that this would result or might result."

15. (B) The passage should be arranged in chronological order. [1] should come first because it describes the first event (the opening of the customs office). [3] should come next because it describes the events that come next in time (Americans were leery of the new office). [2] should be last because it is the final development (the fears turned out to be true).

16. (J) The author does describe events, so *narrative* is a part of the passage. And the author gives a specific example of a ship that was seized: the *Beaver.* The author also gives statistics about wool. The author does not, however, quote from another source.

17. (A) The original is the best choice. The other choices are awkward and needlessly wordy.

18. (H) The original suffers from a lack of parallelism. All three verbs *can step outside, gaze,* and *can become* are governed by the *can,* so the additional *can* in the original creates a series in which the elements do not have the same form. (H) brings the third verb into line with the other two. (G) fails to provide the needed parallelism, and (J) is wrong because *becomes* does not agree in number with the subject, *anyone.*

19. (D) The original is incorrectly punctuated. The comma creates a run-on sentence. (D) solves this problem by starting a new sentence. (B) and (C) fail to solve the problem of the run-on sentence.

20. (G) The original is ambiguous. *Ending* seems to be an adjective modifying *suns,* but the author intends for *ending* to modify *island universe.* (G) corrects this problem by creating a relative clause that modifies *island universe.* (H) too creates a new clause but *ends* does not agree with the antecedent of *that,* which is *universe.* Finally, (J) suffers from the same defect as the original because ended seems to modify *suns.*

21. (A) The original is correct as written. (B) is not idiomatic. Correct English requires the use of the infinitive *to chart* in this situation, not the gerund *charting.* (C) is wrong because there is nothing for a participle like *having charted* to modify. Finally, (D) destroys the logic of the sentence.

22. (G) The verb tense of the original is wrong. The past perfect *had been made* implies that the progress was made at a time in the past completely separated from our own time. But the phrase *in the twentieth century* indicates that the author is describing an action that is still going on. The correct verb tense to show this is the present perfect. *Has been made* correctly implies that the progress began in the past and is still going on. (H) is wrong because the present tense *is made* lacks the implication of a past action. And (J), which uses the future tense, indicates that the progress has not yet been made.

23. (D) In the original, *as such* signals that the second idea is what it is by virtue of the first idea. But the Milky Way is not called the Milky Way because our solar system is a part of it. (B) and (C) also disrupt the logical connection between the two ideas. A new sentence should be used to signal the continuation of the passage development.

24. (H) The material in this sentence belongs with the material in the next paragraph. So this is the point at which a new paragraph should be started, and no new paragraph should be started at the end of the sentence. Only (G) and (J) makes the required change. (J) is wrong because *as* is used to introduce a dependent clause. The result would be a dependent clause with no supporting independent clause.

25. (D) The original is incorrect because a comma and not a semicolon must be used to separate an appositive phrase from the main part of the sentence. The semicolon is too powerful and makes a fragment out of everything that follows it here. (B) is wrong because you must mark the beginning of the phrase placed in quotation marks. (C) is wrong because *is* does not agree with *Clouds,* which is the antecedent of *which.*

26. (F) The original is correct as written. The other choices simply are not idiomatic.

27. (B) The *to* is superfluous and makes the phrasing stilted. Eliminate it. (B) and (C) both make the needed correction, but (C) is wrong because *provide* does not agree with the subject of the sentence, *galaxy*.

28. (F) The original is the best rendering. Study the other choices. You will find that they are stilted or needlessly wordy.

29. (D) The author poses the questions because they are questions about the stars that are still unanswered. He will not provide answers.

30. (J) At first, you might think that *graduated is* intended to be a verb in a phrase such as *graduated from test pilot schools.* Unfortunately, the structure of the sentence doesn't permit that reading. (J) clarifies the issue by making *graduated* a noun. Now *graduates* can function as an appositive for *pilots.* (G) and (H) are wrong because the appositive must be set off by a comma and nothing else.

31. (B) The original contains two errors. First, *were* fails to agree in number with its subject, each. Second, the use of the gerund *having* is not idiomatic. (B) corrects both of these errors. (C) fails to correct the second error. (D) corrects both errors, but the past perfect *had been required* is inconsistent with the other verbs in the paragraph.

32. (G) The original contains low-level usage. Do not use *got* to suggest the passive voice. Use some form of the verb *to be.* (G) makes the needed correction. (H) is a form of the passive voice, but the use of the past perfect is not consistent with the other verbs in the paragraph. (J) is wrong for two reasons. First, the present perfect *has been* is not consistent with the other verbs in the paragraph. Second, *has* is a singular verb, but the subject of the sentence is *seven,* a plural noun.

33. (A) The information contained in the parentheses explains why only seven astronauts were chosen. But it is not vital to the development of the passage. By placing the remark in parentheses, the author signals to the reader that the information is not vital.

34. (J) The original contains a comma splice. (J) corrects the problem of the run-on sentence by starting a new sentence. Neither (G) nor (H) addresses the problem.

35. (B) The second paragraph introduces the topic of failures. (B) provides a good transition by signaling the reader that this will be the topic of the paragraph.

36. (J) The original uses the "ubiquitous they." *They* has no referent. (H) and (J), but not (G), correct the error. However, the usage of *fortunately* is not correct in (H) and (J).

37. (D) The original is needlessly wordy as you can see by comparing it to (D).

38. (F) The author means to say that the failure did not have particularly significant consequences. By using the word *spectacular* to describe the incident, the author is saying "Yes, we made a boo-boo."

39. (A) The original is correct. You need to use an adverb, such as *relatively,* when you modify an adjective, such as *simple*.

40. (J) The underlined verb is not parallel to the other verb to which it is joined: *to ignite* and *shutting down.* (J) corrects the problem: *to ignite and then to shut down*. Neither (G) (*to ignite and then will shut down*) nor (H) (*to ignite and then they shut down*) solves the problem. And (H) suffers from the further defect that *they* doesn't have a referent.

41. (B) This is another example of irony. The rocket was never really launched. The quotation marks signal that the author is using the word *flight* in a non-standard way.

42. (F) The original is correct as written. You should begin a new paragraph here because the author is taking up a new topic. (The passage switches from a discussion of failures in the problem to a discussion of animals in flight.) Because you need a new paragraph, (G), (H), and (J) are wrong.

43. (A) In general, the most concise wording is probably correct. Here it is the original. The other choices are stilted and needlessly wordy.

44. (G) The verb tense of the original is wrong. *Delay* and *leak* belong to the same time frame, so both should be in the same tense.

45. (A) The original is correct. None of the other suggested positions for *unharmed* are idiomatic.

46. (H) *Returning* is not a conjugated verb and therefore cannot be the main verb in a sentence. All three choices supply conjugated verbs, but (H) is the only tense that is consistent with the other verbs in the paragraph.

47. (D) The question mentioned was, at the time, still unanswered. So the choice of verb should reflect that: *could be the case.*

48. (G) The *like* in the original is both superfluous and not idiomatic. (G) corrects the error by eliminating the extra word. (H) and (J) are not idiomatic.

49. (B) The original contains an error of grammar: *longer flights would require that astronauts to have.* The infinitive, however, cannot be the verb for the subject *astronauts.* Instead, you need a conjugated verb. Each of the alternatives supplies a conjugated verb form, but only (B) is consistent with the rest of the sentence. (C) is wrong because the past perfect *had had* suggests a sequence of events that is not supported by the meaning of the sentence. And (D) is wrong because the sentence now reads: *would require that the astronauts are sure to have.*

50. (F) The author emphasizes the successes of the program and downplays its failures. (F) best summarizes this development.

51. (A) The original is correct as written. (B) makes two mistakes. First, it leaves out an essential comma. You must mark the end of the aside begun with *in.* Second, *of* introduces a prepositional phrase that has nothing to modify. (C) is wrong because it fails to mark the close of the aside. And (D) is wrong because *of helping* is not idiomatic.

52. (G) The original is needlessly wordy. *And* and *also* mean the same thing, so you should not use them both. (G) solves this problem by substituting *as well as,* a phrase which also means *and.* (H) is wrong because *with* does not have a meaning that is appropriate in this context. And (J) is wrong because *as opposed to* signals a contrast between two ideas that is not suggested by the content of the sentence.

53. (D) The verb tense of the original is inconsistent with that of the other verb in the sentence: *aided* and *had been emerging.* You should use the simple past: *aided* and *emerged.* Only (D) makes the needed correction.

54. (G) The original is incorrect because the *was enjoying* does not agree with the subject of the sentence, which is *aspects.* (G) makes the needed correction. (H) and (J) are wrong because they are singular, not plural.

55. (B) The original is not idiomatic. The correct idiom is *not only this but that.* (B) supplies the correct idiom. (C) is wrong because *not only this consequently that* is not idiomatic. As for (D), although it supplies the correct idiom, it also contains two errors. First, the comma following *but* illogically disrupts the idiom. Second, the verb *would have* is inconsistent with the other verb in the sentence.

56. (H) The original doesn't contain any grievous errors. You probably should have a comma following *treatment* because the two clauses joined there are fairly long. Additionally, *also* is redundant of *and.* But the main thing that is wrong with the original is excessive wordiness. (H) expresses the thought more concisely, so (H) is a better choice. (G) is wrong because the *but* illogically signals a contrast where none is intended. And (J) destroys the parallelism of the sentence: *the doctor could select and can mitigate.*

57. (A) The original is correct as written. (B) and (C) use inappropriate verb forms: *require that something was available* and *require that something is available.* (The technical explanation for this is that it is one of the last vestiges in English of the subjunctive.) (D) is wrong because *as* does not have the meaning of *to.*

58. (H) The original is wrong because the present tense *presupposes* conflicts with the other past tense verbs in the paragraph. Although (G) also makes the correction, the passive voice is needlessly indirect. (H) makes the same correction and is more concise.

59. (A) The original is correct as written. A new paragraph is required here because the author is taking up a new topic (a discussion of a particular doctor). Therefore, (B) and (D) are wrong. As for (C), *since* is a subordinate conjunction and is used to introduce a dependent clause. The resulting construction would be a dependent clause with no supporting independent clause.

60. (J) The first three paragraphs are a general discussion of medical advances in the nineteenth century. The last two paragraphs are a discussion of a particular advance. The first sentence of the fourth paragraph sets the stage for this transition.

61. (D) The original and (B) and (C) are needlessly wordy. Notice that (D) clearly conveys the idea.

62. (F) The original is correct as written. A new paragraph should not be started here because the following material continues the discussion about Dr. Beaumont. Therefore, (G) and (H) are wrong. (J) is wrong because it is awkward. (Compare the wording of (J) with the more direct wording of the original.)

63. (B) The original is grammatically correct, but the *but* signals a contrast that is inappropriate. The second clause explains the outcome of the first clause. (B) solves this problem. (C) is wrong because the resulting construction would be a comma splice. Finally, (D) is not grammatically incorrect (you could begin a new sentence), but the *but* is out of place.

64. (J) The original suffers from faulty parallelism. The verb *describe* has the same function in the sentence as the verb *demonstrate,* so they should have parallel forms. Only (J) makes the needed correction. The verb forms of (G) and (H) would not create the needed parallelism.

65. (C) The original contains an error of pronoun usage. *Him* refers to *babies.* (C) makes the needed correction by using the plural *them.* (B) and (D) are wrong because, among other things, they use singular pronouns.

66. (H) The original is not idiomatic. The correct idiom is *endowed with.* As for (J), although *endowed by* is idiomatic, it is not appropriate here. It would be used in a different way: *...endowed by their Creator with certain inalienable rights.*

67. (A) The original is correct as written. Although it is not necessary to start a new sentence here, it is acceptable to do so. The other choices, however, are not acceptable. (B) and (C) both create run-on sentences. And (D) destroys the logical structure of the sentence. You need two occurrences of *it,* one to be the object of *hears* and the other to function as the subject of the second clause.

68. (G) In the original, *including* illogically implies that an emotional reaction is a kind of biological reaction. The original intends to state, however, that an infant's cry causes two parallel reactions, one biological and the other emotional. Only a word like *and* will do the trick.

69. (D) The word *unfortunately* has a meaning that is not appropriate here. The last sentence of the paragraph is intended by the author to be a conclusion that is proved by the earlier part of the paragraph: the infant does this and that, *therefore* he is in possession of certain attributes. The *in fact* conveys this idea and adds a special emphasis.

70. (H) The original is needlessly indirect and wordy. (H) comes directly to the point and is more concise. (G), too, is concise, but (G) uses a verb tense that is inconsistent with the other verbs in the paragraph. Finally, (J), like the original, is too wordy. Further, the verb *are* would not agree with the singular subject of the sentence.

71. (C) In English, we sometimes use the present progressive to give special emphasis to an idea: *But Mom, I am doing my homework!* But nothing suggests that the author would want special emphasis here. (C) corrects the problem by using the simple present tense, which is the same tense used for the other verbs. (B) is wrong because the past tense is out of place. (D) is wrong because the subject of *guarantee* is *that,* which in turn refers to the singular *collection.*

72. (G) Although *whether or not* is a perfectly good English idiom, its use here is not idiomatic. The first *whether* in the sentence has set up the comparison: *whether* this or *whether* that. (G) makes the needed correction. (H) and (J) are wrong because *whether if* is not idiomatic.

73. (D) *Although* introduces a long and complex dependent clause that ends with the period. The original is wrong because the dependent clause isn't attached to an independent clause. (D) makes the needed correction.

74. (H) The final sentence serves to summarize in an emphatic way the point the author has been laboring to prove: the newborn infant is not a passive creature.

75. (D) The passage is clearly an argument. The author is trying to persuade the reader that the newborn infant is not a passive creature. And the author uses examples of behavior to prove this point.

TEST 2: MATHEMATICS (p. A-125)

1. (B) Perform the indicated operation: $5.75 - 4.5 = 1.25$.

2. (F) The product of 4 times x is written as $4x$. And 3 less than that would be $4x - 3$.

3. (C) This question really just tests fractions. If $\frac{3}{4}$ of x equals 36, then: $\frac{3}{4}(x) = 36 \Rightarrow x = 36 \cdot \frac{4}{3} = 48$ and $\frac{1}{3}$ of 48 is 16.

4. (J) The measure of the unlabeled angle in the triangle on the right is 90°. The angle vertically opposite it in the right triangle on the left is also equal to 0°. Therefore: $x + y + 90 = 180$ and $x + y = 90$.

5. (E) There are two ways to attack this question. One is to reason that:
   A. $2 + n$ cannot be a multiple of 3. Since n is a multiple of 3, when $2 + n$ is divided by 3 there will be a remainder of 2.
   B. $2 - n$ cannot be a multiple of 3 for the same reason that $2 + n$ cannot be a multiple of 3.
   C. $2n - 1$ cannot be a multiple of 3. Since n is a multiple of 3, $2n$ will also be a multiple of 3, and $2n - 1$ cannot be a multiple of 3.
   D. $2n + 1$ cannot be a multiple for the same reason that $2n - 1$ cannot be a multiple of 3.
   E. $2n + 3$ is a multiple of 3. $2n$ is a multiple of 3; 3 is a multiple of 3; so $2n + 3$ is a multiple of 3.

   You can reach the same conclusion just by substituting an assumed value into the choices. Assuming that $n = 3$,

   A. $2 + n = 2 + 3 = 5$ (Not a multiple of 3.)
   B. $2 - n = 2 - 3 = -1$ (Not a multiple of 3.)
   C. $2n - 1 = 2(3) - 1 = 6 - 1 = 5$ (Not a multiple of 3.)
   D. $2n + 1 = 2(3) + 1 = 6 + 1 = 7$ (Not a multiple of 3.)
   E. $2n + 3 = 2(3) + 3 = 6 + 3 = 9$ (A multiple of 3.)

6. (K) Remember that a ratio is just another way of writing a fraction. So just inspect each of the answer choices. As for (F), $(\frac{1}{5})^2$ is equal to $\frac{1}{25}$, and both 1 and 25 are whole numbers. As for (G), $\frac{1}{5}$ is the ratio of 1 to 5, so (G) is not the correct choice. As for (H), 0.20 is equal to $\frac{1}{5}$, the ratio of two whole numbers. And 5 percent can be written as $\frac{5}{100}$, or $\frac{1}{20}$. Finally, $\sqrt{5}$ is not a whole number, so the expression in (K) is not the ratio of two whole numbers.

7. (D) If you know the area of a square, you can find its perimeter, and vice versa. Area = side • side $= 16 \Rightarrow s^2 = 16 \Rightarrow s = \pm 4$. Distances are always positive. Therefore, the perimeter is equal to $4s$, or $4 \bullet 4 = 16$.

8. (J) Here you have one equation with two variables. It's not possible to solve for x or y individually, but you don't need to. Just rewrite the equation so that you have it in the form $x + y$: $12 + x = 36 - y \Rightarrow x + y = 36 - 12 = 24$.

9. (D) The coefficients are 3, 6, and 2, and 1 is the only common factor of those numbers. The smallest term containing the variable x is simply x. So the greatest factor of those terms is just x. The same is true for the terms containing y and z. So the greatest common factor is xyz.

10. (G) Again, here is a problem for which there is a standard math approach and the Cambridge test-prep approach. You analyze the problem as follows: the sum of $3k$, $4k$, $5k$, $6k$, and $7k$ is $25k$, a number that will be divisible by 7. If, however, the coefficient of k were divisible by 7, then that number would be divisible by 7 regardless of the value of k. If we drop the term $4k$ from the group, the sum of the remaining terms is $21k$. Since 21 is divisible by 7, $21k$ will be divisible by 7 regardless of the value of k.

11. (C) Don't try to convert each of these fractions to decimals to find the value that lies between $\frac{1}{3}$ and $\frac{3}{8}$. Instead, find an escape route. Use a benchmark, approximate, or use whatever else is available.

    First, eliminate (A), because $\frac{1}{2}$ is more than $\frac{3}{8}$. Next eliminate (B). $\frac{3}{15}$ is equal to $\frac{1}{3}$, so $\frac{3}{16}$ is smaller than $\frac{1}{3}$. (A larger denominator makes for a smaller fraction given the same numerator). (C) is close to and slightly less than $\frac{18}{48}$, which is $\frac{3}{8}$. So (C) is the correct choice. But let's finish the line of reasoning. As for (D), $\frac{9}{24}$ is equal to

$\frac{3}{8}$, not less than $\frac{3}{8}$. Finally, $\frac{5}{12}$ is equal to $\frac{10}{24}$, and $\frac{3}{8}$ is equal to $\frac{9}{24}$.

12. (G) By this point in your study you should almost automatically factor the expression $x^2 - y^2$ into $(x + y)(x - y)$. Since $(x - y) = 3$, $(x + y)(3) = 3$, so $x + y = 1$.

13. (E) You can reason this out mathematically. As for (A), whether $n + 1$ is odd or even will depend on whether n is odd or even. The same is true for (B) and (C), because whether $3n$ is odd or even will depend on whether n is odd or even. As for (D), n^2 will be odd or even depending on whether n is odd or even. But (E) is even regardless of whether n is odd or even. If n is even, then the expression $n^2 + n$ is equal to an even number times itself plus itself, which is an even number. And if n is odd, the expression is equal to an odd number times an odd number, which is an odd number, plus an odd number, and the sum of two odd numbers is even.

14. (H) Since the square has an area of 16, it has a side of 4 and a diagonal of $4\sqrt{2}$. The diagonal of the square is also the diameter of the circle. So the circle has a diameter of $4\sqrt{2}$ and a radius of $2\sqrt{2}$. Finally, a circle with a radius of length $2\sqrt{2}$ has an area of $\pi r^2 = \pi(2\sqrt{2})^2 = 8\pi$.

15. (C) First, calculate the sale price: \$120 – (25% of \$120) = \$120 – (0.25 • \$120) = \$120 – \$30 = \$90. Next, calculate the sales tax: Tax = 8% of \$90 = 0.08 • \$90 = \$7.20. So the total price was \$90 + \$7.20 = \$97.20.

16. (G) Use the "this-of-that" formula. The "of that," which forms the denominator of the fraction, is mixture. How much of the mixture is there? 2.5 + 12.5 = 15. So 15 is the denominator of the fraction, and the other number in the problem (the "this"), is the numerator: $\frac{2.5}{15} = \frac{1}{6}$. And $\frac{1}{6}$ is one of the common fraction/decimal equivalents you were encouraged to memorize. Don't divide; just convert by memory: $\frac{1}{6} = 0.16\frac{2}{3} = 16\frac{2}{3}\%$.

17. (D) The triangle has sides of 6, 8, and 10, which you should recognize as multiples of 3, 4, and 5. So the triangle is a right triangle. The sides of 6 and 8 form the right angle, so they can be used as altitude and base for finding the area: Area $= \frac{1}{2}$ • altitude • base $= \frac{1}{2} \cdot 6 \cdot 8 = 24$.

18. (F) Proportions make this calculation easy. First do the calculation for Motorcycle X: $\frac{\text{Fuel Used } X}{\text{Fueld Used } Y} = \frac{\text{Miles Driven } X}{\text{Miles Driven } Y}$. The X and Y here refer to the two different situations, not the motorcycles. Therefore: $\frac{1}{x} = \frac{40}{300} \Rightarrow 300 = 40x \Rightarrow 40x = 300 \Rightarrow x = 7.5$. So Motorcycle X uses 7.5 liters of fuel for the 300-mile trip. Now do the same for Motorcycle Y: $\frac{1}{x} = \frac{50}{300} \Rightarrow 300 = 50x \Rightarrow 50x = 300 \Rightarrow x = 6$. So Motorcycle Y uses 6 liters of fuel for the trip. Since Motorcycle X uses 7.5 – 6 = 1.5 liters more than Motorcycle Y, the fuel for Motorcycle X costs 1.5 • \$2 = \$3 more.

19. (B) First, substitute 3 for x: $f(3) = 3^2 - 2(3) + 1 = 9 - 6 + 1 = 4$. Now substitute 4 for x: $f(4) = 4^2 - 2(4) + 1 = 16 - 8 + 1 = 9$. So $f(f(3)) = 9$.

20. (K) You can factor $6k + 3$: $6k + 3 = 3(2k + 1)$. Or, substitute 1 for k into the choices. The correct one yields the value 9: (K) $6k + 3 = 6(1) + 3 = 6 + 3 = 9$.

21. (E) You can devise the formula as follows. The formula will be x, the cost for the first ounce, plus some expression to represent the additional postage for each additional ounce over the first ounce. The postage for the additional weight is y cents per ounce, and the additional weight is w minus the first ounce, or $w - 1$. So the additional postage is $y(w - 1)$, and the total postage is $x + y(w - 1)$.

You can reach the same conclusion by assuming some numbers to be substituted into the answer choices. Make the ridiculous assumption that the first ounce costs 1 cent and every additional ounce is free. If $x = 1$ and $y = 0$, then a letter, of say, 10 ounces ($w = 10$) will cost 1 cent. Substitute 1 for x, zero for y, and 10 for w into the choices. The correct formula will generate the value 1. Even on these silly assumptions, you can eliminate every choice but (D) and (E). Make another set of assumptions and you'll have the correct answer.

22. (F) Just do the calculation. Since $|-3| = 3$ and $|-\frac{1}{2}| = \frac{1}{2}$: $|-3| \bullet |2| \bullet |-\frac{1}{2}| + |-4| = 3 \bullet 2 \bullet \frac{1}{2} - 4 = 3 - 4 = -1$.

23. (C) The side of the square is also the radius of the circle. Since the square has an area of 2, its side is: $s \bullet s = 2 \Rightarrow s^2 = 2 \Rightarrow s = \sqrt{2}$. And $\sqrt{2}$ is the radius of the circle. So the area of the circle is $\pi r^2 = \pi(\sqrt{2})^2 = 2\pi$.

24. (G) Test each statement. As for statement (I), 2 is the first prime number, and the product of 2 and any other number must be even. So (I) is not part of the correct answer. As for (II), the sum of two prime numbers might be odd, e.g.; $2 + 3 = 5$, but the sum of two prime numbers might also be even, e.g., $3 + 5 = 8$. As for (III), however, the product of two odd numbers is necessarily odd.

25. (A) The coordinates establish that this figure is a rectangle. The width of the rectangle is a, and the length is $b - a$. So the area is $a(b - a)$. You can also assume values and get the same result. Assume that $a = 2$ and $b = 4$. The rectangle has a width of 2; a length of $4 - 2 = 2$; and an area of $2 \bullet 2 = 4$. Substitute 2 for a and 4 for b into the formulas in the answer choices and the correct formula will yield 4.

26. (H) Do the operations: $\sqrt{(43 - 7)(29 + 7)} = \sqrt{(36)(36)} = 36$.

27. (A) Set up a direct proportion: $\frac{\text{Cement } X}{\text{Cement } Y} = \frac{\text{Grit } X}{\text{Grit } Y} \Rightarrow \frac{4}{50} = \frac{20}{x} \Rightarrow 4x = (20)(50) \Rightarrow x = \frac{(20)(50)}{4} = 250$.

28. (G) Let's label the other two angles in the triangle:

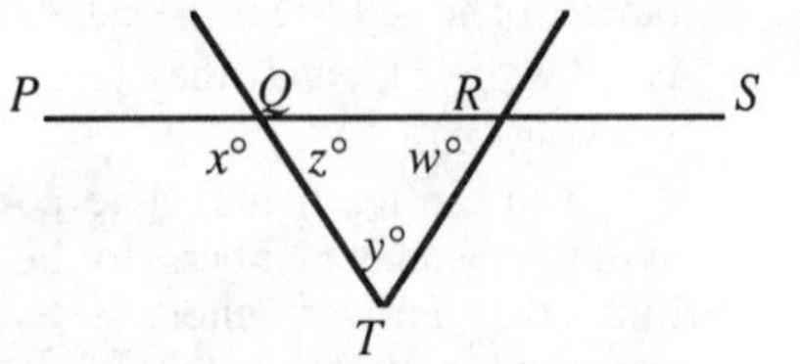

$x + z = 180 \Rightarrow 120 + z = 180 \Rightarrow z = 60$; $z + w + y = 180$. And since $QT = QR$, $y = w$. $60 + y + y = 180 \Rightarrow 2y = 120 \Rightarrow y = 60$.

29. (C) You have only one equation but two variables, so you cannot solve for x and y individually. Instead, look for a way to rewrite the first equation to give you the information you need: $\frac{x}{y} = -1 \Rightarrow x = -y \Rightarrow x + y = 0$.

30. (K) Don't do lengthy calculations. Set up the cost of each fabric as a fraction and compare the fraction directly using a benchmark:

F. $\frac{8}{3}$

G. $\frac{6}{2} = 3$

H. $\frac{9}{4}$

J. $\frac{7}{5}$

K. $\frac{4}{6}$

(K), $\frac{4}{6}$, is less than 1. The other fractions are greater than 1. So (K) is the smallest.

31. (A) Since $PQ \parallel ST$, the "big angle/little angle? theorem establishes that $x = y$. So if we find the value of x, we have found the value of y. $75 + 65 + x + x = 180 \Rightarrow 2x + 140 = 180 \Rightarrow 2x = 40 \Rightarrow x = 20$. So $y = 20$.

32. (J) $\frac{10^3(10^5 + 10^5)}{10^4} = \frac{10(10^4 + 10^4)}{10} = 2(10^4)$.

33. (D) Factor and solve for x: $x^2 - 5x + 4 = 0 \Rightarrow (x - 4)(x - 1) = 0$. So either $x - 4 = 0$ and $x = 4$, or $x - 1 = 0$ and $x = 1$.

Alternatively, you could substitute the values in the choices back into the equation until you found the set that works.

34. (K) Use the method for finding the missing elements of an average. The smallest possible sum for six different positive integers is $1 + 2 + 3 + 4 + 5 + 6 = 21$. The sum of all 7 integers is $7 \bullet 12 = 84$. So the largest the seventh number could be (and the average of the seven numbers still be 12) is $84 - 21 = 63$.

35. (E) To find b in terms of x and y, you will first need to set b equal to x and equal to y:

$x = b + 4$ $\quad$ $y = b - 3$

$x - 4 = b$ $\quad$ $y + 3 = b$

Now combine the two equations by adding:

$b = x - 4$

$+\ b = y + 3$

$2b = x + y - 1$

So $b = \frac{x + y - 1}{2}$.

You can arrive at the same conclusion by substituting some numbers. Let $b = 1$. Then $x = 1 + 4 = 5$, and $y = 1 - 3 = -2$. Substitute 5 for x and -2 for y into the answer choices. The correct choice will yield the value 1.

36. (F) Since $z = 5x = 3y$, and x, y, and z are integers, z is a multiple of both 3 and 5, so z is evenly divisible by 5, 3, and 15. And z is divisible by both x and y individually, but z is not necessarily divisible by the product of x and y. Finally, since $5x = 3y$, and x and y are integers, x is a multiple of 3 (and evenly divisible by 3).

You can reach the same conclusion by substituting some numbers. The most natural assumption is to let $z = 15$, so $x = 3$ and $y = 5$. But on that assumption, every answer choice is an integer. So try the next multiple of 15. Let $z = 30$, so $x = 6$ and $y = 10$. Now (F) is no longer an integer: $30 \div (6 \bullet 10) = \frac{1}{2}$.

37. (B) You can solve the problem by using the formula for finding the area of a rectangle: area of rectangle = width • length ⇒ $48x^2 = w(24x) \Rightarrow w = \frac{48x^2}{24x} = 2x$.

You can reach the same conclusion by substituting numbers. Assume that $x = 2$. Then the area of the rectangle is $48(2^2) = 48(4) = 192$, and the length is 48. So 48 times the width is equal to 192, and the widths $192 \div 48 = 4$. So if $x = 2$, the correct choice will yield the value 4. Only choice (B) works.

38. (H) You can deduce the value for x in the following way. The length of the base of the triangle is $4x - x = 3x$, and the length of the altitude is $3x - 0 = 3x$ (the difference in the y coordinate). Now use the formula for finding the area of a triangle: $\frac{1}{2}(3x)(3x) = 54 \Rightarrow (3x)(3x) = 108 \Rightarrow 9x^2 = 108 \Rightarrow x^2 = 12 \Rightarrow x = \sqrt{12} = 2\sqrt{3}$.

39. (E) Rewrite the equation: $x = \frac{1}{y+1} \Rightarrow x(y + 1) = 1 \Rightarrow y + 1 = \frac{1}{x} \Rightarrow y = \frac{1}{x} - 1 \Rightarrow y = \frac{1-x}{x}$.

40. (K) This question is a little tricky, but it doesn't require any advanced mathematics. If the room were completely dark and you were in a hurry to make sure you got at least one pair of each color, how many socks would you need to pull from the drawer? Well, what's the worst thing that might happen? You could pull 6 blue socks first. You might pull all 10 white socks on the next 10 tries. So far you have only white socks and blue socks, and you have pulled 16 socks. Now there is nothing left in the drawer but green socks. So on the worst assumption, 18 picks will guarantee you a pair of each color.

41. (E) The question stem supplies the area of the shaded part of the figure, which is a portion of the circle. Find what fraction of the circle is shaded, and you can find the value of the unshaded angle at the center of the circle. The area of the entire circle is $\pi r^2 = \pi(4^2) = 16\pi$. So $\frac{14\pi}{16} = \frac{7}{8}$ of the circle is shaded. $\frac{1}{8}$ is unshaded. So the unshaded angle at the circle's center is $\frac{1}{8}$ of $360° = 45°$. Now find x: $x + 45 + 90 = 180 \Rightarrow x + 135 = 180 \Rightarrow x = 45$.

42. (J) This is a composite figure. You will be able to redefine one figure in terms of another. Generally speaking, the diameter of the smaller circle is equal to the side of the square. And the diagonal of the square is the diameter of the larger circle.

Let r be the radius of the smaller circle, so the smaller circle has an area of πr^2. The diameter of the smaller circle is $2r$, which is also the side of the square:

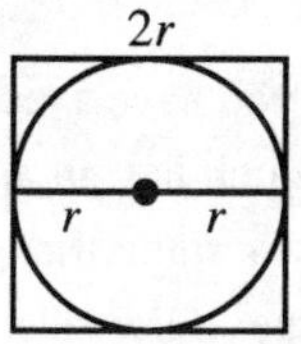

The diagonal of the square creates a 45°-45°-90° triangle with the sides of the square. The hypotenuse of that triangle is equal to the side $s\sqrt{2}$. So the diagonal of the square is equal to $2r \bullet \sqrt{2} = 2\sqrt{2}r$. This is also the diameter of the larger circle. So the larger circle has a radius of $2\sqrt{2}r \div 2 = \sqrt{2}r$, and an area of $\pi(\sqrt{2}r)^2 = 2\pi r^2$. So the ratio is $2\pi r^2 : \pi r^2 = 2:1$ or $\frac{2}{1}$.

43. (D) Just perform the indicated operations:

$2^0 = 1$

$2^3 = 8$

$2^{-2} = \frac{1}{2^2} = \frac{1}{4}$

$1 + 8 - \frac{1}{4} = 8\frac{3}{4}$

44. (J) Since the axis of symmetry of the parabola is given by the equation $x = 0$, the parabola is symmetric about the y-axis. The point symmetric to the point with coordinates

(−1, −2) will have the same y-coordinate, and the x-coordinate of the point will be the same distance from the y-axis but in a positive direction: (1, −2). You might better be able to find the solution if you sketch a graph of the equation:

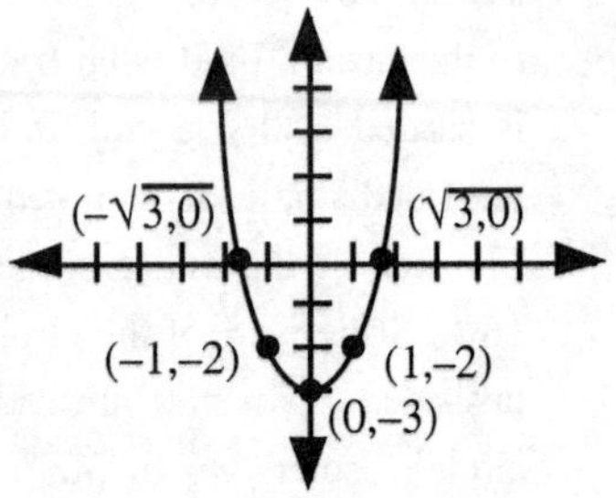

45. (C) If two lines in the coordinate plane are perpendicular to each other, then the product of their slopes is −1.

46. (K) Draw some additional lines to carve the figure up into some more familiar shapes.

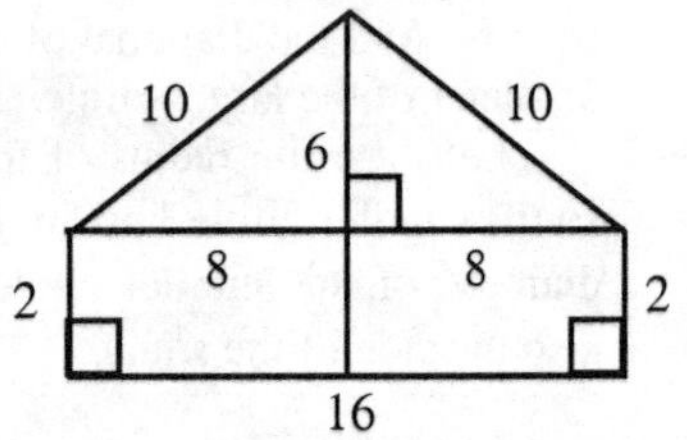

Now you have a rectangle with sides of 2 and 16, which has an area of 2 • 16 = 32. And the two right triangles have sides of 8 and 10, the third side is 6. Using 6 as the altitude of the triangle and 16 as the base, the area of the triangle is $\frac{1}{2} \bullet 6 \bullet 16 = 48$. So the area of the composite figure is 32 + 48 = 80.

47. (D) Rationalize the denominator: $\frac{\sqrt{x}}{2\sqrt{x}-\sqrt{y}} \bullet \frac{2\sqrt{x}+\sqrt{y}}{2\sqrt{x}+\sqrt{y}} = \frac{2x+\sqrt{xy}}{4x+2\sqrt{xy}-2\sqrt{xy}-y} = \frac{2x+\sqrt{xy}}{4x-y}$.

Alternatively, you could have assumed some values for x and y. Since the problem involves square roots, pick a couple of perfect squares, e.g., $x = 9$ and $y = 4$. The expression in the question stem becomes: $\frac{\sqrt{9}}{2\sqrt{9}-\sqrt{4}} = \frac{3}{2(3)-2} = \frac{3}{4}$. Now we substitute 9 for x and 4 for y into the answer choices. The correct choice will generate value $\frac{3}{4}$.

A. $\frac{2\sqrt{x}-\sqrt{y}}{2} = \frac{2\sqrt{9}-\sqrt{4}}{2} = \frac{2(3)-2}{2} = 2$ X

B. $\frac{2\sqrt{x}+\sqrt{y}}{4xy} = \frac{2\sqrt{9}+\sqrt{4}}{4(9)(4)} = \frac{2(3)+2}{144} = \frac{8}{144}$ X

C. $\frac{2\sqrt{x}+\sqrt{xy}}{2x-y} = \frac{2\sqrt{9}+\sqrt{(9)(4)}}{2(9)-4} = \frac{18+6}{14} = \frac{24}{14}$ X

D. $\frac{2x+\sqrt{xy}}{4x-y} = \frac{2(9)+\sqrt{(9)(4)}}{4(9)-4} = \frac{18+6}{32} = \frac{24}{32} = \frac{3}{4}$ √

E. $\frac{4x+\sqrt{xy}}{4x-y} = \frac{4(9)+\sqrt{(9)(4)}}{4(9)-4} = \frac{36+6}{36-4} = \frac{42}{32}$ X

48. (H) Here is one of those geometry questions that requires you to use given information to deduce some further conclusions: Since we have parallel lines l_1 and l_2, and since opposite angles are equal, we deduce:

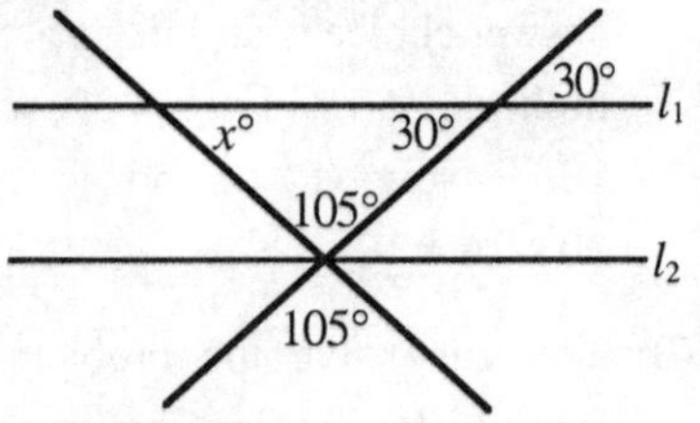

Now we have a triangle with angles 30, 105, and x: $30 + 105 + x = 180 \Rightarrow x = 45$.

49. (D) The graph intersects the y-axis where $x = 0$: $y = 2 \cos 2(0) + 2 = 2 \cos 0 + 2$. Since $\cos 0 = 1$: $y = 2(1) + 2 = 4$.

50. (G) This is a fairly typical "shaded area" question. The shaded area will be the whole square minus the four circles: Shaded Area = □ − (4 • ○). The entire solution statement is: Shaded Area/Square. On the assumption that each circle has a radius of r, the side of the square must be $4r$, and the area of the square is $4r \bullet 4r = 16r^2$. This is the denominator of our solution statement, and it is also an element in our calculation of the shaded area. To complete our calculation of the shaded area, we reason that each circle with radius r has an area of πr^2. So: Shaded area: $16r^2 - 4\pi r^2$. Filling in the solution statement: $\frac{16r^2 - 4\pi r^2}{16r^2} = \frac{4r^2(4-\pi)}{16r^2} = \frac{4-\pi}{4}$.

You should also note that a little common sense goes a long way when applied to the answer choices. We can see from the figure that the shaded area is only about a fifth of the entire square. Yet, (H) asserts that the shaded area is about three-quarters of the area of the square—and (J) and (K) are even larger. In fact, both (J) and (K) are greater than 1, asserting that the shaded area is larger than the square, an absurd conclusion. As for (F), since π is less than 4, (F) is a negative number, and that too is impossible. So common sense goes all the way to solve this problem without having to use the algebraic approach above.

51. (C) One of the Pythagorean Identities is: $\sin^2 \theta + \cos^2 \theta = 1$. Therefore, the expression given in the question stem is equivalent to $\frac{1}{\sin \theta}$. And the reciprocal identity for the sine function is the cosecant function.

Alternatively, you could "get back to the basics." Assume that θ is an acute angle opposite of side a. The other side in the triangle is b, and the hypotenuse is c:

$$\frac{\sin^2 \theta + \cos^2 \theta}{\sin \theta} = \frac{\left(\frac{a}{c}\right)^2 + \left(\frac{b}{c}\right)^2}{\frac{a}{c}} = \frac{\frac{a^2}{c^2} + \frac{b^2}{c^2}}{\frac{a}{c}} = \frac{\frac{a^2 + b^2}{c^2}}{\frac{a}{c}}$$

Since the triangle is a right triangle, $a^2 + b^2 = c^2$:

$$\frac{\frac{c^2}{c^2}}{\frac{a}{c}} = \frac{1}{\frac{a}{c}} = \frac{c}{a}$$

And $\frac{c}{a} = \csc \theta$.

52. (G) $\tan \angle CAB = \frac{\text{opp}}{\text{hyp}} = \frac{6}{AC}$. $1.4 \approx \frac{6}{AC} \Rightarrow AC \approx \frac{6}{1.4} \approx 4.28$.

Alternatively, you could have used your answer sheet to create a ruler. On the edge of a sheet of a paper, mark the distance from BC. That is equal to 6 units. Now divide that distance approximately in half, and compare that to the length of AC. The distance from A to C is more than 3 units but less than 6 units, so (G) is the best answer.

53. (D) When $x = 1$, $x - 1 = 0$, so the entire expression is undefined. Similarly, when $x = -2$, $x + 2$ is 0, and the expression is undefined. When $x = -3$, then $x + 3$ is equal to 0, so the value of the expression is 0.

54. (K) Since the sum of x and y is less than or equal to 6, y will have its maximum value when x has its minimum value. The minimum value for x is 0; therefore, the maximum value of y is 6. And $3(6) = 18$.

Alternatively, you could have tested choices. Since you are looking for the maximum value for y, start with the largest choice—18. If $3y = 18$, then $y = 6$. And: $x + y \le 6 \Rightarrow x + 6 \le 6 \Rightarrow x \le 0$. Since x can be 0, $y = 6$ satisfies the system of inequalities. And since 18 is the largest value available in the choices, we know it must be the largest value possible for $3y$.

55. (D) Find the corresponding values for y:
$y = |(-1)^2 - 3| = |1 - 3| = |-2| = 2$
$y = |(0)^2 - 3| = |-3| = 3$
$y = |(1)^2 - 3| = |1 - 3| = |-2| = 2$
(D) is the correct plotting of the points $(-1, 2)$, $(0, 3)$, and $(1, 2)$.

56. (G) We want to create an equation of the form $y = mx + b$, where m is the slope of the line and b the y-intercept. Begin by calculating the slope: $m = \frac{(-2) + (-4)}{(2) - (-1)} = \frac{-6}{3} = -2$. Therefore: $y = -2x + b$. Now use one of the pairs of coordinates provided in the graph: $4 = -2(-1) + b \Rightarrow 4 = 2 + b \Rightarrow b = 2$.

57. (A) There are at least three different ways of attacking this problem, but one method is clearly superior to the other two. First, you could use the roots to create the equation. If $x = a$ or $x = b$, then $x - a = 0$ or $x - b = 0$. So the factors of the equation are $(x - a)$ and $(x - b)$, and the equation is: $(x - a)(x - b) = x^2 - ax - bx + ab = 0$. Given the roots of this equation, that will take a little time.

Similarly, you could just substitute the solutions into each of the equations to find the equation that will accept both solutions. Again, a lot of work.

The best approach is to see that the roots are expressed in a form that is suggestive of the Quadratic Formula. Thus, $-b = -3$, so $b = 3$. And $a = 1$, and we eliminate (B) and (D). Next, $2a = 2$, so $a = 1$, and we eliminate choice (E). Finally, $b^2 - 4ac = 5$. Since $b = 3$ and $a = 1$: $b^2 - 4ac = 5 \Rightarrow (3)^2 - 4(1)(x) = 5 \Rightarrow 9 - 4c = 5 \Rightarrow 4c = 4 \Rightarrow c = 1$. So the equation is $x^2 + 3x + 1 = 0$.

58. (F) A function is a relationship such that each element of the domain is paired with one and only one element in the range. In the relationship given in the question stem, one element of the domain, *0*, is paired with two different elements in the range—3 and 5. Thus, the relationship given in the question stem is not a function. By dropping the first set of pairs, this duplication is eliminated and the set becomes a function.

59. (D) The trapezoid can be analyzed as a composite figure. Drop a line from point B perpendicular to CD. The trapezoid is a combination of a right triangle and a rectangle. Since the triangle has degree

measures of 30, 60, and 90, the side opposite the 30° angle has a length half that of the hypotenuse or a length of 4. Thus, the rectangle has sides of 4 and 9 and an area of 36. Then, the side of the triangle opposite the 60° angle has a length equal to $4\sqrt{3}$. And the area of the triangle is: $\frac{1}{2}(a)(b) = \frac{1}{2}(4)(4\sqrt{3})$. And the area of the triangle is: $36 + 8\sqrt{3}$.

60. (G) There are several routes by which to reach the right conclusion. Surely, the shortest is just to reason that the cotangent and tangent are reciprocal functions, so if $\cot \theta = \frac{4}{3}$, $\tan \theta = \frac{3}{4}$.

TEST 3: READING (p. A-134)

1. (A) The passage actually makes two points: Who is Josquin, and why have we never heard of him. (A) mentions both of these.

2. (J) (F) is answered in paragraph two ("Solace me, (G) is answered in the final paragraph (sackbut). (H) is answered in the second paragraph (Ockeghem). (J) must be the correct answer, since the author never makes reference to any students.

3. (D) In the third paragraph the author lists certain difficulties in reading a Renaissance score: no tempo specified, missing flats and sharps, and no instrument/voice indication. Since these are regarded as deficiencies of Renaissance scoring, we may infer that modern music notation contains all of these.

4. (G) The support for (G) is found in paragraph 3, where the author discusses the distinction between concept and performance. The author states that music does not exist as printed notes. The notation is just a set of instructions for producing music. So the author would agree with (G).

5. (D) There is some merit to each of the choices, but we are looking for the one answer that is most closely connected with the text. Since the author discusses the lack of funding as one important reason for Josquin's obscurity, an obscurity the author deplores, the argument might be used to support a proposal for funds to promote Josquin's music. That is (D).

6. (G) (H) and (J) are mentioned in the final paragraph. (F) is mentioned in the third paragraph. (G) is never mentioned. The author states that musicians who read modern notation have difficulty reading Renaissance notation—not that these musicians lack talent.

7. (A) The author compares Josquin to Galileo in order to praise Josquin. This suggests the author has a very high opinion of Galileo.

8. (H) The first paragraph states that the dominant theme of liturgical music is reverence.

9. (A) In the third paragraph, the author says that in fine art such as painting and poetry, concept and performance are one. For example, the painting is what it is—a physical object. But in music, the concept exists only during a performance. Ballet is like music in this respect.

10. (H) In the first paragraph, the author states that up to the time of Josquin des Prez, Western music was liturgical. In the second paragraph, the author says that Josquin des Prez wrote both religious and nonreligious music.

11. (C) At the beginning of the story, the child addresses the narrator as Miss Mix. At the end of the story, Mr. Rawjester calls her Mary Jane.

12. (H) As the narrator surmises, the highwayman is in reality Mr. Rawjester. He assumes the role of a robber in order to make sure that he is not suspected of setting the fire.

13. (A) The narrator is employed as a governess by Mr. Rawjester. Apparently, she is required to help Blanche make herself up. This is degrading since the narrator herself has feelings for the master of the house.

14. (H) This can be deduced from the conversation between the narrator and the child. it becomes clear when the narrator identifies herself to the highwayman as a governess.

15. (B) As he leaves the party, he calls his guests idiots under his breath.

16. (G) At the beginning of the story, the child tells the narrator that her father's sweetheart is about to become her mother.

17. (B) Since the narrator survives the encounter with the highwayman, we can infer that she chose to cooperate with him.

18. (J) As we have already noted, the highwayman is a trick designed to allow Mr. Rawjester to dispose of his three crazy wives while avoiding suspicion.

19. (A) Since the highwayman is Mr. Rawjester, he knows about the necklace.

20. (F) Notice that the conversation takes place in a low voice and a whisper.

21. (B) This is the only statement general enough to cover the specific information in the piece. Statement A is contradicted by the text. Statements (C) and (D) are specific details and, therefore, too narrow in scope to be the main idea of the passage.

22. (G) Since the policy approved by the board involves the payment of large bonuses to any management member who is fired after a takeover, the policy by definition is a golden parachute.

23. (C) According to paragraph 2, the defining characteristic of a hostile takeover is the opposition to the takeover by existing management.

24. (F) This statement is supported by the beginning of paragraph 3, which tells of the methods used by raiders to raise the cash they need to buy a targeted company's stock.

25. (D) Paragraph 5 defines the three anti-takeover strategies. Statement (A) defines the greenmail strategy. Statement (B) defines the golden parachute theory. Statement (C) is not supported by anything in the passage.

26. (G) This argument is made at the beginning of the last paragraph. The topics of statements (F), (H), and (J) are all mentioned in the passage, but the text does not support any of these statements.

27. (D) The meaning of a proxy fight is presented in paragraph 2. The other choices are all true but do not involve a proxy battle.

28. (H) This point is explicitly made at the beginning of the last paragraph. All the other choices are properly defined in the paragraph before the last.

29. (B) The rule of the Securities and Exchange Commission is defined in the first sentence of the selection.

30. (H) In the fourth paragraph, the passage states that some people have been convicted of selling inside information about takeovers.

31. (C) In the first sentence of the passage the author says a supernova occurs about twice every century, or about once every fifty years.

32. (J) (F) is stated in the second paragraph. (G) is specifically stated in the first paragraph. (H) is stated in the second paragraph. Although the word galaxy is used in the selection, the author does not say that supernovas are caused by colliding galaxies. So (J) is the one detail not mentioned in the selection.

33. (A) In the first paragraph the author compares a star to a leaky balloon. That is an analogy.

34. (H) The key word for this question is *anomalous.* The author states that the unexpected makeup of the meteorites is evidence that a supernova helped form our solar system. However, this evidence supports the conclusion only if the strange content is foreign to our solar system. Only (H) explains the connection between the theory of the origin of our solar system and the strange makeup of the meteors.

35. (A) In the last two sentences of the second paragraph, the author states that supernovas emit most of their energy as x-rays and notes that x-ray observations provide the most useful insights into the nature of supernovas. He adds that remnants of supernovas have been found using x-ray studies. We can infer from these marks that it is easier to find a supernova using equipment that detects x-rays than it is using equipment for viewing visible light.

36. (J) In the first paragraph, the author describes the start of the sequence of events that leads to a supernova. It begins when a star runs out of fuel and collapses.

37. (B) In the first paragraph, the author describes the collapse of an ordinary star. The result is a neutron star. Then, in the second paragraph, the author describes what follows—a supernova. Thus, the neutron star is an intermediate stage between the ordinary star and its final phase, a supernova.

38. (J) (F), (G), and (H) are all incorrect, and each makes the mistake of elevating a part of the passage to the status of main idea. (J) is the

best description of the passage. The author describes the sequence of events that leads to a supernova and then describes what events follow the supernova.

39. (D) The last paragraph dates the formation of our galaxy at over 4.5 billion years ago.

40. (H) The last paragraph notes that the cosmic radiation generated by supernovas is responsible for many of the genetic mutations that propel evolution.

TEST 4: SCIENCE REASONING (p. A-141)

1. (C) Generally the Wright data show lower lift at a given angle than the Lilienthal data.

2. (H) The highest point on the graph is at 16 degrees (approximately 5.5 pounds/sq. ft.).

3. (A) By extending both lines to the 50° mark, the difference between them is clearly observed to be less than 1 pound/sq. ft.

4. (H) Count the crossing points of the two curves.

5. (C) The widest region is between 18° and 43°.

6. (J) Since plastic beads are not alive, they cannot possibly carry out cellular respiration. This control is designed to detect any atmospheric changes (in the laboratory) that may cause a change in gas volume inside the tubes.

7. (C) Without KOH to remove the carbon dioxide produced during cellular respiration, the same number of gas molecules ($6CO_2$) would always be added to the tube as gas molecules were being consumed in the tube ($6O_2$).

8. (F) Oxygen in the air of the tube is consumed by the peas during cellular respiration (see summary equation).

9. (C) Experiment 2 was conducted at a higher temperature than Experiment 1. The greater decrease in gas in the same time period (15 minutes) demonstrates a faster consumption of oxygen.

10. (G) If results are identical in light (Experiments 1 and 2) and dark, then light/dark conditions are irrelevant to cellular respiration rates in the experiment—only temperature conditions are important.

11. (A) Glucose *must* be consumed in order for cellular respiration to occur. Since cellular respiration *did not* occur at equal rates in Experiments 1 and 2, (A) is the only possible answer. Peas are seeds containing a supply of glucose.

12. (F) Each photon can promote an electron from level 1 to level 2, since the difference in energies is 0.60. (Note that the actual value of level 1 alone, which happens to be 0.60 also, does not determine the answer. Differences in energy are what matter.)

13. (D) There is no way to distinguish between the two emissions, since each releases a photon of equal energy.

14. (J) Only the 3 → 1 emission has an energy difference of 0.92.

15. (D) Each electron can go from level 1 to any of 4 other levels, with each of the four transitions requiring a photon of a different energy.

16. (H) Since absorption of photons occurs first, then emission, electrons must be promoted (gaining the necessary energy from the absorbed photons), then emitted. Transitions between levels 3 and 4 have the necessary energies, namely 0.23.

17. (D) Although 2.07 is the absolute energy of level 5, there is no *difference* of energy levels anywhere on the diagram that equals 2.07; hence, the photons will not be absorbed.

18. (G) Scientist 1 believes that processes associated with sudden events in the past shaped the earth, whereas Scientist 2 believes that the processes are continuing in the present as well.

19. (D) Mountains could not have formed only when *land masses* were raised at the *beginnings* of the earth, if *recent* fossils of *sea creatures* are found at mountain tops. This evidence suggests that the rocks were under water relatively recently.

20. (H) Scientist 1 never refers to time or how old the earth may be. Scientist 2 refers often to "long" or "vast periods of time."

21. (A) If the worldwide ocean precipitated *granite first,* it must be the *lowest layer,* with other precipitated materials covering it later.

22. (F) If the major rock types (three) formed when the worldwide ocean precipitated different materials on three occasions, no further types can be expected since this ocean no longer exists (possibly due to evaporation).

23. (C) Processes cannot be uniform *from the beginning.* Processes that *formed* the earth at its origin must have differed from those that maintain and mold the earth as an existing planet.

24. (G) Scientist 1 refers to three major rock types forming during three separate precipitations. Regions of lava (with no present volcanoes), rivers presently continuing to cut their channels, and "related" fossils that could not have immigrated from other geographic areas are factors that *support* the views of Scientist 2.

25. (D) Ten individuals had their heart rates recorded every 10 minutes during a 30-minute experiment (3 times). Therefore, 30 values were used to calculate the average heart rate for each of the experiments.

26. (G) Since Species B had an increase in heart rate when environmental temperature increased, it is the likely species to be poikilothermic (Species A heart rate stayed about the same).

27. (C) Just by chance alone, any one individual might have an extremely high or extremely low heart rate. The larger the sample of individuals tested, the lower the chances of getting extreme *average* values.

28. (J) Since Species B (poikilothermic) had an increase in average heart rate when environmental temperature increased, a decrease in average heart rate is likely when temperatures drop. Species A should have approximately the same average heart rate at all 3 temperatures.

29. (A) At 22°C, Species A had an average heart rate of 150 beats/minute, while Species B averaged 100 beats/minute.

30. (F) The poikilothermic Species B should have an increase in body temperature in Experiment 2 (35°C conditions in the incubator compared to 22°C in Experiment 1). The homeothermic Species A should have no significant change in body temperature during the experiments.

31. (B) You need to note how θ_1 and θ_2 are defined on the original drawing, then imagine how the diagram will change as the angles become smaller. (Note that (C) would be correct if the angles were defined as those between the ray and the horizontal, not vertical, axis.)

32. (J) Only the last choice fits both experiments.

33. (A) In this question you are asked to interpret the meaning of the diagram.

34. (H) The beam of light only passes into the air for observation in Experiment 2.

35. (C) This response covers all elements of the three diagrams.

36. (H) The number of butterflies captured for marking is found under the heading: *# marked.* Reading across the table for each size group, the dark brown category always has the fewest butterflies marked.

37. (D) By comparing the number of butterflies recaptured to the number marked, students can derive a proportion that represents how easy it is to recapture each type of butterfly. The proportion for small, white butterflies (30/35) is much higher than that for any of the other choices.

38. (G) An examination of the table shows that for all colors, as size increases the number of butterflies marked gets larger.

39. (C) A poisonous chemical will have adverse effects on the butterfly after marking (perhaps by killing or by preventing flight). The group with the lowest number (and proportion) of individuals recaptured in flight (10/30 = 1/3), is the group consisting of large, dark-brown butterflies.

40. (G) For medium-sized butterflies, the proportion of individuals recaptured in each color is as follows: white (15/30 = 1/2), tan (20/40 = 1/2), and dark brown (10/20 = 1/2).

Answer Sheet

Name ______________________ Student ID Number ______________________

Date ______________ Instructor ______________________ Course/Session Number ______________

TEST 1—ENGLISH

1 A B C D	16 F G H J	31 A B C D	46 F G H J	61 A B C D
2 F G H J	17 A B C D	32 F G H J	47 A B C D	62 F G H J
3 A B C D	18 F G H J	33 A B C D	48 F G H J	63 A B C D
4 F G H J	19 A B C D	34 F G H J	49 A B C D	64 F G H J
5 A B C D	20 F G H J	35 A B C D	50 F G H J	65 A B C D
6 F G H J	21 A B C D	36 F G H J	51 A B C D	66 F G H J
7 A B C D	22 F G H J	37 A B C D	52 F G H J	67 A B C D
8 F G H J	23 A B C D	38 F G H J	53 A B C D	68 F G H J
9 A B C D	24 F G H J	39 A B C D	54 F G H J	69 A B C D
10 F G H J	25 A B C D	40 F G H J	55 A B C D	70 F G H J
11 A B C D	26 F G H J	41 A B C D	56 F G H J	71 A B C D
12 F G H J	27 A B C D	42 F G H J	57 A B C D	72 F G H J
13 A B C D	28 F G H J	43 A B C D	58 F G H J	73 A B C D
14 F G H J	29 A B C D	44 F G H J	59 A B C D	74 F G H J
15 A B C D	30 F G H J	45 A B C D	60 F G H J	75 A B C D

TEST 2—MATHEMATICS

1 A B C D E	13 A B C D E	25 A B C D E	37 A B C D E	49 A B C D E
2 F G H J K	14 F G H J K	26 F G H J K	38 F G H J K	50 F G H J K
3 A B C D E	15 A B C D E	27 A B C D E	39 A B C D E	51 A B C D E
4 F G H J K	16 F G H J K	28 F G H J K	40 F G H J K	52 F G H J K
5 A B C D E	17 A B C D E	29 A B C D E	41 A B C D E	53 A B C D E
6 F G H J K	18 F G H J K	30 F G H J K	42 F G H J K	54 F G H J K
7 A B C D E	19 A B C D E	31 A B C D E	43 A B C D E	55 A B C D E
8 F G H J K	20 F G H J K	32 F G H J K	44 F G H J K	56 F G H J K
9 A B C D E	21 A B C D E	33 A B C D E	45 A B C D E	57 A B C D E
10 F G H J K	22 F G H J K	34 F G H J K	46 F G H J K	58 F G H J K
11 A B C D E	23 A B C D E	35 A B C D E	47 A B C D E	59 A B C D E
12 F G H J K	24 F G H J K	36 F G H J K	48 F G H J K	60 F G H J K

TEST 3—READING

1 A B C D	9 A B C D	17 A B C D	25 A B C D	33 A B C D
2 F G H J	10 F G H J	18 F G H J	26 F G H J	34 F G H J
3 A B C D	11 A B C D	19 A B C D	27 A B C D	35 A B C D
4 F G H J	12 F G H J	20 F G H J	28 F G H J	36 F G H J
5 A B C D	13 A B C D	21 A B C D	29 A B C D	37 A B C D
6 F G H J	14 F G H J	22 F G H J	30 F G H J	38 F G H J
7 A B C D	15 A B C D	23 A B C D	31 A B C D	39 A B C D
8 F G H J	16 F G H J	24 F G H J	32 F G H J	40 F G H J

TEST 4—SCIENCE REASONING

1 A B C D	9 A B C D	17 A B C D	25 A B C D	33 A B C D
2 F G H J	10 F G H J	18 F G H J	26 F G H J	34 F G H J
3 A B C D	11 A B C D	19 A B C D	27 A B C D	35 A B C D
4 F G H J	12 F G H J	20 F G H J	28 F G H J	36 F G H J
5 A B C D	13 A B C D	21 A B C D	29 A B C D	37 A B C D
6 F G H J	14 F G H J	22 F G H J	30 F G H J	38 F G H J
7 A B C D	15 A B C D	23 A B C D	31 A B C D	39 A B C D
8 F G H J	16 F G H J	24 F G H J	32 F G H J	40 F G H J

CAMBRIDGE

EDUCATIONAL SERVICES, INC.®

ACT • PLAN • EXPLORE

Appendix A

ACT PRACTICE TEST IV

1 1 1 1 1 1 1 1 1 1 1 1

ENGLISH

45 Minutes—75 Questions

DIRECTIONS: In the five passages that follow, certain parts and phrases are underlined and numbered. In the right-hand column, you will find alternatives for each underlined part. You are to choose the one that best expresses the idea, makes the statement appropriate for standard written English, or is worded more consistently with the style and tone of the passage as a whole. If you think the original version is the best, choose "NO CHANGE."

You will also find questions about a section of the passage, or about the passage as a whole. These questions do not refer to an underlined portion of the passage, but rather are identified with a note.

For each question, choose the alternative you consider best. Read each passage through once before you begin to answer the questions that accompany it. You cannot determine most answers without reading several sentences beyond the question. Be sure that you have read far enough ahead each time you choose an alternative.

Passage I

As befits a nation made up of immigrants from all over the Christian world, Americans have no distinctive Christmas symbols, but [1] we have taken the symbols of all the nations and made them our own. The Christmas tree, the holly and the ivy, the mistletoe, the exchange of gifts, the myth of Santa Claus, the carols of all nations, the plum pudding and the wassail bowl are all elements in the American Christmas of the late twentieth century as we know it today [2]. Though we have no Christmas symbols of our own, the American Christmas still has a distinctive

1. A. NO CHANGE
   B. symbols but
   C. symbols; but
   D. symbols: but

2. F. NO CHANGE
   G. as it is known today
   H. known as it is today
   J. OMIT the underlined portion.

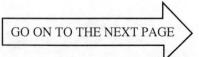

GO ON TO THE NEXT PAGE

aura by virtue of two character[3] elements.

3. A. NO CHANGE
B. characters
C. characterized
D. characteristic

The first of these is when[4], as might be expected in a nation as dedicated to the carrying on of business as the American nation, the dominant role of the Christmas festivities has become[5] to serve as a stimulus to retail business. The themes of Christmas advertising begin to appear as early as September, and the open season on Christmas shopping begins in November. 50 years ago[6], Thanksgiving Day was regarded like it was[7] the opening day of the season for Christmas shopping; today, the season opens immediately after Halloween. Thus, virtually a whole month has been added to the Christmas season—for[8] shopping purposes.

4. F. NO CHANGE
G. is that
H. is which
J. is where

5. A. NO CHANGE
B. have become
C. having become
D. becomes

6. F. NO CHANGE
G. 50 year ago
H. Fifty years ago
J. One time ago

7. A. NO CHANGE
B. like as
C. as
D. like

8. F. NO CHANGE
G. season. For
H. season, for
J. season: for

Second, the Christmas season of festivities has insensibly combined with the New Years[9] celebration into one lengthened period of Saturnalia. This starts with the office parties a few days before Christmas continues[10] on Christmas Eve, now the occasion in America of one of two large-scale revels that mark the Season, and continues in spirited euphoria until

9. A. NO CHANGE
B. New Year's
C. New Years'
D. New Year

10. F. NO CHANGE
G. Christmas, continues
H. as Christmas continues
J. Christmas as continues

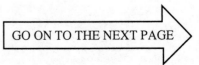

GO ON TO THE NEXT PAGE

New Year's Eve, the second of the large-scale revels. New Year's Day is spent resting, possibly regretting <u>somebody's</u> [11] excesses, watching a football "bowl" game. [12]

11. A. NO CHANGE
 B. everyone's
 C. someone's
 D. one's

12. Is the use of quotation marks appropriate in the passage?
 F. No, because the passage has no dialogue.
 G. No, because commas would be more appropriate.
 H. Yes, because quotation marks are used to set off words used out of context.
 J. Yes, because quotation marks are used around titles of books, plays, and poems.

Passage II

The following paragraphs may or may not be in the most logical order. Each paragraph is numbered in braces, and item 24 will ask you to choose the

[1]

Can you spot a criminal by his physical characteristics? [13] When the science of criminology was founded in the nineteenth century, an imaginative Italian observer decided that criminals are born that way and are <u>distinctly</u> [14] by certain physical marks. They are, he claimed, "a special species, a subspecies having distinct physical and mental characteristics. In general, all criminals have long, large, protruding ears, abundant hair, a thin beard, prominent front sinuses, a

13. Is the use of a question appropriate to begin Paragraph [1]?
 A. No, because questions are not used in formal writing.
 B. No, because the question is not answered.
 C. Yes, because it varies sentence structure and interests the reader.
 D. Yes, because an essay should always begin with a question.

14. F. NO CHANGE
 G. distinguish
 H. distinguished
 J. distinguishing

GO ON TO THE NEXT PAGE

protruding chin, large cheekbones." Rapists, he argued, have "brilliant eyes, delicate faces" and murderers may be distinguished by "cold, glassy eyes, nose always large and frequently aquiline; jaws strong; cheekbones large, hair curly, dark and abundant." [15]

[2]

But the myth doesn't die easily. During the 1930s, a German criminologist, Gustav Aschaffenburg, declared that stout, squat people with large abdomens are more liable to be occasional offenders, while slender builds and slight muscular development are common among habitual offenders. In the 1940s, according to writer Jessica Mitford, a group of Harvard sociologists who study sociology, decided that criminals are most likely to be "mesomorphs," muscular types with large trunks who walk assertively, talk noisily, and behave aggressively. Watch out for those kind of characteristics.

[3]

Around about the turn of the century, a British physician made a detailed study of the faces of three thousand convicts and compared them with a like number of English college students, measuring the

15. Is the use of quotation marks in this paragraph appropriate?
    A. No, because it contains no dialogue.
    B. No, because too much physical detail is confusing.
    C. Yes, because it discusses a theory of criminology.
    D. Yes, because quotation marks are used around direct quotations.

16. F. NO CHANGE
    G. easy
    H. easiest
    J. easier

17. A. NO CHANGE
    B. likely
    C. likely apt
    D. possible

18. F. NO CHANGE
    G. whom study sociological changes
    H. who studied sociology
    J. OMIT the underlined portion.

19. A. NO CHANGE
    B. those sort of
    C. them kind of
    D. those

20. F. NO CHANGE
    G. At about
    H. Around
    J. OMIT the underlined portion.

21. A. NO CHANGE
    B. compare
    C. compares
    D. comparing

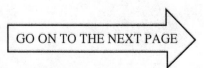

GO ON TO THE NEXT PAGE

noses ears eyebrows and chins[22] of both groups. He could find no correlation among physical types and criminal behavior.

22. F. NO CHANGE
G. noses ears and eyebrows and chins
H. noses; ears; eyebrows and chins
J. noses, ears, eyebrows, and chins

Items 23-24 pose questions about Passage I as a whole.

23. This passage was probably excerpted from:

A. a general sociology textbook.
B. a technical monograph on criminology.
C. a newsmagazine.
D. a biography of Gustav Aschaffenburg.

24. Choose the order of paragraph numbers that will make the essay's structure most logical.

F. NO CHANGE
G. 3, 2, 1
H. 1, 3, 2
J. 2, 3, 1

Passage III

The following paragraphs may or may not be in the most logical order. Each paragraph is numbered in brackets, and item 37 will ask you to choose the

[1]

The history of modern pollution problems show[25] that most have resulted from negligence and ignorance. We have an appalling tendency to interfere with nature before all of the possible consequences of our actions have been studied into completeness[26]. We produce and distribute radioactive substances, synthetic chemicals, and many other potent compounds before fully comprehending their effects[27] on living organisms. Synthetic means manmade. Many of today's fashions are made with synthetic fibers.[28] Our education is dangerously incomplete.

25. A. NO CHANGE
B. shown
C. shows
D. showed

26. F. NO CHANGE
G. a lot
H. for completeness
J. in depth

27. A. NO CHANGE
B. effectiveness
C. affect
D. affects

28. F. NO CHANGE
G. Synthetic fibers are manmade.
H. Many of today's fashions are made with synthetic fibers.
J. OMIT the underlined portion.

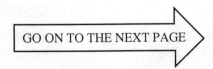

GO ON TO THE NEXT PAGE

[2]

It will be argued that the purpose of science is to move into unknown territory; [29] to explore, and to discover. It can be said that similar risks have been taken before, and that these risks are necessary to technological progress. [30]

29. A. NO CHANGE
B. territory:
C. territory,
D. territory

30. The writer could most effectively bolster the passage at this point by adding which of the following?

F. An example of one of these risks argued by some to be necessary for technological progress.
G. The sentence "The risks are necessary." to gain rhetorical emphasis.
H. A brief description of an unknown territory.
J. A definition of the word "science."

[3]

These arguments overlook an important [31] element. In the past, risks taken in the name of scientific progress were restricted to a small place and brief period of time. The effects of the processes we now strive to master are not either [32] localized nor brief. Air pollution covers vast urban areas. Ocean pollutants have been discovered in nearly every part of the world. Synthetic chemicals spread over huge stretches of forest and farmland may remain in the soil for decades and years to come. [33] Radioactive pollutants will be found in the biosphere for generations. The size and persistent [34] of these problems have grown with the expanding power of modern science.

31. A. NO CHANGE
B. a important
C. importance
D. important

32. F. NO CHANGE
G. either
H. not neither
J. neither

33. A. NO CHANGE
B. for decades.
C. for years to come in decades.
D. for decades and years.

34. F. NO CHANGE
G. persistence
H. persevering
J. persisting

[4]

One might also argue that the hazards of modern

GO ON TO THE NEXT PAGE

pollutants are small comparison for [35] the dangers associated with other human activity. No estimate of the actual harm done by smog, fallout, or chemical residues can obscure the reality that the risks are being taken before being fully understood.

35.
A. NO CHANGE
B. consideration for
C. comparing with
D. compared to

[5]

The importance of these issues lies in the failure of science to predict and control. Human [36] intervention into natural processes. The true measure of the danger is represented by the hazards we will encounter if we enter the new age of technology without first evaluating our responsibility to the environment.

36.
F. NO CHANGE
G. control human
H. control; human
J. control and human

Items 37-38 pose questions about Passage I as a whole.

37. Choose the order of paragraph numbers that will make the essay's structure most logical.

A. NO CHANGE
B. 2, 4, 3, 1, 5
C. 1, 3, 2, 4, 5
D. 5, 1, 2, 3, 4

38. This passage was probably intended for readers who:

F. lack an understanding of the history of technology.
G. are authorities on pollution and its causes.
H. are interested in becoming more aware of our environmental problems and the possible solutions to these problems.
J. have worked with radioactive substances.

Passage IV

The following paragraphs may or may not be in the most logical order. Each paragraph is numbered in brackets, and item 49 will ask you to choose the

[1]

Many researchers can be of greatest service to a company by staying around [39] in the laboratory. A

39.
A. NO CHANGE
B. remaining
C. remaining around
D. staying up

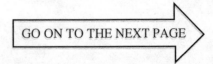

GO ON TO THE NEXT PAGE

single outstanding discovery may of had [40] a far greater impact on the company's profit picture five years hence than the activities of even the most able [41] administrator. It is simply good sense—and good economics—to allow qualified researchers to continue their work. Granting these researchers maximum the freedom to explore their scientific ideas is also eminently good sense.

40. F. NO CHANGE
G. maybe
H. might of had
J. may have

41. A. NO CHANGE
B. most ablest
C. more ablest
D. most abled

[2]

In recent years however [42] this theory has fallen into wide disrepair. [43] Companies find that many researchers continue to be highly productive throughout their careers. There is every reason to allow these researchers to continue their pioneering work.

42. F. NO CHANGE
G. years, however
H. years, however,
J. years however,

43. A. NO CHANGE
B. argument
C. ill repute
D. disrepute

[3]

Some years ago, the theory was rampant that after the age of about 40, the average researcher began losing their [44] creative spark. The chance of one making a major discovery was believed to drop off sharply. Hence, there really wasn't much point to

44. F. NO CHANGE
G. its
H. his
J. theirs

GO ON TO THE NEXT PAGE

encouraging a person of 45 or 50 to do research. [45]

[4]

Companies are also convinced that the traditional guideposts in establishing salaries are not completely valid. In former years <u>of long ago,</u> [46] the size of a man's paycheck was determined primarily by the size of his annual budget. On this basis, the researcher—however brilliant—who had perhaps one assistant and never spent much money made an extremely poor showing. Companies now realize that the two very important criteria that must also <u>be considerable</u> [47] are a man's actual contributions to the company and his creative potential.

[5]

In today's era of scientific manpower shortages, companies have more reason than ever to encourage scientists to do the work for which they are most qualified. They also have greater reason than ever to provide within the laboratory the environment <u>in which</u> [48] the creative processes of research can be carried out most effectively.

45. If, at this point in the passage, the writer wanted to increase the information about creative contributions from researchers. Which of the following additions would be most relevant to the passage as a whole?

A. A bibliography of books about retirement
B. A description of a few of the contributions older researchers have made to science
C. A list of today's most prominent researchers
D. A brief description of a model retirement benefits plan

46. F. NO CHANGE
G. a long time ago
H. long ago,
J. OMIT the underlined portion.

47. A. NO CHANGE
B. be considered
C. most considerable
D. considerable of

48. F. NO CHANGE
G. about which
H. of which
J. into which

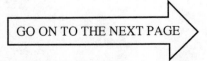

GO ON TO THE NEXT PAGE

Items 49-50 pose questions about Passage I as a whole.

49. Choose the sequence of paragraph numbers that will make the essay's structure most sensible.

A. NO CHANGE
B. 1, 2, 4, 3, 5
C. 1, 2, 3, 5, 4
D. 3, 2, 1, 4, 5

50. Is the author's use of the dash appropriate in the passage?

F. No, because a dash is never used in formal writing.
G. No, because commas would have been as effective for emphasis.
H. Yes, because the dash gives emphasis to the sudden break in thought or interruption in the sentence in which it was used.
J. Yes, because using a dash adds excitement to the passage.

Passage V

The following paragraphs may or may not be in the most logical order. Each paragraph is numbered in brackets, and item 63 will ask you to choose the

[1]

What are those of us whom (51) have chosen careers in science and engineering able to do about meeting our current problems? (52)

51. A. NO CHANGE
B. who
C. whose
D. what

52. F. NO CHANGE
G. problems.
H. problems!
J. problems;

[2]

Second, we can identify the many areas in which science and technology, more considerately used, can be of greatest (53) service in the future than in the past to improve the quality of life. While we can make many speeches, and pass many laws, the quality of our environment will be improved only threw (54) better knowledge and better application of that knowledge.

53. A. NO CHANGE
B. great
C. more great
D. greater

54. F. NO CHANGE
G. through
H. though
J. from

[3]

Third, we can recognize that much of the dissatisfaction we suffer today results from our very

GO ON TO THE NEXT PAGE

successes of former years in the past[55]. We have been so eminently successful in attaining material goals that we are deeply dissatisfied of the fact that[56] we cannot attain other goals more rapidly. We have achieved a better life for most people, but we are unhappy that we have not spread it to all people. We have illuminated many sources of environmental deterioration, because of[57] we are unhappy that we have not conquered all of them. It is our raising[58] expectations rather than our failures which now cause our distress.

[4]

First, we can help destroy the false impression that science and engineering have caused the current world troubles. Quite the contrary,[59] science and engineering have made vast contributions to better living for more people.

55. A. NO CHANGE
B. of the past
C. being in the past
D. OMIT the underlined portion.

56. F. NO CHANGE
G. in the fact that
H. about
J. that

57. A. NO CHANGE
B. despite
C. but
D. also

58. F. NO CHANGE
G. arising
H. rising
J. raised

59. A. NO CHANGE
B. Contrary to,
C. Contrasted with,
D. OMIT the underlined portion.

60. Suppose at this point that the writer wanted to add more information about the benefits of science and engineering. Which of the following additions would be most relevant?

F. A list of the colleges with the best science and engineering degree programs
G. Specific examples of contributions from the areas of science and engineering that have improved the standard of living
H. A brief explanation of the current world troubles
J. The names of several famous scientists and engineers

GO ON TO THE NEXT PAGE

[5]

Granted that many of our current problems must be cured more by social, political, and economic instruments than by science and technology, yet science and technology must still be the tools to make further advances in [61] such things as clean air, clean water, better transportation, better housing, better medical care, more adequate welfare programs, purer food, conservation of resources, and many other areas.

61. A. NO CHANGE
B. advances, in
C. advances. In
D. advances—in

Items 62-63 pose questions about Passage I as a whole.

62. This passage was probably written for readers who

F. are college graduates.
G. are interested in an environmental services career.
H. are in a career or contemplating a career in science or engineering.
J. are frustrated with the current world problems.

63. Choose the sequence of paragraph numbers that will make the essay's structure most logical.

A. NO CHANGE
B. 1, 4, 2, 3, 5
C. 5, 4, 2, 3, 1
D. 4, 2, 3, 1, 5

Passage VI

With increasing prosperity, West European youth am [64] having a fling that is creating distinctive consumer and cultural patterns.

64. F. NO CHANGE
G. youths is
H. youth be
J. youth is

The result has been the increasing emergence in Europe of that phenomenon well known in America as the "youth market." This here [65] is a market in which enterprising businesses cater to the demands of teenagers and older youths in all their rock mania and pop-art forms.

65. A. NO CHANGE
B. here idea
C. here thing
D. OMIT the underlined portion.

GO ON TO THE NEXT PAGE

The evolving European youth market has both <u>similarities</u> [66] and differences from the American youth market.

66. F. NO CHANGE
G. similarity
H. similarities to
J. similar

The <u>markets</u> [67] basis is essentially the same—more spending power and freedom to use it in the hands of teenagers and older youths. Young consumers also make up an <u>increasing high</u> [68] proportion of the population.

67. A. NO CHANGE
B. markets'
C. market's
D. market

68. F. NO CHANGE
G. increasingly high
H. increasing higher
J. high increasing

Youthful tastes in the United States and Europe extend over a similar range of products—records and record players, tapes and CDs, transistor radios, leatherjackets and "wayout" clothing, cosmetics, and soft <u>drinks, generally</u> [69] it now is difficult to tell in which direction, <u>transatlantic</u> [70] teenage influences are flowing.

69. A. NO CHANGE
B. drinks. Generally
C. drinks, in general
D. drinks generally

70. F. NO CHANGE
G. Trans-Atlantic
H. trans-Atlantic
J. Trans-atlantic

As in the United States, where "teen" and "teenager" have become merchandising terms, Europeans also have <u>adapted</u> [71] similar terminology. In Flemish and Dutch it is "tiener" for teenagers. The French have simply adopted the English word "teenagers." In West Germany the key word in advertising addressed to teenagers is "freizeit," meaning holidays or time off.

71. A. NO CHANGE
B. picked up
C. added
D. adopted

GO ON TO THE NEXT PAGE

The most obvious difference among[72] the youth market in Europe and that in the United States is in size. In terms of volume and variety of sales, the market in Europe is only a shadow of its American counterpart, but it's a growing shadow.

72. F. NO CHANGE
    G. betwixt
    H. amongst
    J. between

Items 73-75 pose questions about Passage I as a whole.

73. Is the author's use of quotation marks appropriate in this passage:
    A. No, because quotation marks are used to set off a direct quote.
    B. No, because the passage has no dialogue.
    C. Yes, because quotation marks are used to set off words used in a special sense.
    D. Yes, because quotation marks indicate a conversation.

74. This passage was probably written for readers who
    F. are interested in new trends in the consumer patterns of the world's youth.
    G. are parents of teenagers.
    H. are teenagers.
    J. are interested in the different cultural patterns of West Germany.

75. Is the use of the dash appropriate in this passage?
    A. Yes, because the dash is used to set off interruptions, additions, and illustrations.
    B. No, because the dash is never used in formal writing.
    C. Yes, because the dash adds flair to the passage.
    D. Yes, because the dash is more effective than brackets or parentheses.

IF YOU FINISH BEFORE TIME IS CALLED, YOU MAY CHECK YOUR WORK ON THIS TEST ONLY. DO NOT WORK ON ANY OTHER TEST SECTION. **STOP**

2 2 2 2 2 2 2 2 2 2 2 2

MATHEMATICS

60 Minutes—60 Questions

DIRECTIONS: Solve each problem, choose the correct answer, and then blacken the corresponding oval on your answer sheet. Do not linger over problems that take too much time. Solve as many as you can; then return to the others in time you have left for this test.

Note: Unless otherwise stated, all of the following should be assumed:

1. Illustrative figures are NOT necessarily drawn to scale.
2. Geometry figures lie in a plane.
3. The word *line* means straight line.
4. The word *average* means arithmetic mean.

---

1. What is the additive inverse of $-\frac{2}{3}$?

A. $\frac{2}{3}$
B. $\frac{3}{2}$
C. $-\frac{3}{2}$
D. 1
E. 0

2. Which of the following is an element of the solution set of the equation $x^2 + 6x + 8 = 0$?

F. −8
G. −2
H. 8
J. 6
K. 4

3. In the figure below, if $\angle AOC$ is a central angle and the measure of $\angle AOC = 70°$, what is the measure of $\angle ABC$?

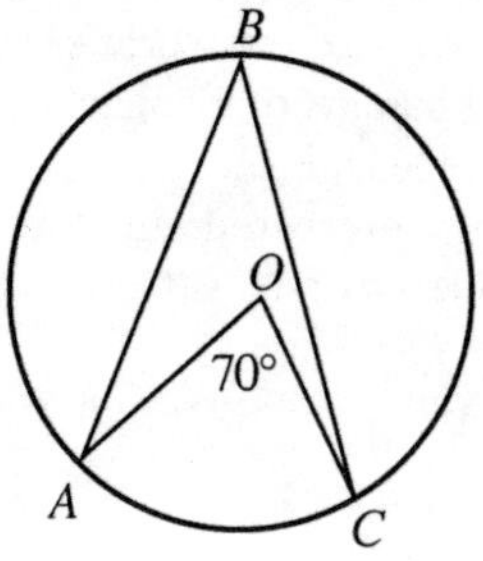

A. 22°
B. 35°
C. 50°
D. 70°
E. 140°

GO ON TO THE NEXT PAGE

4. In the figure below $l_1 \parallel l_2$. If the measure of $\angle x$ = 70° and the measure of $\angle y$ = 105°, what is the measure of $\angle r$?

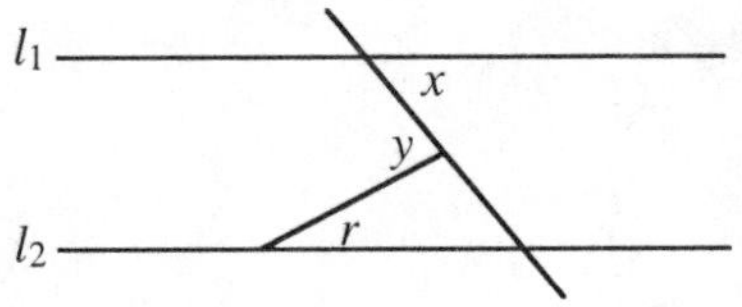

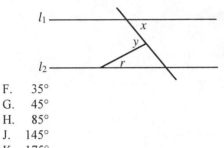

F. 35°
G. 45°
H. 85°
J. 145°
K. 175°

5. $A = \frac{2gr}{g+r}$. What is the value of g, when $r = 1$ and $A = 4$?

A. –2
B. 2
C. 4
D. $\frac{4}{7}$
E. $\frac{8}{5}$

6. The figure below represents which of the following equations?

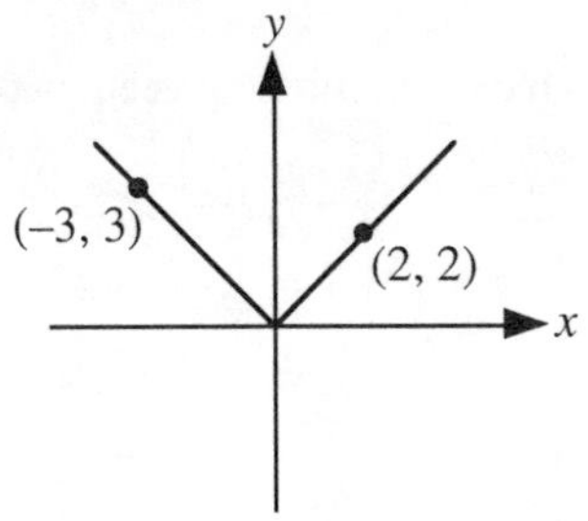

F. $y = x$
G. $y = -x$
H. $y = |x|$
J. $|y| = x$
K. $y = x^2$

7. Which of the following is an illustration of the distributive property?

A. $(12 \bullet 25)(4) = 12(25 \bullet 4)$
B. $7n + 2 - 3n = 7n - 3n + 2$
C. $(17)(b^2)(5) = (17)(5)(b)^2$
D. $ab + ac = ba + ca$
E. $x(x + 2) = x^2 + 2x$

8. Joshua buys a television set for \$600. If the sales tax is 7%, what is the total cost of the purchase?

F. \$4.20
G. \$42.00
H. \$420.00
J. \$604.20
K. \$642.00

9. What is the value of $-x^2 - 2x^3$ when $x = -1$?

A. –3
B. –1
C. 0
D. 1
E. 3

10. What is the average (arithmetic mean) of the numbers represented by $n + 3$, $2n - 1$, and $3n + 4$?

F. $\frac{5n+6}{3}$
G. $2n + 2$
H. $3n + 3$
J. $\frac{6n+7}{3}$
K. $6n + 6$

11. What is the value of $x^0 + x^{1/2} + x^{-2}$ when $x = 9$?

A. $3\frac{1}{81}$
B. $4\frac{1}{81}$
C. $5\frac{7}{18}$
D. $76\frac{1}{2}$
E. $77\frac{1}{2}$

12. $4\sqrt{3} + 3\sqrt{27} = ?$

F. $7\sqrt{30}$
G. $10\sqrt{3}$
H. $13\sqrt{3}$
J. 63
K. 108

GO ON TO THE NEXT PAGE

13. Jessica Dawn received marks of 87, 93, and 86 on three successive tests. What grade must she receive on a fourth test in order to have an average of 90?

A. 90
B. 91
C. 92
D. 93
E. 94

14. In terms of x, what is the total number of cents in $4x$ dimes?

F. $0.04x$
G. $0.4x$
H. $4x$
J. $40x$
K. $400x$

15. Which of the following is shown by the graph below?

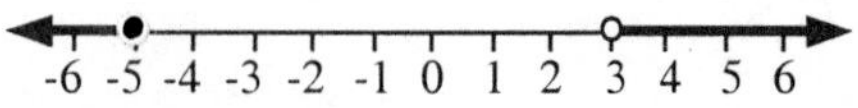

A. $-5 \leq x < 3$
B. $-5 < x$ or $x < 3$
C. $-5 \leq x$ or $x > 3$
D. $-5 \leq x \leq 3$
E. $-5 \geq x$ or $x > 3$

16. $2\frac{2}{5} - 1\frac{7}{8} = ?$

F. $\frac{7}{13}$
G. $\frac{21}{40}$
H. $\frac{11}{40}$
J. $\frac{19}{40}$
K. $1\frac{5}{40}$

17. In a circle with radius 6, what is the measure (in degrees) of an arc whose length is 2π?

A. 20°
B. 30°
C. 60°
D. 90°
E. 120°

18. If $\frac{2x}{3\sqrt{2}} = \frac{3\sqrt{2}}{x}$, what is the positive value of x?

F. 3
G. 9
H. $2\sqrt{3}$
J. $\sqrt{6}$
K. $\sqrt{3}$

19. If $f(x) = 2x - x^2$ and $g(x) = x - 4$, what is the value of $g(f(2))$?

A. −8
B. −4
C. −2
D. 0
E. 3

20. What is the solution set of the equation $|5 - 2x| = 7$?

F. {6, −1}
G. {6}
H. {−1}
J. {1}
K. {}

21. Which of the following is equivalent to $\frac{3 - \frac{3}{x}}{x - 1}$?

A. $\frac{1}{x-1}$
B. $\frac{1}{3}$
C. $x + 1$
D. 3
E. $\frac{3}{x}$

22. What is the slope of the line that passes through the points (−3, 5) and (4, 7)?

F. $\sqrt{53}$
G. 2
H. $\frac{1}{2}$
J. $\frac{2}{7}$
K. $\frac{7}{2}$

GO ON TO THE NEXT PAGE

23. In the figure below, diameter AB is perpendicular to chord CD at E. If chord $CD = 8$ and line $OE = 3$, what is the length of the circle's radius?

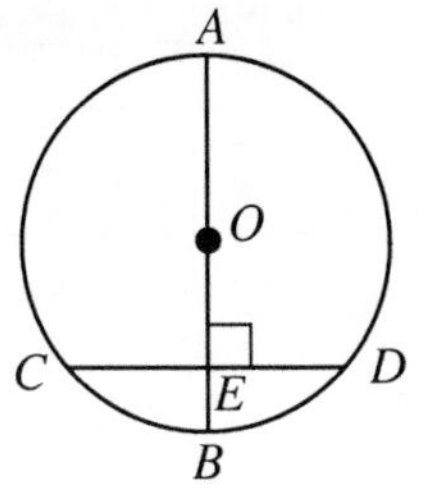

A. $\sqrt{3}$
B. $\sqrt{5}$
C. $\sqrt{7}$
D. $\sqrt{15}$
E. 5

24. The diagonals of parallelogram $ABCD$ intersect at point E. If $DB = 4x + 2$ and $DE = x + 4$, what is the value of x?

F. 3
G. 2
H. 1
J. 0
K. $\frac{2}{3}$

25. If the measure of the central angle of a sector of a circle is 120°, what is the area of the sector if the radius is 6?

A. 4π
B. 6π
C. 8π
D. 10π
E. 12π

26. If the statement "If two triangles are red, then they are equal in area" is true, then which of the following must be true?

F. If the two triangles are not equal in area, then they are not red.
G. If the two triangles are equal in area, then they are red.
H. If the two triangles are equal in area, then they are not red.
J. If the two triangles are not red, then they are not equal in area.
K. If the two triangles are red, then they are not equal in area.

27. If $\frac{a}{b} = \frac{r}{t}$, then which of the following is not necessarily true?

A. $\frac{a}{r} = \frac{b}{t}$
B. $\frac{a}{t} = \frac{b}{r}$
C. $\frac{a+b}{b} = \frac{r+t}{t}$
D. $\frac{b}{a} = \frac{t}{r}$
E. $at = br$

28. If $-2x + 5 = 2 - (5 - 2x)$, then $x = ?$

F. 6
G. 5
H. 4
J. 3
K. 2

29. $\frac{(1 + \sin x)(1 - \sin x)}{(1 + \cos x)(1 - \cos x)}$ is equivalent to which of the following?

A. $\cos x$
B. $\tan x$
C. $\tan^2 x$
D. $\cos^2 x$
E. $\cot^2 x$

30. In the figure below, ΔACB is a right triangle. CE is the median to hypotenuse AB, and $AB = 14$. What is the length of CE?

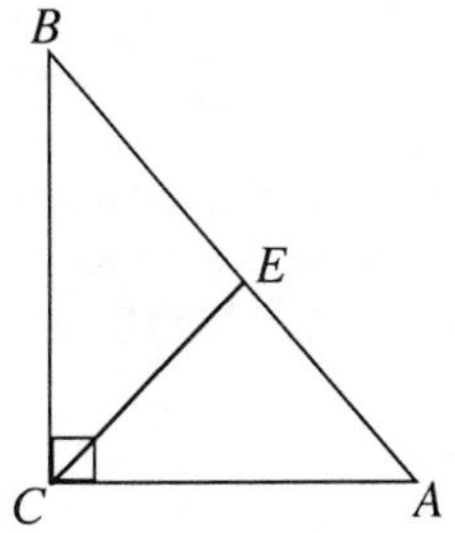

F. 5
G. 6
H. 7
J. 8
K. Cannot be determined from the given information.

GO ON TO THE NEXT PAGE

31. If y varies directly as x, and $y = 10$ when $x = \frac{1}{5}$, what is the value of y when $x = \frac{1}{2}$?

A. 1
B. 4
C. 7
D. 16
E. 25

32. $\frac{(-1)(2)(-3)(4)(-5)}{(5)(-4)(3)(-2)(1)} = ?$

F. 1
G. –1
H. 2
J. –2
K. 3

33. In the diagram below, chords AB and CD of circle O intersect at E. If $AE = 6$, $EB = 4$, $CE = x$, and $ED = 6x$, then $x = ?$

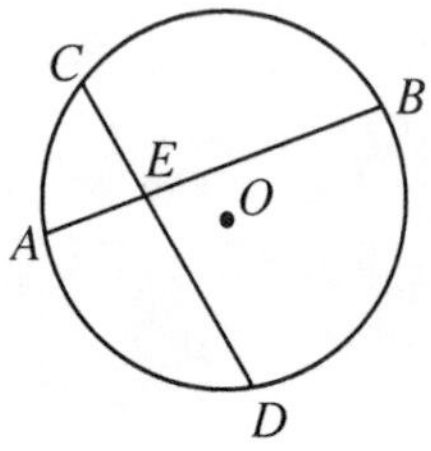

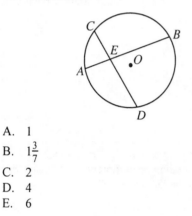

A. 1
B. $1\frac{3}{7}$
C. 2
D. 4
E. 6

34. The measure of the vertex angle of an isosceles triangle is 50 degrees. What is the measure, in degrees, of each base angle?

F. 40°
G. 50°
H. 65°
J. 75°
K. 130°

35. Using the table below, what is the median of the following data?

Score	Frequency
20	4
30	4
50	7

A. 20
B. 30
C. 40
D. 50
E. 60

36. Which of the following is the graph of the solution set of $x^2 - 2x - 3 > 0$?

F. 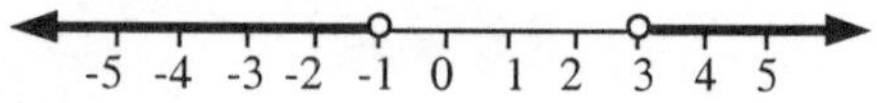

G. 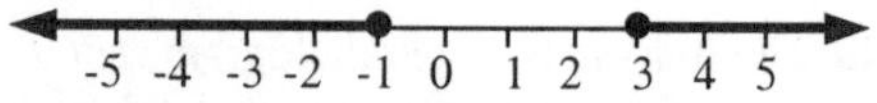

H. 

J. 

K. 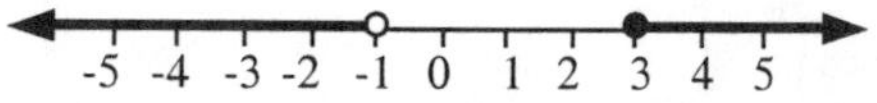

37. The expression $\sin x + \frac{\cos^2 x}{\sin x}$ is equal to which of the following?

A. 1
B. $\sin x$
C. $\cos x$
D. $\frac{1}{\sin x}$
E. $\frac{1}{\cos x}$

38. The value of $(2.5 \cdot 10^5)^2$ is equal to which of the following?

F. $6.25 \cdot 10^7$
G. $6.25 \cdot 10^{10}$
H. $2.5 \cdot 10^7$
J. $2.7 \cdot 10^{10}$
K. $5 \cdot 10^7$

GO ON TO THE NEXT PAGE

39. If $A * B$ is defined as $\frac{AB - B}{-B}$, what is the value of $-2 * 2$?

A. –3
B. –1
C. 0
D. 1
E. 3

40. If one of the roots of the equation $x^2 + kx - 12 = 0$ is 4, what is the value of k?

F. –1
G. 0
H. 1
J. 3
K. 7

41. In the figure below, D is a point on AB and E is a point on BC such that $DE \parallel AC$. If $DB = 4$, $AB = 10$, and $BC = 20$, what is the length of EC?

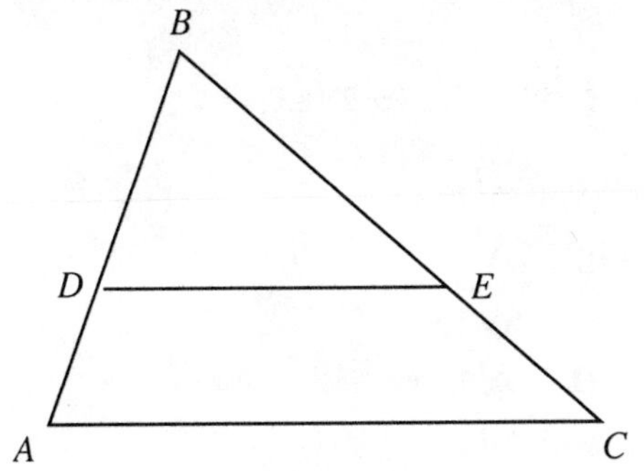

A. 4
B. 6
C. 8
D. 10
E. 12

42. $(x + 2)(x - 4) - (x + 4)(x - 2) = ?$

F. 0
G. $2x^2 + 4x - 16$
H. $-4x$
J. $4x$
K. $-4x - 16$

43. If the sum of the measures of the interior angles of a polygon equals the sum of the measures of the exterior angles, how many sides does the polygon have?

A. 3
B. 4
C. 5
D. 6
E. 7

44. If the perimeter of an equilateral triangle is 12, what is its area?

F. $2\sqrt{3}$
G. $4\sqrt{3}$
H. 8
J. $6\sqrt{3}$
K. $36\sqrt{3}$

45. Two complementary angles are in the ratio of 8:1. What is the number of degrees in the measure of the smaller angle?

A. 10
B. 20
C. 30
D. 40
E. 80

46. GIVEN: a square, a rectangle, a trapezoid, and a circle. If one of the figures is selected at random, what is the probability that the figure has four right angles?

F. 1
G. $\frac{3}{4}$
H. $\frac{1}{2}$
J. $\frac{1}{4}$
K. 0

47. A man travels 320 miles in 8 hours. If he continues at the same rate, how many miles will he travel in the next 2 hours?

A. 6
B. 40
C. 80
D. 120
E. 240

GO ON TO THE NEXT PAGE

48. $\frac{\sin x}{\cos x} + \frac{\cos x}{\sin x} = ?$

F. 1

G. $\sin x$

H. $\frac{1}{\sin x \cos x}$

J. $\tan x$

K. $\frac{\sin x + \cos x}{\sin x \cos x}$

49. The average temperatures for five days were 82°, 86°, 91°, 79°, and 91°. What is the mode for these temperatures?

A. 79°
B. 82°
C. 85.8°
D. 86°
E. 91°

50. A booklet contains 30 pages. If 9 pages in the booklet have drawings, what percent of the pages in the booklet have drawings?

F. 30%

G. 9%

H. 3%

J. 1%

K. $\frac{3}{10}$%

51. Which of the following represents $-7t + 6t^2 - 3$ when it is completely factored?

A. $(3t - 1)(2t + 3)$
B. $(3t + 1)(2t - 3)$
C. $(6t - 1)(t + 3)$
D. $(6t + 1)(t - 3)$
E. $(2t - 1)(3t + 3)$

52. What is the solution set of $2^{x^2 + 2x} = 2^{-1}$?

F. {1}
G. {–1}
H. {1, –1}
J. {2}
K. {}

53. Jessica is 3 years younger than Joshua. If x represents Joshua's age now, what was Jessica's age four years ago in terms of x?

A. $x - 1$
B. $x - 3$
C. $x - 4$
D. $x - 6$
E. $x - 7$

54. In a drama club, x students contributed y dollars each to buy an \$18 gift for their advisor. If three more students had contributed, each student could have contributed one dollar less to buy the same gift. Which of the following sets of equations expresses this relationship?

F. $xy = 18$ and $(x + 3)(y - 1) = 18$
G. $xy = 18$ and $(x - 3)(y + 1) = 18$
H. $xy = 18$ and $(x + 3)(y + 1) = 18$
J. $xy = 18$ and $(x - 3)(y - 1) = 18$
K. $xy = 18$ and $(x + 1)(y - 3) = 18$

55. $\frac{1}{2}\sqrt{112} - \sqrt{28} + 2\sqrt{63} = ?$

A. $6\sqrt{7}$

B. $7\sqrt{7}$

C. $8\sqrt{7}$

D. $9\sqrt{7}$

E. $10\sqrt{7}$

56. What is the value of x for the following set of simultaneous equations?

$$\frac{1}{x} + \frac{1}{y} = \frac{1}{4}$$
$$\frac{1}{x} - \frac{1}{y} = \frac{3}{4}$$

F. 4

G. 2

H. $\frac{1}{2}$

J. $\frac{1}{4}$

K. –4

GO ON TO THE NEXT PAGE

57. Which set could represent the lengths of the sides of a triangle?

A. {1, 3, 6}
B. {2, 4, 7}
C. {2, 10, 12}
D. {4, 6, 8}
E. {4, 4, 10}

58. What is the solution set, in terms of a and b, for the following system of equations?

$$ax + y = b$$
$$2ax + y = 2b$$

F. $\left\{-\frac{b}{a}, 1\right\}$
G. $\{-a, b\}$
H. $\left\{\frac{b}{a}, 0\right\}$
J. $\left\{\frac{b}{a}, \frac{a}{b}\right\}$
K. $\left\{\frac{2a}{b}, \frac{2b}{a}\right\}$

59. In the figure below, $\sin\theta = \frac{r}{4}$. What is the value of $\cos\theta$?

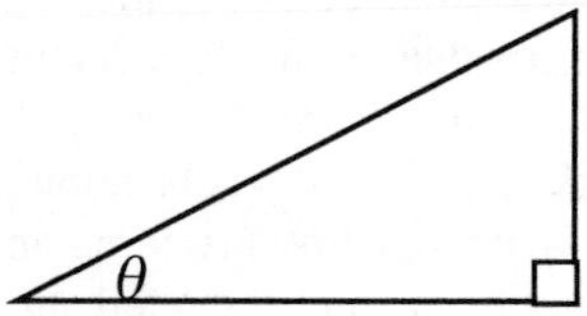

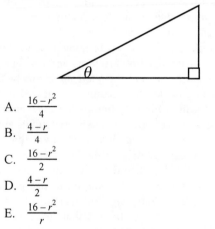

A. $\frac{16-r^2}{4}$
B. $\frac{4-r}{4}$
C. $\frac{16-r^2}{2}$
D. $\frac{4-r}{2}$
E. $\frac{16-r^2}{r}$

60. If 3 copier machines can copy 300 sheets in 3 hours, assuming the same rate, how long (in hours) will it take 6 such copiers to copy 600 sheets?

F. 2
G. 3
H. 4
J. 6
K. 9

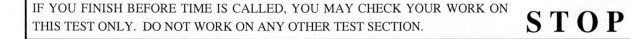

IF YOU FINISH BEFORE TIME IS CALLED, YOU MAY CHECK YOUR WORK ON THIS TEST ONLY. DO NOT WORK ON ANY OTHER TEST SECTION.

STOP

3 3 3 3 3 3 3 3 3 3 3 3

READING

35 Minutes—40 Questions

DIRECTIONS: There are four passages in this test. Each passage is followed by several questions. After reading each passage, choose the best answer to each question and blacken the corresponding oval on your answer sheet. You may refer to the passages as often as necessary.

Passage I (PF): In this passage, the author explores the behavior of Paul, a student who is repeatedly in trouble at school.

It was Paul's afternoon to appear before the faculty of Pittsburgh High School to account for his various misdemeanors. He had been suspended a week ago, and his father had called at the Principal's office and confessed his perplexity about his son. Paul entered the faculty room suave and smiling. His clothes were a trifle outgrown, and the tan velvet on the collar of his open overcoat was frayed and worn; but for all that there was something of the dandy in him, and he wore an opal pin in his neatly knotted black four-in-hand, and a red carnation in his buttonhole. This latter adornment the faculty somehow felt was not properly significant of the contrite spirit befitting a boy under the ban of suspension.

Paul was tall for his age and very thin, with high, cramped shoulders and a narrow chest. His eyes were remarkable for a certain hysterical brilliancy, and he continually used them in a conscious, theatrical sort of way, peculiarly offensive in a boy. The pupils were abnormally large, as though he were addicted to belladonna, but there was a glassy glitter about them which that drug does not produce.

When questioned by the Principal as to why he was there Paul stated, politely enough, that he wanted to come back to school. This was a lie, but Paul was quite accustomed to lying; found it, indeed, indispensable for overcoming friction. His teachers were asked to state their respective charges against him, which they did with such a rancor and aggrievedness as evinced that this was not a usual case. Disorder and impertinence were among the offenses named, yet each of his instructors felt that it was scarcely possible to put into words the real cause of the trouble, which lay in a sort of hysterically defiant manner of the boy's; in the contempt which they all knew he felt for them, and which he seemingly made not the least effort to conceal. Once, when he had been making a synopsis of a paragraph at the blackboard, his English teacher had stepped to his side and attempted to guide his hand. Paul had started back with a shudder and thrust his hands violently behind him. The astonished woman could scarcely have been more hurt and embarrassed had he struck at her. The insult was so involuntary and definitely personal as to be unforgettable. In one way and another he had made all his teachers, men and women alike, conscious of the same feeling of physical aversion. In one class he habitually sat with his hand shading his eyes; in another he always looked out of the window during the recitation; in another he made a running commentary on the lecture, with humorous intention.

His teachers felt this afternoon that his whole attitude was symbolized by his shrug and his flippantly red carnation flower, and they fell upon him without mercy, his English teacher leading the pack. He stood through it smiling, his pale lips parted over his white teeth. (His lips were continuously twitching, and he had a habit of raising his eyebrows that was contemptuous and irritating to the last degree.) Older boys than Paul had broken down and shed tears under that baptism of fire, but his set smile did not once desert him, and his only sign of discomfort was the nervous trembling of the fingers that toyed with the buttons of his overcoat, and an occasional jerking of the other hand that held his hat. Paul was always smiling, always glancing about him, seeming to feel that people might be watching him and trying to detect something. This conscious expression, since it was as far as possible from boyish mirthfulness, was usually attributed to insolence or "smartness."

From "Paul's Case" by Willa Cather

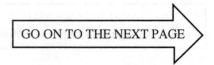

GO ON TO THE NEXT PAGE

1. This short story is subtitled "A Study in Temperament," which suggests that Cather wants to examine:

   A. a certain type of character.
   B. reactions under pressure.
   C. how people change over time.
   D. people and their settings.

2. The introductory phrases "something of the dandy" (line 9), "hysterical brilliancy" (line 17), and "peculiarly offensive" (line 19):

   I. describe Paul's reaction to his peers.
   II. show the narrator's distaste for Paul.
   III. reveal Paul as an unpleasant character.

   F. I only
   G. III only
   H. I and II only
   J. II and III only

3. Cather makes it clear in the first paragraph that the faculty of the high school:

   A. are perplexed by Paul's actions.
   B. find Paul's demeanor inappropriate.
   C. cannot understand Paul's words.
   D. want only the best for Paul.

4. As it is used in lines 17 and 34, "hysterical" and "hysterically" seem to imply:

   F. delirious.
   G. raving.
   H. uncontrolled.
   J. frothing.

5. Cather implies that the most serious flaw Paul has is his:

   A. inability to complete his work.
   B. flippant sense of humor.
   C. drug use.
   D. failure to hide his contempt for others.

6. To keep the reader from sympathizing with the faculty, Cather compares them metaphorically to:

   F. rabbits.
   G. wolves.
   H. dictators.
   J. comedians.

7. Cather uses the phrase "baptism by fire" to denote the:

   A. challenge faced by students in a faculty inquisition.
   B. youthfulness of Paul and his fellow students.
   C. obstacles adolescents confront while growing up.
   D. fury with which Paul faced the faculty.

8. The word "smartness" (line 70) is used to mean:

   F. wit.
   G. intelligence.
   H. impudence.
   J. reasonableness.

9. Which adjective does NOT describe Paul as he is presented in this story?

   A. defiant
   B. proud
   C. flippant
   D. candid

10. By the end of the selection, we find that the faculty:

    F. resent and loathe Paul.
    G. admire and trust Paul.
    H. struggle to understand Paul.
    J. are physically revolted by Paul.

GO ON TO THE NEXT PAGE

Passage II (NS): This passage discusses the production of electromagnetic radiation.

Whenever a changing electric field is produced, electromagnetic radiation is also produced. If you run a comb through your hair, you disturb electrons (negatively charged subatomic particles) in both hair and comb, producing static electricity. Every electron is surrounded by an electric field. Any sudden change in the electron's motion gives rise to *electromagnetic radiation.* If you were to run a comb through your hair while standing near an AM radio, you would produce radio static. These previous examples illustrate an important principle: Whenever you change the motion of an electron, you generate electromagnetic waves.

If you apply this principle to a heated object, you must first determine what is meant by heat. When an object is hot, its atoms are vibrating rapidly. The hotter an object becomes, the faster the atoms vibrate. The vibrating atoms collide with the electrons in the material. Each time the motion of an electron is disturbed, it emits a photon. Therefore, you should expect a heated object to emit electromagnetic radiation. This type of radiation, called *black body radiation,* is very common and is responsible for the light emitted from an incandescent light bulb.

A *spectrum* is an array of electromagnetic radiation in order of wavelength. The spectrum of visible light, such as what you see when you look at a rainbow, is most familiar, but the visible spectrum is just a small segment of the much larger electromagnetic spectrum.

The average wavelength of visible light is about 0.0005 mm. Because this unit is so small (50 light waves could be lined up end to end across the thickness of ordinary plastic wrap), wavelengths are measured in *Angstroms.* One Angstrom (Å) is 10^{-10} m. The wavelength of visible light ranges from 4000 Å to 7000 Å. Light near the short wavelength end of the visible spectrum (4000 Å) looks violet, and light near the long wavelength end (7000 Å) looks red (Figure 1). Beyond the red end of the visible spectrum lies infrared radiation, where wavelengths range from 7000 Å to 1 mm. At wavelengths shorter than violet there is ultraviolet radiation. These wavelengths range from 4000 Å down to about l00 Å. At wavelengths shorter than these are x-rays and gamma rays. Long wavelength radiation (7000 Å to 1 mm) can be observed in "heat lamps," where our skin senses infrared wavelengths as heat. These lower-energy infrared photons can warm you, but because of their low energy, they can't give you a tan. In contrast are the short wavelengths, which contain a high amount of energy. These wavelengths can be dangerous. Small doses can give you a suntan, larger doses produce sunburns, and extreme doses might produce skin cancers.

When a filament is heated, two types of collisions take place among the electrons. Gentle collisions produce low-energy photons with long wavelengths, and violent collisions produce high-energy photons with short wavelengths. A graph of the energy emitted at different wavelengths produces a curve like that in Figure 2. The curve indicates that gentle collisions and violent collisions occur infrequently. Most collisions lie somewhere in between, producing photons of intermediate wavelengths.

The *wavelength of maximum* (λ_{max}) is the wavelength at which an object emits the maximum amount of energy. The wavelength of maximum depends on the object's temperature. As an object is heated, the average collision becomes more violent, producing high-energy, shorter-wavelength photons. The hotter the object is, the shorter the λ_{max} is(Figure 2). Physics shows that λ_{max} in Angstroms equals 30 million divided by the temperature in degrees Kelvin.

$$\lambda_{max} = \frac{30 \cdot 10^6}{T}$$

This is a very important point in astronomy, since with this equation it is possible to determine the temperature of a star from its light. It is also possible to estimate the temperature of a star from the color of light it emits. For a hot star λ_{max} lies in the ultraviolet spectrum and most of the radiation cannot be seen, but in the visible range the star emits more blue than red. Thus a hot star looks blue. In contrast, a cooler star radiates its maximum energy in the infrared. In the visible range of the spectrum it radiates more red than blue and therefore looks red.

The total amount of radiation emitted at all wavelengths depends on the number of collisions per second. If an object's temperature is high, there are many collisions and it emits more light than a cooler object of the same size. Energy is measured in units called *ergs.* The total radiation given off by 1 cm^2 of the object in ergs per second equals a constant number, represented by s [$5.67 \cdot 10^{-5}$ ergs/cm^2 sec degree^4)] times the temperature raised to the fourth power.

$$E = sT^4 \text{ (ergs/sec/cm}^2\text{)}$$

It can be seen from this equation that doubling an object's temperature would radiate 2^4, or 16, times more energy.

GO ON TO THE NEXT PAGE

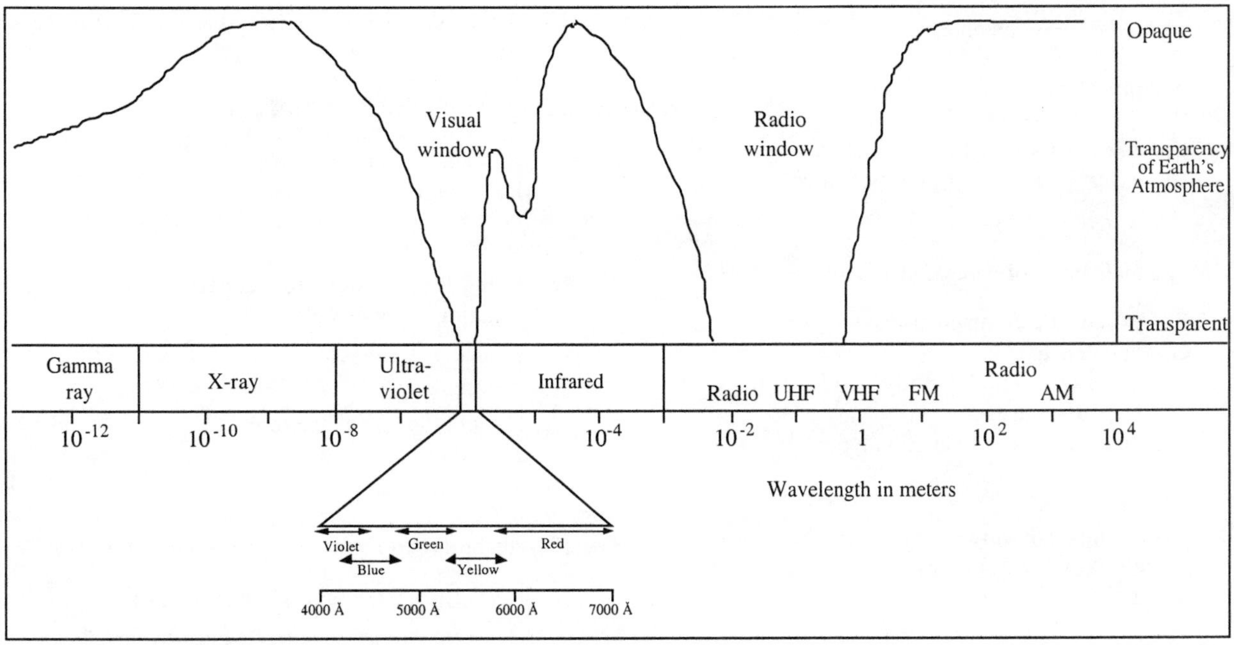

Figure 1: The electromagnetic spectrum includes all wavelengths of electromagnetic radiation. Earth's atmosphere is relatively opaque at most wavelengths. Visual and radio windows allow light and some radio waves to reach Earth's surface.

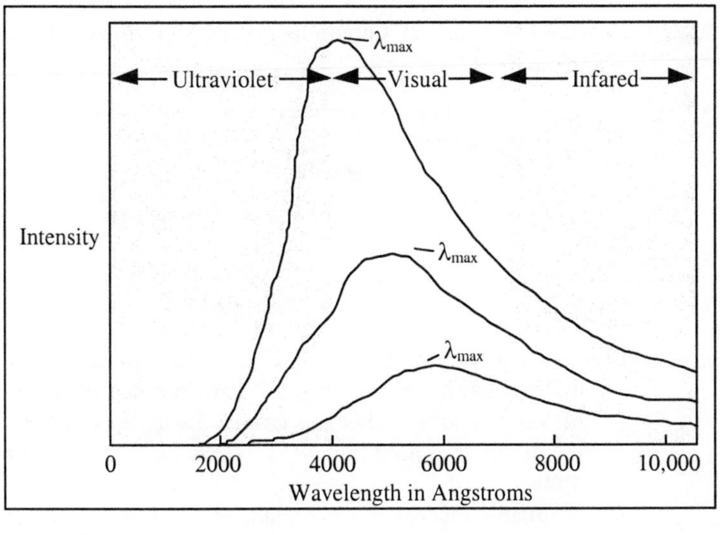

Figure 2: The intensity of radiation emitted by a heated body depends on wavelength, λ_{max} designates the wavelength of maximum intensity. Hotter objects radiate more energy and have shorter λ_{max} than cooler objects. A hot object radiates more blue light than red and therefore looks blue. A cool object radiates more red than blue and therefore looks red.

11. An x-ray has a wavelength shorter than that of:

A. ultraviolet radiation.
B. infrared radiation.
C. 500 Å.
D. all of the above.

12. A short wavelength can be more dangerous than a long wavelength due to its:

F. low energy.
G. high energy.
H. black body radiation.
J. temperature.

GO ON TO THE NEXT PAGE

13. At $\lambda_{max} = \frac{30 \cdot 10^6}{T}$ an object:

A. turns blue.
B. produces gentle collisions of electrons.
C. releases radio static.
D. emits a maximum amount of energy.

14. The main point of paragraph 2 is to:

F. explain electromagnetism.
G. define heat.
H. contrast black body radiation with incandescence.
J. give examples of radiation types.

15. According to Figure 1, which of the following wavelengths would fall within the visible spectrum?

A. 500 Å
B. 1000 Å
C. 5000 Å
D. 10,000 Å

16. In the equation shown in line 97, what is *T*?

F. time
G. wavelength
H. number of photons emitted
J. temperature

17. An astronomer views two stars of different temperatures. Which is hotter?

A. The one that is larger
B. The one that is smaller
C. The one that is redder
D. The one that is bluer

18. Lines 89-90 refers to "collisions per second," meaning collisions of:

F. photons.
G. electrons.
H. photons with electrons.
J. all of the above.

19. According to Figure 2, which statement is true?

A. λ_{max} of a hot object varies with size.
B. Temperature is unrelated to wavelength.
C. A cool object radiates red.
D. Ultraviolet light has a longer wavelength than infrared light.

20. Heating an object from 2000° K to 4000° K would:

F. multiply its radiated energy by 16.
G. decrease its radiated energy by half
H. have no effect on the energy released.
J. cause it to radiate more red light.

Passage III (H): In this selection, the author expresses his opinion regarding the role of philosophy.

Minerva was the goddess of wisdom, but on one occasion she did a very foolish thing; she entered into competition with Juno and Venus for the prize of beauty. It happened thus: At the nuptials of Peleus and Thetis all the gods were invited with the exception of Eris, or Discord. Enraged at her exclusion, the goddess threw a golden apple among the guests, with the inscription, "For the fairest." Thereupon Juno, Venus, and Minerva each claimed the apple. Jupiter, not willing to decide in so delicate a matter, sent the goddesses to Mount Ida, where the beautiful shepherd Paris was tending his flocks, and to him was committed the decision. The goddesses accordingly appeared before him. Juno promised him power and riches, Minerva glory and renown in war, and Venus the fairest of women for his wife, each attempting to bias his decision in her own favour. Paris decided in favour of Venus and gave her the golden apple, thus making the two other goddesses his enemies. Under the protection of Venus, Paris sailed to Greece, and was hospitably received by Menelaus, king of Sparta. Now Helen, the wife of Menelaus, was the very woman whom Venus had destined for Paris, the fairest of her sex. She had been sought as a bride by numerous suitors, and before her decision was made known, they all, at the suggestion of Ulysses, one of their number, took an oath that they would defend her from all injury and avenge her cause if necessary. She chose Menelaus, and was living with him happily when Paris became their guest. Paris, aided by Venus, persuaded her to elope with him, and carried her to Troy, whence arose the famous Trojan war, the theme of the greatest poems of antiquity, those of Homer and Virgil.

Menelaus called upon his brother chieftains of

GO ON TO THE NEXT PAGE

Greece to fulfill their pledge, and join him in his efforts to recover his wife. They generally came forward, but Ulysses, who had married Penelope, and was very happy in his wife and child, had no disposition to embark in such a troublesome affair. He therefore hung back and Palamedes was sent to urge him. When Palamedes arrived at Ithaca Ulysses pretended to be mad. He yoked an ass and an ox together to the plough and began to sow salt. Palamedes, to try him, placed the infant Telemachus before the plough, whereupon the father turned the plough aside, showing plainly that he was no madman, and after that could no longer refuse to fulfill his promise. Being now himself gained for the undertaking, he lent his aid to bring in other reluctant chiefs, especially Achilles. This hero was the son of that Thetis at whose marriage the apple of Discord had been thrown among the goddesses. Thetis was herself one of the immortals, a sea-nymph, and knowing that her son was fated to perish before Troy if he went on the expedition, she endeavored to prevent his going. She sent him away to the court of King Lycomedes, and induced him to conceal himself in the disguise of a maiden among the daughters of the king. Ulysses, hearing he was there, went disguised as a merchant to the palace and offered for sale female ornaments, among which he had placed some arms. While the king's daughters were engrossed with the other contents of the merchant's pack, Achilles handled the weapons and thereby betrayed himself to the keen eye of Ulysses, who found no great difficulty in persuading him to disregard his mother's prudent counsels and join his countrymen in the war.

From "Mythology" by Thomas Bulfinch

21. By describing Jupiter as "not willing to decide in so delicate a matter" (lines 11-12), the author implies that:

    A. Jupiter is usually heavy-handed.
    B. any decision is bound to offend someone.
    C. Jupiter is overly sensitive.
    D. the problems are so obscure that no one can judge them.

22. The word *disposition* (line 40) is used to mean:

    F. inclination.
    G. nature.
    H. integrity.
    J. value.

23. All of the following assertions are examples of the author's inserting himself into the narrative EXCEPT:

    A. Minerva did a foolish thing.
    B. The poems of Homer and Virgil were great.
    C. Helen was the fairest of her sex.
    D. The greatest poems of antiquity were about the Trojan War.

24. The sowing of salt (line 45) is intended to show:

    F. Ulysses' attempt to be found insane.
    G. the difficulty of cultivating in rocky soil.
    H. how the tears of the gods created the sea.
    J. Ulysses' talent as a soldier rather than a farmer.

25. When Palamedes "tries" Ulysses (line 45), he:

    A. finds him guilty.
    B. judges him.
    C. tests him.
    D. attempts to help him.

26. The author reveals that Thetis is a sea-nymph in order to explain:

    F. why she married Peleus.
    G. why she dislikes the idea of war.
    H. the effect of the apple of discord.
    J. her ability to predict the future.

27. Among the chieftains of Greece apparently are:

    A. Juno, Venus, and Minerva.
    B. Paris and Lycomedes.
    C. Ulysses, Achilles, and Menelaus.
    D. Eris and Thetis.

28. Why does Ulysses display arms among the ornaments?

    F. To trick Achilles into revealing himself
    G. As a declaration of war
    H. To mislead the daughters of the king
    J. To complete his disguise as a merchant

GO ON TO THE NEXT PAGE

29. This passage foreshadows which of the following events?

    I. The death of Achilles
    II. The advent of war
    III. The downfall of Paris

    A. I only
    B. II only
    C. I and II only
    D. II and III only

30. A reasonable title for this narrative might be:

    F. "Achilles and Ulysses"
    G. "The Apple of Discord Leads to War"
    H. "Beauty and the Beast"
    J. "The Pettiness of the Gods"

Passage IV (SS): This passage discusses the history of African Americans in Congress.

Only with the enforcement of the Reconstruction Act of 1867 and the ratification of the Fifteenth Amendment to the Constitution—nearly 70 years after the ratification of the U.S. Constitution—did African Americans first win seats in Congress. Hiram Revels of Mississippi became the first African American to serve in Congress when he took his seat in the Senate on February 25, 1870. Joseph Rainey of South Carolina became the first African American member of the House of Representatives later in 1870. In the next 80 years, nearly seventy African Americans served in Congress.

African Americans throughout the South became politically active soon after emancipation and the close of the Civil War. State conventions and local political societies such as the Union League provided an opportunity for freed African Americans to articulate their vision of full participation in the political and economic life of the former slave states. Out of this broad-based political mobilization emerged a generation of African American leaders who nearly unanimously adhered to the Republican Party because it had championed the rights of African Americans. African Americans elected to Congress during Reconstruction found the national legislature an effective forum for the advocacy of political equality. Following the end of federal Reconstruction in 1877, African Americans continued to win election to Congress and carried on the struggle for civil rights and economic opportunity. The African American congressional representatives of the late nineteenth century were the most prominent indication of the persistence of political organization on a local level in the South.

During the 1890s and early 1900s, no African American won election to Congress, in part because of restrictive state election codes in some southern states. During World War I and in the following decade, however, African American migration to northern cities established the foundation for political organization in urban centers. Oscar DePriest's election in 1928 as a representative from Chicago began a slow but steady succession of political victories in the North. Over the next three decades African Americans won congressional seats in New York City, Detroit, and Philadelphia. In the wake of the civil rights movement and the enforcement of the Voting Rights Act of 1965, African Americans regained seats in the South. Since the 1930s, nearly all African American representatives have been Democrats.

Since the nineteenth century African American members of Congress have served as advocates for all African Americans as well as representatives for their constituencies. During Reconstruction and the late nineteenth century, African American representatives called on their colleagues to protect the voting rights of African Americans. These members of Congress, many of them former slaves, also called for expanded educational opportunities and land grants for freed African Americans. In the mid-twentieth century, African American representatives turned to the needs of urban communities and urged federal programs for improved housing and job training. As the most prominent African American officeholders of the time, these representatives served as defenders of the civil rights movement and proponents of legislation to end segregation. In 1971, the establishment of the Congressional Black Caucus offered a formal means of representing the combined interests of African Americans. The caucus has demonstrated a special concern for the protection of civil rights; the guarantee of equal opportunity in education, employment, and housing; and a broad array of foreign and domestic policy issues.

African Americans in Congress have been further united by their shared experience in the African American community. Many of the early Black representatives were born in slavery. The political and

GO ON TO THE NEXT PAGE

economic opportunities of Reconstruction offered these representatives the hope that African Americans might achieve genuine equality in American society, while the opposition of some white Southerners reminded them of the need for federal protection of the liberties won in the aftermath of the Civil War.

Since the victories of the civil rights movement in the 1960s, African American men and women have won election to Congress from increasingly diverse regions of the country. Whether from largely urban districts, suburban areas, or more recently from rural Mississippi, these members of Congress have maintained their common concern with economic issues that affect African Americans and with the protection of civil rights.

The collected biographies of African Americans who served in the House and Senate provide an important perspective on the history of the Congress and the role of African Americans in American politics. Their stories offer eloquent testimony to the long struggle to extend the ideals of the founders to encompass all citizens of the United States.

31. According to the passage, the first African American to serve in the House of Representatives was:

A. Hiram Revels.
B. Joseph Rainey.
C. from Chicago.
D. a former slave.

32. The passage suggests that, in contrast to African Americans elected to Congress during and shortly after Reconstruction, Americans selected to Congress today are more likely to:

F. come from urban areas in the North.
G. be members of the Republican Party.
H. work for full political equality for all African Americans.
J. come from districts in which the majority is African American.

33. One difference between African American congressional representatives in the nineteenth century and those in the mid-twentieth century was:

A. the political party to which they were likely to belong.
B. their commitment to education for African Americans.
C. the strength of their ties to the African American community as a whole.
D. the extent to which they represented all African Americans and not just their constituents.

34. When the African American representatives "turned to" certain issues in the mid-twentieth century (line 62), they:

F. became antagonistic toward those issues.
G. reversed their positions on those issues.
H. devoted themselves to those issues.
J. referred to those issues.

35. According to the passage, one reason African Americans began to be elected to Congress from cities in the northern United States after the 1930s was that:

A. more African Americans lived in northern cities at that time than had been the case previously.
B. African Americans in northern cities had better political organizations than did African Americans in the rural South.
C. African American politicians in the North were more likely to be members of the Democratic party than were those in the South.
D. African American politicians in the North were more likely to focus on voting rights for African Americans than were those in the South.

GO ON TO THE NEXT PAGE

36. Which one of the following is NOT mentioned in the passage as a common concern of African American congressional representatives?

    F. Enforcing voting rights for African Americans
    G. Increasing educational opportunities for African Americans
    H. Ensuring opportunities for employment for African Americans
    J. Protecting people of African descent in other countries

37. One reason cited in the passage for the election of African Americans to Congress from both southern states after Reconstruction and northern states after World War I is the:

    A. success of the civil rights movement.
    B. passage and enforcement of the Fifteenth Amendment.
    C. strength of local African American political organizations.
    D. predominance of African Americans in certain districts.

38. According to the passage, the Congressional Black Caucus:

    F. focused its attention almost exclusively on domestic issues.
    G. was the first organization founded exclusively for African American congressional representatives.
    H. was intended to replace local African American political organizations with one large national organization.
    J. provided a forum in which African American representatives could deal with issues of concern to all African Americans.

39. The last paragraph suggests that this passage might serve as:

    A. a call to political involvement on the part of African Americans.
    B. an introduction to biographies of African American members of Congress.
    C. the conclusion of a history of African Americans in the United States.
    D. part of a longer work on the history of the United States Congress.

40. The author expresses admiration for the African American congressional representatives discussed in the passage for their:

    F. political acumen.
    G. attempts to ensure the rights of all Americans.
    H. single-minded devotion to the struggle for civil rights.
    J. focus on providing economic opportunity for African Americans.

IF YOU FINISH BEFORE TIME IS CALLED, YOU MAY CHECK YOUR WORK ON THIS TEST ONLY. DO NOT WORK ON ANY OTHER TEST SECTION.

STOP

4 4 4 4 4 4 4 4 4 4 4 4

SCIENCE REASONING

35 Minutes—40 Questions

DIRECTIONS: There are seven passages in this test. Each passage is followed by several questions. After reading a passage, choose the best answer to each question and blacken the corresponding oval on your answer sheet. You may refer to the passages as often as necessary.

Passage I

Part of our understanding of the Earth comes from a consideration of its physical properties. A table of selected properties is presented below:

Property	*Value*
Mass	$6 \bullet 10^{24}$ kg
Diameter	$6 \bullet 10^{6}$ m
Orbital Radius	$1.5 \bullet 10^{11}$ m
Period of Revolution	365.3 days
Period of Rotation	24 hours

Below is a table comparing the other planets of the solar system to the Earth.

	Earth	*Jupiter*	*Mars*	*Mercury*	*Neptune*	*Pluto*	*Saturn*	*Uranus*	*Venus*
Diameter	1	10	0.55	0.38	4.3	?	9.4	4.1	0.98
Mass	1	320	0.10	0.58	17	?	95	14	0.83
Surface Gravity	1	2.7	0.40	0.40	1.2	?	1.2	1.1	0.90
Volume	1	1320	0.15	0.58	42	0.729	760	50	0.90
Average Distance to Sun	1	5.3	1.5	0.40	30	40	10	19	0.70
Period of Revolution	1	12	2	0.25	165	248	30	84	0.60
Period of Rotation	1	0.40	1	60	0.50	0	0.40	0.50	240

The following are a few basic equations:

1) density $= \frac{\text{mass}}{\text{volume}}$
2) distance = rate • time
3) volume of a sphere $= \frac{4}{3}\pi r^2$ where r is the radius of the sphere

1. Based on the table above, the approximate ratio of the period of revolution in days to the period of rotation in days for Mercury is:

   A. 240
   B. $\frac{2}{3}$
   C. $\frac{1}{240}$
   D. $\frac{3}{2}$

2. Which planet is as dense as the planet Earth?

   F. Mercury
   G. Venus
   H. Mars
   J. None

3. Which planet orbits the sun at the slowest rate?

   A. Mercury
   B. Jupiter
   C. Neptune
   D. Pluto

GO ON TO THE NEXT PAGE

4. Analysis of the tables above shows that surface gravity most likely depends on:

F. mass alone.
G. distance and mass.
H. density alone.
J. density of the planet and proximity to the sun.

5. Assuming that both the Earth and Pluto are spherical, the diameter of Pluto is:

A. 0.729 • radius of Earth
B. 0.9 • radius of Earth
C. 1.8 • radius of Earth
D. 2.7 • radius of Earth

6. How many millions of miles separate the farthest apart planetary neighbors?

F. 40 • Earth's orbital radius
G. 11 • Earth's orbital radius
H. 9 • Earth's orbital radius
J. 10 • Earth's orbital radius

Passage II

Four groups of 1000 men each were placed on strict diets that contained different intakes of cholesterol. The men stayed on the diet for 40 years, and their history of illness over that time is recorded below.

	Death rate, standardized/1000			
		Men taking in a daily average of		
Illness	*No cholesterol*	0–5 grams	6–20 grams	20+ grams
Cancer				
Colon	0.01	0.03	0.04	0.02
Prostate	2.02	0.06	1.03	4.01
Lung	0.03	0.06	0.40	0.20
Coronary				
Thrombosis	5.02	1.01	4.00	10.05
Arrest	6.00	0.98	5.09	11.00
Cardiovascular	5.96	0.65	4.97	9.08
Cerebral Clot	4.01	0.02	0.50	4.01
Depression	5.01	0.30	0.30	0.30

7. Which of the following statements is best supported by the data?

A. A man ingesting no cholesterol is approximately twice as likely to die of prostate cancer than a man ingesting 10 grams per day.
B. Any ingestion of cholesterol decreases the risk of dying from all three forms of cancer listed here.
C. Ingestion of cholesterol seems unrelated to the probability of coronary disease.
D. Cerebral clots are the most prevalent form of death among the group consuming the most cholesterol.

8. What might one conclude about the relationship between cholesterol ingestion and depression on the basis of the information above?

F. Cholesterol causes depression.
G. Ingestion of cholesterol has no effect on the occurrence of depression.
H. Small amounts of cholesterol are most effective in combating depression.
J. Large and small amounts of cholesterol are equally effective in reducing the depression death rate.

GO ON TO THE NEXT PAGE

9. For which of the following diseases does the highest cholesterol diet increase the probability of death most, compared *relatively* to the non-cholesterol diets (i.e., which increases by the highest percentage)?

   A. Cerebral clots
   B. Coronary arrest
   C. Cardiovascular disease
   D. Coronary thrombosis

10. For which of the following groups of diseases does a daily intake of 0-5 grams of cholesterol reduce the probability of death regardless of initial cholesterol intake?

   F. Cerebral clot, coronary thrombosis, lung cancer
   G. Cerebral clot, depression, colon cancer
   H. Depression, coronary arrest, prostate cancer
   J. Depression, coronary thrombosis, colon cancer

11. What might be involved in determining a standardized death rate for men?

   A. Ignoring deaths that do not conform to the average results
   B. Adjusting death rates according to discrepancies in age
   C. Assuming that the natural death rate is 0 deaths per 1000 men
   D. Comparing data with a similar experiment involving women

---

Passage III

The solubility of materials in liquids depends not only on the nature of the solute and the solvent, but also on temperature. A graph showing the solubilities of several substances in water is presented below.

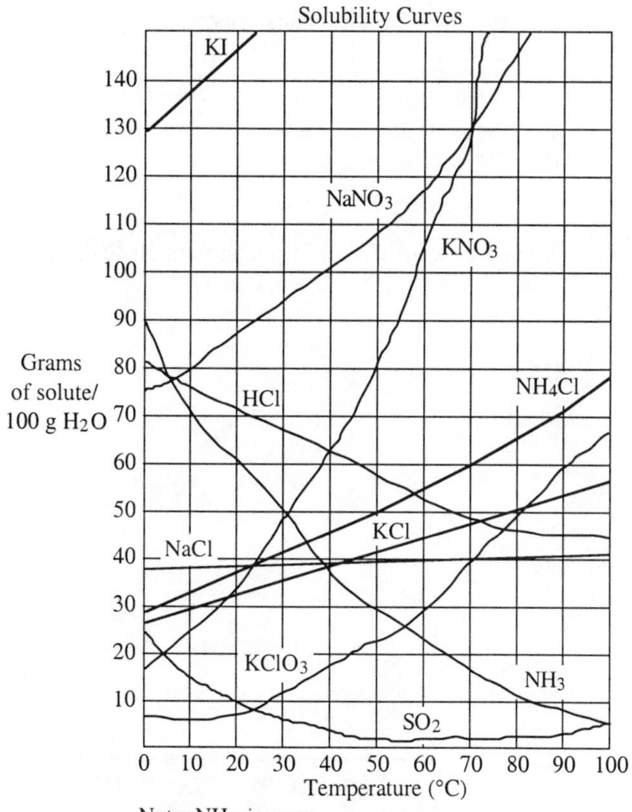

Note: NH_3 is a gas.

12. Which of the following has a solubility most sensitive to temperature throughout the range shown?

   F. $NaNO_3$
   G. KNO_3
   H. NaCl
   J. NH_3

13. The solubility of sodium (Na) salts is:

   A. high because sodium is an alkali metal.
   B. low because sodium combines with anions to make salts.
   C. dependent on what salt it forms.
   D. always greater than 20 grams per 100 grams of water.

14. A 250 ml alcoholic solution of KNO_3 at 500°C contains how many grams KNO_3 at saturation?

   F. 80
   G. 200
   H. 30
   J. Insufficient data is provided.

GO ON TO THE NEXT PAGE

15. A solution containing equal amounts of $NaNO_3$ and KNO_3 is allowed to cool until a white powder begins to appear at the bottom of the flask. That powder is:

A. KNO_3
B. $NaNO_3$
C. A mixture of both
D. Insufficient data is provided.

16. The solubility curve of NH_3 suggests an explanation of why:

F. divers get the bends (nitrogen bubbles in the blood) if they rise too quickly.
G. soda goes flat.
H. warm lemonade is sweeter than cold lemonade.
J. hot air balloons rise.

Passage IV

The resistance (R) of a material is directly proportional to the resistivity (r) of the material, resistivity is measured in ohm-meters. The voltage (V, measured in volts) in a circuit is directly proportional to both the resistance (R, measured in ohms) and the current (I, measured in amperes). Resistors in series act as one resistor according to the formula:

$$R_s = R_1 + R_2 + R_3 + \ldots$$

and resistors in parallel act as one resistor according to the formula:

$$\frac{1}{R_p} = \frac{1}{R_1} + \frac{1}{R_2} + \frac{1}{R_3} + \ldots$$

The resistivities of several materials are listed below.

Substance	*Resistivity (r) (ohm-meters)*
Aluminum	$2.63 \cdot 10^{-8}$
Copper	$1.72 \cdot 10^{-8}$
Germanium	$6.00 \cdot 10^{-1}$
Silicon	$2.30 \cdot 10^{3}$
Silver	$1.47 \cdot 10^{-8}$
Sulfur	$1.00 \cdot 10^{15}$

17. According to the information provided, the best formula for the voltage in a circuit, where voltage is V, current is I, and resistance is R is:

A. $V = \frac{I}{R}$.
B. $V = I + R$.
C. $V = IR$.
D. $V = I - R$.

18. According to the information provided, how would the voltage in a circuit with a silver resistor compare to the voltage in a circuit with a germanium resistor of the same size? (Current is the same in both circuits.)

F. The voltage in the silver circuit would be greater.
G. The voltage in the germanium circuit would be greater.
H. The voltage would be the same in both circuits.
J. Cannot be determined from the information given.

19. Two resistors with $R = 2$ are placed in series. How does the voltage in the circuit compare with the voltage in a circuit with only one resistor, $R = 2$? (Assume current remains constant.)

A. The voltage is doubled.
B. The voltage is halved.
C. The voltage is the same.
D. The voltage is zero.

20. A resistor with $R = 4$ is put in parallel with an identical resistor, $R = 4$. What is R_p?

F. 0
G. $\frac{1}{2}$
H. 1
J. 2

GO ON TO THE NEXT PAGE

21. Power is defined as $P = I^2R$. If R is a constant, then power would increase —— with an increase in the current. (Fill in the blank space with the best answer choice.)

A. Logarithmically
B. Directly
C. Exponentially
D. Inversely

22. In order to keep the current in a circuit constant, if one increases the voltage, one must:

F. lengthen the circuit.
G. shorten the circuit.
H. decrease the resistance.
J. increase the resistance.

Passage V

In order to discover the steps by which a chemical reaction occurs, the dependence of the initial rate of reaction on the concentration of the reactants is determined. Three experiments exploring the mechanism of a reaction are presented below.

Experiment 1

Compound *A* is injected into a rapidly stirred solution of *B* in hexamethyl phosphoramide. As *A* and *B* react, they form a compound that has a characteristic absorption at 520 manometers. The concentration of product, and therefore the rate of reaction, can be calculated by measuring the strength of the absorption. Results are presented below:

Trial	*Concentration* A	*Concentration* B	*Rate*
1	4	4	60
2	2	2	30
3	4	2	30
4	4	8	120

Experiment 2

Compound *A* is injected into a rapidly mixed solution of *B* in carbon tetrachloride. The product of the reaction is identical to the product in the previous experiment. The course of the reaction is followed by spectrophotometric methods as in Experiment 1.

Trial	*Concentration* A	*Concentration* B	*Rate*
1	3	3	27
2	6	6	108
3	6	3	54
4	12	6	216

Experiment 3

Compound *A* is injected in a swirling solution of *B* in a 1:1-by-volume mixture of carbon tetrachloride and hexamethyl phosphoramide. The formation of product, as before, is followed by spectrophotometry.

Trial	*Concentration* A	*Concentration* B	*Rate*
1	9	9	54
2	9	4.5	27
3	4	4.5	18
4	4	9	36

23. Which of the following best describes the effect of concentration *A* on the rate of reaction in Experiment 1?

A. Rate increases with increasing *A*.
B. Rate increases by the square of the concentration of *A*.
C. Rate increases by the square root of the concentration of *A*.
D. Rate is independent of the concentration of *A*.

24. Which of the following best describes the effect of concentration *A* on the rate of reaction in Experiment 2?

F. Rate increases with increasing *A*.
G. Rate increases by the square of the concentration of *A*.
H. Rate increases by the square root of the concentration of *A*.
J. Rate is independent of the concentration of *A*.

GO ON TO THE NEXT PAGE

25. Which of the following best describes the effect of concentration *A* on the rate in Experiment 3?

A. Rate increases with increasing *A*.
B. Rate increases by the square of the concentration of *A*.
C. Rate increases by the square root of the concentration of *A*.
D. Rate is independent of the concentration of *A*.

26. What is the likeliest explanation for the results obtained in Experiment 3?

F. A mechanism intermediate between the ones found in Experiments 1 and 2.
G. Some of the molecules react by Experiment 1's mechanism, others by Experiment 2's mechanism.
H. An entirely different mechanism is responsible.
J. There is an averaging of the mechanisms.

27. What is the best conclusion that can be drawn from this set of experiments?

A. Rate is increased by changing solvents.
B. Reactions may depend on solvent effects as well as on the nature of the reactants.
C. Mechanisms can always be changed by use of an appropriate solvent.
D. Reactions depend on solvent effects as well as on the nature of the reactants.

Passage VI

Acceleration is defined as the change in the velocity of an object divided by the length of time during which that change took place. Contrary to popular belief, Galileo did not base his conclusion on the acceleration of gravity on experiments done with cannonballs dropped from the Leaning Tower of Pisa. Instead, he used the motion of objects moving down an inclined plane to develop his theory. In the following sets of experiments, a student studies the motion of bodies on an inclined plane.

NOTE: For all of the following experiments, time is measured in seconds, distance in meters, and velocity in meters per second. The distance (*d*) an object travels at a constant acceleration (*a*) in time (*t*), assuming it starts from rest, is given by the equation: $d = \frac{1}{2}at^2$.

Experiment 1

A student set up a smooth wooden board at an angle of 30° from horizontal. The board had a length of 10 meters. Using a stroboscope, the student was able to determine the position of a 100-gram steel ball that was rolled down the incline. Velocity was determined by means of a radar gun. The results are presented below:

Time	*Distance*	*Velocity*
0	0	0
0.5	0.44	1.75
1.0	1.75	3.5
1.5	3.94	5.25
2.0	7.00	7.00

Experiment 2

The same 10-meter wooden board was used in Experiment 2. The angle used was again 30°. The object used this time was a 100-gram sled made of the same material as the ball in Experiment 1. The stroboscope and the radar gun were used to determine its position and velocity as it slid down the inclined plane. The results are presented below:

Time	*Distance*	*Velocity*
0	0	0
0.5	1.13	2.45
1.0	2.45	4.90
1.5	5.51	7.35
2.0	9.80	9.80

Experiment 3

The same board at the same angle was used in the third experiment as in the previous two. In this experiment a 100-gram box made of the same material as the ball and the sled was used. The same recording devices were used, and the results are presented below:

GO ON TO THE NEXT PAGE

Time	Distance	Velocity
0	0	0
1.0	0.33	0.66
2.0	1.31	1.32
3.0	2.97	1.98
4.0	5.28	2.64
5.0	8.25	3.30

Experiment 4

The board in the previous experiments was carefully oiled. Once again the board was placed at an angle of 30° from horizontal. Each of the objects was then allowed to move down the inclined plane, and the time required to reach the bottom of the plane is recorded below:

Object	Time
sled	2.02
ball	2.39
box	4.08

28. Which object in the first three experiments has the greatest acceleration?

F. Ball
G. Sled
H. Box
J. Ball and sled are equal.

29. The acceleration of the ball relative to that of the sled is due to the ball's:

A. rolling.
B friction.
C. rolling and friction.
D. being the same mass as the sled, and therefore having the same acceleration.

30. The acceleration of the ball relative to that of the box is due to:

F. the ball's rolling only.
G. the ball's friction only.
H. the ball's rolling and friction.
J. the ball's having the same mass as the box, and therefore having the same acceleration.

31. Based on these four experiments, the ratio of the acceleration of the ball to the acceleration of the sled is:

A. 1
B. $\frac{5}{7}$
C. dependent on amount of friction.
D. time dependent.

32. Based on these four experiments, the ratio of the acceleration of the ball to the acceleration of the box is:

F. 1
G. $\frac{5}{7}$
H. dependent on amount of friction.
J. dependent on time.

Passage VII

What was the fate of Neanderthal man? Two differing views are presented below.

Scientist 1

Neanderthals were very similar to modern humans in appearance. It is true that Neanderthals were somewhat more muscular than modern humans and that the way the muscles seem to have been arranged on the skeleton was, in a few minor ways, different. This we are able to deduce from the places on the surviving bones that mark where the ligaments were once attached. For example, the neck and wrists of Neanderthals were far thicker than is natural to modern humans. Some of the facial structure was also different, especially the protrusion of the brow. But differences between the appearance of Neanderthals and modern humans have been exaggerated, since they are based on the skeleton of one individual who was later discovered to have been suffering from severe arthritis. It is not unlikely that, because of the low population density and the nomadic lifestyle that spread the few individuals over ever-larger areas, Neanderthal and early modern humans interbred and eventually merged into one species. The notion that

GO ON TO THE NEXT PAGE

some sort of "war" broke out between these different species (or, more likely, subspecies) of humans is an attempt to look out of early human eyes with a modern perspective.

Scientist 2

Whenever two species compete for the same niche there is a conflict. In this conflict the loser either moves to a different niche or dies out. It is unusual for two species to interbreed. The difference between early modern humans and Neanderthals physically may not appear great to an anatomist, but to the average man on the street, or prehistoric man in the forest, the differences are not subtle. And it was these individuals, not the anatomists, who had to decide whether or not to mate. And even if early modern humans and Neanderthals did mate, the result—us—would look more like a mix of the two rather than like modern humans. Early modern humans and Neanderthals, because they were so close to each other physically, must have been deadly enemies. The population was thinly dispersed at that time because the resources available would not support a greater population density. There literally was not room enough on the planet for the two species. They could not combine because they were so different in appearance, so only one answer remained. We survived because we killed our cousin.

33. Underlying the hypothesis of Scientist 1 is the assumption that:

A. early modern humans and Neanderthals did not compete for the same kinds of food.
B. early modern humans and Neanderthals were genetically close.
C. early modern humans and Neanderthals did not necessarily live in the same area.
D. early modern humans and Neanderthals often fought.

34. Underlying the hypotheses of both scientists is the assumption that:

F. early modern humans and Neanderthals understood the consequences of their actions.
G. early modern humans and Neanderthals both lived in exactly the same type of environment.
H. early modern humans and Neanderthals both lived in the same geographical regions.
J. early modern humans were more intelligent than Neanderthals.

35. If an isolated community of Neanderthals was discovered, whose hypothesis would be more damaged?

A. Scientist l's because his theory does not allow for such a community to survive.
B. Scientist 2's because early modern human's descendants inhabit all the Earth and therefore there should be no community of Neanderthals.
C. Both hypotheses are disproved.
D. Neither is affected.

36. Which of the following, if true, would most support the hypothesis of Scientist 2?

F. The camps of early modern humans are often close to the camps of Neanderthals.
G. The camps of early modern humans are never close to Neanderthal camps.
H. Bones of Neanderthals and early modern humans are often found near each other.
J. Chipped Neanderthal bones are found with early modern human weapons.

37. The fact that lions and tigers fight when brought together even though they can be interbred supports which hypothesis to the greater extent?

A. Scientist 1's because it proves two species can interbreed.
B. Scientist 1's because two species still exist that share the same niche.
C. Scientist 2's because it suggests that two species that can interbreed may not do so under natural conditions.
D. Scientist 2's because lions and tigers fight when brought together.

38. According to the hypothesis of Scientist 2, what should be the result of interbreeding lions and tigers?

F. The offspring should be infertile.
G. The offspring will resemble one parent only.
H. The offspring will possess a mixture of traits.
J. Scientist 2's hypothesis makes no conjectures on the point because lions and tigers would not interbreed.

GO ON TO THE NEXT PAGE

39. What other assumption do both Scientist 1 and Scientist 2 make about Neanderthals and early modern humans?

A. That early modern humans were directly involved in the disappearance of Neanderthals
B. That early modern humans were the more intelligent of the two
C. That Neanderthals differed little from early modern humans
D. That early modern humans only inhabited regions that were hospitable for Neanderthals

40. If a burial site containing over one hundred early modern humans and Neanderthal remains was discovered, and if two Neanderthal skeletons were found with early modern human spearpoints in them, which hypothesis would be the most strengthened?

F. That of Scientist 1 because spearpoints need not have been what killed the two Neanderthals
G. That of Scientist 2 because two Neanderthals were killed by early modern humans and no early modern humans were killed by Neanderthals.
H. That of Scientist 2 because the spearpoints prove that the early modern humans had more developed weapons
J. That of Scientist 1 because only a couple of the individuals buried together died violently

IF YOU FINISH BEFORE TIME IS CALLED, YOU MAY CHECK YOUR WORK ON THIS TEST ONLY. DO NOT WORK ON ANY OTHER TEST SECTION.

STOP

Answer Key

DIRECTIONS: For the *correct* answers in each ACT Test Subject, check the corresponding unshaded box. (Correct answers correspond to unshaded boxes.) Then, for each test, total the number of checkmarks in each column (subject category) and add to determine the raw scores.

TEST 1: ENGLISH (p. A-170)

#	Answer	UM	RH
1.	C	☐	■
2.	J	■	☐
3.	D	■	☐
4.	G	☐	■
5.	A	☐	■
6.	H	☐	■
7.	C	■	☐
8.	F	☐	■
9.	B	☐	■
10.	G	■	☐
11.	D	☐	■
12.	H	☐	■
13.	C	■	☐
14.	H	■	☐
15.	D	☐	■
16.	F	☐	■
17.	B	☐	■
18.	J	■	☐
19.	D	☐	■
20.	H	☐	■
21.	A	☐	■
22.	J	☐	■
23.	A	■	☐
24.	H	■	☐
25.	C	☐	■
26.	J	■	☐
27.	A	☐	■
28.	J	■	☐
29.	C	☐	■
30.	F	■	☐
31.	A	☐	■
32.	J	☐	■
33.	B	■	☐
34.	G	☐	■
35.	D	■	☐
36.	G	☐	■
37.	A	■	☐
38.	H	■	☐
39.	B	☐	■
40.	J	■	☐
41.	A	☐	■
42.	H	☐	■
43.	D	■	☐
44.	H	☐	■
45.	B	■	☐
46:	J	■	☐
47.	B	■	☐
48.	F	☐	■
49.	D	■	☐
50.	H	■	☐
51.	B	☐	■
52.	F	☐	■
53.	D	☐	■
54.	G	☐	■
55.	D	■	☐
56.	J	■	☐
57.	C	☐	■
58.	H	☐	■
59.	A	■	☐
60.	G	■	☐
61.	A	☐	■
62.	H	■	☐
63.	B	■	☐
64.	J	☐	■
65.	D	■	☐
66.	H	☐	■
67.	C	☐	■
68.	G	■	☐
69.	B	■	☐
70.	F	☐	■
71.	D	☐	■
72.	J	☐	■
73.	C	■	☐
74.	F	■	☐
75.	A	■	☐

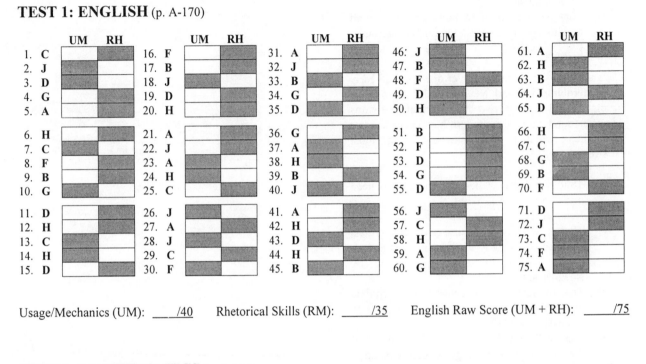

Usage/Mechanics (UM): ____/40 Rhetorical Skills (RM): ____/35 English Raw Score (UM + RH): ____/75

TEST 2: MATHEMATICS (p. A-184)

#	Answer	EA	AG	GT
1.	A	☐	■	■
2.	G	☐	■	■
3.	B	■	■	☐
4.	F	■	■	☐
5.	A	☐	■	■
6.	H	■	☐	■
7.	E	☐	■	■
8.	K	☐	■	■
9.	D	☐	■	■
10.	G	☐	■	■
11.	B	■	☐	■
12.	H	☐	■	■
13.	E	☐	■	■
14.	J	☐	■	■
15.	E	☐	■	■
16.	G	☐	■	■
17.	C	■	■	☐
18.	F	■	☐	■
19.	B	■	☐	■
20.	F	■	☐	■
21.	E	■	☐	■
22.	J	■	☐	■
23.	E	■	■	☐
24.	F	■	■	☐
25.	E	■	■	☐
26.	F	☐	■	■
27.	B	☐	■	■
28.	K	☐	■	■
29.	E	■	■	☐
30.	H	■	■	☐
31.	E	■	☐	■
32.	G	☐	■	■
33.	C	■	■	☐
34.	H	■	■	☐
35.	B	☐	■	■
36.	F	■	☐	■
37.	D	■	■	☐
38.	G	☐	■	■
39.	E	■	☐	■
40.	F	■	☐	■
41.	E	■	■	☐
42.	H	■	☐	■
43.	B	■	■	☐
44.	G	■	■	☐
45.	A	■	■	☐
46.	H	■	☐	■
47.	C	☐	■	■
48.	H	■	■	☐
49.	E	☐	■	■
50.	F	☐	■	■
51.	B	☐	■	■
52.	G	■	☐	■
53.	E	☐	■	■
54.	F	■	☐	■
55.	A	☐	■	■
56.	G	■	☐	■
57.	D	■	■	☐
58.	H	■	☐	■
59.	A	■	■	☐
60.	G	■	☐	■

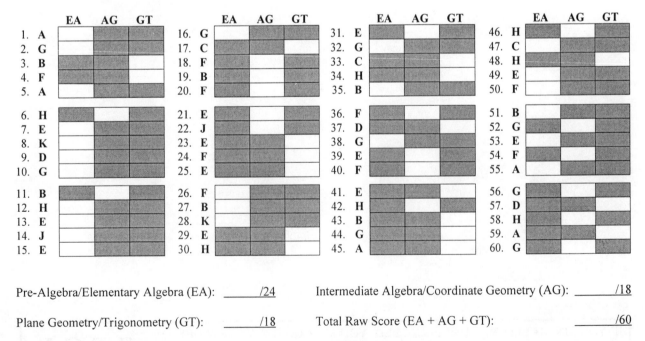

Pre-Algebra/Elementary Algebra (EA): ____/24 Intermediate Algebra/Coordinate Geometry (AG): ____/18

Plane Geometry/Trigonometry (GT): ____/18 Total Raw Score (EA + AG + GT): ____/60

TEST 3: READING (p. A-192)

	SS	S	H	PF
1. A				
2. J				
3. B				
4. H				
5. D				
6. G				
7. A				
8. H				
9. D				
10. F				
11. D				
12. G				
13. D				
14. G				
15. C				
16. J				
17. D				
18. G				
19. C				
20. F				
21. B				
22. F				
23. C				
24. F				
25. C				
26. J				
27. C				
28. F				
29. C				
30. G				
31. B				
32. F				
33. A				
34. H				
35. A				
36. J				
37. C				
38. J				
39. B				
40. G				

Social Studies (SS): ____/10

Sciences (S): ____/10

Humanities (H): ____/10

Prose Fiction (PF): ____/10

Reading Raw Score (SS + S + H + PF): ____/40

TEST 4: SCIENCE REASONING (p. A-201)

	B	C	P	ES
1. D				
2. F				
3. D				
4. G				
5. C				
6. G				
7. A				
8. J				
9. D				
10. H				
11. B				
12. G				
13. C				
14. J				
15. D				
16. G				
17. C				
18. G				
19. A				
20. J				
21. C				
22. J				
23. D				
24. F				
25. C				
26. H				
27. B				
28. G				
29. A				
30. H				
31. B				
32. H				
33. B				
34. H				
35. D				
36. J				
37. C				
38. H				
39. A				
40. G				

Biology (B): ____/5

Chemistry (C): ____/10

Physics (P): ____/11

Earth Science (ES): ____/14

Science Reasoning Raw Score (B + C + P + ES): ____/40

Explanatory Answers

TEST 1: ENGLISH (p. A-170)

1. (C) A semicolon is used between clauses joined by a coordinating conjunction when one or more of the clauses contain commas.
2. (J) This is redundant and not necessary to the sentence.
3. (D) The correct adjective is *characteristic. Characteristic* means distinctive.
4. (G) *When* is not used with *is*. The correct expression is *is that.*
5. (A) *Has become* is correct in both number and tense.
6. (H) Numbers are generally written out, especially at the beginning of a sentence.
7. (C) *As* is the standard usage for comparison.
8. (F) The dash is used for separation and emphasis.
9. (B) The apostrophe is used to show possession.
10. (G) The comma is needed for separation and clarity.
11. (D) *One's* is the correct possessive pronoun.
12. (H) Quotation marks indicate that *bowl* is used in an unusual way.
13. (C) The question gives the reader the main focus of the passage and piques his interest.
14. (H) The correct adjective is *distinguished. Distinguished* means separated from others by extraordinary qualities.
15. (D) The quoted material is the words of the imaginative Italian observer mentioned in the second sentence.
16. (F) *Easily* is the correct adverb modifying the verb *die.*
17. (B) *Likely* should be used to indicate probability. *Liable* implies something undesirable or unwanted.
18. (J) This is redundant and not necessary to the sentence since sociologists, by definition, study sociology.
19. (D) *Those kind of* is a nonstandard expression. *Those* is plural and *kind* is singular.
20. (H) The correct adverb is *around.*
21. (A) The verb *compared* continues the past tense used throughout the sentence.
22. (J) Commas are used to separate items in a list.
23. (A) Criminology is a topic in the study of sociology, but the passage is not technical in nature; thus, (B) is wrong. (C) is too general, while (D) is too specific.
24. (H) Paragraph 1 refers to the nineteenth century, Paragraph 3 to the turn of the century, and Paragraph 2 to twentieth century.
25. (C) *Shows* is necessary for agreement with the singular subject *history.*
26. (J) *In depth* is the correct prepositional phrase.
27. (A) *Effects* is the noun meaning *results.*
28. (J) This information has no relevance to the paragraph, so it should be omitted.
29. (C) A comma is used to separate words, phrases, or clauses in a series.
30. (F) An example of the risks being discussed would make the discussion more concrete to the reader.
31. (A) *An* is used before a word beginning with a vowel.
32. (J) *Neither* agrees with *nor* in the sentence.
33. (B) *And years to come* is redundant and not necessary to the sentence.
34. (G) *Persistence* is the correct noun.
35. (D) *Compared* is the correct verb and *to* is the correct preposition.
36. (G) No punctuation is necessary.
37. (A) Paragraph (1) introduces the topic of the entire essay: modern pollution problems. Thus only (A) and (C) need to be considered. Paragraph (3) starts with *These arguments*, which refers to arguments previously mentioned. This happens only when paragraph (2) comes before paragraph (3) as in (A).

38. (H) The passage discusses pollution problems, not a history of technology; thus (F) is wrong. Because the information presented is general, not technical in nature, (G) is also wrong. (J) is too narrow; the passage covers radioactive substances and more.

39. (B) *Remaining* is the correct gerund. The addition of *around* or *up* is unnecessary.

40. (J) Use of the word *of* in place of *have* is nonstandard. *Maybe* is an adverb, not a verb.

41. (A) *Most* is used correctly to modify the adjective *able*.

42. (H) Commas are used to set off adverbs that compare or contrast some preceding idea.

43. (D) *Disrepute* is the correct noun. It means having a bad reputation.

44. (H) The singular pronoun *his* is needed for agreement with the singular noun *researcher*.

45. (B) The paragraph discusses a theory about the usefulness of the researcher after age 40. Thus discussing contributions of older researchers would now be appropriate. (A) and (D) are irrelevant; (C) is too general. The correct answer is (B).

46. (J) *Of long ago* is redundant and not necessary to the sentence.

47. (B) *Be considered* is the correct verb phrase.

48. (F) *In* is the correct preposition.

49. (D) The most logical order is to contrast views of creativity in the past (3) with those of the present (2) and (1), and then salary guideposts of the past (4) to those of today (5).

50. (H) The correct answer is (H).

51. (B) *Who* is correct as the subject of the verb phrase *have chosen*.

52. (F) Question marks are used after direct questions.

53. (D) *Greater* is the correct comparative adjective. *Greatest* is in the superlative and not required in this sentence.

54. (G) *Through* meaning by means of is the correct preposition. *Threw* is the past tense of the verb *throw*.

55. (D) *In the past* is redundant.

56. (J) The conjunction *that* is the only word needed to introduce the clause that follows.

57. (C) *But* establishes the contrast between the two clauses and parallels the construction of the previous sentence.

58. (H) *Rising*, which means moving upward, is correct. *Raising* means causing to move upward.

59. (A) *Quite the contrary* is the only phrase that makes sense in the sentence.

60. (G) The paragraph discusses the contributions that science and engineering have made. Therefore, specific examples are appropriate.

61. (A) No punctuation is required here.

62. (H) The passage is concerned with solving problems in the fields of science and engineering. It begins by addressing those who have chosen these fields.

63. (B) Paragraph 1 introduces the main concern of this section. Paragraphs 4, 2, and 3 begin with First, Second, and Third, respectively. Paragraph 5 summarizes the author's point of view; hence, it is the conclusion.

64. (J) The singular subject *youth* requires the singular verb *is*.

65. (D) *This here* is nonstandard usage for the pronoun *this*.

66. (H) *Similarities* is not completed by *from*. It requires the preposition *to* (similarities *to* the American market).

67. (C) *Market's* is the correct possessive. The apostrophe followed by an *s* is used to show singular possession.

68. (G) The adverb *increasingly* correctly modifies the adjective *high*.

69. (B) The use of the comma creates a run-on sentence. The two sentences must be separated by a period, and then *generally* must capitalized.

70. (F) *Transatlantic* is one word and an adjective, not a noun. No capitalization is necessary.

71. (D) *Adopted,* meaning to have taken up and practice as one's own, is the correct verb. *Adapted* means to have adjusted.

72. (J) *Between* is used for two persons or things and *among* is used for more than two persons or things.

73. (C) The correct answer is (C).

74. (F) The passage deals with the youth markets of Western Europe and America; therefore, its readers would probably be people interested in the consumer patterns of youth.

75. (A) The correct answer is (A).

TEST 2: MATHEMATICS (p. A-184)

1. (A) If two numbers add up to zero, they are additive inverses. $(a) + (-a) = 0$. The additive inverse is the opposite of the original value. $+\frac{2}{3}$ is the additive inverse of $-\frac{2}{3}$.

2. (G) $x^2 + 6x + 8 = 0 \Rightarrow (x + 4)(x + 2) = 0 \Rightarrow x + 4 = 0$ or $x + 2 = 0$. Therefore, $x = -4$ or -2.

3. (B) $\angle AOC$ is the central angle. Arc $AC = 70°$. A central angle is equal to its intercepted arc. $\angle ABC = 35°$:

   An inscribed angle is equal to $\frac{1}{2}$ the measure of its intercepted arc. $m\angle ABC = \frac{1}{2}m(\text{Arc } AC)$.

4. (F)

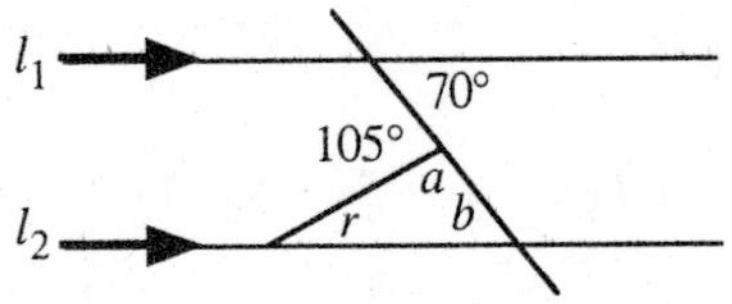

The measure of $\angle b = 70°$. It is an alternate interior angle with angle x. The measure of $\angle a = 75°$. It is the supplement of angle y. $m\angle r + m\angle a + m\angle b = 180°$. They form a triangle. Thus $m\angle r + 75° + 70° = 180°$. Therefore, $m\angle r = 35°$.

5. (A) $A = \frac{2gr}{g+r} \Rightarrow 4 = \frac{2g(1)}{g+(1)} \Rightarrow 4 = \frac{2g}{g+1}$. By cross-multiplication: $4(g + 1) = 2g \Rightarrow 4g + 4 = 2g \Rightarrow 2g = -4 \Rightarrow g = -2$.

6. (H) A V-shaped graph is usually indicative of an absolute value function. By substituting the given coordinates (2, 2), (0, 0), and (–3, 3) into the answer choice, only $y = |x|$ satisfies all the ordered pairs.

7. (E) The distributive property: multiplication over addition ($a(b + c) = ab + ac$) and multiplication over subtraction ($a(b - c) = ab - ac$). Therefore $x(x + 2) = x^2 + 2x$.

8. (K) The sales tax is 7% of \$600. Therefore $\frac{7}{100} \cdot 600 = \frac{7(600)}{100} = \$42$. The total cost is \$600 + \$42 = \$642.

9. (D) Substitute the value -1 for x: $-x^2 - 2x^3 \Rightarrow -(-1)^2 - 2(-1)^3 = -(1) - 2(-1) = -1 + 2 = 1$.

10. (G) Average $= \frac{\text{Sum of the numbers}}{\text{Quantity of numbers}} = \frac{(n+3)+(2n-1)+(3n+4)}{3} = \frac{6n+6}{3} = 2n + 2$.

11. (B) Substitute $x = 9$: $9^0 + 9^{1/2} + 9^{-2} = 1 + \sqrt{9} + \frac{1}{9^2} = 1 + 3 + \frac{1}{81} = 4\frac{1}{81}$.

12. (H) To add radicals, the number in the square root must be the same: $4\sqrt{3} + 3\sqrt{27} = 4\sqrt{3} + 3(3\sqrt{3}) = 4\sqrt{3} + 9\sqrt{3} = 13\sqrt{3}$.

13. (E) Average $= \frac{\text{Sum of the test scores}}{\text{Quantity of tests}} \Rightarrow 90 = \frac{87 + 93 + 86 + x}{4}$. By cross-multiplication: $4(90) = 87 + 93 + 86 + x \Rightarrow 360 = 266 + x \Rightarrow x = 94$.

14. (J) Each dime is 10 cents. Three dimes would be $3(10) = 30$ cents. $4x$ dimes would be $4x(10) = 40x$ cents.

15. (E) The ● indicates either ≥ or ≤. The ○ indicates either > or < without the equal. The arrow to the left indicates less than (<). The arrow to the right indicates greater than (>). The graph indicates $x \leq -5$ or $x > 3$. The answers are connected by an *or*. Therefore, the answer is $x \leq -5$ or $x > 3$.

16. (G) $2\frac{2}{5} - 1\frac{7}{8} = \frac{12}{5} - \frac{15}{8}$. The lowest common denominator is 40. Thus, $\frac{12}{5} - \frac{15}{8} = \frac{96}{40} - \frac{75}{40} = \frac{21}{40}$.

17. (C) Circumference $= 2\pi r = 2\pi(6) = 12\pi$ in length. 2π is $\frac{2\pi}{12\pi} = \frac{1}{6}$ of the circumference. In turn, the central angle is $\frac{1}{6}(360°) = 60°$ or: $\frac{\text{arc length}}{\text{circumference}} = \frac{x°}{360°} \Rightarrow \frac{2\pi}{12\pi} = \frac{x}{360} \Rightarrow \frac{1}{6} = \frac{x}{360} \Rightarrow 6x = 360 \Rightarrow x = 60$.

18. (F) $\frac{2x}{3\sqrt{2}} = \frac{3\sqrt{2}}{x} \Rightarrow 2x(x) = (3\sqrt{2})(3\sqrt{2}) \Rightarrow 2x^2 = 9(2) = 18 \Rightarrow x^2 = 9 \Rightarrow x = \pm 3$. The positive value of x is 3.

19. (B) $f(x) = 2x - x^2 \Rightarrow f(2) = 2(2) - (2)^2 = 4 - 4 = 0$. $g(x) = x - 4 \Rightarrow g(0) = 0 - 4 = -4$. Therefore, $g(f(2)) = g(0) = -4$.

20. (F) Since 7 is set equal to the absolute value of

the equation involving x ($|5 - 2x|$), then that equation equals ± 7. Solve each for the possible values of x: $5 - 2x = -7 \Rightarrow -2x = -12 \Rightarrow x = 6$ and $5 - 2x = 7 \Rightarrow -2x = 2 \Rightarrow x = -1$. Therefore, the possible solution set is $\{6, -1\}$, (F).

21. (E) Multiply the top and bottom of the complex fraction by the lowest common denominator, which is x:

$$\frac{x\left(3-\frac{3}{x}\right)}{x(x-1)} = \frac{x(3)-x\left(\frac{3}{x}\right)}{x(x-1)} = \frac{3x-3}{x(x-1)} = \frac{3(x-1)}{x(x-1)} = \frac{3}{x}$$

22. (J) slope $= m = \frac{y_2 - y_1}{x_2 - x_1} = \frac{7-5}{4-(-3)} = \frac{2}{7}$.

23. (E)

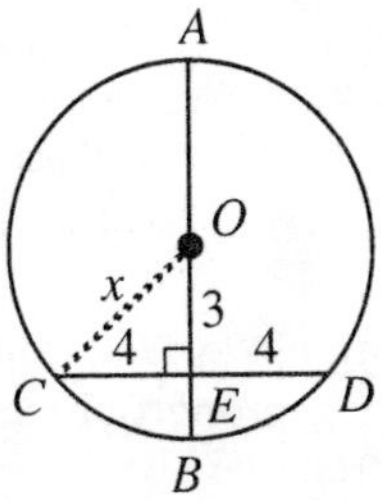

A radius or diameter drawn perpendicular to the chord bisects the chord. Therefore AB bisects CD. A constructed radius OC forms right triangle OEC with OC as the hypotenuse. $(\text{Hypotenuse})^2 = (\text{Leg } 1)^2 + (\text{Leg } 2)^2 \Rightarrow (OC)^2 = (OE)^2 + (CE)^2 \Rightarrow x^2 = 3^2 + 4^2 \Rightarrow x^2 = 25 \Rightarrow x = 5$.

24. (F)

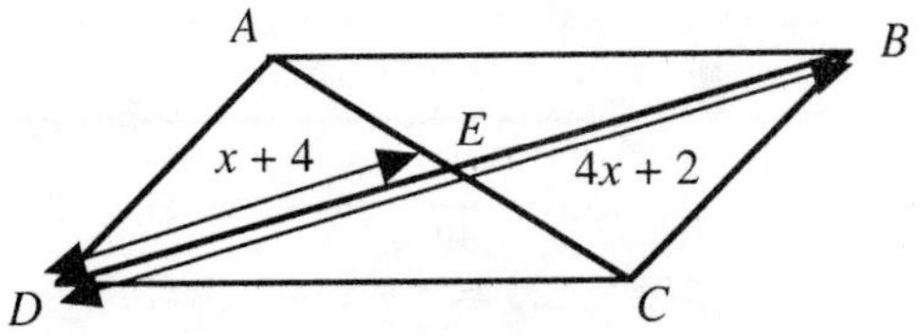

The diagonals of a parallelogram bisect each other. $DB = 2(DE) \Rightarrow 4x + 2 = 2(x + 4) \Rightarrow 4x + 2 = 2x + 8 \Rightarrow 2x = 6 \Rightarrow x = 3$.

25. (E)

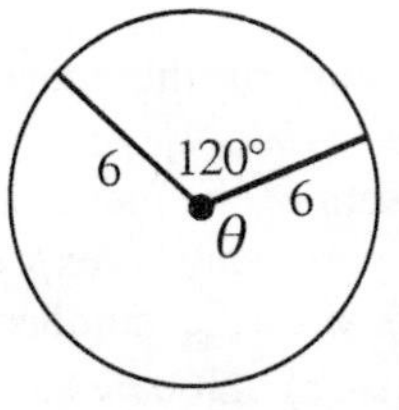

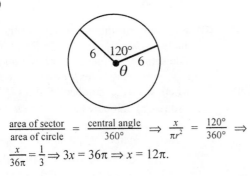

$$\frac{\text{area of sector}}{\text{area of circle}} = \frac{\text{central angle}}{360°} \Rightarrow \frac{x}{\pi r^2} = \frac{120°}{360°} \Rightarrow$$

$\frac{x}{36\pi} = \frac{1}{3} \Rightarrow 3x = 36\pi \Rightarrow x = 12\pi$.

26. (F) If a statement is true, its contrapositive must be true. The contrapositive is the converse of the inverse or the inverse of the converse of the original statement. If the original statement is $p \Rightarrow q$, the contrapositive is "not $q \Rightarrow$ not p."

27. (B) Compare all the answer choices to the original using cross-multiplication:

Original: $\frac{a}{b} = \frac{r}{t} \Rightarrow at = br$

(A) $\frac{a}{r} = \frac{b}{t} \Rightarrow at = br$ √

(B) $\frac{a}{t} = \frac{b}{r} \Rightarrow ar = bt$ X

(C) $\frac{a+b}{b} = \frac{r+t}{t}$
$t(a + b) = b(r + t)$
$at + bt = br + bt$
$at = br$ √

(D) $\frac{b}{a} = \frac{t}{r} \Rightarrow at = br$ √

(E) $at = br$ √

28. (K)
$$\begin{aligned} -2x + 5 &= 2 - (5 - 2x) \\ &= 2 - 5 + 2x \\ &= -3 + 2x \\ (+2x \quad & \quad +2x) \\ 5 &= -3 + 4x \\ (+3 \quad & \quad +3) \\ 8 &= 4x \\ x &= 2 \end{aligned}$$

29. (E) $\frac{(1 + \sin x)(1 - \sin x)}{(1 + \cos x)(1 - \cos x)} = \frac{1 - \sin x + \sin x - \sin^2 x}{1 - \cos x + \cos x - \cos^2 x} = \frac{1 - \sin^2 x}{1 - \cos^2 x}$. From the identity $\sin^2 x + \cos^2 x = 1$, $\sin^2 x = 1 - \cos^2 x$ and $\cos^2 x = 1 - \sin^2 x$. Therefore, by substitution: $\frac{1 - \sin^2 x}{1 - \cos^2 x} = \frac{\cos^2 x}{\sin^2 x} = \left(\frac{\cos x}{\sin x}\right)^2 = \cot^2 x$.

30. (H) The median to the hypotenuse of a right triangle is equal in length to half the hypotenuse: $BE = AE = CE$.

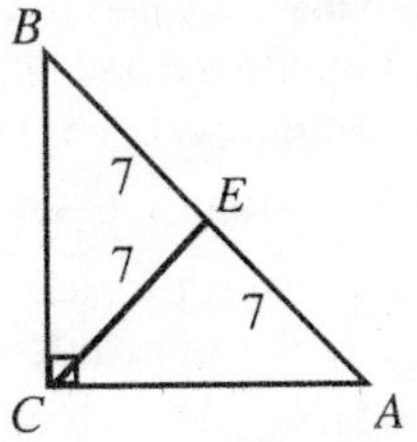

31. (E) y varies directly as x: $\frac{y_1}{x_1} = \frac{y_2}{x_2}$. Therefore: $\frac{10}{\frac{1}{5}} = \frac{y}{\frac{1}{2}} \Rightarrow \frac{1}{2}(10) = \frac{1}{5} \cdot y \Rightarrow 5 = \frac{y}{5} \Rightarrow y = 25$.

32. (G) $\frac{(-1)(2)(-3)(4)(-5)}{(1)(-2)(3)(-4)(5)} = \frac{-120}{120} = -1$.

33. (C) The product of the segments of one chord is equal to the product of the segments of the other.

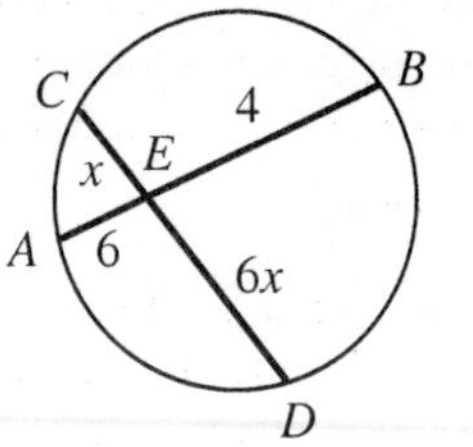

Therefore: (segment CE)(segment ED) = (segment AE)(segment EB) $\Rightarrow x(6x) = 6(4) \Rightarrow 6x^2 = 24 \Rightarrow x^2 = 4 \Rightarrow x = \pm 2$. Since lengths are positive, $x = 2$.

34. (H) An isosceles triangle has two equal sides and two equal angles: $50° + x° + x° = 180° \Rightarrow 50 + 2x = 180 \Rightarrow 2x = 130 \Rightarrow x = 65$.

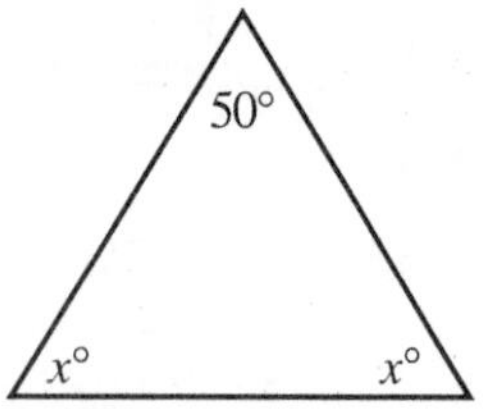

35. (B) The median is the "middle" data element when the data are arranged in numerical order. When the data is arranged numerically (20, 20, 20, 20, 30, 30, 30, 30, 50, 50, 50, 50, 50, 50, 50), the "middle" data element is 30.

36. (F) $x^2 - 2x - 3 > 0 \Rightarrow (x - 3)(x + 1) > 0$. Therefore, x must be larger than 3 or –1. This corresponds to three intervals on a number line: numbers less than –1, numbers between –1 and +3, and numbers greater than +3. Test each interval to determine whether it is part of the solution set.

For the first interval, try $x = -2$: $(x - 3)(x + 1) > 0 \Rightarrow (-2 - 3)(-2 + 1) = 0 \Rightarrow (-5)(-1) > 0 \Rightarrow 5 > 0$. This is true, so values less than –1 are part of the solution set.

For the second interval ($-1 < x < +3$), use $x = 0$: $(x - 3)(x + 1) > 0 \Rightarrow (0 - 3)(0 + 1) > 0 \Rightarrow (-3)(1) > 0 \Rightarrow -3 > 0$. This is false; this interval is not part of the solution set.

For the third interval ($x > 3$), try $x = 4$: $(x - 3)(x + 1) > 0 \Rightarrow (4 - 3)(4 + 1) > 0 \Rightarrow (1)(5) > 0 \Rightarrow 5 > 0$. This is true, so this interval is also part of the solution set.

Finally, since $(x - 3)(x + 1) > 0$ has only a greater than sign (>) and not a greater than or equal sign (≥), the values $x = -1$ and $x = 3$ are not included (represented by hollow circles). The correct representation of the solution set is the number line in choice (F).

37. (D) In order to evaluate $\frac{\sin x}{1}$, a common denominator is required in order to add the fractions. The lowest common denominator is $\sin x$: $\frac{\sin x}{1} \bullet \frac{\sin x}{\sin x} + \frac{\cos^2 x}{\sin x} = \frac{\sin^2 x}{\sin x} + \frac{\cos^2 x}{\sin x} = \frac{\sin^2 x + \cos^2 x}{\sin x}$. Since $\sin^2 x + \cos^2 x = 1$, the expression reduces to $\frac{1}{\sin x}$.

38. (G) $(2.5 \bullet 10^5)^2 = (2.5 \bullet 10^5)(2.5 \bullet 10^5) = 6.25 \bullet 10^{10}$.

39. (E) $A * B = \frac{AB - B}{-B} \Rightarrow -2 * 2 = \frac{(-2)(2) - 2}{-2} = \frac{-4 - 2}{-2} = \frac{-6}{-2} = 3$.

40. (F) Substitute the root into the equation for the value of x: $0 = x^2 + kx - 12 = (4)^2 + k(4) - 12 = 16 + 4k - 12 = 4k + 4 \Rightarrow 4k = -4 \Rightarrow k = -1$.

41. (E) Triangles ΔABC and ΔDBE are similar; create a proportion between the sides of the two triangles. If $AB = 10$ and $BD = 4$, $DA = 6$; if $BC = 20$ and $EC = x$, $BE = 20 - x$.

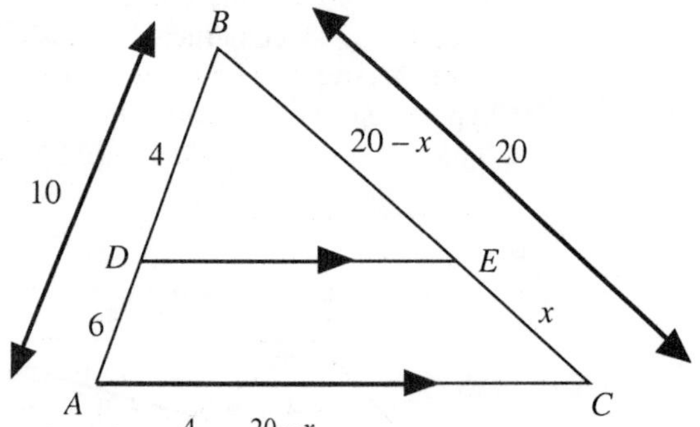

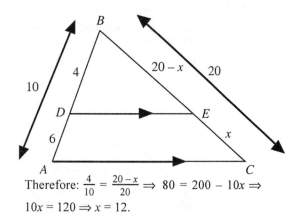

Therefore: $\frac{4}{10} = \frac{20 - x}{20} \Rightarrow 80 = 200 - 10x \Rightarrow 10x = 120 \Rightarrow x = 12$.

42. (H) Simply evaluate the expression using the FOIL (First, Outer, Inner, Last) method: $(x + 2)(x - 4) - (x + 4)(x - 2) = x^2 - 4x + 2x - 8 - (x^2 - 2x + 4x - 8) = x^2 - 2x - 8 - x^2 + 2x - 4x + 8 = (x^2 - x^2) + (-2x + 2x - 4x) + (-8 + 8) = -4x$.

43. (B) The sum of the measures of the exterior angles of a polygon is 360° for all polygons. The sum of the measures of interior angles of a polygon can be expressed as $180°(n - 2)$, where n is the number of sides. Therefore $180(n - 2) = 360 \Rightarrow n - 2 = 2 \Rightarrow n = 4$.

44. (G) If the perimeter = 12, then each side is $\frac{12}{3} = 4$. The area of an equilateral triangle can be

expressed as $A = \frac{s^2}{4}\sqrt{3}$, where s is the length of the side of the equilateral triangle. Therefore, $A = \frac{4^2}{4}\sqrt{3} = 4\sqrt{3}$.

45. (A) Let $8x$ equal the degree measure of one of the angles and x equal the degree measure of the other angle. Since complementary angles add to 90°: $8x + x = 90 \Rightarrow 9x = 90 \Rightarrow x = 10$.

46. (H) A square has four right angles; a rectangle has four right angles; a trapezoid does not have four right angles; a circle has no angles. Thus, the probability of four right angles equals $\frac{\text{number of successes}}{\text{number of possibilities}} = \frac{2}{4} = \frac{1}{2}$.

47. (C) distance = rate • time $\Rightarrow$ rate = $\frac{\text{distance}}{\text{time}} \Rightarrow \frac{320 \text{ miles}}{8 \text{ hrs}} = 40$ mph. Therefore, 40 mph • 2 hrs = 80 miles.

48. (H) Use the common denominator $\sin x \cos x$ to simplify the expression: $\frac{\sin x}{\cos x} \bullet \frac{\sin x}{\sin x} + \frac{\cos x}{\sin x} \bullet \frac{\cos x}{\cos x} = \frac{\sin^2 x}{\sin x \cos x} + \frac{\cos^2 x}{\sin x \cos x} = \frac{\sin^2 x + \cos^2 x}{\sin x \cos x} = \frac{1}{\sin x \cos x}$.

49. (E) The mode is the data element with the greatest frequency—91.

50. (F) $\frac{\text{part}}{\text{whole}} \bullet 100 = \frac{9}{30} \bullet 100 = 30\%$.

51. (B) Rearrange the expression and factor: $-7t + 6t^2 - 3 = 6t^2 - 7t - 3 = (3t + 1)(2t - 3)$.

52. (G) If $2^{x^2 + 2x} = 2^{-1}$, then $x^2 + 2x = -1$. Therefore, $x^2 + 2x + 1 = (x + 1)(x + 1) = 0$. This equation holds true only if $x = -1$.

53. (E) If Joshua is x years old now and Jessica is 3 years younger, then Jessica is now $x - 3$ years old. Four years ago she was $(x - 3) - 4 = x - 7$ years old.

54. (F) The amount collected = (# of students) • (amount each contributed). Therefore, $(x)(y) = 18$ and $(x + 3)(y - 1) = 18$.

55. (A) $\frac{1}{2}\sqrt{112} = \frac{1}{2}\sqrt{16}\sqrt{7} = \frac{1}{2}(4)(\sqrt{7}) = 2\sqrt{7}$. $\sqrt{28} = \sqrt{4}\sqrt{7} = 2\sqrt{7}$. $2\sqrt{63} = 2\sqrt{9}\sqrt{7} = 2(3)\sqrt{7} = 6\sqrt{7}$. Thus, $2\sqrt{7} - 2\sqrt{7} + 6\sqrt{7} = 6\sqrt{7}$.

56. (G) Add the two equations:

$$\begin{array}{r} \frac{1}{x} + \frac{1}{y} = \frac{1}{4} \\ + \frac{1}{x} - \frac{1}{y} = \frac{3}{4} \\ \hline \frac{2}{x} = 1 \\ x = 2 \end{array}$$

57. (D) The sum of the lengths of any two sides of a triangle must exceed the length of the third side. Check each of the answer choices:

(A)	$1 + 3 > 6$	X
(B)	$2 + 4 > 7$	X
(C)	$2 + 10 > 12$	X
(D)	$4 + 6 > 8$	
	$4 + 8 > 6$	
	$6 + 8 > 4$	√
(E)	$4 + 4 > 10$	X

58. (H) To eliminate the variable y, multiply the first equation by –1 and add the equations:

$$\begin{array}{r} -1(ax + y = b) \\ \underline{+\ 2ax + y = 2b} \\ ax = b \\ x = \frac{b}{a} \end{array}$$

Substitute the value of x into the first equation and solve for y: $ax + y = b \Rightarrow a\left(\frac{b}{a}\right) + y = b \Rightarrow b + y = b \Rightarrow y = 0$. Thus, the solution set is: $\left\{\frac{b}{a}, 0\right\}$.

59. (A) From the information given, draw the following figure.

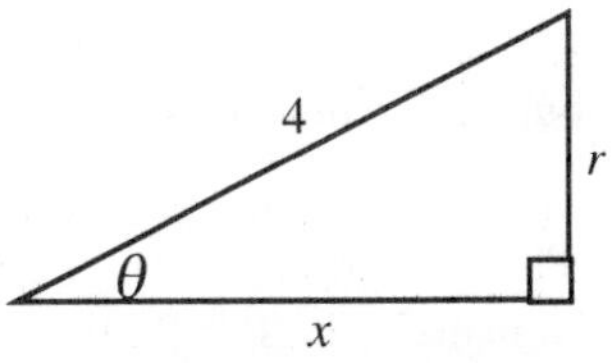

The third side of the triangle, x, is found using the Pythagorean Theorem: $x^2 + r^2 = 4^2 = 16 \Rightarrow x^2 = 16 - r^2 \Rightarrow x = \sqrt{16 - r^2}$. Since $\cos\theta = \frac{\text{side adjacent to } \theta}{\text{hypotenuse}}$, $\cos\theta = \frac{\sqrt{16 - r^2}}{4}$.

60. (G) The number of sheets is directly proportional to the number of machines and also directly proportional to the amount of time. Therefore: $\left(\frac{\text{sheets}}{\text{\# of machines} \bullet \text{time}}\right)_1 = \left(\frac{\text{sheets}}{\text{\# of machines} \bullet \text{time}}\right)_2 \Rightarrow \frac{300}{3(3)} = \frac{600}{6(t)} \Rightarrow \frac{300}{9} = \frac{600}{6t} \Rightarrow \frac{100}{3} = \frac{100}{t} \Rightarrow 100t = 300 \Rightarrow t = 3$.

TEST 3: READING (p. A-192)

1. (A) Only the first choice explains the subtitle. The other choices may be included under the idea "A Study in Temperament," but they are not the main idea.

2. (J) Paul is shown in a very unsympathetic light; one of the interesting things about this passage is the lack of sentiment in the description. Paul is plainly unpleasant, and even the narrator dislikes him.

3. (B) The faculty may be perplexed (A), but the first paragraph focuses on their feeling that Paul's dress and behavior are not properly contrite.

4. (H) Paul seems to be unable to control his odd mannerisms, but he is not actually frenzied, as (F), (G), or (J) would suggest.

5. (D) It is the flaw that has landed Paul in trouble, as evidenced in lines 40-41 and lines 48-49.

6. (G) The faculty "fell upon him without mercy, his English teacher leading the pack" (lines 54-55). The comparison is to a pack of wolves.

7. (A) "Older boys than Paul had broken down and shed tears under that baptism of fire" (lines 59-61). Paul has just undergone an inquisition by the faculty and has borne up without crying, unlike many other students.

8. (H) All of these choices could mean "smartness," but only *impudence* makes sense in context.

9. (D) There is evidence for every other choice in the descriptions of Paul's actions. The point is made in lines 25-26 that Paul often lies; he cannot be called "candid."

10. (F) Paul is physically revolted by the faculty, not *vice versa,* (J). The faculty's attack on Paul indicates their hatred for him.

11. (D) In paragraph 4, lines 43-44 state that x-rays are found at wavelengths shorter than 100 Å, the lower end of ultraviolet radiation, (A). Lines 38-40 state that infrared radiation, (B), has wavelengths longer than 7000 Å. Since (A), (B), and (C) are true, the answer is (D).

12. (G) As stated in lines 48-49, short wavelengths contain a high amount of energy, which makes them more dangerous than long wavelengths.

13. (D) This definition appears in lines 67.

14. (G) The first line of the paragraph states this main idea.

15. (C) The figure clearly shows that the visible spectrum ranges from 4000 Å to 7000 Å.

16. (J) We know from the next line that *T* refers to temperature: "It can be seen from this equation that doubling an object's temperature would radiate 2^4, or 16, times more energy."

17. (D) Lines 81-87 refer to the temperature of stars. Line 84 states that "a hot star looks blue."

18. (G) Returning to lines 55-59 gives you the answer to this question.

19. (C) (A) is never discussed. (B) is certainly not true, as the caption of the figure proves, and (D) is directly contradicted by the graph. Only (C) is true.

20. (F) As stated in lines 98-100: "doubling an object's temperature would radiate 16 times more energy."

21. (B) Jupiter is being asked to decide which of three goddesses is the fairest—it is a no-win decision, since it is bound to anger two of the three.

22. (F) Ulysses has no inclination to embark on the adventure, since he is happy at home with his family.

23. (C) Venus, one of the characters in the narrative, selected Helen as "the fairest of her sex." The other assertions are all opinions of the author.

24. (F) "Ulysses pretended to be mad" (lines 43-44), and one of the methods he chose was to hitch a mismatched team and sow something that could not grow.

25. (C) Palamedes doesn't buy Ulysses' mad act; he thinks up a way to test him. Since Ulysses is unwilling to run over his own son, he is obviously not as mad as he pretends to be.

26. (J) Rather than say that Thetis, being a sea-nymph, can read the future, the author merely mentions her immortal status and expects the reader to understand that this means that she knows "her son was fated to perish."

27. (C) The names in (A) are those of goddesses, Paris, (B), is a "beautiful shepherd." In (D), Eris is the goddess of Discord and Thetis is a sea-nymph.

28. (F) Readers are expected to understand Ulysses' clever ploy without its being spelled out. Achilles is disguised as a woman, but he is inappropriately interested in manly objects.

29. (C) Thetis' foreknowledge predicts Achilles' death, and the preparations for war on the part of the chieftains foreshadow the Trojan conflict.

30. (G) This is an accurate summary of the main themes in the passage.

31. (B) Lines 5-7 say that Hiram Revels was the first African American in Congress, but he was elected to the Senate, not the House of Representatives—thus (A) is false. However, lines 8-10 state that Rainey was the first African American elected to the House. (D) may be true but is not mentioned in the passage.

32. (F) The second paragraph says that the first African American representatives were from the South; the third paragraph describes the shift to northern cities.

33. (A) Compare lines 21-22 and 47-50.

34. (H) The context makes it clear that "turned to" means "concentrated on" or "devoted themselves to."

35. (A) Lines 37-39 indicate that many African Americans moved to northern cities from 1914 to 1930.

36. (J) Voting rights are mentioned or implied in lines 29-30, 57, and 72; educational opportunities in lines 59-60 and 73; and employment in lines 62 and 71.

37. (C) Political organizations in southern states in the nineteenth century are mentioned in lines 15-19 and 30-34; political organizations in northern states in the twentieth century are cited in lines 40-41.

38. (J) This answer is a paraphrase of lines 68-71.

39. (B) The last paragraph specifically mentions "collected biographies of African Americans who served in the House and Senate" and "their stories."

40. (G) In an otherwise factual account, the author expresses admiration only in the last paragraph, where the representatives' "long struggle to extend the ideals of the founders to encompass all citizens of the United States" is cited.

TEST 4: SCIENCE REASONING (p. A-201)

1. (D) Mercury's period of revolution equals 0.25 • (period of revolution for Earth) = 0.25 • (365.3 days) = approximately 90 days. Mercury's period of rotation equals 60 • (period of rotation for Earth) = 60 • (1 day) = 60 days. The ratio of revolution to rotation = $\frac{90}{60}=\frac{3}{2}$.

2. (F) Mercury has a relative density to Earth of 1. Since density equals mass divided by volume, Mercury's density = $\frac{\text{Mercury's mass}}{\text{Mercury's volume}}$ $= \frac{0.58 \cdot \text{Earth's mass}}{0.58 \cdot 0.58 \cdot \text{Earth's volume}} = \frac{\text{Earths's mass}}{\text{Earth's volume}} =$ Earth's density.

3. (D) Rate equals distance divided by time. Divide the average distance to the sun by the period of revolution to get relative rate. The smallest relative rate is the slowest. In this specific case, the planet with the greatest relative period of revolution orbits the sun at the slowest rate.

4. (G) Gravity depends on both the distance between the centers of objects (and thereby the volume—assuming the planets are roughly spherical in shape) and on the mass of the objects. Compare Mars and Mercury to see the effect of volume (by considering their diameters). Mars is more massive, but the smaller size of Mercury gives it an equivalent surface gravity. Density, a ratio of mass and volume, is not enough, because gravity depends on the *amount* of mass and the *amount* of distance, not their ratio.

5. (C) $\frac{\text{Pluto's volume}}{\text{Earth's volume}} = 0.729$

$$\frac{\frac{4}{3}\pi r^3_{\text{Pluto}}}{\frac{4}{3}\pi r^3_{\text{Earth}}} = 0.729$$

$$\frac{r^3_{\text{Pluto}}}{r^3_{\text{Earth}}} = 0.729$$

$$\frac{r_{\text{Pluto}}}{r_{\text{Earth}}} = \sqrt[3]{0.729} = 0.9$$

Pluto's diameter = 2 • (0.9 • Earth's radius) = 1.8 times the Earth's radius.

6. (G) The neighbors farthest from each other are Uranus and Neptune. Relative distances to the sun are as follows:

Mercury	Venus	Earth	Mars	Jupiter
0.4	0.7	1	1.5	5.3
Saturn	Uranus	Neptune	Pluto	
10	19	30	40	

The largest difference (30 – 19) = 11.

7. (A) The death rate for the 6-20 gram/day cholesterol eater from prostate cancer is 1.03, while that for a non-cholesterol eater is 2.02. Thus, (A) is correct. (B) contradicts the data for colon cancer; (C) ignores the direct relationship between coronary deaths and cholesterol intake; and cardiac arrest is a more common form of death than cerebral clots for the 20+ eaters.

8. (J) The death rate for all three groups of cholesterol eaters from depression is 0.30. This number is lower than for non-cholesterol eaters, so (F) and (G) are both wrong. According to the data, large amounts of cholesterol are just as effective in combating depression as small amounts, so (H) is incorrect.

9. (D) Although the 20+ diet increases coronary arrest to the highest absolute death rate, the percentage increase is less than 100% (from 6.00 to 11.00). The percentage increase for coronary thrombosis is greater than 100% (from 5.02 to 10.05).

10. (H) This question merely requires you to read off the chart, and (H) is the only group in which low intake of cholesterol decreases the death rate from all three diseases. Intake of 0-5 grams raises the probability of death for lung and colon cancer only. This question is probably best answered by recognizing that fact and eliminating those choices that include either lung or colon cancer.

11. (B) Standardizing the death rate involves correcting for variables inherent in the subject groups but not involved in the experiment. Age, weight, genetic histories, and accidental deaths are just some of the variables that the scientist must consider when working with human subjects. However, (A) does not correct for intrinsic variables; rather it ignores results that might not conform to a "neat" result. This does not standardize the death rate so much as "fudge" it. (C) involves an arbitrary assumption that is in fact incorrect. Assuming a zero death rate in the male population distorts the result of this experiment and does not correct for variations within the subject groups. (D) is incorrect because this experiment does not consider women at all. It might be valid to compare results with a different experiment involving women, but the actual death rates for men and women for different diseases are not necessarily similar. Consider, for example, the gender-related differences for breast cancer.

12. (G) The sharpest sloping curve is for potassium nitrate (KNO_3).

13. (C) Look at the solubility of NaCl and $NaNO_3$. We observe that the two sodium salts have different solubilities, indicating that their solubility depends on more than the nature of sodium. Therefore, (A) and (B) must be incorrect. (D) is incorrect because we do not know whether we have seen the solubility curves for *all* sodium compounds. (C) is correct because it takes into account the differences in solubilities of different sodium salts.

14. (J) The table gives data only for *aqueous* solutions, not alcoholic.

15. (D) Since the solubility curves cross at 71° F, the temperature needs to be known.

16. (G) Soda goes flat as gas (carbon dioxide) leaves the liquid. The warmer the soda, the faster it goes flat. (F) shows the effect of pressure, not temperature, on solubility. (H) shows solubility of a solid (sugar), which has nothing to do with the solubility characteristics of a gas. (J) deals with relative densities of gases, and not with solubilities.

17. (C) Since voltage is directly related to current, voltage increases by the same factor as current if other variables are held constant. The same applies for resistance; therefore, the only correct formula is (C).

18. (G) According to the formula $V = IR$, the circuit with the greater resistance would have the greater voltage. Since resistance is directly proportional to resistivity, the germanium circuit would have the greater resistance and voltage.

19. (A) The total resistance R_s of the series resistors is $R_1 + R_2 = 2 + 2 = 4$. This resistance is double that of the circuit where $R = 2$. If R doubles, then the voltage doubles as long as the current remains the same.

20. (J) According to the formula for resistors in parallel: $\frac{1}{R_p} = \frac{1}{4} + \frac{1}{4} = \frac{2}{4} = \frac{1}{2} \Rightarrow R_p = 2$.

21. (C) If R is constant, then P increases with I^2; this is a straightforward definition of exponential growth.

22. (J) If $V = IR$, then $I = \frac{V}{R}$. In order to keep I constant, if V increases, then R must be increased.

23. (D) Compare Trials 2 and 3 to see what changing concentration of only one component has on rate. In this case we see no change in rate with change in concentration of A, so rate is independent of concentration.

24. (F) Compare Trials 2 and 4, or Trials 1 and 3.

25. (C) Compare Trials 1 and 4, or Trials 2 and 3.

26. (H) Averaging or intermediate mechanisms do not work because one mechanism has no dependence of A with regard to rate. (G) is unlikely because a well-mixed solution should be homogeneous and have no pockets for mechanism 1 and 2.

27. (B) This is a subtle question. (C) and (D) are incorrect because they overgeneralize from a single case. How can we say for certain that mechanisms can *always* be changed, (C), or that in *every* case the mechanism depends on solvent effects, (D)? (A) is a special case of (D), where we make a claim that *all* reactions are solvent dependent. (B) alone allows for the possibility that solvents need not have an effect (note the word *may*).

28. (G) acceleration $= \frac{D_v}{D_t} = \frac{\text{change in velocity}}{\text{change in time}}$

Experiment 1 (steel ball): The acceleration is constant at 3.50 m/sec^2. This can be demonstrated by choosing a time interval and dividing the corresponding velocity change during the time interval by the length of the time interval. For example, between 1 and 2 seconds the velocity changes from 3.5 m/sec to 7 m/sec; therefore acceleration equals $\frac{\Delta v}{\Delta t} = \frac{7-3.5}{2-1} = \frac{3.5}{1} = 3.5$ m/sec^2.

If we used the time interval from 0.5 seconds to 1 second, the corresponding velocity would change from 1.75 m/sec to 3.5 m/sec; therefore, the acceleration equals $\frac{\Delta v}{\Delta t} = \frac{3.5-1.75}{1-0.5} = \frac{1.75}{0.5} = 3.5\ \text{m/sec}^2$.

Experiment 2 (sled): The acceleration is constant at 4.9 m/sec^2. For example, the change in velocity corresponding to the time interval from 0.5 seconds to 1 second is 4.90 m/sec − 2.45 m/sec = 2.45 m/sec. Therefore, the acceleration $= \frac{\Delta v}{\Delta t} = \frac{4.90-2.45}{1-0.5} = \frac{2.45}{0.5} = 4.9$ m/sec^2.

Experiment 3 (box): The acceleration is constant at 0.66 m/sec^2.

29. (A) When friction is reduced in Experiment 4, the sled and ball still travel at about the same accelerations as in the previous experiments. This can be demonstrated by using the equation $d = 0.5at^2$, which relates the distance an object travels starting from rest to the time (traveling at constant acceleration) it takes to travel the indicated distance. Since the board is 10 meters in length, the distance each travels is 10 meters.

For the sled: $d = \frac{1}{2}at^2$

$$10 = \frac{1}{2}at(2.02)^2 \approx \frac{1}{2}(a)(4)$$

$$a = 5\ \text{m/sec}^2$$

For the ball: $d = \frac{1}{2}at^2$

$$10 = \frac{1}{2}a(2.39)^2 \approx \frac{1}{2}a(5.7)$$

$$a = 3.50\ \text{m/sec}^2$$

Because the ball and sled still travel at about the same accelerations before and after oiling, the differences in their relative accelerations must be due to something other than friction. This difference is the rolling of the ball.

30. (H) Experiment 4 shows that friction affects the relative acceleration between the box and either the sled or ball. Calculating the acceleration for the box in Experiment 4 as we did for the sled and ball in item #29, we get the following for the box: $d = \frac{1}{2}at^2 \Rightarrow 10 = \frac{1}{2}a(4.08)^2 \approx \frac{1}{2}a(16) \Rightarrow a = 1.25\ \text{m/sec}^2$.

Because the oiling in Experiment 4 caused a change in the box's acceleration, friction is a factor. Rolling must also be a factor as per the answer explanation to item #31.

31. (B) The acceleration for the ball is constant at 3.50 m/sec^2 (either Experiment 1 or 4). The acceleration of the sled is constant at 4.90 m/sec^2 (either Experiment 2 and 4). The ratio is: $\frac{3.50}{4.90} = \frac{5}{7}$.

32. (H) Although the acceleration of the ball is relatively insensitive to the amount of friction, the acceleration of the box is very sensitive to friction. Therefore, in a ratio, the effect of changing the amount of friction will change the numerator (ball acceleration) only slightly, whereas the denominator (box acceleration) will change significantly depending on friction. (J) is not correct because within each experiment the acceleration remains constant.

33. (B) Two species genetically distant cannot breed successfully.

34. (H) For early modern humans to completely replace Neanderthals, there could not have been a region containing Neanderthals that did not contain early modern humans as well.

35. (D) Neither hypothesis necessarily rules out isolated communities. Both are concerned about areas where contact occurred.

36. (J) This information suggests that early modern humans killed Neanderthals, which supports Scientist 2.

37. (C) This fact shows that even if two species can breed, they may not do so voluntarily. Scientist 2 can therefore use this case as an example of the fact that two genetically compatible but dissimilar-looking animals choose not to interbreed. (D) is not readily relevant because lions and tigers are brought together artificially. No one disputed the notion that animals can interbreed, so (A) does not enter the argument. (B) is incorrect because lions and tigers do not share the same niche (tigers are solitary forest hunters while lions are group-hunting plains dwellers), and their ranges rarely overlap.

38. (H) The mixing of traits is part of Scientist 2's objections to Scientist 1's hypothesis.

39. (A) Both hypotheses attribute the disappearance of Neanderthals to early modern humans.

40. (G) (F) is a perfectly logical argument but does not strengthen the position of Scientist 1; it only offers a hypothesis that does not strengthen the position of Scientist 2. (J) does not strengthen the position of Scientist 1 since there is no way to prove from the information given whether others also die violently (clubs may have been used, or spearpoints that were used may have been valuable and were taken by the victors). Even if you accept (J), it does not strengthen the position of Scientist 1. It only casts doubt on the position of Scientist 2. (H) is true in general. The only possible answer that *strengthens* a scientist's argument is (G).

Answer Sheet

Name ____________________ Student ID Number ____________________

Date ____________________ Instructor ____________________ Course/Session Number ____________________

TEST 1—ENGLISH

1 A B C D	16 F G H J	31 A B C D	46 F G H J	61 A B C D
2 F G H J	17 A B C D	32 F G H J	47 A B C D	62 F G H J
3 A B C D	18 F G H J	33 A B C D	48 F G H J	63 A B C D
4 F G H J	19 A B C D	34 F G H J	49 A B C D	64 F G H J
5 A B C D	20 F G H J	35 A B C D	50 F G H J	65 A B C D
6 F G H J	21 A B C D	36 F G H J	51 A B C D	66 F G H J
7 A B C D	22 F G H J	37 A B C D	52 F G H J	67 A B C D
8 F G H J	23 A B C D	38 F G H J	53 A B C D	68 F G H J
9 A B C D	24 F G H J	39 A B C D	54 F G H J	69 A B C D
10 F G H J	25 A B C D	40 F G H J	55 A B C D	70 F G H J
11 A B C D	26 F G H J	41 A B C D	56 F G H J	71 A B C D
12 F G H J	27 A B C D	42 F G H J	57 A B C D	72 F G H J
13 A B C D	28 F G H J	43 A B C D	58 F G H J	73 A B C D
14 F G H J	29 A B C D	44 F G H J	59 A B C D	74 F G H J
15 A B C D	30 F G H J	45 A B C D	60 F G H J	75 A B C D

TEST 2—MATHEMATICS

1 A B C D E	13 A B C D E	25 A B C D E	37 A B C D E	49 A B C D E
2 F G H J K	14 F G H J K	26 F G H J K	38 F G H J K	50 F G H J K
3 A B C D E	15 A B C D E	27 A B C D E	39 A B C D E	51 A B C D E
4 F G H J K	16 F G H J K	28 F G H J K	40 F G H J K	52 F G H J K
5 A B C D E	17 A B C D E	29 A B C D E	41 A B C D E	53 A B C D E
6 F G H J K	18 F G H J K	30 F G H J K	42 F G H J K	54 F G H J K
7 A B C D E	19 A B C D E	31 A B C D E	43 A B C D E	55 A B C D E
8 F G H J K	20 F G H J K	32 F G H J K	44 F G H J K	56 F G H J K
9 A B C D E	21 A B C D E	33 A B C D E	45 A B C D E	57 A B C D E
10 F G H J K	22 F G H J K	34 F G H J K	46 F G H J K	58 F G H J K
11 A B C D E	23 A B C D E	35 A B C D E	47 A B C D E	59 A B C D E
12 F G H J K	24 F G H J K	36 F G H J K	48 F G H J K	60 F G H J K

TEST 3—READING

1 A B C D	9 A B C D	17 A B C D	25 A B C D	33 A B C D
2 F G H J	10 F G H J	18 F G H J	26 F G H J	34 F G H J
3 A B C D	11 A B C D	19 A B C D	27 A B C D	35 A B C D
4 F G H J	12 F G H J	20 F G H J	28 F G H J	36 F G H J
5 A B C D	13 A B C D	21 A B C D	29 A B C D	37 A B C D
6 F G H J	14 F G H J	22 F G H J	30 F G H J	38 F G H J
7 A B C D	15 A B C D	23 A B C D	31 A B C D	39 A B C D
8 F G H J	16 F G H J	24 F G H J	32 F G H J	40 F G H J

TEST 4—SCIENCE REASONING

1 A B C D	9 A B C D	17 A B C D	25 A B C D	33 A B C D
2 F G H J	10 F G H J	18 F G H J	26 F G H J	34 F G H J
3 A B C D	11 A B C D	19 A B C D	27 A B C D	35 A B C D
4 F G H J	12 F G H J	20 F G H J	28 F G H J	36 F G H J
5 A B C D	13 A B C D	21 A B C D	29 A B C D	37 A B C D
6 F G H J	14 F G H J	22 F G H J	30 F G H J	38 F G H J
7 A B C D	15 A B C D	23 A B C D	31 A B C D	39 A B C D
8 F G H J	16 F G H J	24 F G H J	32 F G H J	40 F G H J

ACT APPENDIX B: BASIC MATH REVIEW

CAMBRIDGE

EDUCATIONAL SERVICES, INC.®

ACT • PLAN • EXPLORE

Appendix B

BASIC MATH REVIEW

Real Number System

The real number system contains many subsets. You are expected to be familiar with the terminology and numbers contained in several of these subsets so your test preparation is made easier. The following diagram outlines the set of real numbers. Each set is a subset of the one above it; for example, the set of natural numbers is a subset of the set of whole numbers, integers, rational numbers, and real numbers. Natural numbers are whole numbers, integers, rational numbers, and real numbers. Refer back to this diagram as often as necessary.

Real Numbers
All the numbers on the number line including fractions, integers, radicals, negatives, and zero.

Rational Numbers
Numbers that can be expressed as a ratio of two integers (e.g., $\frac{2}{7}, -\frac{8}{2}, \frac{9}{10}$). A rational number can be expressed as a number that terminates (e.g., –1, 0, 35, –5.25, 8.0262) or as a non-terminating decimal with a pattern (e.g., 4.333..., 3.2525..., –0.19621962...).

Irrational Numbers
Numbers that can NOT be expressed as a ratio of two integers. No pattern exists when irrational numbers are expressed as decimals and they do NOT terminate (e.g., $\sqrt{2}$, $-\sqrt{3}$, π).

Integers
Integers are positive and negative whole numbers.
{..., –3, –2, –1, 0, 1, 2, 3, ...}

Whole Numbers
{0, 1, 2, 3, ...}

Natural or Counting Numbers
{1, 2, 3, ...}

Whole Numbers

Whole numbers are the numbers we use for counting, plus the number zero: 0, 1, 2, 3, 4, ...

Operations with Whole Numbers

1. *Terms*

sum or total: The *result* of adding numbers together. The *sum* (or *total*) of 2 and 3 is 5: $2 + 3 = 5$.
difference: The *result* of subtracting one number from another. The *difference* between 5 and 2 is 3: $5 - 2 = 3$.
product: The *result* of multiplying numbers together. The *product* of 2 and 3 is 6: $2 \bullet 3 = 6$.
quotient: The *result* of dividing one number by another. The *quotient* when 6 is divided by 2 is 3: $6 \div 2 = 3$.
remainder: In division, if the quotient is not itself a whole number, the result can be written as a whole number quotient plus a whole number remainder. For example, $7 \div 3 = 2$ plus a *remainder* of 1.

2. *Symbols of Inclusion*

Sets of parentheses, brackets, and braces will tell you in what order operations are to be performed. The inner most symbol of inclusion is done first. Generally, operations in parentheses are done first, operations in brackets second, and operations in braces third. Note that parentheses, brackets, and braces have the same meaning. Three different symbols of inclusion are used so the expressions and equations are easier to read.

EXAMPLES:

1. $(2 + 3) \bullet 4 = 20$
2. $2 + (3 \bullet 4) = 14$
3. $\frac{(2 \bullet 3) \bullet (2 + 1)}{3 \bullet (5 - 4)} = \frac{(6) \bullet (3)}{3 \bullet (1)} = \frac{18}{3} = 6$

A particularly complex statement might use brackets and braces as well.

EXAMPLE:

$[(2 \bullet 3) - 5] + [2 \bullet (4 - 1)]] = [6 - 5] + [2 \bullet 3] = 1 + 6 = 7$

With problems such as these, work from the inside out. Start with the operations within parentheses. Then do the operations within the brackets and finally, finish the problem off.

3. *Order of Operations*

Parentheses, brackets, and braces eliminate ambiguity, but they do not always dictate the order in which operations must be done. You can use the following mnemonic to remember the order of operations for simplifying an expression: ***Please Excuse My Dear Aunt Sally.***

Please: **P**arentheses, brackets, braces
Excuse: **E**xponents, radicals
My: **M**ultiplication*
Dear: **D**ivision*
Aunt: **A**ddition*
Sally: **S**ubtraction*

*Remember, add and subtract in the expression as the operations occur left to right, multiply and divide in the expression as the operations occur left to right.

EXAMPLES:

1. $6 + 4 \cdot 3 - 5 = 6 + 12 - 5 = 18 - 5 = 13$
2. $\{2(3 + 4)\}(3 \cdot 2) = \{2(7)\}(6) = \{14\}(6) = 84$

Finally, we'll end with an example of a very complex expression:

EXAMPLE:

$\{2 + 7 - 8 \cdot 6 \div 2 + 25\}\{[2 + 3(2 - 1)] \div 5\} = \{2 + 7 - 48 \div 2 + 25\}\{[2 + 3(1)] \div 5\} = \{2 + 7 - 24 + 25\}\{[5] \div 5\} = \{9 - 24 + 25\}\{1\} = \{-15 + 25\} = 10$

An important point to make is that even when multiplication and addition are combined, you have a choice about order of operations. In the following example, most people would probably do the addition first and then the multiplication. It is also permissible, however, to do the multiplication first, as the following example illustrates.

EXAMPLE:

$5(2 + 3 + 4) = 5(9) = 45$

$5(2 + 3 + 4) = 2(5) + 3(5) + 4(5) = 10 + 15 + 20 = 45$

We have just seen that $10 + 15 + 20$ is equal to $2(5) + 3(5) + 4(5)$, which in turn equals $5(2 + 3 + 4)$. We might call this reverse multiplication process "de-multiplication." "De-multiplying" can be a tremendous labor-saving device. In the following example, if you had a calculator it would be easiest to first multiply and then subtract. Since the SAT, ACT, and PSAT are the only exams that currently allow calculators, most test-takers will find that when solving expressions by hand, a better way would be to "de-multiply."

EXAMPLE:

$(723)(34) - (723)(33) = 24{,}582 - 23{,}859 = 723$

$(723)(34) - (723)(33) = 723(34 - 33) = 723(1) = 723$

"De-multiplication" can be combined with division for even greater simplifying power.

EXAMPLE:

$\frac{24 + 36}{12} = \frac{12(2 + 3)}{12} = (1)(2 + 3) = 5$

In this case, 12 can be factored from both 24 and 36. Then it is possible to divide 12 by 12, which is 1. This last step is known as canceling.

Factors, Multiples, and Primes

Numbers that evenly divide another number are called the *factors* of that number. If a number is evenly divisible by another number, it is considered to be a multiple of that number. 1, 2, 3, 4, 6, and 12 are all factors of 12. 12 is a *multiple* of 2, a *multiple* of 3, and so on. Some numbers are not evenly divisible except by 1 and themselves. For example, 13 is evenly divisible by 1 and 13, but not by 2 through 12. A number such as this is called a *prime* number.

EXAMPLE:

The following are examples of prime numbers: 2, 3, 5, 7, 11, 13, 17, 19, and 23.

Note: 1 is NOT considered a prime number even though it is not evenly divisible by any other number.

Odds and Evens

An ***even*** number is a number that is divisible by 2; an ***odd*** number is one that is not divisible by 2. Any number the last digit of which is 0, 2, 4, 6, or 8 is divisible by 2 and therefore even. Any number the last digit of which is 1, 3, 5, 7, or 9 is not divisible by 2 and therefore odd. Zero is considered an even number. Here are some important principles that govern the behavior of odd and even numbers:

EVEN + EVEN = EVEN	e.g., $2 + 4 = 6$
EVEN + ODD = ODD	$4 + 3 = 7$
ODD + EVEN = ODD	$3 + 4 = 7$
ODD + ODD = EVEN	$3 + 5 = 8$
EVEN • EVEN = EVEN	$2 \cdot 4 = 8$
EVEN • ODD = EVEN	$2 \cdot 3 = 6$
ODD • EVEN = EVEN	$3 \cdot 2 = 6$
ODD • ODD = ODD	$3 \cdot 5 = 15$

Note: The addition rules apply also to subtraction (which is just the reverse of addition, though you might wind up with a negative number—a topic taken up later). But the rules on multiplication do NOT apply to division. For example, if you divide the even number 4 by the even number 8, the result is $\frac{1}{2}$. Odd and even are characteristics of whole numbers (plus negative integers), but not fractions. A fraction is neither odd nor even.

Consecutive Numbers

Consecutive numbers are ones that immediately follow each other. For example, 3, 4, 5, and 6 are consecutive numbers, but 3, 7, 21, and 45 are not. In a string of consecutive numbers, the next number is always one more than the preceding number. Thus, if n is the first number in a string of consecutive numbers, the second number is $n + 1$, the fourth number is $n + 3$, and so on.

1st	2nd	3rd	4th
3	4	5	6
n	$n + 1$	$n + 2$	$n + 3$

We can also speak of consecutive even numbers and consecutive odd numbers. 2, 4, 6, and 8 are consecutive even numbers; 3, 5, 7, and 9 are consecutive odd numbers. In a string of consecutive even (or odd) numbers, the next number is always two more than the preceding number. Thus, if n is the first number in a string of consecutive even (or odd) numbers, the second number is $n + 2$, the third number is $n + 4$, the fourth number is $n + 6$, and so on.

1st	2nd	3rd	4th
4	6	8	10
n	$n + 2$	$n + 4$	$n + 6$
3	5	7	9
n	$n + 2$	$n + 4$	$n + 6$

Don't be confused by the fact that the sequence for consecutive odd numbers proceeds n, $n + 2$, $n + 4$, etc. Even though 2, 4, etc. are even numbers, $n + 2$, $n + 4$, etc. will be odd numbers when n, the starting point, is odd.

EXERCISE 1

Whole Numbers

DIRECTIONS: Choose the best answer to each of the following questions. Answers are on page B-120.

1. Subtracting 1 from which digit in the number 12,345 will decrease the value of the number by 1,000?

   (A) 1 (B) 2 (C) 3 (D) 4 (E) 5

2. Adding 3 to which digit in the number 736,124 will increase the value of the number by 30,000?

   (A) 7 (B) 3 (C) 6 (D) 2 (E) 4

3. Adding 1 to each digit of the number 222,222 will increase the value of the number by how much?

   (A) 333,333 (B) 111,111 (C) 100,000
   (D) 10 (E) 1

4. (1 • 10,000) + (2 • 1,000) + (3 • 100) + (4 • 10) + (5 • 1) =

   (A) 5,000 (B) 15,000 (C) 12,345
   (D) 54,321 (E) 543,210

5. (1 • 1) + (1 • 10) + (1 • 100) + (1 • 1,000) + (1 • 10,000) =

   (A) 5 (B) 5,000 (C) 11,111
   (D) 111,110 (E) 1,111,100

6. (1 • 100,000) + (2 • 10,000) + (3 • 1,000) =

   (A) 123 (B) 1,230 (C) 12,300
   (D) 123,000 (E) 1,230,000

7. (2 • 1,000) + (3 • 100) + (1 • 10,000) + (2 • 10) + 1 =

   (A) 11,223 (B) 12,132 (C) 12,321
   (D) 23,121 (E) 32,121

8. (9 • 10,000) + (9 • 100) =

   (A) 99 (B) 9,090 (C) 90,009
   (D) 90,090 (E) 90,900

9. (2 • 10,000) + (8 • 1,000) + (4 • 10) =

   (A) 284 (B) 482 (C) 2,084
   (D) 2,840 (E) 28,040

10. What is the sum of 2 and 3?

    (A) 1 (B) 5 (C) 6 (D) 8 (E) 10

11. What is the sum of 5, 7, and 8?

    (A) 12 (B) 15 (C) 20 (D) 25 (E) 28

12. What is the sum of 20, 30, and 40?

    (A) 60 (B) 70 (C) 80 (D) 90 (E) 100

13. What is the difference between 8 and 3?

    (A) 24 (B) 11 (C) 8 (D) 5 (E) 3

14. What is the difference between 28 and 14?

    (A) 2 (B) 7 (C) 14 (D) 42 (E) 392

15. What is the product of 2 and 8?

    (A) 4 (B) 6 (C) 10 (D) 16 (E) 24

16. What is the product of 20 and 50?

    (A) 70 (B) 100 (C) 1,000
    (D) 10,000 (E) 100,000

17. The product of 12 and 10 is

    (A) 2 (B) 22 (C) 120 (D) 240 (E) 300

18. What is the sum of (5 + 1) and (2 + 3)?

    (A) 4 (B) 11 (C) 24 (D) 33 (E) 40

19. What is the difference between (5 + 2) and (3 • 2)?

    (A) 0 (B) 1 (C) 3 (D) 10 (E) 14

20. What is the product of the sum of 2 and 3 and the sum of 3 and 4?

    (A) 6 (B) 12 (C) 35 (D) 48 (E) 72

21. What is the sum of the product of 2 and 3 and the product of 3 and 4?

    (A) 6 (B) 12 (C) 18 (D) 35 (E) 72

22. What is the difference between the product of 3 and 4 and the product of 2 and 3?

    (A) 2 (B) 3 (C) 6 (D) 12 (E) 36

23. What is the remainder when 12 is divided by 7?

    (A) 1 (B) 2 (C) 3 (D) 4 (E) 5

24. What is the remainder when 18 is divided by 2?

    (A) 0 (B) 1 (C) 3 (D) 6 (E) 9

25. What is the remainder when 50 is divided by 2?

    (A) 0 (B) 1 (C) 3 (D) 25 (E) 50

26. What is the remainder when 15 is divided by 8?

    (A) 0 (B) 1 (C) 4 (D) 7 (E) 89

27. What is the remainder when 15 is divided by 2?

    (A) 0 (B) 1 (C) 7 (D) 8 (E) 14

28. When both 8 and 13 are divided by a certain number, the remainder is 3. What is that number?

(A) 4 (B) 5 (C) 6 (D) 7 (E) 8

29. When both 33 and 37 are divided by a certain number, the remainder is 1. What is that number?

(A) 4 (B) 9 (C) 10 (D) 16 (E) 18

30. When both 12 and 19 are divided by a certain number, the remainder is 5. What is that number?

(A) 3 (B) 4 (C) 5 (D) 7 (E) 9

31. $(4 \cdot 3) + 2 =$

(A) 6 (B) 9 (C) 12 (D) 14 (E) 26

32. $(2 \cdot 3) \div (2 + 1) =$

(A) 0 (B) 1 (C) 2 (D) 3 (E) 6

33. $[2 \cdot (12 \div 4)] + [6 \div (1 + 2)] =$

(A) 4 (B) 6 (C) 8 (D) 18 (E) 24

34. $[(36 \div 12) \cdot (24 \div 3)] \div [(1 \cdot 3) - (18 \div 9)] =$

(A) 3 (B) 8 (C) 16 (D) 20 (E) 24

35. $[(12 \cdot 3) - (3 \cdot 12)] + [(8 \div 2) \div 4] =$

(A) 0 (B) 1 (C) 4 (D) 8 (E) 16

36. $(1 \cdot 2 \cdot 3 \cdot 4) - [(2 \cdot 3) + (3 \cdot 6)] =$

(A) 0 (B) 1 (C) 6 (D) 16 (E) 24

37. Which of the following statements is (are) true?

I. $(4 + 3) - 6 = 4 + (6 - 2)$
II. $3(4 + 5) = (3 \cdot 4) + (3 \cdot 5)$
III. $(3 + 5) \cdot 4 = 4 \cdot (5 + 3)$

(A) I only (B) II only (C) III only
(D) II and III only (E) I, II, and III

38. $12 + 24 + 36 =$

(A) $3 \cdot 12$ (B) $12(1 + 2 + 3)$ (C) $12(3 + 4 + 5)$
(D) $6(2) + 6(3) + 6(4)$ (E) $12 \cdot 24 \cdot 36$

39. $25 + 50 + 100 =$

(A) $5(1 + 2 + 3)$ (B) $5(1 + 2 + 4)$
(C) $25(1 + 2 + 3)$ (D) $25(1 + 2 + 4)$
(E) $25(1 + 5 + 10)$

40. $\frac{99(121) - 99(120)}{33} =$

(A) 1 (B) 3 (C) 33 (D) 99 (E) 120

41. $1{,}234(96) - 1{,}234(48) =$

(A) $1{,}234 \cdot 48$ (B) $1{,}234 \cdot 96$
(C) $1{,}234(48 + 96)$ (D) $(1{,}234 \cdot 1{,}234)$
(E) $2 \cdot 1234$

42. How many prime numbers are greater than 20 but less than 30?

(A) 0 (B) 1 (C) 2 (D) 3 (E) 4

43. How many prime numbers are greater that 50 but less than 60?

(A) 0 (B) 1 (C) 2 (D) 3 (E) 4

44. Which of the following numbers are prime numbers?

I. 11
II. 111
III. 1,111

(A) I only (B) II only (C) I and II only
(D) I and III only (E) I, II, and III

45. Which of the following numbers are prime numbers?

I. 12,345
II. 999,999,999
III. 1,000,000,002

(A) I only (B) III only (C) I and II only
(D) I, II, and III (E) Neither I, II, nor III

46. What is the largest factor of both 25 and 40?

(A) 5 (B) 8 (C) 10 (D) 15 (E) 25

47. What is the largest factor of both 6 and 9?

(A) 1 (B) 3 (C) 6 (D) 9 (E) 12

48. What is the largest factor of both 12 and 18?

(A) 6 (B) 24 (C) 36 (D) 48 (E) 216

49. What is the largest factor of 18, 24, and 36?

(A) 6 (B) 9 (C) 12 (D) 15 (E) 18

50. What is the largest factor of 7, 14, and 21?

(A) 1 (B) 7 (C) 14 (D) 21 (E) 35

51. What is the smallest multiple of both 5 and 2?

(A) 7 (B) 10 (C) 20 (D) 30 (E) 40

52. What is the smallest multiple of both 12 and 18?

(A) 36 (B) 48 (C) 72 (D) 128 (E) 216

53. Which of the following is (are) even?

I. 12
II. 36
III. 101

(A) I only (B) II only (C) I and II only
(D) I and III only (E) I, II, and III

54. Which of the following is (are) odd?

I. 24 • 31
II. 22 • 49
III. 33 • 101

(A) I only (B) II only (C) III only
(D) I and III only (D) I, II, and III

55. Which of the following is (are) even?

I. 333,332 • 333,333
II. 999,999 + 101,101
III. 22,221 • 44,441

(A) I only (B) II only (C) I and II only
(D) I and III only (E) I, II, and III

56. If n is an even number, all of the following must also be even EXCEPT

(A) $(n \bullet n) + n$ (B) $n \bullet n - n$ (C) $n + 2$
(D) $3(n + 2)$ (E) $\frac{n}{2}$

57. For any whole number n, which of the following must be odd?

I. $3(n + 1)$
II. $3n + 2n$
III. $2n - 1$

(A) I only (B) II only (C) III only
(D) I and II only (E) I, II, and III

58. If 8 is the third number in a series of three consecutive whole numbers, what is the first number in the series?

(A) 0 (B) 1 (C) 6 (D) 7 (E) 11

59. If 15 is the fifth number in a series of five consecutive odd numbers, what is the third number in the series?

(A) 5 (B) 7 (C) 9 (D) 11 (E) 13

60. If m, n, and o are consecutive whole numbers that total 15, what is the largest of the three numbers?

(A) 4 (B) 5 (C) 6 (D) 14 (E) 17

Fractions

When one whole number is divided by another whole number and the result is *not* a third whole number, the result is a fraction. Thus, when 2 is divided by 3, the result is not a whole number. The result is the fraction $2 \div 3$, which is written $\frac{2}{3}$. Note: A whole number can also be expressed as a fraction (e.g., $\frac{12}{3} = 4$, $7 = \frac{7}{1}$).

The number above the division line in the fraction is called the *numerator*; the number below the line is called the *denominator*.

In a proper fraction, the numerator is *less than* the denominator, so the fraction has a value of less than 1, e.g., $\frac{1}{2}$ and $\frac{3}{4}$, which are both less than 1.

In an improper fraction, the numerator is *greater than* the denominator, so the fraction has a value greater than 1, e.g., $\frac{3}{2}$ and $\frac{4}{3}$ are both greater than 1.

A mixed number consists of both a whole number and a fraction written together. For example: $2\frac{1}{2}$ is equivalent to $2 + \frac{1}{2}$, and $3\frac{4}{5}$ is equivalent to $3 + \frac{4}{5}$.

Working with Mixed Numbers and Improper Fractions

Before you add, subtract, multiply, or divide, change mixed numbers to improper fractions. To convert a mixed number to an improper fraction:

1. Use the denominator of the old fractional part of the mixed number as the new denominator.
2. Multiply the whole number part of the mixed number by its denominator and add to that product the numerator of the old fractional part. This is the new numerator. This is more difficult to describe than it is to do. Take the mixed number $2\frac{3}{7}$. First, the denominator of your new fraction will be 7. Next, multiply 7 by 2, which is 14. Then add 3 to that: $14 + 3 = 17$. 17 is the new numerator, and 7 is the denominator. So the result is $\frac{17}{7}$. In other words: $2\frac{3}{7} \Rightarrow \frac{(2 \cdot 7) + 3}{7} = \frac{14 + 3}{7} = \frac{17}{7}$.

EXAMPLES:

1. $3\frac{1}{4} = \frac{(3 \cdot 4) + 1}{4} = \frac{13}{4}$
2. $6\frac{2}{5} = \frac{(6 \cdot 5) + 2}{5} = \frac{32}{5}$
3. $2\frac{12}{13} = \frac{(2 \cdot 13) + 12}{13} = \frac{38}{13}$

To convert an improper fraction to a mixed number, you reverse the process:

1. Divide the denominator into the numerator. The quotient becomes the whole number part of the mixed number.
2. Using the same denominator, create a fraction the numerator of which is the remainder of the division process in step one.

EXAMPLE:

Convert $\frac{30}{7}$ into a mixed number.

First divide 7 into 30. The result is 4 with a remainder of 2. The 4 is now the whole number part of the mixed number. Next, the numerator of the fraction is the remainder 2, and the denominator is 7. So the result is $4\frac{2}{7}$.

EXAMPLES:

1. $\frac{29}{5}$: 29 ÷ 5 = 5 with a remainder of 4, so $5\frac{4}{5}$.
2. $\frac{31}{6}$: 31 ÷ 6 = 5 with a remainder of 1, so $5\frac{1}{6}$.
3. $\frac{43}{13}$: 43 ÷ 13 = 3 with a remainder of 4, so $3\frac{4}{13}$.

Reducing Fractions

For reasons of convenience, it is customary to reduce all fractions to their lowest terms. When you reduce a fraction to lowest terms, you really are doing nothing but rewriting it in an equivalent form. This is accomplished by eliminating common factors in both the numerator and the denominator of the fraction.

EXAMPLE:

$\frac{8}{16}=\frac{1(8)}{2(8)}=\frac{1}{2}$

There are various ways of describing what goes on when you reduce a fraction. You might think of taking out a common factor, such as 8 in the example above, and dividing 8 into 8 (or canceling the eights). It's also possible to think of the process as dividing both numerator and denominator by the same number:

$\frac{8}{16}=\frac{8 \div 8}{16 \div 8}=\frac{1}{2}$

It doesn't really matter which way you would describe the process, so long as you know how to reduce a fraction to its lowest terms. A fraction is expressed in lowest terms when there is no number (other than 1) that can be evenly divided into both numerator and denominator. For example, $\frac{8}{15}$ is in lowest terms, since there is no number (other than 1) that evenly goes into 8 that also evenly goes into 15. On the other hand, $\frac{8}{12}$ is not in lowest terms, since both 8 and 12 can be evenly divided by 4. Reducing $\frac{8}{12}$ by a factor of 4 gives $\frac{2}{3}$, which is in lowest terms since nothing (other than 1) evenly divides into both 2 and 3.

EXAMPLES:

1. $\frac{12}{36}=\frac{1 \cdot 12}{3 \cdot 12}=\frac{1}{3}$
2. $\frac{42}{48}=\frac{7 \cdot 6}{8 \cdot 6}=\frac{7}{8}$
3. $\frac{50}{125}=\frac{2 \cdot 25}{5 \cdot 25}=\frac{2}{5}$

If a fraction is particularly large, you may need to reduce it in steps. The process is largely a matter of trial and error, but there are a couple of rules that can guide you. Remember that if both numerator and denominator are even numbers, you can reduce the fraction by a factor of 2.

EXAMPLE:

$\frac{32}{64}=\frac{16(2)}{32(2)}=\frac{8(2)}{16(2)}=\frac{4(2)}{8(2)}=\frac{2(2)}{4(2)}=\frac{1}{2}$

If both the numerator and the denominator end in either 0 or 5, they are both divisible by 5.

EXAMPLE:

$\frac{55}{100}=\frac{11(5)}{20(5)}=\frac{11}{20}$

Common Denominators

A common denominator is a number that is a multiple of the denominators of two or more fractions. For example, 12 is a multiple of both 3 and 4 (both 3 and 4 divide evenly into 12), so it is a suitable common denominator for $\frac{1}{3}$ and $\frac{1}{4}$.

Converting a fraction to one with another denominator is the reverse of reducing it to lowest terms.

EXAMPLE:

$\frac{1}{4}=\frac{1 \cdot 3}{4 \cdot 3}=\frac{3}{12}$

When you multiply both the numerator and the denominator by the same number, you are really just multiplying the fraction by 1 ($\frac{3}{3}$ = 1), so you don't change its value.

In the example above, how do we know to use 3? We want to convert a fraction with a denominator of 4, so we ask the question, "What number, when multiplied by 4, yields the product 12?" The answer is found by dividing 12 by 4. Since 12 ÷ 4 = 3, we know we must multiply 4 by 3 to get 12.

To take another example, by what number must you multiply the numerator and denominator of the fraction $\frac{5}{6}$ to get a fraction with a denominator of 30? Since 30 ÷ 6 = 5, you must use 5:

EXAMPLE:

$\frac{5}{6}=\frac{5 \cdot 5}{6 \cdot 5}=\frac{25}{30}$

In grade school you were taught to find the lowest common denominator for fractions. But in truth, any old common denominator will work. The easiest way to find a common denominator is to multiply the two denominators together. Thus, a common denominator for 2 and 3 is 2 • 3, or 6; a common denominator for 3 and 4 is 3 • 4, or 12; a common denominator for 2 and 5 is 2 • 5, or 10.

What, then, was the big deal about *lowest* common denominators? It's the same as reducing fractions to lowest terms: it's easier to work with smaller numbers. Thus, a common denominator for 2 and 8 is 16, but 8 is also a possibility. And it's easier to deal with a fraction of denominator 8 than 16.

In the final analysis, however, you can use any common denominator, because you can always *reduce* a fraction to its lowest terms.

Manipulating Fractions

1. *Addition*

The procedure for adding fractions varies depending on whether or not the fractions already share the same denominator. To add fractions with the same denominator, create a new fraction using that denominator. The new numerator is the sum of the old numerators.

EXAMPLES:

1. $\frac{3}{7}+\frac{2}{7}=\frac{5}{7}$
2. $\frac{2}{5}+\frac{2}{5}=\frac{4}{5}$
3. $\frac{1}{7}+\frac{2}{7}+\frac{3}{7}=\frac{6}{7}$

To add a fraction and a mixed number, change the mixed number to an improper fraction and then add.

EXAMPLE:

$2\frac{1}{3}+\frac{1}{3}=\frac{7}{3}+\frac{1}{3}=\frac{8}{3}=2\frac{2}{3}$

To add fractions with different denominators, you must first find a common denominator and convert the fractions in the manner described above. For example, $\frac{1}{3}$ and $\frac{1}{5}$. Since these fractions have unlike denominators, you must find a common denominator such as 15. Next, you convert each fraction to a fraction with denominator of 15.

EXAMPLES:

1. $\frac{1}{3}+\frac{1}{5}=\frac{1(5)}{3(5)}+\frac{1(3)}{5(3)}=\frac{5}{15}+\frac{3}{15}=\frac{8}{15}$
2. $\frac{1}{3}+\frac{2}{7}=\frac{1(7)}{3(7)}+\frac{2(3)}{7(3)}=\frac{7}{21}+\frac{6}{21}=\frac{13}{21}$
3. $\frac{2}{9}+\frac{4}{5}=\frac{2(5)}{9(5)}+\frac{4(9)}{9(5)}=\frac{10}{45}+\frac{36}{45}=\frac{46}{45}$

If you are adding a fraction and a whole number, you can treat the whole number as a fraction with a denominator of 1.

EXAMPLE:

$2+\frac{1}{5}+\frac{1}{2}=\frac{2}{1}+\frac{1}{5}+\frac{1}{2}=\frac{2(10)}{1(10)}+\frac{1(2)}{5(2)}+\frac{1(5)}{2(5)}=\frac{20}{10}+\frac{2}{10}+\frac{5}{10}=\frac{27}{10}$

2. *Subtraction*

Follow the same procedure for subtraction except that you subtract rather than add. When the fractions have the same denominators, you simply subtract one numerator from the other.

EXAMPLES:

1. $\frac{5}{7}-\frac{2}{7}=\frac{3}{7}$
2. $\frac{4}{5}-\frac{3}{5}=\frac{1}{5}$

When you have fractions with different denominators, it's first necessary to find a common denominator.

EXAMPLES:

1. $\frac{7}{8}-\frac{3}{5}=\frac{7(5)}{8(5)}-\frac{3(8)}{5(8)}=\frac{35}{40}-\frac{24}{40}=\frac{11}{40}$
2. $\frac{5}{6}-\frac{1}{5}=\frac{5(5)}{6(5)}-\frac{1(6)}{5(6)}=\frac{25}{30}-\frac{6}{30}=\frac{19}{30}$
3. $2-\frac{7}{6}=\frac{2}{1}-\frac{7}{6}=\frac{2(6)}{1(6)}-\frac{7(1)}{6(1)}=\frac{12}{6}-\frac{7}{6}=\frac{5}{6}$

A Shortcut

You don't need to worry about finding a lowest common denominator as long as you remember to reduce the result of an operation to lowest terms. This sets up a little trick for adding and subtracting fractions that makes the process a purely mechanical one—one you don't even have to think about. The trick is called the "flying *x*."

To add (or subtract) any two fractions with unlike denominators:

1. Multiply the denominators to get a new denominator.
2. Multiply the numerator of the first fraction by the denominator of the second.
3. Multiply the numerator of the second fraction by the denominator of the first.
4. The new numerator is the sum (or difference) of the results of steps 2 and 3.

Once again, it's more difficult to describe the process than it is to do it. Perhaps the easiest way to learn it is to see it done. Let $\frac{a}{b}$ and $\frac{c}{d}$ be any two fractions (such as $\frac{2}{7}$ and $\frac{1}{5}$). Add them:

$$\frac{a}{b} + \frac{c}{d} = \frac{a}{b} \geq + \leq \frac{c}{d} = \frac{ad + bc}{bd}$$

$$\frac{2}{7} + \frac{1}{5} = \frac{2}{7} \geq + \leq \frac{1}{5} = \frac{10 + 7}{35} = \frac{17}{35}$$

As you can see, the connecting arrows make a figure that looks like an *x* floating above the ground, so we call it the "flying *x*."

The "flying *x*" method also works for subtracting fractions. At step 4 (described above), just subtract instead of add.

EXAMPLES:

1. $\frac{3}{5} - \frac{1}{3} = \frac{3}{5} \geq - \leq \frac{1}{3} = \frac{9-5}{15} = \frac{4}{15}$
2. $\frac{6}{7} - \frac{5}{6} = \frac{6}{7} \geq - \leq \frac{5}{6} = \frac{36-35}{42} = \frac{1}{42}$

Of course, this may not give you the lowest terms of the fractions, so it may be necessary to reduce.

EXAMPLES:

1. $\frac{3}{4} - \frac{1}{8} = \frac{3}{4} \geq - \leq \frac{1}{8} = \frac{24-4}{32} = \frac{20}{32} = \frac{5}{8}$
2. $\frac{2}{3} + \frac{1}{6} = \frac{2}{3} \geq + \leq \frac{1}{6} = \frac{12+3}{18} = \frac{15}{18} = \frac{5}{6}$

3. *Multiplication*

Multiplication of fractions does not require a common denominator. To multiply fractions, just multiply numerators to create a new numerator, and multiply denominators to create a new denominator.

EXAMPLES:

1. $\frac{3}{4} \bullet \frac{1}{5} = \frac{3 \bullet 1}{4 \bullet 5} = \frac{3}{20}$
2. $\frac{2}{3} \bullet \frac{2}{5} = \frac{2 \bullet 2}{3 \bullet 5} = \frac{4}{15}$

4. *Division*

Division is the opposite of multiplication. To divide by a fraction, you invert the divisor (the fraction by which you are dividing) and then multiply.

EXAMPLE:

$$2 \div \frac{1}{4} = \frac{2}{1} \bullet \frac{4}{1} = \frac{8}{1} = 8$$

Follow the same rule when you divide one fraction by another fraction.

EXAMPLES:

1. $\frac{\frac{2}{3}}{\frac{5}{6}} = \frac{2}{3} \bullet \frac{6}{5} = \frac{12}{15} = \frac{4}{5}$
2. $\frac{1}{3} \div \frac{5}{6} = \frac{1}{3} \bullet \frac{6}{5} = \frac{6}{15} = \frac{2}{5}$
3. $\frac{2}{7} \div 2 = \frac{2}{7} \div \frac{2}{1} = \frac{2}{7} \bullet \frac{1}{2} = \frac{2}{14} = \frac{1}{7}$

4. $\frac{1}{5} \div \frac{1}{2} = \frac{1}{5} \bullet \frac{2}{1} = \frac{2}{5}$

5. $3 \div \frac{1}{5} = 3 \bullet \frac{5}{1} = 15$

5. *Comparing Fractions*

We can compare the values of fractions several different ways.

The first method is the one most commonly used but often takes up valuable time. First convert to a decimal equivalent and then compare the values of the fractions to find the least or greatest value.

EXAMPLE:

Find the largest value of the following fractions: $\frac{1}{2}, \frac{2}{3}, \frac{1}{8},$ and $\frac{2}{11}$. Convert each fraction to its decimal equivalent: 0.5, 0.67, 0.125, and 0.19. Compare the values: $\frac{2}{3}$ is the largest.

The second method of comparing fractions is often faster. We use upward cross-multiplication—multiply the denominator of the one fraction with the numerator of the other fraction in an upward direction. The fraction with the greatest product above it has the greatest value.

EXAMPLE:

Find the largest value of the following fractions: $\frac{1}{2}, \frac{2}{3}, \frac{1}{8},$ and $\frac{2}{11}$. Compare $\frac{1}{2}$ with $\frac{2}{3}$ by multiplying (3)(1) and(2)(2) and place the value above each fraction:

$$\begin{matrix} 3 & & 4 \\ \frac{1}{2} & \times & \frac{2}{3} \end{matrix}$$

Since 4 is larger than 3, $\frac{2}{3}$ is larger than $\frac{1}{2}$. We then compare $\frac{2}{3}$ with the other two remaining fractions:

$$\begin{matrix} 16 & & 3 \\ \frac{2}{3} & \times & \frac{1}{8} \end{matrix} \Rightarrow \frac{2}{3} \text{ is larger}$$

$$\begin{matrix} 22 & & 6 \\ \frac{2}{3} & \times & \frac{2}{11} \end{matrix} \Rightarrow \frac{2}{3} \text{ is larger.}$$

Therefore, $\frac{2}{3}$ has the largest value.

EXERCISE 2

Fractions

DIRECTIONS: Choose the best answer to each of the following questions. Answers are on page B-120.

1. $5\frac{3}{8}=$

(A) 1 (B) $\frac{15}{8}$ (C) $\frac{23}{8}$ (D) $\frac{35}{8}$ (E) $\frac{43}{8}$

2. $2\frac{3}{4}=$

(A) $\frac{1}{4}$ (B) $\frac{3}{4}$ (C) $\frac{9}{4}$ (D) $\frac{11}{4}$ (E) $\frac{15}{4}$

3. $3\frac{1}{12}=$

(A) $\frac{13}{12}$ (B) $\frac{37}{12}$ (C) $\frac{41}{12}$ (D) $\frac{53}{12}$ (E) $\frac{71}{12}$

4. $1\frac{1}{65}=$

(A) $\frac{64}{65}$ (B) $\frac{65}{66}$ (C) $\frac{66}{65}$ (D) $\frac{66}{64}$ (E) $\frac{67}{66}$

5. $5\frac{2}{7}=$

(A) $\frac{5}{14}$ (B) $\frac{35}{7}$ (C) $\frac{37}{7}$ (D) $\frac{70}{7}$ (E) $\frac{110}{7}$

6. $\frac{12}{8}=$

(A) 4 (B) 3 (C) $2\frac{1}{2}$ (D) $1\frac{1}{2}$ (E) $1\frac{1}{4}$

7. $\frac{20}{6}=$

(A) $3\frac{1}{3}$ (B) $3\frac{2}{3}$ (C) $4\frac{1}{6}$ (D) $4\frac{1}{3}$ (E) 6

8. $\frac{23}{13}=$

(A) 10 (B) $7\frac{7}{13}$ (C) $1\frac{10}{13}$ (D) $\frac{13}{23}$ (E) $\frac{7}{13}$

9. $\frac{25}{4}=$

(A) $\frac{4}{25}$ (B) $\frac{4}{12}$ (C) $1\frac{1}{8}$ (D) $1\frac{1}{4}$ (E) $6\frac{1}{4}$

10. $\frac{201}{100}=$

(A) $1\frac{1}{100}$ (B) $1\frac{1}{50}$ (C) $2\frac{1}{100}$ (D) $2\frac{1}{50}$ (E) 101

11. $\frac{3}{12}=$

(A) $\frac{1}{6}$ (B) $\frac{1}{4}$ (C) $\frac{1}{3}$ (D) $\frac{1}{2}$ (E) $\frac{3}{4}$

12. $\frac{27}{81}=$

(A) $\frac{1}{9}$ (B) $\frac{2}{9}$ (C) $\frac{1}{3}$ (D) $\frac{4}{9}$ (E) $\frac{2}{3}$

13. $\frac{125}{625}=$

(A) $\frac{1}{10}$ (B) $\frac{1}{5}$ (C) $\frac{2}{5}$ (D) $\frac{7}{10}$ (E) $\frac{4}{5}$

14. $\frac{39}{52}=$

(A) $\frac{1}{5}$. (B) $\frac{1}{4}$ (C) $\frac{1}{3}$ (D) $\frac{1}{2}$ (E) $\frac{3}{4}$

15. $\frac{121}{132}=$

(A) $\frac{1}{11}$ (B) $\frac{1}{10}$ (C) $\frac{9}{10}$ (D) $\frac{10}{11}$ (E) $\frac{11}{12}$

16. $\frac{3}{8}$ is equal to all of the following EXCEPT

(A) $\frac{6}{16}$ (B) $\frac{15}{40}$ (C) $\frac{31}{81}$ (D) $\frac{33}{88}$ (E) $\frac{120}{320}$

17. $\frac{3}{4}$ is equal to all of the following EXCEPT

(A) $\frac{6}{8}$ (B) $\frac{12}{16}$ (C) $\frac{20}{24}$ (D) $\frac{36}{48}$ (E) $\frac{300}{400}$

18. $\frac{4}{25}$ is equal to

(A) $\frac{8}{50}$ (B) $\frac{8}{100}$ (C) $\frac{12}{150}$ (D) $\frac{160}{200}$ (E) $\frac{200}{250}$

19. $\frac{5}{6}$ is equal to all of the following EXCEPT

(A) $\frac{25}{30}$ (B) $\frac{45}{50}$ (C) $\frac{50}{60}$ (D) $\frac{55}{66}$ (E) $\frac{100}{120}$

20. $\frac{1}{6}$ is equal to all of the following EXCEPT

(A) $\frac{2}{12}$ (B) $\frac{3}{18}$ (C) $\frac{4}{24}$ (D) $\frac{5}{30}$ (E) $\frac{6}{40}$

21. $\frac{1}{7}+\frac{2}{7}=$

(A) $\frac{2}{7}$ (B) $\frac{3}{7}$ (C) $\frac{6}{7}$ (D) $\frac{8}{7}$ (E) $\frac{12}{7}$

22. $\frac{5}{8}+\frac{1}{8}=$

(A) $\frac{1}{2}$ (B) $\frac{3}{4}$ (C) $\frac{7}{8}$ (D) $\frac{8}{5}$ (E) $\frac{4}{3}$

23. $\frac{12}{13}+\frac{12}{13}=$

(A) 0 (B) 1 (C) $\frac{12}{26}$ (D) $\frac{24}{13}$ (E) $\frac{26}{13}$

24. $\frac{3}{8}+\frac{5}{8}=$

(A) $\frac{2}{8}$ (B) 1 (C) $\frac{5}{4}$ (D) $\frac{8}{5}$ (E) $\frac{12}{5}$

25. $\frac{1}{11}+\frac{2}{11}+\frac{7}{11}=$

(A) $\frac{4}{11}$ (B) $\frac{7}{11}$ (C) $\frac{10}{11}$ (D) $\frac{11}{10}$ (E) $\frac{11}{7}$

26. $\frac{3}{8}+\frac{5}{6}=$

(A) $\frac{8}{48}$ (B) $\frac{8}{14}$ (C) $\frac{29}{24}$ (D) $\frac{3}{2}$ (E) $\frac{14}{8}$

27. $\frac{1}{8}+\frac{1}{7}=$

(A) $\frac{1}{56}$ (B) $\frac{1}{27}$ (C) $\frac{1}{15}$ (D) $\frac{1}{5}$ (E) $\frac{15}{56}$

28. $\frac{1}{12}+\frac{1}{7}=$

(A) $\frac{19}{84}$ (B) $\frac{19}{42}$ (C) $\frac{10}{19}$ (D) $\frac{20}{19}$ (E) $\frac{5}{4}$

29. $\frac{3}{5}+\frac{2}{11}=$

(A) $\frac{43}{110}$ (B) $\frac{43}{55}$ (C) $\frac{54}{55}$ (D) $\frac{55}{54}$ (E) $\frac{100}{43}$

30. $\frac{1}{2}+\frac{1}{3}+\frac{1}{6}=$

(A) $\frac{1}{36}$ (B) $\frac{1}{12}$ (C) 1 (D) $\frac{7}{6}$ (E) $\frac{7}{3}$

31. $\frac{2}{3}+\frac{3}{6}+\frac{4}{6}=$

(A) $\frac{9}{20}$ (B) $\frac{6}{7}$ (C) $\frac{7}{6}$ (D) $\frac{11}{6}$ (E) $\frac{16}{3}$

32. $\frac{2}{3}-\frac{1}{3}=$

(A) $\frac{1}{6}$ (B) $\frac{1}{3}$ (C) $\frac{2}{3}$ (D) $\frac{4}{3}$ (E) $\frac{6}{3}$

33. $\frac{5}{7}-\frac{4}{7}=$

(A) $\frac{9}{7}$ (B) 1 (C) $\frac{5}{7}$ (D) $\frac{1}{7}$ (E) $\frac{1}{49}$

34. $\frac{9}{10}-\frac{1}{5}=$

(A) $\frac{7}{10}$ (B) $\frac{7}{5}$ (C) $\frac{10}{7}$ (D) $\frac{7}{5}$ (E) $\frac{20}{7}$

35. $\frac{3}{2}-\frac{1}{4}=$

(A) $\frac{5}{4}$ (B) $\frac{4}{5}$ (C) $\frac{3}{4}$ (D) $\frac{2}{3}$ (E) $\frac{1}{3}$

36. $2\frac{1}{2}-\frac{7}{8}=$

(A) $\frac{9}{2}$ (B) $\frac{5}{2}$ (C) $\frac{13}{8}$ (D) $\frac{5}{4}$ (E) $\frac{4}{5}$

37. $2\frac{2}{3}-1\frac{1}{6}=$

(A) $1\frac{1}{6}$ (B) $1\frac{1}{3}$ (C) $1\frac{1}{2}$ (D) $1\frac{2}{3}$ (E) 2

38. $\frac{1}{2}\bullet\frac{2}{3}=$

(A) $\frac{1}{6}$ (B) $\frac{1}{3}$ (C) $\frac{1}{2}$ (D) $\frac{2}{3}$ (E) $\frac{3}{4}$

39. $\frac{2}{7}\bullet\frac{1}{4}=$

(A) $\frac{1}{63}$ (B) $\frac{1}{14}$ (C) $\frac{1}{4}$ (D) $\frac{3}{8}$ (E) $\frac{5}{9}$

40. $\frac{1}{3}\bullet\frac{1}{3}=$

(A) $\frac{1}{9}$ (B) $\frac{1}{6}$ (C) $\frac{1}{3}$ (D) $\frac{2}{3}$ (E) $\frac{3}{2}$

41. $\frac{1}{2}\bullet\frac{1}{2}\bullet\frac{1}{2}=$

(A) $\frac{1}{16}$ (B) $\frac{1}{8}$ (C) $\frac{3}{16}$ (D) $\frac{3}{8}$ (E) $\frac{2}{3}$

42. $\frac{2}{3}\bullet\frac{3}{4}\bullet\frac{4}{5}=$

(A) $\frac{2}{5}$ (B) $\frac{3}{5}$ (C) $\frac{2}{3}$ (D) $\frac{3}{4}$ (E) $\frac{4}{5}$

43. $\frac{1}{4}\bullet\frac{1}{8}\bullet 3=$

(A) $\frac{3}{32}$ (B) $\frac{1}{8}$ (C) $\frac{1}{4}$ (D) $\frac{1}{2}$ (E) $\frac{3}{4}$

44. $\frac{1}{3}\bullet\frac{1}{6}\bullet 12=$

(A) $\frac{1}{3}$ (B) $\frac{2}{3}$ (C) 1 (D) $\frac{3}{2}$ (E) 2

45. $\frac{7}{8}\div\frac{3}{4}=$

(A) $\frac{7}{6}$ (B) 1 (C) $\frac{3}{4}$ (D) $\frac{1}{3}$ (E) $\frac{1}{8}$

46. $\frac{5}{7}\div\frac{1}{7}=$

(A) $\frac{1}{7}$ (B) $\frac{1}{5}$ (C) 5 (D) 7 (E) 12

47. $\frac{1}{12}\div\frac{1}{12}=$

(A) $\frac{1}{144}$ (B) 1 (C) 12 (D) 18 (E) 144

48. $2\div\frac{1}{11}=$

(A) 22 (B) 11 (C) $\frac{11}{2}$ (D) $\frac{11}{22}$ (E) $\frac{1}{22}$

49. $\frac{8}{9}\div\frac{7}{8}=$

(A) $\frac{64}{63}$ (B) $\frac{9}{7}$ (C) $\frac{7}{9}$ (D) $\frac{1}{2}$ (E) $\frac{1}{3}$

50. $\frac{1}{10}\div\frac{3}{5}=$

(A) $\frac{1}{6}$ (B) $\frac{1}{5}$ (C) $\frac{3}{10}$ (D) $\frac{3}{5}$ (E) $\frac{5}{3}$

51. $\left(\frac{1}{4}+\frac{2}{3}\right)\bullet\left(\frac{3}{2}+\frac{1}{4}\right)=$

(A) $\frac{21}{47}$ (B) $\frac{33}{49}$ (C) $\frac{51}{48}$ (D) $\frac{77}{48}$ (E) $\frac{105}{51}$

52. $\left(\frac{2}{3}\bullet\frac{1}{6}\right)\div\left(\frac{1}{2}\bullet\frac{1}{4}\right)=$

(A) $\frac{1}{18}$ (B) $\frac{2}{9}$ (C) $\frac{8}{9}$ (D) $\frac{11}{8}$ (E) $\frac{15}{75}$

53. $\left[\left(\frac{1}{3}+\frac{1}{2}\right)\cdot\left(\frac{2}{3}-\frac{1}{3}\right)\right]\cdot 18 =$

(A) 5 (B) $\frac{7}{8}$ (C) $\frac{5}{6}$ (D) $\frac{4}{5}$ (E) $\frac{2}{3}$

54. $\left[\left(\frac{1}{3}\div\frac{1}{6}\right)\cdot\left(\frac{2}{3}\div\frac{1}{3}\right)\right]\cdot\left(\frac{1}{2}+\frac{3}{4}\right)$

(A) 5 (B) 4 (C) 3 (D) 2 (E) 1

55. Simplify: $8\left(\frac{1}{3}+\frac{3}{4}\right)$

(A) $\frac{1}{3}$ (B) $\frac{4}{3}$ (C) $\frac{16}{3}$ (D) $\frac{19}{3}$ (E) $\frac{26}{3}$

56. Jughead eats $\frac{2}{5}$ pounds of potato chips each day. How many pounds of potato chips does Jughead eat in 3 weeks?

(A) $4\frac{1}{2}$ (B) $5\frac{3}{4}$ (C) $5\frac{1}{5}$ (D) $8\frac{2}{5}$ (E) 10

57. Chompa eats $\frac{3}{8}$ bag of candy per day. How many weeks will 42 bags of candy last Chompa?

(A) 4 (B) 5 (C) 9 (D) 12 (E) 16

58. Simplify: $\frac{1}{4}-\frac{1}{5}$

(A) $\frac{1}{5}$ (B) $\frac{1}{3}$ (C) $\frac{1}{20}$ (D) $\frac{3}{4}$ (E) $\frac{4}{5}$

59. If Chiquita can eat $2\frac{1}{2}$ bananas per day, how many bananas can Chiquita eat in 4 weeks?

(A) 70 (B) 75 (C) 80 (D) 85 (E) 90

60. Simplify: $\left(-\frac{1}{2}\right)^2+\left(\frac{1}{4}\right)^2+(-2)\left(\frac{1}{2}\right)^2$

(A) $-\frac{3}{16}$ (B) $-\frac{1}{5}$ (C) $\frac{1}{3}$ (D) $\frac{3}{4}$ (E) $\frac{4}{5}$

61. Simplify the complex fraction $\dfrac{\frac{4}{9}}{\frac{2}{5}}$.

(A) $7\frac{1}{4}$ (B) $15\frac{3}{4}$ (C) $16\frac{1}{2}$ (D) $17\frac{1}{4}$ (E) $17\frac{1}{2}$

62. Which fraction is largest?

(A) $\frac{9}{16}$ (B) $\frac{7}{10}$ (C) $\frac{5}{8}$ (D) $\frac{4}{5}$ (E) $\frac{1}{2}$

63. One brass rod measures $3\frac{5}{16}$ inches long and another brass rod measures $2\frac{3}{4}$ inches long. Together their length is

(A) $6\frac{9}{16}$ in. (B) $6\frac{1}{16}$ in. (C) $5\frac{1}{2}$ in.
(D) $5\frac{1}{16}$ in. (E) $5\frac{1}{32}$ in.

64. The number of half-pound packages of tea that can be taken out of a box that holds $10\frac{1}{2}$ pounds of tea is

(A) 5 (B) $10\frac{1}{2}$ (C) 11 (D) $20\frac{1}{122}$ (E) 21

65. If each bag of tokens weighs $5\frac{3}{4}$ pounds, how many pounds does 3 bags weigh?

(A) $7\frac{1}{4}$ (B) $15\frac{3}{4}$ (C) $16\frac{1}{2}$ (D) $17\frac{1}{4}$ (E) $17\frac{1}{2}$

66. During one week, a man traveled $3\frac{1}{2}$, $1\frac{1}{4}$, $1\frac{1}{6}$, and $2\frac{3}{8}$ miles. The next week he traveled $\frac{1}{4}$, $\frac{3}{8}$, $\frac{9}{16}$, $3\frac{1}{16}$, $2\frac{5}{8}$, and $3\frac{3}{16}$ miles. How many more miles did he travel the second week than the first week?

(A) $1\frac{37}{48}$ (B) $1\frac{1}{2}$ (C) $1\frac{3}{4}$ (D) 1 (E) $\frac{47}{48}$

67. A certain type of board is sold only in lengths of multiples of 2 feet. The shortest board sold is 6 feet and the longest is 24 feet. A builder needs a large quantity of this type of board in $5\frac{1}{2}$-foot lengths. For minimum waste the lengths to be ordered should be

(A) 6 ft. (B) 12 ft. (C) 22 ft.
(D) 24 ft. (E) 26 ft.

68. A man spent $\frac{15}{16}$ of his entire fortune in buying a car for \$7500. How much money did he possess?

(A) \$6000 (B) \$6500 (C) \$7000
(D) \$8000 (E) \$8500

69. The population of a town was 54,000 in the last census. It has increased $\frac{2}{3}$ since then. Its present population is

(A) 18,000 (B) 36,000 (C) 72,000
(D) 90,000 (E) 108,000

70. If $\frac{1}{3}$ of the liquid contents of a can evaporates on the first day and $\frac{3}{4}$ of the remainder evaporates on the second day, the fractional part of the original contents remaining at the close of the second day is

(A) $\frac{5}{12}$ (B) $\frac{7}{12}$ (C) $\frac{1}{6}$ (D) $\frac{1}{2}$ (E) $\frac{4}{7}$

71. A car is run until the gas tank is $\frac{1}{8}$ full. The tank is then filled to capacity by putting in 14 gallons. The capacity of the gas tank of the car (in gallons) is

(A) 14 (B) 15 (C) 16 (D) 17 (E) 18

Decimals

A decimal is nothing more than a special way of writing fractions using a denominator of ten, or one hundred, or one thousand and so on. For example, the fraction $\frac{3}{10}$ written as a decimal is 0.3, and the fraction $\frac{72}{100}$ written as a decimal is 0.72.

Decimals are written with a decimal point placed to the left of the left-most digit in order to distinguish them from whole numbers.

The positions to the right of the decimal point are called decimal places. Decimal places are analogous to the positions of the digits in whole numbers (units column, tens column, etc.). The number of decimal places indicates the denominator of the fraction. One decimal place indicates a denominator of 10; two places indicate a denominator of 100; three indicate a denominator of 1,000; and so on. We read 0.335 as three hundred thirty-five thousandths and 0.12345 as twelve thousand three hundred forty-five hundred thousandths.

0	.	1	2	3	4	5
		TENTHS	HUNDREDTHS	THOUSANDTHS	TEN THOUSANDTHS	HUNDRED THOUSANDTHS

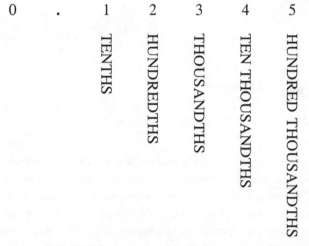

In the examples above, we placed a zero to the left of the decimal point. This has no mathematical significance; it's there just to make the decimals more readable. Without the zero, someone might fail to see the decimal and read .335 as 335. This is the style used by the exam.

Conversion To and From Decimals

If the fraction already has a denominator that is ten, one hundred, one thousand, etc., the conversion is very easy. The numerator of the fraction becomes the decimal. The number of zeros in the denominator governs the placement of the decimal point. Starting just to the right of the last digit of the numerator, you count over one digit to the left for each zero in the denominator. For example, to express $\frac{127}{1,000}$ in decimal form, we take the numerator, 127, as the decimal. Then, starting just to the right of the 7, we count over three places to the left (one for each zero in 1,000). The decimal equivalent is 0.127.

EXAMPLES:

1. $\frac{3}{10} = 0.3$ (One zero in the denominator indicates one decimal place.)
2. $\frac{13}{100} = 0.13$ (Two zeros in the denominator indicates two decimal places.)
3. $\frac{522}{1,000} = 0.522$ (Three zeros in the denominator indicates three decimal places.)

If there are fewer digits in the numerator than zeros in the denominator, add zeros to the *left* of the number until you have enough decimal places. Take $\frac{53}{1,000}$ as an example. The denominator contains three zeros, but 53 is only a two-digit number. So we must add one zero to the left of the 5: $\frac{53}{1,000} = 0.053$. Remember that the zero to the left of the decimal point has no mathematical significance—it's there as a matter of style.

EXAMPLES:

1. $\frac{3}{100} = 0.03$ (Two zeros means two decimal places, but 3 is a single–digit number.)
2. $\frac{71}{10,000} = 0.0071$ (Four zeros means four decimal places, but 71 is a two–digit number.)
3. $\frac{9}{100,000} = 0.00009$ (Five zeros means five decimal places, but 9 is a single–digit number.)

To convert a proper fraction with a denominator other than 10, 100, etc., you first convert the fraction to an equivalent form using a denominator such as ten, one hundred, etc. For example, to convert the fraction $\frac{3}{4}$ to a decimal, you first change it into a fraction with a denominator of 100: $\frac{3}{4} = \frac{3 \cdot 25}{4 \cdot 25} = \frac{75}{100}$. Then you change $\frac{75}{100}$ to 0.75, as described in the previous section.

EXAMPLES:

1. $\frac{2}{5} = \frac{2 \cdot 2}{5 \cdot 2} = \frac{4}{10} = 0.4$
2. $\frac{1}{4} = \frac{1 \cdot 25}{4 \cdot 25} = \frac{25}{100} = 0.25$
3. $\frac{3}{8} = \frac{3 \cdot 125}{8 \cdot 125} = \frac{375}{1,000} = 0.375$
4. $\frac{1}{50} = \frac{1 \cdot 2}{50 \cdot 2} = \frac{2}{100} = 0.02$

To determine which denominator you should use, divide the denominator of the fraction into 10, then into 100, then into 1,000, until you find the first denominator that is evenly divisible by the denominator of the fraction. For example, $\frac{3}{8}$ doesn't have an equivalent form with a denominator of 10, but it does have an equivalent form with a denominator of 1000. This is the same process we used above to find common denominators for fractions. (Note: You can also convert a fraction into a decimal by dividing the numerator of the fraction by its denominator. But this is a method that obviously presupposes you know how to divide decimals. So we will come back to the topic of converting to decimals when we discuss how to divide decimals.)

To change a mixed number to a decimal, convert the fractional part of the mixed number to a decimal as discussed above, and then place the whole number part of the mixed number to the left of the decimal point. For example, in the mixed number $2\frac{3}{4}$, $\frac{3}{4}$ is the fractional part. Convert $\frac{3}{4}$ to a decimal as just shown ($\frac{3}{4} = 0.75$), and then place the whole-number part to the left of the decimal point (2.75). (Notice that the superfluous zero is dropped. There is no reason to write 02.75.)

EXAMPLES:

1. $6\frac{1}{10} = 6.1$ (Convert $\frac{1}{10}$ to 0.1 and then place the 6 to the left of the decimal point.)
2. $12\frac{1}{2} = 12.5$ (Convert $\frac{1}{2}$ to 0.5 and then place the 12 to the left of the decimal point.)
3. $3\frac{7}{8} = 3.875$ (Convert $\frac{7}{8}$ to 0.875 and then place the 3 to the left of the decimal point.)

To convert an improper fraction to a decimal, just treat the improper fraction as a mixed number and follow the procedure just outlined.

EXAMPLES:

1. $\frac{9}{4} = 2\frac{1}{4} = 2.25$
2. $\frac{7}{2} = 3\frac{1}{2} = 3.5$
3. $\frac{8}{5} = 1\frac{3}{5} = 1.6$

Note: It's also possible, and even easier, to convert such fractions to decimals by dividing the numerator by the denominator. Again, we will postpone this part of the discussion until we have studied division of decimals.

To convert a decimal back to a fraction, it is necessary only to create a fraction using the digits of the decimal number as a numerator and a denominator of 1 plus a number of zeros equal to the number of decimal places. Thus, to convert 0.125 back to a fraction, use 125 as the numerator and 1 plus 3 zeros as the denominator: $\frac{125}{1,000}$. Then reduce to lowest terms: $\frac{1}{8}$.

EXAMPLES:

1. $0.04 = \frac{4}{100} = \frac{1}{25}$ (0.04 has two decimal places, so the new denominator is 1 plus two zeros.)
2. $0.25 = \frac{25}{100} = \frac{1}{4}$ (0.25 has two decimal places, so the new denominator is 1 plus two zeros.)
3. $0.005 = \frac{5}{1,000} = \frac{1}{200}$ (0.005 has three decimal places, so the new denominator is 1 plus three zeros.)

Finally, if the decimal consists of both a whole part and a fraction, the conversion will result in a mixed number. The whole part of the mixed number will be the whole part of the decimal. Then convert the fractional part of the decimal as just shown. For example, to convert 2.05 to a mixed number, convert 0.05 to a fraction as just shown: $0.05 = \frac{5}{100} = \frac{1}{20}$. Then create the mixed number: the whole–number part is 2, and the fractional part is $\frac{1}{20}$. Thus, $2.05 = 2\frac{1}{20}$.

EXAMPLES:

1. $1.75 = 1 \text{ plus } \frac{75}{100} = 1 \text{ plus } \frac{3}{4} = 1\frac{3}{4}$
2. $32.6 = 32 \text{ plus } \frac{6}{10} = 32 \text{ plus } \frac{3}{5} = 32\frac{3}{5}$
3. $2.05 = 2 \text{ plus } 0.05 = 2 \text{ plus } \frac{5}{100} = 2 \text{ plus } \frac{1}{20} = 2\frac{1}{20}$
4. $357.125 = 357 \text{ plus } \frac{125}{1,000} = 357 \text{ plus } \frac{1}{8} = 357\frac{1}{8}$

Manipulating Decimals

1. *Addition and Subtraction*

Decimals can be manipulated in very much the same way as whole numbers. You can add and subtract decimals:

EXAMPLES:

0.2 + 0.3 + 0.1 = 0.6

0.7 – 0.2 = 0.5

Adding zeros to the right of a number doesn't change the value of that number. If the decimals don't have the same number of decimal places, add zeros to the right of those that don't until every number has the same number of decimal places. Then line up the decimal points and combine.

EXAMPLE:

What is 0.25 + 0.1 + 0.825?

$$\begin{array}{rcr} 0.25 & \Rightarrow & 0.250 \\ 0.1 & \Rightarrow & 0.100 \\ \underline{+0.825} & \Rightarrow & \underline{+0.825} \\ & & 1.175 \end{array}$$

After filling in the appropriate number of zeros, add. Follow the same process to subtract decimals.

EXAMPLES:

1. $0.75 - 0.1125 = \begin{array}{r} 0.7500 \\ \underline{-0.1125} \\ 0.6375 \end{array}$

2. $0.125 + 0.6 + 0.115 = \begin{array}{r} 0.125 \\ 0.600 \\ \underline{+0.115} \\ 0.840 \end{array}$

3. $0.11 + 0.9 + 0.033 = \begin{array}{r} 0.110 \\ 0.900 \\ \underline{+0.033} \\ 1.043 \end{array}$

4. $2.14 + 0.125 + 0.0005 = \begin{array}{r} 2.1400 \\ 0.1250 \\ \underline{+0.0005} \\ 2.2655 \end{array}$

5. $0.8 - 0.1111 = \begin{array}{r} 0.8000 \\ \underline{-0.1111} \\ 0.6889 \end{array}$

6. $0.999 - 0.000001 = \begin{array}{r} 0.999000 \\ \underline{-0.000001} \\ 0.998999 \end{array}$

7. $2.1 - 1.009 = \begin{array}{r} 2.100 \\ \underline{-1.009} \\ 1.091 \end{array}$

2. *Multiplication*

One can also multiply decimals. As with fractions, there is no need to find a common denominator: the multiplication process generates its own. To multiply decimals, simply multiply as with whole numbers and then adjust the decimal point. To find the correct position for the decimal point, count the total number of decimal places in the numbers being multiplied, count that many places to the left from the right of the final number in the product, and put the decimal point there.

EXAMPLE:

0.25 • 0.2 = ?

In the above example, first multiply as though the numbers were not decimals: 25 • 2 = 50. Next, adjust the decimal point. 0.25 consists of two decimal places, and 0.2 has one decimal place, for a total of three decimal places. Therefore, we count three places to the left, starting at the right of 50, so the final product is 0.050, or just 0.05.

EXAMPLES:

1. 0.1 • 0.2 • 0.3 = 0.006 (1 • 2 • 3 = 6, and there are three decimal places in the multiplication.)
2. 0.02 • 0.008 = 0.00016 (2 • 8 = 16, and there are five decimal places in the multiplication.)
3. 2 • 0.5 = 1 (2 • 5 = 10, and there is one decimal place in the multiplication.)
4. 2.5 • 2.5 = 6.25 (25 • 25 = 625, and there are two decimal places in the multiplication.)
5. 0.10 • 0.10 • 0.10 = 0.001000 = 0.001 (10 • 10 • 10 = 1,000, and there are six decimal places in the problem.)

Note: With regard to this last example, drop the final zeros before multiplying: 0.10 • 0.10 • 0.10 = 0.1 • 0.1 • 0.1 = 0.001. (There are three decimal places.) Dropping final zeros before multiplying makes the process simpler.

3. *Division*

One can also divide decimals. And, like multiplication, division generates a common denominator by a suitable adjustment of zeros. But there are two slightly different situations in division that make things a little tricky. Let's take them one at a time.

First, when the number doing the dividing is a whole number, place the decimal point in the quotient (result of division) immediately above the decimal point in the number being divided. Then, keep dividing until there is no remainder, adding zeros as needed to the right of the number being divided. This is the procedure whenever the number doing the dividing is a whole number—even if the number to be divided is also a whole number.

EXAMPLES:

1. $2.5 \div 2 = 2\overline{)2.50}$ → quotient 1.25
   - -2
   - 0 5
   - -4
   - 10
   - -10
   - 0

2. $1.75 \div 25 = 25\overline{)1.75}$ → quotient 0.07
   - $-1\ 75$
   - 0

3. $1.44 \div 12 = 12\overline{)1.44}$ → quotient 0.12
   - -1.2
   - 24
   - -24
   - 0

4. $9 \div 2 = 2\overline{)9.0}$ → quotient 4.5
   - -8
   - 1 0
   - $-1\ 0$
   - 0

5. $0.25 \div 5 = 5\overline{)0.25}$ → quotient 0.05
   - -25
   - 0

6. $0.1 \div 250 = 250\overline{)0.1000}$ → quotient 0.0004
   - -1000
   - 0

The second situation occurs when the number doing the dividing is a decimal. In these cases, "clear" the fractional part of the decimal by moving the decimal point to the right. For example, if dividing by 0.1 change 0.1 to a whole number, or 1. Or if dividing by 2.11, convert that to 211 by moving the decimal point two places to the right. But when doing this, also move the decimal point of the number being divided by the same number of places to ensure that their relative values aren't changed. Notice in the following examples that both decimal points are moved the same number of places to the right.

EXAMPLES:

1. $5 \div 2.5 = 2.5.\overline{)5.0.}$ → quotient 2.
   - ⇒ ⇒
   - 5 0
   - 0

2. $10 \div 1.25 = 1.25.\overline{)10.00.}$ → quotient 8.
   - ⇒ ⇒
   - -10
   - 0

3. $50 \div 0.05 = 0.05.\overline{)50.00.}$ → quotient 1000.
   - ⇒ ⇒
   - $-50\ 00$
   - 0

There are two final things to say about dividing decimals. First, as was promised above, you can use division of decimals to convert fractions to decimals. Thus, if you need to convert $\frac{9}{2}$ to a decimal number, you just divide 9 by 2, as we did above.

EXAMPLES:

1. $\frac{9}{2} = 2\overline{)9} = 2\overline{)9.0} = 4.5$ (quotient 4.5)
   - -8
   - 1 0
   - 1 0
   - 0

2. $\frac{3}{4} = 4\overline{)3} = 4\overline{)3.0} = 0.75$ (quotient .75)
   - $-2\ 8$
   - 2 0
   - $-2\ 0$
   - 0

Second, some fractions don't have exact decimal equivalents. Try converting $\frac{1}{3}$ to a decimal using the division route. You'll be at it forever, because you keep getting an endless succession of 3s. Or try converting $\frac{1}{9}$ to a decimal using the division method. Again, you wind up with an endless succession of, this time, repeating 1s. By convention, repeating decimals are shown using ellipsis: 0.333....

EXERCISE 3

Decimals

DIRECTIONS: Choose the best answer to each of the following questions. Answers are on page B-121.

1. What is $\frac{7}{10}$ expressed as a decimal?

(A) 70 (B) 7 (C) 0.7 (D) 0.007 (E) 0.0007

2. What is $\frac{73}{100}$ expressed as a decimal?

(A) 73 (B) 7.3 (C) 0.73
(D) 0.073 (E) 0.0073

3. What is $\frac{21}{1{,}000}$ expressed as a decimal?

(A) 0.21 (B) 0.021 (C) 0.0021
(D) 0.00021 (E) 0.000021

4. What is $\frac{557}{1{,}000}$ expressed as a decimal?

(A) 5.57 (B) 0.557 (C) 0.0557
(D) 0.0057 (E) 0.00057

5. What is $\frac{34}{10{,}000}$ expressed as a decimal?

(A) 0.00034 (B) 0.0034 (C) 0.034
(D) 0.34 (E) 3.4

6. What is $\frac{1}{1{,}000{,}000}$ expressed as a decimal?

(A) 0.01 (B) 0.001 (C) 0.0001
(D) 0.00001 (E) 0.000001

7. What is $\frac{30}{100}$ expressed as a decimal?

(A) 3 (B) 0.3 (C) 0.03
(D) 0.003 (E) 0.0003

8. What is $\frac{1{,}000}{4{,}000}$ expressed as a decimal?

(A) 0.25 (B) 0.025 (C) 0.0025
(D) 0.00025 (E) 0.000025

9. Which of the following is (are) equal to $\frac{1}{10}$?

I. 1.0
II. 0.1
III. 0.1000

(A) I only (B) II only (C) III only
(D) I and III only (E) II and III only

10. Which of the following is (are) equal to $\frac{25}{100}$?

I. 0.25
II. 0.025
III. 0.0025

(A) I only (B) I and II only (C) I and III only
(D) II and III only (E) I, II, and III

11. What is $\frac{257}{100}$ expressed as a decimal?

(A) 25.7 (B) 2.57 (C) 0.257
(D) 0.0257 (E) 0.00257

12. What is $\frac{57}{10}$ expressed as a decimal?

(A) 57 (B) 5.7 (C) 0.57
(D) 0.057 (E) 0.0057

13. What is $\frac{5}{8}$ expressed as a decimal?

(A) 0.125 (B) 0.625 (C) 0.850
(D) 1.25 (E) 5.80

14. What is $\frac{4}{5}$ expressed as a decimal?

(A) 0.4 (B) 0.6 (C) 0.8 (D) 1.2 (E) 2.4

15. What is $\frac{1}{20}$ expressed as a decimal?

(A) 0.05 (B) 0.005 (C) 0.0005
(D) 0.00005 (E) 0.000005

16. What is $\frac{1}{50}$ expressed as a decimal?

(A) 0.2 (B) 0.02 (C) 0.002
(D) 0.0002 (E) 0.00002

17. What is $\frac{3}{200}$ expressed as a decimal?

(A) 0.15 (B) 0.015 (C) 0.0015
(D) 0.00015 (E) 0.000015

18. What is $\frac{9}{500}$ expressed as a decimal?

(A) 0.000018 (B) 0.00018 (C) 0.0018
(D) 0.018 (E) 0.18

19. What is $\frac{17}{500}$ expressed as a decimal?

(A) 0.175 (B) 0.034 (C) 0.0175
(D) 0.0034 (E) 0.00034

20. What is $\frac{123}{200}$ expressed as a decimal?
(A) 0.615 (B) 0.256 (C) 0.0615
(D) 0.0256 (E) 0.00615

21. 0.1 + 0.1 =
(A) 0.002 (B) 0.02 (C) 0.2 (D) 2 (E) 20

22. 0.27 + 0.13 + 0.55 =
(A) 0.21 (B) 0.36 (C) 0.47 (D) 0.85 (E) 0.95

23. 0.528 + 0.116 + 0.227 =
(A) 0.871 (B) 0.583 (C) 0.243
(D) 0.112 (E) 0.0012

24. 0.7 + 0.013 + 0.028 =
(A) 0.741 (B) 0.988 (C) 1.02
(D) 1.224 (E) 2.553

25. 1.23 + 0.00001 =
(A) 1.24 (B) 1.2301 (C) 1.23001
(D) 1.2300001 (E) 1.230000001

26. 57.1 + 23.3 + 35.012 =
(A) 412.115 (B) 115.412 (C) 115.0412
(D) 11.5412 (E) 1.15412

27. 0.01 + 0.001 + 0.0001 + 0.00001 =
(A) 1 (B) 0.10 (C) 0.1111
(D) 0.01111 (E) 0.001111

28. 0.9 + 0.09 + 0.009 + 0.0009 =
(A) 0.9999 (B) 0.09999 (C) 0.009999
(D) 0.0009999 (E) 0.0000999

29. 0.27 + 0.36 + 2.1117 + 3.77777 + 1.42 =
(A) 5.44 (B) 7.93947 (C) 8.11143
(D) 12.223479 (E) 14.002785

30. 12,279.1 + 3,428.01 + 3,444.99 =
(A) 19,151.99 (B) 19,152 (C) 19,152.09
(D) 19,152.1 (E) 19,152.11

31. 0.7 – 0.3 =
(A) 0.004 (B) 0.021 (C) 0.04
(D) 0.21 (E) 0.4

32. 0.75 – 0.25 =
(A) 5 (B) 1 (C) 0.5 (D) 0.25 (E) 0.005

33. 1.35 – 0.35 =
(A) 1 (B) 0.35 (C) 0.1
(D) 0.0035 (E) 0.00001

34. 25.125 – 5.357 =
(A) 19.768 (B) 15.432 (C) 12.115
(D) 4.108 (E) 2.288

35. 1 – 0.00001 =
(A) 0.9 (B) 0.99 (C) 0.999
(D) 0.9999 (E) 0.99999

36. 0.2 • 0.1 =
(A) 0.3 (B) 0.2 (C) 0.1 (D) 0.02 (E) 0.006

37. 0.1 • 0.1 • 0.1 =
(A) 0.3 (B) 0.1 (C) 0.01
(D) 0.001 (E) 0.0001

38. 1.1 • 1.1 • 1.1 =
(A) 1.331 (B) 1.111 (C) 0.111
(D) 0.0111 (E) 0.00111

39. 0.11 • 0.33 =
(A) 0.363 (B) 0.0363 (C) 0.00363
(D) 0.000363 (E) 0.0000363

40. 0.2 • 0.5 • 0.2 • 0.5=
(A) 0.1 (B) 0.01 (C) 0.001
(D) 0.0001 (E) 0.00001

41. 5 • 0.25 =
(A) 1.25 (B) 0.125 (C) 0.0125
(D) 0.00125 (E) 0.000125

42. 10 • 0.000001 =
(A) 0.00001 (B) 0.0001 (C) 0.001
(D) 0.01 (E) 0.1

43. 100 • 0.00052 =
(A) 0.0052 (B) 0.052 (C) 5.2
(D) 52 (E) 520

44. 1.2 • 1.2 =
(A) 0.144 (B) 1.44 (C) 14.4
(D) 144 (E) 1,444

45. 1.000 • 1.000 • 1.000 • 1.000 =
(A) 1 (B) 0.1 (C) 0.01
(D) 0.001 (E) 0.0001

46. 6 ÷ 0.2 =
(A) 0.03 (B) 0.3 (C) 3 (D) 30 (E) 300

47. 0.2 ÷ 5 =
(A) 0.4 (B) 0.04 (C) 0.004
(D) 0.0004 (E) 0.00004

48. 1 ÷ 0.001 =
(A) 10,000 (B) 1,000 (C) 100
(D) 0.001 (E) 0.0001

49. 25.1 ÷ 2.51 =
(A) 100 (B) 10 (C) 0.1 (D) 0.01 (E) 0.001

50. $0.25 \div 8 =$

(A) 4 (B) 0.4 (C) 0.03125
(D) 0.004 (E) 0.003125

51. $0.005 \div 0.005 =$

(A) 1 (B) 0.5 (C) 0.005
(D) 0.0005 (E) 0.00005

52. $2 \div 2.5 =$

(A) 8 (B) 5 (C) 0.8 (D) 0.5 (E) 0.008

53. $111 \div 0.111 =$

(A) 1 (B) 10 (C) 11 (D) 110 (E) 1,000

54. $0.12345 \div 0.012345 =$

(A) 100 (B) 10 (C) 1 (D) 0.1 (E) 0.01

55. $0.002 \div 0.00002 =$

(A) 100 (B) 10 (C) 0.1 (D) 0.01 (E) 0.001

56. Express as a decimal: $\frac{3}{5}+\frac{5}{8}$

(A) 1.00 (B) 1.115 (C) 1.225
(D) 1.50 (E) 1.75

57. Find the average of $\frac{2}{3}$ and 0.75.

(A) $\frac{9}{24}$ (B) $\frac{14}{24}$ (C) $\frac{17}{24}$ (D) $\frac{21}{24}$ (E) $\frac{23}{24}$

58. Find the average of 0.1, 0.01, and $\frac{1}{4}$.

(A) 0.10 (B) 0.12 (C) 0.50 (D) 0.75 (E) 1.0

59. Simplify: $\frac{12\frac{1}{3}}{0.2}$

(A) $\frac{1}{50}$ (B) $\frac{3}{40}$ (C) $\frac{85}{2}$ (D) $\frac{185}{3}$ (E) $\frac{225}{4}$

60. Simplify: $0.1\left[\frac{1}{3}-2\left(\frac{1}{2}-\frac{1}{4}\right)\right]$.

(A) $-\frac{2}{15}$ (B) $-\frac{1}{60}$ (C) $-\frac{1}{90}$ (D) $\frac{1}{2}$ (E) $\frac{3}{4}$

61. A boy saved up $4.56 the first month, $3.82 the second month, and $5.06 the third month. How much did he save altogether?

(A) $12.04 (B) $12.44 (C) $13.04
(D) $13.44 (E) $14.44

62. The diameter of a certain rod is required to be 1.51 ± 0.015 inches. The rod's diameter must be between what dimensions?

(A) 1.490 inches to 1.520 inches inclusive
(B) 1.495 inches to 1.520 inches inclusive
(C) 1.495 inches to 1.525 inches inclusive
(D) 1.495 inches to 1.530 inches inclusive
(E) 1.500 inches to 1.530 inches inclusive

63. After an employer figures out an employee's salary of $1 90.57, he deducts $3.05 for social security and $5.68 for pension. What is the amount of the check after these deductions?

(A) $180.84 (B) $181.04 (C) $181.84
(D) $182.04 (E) $182.84

64. If the outer radius of a metal pipe is 2.84 inches and the inner radius is 1.94 inches, the thickness of the metal is

(A) 0.80 in. (B) 0.90 in. (C) 1.00 in.
(D) 1.10 in. (E) 1.20 in.

65. A boy earns $20.56 on Monday, $32.90 on Tuesday, and $20.78 on Wednesday. He spends half of all that he earned during the three days. How much does he left?

(A) $36.12 (B) $36.72 (C) $37.12
(D) $37.72 (E) $38.12

66. The total cost of $3\frac{1}{2}$ pounds of meat at $1.69 a pound and 20 lemons at $.60 a dozen will be:

(A) $5.92 (B) $6.42 (C) $6.92
(D) $7.42 (E) $7.92

67. A reel of cable weighs 1279 pounds. If the empty reel weighs 285 pounds and the cable weighs 7.1 pounds per foot, the number of feet of cable on the reel is:

(A) 140 (B) 150 (C) 160 (D) 170 (E) 180

68. 345 fasteners at $4.15 per hundred will cost:

(A) $13.12 (B) $13.82 (C) $14.12
(D) $14.32 (E) $14.82

Percents

A percent is a special form of a fraction, one that always uses the denominator 100. The percent sign, "%," is shorthand for "$\frac{\quad}{100}$"; for example, 67% = $\frac{67}{100}$.

Conversions

Since a percent is just a special form of a fraction, you can convert both fractions and decimals to percents, and vice versa. The easiest conversion is the one changing a decimal to a percent. To change any decimal to a percent, just move the decimal point two places to the right and add the percent sign.

EXAMPLES:

1. 0.27 = 27%
2. 0.50 = 50%
3. 0.275 = 27.5%

All that this does is substitute the "%" for two decimal places—just a matter of changing things from one form into an equivalent form, a process we have already used in several different ways. To change a percent back to a decimal, just move the decimal point two places to the left and drop the percent sign:

EXAMPLES:

1. 27% = 0.27
2. 50% = 0.50
3. 27.5% = 0.275

You already know the rules for converting fractions to decimals, and vice versa. So to convert a fraction to a percent, just convert the fraction to a decimal and follow the rule above.

EXAMPLES:

1. $\frac{3}{4} = 0.75 = 75\%$
2. $\frac{5}{8} = 0.625 = 62.5\%$
3. $\frac{1}{10} = 0.10 = 10\%$

And to reverse the process, follow the rule given above for turning percentages back into decimals, and then use the procedure outlined in the previous section for converting decimals to fractions.

EXAMPLES:

1. $75\% = 0.75 = \frac{75}{100} = \frac{3}{4}$
2. $62.5\% = 0.625 = \frac{625}{1{,}000} = \frac{5}{8}$
3. $10\% = 0.1 = \frac{1}{10}$

There are two types of percents that are a little tricky: those greater than 100% and those less than 1%. First, it is possible to have a percent that is larger than one hundred. This would be the result of converting a mixed number, such as $2\frac{3}{4}$, to a percent: $2\frac{3}{4} = \frac{11}{4} = 2.75 = 275\%$.

Percents can also be less than 1, in which case they are written with decimals; for example, 0.5%. But these strange numbers follow the general rules outlined above. To convert 0.5% to a fraction: $0.5\% = 0.005 = \frac{5}{1,000} = \frac{1}{200}$. And, conversely, fractions smaller than $\frac{1}{100}$ will yield a percent less than 1: $\frac{1}{2,500} = 0.0004 = 0.04\%$.

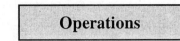

Operations

1. *Addition and Subtraction*

Because percents are fractions, they can be manipulated just like other fractions. Addition and subtraction of percents are easy because you already have a common denominator. Remember that all percentages use 100 as their denominator.

You can add percents: 25% + 15% + 10% = 50%. When would you need to add percents?

EXAMPLE:

Paul originally owned 25 percent of the stock of a certain company. He purchased another 15 percent of the stock privately, and he received a gift of another 10 percent of the stock. What percent of the stock of the company does Paul now own?

25% + 15% + 10% = 50%

And you can subtract percents: 50% – 20% = 30%. When would you need to subtract percents?

EXAMPLE:

In a certain election, Peter and Mary received 50 percent of all the votes that were cast. If Peter received 20 percent of the votes cast in the election, what percent of the votes did Mary receive?

50% – 20% = 30%

2. *Multiplication*

You can also multiply percents. First, convert the percents to decimals, and then multiply, according to the procedure described in the preceding section: 60% • 80% = 0.60 • 0.80 = 0.48. When would you multiply percents?

EXAMPLE:

In a certain group, 80 percent of the people are wearing hats. If 60 percent of those wearing hats are also wearing gloves, what percent of the entire group is wearing both a hat and gloves?

60% of 80% = 60% • 80% = 0.60 • 0.80 = 0.48 = 48%

3. *Division*

Finally, you can also divide percents, by converting them to decimals: 100% ÷ 12.5% = 1 ÷ 0.125 = 8. When would you divide percents?

EXAMPLE:

Peter is purchasing an item on a lay–away plan. If he pays weekly installments of 12.5 percent of the purchase price, how many weeks will he need to pay the entire purchase price?

100% ÷ 12.5% = 8

Common Problems Using Percents

There are three common uses of percents that form the basis of questions on the exams:

- What is x percent of something?
- This is what percent of that?
- What is the percent change from this quantity to that quantity?

1. *What is x percent of something?*

One common problem involving percents has the form "What is x percent of some quantity?" Since a percent is also a fraction, the *of* indicates multiplication.

EXAMPLES:

1. A certain class is made up of 125 students. If 60 percent of the students are men, how many men are in the class?

   60% of 125 = 60% • 125 = 0.60 • 125 = 75

2. If Sam originally had \$25 and gave 25 percent of that amount to his friend Samantha, how much money did Sam give to Samantha?

   25% of \$25 = 25% • 25 = 0.25 • 25 = \$6.25

3. If Paula had 50 marbles and gave 20 percent of them to her friend Paul, how many marbles did Paula give to Paul?

   20% of 50 = 20% • 50 = 0.20 • 50 = 10

2. *What percent is this of that?*

A second common problem involving percents has the form "What percent of this is that?"

EXAMPLE:

What percent is 3 of 12?

$\frac{3}{12} = 0.25 = 25\%$

The question asks that you express the fraction $\frac{3}{12}$ as a percent. To do that, first convert $\frac{3}{12}$ to a decimal (by dividing 3 by 12) and then change that decimal number to a percent.

There are other ways of phrasing the same question:

3 is what percent of 12?
Of 12, what percent is 3?

These questions are equivalent and have the general forms:

What percent is this of that?
This is what percent of that?
Of that, what percent is this?

Although the order of words is different, they ask the same thing: Express a fraction as a percent. Here is a little trick to help you avoid confusion. Notice that in each form of the question there is the phrase *of that* and the word *this*. When you set up your fraction, make sure that *of that* is the denominator and that *this* is the numerator.

EXAMPLES:

1. 5 is what percent of 25?
2. Of 25, what percent is 5?
3. What percent is 5 of 25?
4. Notice that these questions are equivalent. Using our trick: $\frac{\text{This}}{\text{Of that}} = \frac{5}{\text{of } 25} = \frac{5}{25} = \frac{1}{5} = 0.2 = 20\%$.

As long as you remember that the *of that* goes on the bottom of the fraction and the other number goes on the top, you can't make a mistake.

EXAMPLES:

1. What percent is 20 of 50?

$\frac{20}{50}=\frac{2}{5}=0.40=40\%$

2. Of 125, what percent is 25?

$\frac{25}{125}=\frac{1}{5}=0.20=20\%$

3. 12 is what percent of 6?

$\frac{12}{6}=2=200\%$

There is a variation on this theme that can also be attacked using the "of that" trick. For example, what number is 20% of 25? This is very much like the examples just analyzed, except here the percent is given but one of the two numbers is missing. Still, the "of that" trick works. (Here "this" represents "what number"—a slight variation in wording.)

EXAMPLES:

1. What number is 20% of 25?

$\frac{\text{This}}{\text{of that}}=\% \quad \Rightarrow \quad \frac{\text{This}}{\text{of }25}=20\% \quad \Rightarrow \quad \frac{\text{This}}{25}=20\% \quad \Rightarrow \quad \text{This}=0.20\bullet 25=5$

2. 5 is 20% of what number?

$\frac{\text{This}}{\text{of that}}=\% \quad \Rightarrow \quad \frac{5}{\text{of that}}=20\% \quad \Rightarrow \quad \frac{5}{20\%}=\text{That}=\frac{5}{0.20}=25$

No matter how wordy or otherwise difficult such questions get, they are all answerable using the "of that" trick.

EXAMPLE:

John received a dividend check in the amount of $200. Of that amount, he paid Ed $25. Of the original dividend check, John gave Ed what percent?

What's the "of that"? The $200. So the other number is $25. And the solution is: $\frac{25}{200}=\frac{1}{8}=0.125=12.5\%$.

3. *Percent change*

A third type of percent problem involves the change in a quantity over time. This type of question asks you to express the relationship between the change and the original amount in percent terms. To answer, you create a fraction that is then expressed as a percent.

EXAMPLE:

The price of an item increased from $20 to $25. What was the percent increase in the price?

$\frac{\text{Change}}{\text{Original Amount}}=\frac{5}{20}=\frac{1}{4}=0.25=25\%$

Think of this as the "change–over" trick, because the fraction places the change over the original amount.

EXAMPLE:

Mary was earning $16 per hour when she received a raise of $4 per hour. Her hourly wage increased by what percent?

$\frac{\text{Change}}{\text{Original Amount}}=\frac{4}{16}=0.25=25\%$

The "change–over" trick works for decreases as well.

EXAMPLES:

1. The value of a certain stock declined from $50 per share to $45 per share. What was the percent decline in the value of a share?

$\frac{\text{Change}}{\text{Original Amount}}=\frac{5}{50}=\frac{1}{10}=0.10=10\%$

2. Student enrollment at City University dropped from 5,000 students in 1990 to 4,000 students in 2000. What was the percent drop in the number of students enrolled at City University?

$\frac{\text{Change}}{\text{Original Amount}}=\frac{1{,}000}{5{,}000}=\frac{1}{5}=0.20=20\%$

EXERCISE 4

Percents

DIRECTIONS: Choose the best answer to each of the following questions. Answers are on page B-122.

1. What is 0.79 expressed as a percent?
   (A) 0.0079% (B) 0.079% (C) 0.79%
   (D) 7.9% (E) 79%

2. What is 0.55 expressed as a percent?
   (A) 55% (B) 5.5% (C) 0.55%
   (D) 0.055% (E) 0.0055%

3. What is 0.111 expressed as a percent?
   (A) 111% (B) 11.1% (C) 1.11%
   (D) 0.111% (E) 0.0111%

4. What is 0.125 expressed as a percent?
   (A) 125% (B) 12.5% (C) 1.25%
   (D) 0.125% (E) 0.0125%

5. What is 0.5555 expressed as a percent?
   (A) 5555% (B) 555.5% (C) 55.55%
   (D) 5.555% (E) 0.555%

6. What is 0.3 expressed as a percent?
   (A) 30% (B) 3% (C) 0.30%
   (D) 0.03% (E) 0.003%

7. What is 0.7500 expressed as a percent?
   (A) 7500% (B) 750% (C) 75%
   (D) 7.5% (E) 0.75%

8. What is 2.45 expressed as a percent?
   (A) 2,450% (B) 245% (C) 24.5%
   (D) 2.45% (E) 0.245%

9. What is 1.25 expressed as a percent?
   (A) 125% (B) 12.5% (C) 1.25%
   (D) 0.125% (E) 0.0125%

10. What is 10 expressed as a percent?
    (A) 1,000% (B) 100% (C) 10%
    (D) 1% (E) 0.1%

11. What is 0.015 expressed as a percent?
    (A) 15% (B) 1.5% (C) 0.15%
    (D) 0.015% (E) 0.0015%

12. What is 0.099 expressed as a percent?
    (A) 99% (B) 9.9% (C) 0.99%
    (D) 0.099% (E) 0.0099%

13. What is 0.0333 expressed as a percent?
    (A) 3.33% (B) 0.333% (C) 0.0333%
    (D) 0.00333% (E) 0.000333%

14. What is 0.001 expressed as a percent?
    (A) 0.1% (B) 0.01% (C) 0.001%
    (D) 0.0001% (E) 0.00001%

15. What is 0.0100 expressed as a percent?
    (A) 1% (B) 0.01% (C) 0.001%
    (D) 0.0001% (E) 0.1%

16. What is 25 percent expressed as a decimal?
    (A) 25.0 (B) 2.5 (C) 0.25
    (D) 0.025 (E) 0.0025

17. What is 56% expressed as a decimal?
    (A) 5.6 (B) 0.56 (C) 0.056
    (D) 0.0056 (E) 0.00056

18. What is 10% expressed as a decimal?
    (A) 100.0 (B) 10.0 (C) 1.0
    (D) 0.1 (E) 0.001

19. What is 100% expressed as a decimal?
    (A) 100.0 (B) 10.0 (C) 1.0
    (D) 0.1 (E) 0.001

20. What is 250% expressed as a decimal?
    (A) 250.0 (B) 25.0 (C) 2.5
    (D) 0.25 (E) 0.025

21. What is 1,000 percent expressed as a decimal?
    (A) 1,000.0 (B) 100.0 (C) 10.0
    (D) 1.0 (E) 0.01

22. What is 0.25 percent expressed as a decimal?
    (A) 25.0 (B) 0.25 (C) 0.025
    (D) 0.0025 (E) 0.00025

23. What is 0.099 percent expressed as a decimal?
    (A) 99 (B) 0.99 (C) 0.099
    (D) 0.0099 (E) 0.00099

24. What is 0.0988 percent expressed as a decimal?
(A) 0.988 (B) 0.0988 (C) 0.00988
(D) 0.000988 (E) 9.8

25. What is 0.00100 percent expressed as a decimal?
(A) 0.01 (B) 0.001 (C) 0.0001
(D) 0.00001 (E) 0.000001

26. What is $\frac{1}{10}$ expressed as a percent?
(A) 100% (B) 10% (C) 1%
(D) 0.1% (E) 0.01%

27. What is $\frac{3}{100}$ expressed as a percent?
(A) 300% (B) 30% (C) 3%
(D) 0.3% (E) 0.03%

28. What is $\frac{99}{100}$ expressed as a percent?
(A) 99% (B) 9.9% (C) 0.99%
(D) 0.099% (E) 0.0099%

29. What is $\frac{100}{1,000}$ expressed as a percent?
(A) 0.1% (B) 1.0% (C) 10%
(D) 100% (E) 1,000%

30. What is $\frac{333}{100}$ expressed as a percent?
(A) 333% (B) 33.3% (C) 3.33%
(D) 0.333% (E) 0.0333%

31. What is $\frac{9}{1,000}$ expressed as a percent?
(A) 9% (B) 0.9% (C) 0.09%
(D) 0.009% (E) 0.0009%

32. What is $\frac{3}{4}$ expressed as a percent?
(A) 0.0075% (B) 0.075% (C) 0.75%
(D) 7.5% (E) 75%

33. What is $\frac{4}{5}$ expressed as a percent?
(A) 4.5% (B) 8% (C) 45%
(D) 80% (E) 450%

34. What is $\frac{3}{50}$ expressed as a percent?
(A) 60% (B) 6% (C) 0.6%
(D) 0.006% (E) 0.0006%

35. What is $\frac{3}{75}$ expressed as a percent?
(A) 0.004% (B) 0.04% (C) 0.4%
(D) 4% (E) 40%

36. What is $\frac{6}{500}$ expressed as a percent?
(A) 0.012% (B) 0.12% (C) 1.2%
(D) 12% (E) 120%

37. What is $\frac{111}{555}$ expressed as a percent?
(A) 222% (B) 200% (C) 22%
(D) 20% (E) 2%

38. What is $\frac{8}{5,000}$ expressed as a percent?
(A) 16% (B) 0.16% (C) 0.016%
(D) 0.0016% (E) 0.00016%

39. What is $1\frac{1}{10}$ expressed as a percent?
(A) 110% (B) 11% (C) 1.1%
(D) 0.11% (E) 0.011%

40. What is $9\frac{99}{100}$ expressed as a percent?
(A) 999% (B) 99.9% (C) 9.99%
(D) 0.999% (E) 0.0999%

41. What is $3\frac{1}{2}$ expressed as a percent?
(A) 0.35% (B) 3.5% (C) 35%
(D) 350% (E) 3,500%

42. What is $1\frac{3}{4}$ expressed as a percent?
(A) 175% (B) 134% (C) 17.5%
(D) 13.4% (E) 1.75%

43. What is $10\frac{1}{5}$ expressed as a percent?
(A) 10.02% (B) 10.2% (C) 100.2%
(D) 102% (E) 1,020%

44. What is $3\frac{1}{50}$ expressed as a percent?
(A) 302% (B) 30.2% (C) 3.02%
(D) 0.0302% (E) 0.00302%

45. What is $\frac{111}{100}$ expressed as a percent?
(A) 1,110% (B) 111% (C) 11.1%
(D) 1.11% (E) 0.0111%

46. What is $\frac{7}{2}$ expressed as a percent?

(A) 0.35% (B) 3.5% (C) 35%
(D) 350% (E) 3,500%

47. What is $\frac{13}{5}$ expressed as a percent?

(A) 260% (B) 26% (C) 2.6%
(D) 0.26% (E) 0.026%

48. What is $\frac{9}{8}$ expressed as a percent?

(A) 1,125% (B) 112.5% (C) 11.25%
(D) 1.125% (E) 0.1125%

49. What is $\frac{22}{5}$ expressed as a percent?

(A) 440% (B) 44% (C) 4.4%
(D) 0.44% (E) 0.044%

50. What is $\frac{33}{6}$ expressed as a percent?

(A) 550% (B) 53% (C) 5.5%
(D) 5.3% (E) 0.55%

51. Which of the following is equal to 18 percent?
(A) $\frac{18}{1}$ (B) $\frac{18}{10}$ (C) $\frac{18}{100}$ (D) $\frac{18}{1,000}$ (E) $\frac{18}{10,000}$

52. Which of the following is equal to 80 percent?
(A) 80 (B) 8 (C) 0.8 (D) 0.08 (E) 0.008

53. Which of the following is equal to 45 percent?
(A) $\frac{1}{9}$ (B) $\frac{9}{20}$ (C) $\frac{11}{19}$ (D) $\frac{3}{4}$ (E) $\frac{9}{10}$

54. Which of the following is equal to 7 percent?
(A) 0.007 (B) 0.07 (C) 0.7 (D) 7 (E) 70

55. Which of the following is equal to 13.2 percent?
(A) 0.0132 (B) 0.132 (C) 1.32
(D) 13.2 (E) 132

56. Which of the following is equal to 1.111 percent?
(A) 0.001111 (B) 0.01111 (C) 0.11111
(D) 1.111 (E) 11.11

57. Which of the following is equal to 10.101 percent?
(A) 0.0010101 (B) 0.010101 (C) 0.10101
(D) 1.0101 (E) 10.101

58. Which of the following is equal to 33 percent?
(A) $\frac{1}{3}$ (B) $\frac{33}{100}$ (C) $\frac{33}{111}$ (D) $\frac{333}{1,000}$ (E) $\frac{333}{10,000}$

59. Which of the following is equal to 80.1 percent?
(A) $80\frac{1}{10}$ (B) 8.01 (C) $\frac{801}{1,000}$
(D) 0.0801 (E) 0.00801

60. Which of the following is equal to 0.02 percent?
(A) $\frac{1}{5}$ (B) $\frac{1}{50}$ (C) $\frac{1}{500}$ (D) $\frac{1}{5,000}$ (E) $\frac{1}{50,000}$

61. Which of the following is equal to 250 percent?
(A) $\frac{25}{1,000}$ (B) $\frac{25}{100}$ (C) $\frac{1}{4}$ (D) 2.5 (E) 25

62. Which of the following is equal to 1,000 percent?
(A) $\frac{1}{10}$ (B) 1 (C) 10 (D) 100 (E) 1,000

63. 37% + 42% =

(A) 6% (B) 79% (C) 106%
(D) 110% (E) 154%

64. 210% + 21% =

(A) 21,021% (B) 231% (C) 23.1%
(D) 2.31% (E) 0.231%

65. 8% + 9% + 10% + 110% =

(A) 17% (B) 137% (C) 180%
(D) 1,800% (E) 18,000%

66. 254% + 166% + 342% =

(A) 900% (B) 762% (C) 432%
(D) 111% (E) 92%

67. 0.02% + 0.005% =

(A) 7% (B) 2.5% (C) 1%
(D) 0.07% (E) 0.025%

68. 33% – 25% =

(A) 0.08% (B) 0.8% (C) 8%
(D) 80% (E) 800%

69. 100% – 0.99% =

(A) 1% (B) 9.9% (C) 11%
(D) 99.01% (E) 99.99%

70. 222% – 22.2% =

(A) 221.88% (B) 199.8% (C) 22.188%
(D) 19.98% (E) 1.998%

71. If John read 15 percent of the pages in a book on Monday and another 25 percent on Tuesday, what percent of the book did he read on Monday and Tuesday combined?

(A) 7.5% (B) 40% (C) 55%
(D) 75% (E) 80%

72. If from 9:00 AM to noon Mary mowed 35 percent of a lawn, and from noon to 3:00 she mowed another 50 percent of the lawn, what percent of the lawn did she mow between 9:00 AM and 3:00 PM?

(A) 17.5% (B) 60% (C) 74.3%
(D) 85% (E) 98%

Questions 73–75

Schedule for Completing Project X					
	Day by which a portion of work is to be completed				
	Monday	*Tuesday*	*Wednesday*	*Thursday*	*Friday*
Percent to be completed	8%	17%	25%	33%	17%

73. By the end of which day is one–half of the work scheduled to have been completed?

(A) Monday (B) Tuesday (C) Wednesday
(D) Thursday (E) Friday

74. By the end of Tuesday, what percent of the work is scheduled to be completed?

(A) 8% (B) 17% (C) 25% (D) 50% (E) 88%

75. If production is on schedule, during which day will $\frac{2}{3}$ of the project have been completed?

(A) Monday (B) Tuesday (C) Wednesday
(D) Thursday (E) Friday

76. A bucket is filled to 33 percent of its capacity. If an amount of water equal to $\frac{1}{4}$ of the bucket's capacity is added, the bucket is filled to what percent of its capacity?

(A) 8% (B) 25% (C) 33% (D) 58% (E) 75%

77. If Edward spends 15 percent of his allowance on a book and another 25 percent on food, what percent of his allowance remains?

(A) 10% (B) 40% (C) 45%
(D) 60% (E) 80%

78. 50% of 50% =

(A) 1% (B) 2.5% (C) 25%
(D) 100% (E) 250%

79. 1% of 100% =

(A) 0.01% (B) 0.1% (C) 1%
(D) 10% (E) 100%

80. If a jar contains 100 marbles and 66% of those marbles are red, how many marbles in the jar are red?

(A) 6 (B) 34 (C) 66 (D) 660 (E) 6,660

81. If 75 percent of the 240 cars in a certain parking lot are sedans, how many of the cars in the parking lot are sedans?

(A) 18 (B) 24 (C) 60 (D) 180 (E) 210

82. If 0.1 percent of the 189,000 names on a certain mailing list have the initials *B.D.*, how many names on the list have initials *B.D.*?

(A) 1.89 (B) 18.9 (C) 189
(D) 18,900 (E) 189,000

83. What percent of 10 is 1?

(A) 0.1% (B) 1% (C) 10%
(D) 100% (E) 1,000%

84. Of 12, what percent is 3?

(A) 2.5% (B) 3.6% (C) 25%
(D) 36% (E) 400%

85. 50 is what percent of 40?

(A) 125% (B) 90% (C) 80%
(D) 12.5% (E) 8%

86. What number is 10 percent of 100?

(A) 0.01 (B) 0.1 (C) 1 (D) 10 (E) 1,000

87. What number is 250 percent of 12?

(A) 3 (B) 15 (C) 24 (D) 30 (E) 36

88. If Patty's age is 48 and Al's age is 36, then Al's age is what percent of Patty's age?

(A) 7.5% (B) 25% (C) 75%
(D) $133\frac{1}{3}$% (E) 175%

89. If 25 of the employees at a bank are women and 15 are men, then what percent of the bank's employees are women?

(A) 37.5% (B) 40% (C) 60%
(D) 62.5% (E) 90%

90. If the price of an item increases from $5.00 to $8.00, the new price is what percent of the old price?

(A) 20% (B) 60% (C) 62.5%

(D) 92.5% (E) 160%

91. If the price of an item increases from $5.00 to $8.00, the old price is what percent of the new price?

(A) 20% (B) 60% (C) 62.5%

(D) 92.5% (E) 160%

92. If the price of a share of stock drops from $200 to $160, the new price is what percent of the old price?

(A) 20% (B) 25% (C) 50%

(D) 80% (E) 125%

93. If the price of a share of stock drops from $200 to $160, the old price is what percent of the new price?

(A) 20% (B) 25% (C) 50%

(D) 80% (E) 125%

94. If the price of a share of stock drops from $200 to $160, what was the percent decline in the price?

(A) 20% (B) 25% (C) 50%

(D) 80% (E) 125%

Questions 95–99

Enrollments for a One-Week Seminar	
Week Number	*Number of Enrollees*
1	10
2	25
3	20
4	15
5	30

95. The number of people who enrolled for the seminar in Week 1 was what percent of the number of people who enrolled in Week 2?

(A) 5% (B) 40% (C) 50%

(D) 80% (E) 250%

96. The number of people who enrolled for the seminar in Week 4 was what percent of the number of people who enrolled in Week 5?

(A) 15% (B) 25% (C) 50%

(D) 100% (E) 200%

97. The number of people who enrolled for the seminar in Week 5 was what percent of the number of people who enrolled in Week 4?

(A) 15% (B) 25% (C) 50%

(D) 100% (E) 200%

98. What was the percent increase in the number of people enrolled for the seminar from Week 1 to Week 2?

(A) 40% (B) 80% (C) 100%

(D) 150% (E) 250%

99. What was the percent decrease in the number of people enrolled for the seminar from Week 3 to Week 4?

(A) 25% (B) $33\frac{1}{3}\%$ (C) 75%

(D) 125% (E) $133\frac{1}{3}\%$

100. If a textbook costs $35 plus 8% sales tax, what is the tax?

(A) $1.20 (B) $1.80 (C) $2.00
(D) $2.80 (E) $3.20

101. If a textbook costs $30 plus 8.5% sales tax, what is the total cost of one textbook?

(A) $3.55 (B) 12.55 (C) $23.55
(D) $32.55 (E) $33.55

102. How much is 25% of 80?

(A) 2 (B) 8 (C) 20 (D) 40 (E) 45

103. How much is 2.3% of 90?

(A) 1.07 (B) 2.07 (C) 2.17 (D) 2.7 (E) 2.3

104. On a 50-question test, Gertrude got 34 out of the first 40 correct. If she received a grade of 80% on the test, how many of the last 10 did Gertrude have correct?

(A) 6 (B) 8 (C) 10 (D) 12 (E) 34

105. The number of the question you are now reading is what percent of 1,000?

(A) 0.1% (B) 10% (C) 10.5%

(D) 100% (E) 1,050%

106. 40 is what percent of 50?

(A) 5% (B) 25% (C) 80% (D) 90% (E) 95%

107. 80 is what percent of 20?

(A) 4% (B) 8% (C) 40% (D) 200% (E) 400%

108. In the junior class, 300 enrolled in a testprep course, while 500 did not. What percent of the junior class did not enroll in a testprep course?

(A) 7% (B) 35% (C) 62.5% (D) 75% (E) 90%

109. Mary's factory produces pencils at a cost to her company of $0.02 per pencil. If she sells them to a wholesaler at $0.05 each, what is her percent of profit based on her cost of $0.02 per pencil?

(A) 25% (B) 50% (C) 75% (D) 100% (E) 150%

110. In a certain class of 30 students, 6 received A's. What percent of the class did not receive an A?

(A) 8% (B) 40% (C) 60% (D) 80% (E) 90%

111. If the Wildcats won 10 out of 12 games, to the nearest whole percent, what percentage of their games did the Wildcats win?

(A) 3 (B) 8 (C) 38 (D) 83 (E) 94

112. On Thursday, Hui made 86 out of 100 free throws. On Friday, she made 46 out of 50 free throws. What was Hui's free throw percentage for the two days?

(A) 8.8% (B) 12.8% (C) 28% (D) 82% (E) 89%

113. The regular price of a TV set that sold for $118.80 at a 20% reduction sale is

(A) $158.60 (B) $148.50 (C) $138.84
(D) $95.04 (E) $29.70

114. A circle graph of a budget shows the expenditure of 26.2% for housing, 28.4% for food, 12% for clothing, 12.7% for taxes, and the balance for miscellaneous items. The percent for miscellaneous items is

(A) 79.3 (B) 70.3 (C) 68.5 (D) 29.7 (E) 20.7

115. Two dozen shuttlecocks and four badminton rackets are to be purchased for a playground. The shuttlecocks are priced at $.35 each and the rackets at $2.75 each. The playground receives a discount of 30% from these prices. The total cost of this equipment is

(A) $7.29 (B) $11.43 (C) $13.58
(D) $18.60 (E) $19.40

116. A piece of wood weighing 10 ounces is found to have a weight of 8 ounces after drying. The moisture content was

(A) 80% (B) 40% (C) $33\frac{1}{3}$%
(D) 25% (E) 20%

117. A bag contains 800 coins. Of these, 10 percent are dimes, 30 percent are nickels, and the rest are quarters. The amount of money in the bag is

(A) less than $150
(B) between $150 and $300
(C) between $301 and $450
(D) between $450 and $800
(E) more than $800

118. Six quarts of a 20% solution of alcohol in water are mixed with 4 quarts of a 60% solution of alcohol in water. The alcoholic strength of the mixture is

(A) 80% (B) 40% (C) $33\frac{1}{3}$% (D) 25% (E) 10%

119. A man insures 80% of his property and pays a $2\frac{1}{2}$% premium amounting to $348. What is the total value of his property?

(A) $19,000 (B) $18,400 (C) $18,000
(D) $17,400 (E) $13,920

120. A clerk divided his 35-hour work week as follows: $\frac{1}{2}$ of his time was spent in sorting mail; $\frac{1}{5}$ of his time was spent in sorting mail; $\frac{1}{2}$ of his time in filing letters; and $\frac{1}{7}$ of his time in reception work. The rest of his time was devoted to messenger work. The percent of time spent on messenger work by the clerk during the week was most nearly

(A) 6% (B) 10% (C) 14% (D) 16% (E) 20%

121. In a school in which 40% of the enrolled students are boys, 80% of the boys are present on a certain day. If 1152 boys are present, the total school enrollment is

(A) 1440 (B) 2880 C) 3600 (D) 5400 (E) 5760

122. Mrs. Morris receives a salary raise from $25,000 to $27,500. Find the percent of increase.

(A) 19 (B) 10 (C) 90 (D) 151 (E) $12\frac{1}{2}$

123. The population of Stormville has increased from 80,000 to 100,000 in the last 20 years. Find the percent of increase.

(A) 20 (B) 25 (C) 80 (D) 60 (E) 10

124. The value of Super Company Stock dropped from $25 a share to $21 a share. Find the percent of decrease.

(A) 4 (B) 8 (C) 12 (D) 16 (E) 20

125. The Rubins bought their home for $30,000 and sold it for $60,000. What was the percent of increase?

(A) 100 (B) 50 (C) 200 (D) 300 (E) 150

126. During the pre-holiday rush, Martin's Department Store increased its sales staff from 150 to 200 persons. By what percent must it now decrease its sales staff to return to the usual number of salespersons?

(A) 25 (B) $33\frac{1}{3}$ (C) 20 (D) 40 (E) 75

Negative Numbers

Numbers are just positions in a system:

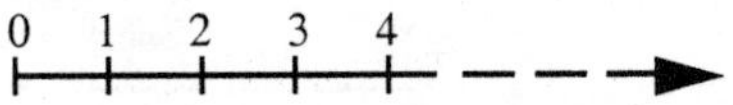

Each number is one greater than the number to its left and one less than the number to its right. And there is no logical objection to continuing this line of numbers to the left as well:

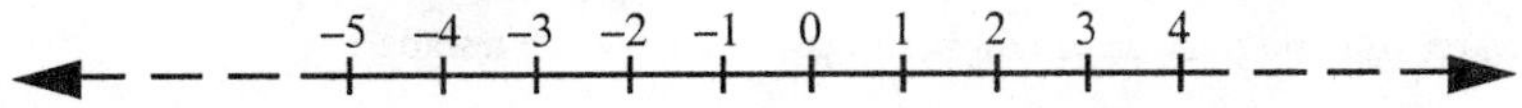

This is only a logical extension of the basic principle of the counting system that each position is one more than the position before it, and one less than the position after it. The number –1 is just one less than zero. And the number –2 is just one less than –1 and one more than –3. The negative numbers plus whole numbers are called integers. So the number line above shows the integer system. The integer system consists of positive integers, zero, and negative integers.

So the negative numbers on this number line don't refer to negative objects. The minus sign indicates the direction in which the number system is moving with reference to zero. If you move to the right, you are going in the positive direction; to the left, in the negative direction.

In fact, there are everyday situations, such as games and banking, in which it is quite natural to use negative numbers. In some games, you might score "minus ten;" or if your checking account is overdrawn, you have a minus balance.

Operations

Negative numbers can be manipulated by the basic operations of addition, subtraction, multiplication, and division. To help explain these operations, we introduce the concept of absolute value.

Absolute value just means the size of a number without regard to its sign. Absolute value is like distance without regard to direction. Five miles in an easterly direction and five miles in a westerly direction are both five miles, but they move in different directions. So, too, –5 and +5 are five units large, but one signifies a change toward the negative, the other a change toward the positive. This idea of value, without regard to direction, should help you understand the operations with negative numbers. Note: The symbol for absolute value is "$|x|$," e.g., $|-10| = 10$.

Addition

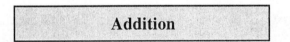

To add a negative number to some other number, just subtract the absolute value of the negative number.

EXAMPLE:

$10 + (-4) = 10 - 4 = 6$

The absolute value of –4 is 4, so just subtract 4 from 10. We can use our number line to illustrate the logic of this.

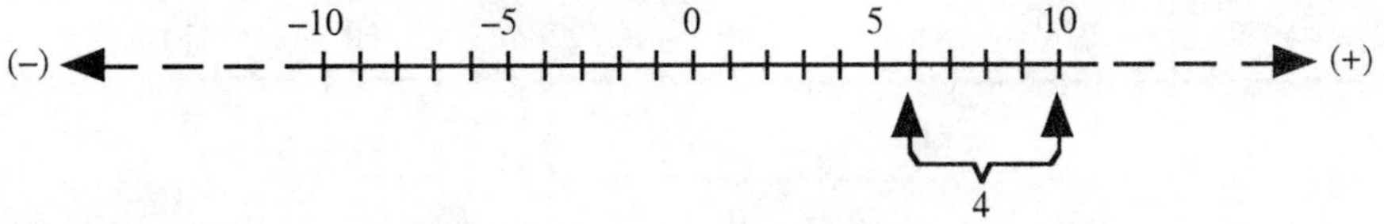

Start at 10 and move the counter four units in the negative direction. The result is 6.

Follow this procedure even if you wind up with a negative result, as the following example illustrates.

EXAMPLE:

10 + (−12) = 10 − 12 = −2

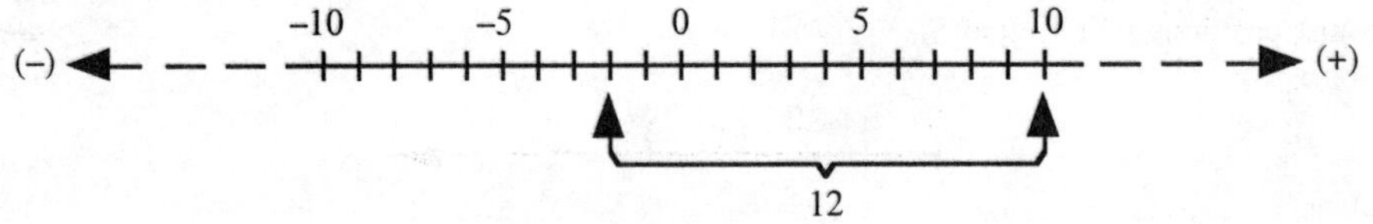

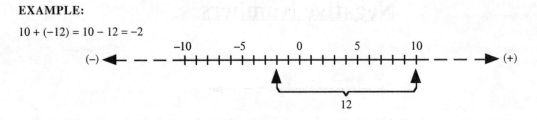

Start at 10 and move the counter 12 units in a negative direction. The result is two units to the left of zero, or −2.

And the procedure works when you add a negative number to another negative number:

EXAMPLE:

−3 + −2 = −3 − 2 = −5

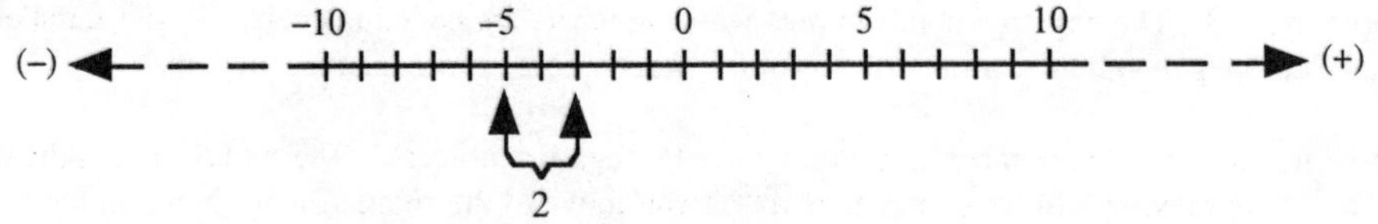

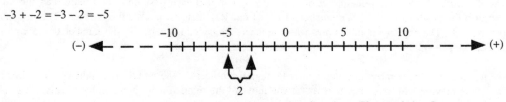

Start off at −3, and move the counter two units in the negative direction. The result is −5.

Subtraction

Subtraction of negative numbers is a little different. When you subtract something you are taking it away, so when you subtract a negative number, you are really adding. This is like a double negative. "It is *not* the case that Ramona is *not* a student" means that Ramona is a student.

To subtract a negative number from another quantity, add the absolute value of the negative number to the other quantity.

EXAMPLE:

10 − (−5) = 10 + 5 = 15

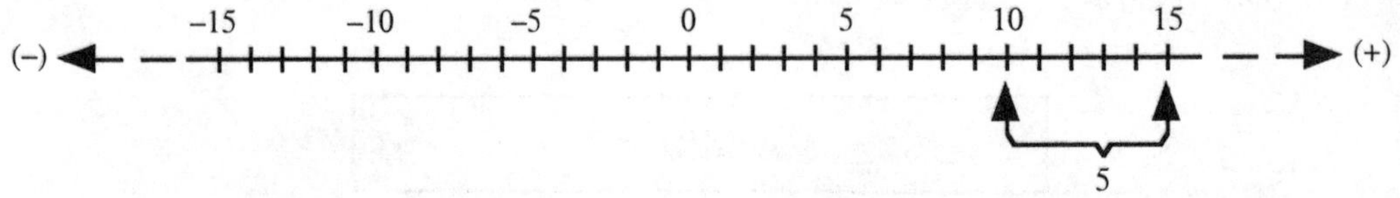

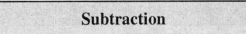

Start at 10, and since you are "eliminating minus points," move the counter in the positive direction.

Follow this procedure no matter where you start—even if you are subtracting a negative number from zero or from another negative number:

EXAMPLE:

−5 − (−10) = −5 + 10 = 5

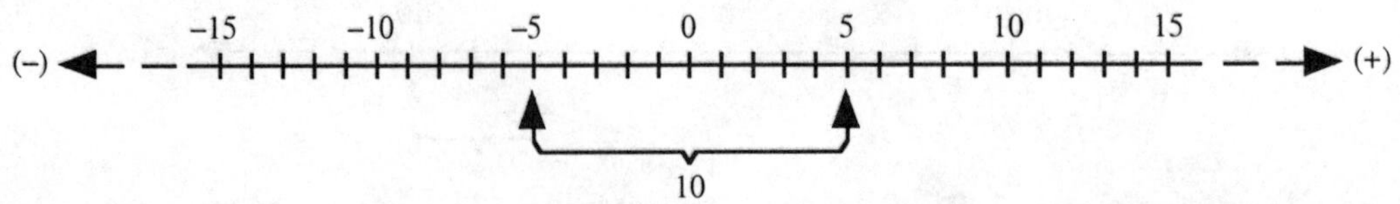

Start at −5. Since you are "eliminating minus points," move the counter in the positive direction.

EXAMPLES:

1. 5 + (−2) = 3
2. 7 + (−7) = 0

3. $4 - (-4) = 4 + 4 = 8$
4. $0 - (-7) = 0 + 7 = 7$
5. $-8 - (-4) = -8 + 4 = -4$

Multiplication

We can also explain the rules for multiplying negative numbers through the concept of absolute value. To multiply a positive number by a negative number, you multiply the absolute values of the two numbers (just as if they were positive), and the product is a negative number.

EXAMPLES:

1. $3 \bullet -6 = -18$
2. $-2 \bullet 4 = -8$

In both examples, the final result is the product of the absolute values of the two numbers, $3 \bullet 6 = 18$ and $2 \bullet 4 = 8$. But both results are negative. A way of remembering this is to think that the minus sign has "tainted" the problem, so the final result must be negative.

To multiply a negative number by a negative number, you multiply the absolute values of the numbers, and the final result is positive.

EXAMPLES:

1. $(-3)(-6) = 18$
2. $(-1)(-4) = 4$

In both examples, the result is the product of the absolute values of the two numbers, $3 \bullet 6 = 18$ and $1 \bullet 4 = 4$. But both results are positive. This is somewhat like saying two wrongs do make a right—a negative times a negative produces a positive.

And if you multiply more than two numbers, the result "toggles" back and forth between positive and negative, like an on/off switch. In multiplication, three negatives produce a negative number, four a positive number, five a negative number, six a positive number, and so on.

EXAMPLES:

1. $-1 \bullet -1 = 1$
2. $-1 \bullet -1 \bullet -1 = -1$
3. $-1 \bullet -1 \bullet -1 \bullet -1 = 1$
4. $-1 \bullet -1 \bullet -1 \bullet -1 \bullet -1 = -1$
5. $-1 \bullet -1 \bullet -1 \bullet -1 \bullet -1 \bullet -1 = 1$

Division

Division is the reverse of multiplication, so the same rules apply. To divide a positive number by a negative number or to divide a negative number by a positive number, divide using absolute values, and the result of the final sign is negative.

EXAMPLES:

1. $6 \div -3 = -2$
2. $-8 \div 2 = -4$

In both examples, we divided using absolute values: 6 ÷ 3 = 2 and 8 ÷ 2 = 4; and in both cases, the sign of the final result is negative.

To divide a negative number by another negative number, divide using absolute values, the final sign is positive.

EXAMPLE:

$-8 \div -4 = 2$

Dividing by using the absolute values of –8 and –2, you get 8 ÷ 4, which is 2, and in this case the "double negative" gives a positive sign to the final result.

These are the rules that govern all operations with signed numbers. But you must be careful how you apply them to more complicated problems. Just take the problem step by step:

EXAMPLE:

$$\frac{(2 \cdot -3) - (-2 + -12)}{(-8 \div 2) \cdot (2 + -4)} = \frac{(-6) - (-14)}{(-4) \cdot (-2)} = \frac{8}{8} = 1$$

Negative Number Principles

Operations with negative numbers depend on how many negative signs appear in a problem. Remember the following principles for ease in simplifying expressions.

- ADDITION OF A NEGATIVE NUMBER IS EQUIVALENT TO SUBTRACTION
- SUBTRACTION OF A NEGATIVE NUMBER IS EQUIVALENT TO ADDITION
- POSITIVE • POSITIVE = POSITIVE
- POSITIVE • NEGATIVE = NEGATIVE
- NEGATIVE • POSITIVE = NEGATIVE
- NEGATIVE • NEGATIVE = POSITIVE
- NEGATIVE • NEGATIVE • NEGATIVE = NEGATIVE
- NEGATIVE • NEGATIVE • NEGATIVE • NEGATIVE = POSITIVE

EXERCISE 5

Negative Numbers

DIRECTIONS: Choose the best answer to each of the following questions. Answers are on page B-123.

Questions 1–15

The following questions use a number line and a counter, as shown below. For each question, select the letter of the correct position for the counter after the indicated operations.

EXAMPLE: 2 + 3 =

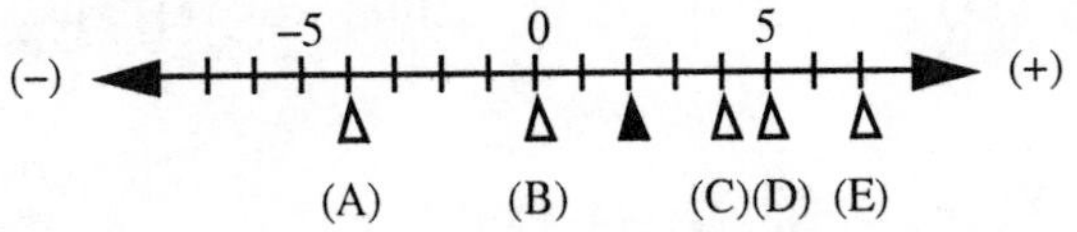

The correct choice is (D). The original position of the counter is 2. If you move it three units in the positive direction, the final result is 5.

1. 3 + 1 =

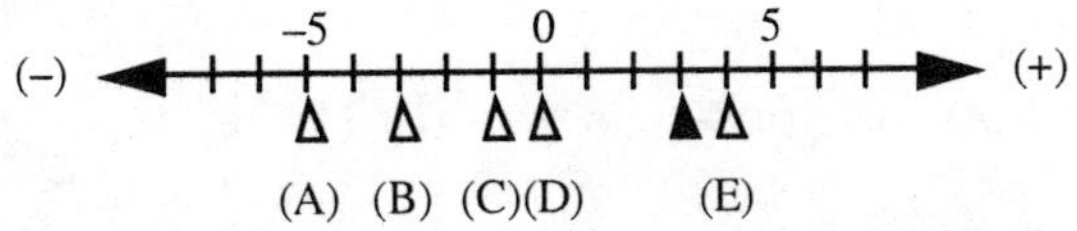

2. 5 – 2 =

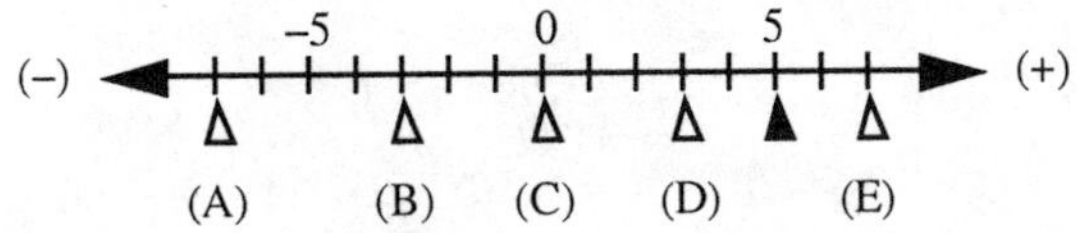

3. 5 + (–2) =

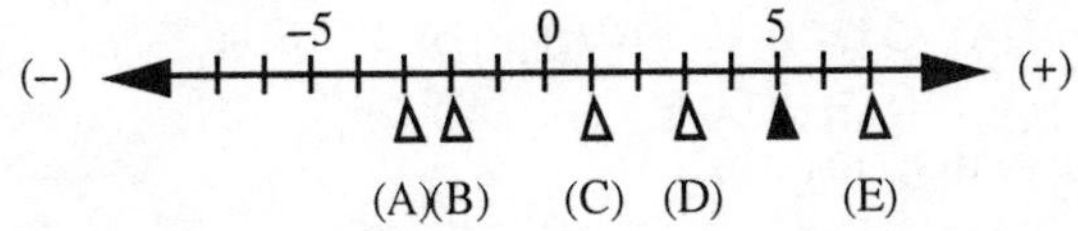

4. 3 + 2 + (–7) =

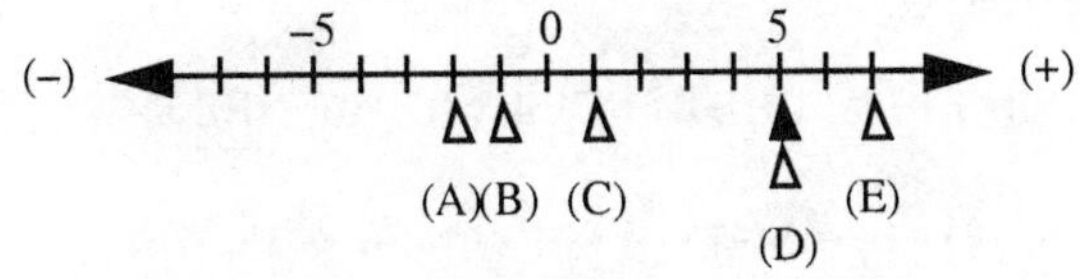

5. 2 + (–4) =

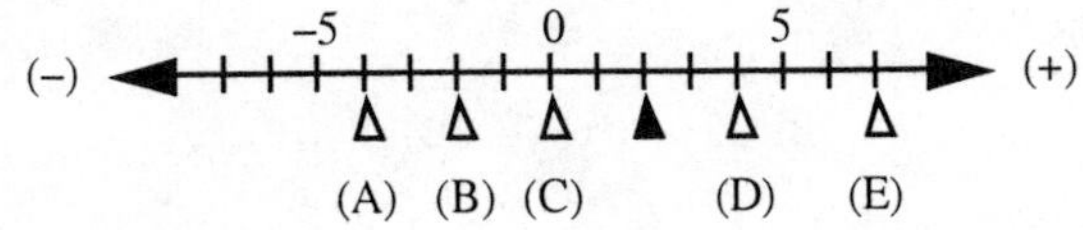

6. –2 + –2 =

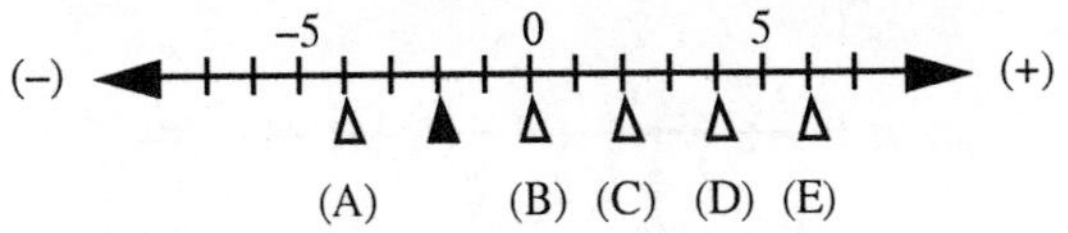

7. 4 + –2 + –2 =

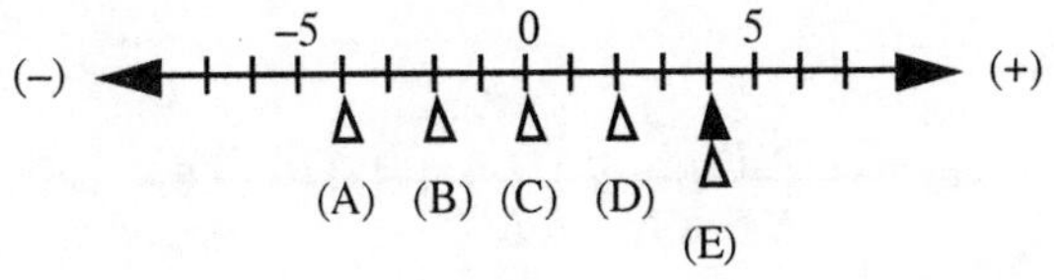

8. –4 + –1 + –1 =

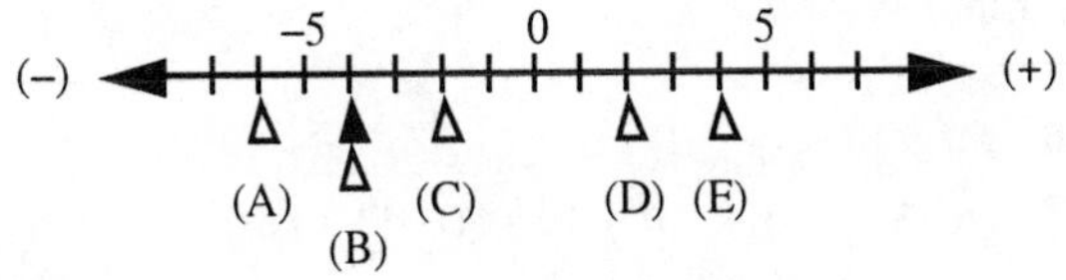

9. –4 + 8 =

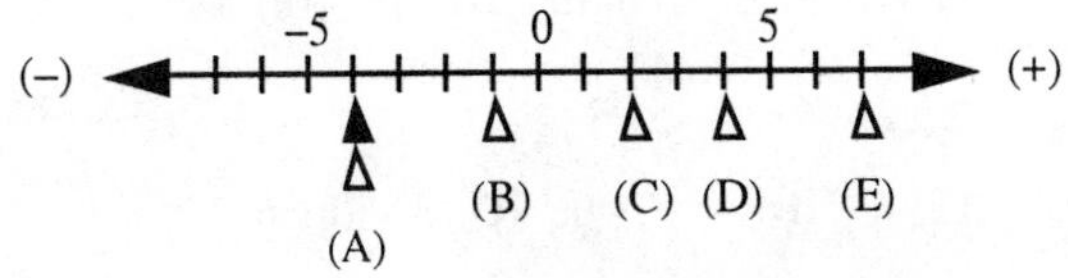

10. –2 + 2 + –1 =

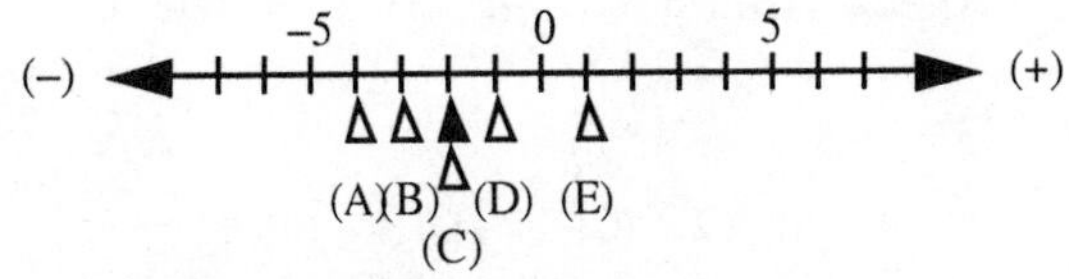

11. 2 – (–1) =

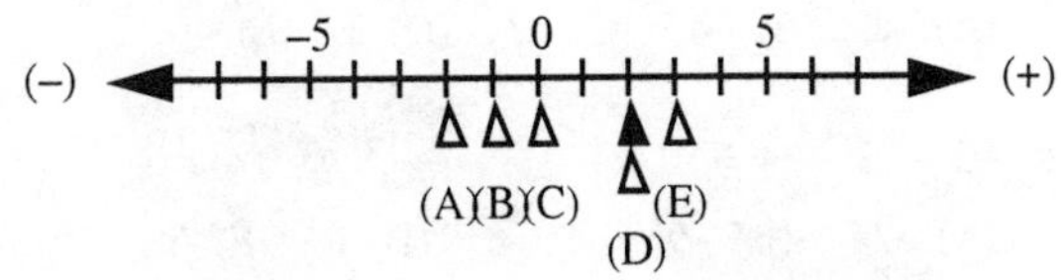

12. 5 – (–2) =

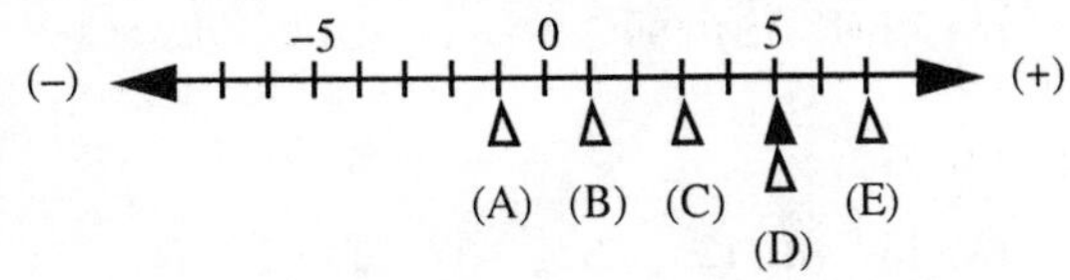

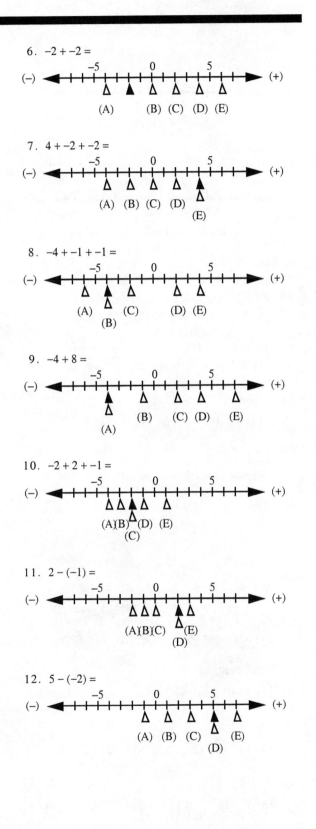

13. 0 − (−4) =

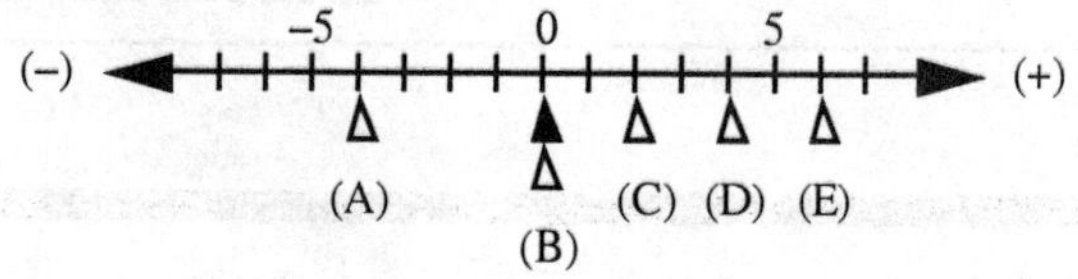

14. −2 − (−1) =

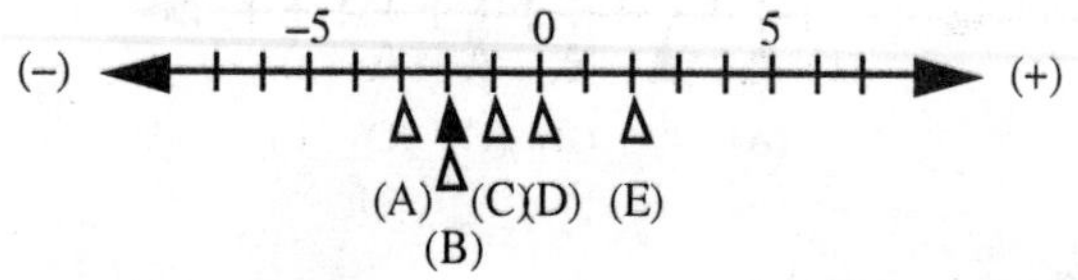

15. −3 − (−1) − (−2) =

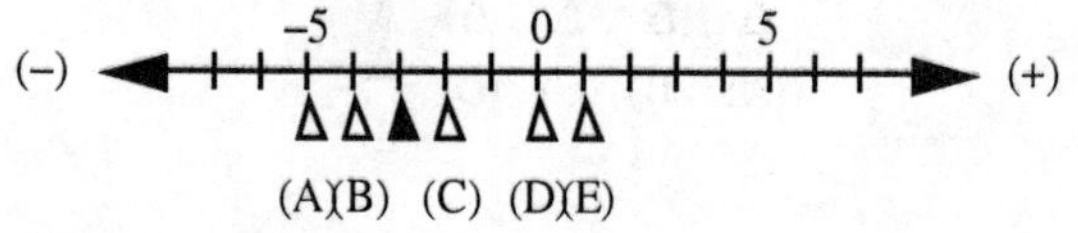

Questions 16–60

16. 5 + 8 + (−2) + (−1) =

(A) 3 (B) 7 (C) 10 (D) 13 (E) 23

17. 12 − 7 + 6 + −1 =

(A) 2 (B) 6 (C) 10 (D) 14 (E) 18

18. 3 + −3 =

(A) −6 (B) −3 (C) 0 (D) 3 (E) 6

19. 0 + −12 =

(A) −12 (B) −6 (C) −1 (D) 0 (E) 12

20. −3 + 1 =

(A) −4 (B) −2 (C) 2 (D) 4 (E) 8

21. −2 + −6 =

(A) −8 (B) −4 (C) −2 (D) 2 (E) 4

22. −2 + −3 + −4 =

(A) −24 (B) −9 (C) −6 (D) 0 (E) 6

23. 100 + (−99) =

(A) −199 (B) −99 (C) −1 (D) 1 (E) 99

24. 14 − (−2) =

(A) 16 (B) 12 (C) 4 (D) −2 (E) −14

25. 2 − (−5) =

(A) 7 (B) 3 (C) −2 (D) −3 (E) −7

26. 0 − (−4) =

(A) −8 (B) −4 (C) 0 (D) 4 (E) −4

27. −2 − (−3) =

(A) −6 (B) −5 (C) −1 (D) 1 (E) 3

28. −5 − (−1) − 1 =

(A) −7 (B) −5 (C) −3 (D) −1 (E) 2

29. (5 − 1) + (1 − 5) =

(A) −5 (B) −3 (C) 0 (D) 3 (E) 5

30. [2 − (−6)] − [−2 + (−1)] =

(A) −2 (B) −1 (C) 1 (D) 5 (E) 11

31. 1 • −2 =

(A) −2 (B) −1 (C) $-\frac{1}{2}$ (D) 1 (E) 2

32. −2 • 1 =

(A) 2 (B) 1 (C) $\frac{1}{2}$ (D) −1 (E) −2

33. −8 • 6 =

(A) −48 (B) −2 (C) 2 (D) 14 (E) 48

34. −2 • −3 =

(A) −6 (B) −5 (C) −1 (D) 6 (E) 12

35. −10 • −10 =

(A) −100 (B) −20 (C) 0 (D) 20 (E) 100

36. −2 • −1 • 1 =

(A) −3 (B) −2 (C) 1 (D) 2 (E) 4

37. −10 • −10 • −10 =

(A) −1,000 (B) −30 (C) −1 (D) 1 (E) 1,000

38. −2 • −2 • −2 • −2 =

(A) −32 (B) −8 (C) 4 (D) 16 (E) 32

39. −1 • −1 • −1 • −1 • −1 • −1 • −1 • −1 • −1 • −1 =

(A) −10 (B) −1 (C) 0 (D) 1 (E) 10

40. 4 ÷ −2 =

(A) −8 (B) −2 (C) $-\frac{1}{2}$ (D) 2 (E) 8

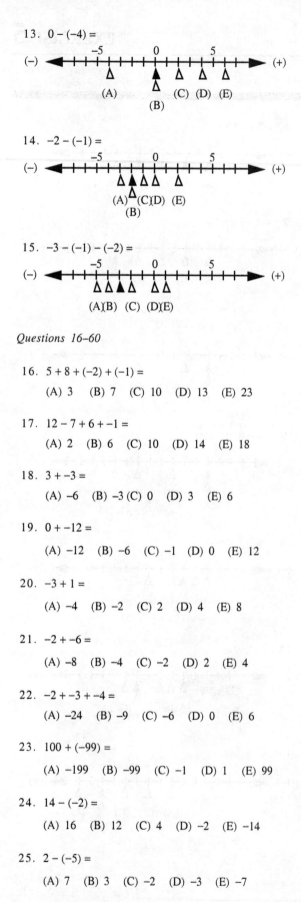

41. $16 \div -1 =$

(A) −16 (B) −1 (C) 1 (D) 8 (E) 16

42. $-12 \div 4 =$

(A) −4 (B) −3 (C) −2 (D) 3 (E) 4

43. $-12 \div -12 =$

(A) −144 (B) −1 (C) 1 (D) 24 (E) 144

44. $(7 - -6) + 3(2 - 4) =$

(A) −2 (B) 0 (C) 7 (D) 12 (E) 23

45. $(2 \bullet -3)(1 \bullet -4)(2 \bullet -1) =$

(A) −48 (B) −16 (C) 2 (D) 28 (E) 56

46. $(6 \bullet -2) \div (3 \bullet -4) =$

(A) −12 (B) −1 (C) 1 (D) 3 (E) 24

47. $(4 - -3 + 7 - -1)(-3 - -2) =$

(A) −25 (B) −15 (C) −7 (D) −1 (E) 8

48. $[(2 \bullet -1) + (4 \div -2)][(-6 + 6) - (2 - 3)] =$

(A) 5 (B) 2 (C) −2 (D) −4 (E) −23

49. $(2 - 3)(3 - 2)(4 - 3)(3 - 4)(5 - 4)(4 - 5) =$

(A) −625 (B) −1 (C) 1 (D) 50 (E) 625

50. $[2(3 - 4)] + [(125 \div -25)(1 \bullet -2)] =$

(A) −12 (B) −8 (C) 2 (D) 8 (E) 125

51. $-\frac{1}{2} \bullet 2 \bullet -\frac{1}{2} \bullet 2 \bullet -\frac{1}{2} \bullet 2 =$

(A) −16 (B) −8 (C) −1 (D) 1 (E) 2

52. $[(2 \bullet 3) \div (-6 \bullet 1)][(21 \div 7) \bullet \frac{1}{3}] =$

(A) −5 (B) −1 (C) 1 (D) 12 (E) 36

53. $(-5 \bullet -2) - (-2 \bullet -5) =$

(A) 0 (B) 2 (C) 10 (D) 12 (E) 18

54. $6 \div -\frac{1}{3} =$

(A) −18 (B) $-\frac{1}{2}$ (C) 2 (D) 3 (E) 18

55. $(-3 - -3) - (-2 - -2) - (-1 - -1) =$

(A) −12 (B) −6 (C) 0 (D) 6 (E) 12

56. If n is any negative number, which of the following must also be negative?

I. $n + n$

II. $n \bullet n$

III. $n - n$

(A) I only (B) II only (C) I and III only
(D) II and III only (E) I, II, and III

57. If n is any negative number, which of the following must also be negative?

I. $n \bullet -n$

II. $-n \bullet -n$

III. $-n + n$

(A) I only (B) II only (C) III only
(D) II and III only (E) I, II, and III

58. If n is any positive number besides zero, which of the following must be negative?

I. $n \bullet -n$

II. $-n + -n$

III. $n - (-n)$

(A) I only (B) II only (C) I and II only
(D) I and III only (E) I, II, and III

59. If n is any positive number, which of the following must be positive?

I. $-n - (-n)$

II. $-n \bullet -n$

III. $n \div (-n \bullet -n)$

(A) I only (B) II only (C) III only
(D) I and III only (E) II and III only

60. Given any number such that $n \neq 0$, which of the following must be equal to 0?

I. $-n \bullet -n \bullet -n \bullet -n \bullet -n \bullet -n$

II. $[(n - n) - n] - [(n - n) - n]$

III. $n \div [(n \div n) \div n]$

(A) I only (B) II only (C) I and II only
(D) I and III only (E) I, II, and III

Mean, Median, and Mode

Averages (or arithmetic mean), medians, and modes are three types of statistics that can be found for a given set of numbers. These statistics give us more information about a particular set of data.

Mean

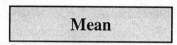

1. *Calculating an Average (or Mean)*

To calculate an ***average***, just add the quantities to be averaged and then divide that sum by the number of quantities involved. For example, the average of 3, 7, and 8 is 6: 3 + 7 + 8 = 18, and 18 ÷ 3 = 6.

EXAMPLE:

A student's final grade is the average of her scores on five exams. If she receives scores of 78, 83, 82, 88, and 94, what is her final grade?

To find the average, add the five grades and divide that sum by 5.

$$\frac{78 + 83 + 82 + 88 + 94}{5} = \frac{425}{5} = 85$$

An average is also called an arithmetic mean, and exam questions that ask for averages may include the phrase *arithmetic mean* in parentheses following the word *average.*

EXAMPLE:

A student's final grade is the average (arithmetic mean) of her scores on five exams. If she receives scores of 78, 83, 82, 88, and 94, what is her final grade?

For the purposes of this review, we will omit the phrase *arithmetic mean*, and on the exam you can just ignore the extra terminology.

It's possible that an easy question might ask that you find the average of a few numbers, as above; but questions about averages can take several other forms. The generalized formula for the arithmetic mean, or average, is:

$$\text{Arithmetic Mean} = \text{Average} = \bar{x} = \frac{x_1 + x_2 + x_3 + \cdots + x_n}{n}$$

2. *Missing Elements of an Average*

Some questions provide the average of a group of numbers and some—but not all—of the quantities involved. You are then asked to find the missing quantity or quantities. For example, if the average of 3, 8, and a third number is 6, what is the value of the third number? Since the average of the three numbers is 6, the sum or total of the three numbers is 3 • 6 = 18. The two numbers we know total 3 + 8 = 11. So the third number must be 7. You can check this solution by averaging 3, 8, and 7: 3 + 8 + 7 = 18, and 18 ÷ 3 = 6.

EXAMPLES:

1. For a certain five-day period, the average high temperature (in degrees Fahrenheit) for Chicago was 30°. If the high temperatures recorded for the first four of those days were 26°, 32°, 24°, and 35°, what was the high temperature recorded on the fifth day?

   The sum of the five numbers is 5 • 30 = 150. The sum for the four days we know about is only 26 + 32 + 24 + 35 = 117. So the fifth day must have had a high temperature of 150 – 117 = 33.

2. The average of Jose's scores on four tests is 90. If three of those scores are 89, 92, and 94, what is his fourth score?

   The sum of all four scores must be 4 • 90 = 360. The three scores that are known total 89 + 92 + 94 = 275. So the remaining score must be 360 – 275 = 85.

A variation on this type of question might ask about more than one missing element.

EXAMPLES:

1. In a group of children, three of the children are ages 7, 8 and 10, and the other two are the same age. If the average of the ages of all five children is 7, what is the age of the other two children?

   We know that the total of the five ages must be 5 • 7 = 35. The known ages total only 7 + 8 + 10 = 25. So the ages of the two other children must total 10. Since there are two of them, each one must be 5 years old.

2. The average of a group of eight numbers is 9. If one of these numbers is removed from the group, the average of the remaining numbers is 7. What is the value of the number removed?

   The sum of the original numbers is 8 • 9 = 72. The sum of the remaining numbers is 7 • 7 = 49. So the value of the number that was removed must be 72 – 49 = 23.

3. *Weighted Averages*

In the average problems discussed thus far, each element in the average has been given equal weight. Sometimes, averages are created that give greater weight to one element than to another.

EXAMPLE:

Cody bought four books that cost $6.00 each and two books that cost $3.00 each. What is the average cost of the six books?

The average cost of the six books is *not* just the average of $6.00 and $3.00, which is $4.50. He bought more of the higher priced books, so our average must take into account that fact. One way of doing the arithmetic is to treat each book as a separate expense:

$$\frac{6+6+6+6+3+3}{6}=\frac{30}{6}=5$$

Another way of arriving at the same result is to "weight" the two different costs: 4(6) + 2(3) = 30.

Median

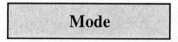

The ***median*** of an odd number of data is the mid-value of the data. The median of an even number of data is the arithmetic mean of the two middle values of the data, when arranged in ascending or descending order.

EXAMPLES:

1. The median of {1, 1, 2, 3, 4, 5, 6, 7, 7, 7, 8, 8, 9} is 6.
2. The median of {7, 9, 10, 16} is 9.5.

Mode

The ***mode*** is the value that appears most frequently in a set of data. Some sets of data have multiple modes. Some sets of data have no modes.

EXAMPLES:

1. The mode of {2, 4, 5, 5, 5, 6, 6, 19.2} is 5.
2. The group of numbers {–3, 5, 6, –3, –2, 7, 5, –3, 6, 5, 5, –3} is bimodal since –3 and 5 each occur four times.

EXERCISE 6

Mean, Median, and Mode

DIRECTIONS: Choose the best answer to each of the following questions. Answers are on page B-123.

1. What is the average of 8, 6, and 16?
(A) 10 (B) 12 (C) 13 (D) 15 (E) 18

2. What is the average of 0 and 50?
(A) 0 (B) 5 (C) 10 (D) 25 (E) 50

3. What is the average of 5, 11, 12 and 8?
(A) 6 (B) 8 (C) 9 (D) 10 (E) 12

4. What is the average of 25, 28, 21, 30, and 36?
(A) 25 (B) 28 (C) 29 (D) 34 (E) 44

5. What is the average $\frac{1}{4}$, $\frac{3}{4}$, $\frac{5}{8}$, $\frac{1}{2}$, and $\frac{3}{8}$?
(A) $\frac{3}{32}$ (B) $\frac{5}{16}$ (C) $\frac{1}{2}$ (D) $\frac{5}{8}$ (E) $\frac{27}{32}$

6. What is the average of $0.78, $0.45, $0.36, $0.98, $0.55, and $0.54?
(A) $0.49 (B) $0.54 (C) $0.56
(D) $0.60 (E) $0.61

7. What is the average of 0.03, 0.11, 0.08, and 0.5?
(A) 0.18 (B) 0.25 (C) 0.28
(D) 0.50 (E) 1.0

8. What is the average of 1,001, 1,002, 1,003, 1,004, and 1,005?
(A) 250 (B) 1,000 (C) 1,003
(D) 2,500 (E) 5,000

9. What is the average of –8, –6, and –13?
(A) –18 (B) –15 (C) –13 (D) –12 (E) –9

10. Jordan receives test scores of 79, 85, 90, 76, and 80. What is the average of these test scores?
(A) 82 (B) 83 (C) 84 (D) 85 (E) 86

11. Mr. Whipple bought five different items costing $4.51, $6.25, $3.32, $4.48, and $2.19. What is the average cost of the five items?
(A) $3.40 (B) $3.80 (C) $3.90
(D) $4.00 (E) $4.15

12. Nadia received scores of 8.5, 9.3, 8.2, and 9.0 in four different gymnastics events. What is the average of her scores?
(A) 8.5 (B) 8.75 (C) 8.9 (D) 9 (E) 9.1

13. Five people have ages of 44, 33, 45, 44, and 29 years. What is the average of their ages in years?
(A) 36 (B) 39 (C) 40 (D) 41 (E) 43

14. In a certain government office, if 360 staff hours are needed to process 120 building permit applications, on the average how long (expressed in hours) does it take to process one application?
(A) 3 (B) 6 (C) 12 (D) 24 (E) 36

15. In a chemical test for Substance X, a sample is divided into five equal parts. If the purity of the five parts is 84 percent, 89 percent, 87 percent, 90 percent, and 80 percent, then what is the overall purity of the sample (expressed as a percent of substance X)?
(A) 83 (B) 84 (C) 86 (D) 87 (E) 88

16. The average of three numbers is 24. If two of the numbers are 21 and 23, what is the third number?
(A) 20 (B) 24 (C) 26 (D) 28 (E) 30

17. The average of three numbers is 5. If two of the numbers are zero, what is the third number?
(A) 1 (B) 3 (C) 5 (D) 10 (E) 15

18. The average of the weight of four people is 166 pounds. If three of the people weigh 150 pounds, 200 pounds, and 180 pounds, what is the weight of the fourth person?
(A) 134 (B) 140 (C) 155 (D) 161 (E) 165

19. For a certain student, the average of five test scores is 83. If four of the scores are 81, 79, 85, and 90, what is the fifth test score?
(A) 83 (B) 82 (C) 81 (D) 80 (E) 79

20. Sue bought ten items at an average price of $3.60. The cost of eight of the items totaled $30. If the other two items were the same price, what was the price she paid for each?
(A) $15.00 (B) $7.50 (C) $6.00
(D) $3.00 (E) $1.50

21. In a certain shipment, weights of 12 books average 2.75 pounds. If one of the books is removed, the weights of the remaining books average 2.70 pounds. What was the weight, in pounds, of the book that was removed?
(A) 1.7 (B) 2.3 (C) 3.0 (D) 3.3 (E) 4.5

22. The average of a group of seven test scores is 80. If the lowest and the highest scores are thrown out, the average of the remaining scores is 78. What is the average of the lowest and highest scores?
(A) 100 (B) 95 (C) 90 (D) 88 (E) 85

23. In a certain group, 12 of the children are age 10, and eight are age 15. What is the average of the ages of all the children in the group?

(A) 9.5 (B) 10.5 (C) 11 (D) 11.5 (E) 12

24. Robert made the following deposits in a savings account:

Amount	Frequency
$15	4 times
$20	2 times
$25	4 times

What was the average of all the deposits Robert made?

(A) $18.50 (B) $20.00 (C) $21.50
(D) $22.00 (E) $22.50

25. The average of the weights of six people sitting in a boat is 145 pounds. After a seventh person gets into the boat, the average of the weights of all seven people in the boat is 147 pounds. What is the weight (in pounds) of the seventh person?

(A) 160 (B) 159 (C) 155 (D) 149 (E) 147

26. Find the mean of the following five numbers: 2, 3, 13, 15, and 1.

(A) 4.6 (B) 6.2 (C) 6.8 (D) 8.6 (E) 16.8

27. Find the mean for the following six numbers: –3, 2, 6, 5, 2, and 0.

(A) 1 (B) 2 (C) 5 (D) 6 (E) 8

28. If the mean for six numbers is 10, what is the sixth number if the five given numbers are –3, 5, 6, 13, and 17?

(A) 12 (B) 16 (C) 18 (D) 20 (E) 22

29. The arithmetic mean of 5 numbers is 56. If two new numbers are added to the list, the average of the 7 numbers is 58. The average of the two new numbers is:

(A) 64 (B) 63 (C) 62 (D) 61 (E) 60

30. Arranged in some order, $3x + 1$, $2x + 4$, and $x + 10$ represent 3 consecutive whole numbers. If x represents a whole number and the arithmetic mean of the 3 numbers is 13, then solve for x.

(A) 2 (B) 4 (C) 6 (D) 8 (E) 10

31. On Monday, Sylvia drove from San Diego to Los Angeles at an average rate of 36 mph. On Wednesday, Sylvia drove the same route at an average of 44 mph. What was her average rate in mph for the 2 trips?

(A) 9 (B) 24 (C) 36 (C) 40 (D) 40.5 (E) 42

32. Julie interviewed 100 female corporate officers and found that 34 of them were 55 years old, 28 were 45 years old, 26 were 35 years old, and 12 of them were 25 years old. What was the arithmetic mean of the women's ages?

(A) 16 (B) 43 (C) 43.4 (D) 44.3 (E) 45

Questions 33-35 refer to the following:

During the last 14 games, a basketball player scored the following points per game: 42, 35, 29, 42, 33, 37, 26, 38, 42, 47, 51, 33, 30, and 40.

33. What is the median score?

(A) 35.4 (B) 35.7 (C) 36 (D) 37.5 (E) 38

34. What is the mode?

(A) 35.4 (B) 37.5 (C) 38 (D) 42 (E) 44

35. If after one more game, the player's arithmetic mean for points per game is exactly 37, how many points did the player score in the fifteenth game?

(A) 30 (B) 37 (C) 37.5 (D) 42 (E) 44

36. Find the median of the following five numbers: 1, 3, 7, 2, and 8.

(A) 1 (B) 2 (C) 3 (D) 4.2 (E) 7

37. Find the median for the following set of numbers: 2, –3, 8, 4, 9, –16, 12, 0, 4, 2, and 1.

(A) 4 (B) 2.1 (C) 2 (D) 1 (E) 0

38. Find the median for the following set of numbers: 2, –3, 8, 4, 9, –16, 12, 8, 4, and 2.

(A) 2 (B) 3 (C) 3.5 (D) 4 (E) 4.2

39. A set of six numbers contains the numbers: 1, 10, 11, 12, $p = x - 3$, and $q = 2x$. If the median of these six numbers is exactly 10 and $p < x < q$, find the sum of $p + q$.

(A) 2 (B) 7 (C) 9 (D) 11 (E) 12

40. Find the mode of the following five numbers: 4, 8, 10, 8, and 15.

(A) 4 (B) 8 (C) 9 (D) 10 (E) 15

41. Find the mode for the following set of numbers: 6, 8, 10, 2, –2, 2, 8, 4, and 2.

(A) 6 (B) 4.4 (C) 4 (D) 2 (E) 1

42. A set of seven numbers contains the numbers: 1, 4, 5, and 6. The other three numbers are represented by $2x + 8$, $x - 4$, and $7x - 4$. If the mode of these seven numbers is a negative even integer, then how many possible values exist for x?

(A) $\frac{1}{2}$ (B) 1 (C) 2 (D) 4 (E) 4.5

43. The grades received on a test by twenty students were 100, 55, 75, 80, 65, 65, 95, 90, 80, 45, 40, 50, 85, 85, 85, 80, 80, 70, 65, and 60. The average of these grades is

(A) 70 (B) 72 (C) 77 (D) 80 (E) 100

44. Arthur purchased 75 six-inch rulers costing 15¢ each, 100 one-foot rulers costing 30¢ each, and 50 one-yard rulers costing 72¢ each. What was the average price per ruler?

(A) $26\frac{1}{8}$¢ (B) $34\frac{1}{3}$¢ (C) 39¢ (D) 42¢ (E) $77\frac{1}{4}$¢

45. What is the average grade for a student who received 90 in English, 84 in Algebra, 75 in French, and 76 in Music, if the subjects have the following weights: English 4, Algebra 3, French 3, and Music 1?

(A) 81 (B) $81\frac{1}{2}$ (C) 82 (D) $82\frac{1}{2}$ (E) 83

Questions 46-48 refer to the following information.

A census shows that on a certain block the number of children in each family is 3, 4, 4, 0, 1, 2, 0, 2, and 2, respectively.

46. Find the average number of children per family.

(A) 4 (B) 3 (C) $3\frac{1}{2}$ (D) 2 (E) $1\frac{1}{2}$

47. Find the median number of children.

(A) 1 (B) 2 (C) 3 (D) 4 (E) 5

48. Find the mode of the number of children.

(A) 0 (B) 1 (C) 2 (D) 3 (E) 4

Ratios and Proportions

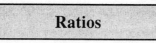

Ratios

1. *What Is A Ratio?*

A ***ratio*** is a statement about the relationship between any two quantities, or we might say a ratio is a statement that *compares* any two quantities. Suppose that in an English class there are five girls and eight boys. We can compare those quantities by saying that the ratio of girls to boys is 5 to 8. Conversely, the ratio of boys to girls is 8 to 5.

Notice that in stating a ratio, order is very important. The order of the numbers in the ratio must reflect the order of the categories you are comparing. Thus, it would be incorrect to say of the above example that the ratio of girls to boys is 8 to 5.

A phrase such as "5 to 8" is one way of stating a ratio, but there are several other ways. A ratio can also be described using a colon: "The ratio of girls to boys is 5:8;" "The ratio of boys to girls is 8:5." Or, we can write the ratio in fraction form:

The ratio $\frac{\text{girls}}{\text{boys}}$ is $\frac{5}{8}$.

The ratio $\frac{\text{boys}}{\text{girls}}$ is $\frac{8}{5}$.

It is also possible to speak of ratios as though they refer to pure numbers instead of a number of objects. Thus, we can speak abstractly of the ratio 5:8, which is the ratio of any set of five things to any set of eight things, e.g., "The ratio of five girls to eight boys is 5:8;" "The ratio of five donuts to eight donuts is 5:8;" and "The ratio of five dogs to eight cats is 5:8."

Since ratios can be treated just as numbers having the form *a*:*b* or *a*/*b*, a ratio can be manipulated in the same way a fraction is manipulated. Just as you would rewrite a fraction to get a form with a different denominator, you can convert a ratio to an equivalent form by multiplying both terms of the ratio by the same number.

$$\frac{5}{8}=\frac{5 \cdot 2}{8 \cdot 2}=\frac{10}{16}$$

$$\frac{8}{5}=\frac{8 \cdot 3}{5 \cdot 3}=\frac{24}{15}$$

It is customary to reduce a ratio to its lowest terms just as you reduce fractions to lowest terms. For example, in a certain classroom there are ten girls and sixteen boys; the ratio of girls to boys is 10/16, which is 5/8.

Although you may not be aware of it, you probably also use ratios in an informal way in ordinary conversation. A common phrase that signifies a ratio is "for every (number)...there are (number)..." For example, in the classroom just described, for every 10 girls there are 16 boys, or in lowest terms, for every 5 girls there are 8 boys. And for every 8 boys there are 5 girls.

Finally, a ratio can also be stated as a rate using the word *per.* If a car travels 200 miles and uses 10 gallons of fuel, the car gets 200 miles per 10 gallons, or 20 miles *per* gallon. Cost, too, is often described as a ratio. If it is possible to purchase a dozen greeting cards for $2.40, the cost of the cards is $2.40 per dozen, or 20 cents *per* card.

2. *Three-Part Ratios*

When a comparison is to be made of three quantities, it can be stated using ordinary ratios. For example, if a bowl of fruit contains two apples, three pears, and five oranges, the ratio of apples to pears is 2:3; the ratio of apples to oranges is 2:5; and the ratio of pears to oranges is 3:5. This same information can be conveyed in a single statement. The ratio of apples to pears to oranges is 2:3:5.

A ***three-part ratio*** depends on the middle term to join the two outside terms. Above, the ratio of apples to pears is 2:3, and the ratio of pears to oranges is 3:5. Since 3 is common to both ratios, it can be the middle term. Sometimes it will be necessary to find a common middle term.

EXAMPLE:

On a certain day, a bank has the following rates of exchange: $\frac{\text{dollar}}{\text{mark}}=\frac{1}{3}$, $\frac{\text{mark}}{\text{pound}}=\frac{6}{1}$. What is the ratio of dollars to pounds?

To find the ratio dollars:pounds, we will use *marks* as the middle term. But the ratio of dollars to marks is 1:3, and the ratio of marks to pounds is 6:1. We must change the first ratio so that it is expressed in terms of six marks rather than three marks. This is like finding a common denominator before adding fractions:

$$\frac{1}{3}=\frac{1 \cdot 2}{3 \cdot 2}=\frac{2}{6}$$

So the ratio of dollars to marks is 2:6, and the ratio of dollars to marks to pounds is 2:6:1. Thus the ratio of dollars to pounds is 2:1.

3. *Dividing A Quantity By A Ratio*

A problem may require that you divide a quantity according to a certain ratio.

EXAMPLES:

1. A $100 prize is to be divided between two contestants according to the ratio 2:3. How much should each contestant receive?

   To solve the problem, add the terms of the ratio to determine how many parts the prize is to be divided into. Divide the prize by that many parts, and multiply the result by the number of parts to be given to each contestant. 2 + 3 = 5, so the prize is to be divided into five parts. Each part is $100 ÷ 5 = $20. One contestant gets 2 • $20 = $40, and the other contestant receives 3 • $20 = $60.

2. Bronze is 16 parts tin and 9 parts copper. If a bronze ingot weighs 100 pounds, what weight (in pounds) is the tin?

   First, the number of parts in the ratio is 16 + 9 = 25. Second, 100 ÷ 25 = 4. So each part is worth 4 pounds. And since there are 16 parts of tin, the tin must weigh 16 • 4 = 64 pounds.

Proportions

1. *What Is A Proportion?*

A ***proportion*** is the mathematical equivalent of a verbal analogy. For example, 2:3::8:12 is read, "two is to three as eight is to twelve." The main difference between a verbal analogy and a mathematical proportion is the precision. Whereas a verbal analogy depends upon words that don't have single unique and precise meanings, mathematical proportions are made up of numbers, which are very exact.

In a mathematical proportion, the first and last terms are called the *extremes* of the *proportion* because they are on the extreme outside, and the two middle terms are called the *means* (*mean* can mean "middle"). In a mathematical proportion, the product of the extremes is always equal to the product of the means:

2:3::8:12
2 • 12 = 3 • 8

Since any ratio can be written as a fraction, a proportion, which states that two ratios are equivalent, can also be written in fractional forms as an equation:

$$\frac{2}{3}=\frac{8}{12} \Rightarrow \frac{2}{3} \times \frac{8}{12} \Rightarrow 2 \cdot 12 = 3 \cdot 8$$

This is the foundation for the process called cross-multiplication, a process useful in solving for an unknown element in a proportion.

EXAMPLES:

1. $\frac{6}{9}=\frac{12}{x} \Rightarrow \frac{6}{9} >\!=\!< \frac{12}{x} \Rightarrow 6x = 108 \Rightarrow x = 18$

   After cross-multiplying, divide both sides of the equality by the number next to the unknown (the numerical coefficient). Then, check the correctness of this solution by substituting 18 back into the original proportion.

   $\frac{6}{9}=\frac{12}{18} \Rightarrow \frac{6}{9} >\!=\!< \frac{12}{18} \Rightarrow 6 \cdot 18 = 9 \cdot 12$

2. $\frac{3}{15}=\frac{x}{45} \Rightarrow \frac{3}{15} >\!=\!< \frac{x}{45} \Rightarrow 3(45) = 15x \Rightarrow x = \frac{3(45)}{15} = 9$

   And you can check this solution by substitution:

   $\frac{3}{15}=\frac{9}{45} \Rightarrow \frac{3}{15} >\!=\!< \frac{9}{45} \Rightarrow 3(45) = 15(9) \Rightarrow 135 = 135$

2. *Problem-Solving With Proportions*

A proportion can be a very powerful problem-solving tool.

EXAMPLE:

If the cost of a dozen donuts is \$3.60, what is the cost of 4 donuts? Assume there is no discount for buying in quantity.

Most people would probably solve this problem by calculating the cost of one donut (\$3.60 ÷ 12 = \$0.30) and then multiplying that cost by four (\$0.30 • 4 = \$1.20). This procedure is mathematically correct, but the same result can be reached in a way that is conceptually simpler.

The more donuts you buy, the greater the total cost, and vice versa. Since the cost of one donut is the same as the cost of any other donut, we say that the total cost increases in *direct proportion* to the number of donuts purchased. This can be described by a mathematical proportion: $\frac{\text{Total Cost } X}{\text{Total Cost } Y}=\frac{\text{Number } X}{\text{Number } Y} \Rightarrow \$3.60(4) = 12x \Rightarrow \$14.40 = 12x \Rightarrow x = \$1.20$.

In this question we set up the proportion by grouping like terms; that is, "cost" is on one side of the proportion and "number" is on the other side. It would be equally correct to set up this proportion: $\frac{\text{Total Cost } X}{\text{Number } X}=\frac{\text{Total Cost } Y}{\text{Number } Y}$. Nor does it make any difference whether "number" goes on the top or bottom. The following is also correct: $\frac{\text{Number } X}{\text{Total Cost } X}=\frac{\text{Number } Y}{\text{Total Cost } Y}$

Although this other form is mathematically correct, it's a good idea to group like terms to avoid confusion. Also, you can simplify the calculation at any stage you choose. Thus, in the example just discussed, you could reduce the right-hand side before cross-multiplying: $\frac{\$3.60}{x}=\frac{12}{4} \Rightarrow \frac{\$3.60}{x}=\frac{3}{1} \Rightarrow \$3.60 = 3x \Rightarrow x = \$1.20$.

But since different people will use different techniques for simplifying, we can't indicate every instance where simplification might be used. Instead, we will explain the problems without simplifying. Here are some other types of problems that can be solved using proportions:

- ***The LONGER the travel time, the GREATER the distance traveled (assuming a CONSTANT speed).***

EXAMPLE:

If a plane moving at constant speed flies 300 miles in 6 hours, how far will the plane fly in 8 hours?

Set up a proportion grouping like terms: $\frac{\text{Time } X}{\text{Time } Y}=\frac{\text{Distance } X}{\text{Distance } Y} \Rightarrow \frac{6}{8}=\frac{300}{x} \Rightarrow 6x = 300(8) \Rightarrow x = \frac{300(8)}{6} \Rightarrow x = 400$.

• ***The LONGER the time of operation, the GREATER the output.***

EXAMPLE:

If a stamping machine operating at a constant rate without interruption can post-mark 320 envelopes in 5 minutes, how long will it take the machine to postmark 480 envelopes?

Set up a proportion grouping like terms: $\frac{\text{Time } X}{\text{Time } Y} = \frac{\text{Output } X}{\text{Output } Y} \Rightarrow \frac{5}{x} = \frac{320}{480} \Rightarrow \quad \frac{5}{x} >=< \frac{320}{480} \Rightarrow 320x = 5(480) \Rightarrow x = \frac{5(480)}{320} = 7.5$ minutes.

• ***The GREATER the number of items, the GREATER the weight.***

EXAMPLE:

If 20 jars of preserves weigh 25 pounds, how much do 15 jars of preserves weigh?

Group like terms: $\frac{\text{Weight } X}{\text{Weight } Y} = \frac{\text{Jars } X}{\text{Jars } Y} \Rightarrow \frac{25}{x} = \frac{20}{15} \Rightarrow \quad \frac{25}{x} >=< \frac{20}{15} \Rightarrow 15(25) = 20x \Rightarrow x = \frac{15(25)}{20} = 18.75$ pounds.

3. *Indirect Proportions*

In the situations just discussed, quantities were related in direct proportion. The more of one, the more of the other—and vice versa. In some situations, quantities are related indirectly; that is, an increase in one results in a decrease in the other. For example, the more workers or machines doing a job, the less time it takes to finish. In this case, quantities are related indirectly or inversely to each other.

To solve problems involving indirect relationships, you must use an indirect or inverse proportion. The procedure is:

1. Set up an ordinary proportion—make sure that you group like quantities.

2. Invert the right side of the proportion.

3. Cross-multiply and solve for the unknown.

EXAMPLE:

Traveling at constant rate of 150 miles per hour, a plane makes the trip from Phoenix to Grand Junction in 4 hours. How long will the trip take if the plane flies at a constant rate of 200 miles per hour? First, set up a proportion grouping like terms:

$\frac{\text{Speed } X}{\text{Speed } Y} = \frac{\text{Time } X}{\text{Time } Y} \Rightarrow \frac{150}{200} = \frac{4}{x}$

Now invert the right side:

$\frac{150}{200} = \frac{x}{4} \Rightarrow \quad \frac{150}{200} >=< \frac{x}{4} \quad \Rightarrow 150(4) = 200x \Rightarrow x = \frac{150(4)}{200} = 3$ hours

Above, we stated that it is possible to set up a direct proportion without grouping like terms—though we advised against it. With an indirect proportion, it is absolutely essential that you group like terms. And this is one reason we recommend always grouping like terms: so you won't make a mistake if the problem involves an indirect proportion.

EXERCISE 7

Ratio and Proportions

DIRECTIONS: Choose the best answer to each of the following questions. Answers are on page 124.

1. If a jar contains three blue marbles and eight red marbles, what is the ratio blue marbles:red marbles?

(A) 3:11 (B) 3:8 (C) 8:3 (D) 11:3 (E) 4:1

2. If a school has 24 teachers and 480 students, what is the ratio of teachers to students?

(A) $\frac{1}{20}$ (B) $\frac{1}{24}$ (C) $\frac{1}{48}$ (D) $\frac{1}{56}$ (E) $\frac{1}{200}$

3. If a library contains 12,000 works of fiction and 3,000 works of nonfiction, what is the ratio of works of fiction to works of nonfiction?

(A) $\frac{1}{9}$ (B) $\frac{1}{5}$ (C) $\frac{1}{4}$ (D) $\frac{4}{1}$ (E) $\frac{5}{1}$

4. Which of the following is equivalent to $\frac{1}{3}$?

I. $\frac{40}{120}$
II. $\frac{75}{100}$
III. $\frac{120}{360}$

(A) I only (B) III only (C) I and III only
(D) II and III only (E) I, II, and III

Questions 5 and 6

Students at Tyler Junior High School	7th Grade	8th Grade
Girls	90	80
Boys	85	75

5. What is the ratio of seventh–grade girls to the total number of girls at Tyler Junior High School?

(A) $\frac{9}{17}$ (B) $\frac{8}{9}$ (C) $\frac{18}{17}$ (D) $\frac{9}{8}$ (E) $\frac{17}{9}$

6. What is the ratio of eighth–grade girls to the total number of students at Tyler Junior High School?

(A) $\frac{8}{33}$ (B) $\frac{9}{33}$ (C) $\frac{8}{15}$ (D) $\frac{8}{17}$ (E) $\frac{17}{30}$

7. If an airplane flies 275 miles on 25 gallons of fuel, then what is the average fuel consumption for the entire trip expressed in miles per gallon?

(A) 25 (B) 18 (C) 15 (D) 11 (E) 7

8. If an assortment of candy contains 12 chocolates, 6 caramels, and 9 mints, what is the ratio of chocolates:caramels:mints?

(A) 4:3:2 (B) 4:2:3 (C) 3:4:2
(D) 3:2:4 (E) 2:4:3

9. If Lucy twice as much money as Ricky, who has three times as much money as Ethel, then what is the ratio of the amount of money Ethel has to the amount of money Lucy has?

(A) $\frac{1}{8}$ (B) $\frac{1}{6}$ (C) $\frac{1}{4}$ (D) $\frac{1}{2}$ (E) $\frac{2}{1}$

10. If three farkels buy two kirns, and three kirns buy five pucks, then nine farkels buy how many pucks?

(A) 2 (B) 5 (C) 8 (D) 10 (E) 17

11. If machine x operates at twice the rate of machine y, and machine y operates at $\frac{2}{3}$ the rate of machine z, then what is the ratio of the rate of operation of machine x to the rate of operation of machine z?

(A) $\frac{4}{1}$ (B) $\frac{3}{1}$ (C) $\frac{4}{3}$ (D) $\frac{3}{4}$ (E) $\frac{1}{3}$

12. If 48 marbles are to be divided between Bill and Carl in the ratio of 3:5, how many marbles should Bill get?

(A) 6 (B) 8 (C) 18 (D) 24 (E) 30

13. If the sum of $10 is to be divided between Janeway and Nelix so that Nelix receives only $\frac{1}{4}$ of what Janeway receives, then how much should Janeway receive?

(A) $10.00 (B) $8.00 (C) $7.50
(D) $6.00 (E) $2.00

14. If a $1,000 reward is to be divided among three people in the ratio of 2:3:5, what is the largest amount that will be given to any one of the three recipients?

(A) $200 (B) $300 (C) $500
(D) $750 (E) $900

15. If $\frac{6}{8}=\frac{x}{4}$ then $x =$

(A) 12 (B) 6 (C) 4 (D) 3 (E) 2

16. If $\frac{14}{x}=\frac{2}{7}$ then $x =$

(A) 7 (B) 14 (C) 28 (D) 49 (E) 343

17. If $\frac{3}{4}=\frac{4}{x}$ then $x =$

(A) $\frac{3}{16}$ (B) $\frac{3}{4}$ (C) $\frac{4}{3}$ (D) $\frac{7}{3}$ (E) $\frac{16}{3}$

18. If 240 widgets cost \$36, what is the cost of 180 widgets?

(A) \$8 (B) \$16 (C) \$24 (D) \$27 (E) \$32

19. If a kilogram of a certain cheese costs \$9.60, what is the cost of 450 grams of the cheese? (1 kilogram = 1,000 grams)

(A) \$2.78 (B) \$3.14 (C) \$3.88
(D) \$4.32 (E) \$5.12

20. If 50 feet of electrical wire cost \$4.80, then \$10.80 will buy how many feet of the wire?

(A) 60 (B) 62.5 (C) 67.25 (D) 75 (E) 112.5

21. In a certain group of people, 100 people have red hair. If only 25 percent of the people have red hair, then how many people do not have red hair?

(A) 75 (B) 125 (C) 300 (D) 400 (E) 500

22. If a certain fundraising project has raised \$12,000, which is 20 percent of its goal, how much money will have been raised when 50 percent of the goal has been reached?

(A) \$60,000 (B) \$30,000 (C) \$18,000
(D) \$15,000 (E) \$4,800

23. If 48 liters of a certain liquid weigh 50 kilograms, then how much (in kilograms) do 72 liters of the liquid weigh?

(A) 25 (B) 60 (C) 75 (D) 90 (E) 120

24. If the trip from Soldier Field to Wrigley Field takes two hours walking at the constant rate of four miles per hour, how long (in hours) will the same trip take walking at a constant rate of five miles per hour?

(A) 2.5 (B) 1.75 (C) 1.6 (D) 1.5 (E) 1.25

25. A swimming pool is filled by either of two pipes. Pipe A supplies water at the rate of 200 gallons per hour and takes eight hours to fill the pool. If Pipe B can fill the pool in five hours, what is the rate (in gallons per hour) at which Pipe B supplies water?

(A) 125 (B) 320 (C) 360 (D) 480 (E) 575

26. What is the ratio of 3 to 8 expressed as a decimal?

(A) 0.125 (B) 0.25 (C) 0.375
(D) 0.50 (E) 1

27. If the ratio of 3 to 4 is the same as the ratio of 15 to x, find x.

(A) 5 (B) 10 (C) 15 (D) 20 (E) 25

28. Annika can solve 10 math problems in 30 minutes. At this rate, how many math problems can she solve in 48 minutes?

(A) 8 (B) 16 (C) 32 (D) 46 (E) 56

29. Seung can walk up 6 flights of stairs in 4 minutes. At this rate, how many flights of stairs could he walk up in 18 minutes?

(A) 4 (B) 10 (C) 14 (D) 20 (E) 27

30. If 4 candy bars cost \$1.04, how much should 6 candy bars cost?

(A) \$0.96 (B) \$1.25 (C) \$1.56
(D) \$1.85 (E) \$2.06

31. If Baby Andrew takes 8 steps to walk 2 yards, how many steps will he take to walk 5 yards?

(A) 5 (B) 10 (C) 15 (D) 20 (E) 25

32. If a 40-inch stick is divided in the ratio of 3:5, how many inches does the short piece contain?

(A) 5 (B) 10 (C) 15 (D) 20 (E) 25

33. When popped, Orville claims that 3 bags of his popcorn will yield 28 ounces. If so, how many ounces will emerge when 5 bags are popped?

(A) 23 (B) $46\frac{2}{3}$ (C) $54\frac{1}{2}$ (D) 64 (E) $64\frac{2}{3}$

34. In a poll of 1000 people, 420 said they would vote for Mason. How many people would be expected to vote for Mason if 60,000,000 people actually vote?

(A) 25,200,000 (B) 25,500,000 (C) 26,000,000
(D) 26,200,000 (E) 26,500,000

35. In 4 days a worm grew from 5 cm to 12 cm. At this rate, how long will the worm be in another 6 days?

(A) 21 cm (B) 22 cm (C) 22.25 cm
(D) 22.5 cm (E) 23 cm

36. Elan can mow 3 lawns in 85 minutes. At this rate how long would he need to mow 5 lawns?

(A) 140 minutes, 20 seconds (B) 141 minutes
(C) 141 minutes, 40 seconds (D) 142 minutes
(E) 142 minutes, 50 seconds

37. Sarah does $\frac{1}{5}$ of the job in 6 minutes. At this rate, what fraction of the job will she do in 10 minutes?

(A) $\frac{1}{4}$ (B) $\frac{1}{3}$ (C) $\frac{1}{2}$ (D) $\frac{3}{4}$ (E) $\frac{3}{2}$

38. A snapshot measures $2\frac{1}{2}$ inches by $1\frac{7}{8}$ inches. It is to be enlarged so that the longer dimension will be 4 inches. The length of the enlarged shorter dimension will be

(A) $2\frac{1}{2}$ in. (B) 3 in. (C) $3\frac{3}{8}$ in.
(D) 4 in. (E) 5 in.

39. Men's white handkerchiefs cost $2.29 for three. The cost per dozen handkerchiefs is

(A) $27.48 (B) $13.74 (C) $9.16
(D) $6.87 (E) $4.5 8

40. A certain pole casts a shadow 24 feet long. At the same time another pole 3 feet high casts a shadow 4 feet long. How high is the first pole, given that the heights and shadows are in proportion?

(A) 18 ft. (B) 19 ft. (C) 20 ft.
(D) 21 ft. (E) 24 ft.

41. The actual length represented by $3\frac{1}{2}$ inches on a drawing having a scale of $\frac{1}{8}$ inch to the foot is

(A) 3.5 ft. (B) 7 ft. (C) 21 ft.
(D) 28 ft. (E) 120 ft.

42. Aluminum bronze consists of copper and aluminum, usually in the ratio of 10:1 by weight. If an object made of this alloy weighs 77 pounds., how many pounds of aluminum does it contain?

(A) 0.7 (B) 7.0 (C) 7.7 (D) 70.7 (E) 77.0

43. It costs 31 cents a square foot to lay vinyl flooring. To lay 180 square feet of flooring, it will cost

(A) $16.20 (B) $18.60 (C) $55.80
(D) $62.00 (E) $180.00

44. If Tuvak earns $352 in 16 days, the amount that he will earn in 117 days is most nearly

(A) $3050 (B) $2575 (C) $2285
(D) $2080 (E) $1170

45. Assuming that on a blueprint $\frac{1}{8}$ inch equals 12 inches of actual length, the actual length in inches of a steel bar represented on the blueprint by a line $3\frac{3}{4}$ inches long is

(A) $3\frac{3}{4}$ (B) 30 (C) 36 (D) 360 (E) 450

46. Blake, James, and Staunton invested $9,000, $7,000, and $6,000, respectively. Their profits were to be divided according to the ratio of their investment. If James uses his share of the firm's profit of $825 to pay a personal debt of $230, how much will he have left?

(A) $30.50 (B) $32.50 (C) $34.50
(D) $36.50 (E) $37.50

Exponents and Radicals

Exponents

1. What Is A Power Of A Number?

A power of a number is the product obtained by multiplying the number by itself a specified number of times. If we multiply 3 by itself five times, the result is $3 \cdot 3 \cdot 3 \cdot 3 \cdot 3 = 243$. So 243 is the fifth power of 3.

EXAMPLES:

1. The second power of 2 is $2 \cdot 2 = 4$.
2. The third power of 2 is $2 \cdot 2 \cdot 2 = 8$.
3. The fourth power of 2 is $2 \cdot 2 \cdot 2 \cdot 2 = 16$.
4. The second power of 3 is $3 \cdot 3 = 9$.
5. The third power of 3 is $3 \cdot 3 \cdot 3 = 27$.

The second power of a number is also called the square of the number:

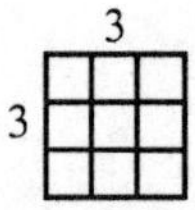

$3 \cdot 3 = 9$

And the third power of a number is also called the cube of the number:

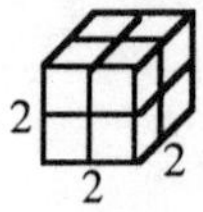

$2 \cdot 2 \cdot 2 = 8$

Beyond the square and the cube, powers are referred to by the number of times the number is multiplied, e.g., fourth, fifth, sixth, and so on.

There is a notation system for powers. To indicate the power of a number, we use a superscript (a small number placed in the upper right–hand corner).

EXAMPLES:

1. 2 to the third power is written 2^3.
2. 3 to the fifth power is written 3^5.
3. 4 to the second power is written 4^2.

The superscript is called an *exponent*, and the number that is being multiplied is called the *base*. The exponent is an instruction to multiply the base by itself the number of times specified by the exponent:

EXAMPLES:

1. Base $\rightarrow 2^{3\leftarrow \text{exponent}} = 2 \cdot 2 \cdot 2$
2. Base $\rightarrow 3^{2\leftarrow \text{exponent}} = 3 \cdot 3$

A number that is not to be multiplied by itself is, of course, just itself, and it is called the first power of the number. But by convention, the 1 is left out.

EXAMPLES:

1. $2^1 = 2$
2. $3^1 = 3$
3. $1{,}000^1 = 1{,}000$

2. *Five Rules For Working With Exponents*

Because powers are written using an exponent, the rules for manipulating numbers don't apply. So you must learn the special rules that apply to exponents. Don't try to memorize them all at once, and don't be put off by our use of letters instead of numbers. Everything will be explained shortly. Here are the five rules:

1. Product Rule: $x^m \cdot x^n = x^{m+n}$
2. Quotient Rule: $x^m \div x^n = x^{m-n}$
3. Power Rule: $(x^m)^n = x^{mn}$
4. Power of a Product Rule: $(xy)^m = (x^m)(y^m)$
5. Power of a Quotient Rule: $\left(\frac{x}{y}\right)^m = \frac{x^m}{y^m}$

• *Product Rule*

The ***product rule*** is used when you have multiplication of powers of the same base. In such cases, add the exponents. *When multiplying like bases, add the exponents.*

EXAMPLE:

$2^2 \cdot 2^3 = 2^{2+3} = 2^5$

The product rule may seem a bit more plausible if we do the multiplication:

$2^2 \cdot 2^3 = (2 \cdot 2) \cdot (2 \cdot 2 \cdot 2) = 2^5$

The simplification done with and without the rule shows that both reach the same result.

EXAMPLES:

1. $3^2 \cdot 3^5 = 3^{2+5} = 3^7$
2. $5^2 \cdot 5^3 \cdot 5^5 = 5^{2+3+5} = 5^{10}$
3. $2^{10} \cdot 2^{10} = 2^{10+10} = 2^{20}$

Notice that in each of the examples there is only one base. In the first example, the base is 3; in the second, it is 5; and in the third, it is 2. This is absolutely essential. The product rule doesn't apply when you have different bases.

EXAMPLE:

$2^4 \cdot 3^4 = ?$

You cannot use the product rule here since 2 and 3 are not the same base. To carry out this simplification, you would have to multiply out the numbers:

$2^4 \cdot 3^4 = (2 \cdot 2 \cdot 2 \cdot 2)(3 \cdot 3 \cdot 3 \cdot 3) = 16 \cdot 81 = 1{,}296$

Nor does the first rule apply to terms that are added, even if they use the same base. For example, $2^2 + 2^3$ is not equal to 2^5, as you can show by multiplying out the numbers: $2^2 + 2^3 = (2 \cdot 2) + (2 \cdot 2 \cdot 2) = 4 + 8 = 12$. But 2^5 is $2 \cdot 2 \cdot 2 \cdot 2 \cdot 2 = 32$.

• ***Quotient Rule***

The ***quotient rule*** is used when you have a power divided by a power of the same base. Subtract the exponents. *When dividing like bases, subtract the exponents.*

EXAMPLES:

1. $2^5 \div 2^3 = 2^{5-3} = 2^2$

The quotient rule may seem more plausible if you actually do the simplification:

$2^5 \div 2^3 = (2 \cdot 2 \cdot 2 \cdot 2 \cdot 2) \div (2 \cdot 2 \cdot 2) = 32 \div 8 = 4$

And 4 equals 2^2, so our manipulation confirms the correctness of the quotient rule.

2. $5^4 \div 5^2 = 5^{4-2} = 5^2$

3. $10^8 \div 10^6 = 10^{8-6} = 10^2$

4. $2^3 \div 2^2 = 2^{3-2} = 2^1 = 2$

Again, notice that in each example the bases are the same, and also that the operation is division (not addition or subtraction).

Since division of powers is accomplished by subtracting exponents, it is possible that you could end up with a zero exponent!

EXAMPLE:

$3^2 \div 3^2 = 3^{2-2} = 3^0$

But what does the zero exponent signify? The zero exponent was the result of dividing a quantity into itself (3^2 and 3^2 are the same number), and you know that the result of such division is always 1. (A number goes into itself exactly one time.) For this reason, we define any number with a zero exponent to be 1.

EXAMPLES:

1. $5^3 \div 5^3 = 5^{3-3} = 5^0 = 1$

2. $3^{12} \div 3^{12} = 3^{12-12} = 3^0 = 1$

In both cases, we are dividing a number into itself, so the result must be simply 1.

It is even possible to end up with a negative exponent!

EXAMPLE:

$2^2 \div 2^3 = 2^{2-3} = 2^{-1}$

The meaning of a negative exponent becomes clearer if we do the problem by first multiplying:

$2^2 \div 2^3 = (2 \cdot 2) \div (2 \cdot 2 \cdot 2) = 4 \div 8 = \frac{1}{2}$

The negative exponent, therefore, does not signify a negative number. Instead, it signifies a fraction. Or, more precisely, the negative exponent indicates the *reciprocal* of the number written.

EXAMPLES:

1. $3^{-2} = \left(\frac{1}{3}\right)^2 = \frac{1}{9}$

2. $2^{-3} = \left(\frac{1}{2}\right)^3 = \frac{1}{8}$

- ***Power Rule***

The ***power rule*** is used when a power is raised to another power. *When raising a power to a power, multiply the exponents.*

EXAMPLES:

1. $(2^2)^3 = ?$

In such situations, according to the Power Rule, we must multiply the exponents:

$(2^2)^3 = 2^{2 \cdot 3} = 2^6$

Again, the power rule gains plausibility if we actually do the multiplication:

$(2^2)^3 = (2 \cdot 2)^3 = 4^3 = 4 \cdot 4 \cdot 4 = 64 = 2^6$

Since $(2^2)^3$ is equal to 2^6, this suggests that the power rule is correct.

2. $(5^2)^3 = 5^{2 \cdot 3} = 5^6$

3. $(3^2)^4 = 3^{2 \cdot 4} = 3^8$

4. $(2^3)^4 = 2^{3 \cdot 4} = 2^{12}$

- ***Power of a Product and Power of a Quotient Rules***

The ***power of a product*** and ***power of a quotient rules*** are really just rules for rewriting expressions using powers, and both say essentially the same thing. An exponent outside parentheses governs all the terms inside the parentheses. The power of a product rule is used when a product is raised to a power. The power of a quotient rule is used when a quotient is raised to a power. *When raising a product or quotient to a power, multiply the exponent on the outside by each exponent on the inside.*

EXAMPLES:

1. $(2 \cdot 3)^2 = 2^2 \cdot 3^2$

2. $\left(\frac{2}{3}\right)^2 = \frac{2^2}{3^2}$

Again, you can verify the correctness of the rules by doing the multiplication or the division.

$(2 \cdot 3)^2 = 2^2 \cdot 3^2 = 4 \cdot 9 = 36$

$(2 \cdot 3)^2 = 6^2 = 36$

$\left(\frac{2}{3}\right)^2 = \frac{2^2}{3^2} = \frac{4}{9}$

$\frac{2}{3} \cdot \frac{2}{3} = \frac{4}{9}$

As you might anticipate, more complex expressions may require the application of two or even more of the rules. And you would be correct. But no matter how complex a problem gets, it can be solved by a series of simple steps following the five rules.

EXAMPLES:

1. $(2^3 \cdot 3^2)^2 = 2^{3 \cdot 2} \cdot 3^{2 \cdot 2} = 2^6 \cdot 3^4$

2. $\left(\frac{3^3 \cdot 5^5}{3^2 \cdot 5^2}\right)^2 = (3^{3-2} \cdot 5^{5-2})^2 = (3^1 \cdot 5^3)^2 = 3^2 \cdot 5^6$

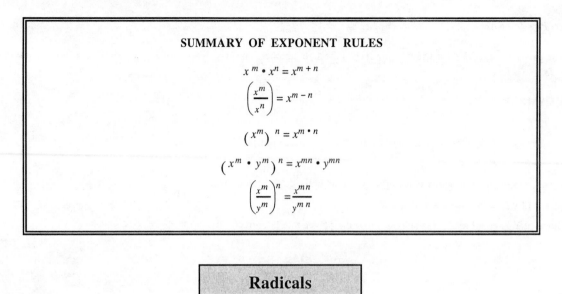

SUMMARY OF EXPONENT RULES

$$x^m \bullet x^n = x^{m+n}$$

$$\left(\frac{x^m}{x^n}\right) = x^{m-n}$$

$$(x^m)^n = x^{m \bullet n}$$

$$(x^m \bullet y^m)^n = x^{mn} \bullet y^{mn}$$

$$\left(\frac{x^m}{y^m}\right)^n = \frac{x^{mn}}{y^{mn}}$$

Radicals

1. *What Is A Root?*

A ***square root*** of a number x is a solution to the equation: $\sqrt{x} = b$, $x = b^2$. When you perform the multiplication indicated by an exponent, you are in effect answering the question, "What do I get when I multiply this number by itself so many times?" Now ask the opposite question, "What number, when multiplied by itself so many times, will give me a certain value?" For example, when you raise 2 to the third power, you find out that $2^3 = 8$. Now ask the question in the other direction. What number, when raised to the third power, is equal to 8?

This reverse process is called "finding the root of a number." Why roots? Look at the following diagram:

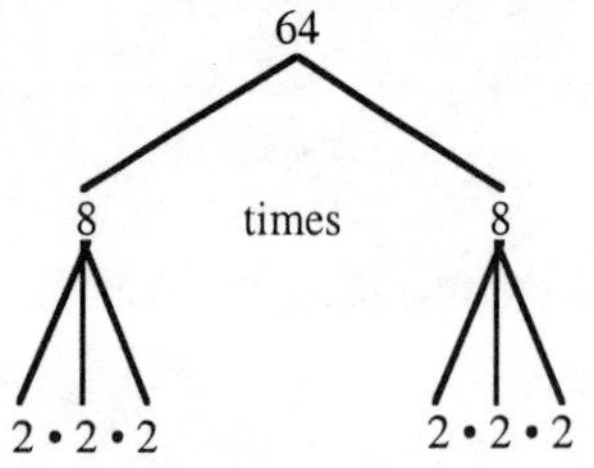

Since $2^6 = 64$, the sixth root of 64 is 2. And the picture is highly suggestive of something like plant roots.

Of course, we rarely deal with sixth roots. Mostly, we deal with numbers that have two roots: $2 \bullet 2 = 4$, so the second or *square* root of 4 is 2; and occasionally with numbers having three roots: $2 \bullet 2 \bullet 2 = 8$, so the third or *cube* root of 8 is 2.

The operation of taking a square root of a number is signaled by the radical sign, $\sqrt{}$. *Radical* comes from the Latin word *rad*, which means "root."

EXAMPLES:

$\sqrt{1} = 1$	$\sqrt{9} = 3$	$\sqrt{25} = 5$	$\sqrt{49} = 7$	$\sqrt{81} = 9$	$\sqrt{121} = 11$
$\sqrt{4} = 2$	$\sqrt{16} = 4$	$\sqrt{36} = 6$	$\sqrt{64} = 8$	$\sqrt{100} = 10$	$\sqrt{144} = 12$

Note: The symbol $\sqrt{}$ always denotes a positive number. Later, when we get to the topic of quadratic equations in algebra, we will run across this sign: $\pm$. But that's another story.

If the radical sign is adorned with a little number, it indicates a different root. The index indicates the root. $\sqrt[n]{a}$: n is the root or index, $\sqrt{}$ is the radical, and a is the radicand.

EXAMPLES:

1. $\sqrt[3]{8} = 2$ (The cube root of 8 is 2.)

2. $\sqrt[3]{27} = 3$ (The cube root of 27 is 3.)

3. $\sqrt[3]{125} = 5$ (The cube root of 125 is 5.)

Theoretically, even greater roots are possible, but you probably won't run across any on the exam.

2. *Extracting Square Roots*

If a number is a perfect square (e.g., 4, 9, 16, etc.), then extracting its square root is easy. You just use the values given in the table above. Not every number, however, has an exact square root. In such cases, you can do one of two things. First, you may be able to find in the number a factor that does have an exact square root and extract that (pull it out) from under the radical sign.

EXAMPLE:

$\sqrt{125} = \sqrt{25 \cdot 5} = \sqrt{25} \cdot \sqrt{5} = 5 \cdot \sqrt{5} = 5\sqrt{5}$

In this case, 125 does not have an exact square root, but 25, which does, is a factor of 125. So we factor 125 into 25 and 5. Then we take the square root of 25, which is 5. The final expression is $5\sqrt{5}$, which means 5 multiplied by the square root of 5.

EXAMPLES:

1. $\sqrt{27} = \sqrt{9 \cdot 3} = \sqrt{9} \cdot \sqrt{3} = 3 \cdot \sqrt{3} = 3\sqrt{3}$
2. $\sqrt{32} = \sqrt{16 \cdot 2} = \sqrt{16} \cdot \sqrt{2} = 4 \cdot \sqrt{2} = 4\sqrt{2}$
3. $\sqrt{52} = \sqrt{4 \cdot 13} = \sqrt{4} \cdot \sqrt{13} = 2 \cdot \sqrt{13} = 2\sqrt{13}$

For non-calculator exams, your second option is to approximate a value for the square root. For the exam, it is useful to know that $\sqrt{2}$ is approximately 1.4 and that $\sqrt{3}$ is approximately 1.7. You can approximate other values by using ranges. For example, $\sqrt{7}$ must be between 2 and 3 ($\sqrt{4} < \sqrt{7} < \sqrt{9}$). And since 7 is closer to 9 than to 4, a good approximation of $\sqrt{7}$ is 2.6 to 2.7. For the test, you would not need greater accuracy.

3. *Manipulating Radicals*

Radicals are really just a form of exponents. In fact, radicals can be written using fractional exponents.

EXAMPLES:

1. $\sqrt{4} = 4^{1/2} = 2$

2. $\sqrt[3]{8} = 8^{1/3} = 2$

The exam doesn't usually make use of fractional exponents; but fractional exponents do make it easier to explain how to simplify radicals, since all of the rules for exponents apply to fractional exponents and therefore to radicals as well.

When you multiply a square root by itself, the result is the number beneath the radical: $\sqrt{2} \cdot \sqrt{2} = 2$. It is explained by the product rule of exponents. Since $\sqrt{2} = 2^{1/2}$, $\sqrt{2}\sqrt{2} = 2^{1/2} \cdot 2^{1/2} = 2^1 = 2$.

The power rules of exponents are the ones you are most likely to use in working with radicals. These are the rules for rewriting expressions. Here is how the power of a product rule applies to radicals:

EXAMPLE:

$$\sqrt{125} = 125^{1/2} = (25 \cdot 5)^{1/2} = 25^{1/2} \cdot 5^{1/2} = \sqrt{25} \cdot \sqrt{5} = 5\sqrt{5}$$

Notice that this is just the process of extracting a square root by finding a factor, but what makes that process work is the power of a product rule of exponents. The power of a quotient rule is used in the following example:

EXAMPLE:

$$\sqrt{\frac{4}{9}} = \left(\frac{4}{9}\right)^{1/2} = \frac{4^{1/2}}{9^{1/2}} = \frac{\sqrt{4}}{\sqrt{9}} = \frac{2}{3}$$

Importantly, since radicals are a form of exponents, you cannot just add radicals. $\sqrt{4} + \sqrt{9}$ is not equal to $\sqrt{13}$, and you can prove this by taking the square root of 4, which is 2, and the square root of 9, which is 3. And 2 + 3 is 5, which does not equal $\sqrt{13}$.

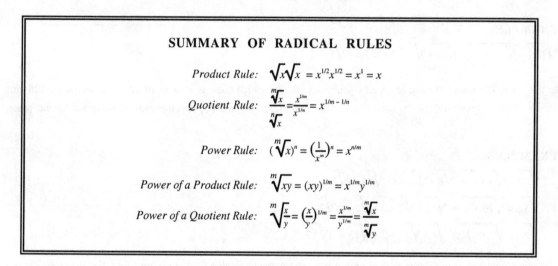

SUMMARY OF RADICAL RULES

Product Rule: $\sqrt{x}\sqrt{x} = x^{1/2}x^{1/2} = x^1 = x$

Quotient Rule: $\dfrac{\sqrt[m]{x}}{\sqrt[n]{x}} = \dfrac{x^{1/m}}{x^{1/n}} = x^{1/m - 1/n}$

Power Rule: $(\sqrt[m]{x})^n = \left(\frac{1}{x^m}\right)^n = x^{n/m}$

Power of a Product Rule: $\sqrt[m]{xy} = (xy)^{1/m} = x^{1/m}y^{1/m}$

Power of a Quotient Rule: $\sqrt[m]{\frac{x}{y}} = \left(\frac{x}{y}\right)^{1/m} = \dfrac{x^{1/m}}{y^{1/m}} = \dfrac{\sqrt[m]{x}}{\sqrt[m]{y}}$

EXERCISE 8

Exponents and Radicals

DIRECTIONS: Choose the best answers to each of the following questions. Answers are on page B-123.

1. What is the third power of 3?
   (A) 1 (B) 3 (C) 9 (D) 15 (E) 27

2. What is the fourth power of 2?
   (A) 2 (B) 4 (C) 8 (D) 16 (E) 32

3. What is the first power of 1,000,000?
   (A) 0 (B) $\frac{1}{1{,}000{,}000}$ (C) 1
   (D) 10 (E) 1,000,000

4. $100^0 =$
   (A) 0 (B) 1 (C) 10 (D) 100 (E) 100,000

5. $2^3 \cdot 2^2 =$
   (A) 6 (B) 8 (C) 2^5 (D) 2^6 (E) 4^6

6. $3^{10} \cdot 10^3 =$
   I. 30^{30}
   II. $300 \cdot 1{,}000$
   III. $30 + 30$
   (A) I, but not II or III (B) II, but not I or III
   (C) I and III, but not II (D) II and III, but not I
   (E) Neither I, II, nor III

7. $5^4 \cdot 5^9 =$
   (A) 25^{36} (B) 5^{36} (C) 5^{13} (D) 5^5 (E) 5

8. $2^3 \cdot 2^4 \cdot 2^5 =$
   (A) 2^{12} (B) 2^{60} (C) 8^{12} (D) 4^{60} (E) 8^{60}

9. $(2 + 3)^{20} =$
   (A) 5^{20} (B) $2^{20} + 3^{20}$ (C) 6^{20} (D) 20^5 (E) 20^6

10. $\frac{2^5}{2^3} =$
   (A) 2^2 (B) 4^4 (C) 2^8 (D) 4^8 (E) 2^{15}

11. $\frac{3^{10}}{3^8} =$
   (A) 3 (B) 3^2 (C) 9^2 (D) 3^{18} (E) 3^{80}

12. $\frac{5^2}{5^2} =$
   I. 0
   II. 1
   III. 5^0
   (A) I and II only (B) I and III only (C) II and III only
   (D) III only (E) Neither I, II, nor III

13. $\frac{3^2}{3^3} =$
   I. 3^{-1}
   II. $\frac{1}{3}$
   III. -1
   (A) I only (B) II only (C) I and II only
   (D) I and III only (E) I, II, and III

14. $(2^2)^3 =$
   (A) 2^5 (B) 2^6 (C) 4^5 (D) 4^6 (E) 6^5

15. $(5^2)^6 =$
   (A) 5^8 (B) 5^{12} (C) 10^4 (D) 10^8 (E) 10^{12}

16. $(7^7)^7 =$
   (A) 21 (B) 7^{14} (C) 7^{49} (D) 21^7 (E) 49^{49}

17. $(3 \cdot 2)^2 =$
   I. 36
   II. $3 \cdot 3 \cdot 2 \cdot 2$
   III. $3^2 \cdot 2^2$
   (A) I only (B) II only (C) III only
   (D) I and III only (E) I, II, and III

18. $(5 \cdot 3)^2 =$
   I. 15^2
   II. $5^2 \cdot 3^2$
   III. 8^2
   (A) I only (B) II only (C) III only
   (D) I and II only (E) I, II, and III

19. $\left(\frac{8}{3}\right)^2 =$
   I. $\frac{64}{9}$
   II. $\frac{8^2}{3^2}$
   III. 11^2
   (A) I only (B) II only (C) I and II only
   (D) I and III only (E) I, II, and III

20. $\left(\frac{4}{9}\right)^2 =$
   (A) $\frac{2}{3}$ (B) $\frac{4}{9}$ (C) $\frac{16}{81}$ (D) $\frac{4^2}{9}$ (E) $\frac{4}{9^2}$

21. $(2 \cdot 2^2 \cdot 2^3)^2 =$
   (A) 2^8 (B) 2^{10} (C) 2^{12} (D) 2^{16} (E) 2^{18}

22. $\left(\frac{2^4 \cdot 5^4}{2^2 \cdot 5^2}\right)^2 =$
   (A) $2^4 \cdot 5^4$ (B) $2^6 \cdot 2^6$ (C) 4^6 (D) 4^8 (E) 24

23. $\frac{3^6 \cdot 5^3 \cdot 7^9}{3^4 \cdot 5^3 \cdot 7^8} =$

(A) $3^2 \cdot 5 \cdot 7$ (B) $3^2 \cdot 5 \cdot 7^2$ (C) $3 \cdot 5 \cdot 7$
(D) $3^2 \cdot 5$ (E) $3^2 \cdot 7$

24. $\left(\frac{5^{12} \cdot 7^5}{5^{11} \cdot 7^5}\right)^2 =$

(A) 25 (B) 49 (C) 5^7 (D) 5^{11} (E) 7^5

25. $\left(\frac{12^{12} \cdot 11^{11} \cdot 10^{10}}{12^{12} \cdot 11^{11} \cdot 10^9}\right)^2 =$

(A) 0 (B) 1 (C) 10 (D) 100 (E) 1,000

26. $\sqrt{36} =$

I. 6
II. −6
III. $3\sqrt{3}$

(A) I only (B) I and II only (C) I and III only
(D) II and III only (E) I, II, and III

27. $\sqrt{81} + \sqrt{4} =$

I. $\sqrt{85}$
II. $\sqrt{9} + \sqrt{2}$
III. 11

(A) I only (B) II only (C) III only
(D) I and II only (E) II and III only

28. $\sqrt{27} =$

(A) 3 (B) $3\sqrt{3}$ (C) $3\sqrt{9}$ (D) 27 (E) 81

29. $\sqrt{52} =$

(A) $\sqrt{5} + \sqrt{2}$ (B) 7 (C) $2\sqrt{13}$
(D) $13\sqrt{4}$ (E) 13^2

30. $\sqrt{\frac{9}{4}} =$

(A) $\frac{\sqrt{3}}{2}$ (B) $\frac{3}{\sqrt{2}}$ (C) $\frac{3}{2}$ (D) 5 (E) $\sqrt{5}$

31. $\frac{\sqrt{81}}{\sqrt{27}} =$

(A) $\sqrt{3}$ (B) 3 (C) $3\sqrt{3}$ (D) 9 (E) $9\sqrt{3}$

32. $2 \cdot \sqrt{2}$ is most nearly equal to
(A) 2.8 (B) 3.4 (C) 4 (D) 7 (E) 12

33. $\sqrt{27}$ is most nearly equal to
(A) 3 (B) 4 (C) 4.5 (D) 5.1 (E) 9

34. $\sqrt{12}$ is most nearly equal to
(A) 2 (B) 3.4 (C) 4 (D) 6 (E) 8

35. $\sqrt{23}$ is most nearly equal to
(A) 4 (B) 4.8 (C) 6 (D) 7 (E) 8

36. Expand and simplify: $(5x + 4y)^2 = ?$
(A) $20x^2 - 40xy + 16y^2$
(B) $25x^2 - 40xy + 16y^2$
(C) $25x^2 + 40xy + 16y^2$
(D) $-25x^2 - 40xy - 16y^2$
(E) $25x^2 + 40xy + 20y^2$

37. Simplify: $\frac{8x^{-4}}{2x} = ?$

(A) $\frac{2}{x^5}$ (B) $\frac{4}{x^4}$ (C) $\frac{3}{x^5}$ (D) $\frac{4}{x^5}$ (E) $\frac{8}{x^5}$

38. Simplify: $\frac{3^{-1}x^5y^2}{2xy} = ?$

(A) $\frac{x^2y}{6}$ (B) $\frac{x^4y}{6}$ (C) $\frac{x^6y^2}{8}$ (D) $\frac{x^6y^4}{6}$ (E) $\frac{x^6y^2}{10}$

39. Simplify: $\frac{6x^{-5}y^2}{3^{-1}x^{-4}y} = ?$

(A) $\frac{12y^4}{x^4}$ (B) $\frac{16y^4}{x^5}$ (C) $\frac{16y^5}{x^4}$
(D) $\frac{18y}{x}$ (E) $\frac{18y^5}{x^6}$

40. Simplify: $\frac{9^2x^3y}{3^{-1}x^{-4}y} = ?$

(A) $243x^7$ (B) $244x^3$ (C) $248x^7$
(D) $252x^2$ (E) $256x$

41. If $x = -2$, $x^2 = ?$
(A) −4 (B) 4 (C) 6 (D) 8 (E) 10

42. If $x = -3$ and $y = 5$, then $x^2y = ?$
(A) −50 (B) −45 (C) 45 (D) 50 (E) 55

43. If $x = -2$ and $y = -3$, then $x^2 - 4xy - x = ?$
(A) −24 (B) −20 (C) − 18 (D) −16 (E) −14

44. Expand and simplify: $(x - y)(x^2 - 2x + 5) = ?$
(A) $x^3 - 2x^2 + 5x - x^2y + 2xy - 5y$
(B) $x^3 + 2x^2 + 5x - x^2y + 2xy - 5y$
(C) $x^3 - 2x^2 - 5x - x^2y + 2xy - 5y$
(D) $x^3 - 2x^2 + 5x + x^2y + 2xy - 5y$
(E) $x^3 - 2x^2 + 5x - x^2y - 2xy - 5y$

45. Expand and simplify: $(2x + \sqrt{3})^2 = ?$

(A) $3x^2 + 3x\sqrt{3} + 3$
(B) $4x^2 - 4x\sqrt{3} + 3$
(C) $4x^2 - 4x\sqrt{3} - 3$
(D) $-4x^2 + 4x\sqrt{3} + 3$
(E) $4x^2 + 4x\sqrt{3} + 3$

46. If $x = -2$ and $y = 3$, then $2x^2 - xy = ?$

(A) 10 (B) 12 (C) 14 (D) 16 (E) 18

47. Simplify: $\left(\frac{x^2y^3x^5}{2^{-1}}\right)^2 = ?$

(A) $4x^{12}y^4$
(B) $4x^{12}y^6$
(C) $4x^{14}y^4$
(D) $4x^{12}y^6$
(E) $4x^{14}y^6$

48. Simplify: $(7 + \sqrt{5})(3 - \sqrt{5}) = ?$

(A) $4 + 4\sqrt{5}$ (B) $4 - \sqrt{5}$ (C) $16 + 4\sqrt{5}$
(D) $16 - 4\sqrt{5}$ (E) 16

49. Simplify: $(5 - \sqrt{2})(3 - \sqrt{2}) = ?$

(A) $17 + \sqrt{2}$ (B) $17 - 8\sqrt{2}$ (C) $17 + \sqrt{8}$
(D) $17 + 8\sqrt{2}$ (E) 25

50. Simplify: $(\sqrt{3} + 1)(2 - \sqrt{3}) = ?$

(A) -1 (B) $-1 - \sqrt{3}$ (C) $-1 + \sqrt{3}$
(D) 1 (E) $1 + \sqrt{3}$

51. Simplify: $\sqrt{2} \cdot 2\sqrt{3} = ?$

(A) $-2\sqrt{6}$ (B) $-\sqrt{6}$ (C) 2 (D) $\sqrt{6}$ (E) $2\sqrt{6}$

52. Simplify: $\sqrt{8} + \sqrt{50} = ?$

(A) $-7\sqrt{2}$ (B) $-\sqrt{2}$ (C) $\sqrt{2}$ (D) $7\sqrt{2}$ (E) 7

53. Simplify: $\sqrt{3^2 + 5^2} = ?$

(A) 6 (B) $\sqrt{34}$ (C) 7 (D) $\sqrt{51}$ (E) 8

54. Simplify: $\sqrt{(2\sqrt{3})^2 + 2^2} = ?$

(A) 1 (B) 2 (C) 3 (D) 4 (E) 5

55. Is $(5 + \sqrt{2})(5 - \sqrt{2})$ rational?

(A) Yes
(B) No
(C) Cannot be determined from the information given.

56. Is $\frac{(5 + \sqrt{2})}{(5 - \sqrt{2})}$ rational?

(A) Yes
(B) No
(C) Cannot be determined from the information given.

57. In terms of π, what is the area of a circle whose radius is $2\sqrt{5}$?

(A) π (B) 4π (C) 10π (D) 20π (E) 40π

58. What is the radius of a circle whose area is 12π?

(A) $\sqrt{3}$ (B) 1 (C) $2\sqrt{3}$ (D) 2 (E) 3

59. What is the radius of a circle if the distance to walk halfway around the rim of the circle is $\sqrt{6}\pi$?

(A) $\sqrt{2}$ (B) $\sqrt{3}$ (C) 2 (D) $\sqrt{6}$ (E) 3

60. If the legs of a right triangle are 2 and 5, what is the hypotenuse?

(A) $\sqrt{22}$ (B) $\sqrt{29}$ (C) $5\sqrt{2}$ (D) $\sqrt{35}$ (E) 6

61. If the hypotenuse of a right triangle is 37 and one leg is 35, what is the length of the other leg?

(A) $4\sqrt{3}$ (B) $6\sqrt{2}$ (C) 12 (D) $14\sqrt{2}$ (E) 16

62. Is the following equality true: $\sqrt{x^2 + y^2} = x + y$?

(A) Yes
(B) No
(C) Cannot be determined from the information given.

63. Is the following equality true: $\sqrt{(x + y)^2} = \sqrt{x^2 + 2xy + y^2}$?

(A) Yes
(B) No
(C) Cannot be determined from the information given.

64. Does $\frac{x}{\sqrt{2x - y}} = x\sqrt{2x + y}$?

(A) Yes
(B) No
(C) Cannot be determined from the information given.

65. Does $\frac{6}{\sqrt{2a - 3c}} = \frac{6\sqrt{2a - 3c}}{(2a - 3c)}$?

(A) Yes
(B) No
(C) Cannot be determined from the information given.

66. Multiply and simplify: $\frac{1}{2}\sqrt{2}(\sqrt{6} + \frac{1}{2}\sqrt{2})$.

(A) $\sqrt{3} + \frac{1}{2}$ (B) $\frac{1}{2}\sqrt{3}$ (C) $\sqrt{6} + 1$
(D) $\sqrt{6} + 1$ (E) $\sqrt{6} + 2$

67. Divide and simplify: $\frac{\sqrt{32b^3}}{\sqrt{8b}}$.

(A) $2\sqrt{b}$ (B) $\sqrt{2b}$ (C) $2b$
(D) $\sqrt{2b^2}$ (D) $b\sqrt{2b}$

68. Divide and simplify: $\frac{15\sqrt{96}}{5\sqrt{2}}$.

(A) $7\sqrt{3}$ (B) $7\sqrt{12}$ (C) $11\sqrt{3}$
(D) $12\sqrt{3}$ (E) $40\sqrt{3}$

69. Simplify $\sqrt{\frac{x^2}{9} + \frac{x^2}{16}}$.

(A) $\frac{25x^2}{144}$ (B) $\frac{5x}{12}$ (C) $\frac{5x^2}{12}$ (D) $\frac{x}{7}$ (E) $\frac{7x}{12}$

70. Simplify $\sqrt{36y^2 + 64x^2}$

(A) $6y + 8x$ (B) $10xy$ (C) $6y^2 + 8x^2$
(D) $10x^2y^2$ (E) Cannot be simplified.

71. Simplify $\sqrt{\frac{x^2}{64} - \frac{x^2}{100}}$

(A) $\frac{x}{40}$ (B) $-\frac{x}{2}$ (C) $\frac{x}{2}$ (D) $\frac{3x}{40}$ (E) $\frac{3x}{80}$

72. Simplify $\sqrt{\frac{y^2}{2} - \frac{y^2}{18}}$

(A) $\frac{2y}{3}$ (B) $\frac{y\sqrt{5}}{3}$ (C) $\frac{10y}{3}$
(D) $\frac{y\sqrt{3}}{6}$ (E) Cannot be simplified.

73. $\sqrt{a^2 + b^2}$ is equal to

(A) $a + b$ (B) $a - b$ (C) $\sqrt{a^2} + \sqrt{b^2}$
(D) $(a + b)(a - b)$ (E) none of these

74. Which of the following radicals are perfect squares?

(A) $\sqrt{0.4}$ (B) $\sqrt{0.9}$ (C) $\sqrt{0.09}$
(D) $\sqrt{0.02}$ (E) $\sqrt{0.025}$

Algebraic Operations

Algebra is that branch of mathematics that uses letter symbols to represent numbers. The letter symbols are in essence place-holders. They function somewhat like English words such as *someone* or *somewhere*. For example, in the English sentence "Someone took the book and put it somewhere," neither the identity of the person in question nor the new location of the book is known. Using letters in the way algebra does, we might say "x put the book in y place." The identity of x is unknown, and the new location of the book is unknown. It is for this reason that letter symbols in algebra are often referred to as "unknowns."

Algebra, like English, is a language, and for making certain statements, algebra is much better than English. For example, the English statement "There is a number such that, when you add 3 to it, the result is 8" can be rendered more easily in algebraic notation: $x + 3 = 8$. In fact, learning the rules of algebra is really very much like learning the grammar of any language.

With this analogy between algebra as a language and English in mind, let us begin by studying the components of the language of algebra.

The Basic Grammar of Algebra

1. *Terms*

The basic unit of the English language is the word. The basic unit of the language of algebra is the *term*. In English, a word consists of one or more letters. In algebra, a term consists of one or more letters or numbers. For example, x, $2z$, xy, N, 2, $\sqrt{7}$, and π are all algebraic terms. A term is a product, quotient, or a single symbol.

In English, a word may have a root, a prefix, a suffix, an ending, and so on. In algebra, a term may have a coefficient, an exponent, and a sign. Of course, algebraic terms also include a variable, also referred to as the base.

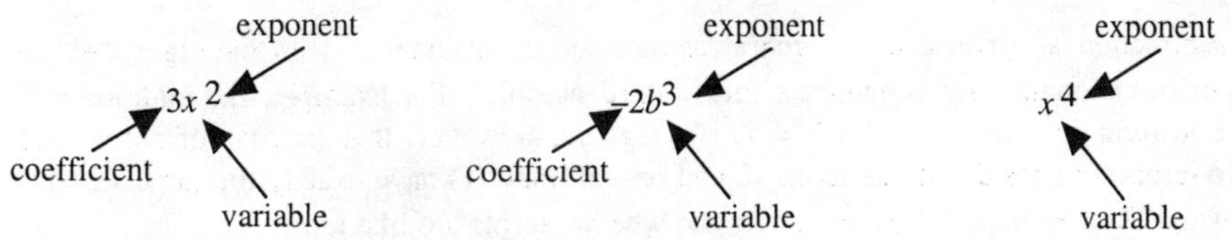

Note: Just as with numbers, when the sign is positive, the "+" is not written but understood, e.g., $3x$ is $+3x$. Also, when the coefficient is 1, it is understood, not written out, e.g., x and not $1x$.

The elements in an algebraic term are all joined by the operation of multiplication. The coefficient (and its sign) is multiplied by the variable. Thus, $-3x$ means -3 times x; $5a$ means $+5$ times a; and $\frac{1}{2}N$ means $\frac{1}{2}$ times N.

The exponent, as you have already learned, also indicates multiplication. Thus, x^2 means x times x; a^3 means a times a times a; and N^5 means N times N times N times N times N. When you are working with algebraic terms, be careful not to confuse the coefficient with the exponent. $3x$ means 3 times x, while x^3 means x times x times x.

Of course, many terms have both a coefficient and an exponent. Thus, $3x^2$ means "3 times x times x," and $-5a^3$ means "-5 times a times a times a."

2. *Expressions*

In English, words are organized into phrases. In algebra, terms are grouped together in *expressions*. An expression is a collection of algebraic terms that are joined by addition, subtraction, or both.

EXAMPLES:

1. $x + y$
2. $-2x + 3x + z$
3. $3x^2 - 2y^2$
4. $x^2 + y^2$

Algebraic expressions are classified according to the number of terms they contain:

- A ***monomial*** is an expression with a single term.
- A ***polynomial*** is any expression with one or more terms.
- A ***binomial*** is a polynomial with exactly two terms.
- A ***trinomial*** is a polynomial with exactly three terms.

3. *Equations*

In algebra, a complete sentence is called an ***equation***. An equation asserts that two algebraic expressions are equal.

EXAMPLE:

$2x + 4 = 3x - 2$

This equation says "2 times a certain unknown plus 4 is equal to 3 times that unknown minus 2."

Basic Algebraic Operations

1. *Addition and Subtraction*

Addition and subtraction are indicated in algebra, as they are in arithmetic, with the signs "+" and "–." In arithmetic, these operations result in the combining of numbers into a third number. For example, the addition of 2 and 3 results in the combining of 2 and 3 to form the number 5: $2 + 3 = 5$. In algebra, however, this process of combining can take place only with *like* terms. Two terms are considered like terms if, and only if, they (1) have exactly the same variable and (2) are raised to exactly the same power. The coefficient does not determine whether terms are like terms.

EXAMPLES:

1. $3x^2$, $40x^2$, $-2x^2$, and $\sqrt{2}x^2$ are like terms.
2. $3x$ and $3x^2$ are not like terms.
3. xy, $5xy$, $-23xy$, and πxy are like terms.
4. xy and x^2y are not like terms.
5. $10xyz$, $-xyz$, and xyz are like terms.
6. xy, yz, and xz are not like terms.

To add or subtract algebraic terms, group like terms and then add or subtract the numerical coefficients.

EXAMPLES:

1. What is $x^2 + 2x^2 + 3x^2$?

   All three terms are like terms: x raised to the second power. To add, simply add the coefficients: $1 + 2 + 3 = 6$. (Remember, a term with no explicit coefficient is understood to have a coefficient of 1.) So the result is $6x^2$.

2. What is $y + 2x + 3y - x$?

   Here we have two different types of terms, x and y terms. First, group like terms together: $(2x - x) + (y + 3y)$.

(Note: The parentheses are not necessary. They are included just so you can see clearly how the like terms are grouped.) Next, add the coefficients for each type of term. For the x terms, the coefficients are $2 - 1 = 1$, and for the y terms, $1 + 3 = 4$. So the final result is $1x + 4y$, which is written as $x + 4y$.

3. What is $x - 3x + 5x - 2x$?

   Here, all of the terms are like terms. Simply add the coefficients: $1 - 3 + 5 - 2 = 1$, so the result is $1x$, or simply x.

4. What is $2x - y - 3x + 4y + 5x$?

   Here, we have both x and y terms. First group similar terms:

   $(2x - 3x + 5x) + (4y - y)$

   Now combine coefficients for each. For the x terms, $2 - 3 + 5 = 4$, and for the y terms, $4 - 1 = 3$. The result is $4x + 3y$.

5. What is $5x^2 + 3x^3 - 2x^2 + 4x^3$?

   Here, we have two different terms, x^2 and x^3. Group like terms:

   $(5x^2 - 2x^2) + (3x^3 + 4x^3)$

   Now combine the coefficients for each term. For the x^2 terms, the result is $5 - 2 = 3$, or $3x^2$. For the x^3 terms, the result is $3 + 4 = 7$, or $7x^3$. The final result is $3x^2 + 7x^3$.

Notice that when you have combined all like terms, it is not possible to carry the addition or subtraction further. For example, $x + y$ is just that, $x + y$.

2. *Rules of Exponents*

The Rules of Exponents apply to algebraic terms just as they apply to numbers in arithmetic. (*See Rules for Working with Powers.*)

1. *Product Rule:* when multiplying like bases, add the exponents: $(x^2)(x^3) = x^{2+3} = x^5$.
2. *Quotient Rule:* when dividing like bases, subtract the exponents: $x^3 \div x^2 = x^{3-2} = x^1 = x$,
3. *Power Rule:* when raising a power to a power, multiply the exponents: $(x^2)^3 = x^{(2)(3)} = x^6$.
4. *Power of a Product Rule:* when raising a product to a power, multiply the exponent on the outside by each exponent on the inside: $(x^2y^3)^2 = x^{(2)(2)}y^{(3)(2)} = x^4y^6$ and $\left(\frac{x^2}{y^3}\right)^2 = \frac{x^{(2)(2)}}{y^{(3)(2)}} = \frac{x^4}{y^6}$.

3. *Multiplication*

Multiplication in algebra can be indicated in four ways: $a \times b$, $(a)(b)$, $a \cdot b$, and ab. To multiply two or more monomial (single) terms, multiply their coefficients and use the Product Rule of Exponents.

EXAMPLES:

1. What is $(4x)(2x)$?

   First, multiply the coefficients: $(4)(2) = 8$. Second, use the Product Rule: $(x)(x) = x^2$. So the final result is $8x^2$.

2. What is $(3x^2)(xy)$?

   First, multiply the coefficients: $(3)(1) = 3$. Second, use the Product Rule: $(x^2)(xy) = x^{2+1}y = x^3y$. So the final result is $3x^3y$.

3. What is $(2xyz)(3xy)(4yz)$?

   First, multiply the coefficients: $(2)(3)(4) = 24$. Next, use Product Rule: $(xyz)(xy)(yz) = x^{1+1}y^{1+1+1}z^{1+1} = x^2y^3z^2$. So the result is $24x^2y^3z^2$.

4. *Division*

To divide one monomial by another, divide coefficients and use the Quotient Rule.

EXAMPLES:

1. What is $4x^3y^4 \div 2xy^3$?

   Divide the coefficients: $4 \div 2 = 2$. Use the Quotient Rule: $x^3y^4 \div xy^3 = x^{3-1}y^{4-3} = x^2y$. So the result is $2x^2y$.

2. What is $2x^4y^3 \div x^2z$?

   Divide exponents: $2 \div 1 = 2$. Use the Quotient Rule: $x^4y^3 \div x^2z = \frac{x^{4-2}y^3}{z} = \frac{x^2y^3}{z}$. So the result is $\frac{2x^2y^3}{z}$.

5. *Fractions*

Addition and subtraction of algebraic fractions, like the addition and subtraction of fractions, require the use of common denominators. When you already have like denominators, simply add the numerators of the fractions, using the existing denominator.

EXAMPLES:

1. $\frac{5}{x}+\frac{3}{x}=\frac{5+3}{x}=\frac{8}{x}$
2. $\frac{2x}{y}-\frac{x}{y}=\frac{2x-x}{y}=\frac{x}{y}$
3. $\frac{a}{cd}+\frac{x}{cd}=\frac{a+x}{cd}$

6. *Unlike Denominators*

To add or subtract algebraic fractions with unlike denominators, you must first find a common denominator.

EXAMPLE:

$\frac{2}{x}+\frac{3}{y}+\frac{4}{z}=\frac{2yz+3xz+4xy}{xyz}$

Usually, this can be accomplished by using the "flying x:"

$\frac{2}{x}+\frac{3}{y}= \frac{2}{x} >+< \frac{3}{y} = \frac{2y+3x}{xy}$

$\frac{2x}{y}+\frac{3y}{x}=\frac{2x}{y} >+< \frac{3y}{x}=\frac{2x^2+3y^2}{xy}$

To multiply fractions, follow the rules for multiplying arithmetic fractions. Multiply terms in the numerators to create a new numerator, and multiply terms in the denominator to create a new denominator.

EXAMPLES:

1. $\frac{2}{x}\bullet\frac{3}{y}=\frac{6}{xy}$
2. $\frac{a}{c}\bullet\frac{b}{d}=\frac{ab}{cd}$
3. $\frac{x^2y^3}{z}\bullet\frac{x^3y^2}{wz}=\frac{x^5y^5}{wz^2}$

To divide algebraic fractions, follow the rule for dividing arithmetic fractions. Invert the divisor and multiply.

EXAMPLES:

1. $\frac{2}{y}\div\frac{3}{x}=\frac{2}{y}\bullet\frac{x}{3}=\frac{2x}{3y}$
2. $\frac{2x^2}{y}\div\frac{y}{x}=\frac{2x^2}{y}\bullet\frac{x}{y}=\frac{2x^3}{y^2}$

Multiplying Polynomials

A polynomial is an algebraic expression with one or more terms involving only the operations of addition, subtraction, and multiplication of variables. The word "polynomial" means "many terms." Although it is possible to get a monomial by adding two polynomials. A multiplication problem such as $(x + y)(x + y)$ requires a special procedure. The fundamental rule for multiplying is that every term of one expression must be multiplied by every term of the other expression. This principle can be illustrated using numbers.

First, take the case in which a polynomial is to be multiplied by a single term; for example, $2(3 + 4 + 5)$. One way of solving the problem is to do the addition first and then multiply

EXAMPLE:

$2(3 + 4 + 5) = 2(12) = 24$

It is also possible, however, to multiply each term in the parentheses by 2, using the Distributive Property and then add. To use the Distributive Property, multiply every term inside the parentheses by the term outside the parentheses. ***The Distributive Property*: $x(y + z) = xy + xz$.**

EXAMPLE:

$2(3 + 4 + 5) = (2)(3) + (2)(4) + (2)(5) = 6 + 8 + 10 = 24$

Notice that the result is the same no matter which method we use.

Now take the case in which it is necessary to multiply two polynomials; for example, $(2 + 3)(1 + 4)$. Again, this can be accomplished by first adding and then multiplying. But it can also be done by first multiplying and then adding, using the Distributive Property:

EXAMPLE:

$(2 + 3)(1 + 4) = (5)(5) = 25$

$(2 + 3)(1 + 4) = (2)(1) + (2)(4) + (3)(1) + (3)(4) = 2 + 8 + 3 + 12 = 25$

You get the same result with either method!

With algebraic expressions such as $(x + y)$, you must use the Distributive Property (multiply and then add), because you cannot add (beyond just saying "$x + y$"). So now we will apply the technique to algebraic expressions.

EXAMPLES:

1. $x(y + z) = xy + xz$
2. $a(b + c + d) = ab + ac + ad$

The multiplication of two binomials (two two-term expressions) presents a special case that arises often enough that you should learn a special technique for handling it. The following diagram illustrates how to multiply two binomials:

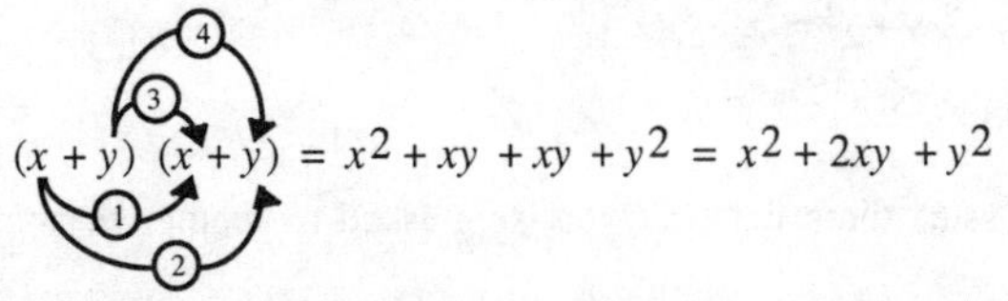

The method described in the diagram is often referred to as the FOIL method. FOIL is an acronym for First, Outer, Inner, and Last. Stated more fully, when multiplying two binomials, e.g., $(x + y)(x + y)$, you first multiply the *first* terms together, then the *outer* terms together, then the *inner* terms together, and then the *last* terms together. Finally, combine like terms.

EXAMPLES:

1. $(x + y)(x + y) =$

   First: $(x)(x) = x^2$; Outer: $(x)(y) = xy$; Inner: $(y)(x) = xy$; Last: $(y)(y) = y^2$. Add: $x^2 + xy + xy + y^2 = x^2 + 2xy + y^2$.

2. $(x-y)(x-y) =$

First: $(x)(x) = x^2$; Outer: $(x)(-y) = -xy$; Inner: $(-y)(x) = -xy$; Last: $(-y)(-y) = y^2$. Add: $x^2 - xy - xy + y^2 = x^2 - 2xy + y^2$.

Three situations, including the ones just shown, arise with sufficient frequency that you should *memorize the results* so you don't have to do the work:

1. $(x+y)^2 = (x+y)(x+y) = x^2 + 2xy + y^2$
2. $(x-y)^2 = (x-y)(x-y) = x^2 - 2xy + y^2$
3. $(x+y)(x-y) = x^2 - y^2$

You might be asked to multiply something more complex than two binomials; for example, $(x+y)^3$. The process is tedious and time–consuming, but ultimately it is executed the same way. First, multiply $(x+y)(x+y)$, as shown above. The result is $x^2 + 2xy + y^2$. Then, complete the multiplication by multiplying every term in that result by both x and y, as follows: $(x+y)(x^2+2xy+y^2) = x(x^2) + x(2xy) + x(y^2) + y(x^2) + y(2xy) + y(y^2) = x^3 + 2x^2y + xy^2 + x^2y + 2xy^2 + y^3 = x^3 + 3x^2y + 3xy^2 + y^3$.

Factoring

Although mention of the term *factoring* strikes fear into the hearts of many, factoring is really nothing more than the reverse of multiplication. For example, if $(x+y)(x+y) = x^2 + 2xy + y^2$, then $x^2 + 2xy + y^2$ can be factored into $(x+y)(x+y)$. Fortunately, for purposes of taking the test, any factoring you might need to do will fall into one of three categories.

1. Finding a Common Factor

If all the terms of an algebraic expression contain a common factor, then that term can be factored out of the expression.

EXAMPLES:

1. $ab + ac + ad = a(b + c + d)$
2. $abx + aby + abz = ab(x+ y+ z)$
3. $x^2 + x^3 + x^4 = x^2(1 + x + x^2)$
4. $3a + 6a^2 + 9a^3 = 3a(1 + 2a + 3a^2)$

2. Reversing a Known Multiplication Problem

Some patterns recur with such frequency on the exam that you must simply *memorize* them.

EXAMPLES:

1. Perfect Square Trinomial: $x^2 + 2xy + y^2 = (x+y)(x+y)$
2. Perfect Square Trinomial: $x^2 - 2xy + y^2 = (x-y)(x-y)$
3. Difference of Two Perfect Squares: $x^2 - y^2 = (x+y)(x-y)$

You will observe that these are the same three patterns you were asked to memorize above while we were studying the FOIL method.

3. Reversing an Unknown Multiplication Process

Occasionally, and only occasionally, you may find it necessary to factor an expression that does not fall into one of the two categories above. The expression will almost surely have the form $ax^2 + bx + c$; for example, $x^2 + 2x + 1$. To factor such expressions, set up a blank diagram: (   )(   ). The diagram is then filled in by answering a series of questions:

1. What factors will produce the first, the x^2, term?

2. What possible factors will produce the last, the c, term?

3. Which of the possible factors from step 2, when added together, will produce the middle, the bx, term?

EXAMPLES:

1. Factor $x^2 + 3x + 2$.
   - What factors will produce the first, the x^2 term? x times x yields x^2, so the factors, in part, are $(x \quad)(x \quad)$.
   - What possible factors will produce the last term? The possibilities are (2, 1) and (–2, –1).
   - Which of the two sets of factors just mentioned, when added together, will produce a final result of $3x$? The answer is (2, 1): $2 + 1 = 3$. You can confirm this by performing the multiplication using the FOIL method:

     $(x + 2)(x + 1) = x^2 + x + 2x + 2 = x^2 + 3x + 2$
2. Factor $x^2 + 4x - 12$.
   - What factors will generate x^2? $(x \quad)(x \quad)$
   - What factors will generate –12? (1, –12), (12, –1), (2, –6) (6, –2), (3, –4), and (4, –3).
   - Which factors, when added together, will produce the middle term of $+ 4x$? The answer is (6, –2): $6 + (-2) = 4$.

   So the factors are $(x + 6)$ and $(x - 2)$, a fact that you can confirm by using the FOIL method to multiply together these two binomials:

   $(x + 6)(x - 2) = x^2 - 2x + 6x - 12 = x^2 + 4x - 12$

EXERCISE 9

Algebraic Operations

DIRECTIONS: Choose the best answers to each of the following questions. Answers are on page B-125.

1. Which of the following pairs of terms are like terms?
   I. $34x$ and $-18x$
   II. $2x$ and $2xy$
   III. x^3 and $3x$

   (A) I only (B) II only (C) I and III only
   (D) II and III only (E) I, II, and III

2. Which of the following pairs of terms are like terms?
   I. $\sqrt{2x}$ and $\sqrt{3x}$
   II. π and 10
   III. x^2 and $2x^2$

   (A) I only (B) II only (C) I and II only
   (D) I and III only (E) I, II, and III

3. $x + 2x + 3x =$

   (A) $6x^6$ (B) x^6 (C) $6x$ (D) $x + 6$ (E) $x - 6$

4. $2x + 3x - x + 4x =$

   (A) $8x^8$ (B) x^8 (C) $8x$ (D) $x + 8$ (E) $x - 8$

5. $a^3 + a^2 + a =$

   (A) $3a^3$ (B) a^3 (C) $2a^2$ (D) a^2 (E) $a^3 + a^2 + a$

6. $z^2 + 2z^2 - 5z^2 =$

   (A) $-9z^2$ (B) $-2z^2$ (C) 0 (D) $2z^2$ (E) $5z^2$

7. $a^3 - 12a^3 + 15a^3 + 2a^3 =$

   (A) $6a^3$ (B) $2a^2$ (C) $6a$ (D) $3a$ (E) a

8. $3c + 2a - 1 + 4c - 2a + 1 =$

   (A) $2a + 4c + 1$ (B) $4a + 3c - 2$ (C) $a + c - 1$
   (D) $2a + 1$ (E) $7c$

9. $-7nx + 2nx + 2n + 7x =$

   (A) 0 (B) $-5nx + 2n + 7x$ (C) $18nx$
   (D) $9nx + 9xn$ (E) $4nx$

10. $c^2 + 2c^2d^2 - c^2 =$

    (A) $4c^2d^2$ (B) $2c^2d^2$ (C) c^2d^2 (D) $2cd$ (E) cd

11. $2x^2 + 2x^2 + 2x^2 =$

    (A) $6x^6$ (B) $2x^6$ (C) $6x^2$ (D) $6x$ (E) 6

12. $3xy + 3x^2y - 2xy + y =$

    (A) $6xy - y$ (B) $x + xy + y$ (C) $3x^2y + xy + y$
    (D) $x^2y^2 + xy$ (E) $3xy + x$

13. $x^2 + 2xy - 3x + 4xy - 6y + 2y^2 + 3x - 2xy + 6y =$

    (A) $x^2 - 2xy + y^2$ (B) $x^2 + y^2 + 3x + 2y$
    (C) $x^2 + 2y^2 + 4xy + 6x + 6y$
    (D) $x^2 + 2y^2 + 4xy + 6x$ (E) $x^2 + 2y^2 + 4xy$

14. $8p + 2p^2 + pq - 4p^2 - 14p - pq =$

    (A) $-2p^2 - 6p$ (B) $-p^2 + 6p$ (C) $2p^2 + 6p$
    (D) $p^2 + 3p$ (E) $3p^2 - pq$

15. $pqr + qrs + rst + stu =$

    (A) $pqrst$ (B) $pq + qr + rs + st + tu$ (C) $pqr + rst$
    (D) $4pqrst$ (E) $pqr + qrs + rst + stu$

16. $(x^2)(x^3) =$

    (A) $x^{2/3}$ (B) x (C) $x^{3/2}$ (D) x^5 (E) x^6

17. $(a)(a^2)(a^3)(a^4) =$

    (A) $10a$ (B) $24a$ (C) a^5 (D) a^{10} (E) a^{24}

18. $y^5 \div y^2 =$

    (A) $3y$ (B) $7y$ (C) $y^{5/2}$ (D) y^3 (E) y^7

19. $(x^2y)(xy^2) =$

    (A) $4xy$ (B) x^3y^3 (C) xy^4 (D) x^4y^4 (E) xy^{16}

20. $(abc)(a^2bc^2) =$

    (A) $4abc$ (B) a^2bc^2 (C) $a^3b^2c^3$
    (D) $a^3b^3c^3$ (E) abc^6

21. $(xy^2)(x^2z)(y^2z) =$

    (A) $8xyz$ (B) x^2y^4z (C) $x^3y^4z^2$
    (D) $x^3y^3z^2$ (E) $x^3y^3z^3$

22. $\dfrac{x^2y^4}{xy} =$

    (A) y^3 (B) xy^3 (C) x^2y^3 (D) x^3y^5 (E) xy^8

23. $\dfrac{a^3b^4c^5}{abc} =$

    (A) $a^2b^3c^4$ (B) $a^3b^4c^5$ (C) $(abc)^3$
    (D) $(abc)^{12}$ (E) $(abc)^{60}$

24. $(x^2y^3)^4 =$
(A) $(xy)^9$ (B) x^6y^7 (C) x^8y^{12} (D) xy^{20} (E) xy^{24}

25. $\left(\frac{a^2}{b^3}\right)^3 =$
(A) $\frac{a^5}{b}$ (B) $\frac{a^6}{b^9}$ (C) a^5b (D) a^6b (E) a^6b^9

26. $\frac{x^3y^4z^5}{x^4y^2z} =$
(A) y^2z^4 (B) xy^2z^4 (C) $\frac{y^2z^4}{x}$ (D) $\frac{y^2z^5}{x}$ (E) $\frac{y^6z^6}{x}$

27. $\left(\frac{c^4d^2}{c^2d}\right)^3 =$
(A) c^5d^3 (B) c^5d^5 (C) c^6d^3 (D) c^6d^4 (E) c^6d^6

28. $\left(\frac{x^2y^3}{xy}\right) \cdot \frac{x^3y^4}{xy} =$
(A) x^2y^3 (B) x^3y^4 (C) x^3y^5 (D) x^5y^6 (E) x^6y^7

29. $\left(\frac{abc^2}{abc^3} \cdot \frac{a^2b^2c}{ab}\right) =$
(A) $\frac{ab}{c}$ (B) $\frac{bc}{a}$ (C) ab (D) c (E) 1

30. $\left(\frac{x^5y^3z^2}{x^4y^2z}\right)^2 \cdot \left(\frac{x^2y^3z^5}{xy^2z^4}\right)^3 =$
(A) xyz (B) $x^2y^2z^2$ (C) $x^5y^5z^5$
(D) $x^6y^6z^6$ (E) xyz^{12}

31. $\frac{a}{c} + \frac{b}{c} =$
(A) $\frac{ab}{c}$ (B) $\frac{a+b}{c}$ (C) $\frac{a+b}{2c}$
(D) $\frac{a+b}{c^2}$ (E) $\frac{a+b}{abc}$

32. $\frac{x}{2} + \frac{y}{2} + \frac{z}{2} =$
(A) $\frac{x+y+z}{2}$ (B) $\frac{x+y+z}{6}$
(C) $\frac{x+y+z}{8}$ (D) $\frac{xyz}{2}$ (E) $\frac{xyz}{8}$

33. $\frac{ab}{x} + \frac{bc}{x} + \frac{cd}{x} =$
(A) $\frac{abcd}{x}$ (B) $\frac{a+b+c+d}{3x}$
(C) $\frac{ab+bc+cd}{x}$ (D) $\frac{ab+bc+cd}{3x}$
(E) $\frac{ab+bc+cd}{x^3}$

34. $\frac{x^2}{k} + \frac{x^3}{k} + \frac{x^4}{k} =$
(A) $\frac{x^9}{k}$ (B) $\frac{x^9}{3k}$ (C) $\frac{x^{24}}{k}$
(D) $\frac{x^2+x^3+x^4}{k}$ (E) $\frac{x^2+x^3+x^4}{3k}$

35. $\frac{2x}{z} - \frac{y}{z} =$
(A) $\frac{2x-y}{z}$ (B) $\frac{2x-y}{2z}$ (C) $\frac{2x-y}{x^2}$
(D) $\frac{2xy}{z}$ (E) $\frac{2xy}{2z}$

36. $\frac{x}{y} + \frac{y}{x} =$
(A) $\frac{xy}{x+y}$ (B) $\frac{x+y}{y+x}$ (C) $\frac{x+y}{xy}$
(D) $\frac{xy+yx}{xy}$ (E) $\frac{x^2+y^2}{xy}$

37. $\frac{a}{b} - \frac{b}{a} =$
(A) $\frac{ab}{a-b}$ (B) $\frac{a-b}{b-a}$ (C) $\frac{a-b}{ab}$
(D) $\frac{ab-ba}{ab}$ (E) $\frac{a^2-b^2}{ab}$

38. $\frac{x^2}{y} + \frac{x^3}{z} =$
(A) $\frac{x^2+x^3}{yz}$ (B) $\frac{x^5}{yz}$ (C) $\frac{x^6}{yz}$
(D) $\frac{x^2+x^3}{yz}$ (E) $\frac{x^2z+x^3y}{yz}$

39. $\frac{x}{a} + \frac{y}{b} + \frac{z}{c} =$
(A) $\frac{xyz}{abc}$ (B) $\frac{x+y+z}{a+b+c}$ (C) $\frac{xbc+yac+zab}{abc}$
(D) $\frac{xbc+yac+zab}{a+b+c}$ (E) $\frac{xa+yb+zc}{abc}$

40. $\frac{x^2}{y^2} - \frac{y^3}{x^3} =$
(A) $\frac{x^2-x^3}{y^5}$ (B) $\frac{x^3-x^2}{y^6}$ (C) $\frac{x^2-y^3}{x^2-y^2}$
(D) $\frac{x^5-y^5}{x^3y^2}$ (E) $\frac{x^6-y^6}{x^3y^2}$

41. $2(x+y) =$
(A) $2xy$ (B) $2x+2y$ (C) $2+x+y$
(D) $4xy$ (E) $2x^2+2y^2$

42. $a(b+c) =$
(A) $ab+bc$ (B) $ab+ac$ (C) $2abc$
(D) ab^2+b^2c (E) $ab+ac+bc$

43. $3(a+b+c+d) =$
(A) $3abcd$ (B) $3a+b+c+d$
(C) $3a+3b+3c+3d$ (D) $3ab+3bc+3cd$
(E) $12a+12b+12c+12d$

44. $2x(3x+4x^2) =$
(A) x^{10} (B) $6x+8x^2$ (C) $5x^2+6x^3$
(D) $6x^2+8x^3$ (E) $6(x^2+x^3)$

45. $3a^2(ab + ac + bc) =$

(A) $3a^3 b^2 c$ (B) $3a^3 + 3b^2 + 3c$
(C) $3a^2b + 3a^2c + 3a^2bc$ (D) $3a^3b + 3a^3c + 3a^2bc$
(E) $3a^5b + 3a^5c$

46. $(x + y)(x + y) =$

(A) $x^2 + y^2$ (B) $x^2 - y^2$ (C) $x^2 + 2xy - y^2$
(D) $x^2 - 2xy + y^2$ (E) $x^2 + 2xy + y^2$

47. $(a + b)^2 =$

(A) $a^2 + b^2$ (B) $a^2 - b^2$ (C) $a^2 + 2ab - b^2$
(D) $a^2 - 2ab + b^2$ (E) $a^2 + 2ab + b^2$

48. $(x - y)^2 =$

(A) $x^2 + 2xy - y^2$ (B) $x^2 + 2xy + y^2$
(C) $x^2 - 2xy + y^2$ (D) $x^2 - 2xy - y^2$ (E) $x^2 + y2$

49. $(a + b)(a - b) =$

(A) $a^2 - b^2$ (B) $a^2 + b^2$ (C) $a^2 + 2ab + b^2$
(D) $a^2 - 2ab + b^2$ (E) $a^2 + 2ab - b^2$

50. $(x - 2)^2 =$

(A) $2x$ (B) $4x$ (C) $x^2 - 4$ (D) $x^2 - 4x + 4$
(E) $x^2 - 4x - 4$

51. $(2 - x)^2 =$

(A) $4 - x^2$ (B) $x^2 + 4$ (C) $x^2 + 4x + 4$
(D) $x^2 - 4x + 4$ (E) $x^2 - 4x - 4$

52. $(ab + bc)(a + b) =$

(A) $a^2b + ab^2 + b^2c + abc$ (B) $a^2b + ab^2 + abc$
(C) $a^2b + ab^2 + a^2bc$ (D) $a^2b + ab + bc + abc$
(E) $a^2 + b^2 + c^2 + abc$

53. $(x - y)(x + 2) =$

(A) $x^2 + 2xy + 2y$ (B) $x^2 + 2xy + x + y$
(C) $x^2 + 2xy + x - 2y$ (D) $x^2 - xy + 2x - 2y$
(E) $x^2 + 2x + 2y - 2$

54. $(a + b)(c + d) =$

(A) $ab + bc + cd$ (B) $ab + bc + cd + ad$
(C) $ac + bd$ (D) $ac + ad + bc + bd$
(E) $ab + ac + ad$

55. $(w + x)(y - z) =$

(A) $wxy - z$ (B) $wy + xy - yz$
(C) $wy - wz + xy + xz$ (D) $wy + wz + xy - xz$
(E) $wy - wz + xy - xz$

56. $(x + y)(w + x + y) =$

(A) $x^2 + wx + wy + xy$ (B) $x^2 + y^2 + wx + wy + 2xy$
(C) $x^2 + y^2 + wxy$ (D) $x^2 + y^2 + wx^2y^2$
(E) $x^2y^2 + wxy$

57. $(2 + x)(3 + x + y) =$

(A) $x^2 + 6xy + 6$ (B) $x^2 + 6xy + 3x + 2y + 6$
(C) $x^2 + 2xy + 6x + 6y + 6$ (D) $x^2 + xy + 5x + 2y + 6$
(E) $x^2 + 3xy + 2x + y + 6$

58. $(x + y)^3 =$

(A) $x^3 + 5x^2y + y^2z + xyz$ (B) $x^3 + 3x^3y + 3xy^3 + y^3$
(C) $x^3 + 3x^2y + 3xy^2 + y^3$ (D) $x^3 + 6x^2y^2 + y^3$
(E) $x^3 + 12x^2y^2 + y^3$

59. $(x - y)^3 =$

(A) $x^3 - 3x^2y + 3xy^2 - y^3$ (B) $x^3 + 3x^2y + 3xy^2 + y^3$
(C) $x^3 + 3x^2y - 3xy^2 - y^3$ (D) $x^3 + 6x^2y^2 + y^3$
(E) $x^3 + 6x^2y^2 - y^3$

60. $(a + b)(a - b)(a + b)(a - b) =$

(A) 1 (B) $a^2 - b^2$ (C) $a^2 + b^2$
(D) $a^4 - 2a^2b^2 + b^4$ (E) $a^4 + 2a^2b^2 + b^4$

61. $2a + 2b + 2c =$

(A) $2(a + b + c)$ (B) $2(abc)$ (C) $2(ab + bc + ca)$
(D) $6(a + b + c)$ (E) $8(a + b + c)$

62. $x + x^2 + x^3 =$

(A) $x(x + 2x + 3x)$ (B) $x(1 + 2x + 3x)$
(C) $x(1 + 2 + 3)$ (D) $x(1 + x + x^2)$ (E) $x(1 + 3x)$

63. $2x^2 + 4x^3 + 8x^4 =$

(A) $2x^2(1 + 2x + 4x^2)$ (B) $2x^2(1 + 2x + 4x^3)$
(C) $2x^2(x + 2x + 4x^2)$ (D) $2x^2(x + 2x^2 + 4x^3)$
(E) $2x^2(x^2 + 2x^3 + 4x^4)$

64. $abc + bcd + cde =$

(A) $ab(c + d + e)$ (B) $ac(b + e)$ (C) $b(a + c + de)$
(D) $c(ab + bd + de)$ (E) $d(a + b + c + e)$

65. $x^2y^2 + x^2y + xy^2 =$

(A) $(x + y)^2$ (B) $x^2 + y^2$ (C) $x^2y^2(x + y)$
(D) $xy(xy + x + y)$ (E) $xy(x + y + 1)$

66. $p^2 + 2pq + q^2 =$

(A) $(p + q)(p - q)$ (B) $(p + q)(p + q)$
(C) $p^2 - q^2$ (D) $p^2 + q^2$ (E) $(p - q)^2$

67. $144^2 - 121^2 =$

(A) 23 (B) $(144 + 121)(144 - 121)$
(C) $(144 + 121)(144 + 121)$ (D) $(23)^2$
(E) $(144 + 121)^2$

68. $x^2 - y^2 =$

(A) $(x + y)(x - y)$ (B) $(x + y)(x + y)$
(C) $(x - y)(x - y)$ (D) $x^2 + y^2$ (E) $2xy$

69. $x^2 + 2x + 1 =$

(A) $(x + 1)(x - 1)$ (B) $(x + 1)(x + 1)$
(C) $(x - 1)(x - 1)$ (D) $x^2 - 1$ (E) $x^2 + 1$

70. $x^2 - 1 =$

(A) $(x + 1)(x + 1)$ (B) $(x - 1)(x - 1)$
(C) $(x + 1)(x - 1)$ (D) $(x - 1)^2$ (E) $(x + 1)^2$

71. $x^2 + 3x + 2 =$

(A) $(x + 1)(x - 2)$ (B) $(x + 2)(x + 1)$
(C) $(x + 2)(x - 1)$ (D) $(x - 2)(x - 1)$
(E) $(x + 3)(x - 1)$

72. $a^2 - a - 2 =$

(A) $(a + 2)(a - 1)$ (B) $(a - 2)(a + 1)$
(C) $(a + 1)(a + 2)$ (D) $(a + 2)(a - 2)$
(E) $(a + 1)(a - 1)$

73. $p^2 + 4p + 3 =$

(A) $(p + 3)(p + 1)$ (B) $(p + 3)(p - 1)$
(C) $(p - 3)(p - 1)$ (D) $(p + 3)(p + 4)$
(E) $(p + 3)(p - 4)$

74. $c^2 + 6c + 8 =$

(A) $(c + 2)(c + 4)$ (B) $(c + 2)(c - 4)$
(C) $(c + 4)(c - 2)$ (D) $(c + 3)(c + 5)$
(E) $(c + 8)(c - 1)$

75. $x^2 + x - 20 =$

(A) $(x + 5)(x - 4)$ (B) $(x + 4)(x - 5)$
(C) $(x + 2)(x - 10)$ (D) $(x + 10)(x - 2)$
(E) $(x + 20)(x - 1)$

76. $p^2 + 5p + 6 =$

(A) $(p + 1)(p + 6)$ (B) $(p + 6)(p - 1)$
(C) $(p + 2)(p + 3)$ (D) $(p - 3)(p - 2)$
(E) $(p + 5)(p + 1)$

77. $x^2 + 8x + 16 =$

(A) $(x + 2)(x + 8)$ (B) $(x + 2)(x - 8)$
(C) $(x - 4)(x - 4)$ (D) $(x + 4)(x - 4)$
(E) $(x + 4)(x + 4)$

78. $x^2 - 5x - 6 =$

(A) $(x + 1)(x + 6)$ (B) $(x + 6)(x - 1)$
(C) $(x + 2)(x + 3)$ (D) $(x - 6)(x + 1)$
(E) $(x - 2)(x - 3)$

79. $a^2 - 3a + 2 =$

(A) $(a - 2)(a - 1)$ (B) $(a - 2)(a + 1)$
(C) $(a + 1)(a - 2)$ (D) $(a - 3)(a + 1)$
(E) $(a + 3)(a + 1)$

80. $x^2 + x - 12 =$

(A) $(x + 6)(x + 2)$ (B) $(x + 6)(x - 2)$
(C) $(x + 4)(x - 3)$ (D) $(x - 4)(x - 3)$
(E) $(x + 12)(x + 1)$

81. $x^2 + 8x + 16 =$

(A) $x + 2$ (B) $x + 4$ (C) $(x + 2)^2$
(D) $(x + 4)^2$ (E) $(x + 4)^3$

82. What number must be added to $12x + x^2$ to make the resulting trinomial expression a perfect square?

(A) 4 (B) 16 (C) 25 (D) 36 (E) 49

83. What number must be added to $4x^2 - 12x$ to make the resulting trinomial expression a perfect square?

(A) 2 (B) 4 (C) 9 (D) 12 (E) 16

84. $x^2 - 8x + 15 =$

(A) $(x + 5)(x + 3)$ (B) $(x - 5)(x + 3)$
(C) $(x + 5)(x - 3)$ (D) $(x - 5)(x - 3)$ (E) $x - 3$

85. $2x^2 + 5x - 3 =$

(A) $(x - 1)(x + 3)$ (B) $(2x - 1)(x + 3)$
(C) $(2x + 1)(x - 3)$ (D) $(3x + 1)(x + 3)$
(E) $(3x - 1)(2x + 3)$

86. $21x + 10x^2 - 10 =$

(A) $(5x - 2)(2x + 5)$ (B) $(5x + 2)(2x + 5)$
(C) $(5x + 2)(2x - 5)$ (D) $(8x + 2)(4x + 5)$
(E) $(10x - 4)(2x - 5)$

87. $ax^2 + 3ax =$

(A) $3ax$ (B) $ax(x - 3)$ (C) $ax(x + 3)$
(D) $ax^2(x - 3)$ (E) $ax^2(x + 3)$

88. $2x^2 - 8x + 3 - (x^2 - 3x + 9) =$

(A) $(x - 6)(x - 1)$ (B) $(x - 6)(x + 1)$
(C) $(x + 6)(x + 1)$ (D) $(2x - 6)(x - 1)$
(E) $(2x + 6)(x + 1)$

89. If $15x^2 + ax - 28 = (5x - 4)(3x + 7)$, then $a =$?

(A) 7 (B) 14 (C) 23 (D) 28 (E) 33

90. $x^2 - 9 =$

(A) $x^2 - 3$ (B) $(x - 3)(x - 3)$ (C) $(x + 3)(x + 3)$
(D) $(x + 3)(x - 3)$ (E) $x - 3$

91. $x^2 - 9y^4 =$

(A) $(x + 3y^2)(x - 3y^2)$ (B) $(x - 3y^2)(x - 3y^2)$
(C) $(x + 3y^2)(x + 3y^2)$ (D) $(2x + 3y^2)(2x + 3y^2)$
(E) $(2x - 3y^2)(2x - 3y^2)$

92. $x^2 - 3(6 - x) + 2(x - 4)(-(1 - x)) =$

(A) $(x - 9)(x - 9)$ (B) $(x - 9)(x - 3)$
(C) $(x - 3)(x - 3)$ (D) $(x + 9)(x + 3)$
(E) $(x + 9)(x - 3)$

93. Find the sum of $\frac{n}{6} + \frac{2n}{5}$.

(A) $\frac{13n}{30}$ (B) $17n$ (C) $\frac{3n}{30}$ (D) $\frac{17n}{30}$ (E) $\frac{3n}{11}$

94. Combine into a single fraction: $1 - \frac{x}{y}$.

(A) $\frac{1-x}{y}$ (B) $\frac{y-x}{y}$ (C) $\frac{x-y}{y}$
(D) $\frac{1-x}{1-y}$ (E) $\frac{y-x}{xy}$

95. Divide $\frac{x-y}{x+y}$ by $\frac{y-x}{y+x}$.

(A) 1 (B) –1 (C) $\frac{(x-y)^2}{(x+y)^2}$
(D) $-\frac{(x-y)^2}{(x+y)^2}$ (E) 0

96. Simplify: $\frac{1+\frac{1}{x}}{\frac{y}{x}}$.

(A) $\frac{x+1}{y}$ (B) $\frac{x+1}{x}$ (C) $\frac{x+1}{xy}$
(D) $\frac{x^2+1}{xy}$ (E) $\frac{y+1}{y}$

97. Find an expression equivalent to $\left(\frac{2x^3}{y}\right)^2$.

(A) $\frac{8x^5}{3y}$ (B) $\frac{6x^6}{y^3}$ (C) $\frac{6x^5}{y^3}$ (D) $\frac{8x^5}{y^3}$ (E) $\frac{8x^6}{y^3}$

98. Simplify: $\frac{\frac{1}{x}+\frac{1}{y}}{3}$.

(A) $\frac{3x+3y}{xy}$ (B) $\frac{3xy}{x+7}$ (C) $\frac{xy}{3}$
(D) $\frac{y+x}{3xy}$ (E) $\frac{y+x}{3}$

99. $\frac{1}{a} + \frac{1}{b} = 7$ and $\frac{1}{a} - \frac{1}{b} = 3$. Find $\frac{1}{a^2} - \frac{1}{b^2}$.

(A) 10 (B) 7 (C) 3 (D) 21 (E) 4

100. If $\frac{3}{4}(x) = 1$, then $\frac{2}{3}(x) = ?$

(A) $\frac{1}{3}$ (B) $\frac{1}{2}$ (C) $\frac{2}{3}$ (D) $\frac{8}{9}$ (E) 2

101. If $x = \frac{y}{7}$ and $7x = 12$, then $y = ?$

(A) 3 (B) 5 (C) 7 (D) 12 (E) 72

102. If $x = k + \frac{1}{2} = \frac{k+3}{2}$, then $x =$

(A) $\frac{1}{3}$ (B) $\frac{1}{2}$ (C) 1 (D) 2 (E) $\frac{5}{2}$

103. If $7 - x = 0$, then $10 - x = ?$

(A) –3 (B) 0 (C) 3 (D) 7 (E) 10

Equations and Inequalities

Pursuing the analogy between English and algebra as a language (see *Algebraic Operations*), the algebraic analogue of a complete sentence in English (with subject and verb) is an equation. An equation is an algebraic statement that two expressions are equivalent.

EXAMPLES:

English:	Ed is three years older than Paul.	*Algebra:* $E = P + 3$
	Paul is twice as old as Mary.	$P = 2M$
	Ned has \$2 more than Ed.	$N = E + \$2$
	Bill has three times as much money as Ted.	$B = 3T$

Solving Linear Equations

An equation containing variables of just the first power is called a first degree or linear equation. Although a linear equation can in principle contain any number of variables, in practice, equations on the exam usually contain only one variable. (Those containing two variables will be discussed in *Simultaneous Equations*.)

The fundamental rule for working with equations is that you can add, subtract, multiply, and divide both sides of the equation by any value without changing the statement of equality. (The one exception is that you cannot multiply or divide by zero.)

EXAMPLE:

$5 = 5$

This is obviously a true statement. And you can add any value to both sides of the equation, say 10, and the statement will remain true:

Add 10: $5 + 10 = 5 + 10$

$15 = 15$

You can also subtract the same value from both sides, say, 7:

$15 - 7 = 15 - 7$

$8 = 8$

And you can multiply both sides by the same value (except zero), say, –2:

$8 \cdot -2 = 8 \cdot -2$

$-16 = -16$

And finally, you can divide both sides by the same value (except zero), for example, –4:

$-16 \div -4 = -16 \div -4$

$4 = 4$

This principle holds true for variables as well.

EXAMPLE:

$5 = 5$

Add x: $5 + x = 5 + x$

Whatever x is, since it appears on both sides of the equation, both sides of the equation must still be equal. Now subtract a value, say, y:

$5 + x - y = 5 + x - y$

Again, since y appears on both sides of the equation, the statement that the two expressions are equal remains true. And you can surely see by now that you can multiply and divide (so long as you don't do it by zero) without changing the truth of the equality.

This fundamental rule for working with equations is the key to solving linear equations containing just one variable. To solve for an unknown, isolate the unknown on one side of the equation.

EXAMPLES:

1. If $2x + 3 = x + 1$, what is x?

   To solve, subtract x from both sides of the equation:

   $2x + 3 - x = x + 1 - x$
   $x + 3 = 1$

   Next, subtract 3 from both sides of the equation:

   $x + 3 - 3 = 1 - 3$
   $x = -2$

2. If $4x + 2 = 2x + 10$, what is x?

   First, subtract $2x$ from both sides of the equation:

   $4x + 2 - 2x = 2x + 10 - 2x$
   $4x - 2x + 2 = 2x - 2x + 10$
   $2x + 2 = 10$

   Now subtract 2 from both sides of the equation:

   $2x + 2 - 2 = 10 - 2$
   $2x = 8$

   Now, to isolate a single x on the left side of the equation, divide both sides of the equation by 2:

   $2x \div 2 = 8 \div 2$
   $x = 4$

A Shortcut

So far, we have been very formal in following the fundamental rule for solving equations. Now it is time to introduce a shortcut called "transposition." Transposing is the process of moving a term or a factor from one side of the equation to the other by changing it into its mirror image.

To transpose a term that is added or subtracted, move it to the other side of the equation and change its sign. Thus, a term with a positive sign on one side is moved to the other side and becomes negative, and vice versa. *Change sides, change signs.*

EXAMPLES:

1. $x + 5 = 10$

   Rather than thinking "subtract 5 from both sides," just transpose the 5, that is, move it from the left side to the right side and change the sign from "+" to "–":

   $x = 10 - 5$
   $x = 5$

2. $x - 5 = 10$

   Transpose the –5 by moving it to the right side of the equation and changing the sign from "+" to "–":

   $x = 10 + 5$
   $x = 15$

3. $3x = 5 + 2x$

   Transpose the + $2x$ by moving it from the right side of the equation to the left side and changing "–" to "+":

   $3x - 2x = 5$
   $x = 5$

To transpose a *factor*, move the factor to the other side of the equation and invert it (its reciprocal).

EXAMPLE:

$\frac{2x+6}{2} = 9$

In this equation, you may not transpose the 6 without first taking care of the 2, because the 6 is really 6 divided by 2. So you first transpose the 2. Instead of thinking "multiply both sides of the equation by 2," simply move the 2, which is really $\frac{1}{2}$ to the right side and invert it. The $\frac{1}{2}$ becomes 2: $2x + 6 = 9(2) = 18 \Rightarrow 2x = 18 - 6 = 12$. Finally, solve for x by transposing the 2: $x = 12(\frac{1}{2}) = 6$.

Solving Simultaneous Equations

Ordinarily, if an equation has more than one variable, it is not possible to find specific solutions for those variables. For example, the equation $x + y = 10$ does not have one, unique solution set for x and y. x and y could be 1 and 9, 5 and 5, −2 and 12, and so on.

There is a situation, however, in which it is possible to find specific values for x and y: when two equations are taken together.

EXAMPLE:

$x + y = 10$
$x - y = 6$

If we treat both of the equations as making true statements at the same time, then there is only one solution set for x and y, for there is only one pair of numbers that will satisfy both equations, $x = 8$ and $y = 2$. This technique is called "solving simultaneous equations," because both equations are taken to be true at the same time or simultaneously.

How do you find that one solution set? There are three methods: substitution, elimination, and calculator.

1. Substitution

The following are the steps for *substitution*:

1. In one of the two equations, define one variable in terms of the other.
2. Substitute that value for the defined variable in the other equation and solve.
3. Substitute your solution back into either equation to solve for the remaining variable.

EXAMPLE:

$2x + y = 13$
$x - y = 2$

1. Choose either equation. Let's take the first. Redefine either variable in terms of the other. Since we already have a single y variable (as opposed to a $2x$ variable), let's define y in terms of x: $y = 13 - 2x$.
2. Substitute $13 - 2x$ for y in the second equation: $x - (13 - 2x) = 2$. Now you have an equation with a single variable. Combine like terms and solve for x:

   $x - (13 - 2x) = 2$
   $x - 13 + 2 = 2$
   $x + 2x - 13 = 2$
   $3x - 13 = 2$
   $3x = 2 + 13$
   $3x = 15$
   $x = 15(\frac{1}{3}) = 5$

3. Solve for y by substituting 5 for x in either equation: $2x + y = 13 \Rightarrow 2(5) + y = 13 \Rightarrow 10 + y = 13 \Rightarrow y = 13 - 10 \Rightarrow y = 3$.

EXAMPLE:

$3x + 2y = 16$

$2x - y = 6$

1. Choose either equation, and define either variable in terms of the other. In this case, since you have a simple y term in the second equation, it will be easier to use the second equation. Define y in terms of x: $2x - y = 6 \Rightarrow -y = 6 - 2x \Rightarrow y = 2x - 6$.
2. Substitute this for y in the first equation and solve for x: $3x + 2(2x - 6) = 16 \Rightarrow 3x + 4x - 12 = 16 \Rightarrow 7x - 12 = 16 \Rightarrow 7x = 28 \Rightarrow x = 4$.
3. Substitute 4 for x into either equation: $2x - y = 6 \Rightarrow 2(4) - y = 6 \Rightarrow 8 - y = 6 \Rightarrow y = 2$.

2. *Elimination*

The second method for attacking simultaneous equations is *elimination*. Eliminate one of the two variables by adding or subtracting.

EXAMPLE:

$2x + y = 8$

$x - y = 1$

In this pair of simultaneous equations, you have a "$+y$" term in one equation and a "$-y$" term in the other. Since $+y$ and $-y$ added together yield zero, you can eliminate the y term by adding the two equations together. (Actually, you will be adding the left side of the second equation to the left side of the first equation and the right side of the second to the right side of the first, but it is easier to speak of the process as "adding equations.")

$2x + y = 8$

$\underline{+(x - y = 1)}$

$3x = 9$

$x = 3$

Now you can find the value of y by substituting 3 for x in either equation.

EXAMPLE:

$4x + 3y = 17$

$2x + 3y = 13$

In this pair, each equation has a $+3y$ term, which you can eliminate by subtracting the second equation from the first:

$4x + 3y = 17$

$\underline{-(2x + 3y = 13)}$

$2x = 4$

$x = 2$

Finally, you can solve for y simply by substituting 2 for x in either equation.

$4x + 3y = 17 \Rightarrow 4(2) + 3y = 17 \Rightarrow 8 + 3y = 17 \Rightarrow 3y = 9 \Rightarrow y = 3$

3. *Calculator*

The SAT, PSAT, and ACT allow calculators: a graphing calculator may be used to quickly solve simultaneous equations. There are several methods to solve equations: (1) Use a system solver program in your calculator or in each equation, (2) Solve for y in terms of x, graph both equations simultaneously, and find the point of intersection, (x, y), and (3) Use inverse matrices.

EXAMPLE:

$2x - y = 6; -y = 6 - 2x; y = \frac{(6 - 2x)}{-1}$

$3x + 2y = 16; 2y = 16 - 3x; y = \frac{(16 - 3x)}{2}$

Graph both equations; the point of intersection is found at (4, 2), $x = 4$, $y = 2$.

Solving Quadratic Equations

Equations that involve variables of the second power (e.g., x^2) are called quadratic equations. Unlike a linear equation with a single variable, which has a single solution, a quadratic may have two solutions. By convention, quadratic equations are written so that the right side of the equation is equal to zero. The general form is: $ax^2 + bx + c = 0$.

EXAMPLES

$x^2 + x - 2 = 0$

To solve a quadratic equation, factor the expression on the left side: $x^2 + x - 2 = 0 \Rightarrow (x + 2)(x - 1) = 0$.

Since $(x + 2)$ times $(x - 1)$ is equal to zero, either $(x + 2)$ or $(x - 1)$ must be equal to zero. If $x + 2$ is equal to zero, then x is equal to -2 $(-2 + 2 = 0)$, and if $x - 1$ is equal to zero, then $x = 1$ $(1 - 1 = 0)$. We conclude, therefore, that *either* x is equal to -2 or x is equal to $+1$. There are two possible values for x, so this quadratic equation has two solutions.

This last example illustrates the *Zero Product Property:* if $xy = 0$, then $x = 0$ or $y = 0$.

EXAMPLE:

$x^2 - 3x - 4 = 0$

Factor the left side of the equation: $(x + 1)(x - 4) = 0$.

Either $x + 1 = 0$, in which case $x = -1$, or $x - 4 = 0$, in which case $x = 4$. So the two solutions to this quadratic equation are -1 and $+4$.

Not every quadratic equation has two different solutions.

EXAMPLE:

$x^2 + 2x + 1 = 0$

Factor the left side of the equation: $(x + 1)(x + 1) = 0$.

Since the two factors are the same, the equation has but a single solution, -1.

If you encounter a quadratic equation that is not written in standard form, you must first rearrange its elements using the rules already studied to put it in standard form.

EXAMPLE:

$2x^2 + 12 - 3x = x^2 + 2x + 18$

To find the solution of this quadratic equation, you must first rewrite the equation, putting it in standard form:

$2x^2 + 12 - 3x = x^2 + 2x + 18 \Rightarrow (2x^2 - x^2) + (-3x - 2x) + (12 - 18) = 0 \Rightarrow x^2 - 5x - 6 = 0$

Now factor the left side: $(x - 6)(x + 1) = 0$.

So either $x - 6 = 0$, in which case $x = 6$, or $x + 1 = 0$, in which case $x = -1$. So the two solutions are 6 and -1.

Alternatively, the quadratic formula, $x = \frac{-b \pm \sqrt{b^2 - 4ac}}{2a}$, may also be used to solve quadratic equations.

EXAMPLE:

$3 - x = 2x^2 \Rightarrow 2x^2 + x - 3 = 0$

$a = 2$, $b = 1$, and $c = -3$

$$x = \frac{-b \pm \sqrt{b^2 - 4ac}}{2a} = \frac{-1 \pm \sqrt{1^2 - 4(2)(-3)}}{2(2)}$$

$$x = \frac{-1 \pm \sqrt{1 + 24}}{4} = \frac{-1 \pm 5}{4}$$

$x = 1$ or $x = -\frac{3}{2}$

The SAT, PSAT, and ACT allow calculators: a graphing calculator may be used to quickly solve quadratic equations. A quadratic formula program must be entered into your calculator.

Inequalities

An inequality is very much like an equation except, as the name implies, it is a statement that two quantities are not equal. Four different symbols are used to make statements of inequality:

- $>$ greater than
- $<$ less than
- $\geq$ greater than or equal to
- $\leq$ less than or equal to

EXAMPLES:

$5 > 1$......... 5 is greater than 1.
$2 > -2$....... 2 is greater than -2.
$x > 0$......... x is greater than zero.
$x > y$.......... x is greater than y.
$8 < 9$......... 8 is less than 9.
$-4 < -1$...... -4 is less than -1.
$x < 0$......... x is less than zero.
$y < x$......... y is less than x.
$x \geq 0$......... x is greater than or equal to zero. (x could be zero or any number larger than zero.)
$x \geq y$.......... x is greater than or equal to y. (Either x is greater than y, or x and y are equal.)
$x \leq 0$......... x is less than or equal to zero. (x could be zero or any number less than zero.)
$x \leq y$.......... x is less than or equal to y. (Either x is less than y, or x and y are equal.)

The fundamental rule for working with inequalities is similar to that for working with equalities. You can add or subtract the same value to each side of an inequality without changing the inequality, and you can multiply or divide each side of an inequality *by any positive value* without changing the inequality. To illustrate the rule, let's start with a statement of inequality that we know to be true:

EXAMPLES:

1. $5 > 2$

   You can add any value to both sides without changing this statement:

   $5 + 25 > 2 + 25$
   $30 > 27$

   You can subtract any value from both sides without changing this statement:

   $30 - 6 > 27 - 6$
   $24 > 21$

   You can multiply both sides of the inequality by the same *positive* number:

   $24(2) > 21(2)$
   $48 > 42$

   And you can divide both sides of the inequality by the same *positive* number:

   $48 \div 6 > 42 \div 6$
   $8 > 7$

   If you should multiply or divide by a *negative* number, however, you will change the direction of the inequality:

2. $4 > 3$
   $4(-2) > 3(-2)$ X
   $-8 > -6$ X

   You can multiply or divide by a negative number, so long as you remember to change the direction of the inequality.

   $4 > 3$
   $4(-2) < 3(-2)$
   $-8 < -6$

EXERCISE 10

Equations and Inequalities

DIRECTIONS: Choose the best answer to each of the following questions. Answers are on page B-125.

1. If $3x = 12$, then $x =$

(A) 2 (B) 3 (C) 4 (D) 6 (E) 10

2. If $2x + x = 9$, then $x =$

(A) 0 (B) 1 (C) 3 (D) 6 (E) 9

3. If $7x - 5x = 12 - 8$, then $x =$

(A) 0 (B) 1 (C) 2 (D) 3 (E) 4

4. If $3x + 2x = 15$, then $x =$

(A) 2 (B) 3 (C) 5 (D) 6 (E) 9

5. If $a - 8 = 10 - 2a$, then $a =$

(A) –2 (B) 0 (C) 2 (D) 4 (E) 6

6. If $p - 11 - 2p = 13 - 5p$, then $p =$

(A) –4 (B) –1 (C) 1 (D) 2 (E) 6

7. If $12x + 3 - 4x - 3 = 8$, then $x =$

(A) –5 (B) –1 (C) 0 (D) 1 (E) 5

8. If $5x - 2 + 3x - 4 = 2x - 8 + x + 2$, then $x =$

(A) –5 (B) 0 (C) 1 (D) 3 (E) 6

9. If $a + 2b - 3 + 3a = 2a + b + 3 + b$, then a

(A) –1 (B) 0 (C) 2 (D) 3 (E) 6

10. If $4y + 10 = 5 + 7y + 5$, then $y =$

(A) –2 (B) –1 (C) 0 (D) 4 (E) 8

11. If $-4 - x = 12 + x$, then $x =$

(A) –8 (B) –2 (C) 1 (D) 2 (E) 4

12. If $\frac{1}{2}x + x = 3$, then $x =$

(A) $\frac{1}{2}$ (B) $\frac{2}{3}$ (C) 1 (D) 2 (E) 3

13. If $\frac{2}{3}x + \frac{1}{4}x + 4 = \frac{1}{6}x + 10$, then $x =$

(A) $\frac{11}{12}$ (B) $\frac{3}{2}$ (C) 5 (D) 8 (E) 20

14. If $\frac{a}{2} - \frac{a}{4} = 1$, then $a =$

(A) $\frac{1}{2}$ (B) $\frac{2}{3}$ (C) 1 (D) 2 (E) 4

15. If $\frac{1}{p} + \frac{2}{p} + \frac{3}{p} = 1$, then $p =$

(A) $\frac{2}{3}$ (B) $\frac{3}{4}$ (C) 1 (D) 2 (E) 6

16. If $\frac{2x - 6}{3} = 8$, then $x =$

(A) 1 (B) 3 (C) 6 (D) 15 (E) 18

17. If $\frac{5 - x}{5} = 1$, then $x =$

(A) –5 (B) –1 (C) 0 (D) 1 (E) 5

18. If $\frac{2 - x}{10} = 1$, then $x =$

(A) –8 (B) –1 (C) $-\frac{1}{5}$ (D) 1 (E) 5

19. If $\frac{5}{x + 1} + 2 = 5$, then $x =$

(A) $-\frac{2}{7}$ (B) $\frac{2}{3}$ (C) $\frac{7}{2}$ (D) 7 (E) 10

20. If $\frac{x}{2} + \frac{x}{3} = \frac{1}{2} + \frac{1}{3}$, then $x =$

(A) $\frac{1}{3}$ (B) $\frac{2}{3}$ (C) 1 (D) 2 (E) 3

21. If $3x + y = 10$ and $x + y = 6$, then $x =$

(A) 1 (B) 2 (C) 3 (D) 4 (E) 5

22. If $2x + y = 10$ and $x + y = 7$, then $y =$

(A) 3 (B) 4 (C) 5 (D) 6 (E) 9

23. If $x + 3y = 5$ and $2x - y = 3$, then $x =$

(A) 2 (B) 4 (C) 5 (D) 6 (E) 9

24. If $x + y = 2$ and $x - y = 2$, then $y =$

(A) –2 (B) –1 (C) 0 (D) 1 (E) 2

25. If $a + b = 5$ and $2a + 3b = 12$, then $b =$

(A) 1 (B) 2 (C) 3 (D) 4 (E) 6

26. If $5x + 3y = 13$ and $2x = 4$, then $y =$

(A) 1 (B) 2 (C) 3 (D) 4 (E) 5

27. If $K - n = 5$, and $2K + n = 16$, then $K =$

(A) –3 (B) 0 (C) 1 (D) 5 (E) 7

28. If $T = K - 5$ and $K + T = 11$, then $K =$

(A) 2 (B) 3 (C) 8 (D) 11 (E) 14

29. If $a + 5b = 9$ and $a - b = 3$, then $a =$

(A) 1 (B) 4 (C) 5 (D) 7 (E) 11

30. If $8 + x = y$ and $2y + x = 28$, then $x =$

(A) 2 (B) 4 (C) 6 (D) 12 (E) 18

31. If $\frac{x+y}{2} = 4$ and $x - y = 4$, then $x =$

(A) 1 (B) 2 (C) 4 (D) 6 (E) 8

32. If $\frac{x+y}{2} = 7$ and $\frac{x-y}{3} = 2$, then $x =$

(A) 2 (B) 4 (C) 8 (D) 10 (E) 14

33. If $x + y + z = 10$ and $x - y - z = 4$, then $x =$

(A) 2 (B) 3 (C) 6 (D) 7 (E) 12

34. If $x + 2y - z = 4$ and $2x - 2y + z = 8$, then $x =$

(A) –2 (B) 0 (C) 4 (D) 6 (E) 8

35. If $x + y + z = 6$, $x + y - z = 4$, and $x - y = 3$, then $x =$

(A) –2 (B) 0 (C) 4 (D) 6 (E) 8

36. If $x^2 - 3x + 2 = 0$, then $x =$

(A) –2 or 1 (B) 2 or 1 (C) –1 or 2
(D) –1 or 4 (E) 2 or 4

37. If $x^2 - 3x - 4 = 0$, then $x =$

(A) –4 or 1 (B) –2 or 2 (C) –1 or 2
(D) 4 or –1 (E) 6 or –1

38. If $x^2 + 5x + 6 = 0$, then $x =$

(A) –3 or –2 (B) –3 or 2 (C) –1 or 6
(D) 1 or –6 (E) 6 or –2

39. If $x^2 + 3x + 2 = 0$, then $x =$

(A) –2 or –1 (B) –1 or 2 (C) 1 or 2
(D) 2 or 3 (E) 3 or 5

40. If $x^2 + 3x + 2 = 0$, then which of the following are possible values of x?

I. 1
II. –1
III –2

(A) I only (B) II only (C) III only
(D) I and II only (E) II and III only

41. If $x^2 + 5x = -4$, then $x =$

(A) –1 or –4 (B) –1 or –2 (C) 1 or 2
(D) 1 or 4 (E) 2 or 6

42. If $x^2 - 8 = 7x$, then $x =$

(A) –8 and –1 (B) –4 and 1 (C) –1 and 8
(D) 1 and 4 (E) 1 and 8

43. If $k^2 - 10 = -3k$, then $k =$

(A) –10 and –1 (B) –10 and 1 (C) –5 and 3
(D) –3 and 5 (E) 2 and –5

44. If $x^2 = 12 - x$, then $x =$

(A) –4 and –3 (B) –4 and 3 (C) –3 and 4
(D) –2 and 6 (E) 1 and 6

45. If $x^2 = 6x - 8$, then $x =$

(A) –8 and –2 (B) –4 and –2 (C) –2 and 2
(D) 2 and 4 (E) 2 and 8

46. If $(x - 8)(x + 2) = 0$, then $x =$

(A) –8 or –2 (B) –4 or –2 (C) 4 or –2
(D) 8 or –2 (E) 10 or –5

47. If $9 - 3(6 - x) = 12$, then $x =$

(A) 4 or –2 (B) 7 or –2 (C) 4 (D) 6 (E) 7

48. If $\frac{1}{4}(x + 5) = 17$, then $x =$

(A) 13 or 25 (B) 54 (C) 63
(D) 75 or –24 (E) 124

49. If $\frac{1}{2}(x) - \frac{1}{3}(x - 2) = 0.4$, then $x =$

(A) –1 or 1.4 (B) –1.6 (C) 2 or –1.6
(D) 2.4 (E) 2.6

50. If $0.02x + 1.44 = x - 16.2$, then $x =$

(A) 18 (B) 16 (C) 14 (D) 12 (E) 10

51. If $3 - 2(x - 5) = 3x + 4$, then $x =$

(A) $\frac{1}{2}$ or $\frac{1}{4}$ (B) $-\frac{9}{5}$ (C) $\frac{9}{5}$ (D) 1 or 3 (E) 5

52. If $x^2 - 9x = 22$, then $x =$

(A) –11 or 2 (B) 3 (C) 2 or 3
(D) 11 or –2 (E) 11

53. If $(x + 8)(x + 1) = 78$, then $x^2 + 9x =$

(A) 50 (B) 55 (C) 60 (D) 65 (E) 70

54. If $2x + 3y = 12$ and $x = -6$, then $y =$

(A) 2 (B) 4 (C) 8 (D) 10 (E) 12

55. At what point does the line $5x + 2y = 20$ intersect the x-axis? (Hint: What must the y-coordinate be?)

(A) (–4,0) (B) (–2,0) (C) (0,0)
(D) (4,0) (E) (4,2)

56. If $3x + 5y = 10$, then $y =$

(A) $-0.6x - 2$ (B) $-0.4x + 2$ (C) $0.5x - 4$
(D) $0.6x - 2$ (E) $-0.6x + 2$

57. If $x = ay + 3$, $y =$

(A) $\frac{x-2}{4a}$ (B) $\frac{x-3}{a}$ (C) $\frac{a}{x-3}$ (D) $\frac{x+a}{3}$ (E) $\frac{a}{3x}$

58. If $8x + 16 = (x + 2)(x + 5)$, then $x =$

(A) 3 or -2 (B) -3 (C) -2 (D) 2 or 3 (E) 3

59. If $\frac{x+5}{0.2} = 0.3x$, then $x =$

(A) $-\frac{125}{23}$ (B) -76 (C) $-\frac{250}{47}$ (D) $\frac{47}{250}$ (E) $\frac{250}{47}$

60. If $\frac{0.2+x}{3} = \frac{\frac{5}{6}}{4}$, then $x =$

(A) $-\frac{40}{17}$ (B) $-\frac{17}{40}$ (C) 0 (D) $\frac{17}{40}$ (E) $\frac{40}{17}$

61. If x is an integer and $6 < x < 8$, then what is the value of x?

(A) 4 (B) 5 (C) 7 (D) 9 (E) 10

62. If x is an integer and $5 \le x \le 7$, which of the following are possible values of x?

I. 5
II. 6
III. 7

(A) II only (B) I and II only (C) I and III only
(D) II and III only (E) I, II, and III

63. If x and y are integers such that $2 < x < 4$ and $8 > y > 6$, then what is the value of xy?

(A) 12 (B) 16 (C) 21 (D) 24 (E) 32

64. If x and y are integers, $5 > x \ge 2$, and $6 < y \le 9$, then what is the *minimum* value of xy?

(A) 14 (B) 18 (C) 20 (D) 45 (E) 54

65. If $1 \le x \le 3$, then which of the following are possible values of x?

I. $\frac{5}{2}$
II. $\frac{7}{2}$
III. $\frac{3}{2}$

(A) I only (B) II only (C) I and II only
(D) I and III only (E) I, II, and III

Geometry

If you have ever taken a basic course in geometry, you probably remember having to memorize theorems and do formal proofs. Fortunately, you won't be asked to do any formal proofs on the exam, and the formulas you need to know are fairly few in number and relatively simple.

Most often, test questions involve things like finding the measure of an angle, the length of a line, or the area of a figure.

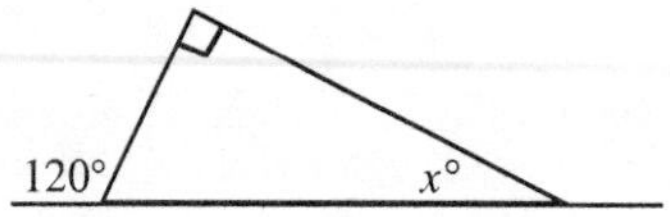

EXAMPLE:

In the figure above, $x =$

(A) 15 (B) 30 (C) 45 (D) 60 (E) 90

The answer is (B). The unmarked angle plus the 120° angle form a straight line, so their sum must be 180°:

120 + unmarked angle = 180
unmarked angle = 180 – 120
unmarked angle = 60

Then, since the unmarked angle is contained in a triangle:

$90 + 60 + x = 180$
$150 + x = 180$
$x = 180 - 150$
$x = 30$

This is a fairly easy test question, but it does illustrate the kind of principles you need to know.

In this section, we cover some of the most important concepts of geometry.

Line and Angles

For purposes of our discussion (and for test–taking purposes), the word ***line*** means a straight line:

The line above is designated line l. The portion of line l from point P to point Q is called "line segment PQ."

When two lines intersect, they form an ***angle***, and their point of intersection is called the ***vertex*** of that angle.

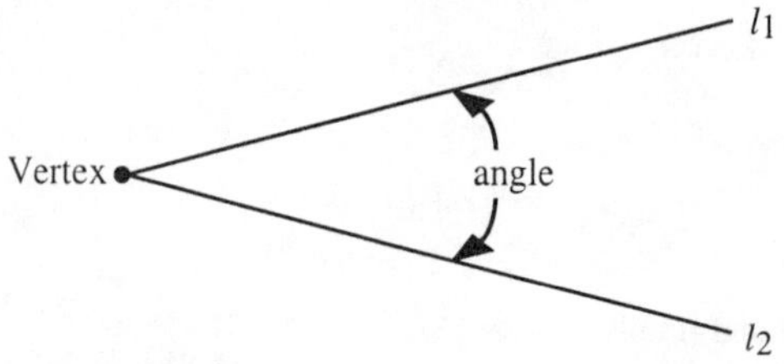

The size of an angle is measured in ***degrees***. Degrees are defined by reference to a circle. By convention, a circle is divided into 360 equal parts, or degrees.

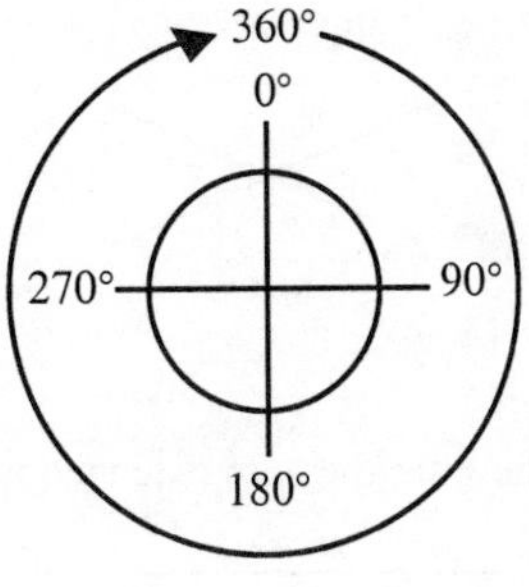

A 90° angle is also called a ***right angle***. A right angle is often indicated in the following way:

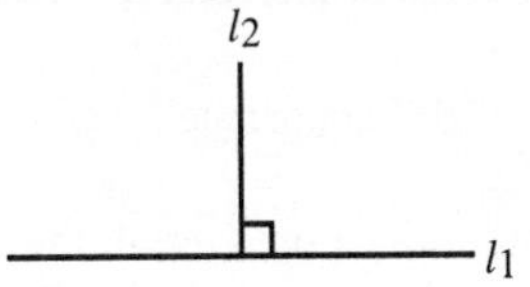

Two right angles form a straight line:

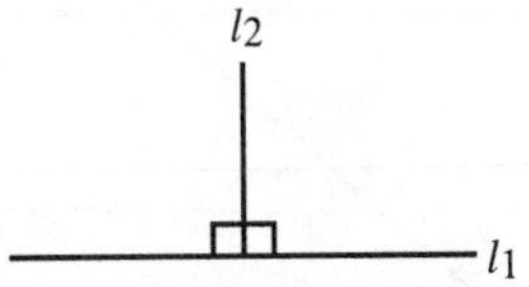

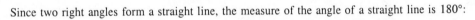

Since two right angles form a straight line, the measure of the angle of a straight line is 180°:

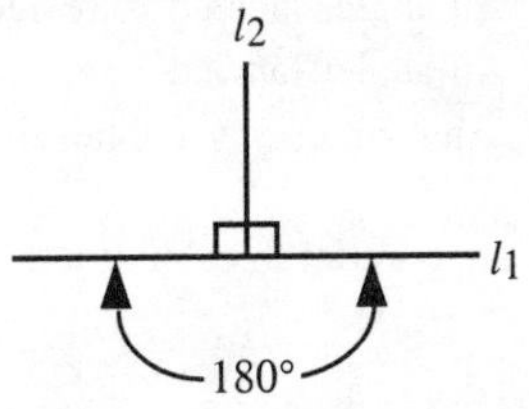

An angle that is less than 90° is called an ***acute angle***:

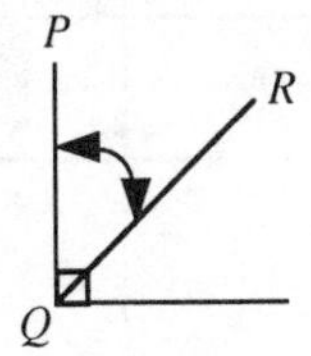

In the figure above, angle *PQR* is an acute angle.

An angle that is greater than 90° but less than 180° is called an ***obtuse angle***:

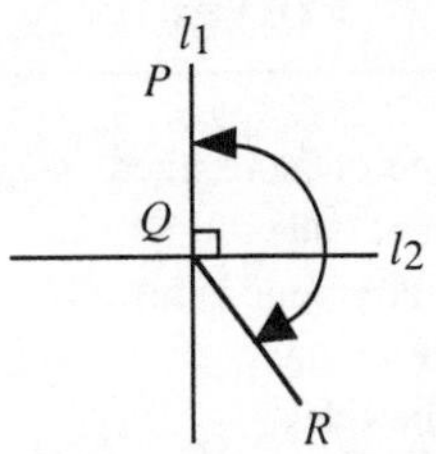

In the figure above, angle *PQR* is an obtuse angle.

When two lines intersect, the opposite (or vertical) angles created by their intersection are equal:

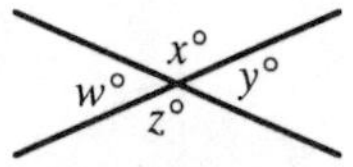

$w = y$
$x = z$

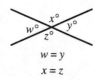

Two lines that do not intersect regardless of how far they are extended are parallel to each other:

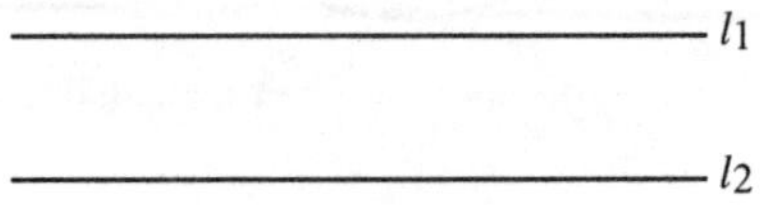

In the figure above, the symbol || indicates that l_1 and l_2 are parallel, *e.g.*, $l_1 \parallel l_2$.

When parallel lines are intersected by a third line, a transversal, the following angle relationships are created:

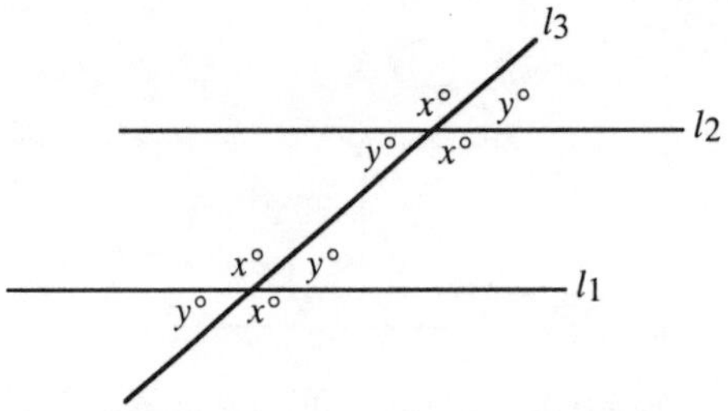

All angles labeled x are equal.
All angles labeled y are equal.
Any x plus any y totals 180.

Two lines that are perpendicular to the same line are parallel to each other:

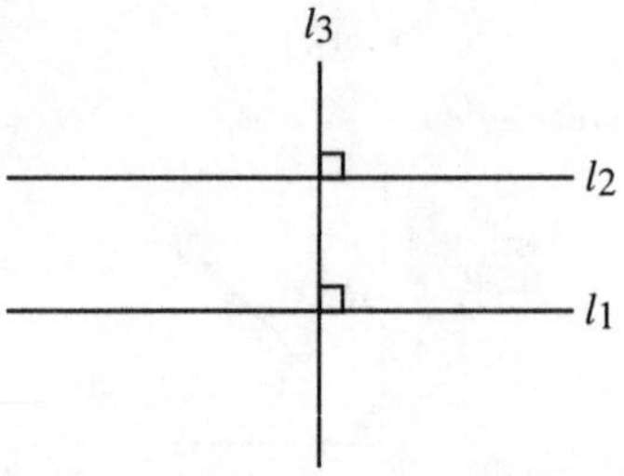

Since l_1 and l_2 are both perpendicular to l_3, we can conclude that l_1 and l_2 are parallel to each other.

Polygons

- A ***polygon*** is a closed figure created by three or more lines.
- A ***triangle*** is any polygon with exactly three sides.
- A ***quadrilateral*** is any polygon with exactly four sides.
- A ***pentagon*** is any polygon with exactly five sides.
- A ***hexagon*** is any polygon with exactly six sides.

A polygon with more than six sides is usually referred to just as a polygon with a certain number of sides; for example, a polygon with ten sides is called a ten–sided polygon.

Every polygon has both a ***perimeter*** (the sum of the lengths of all of its sides) and an area. A regular polygon is a polygon with equal sides and equal angles (e.g., a square).

The sum of the measures of the exterior angles of a polygon is 360°. The sum of the measures of interior angles of a polygon can be expressed as $180°(n - 2)$.

Triangles

A ***triangle*** is a three–sided figure. Within a given triangle, the larger the angle, the longer the opposite side; and, conversely, the longer the side, the larger the opposite angle.

EXAMPLES:

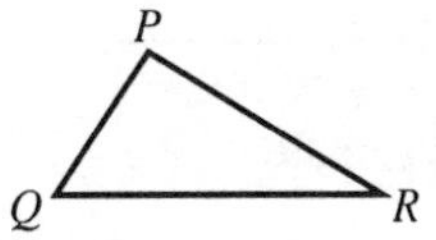

1. Since angle $P >$ angle $Q >$ angle R, $QR > PR > PQ$.

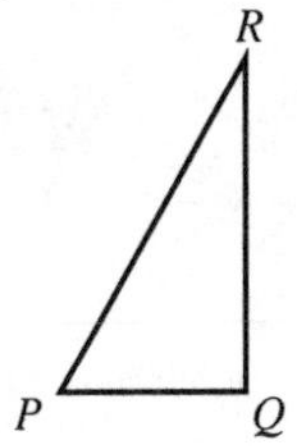

2. Since $PR > QR > PQ$, angle $Q >$ angle $P >$ angle R.

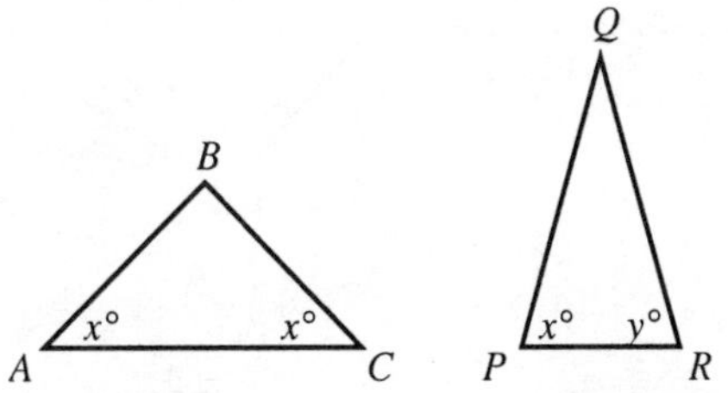

$AB = BC$ $\quad$ $PQ = QR \Rightarrow x = y$

Within a given triangle, if two sides are equal their opposite angles are equal, and vice versa:

A triangle with exactly two equal sides is called an ***isosceles*** triangle. A triangle with exactly three equal sides is called an ***equilateral*** triangle.

EXAMPLE:

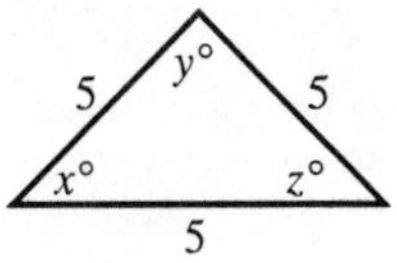

Since the equilateral triangle has three equal sides, all angles are also equal: $x = y = z$. Since all angles are equal in an equilateral triangle, each angle is 60°.

A triangle with a right angle is called a ***right triangle***. The longest side of the right triangle, which is opposite the 90° angle, is called the ***hypotenuse***.

The sides of every right triangle fit a special relationship called the ***Pythagorean Theorem***: The square of the hypotenuse is equal to the sum of the squares of the other two sides. This is easier to understand when it is summarized in a formula:

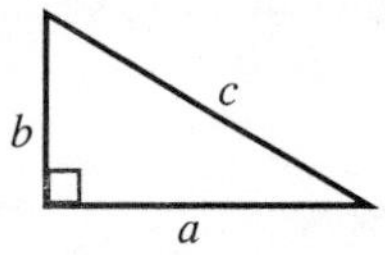

In the right triangle above, $c^2 = a^2 + b^2$.

The ***perimeter*** of a triangle is the sum of the lengths of the three sides:

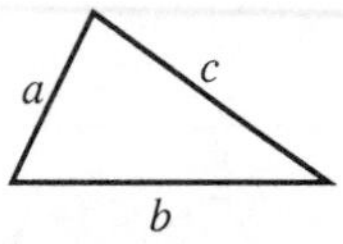

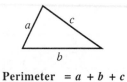

Perimeter $= a + b + c$

The ***altitude*** of a triangle is a line drawn from a vertex perpendicular to the opposite side:

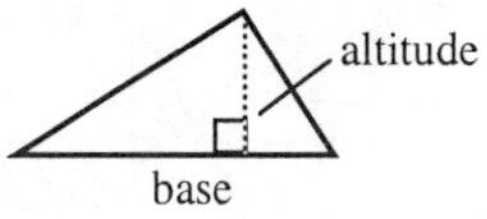

The formula for finding the ***area*** of a triangle is $\frac{1}{2}$ times the altitude times the base: $\frac{1}{2}(a)(b)$, or ***area*** $= A = \frac{ab}{2}$.

EXAMPLE:

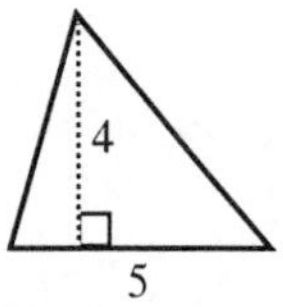

The area of the triangle above is $\frac{1}{2}(4)(5) = 10$.

Two right triangles deserve special mention. First, in a triangle with angles of 45°–45°–90°, the length of the hypotenuse is equal to the length of either side multiplied by the square root of two:

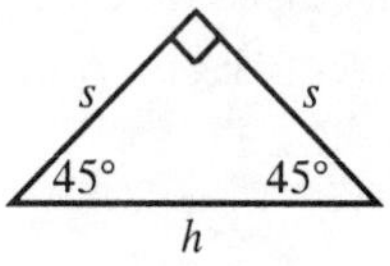

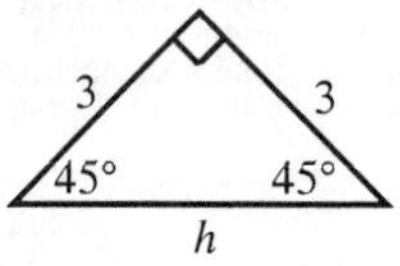

$h = s \cdot \sqrt{2}$ $\quad$ $h = 3 \cdot \sqrt{2} = 3\sqrt{2}$

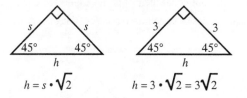

Conversely, in a ***45°–45°–90° triangle***, the length of each of the two sides is equal to one–half the length of the hypotenuse multiplied by the square root of two.

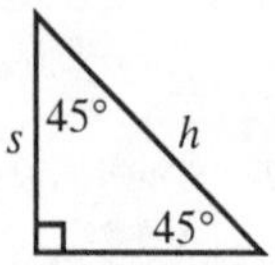

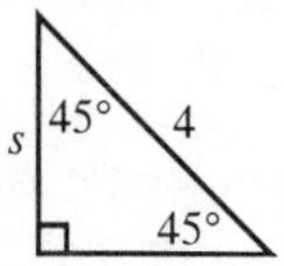

$s = \frac{1}{2} \cdot h \cdot \sqrt{2}$ $\quad$ $s = \frac{1}{2} \cdot 4 \cdot \sqrt{2} = 2\sqrt{2}$

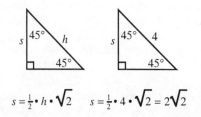

In a ***30°–60°–90° triangle***, the length of the side opposite the 30° angle is equal to one–half the length of the hypotenuse and the length of the side opposite the 60° angle is equal to one–half the length of the hypotenuse multiplied by $\sqrt{3}$

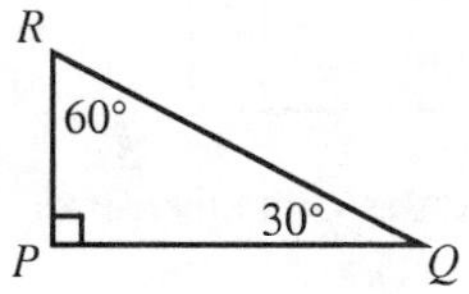

$PR = \frac{1}{2}QR$

$PQ = \frac{1}{2}QR \cdot \sqrt{3} = \frac{\sqrt{3}}{2}QR$

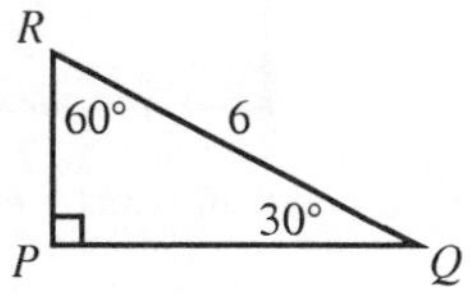

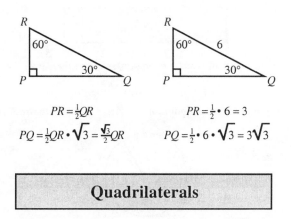

$PR = \frac{1}{2} \cdot 6 = 3$

$PQ = \frac{1}{2} \cdot 6 \cdot \sqrt{3} = 3\sqrt{3}$

Quadrilaterals

A ***quadrilateral*** is a closed, four-sided figure in two dimensions. Common quadrilaterals are the parallelogram, rectangle, and square. The sum of the four angles of a quadrilateral is 360°.

A ***parallelogram*** is a quadrilateral in which both pairs of opposite sides are parallel.

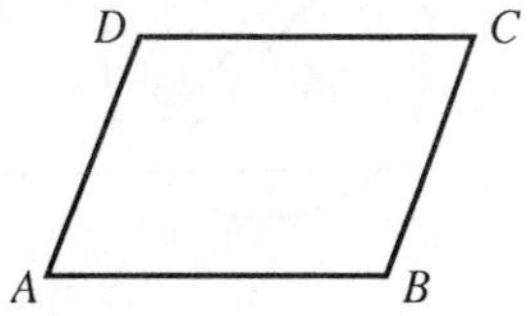

Opposite sides of a parallelogram are also equal. Similarly, opposite angles of a parallelogram are also equal.

A ***rectangle*** is any four–sided figure that has four right angles. Since the opposite sides of a rectangle are equal, it is customary to speak of the *two* dimensions of a rectangle, width and length:

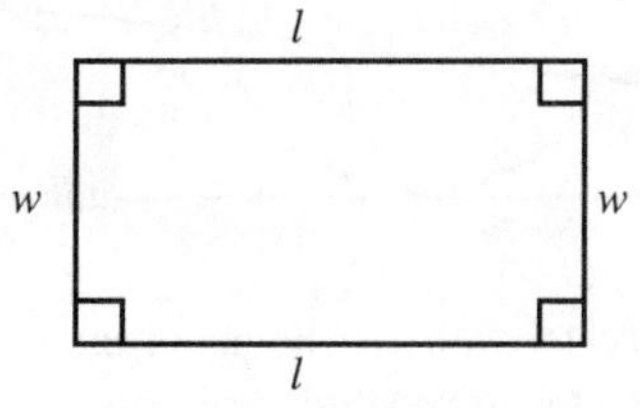

A ***square*** is a rectangle with four equal sides:

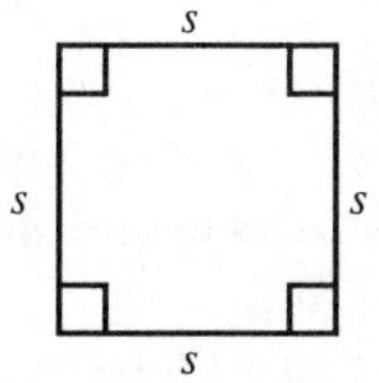

To find the perimeter of either a rectangle or a square, simply add the lengths of the four sides. To find the area of a rectangle, multiply the width times the length. In a square, the sides are all equal, so there is no difference between length and width. So to find the area of a square, just multiply: side • side.

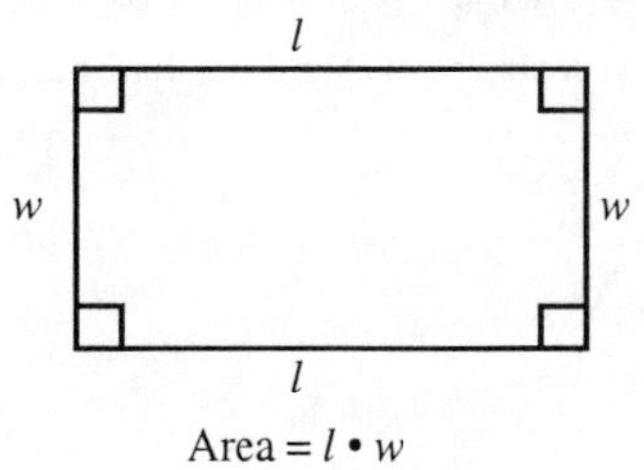

Area = $l \cdot w$

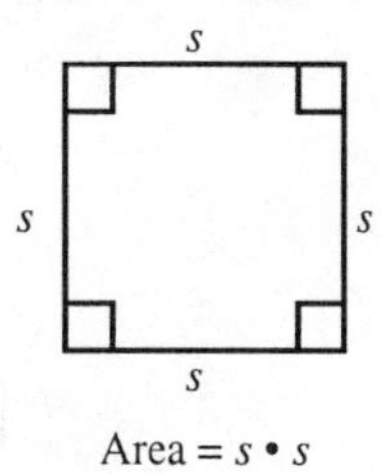

Area = $s \cdot s$

Circles

A ***circle*** is a closed plane curve, all points of which are equidistant from the center. A complete circle contains 360° and a semicircle contains 180°.

The distance from the center of the circle to any point on the circle is called the ***radius***:

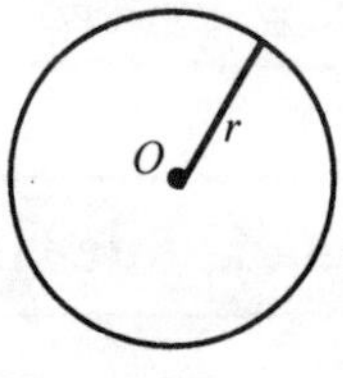

A line segment with end points on the circle which passes through the center of the circle is called the ***diameter***:

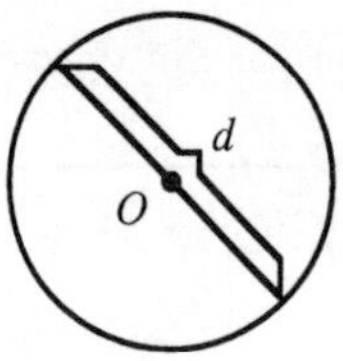

The diameter of a circle is twice the radius.

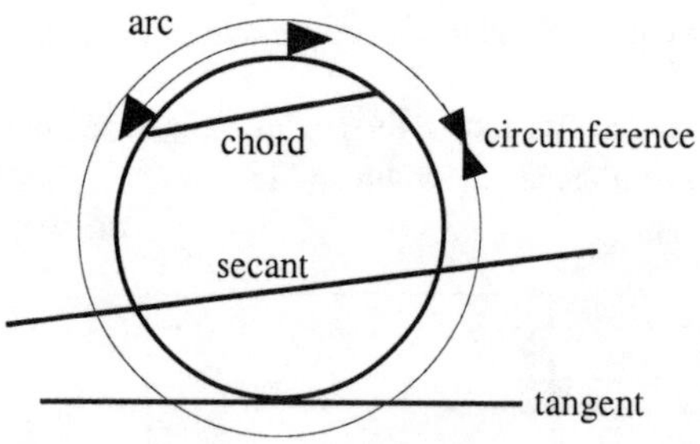

A ***chord*** is a line segment connecting the center with any point on the circle. A ***secant*** is a chord extended in either one or both directions. A ***tangent*** is a line touching a circle at one and only one point. The ***circumference***, or perimeter, is the curved line bounding the circle. An ***arc*** of a circle is any part of the circumference.

The formula for calculating the ***circumference*** of a circle is 2 times π times the radius: ***circumference*** $= C = 2\pi r$. The formula for calculating the *area* of a circle is π times the radius squared: ***area*** $= A = \pi r^2$. π (pi) is approximately equal to $\frac{22}{7}$, or 3.14

A ***central angle***, as $\angle AOB$ in the next figure, is an angle whose vertex is the center of the circle and whose sides are radii. A central angle is equal to, or has the same number of degrees as, its intercepted arc.

An ***inscribed angle***, as $\angle MNP$, is an angle whose vertex is on the circle and whose sides are chords. An inscribed angle has half the number of degrees of its intercepted arc. $\angle MNP$ intercepts arc MP and has half the degrees of arc MP.

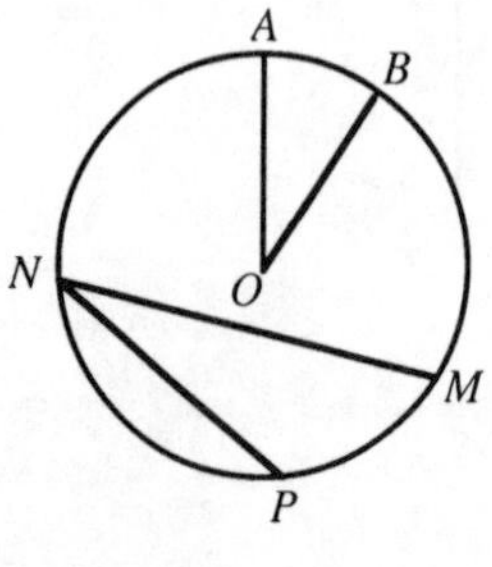

Solids

In a three-dimensional figure, the total space contained within the figure is called the *volume*; it is expressed in *cubic denominations* (*e.g.*, cm^3). The total outside surface is called the *surface area;* it is expressed in *square denominations* (*e.g.*, cm^2). In computing volume and surface area, all dimensions must be expressed in the same denomination.

A ***rectangular solid*** is a figure of three dimensions having six rectangular faces meeting each other at right angles. The three dimensions are length, width, and height.

To find the ***volume of a rectangular solid***, simply multiply the three dimensions: ***Volume*** $= V = w \bullet l \bullet h$.

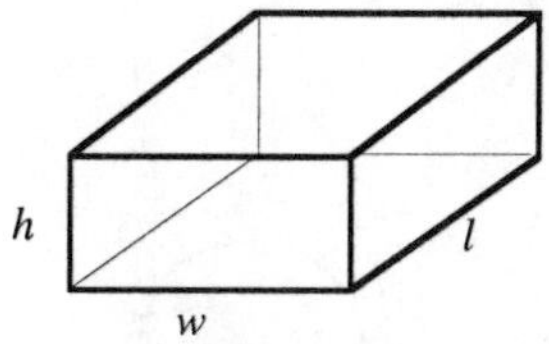

Volume = $w \bullet l \bullet h$

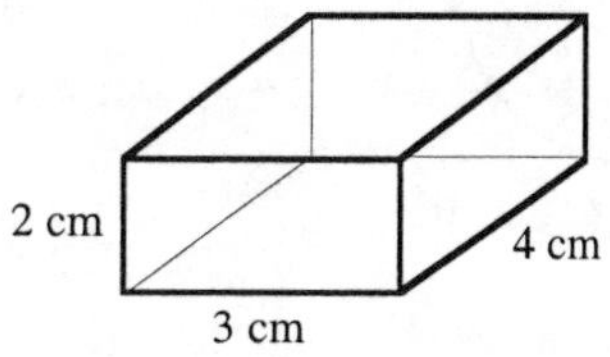

Volume = 3 cm • 4 cm • 2 cm = 24 cm^3

A ***cube*** is a rectangular solid whose edges are equal. The figure below is a cube; the length, width, and height are all equal to "*e.*"

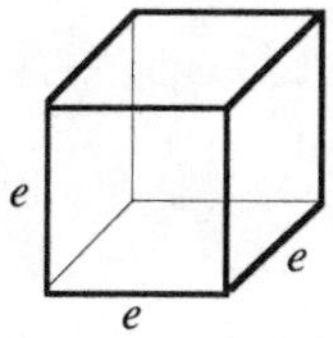

The ***volume of a cube*** is equal to the side cubed: ***volume*** $= V = e^3$. The ***surface area of a cube*** is equal to the area of any side multiplied by 6: ***surface area*** $= SA = 6e^2$.

The ***volume of a circular cylinder*** is equal to the product of π, the radius squared, and the height.

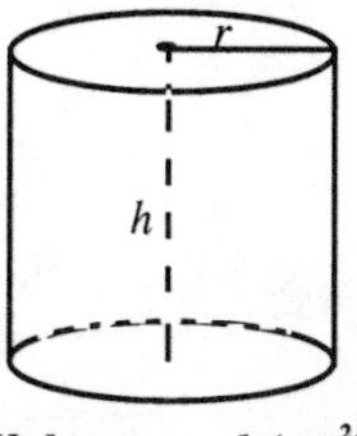

Volume $= h(\pi r^2)$

The ***volume of a sphere*** is four-thirds times π times the radius cubed.

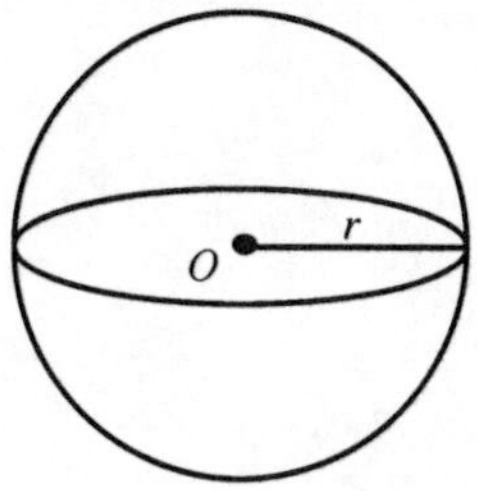

Volume $= \frac{4}{3}(\pi r^3)$

EXERCISE **11**

Geometry

DIRECTIONS: Choose the best answer to each of the following questions. Answers are on page B-126.

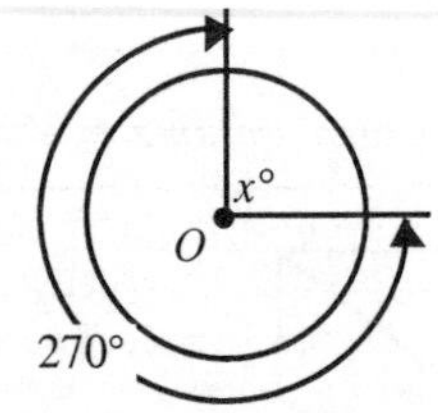

O is the center of the circle.

1. In the figure above, $x =$

   (A) 30 (B) 60 (C) 90 (D) 120 (E) 270

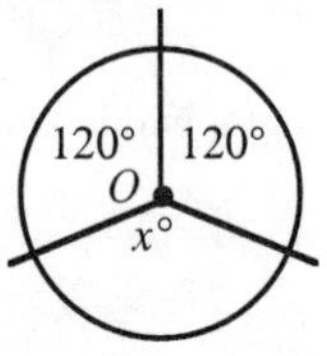

O is the center of the circle.

2. In the figure above, $x =$

   (A) 45 (B) 60 (C) 90 (D) 120 (E) 150

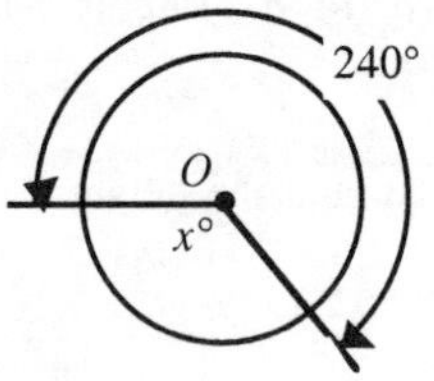

O is the center of the circle.

3. In the figure above, $x =$

   (A) 60 (B) 90 (C) 120 (D) 150 (E) 180

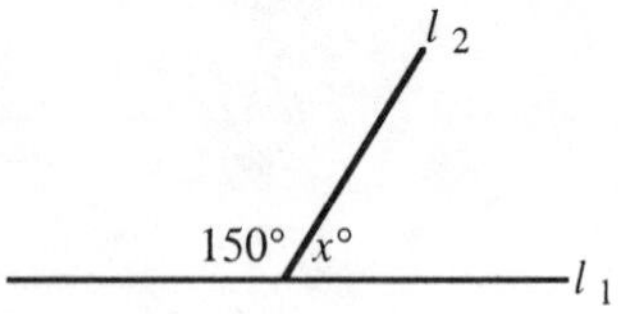

4. In the figure above, $x =$

   (A) 15 (B) 30 (C) 45 (D) 90 (E) 120

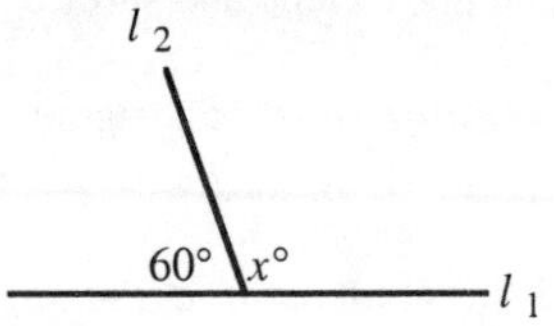

5. In the figure above, $x =$

   (A) 15 (B) 30 (C) 45 (D) 90 (E) 120

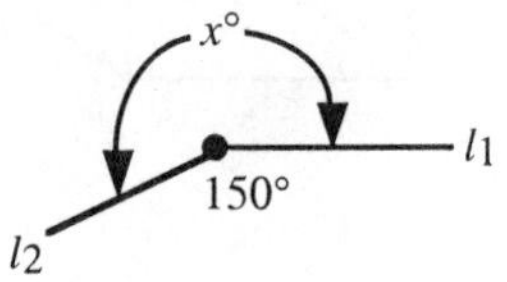

6. In the figure above, $x =$

   (A) 210 (B) 180 (C) 150 (D) 135 (E) 120

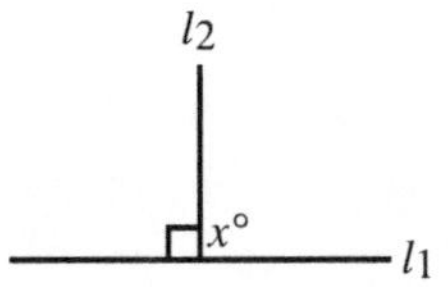

7. In the figure above, $x =$

   (A) 15 (B) 30 (C) 45 (D) 60 (E) 90

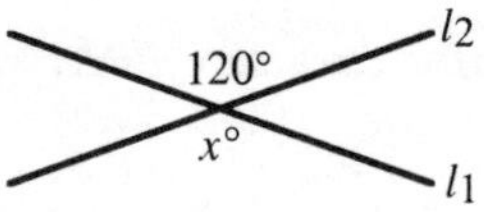

8. In the figure above, $x =$

   (A) 15 (B) 30 (C) 45 (D) 60 (E) 90

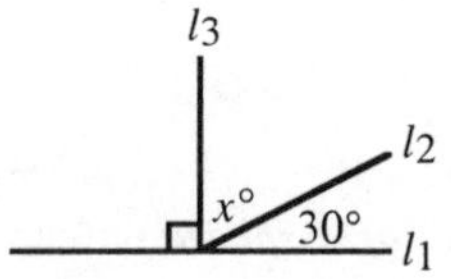

9. In the figure above, $x =$

   (A) 45 (B) 60 (C) 75 (D) 90 (E) 120

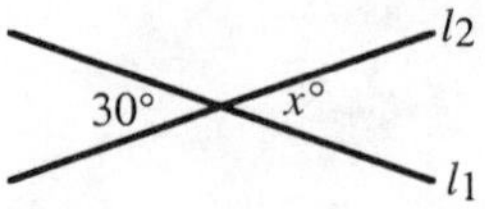

10. In the figure above, $x =$

    (A) 30 (B) 45 (C) 55 (D) 65 (E) 80

Questions 11 through 15 are based on the following figure.

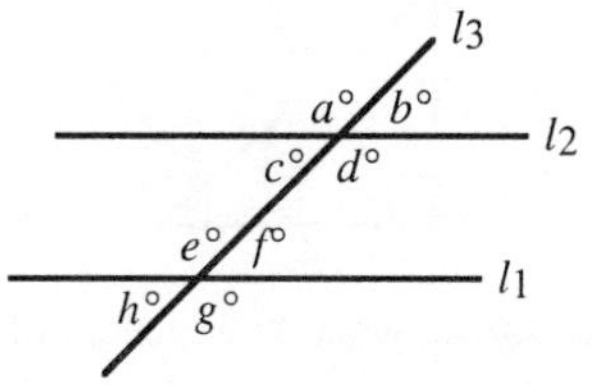

$l_1 \parallel l_2$

11. Which of the following is (are) necessarily true?
    I. $a = b$
    II. $b = c$
    III. $g = h$

    (A) I only (B) II only (C) I and II only
    (D) II and III only (E) I, II, and III

12. Which of the following is (are) necessarily true?
    I. $b = c$
    II. $d = c$
    III. $g = e$

    (A) I only (B) III only (C) I and III only
    (D) II and III only (E) I, II, and III

13. Which of the following is (are) necessarily true?
    I. $c + d = 180$
    II. $c + a = 180$
    III. $b + g = 180$

    (A) I only (B) III only (C) I and III only
    (D) II and III only (E) I, II, and III

14. If $e = 120$, then $g =$

    (A) 60 (B) 90 (C) 120 (D) 150 (E) 180

15. If $d = 60$, then $h =$

    (A) 60 (B) 90 (C) 120 (D) 150 (E) 180

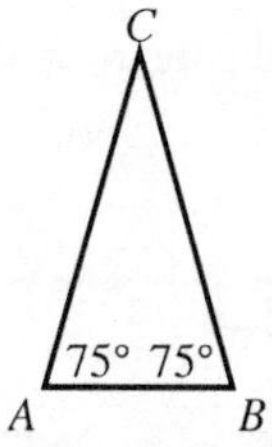

16. Which of the following is (are) true of the figure above?
    I. $AB = BC$
    II. $BC = AC$
    III. $AC = AB$

    (A) I only (B) II only (C) I and II only
    (D) I and III only (E) I, II, and III

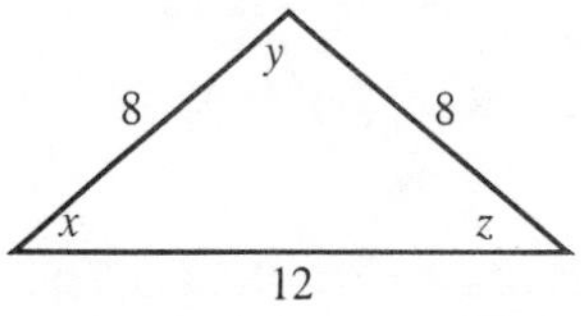

17. Which of the following is (are) true of the figure above?
    I. $x = y$
    II. $y = z$
    III. $x = z$

    (A) I only (B) II only (C) III only
    (D) I and II only (E) I, II, and III

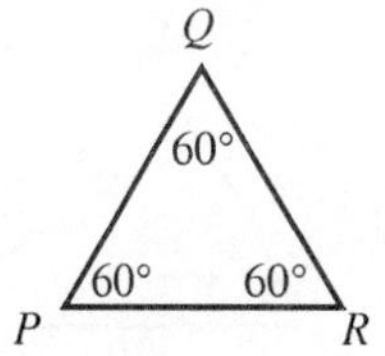

18. Which of the following is (are) true of the figure above?
    I. $PQ = QR$
    II. $QR = PR$
    III. $PR = PQ$

    (A) I only (B) III only (C) I and II only
    (D) II and III only (E) I, II, and III

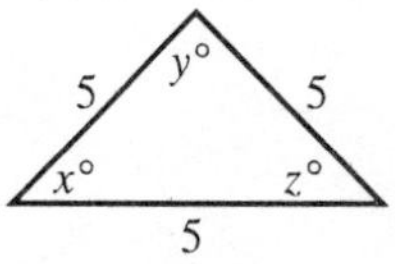

19. Which of the following is (are) true of the figure above?
    I. $x = y$
    II. $y = z$
    III. $z = x$

    (A) I only (B) I and II only (C) I and III only
    (D) II and III only (E) I, II, and III

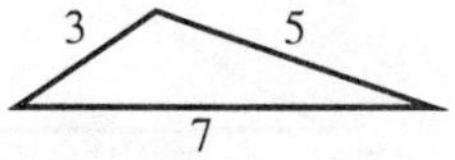

20. What is the perimeter of the triangle above?

    (A) 3 (B) 5 (C) 15 (D) 20 (E) 30

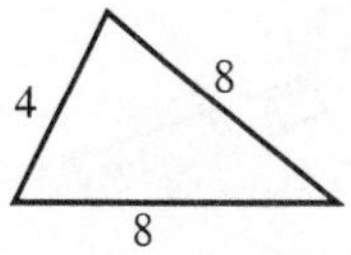

21. What is the perimeter of the triangle above?

    (A) 20 (B) 18 (C) 12 (D) 10 (E) 8

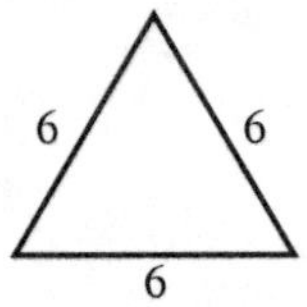

22. What is the perimeter of the triangle above?
(A) 6 (B) 12 (C) 18 (D) 21 (E) 24

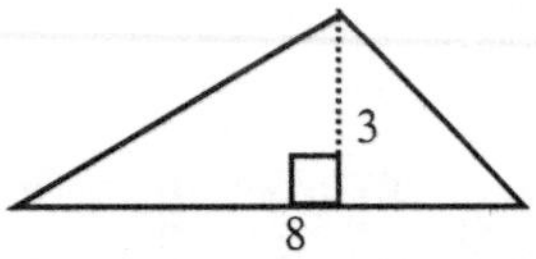

23. What is the area of the triangle above?
(A) 3 (B) 6 (C) 12 (D) 18 (E) 24

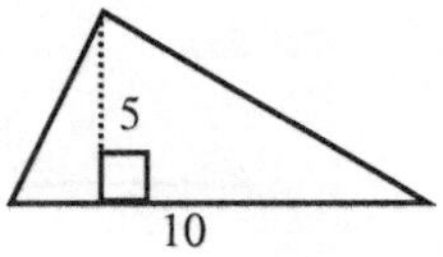

24. What is the area of the triangle above?
(A) 5 (B) 10 (C) 12 (D) 15 (E) 25

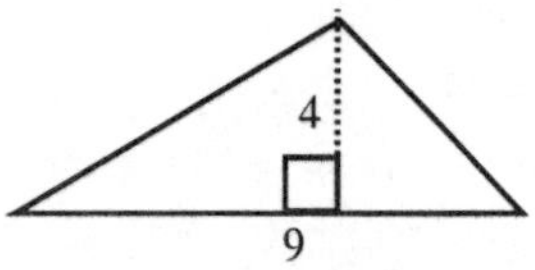

25. What is the area of the triangle above?
(A) 6 (B) 12 (C) 15 (D) 18 (E) 24

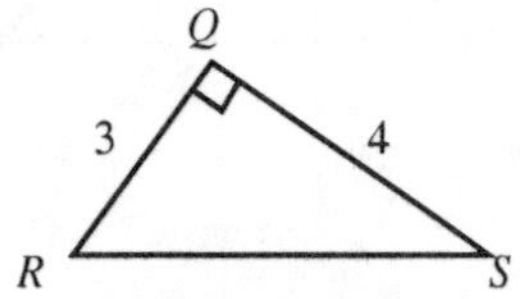

26. In the figure above, what is the length of *RS*?
(A) 3 (B) 5 (C) 8 (D) 12 (E) 16

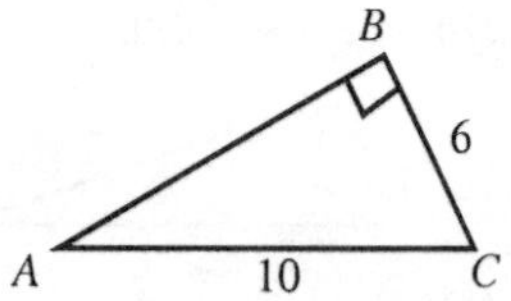

27. In the figure above, what is the length of *AB*?
(A) 4 (B) 8 (C) 12 (D) 16 (E) 24

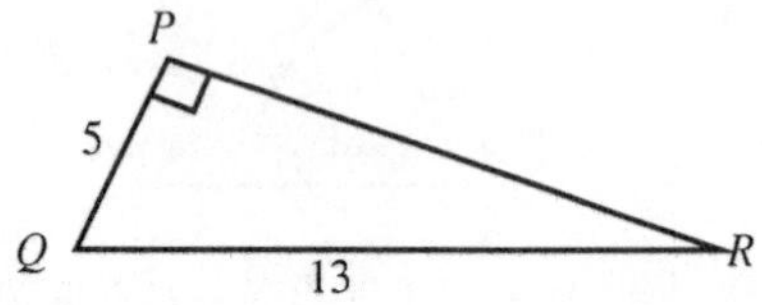

28. In the figure above, what is the length of *PR*?
(A) 12 (B) 23 (C) 27 (D) 36 (E) 48

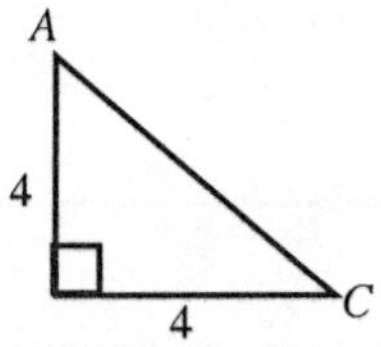

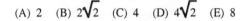

29. In the figure above, what is the length of *AC*?
(A) 2 (B) $2\sqrt{2}$ (C) 4 (D) $4\sqrt{2}$ (E) 8

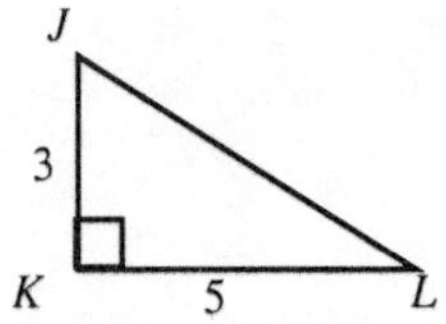

30. In the figure above, what is the length of *JL*?
(A) $\sqrt{2}$ (B) $2\sqrt{2}$ (C) $\sqrt{15}$ (D) $2\sqrt{6}$ (E) $\sqrt{34}$

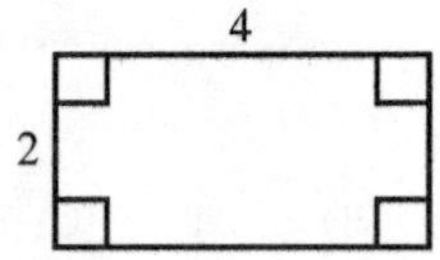

31. What is the perimeter of the figure above?
(A) 6 (B) 8 (C) 10 (D) 12 (E) 16

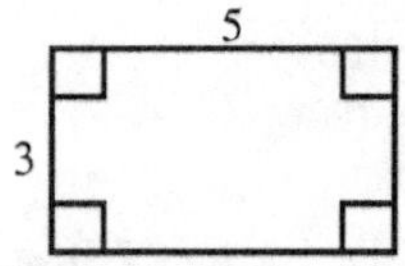

32. What is the perimeter of the figure above?
(A) 8 (B) 12 (C) 14 (D) 15 (E) 16

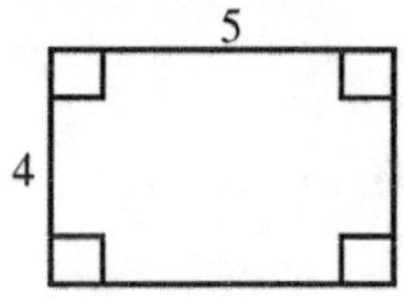

33. What is the area of the figure above?
(A) 10 (B) 15 (C) 16 (D) 18 (E) 20

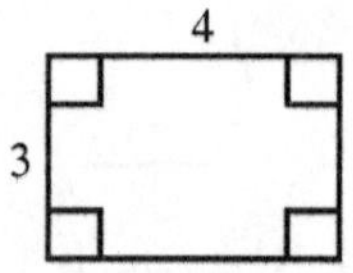

34. What is the area of the figure above?
(A) 6 (B) 8 (C) 12 (D) 16 (E) 24

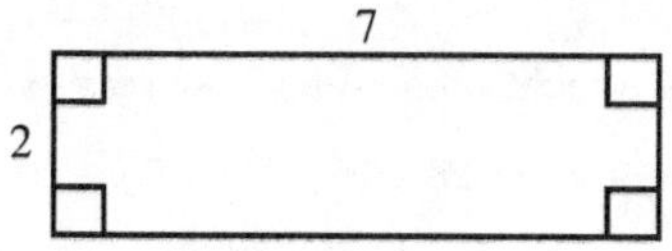

35. What is the area of the figure above?

(A) 5 (B) 9 (C) 14 (D) 25 (E) 81

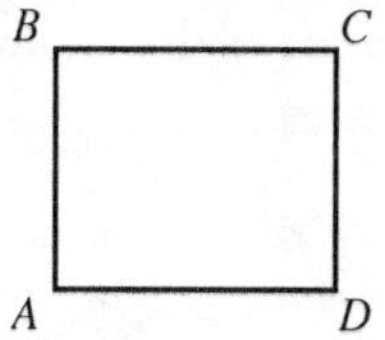

ABCD is a square.

36. In the figure above, if $AB = 5$, what is the area of *ABCD*?

(A) 5 (B) 10 (C) 20 (D) 25 (E) 40

37. If the radius of a circle is 2, then the diameter is

(A) 1 (B) 2 (C) 3 (D) 4 (E) 8

38. If the diameter of a circle is 10, what is the radius?

(A) 2 (B) 5 (C) 8 (D) 15 (E) 20

39. If the radius of a circle is 3, what is the circumference?

(A) 2π (B) 3π (C) 6π (D) 9π (E) 12π

40. If the radius of a circle is 5, what is the circumference?

(A) 5π (B) 10π (C) 15π (D) 20π (E) 24π

41. If the diameter of a circle is 8, what is the circumference?

(A) 8π (B) 6π (C) 4π (D) 2π (E) π

42. If the radius of a circle is 3, what is the area?

(A) π (B) 3π (C) 6π (D) 9π (E) 12π

43. If the radius of a circle is 5, what is the area?

(A) 25π (B) 21π (C) 18π (D) 2π (E) π

44. If the diameter of a circle is 8, what is the area?

(A) 16π (B) 12π (C) 10π (D) 8π (E) 4π

45. If the diameter of a circle is 12, what is the area?

(A) 18π (B) 24π (C) 30π (D) 32π (E) 36π

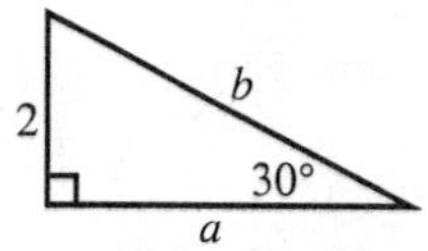

46. In the figure above, what are *a* and *b*?

(A) $a = \sqrt{3}, b = 2$ (B) $a = 2\sqrt{3}, b = 4$

(C) $a = 2, b = 2$ (D) $a = 4, b = 2\sqrt{3}$

(E) $a = 4, b = 4\sqrt{3}$

47. In the figure above, what are *c* and *d*?

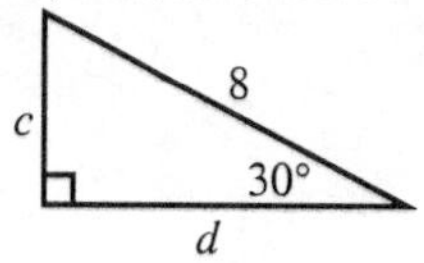

(A) $c = 2, d = \sqrt{3}$ (B) $c = 2\sqrt{2}, d = 3$ (C) $c = 4, d = 4\sqrt{3}$ (D) $c = 4\sqrt{2}, d = 2$ (E) $c = 3, d = 2\sqrt{3}$

48. In the figure above, what are *e* and *f*?

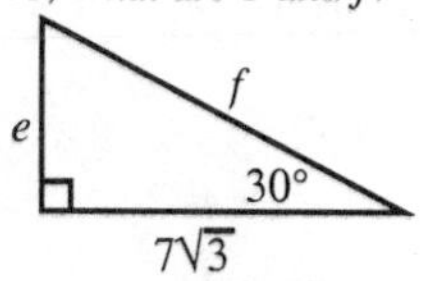

(A) $e = 2, f = 6$ (B) $e = \sqrt{2}, f = 8$ (C) $e = 4, f = 3\sqrt{5}$
(D) $e = 7, f = 10$ (E) $e = 7, f = 14$

49. In the figure above, what are *g* and *h*?

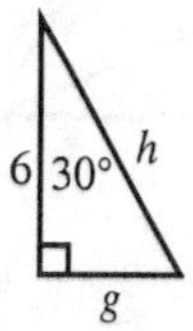

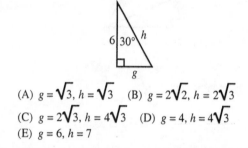

(A) $g = \sqrt{3}, h = \sqrt{3}$ (B) $g = 2\sqrt{2}, h = 2\sqrt{3}$

(C) $g = 2\sqrt{3}, h = 4\sqrt{3}$ (D) $g = 4, h = 4\sqrt{3}$

(E) $g = 6, h = 7$

50. What is the altitude of an equilateral triangle whose perimeter is 24?

(A) $2\sqrt{3}$ (B) $4\sqrt{3}$ (C) 6 (D) $4\sqrt{5}$ (E) 8

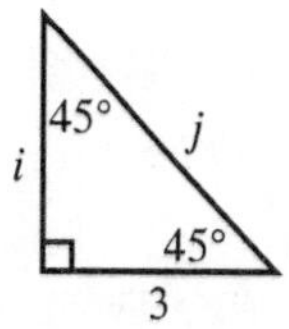

51. In the figure above, what are *i* and *j*?

(A) $i = 3, j = 3\sqrt{2}$ (B) $i = 3, j = 3$ (C) $i = 4\sqrt{2}, j = 4$

(D) $i = 5, j = 3\sqrt{3}$ (E) $i = 4, j = 5$

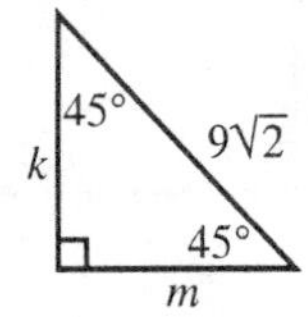

52. In the figure above, what are k and m?

(A) $k = 3, m = 3$ (B) $k = 2\sqrt{3}, m = 3$
(C) $k = 4, m = 6$ (D) $k = 9, m = 9$
(E) $k = 3, m = 9$

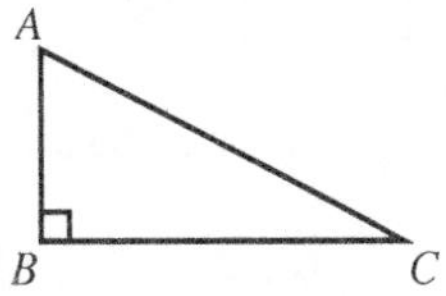

53. In the figure above, $AB = BC = \sqrt{6}$. What is the length of AC?

(A) 2 (B) $2\sqrt{3}$ (C) 3 (D) $3\sqrt{2}$ (E) 4

54. If the perimeter of a square is equal to 40, what is the length of the diagonal?

(A) $10\sqrt{2}$ (B) $5\sqrt{3}$ (C) 10 (D) $3\sqrt{5}$ (E) 14

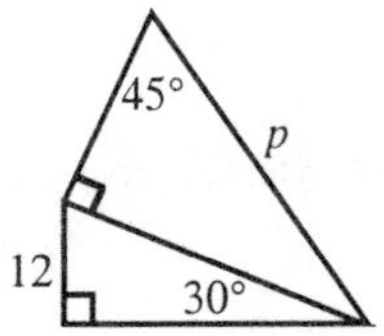

55. In the figure above, what is p equal to?

(A) $2\sqrt{2}$ (B) $2\sqrt{3}$ (C) $10\sqrt{2}$
(D) $20\sqrt{3}$ (E) $24\sqrt{2}$

56. If $\frac{10}{12 + 5x} = \frac{30}{4 - x}$, then $7 + x$ is equal to:

(A) −2 (B) 5 (C) 7 (D) 9 (E) 11

57. If on a road map $1\frac{5}{8}$ inches represents 10 miles, how many miles does 2.25 inches represent?

(A) $\frac{180}{13}$ miles (B) $\frac{53}{4}$ miles (C) $\frac{57}{4}$ miles
(D) $\frac{27}{2}$ miles (E) 3 miles

58. Jake and Jessie are standing next to each other in the sun. If Jake's shadow is 48 inches, and he is 72 inches tall, how many inches are there in Jessie's shadow if she is 66 inches tall?

(A) 42 (B) 43 (C) 44 (D) 45 (E) 46

59. A blueprint allows 1 inch for every 12 feet. At that rate, 7 inches represents how many yards?

(A) $\frac{28}{3}$ (B) 28 (C) 84 (D) 252 (E) 336

60. A bug crawls around the outside rim of a clock from the 12 to the 4 and travels 7 inches. If a second bug crawls around the outside rim from the 6 to the 11, how many inches did the bug travel?

(A) 7.75 (B) 8 (C) 8.25 (D) 8.5 (E) 8.75

61. The number of degrees in the angle formed by the minute and hour hands of a clock at 2:20 is:

(A) 60° (B) 40° (C) 45° (D) 50° (E) 55°

62. The radius of a circle with an area of 49 is:

(A) 7 (B) 7π (C) $\frac{7}{\sqrt{\pi}}$ (D) $\frac{7}{\pi}$ (E) π^2

63. The area of a circle with a circumference of $\frac{22}{3}\pi$ is:

(A) $\frac{484}{9}\pi$ (B) $\frac{121}{9}\pi$ (C) $\frac{121}{3}\pi$ (D) $\frac{484}{3}\pi$ (E) $\frac{556}{4}\pi$

64. A circle has an area of $36\pi^3$. The radius of the circle is:

(A) 6 (B) 6π (C) $6\pi^2$ (D) $6\pi^3$ (E) $6\pi^4$

65. If the radius of a circle is 8, then the circumference of the circle is:

(A) 4π (B) 8π (C) 12π (D) 14π (E) 16π

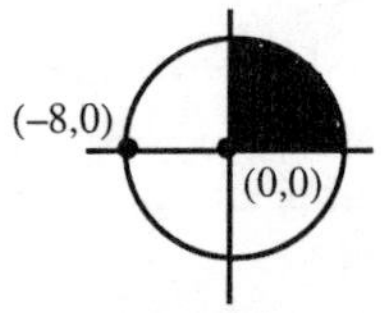

66. In the figure above, the shaded area is equal to:

(A) 16π (B) 32π (C) 64π (D) 66π (E) $16\pi^2$

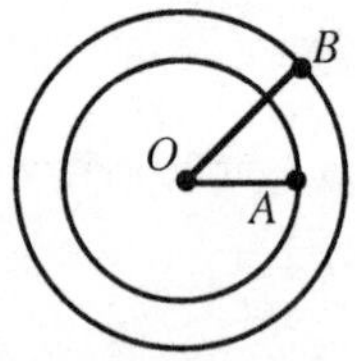

67. In the figure above, $OA = 2$ and $OB = 3$. The area between the two circles is equal to:

(A) 4π (B) 5π (C) 6π (D) 7π (E) 8π

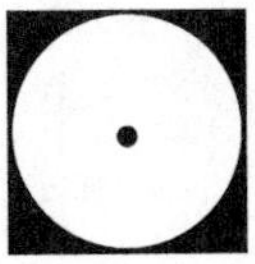

68. In the figure above, a circle with an area of 144π is inscribed in a square. What is the area of the shaded region?

(A) $576 - 144\pi$ (B) $216 - 72\pi$ (C) $144 - 24\pi$
(D) $1728 - 144\pi$ (E) $256 - 24\pi$

69. A square has a perimeter of 40. A second square has an inscribed circle with an area of 64π. The ratio of the length of a side of the first square to the length of a side of the second square is:

(A) 5:8 (B) 5:4 (C) 5:16 (D) $10:8\pi$ (E) $12:\pi$

70. The area of a square is $64x^2y^{16}$. The length of a side of the square is:

(A) $8xy^8$ (B) $8xy^4$ (C) $8x^2y^{16}$
(D) $16x^2y^{16}$ (E) $20x^2y^4$

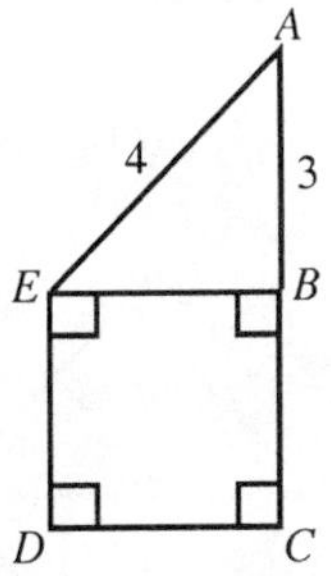

71. In the figure above, the area of the square *BCDE* is equal to:

(A) 5 (B) 7 (C) 12 (D) 24 (E) 49

72. The area of a right triangle with legs of 4 and 5 is equal to:

(A) 6 (B) 10 (C) 12 (D) 20 (E) 24

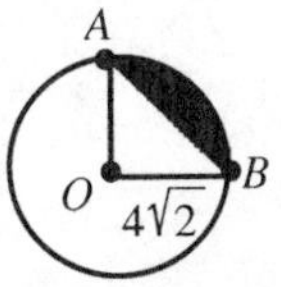

73. In the figure above, if $\angle OAB$ is 45°, then the area of the shaded segment is equal to:

(A) $32\pi - 16\sqrt{2}$ (B) $32\pi - 8$ (C) $4\pi - 8$
(D) $8\pi - 16$ (E) $8\pi - 8$

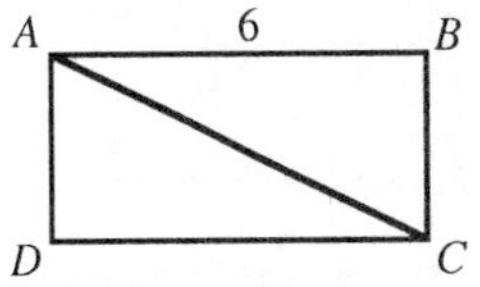

74. In the figure above, rectangle *ABCD* has an area of 15. What is the diagonal, *AC*, equal to?

(A) 4 (B) 5 (C) 6.5 (D) 7 (E) 7.5

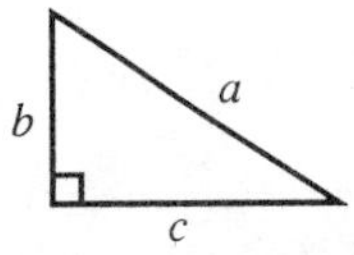

75. Regarding the figure above, which one of the following statements is true?

(A) $a^2 + b^2 = c^2$ (B) $a + b = c$ (C) $b + c = a$
(D) $b^2 + c^2 = a^2$ (E) $a + c = b$

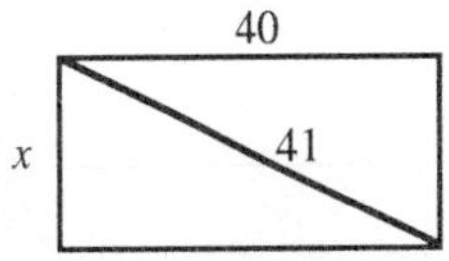

76. At 12 cents per square foot, how much will it cost to paint the rectangular slab in the figure above?

(A) \$43.20 (B) \$46.40 (C) \$98.40
(D) \$196.80 (E) \$201.50

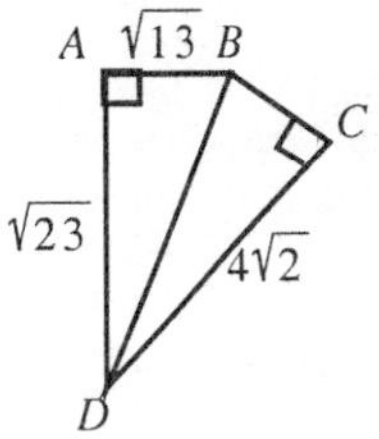

77. In the figure above, *BC* is equal to:

(A) 1 (B) 2 (C) 3 (D) 4 (E) 5

78. If the diagonal of a square is $5\sqrt{2}$, the area of the square is equal to:

(A) 10 (B) 20 (C) 25 (D) 30 (E) 35

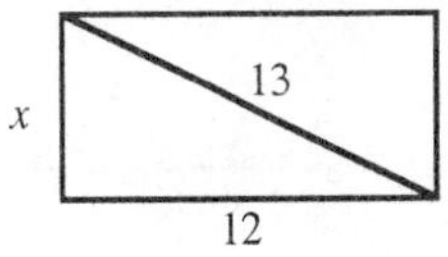

79. What is the area of the rectangle in the above figure?

(A) 156 (B) 78 (C) 72 (D) 66 (E) 60

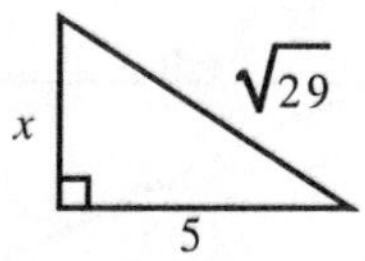

80. In the figure above, x is equal to:

(A) $\sqrt{29}-5$ (B) $\sqrt{24}$ (C) 24 (D) 2 (E) $\sqrt{2}$

81. On a coordinate graph, the distance between points (5, 6) and (6, 7) is equal to:

(A) $\sqrt{2}$ (B) 1 (C) 2 (D) 4 (E) $6\sqrt{2}$

82. On a coordinate graph, the distance between points (–1, 4) and (2, 8) is equal to:

(A) 3 (B) 4 (C) 5 (D) 6 (E) 8

83. If $2\sqrt{3}$ is the diagonal of a square, then the perimeter of the square is:

(A) $4\sqrt{6}$ (B) 8 (C) $6\sqrt{3}$ (D) 12 (E) 14

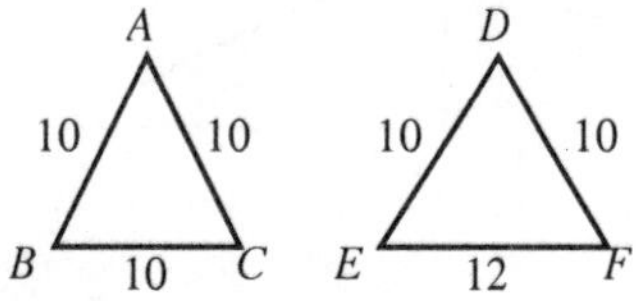

84. In the figure above, the ratio of the perimeter of ΔABC to the perimeter of ΔDEF is:

(A) 1:1 (B) 5:6 (C) 15:16 (D) 6:5 (E) 7:3

85. If $2\sqrt{12}$, $3\sqrt{6}$, and $4\sqrt{3}$ are the dimensions of a rectangular solid, the volume of the solid is:

(A) $216\sqrt{24}$ (B) $\sqrt{5184}$ (C) $144\sqrt{6}$
(D) 5184 (E) $\sqrt{24}$

86. A cylinder with an altitude of 10 and a circumference of $\sqrt{128\pi}$ has a volume equal to:

(A) $\sqrt{1280\pi}$ (B) 320π (C) 640π
(D) 1280π (E) 3460π

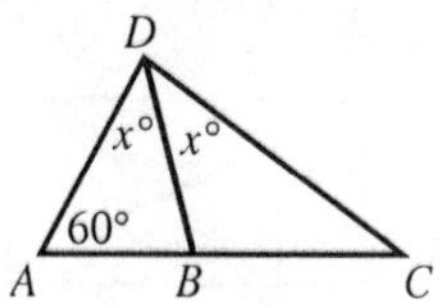

87. In the figure above, x is equal to:

(A) 30° (B) 32° (C) 35° (D) 40° (E) 70°

88. If the ratio of the angles of a triangle are 1:2:3, and the length of the smallest side is 5, the length of the largest side is:

(A) 10 (B) 12 (C) $8\sqrt{3}$ (D) 15 (E) 20

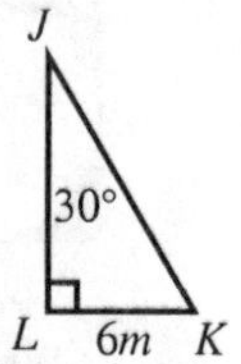

89. In the figure above, JK is equal to:

(A) $6m\sqrt{3}$ (B) $9m$ (C) $12m$
(D) $12m\sqrt{3}$ (E) $14m$

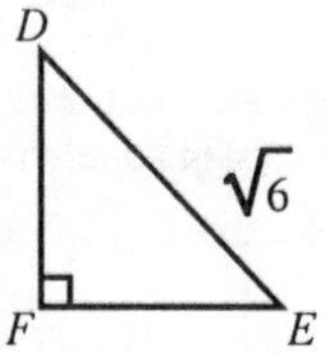

90. In the isosceles triangle above, DF is equal to:

(A) $2\sqrt{6}$ (B) $6\sqrt{2}$ (C) $\sqrt{3}$ (D) 12 (E) $12\sqrt{2}$

91. The area of a 30°-60°-90° triangle whose longest side is $2\sqrt{3}$ is:

(A) 8 (B) 4 (C) $1.5\sqrt{3}$ (D) 2 (E) 1

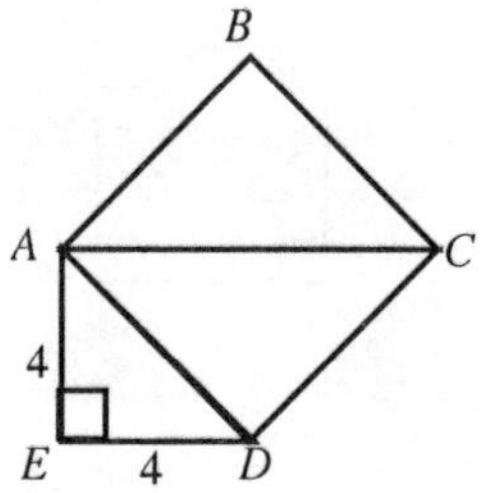

92. In the figure above, the diagonal AC of square $ABCD$ is equal to:

(A) $4\sqrt{2}$ (B) 8 (C) $8\sqrt{2}$ (D) 16 (E) $32\sqrt{2}$

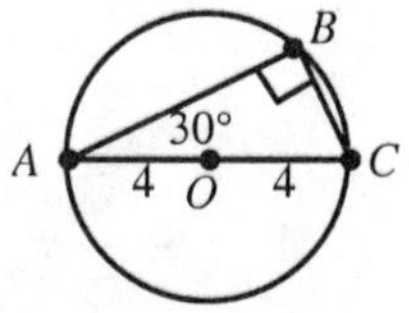

93. In the figure above, if arc BC is equal 60°, then the area of ΔABC is:

(A) 16 (B) $4\sqrt{3}$ (C) $8\sqrt{3}$ (D) 12 (E) $10\sqrt{2}$

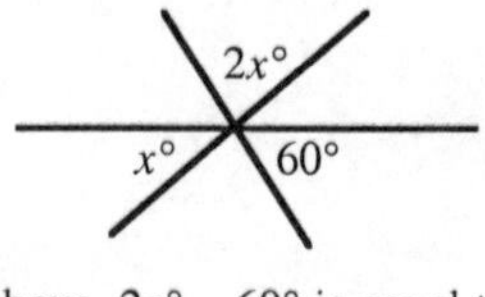

94. In the figure above, $2x° - 60°$ is equal to:

(A) 80° (B) 40° (C) 30° (D) 20° (E) 10°

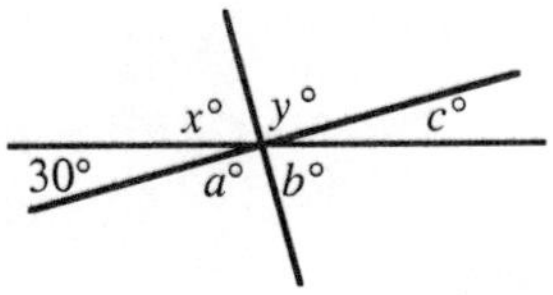

95. In the figure above, a does NOT always equal:

(A) y (B) $150 - x$ (C) $180 - b - c$
(D) $150 - b$ (E) $180 - x - y$

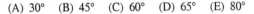

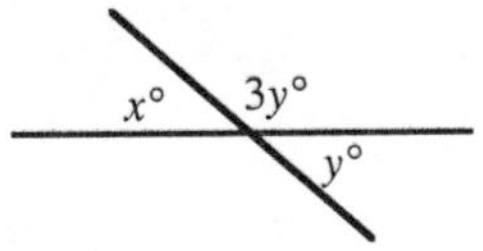

96. In the figure above, what is the value of x?

(A) 30° (B) 45° (C) 60° (D) 65° (E) 80°

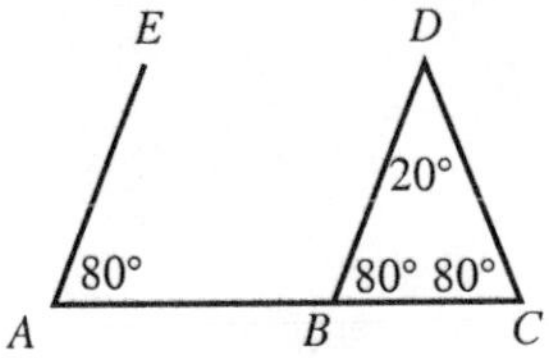

97. In the figure above, if $AE \parallel BD$, $BD = DC$, $\angle BDC$ is:

(A) 10° (B) 15° (C) 18° (D) 20° (E) 24°

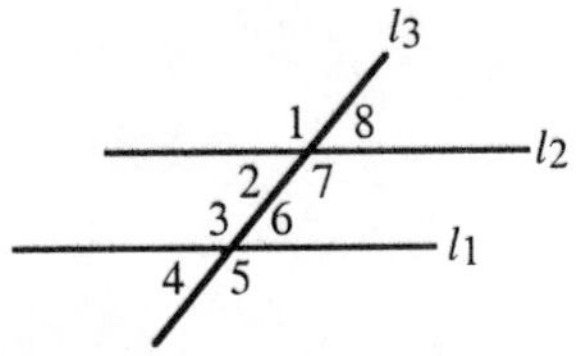

98. In the figure above, $l_1 \parallel l_2$ and $\angle 7 = 117°$, which other angles must also equal 117°?

(A) 1, 3, 5 (B) 1, 2, 8 (C) 2, 3, 6
(D) 5, 6, 8 (E) 1, 2, 3, 4

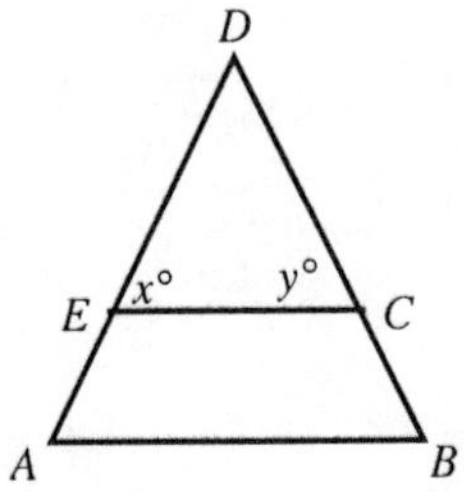

99. In the figure above, if $EC \parallel AB$ and $AD = BD$, then the sum of the degree measures of $\angle A + \angle B + \angle BCE$ is:

(A) $x + 2y$ (B) $3x$ (C) $180 + x$
(D) $180 - 2x$ (E) $360 - 180y$

100. If the perimeter of a rectangle is 68 yards and the width is 48 feet, the length is:

(A) 10 yd. (B) 18 yd. (C) 20 ft.
(D) 46 ft. (E) 56 ft.

101. The total length of fencing needed to enclose a rectangular area 46 feet by 34 feet is:

(A) 26 yd. 1 ft. (B) $26\frac{2}{3}$ yd. (C) 48 yd.
(D) 52 yd. 2 ft. (E) $53\frac{1}{3}$ yd.

102. An umbrella 50" long can lie on the bottom of a trunk whose length and width are, respectively:

(A) 26", 30" (B) 39", 36" (C) 31", 31"
(D) 40", 21" (E) 40", 30"

103. A road runs 1200 ft. from A to B, and then makes a right angle going to C, a distance of 500 ft. A new road is being built directly from A to C. How much shorter will be new road be?

(A) 400 ft. (B) 609 ft. (C) 850 ft.
(D) 1000 ft. (E) 1300 ft.

104. A certain triangle has sides that are, respectively, 6 inches, 8 inches, and 10 inches long. A rectangle equal in area to that of the triangle has a width of 3 inches. The perimeter of the rectangle, expressed in inches, is:

(A) 11 (B) 16 (C) 22 (D) 24 (E) 30

105. A ladder 65 feet long is leaning against the wall. Its lower end is 25 feet away from the wall. How much farther away will it be if the upper end is moved down 8 feet?

(A) 60 ft. (B) 52 ft. (C) 14 ft.
(D) 10 ft. (E) 8 ft.

106. A rectangular bin 4 feet long, 3 feet wide, and 2 feet high is solidly packed with bricks whose dimensions are 8 inches, 4 inches, and 2 inches. The number of bricks in the bin is

(A) 54 (B) 320 (C) 648
(D) 848 (E) none of these

107. If the cost of digging a trench is \$2.12 a cubic yard, what would be the cost of digging a trench 2 yards by 5 yards by 4 yards?

(A) \$21.20 (B) \$40.00 (C) \$64.00
(D) \$84.80 (E) \$104.80

108. A piece of wire is shaped to enclose a square, whose area is 121 square inches. It is then reshaped to enclose a rectangle whose length is 13 inches. The area of the rectangle, in square inches, is

(A) 64 (B) 96 (C) 117 (D) 144 (E) 234

109. The area of a 2-foot-wide walk around a garden that is 30 feet long and 20 feet wide is

(A) 104 sq. ft. (B) 216 sq. ft. (C) 680 sq. ft.
(D) 704 sq. ft. (E) 1416 sq. ft.

110. The area of a circle is 49π. Find its circumference, in terms of π.

(A) 14π (B) 28π (C) 49π (D) 98π (E) 147π

111. In two hours, the minute hand of a clock rotates through an angle of:

(A) 90 (B) 180 (C) 360 (D) 720 (E) 1080

112. A box is 12 inches in width, 16 inches in length, and 6 inches in height. How many square inches of paper would be required to cover it on all sides?

(A) 192 (B) 360 (C) 720 (D) 900 (E) 1440

113. If the volume of a cube is 64 cubic inches, the sum of its edges is:

(A) 48 in (B) 32 in. (C) 24 in. (D) 16 in. (E) 12 in.

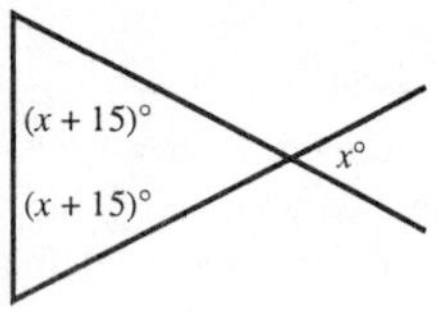

114. In the figure above, $x = ?$

(A) 20 (B) 35 (C) 50 (D) 65 (E) 90

115. What is the difference of the areas of two squares with sides of 5 and 4, respectively?

(A) 3 (B) 4 (C) 9 (D) 16 (E) 91

116. A triangle with sides of 3, 6, and 9 has the same perimeter as an equilateral triangle with sides of length:

(A) 2 (B) $\frac{3}{2}$ (C) 3 (D) 6 (E) 8

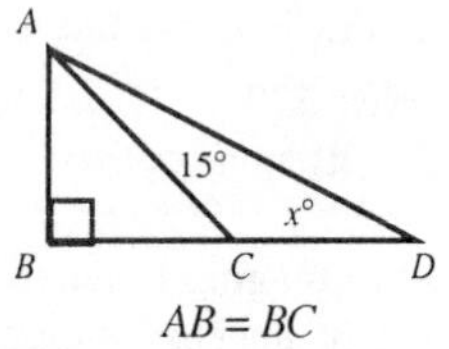

$AB = BC$

117. In the figure above, $x =$

(A) 15 (B) 30 (C) 40 (D) 60 (E) 75

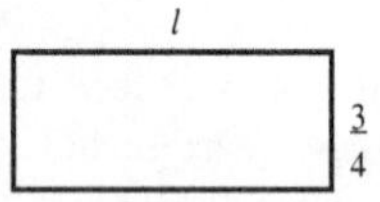

118. If the area of the rectangle shown above is equal to 1, then $l = ?$

(A) $\frac{4}{9}$ (B) 1 (C) $\frac{4}{3}$ (D) $\frac{9}{4}$ (E) 2

(E) Cannot be determined from the information given.

Coordinate Geometry

The easiest way to understand the coordinate axis system is as an analog to the points of the compass. If we take a plot of land, we can divide it into quadrants:

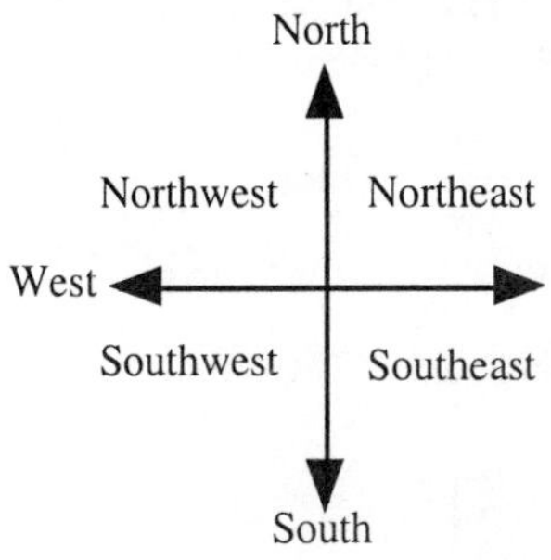

Now, if we add measuring units along each of the directional axes, we can actually describe any location on this piece of land by two numbers.

EXAMPLE:

Point *P* is located at 4 units East and 5 units North. Point *Q* is located at 4 units West and 5 units North. Point *R* is located at 4 units West and 2 units South. And Point *T* is located at 3 units East and 4 units South.

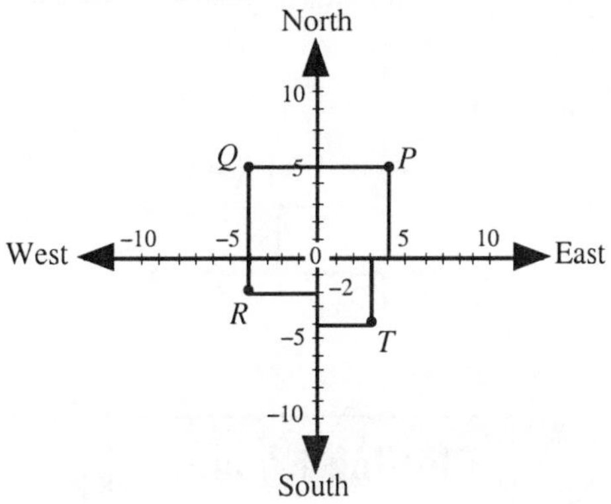

Negative and Positive Regions

The coordinate system used in coordinate geometry differs from our map of a plot of land in two respects. First, it uses *x*- and *y*-axes divided into negative and positive regions.

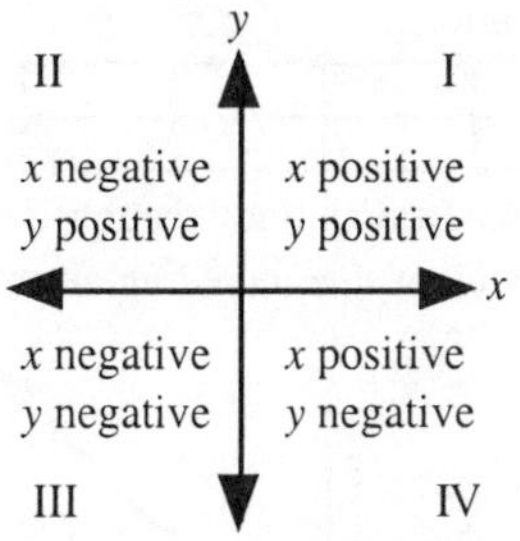

It is easy to see that Quadrant I corresponds to our Northeast quarter, and in it the measurements on both the *x*- and *y*-axes are positive. Quadrant II corresponds to our Northwest quarter, and in it the measurements on the *x*-axis are negative and the measurements on the *y*-axis are positive. Quadrant III corresponds to the Southwest quarter, and in it both the *x*-axis measurements and the *y*-axis measurements are negative. Finally, Quadrant IV corresponds to our Southeast quarter, and there the *x*-values are positive while the *y*-values are negative.

Ordered Pairs

Second, mathematicians adopt a convention called ordered pairs to eliminate the necessity of specifying each time whether one is referring to the x-axis or the y-axis. An ordered pair of coordinates has the general form (a, b). The first element refers to the x-value (distance left or right of the *origin,* or intersection, of the axes) while the second element gives the y-value (distance up or down from the origin).

EXAMPLE:

Plot (3, 2).

Begin by moving to the positive 3 value on the x-axis. Then from there move up two units on the y-axis.

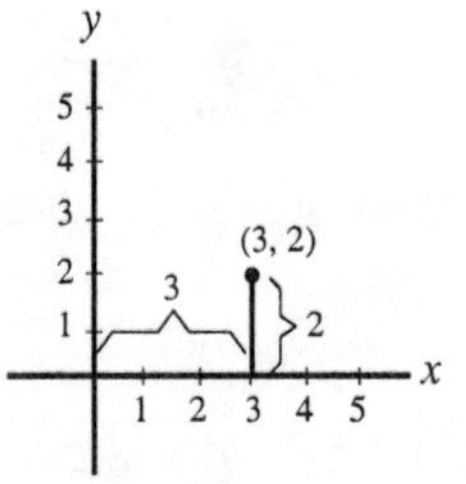

An alternative way of speaking about this is to say that the point (3, 2) is located at the intersection of a line drawn through the x-value 3 parallel to the y-axis and a line drawn through the y-value 2 parallel to the x-axis.

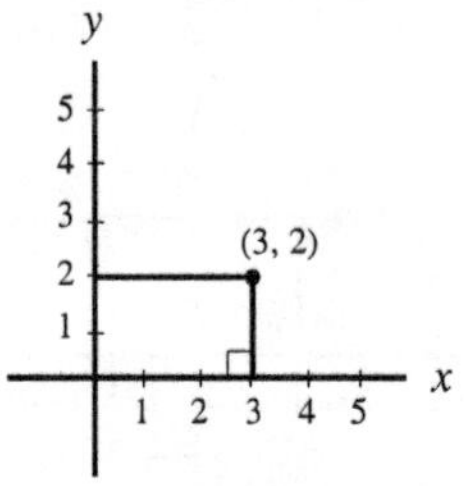

Plotting Equations

One important use of the coordinate axis system is that it can be used to draw a picture of an equation. An important equation to remember is that for a straight line. ***The Slope-Intercept Form:*** $y = mx + b$, where m is the slope and b is the y-intercept when $x = 0$.

EXAMPLE:

Plot the equation $x = y$.

This equation has an infinite number of solutions:

x	1	2	3	5	0	−3	−5	...
y	1	2	3	5	0	−3	−5	...

Plot these pairs of x and y on the axis system. Draw a line through them to produce a plot of the original equation. The complete picture of the equation $x = y$ is a straight line including all the real numbers such that x is equal to y.

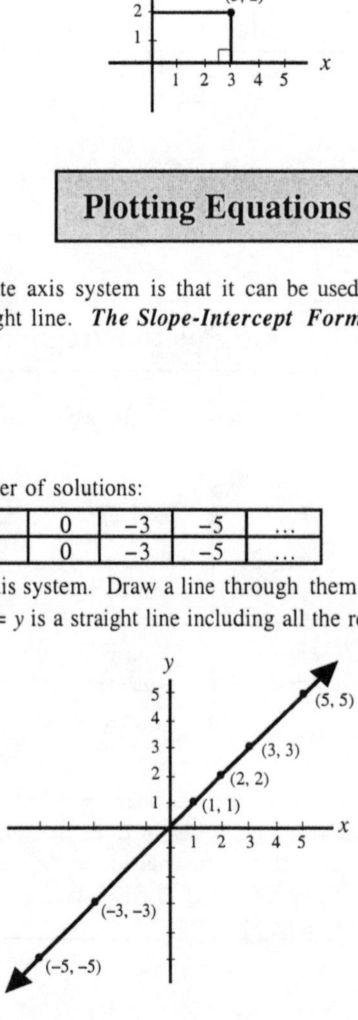

EXAMPLE:

Graph the equation $y = 2x$:

x	−4	−2	−1	0	1	2	4	...
y	−8	−4	−2	0	2	4	8	...

After entering these points on the graph, complete the picture:

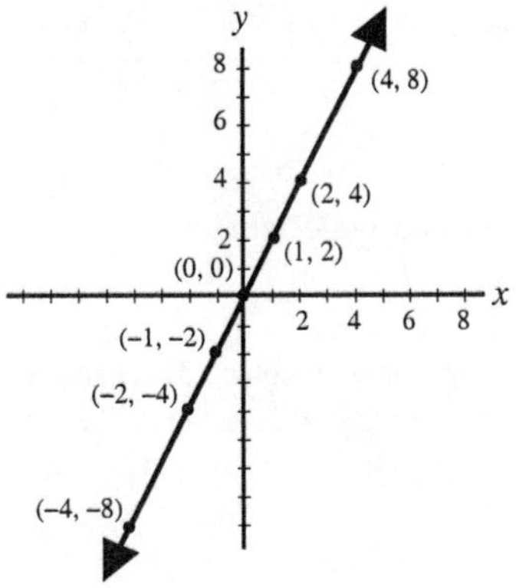

It too is a straight line, but it rises at a more rapid rate than does $x = y$.

Graphing Figures

A final use one might have for the coordinate system is graphing geometric figures. The following figure is a graph of a square whose vertices are (0, 0), (4, 0), (4, 4) and (0, 4).

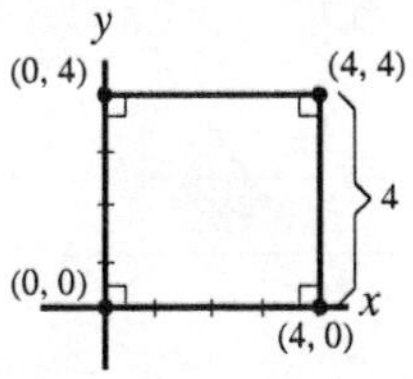

Each side of the square must be equal to 4 since each side is four units long (and parallel to either the x- or y-axis). Since all coordinates can be viewed as the perpendicular intersection of two lines, it is possible to measure distances in the system by using some simple theorems.

EXAMPLES:

What is the area of the circle?

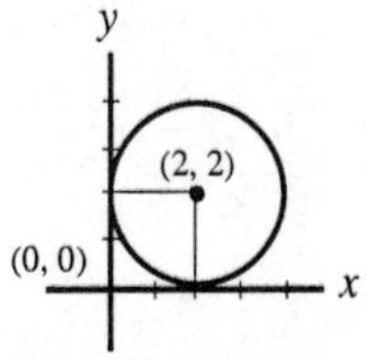

To solve this problem, find the radius of the circle. The center of the circle is located at the intersection of $x = 2$ and $y = 2$, or the point (2, 2). So we know the radius is 2 units long and the area is 4π.

What is the length of PQ?

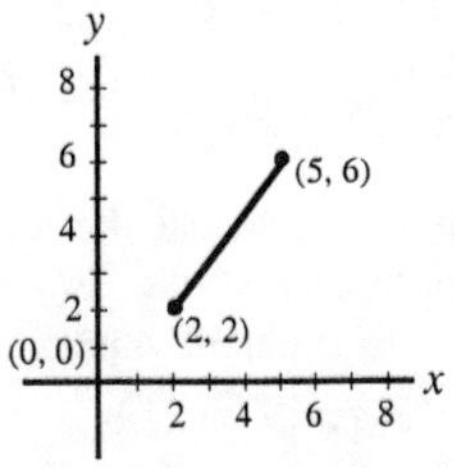

Find the length of *PQ* by constructing a triangle:

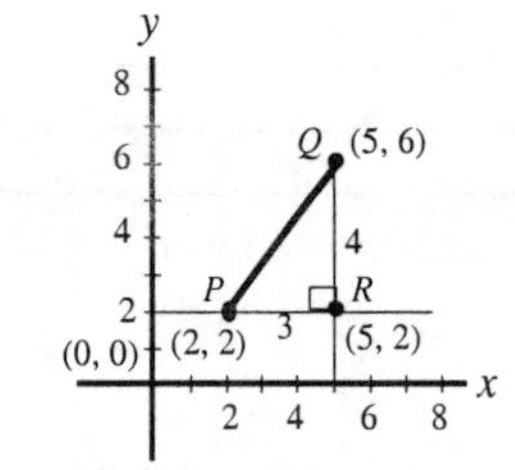

QR runs from (5, 6) to (5, 2), so it must be 4 units long. *PR* runs from (2, 2) to (5, 2) so it is 3 units long. Use the Pythagorean Theorem ($leg^2 + leg^2 = hypotenuse^2$) to determine that *PQ*, which is the hypotenuse of our triangle, is 5 units long ($3^2 + 4^2 = 9 + 16 = 25$, so hypotenuse $= \sqrt{25} = 5$).

It is actually possible to generalize on the last example. Take any two points on the graph (for simplicity's sake, confine the discussion to the First Quadrant, but the method is generally applicable, that is, will work in all quadrants and even with lines covering two or more quadrants) *P* and *Q*. Assign the value (x_1, y_1) to *P* and (x_2, y_2) *to Q*.

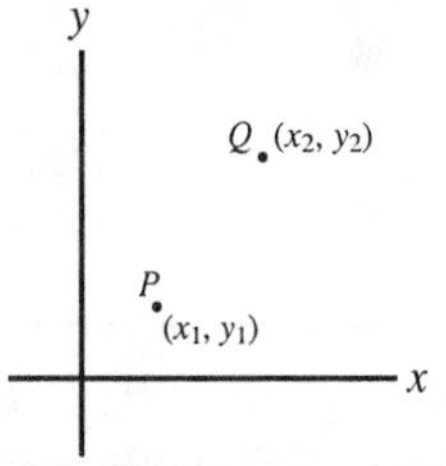

Then, following the method above, a triangle may be constructed so as to use the Pythagorean Theorem:

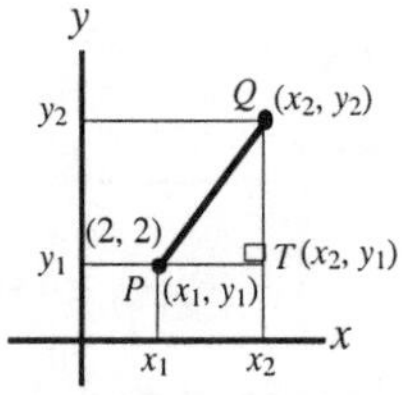

Point *T* now has the coordinates (x_2, y_1). Side *PT* will be $x_2 - x_1$ units long (the *y*-coordinate does not change, so the length is only the distance moved on the *x*-axis), and *QT* will be $y_2 - y_1$ (again, the distance is purely vertical, moving up from y_1 to y_2, with no change in the *x*-value). Using the Pythagorean Theorem:

$$PQ^2 = PT^2 + QT^2 = (x^2 - x^1)^2 + (y^2 - y^1)^2$$

$$PQ = \sqrt{(x_2 - x_1)^2 + (y_2 - y_1)^2}$$

And we have just derived what is called the ***Distance Formula.*** We can find the length of any straight line segment drawn in a coordinate axis system (that is, the distance between two points in the system) using this formula.

EXAMPLE:

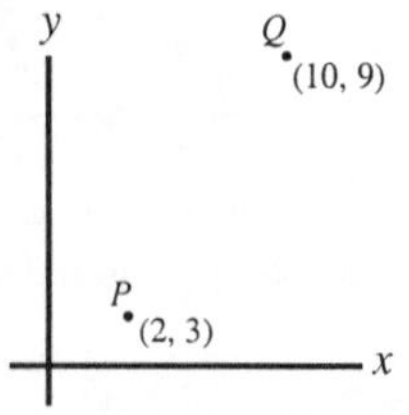

What is the distance between *P* and *Q?*

Point *P* has coordinates (2, 3) and *Q* has coordinates (10, 9): $PQ = \sqrt{(10 - 2)^2 + (9 - 3)^2} = \sqrt{64 + 36} = \sqrt{100} = 10$.

For those who find the Distance Formula a bit too technical, be reassured that the Pythagorean Theorem (which is more familiar) will work just as well on the test. In fact, as a general rule, any time one is asked to calculate a distance which does not move parallel to one of the axes, the proper attack is to use the Pythagorean Theorem.

EXERCISE 12

Coordinate Geometry

DIRECTIONS: Choose the best answer to each of the following questions. Answers are on page 128.

1. AB is the diameter of a circle whose center is O. If the coordinates of A are (2, 6) and the coordinates of B are (6, 2), find the coordinates of O.

   (A) (4, 4) (B) (4, –4) (C) (2, –2)
   (D) (0, 0) (E) (2, 2)

2. AB is the diameter of a circle whose center is O. If the coordinates of O are (2, 1) and the coordinates of B are (4, 6), find the coordinates of A.

   (A) $(3, 3\frac{1}{2}$ (B) $(1, 2\frac{1}{2}$ (C) (0, –4)
   (D) $(2\frac{1}{2}, 1)$ (E) $9–1, -2\frac{1}{2})$

3. Find the distance from the point whose coordinates are (4, 3) to the point whose coordinates are (8, 6).

   (A) 5 (B) 25 (C) •7 (D) $\sqrt{67}$ (E) 15

4. The vertices of a triangle are (2, 1), (2, 5), and (5, 1). The area of the triangle is:

   (A) 12 (B) 10 (C) 8 (D) 6 (E) 5

5. The area of a circle whose center is at (0, 0) is 16π. The circle passes through each of the following points *except*:

   (A) (4, 4) (B) (0, 4) (C) (4, 0)
   (D) (–4, 0) (E) (0, –4)

6. If point P has coordinates (–2, 2) and point Q has coordinates (2, 0), what is the distance from P to Q?

   (A) –4 (B) $2\sqrt{5}$ (C) $4\sqrt{5}$
   (D) 4 (E) 6

7. If point R has coordinates (x, y) and point S has coordinates $(x + 1, y + 1)$, what is the distance between R and S?

   (A) $\sqrt{2}$ (B) 2 (C) $\sqrt{x^2 + y^2}$
   (D) $\sqrt{x^2 + y^2 + 2}$ (E) $x + y + 1$

8. Will is standing 40 yards due north of point P. Grace is standing 60 yards due west of point P. What is the shortest distance between Will and Grace?

   (A) 20 yards (B) $4\sqrt{13}$ yards (C) $20\sqrt{13}$ yards
   (D) 80 yards (E) $80\sqrt{13}$ yards

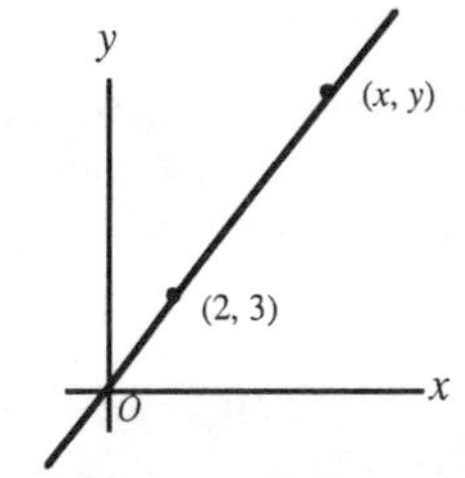

9. In the rectangular coordinate system above, if $x = 4.2$, then y = ?

   (A) 2.8 (B) 3.4 (C) 4.8 (D) 6.2 (E) 6.3

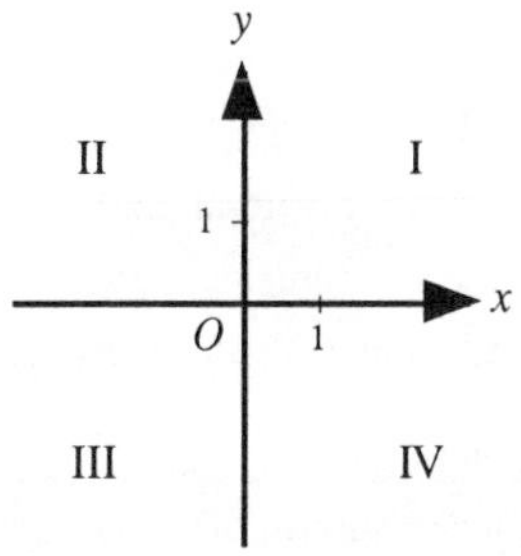

10. Points $(x, -4)$ and $(-1, y)$, not shown in the figure above, are in quadrants III and II, respectively. If x and $y \neq 0$, in which quadrant is point (x, y)?

    (A) I (B) II (C) III (D) IV
    (E) Cannot be determined from the information given.

11. If Sam lives 8 miles west of Jeni, and Molly lives 10 miles north of Jeni, approximately how many miles less would Molly walk if she walk's directly to Sam's house, rather than first to Jeni's house and then to Sam's house?

    (A) 1 (B) 2 (C) 3 (D) 4 (E) 5

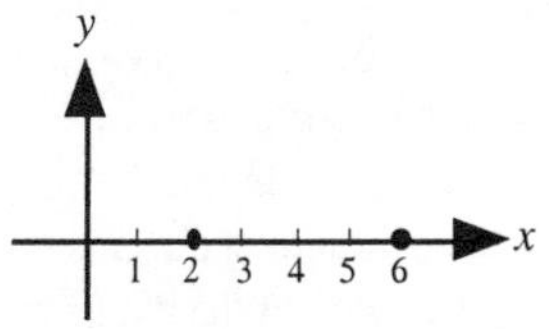

12. Point B (not shown in the above figure) lies below the x-axis at point (4, –4), the area of ΔABC is:

    (A) 2 (B) 4 (C) 6 (D) 8 (E) 16

Problem-Solving

Problem-solving questions present multiple-choice problems, in which the task is to solve the problem and choose the correct answer from among the answer choices. Typically, these problems are presented in the form of a story (hence the term *story problems* is often used in reference to these types of problems) and may test everything from arithmetic to algebra and geometry.

You should have everything you need to solve these problems from your review of this Basic Math Review. However, if a problem-solving math question stumps you, work backwards from the answers. The right answer has to be on of the choices. Since quantitative (*i.e.,* numerical value) choices are arranged in size order, starting with (C) will result in the fewest calculations.

In solving verbal (story) problems, the most important technique is to read accurately. Be sure you understand clearly what you are asked to find. Then evaluate the problem in common sense terms; use this to eliminate answer choices. For example, If two people are working together, their combined speed is greater than either one, but not more than twice as fast as the fastest one.

Be alert for the "hidden equation." This is some necessary information so obvious in the stated situation that the question assumes that you know it.

EXAMPLES:

1. boys plus girls = total class
2. imported wine plus domestic wine = all wine
3. wall and floor make a right angle (Pythagorean Theorem)

When the "hidden equation" involves rates, then multiplication can make finding this equation more difficult. Utilize the given units and make sure in the final equation the units work out right. You can manipulate it for the unit value for which you are looking.

Below are some of the frequently encountered types of problem-solving problems, although not every problem you may get will fall into one of these categories. However, thoroughly familiarizing yourself with the types of problems that follow will help you to translate and solve all kinds of verbal problems.

Coin Problems

In solving coin problems, it is best to change the value of all monies involved to cents before writing an equation. Thus, the number of nickels must be multiplied by 5 to give their value in cents; dimes must be multiplied by 10; quarters by 25; half-dollars by 50; and dollars by 100.

EXAMPLE:

Richard has $3.50 consisting of nickels and dimes. If he has 5 more dimes than nickels, how many dimes does he have?
Let x = the number of nickels
$x + 5$ = the number of dimes
$5x$ = the value of the nickels in cents
$10x + 50$ = the value of the dimes in cents
350 = the value of the money he has in cents
$5x + 10x + 5 = 350$
$15x = 300$
$x = 20$
Therefore, he has 20 nickels and 25 dimes.

In a problem such as this, you can be sure that 20 would be among the multiple-choice answers. You must be sure to read carefully what you are asked to find and then continue until you have found the quantity sought.

Consecutive Integer Problems

Consecutive integers are one apart and can be represented by x, $x + 1$, $x + 2$, etc. Consecutive even or odd integers are two apart and can be represented by x, $x + 2$, $x + 4$, etc.

EXAMPLE:

Three consecutive odd integers have a sum of 33. Find the average of these integers.

Represent the integers as x, $x + 2$, and $x + 4$. Write an equation indicating the sum is 33:

$3x + 6 = 33$

$3x = 27$

$x = 9$

The integers are 9, 11, and 13. In the case of evenly spaced numbers such as these, the average is the middle number, 11. Since the sum of the three numbers was given originally, all we really had to do was to divide this sum by 3 to find the average, without ever knowing what the numbers were.

Age Problems

Problems of this type usually involve a comparison of ages at the present time, several years from now, or several years ago. A person's age x years from now is found by adding x to his present age. A person's age x years ago is found by subtracting x from his present age.

EXAMPLE:

Michelle was 12 years old y years ago. Represent her age b years from now.

Her present age is $12 + y$. In b years, her age will be $12 + y + b$.

Interest Problems

The annual amount of interest paid on an investment is found by multiplying the amount of principal invested by the rate (percent) of interest paid.

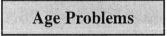

Principal • Rate = Interest Income

EXAMPLE:

Mr. Krecker invests $4,000, part at 6% and part at 7%. His income from these investments in one year is $250. Find the amount invested at 7%.

Represent each investment:

Let x = the amount invested at 7% (Always try to let x represent what you are looking for.)

$4000 - x$ = the amount invested at 6%

$0.07x$ = the income from the 7% investment

$0.06(4000 - x)$ = the income from the 6% investment

$0.07x + 0.06(4000 - x) = 250$

$7x + 6(4000 - x) = 25000$

$7x + 24000 - 6x = 25000$

$x = 1000$

Thus, he invested $1,000 at 7%.

Mixture Problems

There are two kinds of mixture problems with which you should be familiar. These problems are rare, so this is best regarded as an extra-credit section and not given top priority. The first is sometimes referred to as dry mixture, in which we mix dry ingredients of different values, such as nuts or coffee. Also solved by the same method are problems such as those dealing with tickets at different prices. In solving this type of problem, it is best to organize the data in a chart of three rows and three columns labeled as illustrated in the following problem.

EXAMPLE:

A dealer wishes to mix 20 pounds of nuts selling for 45 cents per pound with some more expensive nuts selling for 60 cents per pound, to make a mixture that will sell for 50 cents per pound. How many pounds of the more expensive nuts should he use?

	No. of lbs. ×	Price/lb. =	Total Value
Original	20	0.45	0.45(20)
Added	x	0.60	$0.60(x)$
Mixture	$20 + x$	0.50	$0.50(20 + x)$

The value of the original nuts plus the value of the added nuts must equal the value of the mixture. (Almost all mixture problems require an equation that comes from adding the final column).

$0.45(20) + 0.60(x) = 0.50(20 + x)$

$45(20) + 60(x) = 50(20 + x)$

$900 + 60x = 1000 + 50x$

$10x = 100$

$x = 10$

Therefore, he should use 10 lbs. of 60-cent nuts.

In solving the second type, or chemical mixture problem, we are dealing with percents rather than prices, and amounts instead of value.

EXAMPLE:

How much water must be added to 20 gallons of solution that is 30% alcohol to dilute it to a solution that is only 25% alcohol?

	No. of gals.	% alcohol =	Amt. alcohol
Original	20	0.30	0.30(20)
Added	x	0	0
Mixture	$20 + x$	0.25	$0.25(20 + x)$

Note that the percent of alcohol in water is 0. Had pure alcohol been added to strengthen the solution, the percent would have been 100. The equation again comes from the last column. The amount of alcohol added (none in this case) plus the original amount must equal the amount of alcohol in the new solution:

$0.30(20) = 0.25(20 + x)$

$30(20) = 25(20 + x)$

$600 = 500 + 25x$

$100 = 25x$

$x = 4$ gallons

Motion Problems

The fundamental relationship in all motion problems is that Rate • Time = Distance. The problems at the level of this examination usually derive their equation from a relationship concerning distance. Most problems fall into one of three types.

1. Motion in Opposite Directions

When two objects moving at the same speed start at the same time and move in opposite directions, or when two objects start at points at a given distance apart and move toward each other until they meet, then the distance the second travels will equal one-half the total distance covered.

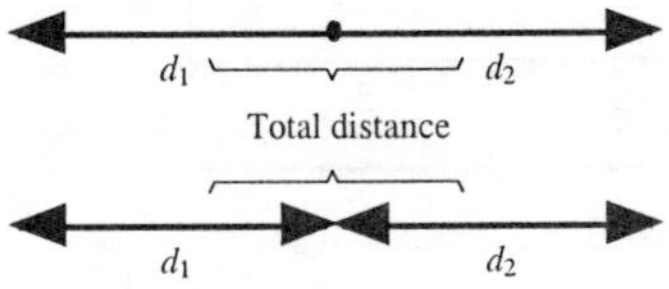

In either of the above cases, $d_1 + d_2 =$ Total distance.

2. Motion in the Same Direction

This type of problem is sometimes called the "catch-up" problem. Two objects leave the same place at different times and different rates, but one "catches up" to the other. In such a case, the two distances must be equal.

3. Round Trip

In this type of problem, the rate going is usually different from the rate returning. The times are also different. But if we go somewhere and then return to the starting point, the distances must be the same.

To solve any motion problem, it is helpful to organize the data in a box with columns for rate, time, and distance. A separate line should be used for each moving object. Remember that if the rate is given in *miles per hour,* the time must be in *hours* and the distance in *miles.*

EXAMPLES:

1. Two cars leave a restaurant at 1 p.m., with one car traveling east at 60 miles per hour and the other west at 40 miles per hour along a straight highway. At what time will they be 350 miles apart?

	Rate ×	Time =	Distance
Eastbound	60	x	$60x$
Westbound	40	x	$40x$

Notice that the time is unknown, since we must discover the number of hours traveled. However, since the cars start at the same time and stop when they are 350 miles apart, their times are the same: $60x + 40x = 350 \Rightarrow 100x = 350 \Rightarrow x = 3\frac{1}{2}$. Therefore, in $3\frac{1}{2}$ hours, it will be 4:30 p.m.

2. Gloria leaves home for school, riding her bicycle at a rate of 12 m.p.h. Twenty minutes after she leaves, her mother sees Gloria's English paper on her bed and leaves to bring it to her. If her mother drives at 36 m.p.h, how far must she drive before she reaches Gloria?

	Rate ×	Time =	Distance
Gloria	12	x	$12x$
Mother	36	$x-\frac{1}{3}$	$40x$

Notice that 20 minutes has been changed to $\frac{1}{3}$ of an hour. In this problem the times are not equal, but the distances are: $12x = 36(x-\frac{1}{3}) = 36x - 12 \Rightarrow 12 = 24x \Rightarrow x = \frac{1}{2}$. Therefore, if Gloria rode for $\frac{1}{2}$ hour at 12 m.p.h., the distance covered was 6 miles.

3. Nisha leaves home at 11 a.m. and rides to Andrea's house to return her bicycle. She travels at 12 miles per hour and arrives at 11:30 a.m. She turns right around and walks home. How fast does she walk if she returns home at 1 p.m.?

	Rate ×	Time =	Distance
Going	12	$\frac{1}{2}$	6
Return	x	$1\frac{1}{2}$	$\frac{3}{2}(x)$

The distances are equal: $6 = \frac{3}{2}(x) \Rightarrow 12 = 3x \Rightarrow x = 4$ m.p.h.

Variation Problems

Variation in mathematics refers to the interrelationship of variables in such a manner that a change of value for one variable produces a corresponding change in another. There are three basic types of variation: direction, inverse, and joint.

1. *Direct Variation*

The expression "x varies directly as y" can be described by any of the following equations:

$$\frac{x}{y} = \textbf{constant} \qquad \frac{x_1}{y_1} = \frac{x_2}{y_2} \qquad \frac{x_1}{y_2} = \frac{x_1}{y_2}$$

Two quantities are said to vary directly if they change in the same direction. As one increases, the other increases and their ratio is equal to the positive constant.

For example, the amount you must pay for milk varies directly with the number of quarts of milk you buy. The amount of sugar needed in a recipe varies directly with the amount of butter used. The number of inches between two cities on a map varies directly with the number of miles between these cities.

EXAMPLE:

If x varied directly as the square of m and $x = 12$ when $m = 2$, what is the value of x when $m = 3$?

$$\frac{x_1}{y_1^2} = \frac{x_2}{y_2^2} \Rightarrow \frac{x}{(3)^2} = \frac{12}{(2)^2} \Rightarrow \frac{x}{9} = \frac{12}{4} \Rightarrow \frac{x}{9} = 3 \Rightarrow x = 27$$

2. *Inverse Variation*

The expression "x varies inversely as y" can be described by any of the following equations:

$$\frac{x}{y} = \textbf{constant} \qquad \frac{x_1}{y_1} = \frac{x_2}{y_2} \qquad \frac{x_1}{y_2} = \frac{x_2}{y_1}$$

Two quantities are said to vary inversely if they change in opposite directions. As one increases, the other decreases.

For example, the number of people hired to paint a house varies inversely with the number of days the job will take. A doctor's stock of flu vaccine varies inversely with the number of patients she injects. The number of days a given supply of cat food lasts varies inversely with the number of cats being fed.

EXAMPLE:

The time t to empty a container varies inversely as the square root of the number of men m working on the job. If it takes, 3 hours for 16 men to do the job, how long will it take 4 men working at the same rate to empty the container?

$$t_1\sqrt{m_1} = t_2\sqrt{m_2} \Rightarrow 3\sqrt{16} = t\sqrt{4} \Rightarrow 3(4) = t(2) \Rightarrow 2t = 12 \Rightarrow t = 6$$

3. *Joint Variation*

The expression "x varies jointly as y and z" can be described by any of the following equations:

$$\frac{x}{yz} = \text{constant} \qquad \frac{x_1}{y_1z_1} = \frac{x_2}{y_2z_2} \qquad \frac{x_1}{y_2} = \left(\frac{y_1}{y_2}\right)\left(\frac{z_1}{z_2}\right)$$

EXAMPLE:

The area A of a triangle varies jointly as the base b and the height h. If $A = 20$ when $b = 10$ and $h = 4$, find the value of A when $b = 6$ and $h = 7$.

$\frac{A_1}{b_1h_1} = \frac{A_2}{b_2h_2} \Rightarrow \frac{20}{(10)(4)} \Rightarrow \frac{A_2}{(6)(7)} \Rightarrow \frac{20}{40} = \frac{A_2}{42} \Rightarrow \frac{1}{2} = \frac{A_2}{42} \Rightarrow A_2 = 21$

Percent Problems

Many problem-solving questions involve percents. Certain types of business situations make for excellent applications involving percents on the test.

1. *Percent of Increase or Decrease*

The percent of increase or decrease is found by putting the amount of increase or decrease over the original amount and changing this fraction to a percent as explained in a previous situation.

EXAMPLES:

A company normally employs 100 people. During a slow spell, it fired 20% of its employees. By what percent must it know increase its staff to return to full capacity?

$20\% = \frac{1}{5} \cdot \frac{1}{5} \cdot 100 = 20$. The company now has $100 - 20 = 80$ employees. If it then increases by 20, the percent of increase is $\frac{20}{80} = \frac{1}{4}$, or 25%.

2. *Discounts*

A discount is usually expressed as a percent of the marked price, which will be deducted from the marked price to determine the sale price.

EXAMPLES:

Bill's Hardware offers a 20% discount on all appliances during a sale week. How much must Mrs. Russell pay for a washing machine marked at $280?

You can solve this problem two ways, a long way and short way. First the long way: $20\% = \frac{1}{5} \Rightarrow \frac{1}{5} \cdot 280 =$ $56 discount $\Rightarrow$ $280 – $56 = $224 sale price.

The shortcut method: if there is a 20% discount, Mrs. Russell will pay 80% of the marked price: $80\% = \frac{4}{5} \Rightarrow \frac{4}{5} \cdot 280 = \$224$ sale price.

A store offers a television set marked at $340 less consecutive discounts of 10% and 5%. Another store offers the same set with a single discount of 15%. How much does the buyer save buying at the better price?

In the first store, the initial discount means the buyer pays 90% or $\frac{9}{10}$ of 340, which is $306. The additional 5% discount means the buyer pays 95% of $306, or $290.70. Note that the second discount must be figured on the first sale price. Taking 5% of $306 is a smaller amount than talking the additional 5% off $340. The second store will therefore have a longer sale price. In the second store, the buyer will pay 85% of $340, or $289, making the price $1.70 less than in the first store.

3. *Commission*

Many salespeople earn money on a commission bases. In order to inspire sales, they are paid a percentage of the value of goods sold. This amount is called a commission.

EXAMPLES:

Mr. Saunders works at Brown's Department Store, where he is paid \$80 per week in salary plus a 4% commission on all his sales. How much does he earn in a week in which he sells \$4,032 worth of merchandise?

Find 4% of \$4,032 and add this amount to \$80: $4032 \cdot 0.04 = \$161.28 \Rightarrow \$161.28 + \$80 = \$241.28$.

Bill Olson delivers newspapers for a dealer and keeps 8% of all money collected. One month he was able to keep \$16. How much did he forward to the dealer?

First, find how much he collected by asking 16 is 8% of what number: $16 = 0.08x \Rightarrow 1600 = 8x \Rightarrow x = 200$.

4. *Taxes*

Taxes are a percent of money spent or money earned.

EXAMPLES:

Dane County collects a 7% sales tax on automobiles. If the price of a used Ford is \$5,832 before taxes, what will it cost when the sales tax is added in?

Find 7% of \$5,832 to find tax and then add it to \$5,832. This can be done in one step by finding 107% of \$5,832: $5832 \cdot 1.07 = \$6240.24$.

If income is taxed at the rate of 10% for the first \$10,000 of earned income, 15% for the next \$10,000, 20% of the next \$10,000 and 25% for all earnings over \$30,000, how much income tax must be paid on a yearly income of \$36,500?

10% of first \$10,000 = \$1,000
15% of next \$10,000 = \$1,500
20% of next \$10,000 = \$2,000
\+ 25% of \$6,500 = \$1,625
Total tax = \$6,125

EXERCISE 13

Problem-Solving

DIRECTIONS: Choose the best answer to each of the following questions. Answers are on page 129.

1. A suit is sold for \$68 while marked at \$80. What is the rate of discount?

   (A) 15% (B) 12% (C) $17\frac{11}{17}$%
   (D) 20% (E) 24%

2. Lilian left home with \$60 in her wallet. She spent $\frac{1}{3}$ of that amount at the supermarket, and she spent $\frac{1}{2}$ of what remained at the drugstore. If Lilian made no other expenditures, how much money did she have when she returned home?

   (A) \$10 (B) \$15 (C) \$20 (D) \$40 (E) \$50

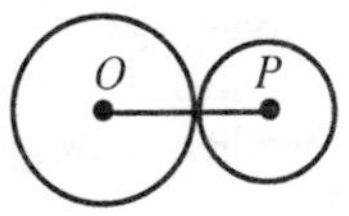

3. In the figure above, circle O and circle P are tangent to each other. If the circle with center O has a diameter of 8 and the circle with center P has a diameter of 6, what is the length of segment OP?

   (A) 7 (B) 10 (C) 14 (D) 20 (E) 28

4. A man buys a radio for \$70 after receiving a discount of 20%. What was the marked price?

   (A) \$84 (B) \$56 (C) \$87.50
   (D) \$92 (E) \$90

5. Colin and Shaina wish to buy a gift for a friend. They combine their money and find they have \$4.00, consisting of quarters, dimes, and nickels. If they have 35 coins and the number of quarters is half the number of nickels, how many quarters do they have?

   (A) 5 (B) 10 (C) 20 (D) 3 (E) 6

6. Willie receives r% commission on a sale of s dollars. How many dollars does he receive?

   (A) rs (B) $\frac{r}{s}$ (C) $100rs$ (D) $\frac{r}{100s}$ (E) $\frac{rs}{100}$

7. Three times the first of three consecutive odd integers is 3 more than twice the third. Find the third integer.

   (A) 9 (B) 11 (C) 13 (D) 15 (E) 7

8. A refrigerator was sold for \$273, yielding a 30% profit on the cost. For how much should it be sold to yield only a 10% profit on the cost?

   (A) \$210 (B) \$231 (C) \$221
   (D) \$235 (E) \$240

9. If 60 feet of uniform wire weigh 80 pounds, what is the weight of 2 yards of the same wire?

   (A) $2\frac{2}{3}$ (B) 6 (C) 2400
   (D) 120 (E) 8

10. What single discount is equivalent to two successive discounts of 10% and 15%?

    (A) 25% (B) 24% (C) 24.5%
    (D) 23.5% (E) 22%

11. Robert is 15 years older than his brother Stan. However, y years ago Robert was twice as old as Stan. If Stan is now b years old and $b > y$, find the value of $b - y$.

    (A) 13 (B) 14 (C) 15 (D) 16 (E) 17

12. The net price of a certain article is \$306 after successive discounts of 15% and 10% have been allowed on the marked price. What is the marked price?

    (A) \$234.09 (B) \$400 (C) \$382.50
    (D) \$408 (E) None of these

13. A gear 50 inches in diameter turns a smaller gear 30 inches in diameter. If the larger gear makes 15 revolutions, how many revolutions does the smaller gear make in that time?

    (A) 9 (B) 12 (C) 20 (D) 25 (E) 30

14. If a merchant makes a profit of 20% based on the selling price of an article, what percent does he make on the cost?

    (A) 20 (B) 40 (C) 25
    (D) 80 (E) None of these

15. How many ounces of pure acid must be added to 20 ounces of a solution that is 5% acid to strengthen it to a solution that is 24% acid?

    (A) $2\frac{1}{2}$ (B) 5 (C) 6 (D) $7\frac{1}{2}$ (E) 10

16. If x men can do a job in h days, how long would y men take to do the same job?

(A) $\frac{x}{h}$ (B) $\frac{xh}{y}$ (C) $\frac{hy}{x}$ (D) xyh (E) $\frac{x}{y}$

17. A certain radio costs a merchant $72. At what price must he sell it if he is to make a profit of 20% of the selling price?

(A) $86.40 (B) $92 (C) $90
(D) $144 (E) $148

18. A dealer mixes a lbs. of nuts worth b cents per pound with c lbs. of nuts worth d cents per pound. At what price should he sell a pound of the mixture if he wishes to make a profit of 10 cents per pound?

(A) $\frac{ab+cd}{a+c}+10$ (B) $\frac{ab+cd}{a+c}+0.10$ (C) $\frac{b+d}{a+c}+10$
(D) $\frac{b+d}{a+c}+0.10$ (E) $\frac{b+d+10}{a+c}$

19. If a furnace uses 40 gallons of oil in a week, how many gallons, to the nearest gallon, does it use in 10 days?

(A) 57 (B) 4 (C) 28 (D) 400 (E) 58

20. Nell invests $2,400 in the Security National Bank at 5%. How much additional money must she invest at 8% so that the total annual income will be equal to 6% of her entire investment?

(A) $2,400 (B) $3,600 (C) $1,000
(D) $3,000 (E) $1,200

21. A baseball team has won 40 games out of 60 played. It has 32 more games to play. How many of these must the team win to make its record 75% for the season?

(A) 26 (B) 29 (C) 28 (D) 30 (E) 32

22. A recipe requires 13 oz. of sugar and 18 oz. Of flour. If only 10 oz. of sugar are used, how much flour, to the nearest ounce, should be used?

(A) 13 (B) 23 (C) 14 (D) 14 (E) 15

23. Ivan left Austin to drive to Boxville at 6:15 p.m. and arrived at 11:45 p.m. If he averaged 30 miles per hour and stopped one hour for dinner, how far is Boxville from Austin?

(A) 120 (B) 135 (C) 180 (D) 165 (E) 150

24. If prices are reduced 25% and sales increase 20%, what is the net effect on gross receipts?

(A) The increase by 5%.
(B) They decrease by 5%.
(C) They remain the same.
(D) They increase by 10%.
(E) They decrease by 10%.

25. If a car can drive 25 miles on two gallons of gasoline, how many gallons will be needed for a trip of 150 miles.

(A) 12 (B) 3 (C) 6 (D) 7 (E) 10

26. A plane traveling 600 miles per hour is 30 miles from Kennedy Airport at 4:58 p.m. At what time will it arrive at the airport?

(A) 5:00 p.m. (B) 5:01 p.m. (C) 5:02 p.m.
(D) 5:20 p.m. (E) 5:03 p.m.

27. A salesperson earns a commission of 5% on all sales between $200 and $600, and 8% on all sales over $600. What is the commission earned in a week in which sales total $800?

(A) $20 (B) $46 (C) $88 (D) $36 (E) $78

28. A school has enough bread to last 30 children 4 days. If 10 children are added, how many days will the bread last?

(A) $5\frac{1}{3}$ (B) $1\frac{1}{3}$ (C) $2\frac{2}{3}$ (D) 12 (E) 3

29. Mr. Bridges can wash his car in 15 minutes, while his son Dave takes twice as long to do the same job. If they work together, how many minutes will the job take them?

(A) 5 (B) $7\frac{1}{2}$ (C) 10 (D) $22\frac{1}{2}$ (E) 30

30. At cents per pound, what is the cost of a ounces of salami?

(A) $\frac{c}{a}$ (B) $\frac{a}{c}$ (C) ac (D) $\frac{ac}{16}$ (E) $\frac{16c}{a}$

31. The value of a fraction is $\frac{2}{5}$. If the numerator is decreased by 2 and the denominator increased by the resulting fraction is equivalent to $\frac{1}{4}$. Find 4 the numerator of the original fraction.

(A) 23 (B) 4 (C) 6 (D) 10 (E) 15

32. If 3 miles are equivalent to 4.83 kilometers, then 11.27 kilometers are equivalent to how many miles?

(A) $7\frac{1}{3}$ (B) $2\frac{1}{3}$ (C) 7 (D) 5 (E) $6\frac{1}{2}$

33. If enrollment at City University grew from 3,000 to 12,000 in the last 10 years, what was the percent of increase in enrollment?

(A) 125% (B) 25% (C) 300%
(D) 400% (E) 3%

34. At a certain printing plant, each of m machines prints 6 newspapers every s seconds. If all machines work together but independently without interruption, how many minutes will it take to print an entire run of 18,000 newspapers?

(A) $\frac{180s}{m}$ (B) $\frac{50s}{m}$ (C) $50ms$ (D) $\frac{ms}{50}$ (E) $\frac{300m}{s}$

35. If p pencils cost d dollars, how many pencils can be bought for c cents?

(A) $\frac{100pc}{d}$ (G) $\frac{pc}{100d}$ (C) $\frac{pd}{c}$ (D) $\frac{pc}{d}$ (E) $\frac{cd}{p}$

36. A car dealer who gives a customer a 20 percent discount on the list price of a car still realizes a net profit of 25 percent of cost. If the dealer's cost is $4800, what is the usual list price of the car?

(A) $6000 (B) $6180 (C) $7200
(D) $7500 (E) $8001

37. m varies directly as the square of t. If m is 7 when t = 1, what is the value of m when t = 2?

(A) 28 (B) 14 (C) 7 (D) $3\frac{1}{2}$ (E) 2

38. 6 students in a class failed algebra. This represents $16\frac{2}{3}\%$ of the class. How many students passed the course?

(A) 48 (B) 36 (C) 42 (D) 30 (E) 32

39. If the value of a piece of property decreases by 10 percent while the tax rate on the property increases by 10 percent, what is the effect on taxes?

(A) Taxes increase by 10 percent.
(B) Taxes increase by 1 percent.
(C) There is no change in taxes.
(D) Taxes decrease by 1 percent.
(E) Taxes decrease by 10 percent.

40. m varies jointly as r and l. If m is 8 and when r and l are each 1, what is the value of m when r and l are each 2?

(A) 64 (B) 32 (C) 16 (D) 4 (E) 2

41. A rectangular box with a top is created by folding the figure above along the dotted lines. What is the volume of the box in cubic feet?

(A) 6 (B) 9 (C) 12 (D) 18 (E) 24

42. 95% of the residents of Coral Estates live in private homes. 40% of those live in air-conditioned homes. What percent of the residents of Coral Estates live in air-conditioned homes?

(A) 3% (B) 30% (C) 3.8% (D) 40% (E) 38%

43. If the spaces between the lettered points in the figure above are all equal, then $\frac{PT}{2} - \frac{QS}{2}$ is equal to which of the following?

(A) $PS - QR$ (B) $QR - QS$ (C) PR (D) QT (E) ST

44. Exactly three years before the year in which Anna was born, the year was 1980 – x. In terms of x, on Anna's twentieth birthday, the year will be

(A) $1977 + x$ (B) $1997 + x$ (C) $2003 - x$
(D) $2003 + x$ (E) $2006 + x$

45. Mr. Carlson receives a salary of $500 a month and a commission of 5% on all sales. What must be the amount of 5% on all sales. What must be the amount of his sales in July so that his total monthly income is $2,400?

(A) $48,000 (B) $38,000 (C) $7,600
(D) $3,800 (E) $25,000

46. John can wax his car in 3 hours. Jim can do the same job in 5 hours. How long will it take them if they work together?

(A) $\frac{1}{2}$ hours (B) $1\frac{7}{8}$ hours (C) 2 hours

(D) $2\frac{7}{8}$ hours (E) 8 hours

Answer Key

EXERCISE 1—WHOLE NUMBERS (p. B-7)

1. B	11. C	21. C	31. D	41. A	51. B
2. B	12. D	22. C	32. C	42. C	52. A
3. B	13. D	23. E	33. C	43. C	53. C
4. C	14. C	24. A	34. E	44. A	54. C
5. C	15. D	25. A	35. B	45. E	55. C
6. D	16. C	26. B	36. A	46. A	56. E
7. C	17. C	27. B	37. D	47. B	57. C
8. E	18. B	28. B	38. B	48. A	58. C
9. E	19. B	29. A	39. D	49. A	59. D
10. B	20. C	30. D	40. B	50. B	60. C

EXERCISE 2—FRACTIONS (p. B-16)

1. E	11. B	21. B	31. D	41. B	51. D
2. D	12. C	22. B	32. B	42. A	52. C
3. B	13. B	23. D	33. D	43. A	53. A
4. C	14. E	24. B	34. A	44. B	54. A
5. C	15. E	25. C	35. A	45. A	55. E
6. D	16. C	26. C	36. C	46. C	56. D
7. A	17. C	27. E	37. C	47. B	57. E
8. C	18. A	28. A	38. B	48. A	58. C
9. E	19. B	29. B	39. B	49. A	59. A
10. C	20. E	30. C	40. A	50. A	60. A

61. (E) To simplify a complex fraction, divide the numerator by the denominator: $\frac{4}{9} \div \frac{2}{5} = \frac{\cancel{4}^{2}}{9} \cdot \frac{5}{\cancel{2}_{1}} = \frac{10}{9} = 1\frac{1}{9}$.

62. (D) Write all of the fractions with the same denominator. The lowest common denominator equals 80.

(A) $\frac{9}{16} = \frac{45}{80}$ X

(B) $\frac{7}{10} = \frac{56}{80}$ X

(C) $\frac{5}{8} = \frac{50}{80}$ X

(D) $\frac{4}{5} = \frac{64}{80}$ √

(E) $\frac{1}{2} = \frac{40}{80}$ X

This makes it clear that (D) is the largest.

63. (B)

$$\begin{array}{rcl} 3\ 5/16 & = & 3\ 5/16 \\ \underline{+\ 2\ 3/4} & = & \underline{+\ 2\ 12/16} \\ & & 5\frac{17}{16} = 6\frac{1}{16} \end{array}$$

64. (E) $10\frac{1}{2} \div \frac{1}{2} = \frac{21}{2} \div \frac{1}{2} = \frac{21}{2} \cdot \frac{2}{1} = 21.$

65. (D) $5\frac{3}{4} \cdot 3 = \frac{23}{4} \cdot \frac{3}{1} = \frac{69}{4} = 17\frac{1}{4}.$

66. (A) First week: lowest common denominator = 24.

$$\begin{array}{rcl} 3 & = & 3\ 12/24 \text{ miles} \\ 1\ 1/4 & = & 1\ 6/24 \\ 1\ 1/6 & = & 1\ 4/24 \\ \underline{+\ 2\ 3/8} & = & \underline{+2\ 9/24} \\ & & 7\frac{31}{24} = 8\frac{7}{24} \text{ miles} \end{array}$$

Second week: lowest common denominator = 16.

$\frac{1}{4} = \frac{4}{16}$ miles

$\frac{3}{8} = \frac{6}{16}$

$\frac{9}{16} = \frac{9}{16}$

$$\begin{array}{rcl} 3\ 1/16 & = & 3\ 1/16 \\ 2\ 5/8 & = & 2\ 10/16 \\ +\ 3\ 3/16 & = & +\ 3\ 3/16 \\ \hline & & 8\frac{33}{16} = 10\frac{1}{16} \text{ miles} \end{array}$$

The lowest common denominator for both the first and second weeks is 48.

$$\begin{array}{rcll} 10\ 1/16 & = & 9\ 51/48 & \text{miles second week} \\ -\ 8\ 7/24 & = & -\ 8\ 14/48 & \text{miles first week} \\ \hline & & 1\frac{37}{48} & \text{more miles traveled} \end{array}$$

67. (C) Consider each choice:

(A) Each 6-ft. board yields one $5\frac{1}{2}$ft. board with $\frac{1}{2}$ ft. waste.

(B) Each 12-ft. board yields two $5\frac{1}{2}$ft. boards with 1 ft. waste ($2 \cdot 5\frac{1}{2} = 11$; $12 - 11 = 1$ ft. waste).

(C) Each 24-ft. board yields four $5\frac{1}{2}$ft. boards with 2 ft. waste ($4 \cdot 5\frac{1}{2} = 22$; $24 - 22 = 2$ ft. waste).

(D) Each 22 ft. board may be divided into four $5\frac{1}{2}$ft. boards with no waste ($4 \cdot 5\frac{1}{2} = 22$ exactly).

Therefore, the correct choice is (C), 22 ft.

68. (D) $\frac{15}{16}$ of fortune is \$7500. Therefore, his fortune = $7500 \div \frac{15}{16} = \frac{7500}{1} \cdot \frac{16}{15} = \frac{500}{1} \cdot \frac{16}{1} = 8000$.

69. (D) $\frac{2}{3}$ of 54,000 = increase. Therefore: Increase = $\frac{2}{3} \cdot 54{,}000 = \frac{2}{1} \cdot 18{,}000 = 36{,}000$. Present population = $54{,}000 + 36{,}000 = 90{,}000$.

70. (C) First day: $\frac{1}{3}$ evaporates, $\frac{2}{3}$. Second day: $\frac{3}{4}$ of $\frac{2}{3}$ evaporates, $\frac{1}{4}$ of $\frac{2}{3}$ remains. Remainder = $\frac{1}{4} \cdot \frac{2}{3} = \frac{1}{2} \cdot \frac{1}{3} = \frac{1}{6}$ of original.

71. (C) $\frac{7}{8}$ of capacity = 14 gallons. Therefore, capacity = $14 \div \frac{7}{8} = \frac{14}{1} \cdot \frac{8}{7} = \frac{2}{1} \cdot \frac{8}{1} = 16$ gallons.

EXERCISE 3—DECIMALS (p. B-24)

1. C	11. B	21. C	31. E	41. A	51. A
2. C	12. B	22. E	32. C	42. A	52. C
3. B	13. B	23. A	33. A	43. B	53. E
4. B	14. C	24. A	34. A	44. B	54. B
5. B	15. A	25. C	35. E	45. A	55. A
6. E	16. B	26. B	36. D	46. D	56. C
7. B	17. B	27. D	37. D	47. B	57. C
8. A	18. D	28. A	38. A	48. B	58. B
9. E	19. B	29. B	39. B	49. B	59. D
10. A	20. A	30. D	40. B	50. C	60. B

61. (D) Add the savings for each month:

$$\begin{array}{r} \$4.56 \\ 3.82 \\ +5.06 \\ \hline \$13.44 \end{array}$$

62. (C)

$$\begin{array}{r} 1.51 \\ +0.015 \\ \hline 1.525 \end{array} \qquad \begin{array}{r} 1.510 \\ -0.015 \\ \hline 1.495 \end{array}$$

Therefore, the rod may have a diameter of 1.495 inches to 1.525 inches inclusive.

63. (C) Add to find total deductions:

$$\begin{array}{r} \$3.05 \\ +5.68 \\ \hline \$8.73 \end{array}$$

Subtract total deductions from salary to find amount of check:

$$\begin{array}{r} \$190.57 \\ -\ 8.73 \\ \hline \$181.84 \end{array}$$

64. (B) Outer radius minus inner radius equals thickness of metal: 2.84 – 1.94 = 0.90.

65. (C) Add daily earnings to find total earnings: \$20.56 + 32.90 + 20.78 = \$74.24. Divide total earnings by 2 to find out what he has left:

$$2\overline{)\$74.24}\quad = \$37.12$$

66. (C) Find the cost of $3\frac{1}{2}$ pounds of meat: \$1.69 • 3.5 ≈ \$5.92. Find the cost of 20 lemons: \$0.60 ÷ 12 = \$0.05 for 1 lemon and \$0.05 • 20 = \$1.00 for 20 lemons. Add the cost of meat and the cost of lemons: \$5.92 + \$1.00 = \$6.92.

67. (A) Subtract the weight of the empty reel from the total weight to find the weight of the cable: 1279 lb. – 285 lb. = 994 lb. Each foot of cable weighs 7.1 lb. Therefore, to find the number of feet of cable on the reel, divide 994 by 7.1:

```
      14 0.
7.1.)994. 0.
     71
     284
     284
       0.0
```

68. (D) Each fastener costs: \$4.15 ÷ 100 = \$0.0415. Thus, 345 fasteners cost: 345 • 0.0415 = \$14.32.

EXERCISE 4—PERCENTS (p. B-31)

1. E	20. C	39. A	58. B	77. D	96. C
2. A	21. C	40. A	59. C	78. C	97. E
3. B	22. D	41. D	60. D	79. C	98. D
4. B	23. E	42. A	61. D	80. C	99. A
5. C	24. D	43. E	62. C	81. D	100. D
6. A	25. D	44. A	63. B	82. C	101. D
7. C	26. B	45. B	64. B	83. C	102. C
8. B	27. C	46. D	65. B	84. C	103. B
9. A	28. A	47. A	66. B	85. A	104. A
10. A	29. C	48. B	67. E	86. D	105. C
11. B	30. A	49. A	68. C	87. D	106. C
12. B	31. B	50. A	69. D	88. C	107. E
13. A	32. E	51. C	70. B	89. D	108. C
14. A	33. D	52. C	71. B	90. E	109. E
15. A	34. B	53. B	72. D	91. C	110. D
16. C	35. D	54. B	73. C	92. D	111. D
17. B	36. C	55. B	74. C	93. E	112. E
18. D	37. D	56. B	75. D	94. A	
19. C	38. B	57. C	76. D	95. B	

113. (B) Since \$118.80 represents a 20% reduction, \$118.80 = 80% of the regular price. Regular price = $\frac{\$118,80}{80\%}$ = \$118.80 ÷ 0.80 = \$148.50.

114. (E) All the items in a circle graph total 100%. Add the figures given for housing, food, clothing, and taxes: 26.2 + 28.4% + 12.0% + 12.7% = 79.3%. Subtract this total from 100% to find the percent for miscellaneous items: 100.0% – 79.3% = 20.7%.

115. (C) Price of shuttlecocks = 24 • \$0.35 = \$8.40. Price of rackets = 4 • \$2.75 = \$11.00. Total price = \$8.40 + \$2.75 = \$19.40. Discount is 30%, and 100% – 30% = 70%. Actual cost = 70% of 19.40 = 0.70 • 19.40 = 13.58.

116. (E) Subtract weight of wood after drying from original weight of wood to find amount of moisture in wood: 10 – 8 = 2 ounces of wood. Moisture content = $\frac{\text{2 ounces}}{\text{10 ounces}}$ = 0.2 = 20%.

117. (A) Find the number of each kind of coin: 10% of 800 = 0.10 • 800 = 80 dimes
30% of 800 = 0.30 • 800 = 240 nickels
60% of 800 = 0.60 • 800 = 480 quarters

Find the value of the coins:
80 dimes = 80 • 0.10 = \$8.00
240 nickels = 240 • 0.05 = 12.00
480 quarters = 480 • 0.25 = 120.00
Total = \$140.00

118. (C) First solution contains 20% of 6 quarts of alcohol. Alcohol content = 0.20 • 6 = 1.2 quarts. Second solution contains 60% of 4 quarts of alcohol. Alcohol content = 0.60 • 4 = 2.4 quarts. Mixture contains: 1.2 + 2.4 = 3.6 quarts alcohol; 6 + 4 = 10 quarts liquid; alcoholic strength of mixture $= \frac{3.6}{10} = 36\%$.

119. (D) $2\frac{1}{2}\%$ of insured value = \$348. Insured value $= \frac{342}{2\frac{1}{2}\%} = 348 \div 0.025 = 13{,}920$. \$13,920 is 80% of total value: total value $= \frac{\$13{,}920}{80\%} = \$13{,}920 \div 0.80 = \$17{,}400$.

120. (D) $\frac{1}{5} \cdot 35 = 7$ hr. sorting mail; $\frac{1}{2} \cdot 35 = 17\frac{1}{2}$ hr. filing; $\frac{1}{7} \cdot 35 = 5$ hr. reception; $29\frac{1}{2}$ hr. accounted for; $35 - 29\frac{1}{2} = 5\frac{1}{2}$ hr. left for messenger work; % spent on messenger work: $\frac{5\frac{1}{2}}{35} = 5\frac{1}{2} \div 35 = \frac{11}{2} \cdot \frac{1}{35} = \frac{11}{70} = 0.15\frac{5}{7} = 15\frac{5}{7}\%$.

121. (C) 80% of the boys = 1152. Number of boys $= \frac{1152}{80\%} = 1152 + 0.80 = 1440$. 40% of students = 1440. Total numbers of students $= \frac{1440}{40\%} = 1440 + 0.40 = 3600$.

122. (B) Amount of increase = \$2500. Percent of increase $= \frac{\text{amount of increase}}{\text{original}} = \frac{2500}{25{,}000} = \frac{1}{10} = 10\%$.

123. (B) Amount of increase = 20,000. Percent of increase $= \frac{20{,}000}{80{,}000} = \frac{1}{4} = 25\%$.

124. (D) Amount of decrease = \$4. Percent of decrease $\frac{4}{25} = \frac{16}{100} = 16\%$.

125. (A) Amount of increase = \$30,000. Percent of increase $= \frac{30{,}000}{30{,}000} = 1 = 100\%$.

126. (A) Amount of decrease = 50. Percent of decrease $= \frac{50}{200} = \frac{1}{4} = 25\%$.

EXERCISE 5—NEGATIVE NUMBERS (p. B-41)

1. E	11. E	21. A	31. A	41. A	51. C
2. D	12. E	22. B	32. E	42. B	52. B
3. D	13. D	23. D	33. A	43. C	53. A
4. A	14. C	24. A	34. D	44. C	54. A
5. B	15. D	25. A	35. E	45. A	55. C
6. A	16. C	26. D	36. D	46. C	56. A
7. C	17. C	27. D	37. A	47. B	57. A
8. A	18. C	28. B	38. D	48. D	58. C
9. D	19. A	29. C	39. D	49. B	59. E
10. D	20. B	30. E	40. B	50. D	60. B

EXERCISE 6—MEAN, MEDIAN, AND MODE (p. B-46)

1. A	8. C	15. C	22. E	29. B	36. C
2. D	9. E	16. D	23. E	30. B	37. C
3. C	10. A	17. E	24. B	31. C	38. D
4. B	11. E	18. A	25. B	32. C	39. E
5. C	12. B	19. D	26. C	33. D	40. B
6. E	13. B	20. D	27. B	34. D	41. D
7. A	14. A	21. D	28. E	35. A	42. C

43. (B) Sum of the grades = 1440 $\Rightarrow \frac{1440}{20} = 72$.

44. (B)
75 • 15¢ = 1125¢
100 • 30¢ = 3000¢
50 • 72¢ = 3600¢
225 7725¢
Therefore, $\frac{7725¢}{225} = 34\frac{1}{3}¢$

45. (E) Multiply the grade in each course by the weight given it in the final average: (90 • 4) + (84 • 3) + (75 • 3) + (76 + 1) = 360 + 252 + 225 + 76 = 913. Total weight = 4 + 3 + 3 + 1 = 11. Therefore, the average = 913 ÷ 11 = 83.

46. (D) Average $= \frac{3+4+4+0+1+2+0+2+2}{9} = \frac{18}{9} = 2$.

47. (B) Arrange the numbers in order: 0, 0, 1, 2, 2, 2, 3, 4, 4. Of the 9 numbers, the fifth (middle) number is 2.

48. (C) The number appearing most often is 2.

EXERCISE 7—RATIOS AND PROPORTIONS (p. B-53)

1. B	8. B	15. D	22. B	29. E	36. C
2. A	9. B	16. D	23. C	30. C	37. B
3. D	10. D	17. E	24. C	31. D	
4. C	11. C	18. D	25. B	32. C	
5. A	12. C	19. D	26. C	33. B	
6. A	13. B	20. E	27. D	34. A	
7. D	14. C	21. C	28. B	35. D	

38. (B) $\frac{2\frac{1}{2}}{4} = \frac{1\frac{7}{8}}{s} \Rightarrow s = \frac{4 \cdot 1\frac{7}{8}}{2\frac{1}{2}} = \frac{4 \cdot \frac{15}{8}}{2\frac{1}{2}} = \frac{1 \cdot \frac{15}{2}}{2\frac{1}{2}} = \frac{15}{2} \div 2\frac{1}{2} = \frac{15}{2} \div \frac{5}{2} = \frac{15}{2} \cdot \frac{2}{5} = 3$ inches.

39. (C) If p is the cost per dozen (12): $\frac{3}{12} = \frac{2.29}{p} \Rightarrow p = \frac{12 \cdot 2.29}{3} = \frac{4 \cdot 2.29}{1} = 9.16$.

40. (A) If f is the height of the first pole, the proportion is: $\frac{f}{24} = \frac{3}{4} \Rightarrow f = \frac{24 \cdot 3}{4} = \frac{6 \cdot 3}{1} = 18$ ft.

41. (D) If y is the unknown length: $\frac{3\frac{1}{2}}{\frac{1}{8}} = \frac{y}{1} \Rightarrow y = \frac{3\frac{1}{2} \cdot 1}{\frac{1}{8}} = 3\frac{1}{2} \div \frac{1}{8} = \frac{7}{2} \cdot \frac{8}{1} = \frac{7}{1} \cdot \frac{4}{1} = 28$ ft.

42. (B) Only two parts of a proportion are known the problem must be solved by the ratio method. The ratio 10:1 means that if the alloy were separated into equal parts, 10 of those parts would be copper and 1 would be aluminum, for a total of $10 \div 1 = 11$ parts. $77 \div 11 = 7$ lb. per part. The allow has 1 part aluminum. $7 \cdot 1 = 7$ lb. aluminum.

43. (C) The cost, c, is proportional to the number of square feet: $\frac{\$0.31}{c} = \frac{1}{180} \Rightarrow c = \frac{\$0.31 \cdot 180}{1} = \$55.80$.

44. (B) The amount earned is proportional to the number of days worked: $\frac{\$352}{a} = \frac{16}{117} \Rightarrow a = \frac{\$352 \cdot 117}{16} = \$2574$.

45. (D) If n is the unknown length: $\frac{\frac{1}{8}}{3\frac{3}{4}} = \frac{12}{n} \Rightarrow n = \frac{12 \cdot 3\frac{3}{4}}{\frac{1}{8}} = \frac{12 \cdot \frac{15}{4}}{\frac{1}{8}} = \frac{3 \cdot \frac{15}{1}}{\frac{1}{8}} = \frac{45}{\frac{1}{8}} = 45 \div \frac{1}{8} = 45 \cdot \frac{8}{1} = 360$.

46. (B) The ratio of investment is: 9,000:7,000:6,000 or 9:7:6. $9 + 7 + 6 = 22$. $\$825 \div 22 = \$37.20$ each share of profit. $7 \cdot \$37.50 = \$262.40$, B's share of profit. $\$262.50 - 230.00 = \$32.50$, the amount B has left.

EXERCISE 8—EXPONENTS AND RADICALS (p. B-63)

1. E	12. C	23. E	34. B	45. E	56. B
2. D	13. C	24. A	35. B	46. C	57. D
3. E	14. B	25. D	36. C	47. E	58. C
4. B	15. B	26. A	37. D	48. D	59. D
5. C	16. C	27. C	38. B	49. B	60. B
6. E	17. E	28. B	39. D	50. C	61. C
7. C	18. D	29. C	40. A	51. E	62. B
8. A	19. C	30. C	41. B	52. D	63. A
9. A	20. C	31. A	42. C	53. B	64. B
10. A	21. C	32. A	43. C	54. D	65. A
11. B	22. A	33. D	44. A	55. A	

66. (A) Using the distributive law, we have $\frac{1}{2}\sqrt{12} + \frac{1}{4} \cdot 2 = \frac{1}{2}\sqrt{4}\sqrt{3} + \frac{1}{2} = \sqrt{3} + \frac{1}{2}$.

67. (D) Dividing the numbers in the radical sign, we have $\sqrt{4b^2} = 2b$.

68. (D) $3\sqrt{48} = 3\sqrt{16}\sqrt{3} = 12\sqrt{3}$.

69. (B) $\sqrt{\frac{16x^2 + 9x^2}{144}} = \frac{25x^2}{144} = \frac{5x}{12}$.

70. (E) The terms cannot be combined, and it is not possible to take the square root of separated terms.

71. (D) $\sqrt{\frac{100x^2 - 64x^2}{6400}} = \sqrt{\frac{36x^2}{6400}} = \frac{6x}{80} = \frac{3x}{40}$.

72. (A) $\sqrt{\frac{18y^2 - 2y^2}{36}} = \frac{16y^2}{36} = \frac{4y}{6} = \frac{2y}{3}$.

73. (E) It is not possible to find the square root of separate terms.

74. (C) In order to take the square root of a decimal, it must have an even number of decimal places so that its square root will have exactly half as many. In addition to this, the digits must form a perfect square ($\sqrt{0.09} = 0.3$).

EXERCISE 9—ALGEBRAIC OPERATIONS (p. B-74)

1. A	17. D	33. C	49. A	65. D	81. D
2. D	18. D	34. D	50. D	66. B	82. D
3. C	19. B	35. A	51. D	67. B	83. C
4. C	20. C	36. E	52. A	68. A	84. D
5. E	21. C	37. E	53. D	69. B	85. B
6. B	22. B	38. E	54. D	70. C	86. A
7. A	23. A	39. C	55. E	71. B	87. C
8. E	24. C	40. D	56. B	72. B	88. B
9. B	25. B	41. B	57. D	73. A	89. C
10. B	26. C	42. B	58. C	74. A	90. D
11. C	27. C	43. C	59. A	75. A	91. A
12. C	28. C	44. D	60. D	76. C	92. E
13. E	29. C	45. D	61. A	77. E	
14. A	30. C	46. E	62. D	78. D	
15. E	31. B	47. E	63. A	79. A	
16. D	32. A	48. C	64. D	80. C	

93. (D) $\frac{n}{6} + \frac{2n}{5} = \frac{5n + 12n}{30} = \frac{17n}{30}$.

94. (B) $\frac{1}{1} - \frac{x}{y} = \frac{y - x}{y}$.

95. (B) $\frac{x-y}{x+y} \bullet \frac{y+x}{y+x}$. Since addition is commutative, we may cancel $x + y$ with $y + x$, as they are the same quantity. However, subtraction is not commutative, so we may not cancel $x - y$ with $y - x$, as they are *not* the same quantity. We can change the form of $y - x$ by factoring out -1. Thus, $y - x = (-1)(x - y)$. In this form, we cancel $x - y$, leaving an answer of $\frac{1}{-1}$, or -1.

96. (A) Multiply every term in the fraction by x, giving $\frac{x+1}{y}$.

97. (E) $\frac{2x^2}{y} \bullet \frac{2x^2}{y} \bullet \frac{2x^2}{y} = \frac{8x^6}{y^3}$.

98. (D) Multiply every term of the fraction by xy, giving $\frac{y+x}{3xy}$.

99. (D) $\frac{1}{a^2} - \frac{1}{b^2}$ is equivalent to $(\frac{1}{a} + \frac{1}{b})(\frac{1}{a} - \frac{1}{b})$. We therefore multiply 7 by 3 for an answer of 21.

100. (D) Solve for x: $\frac{3}{4}x = 1 \Rightarrow x = \frac{4}{3}$. Then substitute this for x in the expression $\frac{2}{3}(x)$: $\frac{2}{3}(\frac{4}{3}) = \frac{8}{9}$.

101. (D) Treat the two equations as simultaneous equations—substitute $\frac{y}{7}$ for x in the second equation: $7(\frac{y}{7}) = 12$, so $y = 12$.

102. (E) There are really two equations given: $x = k + \frac{1}{2}$ and $k + \frac{1}{2} = \frac{k+3}{2}$. Solve for k: $k + \frac{1}{2} = \frac{k+3}{2} \Rightarrow 2 = (k + \frac{1}{2}) = k + 3 \Rightarrow 2k + 1 = k + 3 \Rightarrow k = 2$. Now substitute 2 for k: $k = k + \frac{1}{2} = 2 + \frac{1}{2} = \frac{5}{2}$.

103. (C) Solve for x: $7 - x = 0$, so $7 = x$. Then substitute 7 for x in the expression $10 - x$: $10 - 7 = 3$.

EXERCISE 10—EQUATIONS AND INEQUALITIES (p. B-85)

1. C	12. D	23. A	34. C	45. D	56. E
2. C	13. D	24. C	35. C	46. D	57. B
3. C	14. E	25. B	36. B	47. E	58. A
4. B	15. E	26. A	37. D	48. C	59. C
5. E	16. D	27. E	38. A	49. B	60. D
6. E	17. C	28. C	39. A	50. A	61. C
7. D	18. A	29. B	40. E	51. C	62. E
8. B	19. B	30. B	41. A	52. D	63. C
9. D	20. C	31. D	42. C	53. E	64. A
10. C	21. B	32. D	43. E	54. C	65. D
11. A	22. A	33. D	44. B	55. D	

EXERCISE 11—GEOMETRY (p. B-96)

1. C	18. E	35. C	52. D	69. A	86. B
2. D	19. E	36. D	53. B	70. A	87. C
3. C	20. C	37. D	54. A	71. B	88. A
4. B	21. A	38. B	55. E	72. B	89. C
5. E	22. C	39. C	56. B	73. D	90. C
6. A	23. C	40. B	57. A	74. C	91. C
7. E	24. E	41. A	58. C	75. D	92. B
8. D	25. D	42. D	59. B	76. A	93. C
9. E	26. B	43. A	60. E	77. B	94. D
10. A	27. B	44. A	61. D	78. C	95. E
11. B	28. A	45. E	62. C	79. E	96. B
12. C	29. D	46. B	63. B	80. D	97. D
13. E	30. E	47. C	64. B	81. A	98. A
14. C	31. D	48. E	65. E	82. C	99. C
15. C	32. E	49. C	66. A	83. A	
16. B	33. E	50. B	67. B	84. C	
17. C	34. C	51. A	68. A	85. C	

100. (E) Perimeter = 68 yards; each width = 48 feet = 16 yards; both widths = 16 yd. + 16 yd. = 32 yd.; perimeter = sum of all sides. The remaining two sides must total 68 – 32 = 36 yards. Since the remaining two sides are equal, they are each 36 ÷ 2 = 18 yards.

101. (E) Perimeter = 2(46 + 34) feet = 2 • 80 feet = 160 feet. 160 feet = 160 ÷ 3 yards = $53\frac{1}{3}$ yards.

102. (E) The umbrella would be the hypotenuse of a right triangle whose legs are the dimensions of the trunk.

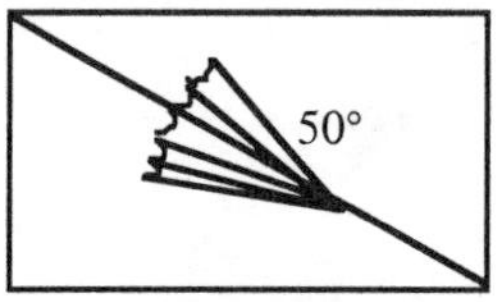

The Pythagorean Theorem states that in a right triangle, the square of the hypotenuse equals the sum of the squares of the legs. Therefore, the sum of the dimensions of the trunk squared must at least equal the length of the umbrella squared, which is 50^2 or 2500. The only set of dimensions filling this condition is (E): $40^2 + 30^2 = 1600 + 900 = 2500$.

103. (A) The new road is the hypotenuse of a right triangle, whose legs are the old road.

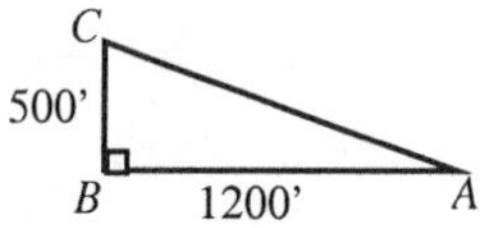

$AC^2 = AB^2 + BC^2 \Rightarrow AC = \sqrt{500^2 + 1200^2} = \sqrt{250{,}000 + 1{,}440{,}000} = \sqrt{1{,}690{,}000}$. The old road = 1200 + 500 = 1700 feet. The new road = 1300 feet. Therefore, the difference is 400 feet.

104. (C) Since $6^2 + 8^2 = 10^2 (36 + 64 = 100)$, the triangle is a right triangle. The area of the triangle is $\frac{1}{2} \cdot 6 \cdot 8 = 24$ square inches. Therefore, the area of the rectangle is 24 square inches. If the width of the rectangle is 3 inches, the length is 24 ÷ 3 = 8 inches. Then the perimeter of the rectangle is 2(3 + 8) = 2 • 11 = 22 inches.

105. (C) The ladder forms a right triangle with the wall and the ground.

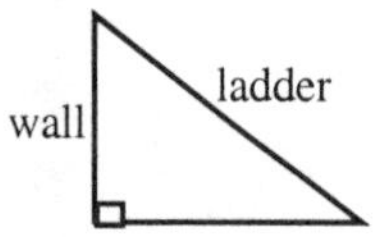

First, find the height that the ladder reaches when the lower end of the ladder is 25 feet from the wall: $65^2 = 4225 \Rightarrow 25^2 = 625 \Rightarrow 65^2 - 25^2 = 3600 \Rightarrow \sqrt{3600} = 60$. The ladder reaches 60 feet up the wall when its lower end is 25 feet from the wall.

If the upper end is moved down 8 feet, the ladder will reach a height of 60 – 8 = 52 feet. The new triangle formed has a hypotenuse of 65 feet of one leg of 52 feet. Find the other leg: $65^2 = 4225 \Rightarrow 52^2 = 2704 \Rightarrow 65^2 - 52^2 = 1521 \Rightarrow$

$\sqrt{1521} = 39$. The lower end of the ladder is now 39 feet from the wall. This is 39 – 25 = 14 feet farther than it was before.

106. (C) Convert the dimensions of the bin to inches: 4 feet = 48 inches, 3 feet = 36 inches, 2 feet = 24 inches. Thus the volume of the bin = 48 in. • 36 in. • 24 in. = 41,472 cubic inches. The volume of each brick = 8 in. • 4 in. • 2 in. = 64 cubic inches. Therefore, 41,472 ÷ 64 = 648 bricks.

107. (D) The trench contains 2 yd. • 5 yd. • 4 yd. = 40 cubic yards ⇒ 40 • \$2.12 = \$84.80.

108. (C) Find the dimensions of the square: if the area of the square is 121 square inches, each side is $\sqrt{121} = 11$ inches, and the perimeter is 4 • 11 = 44 inches. Next, find the dimensions of the rectangle: the perimeter of the rectangle is the same as the perimeter of the square, since the same length of wire is used to enclose either figure. Therefore, the perimeter of the rectangle is 44 inches. If the two lengths are each 13 inches, their total is 26 inches, and 44 – 26 inches, or 18 inches, remain for the two widths. Each width is equal to 18 ÷ 2 = 9 inches. Thus, the area of a rectangle with length 13 in. and width 9 in. 13 • 9 = 117 sq. in.

109. (B)

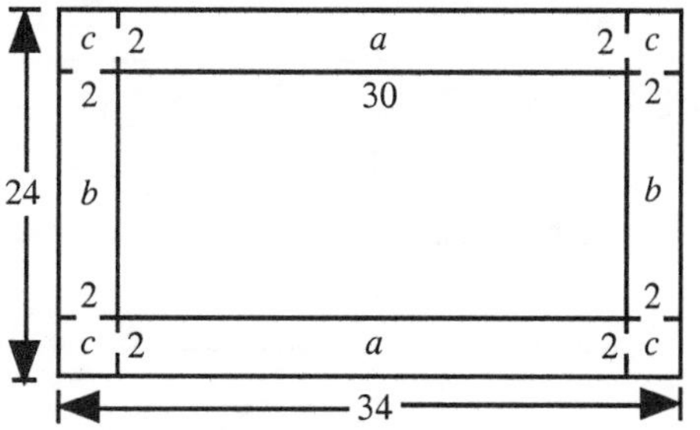

The walk consists of:

a. 2 rectangles of length 30 feet and width 2 feet.
Area of each rectangle = 2 • 30 = 60 sq. ft.
Area of both rectangles = 120 sq. ft.

b. 2 rectangles of length 20 feet and width 2 feet.
Area of each = 2 • 20 = 40 sq. ft.
Area of both = 80 sq. ft.

c. 4 squares, each having sides measuring 2 feet.
Area of each square = 2 • 2 = 4 sq. ft.
Area of 4 squares = 16 sq. ft.

Therefore, the total area of walk = 120 + 80 + 16 = 216 sq. ft.
Alternatively, you could solve this problem by subtraction: Area of walk = Area of large rectangle – Area of small rectangle = (34 • 24) – (30 • 20) = 816 – 600 = 216 sq. ft.

110. (A) If the area of a circle is 49π, its radius is $\sqrt{49} = 7$. Then, the circumference is equal to $2 \cdot 7 \cdot \pi = 14\pi$.

111. (D) In one hour, the minute hand rotates through 360°. In two hours, it rotates through 2 • 360° = 720°.

112. (C) Find the area of each surface: Area of top = 12 • 16 = 192 in.^{2}; Area of bottom = 12 • 16 = 192 in.^{2}; Area of front = 6 • 16 = 96 in.^{2}; Area of back = 6 • 16 = 96 in.^{2}; Area of right side = 6 • 12 = 72 in.^{2}; Area of left side = 6 • 12 = 72 in.^{2}. Therefore, total surface area = 2 • 192 + 2 • 96 + 2 • 72 = 720 in.^{2}

113. (A) For a cube, $V = e^3$. If the volume is 64 cubic inches, each edge is $\sqrt[3]{64} = 4$ inches. A cube has 12 edges. If each edge is 4 inches, the sum of the edges is 4 • 12 = 48 inches.

114. (C) The unlabeled angle inside the triangle is equal to x: $(x + 15) + (x + 15) + x = 180 \Rightarrow 3x + 30 = 180 \Rightarrow x = 50$.

115. (C) The question asks for: "Area of square with side 5" minus "Area of square with side 4" = (5 • 5) – (4 • 4) = 25 – 16 = 9.

116. (D) A triangle with sides of 3, 6, and 9 has a perimeter of 3 + 6 + 9 = 18. An equilateral triangle with the same perimeter would have a side of 18 ÷ 3 = 6.

117. (B) Since $AB = BC$, ABC is a 45-45-90 triangle. Angle ABD is 45° + 15° = 60°. And x = 180° – 90° – 60° = 30°. You should also be able to estimate the angle as 30°.

118. (C) Just use the formula for the area of a rectangle: l • **Error!**) = 1, so l = **Error!**.

EXERCISE 12—COORDINATE GEOMETRY (p. B-117)

1. (A) Find the midpoint AB by averaging the x-coordinates and averaging the y-coordinates: $(\frac{6+2}{2}, \frac{2+6}{2}) = (4, 4)$.

2. (C) O is the midpoint of AB. $\frac{x+4}{2} = 2 \Rightarrow x + 4 = 4 \Rightarrow x = 0$. $\frac{y+6}{2} = 1 \Rightarrow y + 6 = 2 \Rightarrow y = -4$. Therefore, (x, y) is $(0, -4)$.

3. (A) $d = \sqrt{(8-4)^2 + (6-3)^2} = \sqrt{4^2 + 3^2} = \sqrt{16+9} = \sqrt{25} = 5$.

4. (D) Sketch the triangle:

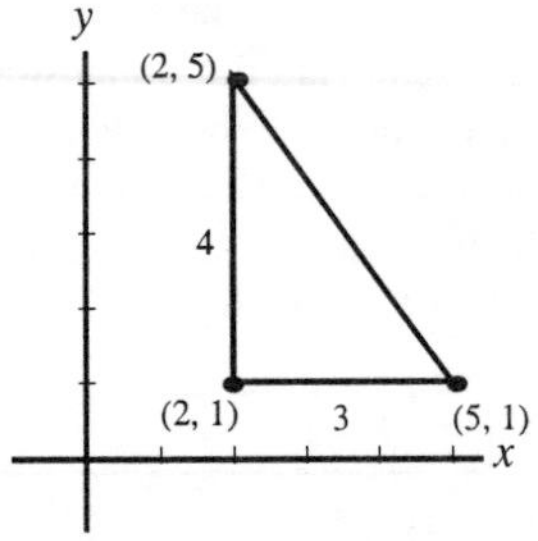

Area $= \frac{1}{2} \cdot b \cdot h = \frac{1}{2} \cdot 4 \cdot 3 = 6$.

5. (A) Area of a circle $= \pi r^2 = 16\pi$, $r = 4$. Points B, C, D, and E are all 4 units from the origin, Point A is not. Therefore, the answer is (4, 4).

6. (B) Since no drawing is provided, sketch the coordinate system and enter points P and Q:

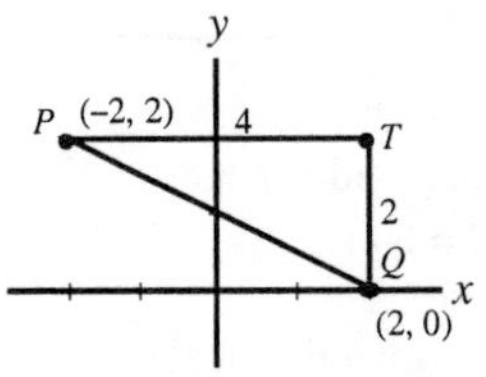

Find the distance between the two points by using the Pythagorean Theorem: $PT^2 + TQ^2 = PQ^2 \Rightarrow 4^2 + 2^2 = 16 + 4 = 20$. Therefore, $PQ = \sqrt{20} = \sqrt{4 \cdot 5} = 2\sqrt{5}$.

Alternatively, the Distance Formula may be used: $d = \sqrt{(x_2 - x_1)^2 + (y_2 - y_1)^2} = \sqrt{(2-0)^2 + (-2-2)^2} = \sqrt{2^2 + -4^2} = \sqrt{4+16} = \sqrt{20} = 2\sqrt{5}$.

7. (A) Use the distance formula: $d = \sqrt{(x_2 - x_1)^2 + (y_2 - y_1)^2} = \sqrt{(x+1-x)^2 + (y+1-y)^2} = \sqrt{1^2 + 1^2} = \sqrt{2}$.

8. (C) A quick sketch of the information provided in the problem shows that we need to employ the Pythagorean Theorem: The shortest distance from Will to Grace is the hypotenuse of this right triangle: $h^2 = 60^2 + 40^2 = 3600 + 1600 = 5200$. Solve for h: $h = \sqrt{5200} = \sqrt{4 \cdot 1300} = \sqrt{4 \cdot 4 \cdot 325} = \sqrt{16 \cdot 25 \cdot 13} = 4 \cdot 5\sqrt{13} = 20\sqrt{13}$.

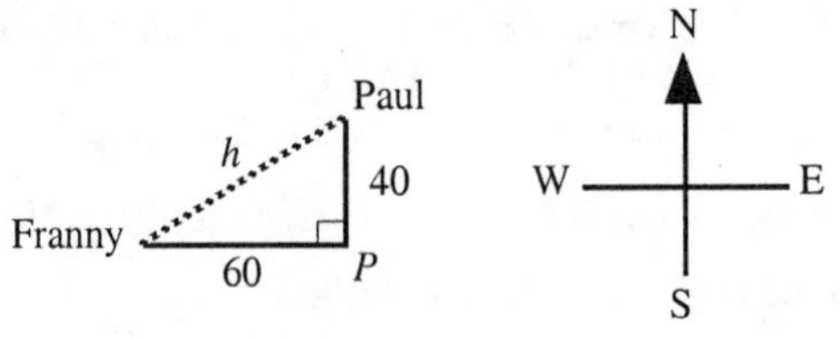

9. (E) Since the graph is of a straight line, plug the values given in the question into the straight line equation, $y = mx + b$ (m is the slope and b is the y-intercept when x is zero), and solve for y: $y_{x=0} = 0 = m(0) + b \Rightarrow b = 0$; $y_{x=2} = 3 = m(2) \Rightarrow m = \frac{3}{2}$. Therefore the equation for the plotted line is: $y = \frac{3}{2}m$. Therefore, $y_{x=4.2} = \frac{3}{2}(4.2) = \frac{12.6}{2} = 6.3$.

10. (B) If $(x, -4)$ is in quadrant III, then x is negative. If $(-1, y)$ is in quadrant II, y is positive. Therefore (x, y), or $(-, +)$, is in quadrant II.

11. (E) Since a figure is not provided, draw one:

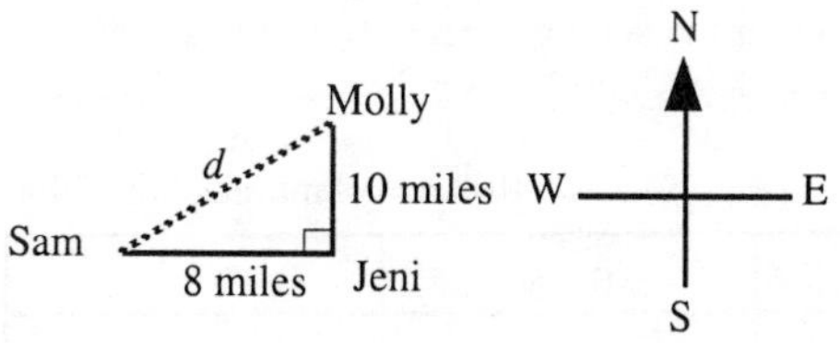

Therefore, the approximate distance between Molly's house and Sam's house is (using Pythagorean Theorem): $d = \sqrt{8^2 + 10^2} = \sqrt{64 + 100} = \sqrt{164} = \sqrt{4 \cdot 41} \approx \sqrt{4 \cdot 40} = \sqrt{4 \cdot 4 \cdot 10} \approx \sqrt{16 \cdot 9} = 4 \cdot 3 = 12$. Therefore the approximate difference between the two paths is: 18 miles – 12 miles, or 6 miles. Since this is not an answer choice, choose (E), or 5 miles (the largest answer choice). We over estimated the difference because in our approximating, we rounded down twice.

12. (D) Since the figure provided is not complete, fill it in:

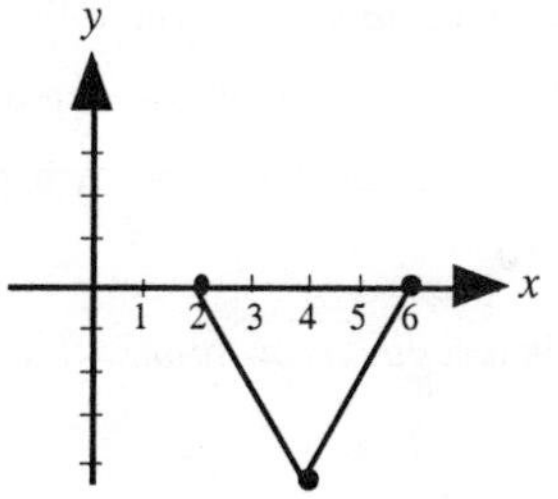

Area of $\Delta ABC = \frac{1}{2} \cdot$ base $\cdot$ height $= \frac{1}{2} \cdot 4 \cdot 4 = 8$.

EXERCISE 13—PROBLEM-SOLVING (p. B-117)

1. (A) The amount of the discount is \$12. Rate of discount is figured on the original price: $\frac{12}{80} = \frac{3}{20} \Rightarrow \frac{3}{20} \cdot 100 = 15\%$.
2. (C) Lilian spent $\frac{1}{3}$ of \$60, or \$20, at the supermarket, leaving her with \$40. Of the \$40 she spent $\frac{1}{2}$, or \$20, at the drugstore, leaving her with \$20 when she returned home.
3. (A) The segment OP is made up of the radius of circle O and the radius of circle P. To find the length of OP, you need to know the lengths of the two radii. Since the length of the radius is one-half that of the diameter, the radius of the circle O is $\frac{1}{2}(8)$ or 4, and the radius of circle P is $\frac{1}{2}(6)$ or 3. So the length of OP is $3 + 4 = 7$.
4. (C) \$70 represents 80% of the marked price: $70 = 0.80x \Rightarrow 700 = 8x \Rightarrow \$87.50 = x$.
5. (B) Let x= number of quarters; $2x$ = number of nickels; $35 - 3x$ = number of dimes. Write all money values in cents: $25(x) + 5(2x) + 10(35 - 3x) = 400 \Rightarrow 25x + 10x + 350 - 30x = 400 \Rightarrow 5x = 50 \Rightarrow x = 10$.
6. (E) $r\% = \frac{r}{100}$. Commission is $\frac{r}{100} \cdot s = \frac{rs}{100}$.
7. (D) Let x = first integer; $x + 2$ = second integer; $x + 4$ = third integer. $3(x) = 3 + 2(x + 4) = 3 + 2x + 8 \Rightarrow x = 11$. Therefore, the third integer is $11 + 4 = 15$.
8. (B) \$273 represents 130% of the cost: $1.30x = 273 \Rightarrow 13x = 2730 \Rightarrow x = \$87.50$
9. (E) We are comparing *feet* with *pounds*. The more feet, the more pounds. This is *direct variation*. Change yards to feet: $\frac{60}{80} = \frac{6}{x} \Rightarrow \frac{3}{4} = \frac{6}{x} \Rightarrow 3x = 24 \Rightarrow x = 8$.
10. (D) Work with a simple figure, such as 100: first sale price is 90% of \$100, or \$90; final sale price is 85% of \$90, or \$76.50; total discount was \$100 – \$76.50 = \$23.50. Therefore, percent of discount $= \frac{23.50}{100}$, or 23.5%.
11. (C) b= Stan's age now; $b + 15$ = Robert's age now; $b - y$ = Stan's age y years ago; $b + 15 - y$ = Robert's age y years ago. Therefore, $b + 15 - y = 2(b - y) \Rightarrow b + 15 - y = 2b - 2y \Rightarrow 15 = b - y$.
12. (B) If marked price = m, first sale price = $0.85m$ and net price = $0.90(0.85m) = 0.765m$. Therefore, $765m = 306 \Rightarrow m =$ \$400. In this case, it would be easy to work from the answers: 15% of \$400 is \$60, making a first sale price of \$340; 10% of this price is \$34, making the net price \$306. (A), (C), and (D) would not give a final answer in whole dollars.
13. (D) The larger a gear, the fewer times it revolves in a given period of time. This is *inverse variation*: $50 \cdot 15 = 30 \cdot x \Rightarrow 750 = 3x \Rightarrow 25 = x$.

14. (C) Use an easy amount of $100 for the selling price. If profit is 20% of the selling price, or $20, cost is $80. Profit based on cost is $\frac{20}{80} = \frac{1}{4} = 25\%$.

15. (B)

	No. of oz. ×	% acid ÷ 100 =	Amt. alcohol Value
Original	20	0.05	1
Added	x	1.00	x
Mixture	$20 + x$	0.24	$0.24(20 + x)$

$1 + x = 0.24(20 + x)$. Multiply by 100 to eliminate decimal: $100 + 100x = 480 + 24x \Rightarrow 76x = 380 \Rightarrow x = 5$.

16. (B) The more men, the less days. This is *inverse variation*: $x \cdot h = y \cdot ? \Rightarrow \frac{xh}{y} = ?$.

17. (C) If profit is to be 20% of selling price, cost must be 80% of selling price: $72 = 0.80x \Rightarrow 720 = 8x \Rightarrow x = \$90$.

18. (A) The a lbs. of nuts are worth a total of ab cents. The c lbs. of nuts are worth a total of cd cents. The value of the mixture is $ab + cd$ cents. Since there are $a + c$ pounds, each pound is worth $\frac{ab + cd}{a + c}$ cents. Since the dealer wants to add 10 cents to each pound for profit, and the value of each pound is in cents, add 10 to the value of each pound. Therefore, the answer is $\frac{ab + cd}{a + c} + 10$.

19. (A) The more days, the more oil. This is a *direct variation*. Remember to change a week to days: $\frac{40}{7} = \frac{x}{10} \Rightarrow 13x = 180 \Rightarrow x = 13\frac{11}{13}$.

20. (E) If Nell invests x additional dollars at 8%, her total investment will amount to $2400 + x$ dollars. $0.05(2400) + .08(x) = 0.06(2400 + x) \Rightarrow 5(2400) + 8(x) = 6(2400 + x) \Rightarrow 12{,}000 + 8x = 14400 + 6x \Rightarrow 2x = 2400 \Rightarrow x = \$1{,}200$.

21. (B) The team must win 75%, or $\frac{3}{4}$, of the games played during the entire season. With 60 games played and 32 more to play, the team must win $\frac{3}{4} \cdot 92 = 69$. Since 40 games have already been won, the team must win 29 additional games.

22. (D) The more sugar, the more flour. This is *direct variation*: $\frac{13}{18} = \frac{10}{x} \Rightarrow 13x = 180 \Rightarrow x = 13\frac{11}{13}$.

23. (B) Total time, elapsed is $5\frac{1}{2}$ hours. However, one hour was used for dinner. Therefore, Ivan drove at 30 m.p.h. for 41 hours, covering 135 miles.

24. (E) Let original price = p, and the original sales = s. Therefore, original gross receipts = ps. Let the new price = $0.75p$, and new sales = $1.20s$. Therefore, new gross receipts = $0.90ps$. Gross receipts are only 90% of what they where.

25. (A) The more miles, the more gasoline. This is a *direct variation*: $\frac{25}{2} = \frac{150}{x} \Rightarrow 25x = 300 \Rightarrow x = 12$.

26. (B) Time $= \frac{\text{Distance}}{\text{Rate}} = \frac{30}{600} = \frac{1}{20}$ hour, or 3 minutes. Therefore the arrival time is 5:01 p.m.

27. (D) 5% of sales between $200 and $600 is 0.05(400) = $20. 8% of sales over $600 is 0.08(200) = $16. Total commission is $20 + $16 = $36.

28. (E) The more children, the fewer days. This is *inverse variation*: $30 \cdot 4 = 40 \cdot x \Rightarrow 120 = 40x \Rightarrow 3 = x$.

29. (C) Dave takes 30 minutes to wash the car alone. $\frac{x}{15} + \frac{x}{30} = 1 \Rightarrow 2x + x = 30 \Rightarrow 3x = 30 \Rightarrow x = 10$.

30. (D) The more children, the fewer days. This is *inverse variation*: $\frac{c}{16} = \frac{x}{a} \Rightarrow x = \frac{ac}{16}$.

31. (C) Let $2x$= original numerator; $5x$ = original denominator. $\frac{2x - 2}{5x + 1} = \frac{1}{4} \Rightarrow 8x - 8 = 5x + 1 \Rightarrow 3x = 9 \Rightarrow x = 3$. Therefore, the original numerator is 2(3), or 6.

32. (C) The more miles, the greater kilometers. This is *direct variation*: $\frac{\text{miles}}{\text{kilometers}} = \frac{\text{miles}}{\text{kilometers}} \Rightarrow \frac{3}{4.83} = \frac{x}{11.27} \Rightarrow 4.83x = 33.81 \Rightarrow x = 7$.

33. (C) The increase is 9000. Percent of increase is figured on original. $\frac{9000}{3000} = 3 = 300\%$.

34. (B) By paying attention to how the units cancel out and what value we are looking for, it is easy to find the "hidden equation"—just write out the information given, arranging it so like units cancel: 18,000 newspapers $= m \cdot \frac{6 \text{ newspapers}}{s \text{ seconds}} \cdot \frac{60 \text{ seconds}}{1 \text{ minute}} \cdot x$ minutes $\Rightarrow x$ minutes $= \frac{m18{,}000 \text{ newspapers } s}{6 \text{ newspapers} \cdot m \cdot 60} = \frac{50s}{m}$.

Alternatively, since the information is given algebraically, the letters could stand for any numbers (so long as you don't divide by 0). Pick some values for m and s and see which answer choice works. Start with easy numbers. Assume the plant has 2 machines, $m = 2$. Assume $s = 1$ (each machine produces 6 newspapers per second). Thus, each machine prints 360 papers per minute; with two, the capacity doubles to 720 papers per minute. To find how long it will take the plant to do the work, divide 18,000 by 720, or 25 minutes. Therefore, the correct formula should produce the number 25:

(A) $\frac{180s}{m} = 180(1)/2 \neq 25$ X
(B) $\frac{50s}{m} = 50(1)/2 = 25$ √
(C) $50ms = 50(2)(1) \neq 25$ X
(D) $\frac{ms}{50} = (2)(1)/50 \neq 25$ X
(E) $\frac{300m}{s} = 300(2)/(1) \neq 25$ X

35. (B) The more pencils, the greater cost. The is *direct variation*. Remember to change dollars to cents: $\frac{\text{pencils}}{\text{cents}} = \frac{\text{pencils}}{\text{cents}} \Rightarrow \frac{p}{100d} = \frac{x}{c} \Rightarrow x = \frac{pc}{100d}$.

36. (D) First the conventional way: Final Selling Price = Usual List Price – 20% of Usual List Price or, $f = l - 0.20l$; Profit = Final Selling Price – Cost, or $f = p + c$. We are told that the cost is \$4,800 and the profit is equal to 25% of the cost, or $0.25c$. Therefore $f = 0.25c + c$. Thus: $l - 0.20l = 0.25c + c \Rightarrow 0.80l = 1.25c \Rightarrow l = \frac{1.25 \cdot 4{,}800}{0.80} = \$7{,}500$.

Alternatively, test each one until you find the correct one. Start with (C). If the usual list price is \$7,200, the actual sell price after the 20% discount is \$7,200 – (0.20 • 7,200) = \$7,200 – \$1,440 = \$5760. On that assumption, the dealer's profit would be: Profit = Final Selling Price – Cost = \$5,760 – \$4,800 = \$960. Is that a profit of 25%? 960/4800 is less than one-quarter, so (C) is wrong.

Our choice of (C) resulted in the profit being too small. Therefore, pick the larger price to generate a larger profit. So try (D). The price is \$7,500 – (0.20)(\$7,500) = \$6,000. The profit is thus \$1,200. Since \$1,200/\$4,800 = 25%, (D) is the correct answer.

37. (A) m varies directly as the square of t can be expressed mathematically as: $\frac{m_1}{t_1^2} = \frac{m_2}{t_2^2} \Rightarrow \frac{7}{(1)^2} = \frac{m}{(2)^2} \Rightarrow \frac{7}{1} = \frac{m}{4} \Rightarrow m = 28$.

38. (D) $16\frac{2}{3}\% = \frac{1}{6} \Rightarrow 6 = \frac{1}{6}x \Rightarrow x = 36$.

39. (D) First the conventional method—turn the story into algebraic equations: $\text{value}_2 = \text{value}_1 - (0.10 \cdot \text{value}_1) \Rightarrow v_2 = 0.90v_1$; $\text{rate}_2 = \text{rate}_1 + (0.10 \cdot \text{rate}_1) \Rightarrow r_2 = 1.10r_1$. Since *tax = value • tax rate:* $\text{tax}_2 = \text{value}_2 \cdot \text{rate}_2 = 0.90v_1 \cdot 1.10r_1 = (0.90 \cdot 1.10) \cdot \text{tax}_1 = 0.99 \cdot \text{tax}_1$, or a 1% decrease.

Alternatively, since no numbers are supplied, supply your own. Assume the piece of property has a value of \$1,000 and assume that the original tax rate is 10%. On the basis of those assumptions, the tax bill is originally 10% of \$1,000 or \$100. Now make the specified adjustments. The value of the property drops by 10%, from \$1000 to \$900, but the tax rate goes up by 10%, from 10% to 11%. The new tax bill is 11% of \$900, or \$99. The original tax bill was \$100; the new tax bill is \$99; the net result is a decrease of \$1 out of \$100, or a 1% decrease.

40. (B) m varies jointly as r and l can be expressed mathematically as: $\frac{m_1}{r_1l_1} = \frac{m_2}{r_2l_2} \Rightarrow \frac{8}{(1)(1)} = \frac{m}{(2)(2)} \Rightarrow \frac{8}{1} = \frac{m}{4} \Rightarrow m = 32$.

41. (A) The box when assembled looks like this:

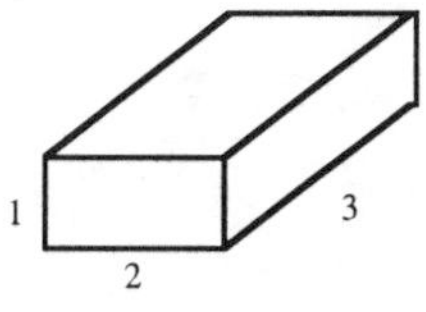

Its volume is 1 • 2 • 3 = 6.

42. (E) $40\% = \frac{2}{5} \Rightarrow \frac{2}{5}$ of $95\% = 38\%$.

43. (E) $\frac{PT}{2}$ is $\frac{1}{2}$ the length of the entire segment. QS is $\frac{1}{2}$ the length of the segment, and $\frac{QS}{2}$ is $\frac{1}{4}$ of the segment. So $\frac{PT}{2} - \frac{QS}{2}$ is $\frac{1}{2}$ of the segment minus $\frac{1}{4}$ of the length of the segment. Only (E) is $\frac{1}{4}$ the length of the segment.

You can also assign numbers to the lengths. Assume that each segment is equal to 1. The PT is 4, and $\frac{PT}{2} = 2$. And QS is 2, and $\frac{QS}{2} = 1$. Finally, $2 - 1 = 1$. So the correct answer choice should have a length of 1:

(A) $3 - 1 = 2$ X
(B) $1 - 2 = -1$ X
(C) 2 X
(D) 3 X
(E) 1 √

44. (C) Create a formula. Anna was born three years after $1980 - x$, so she was born in $1980 - x + 3$. 20 years later the later will be $1980 - x + 3 + 20 = 2003 - x$.

You can also substitute numbers. Assume $x = 1$. And then assume Anna was born three years after $1980 - 1 = 1979$, so she was born in 1982. So she will turn 20 in 2002. Substituting 1 for x in each of the answer choices:

(A) $1977 + 1 = 1978$ X
(B) $1997 + 1 = 1998$ X
(C) $2003 - 1 = 2002$ √
(D) $2003 + 1 = 2004$ X
(E) $2006 + 1 = 2007$ X

45. (B) $\$500 + 0.05x = \$2{,}400 \Rightarrow 0.05s = 1{,}900 \Rightarrow 5s = 190{,}000 \Rightarrow s = \$38{,}000$.

46. (B) The correct answer must be smaller than the shortest time give, for no matter how slow a helper may be, he does do part of the job and therefore it will be completed in less time. $\frac{\text{Time spent}}{\text{Total time needed to do job alone}} = \frac{x}{3} + \frac{x}{5} = 1$. Multiply by 15 to eliminate fractions: $5x + 3x = 15 \Rightarrow 8x = 15 \Rightarrow x = 1\frac{7}{8}$ hours.

CAMBRIDGE
EDUCATIONAL SERVICES, INC.®

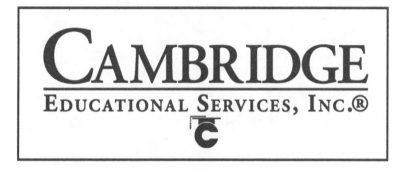

ACT • PLAN • EXPLORE
Appendix B

MATH EXPRESS

I. ARITHMETIC SUMMARY

1. **Real Numbers:** Real numbers are all the numbers on the number line, including integers, decimals, fractions, and radical numbers.

   e.g., $-\frac{1}{2}, 0, \frac{2}{3}, \sqrt{2}, \pi$

   A real number is *rational* if it can be written as the ratio of two integers where the denominator does not equal zero. Natural numbers, whole numbers, and integers are all rational numbers.

   e.g., $-\frac{1}{2}, 0, 0.75, \frac{2}{3}$

   A real number is *irrational* if it cannot be written as the ratio of two integers. Irrational numbers have infinite nonrepeating decimal representations.

   e.g., $\sqrt{2}, \pi$

   Properties of real numbers:
   $(+)(+) = (+)$
   $(-)(-) = (+)$
   $(+)(-) = (-)$
   $(-)^2 = (+)$
   m, $m + 0 = m$, where m is a real number
   $m \cdot 0 = 0$, where m is a real number

   e.g., $(\frac{1}{2})(4) = 2$
   $(-2)(-\frac{4}{5}) = \frac{8}{5}$
   $(2)(-4) = -8$
   $(-\frac{3}{4})(4) = -3$
   $(-2)^2 = 4$
   $2 + 0 = 2$
   $(2)(0) = 0$

2. **Natural Numbers:** Natural numbers are the set of positive integers and are also referred to as counting numbers: 1, 2, 3, 4, 5, ...

3. **Whole Numbers:** Whole numbers are the set of numbers used for counting, plus the number zero: 0, 1, 2, 3, 4, ...

   e.g., 0, 5, 56, 490

4. **Integers:** An integer is a positive or negative whole number.

   e.g., $-568, -45, 0, 6, 67, 2345, \frac{16}{2}$

5. **Working with Positive and Negative Integers:** If the signs of the two numbers being added or subtracted are *different,* subtract the smaller number from the larger number and keep the sign of the larger.

   e.g., $-3 + 2 = -1$
   $-4 + 6 = 2$

   If the signs of the two numbers being added or subtracted are the *same*, add the two numbers and keep the same sign.

   e.g., $-5 - 3 = -8$
   $4 + 8 = 12$

6. **Even and Odd Integers:** An *even* integer is evenly divisible by 2, whereas an *odd* integer is not evenly divisible by 2. 0 is an even integer.

   e.g., Even integers: –50, –4, 0, 2, 34
   Odd integers: –45, –3, 9, 15

   Important properties of even and odd integers:

even + even = even	*e.g.,*	$2 + 4 = 6$
even + odd = odd		$4 + 3 = 7$
odd + odd = even		$3 + 5 = 8$
odd + even = odd		$3 + 4 = 7$
even • even = even		$2 \cdot 4 = 8$
even • odd = even		$2 \cdot 3 = 6$
odd • odd = odd		$3 \cdot 5 = 15$
odd • even = even		$3 \cdot 2 = 6$

7. **Factor:** A factor is a number that divides evenly into another number.

   e.g., 1, 2, 3, 4, 6, and 12 are factors of 12

8. **Prime:** A prime number is a natural number that is divisible only by 1 and itself. (1 is not a prime number.)

   e.g., 2, 3, 5, 7, 11, 13, 17, 19

9. **Prime Factors:** All natural numbers can be expressed as the product of prime numbers which are called the prime factors of that number.

   e.g., $3 = (3)(1)$
   $4 = (2)(2)$
   $12 = (2)(2)(3)$

10. **Consecutive Integers:** Consecutive integers are in continuous sequence. If the first integer of a consecutive sequence is m, the sequence is m, $m + 1$, $m + 2$, *etc.*

    e.g., 4, 5, 6, 7, ...
    –10, –9, –8, –7, ...

    Consecutive even or odd integers are in continuous sequence of even or odd integers, respectively. An even or odd sequence is m, $m + 2$, $m + 4$, $m + 6$, *etc.*

    e.g., –4, –2, 0, 2, ...;
    7, 9, 11, 13, ...

11. **Miscellaneous Symbols:**

$=$ ⇔ is equal to

$\neq$ ⇔ is not equal to

$<$ ⇔ less than

$>$ ⇔ is greater than,

$\leq$ ⇔ is less than or equal to

$\geq$ ⇔ is greater than or equal to

$|x|$ ⇔ absolute value of x

(Absolute value is always non-negative.)

e.g., $3 = 3$

$\frac{3}{4} \neq \frac{5}{6}$

$-3 < 6$

$5 > 4$

$m - 3 \leq -3$, for $m = \ldots, -3, -2, -1, 0$

$m + 3 \geq 3$, for $m = 0, 1, 2, 3, \ldots$

$|-5| = 5$

12. **Terms:** The *sum* or *total* is the result of adding numbers together. The *difference* is the result of subtracting one number from another. The *product* is the result of multiplying numbers together. The *quotient* is the result of dividing one number by another. The *remainder* is the number remaining after one number is divided into another number.

e.g., The sum (or total) of 2 and 3 is 5: $2 + 3 = 5$.
The difference between 5 and 2 is 3: $5 - 2 = 3$.
The product of 2 and 3 is 6: $(2)(3) = 6$.
The quotient of 6 divided by 2 is 3: $6 \div 2 = 3$.
The remainder of 7 divided by 3 is 1: $7 \div 3 =$ 2 plus a remainder of 1.

13. **Fractions:** When one whole integer is divided by another whole integer (other then zero) and the result is not a third whole integer, the result is a fraction, or ratio. The top number is called the *numerator*; and the bottom number is called the *denominator*.

e.g., When 2 is divided by 3, the result is not a whole number. The result is the fraction $2 \div 3$, which is written $\frac{2}{3}$.

Proper fractions have a numerator of lower value than the denominator and therefore have a value less than 1.

e.g., $\frac{1}{2}$ and $\frac{3}{4}$ are both < 1

Improper fractions have a numerator of greater value than the denominator, and therefore have a value greater than 1.

e.g., $\frac{3}{2}$ and $\frac{4}{3}$ are both > 1

A *mixed number* consists of both a whole number and a fraction written together.

e.g., $2\frac{1}{2} = 2 + \frac{1}{2}$

$3\frac{4}{5} = 3 + \frac{4}{5}$

Before adding, subtracting, multiplying, or dividing fractions, convert mixed numbers to improper fractions using this method:

a. Use the denominator of the old fractional part of the mixed number as the new denominator.

b. Multiply the whole number part of the mixed number by its denominator and add to that the numerator of the old fractional part. This is the new numerator.

e.g., $3\frac{1}{4} = \frac{(3 \bullet 4) + 1}{4} = \frac{13}{4}$

$6\frac{2}{5} = \frac{(6 \bullet 5) + 2}{5} = \frac{32}{5}$

$2\frac{12}{13} = \frac{(2 \bullet 13) + 12}{13} = \frac{38}{13}$

To convert an improper fraction to *a mixed number*, reverse the process:

a. Divide the denominator into the numerator. The integer part of the quotient becomes the whole number part of the mixed number.

b. With the same denominator, create a fraction with the numerator equal to the remainder of the first step.

e.g., $\frac{29}{5}$: $29 \div 5 = 5$ with a remainder of $4 = 5\frac{4}{5}$

$\frac{31}{6}$: $31 \div 6 = 5$ with a remainder of $1 = 5\frac{1}{6}$

$\frac{43}{13}$: $43 \div 13 = 3$ with a remainder of $4 = 3\frac{4}{13}$

14. **Reducing Fractions:** It is convention to reduce all fractions to lowest terms. To reduce a fraction to lowest terms, eliminate redundant factors in both the numerator and the denominator. Either remove a common factor out of both or divide both by a common factor—each is the same.

e.g., $\frac{8}{16} = \frac{1(8)}{2(8)} = \frac{1}{2} \Leftrightarrow \frac{8}{16} = \frac{8 \div 8}{16 \div 8} = \frac{1}{2}$

A fraction is expressed in *lowest terms* when there is no number (other than 1) that can be divided evenly into both numerator and denominator.

e.g., $\frac{8}{15}$ is in lowest terms, since there is no number (other than 1) that divides evenly into 8 and 15.

15. **Complex Fractions:** A complex fraction is a fraction in which either the numerator or the denominator, or both, contain fractions. There are two methods for simplifying complex fractions.

Method I: Multiply both the numerator and the denominator by the reciprocal of the denominator and simplify.

e.g., $\frac{\frac{1}{2}}{\frac{3}{4}} = \frac{\left(\frac{1}{2}\right)\left(\frac{4}{3}\right)}{\left(\frac{3}{4}\right)\left(\frac{4}{3}\right)} = \frac{\frac{4}{6}}{1} = \frac{4}{6} = \frac{2}{3}$

Method II: Multiply both the numerator and the denominator by the least common denominator for the terms in the numerator and denominator of the complex fractions and simplify.

e.g., $\frac{\frac{1}{2}}{\frac{3}{4}} \bullet \frac{(4)}{(4)} = \frac{\frac{4}{2}}{\frac{12}{4}} = \frac{2}{3}$

16. Common Denominators: A common denominator is a number that is a multiple of the denominators of two or more fractions.

e.g., 12 is a multiple of both 3 and 4 (both 3 and 4 divide into 12 evenly), so it is a suitable common denominator for $\frac{1}{3}$ and $\frac{1}{4}$

Converting a fraction to another denominator is the reverse of reducing it to lowest terms. Multiplying the numerator and denominator of a fraction by the same number is the same as multiplying the fraction by 1, so the value is not changed.

e.g., $\frac{1}{4} = \frac{(1)(3)}{(4)(3)} = \frac{3}{12}$

$\frac{2}{3} = \frac{(2)(4)}{(3)(4)} = \frac{8}{12}$

17. Adding Fractions: The procedure for adding fractions varies depending on whether or not the fractions already share the same denominator.

To add fractions with the *same denominator,* create a new fraction using the common denominator. The new numerator is the sum of the old numerators.

e.g., $\frac{3}{7} + \frac{2}{7} = \frac{5}{7}$

To add fractions with *different denominators*, find a common denominator and convert the fractions in the manner described above.

e.g., $\frac{1}{3} + \frac{1}{5} = \frac{1(5)}{3(5)} + \frac{1(3)}{5(3)} = \frac{5}{15} + \frac{3}{15} = \frac{8}{15}$

$\frac{1}{3} + \frac{2}{7} = \frac{1(7)}{3(7)} + \frac{2(3)}{7(3)} = \frac{7}{21} + \frac{6}{21} = \frac{13}{21}$

To add a fraction and a *whole number,* treat the whole number as a fraction with a denominator of 1.

e.g., $2 + \frac{1}{5} + \frac{1}{2} = \frac{2}{1} + \frac{1}{5} + \frac{1}{2} = \frac{2(10)}{1(10)} + \frac{1(2)}{5(2)} + \frac{1(5)}{2(5)}$

$= \frac{20}{10} + \frac{2}{10} + \frac{5}{10} = \frac{27}{10}$

To add a fraction and a *mixed number*, change the mixed number to an improper fraction and then add.

e.g., $2\frac{1}{3} + \frac{1}{3} = \frac{7}{3} + \frac{1}{3} = \frac{8}{3} = 2\frac{2}{3}$

18. Subtracting Fractions: Follow the same procedure for addition, except subtract rather than add. To subtract fractions with the *same denominator*, simply subtract the second numerator from the first.

e.g., $\frac{5}{7} - \frac{2}{7} = \frac{3}{7}$

To subtract fractions with *different denominators*, first find a common denominator.

e.g., $\frac{7}{8} - \frac{3}{5} = \frac{7(5)}{8(5)} - \frac{3(8)}{5(8)} = \frac{35}{40} - \frac{24}{40} = \frac{11}{40}$

19. Flying *X* Method for Adding and Subtracting Fractions: If the result of adding or subtracting fractions is reduced to lowest terms, finding the lowest common denominator of the two initial fractions is not necessary. The trick is called the "flying *x*."

$\frac{a}{b} + \frac{c}{d} = \frac{a}{b} \geq + \leq \frac{c}{d} = \frac{ad + bc}{bd}$

a. Multiply the denominators to get a new denominator.

b. Multiply the numerator of the first fraction by the denominator of the second.

c. Multiply the numerator of the second fraction by the denominator of the first.

d. The new numerator is the sum (or difference) of the results of steps 2 and 3.

e.g., $\frac{2}{7} + \frac{1}{5} = \frac{2}{7} \geq + \leq \frac{1}{5} = \frac{10 + 7}{35} = \frac{17}{35}$

$\frac{3}{5} - \frac{1}{3} = \frac{3}{5} \geq + \leq \frac{1}{3} = \frac{9 - 5}{15} = \frac{4}{15}$

20. Multiplying Fractions: Multiplication of fractions does not require a common denominator. Just multiply numerators to create a new numerator, and multiply denominators to create a new denominator.

e.g., $\left(\frac{3}{4}\right)\left(\frac{1}{2}\right) = \frac{(3)(1)}{(4)(2)} = \frac{3}{8}$

$\left(\frac{2}{3}\right)\left(\frac{2}{5}\right) = \frac{(2)(2)}{(3)(5)} = \frac{4}{15}$

21. Dividing Fractions: To divide by a fraction, take the reciprocal of the divisor (the fraction doing the dividing) and then multiply.

e.g., $2 \div \frac{1}{4} = (2)\left(\frac{4}{1}\right) = \frac{8}{1} = 8$

$\frac{\frac{2}{3}}{\frac{5}{6}} = \left(\frac{2}{3}\right)\left(\frac{6}{5}\right) = \frac{12}{15} = \frac{4}{5}$

22. Converting Fractions To Decimals: If the fraction already has a denominator that is 10, 100, 1000, etc., the conversion is easy. The numerator of the fraction becomes the decimal. The placement of the decimal point is governed by the number of zeros in the denominator.

e.g., To express $\frac{127}{1000}$ in decimal form, start with the numerator, 127. From the right of the 7, count over three places to the left (one for each zero in 1,000). The decimal equivalent is 0.127.

If there are fewer numbers in the numerator than there are decimal places, add zeros to the left of the number until you have enough decimal places.

e.g., $\frac{3}{100} = 0.03$ (Two zeros mean two decimal places, but 3 is a single–digit number.)

To convert a proper fraction with a denominator other than 10, 100, etc., first convert the fraction to the equivalent form using a denominator such as 10, 100, etc. To determine which denominator to use, divide the denominator of the fraction into 10, then into 100, then into 1000, until a denominator that is evenly divisible by the denominator of the original fraction is found.

e.g., $\frac{2}{5} = \frac{(2)(2)}{(5)(2)} = \frac{4}{10} = 0.4$

$\frac{1}{4} = \frac{(1)(25)}{(4)(25)} = \frac{25}{100} = 0.25$

$\frac{3}{8} = \frac{(3)(125)}{(8)(125)} = \frac{375}{1000} = 0.375$

When converting proper fractions to decimals there is a second method that is usually easier. Simply divide the denominator into the numerator.

e.g., $\frac{2}{5} = 5\overline{)2.00}$ with quotient 0.40 $= 0.4$

$\frac{3}{8} = 8\overline{)3.000}$ with quotient 0.375 $= 0.375$

To convert a *mixed number* into a decimal, convert the fractional part of the mixed number to a decimal fraction as just discussed, and then place the whole number part of the mixed number to the left of the decimal point.

e.g., $6\frac{1}{10} = 6.1$ (Convert $\frac{1}{10}$ to 0.1 and then place the 6 to the left of the decimal point.)

$3\frac{7}{8} = 3.875$ (Convert $\frac{7}{8}$ to 0.875 and then place the 3 to the left of the decimal point.)

To convert an *improper fraction* to a decimal, just treat the improper fraction as a mixed number and follow the procedure just outlined.

e.g., $\frac{9}{4} = 2\frac{1}{4} = 2.25$

23. Converting Decimals To Fractions: The numerator of the fraction is the digits to the right of the decimal point. The denominator of the fraction is 1 plus a number of zeros equal to the number of decimal places (to the right of the decimal point).

e.g., $0.005 = \frac{5}{1000} = \frac{1}{200}$ (0.005 has three decimal places, so the new denominator is 1 plus three zeros.)

If a decimal has numbers to both the right and left of the decimal point, the conversion to a fraction will result in a mixed number. The whole part of the mixed number will be the whole part of the decimal.

e.g., $1.75 = 1 \text{ plus } \frac{75}{100} = 1 \text{ plus } \frac{3}{4} = 1\frac{3}{4}$

$357.125 = 357 \text{ plus } \frac{125}{1000} = 357 \text{ plus } \frac{1}{8} = 357\frac{1}{8}$

Memorize these values:

$\frac{1}{2} = 0.5$	$\frac{1}{3} = 0.3\overline{3}$	$\frac{1}{4} = 0.25$	$\frac{1}{5} = 0.20$
$\frac{1}{6} = 0.1\overline{66}$	$\frac{1}{7} = 0.1428$	$\frac{1}{8} = 0.125$	$\frac{1}{9} = 0.1\overline{1}$

24. Adding and Subtracting Decimals: When adding and subtracting decimals, simply line up the decimal points, fill in the appropriate number of zeros, and add (or subtract).

e.g.,
$$0.25 + 0.1 + 0.825 = \begin{array}{r} 0.25 \\ 0.1 \\ +0.825 \\ \hline \end{array} = \begin{array}{r} 0.250 \\ 0.100 \\ +0.825 \\ \hline 1.175 \end{array}$$

25. Multiplying Decimals: When multiplying, simply multiply as with whole numbers and then adjust the decimal point. To find the correct position for the decimal point, count the total number of decimal places in the numbers being multiplied, count that many places to the left from the right of the final number in the product, and put the decimal point there.

e.g., $(0.1)(0.2)(0.3) = 0.006$
($1 \cdot 2 \cdot 3 = 6$, and there are three decimal places in the multiplication.)

$(0.10)(0.10)(0.10) = 0.001000 = 0.001$
($10 \cdot 10 \cdot 10 = 1{,}000$, and there are six decimal places in the problem.)

26. Dividing Decimals: When the divisor is a whole number, place a decimal point in the quotient immediately above the decimal point in the dividend. Then, keep dividing until there is no remainder, adding zeros as needed to the right of the divisor.

e.g., $2.5 \div 2 = $

$$\begin{array}{r} 1.25 \\ 2\,\overline{)\,2.50} \\ \underline{-2} \\ 0\,5 \\ \underline{-4} \\ 10 \\ \underline{-10} \\ 0 \end{array}$$

When the divisor is a *decimal*, "clear" the fractional part of the decimal by moving both the divisor and dividend decimal points the same number of spaces to the right.

e.g., $5 \div 2.5 = $

$$\begin{array}{r} 2. \\ 2.5.\,\overline{)\,5.0.} \\ \rightarrow \quad \rightarrow \\ \underline{-5\,0} \\ 0 \end{array}$$

27. Ratios: A ratio is a statement about the relationship between any two quantities. The ratio of two quantities, x and y, can be expressed as $x \div y$, x/y, or $x{:}y$.

e.g., $\frac{2}{5} = 2{:}5$

$\frac{\text{boys}}{\text{girls}}$ = boys:girls = ratio of boys to girls

$\frac{\text{miles}}{\text{hour}}$ = miles:hour

28. Proportions: A proportion is a statement of equality between two ratios.

e.g., $\frac{3}{4} = \frac{9}{12}$

Direct proportions are proportions that are directly related; the more of one, the more of the other and vice versa.

e.g., If the cost of a dozen donuts is \$3.60, what is the cost of four donuts?

$\frac{\text{Total Cost } X}{\text{Total Cost } Y} = \frac{\text{Number } X}{\text{Number } Y} \Rightarrow \frac{\$3.60}{Y} = \frac{12}{4}$

$\$3.60(4) = 12Y$

$Y = 3.60(4) \div 12$

$Y = \$1.20$

With *indirect proportions* the quantities are related indirectly; an increase in one results in a decrease in the other. Use the following method to solve problems involving indirect relationships:

a. Set up an ordinary proportion, making sure that you group like quantities.

b. Take the reciprocal of the right side of the proportion.

c. Cross-multiply and solve for the unknown.

e.g., Traveling at a constant rate of 150 miles per hour, a plane makes the trip from City P to City Q in four hours. How long will the trip take if the plane flies at a constant rate of 200 miles per hour?

$\frac{\text{Speed } X}{\text{Speed } Y} = \frac{\text{Time } X}{\text{Time } Y} \Rightarrow \frac{150 \text{ mph}}{200 \text{ mph}} = \frac{4 \text{ hours}}{Y \text{ hours}}$

$\frac{150}{200} = \frac{Y}{4}$

$Y = 4(150) \div 200$

$Y = 3$ hours

29. Percentage Conversions: To change any *decimal* to a percent, move the decimal point two places to the right and add a percent sign. To change a percent to decimal, reverse the process.

e.g., 0.275 = 27.5%

0.03 = 3%

0.02% = 0.0002

120% = 1.20

To convert a *fraction* to a percent, first convert the fraction to a decimal. Reverse the process for converting percents to fractions.

e.g., $\frac{3}{4} = 0.75 = 75\% = 0.75 = \frac{75}{100} = \frac{3}{4}$

$\frac{5}{8} = 0.625 = 62.5\% = 0.625 = \frac{625}{1000} = \frac{5}{8}$

30. Common Percentage Problems: The following questions are equivalent and have the same general form:

"What percent is this of that?"
"This is what percent of that?"
"Of that, what percent is this?"

Percentage problems can be solved using several different methods. Two methods are outlined below.

Method I: Write the given statement as an equation, rewriting "what percent" as $x/100$ and solve for the unknown.

e.g., What number is 20% of 25?

$x = \left(\frac{20}{100}\right)\left(\frac{25}{1}\right)$

x = 5; therefore 5 is 20% of 25.

Method II: There are three parts to all percentage problems: is, of, and %. Use the following equation to solve for the unknown:

$$\frac{\text{is}}{\text{of}} = \frac{\%}{100}$$

e.g., What percent is 20 of 50?

% = x, is = 20, of = 50

$\frac{\text{is}}{\text{of}} = \frac{\%}{100}$

$\frac{20}{50} = \frac{x}{100}$

$\frac{(20)(100)}{50} = 40\%$

What number is 20% of 25?

% = 20, is = x, of = 25

$\frac{\text{is}}{\text{of}} = \frac{\%}{100} \Leftrightarrow \frac{x}{25} = \frac{20}{100}$

$x = \frac{(20)(25)}{(100)} = 5$

Another common type of percent problem involves the *change in a quantity over time.*

$$\frac{|\text{New Price} - \text{Old Price}|}{\text{Old Price}} = \text{Percentage Change}$$

Absolute value is used so that price decreases can be dealt with as well.

e.g., An item's price is increased from \$20 to \$25. What is the percent increase in the price?

$$\frac{|\text{New Price} - \text{Old Price}|}{\text{Old Price}} = \frac{25-20}{20} = \frac{5}{20} = \frac{1}{4} = 25\%$$

31. Averages: To calculate an average (or mean), add the quantities to be averaged and then divide that sum by the number of quantities added.

e.g., Average of 3, 7, and 8 is 6: $3 + 7 + 8 = 18$ and $18 \div 3 = 6$.

If solving for a *missing element* of an average, set up the average equation and solve for the unknown.

e.g., The average score on four tests is 90. Three scores are 89, 92, and 94: what is the fourth?

$$\frac{89 + 92 + 94 + x}{4} = 90 \Rightarrow x = 85$$

In *weighted averages*, greater weight is given to one element than to another.

e.g., Four books cost \$6.00 each and two books cost \$3.00 each. What is the average cost of the six books?

$$\frac{(4)(6) + (2)(3)}{4 + 2} = \frac{24 + 6}{6} = \frac{30}{6} = 5$$

32. Median: The median is the middle value of a set of numbers when arranged in ascending or descending order. The median of an even number is the arithmetic mean of the two middle values, when the numbers are arranged in ascending or descending order.

e.g., The median of 8, 6, 34, 5, 62, 17, 23, and 2 is 12.5.

33. Mode: The value that appears most frequently in a set of numbers is the mode.

e.g., The mode of 2, 4, 5, 3, 4, 5, 1, 2, 3, 6, 4, 6, and 7 is 4.

34. Counting Principle: To determine the number of ways particular events can occur, multiply the number of ways each event can occur.

e.g., If a math class has 15 girls and 13 boys, how many ways can you select one boy and one girl?

(15)(13) = 195 ways

In how many ways can five students sit in a row with five chairs?

(5)(4)(3)(2)(1) = 120 ways

In how many ways can you fill three chairs given five students?

(5)(4)(3) = 60 ways

II. ALGEBRA SUMMARY

1. **Basic Operations:**

Addition: $n + n = 2n$

$n + m = n + m$

Subtraction: $3n - 2n = n$

$n - m = n - m$

Multiplication: n times $m = (n)(m) = nm$

$(n)(0) = 0$

Division: n divided by $m = n \div m = \frac{n}{m}$

$n \div 0 =$ undefined

2. **Powers:** A power of a number is the product obtained by multiplying the number by itself a specified number of times.

e.g., 3 raised to the fifth power is 3 multiplied by itself five times: (3)(3)(3)(3)(3) = 243.

3. **Exponents:** Exponents are used as notation for powers. To indicate the power of a number, we use a superscript, or *exponent.* The number being multiplied is the *base.* The base is multiplied the number of times indicated by the exponent.

e.g., $2^3 = (2)(2)(2) = 8$

$5^4 = (5)(5)(5)(5) = 625$

Exponent Rules:

a. $x^m \cdot x^n = x^{m+n}$
b. $x^m \div x^n = x^{m-n}$
c. $(x^m)^n = x^{mn}$
d. $(xy)^m = x^m y^m$
e. $\left(\frac{x}{y}\right)^m = \frac{x^m}{y^m}$
f. $x^1 = x$, for any number x
g. $x^0 = 1$, for any number x, such that $x \neq 0$
h. 0^0 is undefined.

e.g., $(2^3)(2^2) = (2 \cdot 2 \cdot 2)(2 \cdot 2) = 2^{3+2} = 2^5$

$(3^2)(3^3)(3^5) = 3^{2+3+5} = 3^{10}$

$2^4 \div 2^2 = \frac{(2)(2)(2)(2)}{(2)(2)} = 2^{4-2} = 2^2$

$5^3 \div 5^5 = 5^{3-5} = 5^{-2} = \left(\frac{1}{5}\right)^2 = \frac{1}{25}$

$(2^2)^3 = (2 \cdot 2)^3 = (2 \cdot 2)(2 \cdot 2)(2 \cdot 2)$
$= 2^{2 \cdot 3} = 2^6$

$(2 \cdot 3)^2 = (2 \cdot 3)(2 \cdot 3) = (2 \cdot 2)(3 \cdot 3)$
$= 2^2 \cdot 3^2 = 4 \cdot 9 = 36$

$(2^3 \cdot 3^2)^2 = 2^{3 \cdot 2} \cdot 3^{2 \cdot 2} = 2^6 \cdot 3^4$

$\left(\frac{2}{3}\right)^2 = \frac{2^2}{3^2} = \frac{4}{9}$

$\left(\frac{3^3 \cdot 5^5}{3^2 \cdot 5^2}\right)^2 = (3^{3-2} \cdot 5^{5-2})^2 = (3^1 \cdot 5^3)^2 = (3^2)(5^6)$

A negative exponent signifies a fraction, indicating the *reciprocal* of the base.

e.g., $x^{-1} = \frac{1}{x}$

$2x^{-1} = \frac{2}{x}$

$4^{-2} = \left(\frac{1}{4}\right)^2 = \frac{1}{16}$

4. **Roots:** The root of a number is a number that is multiplied a specified number of times to give the original number. $m^{1/2} = \sqrt{m} =$ square root, and $m^{1/3} = \sqrt[3]{m} =$ cube root.

e.g., $\sqrt{4} = 4^{1/2} = 2$

$\sqrt[3]{8} = 8^{1/3} = 2$

$\sqrt{125} = 125^{1/2} = (25 \cdot 5)^{1/2} = (25^{1/2})(5^{1/2})$
$= (\sqrt{25})(\sqrt{5}) = 5\sqrt{5}$

$\sqrt{\frac{4}{9}} =$

$\left(\frac{4}{9}\right)^{1/2} = \frac{4^{1/2}}{9^{1/2}} = \frac{\sqrt{4}}{\sqrt{9}} = \frac{2}{3}$

5. **Basic Algebra Operations:** Algebraic operations are the same as for arithmetic, with the addition of unknown quantities. Manipulate operations in the same way, combining (adding and subtracting) only like terms. Like terms have the same variables with the same exponents.

e.g., $x^2 - 3x + 5x - 3x^2 = -2x^2 + 2x$

$(x^2)(x^3) = x^{2+3} = x^5$

$4x^3y^4 \div 2xy^3 = 2x^2y$

$\frac{5}{x} + \frac{3}{x} = \frac{5+3}{x} = \frac{8}{x}$

$\left(\frac{x^2y^3}{z}\right)\left(\frac{x^3y^2}{wz}\right) = \frac{x^5y^5}{wz^2}$

6. **Multiplying Polynomials:** A polynomial is an algebraic expression with more than one term. When multiplying polynomials, use the FOIL (First, Outer, Inner, Last) Method:

$(x + y)(x + y) =$
Multiply First Terms: x times $x = x^2$
Multiply Outer Terms: x times $y = xy$
Multiply Inner Terms: y times $x = yx = xy$
Multiply Last Terms: y times $y = y^2$
Group and combine like terms:
$(x + y)(x + y) = x^2 + 2xy + y^2$

e.g., $(x - y)(x - y) =$
First: $(x)(x) = x^2$
Outer: $(x)(-y) = -xy$
Inner: $(-y)(x) = -xy$
Last: $(-y)(-y) = y$
Combine: $x^2 - xy - xy + y^2 = x^2 - 2xy + y^2$

e.g., $(x + y)(x^2 + 2xy + y^2) = x(x^2) + x(2xy)$
$+ x(y^2) + y(x^2) + y(2xy) + y(y^2)$
$= x^3 + 2x^2y + xy^2 + x^2y + 2xy^2 + y^3$
$= x^3 + 3x^2y + 3xy^2 + y^3$

Memorize these Common Patterns:
$(x + y)^2 = (x + y)(x + y) = x^2 + 2xy + y^2$
$(x - y)^2 = (x - y)(x - y) = x^2 - 2xy + y^2$
$(x + y)(x - y) = x^2 - y^2$

7. **Factoring:** Factoring is the reverse of multiplication. There are three factoring situations.

a. If all the terms of an algebraic expression contain a common factor, then that term can be factored out of the expression.

e.g., $ab + ac + ad = a(b + c + d)$
$x^2 + x^3 + x^4 = x^2(1 + x + x^2)$
$3xy + xz + 4x = x(3y + z + 4)$

b. Expressions are one of the three common patterns.

e.g., $x^2 + 2xy + y^2 = (x + y)(x + y) = (x + y)^2$
$x^2 - 2xy + y^2 = (x - y)(x - y) = (x - y)^2$
$x^2 - y^2 = (x - y)(x + y)$

c. Occasionally expressions do not fall into one of the two categories above. To factor the expression, usually of the form $ax^2 + bx + c$, set up a blank diagram: ( )( ). The diagram is filled in by asking the following questions:

- What factors produce the first term, ax^2?
- What possible factors produce the last term, c?
- Which of the possible factors, when added together, produce the middle term, bx?

e.g., $x^2 + 3x + 2 = (x + 2)(x + 1)$
$x^2 + 4x - 12 = (x + 6)(x - 2)$

8. **Solving Linear Equations:** An equation containing variables of just the first power is called a linear equation. You can add, subtract, multiply, and divide both sides of an equation by any value without changing the statement of equality. (You cannot multiply or divide by zero.) To find the value of a variable, isolate the variable on one side of the equation and solve.

e.g., $4x + 2 = 2x + 10$
$(4x + 2) - 2x = (2x + 10) - 2x$
$2x + 2 = 10$
$(2x + 2) - 2 = (10) - 2$
$2x = 8$
$\frac{(2x)}{2} = \frac{(8)}{2}$
$x = 4$

e.g., $\frac{2x + 6}{2} = 9$
$2x + 6 = 9(2)$
$2x = 18 - 6$
$x = \frac{12}{2} = 6$

9. **Solving Quadratic Equations:** Equations that involve variables of the second power are called quadratic equations and may have zero, one, or two real solutions.

a. If possible take the square root of both sides.

e.g., $x^2 = 25$
$x = \pm 5$

b. Otherwise arrange all terms on the left side of equation so that the right side of equation is zero; $ax^2 + bx + c = 0$. Factor the left side of the equation and set each binomial equal to zero. Solve for the unknown.

e.g., $x^2 - 2x = 3$
$x^2 - 2x - 3 = 0$
$(x - 3)(x + 1) = 0$
$x = 3$ or $x = -1$

$x^2 - 3x = 4$
$x^2 - 3x - 4 = 0$
$(x - 4)(x + 1) = 0$
$x = 4$ or $x = -1$

c. The quadratic formula, $x = \frac{-b \pm \sqrt{b^2 - 4ac}}{2a}$, may also be used to solve quadratic equations.

e.g., $3 - x = 2x^2$
$2x^2 + x - 3 = 0$
$a = 2$, $b = 1$, and $c = -3$
$x = \frac{-b \pm \sqrt{b^2 - 4ac}}{2a} = \frac{-1 \pm \sqrt{1^2 - 4(2)(-3)}}{2(2)}$
$x = \frac{-1 \pm \sqrt{1 + 24}}{4} = \frac{-1 \pm 5}{4}$
$x = 1$ or $x = -\frac{3}{2}$

d. The SAT, PSAT, and ACT allow calculators: a graphing calculator may be used to quickly solve quadratic equations. A quadratic formula program must be entered into your calculator.

10. **Solving Simultaneous Equations:** Given two equations with two variables, the equations may be solved simultaneously for the values of the two variables. There are several methods for

solving simultaneous equations and four are outlined below.

Method 1 (Substitution): Solve one equation for one variable and substitute the result into the other equation to find the other variable. Plug back into the first variable equation.

e.g., Given: $2x - y = 6$ and $3x + 2y = 16$

Solve for y: $-y = 6 - 2x$

$y = 2x - 6$

Substitute: $3x + 2(y) = 16$

$3x + 2(2x - 6) = 16$

$3x + 4x - 12 = 16$

$7x = 28$

$x = 4$

Substitute: $y = 2(x) - 6$

$y = 2(4) - 6$

$y = 2$

Therefore: $x = 4$ and $y = 2$

Method 2 (Elimination): Make the coefficients of one variable equal and then add (or subtract) the two equations to eliminate one variable.

e.g., Given: $2x - y = 6$ and $3x + 2y = 16$

Multiply: $2(2x - y = 6)$

$4x - 2y = 12$

Add Equations: $4x - 2y = 12$

$\underline{+\ 3x + 2y = 16}$

$7x = 28$

$x = 4$

Substitute: $2(x) - y = 6$

$2(4) - y = 6$

$-y = -2$

$y = 2$

Method 3 (Calculator): The SAT, PSAT, and ACT allow calculators: a graphing calculator may be used to quickly solve simultaneous equations. In each equation, solve for y in terms of x. Graph both equations simultaneously—the point of intersection is (x, y).

e.g., $2x - y = 6$; $-y = 6 - 2x$; $y = \frac{(6 - 2x)}{-1}$

$3x + 2y = 16$; $2y = 16 - 3x$; $y = \frac{(16 - 3x)}{2}$

Graph both equations—the intersection is found at (4,2).

Method 4 (Calculator): The SAT, PSAT, and ACT allow calculators: a graphing calculator may be used to quickly solve simultaneous equations. A system solver program must be entered into your calculator.

11. **Inequalities:** The fundamental rule for working with inequalities is similar to that for working with equalities. The same value may be added or subtracted to each side of an inequality without changing the inequality. Each side may be multiplied or divided by the same *positive* value without changing the inequality.

e.g., $5 > 2$

$5 + 25 > 2 + 25$

$30 > 27$

$24 > 20$

$24(2) > 20(2)$

$48 > 40$

$24 > 20$

$24 \div 4 > 20 \div 4$

$6 > 5$

To multiply or divide by a *negative* number, reverse the direction of the inequality.

e.g., $4 > 2$

$4(-2) > 2(-2)$

$-8 < -4$

$4 > 2$

$4 \div (-2) > 2 \div (-2)$

$-2 < -1$

12. **Slope:** The slope, m, of a line describes its steepness. It is defined as the change in y-values divided by the change in x-values, or rise over run.

$$m = \frac{y_2 - y_1}{x_2 - x_1} = \frac{\text{rise}}{\text{run}} = \frac{\Delta y}{\Delta x}$$

e.g., The slope of the line that contains (–3, 5) and (2, 7) is $\frac{7-5}{2-(-3)} = \frac{2}{5}$.

13. **Linear Equations:**

Slope-Intercept Form: $y = mx + b$

$$m = \text{slope} = \frac{\Delta y}{\Delta x} = \frac{y_2 - y_1}{x_2 - x_1}$$

Point-Slope Form: $y - y_1 = m(x - x_1)$

Standard Form: $Ax + By = C$; $m = -\frac{A}{B}$

14. **Distance Formula:** The distance between two points can be found using the distance formula:

$$d = \sqrt{(x_2 - x_1)^2 + (y_2 - y_1)^2}$$

where (x_1, y_1) and (x_2, y_2) are the given points.

e.g., The distance between (–1, 4) and (7, 3) is equal to:

$$d = \sqrt{(7 - (-1))^2 + (3 - 4)^2} = \sqrt{64 + 1} = \sqrt{65}$$

III. COMMON EQUATIONS SUMMARY

1 . **Distance:** Distance = (Rate)(Time). Given two of the three values, any unknown may be solved for by rearranging the equation.

e.g., After driving constantly for four hours, we reached our destination—200 miles from where we started. What was our average rate of travel?

Distance = (Rate)(Time)

$\text{Rate} = \frac{\text{Distance}}{\text{Time}} = \frac{200 \text{ miles}}{4 \text{ hours}} = 50 \text{ mph}$

2 . **Simple Interest:** $I_s = Prt$, where P is the principle, r is the rate, and t is the time period.

e.g., With a principle of $1,200 and a rate of 10% per year, what was the interest earned over one month?

$I_s = Prt = (\$1200)\left(\frac{0.10}{\text{year}}\right)\left(\frac{1 \text{ year}}{12 \text{ months}}\right) = \$10$

3 . **Compound Interest:** $I_c = P(1 + r)^n - P$, where P is the principle, r is the rate, and n is the number of periods.

e.g., With a principle of $1000 and an compound interest rate of 15% per year, how much compound interest was earned over 5 years?

$I_c = P(1 + r)^n - P = (\$1{,}000)(1 + 0.15)^5 - (\$1{,}000) = \$2{,}011 - \$1{,}000 = \$1{,}011$

4 . **Combined Work Rates:** $\text{Rate}_1 + \text{Rate}_2 = \text{Rate}_3$

e.g., Machine I washes four loads in 60 minutes and Machine II washes one load in 30 minutes. How many loads will both machines working together wash in 20 minutes?

$\left(\frac{4 \text{ loads}}{60 \text{ minutes}}\right) + \left(\frac{1 \text{ loads}}{30 \text{ minutes}}\right) = \left(\frac{x \text{ loads}}{20 \text{ minutes}}\right)$

$\frac{4}{60} + \frac{1}{30} = \frac{x}{20}$

$\frac{4(1)}{60} + \frac{1(2)}{60} = \frac{x}{20}$

$\frac{4+2}{60} = \frac{x}{20}$

$x = \frac{6(20)}{60} = 2 \text{ loads}$

5 . **Mixed Denominations:** When a problem gives mixed denominations (*e.g.,* different prices for same item, tickets, colors, etc.) set up simultaneous equations and solve the equations.

e.g., The store sold apples for $0.20 and oranges for $0.50 each. A total of 50 apples and oranges were bought for $19. How many apples and how many oranges were bought?

x = # of apples; y = # of oranges

$x + y = 50$; $(0.20)x + (0.50)y = 19$

$x = 50 - y$

$0.2(50 - y) + 0.5y = 19$

$10 - 0.2y + 0.5y = 19$

$0.3y = 9$

$y = 30$ = 30 oranges

$x = 50 - y = 50 - 30 = 20$ apples

6 . **Mixture of Concentrations or Values:** A mixture problem is one in which two quantities of different items with different concentrations or values are mixed together and a new quantity (the sum of the two) and concentration or value is created.

$$Q_1C_1 + Q_2C_2 = (Q_1 + Q_2)C_3$$

e.g., How many liters of a juice which is 10% orange juice must be added to three liters of another juice that is 15% orange juice to produce a mixture that is 12% orange juice?

$Q_1C_1 + Q_2C_2 = (Q_1 + Q_2)C_3$

$Q(0.10) + (3)(0.15) = (Q + 3)(0.12)$

$0.1Q + 0.45 = 0.12Q + 0.36$

$0.45 - 0.36 = 0.12Q - 0.1Q$

$0.09 = 0.02Q$

$Q = 4.5$

7 . **Markup, Cost, and Revenue:** $R = (1 + M)C$, where R is the revenue, M is the markup, and C is the cost.

e.g., The revenue from an item is $120. With a markup in cost of 25%, what is the original cost?

$C = \frac{R}{1+M}$

$\text{Cost} = \frac{120}{1 + 0.25} = \$96$

IV. GEOMETRY SUMMARY

1. Lines and Angles

a. Symbols:

$\overline{AB}$ = line segment

$l_1 \parallel l_2$ = parallel lines

$\perp$ = perpendicular

∟ = right angle

b. Facts About Lines and Angles:

Vertical angles are equal:

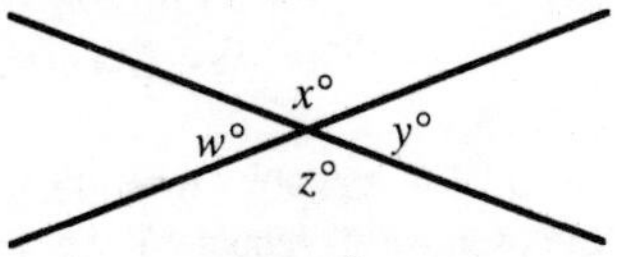

$w = y$ and $x = z$

Two extended lines that do not intersect regardless of length are parallel to each other:

Parallel lines intersected by a third line, the transversal, creates the following angles:

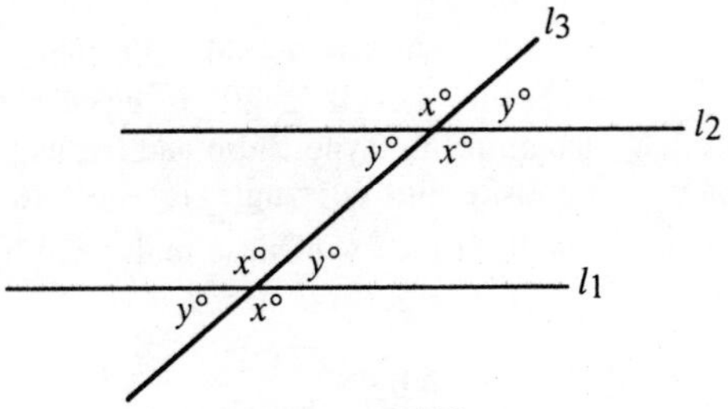

$x = x$; $y = y$; $x + y = 180$

Two lines perpendicular to the same line are parallel to each other:

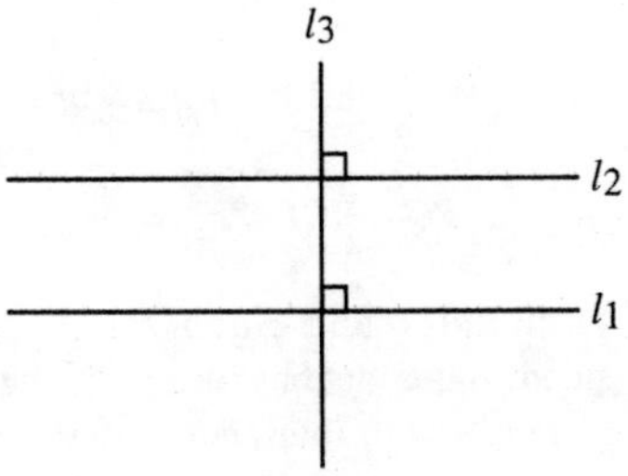

$l_1 \parallel l_2$

There are 180° in a straight line:

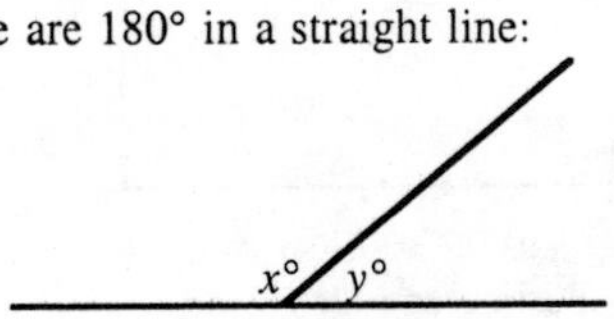

$x + y = 180$

There are 90° in a right angle and two right angles form a straight line:

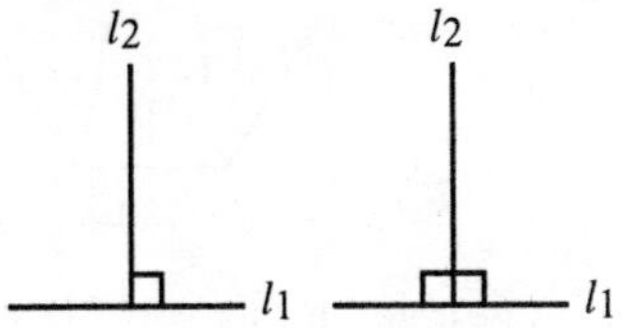

An angle less than 90° is an acute angle:

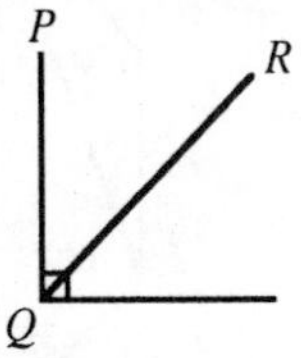

In the figure above, ∠PQR is an acute angle.

An angle greater than 90° is an obtuse angle:

In the figure above, ∠PQR is an obtuse angle.

2. Polygons:

A *polygon* is a closed figure created by three or more lines. The sum of the interior angles of any polygon is $180(n - 2)$, where n = the number of sides of the polygon. The sum of the measures of the exterior angles of a polygon is 360° for all polygons.

A *triangle* is any polygon with exactly three sides.

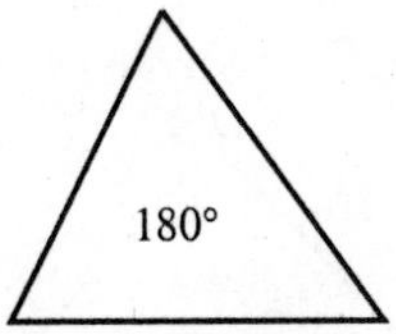

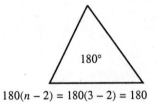

$180(n - 2) = 180(3 - 2) = 180$

A *quadrilateral* is any polygon with exactly four sides. Opposite sides of a parallelogram are equal and parallel.

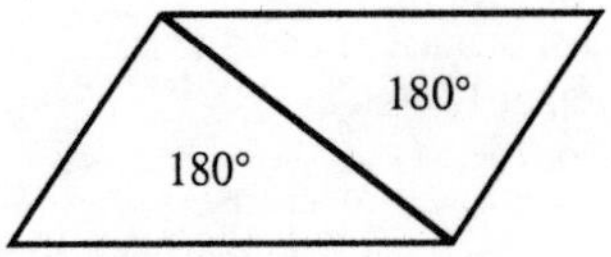

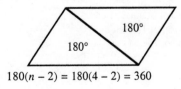

$180(n - 2) = 180(4 - 2) = 360$

A *pentagon* is any polygon with exactly five sides.

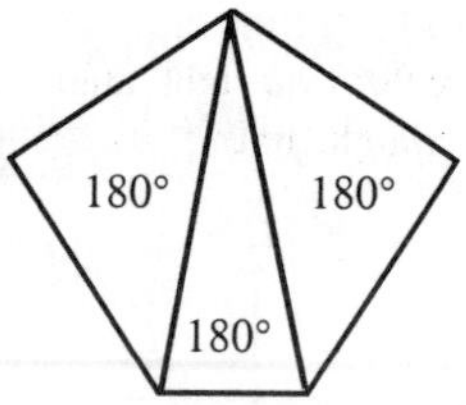

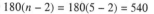

$180(n - 2) = 180(5 - 2) = 540$

A *hexagon* is any polygon with exactly six sides.

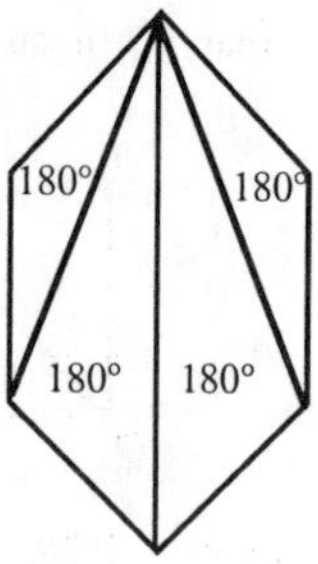

$180(n - 2) = 180(6 - 2) = 720$

3. **Triangles:** A triangle is a 3-sided figure. Within a given triangle, the larger the angle, the longer the opposite side; and conversely, the longer the side, the larger the opposite angle.

A triangle with two equal sides is an *isosceles* triangle. A triangle with three equal sides is an *equilateral* triangle.

Within a given triangle, if two sides are equal, their opposite angles are equal, and vice versa:

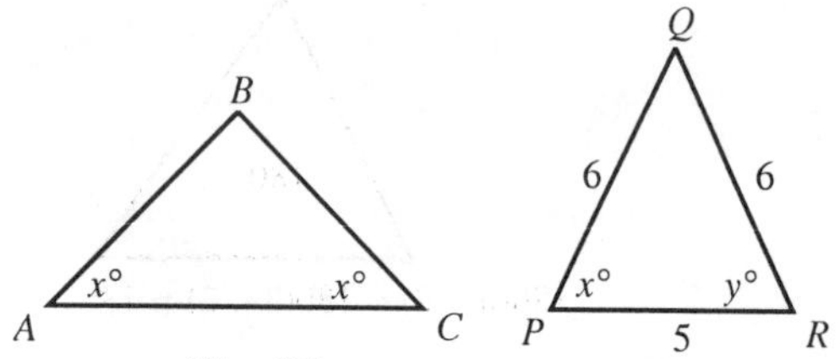

$AB = BC$ $x = y$

The sides of every right triangle follow the *Pythagorean Theorem*: the square of the hypotenuse is equal to the sum of the squares of the other two sides.

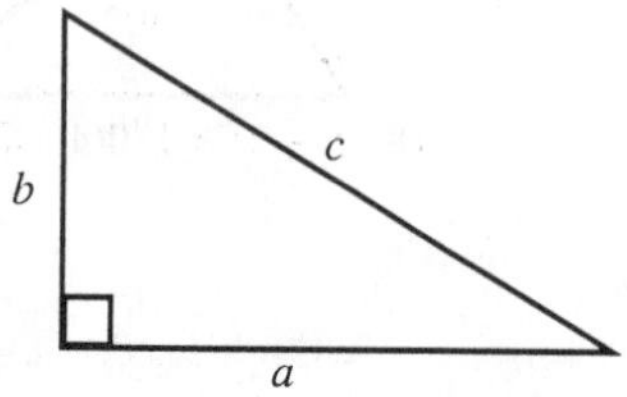

$c^2 = a^2 + b^2$

The perimeter of a triangle is the sum of the lengths of the three sides:

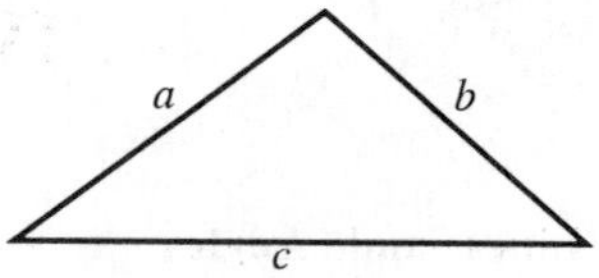

Perimeter = $a + b + c$

The area of a triangle is one-half times the base times the height:

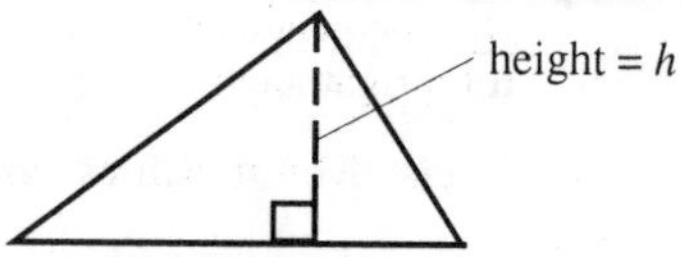

base = b

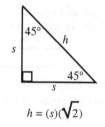

$$\text{Area} = \frac{1}{2}(bh) = \frac{bh}{2}$$

In a 45°-45°-90° triangle, the length of the hypotenuse is equal to the length of either side multiplied by the square root of two:

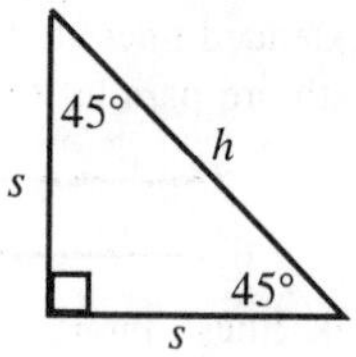

$$h = (s)(\sqrt{2})$$

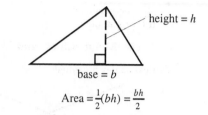

In a 30°-60°-90° triangle, the length of the side opposite the 30° angle is equal to one-half the length of the hypotenuse and the length of the side opposite the 60° angle is equal to one-half the length of the hypotenuse multiplied by $\sqrt{3}$:

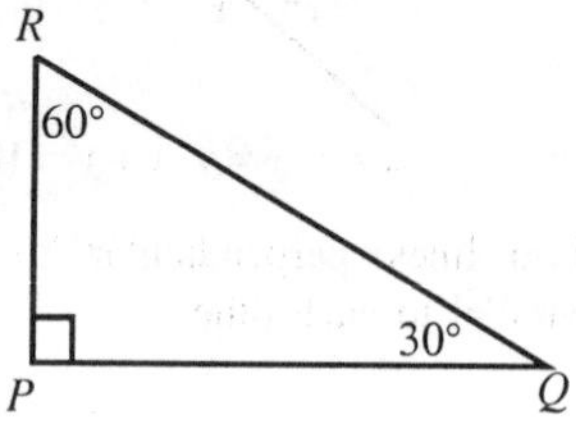

$$PR = \frac{1}{2}QR$$

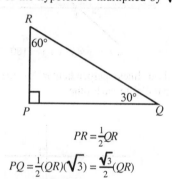

$$PQ = \frac{1}{2}(QR)(\sqrt{3}) = \frac{\sqrt{3}}{2}(QR)$$

4. **Rectangles and Squares:** A rectangle is any 4-sided figure that has four right angles. A square is a rectangle with four equal sides:

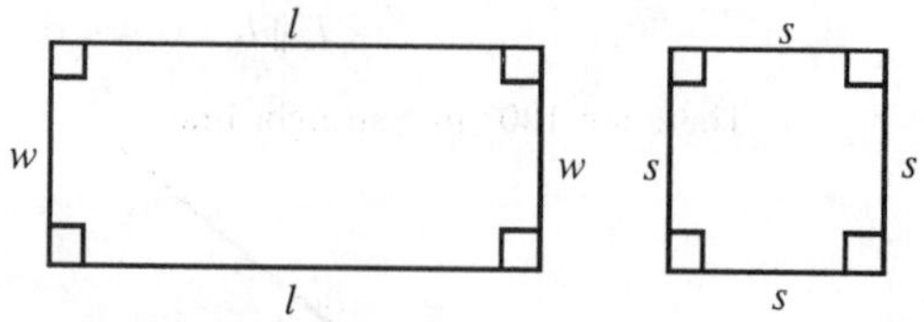

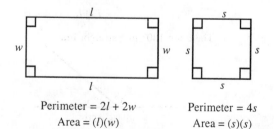

Perimeter = $2l + 2w$
Area = $(l)(w)$

Perimeter = $4s$
Area = $(s)(s)$

5. **Circles:** The distance from the center of a circle to any point on the circle is the *radius*. A line segment with end points on the circle which passes through the center of the circle is called the *diameter*. The diameter of a circle is twice the radius.

There are 360° of arc in a circle:

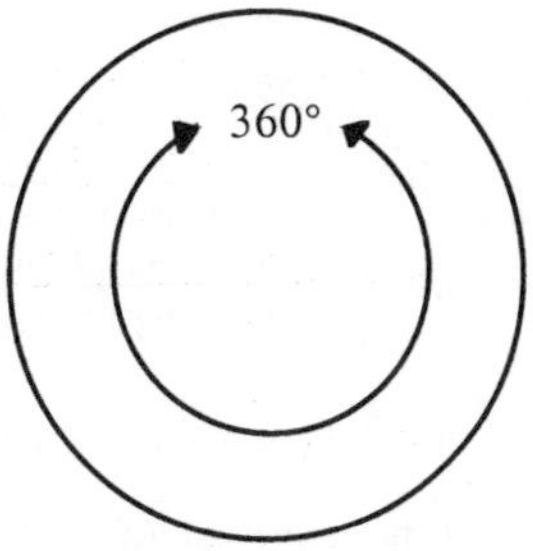

An angle inscribed in a circle intercepts twice its arc:

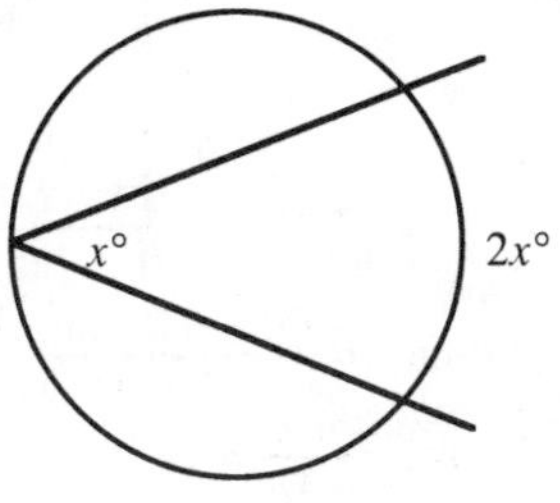

An angle whose vertex is at the center of a circle intercepts its arc:

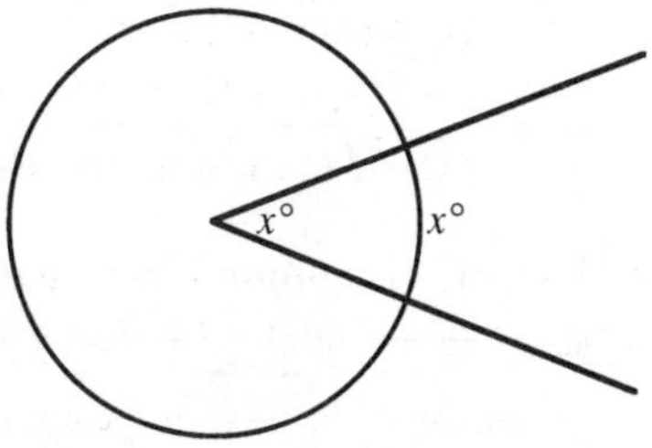

The circumference of a circle is the radius times 2π. The area is the radius squared times π.

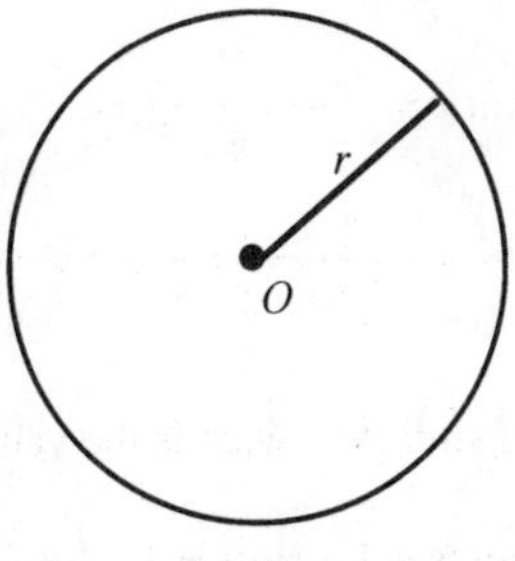

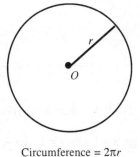

Circumference $= 2\pi r$

Area $= \pi r^2$

6. **Solid Geometry:** Solid geometry refers to three-dimensional figures. Volume is a three dimensional quantity.

The volume of a rectangular solid is the length times the width times the height:

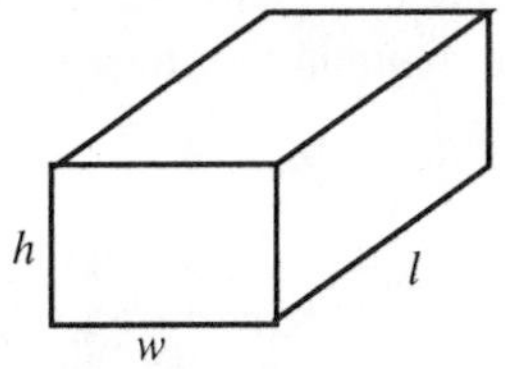

Volume $= (l)(w)(h)$

The volume of a cylinder is the height times the radius squared times π.

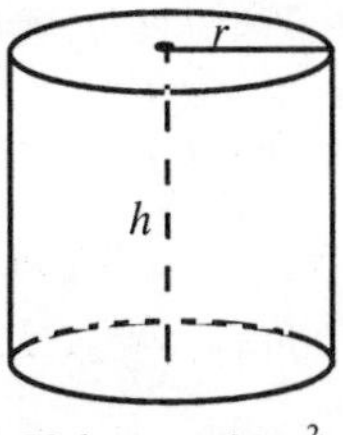

Volume $= h(\pi r^2)$

The volume of a sphere is four-thirds times π times the radius cubed.

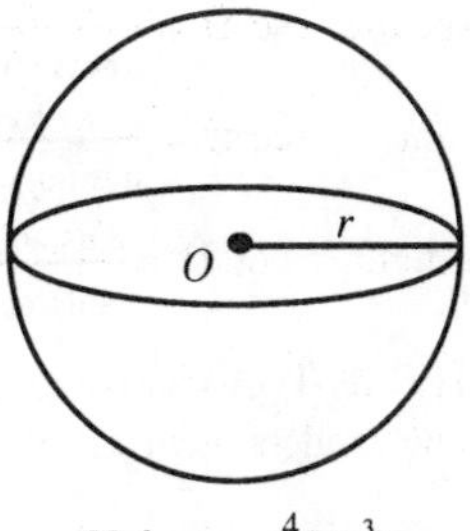

Volume $= \frac{4}{3}(\pi r^3)$

V. TRIGONOMETRY SUMMARY

(ACT only)

1 . **Basic Trigonometric Functions:** The three basic trigonometric functions are sine, cosine, and tangent. The functions can be viewed in relationship to a right triangle.

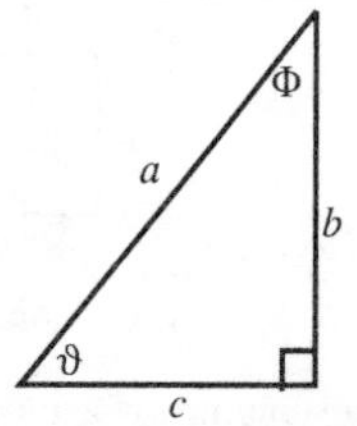

The *hypotenuse* is the side opposite the right angle. The *side opposite* is the side opposite the referenced angle. The *side adjacent* is the side next to the referenced angle, but not the hypotenuse.

Memorize these Trigonometric Definitions:

sine: $\sin \vartheta = \dfrac{\text{Side Opposite angle } \vartheta}{\text{Hypotenuse}} = \dfrac{b}{a}$

cosine: $\cos \vartheta = \dfrac{\text{Side Adjacent angle } \vartheta}{\text{Hypotenuse}} = \dfrac{c}{a}$

tangent: $\tan \vartheta = \dfrac{\text{Side Opposite angle } \vartheta}{\text{Side Adjacent angle } \vartheta} = \dfrac{b}{c}$

cosecant: $\csc \vartheta = \dfrac{\text{hypotenuse}}{\text{side opposite angle } \vartheta} = \dfrac{a}{b}$

secant: $\sec \vartheta = \dfrac{\text{hypotenuse}}{\text{side adjacent to angle } \vartheta} = \dfrac{a}{c}$

cotangent: $\cot \vartheta = \dfrac{\text{side adjacent to angle } \vartheta}{\text{side opposite angle } \vartheta} = \dfrac{c}{b}$

SOH-CAH-TOA can be used to memorize the sine, cosine, and tangent ratios.

e.g., Find the values of sin *A*, cos *A*, tan *A*, csc *A*, sec *A*, cot *A*, sin *C*, cos *C*, tan *C*, csc *C*, sec *C*, and cot *C* in the triangle below.

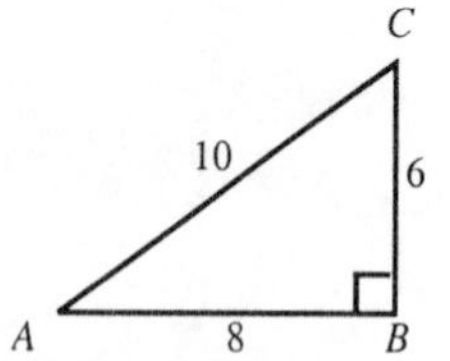

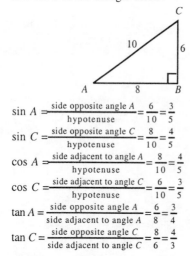

$\sin A = \dfrac{\text{side opposite angle } A}{\text{hypotenuse}} = \dfrac{6}{10} = \dfrac{3}{5}$

$\sin C = \dfrac{\text{side opposite angle } C}{\text{hypotenuse}} = \dfrac{8}{10} = \dfrac{4}{5}$

$\cos A = \dfrac{\text{side adjacent to angle } A}{\text{hypotenuse}} = \dfrac{8}{10} = \dfrac{4}{5}$

$\cos C = \dfrac{\text{side adjacent to angle } C}{\text{hypotenuse}} = \dfrac{6}{10} = \dfrac{3}{5}$

$\tan A = \dfrac{\text{side opposite angle } A}{\text{side adjacent to angle } A} = \dfrac{6}{8} = \dfrac{3}{4}$

$\tan C = \dfrac{\text{side opposite angle } C}{\text{side adjacent to angle } C} = \dfrac{8}{6} = \dfrac{4}{3}$

$\csc A = \dfrac{\text{hypotenuse}}{\text{side opposite to angle } A} = \dfrac{10}{6} = \dfrac{5}{3}$

$\csc C = \dfrac{\text{hypotenuse}}{\text{side opposite to angle } C} = \dfrac{10}{8} = \dfrac{5}{4}$

$\sec A = \dfrac{\text{hypotenuse}}{\text{side adjacent to angle } A} = \dfrac{10}{8} = \dfrac{5}{4}$

$\sec C = \dfrac{\text{hypotenuse}}{\text{side adjacent to angle } C} = \dfrac{10}{6} = \dfrac{5}{3}$

$\cot A = \dfrac{\text{side adjacent to angle } A}{\text{side opposite angle } A} = \dfrac{8}{6} = \dfrac{4}{3}$

$\cot C = \dfrac{\text{side adjacent to angle } C}{\text{side opposite angle } C} = \dfrac{6}{8} = \dfrac{3}{4}$

e.g., In the right triangle below, $\sin x = \frac{3}{4}$. What is the length of $\overline{AC}$?

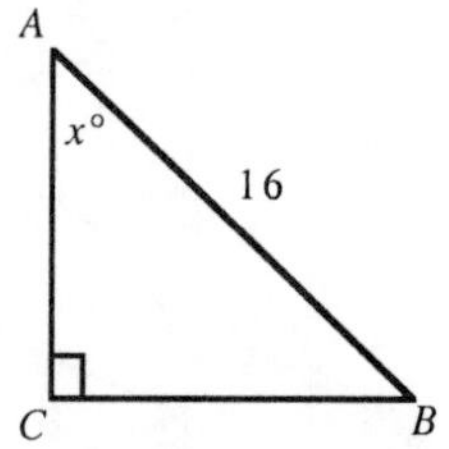

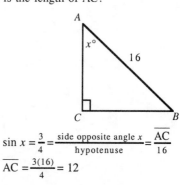

$\sin x = \dfrac{3}{4} = \dfrac{\text{side opposite angle } x}{\text{hypotenuse}} = \dfrac{\overline{AC}}{16}$

$\overline{AC} = \dfrac{3(16)}{4} = 12$

Or using the Pythagorean Theorem:

$(\overline{AB})^2 = (\overline{AC})^2 + (\overline{CB})^2$

$16^2 = (\overline{AC})^2 + 12^2$

$(\overline{AC})^2 = 16^2 - 12^2 = 256 - 144 = 112$

$\overline{AC} = \sqrt{112} = \sqrt{16(7)} = 4\sqrt{7}$

2 . **Useful Trigonometric Relationships:**

$\sin x = \dfrac{1}{\csc x},\ \cos x = \dfrac{1}{\sec x},\ \tan x = \dfrac{1}{\cot x},\ \tan x = \dfrac{\sin x}{\cos x}$

$\sin^2 x + \cos^2 x = 1;\ 1 + \cot^2 x = \csc^2 x;\ \tan^2 x + 1 = \sec^2 x$

e.g., If $\sin x = \frac{3}{5}$ and $\cos x = \frac{4}{5}$, what is the value of tan *x*, csc *x*, sec *x*, and cot *x*?

$\tan x = \dfrac{\sin x}{\cos x} = \dfrac{\frac{3}{5}}{\frac{4}{5}} = \dfrac{3}{4},\ \csc x = \dfrac{1}{\sin x} = \dfrac{1}{\frac{3}{5}} = \dfrac{5}{3}$

$\sec x = \dfrac{1}{\cos x} = \dfrac{1}{\frac{4}{5}} = \dfrac{5}{4},\ \cot x = \dfrac{1}{\tan x} = \dfrac{1}{\frac{3}{4}} = \dfrac{4}{3}$

e.g., If $\sin^2 x = \frac{1}{4}$, what is the value of cos *x*?

$\cos^2 x = 1 - \sin^2 x = 1 - \frac{1}{4} = \frac{3}{4},\ \cos x = \dfrac{\sqrt{3}}{2}$

ARITHMETIC FORMULAS

Price Percentage Change = $\frac{|\text{New Price} - \text{Old Price}|}{\text{Old Price}}$

Average = $\frac{a+b+c+\ldots}{n}$; a, b, c, etc., = values, n = total number

Distance = Rate • Time

Slope = $m = \frac{y_2 - y_1}{x_2 - x_1}$

Slope-Intercept Linear Equation $y = mx + b$

Simple Interest = Principle • Rate • Time

Compound Interest = $(\text{Principle})(1 + \text{rate})^{\#\text{ of periods}} - \text{Principle}$

Revenue = (1 + Markup)(Cost)

Combined Work Rate: $\text{Rate}_3 = \text{Rate}_1 + \text{Rate}_2$

Percentage Problems: $\frac{\text{is}}{\text{of}} = \frac{\%}{100}$

Mixture: $(Q_1 + Q_2)C_3 = Q_1C_1 + Q_2C_2$; Q = quantities, C = concentrations

GEOMETRY FORMULAS

Perimeter of a Square: $P = 4s$; s = side

Perimeter of a Rectangle: $P = 2l + 2w$; l = length, w = width

Perimeter of a Triangle: $P = a + b + c$; a, b, and c are the sides

Circumference of a Circle: $C = 2\pi r$; $\pi \approx 3.14$, r = radius

Area of a Square: $A = s^2$; s = length of side

Area of a Rectangle: $A = lw$; l = length, w = width

Area of a Triangle: $A = \frac{1}{2}bh$; b = base, h = height

Area of a Circle: $A = \pi r^2$; r = radius, $\pi \approx 3.14$

Volume of a Cube: $V = s^3$; s = side

Volume of a Rectangle Solid: $V = lwh$; l = length, w = width, h = height

Volume of a Cylinder: $V = h(\pi r^2)$; h = height, $\pi \approx 3.14$, r = radius

Volume of a Sphere: $V = \frac{4}{3}\pi r^3$; $\pi \approx 3.14$, r = radius

POLYGON FORMULAS

45°-45°-90° Triangle: $h = s\sqrt{2}$; h = hypotenuse, s = length of either leg

30°-60°-90° Triangle: $a = \frac{1}{2}h$; a = side opposite 30° angle

$b = \frac{\sqrt{3}}{2}h$; b = side opposite 60° angle

Pythagorean Theorem (Right Triangles): $c^2 = a^2 + b^2$; c = hypotenuse, a and b = legs

Sum of Interior Angles of Polygon: $S = 180(n - 2)$; n = number of sides of the polygon

TRIGONOMETRY FORMULAS
(ACT Only)

$\sin A = \frac{\text{opp}}{\text{hyp}}$ $\cos A = \frac{\text{adj}}{\text{hyp}}$ $\tan A = \frac{\text{opp}}{\text{adj}}$ $\csc A = \frac{\text{hyp}}{\text{opp}}$ $\sec A = \frac{\text{hyp}}{\text{adj}}$ $\cot A = \frac{\text{adj}}{\text{opp}}$

$\sin^2 A + \cos^2 A = 1$ $1 + \cot^2 A = \csc^2 A$ $\tan^2 A + 1 = \sec^2 A$

ACT APPENDIX C: BASIC GRAMMAR TUTOR

CAMBRIDGE
EDUCATIONAL SERVICES, INC.®

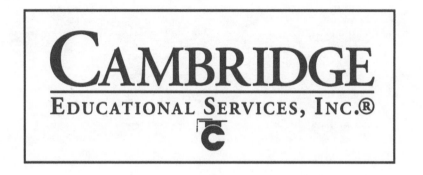

ACT • PLAN • EXPLORE
Appendix C

BASIC GRAMMAR REVIEW

Parts of Speech

Nouns

A ***noun*** is a word that refers to one of the following: persons, animals, plants, objects, times, places, and ideas.

EXAMPLES:

Persons: Bob, woman, niece, student, doctor, men, brothers, teachers
Animals: dog, mouse, cow, cats, elephants, birds
Plants: grass, tree, bushes, oaks
Objets: glove, car, building, sidewalk, desks, buses
Times: hour, yesterday, Thanksgiving, Mondays, weekends
Places: home, office, city, Puerto Rico, Poland, Africa
Ideas: democracy, love, youth, sisterhood, dreams

Pronouns

A ***pronoun*** is a word that can substitute for a noun.

EXAMPLES:

Hernandez hit a home run. *He* waved to the crowd.
The woman went into the store. *She* bought a book.
My sisters live in St. Louis. *They* are coming to visit.
The bull escaped from the pasture. The farmer caught *him*.
The bush seems dry. Julie should water *it*.

Verbs

A ***verb*** is a word that describes activity, change, feeling, or existence.

EXAMPLES:

The dog *is running* down the street.
Mary *wrote* a letter.
Kevin *sewed* a button on the shirt.
The weather *became* cold.
The sky *darkened*.
John *likes* Mary.
Carl *worries* that he might not pass the test.
The house *is* green.
The letter *was* several days late.

Modifiers

A ***modifier*** gives further detail to nouns and verbs.

EXAMPLES:

The *blue* car ran into the *red* car.
The *tall* woman was carrying an *expensive* umbrella.

The farmer *patiently* waited for the cows.
Margaret walked *quickly* into the kitchen.

Conjunctions

A ***conjunction*** joins ideas together.

EXAMPLES:

Paul *and* Mary ate dinner.
I like coffee, *but* George likes tea.
You can take the subway *or* the bus.
Harry played *while* Sam sang.
Although Ed had not arrived, we ate anyway.

Prepositions

Prepositions show the relationship between some idea and some noun in the sentence.

EXAMPLES:

Patty sat *on* the chair.
Cliff gave the apples *to* Tom.
Geneva is the owner *of* the dinner.
The mop is *in* the closet *beside* the broom.

EXERCISE 1

Parts of Speech

DIRECTIONS: In questions #1-20, identify the part of speech of the words underlined in the sentences below. Use the following key:

N = Noun	V = Verb
Pro = Pronoun	M = Modifier
C = Conjunction	Prep = Preposition

Answers are on page C-64.

1. The ambulance weaved in and out of traffic as it hurried to the hospital.

   ambulance _____ it _____ hospital _____

   traffic _____ hurried _____

2. The movers unloaded the sofa and put it in the living room.

   movers _____ and _____ in _____

   unloaded _____ it _____

3. The dark clouds completely blocked our view of the mountains and the lake.

   dark _____ blocked _____ and _____

   clouds _____ our _____

4. After dinner we cleared the dishes from the table, put them in the kitchen sink, and sat down to watch the game.

   dinner _____ table _____ sat _____

   cleared _____ and _____

5. One room in the library was filled with books written by authors of Polish ancestry.

   room _____ with _____ Polish _____

   was filled _____ authors _____

6. Some of the first television shows were adaptations of earlier radio versions of the same program.

   first _____ were _____ program _____

   shows _____ earlier _____

7. When the waiter arrived, Victor ordered pie with ice cream, chocolate syrup, and a cherry.

   waiter _____ Victor _____ and _____

   arrived _____ ordered _____

8. The building inspector finally approved the plans and allowed the construction to continue.

   inspector _____ approved _____ allowed _____

   finally _____ and _____

9. The superintendent notified the tenants in the building that the water would be off for two hours.

   notified _____ water _____ hours _____

   in _____ would be _____

10. Just as the band finished the number, the crowd burst into a loud applause.

    band _____ crowd _____ loud _____

    finished _____ burst _____

11. Carlos telephoned Iris to tell her that he would be late for their date.

    telephoned _____ would be _____ date _____

    her _____ their _____

12. The cat was sleeping on the windowsill in the warmth of the afternoon sun.

    cat _____ warmth _____ sun _____

    was sleeping _____ of _____

13 As the train pulled into each station, the conductor called out the name of that station and the name of the station coming next.

    train _____ called _____ and _____

    pulled _____ name _____

14. By the time we got to Woodstock, the children were sound asleep in the rear of the car.

    we _____ were _____ rear _____

    children _____ in _____

15 . Before they leave the camp, the guides teach the hikers how to identify poison ivy and warn them to avoid it.

    they _____ teach _____ and _____

    leave _____ hikers _____

16. Chuck covered the steaming hot pancakes with plenty of melted butter and sweet, sticky syrup.

covered _____ melted _____ syrup _____

steaming _____ sticky _____

17. Last weekend, we made a special trip to the mountains to see the brilliant colors of the beautiful fall leaves.

weekend _____ special _____ beautiful _____

made _____ brilliant _____

18. After that eventful afternoon, Art wrote several times to Cathy, but his letters all came back unopened.

eventful _____ but _____ unopened ____

wrote _____ his _____

19. Through the morning mist, we could just barely make out the headlights of the bus as it turned off the highway.

barely _____ bus _____

make out _____ as _____

20. Our host offered us a choice of coffee or tea and served some little cakes, which were delicious.

offered _____ or _____ delicious _____

us _____ were _____

Common Grammatical Errors

Subject-Verb Agreement

One common grammatical error is lack of agreement between subject and verb. The simplest subject-verb disagreements are usually highly evident, as in the following examples:

EXAMPLES:

The books *is* on the shelf. X
The books *are* on the shelf. √

The teacher *tell* the class to calm down. X
The teacher *tells* the class to calm down. √

In order to make exam questions a bit subtler, a question writer who wants to test your ability to spot such errors might use one of three tricks:

TRICKS FOR OBSCURING SUBJECT-VERB AGREEMENT

1. Insertion of material between subject and verb,
2. Inversion of sentence structure, and
3. Use of compound subjects.

1. Material Inserted Between Subject and Verb

The first technique used to obscure the connection between the subject and the verb is the insertion of material between the two. If you are not careful, by the time you reach the verb, you will have forgotten the subject and will have no way of knowing whether the verb does or does not agree with the subject. Consider the following examples:

EXAMPLES:

Star performers in the movies or on television usually *earns* substantial income from royalties. X

One school of thought maintains that the federal deficit, not exorbitant corporate profits and excessively high wages, *cause* most of the inflation we are now experiencing. X

A recent survey shows that a household in which both the wife and the husband are pursuing careers *stand* a better chance of surviving intact than one in which only the husband works. X

In each of the three sentences there is a failure of agreement between subject and verb: *performers...earns, deficit...cause,* and *household...stand.* The errors may not be immediately evident, however, because of the intervening material. In the first sentence the subject is separated from the verb by prepositional phrases. In the second, the subject and verb are separated by a parenthetical expression. In the third, a clause intervenes between the subject and verb.

The plausibility of the incorrect verb choice, and therefore the chance that the error will go unnoticed, is strengthened by placing a word or phrase near the verb that might be mistaken for the subject: *television...earns, profits and wages...cause,* and *careers...stand.* If the first word of each of these pairs had been the subject, then there would have been no failure of agreement.

2. Inverted Sentence Structure

A second common problem of subject-verb agreement is inverted sentence structures. An inverted sentence has the subject preceded by the verb. You should pay careful attention to the connection between subject and verb, no matter how those elements are presented.

EXAMPLES:

Although the first amendment to the Constitution does guarantee freedom of speech, the Supreme Court has long recognized that there *has* to be some restrictions on the exercise of this right. X

Jennifer must have been doubly pleased that day, for seated in the gallery to watch her receive the award *was* her brother, her parents, and her husband. X

In both of these sentences we have a failure of agreement between subject and verb. The relationships are obscured by the order in which the elements appear in the sentence—verbs come before the subjects. These sentences should read:

Although the first amendment to the Constitution does guarantee freedom of speech, the Supreme Court has long recognized that there *have* to be some restrictions on the exercise of this right. √

Jennifer must have been doubly pleased that day, for seated in the gallery to watch her receive the award *were* her brother, her parents, and her husband. √

WATCH FOR INVERTED SENTENCE STRUCTURES

Regardless of the order of the sentence—subject-verb or verb-subject—the verb must always agree with the subject to which it refers. It often helps to isolate each element to make sure that the needed agreement is there.

3. Compound Subjects

Finally, be alert for compound subjects. Usually when the subject of a sentence consists of two or more elements joined by the conjunction *and,* the subject is considered plural and requires a plural verb. Consider the following:

EXAMPLE:

Of the seven candidates, only John, Bill, and he *was* past office holders. X

The subject, *John, Bill, and he,* is compound (joined by *and*) and requires the plural verb *were*—even though *he* itself is singular.

WATCH FOR COMPOUND SUBJECTS

Compound subjects, typically two or more subject joined by *and* are plural and need a plural verb.

Be careful not to confuse the compound subject with the disjunctive subject. When elements of the subject are joined by *or*, the verb must agree with the element nearest to it. Replacing *and* with *or* changes our previous example:

EXAMPLE:

Of the seven candidates, John, Bill, or he *is* likely to win. √

Now the elements are joined by *or*, so the verb must agree with *he*. Therefore, the verb *is* correctly agrees with the disjunctive subject, *he*.

Additionally, watch out for subjects that are designed to look like they are compound subjects but are actually singular. Typically, these subjects are disguised using pronouns.

EXAMPLE:

Neither one of those fools even *know* how to change a light bulb. X

The subject above is not *those fools*, but instead is the singular subject *neither one*. Thus the singular verb *knows* is required.

WATCH FOR DISJUNCTIVE AND SINGULAR SUBJECTS

1. If the elements of the subject are joined by *or,* the subject is disjunctive. The verb should be singular and agree with the closest element of the subject.
2. Be alert for singular subjects that appear to be plural (typically pronouns).

Pronoun Usage

The rules for pronoun usage are summarized as follows:

PRONOUN USAGE RULES

1. A pronoun must have an *antecedent* (referent) to which it refers.
2. The pronoun must refer *clearly* to the antecedent.
3. The pronoun and antecedent must *agree.*
4. The pronoun must have the appropriate *case.*

1. Pronoun Must Have An Antecedent

A pronoun is used as a substitute for a noun. The noun it replaces is called its antecedent or what it refers to, its referent. With the exception of certain idioms such as "*It* is raining," a pronoun that does not have an antecedent is used incorrectly.

EXAMPLES:

Although Glen is president of the student body, he has not yet passed his English exam, and because of *it,* he will not graduate with the rest of his class. X

The damage done by Senator Smith's opposition to the policy of equal employment is undeniable, but *that* is exactly what he attempted to do in his speech on Thursday. X

In the first example, what is the antecedent of *it*? It is not *he has not yet passed his English exam,* because that is a complete thought, or clause, not just a noun. *It* is not a pronoun substitute for that entire thought. You would do better by responding that *it* refers to Glen's *failure* to pass the exam—thereby providing *it* with the required antecedent. But *failure* does not appear in noun form in the sentence. In other words, *it* wants to refer to a noun, but there is no noun to function as its point of reference. The sentence must be rewritten: *because of that fact, he will not graduate....*

In the second example, *that* functions as a relative pronoun—it relates something in the first clause to the second clause. But to what does *that* refer? Test possibilities by substituting them for *that* in the second clause. After all, if the sentence makes sense using the pronoun *that,* it should also make sense when you substitute the pronoun's antecedent for the pronoun. Is the antecedent *damage*? This attempt fails:

but *the damage* is exactly what he attempted to do....

Perhaps, then, the antecedent is *opposition* or *undeniable*:

but the *opposition* is exactly what he attempted to do....
but the *undeniable* is exactly what he attempted to do....

There are no other candidates for antecedent, so we must conclude that the use of *that* is incorrect. Most likely, what the writer intended to say was that the Senator attempted to deny the damage:

The damage done by Senator Smith's opposition to the policy of equal employment is undeniable, but he attempted to deny that damage in his speech on Thursday. √

PRONOUNS MUST HAVE ANTECEDENTS

Except for a few idiomatic expressions—*It is getting late*—all pronouns must have an antecedent. An antecedent must be a noun, not a thought or phrase. First identify a pronoun's antecedent and then make sure you are correct by substituting the antecedent for the pronoun.

2. *Antecedents Must Be Clear*

Secondly, the antecedent of a pronoun must be clear from the structure of the sentence. Consider these examples:

EXAMPLES:

Edward's father died before *he* reached his 20th birthday, so *he* never finished his education. X

In 1980, the University Council voted to rescind Provision 3, *which* made it easier for some students to graduate. X

In the first example, it is not clear whether the father died before he reached the age of 20 or before Edward reached the age of 20. Furthermore, it is not entirely clear whose education remained unfinished.

Similarly, in the second example, the antecedent of *which* is not made clear. *Which* may refer to Provision 3 or it may refer to the University Council's vote to rescind Provision 3.

WATCH FOR UNCLEAR ANTECEDENTS

The antecedent of a pronoun must be clearly identified by the structure of the sentence.

EXAMPLES:

The letter is on the desk *that* we received yesterday. X
The *letter that* was received yesterday is on the desk. √

When you have finished the book and written your summary, please return *it* to the library. X
When you have finished the book and written your summary, please return *the book* to the library. √

Finally, the impersonal use of *it*, *they*, and *you*—tends to produce vague, wordy sentences.

EXAMPLES:

In the manual *it* says to make three copies. X
The manual says to make three copies. √

They say we are in for a cold, wet winter. X
The almanac predicts a cold, wet winter. √

3. *Pronoun-Antecedent Agreement*

The third rule for pronoun usage is that the pronoun must agree with its antecedent. Consider the following example:

EXAMPLE:

Historically, the dean of a college was also a professor, but today *they* are usually administrators. X

In the example, *they* must refer to *dean*, but *dean* is singular and *they* is plural—an error. The sentence can be corrected in either of two ways: by changing the first clause to the plural or by changing the second clause to the singular:

Historically, college deans were also professors, but today the dean is usually an administrator. √

WATCH FOR PRONOUN-ANTECEDENT AGREEMENT

If the antecedent is singular, the pronoun must be singular; if the antecedent is plural, the pronoun must be plural.

Finally, it is incorrect to use different forms of the same pronoun to refer to an antecedent. This error results in the sentence having different antecedents and therefore a "shifting subject."

WATCH FOR SHIFTING SUBJECT

Watch for shifting subject errors. These errors occur when different forms of the same pronoun are used to refer to the antecedent.

EXAMPLE:

The teacher told John that *he* thought *his* work was improving. X

Does the teacher think that his own work is improving, or that John's work is improving? The correct sentence reads:

John was told by *his* teacher that *his* work was improving. √

4. Pronouns Must Have Proper Case

A pronoun must agree with its antecedent in case, number, and person. The pronoun's function in a sentence determines which case should be used. There are three types of pronoun case: nominative (or subjective), objective, and possessive.

TYPES OF PRONOUN CASE

1. *Nominative* (or *subjective*) case pronouns are used as subjects of sentences.
2. *Objective* case pronouns are used as objects: direct objects, indirect objects, and objects of prepositions. If a prepositional phrase ends with a pronoun, it must be an objective pronoun.
3. *Possessive* case pronouns are used to show possession. Use a possessive pronoun preceding a gerund. A gerund is the *-ing* form of a verb that is used as a noun.

The following examples illustrate the correct use of pronoun case:

EXAMPLES:

Nominative: *I* thought *he* would like the gift *we* bought. √

Objective: The choice for the promotion is between Bob and *me*. √
(The object pronoun *me* follows the preposition *between.)*

Possessive: Do you mind *my* using your computer? √
(The possessive pronoun *my* precedes the gerund *using*.)

EXAMPLES OF PRONOUN CASE

	NOMINATIVE CASE		OBJECTIVE CASE		POSSESSIVE CASE	
	Singular	*Plural*	*Singular*	*Plural*	*Singular*	*Plural*
1st Person:	I	we	me	us	my	our
2nd Person:	you	–	you	you	–	your
3rd Person:	he, she, it	they	him, her, it	them	his, her, its	their
Interrogative:	who	who	whom	whom	whose	whose

The following are additional examples of the nominative, or subjective, pronoun case.

EXAMPLES:

John and *him* were chosen. X
John and *he* were chosen √ (*He* is the subject of the verb; we certainly would not say that *him* was chosen.)

It was *her* who was chosen. X
It was *she* who was chosen. √

Us student-workers decided to organize into a union. X
We student-workers decided to organize into a union. √

He is as witty as her. X
He is as witty *as she.* √

Whom do you suppose will win the election? X
Who do you suppose will win the election? √

The following are additional examples of the objective pronoun case.

EXAMPLES:

They accused Tom and *he* of stealing. X
They accused Tom and *him* of stealing. √ (*Him* is the object of the verb *accused*; they accused *him*, not *he*.)

The tickets were given to Bill and *I.* X
The tickets were given to Bill and *me.* √ (*Me* is the object of *to*; the tickets were given to *me*, not to *I*.)

Who did you see? X
Whom did you see? √ (*Hint:* Make this a declarative sentence: You saw *him*–you wouldn't say *You saw he.*)

An easy way to remember when to use *who* versus *whom* is that in those situations that hi*m* (or her) would be appropriate, who*m* should be used; in those situations that he (or she) would be appropriate, who should be used.

Finally, personal pronouns that express ownership never require an apostrophe. Also, a pronoun that precedes a gerund (*-ing* verb form) is usually the possessive case. The following possessive pronoun examples illustrate these last two points.

EXAMPLES:

This book is *your's*, not *her's*. X
This book is *yours*, not *hers*. √

He rejoiced at *him* going to the party. X
He rejoiced at *his* going to the party. √

Some pronouns are singular or plural, while others can be both. The structure and intended meaning of the sentence indicate whether the pronoun is singular or plural.

SINGULAR AND/OR PLURAL PRONOUNS

Singular:	anybody, another, everybody, everything, somebody, something, nobody, one, anyone, everyone, someone, no one, each, every, neither, either, much,
Plural:	both, few, many, most, several
Singular & Plural:	all, any, half, more, none, some

Technically, pronouns are divided into the following eight formal categories:

FORMAL CATEGORIES OF PRONOUNS

Personal:	I, we, my, mine, our, ours, me, us, you, your, yours, he, she, it, they, his, hers, its, their, theirs, him, her, it, them
Demonstrative:	this, these, that, those
Indefinite:	all, any, anything, both, each, either, one, everyone, everybody, everything, few, many, more, neither, none, somebody, someone, something
Relative:	who, whose, whom, which, of which, that, of that, what, of what
Interrogative:	who, whose, whom, which, of which, what, of what
Numerical:	one, two, three, first, second, third
Reflexive/Intensive:	myself, ourselves, yourself, yourselves, himself, herself, itself, themselves
Reciprocal:	each other, one another

It is not necessary for test purposes that you know the names of the individual categories and which pronouns belong in which categories. However, through your experience in conversation and writing, you should be able to correctly use each type of pronoun and you should have the ability to spot when each type of pronoun is incorrectly used.

EXAMPLE:

Many of the students *which* were participating in the spelling bee had been finalists last year. X

In the above example, the pronoun *which* refers to *Many of the students* and is the incorrect pronoun choice. Instead, the sentence should read: *Many...who were participating....*

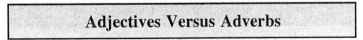

Adjectives Versus Adverbs

Adjectives are used to modify nouns, while adverbs are used to modify verbs or adjectives.

EXAMPLE:

No matter how *quick* he played, Rich never beat Julie when playing "speed." X

In the above example *quick* is intended to modify the speed with which Rich played cards. However, *quick* is an adjective and therefore cannot be used to modify a verb. By adding *-ly* to the end of *quick* we can transform it into an adverb and the sentence reads: *No matter how quickly he played....*

1. *Linking Verbs*

Linking verbs are followed by adjectives, not adverbs. Here is a list of common linking verbs:

COMMON LINKING VERBS				
be	become	appear	look	seem
remain	feel	smell	sound	taste

Note that some of the verbs listed as linking verbs may sometimes function as verbs of action. The following examples illustrate this.

EXAMPLES:

Adjectives: I feel *tired.*
He looked *angry.*
The pie tastes *delicious.*

Adverbs: I felt my way *slowly* in the darkness
He looked about the room *angrily.*
She tasted the pie *cautiously.*

2. *Adjectives Modify Nouns, Adverbs Modify Verbs*

Adverbs are used to modify verbs and adjectives are used to modify nouns. The following examples illustrate the proper use of adjectives and adverbs.

EXAMPLES:

Adverbs: Mr. Jackson teaches *well.*
He drives *badly.*
The weather has changed *considerably.*
My sister dances *superbly.*
The teacher explained the problem *quickly.*
This exercise must be done *slowly.*

Adjectives: Mr. Jackson is a *good* teacher.
Her brother is a *bad* driver.
There has been a *considerable* change in the weather.
My sister is a *superb* dancer.
The teacher gave a *quick* explanation of the problem.
This is a *slow* exercise.

The following examples underscore that adverbs, not adjectives, must be used to modify verbs and adjectives.

EXAMPLES:

I felt *badly* about forgetting the appointment. X
I felt *bad* about forgetting the appointment. √

We all agreed that the new film was *real* good. X
We all agreed that the new film was *really* good. √

The students found the physics examination *extreme* difficult. X
The students found the physics examination *extremely* difficult. √

If you speak firm, he will listen to you. X
If you speak firmly, he will listen to you. √

He made considerable more progress than I. X
He made considerably more progress than I. √

The professor presented an obvious important point in class. X
The professor presented an obviously important point in class. √

He said that the medicine tasted terribly. X
He said that the medicine tasted terrible. √

It rained steady all day yesterday. X
It rained steadily all day yesterday. X

The dog remained faithfully to its master until the end. X
The dog remained faithful to its master until the end. √

He can do the job easier than you can. X
He can do the job more easily than you can. √

The problem seemed exceeding complex to me. X
The problem seemed exceedingly complex to me. √

3. *Watch for Adjectives Posing as Adverbs*

WATCH FOR ADJECTIVE-ADVERB SWITCHING

Be alert for adjectives posing in place of adverbs and vice versa. Adjectives can usually be transformed into adverbs by adding *-ly* to the end of the adjective. However, verbs must be modified by adverbs, not simply an adjective posing as an adverb!

EXAMPLES:

The girl looks *intelligently.* X
The girl looks *intelligent.* √

That perfume smells *sweetly*, doesn't it? X
That perfume smells *sweet,* doesn't it? √

The physician appeared *nervously* when he talked to the patient. X
The physician appeared *nervous* when he talked to the patient. √

This bed seems very *comfortably.* X
This bed seems very *comfortable.* √

Several people arrived too *lately* to be admitted to the performance. X
Several people arrived too *late* to be admitted to the performance. √

The horse ran *fastly* enough to win the race. X
The horse ran *fast* enough to win the race. √

The architect worked *hardly* to finish his drawings by the next day. X
The architect worked *hard* to finish his drawings by the next day. √

Double Negatives

It is true that we all hear and sometimes say double negatives in daily conversation. However, double negatives are not acceptable in standard written English.

EXAMPLE:

I *hadn't hardly* begun to understand Spanish when I had to move again. X

The phrase *hadn't hardly* is a double negative. The sentence should read: *I had hardly begun to understand....*

WATCH FOR DOUBLE NEGATIVES

Be alert for double negatives (*not barely, hardly nothing*)—they are always incorrect.

Nouns and Noun Clauses

Nouns are names of people, places, things, or ideas; they are used to indicate what the sentence is about. Like pronouns, nouns have case.

TYPES OF NOUN CASE

1. *Objective* case is used when the noun is an indirect or direct object or is the object of a preposition.
2. *Nominative* case is used when the noun is the subject of the sentence.
3. *Possessive* case is used when nouns are intended to show possession.

Sometimes the place of the noun in a sentence is filled by a noun clause instead of a single noun. A noun clause is a dependent clause.

EXAMPLE:

That Judy was chosen for the promotion is not surprising. √

The failure to properly introduce a noun clause is an error of sentence structure. *That* by itself is not the noun, nor is *Judy was chosen for the promotion* a noun. However, the two combined create a noun clause and function as the noun.

RULE FOR INTRODUCING NOUN CLAUSES

A noun clause is a group of words that functions as the subject (or another noun use) of a sentence. *That* is often the best word to use to introduce noun clauses.

EXAMPLES:

The reason the saxophone is a popular jazz instrument is *because* the timbre of the saxophone can approximate that of the human voice. X

Many people believe happiness is *when* you have reached the age of retirement, raised a family and completed a career. X

These examples make the error of introducing a noun clause with *because* and *when.* In both sentences, a noun clause is required, so *that* should be used in both cases.

The reason the saxophone is a popular jazz instrument is *that* the timbre of the saxophone can approximate that of the human voice. √

Many people believe happiness is *that* you have reached the age of retirement, raised a family and completed a career. √

WATCH FOR *BECAUSE* AND *WHEN* AS NOUN CLAUSE INTRODUCTIONS

Noun clauses must be introduced by *that*, not *because* and *when*.

Do not use *where* for *that* in object clauses:

EXAMPLE:

I saw in the bulletin *where* Mrs. Wagner's retirement was announced. X
I saw in the bulletin *that* Mrs. Wagner's retirement was announced. √

However, if the subject of the sentence is actually about where something is, then *where* is the right word to use:

EXAMPLES:

Where he went is not known now. √
Where the wedding had initially been planned for is not where it ended up being held. √
All I want to know is *where* we are supposed to go for homeroom attendance. √

EXERCISE 2

Common Grammatical Errors

DIRECTIONS: The following exercise contains 25 sentences. Each sentence makes a grammatical error of the sort just reviewed. Circle the letter of the underlined part of the sentence containing the error. Answers are on page C-64.

1. The professor deals harsh (A) with students who are not prepared (B), and he is (C) even more severe (D) with those who plagiarize.

2. A recent study indicates (A) that the average person ignores (B) most commercial advertising and does not buy (C) products because of them (D).

3. Despite the fact (A) that New York City is one of the most (B) densely populated areas in the world, there are (C) many parks where one can sit on a bench under the trees and you can (D) read a book.

4. Charles Dickens wrote (A) about the horrifying (B) conditions in the English boarding schools which (C) he learned about on one of his (D) trips to Yorkshire.

5. André Breton initiated (A) the Surrealist movement with the publication (B) of a manifesto, and it (C) incorporated the theories of Freud as well as (D) his own.

6. The review of the concert published (A) in the morning's paper mentioned that the soloist is (B) a very promising talent and that (C) the orchestra played capable (D).

7. During the war (A), there were many people in the Polish countryside that (B) sheltered those (C) who had escaped (D) from concentration camps.

8. The dean lectured (A) to we students (B) on the privilege and (C) responsibility of attending (D) the university.

9. You taking the initiative (A) in the negotiations (B) will (C) profit the company to a great degree (D).

10. The members of the club insisted that (A) I be (B) the representative of the organization at the conference which (C) was something I had hoped (D) to avoid.

11. No one (A) knows for sure whether there was (B) a real person about which (C) Shakespeare wrote (D) his sonnets.

12. Although (A) the director of the zoo takes (B) great pains to recreate (C) the natural habitats of the animals, few of the exhibits is completely (D) accurate in every detail.

13. Climatic differences between the north and south of some (A) countries helps to (B) account for the differences (C) in temperament of the inhabitants of the two (D) regions.

14. The month of August was particularly cold (A); hardly no daily temperatures (B) were recorded (C) above 80 degrees, and only one was (D) recorded above 90 degrees.

15. The diaries of Stendhal, which make entertaining reading, (A) also provides (B) a great wealth of information about musical taste (C) and performance practice in the last century (D).

16. Given the evidence (A) of the existence of a complicated system of communication used by whales, (B) it is necessary to (C) acknowledge its (D) intelligence.

17. Him being at the rally (A) does not necessarily mean (B) that (C) the congressman agrees (D) with the president's entire platform.

18. Although there is no perfect form of government, representative democracy, as it is practiced in America, (A) is a system (B) that is working well (C) and more than satisfactory (D).

19. Alfred Stieglitz launched (A) the career of Georgia O'Keeffe, who (B) he (C) later married (D), by exhibiting her paintings in his gallery.

20. After driving past Trinity Church (A), the bus stopped at the recent constructed (B) World Trade Tower, the tallest (C) building in the world, to allow the passengers to take (D) the special elevators to the observation tower.

21. The student senate passed (A) the resolution banning smoking in the cafeteria (B) with scarcely any (C) dissenting votes which angered (D) many members of the faculty.

22. Most employers assume (A) that one's professional personality and work habits are formed (B) as a result of (C) your (D) early work experience.

23. Only a small number (A) of taxi drivers fail to insure (B) their vehicles, but usually these are the ones (C) who need it (D) most.

24. Angered (A) by the double standard society imposed on (B) women, Edna St. Vincent Millay wrote candid about (C) her (D) opinions and her personal life.

25. Unless they (A) hire players who (B) are (C) better hitters, the fans will gradually lose (D) interest in the team despite the fine efforts of the pitching staff.

Analyzing Sentence Structure

When analyzing the structure of a sentence, ask yourself five things:

CHECKLIST FOR ANALYZING SENTENCE STRUCTURE

1. Is the sentence a run-on sentence?
2. Are the elements of the sentence parallel?
3. Are there any incomplete split constructions?
4. Do the verb tenses correctly reflect the sequence of events?

Run-On Sentences

Be aware of sentences that carelessly run main clauses together without appropriate punctuation or connectors. Run-on sentences can be corrected in one of three ways.

The most common way to correct a run-on sentence is to divide the sentence using end-stop punctuation.

EXAMPLES:

The lecture was dull you almost fell asleep. X
The lecture was dull. You almost fell asleep. √

Was the lecture dull you almost fell asleep. X
Was the lecture dull? You almost fell asleep. √

The lecture was incredibly dull you almost fell asleep. X
The lecture was incredibly dull! You almost fell asleep. √

The comma is not an end-mark. It cannot be used by itself to separate two sentences.

EXAMPLE:

Close the window, there is a draft in the room. X
Close the window. There is a draft in the room. √

Sometimes two sentences are very closely related in meaning and full end-stop punctuation may seem too strong. A semicolon can then be used to divide the two sentences.

EXAMPLE:

It was a beautiful day there was not a cloud in the sky. X
It was a beautiful day; there was not a cloud in the sky. √

A third way to correct the run-on is to use a connector (conjunction) such as *and, but, for, or,* and *nor* if the two sentences are equal in importance. It is usually advisable to place a comma before these connectors.

EXAMPLE:

I like to ski, my friend prefers to sit by the fire. X
I like to ski, but my friend prefers to sit by the fire. √

Particular problem words that may cause run-ons are *however, therefore, consequently,* and *moreover.* These words are not sentence connectors, and when they follow a complete thought, they should be preceded by either a period or a semicolon.

Faulty Parallelism

Faulty parallelism is a grammatical error quite common for writers. Whenever elements of a sentence perform similar or equal functions, they should have the same form. Consider the following faulty sentences—they are missing necessary words:

EXAMPLES:

At most colleges, the dominant attitude among students is that gaining admission to professional graduate school is more important than *to obtain* a well-rounded education. X

To demand that additional seasonings be placed on the table *is insulting* the chef's judgment on the proper balance of ingredients. X

The review was very critical of the film, citing the poor photography, the weak plot, and the dialogue *was stilted.* X

In the first example, *gaining admission* and *to obtain* must both have the same form. Either both must be in the infinitive form or both must be in the gerund form. For example: *gaining admission...is more important than obtaining....*

In the second example, the subject (*to demand*) and the predicated complement (*insulting*) must both have the same form: *To demand...is to insult....*

In the third example, each element in the series of bad features should have the same form: *the poor photography, the weak plot, and the stilted dialogue.*

ALL ELEMENTS OF A SENTENCE MUST BE PARALLEL

Check that all elements of a sentence are parallel; including verb forms, noun forms, and word pairs such as *this... that, either...or,* and *neither...nor.*

EXAMPLES:

He spends his time playing cards, swimming, going to the theater, and at school. X
He spends his time *playing* cards, *swimming*, *going* to the theater and *going* to school. √

He manages his business affairs with knowledge, with ease, and confidently. X
He manages his business affairs *with knowledge*, *with ease*, and *with confidence.* √

He was required by the instructor to go to the library, to take out several books on the Vietnam War, and that he should report to the class on what he had learned. X
He was required by the instructor *to go* to the library, *to take* out several books on the Vietnam War, and *to report* to the class on what he had learned. √

I am studying the sources of educational theory and how educational theory has evolved. X
I am studying *the sources* and *the evolution of educational theory.* √

He was not only sympathetic but also knew when to be considerate. X
He was *not only sympathetic but also considerate.* √

Not only did he enjoy the movie but also the play. X
He enjoyed *not only the movie but also the play.* √

I was concerned about the price of the car and if it was comfortable. X
I was concerned about *the price* and *the comfort of the car.* √

Neither does he speak Spanish nor Helen. X
Neither he nor Helen speaks Spanish. √

Incomplete Split Constructions

Split constructions refer to phrases in which a thought, interrupted by intervening material, is completed later in the sentence.

EXAMPLE:

The officials were not only aware of, but actually encouraged, the misreporting of scores. √

This sentence contains a perfectly acceptable split construction. Ordinarily, the object of a preposition closely follows the preposition: *...aware of the misreporting.* Here, the object of the preposition is separated from the preposition by the phrase *but actually encouraged.* This is unobjectionable as long as the thought is properly completed. There is a danger, however, that the intervening material will throw something off.

SPLIT CONSTRUCTIONS MUST BE COMPLETED

A split construction is a sentence structure in which two otherwise separate ideas are joined together by a later element. Be alert for split constructions and check that any interrupted thought is correctly completed.

Consider the following *faulty* sentences—they are incomplete split constructions.

EXAMPLES:

Opponents of the President's foreign policy disclosed yesterday that the CIA not only knew but tacitly encouraged terrorist activities in Central America. X

Her colleagues always speak of Professor Collins as a person who has and will always be sensitive to the needs of younger students. X

Judging from the pricing policies of many large corporations, maintaining a stable share of the market is as important, if not more important than, making a large profit. X

In each of these examples there is an error of split construction. There is a missing preposition in the first sentence. The CIA did not know the terrorist activities, rather it knew *of* the activities.

In the second sentence, the error is in the verb. The auxiliary verb *has* needs the verb *been*, but *been* does not appear in the sentence. The sentence could be corrected by completing the construction: *...has been and will always be....*

In the third sentence, the error is an incomplete comparison. The sentence should read: *...as important as, if not more important than....*

CHECKING FOR SPLIT CONSTRUCTIONS

It is the intervening material that makes errors of split construction difficult to spot. Therefore, when checking split constructions, read the sentence without the intervening material—it should make sense, be grammatically correct, and be a complete sentence.

Verb Tense

The same verb tense should be used whenever possible within a sentence or paragraph. Avoid shifts in verb tense unless there is a valid reason.

EXAMPLE:

Joan *came* home last week and *goes* to her home in the country where she *spends* the last weekend of her vacation. X
Joan *came* home last week and *went* to her home in the country where she *spent* the last weekend of her vacation. √

1. *Principal Parts of Verbs*

We indicate tense by changing the verb itself or by combining certain forms of the verb with auxiliary verbs. The verb tenses from which we derive every form of a verb are called the principal parts. The principal parts of a verb are:

VERB PRINCIPAL PARTS

1. The Present Tense: talk, write
2. The Past Tense: talked, wrote
3. The Present Perfect: have talked, has written
4. The Future Perfect: will have talked, will have written

Verbs are classified as regular (or *weak)* and irregular (or strong), according to the way in which their principle parts are formed. Regular verbs form their past tense and present perfect tense by the addition of *-ed* to the infinitive,

EXAMPLES:

Present Tense	*Past Tense*	*Present Perfect Tense*	*Future Perfect Tense*
talk	talked	has (have) talked	will have talked
help	helped	has (have) helped	will have helped
walk	walked	has (have) walked	will have walked

The principal parts of irregular verbs are formed by changes in the verb itself:

EXAMPLES:

Present Tense	*Past Tense*	*Present Perfect Tense*	*Future Perfect Tense*
see	saw	has (have) seen	will have seen
say	said	has (have) said	will have said
go	went	has(have)gone	will have gone

PRINCIPAL PARTS OF COMMON IRREGULAR VERBS

Present	*Past*	*Past Participle*
arise	arose	arisen
be	was, were	been
bear	bore	borne
become	became	become
begin	began	begun
bid	bade	bid, bidden
blow	blew	blown
break	broke	broken
bring	brought	brought
build	built	built
buy	bought	bought
catch	caught	caught
choose	chose	chosen
cling	clung	clung
come	came	come
cut	cut	cut
do	did	done
draw	drew	drawn
drink	drank	drunk
drive	drove	driven
eat	ate	eaten
fall	fell	fallen
feed	fed	fed
feel	felt	felt
fight	fought	fought

PRINCIPAL PARTS OF COMMON IRREGULAR VERBS, CONTINUED

Present	*Past*	*Past Participle*
find	found	found
flee	fled	fled
fling	flung	flung
fly	flew	flown
forget	forgot	forgotten
forgive	forgave	forgiven
freeze	froze	frozen
get	got	gotten
give	gave	given
go	went	gone
grow	grew	grown
hang (a person)	hanged	hanged
hang (an object)	hung	hung
hear	heard	heard
hide	hid	hidden
hold	held	held
hurt	hurt	hurt
keep	kept	kept
know	knew	known
lay	laid	laid
lead	led	led
leave	left	left
lend	lent	lent
lie	lay	lain
light	lit, lighted	lit, lighted
lose	lost	lost
make	made	made
meet	met	met
read	read	read
ride	rode	ridden
ring	rang	rung
rise	rose	risen
run	ran	run
see	saw	seen
send	sent	sent
sew	sewed	sewn
shake	shook	shaken
shoot	shot	shot
shrink	shrank, shrunk	shrunk, shrunken
sit	sat	sat
slay	slew	slain
sleep	slept	slept
slide	slid	slid
speak	spoke	spoken
spend	spent	spent
spin	spun	spun
spring	sprang, sprung	sprung
stand	stood	stood
steal	stole	stolen
sting	stung	stung
strive	strove	striven
swear	swore	sworn
take	took	taken
teach	taught	taught
tear	tore	torn
tell	told	told
think	thought	thought
throw	threw	thrown
wake	waked, woke	waked, woken
wear	wore	worn
weave	wove	woven
win	won	won
wring	wrung	wrung
write	wrote	written
swim	swam	swum
swing	swung	swung

2. *When to Use the Perfect Tenses*

Use the *present perfect* for an action begun in the past and extended to the present.

EXAMPLE:
I am glad you are here at last; *I have waited* an hour for you to arrive. √

In this case, *I waited* would be incorrect. The action *have waited* (present perfect) began in the past and extended to the present.

Use the *past perfect* for an action begun and completed in the past before some other past action.

EXAMPLE:
The foreman asked what *had happened* to my eye. √

In this case, *what happened* would be incorrect. The action *asked* and the action *had happened* (past perfect) are used because one action (regarding the speaker's eye) is "more past" than the other (the foreman's asking).

Use the *future perfect* for an action begun at any time and completed in the future.

EXAMPLE:
When I reach Chicago tonight, my uncle *will have left* for Los Angeles. √

In this case the action *will have left* is going to take place before the action *reaches,* although both actions will occur in the future.

When there are two future actions, the action completed first is expressed in the future perfect tense.

EXAMPLES:
When he spoke, all the people *cheer* him. X
When he spoke, all the people *cheered* him. √

Since he *is* late, he didn't receive a gift. X
Since he *was* late, he didn't receive a gift. √

I am told that you *had completed* the job. X
I am told that you *have completed* the job. √

I was told that you *have completed* the job. X
I was told that you *had completed* the job. √

We were taught that vitamins *were* important for our well-being. X
We were taught that vitamins *are* important for our well-being. X

In the last example, the verb tense *are* is used because when you are expressing a permanent fact, the *present tense* is used.)

3. *The Subjunctive Mood*

The subjunctive expresses a condition contrary to fact, a wish, a supposition, or an indirect command.

WHEN TO USE THE SUBJUNCTIVE MOOD

The subjunctive mood verb forms should be used in the following situations:

1. To express a wish not likely to be fulfilled or impossible to be realized,
2. In a subordinate clause after a verb that expresses a command, a request, or a suggestion,
3. To express a condition known or supposed to be contrary to fact, and
4. After *as if* or *as though.*

EXAMPLES:

I wish it *were* possible for us to approve his transfer at this time.

He asked *that* the report *be* submitted in duplicate.
It is recommended *that* this office *be* responsible for preparing the statements.
We suggest *that* he *be* relieved of the assignment.

If *I were* in St. Louis, I should be glad to attend.
If this *were* a simple case, we would easily agree on a solution.
If I *were* you, I should not mind the assignment.

In formal writing and speech, *as if* and *as though* are followed by the subjunctive, since they introduce as supposition something not factual. In informal writing and speaking, the indicative is sometimes used.

EXAMPLES:

He talked *as if he were* an expert on taxation. (He's not.)

This report looks *as though* it *were* the work of a college freshman.

Avoid shifts in mood. Once you have decided on the mood that properly expresses your message, use that mood throughout the sentence or the paragraph. A shift in mood is confusing to the listener or reader; it indicates that the speaker or writer himself has changed his way of looking at the conditions.

EXAMPLE:

It is requested that a report of the proceedings *be* prepared and copies *should be* distributed to all members. (*Be* is subjunctive; *should be,* indicative.) X
It is requested that a report of the proceedings *be* prepared and that copies *be* distributed to all members. √

EXERCISE 3

Analyzing Sentence Structure

DIRECTIONS: In sentences #1-35, circle the correct verb choice. Answers are on page C-65.

1. Each year, many people who did not graduate from high school (receive, receives) a GED diploma.
2. The books on the top shelf (was, were) all written by Emily Bronte.
3. The stores in the downtown sector's newly renovated mall (offer, offers) brand name fashions at reduced prices
4. Only a few dust covered bottles of the vintage wine (remain, remains) in the cellar.
5. Each tourist who visits the caverns (is, are) given a guidebook.
6. Underneath the leaf covering (was, were) several different species of insects.
7. The young boys, who had never before been in trouble with the law, (was, were) worried about what their parents would say.
8. Several barrels containing a highly toxic liquid (has, have) been discovered at the abandoned factory.
9. The sponsors of the arts and crafts fair (hope, hopes) that it will attract several thousand visitors.
10. Dawn, Harriet, and Gloria, who have formed their own singing group, (is, are) auditioning for jobs.
11. According to insiders, the mayor, whose administration has been rocked by several crises, (worry, worries) that more layoffs are inevitable.
12. There (has, have) been several acts of vandalism in the cemetery in recent months.
13. Rock musicians who perform in front of large amplifiers often (loses, lose) part of their hearing.
14. The leaves from the branches of the tree that hang over the fence (falls, fall) into the neighbor's yard.
15. The computer and the printer, which are sitting on James' desk, (has, have) never been used.
16. Theresa, wearing her hip length waders, (was, were) fishing in the middle of the stream.
17. The film critic for the New York Times (write, writes) that the film is very funny and entertaining.
18. Several of the ingredients that are used in the dish (has, have) to be prepared in advance.
19. The computer that controls the temperature of the living quarters of the ship (was, were) malfunctioning.
20. There (has, have) been some support for a proposal to build a new courthouse in the center of town.
21. Bill and Jean (is, are) going to the game tomorrow.
22. Either Jay or his friends (have, has) the answer key.
23. There (was, were) several students absent last week.
24. I hope that no one has left (his, their) homework at home.
25. Each of the sisters celebrated (her, their) birthday at the Plaza.
26. The music of Verdi's operas (is, are) filled with dramatic sweep.
27. All the musicians tuned (his, their) instruments.
28. Neither Mark nor the twins (know, knows) the correct answer.
29. Either Mrs. Martinez or Carlos (go, goes) to church each week.
30. However, neither the seller nor the buyers (is, are) satisfied with the arrangement.
31. When he spoke, all the people (cheer, have cheered, cheered) him.
32. Since he (is, was, be) late, he didn't receive a gift.
33. I am told that you (had completed, have completed) the job.
34. I was told that you (had completed, have completed) the job.
35. We were taught that vitamins (are, were) important for our well-being.

DIRECTIONS: For questions #36-60, choose the correct form of the verb in the space provided. Answers are on page C-65.

36. A gentleman has _______ to see you.

(A) to come
(B) came
(C) come
(D) coming
(E) will come

37. Bill was _______ to telephone you last night.

(A) to suppose
(B) supposed
(C) suppose
(D) supposing
(E) will suppose

38. My friend has _______ to get impatient.

(A) to begin
(B) began
(C) begin
(D) beginning
(E) begun

39. He has _______ a serious cold.

(A) to catch
(B) caught
(C) catch
(D) catching
(E) will catch

40. He could _______ before large groups if he were asked to.

(A) sing
(B) sang
(C) sung
(D) singed
(E) singing

41. She has _______ before large groups several times.

(A) sing
(B) sang
(C) sung
(D) singed
(E) singing

42. They have already _______ to the theater.

(A) go
(B) goes
(C) going
(D) gone
(E) will go

43. He has _______ me excellent advice.

(A) give
(B) gave
(C) to give
(D) giving
(E) given

44. He is _______ to his parents.

(A) to devote
(B) devote
(C) devoted
(D) devoting
(E) will devote

45. The engineer has designed and _______ his own home.

(A) to build
(B) builds
(C) building
(D) built
(E) had built

46. He _______ as he ran onto the stage following the clown and the magician.

(A) to laugh
(B) laughing
(C) laughed
(D) laughs
(E) had laughed

47. She _______ the high-jump so well at trials that she is going to the Olympics this summer.

(A) had jumped
(B) to jump
(C) jumping
(D) jumps
(E) jumped

48. It _______ that she continued to blame me even after she knew it wasn't my fault.

(A) hurt
(B) hurts
(C) has hurt
(D) hurting
(E) will hurt

49. The man _______ the murder occur if he had really been on that street corner when he said he was.

(A) see
(B) sees
(C) would have saw
(D) seen
(E) would have seen

50. The child _______ everywhere now that she is able to stand up by herself.

(A) to walk
(B) walks
(C) walked
(D) walking
(E) had walked

51. Tomorrow morning, Sam _______ his sister.

(A) was calling
(B) called
(C) calling
(D) has called
(E) will call

52. After she had completed her investigation, the state trooper _______ her report.

(A) was writing
(B) wrote
(C) has written
(D) writes
(E) will write

53. When I was growing up, we _______ every summer at my grandmother's home in the country.

(A) spend
(B) will spend
(C) have spent
(D) were spending
(E) spent

54. Whenever we get a craving for a late night snack, we _______ a pizza.

(A) order
(B) ordered
(C) had ordered
(D) have ordered
(E) were ordering

55. For years now, John _______ his milk at the corner grocery.

(A) buys
(B) will buy
(C) has bought
(D) is buying
(E) bought

56. We were just leaving, when the telephone _______.

(A) rang
(B) will ring
(C) was ringing
(D) has rung
(E) had rung

57. We got to the house by noon, but the wedding _______ over.

(A) is
(B) will be
(C) had been
(D) has been
(E) was

58. We _______ to drive to the game, but our car broke down.

(A) plan
(B) will plan
(C) had planned
(D) are planning
(E) have planned

59. The roofers were putting the last shingles on the top of the house while the plumber _____ the water lines.

(A) is testing
(B) was testing
(C) tests
(D) will test
(E) had tested

60. A large flock of Canada Geese _____ over the meadow and landed in the pond.

(A) will fly
(B) were flying
(C) fly
(D) flew
(E) are flying

DIRECTIONS: For questions #61-83, circle the letter of the underlined part of the sentence containing the error. Answers are on page C-65.

61. The owner of the collection requested that (A) the museum require (B) all people with a camera (C) to leave (D) them at the door.

62. The young comic found (A) that capturing the audience's attention was easy, but to maintain (B) their (C) interest was (D) difficult.

63. The whale had been laying (A) on the beach for over two hours before the rescue teams were able to begin (B) moving (C) it back into (D) the water.

64. The praying mantis is welcomed by (A) homeowners for its (B) ability to control (C) destructive garden pests, unlike the cockroach which serves no useful function (D).

65. The newly (A) purchased (B) picture was hanged (C) on the back wall nearest (D) the bay window.

66. The opening scene (A) of the film was a grainy, black-and-white (B) shot of an empty town square in which (C) an outlaw was hung (D).

67. We spent (A) an exhausting day shopping (B) we could (C) hardly wait to get (D) home.

68. The fact that she is bright, articulate, and has charisma (A) will serve (B) her well in her campaign for governor, particularly (C) since her opponent has none (D) of those qualities.

69. Puritans such as William Bradford displaying (A) the courage and piety needed to survive (B) in the New World, a world both (C) promising and threatening which (D) offered unique challenges to their faith.

70. The woman to whom (A) I take my clothes for tailoring (B) has sown (C) the hem on this skirt perfectly (D).

71. Unfortunately, before (A) cures are found for diseases such as cancer, many lives would have been (B) lost and millions of dollars in medical services spent to (C) treat symptoms rather than (D) provide a cure.

72. The house on (A) the corner was completely (B) empty, no (C) one came (D) to the door.

73. For many people it is difficult to accept (A) compliments graciously and is even more difficult (B) taking (C) criticism graciously (D).

74. Due (A) to the extremely warm (B) weather this winter, the water has not froze (C) on the pond sufficiently (D).

75. The French poet Artaud believed (A) that, (B) following (C) the climax of a drama, the audience experienced (D) a violent catharsis and is thereby "reborn."

76. Where (A) had everyone (B) gone all (C) the lights were off (D).

77. Rather (A) than declaring (B) bankruptcy, he applied (C) for a loan and the bank loaned (D) him the money.

78. Wagering (A) on the Kentucky Derby favorite is (B) a bad betting (C) proposition, for in the last fifteen years, the horse that was the crowd favorite at post time of the Kentucky Derby loses (D) the race.

79. We entered the cave very (A) slowly almost (B) afraid of what we might find (C) there (D).

80. After he had learned (A) of (B) her suicide, he drunk (C) all of the poison from the vial (D).

81. During the years (A) she spent searching for a cure (B) for the disease, Dr. Thompson interviewed hundreds of patients, ran thousands of tests, and cross-checking (C) millions of bits of data (D).

82. After struggling with the problem (A) for most of the afternoon, he finally flinged (B) the papers on (C) the desk and ran out of the room (D).

83. Suddenly (A) I felt that something was going to (B) happen (C) my heart began to beat furiously (D).

Problems of Logical Expression

Ask yourself the following five questions when checking the logical expression of a sentence:

CHECKLIST FOR LOGICAL EXPRESSION ERRORS

1. Does the sentence contain a faulty or illogical comparison?
2. Does the sentence maintain consistent verb tenses?
3. Does the sentence contain any misplaced modifiers?
4. Does the sentence actually convey the intended meaning?
5. Is the sentence clear and concise?

Faulty or Illogical Comparisons

One problem of logical expression is faulty or illogical comparisons. A faulty comparison is the attempt to compare two things that cannot logically be compared. Consider the following *faulty* examples:

EXAMPLES:

Today, life expectancies of both men and women are much higher compared to the turn of the century when living conditions were much harsher. X

The average salary of a professional basketball player is higher than the top-level management of most corporations. X

A comparison can only be made between like items. Yet, in the first sentence we see an attempt to compare *life expectancies* with *the turn of the century*—two dissimilar concepts. The sentence is corrected by simply adding the phrase *those of*. Now we have life expectancies compared to life expectancies, and that is a logical comparison.

The same error occurs in the second sentence. There, an attempt is made to compare *average salary* to *management*. The error can be corrected in the same way as in the first example: *...is higher than those of the top-level management....*

WATCH FOR ILLOGICAL COMPARISONS

Be alert for sentences that attempt to make an illogical comparison between two dissimilar items.

When two things are being compared, the comparative form of the adjective is used. The comparative is formed in one of two ways.

COMPARISONS BETWEEN TWO OBJECTS

Comparisons are made by using *one* of the following methods:

1. Either add *–er* to the adjective, or
2. place *more* before the adjective.

EXAMPLES:

She is *more pretty* than her sister. X
She is *prettier* than her sister. √

Jeremy is *more wiser* than we know. X
Jeremy is *wiser* (or *more wise)* than we know. √

When three or more things are being compared, the superlative form of the adjective is used. The superlative is formed in one of two ways.

COMPARISONS AMONG THREE OR MORE OBJECTS

Comparisons are made by using *one* of the following methods:

1. Either add *–est* to the adjective, or
2. place *most* before the adjective.

EXAMPLES:

Of all the books, this one is the *most* difficult.
Which is the *shortest* of all of Shakespeare's plays?

Mary is the *shorter* of all of her friends. X
Mary is the *shortest* of all of her friends. √

This is the *most sharpest* knife I have. X
This is the *sharpest* knife I have. √

Some modifiers are compared by changes in the words themselves. A few of these irregular comparisons are given below; consult your dictionary whenever you are in doubt about the comparisons of any adjective or adverb.

MODIFIERS REQUIRING A CHANGE

Positive	*Comparative*	*Superlative*
good	better	best
well	better	best
bad (evil, ill)	worse	worst
badly	worse	worst
far	farther, further	farthest, furthest
late	later, latter	latest, last
little	less, lesser	least
many, much	more	most

Some adjectives and adverbs express qualities that go beyond comparison. They represent the highest degree of a quality and, as a result, cannot be improved. Some of these words are listed below.

MODIFIERS THAT DO NOT CHANGE

complete	preferable	horizontally	supreme	totally
correct	round	secondly	immortally	unique
dead	deadly	square	infinitely	uniquely
perfectly	exact	squarely	perfect	universally
perpendicularly				

The use of the comparative in such an expression as *"This thing is better than any other,"* implies that *this thing* is separate from the group or class to which it is being compared. In these expressions a word such as *other or else* is required to separate the thing being compared from the rest of the group of which it is a part.

EXAMPLE:

Our house is cooler than any house on the block. X

The mistake here is not separating the item being compared—house—from the group to which it is being compared. While *our house* is one of the houses on the block, it should not be included in the comparison. The sentence should read:

Our house is cooler than any *other* house on the block. √

EXAMPLE:

He has a better record than any salesman in our group. X

Since *he* is himself one of the salesmen in the group, the comparison must separate him from the group. The sentence should read:

He has a better record than any *other* salesman in our group. √

Finally, be careful of incomplete comparisons. The result is illogical and confusing.

EXAMPLES:

The plays of Shakespeare are as good as Marlowe. X
The plays of Shakespeare are as good as *those* of Marlowe. √

His skill in tennis is far better than other athletes his age. X
His skill in tennis is far better than *that* of other athletes his age. √

His poetry is as exciting, if not more exciting than, the poetry of his instructor. X
His poetry is as exciting *as*, if not more exciting than, the poetry of his instructor. √

Sequence and Verb Tense

A second fairly common problem of logical expression is poor choice of verb tense.

WATCH FOR INCONSISTENT VERB TENSES

Make sure that verb tenses properly reflect the order and duration of action described.

The choice of verb tense in a correctly written sentence reflects the sequence of events described. The following examples contain verb tense errors:

EXAMPLES:

As soon as Linda finished writing her dissertation, she *will take* a well-earned vacation in Paris. X

A recent study shows that many mothers reenter the labor force after their children *left* home. X

In the first example, both the *writing* and the *vacation* must be placed in the same time frame. As written, the sentence places the two actions in different, unconnected time frames. Depending on whether Linda has already completed the dissertation, the sentence could be corrected in either of two ways:

As soon as Linda finishes writing her dissertation, she will take a well-earned vacation in Paris. √
As soon as Linda finished writing her dissertation, she took a well-earned vacation in Paris. √

The first sentence states that neither event has yet occurred and that the writing will precede the vacation. The second sentence states that the events are completed and that the writing preceded the vacation.

In the second example, the verb *left* is incorrect. The verb *reenter* is describing a present, ongoing action. The sentence can be corrected by making it clear that children leaving home is also a present phenomenon:

A recent study shows that many mothers reenter the labor force after their children leave home. √
A recent study shows that many mothers reenter the labor force after their children have left home. √

Either sentence is acceptable since both make it clear that the leaving home is not a completed past action but an ongoing phenomenon.

> **WATCH FOR SHIFTING VERB TENSE**
>
> Make sure that verb tenses properly reflect the sequence, as well as the duration, of any action described in the sentence.

EXAMPLES:
Joan came home last week and *goes* to her home in the country where she *spends* the last weekend of her vacation. X
Joan came home last week and *went* to her home in the country where she *spent* the last weekend of her vacation. √

Unintended Meanings

Another problem in the category of logical expression is whether the sentence actually says what it intends to say. Often, sentences will intend to say one thing but actually say another:

EXAMPLES:

A childless charwoman's daughter, Dr. Roberts was a self-made woman. X

If the present interest rates fall drastically, the dollar will lose much of its value on the foreign exchange. X

Both of these sentences may seem at first plausible, but a closer reading will show that each contains an error of logical expression. The first example is actually self-contradictory. As written, it asserts that Dr. Roberts was the daughter of a childless charwoman. In that case, Dr. Roberts would indeed have been a self-made woman! What the sentence intends to say about Dr. Roberts is that she was both childless and the daughter of a charwoman:

A charwoman's daughter and childless, Dr. Roberts was a self-made woman. √

The second sentence is a bit subtler. It suggests that present interest rates can change, but that is internally inconsistent, for if the interest rate changes, the result is a new interest rate—not a changed *present* rate. The sentence can easily be corrected by deleting the word *present*:

If the interest rates fall drastically, the dollar will lose much of its value on the foreign exchange. √

In this category, there are as many possible examples as there are possible errors in human reasoning. Therefore, when checking for intended meaning, just ask yourself what the logic of the sentence implies.

> **SENTENCE STRUCTURE MAY OBSCURE INTENDED MEANING**
>
> Determine if the sentence asserts what it intends to say from the logical structure of the sentence.

Conciseness

There are endless possibilities for conciseness errors. Several examples are illustrated below.

1. *Avoid Awkward Sentences and Passive Verbs*

A sentence may be grammatically and logically correct and yet be in need of correction because it is awkward.

EXAMPLES:

The giant condor is able to spread its wings up to 25 feet. X
The giant condor has a wingspan of up to 25 feet. √

Although most students would benefit from further study of the sciences, doing so is frightening to most of them in that science courses are more difficult than liberal arts courses. X
Although most students would benefit from further study of the sciences, most of them are afraid to take such courses because they are more difficult than liberal arts courses. √

Given that the Incas lacked the wheel, the buildings at Machu Picchu are more astonishing than any Greek temples that are comparable as an achievement. X
Given that the Incas lacked the wheel, the buildings at Machu Picchu are more astonishing than any comparable Greek temple. √

In each case, the second sentence is less awkward and clearly renders the intended thought.

A common error among writers is the use of the passive verb. Each of the following examples containing the use of the weak passive verb is then followed by a suggested correction that renders the sentence both clear and concise.

EXAMPLES:

The unemployment rate being 4%, there are as many open jobs as there are job seekers. X
When the unemployment rate is 4%, there are as many open jobs as there are job seekers. √

Aliens, unlike citizens, being unable to vote, have little voice in American politics. X
Because aliens, unlike citizens, are not able to vote, they have little voice in American politics. √

One-fourth of the market was captured by the new computer firm. X
The new computer firm captured one-fourth of the market. √

AVOID PASSIVE VERBS

Any verb construction using a form of the verb *be* in addition to the active verb is called a passive verb. Use of the passive verb is unacceptable and should be avoided.

2. *Avoid Needlessly Wordy Sentences*

Occasionally, an original sentence will be incorrect simply because it is needlessly wordy.

EXAMPLES:

The protracted discussion over which route to take continued for a long time. (Wordy)
The discussion over which route to take continued for a long time. √

A aim of the proposal is chiefly to ensure and guarantee the academic freedom of students. (Wordy)
A aim of the proposal is to guarantee the academic freedom of students. √

To be *protracted* is to be *continued for a long time* and to *ensure* is to *guarantee*. Therefore each original is needlessly wordy.

Misplaced Modifiers

Another error of logical expression is the infamous misplaced modifier. Generally, a modifier should be placed as close to what it modifies as possible. A modifier too far from what it intends to modify or too close to some other important element will seem to modify the wrong part of the sentence. Consider the following faulty sentences:

EXAMPLES:

Stuffed with herb dressing, trussed neatly, and baked to a golden hue, Aunt Fannie served her famous holiday turkey. X

The doctor said gently to the patient that there was nothing wrong with a smile. X

At the tailgate party, Fred served cold beer to his thirsty guests in paper cups. X

As for the first example, poor Aunt Fannie! The proximity of the introductory modifier to Aunt Fannie suggests that Aunt Fannie was stuffed, trussed, and baked. The sentence can be corrected by relocating the modifying phrase: *Aunt Fannie served her famous holiday turkey, stuffed with herb dressing, trussed neatly, and baked to a golden hue.*

The second example is ambiguous and could mean either that there is nothing wrong with smiling or that the doctor said with a smile that nothing was wrong with the patient.

Finally, in the third example, the location of the prepositional phrase *in paper cups* implies that it is the guests who are in the paper cups, not the beer. The sentence can be corrected by repositioning the modifying phrase so that it is closer to what it is intended to modify: *At the tailgate party, Fred served cold beer in paper cups to his thirsty guests.*

WATCH FOR MISPLACED MODIFIERS

Be alert for sentences with ambiguous or incorrect modification. Correct misplaced modifiers by placing them as close as possible to what the modifier modifies.

EXAMPLES:

I bought a piano from an old lady with intricate carvings. X
I bought a piano with intricate carvings from an old lady. √

I read about the destruction of Rome in my history class. X
In my history class, I read about the destruction of Rome. √

The word *only* often causes confusion. Examine the following confusing sentences.

EXAMPLES:

Only he kissed her.
He *only* kissed her.
He kissed *only* her.

All three sentences are possible, but a different meaning is conveyed in each, depending on the positioning of the word only.

Finally, problems may be created by the placement of a participle phrase.

EXAMPLE:

Answering the doorbell, the cake remained in the oven. X

As written, it sounds as though the *cake* answered the doorbell! Correct this sentence by adding a subject to which the phrase can refer:

Answering the doorbell, *we* forgot to take the cake from the oven. √

EXAMPLE:

Falling on the roof, we heard the sound of the rain. X
We heard the sound of the rain falling on the roof. √

EXERCISE 4

Problems of Logical Expression

DIRECTIONS: Read the following passage. In questions #1-14, choose the best answer that corrects the sentence without changing its meaning or intent. When correcting the sentences, you must look at the sentence in the context of the passage in order to check for consistency and logical expression. Answers are on page C-66.

(1) When I was a child, my grandmother's kitchen was the scene of feverish activity during the early fall. (2) Each morning, she would go to the farmers' market and returns with baskets of fruits and vegetables. (3) Then, she would spend the rest of the day preparing the food for the widemouthed canning jars that would preserve them through the winter. (4) By late fall, the pantry shelves are lined with rows of jars containing pickled peaches, creamed corn, and many varieties of jams and jellies.

(5) Today, we are able to buy fresh fruits and vegetables at the local grocery store even during the winter. (6) Indeed, years ago, home canning was a practical solution to one of nature's dilemmas. (7) On the one hand, the harvest produced more fruits and vegetables than could be consumed immediately, so without some way to preserve the produce, they would spoil. (8) On the other hand, during the winter months, fresh produce was not available, so it was important to have preserved foods available.

(9) There are nothing mysterious about home-canning. (10) Fruits or vegetables are packed into special canning jars, fitted with self-sealing lids, and you submerge them in boiling water. (11) The sustained high heat kills dangerous organisms causing the food to spoil. (12) As it gradually cools, a vacuum pulls the lid down against the mouth of the jar to make an air-tight seal. (13) Unless the seal is broken, no organisms can enter the jar to cause spoilage.

(14) Although we no longer depend on home-canning, home-canning can be fun. (15) Jams and jellies spread over hot toast on a cold winter morning seems to taste better when you have made them yourself (16) You also enjoy giving home-made preserves to friends and relatives as gifts. (17) All one needs to do to get started is to find a book about home-canning at the local library or bookstore and follow the directions.

1. Sentence (2), Each morning, she would go to the farmers' market and <u>returns</u> with baskets of fruits and vegetables.

   Which is the best way to write the underlined portion of this sentence? If you think the original is the best way, choose (A).

   (A) returns
   (B) is returning
   (C) would return
   (D) was returning
   (E) have returned

2. Sentence (3): Then, she would spend the rest of the day preparing the food for the widemouthed canning jars that <u>would preserve them</u> through the winter.

   Which is the best way to write the underlined portion of this sentence? If you think the original is the best way, choose (A).

   (A) would preserve them
   (B) would preserve it
   (C) preserved them
   (D) was preserving them
   (E) preserves it

3. Sentence (4): By late fall, the pantry shelves <u>are lined</u> with rows of jars containing pickled peaches, creamed corn, and many varieties of jams and jellies.

   Which is the best way to write the underlined portion of this sentence? If you think the original is the best way, choose (A).

   (A) are lined
   (B) is lines
   (C) were lined
   (D) was lined
   (E) might be lined

4. Sentence (6): <u>Indeed</u>, years ago, home-canning was a practical solution to one of nature's dilemmas.

   Which is the best way to write the underlined portion of this sentence? If you think the original is the best way, choose (A).

   (A) Indeed,
   (B) Indeed
   (C) Furthermore,
   (D) Moreover,
   (E) However,

5. Sentence (7): On the one hand, the harvest produced more fruits and vegetables than could be consumed immediately, so without some way to preserve the produce, <u>they would spoil</u>.

   Which is the best way to write the underlined portion of this sentence? If you think the original is the best way, choose (A).

   (A) they would spoil
   (B) it would spoil
   (C) they spoil
   (D) it spoils
   (E) it spoiled

6. Sentence (8): On the other hand, during the winter months, fresh produce was not available, so it was important to have preserved food available.

   Which is the best way to write the underlined portion of this sentence? If you think the original is the best way, choose (A).

   (A) was
   (B) is
   (C) has been
   (D) could be
   (E) can be

7. Sentence (9): There are nothing mysterious about home-canning.

   Which is the best way to write the underlined portion of this sentence? if you think the original is the best way, choose (A).

   (A) are
   (B) is
   (C) was
   (D) were
   (E) has been

8. Sentence (10); Fruits or vegetables are packed into special canning jars, fitted with self-sealing lids, and you submerge them in boiling water.

   Which is the best way to write the underlined portion of this sentence? If you think the original is the best way, choose (A).

   (A) you submerge them
   (B) you submerge it
   (C) you submerged them
   (D) you submerged it
   (E) submerged

9. Sentence (11): The sustained high heat kills dangerous organisms causing the food to spoil.

   Which is the best way to write the underlined portion of this sentence? If you think the original is the best way choose (A).

   (A) causing
   (B) that caused
   (C) that could cause
   (D) to cause
   (E) which caused

10. Sentence (12): As it gradually cools, a vacuum pulls the lid down against the mouth of the jar to make an air-tight seal.

    Which is the best way to write the underlined portion of this sentence? If you think the original is the best way, choose (A).

    (A) As it gradually cools,
    (B) As they gradually cool,
    (C) Gradually cooling,
    (D) Gradually cooled,
    (E) As the jars gradually cool,

11. Sentence (13): Unless the seal is broken, no organisms can enter the jar to cause spoilage.

    Which is the best way to write the underlined portion of this sentence? If you think the original is the best way, choose (A).

    (A) can enter
    (B) are entering
    (C) entered
    (D) have entered
    (E) had entered

12. Sentence (15): Jams and jellies spread over hot toast on a cold winter morning seems to taste better when you have made them yourself.

    Which is the best way to write the underlined portion of this sentence. If you think the original is the best way, choose (A).

    (A) seems to taste
    (B) seem to taste
    (C) seems tasting
    (D) will seem to taste
    (E) seemed to taste

13. Sentence (16): You also enjoy giving home-preserves to friends and relatives as gifts.

    Which is the best way to write the underlined portion of this sentence? If you think the original is the best way, choose (A).

    (A) enjoy giving
    (B) will enjoy giving
    (C) enjoyed giving
    (D) enjoy to give
    (E) enjoys giving

14. Sentence (17): All one needs to do to get started is to find a book about home-canning at the local library or bookstore and follow the directions.

    Which is the best way to write the underlined portion of this sentence? If you think the original is the best way, choose (A).

    (A) one needs
    (B) you needs
    (C) you need
    (D) people need
    (E) the reader needs

DIRECTIONS: In questions #15-29, circle the letter of the underlined part of the sentence containing the error. Answers are on page C-66.

15. Written in almost total isolation from the world, (A) Emily Dickinson spoke of (B) love and (C) death in her (D) poems.

16. Early in his career, (A) the pianist entertained thoughts of becoming (B) a composer; but after receiving bad reviews for his own work, he (C) had given it up (D).

17. The baseball game was halted due to rain and rescheduled for the following day, even though (A) the (B) fans (C) would not leave (D) the stadium.

18. Being highly qualified for the position, (A) the bank president will conduct (B) a final interview of the new candidate tomorrow, after which (C) he will make (D) her a job offer.

19. The literature of Native Americans has been overlooked (A) by most (B) scholars, and the reason is because (C) most university courses in literature are taught (D) in departments that also teach a language, such as French.

20. In broken English, (A) the police officer patiently listened to the tourist ask for directions to Radio City Music Hall, after which (B) she motioned (C) the tourist and his family into the squad car and drove them (D) to their destination.

21. Bullfighting remains (A) a controversial sport and many (B) are repulsed by it, since (C) Hemingway was an aficionado of the sport and glorified it (D) in his writing.

22. Following the recent crash of the stock market, (A) Peter bought (B) a book on portfolio management in order to learn (C) methods to protect his investments from a well-known investment banker (D).

23. Since (A) we have a broader (B) technological base, American scientists believe that our space program will ultimately prove (C) superior to the Soviet Union (D).

24. Although a person may always represent himself (A) in a judicial proceeding, licensed lawyers only (B) may represent others (C) in such (D) proceedings for a fee.

25. Unlike the pale and delicately built ballerinas of romantic ballet, (A) (B) Judith Jamison's movement seems more African than (C) European-American, and her physical appearance reinforces (D) the contrast.

26. Market experts predict (A) that in ten years, when the harmful effects of caffeine become more generally known, (B) the number of tons of decaffeinated coffee consumed by (C) Americans each year will exceed coffee containing caffeine (D).

27. Illiteracy, a widespread problem in the United States, (A) undermines (B) productivity because many mistakes are (C) made by workers who do not know how to read on (D) the job.

28. As sailors are often assigned (A) to ships that remain (B) at sea for months at a time, men in the Navy spend (C) more time away from home than any branch of the service (D).

29. Like A.J. Ayer, (A) much of Gilbert Ryle's philosophical argumentation relies (B) on analysis of the way people (C) ordinarily (D) use language.

DIRECTIONS: Rewrite sentences #30-49 so that the word being modified is clear. Answers are on page C-68.

30. He tripped on a crack in the pavement going to school.

____

____

31. Mary only failed the test.

____

____

32. Did you see the film about the five on the boat on television?

____

____

33. The police officer ordered the man to stop in his patrol car.

____

____

34. Upon picking up the phone, the noise became muted.

____

____

35. While swimming, a fish nibbled on my toe.

____

____

36. He went to the old church to pray for the people on Cemetery Hill.

____

____

37. Of all his admirers, his wife only loved him.

____

____

38. Upon entering the class, the blackboard came into view.

____

____

39. The baby was pushed by his, mother in a stroller.

____

____

DIRECTIONS: Some of sentence #40-49 are correct, but most are incorrect. Rewrite each incorrect sentences. Answers are on page C-67.

40. She likes tennis, golf, and to go swimming.

____

____

41. He could not deliver the supplies. Because the roads had not yet been plowed.

____

____

42. If you want to succeed, one must be willing to work hard.

____

____

43. Jeff is taller than any boy in his class.

____

____

44. To get to school we nearly walked two miles.

____

____

45. The heroine was unbelievable naive.

____

____

46. Drive carefully. There may be ice on the roads.

____

____

47. Leaning out the window, the garden could be seen below.

____

____

48. The hotel room was clean and comfortable that we had reserved.

____

____

49. This book is heavier in weight than that one.

____

____

Idioms and Clarity of Expression

Standard English contains numerous idioms and two-word verbs that are perfectly acceptable to use. The following is a list of commonly accepted idioms and two-word verbs.

IDIOMS AND TWO-WORD VERBS

about time, about to
above all
act up
add up (*make sense*)
a good deal of
an arm and a leg
at the drop of a hat
back out (of)
bank on
be about to
be an old hand (at)
be out of the question
be a question of
beat around the bush
be bound to
be broke
be fed up (with)
be off
be out of something
be over
be short for, be short of
be the picture of
be up to someone
be warm
bite off more than one can chew
break down, break the ice
break the news (to)
bring about
broken English
brush up on
by and large
by heart, by no means
call off
call on
care for
catch on, catch up (with)
come across, come down with
come out smelling like a rose
cost an arm and a leg
count on, count out
cut down on, cut it close
cut out, cut out for
day in and day out
die down
do over, do with, do without
dream up
do without
drop in (on), drop off
every other
fall behind, fall through
a far cry from
feel free
feel like a million bucks
feel up to
few and far between
fill in (for)
fly off the handle
follow in someone's footsteps
for good
get the hang of
get in one's blood
get in the way
get off, get on, get over, get to
get rid of
get the better of
get under way
give a hand (to, with)
go on (with)
go without saying
hand in, hand out
hang up
have a heart
have in mind
have over
hear first hand (from)
hear from, hear of
hit it off
hold on, hold on (to), hold still, hold up
how come?
in the dark, in hot water
in the long run, in no time
jump to conclusions
keep an eye on, keep an eye out (for)
keep from, keep on one's toes
keep on (with), keep up (with)
knock it off
lay off
lean the ropes
leave out
let (somebody) alone, let (somebody) know
let go of
look after, look for, look forward to
look into, look out (for)
look up, look up (to)
make a difference, make a point of
make ends meet, make out
make sense of, make way for
make up, make up one's mind
mark up, mark down
may as well, might as well
mean to
move on, move up
next to nothing
nose something out
now and then
odds and ends
open up
on a shoestring, on its last leg
on the go, on the go
on one's last leg, on one's toes
on pins and needles
on second thought, on the go
on the mend, on the road, on the run
on the tip of one's tongue
on the whole
out of order, out of sorts
out of this world, out to win
over and over
part with
pass up
pat oneself on the back
pay off, pay someone a visit
pick out, pick up (lean)
pick up the tab (for)
a piece of cake
play by ear
point out
pull one's leg
put aside, put off
put one's best foot forward
put together, put up, put up (with)
rave about
rough it
rule out
run into, run out of, run short (of)
save one's breath
search me
see off, see to
serve one right
set out
settle down, settle on
sing another tune
show around, show up
shut down

IDIOMS AND TWO-WORD VERBS, CONTINUED

size up	take it easy, take off (*leave*)	up against
sleep on it	take one's mind off, take one's time,	ups and downs
snap out of	take over, take pains, take turns	up-to-date
speak up (*say something,*	talk over	use up
speak more loudly)	tangle with	wait for, wait on
spell out (for)	tell apart	warm up (to)
spick and span	think much of	watch out (for)
stand a chance, stand for, stand out	think over	wear out
start up	throw cold water on	a whole new ballgame
stay out, stay up	tie up, tie into	with flying colors
a stone's throw (from)	trade in	without a hitch
straighten up	turn down, turn up, turn into	work out (*exercise, solve*)
take a chance, take advantage (of)	turn off, turn on, turn out, turn in	write out
take after, take in, take into account	under the weather	zero in (on)

An expression that is not idiomatic is one that is not acceptable English for any of several reasons.

CHECKLIST FOR IDIOMATIC EXPRESSION ERRORS

1. Wrong Prepositions
2. Diction
3. Gerund versus Infinitive
4. Ambiguity in Scope
5. Low-level Usage

Wrong Prepositions

In standard written English, only certain prepositions can be used with certain verbs. Students should have knowledge of which prepositions to use with which verbs due to daily conversation and writing in standard written English.

EXAMPLE:

I asked him repeatedly if he was from *about* here, but he never answered me. X

The phrase *was from about here* is not correct. You should recognize the correct phrasing: *he was from around here....*

Diction

The second category of idiomatic expression errors involves diction, i.e., word choice. Sometimes a sentence will be incorrect because a word is used incorrectly. This occurs when a construction is simply not idiomatic: the phrase is not acceptable according to standard usage.

EXAMPLE:

The techniques of empirical observation in the social sciences are different *than* those in the physical sciences. X

This example is improved by replacing *than* with *from*. Rewritten, the sentence reads: *The techniques of empirical observation in the social sciences are different from those in the physical sciences.*

A variation on this theme uses pairs of words that are often incorrectly used:

EXAMPLES:

John expressed his intention to make the trip, but *if* he will actually go is doubtful. X
John expressed his intention to make the trip, but *whether* he will actually go is doubtful. √

Herbert divided the cake *among* May and Sally. X
Herbert divided the cake *between* May and Sally. √

Herbert divided the cake *between* Mary, Sally, and himself. X
Herbert divided the cake *among* Mary, Sally, and himself. √

The *amount* of students in the class declined as the semester progressed. X
The *number* of students in the class declined as the semester progressed. √

There are *less* students in Professor Smith's class than there are in Professor Jones' class. X
There are *fewer* students in Professor Smith's class than there are in Professor Jones' class. √

Some sentences are incorrect because they use a word that does not mean what is intended. The confusion is understandable because of the similarity between the correct word and the chosen word.

WATCH FOR INAPPROPRIATE DICTION

Be alert for non-idiomatic usage and commonly misused words.

The following is an extended summary of commonly confused word groups.

CONFUSING WORD GROUPS

accede—*to agree with*	They will *accede* to your request for more information.
exceed—*to be more than*	Unfortunately, her expenditures now *exceed* her income.
concede—*to yield* (not necessarily in agreement)	They *concede* that more information is necessary.
accept—*to receive* or *to agree* to something	*I'll accept* the gift from you.
except—*to exclude* or *excluding*	Everyone *except* my uncle went home.
access—*availability*	The lawyer was given *access* to the grand jury records.
excess—*state of surpassing specified limits* (noun), or	Expenditures this month are far in *excess* of income.
more than usual (adjective)	The airline charged him fifty dollars for *excess* baggage.
adapt—*to adjust* or *change*	Children can *adapt* to changing conditions very easily.
adept—*skillful*	Proper instruction makes children *adept* in various games.
adopt—*to take as one's own*	The war orphan was *adopted* by the general and his wife.
adapted to—*original* or *natural suitability*	The gills of the fish are *adapted to* underwater breathing.
adapted for—*created suitability*	Atomic energy is constantly being *adapted for* new uses.
adapted from—*changed to be made suitable*	Many of Wagner's opera librettos were *adapted from* old Norse sagas.
addition—*the act or process of adding*	In *addition* to a dictionary, he always used a thesaurus.
edition—*a printing of a publication*	The first *edition* of Shakespeare's plays appeared in 1623.
advantage—*a superior position*	He had an *advantage* in experience over his opponent.
benefit—*a favor conferred or earned* (profit)	The rules were changed for his *benefit*.
adverse—*unfavorable*	He was very upset by the *adverse* decision.
averse—*having a feeling of repugnance or dislike*	Many writers are *averse* to criticism of their work.
advice—*counsel* (noun), *opinion*	Let me give you some free *advice*.
advise—*to offer advice* (verb)	*I'd advise* you to see your doctor.
affect—*to influence* (verb)	The pollution *affected* our health.
effect—*to cause* or *bring about* (verb), or	Our lawsuit *effected* a change in the law.
a result (noun)	The *effect* of the storm could not be measured.
all ready—*everybody* or *everything ready*	They were *all ready* to write when the test began.
already—*previously*	They had *already* written the letter.
all together—*everybody* or *everything together*	The boys and girls stood *all together* in line.
altogether—*completely*	His action was *altogether* strange for a person of his type.
allude—*to make a reference to*	In his essay, he *alludes* to Shakespeare's puns.
elude—*to escape from*	The burglar *eluded* the police.

CONFUSING WORD GROUPS, CONTINUED

allusion—an *indirect reference*	The poem is an *allusion* to one of Shakespeare's sonnets.
illusion—an *erroneous concept* or *perception*	My mirror created the *illusion* of space in the narrow hall.
alongside of—*side by side with*	Bill stood *alongside* of Henry.
alongside—*parallel to the side*	Park the car *alongside* the curb.
among—used with more than two persons or things	The inheritance was equally divided *among* the four kids.
between—used with two persons or things	The inheritance was divided *between* the two kids.
angel—a *heavenly creature*	She has been an *angel* in these difficult times.
angle—a *point at which two lines meet,* or an *aspect seen from a particular point of view*	A line perpendicular to another line forms a right angle.
ante—a prefix meaning *before*	The *antechamber* is the small room before the main room.
anti—a prefix meaning *against*	He is known to be *anti*-American.
assistance—*the act of assisting, aid*	I needed his *assistance* when I repaired the roof.
assistants—*helpers, aides*	The chief surgeon has four *assistants.*
breath—an *intake of air*	Before you dive in, take a very deep *breath.*
breathe—*to draw air in* and *give it out*	It is difficult to *breathe* when you have a bad cold.
breadth—*width*	The canvas was twice greater in length than in *breadth.*
build—*to erect, construct* (verb), or	I want to *build* a sandcastle.
the physical makeup of a person (noun)	She has a very athletic *build.*
built—the past tense of *build*	We *built* a moat around the sandcastle.
buy—*to purchase*	I want to *buy* a new tie.
by—near, by means *of,* or *before*	He comes to school by public transportation.
canvas—a *heavy, coarse material*	The *canvas* sails were very heavy.
canvass—*to solicit, conduct a survey*	The politicians are going to *canvass* our neighborhood.
capital—*place of government,* or	Paris is the *capital* of France.
wealth	It takes substantial *capital* to open a restaurant.
capitol—*building* which houses legislatures	Congress convenes in the *Capitol* in Washington, D.C.
carat—*a unit of weight*	The movie star wears a ten-*carat* diamond ring.
caret—*a proofreading symbol,* indicating where something is to be inserted	He added a phrase in the space above the *caret.*
carrot is a *vegetable*	Does he feed his pet rabbit a *carrot* every other day?
click—a *brief, sharp sound*	The detective drew his gun when he heard the lock *click.*
clique—*an exclusive group of people, a circle* or *set*	In high school, I was not part of any *clique.*
cease—*to end*	Please *cease* making those sounds.
seize—*to take hold of*	*seize* him by the collar as he comes around the corner.
choice—a *selection*	My *choice* for a career is teaching.
choose—*to select*	We may *choose* our own advisors.
chose—the past tense of *choose*	I finally *chose* my wedding dress.
cite—*to quote*	He enjoys *citing* Shakespeare to illustrate his views.
sight—*seeing, what is seen*	The *sight* of the accident was appalling.
site—a *place where something is located or occurs*	We are seeking a new *site* for the baseball field.
cloth—*fabric* or *material*	The seats were covered with *cloth,* not vinyl.
clothe—*to put on clothes, to dress*	Her job is to *clothe* the actors for each scene.
coarse—*vulgar,* or	He was shunned because of his *coarse* behavior.
harsh	The sandpaper was very *coarse.*
course—*a path,* or	The ship took its usual *course.*
a plan of study	How many *courses* are you taking this term?
complement—*a completing part*	His wit was a *complement* to her beauty.
compliment—*an expression of praise or admiration*	He received many *compliments* for his fine work.
confidant—*one to whom private matters are confided* (noun)	His priest was his only *confidant.*
confident—*being sure, having confidence in oneself* (adjective)	Her success in business has given her a *confident* manner.
confidence—*a feeling, of assurance or certainty, trust* (noun)	The ballplayer is developing *confidence* in his ability.
conscience—*the ability to recognize the difference between right and wrong*	The attorney said the criminal lacked a *conscience.*
conscious—*aware*	He was *conscious* that his actions had *consequences.*
consul—a *government representative*	Americans abroad should keep in touch with the *consuls.*
council—*an assembly that meets for deliberation*	The student *council* met to discuss a campus dress code.
counsel—*advice* (counselor)	The defendant heeded the *counsel* of his friends.
decent—*suitable*	The *decent* thing to do is to admit your error.
descent—*going down*	The *descent* into the cave was dangerous.
dissent—*disagreement*	Two of the justices filed a *dissenting* opinion.

CONFUSING WORD GROUPS, CONTINUED

desert (DEZZ-ert)—an *arid area*	I have seen several movies set in the Sahara *desert.*
desert (di-ZERT)—*abandon*, or	The soldier was warned not to *desert* his company.
a *reward* or *punishment* (usually plural)	We're certain that execution is a just *desert* for his crime. He received his just *deserts.*
dessert (di-ZERT)—the *final course of a meal*	We had strawberry shortcake for *dessert.*
disburse—*to pay out*	This week the bank has *disbursed* a million dollars.
disperse—*to scatter, distribute widely*	The defeated army began to *disperse.*
discomfit—*to upset*	The general's plan was designed to *discomfit* the enemy.
discomfort—*lack of ease*	This starched collar causes *discomfort.*
dual—*double*	Dr. Jekyll had a *dual* personality.
duel—a *contest between two persons or groups*	Aaron Burr and Alexander Hamilton engaged in a *duel.*
elicit—*to draw forth, evoke*	Her performance *elicited* tears from the audience.
illicit—*illegal, unlawful*	He was arrested because of his *illicit* business dealings.
emigrate—*to leave a country*	They *emigrated* from Norway in the nineteenth century.
immigrate—*to enter a country*	Many Norwegian *immigrants* settled in the Midwest.
eminent—*of high rank, prominent, outstanding*	He was the most *eminent* physician of his time.
imminent—*about to occur, impending*	His nomination to the board of directors is *imminent.*
epitaph—*a memorial inscription on a tombstone or monument*	His *epitaph* was taken from a section of the Bible.
epithet—a term used to describe or characterize *the nature of a person or thing*	The drunk was shouting *epithets* at the passersby.
expand—*to spread out*	As the staff increases, we can *expand* our office space.
expend—*to use up*	Don't *expend* all your energy on one project.
farther—*used to express distance*	John ran *farther* than Bill walked.
further—*used to express time or degree*	Please go no *further* in your argument.
fair—*light in color, reasonable, pretty*	Your attitude is not a *fair* one.
fare—a *set price*	The *fare* is reduced for senior citizens.
faze—*to worry* or *to disturb*	I tried not to let his mean look *faze* me.
phase—*an aspect*	A crescent is a *phase* of the moon.
formally—in *a formal way*	He was dressed *formally* for the dinner party.
formerly—*at an earlier time*	He was *formerly* a delegate to the convention.
fort—*a fortified place*	A small garrison was able to hold the *fort.*
forte (fort)—*a strong point*	Conducting Wagner's music was Toscanini's *forte.*
forte (for-TAY)—*a musical term that means loudly*	The final movement of the musical composition was meant to be played *forte.*
fine—*good, well, precise,* or *a penalty*	He is a *fine* cook.
find—*to locate*	Can you *find* the keys?
fined—*penalized*	The judge *fined* him twenty dollars.
idle—*unemployed* or *unoccupied*	He didn't enjoy remaining *idle* while he recuperated.
idol—*image* or *object of worship*	Rock musicians are the *idols* of many teenagers.
in—*indicates inclusion, location,* or	The spoons are *in* the drawer.
motion within limits	We were walking *in* the room.
into—*motion toward* one place *from* another	I put the spoons *into* the drawer.
incidence—*to the extent,* or *frequency of an occurrence*	The *incidence* of rabies has decreased since last year.
incidents—*to occurrences, events*	Luckily, the accidents were just minor *incidents.*
it's—the contraction of *it is*, or *it has*	*It's* a very difficult assignment.
its—possessive pronoun meaning *belonging to it*	We tried to analyze its meaning.
knew—the past tense of *know*	I *knew* her many years ago.
new—*of recent origin*	I received a *new* bicycle for my birthday.
know—*to have knowledge* or *understanding*	I *know* your brother.
no—a negative used to express *denial* or *refusal*	There are *no* more books available.
later—*after a certain time*	I'll see you *later.*
latter—*the second of two*	Of the two speakers, the *latter* was more interesting.
lay—*to put*	I (*lay, laid, have laid*) the gift on the table.
lie—*to recline*	I (*lie, lay, have lain*) on my blanket on the beach.
let—the third person singular present of *let*	He *lets* me park my car in his garage.
let's—contraction for *let us*	*Let's* go home early today.
lightening—*making less heavy (from to lighten)*	Removing the books will succeed in *lightening* your bag.
lightning—*electric discharge in the atmosphere, flashes of light, moving with great speed*	Thunderstorms often produce startling *lightning* bolts.
mine—*a possessive, showing ownership*	Use your own sled; that one is *mine.*
mind—*human consciousness* (noun), or	Make up your *mind* which record you want.
to object, to watch out for (verb)	We don't *mind* if you bring a friend.

CONFUSING WORD GROUPS, CONTINUED

loose—*not fastened* or *restrained,* or *not tightfitting*	The dog got *loose* from the leash.
lose—*to mislay, to be unable to keep, to be defeated*	Try not *to lose* your umbrella.
moral—*good* or *ethical* (adjective), or	The trust administrator had a *moral* obligation to the *heirs.*
a lesson to be drawn (noun)	The *moral* of the story is that it pays to be honest.
morale—*spirit*	The team's *morale* improved after the coach's speech.
passed—the past tense of *to pass*	The week *passed* very quickly.
past—*just preceding* or an *earlier time*	The *past* week was a very exciting one.
patience—*enduring calmly, with tolerant understanding*	He has very little *patience* with fools.
patients—*people under medical treatment*	There are twenty *patients* waiting to see the doctor.
personal—*an individual's character, conduct, private affairs*	He took a *personal* interest in each of the students.
personnel—*an organized body of individuals*	The store's *personnel* department is on the third floor.
precede—*to come before*	What events *preceded* the attack?
proceed—*to go ahead*	We can *proceed* with our next plan.
prophecy—*prediction* (noun, rhymes with *sea)*	What is the fortune-teller's *prophecy?*
prophesy—*to predict* (verb, rhymes with *sigh)*	What did the witches *prophesy?*
principal—*chief* or *main* (adjective), or	His *principal* support comes from the real estate industry.
a leader, or	The school *principal* called a meeting of the faculty.
a sum of money (noun)	He earned 10% interest on the *principal* he invested.
principle—a fundamental *truth,* or *belief*	As a matter of *principle,* he didn't register for the draft.
quiet—*silent, still*	My brother is very shy and *quiet.*
quit—*to give* up or *discontinue*	I *quit* the team last week.
quite—*very* or *exactly, to the greatest extent*	His analysis is *quite* correct.
raise—*to lift, to erect*	The neighbors helped him *raise* a new barn.
raze—*to tear down*	The demolition crew *razed* the old building.
rise—*to increase in value, to get up to move from a lower to a higher position*	The price of silver will *rise* again this month.
seem—*to appear*	He *seems* to be sleeping.
seen—the past participle of *see*	Have you *seen* your sister lately?
set—*to place something down* (mainly)	He (*sets, set, has set*) the lamp on the table.
sit—*to seat oneself* (mainly)	He (*sits, sat, has sat*) on the chair.
stationary—*standing still*	Long ago, people thought that the earth was *stationary.*
stationery—*writing material*	We bought our school supplies at the *stationery* store.
suppose—*to assume* or *guess*	I *suppose* you will be home early.
supposed—past tense and past participle *of suppose*	I (*supposed, had supposed*) you would be home early.
supposed—*ought to* or *should* (when followed by *to)*	I *am supposed* to be in school tomorrow.
than—used to express *comparison*	Jim ate more *than* we could put on the large plate.
then—used to express *time* or a *result,* or	I knocked on the door, and *then* I entered.
consequence	If you go, *then* I will go too.
their—*belonging to them*	We took *their* books home with us.
there—*in that place*	Your books are over *there* on the desk.
they're—the contraction for *they are*	*They're* coming over for dinner.
though—*although or as if*	*Though* he's my friend, I cannot recommend him.
thought—past tense of *to think,* or *an idea* (noun)	I *thought* you were serious!
through—*in one side and out another, by way of, finished*	We enjoyed running *through* the snow.
to—in *the direction of* (preposition), and	We shall go *to* school.
used before a verb to indicate the *infinitive*	I like *to* swim.
too—*very, also*	It is *too* hot today.
two—the numeral 2	I ate *two* sandwiches for lunch.
use—*to employ, put into service*	I want to *use* your chair.
used—past tense and the past participle of *use*	I *used* your chair.
used—in *the habit of* or *accustomed to,* is followed by to	I am *used* to your comments.
used— an adjective meaning not new	I bought a used car.
weather—atmospheric conditions	I don't like the weather in San Francisco.
whether—introduces a choice; should not be preceded by of or as to	He inquired whether we were going to the dance.
were—a past tense of be	They were there yesterday.
we're—a contraction of we are	We're in charge of the decorations.
where—place or location	Where are we meeting your brother?
who's—the contraction for who is (or who has)	Who's the next batter?
whose—of whom, implying ownership	Whose notebook is on the desk?
your—a possessive, showing ownership	Please give him your notebook.
you're—a contraction for you are	You're very sweet.

Gerunds Versus Infinitives

The infinitive is the to form of a verb and the gerund is the *-ing* form of a verb. Both may be used as nouns. In some circumstances you can use either:

EXAMPLES:
Adding an extra room to the house is the next project. √
To add an extra room to the house is the next project √

In this example, each sentence is correct. However, in some circumstances, gerund and infinitive are not interchangeable.

WATCH FOR GERUND-INFINITIVE SWITCHING

Be alert for situations in which the infinitive form of the verb has been switched with the gerund form, or vice versa, when it is not appropriate usage in standard written English.

The following is a summary of common verbs often followed by infinitives.

VERBS OFTEN FOLLOWED BY *TO* VERB FORMS

advise**	care	encourage**	implore**	prefer*	teach**
afford	cause**	endeavor	instruct**	prepare	teach...how**
agree	caution**	expect*	intend*	pretend	tell**
allow**	challenge**	fail	invite**	proceed	tend
appear	claim	forget	learn	promise*	threaten
appoint**	come	forbid**	manage	prove	urge**
arrange	command**	force**	mean	refuse	use**
ask*	compel**	get (manage,	motivate**	remind**	volunteer
attempt	consent	have the opportunity)	need*	request**	wait
be	convince**	get** (persuade)	oblige**	require**	want*
be supposed	dare*	happen	offer	seem	warn**
beg*	decide	help*	order**	serve	wish*
begin	demand	hesitate	pay*	show...how**	would like*
believe**	deserve	hire**	permit**	struggle	would love*
can't afford	direct**	hope	persuade**	swear	would prefer*
can't wait	enable**	hurry	plan		

* verb + (noun or pronoun) + infinitive   ** verb + noun *or* pronoun + infinitive

EXAMPLES:
Our new physics professor *prefers* to teach by example; that is, by laboratory experience, rather than by theory. √
Our dinner reservations were at such an exclusive restaurant, the host *required* my date to wear a coat and tie. √

The following is a summary of common verbs often followed by gerunds.

VERBS OFTEN FOLLOWED BY *-ING* VERB FORMS

acknowledge	defer	escape	keep (continue)	recommend
admit	delay	excuse	mention	regret
anticipate	deny	explain	mind (object to)	resent
appreciate	detest	feel like	report	risk
avoid	discontinue	finish	miss	spend time
be worth	discuss	forgive	postpone	suggest
can't help	dislike	give up (stop)	practice	tolerate
can't stand	dispute	go (*idiom*)	prevent	understand
celebrate	dread	imagine	prohibit	
complete	endure	involve	quit	
consider	enjoy	justify	recall	

EXAMPLES:

My brother *recommended* bicycling to relieve the knee pain normally caused by running. √

I must *consider* filing my taxes √

Either infinitives or gerunds may follow the following verbs with no change in the original meaning of the verb:

VERBS FOLLOWED BY EITHER INFINITIVES OR GERUNDS WITHOUT CHANGE IN MEANING

attempt	can't stand	intend	neglect
begin	continue	like	prefer
can't bear	hate	love	start

EXAMPLES:

Following the divorce, she *attempted* to bring her ex-husband to court on charges of failure to pay alimony. √

I had to admit, I *preferred* eating out at a restaurant rather than eating at home when he was cooking! √

However, the meanings of the following verbs change when followed by infinitives or gerunds:

VERBS FOLLOWED BY EITHER INFINITIVES OR GERUNDS WITH CHANGE IN MEANING

forget	propose	regret	stop
mean	quit	remember	try

EXAMPLES:

You can *forget* having the party here. √

I *forgot* to have the electricity connected by the time we moved into the new house. √

Ambiguity in Scope

Watch for ambiguity in scope. This occurs when there is no clear division between two ideas, so that the ideas seem to merge. Consider the following incorrect sentences:

EXAMPLES:

After the arrest, the accused was charged with resisting arrest and criminal fraud. X

The recent changes in the tax law will affect primarily workers who wait tables in restaurants, operate concessions in public places, and drive taxis. X

In the first example, the scope of *resisting* is not clear. The sentence can be read to assert that the accused was charged with resisting criminal fraud. The intended scope can be made clear by inserting *with*: *...charged with resisting arrest and with criminal fraud.* This indicates that there are two separate ideas, not one.

In the second example, the use of *and* seems to tie three separate ideas together; that is, it is those workers who do all three jobs who will be affected—clearly not the intent of the sentence. That these are three separate ideas can be made clear by changing *and* to *or*, or by making a series of parallel ideas: *...workers who wait tables in restaurants, workers who operate concessions in public places, and workers who drive taxis.*

WATCH FOR AMBIGUITY IN SCOPE

Be alert for sentences that run two or more ideas together. Usually the error can be corrected by adding words to clarify the two ideas as distinct and to separate them from one another.

Low-Level Usage

There are a few expressions that are heard frequently in conversation that are regarded as low-level usage and are unacceptable in standard written English. Because nonstandard English includes illiteracies, ungrammatical constructions, slang, jargon, and obsolete words, you should avoid using nonstandard English unless you are aware that you are using a word or phrase that will not be acceptable or understood by a majority of readers. Colloquialisms are sometimes called informalisms, and while they be appropriate to relaxed conversation, they usually should be avoided in writing.

Most tests measure the student's ability to recognize the difference between standard and nonstandard writing. Nonstandard forms should be avoided in formal essay writing.

EXAMPLE:

She *sure* is pretty! (Low-level usage)
She *certainly* is pretty! √

AVOID "LOW-LEVEL" USAGE

Instead of:	*Say:*
ain't	am not; are not; is not
aren't I	am I not
around (2 P.M.)	about (2 P.M.)
being that	since
between you and I	between you and me
bunch (of people)	group (of people)
but that	that
cannot seem	seems unable
different than	different from
else than	other than
equally as good	equally good; just as good
have got	have
having took	having taken
in back of	behind
kind of	somewhat; rather
may of	may have
might of	might have
must of	must have
off of	off
on account of	because
plan on	plan to
put in	spend, make; or devote
quite a few	many
same as	in the same way as; just as
sort of	somewhat; rather
theirselves	themselves
try and	try to
unbeknownst to	without the knowledge of
upwards of	more than
should of	should have
worst kind	very badly
worst way	extremely
would of	would have

EXERCISE 5

Idioms and Clarity of Expression

DIRECTIONS: In sentences #1-104, circle the correct word choice. Answers are on page C-68.

1. He is the (principal, principle) backer of the play.
2. I hope your company will (accept, except) our offer.
3. We hope to have good (weather, whether) when we are on vacation.
4. Put the rabbit back (in, into) the hat.
5. The attorney will (advice, advise) you of your rights.
6. She is far taller (than, then) I imagined.
7. Are they (all ready, already) to go?
8. She answered the letter on shocking pink (stationary, stationery).
9. What is the (affect, effect) you are trying to achieve?
10. I want to (set, sit) next to my grandfather.
11. He's going to (lay, lie) down for a nap.
12. I'm (all together, altogether) tired of his excuses.
13. He saluted when the flag (passed, past) by.
14. I'd like another portion of (desert, dessert).
15. Try not to (loose, lose) your good reputation.
16. How much will the final examination (effect, affect) my grade.
17. What is it (you're your) trying to suggest.
18. She's not (use, used) to such cold weather.
19. The cost of the coat will (raise, rise) again.
20. You are (suppose, supposed) to be home at six o'clock.
21. Her cat ran straight for (its, it's) bowl of food.
22. Are you (conscience, conscious) of what you are doing?
23. It will (seen, seem) that we are afraid.
24. His essays are filled with literary (allusions, illusions).
25. This wine will be a good (complement, compliment) to the meal.
26. It's (later, latter) than you think!
27. My cousin has a swimmer's (build, built).
28. I never (knew, new) him before today.
29. She asked her for a (personal, personnel) question.
30. The golf (coarse, course) was very crowded.
31. The costume was made from old (cloth, clothe) napkins.
32. The ballcarrier was trying to (allude, elude) the tacklers.
33. There are (know, no) more exhibitions planned.
34. I'll wait for you in the (ante, anti) room.
35. Her (moral, morale) is very low.
36. Begin the sentence with a (capital, capitol) letter.
37. The fact that he nearly had an accident didn't even (faze, phase) him.
38. He earns royalties in (access, excess) of a million dollars a year.
39. Now may we (precede, proceed) with the debate?
40. Her (fort, forte) is writing lyrics for musical comedy.
41. They wondered how they were going to (disburse, disperse) the huge crowd.
42. Everyone was dressed (formally, formerly) for the dinner party.
43. I am not (adverse, averse) to continuing the discussion at another time.
44. Can something be done to retard the (incidence, incidents) of influenza in that area?
45. "Seeing the film in class will serve a (dual, duel) purpose," he explained.
46. I'm not sure I want to (expand, expend) so much energy on that project.
47. Imagine my (discomfit, discomfort) when she showed up at the party too!
48. He was a famous matinee (idle, idol) many years ago.
49. When did they (emigrate, immigrate) from New York to Paris?

50. I think she is part of a (click, clique) of snobs and creeps.

51. She paid little attention to the fortune-teller's (prophecy, prophesy).

52. The lights went out when the (lightning, lightening) hit the house.

53. I'll provide you (what ever, whatever) assistance you require.

54. We are in (eminent, imminent) danger of losing our reservations.

55. Will she be able to (adapt, adopt) to our way of performing the operation?

56. As we went through the old cemetery, we were fascinated by some of the (epitaphs, epithets).

57. He shared the riches (between, among) Laura, Millie and Ernestine.

58. The housing law was rewritten for his (advantage, benefit).

59. (Alot, a lot) of the time, he falls asleep at nine o'clock.

60. It was hard to keep track of the (amount, number) of people who visited him last week.

61. I see him in the park (almost, most) every day.

62. Are you certain that he is (alright, all right) now?

63. She is just beginning to (aggravate, annoy) her mother.

64. He is the school's oldest living (alumni, alumnus).

65. He guided the canoe (alongside, alongide of) the riverbank.

66. (Being as, Since) it is Wednesday, we are going to a Broadway matinee.

67. He is (anxious, eager) to be finished with the dental treatment.

68. Where do you want to (meet, meet at)?

69. My aunt just went inside to rest (awhile, a while).

70. It was (about, around) noon when we met for lunch.

71. I brought a (couple, couple of) books for you; both are historical novels.

72. Between (you and I, you and me), I think that her hat is very unbecoming.

73. The (continual, continuous) ticking of the clock was very disconcerting.

74. She (cannot seem, seems unable) to get up early enough to eat breakfast with him.

75. I (assume, expect) that you really earned your salary today.

76. I'm truly (disinterested, uninterested) in seeing that movie.

77. You must be (every bit, just as) sleepy as I am.

78. I doubt (that, whether) it will snow today.

79. (Because of, Due to) the star's illness, the understudy performed the role.

80. Sam, Joe, Lou, and Artie have worked with (each other, one another) before.

81. She asked him (if, whether) he wanted to have lunch with her or with her sister.

82. All (humans, human beings) need to take a certain amount of water into their bodies every week.

83. I (guess, suppose) he is a good person.

84. We hope to (conclude, finalize) the deal this month.

85. We were upset when she (flaunted, flouted) her mother's orders.

86. His girlfriend only eats (healthful, healthy) foods.

87. He said such terrible things about her that she is suing him for (libel, slander).

88. I would like to see you in (regard, regards) to the apartment you plan to rent.

89. She is always late for work, (irregardless, regardless) of how early she wakes up in the morning.

90. He'll (loan, lend) you the money for carfare.

91. He stayed indoors (because, on account) of the weather.

92. The media (are, is) doing the job poorly.

93. The art director was taken (off, off of) the most profitable gallery show.

94. I hope that she will (quit, stop) sending us the job applications.

95. The reason the baby is crying is (because, that) she is hungry.

96. Does he (manage, run) the department efficiently?

97. Anyone who wants to have (his, their) conference with me today is invited to meet in my office at ten o'clock.

98. She scored more points than (any, any other) player on the team.

99. His room is very neat (but, while) hers is very messy.

100. He will (try and, try to) be more pleasant to his sister.

101. (Unbeknownst to, Without the knowledge of) the manager, the men in the shipping department decided to have a party today.

102. (More than, Upwards of) one hundred students attended the lecture this morning.

103. I shall give it to (whoever, whomever) arrives first.

104. This time, we will not wait (for, on) you for more than ten minutes.

DIRECTIONS: Sentences #105-119 each make a grammatical error of the sort just reviewed. Circle the letter of the underlined part of the sentence containing the error. Answers are on page C-68.

105. Economists have established (A) that there is a relation (B)—albeit an indirect one—between the amount (C) of oil imported into this country and the number (D) of traffic accidents.

106. Ironically, today Elizabeth I and her (A) rival for the English throne, Mary Stuart, whom (B) Elizabeth had (C) executed, lay (D) side by side in Westminster Abbey.

107. Although the script is interesting and well-written, it is not clear whether (A) it can be adopted (B) for television since the original story contains scenes that could not be broadcast (C) over (D) the public airwaves.

108. If he had known (A) how difficult law school would be, he would of chosen (B) a different profession or perhaps even have followed (C) the tradition (D) of going into the family business.

109. When shopping malls and business complexes get built, (A) quite often the needs of the handicapped are (B) not considered; as a result, it later becomes necessary to make costly (C) modifications to structures to make them accessible (D) to persons of impaired mobility.

110. Researchers have found (A) that children experience (B) twice as much deep sleep than (C) adults, a fact which (D) may teach us something about the connection between age and learning ability.

111. Despite (A) the ample evidence that smoking is (B) hazardous to one's health, many (C) people seem to find the warnings neither frightening or (D) convincing.

112. No matter how many (A) encores the audience demands, Helen Walker is always willing (B) to sing yet (C) another song which pleases (D) the audience.

113. In light of recent (A) translations of stone carvings describing (B) scenes of carnage, scholars are now questioning as to whether (C) the Incas were really (D) a peace-loving civilization.

114. In galleries containing works of both Gauguin and Cézanne, you will find an equal number (A) of admirers in front of (B) the works of each, (C) but most art critics agree that Gauguin is not of the same artistic stature with (D) Cézanne.

115. The Board of Education $\underline{\text{will never be}}_{A}$ $\underline{\text{fully}}_{B}$ $\underline{\text{responsive}}_{C}$ to the needs of Hispanic children in the school system so long $\underline{\text{that}}_{D}$ the mayor refuses to appoint a Hispanic educator to the Board.

116. The judge $\underline{\text{sentenced}}_{A}$ the president of the corporation to ten years in prison for $\underline{\text{embezzling}}_{B}$ corporate funds but $\underline{\text{gave}}_{C}$ his partner in crime $\underline{\text{less of a sentence}}_{D}$.

117. Scientists $\underline{\text{have recently discovered}}_{A}$ that mussels $\underline{\text{secrete}}_{B}$ a powerful adhesive that allows them $\underline{\text{attaching}}_{C}$ themselves to rocks, concrete pilings, and $\underline{\text{other}}_{D}$ stone or masonry structures.

118. Wall paintings found recently in the caves of Brazil are $\underline{\text{convincing}}_{A}$ evidence that cave art $\underline{\text{developed}}_{B}$ in the Americas at an earlier time $\underline{\text{as}}_{C}$ $\underline{\text{it}}_{D}$ did on other continents.

119. The $\underline{\text{drop}}_{A}$ in oil prices and the slump in the computer industry $\underline{\text{account for}}_{B}$ the recent $\underline{\text{raise}}_{C}$ in unemployment in Texas and the $\underline{\text{associated}}_{D}$ decline in the value of real estate in the region.

Punctuation

Although punctuation is stressed less than other aspects of writing on the test, it is important to be aware of the principal rules governing punctuation. This section is not intended to give a definitive set of rules, but rather only to provide a basic framework for writing.

Commas

Correct use of the comma is essential for effective writing. Follow these rules when using commas.

A comma is not generally used before a subordinate clause that ends a sentence, but in long, unwieldy sentences, use of such comma is optional.

USE A COMMA BEFORE COORDINATING CONJUNCTIONS

Coordinating conjunctions (*and, but, nor, or, for, yet, so*) join two independent clauses. Use a comma before coordinating conjunctions unless the two clauses are very short.

EXAMPLES:

The boy wanted to borrow a book from the library, *but* the librarian would not allow him to take it until he had paid his fines. √

Joe has been very diligent about completing his work, *but* he has had many problems concerning his punctuality. √

I sincerely hope that these exercises prove of assistance to you, *and* I believe that they will help you to make a better showing on your examinations. √

Remember, if the two clauses are very short, the separating comma may be omitted.

EXAMPLES:

Roy washed his dishes *and* Helen dried. √

I saw him *and* I spoke to him. √

A *restrictive* phrase or clause is vital to the meaning of a sentence and cannot be omitted. Do *not* set it off with commas.

EXAMPLE:

A sailboat without sails is useless. √

USE COMMAS FOR CLARITY

1. Use a comma if the sentence might be subject to different interpretations without it.
2. Use a comma if a pause would make the sentence clearer and easier to read.

The following examples show how commas change the interpretation of the sentences:

EXAMPLES:

The banks which closed yesterday are in serious financial difficulty. (Some banks closed yesterday and those banks are in trouble.)

The banks, which closed yesterday, are in serious financial difficulty. (All banks closed yesterday and all are in trouble.)

My brother Bill is getting married. (The implication is that I have more than one brother.)

My brother, Bill, is getting married. (Here *Bill* is an appositive. Presumably he is the only brother.)

Inside the people were dancing. (Confusing)
Inside, the people were dancing. √

After all crime must be punished. (Confusing)
After all, crime must be punished. √

The pause rule is not infallible, but it is your best resort when all other rules governing use of the comma fail you.

USE COMMAS TO SEPARATE COORDINATE ADJECTIVES, WORDS IN A SERIES, AND NOUNS IN DIRECT ADDRESS

1. Coordinate adjectives are adjectives of equal importance and precede the noun they describe.

2. Use a comma between words in a series when three or more elements are present. If the series ends in *etc.*, use a comma before *etc.* Do NOT use a comma after *etc.* in a series, even if the sentence continues.

3. Use commas to set off nouns in direct address. The name of the person addressed is separated from the rest of the sentence by commas.

EXAMPLES:

The jolly, fat man stood at the top of the stairs.
He is a wise, charming man.
She is a slow, careful reader.

Coats, umbrellas, and boots should be placed in the closet at the end of the hall.
Pencils, scissors, paper clips, etc. belong in your top desk drawer.

Bob, please close the door.
I think, José, that you are the one who was chosen.

The use of a comma before *and* and *or* is optional. However, you should be consistent in your choice.

If you can add the word *and* between the adjectives without changing the sense of the sentence, then use commas.

USE A COMMA TO SEPARATE QUOTATIONS & INTRODUCTORY PHRASES

1. Commas should be used to separate a short direct quotation from the speaker.

2. Place a comma after an introductory phrase of five or more words.

3. Use a comma after a short introductory phrase whenever the comma would aid clarity.

4. Regardless of their length, use a comma after introductory gerunds, participles, and infinitives.

However, if the subordinate clause follows the main clause, you do not need to set it off with a comma.

EXAMPLES:

She said, "I must leave work on time today."
"Tomorrow I begin my summer job," he told us.

As a child she was a tomboy. (The comma is unnecessary.)

To Dan, Phil was a friend as well as a brother. (The comma clarifies.)
In 1978, 300 people lost their lives in one air disaster. (The comma clarifies.)

When you come home, please ring the bell before opening the door.

Because the prisoner had a history of attempted jailbreaks, he was put under heavy guard. (The comma clarifies.)

Commas must be used in situations to set off a phrase or to interrupt the flow of the sentence.

USE PAIRS OF COMMAS TO SET OFF APPOSITIVE, PARENTHETICAL, AND NONRESTRICTIVE ELEMENTS

1. An appositive phrase follows a noun or pronoun and means the same as that noun or pronoun.

2. Parenthetical expressions are words that interrupt the flow of the sentence, such as *however, though, for instance, by the way, to tell the truth, believe me, it appears to me, I am sure,* and *as a matter of fact,* without changing the meaning of the sentence.

3. A nonrestrictive element supplies material not essential to the sentence and, if removed, will not change the meaning of the original sentence.

EXAMPLES:

Mr. Dias, our lawyer, gave us some great advice.
Bob, an industrious and hard-working student, will run for class treasurer.
Shrill and loud, her voice grated on our ears.
This book, I believe, is the best of its kind.
As a matter of fact, it was not my turn to take out the garbage.
Sam, who is a very well-behaved dog, never strays from the front yard.
Millie, who is a fine student, has a perfect attendance record.

Test for placement of commas in a parenthetical expression by reading aloud. If you would pause before and after such an expression, then it should be set off by commas.

USE COMMAS TO SEPARATE DATES AND ADDRESSES

Commas, including a comma after the last item, separate the different parts of a date and address.

EXAMPLES:

The train will arrive on Friday, February 13, 1992, if it is on schedule.
My daughter traveled from Cambridge, Massachusetts, to Albany, New York, in three hours.

In general, if you can omit the material without changing the meaning of the main clause, then the material is nonrestrictive and should be set off by commas.

Finally, a comma must be used to separate dates and addresses.

The above rules summarize the most important uses of commas. If you use them in just these situations, then you won't make a mistake in their use.

SITUATIONS IN WHICH *NOT* TO USE COMMAS

1. Do not use a comma to separate a subject from its verb.

2. Do not use commas to set off restrictive or necessary clauses or phrases.

3. Do not use a comma in place of a conjunction.

Semicolons

USE A SEMICOLON TO SEPARATE TWO COMPLETE IDEAS

A semicolon may be used to separate two complete ideas (independent clauses) in a sentence when the two ideas have a close relationship and they are *not* connected with a coordinating conjunction.

EXAMPLE:

The setting sun caused the fields to take on a special glow; all was bathed in a pale light.

The semicolon is often used between independent clauses connected by conjunctive adverbs such as *consequently, therefore, also, furthermore, for example, however, nevertheless, still, yet, moreover,* and *otherwise*. However, do not use the semicolon between an independent clause and a phrase or subordinate clause.

EXAMPLE:

He waited at the station for well over an hour; however, no one appeared.

USE A SEMICOLON TO SEPARATE A SERIES OF PHRASES CONTAINING COMMAS OR A SERIES OF NUMBERS

1. Use a semicolon to separate a series of phrases or clauses, each of which contain commas.

2. Use a semicolon to avoid confusion with numbers.

EXAMPLES:

The old gentleman's heirs were Margaret Whitlock, his half-sister; James Bagley, the butler; William Frame, companion to his late cousin, Robert Bone; and his favorite charity, the Salvation Army.

Add the following: $.25; $7.50; and $12.89.

USE A SEMICOLON TO SEPARATE INDEPENDENT CLAUSES

1. You may use a semicolon to separate two short, related independent clauses in a sentence when the two ideas have a close relationship and they are *not* connected with a coordinating conjunction.

2. The semicolon is often used between independent clauses connected by conjunctive adverbs such as *consequently, therefore, also, furthermore, for example, however, nevertheless, still, yet, moreover, otherwise.* Note: the adverb must be followed by a comma.

EXAMPLES:

Anne is working at the front desk on Monday; Ernie will take over on Tuesday.

She waited for her check to arrive in the mail for two weeks; however, the check never appeared.

You may use a semicolon to separate this clause from the next; however, you will not be incorrect if you choose to write two separate sentences.

Two main clauses should be separated by a conjunction *or* by a semicolon *or* they must be written as two sentences. The same two clauses may be written in any one of three ways, as the following example shows:

EXAMPLE:

Autumn had come and the trees were almost bare.
Autumn had come; the trees were almost bare.
Autumn had come. The trees were almost bare.

If you are uncertain about how to use a semicolon to connect independent clauses, write two sentences instead.

USE SEMICOLONS ONLY FOR INDEPENDENT CLAUSES

Unless each clause can function as an independent sentence, it is probably wrong to use a semicolon.

Colons

The colon is always used in the following situations:

SITUATIONS REQUIRING A COLON

1. A colon should be placed after the salutation in a business letter.
2. Use a colon to separate hours from minutes.
3. The colon is used to precede a list of three or more items or a *long quotation*.
4. A colon should be used to introduce a question.

EXAMPLES:

Dear Board Member:

The eclipse occurred at 10:36 A.M.

Many people refer to four, rather than three, branches of government: the executive, the judicial, the legislative, and the media.

My question is this: Are you willing to punch a time clock?

Avoid using the colon directly after a verb. Avoid using the colon to interrupt the natural flow of language.

EXAMPLES:

We played: volleyball, badminton, football, and tag. X
We played volleyball, badminton, football, and tag. √

We purchased: apples, pears, bananas, and grapes. X
We purchased apples, pears, bananas, and grapes. √

USE COLONS TO CALL ATTENTION, BUT NOT IF ALREADY SIGNALLED

A colon may be used to introduce or to call attention to elaboration or explanation. Be careful not to use a colon to introduce or call attention to material that is already signaled by some other element of the sentence.

End-Stop Punctuation

There are three types of punctuation used to end a sentence.

END-STOP PUNCTUATION

1. A *period* is used at the end of a sentence that makes a statement.
2. A *question mark* is used after a direct question. A period is used after an indirect question.
3. A *exclamation mark* is used after an expression that shows strong emotion or issues a command. It may follow a word, a phrase, or a sentence.

EXAMPLES:

He is my best friend.
There are thirty days in September.

Did you take the examination on Friday?
The instructor wanted to know if you took the examination on Friday.

Wonderful! You won the lottery!
Oh, no! I won't go!
Do it!

Dashes

SITUATIONS REQUIRING A DASH

1. Use a dash (or parentheses) for emphasis or to set off an explanatory group of words.
2. A dash is used before a word group to indicate a summation or reversal of what preceded it.
3. Use a dash to mark a sudden break in thought that leaves a sentence unfinished.

The material following the dash usually directs the attention of the reader to the content preceding it. Unless the set-off expression ends a sentence, dashes, like parentheses, must be used in pairs.

EXAMPLES:

The tools of his trade—probe, mirror, cotton swabs—were neatly arranged on the dentist's tray.

Patience, sensitivity, understanding, and empathy—these are marks of a friend.

He was not pleased with—in fact, he was completely hostile to—the take-over.

Dashes in sentences have a function similar to commas when they are used to set off parenthetical remarks. The difference between the two is a matter of emphasis. The dashes mark a more dramatic shift or interruption of thought. Do not, however, mix dashes and commas.

Hyphens

SITUATIONS REQUIRING A HYPHEN

1. Use a hyphen with a compound modifier that precedes the noun.
2. The hyphen is also used with fractions that serve as adjectives or adverbs.

The next examples demonstrate those situations in which it is correct to use a hyphen and those situations in which it is not.

EXAMPLES:

There was a *sit-in* demonstration at the office.
We will *sit in* the auditorium.

I purchased a *four-cylinder* car.
I purchased a car with *four cylinders.*

Quotation Marks

WHEN TO USE QUOTATION MARKS

1. Use question marks to enclose the actual words of the speaker or writer,
2. to emphasize words used in a special or unusual sense, and
3. to set off titles of short themes or parts of a larger work.

EXAMPLES:

Jane said, "There will be many people at the party."

He kept using the phrase "you know" throughout his conversation.

WHEN *NOT* TO USE QUOTATION MARKS

1. Do not use quotation marks for indirection quotations.
2. Do not use quotation marks to justify your own poor choice of words.

EXAMPLES:

He said that "he would be happy to attend the meeting." X
He said that he would be happy to attend the meeting. √

Any periods and commas are placed *inside* the quotation marks; any colons and semicolons are placed *outside* the quotation marks.

EXAMPLES:

My favorite poem is "My Last Duchess," a dramatic monologue written by Robert Browing. √

My favorite poem is "My Last Duchess"; this poem is a dramatic monologue written by Robert Browning. √

EXERCISE 6

Punctuation

DIRECTIONS: Punctuate sentences #1-35 with additional commas, semicolons, periods, exclamation marks, question marks, quotes, dashes, and hyphens *if necessary*. Answers are on page C-69.

1. He was not aware that you had lost your passport
2. Did you report the loss to the proper authorities
3. I suppose you had to fill out many forms
4. What a nuisance
5. I hate doing so much paper work
6. Did you ever discover where the wallet was
7. I imagine you wondered how it was misplaced
8. Good for you
9. At least you now have your passport
10. What will you do if it happens again
11. Neurology is the science that deals with the anatomy physiology and pathology of the nervous system
12. He was not aware that you had lost your wallet
13. Nursery lore like everything human has been subject to many changes over long periods of time
14. Bob read Tennyson's Ulysses to the class everyone seemed to enjoy the reading.
15. In order to provide more living space we converted an attached garage into a den
16. Because he is such an industrious student he has many friends
17. Begun while Dickens was still at work on *Pickwick Papers Oliver Twist* was published in 1837 and is now one of the author's most widely read works
18. Given the great difficulties of making soundings in very deep water it is not surprising that few such soundings were made until the middle of this century
19. Did you report the loss to the proper authorities
20. The root of modern Dutch was once supposed to be Old Frisian but the general view now is that the characteristic forms of Dutch are at least as old as those of Old Frisian
21. Moose once scarce because of indiscriminate hunting are protected by law and the number of moose is once again increasing
22. He ordered a set of books several records and a film almost a month ago
23. Perhaps the most interesting section of New Orleans is the French Quarter which extends from North Rampart Street to the Mississippi River
24. Writing for a skeptical and rationalizing age Shaftesbury was primarily concerned with showing that goodness and beauty are not determined by revelation authority opinion or fashion
25. We tried our best to purchase the books but we were completely unsuccessful even though we went to every bookstore in town
26. A great deal of information regarding the nutritional requirements of farm animals has been accumulated over countless generations by trial and error but most recent advances have come as the result of systematic studies at schools of animal husbandry
27. *Omoo* Melville's sequel to *Typee* appeared in 1847 and went through five printings in that year alone.
28. I imagine you wondered how it was misplaced
29. Although the first school for Blacks was a public school established in Virginia in 1620 most educational opportunities for Blacks prior to the Civil War were provided by private agencies
30. As the climate of Europe changed the population became too dense for the supply of food obtained by hunting and other means of securing food such as the domestication of animals were necessary
31. In Faulkner's poetic realism the grotesque is somber violent and often inexplicable in Caldwell's writing it is lightened by a balladlike humorous sophisticated detachment
32. The valley of the Loire a northern tributary of the Loire at Angers abounds in rock villages and they occur in many other places in France Spain and northern Italy
33. The telephone rang several times as a result his sleep was interrupted
34. He has forty three thousand dollars to spend however once that is gone he will be penniless
35. Before an examination do the following review your work get a good nights sleep eat a balanced breakfast and arrive on time to take the test

Explanatory Answers

EXERCISE 1—PARTS OF SPEECH (p. C-5)

1. ambulance = noun
it = pronoun
hospital = noun
traffic = noun
hurried = verb

2. movers = noun
and = conjunction
in = preposition
unloaded = verb
it = pronoun

3. dark = modifier
blocked = verb
and = conjunction
clouds = noun
our = pronoun

4. dinner = noun
table = noun
sat = verb
cleared = verb
and = conjunction

5. room = noun
with = preposition
Polish = modifier
was filled = verb
author = noun

6. first = modifier
were = verb
program = noun
shows = noun
earlier = modifier

7. waiter = noun
Victor = noun
and = conjunction
arrived = verb
ordered = verb

8. inspector = noun
approved = verb
allowed = verb
finally = modifier
and = conjunction

9. notified = verb
water = noun
hours = noun
in = preposition
would be = verb

10. band = noun
crowd = noun
loud = modifier
finished = verb
burst = verb

11. telephoned = verb
would be = verb
date = noun
her = pronoun
their = pronoun

12. cat = noun
warmth = noun
sun = noun
was sleeping = verb
of = preposition

13. train = noun
called = verb
and = conjunction
pulled = verb
name = noun

14. we = pronoun
were = verb
rear = noun
children = noun
in = preposition

15. they = pronoun
teach = verb
and = conjunction
leave = verb
hikers = noun

16. covered = verb
melted = modifier
syrup = noun
steaming = modifier
sticky = modifier

17. weekend = noun
special = modifier
beautiful = modifier
made = verb
brilliant = modifier

18. eventful = modifier
but = conjunction
unopened modifier
wrote = verb
his = pronoun

19. barely = modifier
bus = noun
make out = verb
as = conjunction

20 offered = verb
or = conjunction
delicious = modifier
us = pronoun
were = verb

EXERCISE 2—COMMON GRAMMAR PROBLEMS (p. C-18)

1. (A) *Harsh* is intended to modify *deals,* a verb. The adverb *harshly* is needed here.

2. (D) *Them* is intended to be a pronoun substitute for *advertising,* but *advertising* is singular, not plural. *It* should replace *them.*

3. (D) *You* is intended to refer to *one,* but *one* is in the third person while *you* is in the second person. The sentence could be corrected simply by omitting the second pronoun *you* altogether: "...and read a book."

4. (C) *Which* has no clear referent. *Which* might refer either to *horrifying conditions* or to *English boarding schools.* The ambiguity could be avoided by rewording the sentence: "...about the horrifying conditions in the English boarding schools, conditions which he learned about...."

5. (C) *It* has no clear referent. It might refer either to the movement or to the manifesto. The sentence can be corrected by including an appropriate noun to clarify the speaker's meaning; e.g., "...of a manifesto, a work that incorporated...."

6. (D) *Capable* is intended to modify *played,* a verb. So the adverb form must be used: "...played capably."

7. (B) *Who* and *whom* are the correct pronouns to use for people: "...countryside who sheltered...."

8. (B) *We* cannot be used as the object of *to.* The correct choice of pronoun is *us.*

9. (A) When a pronoun is used to modify a gerund, the pronoun must be in the possessive case: "Your taking the initiative...."

10. (C) *Which* has no clear antecedent. Had the speaker hoped to avoid the conference or just being selected to be the representative of the group at the conference? To avoid the ambiguity, the sentence will have to be substantially revised: "...at the conference, and I had hoped to avoid the conference altogether."

11. (C) *Whom* should be used here instead of *which,* since the pronoun refers to *.person.*

12. (D) The subject of the main clause is *few,* a plural pronoun, so the verb should be *are* rather than *is.*

13. (B) The subject of the sentence is *differences,* a plural noun, so the verb should be *help* rather than *helps.*

14. (B) *Hardly no* is a double negative. The sentence should read *hardly any.*

15. (B) The subject of the sentence is *diaries,* a plural noun. So the verb should be *provide* rather than *provides.*

16. (D) *Its* intends to refer to *whales,* so the sentence should use the plural pronoun *their.*

17. (A) A pronoun used to modify a gerund must be in the possessive case: "His being at the rally."

18. (D) *Satisfactory* is either intended to modify *working* or *system.* If it modifies *working,* then the adverb should be used: "...and more than satisfactorily." If the word modifies *system,* then another verb is required: "...and is more than satisfactory."

19. (B) *Who* is intended to be the object of the verb *married,* so the objective case pronoun *whom* is required.

20. (B) *Recent* is intended to modify *constructed,* an adjective. But an adjective cannot be used to modify another adjective. Here the adverb *recently* should be used.

21. (D) *Which* has no clear referent. Were the faculty angry because the resolution passed or because it passed with few dissenting votes? The sentence must be rewritten to clarify the speaker's intention.

22. (D) *Your* is intended to refer to *one's,* so you need some kind of third person pronoun, for example, *his or her.*

23. (D) *It* lacks a referent. *It* seems to refer to something like *insurance,* but there is no such noun in the sentence. The sentence could be corrected by using the noun *insurance* in place of the pronoun *it.*

24. (C) *Candid* is intended to modify *wrote,* so the sentence must use the adverb *candidly.*

25. (A) The sentence commits the error of the "ubiquitous they." The sentence can be corrected by using a noun such as *the team* or in place of *they.*

EXERCISE 3—ANALYZING SENTENCE STRUCTURE (p. C-27)

1. receive	10. are	19. was	28. know
2. were	11. worries	20. has	29. goes
3. offer	12. have	21. are	30. are
4. remain	13. lose	22. have	31. cheered
5. is	14. fall	23. were	32. was
6. were	15. have	24. his	33. have completed
7. were	16. was	25. her	34. had completed
8. have	17. writes	26. is	35. are
9. hope	18. have	27. their	

36. C	43. E	49. E	55. C
37. B	44. C	50. B	56. A
38. E	45. D	51. E	57. E
39. B	46. C	52. B	58. C
40. A	47. E	53. E	59. B
41. C	48. A	54. A	60. D
42. D			

61. (C) The sentence commits an error of logical expression, because it implies that all the people coming into the museum have but a single camera. It could be corrected by changing *camera* to *cameras.*

62. (B) The sentence is flawed by faulty parallelism. It could be corrected by changing *to maintain* to *maintaining.*

63. (A) The sentence contains the incorrect form of the irregular verb *to lay.* The sentence is correct by changing *laying* to *lying.*

64. (D) The final phrase is out of place. As written, the sentence implies that the cockroach is unlike destructive garden pests, but the speaker means to say that the cockroach is not like the praying mantis. The sentence can be corrected by relocating the offending phrase closer to the noun it modifies: "The praying mantis, unlike the cockroach, which serves no useful function, is welcomed by homeowners...."

65. (C) The incorrect form of the verb *to hang* is used in the original sentence. Instead, the sentence should read: "...picture was hung...."

66. (D) Unlike in the previous item in which the correct sentence read: "...picture was hung...", when one is talking about the hanging of a person, the correct verb form is *hanged,* not *hung.*

67. (B) The original sentence is a run-on sentence. It can be correct by adding end-stop punctuation: "It was an exhausting day shopping. We could hardly wait to get home."

68. (A) The sentence is flawed by a lack of parallelism, an error that can be corrected by substituting the adjective *charismatic* for the phrase *has charisma.*

69. (A) This item is a sentence fragment that lacks a conjugated verb. The fragment can be changed into a complete sentence by substituting *displayed* for *displaying.*

70. (C) The improper form of *to sew* is used in the original sentence. The sentence should read: "The woman...has sewn the skirt perfectly...."

71. (B) The use of the subjunctive *would have been* is illogical. The use of the subjunctive incorrectly implies that the loss of lives and money is contingent upon some event, but no such event is mentioned in the sentence. The sentence can be corrected by substituting *will have been.*

72. (C) This is a run-on sentence. It should read: "The house on the corner was completely empty. No one came to the door."

73. (C) The sentence suffers from a lack of parallelism. This deficiency can be corrected by changing *taking to* to *take.* (In any event, the use of the gerund, *taking,* instead of the infinitive, *to take,* is not idiomatic.)

74. (C) The incorrect verb tense of *to freeze* is used in the original sentence. The sentence can be corrected by substituting *frozen* for *froze.*

75. (D) The tense of the first verb is not consistent with the tense of the second verb. The sentence can be corrected by substituting *experiences* for *experienced.*

76. (C) This is a run-on sentence. It can be corrected by adding a question mark: "Where had everyone gone? All the lights were off."

17. (D) The original sentence contains an incorrect verb form. The sentence should read: "...the bank lent him the money."

78. (D) The use of the present tense *loses* is illogical and inconsistent with the use of the past tense *was* earlier in the sentence. The error can be corrected by substituting *lost* for *loses.*

79. (B) This is a run-on sentence. The sentence is correct if a comma is added between *slowly* and *almost.* The correct sentence reads: "We entered the cave very slowly, almost afraid of what we might find there."

80. (C) The original sentence contains the incorrect form of the verb *to drink.* The corrected sentence reads: "...he drank all of the poison from the vial."

81. (C) The elements of the sentence are not parallel. The sentence would be correct if *cross-checked* were substituted for *cross-checking.*

82. (B) The sentence contains an incorrect form of the verb *to fling.* The sentence can be corrected by changing *flinged* to *flung.*

83. (C) The sentence is a run-on sentence. The sentence may be corrected one of two ways, both changes occurring between *happen* and *my.* First, end-stop punctuation may be added: "...was going to happen. My heart...." Second, an exclamation mark could be used instead of a period: "...was going to happen! My hear...."

EXERCISE 4—PROBLEMS OF LOGICAL EXPRESSION (p. C-38)

1. C	4. E	7. B	10. E	13. B
2. B	5. B	8. E	11. A	14. C
3. C	6. A	9. C	12. B	

15. (A) The sentence is afflicted with a dangling modifier. As written, the sentence implies that Emily Dickinson herself was written. To correct this error, it would have to be rewritten to bring the introductory modifier closer to the noun it modifies (poems): "The poems by Emily Dickinson, written in almost total isolation from the world, spoke of love and death."

16. (D) The use of the perfect tense *had given up* is not consistent with the use of the past tense *entertained,* for the use of the perfect tense implies that the pianist gave up his attempt to become a composer before he even entertained the idea of becoming one. The sentence can be corrected by substituting *gave up* for *had given up.*

17. (B) The sentence commits an error of illogical expression, for, as written, it implies that the fans' leaving the stadium would ordinarily be sufficient to halt a game and reschedule it for later. The problem of illogical expression can be corrected by substituting the conjunction *but* for *even though.* (This particular error of logical expression is called illogical subordination.)

18. (A) The sentence is afflicted with a dangling modifier. As written, it implies that the bank president is highly qualified for the position. The sentence needs substantial revision: "The bank president will conduct a final interview of the new candidate tomorrow. Since the candidate is highly qualified for the position, the president will make her a job offer after the interview."

19. (C) The sentence commits an error of logical expression by implying that the *reason* is an effect of some other cause, when the speaker really means to say that the *reason* and the *cause* are the same thing, the explanation for the phenomenon. The error can be corrected by substituting *that* for *because.* (Note: This use of *because* to introduce a noun clause can also be considered an example of an expression that is not acceptable in English usage.)

20. (A) The sentence contains a dangling modifier. As written, it implies that the police officer is listening in broken English (not listening to broken English). The sentence can be corrected by relocating the modifier: "The police officer patiently listened to the tourist ask in broken English for directions to Radio City Music Hall,...."

21. (C) The choice of *since* is illogical, because *since* implies that there is a causal or explanatory connection between Hemingway's view of bullfighting and the fact that bullfighting is a controversial sport that repulses some people. The problem of illogical subordination can be corrected by substituting *but* for *since.*

22. (D) The sentence contains a misplaced modifier. As written, it implies that Peter hopes to learn how to protect his investments from the threat posed by a well-known investment banker. The sentence must be rewritten: "...in order to learn from a well-known investment banker methods to protect his investments."

23. (D) The sentence makes an error of logical expression, for it seems to compare our space program to the Soviet Union. The error can be eliminated by using the phrase *to that of* instead of *to* after *superior.*

24. (B) The sentence contains a misplaced modifier. The placement of *only* seems to imply a restriction on the verb rather than on the subject. The sentence can be easily corrected by moving *only* and placing it just before *licensed lawyers.*

25. (A) The sentence contains a dangling modifier and seems to compare ballerinas of the romantic ballet with the movement of Judith Jamison. To correct this error, the sentence would have to be substantially rewritten: "Judith Jamison's movement seems more African than European-American, and her physical appearance, which is unlike that of the pale and delicately built ballerinas of romantic ballet, reinforces the contrast."

26. (D) The sentence contains an error of logical expression. It attempts to compare an amount of decaffeinated coffee with coffee containing caffeine. The sentence can be corrected by inserting clarifying phrases: ...the number of tons of coffee containing caffeine consumed by Americans."

27. (D) The sentence contains a misplaced modifier. As written, it implies that the workers are illiterate because they don't know how to read on the job. The sentence can be corrected by relocating the offending phrase so that it is closer to the noun it modifies: "Many mistakes are made *on the job* by workers."

28. (D) The sentence makes an illogical statement. It attempts to compare *time* and *branch of the service.* The sentence can be corrected by inserting a clarifying phrase: "...than do men in any other branch...."

29. (A) The sentence contains a dangling modifier. As written, it implies a comparison between A.J. Ayer, the person, and the philosophical writings of Gilbert Ryle. The error can be corrected in the following way: "Like the writing of A.J. Ayer, much of...."

30. Going to school, he tripped on a crack in the pavement.

31. Only Mary failed the test.

32. Did you see the film on television about the five on the boat?

33. The police officer in his patrol car ordered the man to stop.

34. When we picked up the phone, the noise became muted.

35. While I was swimming, a fish nibbled on my toe.

36. He went to the old church on Cemetery Hill to pray for the people.

37. Of all his admirers, only his wife loved him.

38. When we entered the class, the blackboard came into view.

39. The baby was in a stroller pushed by his mother.

40. She likes tennis, golf, and swimming.

41. He could not deliver the supplies because the roads had not yet been plowed.

42. If you want to succeed, you must be willing to work hard.

43. Jeff is taller than any other boy in his class.

44. To get to school we walked nearly two miles.

45. The heroine was unbelievably naive.

46. Drive carefully. There may be ice on the roads..

47. Leaning out the window, she could see the garden below.

48. The hotel room that we had reserved was clean and comfortable.

49. This book is heavier than that one.

EXERCISE 5—IDIOMS AND CLARITY OF EXPRESSION (p. C-52)

1. principal
2. accept
3. weather
4. into
5. advise
6. than
7. all ready
8. stationery
9. effect
10. sit
11. lie
12. altogether
13. passed
14. dessert
15. lose
16. affect
17. you're
18. used
19. rise
20. supposed
21. its
22. conscious
23. seem
24. allusion
25. complement
26. later
27. build
28. knew
29. personal
30. course
31. cloth
32. elude
33. no
34. ante
35. morale
36. capital
37. faze
38. excess
39. proceed
40. forte
41. disperse
42. formally
43. averse
44. incidence
45. dual
46. expend
47. discomfort
48. idol
49. emigrate
50. clique
51. prophecy
52. lightning
53. what ever
54. imminent
55. adapt
56. epitaphs
57. among
58. benefit
59. A lot
60. number
61. almost
62. all right
63. annoy
64. alumnus
65. alongside
66. Since
67. eager
68. meet
69. awhile
70. about
71. couple of
72. you and me
73. continuous
74. seems unable
75. assume
76. uninterested
77. just as
78. that
79. Because of
80. one another
81. whether
82. human beings
83. suppose
84. conclude
85. flouted
86. healthful
87. slander
88. regard
89. regardless
90. lend
91. because
92. is
93. off
94. stop
95. that
96. manage
97. his
98. any other
99. but
100. try to
101. Without the knowledge of
102. More than
103. Whoever
104. for

105. (B) Substitute *relationship.*

106. (D) Substitute *lie.*

107. (B) Substitute *adapted.*

108. (B) Substitute *would have chosen.*

109. (A) Substitute *are built.*

110. (C) Substitute as.

111. (D) Substitute *nor.*

112. (D) Substitute *to please.*

113. (C) Substitute *whether.*

114. (D) Substitute *as.*

115. (D) Substitute *as.*

116. (D) Substitute *a lesser sentence.*

117. (C) Substitute *to attach.*

118. (C) Substitute *than.*

119. (C) Substitute *rise.*

EXERCISE 6—PUNCTUATION (p. C-63)

1. He was not aware that you had lost your passport.
2. Did you report the loss to the proper authorities?
3. I suppose you had to fill out many forms.
4. What a nuisance!
5. I hate doing so much paper work!
6. Did you ever discover where the wallet was?
7. I imagine you wondered how it was misplaced.
8. Good for you!
9. At least you now have your passport.
10. What will you do if it happens again?
11. Neurology is the science that deals with the anatomy, physiology, and pathology of the nervous system.
12. He was not aware that you had lost your wallet.
13. Nursery lore, like everything human, has been subject to many changes over long periods of time.
14. Bob read Tennyson's *Ulysses* to the class; everyone seemed to enjoy the reading.
15. In order to provide more living space, we converted an attached garage into a den.
16. Because he is such an industrious student, he has many friends.
17. Begun while Dickens was still at work on *Pickwick Papers, Oliver Twist* was published in 1837 and is now one of the author's most widely read works.
18. Given the great difficulties of making soundings in very deep water, it is not surprising that few such soundings were made until the middle of this century.
19. Did you report the loss to the proper authorities?
20. The root of modern Dutch was once supposed to be Old Frisian, but the general view now is that the characteristic forms of Dutch are at least as old as those of Old Frisian.
21. Moose, once scarce because of indiscriminate hunting, are protected by law; and the number of moose is once again increasing. (You could use a comma in place of the semicolon.)
22. He ordered a set of books, several records, and a film almost a month ago.
23. Perhaps the most interesting section of New Orleans is the French Quarter, which extends from North Rampart Street to the Mississippi River.
24. Writing for a skeptical and rationalizing age, Shaftesbury was primarily concerned with showing that goodness and beauty are not determined by revelation, authority, opinion, or fashion. (The final comma is optional.)
25. We tried our best to purchase the books, but we were completely unsuccessful even though we went to every bookstore in town.
26. A great deal of information regarding the nutritional requirements of farm animals has been accumulated over countless generations by trial and error; but most recent advances have come as the result of systematic studies at schools of animal husbandry.
27. *Omoo*, Melville's sequel to *Typee*, appeared in 1847 and went through five printings in that year alone.
28. I imagine you wondered how it was misplaced?

27\. Although the first school for Blacks was a public school established in Virginia in 1620, most educational opportunities for Blacks prior to the Civil War were provided by private agencies.

29. As the climate of Europe changed, the population became too dense for the supply of food obtained by hunting; and other means of securing food, such as the domestication of animals, were necessary. (Here, given the complexity of the independent clauses, you should use a semicolon and not a comma.)
30. As the climate of Europe changed, the population became too dense for the supply of food obtained by hunting; and other means of securing food, such as the domestication of animals, were necessary.

31. In Faulkner's poetic realism, the grotesque is somber, violent, and often inexplicable; in Caldwell's writing, it is lightened by a balladlike, humorous, sophisticated detachment. The comma following violent is optional, but the comma following *humorous* is required—because there is no conjunction between *humorous* and *sophisticated.* The semicolon is required here. A comma would create a comma splice because there is no conjunction to join the two clauses.

32. The valley of the Loire, a northern tributary of the Loire at Angers, abounds in rock villages; and they occur in many other places in France, Spain, and northern Italy.

33. The telephone rang several times; as a result, his sleep was interrupted.

34. He has forty-three thousand dollars to spend; however, once that is gone, he will be penniless.

35. Before an examination, do the following: review your work, get a good night's, sleep, eat a balanced breakfast, and arrive on time to take the test.